Early Television

GARLAND REFERENCE LIBRARY OF SOCIAL SCIENCE
VOLUME 582

Early Television
A Bibliographic Guide to 1940

Compiled by George Shiers
Assisted by May Shiers

Edited and Indexed
by Diana Menkes

Project Manager
Christopher H. Sterling

Editorial Associate
Elliot N. Sivowitch

Garland Publishing, Inc.
New York and London
1997

Copyright © 1997 by Christopher Sterling
All rights reserved

Library of Congress Cataloging-in-Publication Data

Shiers, George, 1908–1983.
    Early television : a bibliographic guide to 1940 / by George Shiers and May Shiers, 1915–1990.
        p.   cm. — (Garland reference library of social science ; v. 582)
    Includes indexes.
    ISBN 0-8240-7782-2 (alk. paper)
    1. Television—History—Bibliography. 2. Television broadcasting—History—Bibliography. I. Shiers, May. II. Title. III. Series.
Z7711.S49   1997
[TK6637]
621.388'009'09041—dc20   96-19445
                                                            CIP

Printed on acid-free, 250-year-life paper
Manufactured in the United States of America

List of Tables

1	Chronology: 1817–1877	*2*
2	Chronology: 1878–1884	*14*
3	Chronology: 1885–1900	*25*
4	From Telectroscopy to Television: Components and Techniques	*39*
5	Chronology: 1901–1918	*40*
6	The Postwar Art	*62*
7	Chronology: 1919–1924	*65*
8	To See by Radio	*81*
9	Chronology: 1925–1926	*84*
10	For Transmitting Images	*105*
11	Contributors to the Development of Television: 1878–1927	*108*
12	Chronology: 1927	*111*
13	Chronology: 1928	*136*
14	Chronology: 1929	*178*
15	Corporate Patents: 1929–1930	*211*
16	Chronology: 1930	*214*
17	Corporate Patents: 1930–1931	*252*
18	Chronology: 1931	*256*
19	Chronology: 1932	*294*
20	Chronology: 1933	*326*
21	Corporate Patents: 1932–1933	*327*
22	Chronology: 1934	*357*
23	Corporate Patents: 1933–1934	*358*
24	Chronology: 1935	*388*
25	Corporate Patents: 1935	*389*

Contents

Foreword by T.H. Bridgewater	*v*
Preface	*vii*
Understanding a Century of Television	*x*
User Notes	*xiii*
Periodical Titles and Abbreviations	*xiv*

1	Inventions and Discoveries (1817–1877)	*1*
2	Seeing by Electricity (1878–1884)	*12*
3	Era of Telectroscopes (1885–1900)	*24*
4	Distant Electric Vision (1901–1918)	*37*
5	Broadcasting and Pictures (1919-1924)	*61*
6	Images and Promises (1925–1926)	*80*
7	By Radio and by Wire (1927)	*104*
8	A Very Good Year (1928)	*131*
9	Designs for Tomorrow (1929)	*173*
10	On Stage (1930)	*209*
11	Big Pictures and Tiny Beams (1931)	*250*
12	The Derby and All That (1932)	*294*
13	A Matter for Big Business (1933)	*326*
14	High Noon of Low Definition (1934)	*357*
15	Race for Success (1935)	*388*
16	End of an Era (1936)	*436*
17	Battle of the Systems (1937)	*480*
18	International Scene (1938)	*512*
19	The Video Art (1939)	*538*
20	Distant View (1940–1995)	*561*

Name Index	*575*
Subject Index	*603*

Foreword

T.H. Bridgewater

Thornton Howard (Tony) Bridgewater *joined the Baird Company at Long Acre in 1928 and helped to develop 30-line mechanical television. He moved to the BBC (one of three television engineers) when the Corporation took over most Baird operations in 1930 and played an active part in the development of the Alexandra Palace studios for the inception of regular BBC television in November 1936. After wartime work in radar and signals for the RAF, Bridgewater returned to the BBC in 1946 as engineer-in-charge of outside (remote) television broadcasts. He was in overall charge of BBC coverage of Queen Elizabeth's June 1953 coronation. From 1962 until his retirement in 1968, Bridgewater served as chief engineer for BBC Television. He is a fellow of the Royal Television Society and has written a number of historical papers on television including a 1982 monograph on the life and work of A.A. Campbell Swinton.*

In my lifetime and that of George Shiers, television evolved from small corners in a few bright minds to an accompaniment to everyday life almost as natural as food and drink. Whether the nourishment provided is always healthful is a subject often analyzed, but that is not our concern; the means and the product are often quite separate applications of human ingenuity. Our attention here is directed solely to the early researches and discoveries from which the technology of modern television has taken its pick at one time or another.

Who invented television? Despite numerous claims, no one person has been universally credited. Television is more in the nature of a system formed by the agglomeration of many different inventions and ideas. There is room for debate on the relative importance of these ingredients, but reliable facts are needed before a clear assessment of validity and priorities can be reached. All these facts are now close at hand, thanks to the labors of George and May Shiers. Of course, opinions can still differ, and indeed history itself has been defined as "an opinion of the past." The history of television may not be exempt from that qualification, but I confidently suggest that greater agreement will result from use of the unique encyclopedia on the following pages. Once and for all we can surely settle: who did what, when, and sometimes why?

This work carries television's story up to 1940. Much has happened since then and television has taken huge strides, but by that year all the main foundations had been well and truly laid. More than that, the edifice was rising fast. I had the privilege of working in television for 40 years, beginning in 1928 with John Logie Baird. Those were days of whirling disks and dim, flickering, blurred, unsteady, tiny pink images composed of but 30 lines. Yet the first sight out of a receiver of one of my colleagues in another room faintly grimacing gave as much excitement as anything I have experienced from all the wonders and innovations in the subsequent progress of television.

Who now remembers or knows that television broadcasting began, in my country at least, in 1929? And who now would think it worth while to wait until midnight for the half-hour program to appear? And who would now be excited to see only a gesticulating face unaccompanied by any sound? Yet that is how television for public viewing subsisted for six months until a second channel became available. Thereafter, and for another two years, programs were regularly transmitted at that same late hour on several nights a week, with a few short morning turns as well. The crude images that came through to the home—usually no more than the head and shoulders of a performer—would be watched by an enthusiastic band of experimenters on their homemade receivers as well as by those who had installed the factory-built set that first came on the market in 1930—maybe a few thousand viewers in total.

The present generation may well smile at our simple pleasures of those days, but pioneering can be fun, and we certainly enjoyed and profited by our practice on the nursery slopes of television. Although we could not clearly foresee our destination, there was no worry about our direction: we would get somewhere soon. We were happy and our audience never grumbled about our modest offering.

Some changes and improvements were introduced in 1932 when the BBC took over from Baird the responsibility for studio operations and programming. One welcome change was an earlier starting time—11 pm instead of midnight—while the programs were more imaginatively planned and staged. Despite improvements at both ends, camera and receiver, the primitive transmission system was essentially the same. Nonetheless the service continued tenaciously until 1935.

Then came the miracle. Almost overnight, it seemed—though actually after a year of preparation—television broadcasting was totally transformed. Just imagine the stunning impact of some of these changes:

- scanning disks replaced by cathode ray tubes
- dim and unsteady images converted to bright and steady ones
- 30 lines of picture definition increased to 400
- 12.5 fields per second increased to 50 to eliminate flicker
- small screens replaced by large
- dark studios with spotlights replaced by flood-lit studios
- one fixed camera superseded by several that could be moved
- 15 kHz of broadcast bandwidth in medium frequencies giving way to 3 MHz of space in the very high frequencies.

Such a list can be endless, but one must not omit the special bonus for viewers: two daily programs of over one hour each, beginning at the more civilized hours of 3 and 9 pm. And soon even Sundays were included.

As to the end product, we were now able to offer our customers almost any entertainment within the range of a producer's imagination, whether from the studio or elsewhere. After a few months the King's coronation procession was brought from the streets of London into the homes of the people. To us at the time, such wonders had hitherto been the perogative only of Aladdin; yet here we were in their midst.

How this scene change came about has been told many times, and confirmation in detail will be found in the pages that follow. Many today may not realize that this new television was, in fact, the culmination of an idea first put forward by the British scientist A.A. Campbell Swinton in 1908. He proposed that electron beams should replace mechanical scanning. Researchers on both sides of the Atlantic slowly valued that guidance and through the later 1920s and the 1930s worked to achieve a practical result. While the greater credit must by conceded to the U.S., we were part of that effort and the first to launch a regular high-definition service. This was the birth of modern television. Technologically, operationally, and in nearly every other way, today's television has grown directly from that offspring.

In other countries too, parallel developments were soon taking place, until today television is truly international. The same methods, equipment, and to a considerable extent programs, pervade the world. The most significant advancements in recent years would include the introduction of color, worldwide intercommunication by satellite, and the still-developing digital higher-definition television. While the majority of programs are now pre-recorded, I reflect that during my early association with television broadcasting there was little demand for recording. We would not have regarded such a thing as "real" television. Seeing events while they were happening, now that was the stuff, the appeal, the thrill of television. And back then it *was* a thrill.

None of us can foretell what the future holds, but George and May Shiers saw to it that the past was safely preserved; and now the vaults are open to us all. I had the privilege of knowing George Shiers during the later years of his life, and in the course of regular correspondence we became close friends. Not only was I a beneficiary of his humanity and kindness, but also an admirer of his dedication to truth (whole and nothing but) and accuracy. I am certain that these qualities will render his work an enduring and infallible resource.

East Twickenham, Middlesex

Preface

This is the most comprehensive bibliography on television history until 1940 published to date. Yet despite its size (nearly 9,000 citations, many of them annotated), the book remains an incomplete record for two reasons. Given its intent—to index every patent and the more important publications concerning television's development before World War II—many citations are bound to have slipped through the research filter. More sadly, it is incomplete because of the premature death of its author when only half the volume was in draft manuscript.

How This Book Came To Be

Building on his career in electronics, part-time teaching, and writing (see below), author George Shiers began to focus his research and writing on telecommunications, and especially television history. While working on many other journal and book projects, he began to develop a history of electronics. By the mid-1970s that project had carved down its focus to the development of television.

Long fascinated with patents, Shiers developed a hand-compiled data base of American, British, and other patents on early television schemes. Working from his own extensive research library as well as in major academic libraries in Southern California, Shiers and his wife May developed an extensive handwritten card file of patent, journal, and book citations on television in many languages, focusing on the developmental period up to 1940. Shiers would draft the manuscript and his wife May would convert that to typewritten copy (how a computerized data base would have aided such a process!). Active writing began in 1978 and had progressed through Chapter 11 by the time of the author's final illness five years later.

Before Shiers' death, the undersigned promised to see the project through to completion and publication. We had come to know each other in the early 1970s, working on a series of projects reprinting important early telecommunications books. Working closely with the Smithsonian's Elliot Sivowitch and others making up a project team, we prepared for publication as much as possible of the work Shiers had accomplished. That included working with only hand-written citations on paper slips for most of the material after 1931. At the same time we sought funding for manuscript processing, and a publisher. All of that, unfortunately, took far longer than intended or expected.

Coverage and Limitations

George Shiers designed *Early Television* to be a complete historical reference source guide to the many strains of television development, mechancial and electronic, in the years leading to World War II. He includes extensive citations to material in German and French as well as English. Material through 1925 is divided among several initial chapters. By 1926 sufficient information exists that chapters beyond that point are each devoted to a single year's published output. A brief final chapter surveys the historical literature issued since 1940.

Through chapter 11, which covers events of 1931, *Early Television* appears as its author intended. That is, chapters begin with an historical narrative relating key events of the year to those before and those yet to come. A detailed chronology highlights the year of that chapter, and further tables detail patent activity. Within the citations are extensive annotations as well as textual extracts of important eye-witness accounts of television experiments and innovations.

Because of the author's death prior to the book's completion, chapters 12 through 20 are less complete than the usually meticulous Shiers intended. Chapters 12 through 15 (1932–35) include the same detailed entries as earlier chapters, missing only Shiers' intended historical narrative introduction to each. Chapters 16–19 (1936–39) lack most citations from the New York *Times* (especially 1938–39), have few annotations and virtually no extracts, and some entries are not fully complete. They also lack most linking cross-reference numbers to the rest of the book. Despite these shortcomings, they have been included in an attempt to bring to the research community as much of Shiers' work as possible. To have attempted to fill out these chapters to match the others would have even further delayed publication. We also lack some of the overall introduction to this book that Shiers, with his years of experience in the vineyards of television history, fully intended to write.

Specific conventions of style and approach are detailed in the "User Notes," found on p. xiii.

About the Author

In the years he worked on this book, George Shiers was a free-lance technical writer and part-time college teacher living in Santa Barbara, California. Born in Coventry, England in 1908, Shiers was educated in London and worked in the electrical industry before the war. After wartime service he worked in electronics, moving to the United States in 1948. He continued working in electronics for another decade (moving to California in 1954), and then turned to free-lance writing and teaching at the Santa Barbara City College, the University of California at Santa Barbara, and for various U.S. Navy installations.

Among his eight books were long-standard texts on electronic drafting, *Bibliography of the History of Electronics* (Scarecrow Press, 1972), and several anthologies on aspects of telecommunication history. As he focused more on historical work in his later years, Shiers authored a series of important scholarly articles on electrical communications history in, among other places, *Scientific American*, *IEEE Spectrum*, and the *Journal of the Royal Television Society*. Many are cited herein. Shiers was a life member of the IEEE, a member of the Royal Television Society, and a member of the Society of Motion Picture and Television Engineers. When he died in April 1983 at age 74, he and his wife May (a childhood friend whom he married in 1936 and who assisted in all of the research) had been married for 46 years. May Shiers died in January 1990.

Acknowledgements

That this book exists in published form is thanks largely to the efforts of many individuals over the years since George Shiers' death. Doubtless there are many librarians in California and elsewhere George would have thanked, but we lack any record of those names. Rest assured, he could not have accomplished all this without their unsung assistance.

Certainly three long-term friends of George Shiers helped along the way with citations, ideas, and encouragement. Elliot Sivowitch, Museum Specialist with the Division of Information Technology & Society of the Smithsonian Institution, provided information for nearly 20 years, and worked closely with the undersigned in moving the incomplete manuscript through editing and publication. Albert Abramson, noted television historian whose work is cited herein, offered ideas and assistance along the way. And while they never met face-to-face, years of correspondence between George and T.H. "Tony" Bridgewater, who supplies a foreword to this volume, were welcome inputs and updates on what was going on in Britain.

For a year or so before and after George died, Hans Camenzind provided considerable help in pulling together and beginning to standardize the hundreds of periodical citations.

Editing and otherwise preparing a book of this scope for publication is an expensive proposition. Several people provided funds in the years after the author's death, enabling the project to proceed. The Institute of Electrical and Electronics Engineers Foundation in New York provided a substantial grant in 1989 that got a stalled project moving again. Any royalties derived from sales of *Early Television* will go to the IEEE Foundation to help support further work. In addition, the late Mrs. A. B. Slee of Appledore in England, a lifelong friend of the Shiers, helped earlier with a major donation. The final push to completion (final design and typesetting) was made possible thanks to the proceeds of an earlier generous grant by the Shiers to George Washington University's graduate telecommunication program, directed by the undersigned.

The difficult job of defining a standard style for this volume, based in large part on the author's specific desires, was undertaken by Mrs. Diana Menkes who with deft tact and sure hand brought the manuscript in all its formats into a cohesive whole. She also undertook the killing job of indexing nearly 9,000 entries.

Word processing services through chapter 15 were provided by Mrs. Jo Harrop and Mrs. Pat Kaenel while Ms. Rosemary Regan completed the task. All of these people often had to work from hand-written manuscript (luckily, George Shiers had wonderfully clear hand-writing!). Further computer assistance was provided by Nance Briscoe. The final design and typography of the volume was done by Jennifer Anne Sterling of Spot Color.

On behalf of George and May Shiers—and the project team since—our sincere thanks!

Christopher H. Sterling
George Washington University
Washington D.C.

Understanding a Century of Television

George Shiers

After his death in 1983, manuscript copy for this commentary was found among the author's papers. Though incomplete (he had not written about the final or seventh historical period in his conception of TV development), the brief essay reflected Shiers' thinking after several decades of study on the development of television.

Television is a composite of many inventions and, contrary to popular belief, is much older than radio. In the years before the introduction of wireless telegraphy in 1896, the art of "seeing by electricity" implied the sending of images along wires. After the late 1870s these images were intended to be both moving and instantaneous, producible by schemes generally referred to as "telectroscopes." Before that time, an image transmitted by telegraph was simply a kind of printed reproduction. This sort of pictorial transmission, later known as phototelegraphy, provided a facsimile or exact copy of the original graphic message or design.

The technical progress of television is such that seven periods can be discerned with reasonable justification, beginning with Bain's invention of the first copying telegraph in 1843 and ending, for present purposes, in 1939. During the **first period (to 1876)**, several copying or facsimile telegraphs were designed and even put into brief service. They all depended on some form of on-off contact to translate the design at the sender, or the electrochemical effect to reproduce the design at the receiver, or clockwork to drive the apparatus, and pendulums and contacts for timing and synchronous control.

The discovery of several electro-optical effects during the 1870s provided new means for seeing by electricity. The prime discovery (in 1873) that light affected the electrical resistance of selenium opened up exciting prospects and stimulated a crop of schemes that, on paper at least, constituted the first television boom. A spate of ideas, all relying to varying degrees upon telegraphic devices and techniques, came from many quarters during the years 1877–1892. Electrical engineers, physicists, and other would-be inventors boldly suggested ways in which the magic mirror of ancient fable and legend could be reduced to practice with the aid of modern technology. Almost without exception, however, these proposals for seeing by electricity were more allied with facsimile recording than with the transmission of moving images. This **second period (1877–1884)** lasted until Nipkow applied for the first patent in the new art, one that disclosed his invention of the all-important scanning disk.

Some two dozen new proposals for telectroscopy and kindred systems appeared during the next 20 years. More important for the future, however, was the discovery of the photoelectric effect and Braun's invention of the cathode-ray indicator tube. This **third period (1885–1906)** also witnessed the discovery of the electron, the introduction of thermionic tubes, the rise of practical wireless telegraphy, the introduction of the word "television," and the use of a cathode-ray tube for displaying graphic images. Though not so called for another quarter of a century, the electronic era of television had begun.

Among the dozen or so solutions to the problems of television brought forward during the **fourth period (1907–1926)** the most notable was Rosing's semi-electronic system of 1907, which also used a cathode-ray tube as a receiver. A glimpse of the future appeared in print the following year when Swinton suggested an all-electric approach employing "two synchronized beams of kathode rays" as a means for overcoming mechanical difficulties. Both men dominate the early years. Rosing demonstrated his "electric eye" and came out with another version in 1911. Swinton followed with a full description of his revolutionary electronic tube near the end of that year.

Television passed through a quiescent stage during the rest of that decade, partly because of the turmoil of the Great War (1914–1918) and partly because of technical limitations. Meanwhile, radical advances in electron tubes and radio circuits as well as in cathode-ray developments and photo-sensitive devices provided a new pool of technical resources. The new hardware and techniques available after the war, along with the rise of popular broadcast radio after 1920, revived interest in the challenge of distant electric vision.

Accounts of experiments in television began to multiply toward the mid-1920s. Jenkins, an American inventor, Mihaly, a Hungarian engineer, and Baird in London were all anticipating success. It seemed, at least to journalists, as if "radio vision" by mechancial means was almost if not already a practicality. Headlines declared that television had arrived, that one could indeed see by radio, and that motion pictures sent by ether waves would very soon compete with radio in the home. Success appeared imminent from time to time, but nothing more than the transmission of silhouettes was achieved before 1926. Swinton, always a sharp critic of mechanical proposals, thought otherwise. In 1924 he outlined his definitive plan showing the possibilities for all-electric television by wire and by radio. Though basically known at that time, the electronic camera tube that he had clearly envisioned in 1911 had already been introduced in a rudimentary form by Zworykin in America.

When Baird publicly demonstrated true television early in 1926, he put the seal of success on a half-century of inventive endeavors. This event marked the end of the speculative era, the beginning of television as a new field of engineering, and the start of another period of intensive development. The roster of inventors grew ever longer in the next few years, first as independent workers and then as large manufacturers entered what soon became an international race.

In the later years of the twenties, low-definition mechanical systems advanced to a level of perfection that equalled the earlier reportorial optimism. Visual images, both live and on film, were dissected and reconstituted with fair success by mirrors and drums and lenses and flying beams of light as well as by the spinning disk. Flickering neon-hued pictures, always tiny and generally elusive, became daily fare, at least during the inconvenient hours alloted to experimental broadcasts, for enterprising amateurs who had to build their own receivers.

In keeping with the mood of the times, during the **fifth period (1927–1930)**—when anything seemed possible and often was—new lines of development reached out in all directions, even before there was a sound commercial foundation. Television by infrared and disk recording was demonstrated. Pictures were sent long distance over telephone lines and by radio, even across the Atlantic. Television in color, stereoscopic television, daylight television and two-way television appeared on the scene, along with simultaneous transmission of sight and sound. There were demonstrations of tele-talkies, or the transmission of motion pictures with sound, of intermediate-film recording and of large-screen reception for theaters. Spurred by the commercial prospects for home entertainment and the domestic market for receivers, television became big business for a while and then subsided somewhat with the coming of the worldwide economic depression.

During these years of peak activity, the Television Society was founded in London and the first periodical devoted solely to television appeared. More than a dozen books were published to suit the interests of laymen, amateurs and students alike. Magazines and daily papers carried a feast of words and pictures that covered the spectrum: brief notes on current events, news of developments at home and abroad, theoretical and constructional articles, popular explanations and practical hints and tips, exhibition reports, business and trade news, program schedules, all intermixed with criticism, responses, and editorials on the current status, problems, possibilities and future trends of this thing called television.

Complete receivers (radiovisors, televisors) were advertised, along with a range of parts as well as kits suitable for home construction. As a token of progress, viewing areas and image screens grew out of the peephole stage with more reasonable dimensions: about 20 square inches by 1930 or even larger with a magnifying lens. But the anticipated amateur boom like that of radio in the early twenties never materialized. Despite the flood of promotional prose and corporate efforts, most receiver assemblies stayed in the experimental workshop; few entered the living room. But a new technology had arisen and a new art form had been born. The telecommunication family had, in fact, acquired a promising new member, one destined to transform the lifestyle of millions within the coming quarter-century.

The **sixth period (1931–1936)** is marked by the rise of electronic systems, the production of highly engineered mechanical apparatus, and the beginning of high-definition broadcasting. The cathode-ray tube slowly replaced moving parts in receivers. With the rapid advances made in radio engineering, transmissions shifted first to the more spacious short-wave band then climbed to the ultra-short-wave region. The number of scanning lines increased almost tenfold in the trend toward high definition and viewing screens of home receivers doubled in size from the skimpy dimensions of 1930.

Economic restraints of the early 1930s did not stop television research. Several large concerns pushed the development of new forms of mechanical apparatus, even as electronic methods were approaching the practical stage. The scope of public interest widened as broadcast programs became more interesting and of better quality. More frequent exhibitions and commercial demonstrations also boosted interest. By 1933 the erstwhile Cinderella was an attractive feature in radio exhibitions where the visitor could examine a dozen or so commercial products, though many were scarcely ready for the market.

Receiver displays, often unstable and sometimes distorted, were generally bright and clear with good to excellent detail and little flicker—as measured by the standards of the times. Picture tints ranged from the classical neon-pink to pale yellow, yellow-green, pale blue, and white, according to the light source and scanner—disk, mirror screw, drum or ring—and the phosphor coatings of the new picture tubes. Within the next three years the cathode-ray tube replaced opto-mechanical devices in almost all receivers, in some of which the image was viewed via a tilted mirror in the cabinet lid.

Whisperings of the "electric eye" began to circulate in the late twenties. But with almost everyone knee-deep in mechanical apparatus, the barest details that were released about the electronic camera seemed little more than science fiction. By 1930, however, it became more clear that perhaps, after all, the "crystal globe" and the "electric pencil" would some day work together and eliminate all moving parts.

Technical details of Farnsworth's image dissector camera tube and oscillite receiver were released in the spring of 1931. One electronic solution had arrived. News of RCA's electronic system appeared in the summer of 1933 with a description of the inconoscope camera tube invented by Zworykin. Full disclosure of the Farnsworth system was published the next year. Another electronic system was also reaching the practical stage at the EMI Laboratories in England at the same time. Like a brash adolescent, the electron-beam camera now challenged the time-honored mechanical art.

User Notes

Given the massive amount of information detailed here, a number of standardized conventions have been adopted to make the most efficient use of space.

Names: Where known, the full personal names for authors, scientists, or other figures are given in the first entry together with their biographical dates when these could be determined. Initials are used in subsequent entries.

Journal Entries: Each shows author, title, journal name or abbreviation in capital letters, volume number, date, and pages. For foreign-language articles, the English title is given in brackets. Journals published monthly, like SCIENTIFIC AMERICAN, are arranged alphabetically at the beginning of each month. Weekly journals, like NATURE, are entered before newspaper items of the same date. (See the separate listing of all periodical titles and their abbreviations on the following pages.)

Newspaper Entries: Each shows headline(s), name or abbreviation of the newspaper in capital letters, page, date and column(s). Sunday issues have sections indicated in roman numerals which precede the page number:

2976   "Latest television receiver which produces the image on an eight-inch screen." N.Y.T. IX, 11 (June 28):5,6.

Book Entries: Unless the exact publication date is known, these are presented at the end of the year in alphabetical sequence by author's name. Each provides author, title in capital letters, place of publication, publisher, date, number of pages, and number of illustrations. If the book is in a foreign language, the English title is given in brackets immediately after the original title. The annotations describe contents with a degree of detail depending on the book's importance.

Patent Entries: In the daily chronological order, patents, listed by the earliest application date, follow journal and newspaper entries. Two or more patents with the same date are listed alphabetically by the first patentee name. Basic elements provided for patents include the patentee name, title of the patent, patent number prefixed by Br. (British) or U.S., application date, and (for the U.S.) a publication date. Other elements may include a reissue date, name of assignee, country of origin and date.

Patentee Names: All American patents are filed in an individual's name. Otherwise a personal name is given only in the case of independent inventors. In some instances a British patent gives a person's name even though he is affiliated with a company. The respective company name, if known, is given in parentheses after the final date. Some British patents of German origin give only a company name. Composite names (company and person) in British patents are given in the order shown in the official abridgment. All the individual and company names appearing in a patent entry have been indexed.

Link Numbers: The numbers appearing separately in parentheses at the end of some bibliographic entries refer to the nearest prior and subsequent entries under the same individual's or organization's name.

Chronologies: Appearing just before the bibliographic entries, these list the highlights of events for each year.

Periodical Titles and Abbreviations

Included here are all periodical titles used in EARLY TELEVISION. They are listed in order of the abbreviated form (or, as relevant, full title) used in the body of the bibliography.

ALTA FREQ.   Alta Frequenza
AM. J. PHYS.   American Journal of Physics
AM. J. SCI.   American Journal of Science
AM. MON. REV. REV.   American Monthly Review of Reviews
ANN. CHIM. PHYS.   Annales de Chimie et de Physique
ANN. PHYS.   Annalen der Physik
ANN. POSTES   Annales des Postes, Télégraphes et Téléphones
ANN. TELEGR.   Annales Télégraphiques
ANNALS   Annals of the American Academy of Political and Social   Science
ARCH. ELEKT.   Archive der Elektrischen Ubertragung
ARCH. F. ELEKT.   Archiv für Electrotechnik
ARCH. POST- FERNMELD.   Archiv für das Post und Fernmeldesesen
ARCH. POST TELEGR.   Archiv für Post und Telegraphie
ARCH. SCI PHYS. NAT.   Archives des Sciences Physiques et Naturelles
ASTROPHYSICS J.   Astrophysics Journal
ATHENAEUM
AV INST.   Audiovisual Instruction

BAYR. IND. GEWER.   Bayrisches Industrie- und Gewerbeblatt,   München
BELL LAB RECORD
BOLL. COLL. ING. ARCH. NAPOLI   Bolletino del Collegio degl'Ingegneri ed Architetti Napoli
BR. ASSOC. REP.   British Association Reports
BR. INST. RAD. ENG. J.   British Institute of Radio Engineers
J. BR. J. PHOTOGRAPHY   British Journal of Photography
BROADCASTING
B.S.T.J.   Bell System Technical Journal

CASSIRER'S MAG.   Cassirer's Magazine
CHAMBERS J.   Chambers Journal
CIT. RAD. CALL BOOK   Citizens Radio Call Book Magazine
COMM   Communications
COMM. & BRDCAST. ENG.   Communication and Broadcast Engineering
COSMOS
C.R.   Comptes Rendu Hebdomadaires des Séances de l'Académie des Sciences
CURRENT HIST.   Current History

DAILY CHRONICLE
DAILY EXPRESS

DAILY HERALD
DAILY MAIL
DAILY NEWS
DAILY TELEGRAPH
DER MECH.   Der Mechaniker
DESIGN AND WORK
DEUT. PHYS. GES.   Deutsche Physikalische Gesellschaft
DIE UMSCHAU
DISCOVERY

ECL. ELECT.   L'Eclairage Electrique
EDINBURGH NEW PHIL.   Edinburgh New Philosophical Journal
ELECT.   Electrician
ELECT. BULL.   Electrical Bulletin
ELECT. COMM.   Electrical Communication
ELECT. DES.   Electronic Design
ELECT. ENG.   Electrical Engineering
ELECT. ENGINEER   Electrical Engineer
ELECT. EXPER.   Electrical Experimenter
ELECT. MFG   Electronics Manufacturing
ELECT. & POWER   Electronics and Power
ELECT. REV.   Electrical Review
ELECT. W.   Electrical World
ELECTRICITY
ELECTRONIC IMAGING
ELECTRONICS
ELEKT. ANZ.   Elektrotechnischer Anzeiger
ELEKTRICHESTVO
ELETTRICISTA
ELETTROTECNIA
ENG. MECH.   English Mechanic and World of Science
ENG. NEWS   Engineering News
ENG. PROG.   Engineering Progress
ENGINEER
ENGINEERING
E.N.T.   Elektrische Nachrichten-Technik
E.T.Z.   Elektrotechnische Zeitschrift
EXP. W.   Experimental Wireless and the Wireless Engineer
EXPERIMENTER

FERN.   Fernsehen
FERN.U.TON.   Fernsehen und Tonfilm
FREQUENZ
FORTUNE
FUNKSCHAU

G.E. REV.   General Electric Review
GENIE CIVIL
GRAPHIC

HAM RADIO
HARPER'S WEEKLY

HOCH. ELEKT.   Hochfrequenztechnik und Elektroakustik

IEEE COMMUNICATIONS   Institute of Electrical and Electronic Engineers Communications Society Magazine
IEEE SPECTRUM
IEEE TRANS.   IEEE Transactions
ILLUS. LONDON NEWS   Illustrated London News
L'ILLUSTRATION
INT. BRD. ENG.   International Broadcast Engineering
INT. TELEV. TECH. REV.   International Television Technical Review

J. APP. PHYS.   Journal of Applied Physics
J. BR. KINE.   Journal of the British Kinematography, Sound and Television Society
J. BROADCASTING   Journal of Broadcasting (later Journal of Broadcasting and Electronic Media)
J. F.I.   Journal of the Franklin Institute
J. IEE   Journal of the Institution of Electrical Engineers
J. IEE JAPAN   Journal of the IEE, Japan
J. OSA   Journal of the Optical Society of America
J. POLITICAL ECONOMY   Journal of Political Economy
J. RONTGEN SOC   Journal of the Röntgen Society
J. ROY. SOC. EE   Journal of the Royal Society of Electrical Engineers
J. ROY. SOC. ARTS   Journal of the Royal Society of the Arts
J. ROY. TELEV. SOC.   Journal of the Royal Television Society
J. SCI. INST.   Journal of Scientific Instruments
J. SMPE   Journal of the Society of Motion Picture Engineers
J. SMPTE   Journal of the Society of Motion Picture and Television Engineers
J. SOC. ARTS   Journal of the Society of Arts
J. SOC. TEL. ENGRS   Journal of the Society of Telegraph Engineers
J. TELEV. SOC.   Journal of the Television Society (later Royal Television Society)

KINE. WKLY.   Kinematograph Weekly

LA EPOCA
LA NATURE
LES MONDES
LUM. ELECT.   La Lumière Electrique

MAN. GUARD.   Manchester Guardian
MOD. ELECT.   Modern Electricity
MONATSBER AKAD. WISS BERLIN   Monatsberichte der Deutschen Akademie der Wissenschaften zu Berlin
MON. KOEN. PREUS. AKAD.   Monatsschrift der Königlichen Preussischen Akademie
MORNING POST
MOTION PICTURE HERALD

NATUR
NATURE
NEW ENG. J. EDUC.   New England Journal of Education
NEW SCIENTIST
NOTES & RESEARCHES ROY. SOC.   Notes and Researches of the Royal Society
N.Y. HERALD   New York Herald
N.Y.P.L. BULL.   New York Public Library Bulletin

N.Y.T   New York Times

OBSERVER
O INSTITUTO
OBSERVER MAG.   Observer Magazine
ONDE ELECT.   Onde Electrique

PEARSON'S MAG.   Pearson's Magazine
PHIL. MAG.   The London, Edinburgh, and Dublin Philosophical Magazine and Journal of Science
PHIL. TECH. REV.   Philips Technical Review
PHIL. TRANS.   Philosophical Transactions of the Royal Society
PHOTOGRAPHIC J.   Photographic Journal
PHYS. BER.   Physikalische Berichte
PHYS. REV.   Physical Review
PHYS. SOC.   Physical Society of London
PHYS. Z.   Physikalische Zeitschrift
PHYSICA
P.O. EE J.   Post Office Electrical Engineers Journal
POLYTECH. J.   Polytechnic Journal
POP. MECH.   Popular Mechanics
POP. RADIO   Popular Radio
POP. SCI.   Popular Science
POP. SCI. MON.   Popular Science Monthly
POP. SCI. REV.   Popular Science Review
POP. W.   Popular Wireless and Wireless Review
PRAC. ELECT.   Practical Electrics
PRAT. IND. MECH.   Practique des Industries Méchaniques
PROC. AM. ACAD.   Proceedings, American Academy of Arts and Sciences
PROC. AM. ASSOC.   Proceedings, American Association for the Advancement of Science
PROC. IEEE   Proceedings, Institute of Electrical and Electronics Engineers
PROC. IRE   Proceedings, Institute of Radio Engineers
PROC. PHIL. SOC. GLASGOW   Proceedings, Philosophical Society of Glasgow
PROC. PHYS. SOC.   Proceedings, Physical Society of London
PROC. ROY. INST.   Proceedings, Royal Institution of Great Britain
PROC. ROY. SOC.   Proceedings, Royal Society
PROC. SOC. INFO. DISPLAY   Proceedings, Society for Information Display
PROC. U.S. NAVAL INST.   Proceedings, U.S. Naval Institute
PROJ. ENG.   Projection Engineering
PROMETHEUS

QST
QSTF   QST Francais et Radioélectricité Reunis
QUART. REV.   Quarterly Review
QUEEN'S QUART.   Queen's Quarterly

RADIO
RADIO BRD.   Radio Broadcast
RADIO CALL BOOK
RADIO-CRAFT
RADIOELECTRICITE
RADIO-ELECTRONICS
RADIO & ELECT. ENG.   Radio and Electronic Engineer

RADIO ENG.   Radio Engineering
RADIO INDEX
RADIO INDUSTRIES
RADIO LISTENER'S GUIDE   Radio Listener's Guide and Call Book
RADIO N.   Radio News
RADIO & TELEV.   Radio and Television
RADIO TIMES
RADIOTEKHNIKA
REALE ACCAD. SCI. TORINO   Reale Accademia delle Scienze di Torino
RCA REV.   RCA Review
REV. GEN.   Revue Génerale de l'Electricité
REV. GEN. SCI.   Revue Generale des Sciences Pures et Appliquees
REV. IND.   Revue Industrielle
REV. SCI. INSTS   The Review of Scientific Instruments
REVUE DES REVUES
RMA ENG.   Radio Manufacturers Association Engineer

SCIENCE
SCI. AM.   Scientific American
SCI. AM. SUPP.   Scientific American Supplement
SCI. & INV.   Science and Invention
SCI. MON.   Scientific Monthly
SCI. N. LETTER   Science News Letter
SCI. PROG.   Scientific Progress
S.F. CHRONICLE   San Francisco Chronicle
SHORT WAVE & TELEV.   Short Wave and Television
SITZ. KON. AKAD. WISS.
SITZ. KON. PREUSS. AKAD. Sitzungsberichte. Koeniglich-Preussische Akademie der Wissenschaften
SITZUNGBER. PHYS. MED. SOZ. ERLANGEN   Sitzunberichte der Physikalische-Medizinischen Sozietät zu Erlangen
SITZUNGBER. WURZBURG. PHYS. MED. GES.   Sitzunberichte der Würzburger Physikalischen-Medizinischen Gesellschaft
SMITH. INST. ANN. REP.   Smithsonian Institution Annual Report
SOC. FR. ELECT. BULL.   Société Française des Electriciens, Bulletin
SOC. TELEG. ENGRS.   Society of Telegraph Engineers
SPHERE
SUNDAY STAR

TECH. ENG. NEWS   Tech Engineering News
TECH. MOD.   Technique Moderne
TECH. PHYS. OF USSR   Technical Physics of the USSR
TECH. REV.   Technology Review
TEKH. KINO I TELEV.   Tekhnika Kino i Televideniya
TELEG. J. & ELECT. REV.   Telegraphic Journal and Electrical Review
T.F.T   Telegraphen und Fernsprech-Technik
TELEV.   Television
TELEV. & S.W.W.   Television and Short-Wave World
TELEV. QUARTERLY   Television Quarterly
TIMES   The [London] Times
TRANS. AIEE   Transactions, American Institute of Electrical Engineers

TRANS. INST. ENGRS & SHPBLDERS. SCOT.   Transactions, Institute of Engineers and Shipbuilders in Scotland
TRANS. ROY. DUBLIN SOC.   Transactions, Royal Dublin Society
TRANS. ROY. IRISH. ACAD. Transactions, Royal Irish Academy
TRANS. SMPE   Transactions, Society of Motion Picture Engineers
TWENTIETH CENTURY

UNTERRICHTSBL. MATH. NATUR   Unterrichtsblätter für Mathematik und Naturwissenschaften

V.D.I.Z.   Verein Deutscher Ingenieure Zeitschrift

W. AGE   Wireless Age
W. CONSTRUCTOR   Wireless Constructor
W. ENG.   Wireless Engineer
W. REV.   Wireless Review
W. W.   Wireless World
WIRELESS & GRAMOPHONE TRADER
WELTALL
WEST. ELECT.   Western Electrician
WINDSOR MAG.   Windsor Magazine
WORLD RADIO
WORLD TODAY

Z.F. FERN   Zeitschrift für Fernmeldetechnik
Z.F. HOCHFREQUENZTECH   Zeitschrift für Hochfrequenztechnik
Z.F. PHYS.   Zeitschrift für Physik
Z.F. SCHWACH.   Zeitschrift für Schwachstromtechnik
Z. PHYS. CHEM. UNT.   Zeitschrift für den physikalischen und Chemischen Unterricht
Z. SCHWAB
Z. TECH. PHYS.   Zeitschrift für technische Physik

CHAPTER 1

INVENTIONS AND DISCOVERIES: 1817–1877

The idea of seeing by electricity did not arise until the end of the period covered in this chapter, but at least ten specific advances in science and technology made during these years were cardinal features in proposals that appeared before the close of the century. The chief stimulus to inventors came from the discovery that metallic selenium is electrically sensitive to light, a remarkable property that opened the way for conversion of optical images into electric currents.

Legacies of this early period that came from scientific research include Faraday's discovery of the magnetic rotation of polarized light (13), Nicol's polarizing prism (3), and Kerr's discovery of electrostatic birefringence (62). Embodied in practical devices, these discoveries were applied for varying, or modulating, the intensity of light in receivers. Other proposals for modulators incorporated the principle of König's manometric flame (38), variable apertures, and Bell's telephone (66). Together these gave inventors a range of approaches utilizing electricity, magnetism, optics, and acoustics. Concerning his discovery of a relation between magnetism and light, Faraday wrote, "This fact will most likely prove exceedingly fertile and of great value...," a remark that could be applied to the other discoveries in relation to television.

Early electric telegraphs developed during the 1830s employed a code sequence of signals in the transmission of a message. The advantages of recording a message in graphic form, directly readable as a page of type, were perceived in 1843 by Bain (11). This first proposal for an electrochemical copying telegraph was followed by the inventions of Bakewell (15), Caselli (23), Bonelli (31), d'Arlincourt (46), and others. These and other advances in the telegraph art depended on accurate synchronism between moving parts effected by pendulums, clockwork, and various mechanisms, usually incorporating electromagnets. Later rendered practicable by the use of electromagnetic tuning forks, by phonic wheels or synchronous motors, and by some form of distributor (15) or commutator, automatic telegraph instruments of the 1870s embodied these and other techniques that were adopted in some of the earlier proposals for telectroscopes.

The roots of electronic television can be found in the researches into electric discharges in rarefied gases. Beginning with the experiments of Francis Hauksbee (1666–1713) in 1705, more than one hundred investigations were carried out with various forms of exhausted tubes during the eighteenth century. This branch of science attracted the attention of Faraday (6), Abria (12), Gassiot (25), Plücker (26), De la Rive (35), Hittorf (45), De la Rue (57), Spottiswoode (58), Goldstein (70), and others whose work became the foundation of cathode-ray-tube technology, which led much later to electron physics. These investigations were aided considerably by the skills of glassblowers and particularly by the invention and development of more efficient vacuum pumps, notably those due to Geissler (28), Toepler (33), and Sprengel (39).

The prime researches of Faraday and Joseph Henry (1797–1878) into electromagnetic induction in 1831 soon led to the inception of induction coils by Page (4) and Callan (5). Improved by Ruhmkorff (22) and others, induction coils became essential components in electrotechnology, in the study of electric conduction in rarefied gases, and in numerous schemes for telectroscopes well past the turn of the century. The investigations of Becquerel on the photovoltaic effect (9), of Stokes (19) and others on fluorescence and phosphors, and theories concerning the nature of cathode rays by Varley (48) and other workers with electricity in vacuo were some of the stepping stones to the threshold of electronic science of later years.

Although there had been only sporadic interest in selenium following its discovery by Berzelius in 1817, once Smith (50) announced in 1873 his discovery of selenium's property of photosensitivity, it was studied intensively. By 1877 several men had realized that selenium could be put to use for seeing by electricity, a notion that was promoted by the introduction of the telephone. A survey of the schemes of later years shows how much dependence was placed upon the discoveries and inventions of this period. As the level of physical science and telecommunications was raised, new devices and approaches expanded the field for would-be inventors of telectroscopes and later television systems. Nevertheless, the apparatus and techniques born during this early period remained more or less staples, even into the early decades of the present century: Nicol prisms, induction coils, Kerr cells, manometric flames, telephone actuators, tuning forks, electromagnetic devices, and of course the ubiquitous selenium cell.

TABLE 1   CHRONOLOGY: 1817–1877

1817	Berzelius	Discovery of selenium
1829	Nicol	Polarizing prism
1836	Page	Autotransformer
	Callan	Induction coil
	Faraday	Cathode rays
1838	Page	Induction coil
1839	Becquerel	Photovoltaic effect
1843	Bain	Copying telegraph
1845	Faraday	Magneto-optic effect
1847	Caselli	Copying telegraph
1848	Bakewell	Copying telegraph, distributor
1852	Stokes	Fluorescence
1855	Ruhmkorff	Induction coil
	Geissler	Vacuum pump, sealed tubes
1858	Plücker	Cathode rays
1860	Bonelli	Copying telegraph
1862	Toepler	Vacuum pump
1863	De la Rive	Cathode rays
1864	König	Manometric flame
	Maxwell	Electromagnetic theory
1865	Sprengel	Vacuum pump
1869	Hittorf	Cathode rays
	d'Arlincourt	Tuning fork control
1871	Varley	Cathode rays
1873	Smith	Light-sensitivity of selenium
1875	De la Rue, et al.	Cathode rays
	Kerr	Electrostatic birefringence
	Kerr	Magneto-optic effect
1877	Edison	Phonograph

BIBLIOGRAPHY: 1817–1877

1 Berzelius, Jöns Jakob (1779–1848). "Lettre de M. Berzelius à M. Berthollet sur deux métaux nouveaux" [Letter from Mr. Berzelius to Mr. Berthollet concerning two new metals]. ANN. CHIM. PHYS. 7 (1817): 199–207. (2)

2 Berzelius, J.J. "Recherches sur un nouveau corps minéral trouvé dans le soufre fabriqué à Fahlun" [Research on a new mineral body found in the sulfur working at Fahlun]. ANN. CHIM. PHYS. 9 (1818): 160–80, 225–67, 337–65. Berzelius, professor of chemistry at Stockholm and secretary of the Swedish Academy of Sciences, isolated a new substance from the sulfuric acid deposits of copper ore at Fahlun. "I then discovered an unknown substance with properties closely resembling those of tellurium. This resemblance induced me to call it Selenium, from the Greek word [Selene] which signifies the moon, while Tellus is the name of our own planet." (1, 636)

3 Nicol, William (1768–1851). "On a method of so far increasing the divergency of the two rays in calcareous spar that only one image may be seen at a time." EDINBURGH NEW PHIL. J. 6 (1829): 83, 84. The popular form of Nicol's polarizing prism consists of a block of Iceland spar (calcite) split along a diagonal plane, with the cut surfaces polished and cemented together with Canada balsam, a transparent resin. "Ordinary" (non-polarized) light entering one end face is divided into two rays: the "ordinary ray" strikes the plane of intersection and is reflected to and absorbed by one side of the prism, while the "extraordinary ray" passes through the intersection and emerges at the far end parallel with the original beam. Two crossed Nicols (polarizer, analyzer), with the plane of polarization at right angles, were important elements in many television proposals (127, 167, 181, 213) and were used in several practical electromechanical systems.

4 Page, Charles Grafton (1812–1868). "Method of increasing shocks, and experiments, with Professor Henry's apparatus for obtaining sparks and shocks from the calorimotor." AM. J. SCI. 31 (1837): 137–41. Letter on the autotransformer, May 12, with postscript on a spur wheel interrupter, June 8. Page was a pioneer inventor of electromechanical apparatus in the United States. (7, 220)

5 Callan, Nicholas Joseph (1799–1864). "On a new galvanic battery." PHIL. MAG. 9 (Dec. 1836): 472–8. Description of an induction coil and experiments, dated Aug. 23. Also ANN. PHYS. 39 (1836): 407–10. Callan was a priest and professor of natural philosophy at St. Patrick's College, Maynooth, near Dublin. (220)

6 Faraday, Michael (1791–1867). "Experimental researches in electricity, 13th Series. Discharges in air and gases at varying pressures; the negative glow, the positive column and the dark space." PHIL. TRANS. 128 (1838): 125–68. Paper read Mar. 15, 1838. Experiments made June 21, 1836. Further experiments, DIARY, Vol. III, pp. 234–6, Jan. 4, 5; pp. 242–57, Jan. 25, 26; pp. 269–71, Mar. 15, 1838 (3759). Also ANN. PHYS. 48 (1839): 269–86, 424–60, 513–39. EXPERIMENTAL RESEARCHES, Vol. I (1839), pp. 473–532. (8)

7 Page, C.G. "Magneto-electric and electromagnetic apparatus and experiments." AM. J. SCI. 35 (1839): 252–68. An illustration shows a prototype induction coil said to have been completed Apr. 1838. (4, 220)

8 Faraday, M. EXPERIMENTAL RESEARCHES IN ELECTRICITY. Reprinted from PHIL. TRANS., 1831–1838. Vol. I, London: Richard & John Edward Taylor, 1839. Vol. II, 1844, Vol. III, 1855. (6, 13)

9 Becquerel, Alexandre Edmond (1820–1891). "Recherches sur les effets de la radiation chimique de la lumière solaire au moyen des courants électriques" [Research on the effects of chemical radiation of sunlight by means of electrical currents]. C.R. 9 (July 1839): 145–9. Also ANN. PHYS. 54 (1841): 18–34. (10)

10 Becquerel, A.E. "Mémoire sur les effets electriques produits sous l'influence des rayons solaires" [Notes on the electrical effects produced under the influence of solar rays]. C.R. 9 (Nov. 1839): 561–7. Also ANN. PHYS. 54 (1841): 35–42. Discovery of a photovoltaic effect whereby a potential difference is generated between a pair of silver electrodes in an electrolyte when one plate is illuminated. Though of scientific importance, electrolytic cells were not of practical use in television developments. (9, 20)

11 Bain, Alexander (1810–1877). "Electric time-pieces and telegraphs." Br. 9745, May 27, Nov. 27, 1843. The first proposal for a copying telegraph is contained in this composite specification under two sections: for electric clocks and the manner of "making pendulums regulate each other," and an instrument "for taking copies of surfaces at distant places by means of electricity." The apparatus embodies the principle of sequential scanning line by line, automatic synchronous control, and transmission along a single wire with a ground return. Bain was a Scottish clockmaker, telegraph pioneer, and inventor of electric clocks. (40)

12 Abria, Jérémie Joseph Benôit (1811–1892). "Recherches sur les lois de l'induction des courants par les courants" [Research on the laws of induction of currents by currents]. ANN. CHIM. PHYS. 7 (1843): 462–88. Experiments with striated discharges in vacua. The general phenomena of electric discharges in rarefied air were studied intensively during the eighteenth century. Edward Nairne discovered striations in 1777.

13 Faraday, M. "Experimental researches in electricity, 19th series. On the magnetization of light and the illumination of magnetic lines of force." PHIL. TRANS. 136 (1846): 1–20. Paper read Nov. 20, 1845. DIARY, Vol. IV, pp. 263–7, experiments Sept. 13, 1845 (3759). EXPERIMENTAL RESEARCHES, Vol. III, pp. 1–26 (8). PHIL. MAG. 28 (1846): 294–317, 396–406, 455–68; ANN. PHYS. 68 (1846): 105–35. Discovery of the magnetic rotation of polarized light (Faraday effect): a magnetic field, with the lines of force parallel with a beam of polarized light, produces rotation of the plane of polarization. This arrangement of a coil between Nicol prisms (Faraday cell) was incorporated as a modulator or light valve in Nipkow's television patent of 1884 (181), but the Kerr cell (62) was more often preferred and was used in practical systems up to the 1930s. Kerr discovered a related effect in 1876 (74). (8, 21)

14 Caselli, Luigi. IL TELEGRAFO ELETTRICO. Rome, 1847. Pamphlet, 22 pp., 2 plates. On his brother's facsimile telegraph. (23)

15 Bakewell, Frederick Collier (1800–1869). "Electric telegraphs, improvements in making communications from one place to another by means of electricity." Br. 12,352, Dec. 2, 1848, June 2, 1849. His cylinder machine was the first practicable electrochemical copying telegraph. The specification also discloses the use of a distributor that permits multipoint scanning with sequential signals being transmitted along a single line, one of the important features of later television proposals. (16)

16 Bakewell, F.C. "On the copying telegraph." AM. J. SCI. 12 (Nov. 1851): 278. From British Association Report, paper read at the Ipswich meeting, July 2. (15)

17 Hittorf, Johann Wilhelm (1824–1914). "Uber das elektrische Leitungsvermögen des Schwefelsilbers und Halbschwefelkupfers" [On the electric conductivity of sulfuric silver and half-sulfuric copper]. ANN. PHYS. 84 (1851): 1–27. Also, "Uber die Allotropie des Selens" [About the allotropy of selenium]. ANN. PHYS. 84 (1851): 214–20. Early research on selenium. (45)

18 Grove, (Sir) William Robert (1811–1896). "On the electro-chemical polarity of gases, including the striae in electrical discharges." PHIL. TRANS. 142 (1852): 87–102. Grove employed an induction coil made by Ruhmkorff. (22)

19 Stokes, (Sir) George Gabriel (1812–1903). "On the change of refrangibility of light."

PHIL. TRANS. 142 (1852): 463–562; 143 (1853): 385–96. Cardinal paper on fluorescence, a word coined by Stokes from fluorspar. PROC. ROY. SOC. 6: 195–200, 333–5; ANN. PHYS. 87: 480–90.

20 Becquerel, A.E. "Recherches sur la conductibilité électrique des gaz à des températures élevées" [Research on the electrical conductivity of gases at elevated temperatures]. C.R. 37 (1853): 20–4; ANN. CHIM. PHYS. 39 (1853): 355–402. (10, 44)

21 Faraday, M. "On Ruhmkorff's induction apparatus." PROC. ROY. INST. 2 (1855): 139–42. Lecture, June 8. Heinrich Daniel Ruhmkorff (1803–1877), a German instrument maker in Paris, was awarded Le Prix Volta (50,000 francs) for his development of the induction coil. (13, 24, 220)

22 Du Moncel, Théodose Achille Louis (1821–1884). NOTICE SUR L'APPAREIL D'INDUCTION ÉLECTRIQUE DE RUHMKORFF ET LES EXPERIENCES QUE L'ON PEUT FAIRE AVEC CET INSTRUMENT [Note on the electrical induction apparatus of Ruhmkorff and the experiments which one can make with that instrument]. Paris: Hachette, 1855. 152 pp. See Fig 3. (36, 220)

23 Caselli, Giovanni (1815–1891). "Electric telegraphs, improvements in transmitting facsimile copies of writings and drawings by means of electric currents." Br. 2532, Nov. 10, 1855, May 10, 1856. Filed by Alfred Vincent Newton, as agent. (14, 32)

24 Faraday, M. (Experiments on electric discharges in vacuum tubes.) DIARY, Vol. VII, pp. 412–61 (3759). Detailed description of a wide series of experiments made at the Royal Institution and at Gassiot's (25) private laboratory at Clapham Common from Jan. 23 to Mar. 18, 1858. The pages contain 86 diagrams of tubes and arrangements, and some letters from Gassiot to Faraday. (21)

25 Gassiot, John Peter (1797–1877). "On the stratifications and dark band in electrical discharges as observed in Torricellian vacua (Bakerian lecture)." PHIL. TRANS. 148 (1858): 1–16. Paper read Mar. 4. Plate with 15 diagrams showing induction coil, apparatus, tubes and striae. Gassiot was vice-president of the Royal Society. (29)

26 Plücker, Julius (1801–1868). "Uber die Einwirkungen des Magneten auf die elektrischen Entladungen in verdünnten Gasen." ANN. PHYS. 103 (1858): 88–106, 151–7. Trans. by F. Guthrie: "On the action of the magnet upon the electrical discharge in rarefied gases." PHIL. MAG. 16 (Aug. 1858): 119–35. Article dated Bonn, Dec. 27, 1857, and Jan. 25, 1858. (27)

27 Plücker, J. "Fortgesetzte Beobachtung über die elektrische Entladung durch gasverdünnte Räume." ANN. PHYS. 104 (1858): 113–28, 622–30; 105 (1858): 67–84; 107 (1858): 77–113. Trans. by F. Guthrie: "Observations on the electrical discharge through rarefied gases." PHIL. MAG. 16 (Dec. 1858): 408–18. "Observations on the electric discharge; on the action of the magnet upon the electric current, from a new point of view." PHIL. MAG. 18 (July 1859): 1–7. "Observations on the electric discharge, on the spectra in highly rarefied gases of different kinds during the passage of the electric discharge." PHIL. MAG. 18 (July 1859): 7–20. Articles dated Bonn, Mar. 30, July 15, Aug. 25, 1858. Plate with 14 diagrams shows tubes and apparatus with 7 patterns of the striated discharge. Plücker noted how the glow discharge formed lines of light coincident with the lines of force from a magnet, fluorescence of the glass, various striae, the Faraday dark space, and the spectra of different gases. His experiments were made possible by highly evacuated glass tubes with sealed-in electrodes made by Geissler, who also invented an improved form of vacuum pump (28). See Fig. 4. (26, 30)

28 Geissler, Heinrich (1815–1879). UBER DAS GESCHICHTE ELEKTRISCHE LICHT. Berlin: W.H.T. Meyer, 1858. Pamphlet describing the mercurial vacuum pump which Geissler invented in 1855. (199)

29 Gassiot, J.P. "On the stratifications in electrical discharges, as observed in Torricellian and other vacua; second communication."

PHIL. TRANS. 149 (1859): 137–60. Paper read Jan. 13. 11 diags. (25, 34)

30 (Plücker, J.) "Abstract of a series of papers and notes concerning the electric discharge through rarefied gases and vapours." By Sir Benjamin C. Brodie. PROC. ROY. SOC. 10 (1859–1860): 256–69. Dated Dec. 6, 1859. 3 diags. (27)

31 Bonelli, Gaetano (1815–1867). "Apparatus for transmitting telegraphic dispatches." Br. 2383, Oct. 2, 1860, provisional. A facsimile system employing multiple brushes (combs) with multiwire connections between stations. (41)

32 Caselli, G. "Telegraphic apparatus, improvements in the construction of and mode of working telegraphic apparatus." Br. 2395, Sept. 25, 1861, Mar. 25, 1862. Filed by Alfred Vincent Newton, as agent. This patent discloses the instruments substantially as used in service in France during the 1860s. (23) Problems with synchronism, electrical interference on the lines, frequent illegibility of the reproductions, and the lack of commercial demand led to abandonment of the system. (37)

33 Toepler, August Joseph Ignaz (1836–1912). "Uber eine einfache Barometer-Luftpumpe ohne Hähne, Ventile, und schädlichen Raum" [About a simple barometer air pump without faucets, valves, and residual space]. POLYTECH. J. 163 (1862): 426. (199)

34 Gassiot, J.P. "Experimental investigations on the stratified appearance of electrical discharges. Effect obtained by varying the resistance." PROC. ROY. SOC. 12 (Dec. 11, 1862): 329–40. (29)

35 De la Rive, August Arthur (1801–1873). "Recherches sur les phénomènes qui caractérisent et accompagnent la propagation de l'électricité dans les fluides élastiques très raréfiés" [Researches on the phenomena which characterize and accompany the propagation of electricity in highly rarefied elastic fluids]. C.R. 56 (1863): 669–77. SMITH. INST. ANN. REP. for 1863 (1872): 169–92. From Mémoires de la Société de Physique et d'Historie Naturelle de Geneva, Vol. XVII, 1863. Other articles: C.R. 48 (1859): 1011–16; 54 (1862): 1171–5. (42)

36 Du Moncel, T.A.L. "Description des télégraphs électro-chemiques de Caselli et Bonelli." ANN. TELEGR. 6 (1863): 209–45. On Caselli's Pantelegraph and Bonelli's Typotelegraph. (31, 32). (22, 135)

37 Culley, Richard Spelman. "On printing telegraphs." POP. SCI. REV. 3 (1864): 293–303. Caselli's copying telegraph, with several specimens of facsimiles. (32)

38 König, Karl Rudolph (1832–1901). "Uber ein Mittel den wechselnden Dichtigkeitszustand der Luft in tönenden Orgelpfeifen sichtbar darzustellen" [About a means to make visible the changing state of density of the air in sounding organ pipes]. ANN. PHYS. 122 (1864): 242–5, 660. The change of flame intensity according to the change of pressure in a gas chamber—or manometric flame—was applied as a light modulator in numerous television schemes. (151, 204, 234)

39 Sprengel, Hermann Johann Philipp (1834–1906). "Researches on the vacuum." J. CHEM. SOC. 3 (1865): 9–21; also ANN. PHYS. 129 (1865): 564. Vacuum pumps designed by Geissler (28), Toepler (33), and Sprengel were the better-known kinds of many varieties developed during these years. (166, 199)

40 Bain, A. "Automatic telegraphy." J. SOC. ARTS 14 (1866): 138–46. Paper read Jan. 17. ENG. MECH. 2 (Feb. 9, 1866): 273, 274. Includes description of his copying telegraph of 1843. (11)

41 Bonelli, G. "Telegraphic printing apparatus." Br. 1504, May 29, 1866, provisional. Filed by Christine Temple Bowdoin, as agent. ENG. MECH. 2 (Mar. 16, 1866): 369. (31)

42 De la Rive, A.A. "Recherches sur la propagation de l'électricité dans les fluides élastiques très raréfiés et particulièrement sur les stratifications de la lumière électrique qui accompagnent cette propagation." ARCH. SCI. PHYS. NAT. 26 (1866): 177–208. "On the propagation of electricity in highly rar-

efied elastic fluids and in particular on the stratifications of the electric light in very rare media." PHIL. MAG. 33 (1867): 241–61. (35, 43)

43 De la Rive, A.A. "Recherches sur l'action qu'exerce le magnétisme sur les jets électriques qui se propagant dans les milieux gazeux très raréfiés." ARCH. SCI. PHYS. NAT. 27 (1866): 289–316. "On the action of magnetism upon the electric discharge in highly rarefied gaseous media." PHIL. MAG. 33 (1867): 512–30. (42, 47)

44 Becquerel, A.E. "Note sur la passage des courants électriques au travers des gaz incandescents" [Note on the passage of electric current through glowing gases]. C.R. 65 (1867): 1097–9. PHIL. MAG. 35 (1868): 319, 320. (20)

45 Hittorf, J.W. "Uber die Elektrizitätsleitung der Gase" [On the conduction of electricity by gases]. ANN. PHYS. 136 (Jan. 27, 1869): 1–31; (Mar. 2. 1869): 197–234. Experiments with cold electrodes in rarefied gases. A student and associate of Plücker (26, 27, 30) at the University of Bonn, Hittorf continued research with vacuum tubes containing cold and hot electrodes until the 1880s. He discovered how the cathode glow spread toward the anode, how solid objects placed near the cathode would cast shadows in the phosphorescent glow in the glass, and that this glow was produced by raylike emanations that traveled in straight lines from the cathode. (17, 125)

46 d'Arlincourt, Ludovic Charles Adrien Joseph Guyot. "Improvements in electric telegraphic apparatus." Br. 1920, June 23, Dec. 20, 1869. Filed by Alexander Melville Clark, as agent. An electrochemical facsimile telegraph system employing induction coils, and tuning forks for synchronous control. (107)

47 De la Rive, A.A., and Edouard Sarasin (1843–1890). "De l'action du magnétisme sur les gaz traversés par des décharges électriques" [On the action of magnetism on gas traversed by electrical discharge]. ARCH. SCI. PHYS. NAT. 41 (1871): 5–26. PHIL. MAG. 42 (1871): 211–23. (43, 49)

48 Varley, Cromwell Fleetwood (1828–1883). "Some experiments on the discharge of electricity through rarefied media and the atmosphere." PROC. ROY. SOC. 19 (1871): 236–42. Deflection of cathode rays by an electrostatic field. The rays consist of attenuated particles of metal projected from the cathode.

49 De la Rive, A.A., and E. Sarasin. "Sur la rotation sous l'influence magnétique de la décharge électrique dans les gaz raréfiés, et sur l'action mécanique que peut exercer cette décharge dans sou mouvement de rotation" [On the rotation under the magnetic influence of the electrical discharge in rarefied gases, and on the mechanical action which can achieve that discharge in its rotational movement]. ARCH. SCI. PHYS. NAT. 45 (1872): 387–407. (47)

50 Smith, Willoughby (1828–1891). "Effect of light on selenium during the passage of an electric current." NATURE 7 (Feb. 20, 1873): 303. Also AM. J. SCI. 5 (Jan.–June 1873): 301. "The action of light on selenium." J. SOC. TEL. ENGRS. 2 (1873): 31. Letter to Latimer Clark, vice-president of the Society, dated Feb. 4, read Feb. 12, announcing the discovery that the resistance of metallic selenium is decreased by illumination. This characteristic, of great importance in almost all proposals and systems for television from 1878 to the 1920s, was discovered during special tests set up for the purpose at the Greenwich Works of the Telegraph Construction and Maintenance Company. Smith was then the company's chief electrician; the tests were conducted under his direction by Joseph May, his chief assistant at the cable works and his colleague on many cable-laying expeditions. (68, 83, 228)

"Being desirous of obtaining a more suitable high resistance for use at the Shore Station in connection with my system of testing and signalling during the submersion of long submarine cables, I was induced to experiment with bars of selenium, a known metal of very high resistance. I obtained several bars varying in length from 5 to 10 centimetres, and of a diameter from 1 to 1 1/2 millimetres. Each bar was hermetically sealed in a glass tube, and a platinum wire projected from each end for the purpose of connection.

"The early experiments did not place the selenium in a very favorable light for the purpose required; for although the resistance was all that could be desired—some of the bars giving 1,400 meg-ohms absolute—yet there was a great discrepancy in the tests, and seldom did different operators obtain the same results. While investigating the cause of so great differences in the resistance of the bars, it was found that the resistance altered materially according to the intensity of light to which they were subjected. When the bars were fixed in a box with a sliding cover, so as to exclude all light, their resistance was at its highest, and remained constant, fulfilling all the conditions necessary to my requirements; but immediately the cover of the box was removed, the conductivity increased from 15 to 100 per cent, according to the intensity of the light falling on the bar. Merely intercepting the light by passing the hand before an ordinary gas-burner placed several feet from the bar increased the resistance from 15 to 20 per cent. If the light be intercepted by rock salt or by glass of various colours, the resistance varies according to the amount of light passing through the glass.

"To ensure that temperature was in no way affecting the experiments, one of the bars was placed in a trough of water so that there was about an inch of water for the light to pass through, but the results were the same; and when a strong light from the ignition of a narrow band of magnesium was held about nine inches above the water the resistance immediately fell more than two-thirds, returning to its normal condition immediately the light was extinguished."

51 Draper, Harry Napier. "Effect of light on the electric conductivity of selenium." NATURE 7 (Mar. 6, 1873): 340. Questions on Smith's letter. (50)

52 Smith, W. "Selenium." NATURE 7 (Mar. 13, 1873): 361. Letter on experiments with note on selenium, size of bars, etc. (50, 68)

53 Sale, M.L. "The action of light on the electrical resistance of selenium." PROC. ROY. SOC. 21 (May 8, 1873): 283–5; PHIL. MAG. 47 (1874): 216–8; ANN. PHYS. 150 (1873): 333–6; J. SOC. TEL. ENGRS. 2 (1873): 152–4. See also NATURE 7 (Mar. 6, 1873): 340; 8 (June 12, 1873): 134.

54 Draper, H.N., and Richard Jackson Moss (1847–1934). "On some forms of selenium, and on the influence of light on the electrical conductivity of this element." PROC. ROY. IRISH ACAD. 1 (Nov. 10, 1873): 529–33. (51, 61, 116)

55 Rosse, 4th Earl (Parsons, Sir Laurence, 1840–1908). "On the electrical resistance of selenium." PHIL. MAG. 47 (Mar. 1874): 161–4; J. SOC. TEL. ENGRS. 3 (1874): 356; AM. J. SCI. 7 (1874): 513.

56 Siemens, Ernst Werner (1816–1892). "Uber den Einfluss der Beleuchtung auf die Leitungsfähigkeit des krystallinischen Selens" [On the influence of illumination on the conductivity of crystalline selenium]. MONATSBER. AKAD. WISS. BERLIN (1875): 280–1. ANN. PHYS. 156 (1875): 344, 5; PHIL. MAG. 50 (Nov. 1875): 416. (64)

57 De la Rue, Warren (1815–1889), Hugo W. Müller, and William Spottiswoode (1825–1883). "Experiments to ascertain the cause of stratification in electrical discharges in vacuo." PROC. ROY. SOC. 23 (Apr. 8, 1875): 356–61; J. SOC. TEL. ENGRS. 4 (1875): 246–52; PHIL. MAG. 1 (1876): 239–44. Spottiswoode carried on separate researches (58); the others continued their joint investigations up to 1883. (80)

58 Spottiswoode, W. "Experiments on stratification in electrical discharges through rarefied gases." PROC. ROY. SOC. 23 (June 10, 1875): 455–62. These researches were continued up to 1882. (57, 72)

59 Adams, William Grylls (1836–1915). "The action of light on selenium." PROC. ROY. SOC. 23 (June 17, 1875): 535–9; PHIL. MAG. 1 (1876): 155–9; ANN. PHYS. 159 (1876): 622–9. (65)

60 Gordon, James Edward Henry (1852–1893). "Anomalous behaviour of selenium." NATURE 12 (July 8, 1875): 187. Letter on experiments at the Cavendish Laboratory, Cambridge. (128)

61 Moss, R.J. "Properties of selenium," NATURE 12 (Aug. 12, 1875): 291. Letter on experiments and results. (54, 116)

62 Kerr, John (1824–1907). "A new relation between electricity and light; dielectrified media birefringence." PHIL. MAG. 50 (Nov. 1875): 337–48; (Dec. 1875): 446–58. Announcement of discovery of electrostatic birefringence: an electric potential applied to certain dielectrics causes rotation of the plane of polarized light. In the practical form, or Kerr cell, a liquid dielectric such as bisulfide of carbon or nitrobenzol is placed between two parallel electrodes. This cell was introduced as a light valve or modulator in 1890 by Sutton (213) and was of considerable value in practical systems around 1930. (74)

63 W. (Correspondent in Germany). "Science in Germany." NATURE 13 (Dec. 9, 1875): 112. Note on E.W. Siemens' experiments with selenium.

64 Siemens, E.W. "Uber die Abhängigkeit der elektrischen Leitungsfähigkeit des Selens von Wärme und Licht" [On the dependency of electrical conductivity of selenium on heat and light]. MONATSBER. AKAD. WISS. BERLIN (1876): 95–116; (1877): 299–326. Also ANN. PHYS. 159 (1876): 117–41; (1877): 521–50. (56)

65 Adams, W.G. "On the action of light on tellurium and selenium." PROC. ROY. SOC. 24 (Jan. 6, 1876): 163, 164; NATURE 13 (Jan. 20, 1876): 238. Also ANN. PHYS. 159 (1876): 629–32. Details of experiments and results. (59, 69)

66 Bell, Alexander Graham (1847–1922). "Improvements in telegraphy." U.S. 174,465, Feb. 14, Mar. 7, 1876. This famous patent describes the method and apparatus for transmitting and receiving musical and vocal sounds by means of undulatory currents. Also Br. 4765, Dec. 9, 1876. (148) Bell's successful telephone, along with the sensitivity of selenium to light, promoted early ideas for seeing by electricity. Light modulators operated by telephones were favored in numerous plans for television receivers. (71)

67 Siemens, (Sir) Charles William (Carl Wilhelm) (1822–1883). "The action of light on selenium." PROC. ROY. INST. 8 (1876): 68–79. Paper read Feb. 18. Also NATURE 13 (Mar. 23, 1876): 407, 408. This report refers to the discovery of the light sensitivity of selenium as being "an observation made first by Mr. May, a telegraph clerk at Valentia...." William Siemens, the younger brother of Werner (56) immigrated to England at the age of twenty. (50, 68)

68 Smith, W. "Original communications, letter on the electrical conductivity of selenium." J. SOC. TEL. ENGRS. 5 (1876): 183, 184. Dated Mar. 3, read Mar. 8. This letter somewhat clarifies the original announcement. (52, 83)

"On February 4, 1873, I brought before the notice of the scientific world, through the Society of Telegraph Engineers, the effect which light has on the electrical conductivity of selenium. Since that time the subject has been investigated by several scientific gentlemen, and although nothing new has been brought forward it is satisfactory to find that they all confirm my statement that the phenomena are due solely to the action of light. The subject is now attracting the attention of scientific gentlemen of other countries, and I have had my attention drawn to several inaccuracies which have occurred in reported statements made by those gentlemen. I therefore think it be well if the Society to whom I first communicated what in time may prove a very important discovery will allow me to place on record a few particulars as regards the actual discovery of the action of light on selenium.

"While in charge of the electrical department of the laying of the cable from Valentia to Heart's Content in 1866 I introduced a new system by which ship and shore could communicate freely with each other during the laying of the cable without interfering with the necessary electrical tests. To work this system it was necessary that a resistance of about one hundred megohms should be attached to the shore-end of the conductor of the cable. The resistance which I first employed was composed of alternate sheets of tinfoil and gelatine, and, although they answered the purpose, still the resistance was not constant enough to be satisfactory. While searching for a more suitable material the high resistance of selenium was brought to my notice, but at the same time I was informed that it was doubtful whether it would answer my purpose as it was not constant in its resistance. I obtained several specimens of selenium and instructed Mr. May, my chief assistant at our works at Greenwich, to fit up the system we adopt on shore during the laying of cables, using selenium as the high resistance, and employ the spare members of the staff as though they were on shore duty and report to me on the subject. It was while these experiments were going on that it was noticed that the deflections varied according to the intensity of light falling on the selenium."

69 Adams, W.G. "The influence of light and heat on the electrical conductivity of selenium." NATURE 13 (Mar. 23, 1876): 419, 420. Lecture at the Physical Society, March 11. (65, 73)

70 Goldstein, Eugen (1850–1930). "Vorläufige Mittheilungen über elektrische Entladungen in verdünnten Gasen" [Preliminary notes on the electrical discharges in rarefied gases]. MONATSBER. AKAD. WISS. BERLIN (May 4, 1876): 279–95. Also PHIL. MAG. 4 (1877): 353–63. Goldstein carried out extensive experiments with vacuum tubes and introduced the term "cathode ray" in this paper. (189)

71 Bell, A.G. "Researches in telephony." PROC. AM. ACAD. 12 (1877): 1–10. Paper read May 10, 1876. This brief survey of telephonic phenomena includes some historical background, with 29 refs.

72 Spottiswoode, W. "On stratified discharges. II. Observations with a revolving mirror." PROC. ROY. SOC. 25 (1877): 73–82. Paper read May 18, 1876. Also "Experiments on striae with revolving mirror." PHIL. MAG. 3 (1877): 144–53. (58, 77)

73 Adams, W.G., and Richard Evan Day. "The action of light on selenium." PHIL. TRANS. 167 (1876): 313–49; PROC. ROY. SOC. 25 (1876): 113–17; PHIL. MAG. 3 (1877): 295–300. Paper read June 15, 1876. (69)

74 Kerr. J. "On the rotation of the plane of polarization by reflection from a magnetic pole." BR. ASSOC. REP. Abstract (1877): 40, 41. Paper read at the Glasgow meeting, Sept. 1876. This discovery, known as the Kerr effect, is related to the Faraday effect (13). A suggestion that the effect could be applied for a television system was made in 1880 by Ayrton and Perry (127). (62, 76)

75 (Bell, A.G.) "Bell's articulating telephone." ENGINEERING 22 (Dec. 22, 1876): 518, 519. An illustrated description. (71, 81)

76 Kerr, J. "On rotation of the plane of polarization by reflection from the pole of a magnet." PHIL. MAG. 3 (May 1877): 321–43. Full report of the original disclosure (74). (91)

77 Spottiswoode, W. "On stratified discharges. III. On a rapid contact breaker, and the phenomena of the flow." PROC. ROY. SOC. 25 (1877): 547–50; PHIL. MAG. 3 (1877): 535–8. (72, 78)

78 Spottiswoode, W. "On stratified discharges. IV. Stratified and unstratified forms of the jar-discharge." PHIL. MAG. 4 (1877): 231–4; PROC. ROY. SOC. 26 (1878): 90–3. (77, 79)

79 Spottiswoode, W. "Photographic image of stratified discharges." PROC. ROY. SOC. 26 (1877): 323. (78, 96)

80 De la Rue, W., and H.W. Müller. "Experimental researches on the electric discharge with the chloride of silver battery." PROC. ROY. SOC. 26 (Aug. 23, 1877): 519–23; PHIL. TRANS. 169 (1878): 55–121. This

series of papers contains a number of outstanding early photographs of striated discharges. (57, 97)

81 Bell, A.G. "Researches in electric telephony." J. SOC. TEL. ENGRS. 6 (1877): 385–416. Paper read Oct. 31. (75, 82)

82 Bell, A.G. "The telephone." J. SOC. ARTS 26 (1877): 17–24. Paper read Nov. 30. (81, 84)

83 Smith, W. "Selenium, its electrical qualities, and the effect of light thereon." J. SOC. TEL. ENGRS. 6 (Nov. 1877): 423–40. Also pamphlet, London: Hayman Bros. & Lilly, 1877. 21 pp. (68, 228)

84 Bell. A.G. "Societies and academies, Physical Society, Dec. 1." NATURE 17 (Dec. 13, 1877): 135. Report on meeting, and Bell telephone exhibit. (82, 126)

85 Edison, Thomas Alva (1847–1931). "Improvement in phonograph or speaking machine." U.S. 200,521, Dec. 24, 1877, Feb. 19, 1878. Metallic foil on a cylinder, "to record in permanent characters the human voice and other sounds, from which characters such sounds may be reproduced and rendered audible again at a future time." (86)

86 Edison, T.A.. "A wonderful invention, speech capable of indefinite repetition from automatic records." SCI. AM. 37 (Nov. 17, 1877): 304. "The talking phonograph." SCI. AM. 37 (Dec. 22, 1877): 384, 385. Engraving of the first cylinder machine. (85, 123)

87 Obach, Eugen Friedrich August (1852–1898). "Researches on selenium." J. SOC. TEL. ENGRS. 6 (1877): 498–506. (141)

CHAPTER 2

SEEING BY ELECTRICITY: 1878–1884

Researches on electricity in rarefied gases and selenium continued during the period 1878–1884. The work of Crookes (99), his lectures (120), and his bold views on the fourth state of matter, along with the researches and contrasting theories of Wiedemann (150) and his compatriots, prompted more intensive researches into the nature of cathode rays. Refinements in the design of vacuum pumps by Gimingham (99) and others provided the ever-lower pressures necessary for progress in this work.

Incandescent lamps by Edison (123) and by Joseph Wilson Swan (1828–1914), which appeared in 1879, were also dependent on high-vacuum techniques. Experiments with electricity in vacuum tubes, hitherto confined to the laboratory and lecture room, now had a practical end which also led to further discoveries with incandescent filaments. Conduction between a heated filament and an isolated cold electrode inserted in a lamp was observed by Edison in 1880 (183). This phenomenon, later known as the Edison effect, was further studied by the inventor and by Fleming (174), Elster and Geitel (178), Hittorf (184), and others.

Advances in the telegraph of present interest include the introduction of the phonic wheel by La Cour, his use of electromagnetic tuning forks for synchronous control (102), and the appearance of writing (autographic) telegraphy by Cowper (110), Dolbear (118), and others. The employment of selenium as a pickup element in a facsimile system was proposed by Perosino (112) and developed experimentally by Bidwell (155). Selenium and the autographic method were combined in a proposal for a facsimile system by Senlecq (106), which also incorporated a telephone receiver. Carey also was working on a facsimile system with selenium (115), and Middleton proposed a thermoelectric method (129).

One year after de Paiva's paper (88) on selenium and the electric telescope, Redmond described his experiments with a mosaic assembly (108). The dawning interest in seeing by electricity was stimulated by news (126) early in 1880 of an invention by Bell which was revealed several months later as the Photophone (137). A prophetic cartoon by Dumaurier (100), combined with the news of Bell's secret invention, spurred Ayrton and Perry to outline their mosaic schemes (127), one of which made use of the Kerr effect. This was in April 1880—a very good year indeed for the infant telectroscope.

Details of Carey's proposed instruments (133) that appeared in June were followed by Sawyer's plan (134) and his evaluation of the problems. Carey's proposals referred to facsimile methods, one with mosaics and one with a spiral scan, with the alternative suggestion of an incandescent mosaic for visual reproduction. Sawyer also suggested a spiral scan in a system employing an induction coil and a helically rotating spark gap. Near the end of the year Leblanc disclosed a range of ideas concerning the transmission of luminous images (145). His proposal to use vibrating mirrors for analyzing and recomposing an image in a back-and-forth linear scan reappeared in numerous later schemes. The idea of modulating light by a variable-aperture shutter operated by a telephone is another innovation that persisted in the art.

Early in 1881 Senlecq proposed another facsimile system (154) employing mosaics which included a suggestion for an incandescent receiver that would display a momentary luminous image. A falling slider, or linear distributor, scanned the selenium contacts and also operated another distributor in the receiver by pulses in a rudimentary form of synchronous control. Based on their alternative suggestions for an incandescent display, Senlecq and Carey have been regarded as early pioneers in the television art, though their proposals were basically for facsimile. Carey's mosaic scheme with incandescent filaments has commonly been taken as the first suggestion of its kind, credited by him in 1875, even though he did not publish any details until 1880. Senlecq, Carey, and Sawyer all claimed that their inventions dated from 1877; but the sequence of actual disclosures of schemes intended to display luminous images is Redmond in 1879, Ayrton and Perry, Carey, Sawyer, and Le-blanc in 1880, and Senlecq in 1881.

Lecture demonstrations by Ayrton and Perry (156, 160) in March 1881 were probably the first public exhibits of apparatus related to the transmission of luminous patterns. Redmond earlier had claimed some success with his private mosaic experiments. In 1881 Bidwell successfully demonstrated his facsimile apparatus (158). Later than year he exhibited a modified version (162) which employed a vertical scan with automatic flyback between closely spaced lines. Continuous scanning appears in the optical receiver proposal by Lucas (167), in which he describes a back-and-forth horizontal scan with flyback between frames from corner to corner. These techniques of line and frame flyback are the basics of continuous linear scanning methods which were later incorporated in practical systems.

Some vivid forecasts of the future applications of technology, including electricity and the telectroscope, came from Robida (180) during the 1880s. With the recent wonders of the telephone, electric light, and public power supplies in the larger cities, it seemed that anything was possible in the new electrical age—even distant sight along telegraph wires. The future even then was close at hand; after only six years from the tentative beginning, the first near-practicable scheme for an electric telescope was devised by Nipkow (181) at the end of 1883. His premier patent on television incorporated a modulator based on Faraday's magneto-optic effect combined with Nicol prisms. The most important part of this invention, however, is the spinning disk with a spiral of holes near the edge, a scanning device that was destined to become as universal as the selenium cell.

The future pattern of the art is apparent in the proposals of these formative years. Often considered as merely a conjectural period, the technical score is nevertheless impressive; among the electrical, mechanical, and optical solutions that were brought forward there exist the foundations of a new technology. Two basic approaches had been realized: the simple arrangements of mosaics with multiple connections and the more complex single-circuit system which required accurately synchronized scanning means for exploring and reconstituting the image.

Disadvantages of a multitude of wires were realized by Redmond and others, but the more desirable single-circuit system was beyond reach—despite some optimistic suppositions—since the prevailing level of technology did not offer practicable means for rapid synchronous control. Senlecq, however, introduced an alternative method with mosaics scanned by distributors for sequential transmission along a single wire. Synchronism between the stations was by the simultaneous transmission of pulses along another line. Like the Sawyer plan and one of Carey's, this proposal lacked the means of continuous viewing, since it was limited to a one-shot scan. It is interesting to note that this approach is the predecessor of modern television wherein photoelectric and electroluminescent mosaics are scanned by electron beams that also serve as distributors for sequential transmission of visual signals.

It is also interesting to see the varied backgrounds of the proponents. These range from technical specialists to their pupils: Ayrton, Perry, and Sawyer, electrical engineers; de Paiva, physics professor; Senlecq, lawyer; Carey, employee in a surveyor's office; Leblanc, Lucas, and Nipkow, students; and Redmond, a private experimenter. The technical features similarly cover a wide range. Borrowed from physical science and electrical engineering, and refined by the inventive touch, the elements of the various schemes include selenium and incandescent mosaics, electromagnetic shutters, telephone actuators, distributors, induction coils, Kerr reflecting pole pieces, light pipes, rotary spark displays, autographic mechanisms, variable-aperture shutters, vibrating mirrors, Nicol prisms, polarized light, Faraday effect, scanning disks, linear and spiral scans, line and frame flyback, continuous scan, pulse control, and even color TV.

This diversity of technical approaches is matched by the national origins of individuals mostly working alone in different countries, linked only by sporadic accounts in newspapers and journals. Contributions came from America, England, France, Germany, Ireland, and Portugal, a mixture of sources that presaged the international character that prevailed in future years.

TABLE 2 CHRONOLOGY: 1878–1884

Year	Person	Contribution
1878	de Paiva	Suggestion for electric telescope
	Hughes	Microphone
	Perosino	Phototelegraph
	Crookes	Cathode rays
	La Cour	Phonic wheel
1879	Senlecq	Phototelegraph
	Redmond	Mosaic experiments
	Cowper	Autographic telegraph
	Swan	Incandescent lamp
	Edison	Filament lamp patent
1880	Edison	First "Edison effect" experiment
	Ayrton, Perry	Visual mosaic receivers
	Carey	Mosaic system, visual receiver
	Sawyer	Single-circuit, spiral scan, spark receiver
	Bell	Photophone
	de Paiva	Booklet on electric telescope
	Leblanc	Vibrating mirror, linear scan, variable-aperture modulator, color suggestion
	Wiedemann	Cathode rays
1881	Senlecq	Double-circuit, distributor, pulse sync, one-shot scan, visual receiver
	Ayrton, Perry	Public demonstration of elemental system
	Bidwell	Phototelegraph, line flyback
1882	Lucas	Optical receiver, linear scan, frame flyback, screen projection
	La Cour	Phonic wheel and tuning fork sync
	Elster, Geitel	Conductivity of flames
1883	Fleming	Molecular radiation
	Edison	Electrical indicator patent
1884	Nipkow	Electric telescope patent, perforated disk
	Schuster	Cathode rays

BIBLIOGRAPHY: 1878–1884

88 de Paiva, Adriano (1847–1907). "A telephonia, a telegraphia e a telescopia." O INSTITUTO 25 (Mar. 1878): 414–21. University Press, Coimbra. Article dated Feb. 20. A Portuguese professor of physics at the Academia Polytechnica in Oporto, de Paiva compares the telegraph, telephone, and telescope. Considering selenium as a means for visual pickup and a galvanometer as an indicator, he advances ideas concerning an electric telescope, or telectroscope, as an instrument for long-distance vision over wires. (89)

89 (de Paiva, A.) "Other accounts of the electric telescope." COMMERCIO DA PORTUGUEZ, Oporto, Apr. 27, 1878; Oct. 4, 7, 1879.

LA NATURE, Aug. 23, 1879. LA EPOCA 31 (Sept. 27, 1879): 790. (88, 142)

90 Preece, (Sir) William Henry (1834–1913). "The phonograph." J. SOC. TEL. ENGRS. 7 (1878): 68–73. (139)

91 Kerr, J. "On reflection of polarized light from the equatorial surface of a magnet." PHIL. MAG. 5 (1878): 161–77. Further experiments on the rotation of the plane of polarization by magnetism. (76)

92 Sabine, Robert (1837–1884). "Some electrical experiments with crystalline selenium." PHIL. MAG. 5 (1878): 401–15. (93)

93 Sabine, R. "Action of light on a selenium (galvanic) element." NATURE 17 (Apr. 25, 1878): 512, 513. Report on experiments. (92)

94 Rayleigh, Lord (Strutt, John William, 1842–1919). "Societies and Academies, Physical Society, March 20." NATURE 18 (May 23, 1878): 111. Report of the Physical Society meeting and exhibition, with description of a phonic motor employed by Rayleigh to obtain uniform motion in acoustical experiments. (102)

95 Hughes, David Edward (1831–1900). " On the physical action of the microphone." PHIL. MAG. 6 (July 1878): 44–50. Read June 8. Reprinted in George Shiers, ed. THE TELEPHONE: AN HISTORICAL ANTHOLOGY. New York: Arno Press, 1977. "On the action of sonorous vibrations in varying the force of an electric current." PROC. ROY. SOC. 27 (May 9, 1878): 362–9.

96 Spottiswoode, W. "On stratified discharges. V. Discharge from a condenser of large capacity." PROC. ROY. SOC. 27 (1878): 60–2. (79, 113)

97 De la Rue, W. and H.W. Müller. "Experimental researches on the electric discharge with the chloride of silver battery. II. The discharge in exhausted tubes." PROC. ROY. SOC. 27 (1878): 374–81; PHIL. TRANS. 169 (1878): 155–241. (80, 117)

98 Dolbear, Amos Emerson (1837–1910). "Researches in telephony." PROC. AM. ACAD. 14 (1879): 77–91. Presented Nov. 13, 1878. Reprinted in George Shiers, ed. THE TELEPHONE: AN HISTORICAL ANTHOLOGY. New York: Arno Press, 1977.

99 Crookes, (Sir) William (1832–1919). "On the illumination of lines of molecular pressure, and the trajectory of molecules." PHIL. TRANS. 170 (Dec. 1878): 135–64. A classic paper, read Nov. 30. Also PROC. ROY. SOC. 28 (1879): 103–11; PHIL. MAG. 7 (1879): 57–64. In a series of brilliant experiments with vacuum tubes at low pressures (which extended the researches of Plücker, Hittorf, and Goldstein) Crookes examined the colored phosphorescence of the glass, the rectilinear projection of molecular shadows, the mechanical and thermal effects of projected molecules (cathode rays), and magnetic deflection, and he discovered an extended dark space, since known by his name. He advanced the theory of an ultra-gaseous, or fourth, state of matter, with reference to the long free path of molecules which exists in a highly exhausted tube. In this work he was assisted by Charles H. Gimingham, who improved the vacuum pump (199) and also made the intricate glasswork needed for the experiments. (114)

100 Dumaurier, George (Busson, Louis Palmella, 1834–1896). "Edison's Telephonoscope (transmits light as well as sound)." ALMANACK FOR 1879, PUNCH 75 (Dec. 9, 1878). Cartoon showing an elderly couple in their home in London watching a wide-view screen over the mantle displaying a view of their daughter talking to them by telephone on a tennis court in Ceylon. This prophetic illustration stimulated Ayrton and Perry to think about how seeing by electricity could be accomplished (127). (180)

101 Gray, Elisha (1835–1901). EXPERIMENTAL RESEARCHES IN ELECTRO-HARMONIC TELEGRAPHY AND TELEPHONY: 1867–1878. New York: Russell Bros., 1878. 96 pp., 40 illus.

102 La Cour, Poul (1846–1908). LA ROUE PHONIQUE. Copenhagen: K. Schoenberg; Paris: R. Nilson, 1878. 72 pp. La Cour in-

vented the phonic wheel (a synchronous motor operated by pulsating current), which he applied with the electromagnetic tuning fork for synchronous control in telegraph systems. (94, 170). Both components were important features in many proposals for telectroscopes (190, 213, 234) and in some electromechanical television systems. (103)

103 "La Cour's phonic wheel." ENG. MECH. 28 (Jan. 3, 1879): 410–411. 4 illus. (102, 170)

104 (Senlecq, Constantin.) (Article on the telectroscope.) LES MONDES 48 (Jan. 16, 1879): 90. (105)

105 (Senlecq, C.) "Notes." NATURE 19 (Jan. 23, 1879): 278. Brief note on Senlecq's facsimile system, from LES MONDES. (104, 106)

106 (Senlecq, C.) "The telectroscope." TIMES (Jan. 27, 1879): 4f. Description of Senlecq's plan for reproducing telegraphically the images obtained in a camera obscura. A lawyer in Ardres, near Calais, the inventor intended to explore the image with a piece of selenium, and to reproduce the picture with a black-lead pencil operated by a telephone receiver. The motions of the selenium and the pencil were vaguely supposed to be effected by "any system of autographic transmission." Also ENG. MECH. 28 (Jan. 31, 1879): 509; SCI. AM. 40 (Mar. 8, 1879): 143. Senlecq's second plan appeared early in 1881. (105)

107 d'Arlincourt, L. "Facsimile telegraph instruments." J. SOC. TEL. ENGRS. 8 (1879): 15. (46)

108 Redmond, Denis D. "An electric telescope." ENG. MECH. 28 (Feb. 7, 1879): 540. Letter describing experiments "with the object of transmitting a luminous image by electricity." Redmond, of Belmont Lodge, Sandford, Dublin, used a multiwire mosaic arrangement consisting of "a number of circuits, each containing selenium and platinum" and claimed some success. Realizing the drawback of many connecting wires, he also tried unsuccessfully to get results with a single circuit employing the principle of the copying telegraph. This is the earliest description in English of a plan for transmitting visual images. (131)

"To transmit light alone all that is required is a battery circuit with a piece of selenium introduced at the transmitting end, the resistance of which falling as it is exposed to light increased the strength of the current, and renders a piece of platinum incandescent at the receiving end thus reproducing the light at the distant station.

"By using a number of circuits, each containing selenium and platinum arranged at each end, just as the rods and cones are in the retina, the selenium end being exposed in a camera, I have succeeded in transmitting built-up images of very simple luminous objects.

"An attempt to reproduce images with a single circuit failed through the selenium requiring some time to recover its resistance. The principle adopted was that of the copying telegraph, namely, giving both the platinum and selenium a rapid synchronous movement of a complicated nature, so that every portion of the image of the lens should act on the circuit ten times in a second, in which case the image would be formed just as a rapidly-whirled stick forms a circle of fire. Though unsuccessful in the latter experiment, I do not despair of yet accomplishing my object, as I am at present on the track of a more suitable substance than selenium."

109 "Electric telescope." ENG. MECH. 28 (Feb. 21, 1879): 586. Letters by F.H. Glew and W. Morshed in response to Redmond's letter (108), in which both declare that they had similar ideas in mind. (132)

110 Cowper, Edward Alfred (1820–1893). "The writing telegraph." J. SOC. TEL. ENGRS. 8 (1879): 141–7. Paper read Feb. 26. An autographic system for the direct transmission of handwriting in which the coordinate motions of a pen are converted into variable currents for transmission over separate circuits. The same principle of autographic transmission, with automatic synchronous motion of the parts, was a basic feature in several plans for telectroscopes. (111)

111 "Cowper's writing telegraph." ENG. MECH. 28 (Mar. 7, 1879): 623, 624. An illustrated description from ENGINEERING. (110, 121)

112 Perosino, Carlo Mario. "Su d'un telefotografo ad un solo fils." REALE ACCAD. SCI. TORINO 14 (1879): 574–85. Mar. 1878. A cylinder facsimile system, like Bakewell's (15), with selenium as a pickup element instead of on-off contacts. (155)

113 Spottiswoode, W., and John Fletcher (Lord) Moulton (1844–1921). "On the sensitive state of electrical discharges through rarefied gases." PROC. ROY. SOC. 29 (1879): 21–4. April 2. First of a series of papers on these researches. Also PHIL. TRANS. 170 (1880): 165–229. (96, 149)

114 Crookes, W. "Contributions to molecular physics in high vacua; magnetic deflection of molecular trajectory; laws of magnetic rotation in high and low vacua; phosphorogenic properties of molecular discharge." PROC. ROY. SOC. 28 (1879): 477–82; PHIL. TRANS. 170 (1879): 641–62. Lecture at Royal Institution, Apr. 4. A noteworthy addition to his previous disclosure (99). (120)

115 (Carey, George R.) "The telectroscope." SCI. AM. 40 (May 17, 1879): 309. A short editorial note on the "invention of Mr. George R. Carey, of Boston, Mass.," referring to an electrochemical facsimile system. Most accounts of the origins of television credit Carey as being the first to propose a system in 1875, but this editorial preview is the first published notice of his work. (133, 249)

116 Draper, H.N., and R.J. Moss. "Report on the allotropism of selenium, and on the influence of light on the electrical conductivity of this element." TRANS. ROY. IRISH ACAD. 26 (1879): 231–48. Experiments on conductivity at different temperatures. (61)

117 De la Rue, W., and H.W. Müller. "The electric discharge with the chloride of silver battery." NATURE 20 (June 19, 1879): 174–8; (June 26,1879): 199–204, 21 diags., plate with 12 photos of the striated discharge. From PHIL. TRANS. 1878. (97, 119)

118 Dolbear, A.E. "Professor Dolbear's writing telegraph." ENG. MECH. 29 (June 27, 1879): 330. Diag. Report from NEW ENG. J. EDUC. An autographic system similar to Cowper's (110). (98)

119 De La Rue, W., and H.W. Müller. "Experimental researches on the electric discharge with the chloride of silver battery. III." PROC. ROY. SOC. 29 (1879): 281–90; 30 (1880): 563–72; PHIL. TRANS. 171 (1880): 65–116. Paper read Aug. 7. (117, 175)

120 Crookes, W. "On radiant matter." NATURE 20 (Aug. 28, 1879): 419–23; (Sept. 4, 1879): 436–40. 21 illus. A lecture at the Sheffield meeting of the British Association, Aug. 22. A popular demonstration of different vacuum tubes and the various effects of gaseous discharges. AM. J. SCI. 18 (Oct. 1879): 241–62. 15 illus. (114, 136)

121 "Cowper's writing telegraph." ENG. MECH. 30 (Sept. 12, 1879): 17. 2 diags. (111, 122)

122 W.B.B. "Cowper's writing telegraph." ENG. MECH. 30 (Dec. 12, 1879): 325, 326. Letter from Dunedin, New Zealand; a system similar to Cowper's. (121)

123 Edison, T.A. "Electric lamp." U.S. 223,898, Nov. 4, 1879, Jan. 27, 1880. Famous patent for an incandescent lamp with a carbon filament. (86, 124)

124 Fox, Marshall. "Edison's light." N.Y. HERALD (Dec. 21, 1879). First public announcement of the successful incandescent filament lamp. (123, 176)

125 Hittorf, J.W. "Uber die Elektrizitätsleitung der Gase" [On the conduction of electricity in gases]. ANN. PHYS. 7 (1879): 533–561. Experiments with cold electrodes in rarefied gases. (45, 179)

126 "Physical notes." NATURE 21 (Apr. 15, 1880): 576. On the rumor of a mysterious "telephote" or "diaphote" by rival American inventors (Hicks, Connelly, McTighe) re-

cently in the news. See N.Y.T. Feb. 25, Mar. 2, and LUM. ELECT. 2:140. Bell's sealed package is also noted. Bell and Charles Sumner Tainter (1854–1940) had started experiments on the Photophone in December 1879. Early in March 1880 they deposited a sealed box containing a model and an account of their work at the Smithsonian Institution. Particulars of the Photophone and its principles were not revealed until Bell gave his famous lecture at Boston in August 1880. Meanwhile, suppositions about the invention stimulated ideas on seeing by electricity. (84, 137)

127 Perry, John (1850–1920), and William Edward Ayrton (1847–1908). "Seeing by electricity." NATURE 21 (Apr. 22, 1880): 589; TIMES (Apr. 22, 1880): 13b; ELECT. 4 (Apr. 24, 1880): 268; ENG. MECH. 31 (Apr. 30, 1880): 177, 178. After referring to Bell's sealed package (126) and the cartoon in PUNCH (100), the writers propose two schemes employing mosaics and multiwire connections. One receiver would have apertures fitted with magnetically operated shutters, the other would use the Kerr effect (74), with polarized light reflected from the poles of magnet cores viewed through an optical analyzer. Well-known electrical engineers and educators, they rightly emphasized the "elaborate nature" and the "expensive character" of their plans. This letter did much to stimulate interest in the subject during succeeding months. (130)

128 Gordon, J.E.H. "Seeing by electricity." NATURE 21 (Apr. 29, 1880): 610. Critical comments on the Perry and Ayrton letter (127) with reference to the ineffectiveness of the Kerr effect with "little magnets" and tiny currents. (60, 127, 130)

129 "Seeing by telegraph." ENG. MECH. 31 (Apr. 30, 1880): 178. Report on a lecture by Henry Middleton before the Cambridge Philosophical Society, Mar. 8. Proposal for mosaic system employing thermopile elements, essentially facsimile.

130 Perry, J., and W.E. Ayrton. "Seeing by telegraphy." NATURE 22 (May 13, 1880): 31. This reply to Gordon's letter (128) contains the first suggestion of a solid-state electroluminescent receiver. "There must be some bodies, presumably of the sulphur selenium order, which, when properly employed, will convert a portion of the current energy into visible luminous vibrations, and may therefore be used as receivers in a sight telegraph." (127, 128, 156)

131 Redmond, D.D. "Seeing by telegraph." TIMES (May 13, 1880): 10d. Redmond calls attention to his earlier letter (108) and his apparatus: "I think this of interest to the public, as I have not patented it."

132 Bolton, H.E. "Seeing by electricity." ENG. MECH. 31 (May 14, 1880): 235. Reference to Redmond's original letter (108), with extracts. (109)

133 Carey, G.R. "Seeing by electricity." SCI. AM. 42 (June 5, 1880): 355; ENG. MECH. 31 (June 18, 1880): 345, 346; DESIGN AND WORK 8 (June 26, 1880): 569. 9 diags. Two proposed facsimile instruments, one multiwire mosaic and the other single wire with mechanisms for spiral scans. In an alternative multiwire receiver the recording points are replaced by "platinum or carbon points, covered with a glass cap," in an evacuated space, equivalent to a bank of incandescent filaments. (115) A virtual reprint of this article appeared in 1895 (249). (134)

134 Sawyer, William Edward. "Seeing by electricity." SCI. AM. 42 (June 12, 1880): 373. A reference to Carey's article is followed by a critical view of the overall problem: the slow reaction time of selenium and its low sensitivity, the need for a very large number of selenium points (10,000), and the problem of isochronism. "There is no likelihood of any plan of this kind ever being reduced to practice." Sawyer then proposes a system with a light pipe scanning a helix of selenium wire in a camera, with a similarly rotating spark gap actuated by an induction coil at the receiver. (133)

135 Du Moncel, T.A.L. "Le téléphote et le diaphote." LUM. ELECT. 2 (1880): 267, 268.

Mainly on Sawyer's article, with mention of Carey and Ayrton and Perry. See also 2 (June 15, 1880): 240. (36, 143)

136 Crookes, W. "Contributions to molecular physics in high vacua." NATURE 22 (June 3, 1880): 101–4; (June 10, 1880): 125–8. 15 illus. Extracts from PROC. ROY. SOC. lecture, Apr. 1879 (114). (120, 177)

137 Bell, A.G. "On the production and reproduction of sound by light." AM. J. SCI. 20 (Oct. 1880): 305–24. Paper read at the American Association meeting at Boston, Aug. 27. J. SOC. TEL. ENGRS. 9 (1880): 404–26; PROC. AM. ASSOC. 29 (1881): 115–36. Bell reveals the nature of his "secret" invention—the Photophone. (126, 138)

138 Bell, A.G. "Professor A.G Bell on selenium and the Photophone." ELECT. 5 (Sept. 18, 1880): 214, 215; (Sept. 25, 1880): 220, 221; (Oct. 2, 1880): 237. 10 illus. NATURE 22 (Sept. 23, 1880): 500–3; ENGINEERING 30 (1880): 240–2; 253, 254; 407–9; J. SOC. TEL. ENGRS. 9 (1880): 375–87. (137, 140)

139 Preece, W.H. "The Photophone and the conversion of radiant energy into sound." J. SOC. TEL. ENGRS. 9 (1880): 363–75. (90, 161)

140 (Bell, A.G.) "Other papers on the Photophone." E.T.Z. 1 (1880): 391–6; J. SOC. ARTS 28 (1880): 847, 848; 29 (1880): 60–2; C.R. 91 (1880–1881): 595–8; 726, 727; 929–31, 982; 82 (1880–1881): 409–12; 450, 451; 1224–7. (138, 146)

141 Obach, E.F.A. "Action of phosphorescent light on selenium." NATURE 22 (Sept. 23, 1880): 496, 497. (87)

142 de Paiva, A. LA TELESCOPIE ELECTRIQUE BASEE SUR L'EMPLOI DU SELENIUM [The electric telescope based on the use of selenium]. Oporto: A.J. da Sylva, 1880. 48 pp. The first publication of its kind on "television." (89)

143 Du Moncel, T.A.L. "La télescopie électrique." LUM. ELECT. 2 (1880): 398, 399. Review of de Paiva's booklet (142) with mention of earlier events (89). (135, 159)

144 A.T.F. "Selenium." NATURE 22 (Oct. 21, 1880): 585. On preparing thin transparent sheets of selenium capable of conducting electricity for camera pictures. Letter from London.

145 Leblanc, Maurice (1857–1923). "Etude sur la transmission électrique des impressions lumineuses" [Study on the electrical transmission of luminous impressions]. LUM. ELECT. 2 (1880): 477–81. Letter dated Nov. 2, 1880, Ecole Polytechnique, Paris. 11 diags. In this important article Leblanc surveys the problems and suggests how various devices and effects could be used for visual pickup, picture analysis, and light modulation. He considers the pressure of light, modulation of an arc, use of sparks, and the phosphorescent effect of cathode rays. A mirror vibrating on two axes at different rates, arranged to give a continuous linear back-and-forth scan, for analyzing and recomposing an image is his most well-known contribution. A variable-aperture-shutter modulator operated by a telephone is another original proposal that was embodied in several later schemes. He also considered color transmission and suggested the use of seven selenium cells separately connected to modulators operating in conjunction with lenses, prisms, and shutters.

146 "Bell's Photophone." NATURE 23 (Nov. 4, 1880): 15–9. 7 illus. (140, 148)

147 Bidwell, Shelford (1848–1909). "The Photophone." NATURE 23 (Nov. 18, 1880): 58, 59. Details of a selenium cell. (155)

148 Bell, A.G., and C.S. Tainter. U.S. 235,199; 235,496; 235,497; 235,590; 235,616, Dec. 1880. A few early patents (among many others) on Photophone apparatus applied for by one or both inventors. (146, 153)

149 Spottiswoode, W., and J.F. Moulton. "On the sensitive state of vacuum discharges. II." PROC. ROY. SOC. 30 (1880): 302–4; PHIL. TRANS. 171 (1881): 561–652. (113, 163)

150 Wiedemann, Eilhard Ernst Gustav (1852–1928). "Uber das thermische und optische

Verhalten von Gasen unter dem Einflusse elektrischer Entladungen" [On the thermal and optical behavior of gases under the influence of electrical discharges]. ANN. PHYS. 10 (1880): 202–57. Also PHIL. MAG. 10 (1880): 357–80, 407–27. Most German physicists, such as Wiedemann, Goldstein, and Hertz, subscribed to the wave theory of electric discharges in rarefied gases, in opposition to Crookes and others who held to the molecular or particle theory.

151 Jamieson, Andrew. "The history of selenium, and its action in the Bell Photophone, with description of a recently designed form." PROC. PHIL. SOC. GLASGOW 13 (1881): 109–21. Experiments with manometric flame apparatus shown at a meeting of the Society, Jan. 19. Also "Photophone experiments." NATURE 23 (Feb. 10, 1881): 354. 2 illus. (38)

152 Lodge, (Sir) Oliver Joseph (1851–1940). "The relation between electricity and light." NATURE 23 (Jan. 27, 1881): 302–4. Lecture at the London Institution, Dec. 16. "In conclusion I must just allude to what may very likely be the next striking popular discovery, viz., the transmission of light by electricity; I mean the transmission of such things as views and pictures by means of the electric wire. It has not yet been done, but it seems already theoretically possible, and it may very soon be practically accomplished." (243)

153 "Bell's Photophone." ELECT. 6 (Feb. 5, 1881): 136–8. 9 illus. (148)

154 (Senlecq, C.) "The telectroscope of Mons. Senlecq, of Ardres." ELECT. 6 (Feb. 5, 1881): 141, 142; ENG. MECH. 32 (Feb. 11, 1881): 534, 535. 5 diags. Entirely different from the earlier proposal (106), this mosaic facsimile system has a falling contact slider at the transmitter and a stepping selector switch at the receiver, with two line wires and ground return, for a one-shot scan. The suggestion is made that by using incandescent platinum wires at the receiver "a picture of a fugitive kind" can be obtained. A statement credits Senlecq with inventing the apparatus "in the early part of 1877." This is the first scheme employing a distributor as suggested by Bakewell (15) and the first to incorporate a positive form of pulse control. (165) The inventor patented an entirely different system in 1907. (354)

155 Bidwell, S. "Telephotography." NATURE 23 (Feb. 10, 1881): 344–6. 4 diags. Description of experiments with cylinder machines. This facsimile system, employing selenium instead of on-off contacts, though only experimental, was the prototype for phototelegraphic developments for forty years. (147, 157)

156 Ayrton, W.E., and J. Perry. "Seeing by electricity." NATURE 23 (Mar. 3, 1881): 423, 424. Report of a meeting and experiments at the Physical Society, Feb. 26. The authors demonstrated the principle of a single shutter, as in their earlier proposal (127). They also explained how "thirty or forty selenium cells on a revolving arm would enable them to transmit electrically a complete picture of even moving objects." (130, 160)

157 Bidwell, S. "Selenium and its applications to the Photophone and telephotography." PROC. ROY. INST. 9 (1881): 524–35; ENG. MECH. 33 (Apr. 22, 1881): 158, 159; (Apr. 29, 1881): 180, 181. 4 diags. Lecture at the Royal Institution, Mar. 11 (155, 158)

158 Bidwell, S. "On telegraphic photography." J. SOC. TEL. ENGRS. 10 (1881): 354–60. Meeting of the Society at University College, London, Apr. 11. Also NATURE 23 (Apr. 14, 1881): 563. On Bidwell's telephotographic machine: "Perhaps the most interesting experiment of the evening was the transmission of pictures of natural objects by telegraphy, the picture of a butterfly being most beautifully transmitted by means of a selenium plate." (157, 162)

159 Du Moncel, T.A.L. "La téléphotographie." LUM. ELECT. 3 (1881): 209–11. (143)

160 Perry J. "The future development of electrical appliances." ELECT. 6 (May 14, 1881): 339. Fifth part of a paper read to the Society of Arts, Mar. 24. Perry repeated the earlier

experiment (156) showing how a tube with a shutter could display modulated light representing a single square of a mosaic screen and produce an image "as a distinct picture in black, and grey, and white, just like a photograph." He also described how, with a number of rotating cells, "it would actually be possible to show at London, not merely an image of a girl at York, but an image of a girl skipping."

161 Preece, W.H. "Radiophony." ENGINEERING 32 (July 8, 1881): 29–33; J. SOC. TEL. ENGRS. 10 (1881): 212–28. On the Photophone. (139, 186)

162 Bidwell, S. "Telegraphic photography." ELECT. 7 (Oct. 1, 1881): 310. Diag. Paper read at the Paris meeting of the Society of Telegraph Engineers, Sept. 24. In this modified apparatus the transmitting cylinder is replaced by a box containing a peephole in front of a selenium cell. The box moved up and down through 2 in. and laterally in 1/64-in. steps, thereby providing a vertical scan with line-by-line flyback. Though only an experimental model, it was believed that if perfected, it would be possible to obtain monochromatic (brown-white) reproductions of natural objects, rather than artificial drawings, on the electrochemical receiver. (158, 173)

163 Spottiswoode, W., and J.F. Moulton. "On stratified discharges. VI. Shadows of striae." PROC. ROY. SOC. 32 (1881): 385–7. (149, 164)

164 Spottiswoode, W., and J.F. Moulton. "On stratified discharges. VII. Multiple radiations from the negative terminal." PROC. ROY. SOC. 32 (1881): 388–90. (163, 171)

165 Senlecq, C. LE TELECTROSCOPE. Saint-Omer: H. d'Homont, 1881. 28 pp. This booklet on the author's second scheme (154) was also published in Paris and London. (354)

166 Sprengel, H.J.P. SPRENGEL'S VACUUM PUMP, COMMONLY CALLED BUNSEN'S PUMP. London: E. & F.N. Spon, 1881. 12 pp. (39, 199)

167 Lucas, William (1863–1945). "The telectroscope, or 'seeing by electricity.'" ENG. MECH. 35 (Apr. 21, 1882): 151, 152. Suggestion for an optical receiver. Light from a local source is modulated by electromagnetically operated Nicol prisms (3) and deflected by separate movable prisms to cast a spot moving back and forth in a horizontal scan, with flyback from the bottom of the screen to the top left-hand corner. This plan, which is closely equivalent to a cathode-ray tube, contains the essentials needed to receive continuously moving images. (162, 205)

168 Soward, Alfred W. "Seeing by electricity." ENG. MECH. 35 (Apr. 28, 1882): 177. Reference to Lucas letter (167), and the one by Ayrton and Perry. (127)

169 Atkinson, Llewelyn Birchall (1863–1939). "The telectroscope." ENG. MECH. 35 (May 5, 1882): 194. Letter on the Lucas plan (167) pointing out that the inertia of the moving parts "would render it impracticable." Atkinson built some experimental apparatus this year but did not publish any details (20). (205)

170 La Cour, P. "Obtaining synchronous movements." Br. 4779, Oct. 7, 1882, Apr. 3, 1883. Communicated to Frederik Wolff of the International Patent Office, Copenhagen, Denmark, as agent. Application of phonic wheels and electromagnetic tuning forks in telegraph systems. (103)

171 Spottiswoode, W., and J.F. Moulton. "On the movement of gases in vacuum discharges." PROC. ROY. SOC. 33 (1882): 453–5. (164)

172 Elster, Johann Philipp Ludwig Julius (1854–1920), and Hans Friedrich Karl Geitel (1855–1923). "Uber die Elektrizität der Flamme" [On the electricity of flames]. ANN. PHYS. 16 (1882): 193–222. PHIL. MAG. 14 (1882): 161–84. The first of several reports on the unsymmetrical conductivity of flames. (178)

173 Bidwell, S. "The electrical resistance of selenium cells." PHIL. MAG. 15 (1883): 31–5. PROC. PHYS. SOC. 5 (1884): 167–72. (162, 188)

174 Fleming, (Sir) John Ambrose (1849–1945). "On a phenomenon of molecular radiation in incandescent lamps." PHIL. MAG. 16 (1883): 48, 49. PROC. PHYS. SOC. 5 (1884): 283–5. Report of May 26 on the shadow of a filament in the carbon deposit on the glass of used lamps. First of numerous papers on his researches that led to the invention of the two-electrode thermionic valve in 1904. (187)

175 De la Rue, W., and H.W. Müller. "Experimental researches on the electric discharge with the chloride of silver battery. VI." PROC. ROY. SOC. 35 (1883): 292–300; 36 (1884): 151–7. NATURE 28 (Aug. 16, 1883): 381–8. Abstract, 8 illus. (119)

176 Edison, T.A. "Electrical Indicator." U.S. 307,031, Nov. 15, 1883. Oct. 21, 1884. First patent for an electronic instrument, intended to indicate changes of supply voltage via a galvanometer in series with an Edison-effect lamp. (124, 183)

177 Crookes, W. "Societies and academies; recent discoveries in high vacua." NATURE 29 (Nov. 22, 1883): 95, 96. Lecture at the Western Microscopical Club, Nov. 5. (136, 218)

178 Elster, J., and H. Geitel. "Uber Elektrizitätserregung beim Contact von Gasen und glühenden Körpern" [On the excitation of electricity by the contact of gases and glowing bodies]. ANN. PHYS. 19 (1883): 588–624. (172, 185)

179 Hittorf, W. "Uber die Elektrizitätsleitung der Gase" [On the conduction of electricity in gases]. ANN. PHYS. 20 (1883): 705–55. Experiments with cold electrodes in rarefied gases. (125, 184)

180 Robida, Albert (1848–1926). LE VINGTIEME SIECLE. Paris: G. Decaux, 1883. 404 pp. LA VIE ELECTRIQUE (LE VINGTIEME SIECLE) [The life of electricity, the twentieth century]. Paris: Libraire Illustrée, 1892. 234 pp. In these and later editions, the noted French author and artist forecast life in the twentieth century in prose and line, including uses for the Telephonoscope. He foresaw the elimination of books and reading by phonograph recordings distributed over telephone lines, private study in the home via the telephone and the telectroscope, home entertainment with stage shows and dancing girls by the same audiovisual means, and a public booth with a telephone and an image screen. (100)

181 Nipkow, Paul Gottlieb (1860–1940). "Elektrisches Teleskop." Ger. 30,105, Jan. 6, 1884, Jan. 15, 1885. The spinning perforated disk for analyzing and recomposing an image was introduced in this premier television patent. Modulation of light at the receiver was by a light valve employing the Faraday magneto-optic effect (13), consisting of a block of flint glass placed inside a coil between two crossed Nicol prisms (3). This specification gives the first detailed description of a complete single-circuit system. The inventor, then a 23-year-old student of physics in Berlin, did not construct any apparatus and allowed the patent to lapse. First used again in 1890 by Sutton (213), Nipkow's disk was the favored scanning device in many schemes for more than forty years. (190) In 1933 Paul Nipkow was interviewed by Orrin E. Dunlap, Jr. N.Y.T. (Aug. 6, 1933):

"One raw winter evening I was cheered by receiving from the post-office the loan of a genuine Bell telephone for two hours. I lived in one room, which served as a living room, sleeping chamber, laboratory and workshop. The remarkable simplicity of the telephone astounded me. It gave me an idea and I constructed a microphone, using nails. It was successful in transmitting noises and words from one attic to another. This experience is what started me thinking about the problem of television. That puzzle stayed with me from then on, even during the lectures of Helmholtz and Slaby in Berlin. Thus a sort of mental training along this line was developed in me and finally, on Christmas Eve, 1883, the solution came to me!

"It was the general idea of television. And the details included the perforated spiral distribution disk. The mental experiment was a complete success. The ideas of the invention were automatically at hand, as all everyday ideas are. How sure I was of having made a discovery may be seen from the fact that, despite serious financial difficulties, I did not hesitate to spend the money needed to apply for a patent."

182 Schuster, Arthur (1851–1934). "Experiments on the discharge of electricity through gases. Sketch of a theory (Bakerian Lecture)." PROC. ROY. SOC. 37 (1884): 317–39, 495. Experiments at Owens College, University of Manchester, on ionization in rarefied gases and magnetic deflection of cathode rays. (197)

183 Houston, Edwin James (1847–1914). "Notes on phenomena in incandescent lamps." TRANS. AIEE 1 (Oct. 1884): 1–8. 3 diags. This paper, presented at the International Electrical Exhibition in Philadelphia, was the first to be printed in the TRANSACTIONS of the newly formed American Institute of Electrical Engineers. It is also the first technical paper dealing with Edison's experiments with different lamps containing an incandescent filament and added electrode to investigate what Edison called "electric carrying," later known as the Edison effect. Generally assigned to the year 1883, the first experiment on this phenomenon is recorded in an Edison notebook as Experiment No. 1, dated Feb. 13, 1880. (176, 186)

184 Hittorf, W. "Uber die Elektrizitätsleitung der Gase" [On the conduction of electricity in gases]. ANN. PHYS. 21 (1884): 90–139. Experiments with heated spiral filament and two cold electrodes. Conductivity increases with increase of filament temperature and with a lower gas pressure. (179)

185 Elster, J., and H. Geitel. "Uber die Elektrizität der Flamme" [On the electricity of flames]. ANN. PHYS. 22 (1884): 123–8. (178, 191)

CHAPTER 3

ERA OF TELECTROSCOPES: 1885–1900

The prolific years 1885–1900 are noteworthy for advances in electrophysics, particularly discharges in vacua, the electron theory, electron emission from heated elements, photoelectric phenomena, electromagnetic waves, and X rays. Continuing studies of electricity in rarefied gases revealed the particulate nature of cathode rays, which led to a clearer understanding of electricity and of the structure of matter. Highlights are the discoveries of X rays by Röntgen (254) in 1895 and of the electron by Thomson (266) in 1897. These successes arose from experimental and theoretical work centered on cathode rays carried out by others, notably Goldstein (193), Schuster (197), Hertz (229), Lenard (239), Fitzgerald (240), and Perrin (252), as well as Thomson's earlier investigations (237) and the theories of Stoney (223) and their contemporaries.

The rudimentary discharge tube—variously known as a Geissler tube, Hittorf tube, or Crookes tube—became a more refined piece of apparatus designed for studying electrostatic and magnetic effects on cathode rays. Another kind of cathode-ray tube appeared with Braun's invention of the indicator tube (263) in 1897. Intended for the visual study of alternating current, this new laboratory tool was a significant advance in oscillographic techniques, at that time limited to low-frequency electromechanical methods. The forerunner of electron-beam devices that today serve a vast range of uses for instrumentation and display, Braun's tube in its modern form is now as well known as the electric lamp and the telephone.

Further experiments on conduction with heated filaments in a vacuum were undertaken by Preece (186), Fleming (187), and Elster and Geitel (191). Fleming's work culminated in his development of the oscillation valve in 1904. Meanwhile, in 1889 the famous co-workers Elster and Geitel began a long series of studies on photoelectricity (207), following the discovery of the photoelectric effect by Hertz (196) and the experiments of Hallwachs (200). This new branch of physics, which attracted the attention of Stolëtov (208) and other investigators, was a fundamental advance in pure science and a key to the development of television as the phototube and the Braun tube became companions in the art early in the twentieth century.

Other events of current interest to be noted comprise a miscellany of scientific researches and technological innovations that are relevant in the history of television. The electromagnetic theory of light propounded by James Clerk Maxwell (1831–1879) in 1863 (published in 1864) formed the basis for the pioneer work of Hertz (195) and others (243) on electromagnetic waves, one of the practical results being the inception of wireless telegraphy by Marconi (258). Ramsay's discovery of neon (270) was to be of practical value in the development of glow tubes and their application in experimental television of later years. The recording disk by Berliner (198), Poulsen's magnetic recorder (281), and the beginning of cinematography are other pointers to future technologies that would play a part in television.

Though of little consequence compared with the impressive achievements of physical science already mentioned, the art of telectroscopy continued to advance on an expanded international base. Contributions came from twenty individuals in nine countries: America, Australia, England, France, Germany, Italy, Poland, Russia, and Sweden. Some isolated speculations on sending visual images over wires reveal a slowly growing interest in the subject. Interesting comments on the possibilities were made in an editorial (211) in 1890, a brilliant forecast of television in the future (236) appeared in 1893, and the period closed with another prophetic view (290) of long-distance transmission of sight and sound in the mid-twentieth century.

The technical scene radically changed during these years with the introduction of new scanning methods and proposals for screen projection, color reproduction, radio transmission, and recording.

Morse (235), Rabourdin (244), and Jenkins (245) retained the mosaic method, but the clear favorites were single-channel transmission and linear scanning. Bakhmet'yev (192) and a Swedish inventor (253) selected spiral scanning, and Szczepanik (262) introduced the zigzag scan. The mirror drum by Weiller (204), the lensed disk by Brillouin (219), slotted disks by Majorana (248), and Polumordvinov's slotted cylinders with color filters (285) are important additions to scanning techniques.

Nipkow's disk appears in the systems of Sutton (213), Le Pontois (234), Dussaud (271), and Vol'fke (276). Two vibrating mirrors for scanning were adopted by Szczepanik. Both Weiller and Le Pontois employed manometric modulators, but the most significant innovation for light control is the Kerr-cell modulator in Sutton's plan. Variable-aperture control appears in the proposals of Brillouin, Blondin (233), and Dussaud.

In addition to the inventions that belong solely to television, such as scanners and modulators, some ideas from current technology as well as older ones were put to use by the proponents. Examples of well-known devices in their schemes are induction coils or transformers (Sutton, Morse, Szczepanik, Dussaud, Vol'fke), shutters (Blondin, Rabourdin), and phonic wheels and tuning forks, introduced by Nipkow (190) and used by Sutton and Le Pontois. The rise of electrical engineering from the early 1880s had an influence in some of the proposals; for example, the pulsating-current drive and synchronizing circuit of Le Pontois, Jenkins' dynamo power source, and the arc lamp by Dussaud. The advent of cinematography during the mid-1890s similarly influenced Dussaud's use of a camera assembly and a magic lantern for screen projection, and Lardeur's arrangement for transmitting pictures from transparencies. Adaptations of the old and the new are also represented by Vol'fke's gas tube modulator, his radio transmission, and Lardeur's phonographic method for signal storage and playback.

During the final years of the century a burst of publicity (273) brought the telectroscope into the news, largely as a result of the promotional efforts by and on behalf of Szczepanik. Even Mark Twain (274) supported the young inventor with a few paragraphs. There were optimistic plans for displaying Szczepanik's apparatus and that of Dussaud at the Paris Exposition in 1900, but they never materialized. The topic was of sufficient interest by now, however, for a report to be given to a meeting of the International Electricity Congress at the Exposition on August 24, in which the term "télévision" was introduced in a survey of various proposals (288). The world now had a new and permanent name for the art of seeing by electricity, even though no practicable telectroscopes had yet been demonstrated.

TABLE 3 CHRONOLOGY: 1885–1900

1885	Bakhmet'yev	Telephotograph, single circuit, spiral scan
1886	Goldstein	Canal rays
1887	Hertz	Electromagnetic waves, photoelectric effect
	Berliner	Gramophone
1888	Hallwachs	Photoelectric effect
1889	Weiller	Phoroscope, mirror drum, telephone/manometric modulator
	Elster, Geitel	Phototube
	Stolëtov	Photoelectric effect
1890	Sutton	Telephane, Nipkow disk, Kerr cell, phonic wheel, tuning fork
1891	Brillouin	Lens disk, variable-aperture modulator, picture analysis
	Liesegang	Matrix system
1892	Hertz	Cathode rays, thin metallic film

Table continued on next page.

TABLE 3 (continued)

Year	Name	Description
1893	Blondin	Téléphote, mirror wheel, shutter modulator
	Le Pontois	Telectroscope, Nipkow disk, manometric modulator, phonic wheel, tuning fork
	Morse	Multicircuit mosaic, high voltage
1894	Amstutz	Phonoscope, apertured cylinders, two-way
	Lenard	Cathode rays, thin metallic film
	Rabourdin	Mosaic shutter receiver
	Jenkins	Mosaic system, multifilament receiver
	Stoney	"Electron"
	Majorana	Slotted disk scanner
1895	Perrin	Cathode rays, negative charges
	Swedish	Telephotograph, single-circuit, spiral scan
	Röntgen	Discovery of X rays
1896	Fleming	Edison-effect experiments, unilateral conductivity
	Marconi	Wireless telegraph patent
1897	Szczepanik	Telectroscope, vibrating mirrors, zigzag scan
	Braun	Cathode-ray oscilloscope
	Thomson	Discovery of the electron
1898	Ramsay, Travers	Discovery of neon
	Dussaud	Téléoscope, Nipkow disk, shutter modulator, screen projection
	Lardeur	Slotted disks, diaphragm receiver, phonograph recording
	Vol'fke	Nipkow disk, radio transmission, Geissler tube receiver
	Schöffler	Electric television
	Poulsen	Magnetic recording
1899	Polumordvinov	Slotted disks, concentric cylinders, color filters
1900	Perskyi	"Television"

BIBLIOGRAPHY: 1885–1900

186 Preece, W.H. "On a peculiar behaviour of glow-lamps when raised to high incandescence." PROC. ROY. SOC. 38 (Mar. 1885): 219–30. ELECT. 14 (Apr. 4, 1885): 436–8. 5 diags. Tables of 8 experiments. Discussion of the conduction between a glowing filament and a positively charged electrode inserted in lamps of different shapes, as discovered by Edison in 1880, and here named the "Edison effect," and of the "blue glow" produced by ionization of the residual gas at higher voltages. (161, 183)

187 Fleming, J.A. "On molecular shadows in incandescent lamps." PHIL. MAG. 20 (1885): 141–4. PROC. PHYS. SOC. 7 (1886): 178–81. Paper read June 27. (174, 209)

188 Bidwell, S. "On the sensitiveness of selenium to light, and the development of a similar property in sulphur." PHIL. MAG. 20 (Aug. 1885): 178–91; ELECT. 15 (Sept. 18, 1885): 356–9. PROC. PHYS. SOC. 7 (1886): 129–45. Paper read at the British Association meeting at Aberdeen. (173, 350)

189 Goldstein, E. "Uber elektrische Leitung im Vakuum" [On electric conduction in vacu-

um]. ANN. PHYS. 24 (1885): 79–92. (70, 193)

190 Nipkow, P. "Der Telephotograph und des elektrische Teleskop." E.T.Z. 6 (1885): 419–25. Proposal for phonic wheel and tuning fork control (102). (181, 632)

191 Elster, J., and H. Geitel. "Uber die unipolare Leitung erhitzer Gase" [On the unipolar conductivity of heated gases]. ANN. PHYS. 26 (1885): 1–9. (185, 194)

192 Bakhmet'yev, P.I. (The new telephotograph.) ELEKTRICHESTVO No. 1 (1885). Proposal for a single-channel television system with single selenium cell, single light source, and spiral scan. According to Gorokhov, this proposal originated earlier in the de Paiva-Senlecq period.

193 Goldstein, E. "Uber eine noch nicht untersuchte Strahlungsform an der Kathode inducirter Entladungen" [About a not yet investigated radiation caused by induced discharges at the cathode]. SITZUNGBER. PREUSS. AKAD. WISS. BERLIN 2 (July 29, 1886): 691–9. ANN. PHYS. 64 (1886): 38–48. Discovery of faintly luminous rays that passed through a perforated cathode; called Kanalstrahlen (channel, or canal, rays), composed of positive ions. (189)

194 Elster, J., and H. Geitel. "Uber die Elektrisierung der Gase durch glühende Körper" [On the electrification of gases by glowing bodies]. ANN. PHYS. 31 (1887): 109–26. (191, 203)

195 Hertz, Heinrich Rudolf (1857–1894). "Uber sehr schnelle elektrische Schwingungen" [About very fast electrical oscillations]. ANN. PHYS. 31 (1887): 421–48, 543, 544. Includes the first observation of the photoelectric effect of one spark discharge upon another. (196)

196 Hertz, H.R. "Uber einen Einfluss des ultravioletten Lichtes auf die elektrische Entladung" [On the influence of ultraviolet light upon the electric discharges]. ANN. PHYS. 31 (June 1887): 983–1000. The beginning of research on photoelectric phenomena. (195, 201)

197 Schuster, A. "Experiments on the discharge of electricity through gases." ELECT. 19 (Sept. 2, 1887): 352, 355. Second paper with same title, PROC. ROY. SOC. 42 (1887): 371–9. On the general theory of electric discharges and ionization in rarefied gases, this paper was read at the British Association meeting at Manchester. (182, 212)

198 Berliner, Emile (1851–1929). "Gramophone." U.S. 372,786, May 4, Sept. 26, Nov. 8, 1887. This specification covers the lateral cut method of recording. Style cuts groove in lampblack, which is then fixed with varnish. Permanent records are then made from the master by photoengraving.

199 Thompson, Silvanus Phillips (1851–1916). "The development of the mercurial air pump." TELEG. J. & ELECT. REV. 21 (Dec. 2, 1887): 556–9; (Dec. 9, 1887): 587–90; (Dec. 16, 1887): 610–3; (Dec. 23, 1887): 632–4; (Dec. 30, 1887): 659–65. 36 illus. 104 refs. This important historical paper was read before the Royal Society of Arts, Nov. 23. (202)

200 Hallwachs, Wilhelm Ludwig Franz (1859–1922). "Uber den Einfluss des Lichtes auf Elektrostatisch Geladene Körper" [About the influence of light on electrostatically charged bodies]. ANN. PHYS. 33 (Jan. 1888) 301–12. On the electrification of metal plates by irradiation with electrical light. PHIL. MAG. 26 (July 1888): 78–80. Discharge of electricity by ultraviolet light.

201 (Hertz, H.R.) "Our electrical column." NATURE 37 (Feb. 9, 1888): 355. Note on experiments on the effect of ultraviolet light on spark discharges. (196, 229)

202 Thompson, S.P. THE DEVELOPMENT OF THE MERCURIAL AIR PUMP. London: E. & F.N. Spon, 1888. 37 pp. Reprint of the article (199) with additions.

203 Elster, J., and H. Geitel. "Uber die Elektrizitätserregung beim Contact verdünnter Gase mit galvanische glühenden Drähten" [On the excitation of electricity by the contact of rarefied gases with galvanically glowing

wires]. ANN. PHYS. 37 (Mar. 1889): 315–29. (194, 206)

204 Weiller, Jean Lazare. "Sur la vision à distance par l'électricité." GENIE CIVIL 15 (1889): 570–3; LUM. ELECT. 34 (1889): 334–6. In this plan for a Phoroscope, the inventor introduced the mirror drum as a new scanning device, and a telephone-operated manometric flame (38) as a light modulator. The circuit includes one line for visual signals, and one line for speed regulation or synchronism of the rotating mirror wheels, with ground returns for both circuits. The mirror drum was featured in several practical systems around 1930. As revealed much later, Atkinson in 1882 had built some experimental apparatus with mirror drums and a manometric flame modulator. (205)

205 Atkinson, L.B. (Note on seeing to a distance by electricity.) TELEG. J. & ELECT. REV. 25 (Dec. 13, 1889): 683. Reference to the Lucas plan (167) of 1882. (169, 204, 1804)

206 Elster, J., and H. Geitel. "Einige Demonstrationversuche zum Nachweis einseitiger Elektrizitätsbewegung in verdünnten Gasen bei Anwendung glühender Elektroden" [Some demonstrations to show unilateral conductivity of electricity in rarefied gases by application of glowing electrodes]. ANN. PHYS. 38 (1889): 27–39, 676. (203, 207)

207 Elster, J., and H. Geitel. "Notiz über die Zerstreuung der negativen Elektrizität durch das Sonnen- und Tageslicht" [On the dissipation of negative electricity by sun- and daylight]. ANN. PHYS. 38 (1889): 40, 41; also 497–514. The first of a long series of papers by this noted team on their researches into photoelectric phenomena. (206, 214)

208 Stolětov, Aleksandr Grigorjevic (1839–1896). (Actino-electrical investigations.) J. RUSS. PHYS. CHEM. SOC. 21 (1889): 159–206; PHIL. MAG. 30 (1890): 436–8. "Sur les phénomènes actino-électriques." C.R. 108 (1889): 1241–3. See also C.R. 106 (1888): 1593.

209 Fleming, J.A. "On electric discharge between electrodes at different temperatures in air and in high vacua." PROC. ROY. SOC. 47 (Jan. 9, 1890): 118–26. (187, 210)

210 Fleming, J.A. "Problems in the physics of an electric lamp." PROC. ROY. INST. 13 (Feb. 14, 1890): 34–49. 17 diags. Thorough examination of the Edison effect, or unilateral conductivity, with a variety of tube and electrode geometries. Fleming gives credit to the prior work of Hittorf, Goldstein, Preece, and Elster and Geitel. Referring to the experiments and brief expositions given in the lecture, he believes the subject field "is a region abounding in interesting facts and problems in molecular physics." ELECT. 24 (Feb. 21, 1890): 393–5; (Feb. 28, 1890): 417–20; correction note p. 413; SCI. AM. SUPP. 30 (Aug. 23, 1890): 12204–6. (209, 220)

211 "Seeing by electricity." ELECT. 24 (Mar. 7, 1890): 448–50. Editorial discussion of the problems of and possibilities for sending visual images over wires. A multiwire mosaic system is called a "gigantic electric eye" and is dismissed as a possible solution to the question, "Shall we ever see by electricity?" Prophetically, two statements refer to the conception of new means for photoelectric pickup and for optical display. "Perhaps one day some sort of electro-optic action may be discovered," and "It is possible to conceive of some as yet uninvented glow lamp of extraordinary delicacy that may serve the purpose." The Elster and Geitel phototube (215) was introduced that year, and the Braun tube (263) came along in 1897. But the writer concluded, "There is more hope of seeing through the proverbial brick wall than of seeing through a copper wire."

212 Schuster, A. "The discharge of electricity through gases." NATURE 42 (Oct. 16, 1890): 591, 592. PROC. ROY. SOC. 47 (1890): 526–59. Preliminary communication (Bakerian Lecture). (197)

213 Sutton, Henry. "Tele-Photography." TELEG. J. & ELECT. REV. 27 (Nov. 7, 1890): 549–51. This Australian plan for a Telephane, as Sutton called it, employs Nipkow

disks (181), and a Kerr cell (62) as a light valve at the receiver. A transformer in the selenium cell circuit furnishes the high voltage required to operate the Kerr cell. Phonic wheels and tuning forks are provided for synchronous control (102). The inventor declared that with the exception of the disks, "the whole design is original and was devised at Ballarat, Victoria." Like the mirror drum, the Kerr cell came into favor around 1930. This article was reprinted in 1910 (391). See also LUM. ELECT. 38 (1890): 538; SCI. AM. SUPP. 31 (1891): 12645.

214 Elster, J., and H. Geitel. "Uber einen hemmenden Einfluss der Belichtung auf elektrische Funken- und Büschelentladungen" [About an impending influence of illumination on electric spark and brush discharge]. ANN. PHYS. 39 (1890): 332–5. (207, 215)

215 Elster, J., and H. Geitel. "Uber die Verwendung des Natriumamalgames zu Lichtelektrischen Versuchen" [On the use of sodium amalgam in photoelectric experiments]. ANN. PHYS. 41 (1890): 161–5. Description of first phototube constructed in 1889. (214, 216)

216 Elster, J., and H. Geitel. "Uber den hemmenden Einfluss des Magnetismus auf Lichtelektrische Entladungen in verdünnten Gasen" [About the impending influence of magnetism on photoelectric discharge in rarefied gases]. ANN. PHYS. 41 (1890): 166–76. (215, 225)

217 Stephan, Walther. "Elektrischer Fernseher" [Electric television]. E.T.Z. 11 (1890): 260, 261, 308. (333)

218 Crookes, W. "Electricity in transitu; from plenum to vacuum (Inaugural address)." J. IEE 20 (1891): 4–49; ELECT. 26 (Jan. 16, 1891): 323–7; (Jan. 23, 1891): 354–60; (Jan. 30, 1891): 382–92. 30 illus. Crookes reviews his earlier work on electricity in rarefied gases. (177)

219 Brillouin, Louis Marcel (1854–1948). "La photographie des objets à très grande distance" [The photography of objects at a very great distance]. REV. GEN. SCI. 2 (Jan. 30, 1891): 33–8. Suggestions include a new kind of scanner consisting of two lensed disks rotating at very different speeds, and a variable-aperture control employing a mirror galvanometer for modulating light at the receiver. One important feature is the analysis of picture definition in comparison with the half-tone printing process. Brillouin concluded that about one-quarter million picture points per square inch would be necessary for acceptable reproduction. Lensed disks appeared in numerous proposals after 1920. See also LUM. ELECT. 48 (1893): 264.

220 Fleming, J.A. "The historical development of the induction coil and transformer." ELECT. 26 (Jan. 30, 1891): 396, 397; (Feb. 6, 1891): 416, 417; 27 (June 26, 1891): 211–3; (July 3, 1891): 246–8; (July 17, 1891): 300–2; (July 31,1891): 359–61; (Aug. 21, 1891): 433–5. (4, 5, 7, 21, 22) (210, 257)

221 Liesegang, Raphael Eduard. BEITRAGE ZUM PROBLEM DES ELEKTRISCHEN FERNSEHENS [Contributions to the problem of electric television]. Düsseldorf: E. Liesegang, 1891. x + 130 pp. Introduction of the word "Fernsehen."

222 "Transmission of images, seeing, and photographing by telegraph." BR. J. PHOTOG. 38 (Apr. 10, 1891): 226, 227; (Apr. 17, 1891): 242, 243; (May 1, 1891): 273–5. General discussion of photosensitive discoveries, methods, and devices centered on Liesegang's book (221) with mention of his matrix connections for reducing the number of line wires between stations.

223 Stoney, George Johnstone (1826–1911). "On the cause of double lines and of equidistant satellites in the spectra of gases." SCI. TRANS. ROY. DUBLIN SOC. 4 (July 1891): 563–608. The word "electron" is suggested as a name for the natural unit of electricity. "A charge of this amount is associated in the chemical atom with each bond. There may accordingly be several such charges in one chemical atom, and there appear to be at least two in each atom. These charges, which it will be convenient to call electrons, cannot be removed from the atom;

but they become disguised when atoms chemically unite." See also PHIL. MAG. 33 (1891): 503–16. (247)

224 Thomson, (Sir) Joseph John (1856–1940). "On the discharge of electricity through exhausted tubes without electrodes." PHIL. MAG. 32 (Oct. 1891): 321–36; (Nov. 1891): 445–64. SMITH. INST. ANN. REP. for 1892 (1893): 229–54. (237)

225 Elster, J., and H. Geitel. "Notiz über eine neue Form der Apparate zur Demonstration der Lichtelektrischen Entladung durch Tageslichte" [Notice about a new form of apparatus for demonstrating photoelectric discharge by means of daylight]. ANN. PHYS. 42 (1891): 564–7.

226 Elster, J., and H. Geitel. "Uber die Abhängigkeit der durch das Licht bewirkten Elektrizitäts-zerstreuung von der Natur der belichteten Oberfläche" [On the dependence of the discharging action of light on the nature of the illuminated surface]. ANN. PHYS. 43 (1891): 225–40. Tests with various metals.

227 Elster, J., and H. Geitel. "Uber die durch Sonnenlichte bewirkte elektrische Zerstreuung von mineralischen Oberflächen" [On the dissipation of electric charge from mineral surfaces by sunlight]. ANN. PHYS. 44 (1891): 722–36. (226, 230)

228 Smith, W. THE RISE AND EXTENSION OF SUBMARINE TELEGRAPHY. London: J.S. Virtue, 1891. Reprint, New York: Arno Press, 1974. xii + 390 pp., illus. Largely autobiographical, with details of various cables, cable developments, and accounts of many cable-laying expeditions around the world. Includes mention of the discovery of the photosensitive property of selenium. (83)

229 Hertz, H. "Uber den Durchgang der Kathodenstrahlen durch dünne Metallschichten." ANN. PHYS. 45 (1892): 28–32. "On the passage of cathode rays through thin metallic films." ELECT. 32 (Apr. 27, 1894): 722, 723. (201, 239)

230 Elster, J., and H. Geitel. "Lichtelektrische Versuche" [Photoelectric experiments]. ANN. PHYS. 46 (1892): 281–91. Alkali metal cathodes in vacuum tubes, photoelectric discharge in a magnetic field, measurement of current in potassium cells. (227, 231)

231 Elster, J., and H. Geitel. "Beobachtungen des atmosphärischen Potentialgefälles und der ultravioletten Sonnenstrahlung" [Experiments on the gradient of atmospheric potential and ultraviolet solar radiation]. ANN. PHYS. 48 (1892): 338–73. (230, 232)

232 Elster, J., and H. Geitel. "Uber die Vergleichung von Lichtstärken auf photoelektrischen Wege" [On the photoelectric comparison of light intensities]. ANN. PHYS. 48 (1893): 625–35. (231, 242)

233 Blondin, Jules. "Le téléphote." LUM. ELECT. 48 (1893): 259–66. Proposal incorporating a mirror wheel, electromagnetic mirror, and shutter modulator.

234 Le Pontois, Leon. "The telectroscope." SCI. AM. SUPP. 35 (June 10, 1893): 14546, 14547. 3 diags. This apparatus for transmitting "pictures or views of moving or stationary objects at great distances" was described to the Pittsburgh Electric Club. It incorporated scanning disks, pulsating-current motor drive with tuning for control (102), and an involved manometric flame (38) modulator comprising relays and pressure chambers supplied with oxygen and hydrogen. The selenium cell, designed to react to heat as well as light, was protected by a cooling system, but the unfortunate subject was simply flooded with "hot light."

235 Morse, George H. "Seeing by electricity." ENG. MECH. 58 (Nov. 10, 1893): 258, 259, from ELECT. W. In this extraordinary mosaic system, selenium surfaces formed on the ends of a cable were enclosed in evacuated glass cylinders containing wire or mesh electrodes in front of the selenium. Operated by an induction coil, the high voltage would produce a phosphorescent glow at the receiver. The cylinders, identical except for a lens or an eyepiece, were connected by "many thousands of small insulated wires."

Morse believed this arrangement "would appear to be a practical form." (1836)

236 Munro, John. THE ROMANCE OF ELECTRICITY. London: Religious Tract Society, 1893. 320 pp., illus. Chapter 14, "Electricity in the future," pp. 300–1, contains a vivid picture of television in the years to come:

"There is also some prospect of a "telephote," as it is called in advance, that is to say, an instrument for transmitting light by wire, as the telephone transmits sound. It is becoming, however, to speak with all reserve of this hypothetical invention. A number of crude experiments have already been made in this direction; but as yet they are hopelessly defective. Still, if we bear in mind how much has been achieved in the past, and consider that light and electricity are forms of energy which are intimately related and mutually convertible, we may be justified in entertaining hopes that some day a means will be found of transforming a luminous image into electricity, and after transmitting that to a distance, reproducing the original image. If this is done, there will be little or no need of the magic lantern and the photograph, since a speaker by telephone will be rendered visible by an auxiliary telephone.

"Lovers will be able to see each other, while conversing at a distance. Doctors will examine their patient's tongues in another town. The drama will be 'switched on' to private houses; and on Sundays and holidays even the poor will be able to enjoy a visual trip to wherever their fancy may incline. In hot weather a man will be able to refresh himself with a glimpse of the Alpine glaciers, or the icebergs of the Arctic Circle, and in the rigours of a north-east wind he may taste the pleasures of imagination, by gloating over the palms and orchids of the tropics. Think of paying your shilling for a view of the geysers of the Yellowstone, or an eruption of Vesuvius, or a peep at the Yosemite Falls!"

237 Thomson, J.J. NOTES ON RECENT RESEARCHES IN ELECTRICITY AND MAGNETISM, INTENDED AS A SEQUEL TO PROFESSOR CLERK MAXWELL'S TREATISE ON ELECTRICITY AND MAGNETISM. Oxford: Clarendon Press, 1893. Reprint, London: Dawsons, 1968. xvi + 578 pp., 144 illus. A full survey of advanced electromagnetic theories, with a comprehensive account of the discharge of electricity in gases. (224, 266)

238 Amstutz, Noah W. "Visual telegraphy." ELECTRICITY 6 (Feb. 28, 1894): 77–80; (Mar. 14, 1894): 110, 111. 13 illus. Survey of selenium and early proposals, discussion of lines and picture points. Outline of the author's proposal for a Phonoscope, an instrument combining the telephone and telectroscope adaptable for two-way communication, based on a scheme by H.C. Johnson employing cylinders with a series of staggered openings.

239 Lenard, Philipp Eduard Anton von (1862–1947). "Uber Kathodenstrahlen in Gasen von atmosphärischen Druck und im äussersten Vakuum" [On cathode rays in gases under atmospheric pressure and in extreme vacua]. ANN. PHYS. 51 (1894): 225–67. ELECT. 32 Mar. 23, 1894): 574–7; (Mar. 30, 1894): 613–6; (Apr. 6, 1894): 630–3. 11 illus., 4 tables. Cathode rays penetrate thin aluminum windows. Lenard received the Nobel Prize for 1905. (241, 229)

240 Fitzgerald, George Francis (1851–1901). "On cathode rays in gases under atmospheric pressure and in extreme vacua." ELECT. 32 (Mar. 23, 1894): 573, 574. (267)

241 Lenard, P. "Uber die magnetische Ablenkung der Kathodenstrahlen" [On the magnetic deflection of cathode rays]. ANN. PHYS. 52 (1894): 23–33. (239, 332)

242 Elster, J., and H. Geitel. "Weitere lichtelektrische Versuche" [Further photoelectric experiments]. ANN. PHYS. 52 (1894): 433–54. With various metals, sunlight, and ultraviolet. (232, 243)

243 Lodge, O.J. "The work of Hertz." NATURE 50 (June 7, 1894): 133–9. The work of Hertz and his successors. ELECT. 33 (June 8–July

27, 1894): 153–5, 186–90, 204, 205, 271, 272, 362, 25 illus. Lecture at the Royal Institution, June 1. Also in book form: THE WORK OF HERTZ. London: "The Electrician" Printing & Publishing Co., 1894. i + 58 pp. 2nd ed. (1897), 73 pp. Rev. 2nd ed. (1898). SIGNALLING THROUGH SPACE WITHOUT WIRES; BEING A DESCRIPTION OF THE WORK OF HERTZ AND HIS SUCCESSORS. 58 pp. 3rd ed. (1900), ii + 133 pp., 73 illus. Reprint, New York: Arno Press, 1974. Appendix IV, pp. 115–26, On the diselectrification of metals and other bodies by light, contains abstracts of 12 papers by Elster and Geitel on their photoelectric researches, published in ANN. PHYS. 38–52, 1889–94. (207, 214–216, 224–226, 230, 232, 242, also 246) (152, 302)

244 Rabourdin. (Television receiver.) COSMOS 28 (1894): 361. Proposed use of electromagnetic shutters to control light from a bank of glow lamps.

245 Jenkins, Charles Francis (1867–1934). "Transmitting pictures by electricity." ELECT. ENGINEER 18 (July 25, 1894): 62, 63. A mosaic system with a multifilament receiver in the form of a "flat electric lamp of ground glass." Also, glow lamp receiver. COSMOS 29 (1894): 161. Jenkins invented a moving film projector at this time and became a pioneer in radio movies during the 1920s. (425)

246 Elster, J., and H. Geitel. "Photo-electric phenomena." NATURE 50 (Sept. 6, 1894): 451, 452. In this letter the authors summarize the results of experiments with many different substances and give the following references to Wiedemann's ANN. PHYS.: 38:40, 497; 39:332; 41:161, 166; 42:564; 43:225; 44:772; 46:281; 48:625; 52:433. (243, 250)

247 Stoney, G.J. "Of the 'electron,' or atom of electricity." PHIL. MAG. 38 (Oct. 1894): 418–20. Following the original suggestion (223), this paper gives prominence to the name for the corpuscle which J.J. Thomson identified in 1897 as a subatomic particle. (223, 266)

248 Majorana, Quirino (1871–1957). (Disk scanner.) ELETTRICISTA 3 (1894): 3. The suggested scanner, two disks with intersecting radial slots, appeared in numerous proposals and patents (275), especially in the 1920s.

249 Carey, G.R. "Transmitting, recording and seeing by electricity." ELECT. ENGINEER 19 (Jan. 16, 1895): 57, 58. With minor changes, this is a reprint of the original which appeared in 1880 (133). Carey states that "in 1877 I invented the following instruments," but he does not refer to the first publication, nor claim that the apparatus was constructed or that any experiments were carried out.

250 Elster, J., and H. Geitel. "Lichtelektrische Untersuchungen an polarisirtem Lichte" [Photoelectric investigation on polarized light]. ANN. PHYS. 55 (1895): 687–700. (246, 251)

251 Elster, J., and H. Geitel. "Uber bewegliche Lichterscheinungen in verdünnten Gasen, verursacht durch elektrische Schwingungen." ANN. PHYS. 56 (1895): 733–40. "On the motions of the luminous glow in rarefied gases produced by electric oscillations." ELECT. 36 (Jan. 17, 1896): 387, 388. 10 illus. Experiments give further proof of the wave theory. (250, 260)

252 Perrin, Jean Baptiste (1870–1942). "Nouvelles propriétés des rayons cathodiques." C.R. 121 (1895): 1130–4. "New properties of cathode rays." ELECT. 36 (Feb. 14, 1896): 523, 524. 2 diags. Cylinder experiment proving that cathode rays carry negative charges. Perrin received the Nobel Prize in 1926. (824)

253 "The telephotograph." ELECT. 35 (Sept. 5, 1895): 600. Quote from ENGINEERING on a Swedish inventor of a single-circuit system with selenium cell, incandescent lamp, and spiral scanning.

254 Röntgen, Wilhelm Konrad (1845–1925). "Eine neue Art von Strahlen." SITZUNGSBER. WURZBURG. PHYS. MED. GES. (Dec. 1895). "On a new kind of rays." Trans. Arthur Stanton. NATURE 53 (Jan. 23, 1896): 274–6. A preliminary communication on the discovery of X rays. Also, "On a

new form of radiation." ELECT. 36 (Jan. 24): 415–7. (256)

255 Swinton, Alan Archibald Campbell (1863–1930). "Professor Röntgen's discovery." NATURE 53 (Jan. 23, 1896): 276, 277. First of many papers by Swinton on this subject and an early one in the flood of literature abut Röntgen's new rays that appeared that year. Includes photo of a hand taken with a Crookes tube. (259)

256 Röntgen, W.K. "Second paper on the new kind of rays." Published by the Physical Medical Society of Würzburg, Mar. 9. ELECT. 36 (Apr. 24, 1896): 850, 851. SMITH. INST. ANN. REP. for 1897 (1898): 137–155. (254)

257 Fleming, J.A. "A further examination of the Edison effect in glow lamps." PROC. PHYS. SOC. 14 (1896): 187–242. This extensive paper (read Mar. 27) gives detailed descriptions of 29 experiments, has 22 illustrations of experimental lamps with different electrode arrangements, 13 tables of results, and 6 graphs relating to unilateral conductivity, rectifying action, and the phenomenon of "molecular electrovection." (220, 261)

258 Marconi, Guglielmo (1874–1937). "Improvements in transmitting electrical impulses and signals, and in apparatus therefor." Br. 12,039, June 2, 1896, July 2, 1897. First patent on wireless telegraphy employing electromagnetic radiations in space. Marconi and Braun shared the Nobel Prize in 1909. (377)

259 Swinton, A.A.C. "The effects of a strong magnetic field upon electric discharges in vacuo." PROC. ROY. SOC. 60 (June 18, 1896): 179–82. ELECT. 37 (July 10, 1896): 349, 350. Electromagnetic focusing with axial coil and the dispersion of fluorescence on the end of a Crookes tube by a magnet. (255, 264)

260 Elster, J., and H. Geitel. "Uber eine lichtelektrische Nachwirkung der Kathodenstrahlen." ANN. PHYS. 59 (1896): 487–96. "A residual photo-electric effect of cathode rays." ELECT. 38 (Dec. 4, 1896): 183, 184. (251, 268)

261 Fleming, J.A. "An experiment showing the deflection of cathode rays by a magnetic field." ELECT. 38 (Jan. 1, 1897): 302. 4 illus. Distortion of the shadow of a cross on the fluorescent face of a Crookes tube by the field from an axial coil. Swinton's paper (259) prompted this experiment. (257, 265)

262 Szczepanik, Jan (1872–1926), and Ludwig Kleinberg. "Method and apparatus for reproducing pictures and the like at a distance by means of electricity." Br. 5031, Feb. 24, 1897, Feb. 24, 1898. Two mirrors vibrating in planes at right angles produce a zigzag scan. Signals from an annular selenium cell (slowly rotating to eliminate fatigue) move a prism and also vary the intensity of light from a filament lamp at the receiver. Electromagnets operating the mirrors are supplied with interrupted current from induction coils to maintain "perfect synchronism." Claims include reproduction of a scene or object in natural colors and the use of telephones for speaking as well as seeing at a distance. The use of direct sunlight instead of an incandescent lamp at the receiver is suggested but not claimed. (269)

263 Braun, Karl Ferdinand (1850–1918). "Uber ein Verfahren zur Demonstration und zum Studium des zeitlichen Verlaufes variabler Strome" [On a method for the demonstration and study of currents varying with time]. ANN. PHYS. 60 (Feb. 1897): 522–9. 6 illus. Cold cathode tube with side anode, annular diaphragm to control spot size, and built-in fluorescent screen. Beam deflection by one external coil with the trace viewed indirectly in a rotating mirror, or by two coils at right angles for direct viewing. Excitation by hand-drive influence machine (friction generator) or by an induction coil. This "indicator tube," which enabled Braun to demonstrate how a variety of periodic and transient electrical phenomena could be visually examined, is the ancestor of electronic oscilloscopes, television picture tubes, and other modern electron-beam display de-

vices. Braun and Marconi shared the Nobel Prize in 1909.

264 Swinton, A.A.C. "Some experiments with cathode rays." NATURE 55 (Apr. 15, 1897): 568–71. Paper read to the Royal Society, Mar. 11. 24 illus. PROC. ROY. SOC. 61 (1897): 79–95. ELECT. 38 (Apr. 23, 1897): 868–72. Investigations of hollow cones of cathode rays in pumped-down tubes with concave cathodes, carbon targets, interposed objects, and magnetic deflection. (259, 286)

265 Fleming, J.A. "Cathode rays in an alternating magnetic field." ELECT. 38 (Apr. 23, 1897): 864. Diag. Repetition of earlier experiment (261) with a-c in the axial coil, showing rotation of the shadow of a cross projected on the fluorescence on the end of the tube. (294)

266 Thomson, J.J. "Cathode rays." ELECT. 39 (May 21, 1897): 104–9. 10 illus. Lecture at the Royal Institution, Apr. 30. PHIL. MAG. 44 (Oct. 1897): 293–316; SMITH. INST. ANN. REP. for 1897 (1898): 157–68. PROC. ROY. INST. 15 (1899): 419–32. Description of apparatus and experiments for investigating the nature of cathode rays. With a cold cathode tube fitted with internal plates for electrostatic deflection and external coils for electromagnetic deflection, Thomson discovered the particulate nature of the discharge and determined the ratio of charge to mass (e/m) of the "corpuscles," or electrons. Thomson received the Nobel Prize in 1906 (340). (237, 247, 280)

267 Fitzgerald, G.F. "Dissociation of atoms." ELECT. 39 (May 21, 1897): 103, 104. In this commentary on Thomson's lecture (266), the author speaks of "free electrons" in cathode rays. (240)

268 Elster, J., and H. Geitel. "Uber die Abhängigkeit des photoelektrischen Strömes vom Einfallswinkel und der Schwingungsrichtung des erregenden Lichtes und seine Beziehung zu der Absorption des Lichtes an der Kathode" [On the dependence of photoelectric currents on the angle of incidence and the direction of oscillation of the existing light and its relation to the absorption of the light at the cathode]. ANN. PHYS. 61 (1897): 445–65. (260, 385)

269 Horowitz, J. (Szczepanik's telectroscope.) N.Y.T. 22 (Apr. 3, 1898): 3. (262, 272)

270 Ramsay, (Sir) William (1852–1916), and Morris William Travers (1872–1961). "Companions of argon." NATURE 58 (June 23, 1898): 182, 183. PROC. ROY. SOC. 63 (1898): 437–40. C.R. 126 (1898): 1762, 1763. Read to the Society on June 16, this paper announced the discovery of neon ("new gas") on June 13. In collaboration with Lord Rayleigh, Travers, and others, Ramsay also discovered rare gases of the atmosphere: argon, helium, krypton, radon, xenon. Practical discharge tubes containing low-pressure neon were introduced by Georges Claude in 1910 (393). Two-electrode lamps containing neon were essential as modulated light sources in most mechanical television receivers of the 1920s. Ramsay received the Nobel Prize in Chemistry in 1904.

271 "The Dussaud téléoscope." SCI. AM. SUPP. 46 (July 2, 1898): 18793. 2 illus. A report by M. Armengaud, from LA NATURE. Invented by Frantz Dussaud (1870–1953), a Swiss physicist, this apparatus has Nipkow disks, an induction coil, and a variable-aperture grid shutter operated by a telephone. A magic lantern with a carbon arc provides large-screen projection. Also C.R. 127 (1898): 417. (297)

272 (Szczepanik, J.) "The telectroscope and the problem of electrical vision." SCI. AM. SUPP. 46 (July 30, 1898): 18889, 18890, 10 illus. ELECT. ENGINEER 26 (1898): 14; ELECT. REV. (N.Y.) 33 (1898): 72. Description of apparatus essentially as given in the British patent (262). "For some weeks past rumors have been rife that an apparatus has been invented in Europe by means of which events could be seen which were taking place miles away." (269, 273)

273 (Szczepanik, J.) "The telectroscope and its inventor." AM. MON. REV. REV. 18 (July 1898): 93, 94. Mentions an article by Jacques Boyer in the REVUE DES REVUES, April 1, another in the HUMANITARIAN for May, and items in VOM FELS

ZUM MEER by Dr. Kruesser and by Gustav Klitscher, the last on Maximilian Plessner, said to be a pioneer in the invention of the telectroscope. "But it has been left to Jan Szczepanik to startle the world with the apparatus by which objects in the natural colors can be seen hundreds of miles away." It is also reported that "the authorities of the Paris Exposition of 1900 have paid him a million and a quarter of dollars not to part with his rights in this new apparatus till the exposition is over." (272, 274, 407)

274 Twain, Mark (Samuel Langhorne Clemens, 1835-1910). "The Austrian Edison keeping school again." CENTURY 34 (Aug. 1898): 630, 631. Szczepanik, former teacher of a village school in Krosno, Poland, returns there to teach periodically. The noted author said he knew the inventor very well: "His most picturesque achievement is his telectroscope." (273, 282)

275 Lardeur, Alfred Edouard. "Apparatus for the conversion of light waves into electrical waves, for the transmission of such electrical waves to a distance, and for the reconversion of such electrical waves into light waves; also for recording such waves upon suitably prepared surfaces." Br. 5339, Oct. 27, 1898, Oct. 27, 1899.

"Intended for transmitting pictures from transparencies, the camera contains selenium on a copper wire screen which is scanned by clockwork-driven concentric disks with radial slots (248) and radial perforations. A magnetically moved metal foil diaphragm in the receiver provide an image which can be observed directly or projected upon a screen. Signals can be recorded electrochemically by an array of metal pins or by an electromagnetically operated style on a phonograph cylinder. Signals can be played back from the cylinder in a separate reproducer via a contact breaker. Synchronous control is mentioned but not specified. Evidently this is the first attempt to incorporate means for storing and reproducing picture signals."

276 Vol'fke, M. (Device for the electrical transmission of images without wires.) Russ. 4498, Nov. 24, 1898. Scanning by Nipkow disks, Geissler tube in receiver, and induction coil for radiating electromagnetic waves. Radio transmission and the gas discharge tube as a modulated light source are notable innovations.

277 "Fernseher." V.D.I.Z. 42 (1898): 682, 683. (2705)

278 Lehmann, Otto (1855-1922). ELEKTRISCHE LICHTERSCHEINUNGEN ODER ENTLADUNGEN BEZEICHNET GLIMMEN, BUSCHEL, FUNKEN, UND LICHTBOGEN, IN FREIER LUFT UND IN VAKUUMROHREN, ETC. [Electric light phenomena or discharges designated glow, brush, spark and arc, in free air and in vacuum tubes, etc.]. Halle a.S.: W. Knapp, 1898. viii + 569 pp., 370 illus. Full coverage of the phenomena of electroluminescence and related topics that were so prominent in electrical researches during the last quarter of the century.

279 Schöffler, B. DIE PHOTOTELEGRAPHIE UND DAS ELEKTRISCHE FERNSEHEN. Vienna: W. Braumüller, 1898. 27 pp.

280 Thomson, J.J. THE DISCHARGE OF ELECTRICITY THROUGH GASES. London: A. Constable, 1898. x + 203 pp., 41 illus. First of a series of classic works solely devoted to the subject. Reissued in 1903. (266, 311)

281 Poulsen, Valdemar (1869-1942). "Method of recording and reproducing sounds or signals." U.S. 661,619, July 8, 1899, Nov. 13, 1900. In Denmark, Dec. 1, 1898. Patents also filed in 12 other countries. Poulsen's Telegraphone, the first magnetic recorder, was shown but not operated at the Paris Exposition in 1900 and obtained a Grand Prix. (287, 291)

282 Szczepanik, J. "Das telektroscope." V.D.I.Z. 43 (1899): 1139-42. (274, 283)

283 Moffett, Cleveland. "Seeing by wire; the first authentic account of a young Pole's marvellous invention." PEARSON'S MAG.

8 (July–Dec. 1899): 490–6. Interview with Szczepanik. (282, 284)

284 "Notes." ELECT. 43 (Oct. 20, 1899): 900. On the report in PEARSON'S (283), in which the inventor said he had achieved success in 1896 and had worked his apparatus over 40 miles. A contract with a French syndicate prevents further release of news until the apparatus is displayed at the Paris Exposition in 1900. The editor feels justified in treating the sensational notices with the utmost skepticism. See ENG. MECH. 70 (Oct. 20, 1898): 230; also (Oct. 27, 1898): 253–5; (Dec. 1, 1898): 361 for three letters and ELECT. 41 (July 2, 1898): 378. (330)

285 Polumordvinov, A.A. Russ. 10,738, Dec. 23, 1899. A specification for monochrome and color. Two slotted disks, rotating at different speeds, for black-and-white scanning. Two concentric cylinders with slots covered alternately by red, green, and violet filters for color scanning. This is the first proposal incorporating slotted cylinders and rotating color filters.

286 Swinton, A.A.C. "On the luminosity of the rare earths when heated in vacuo by means of cathode rays." PROC. ROY. SOC. 65 (June 1900): 115–9. (264, 366)

287 Poulsen, V. "The Telegraphone." SCI. AM. SUPP. 50 (Aug. 25, 1900): 20616. 2 illus. From LA NATURE. See also ELECT. 45 (May 4, 1900): 39; (July 13, 1900): 441, 442. (281, 289)

288 (Perskyi, Constantin.) "The International Electricity Congress." ELECT. 45 (Sept. 21, 1900): 820–2. The last paragraph of this report states: "At the afternoon sitting on Friday, M.C. Perskyi read a communication on 'Television,' describing a number of apparatus based on the magnetic properties of selenium." In an errata notice the following week (p. 840), the word "magnetic" is corrected to "electrical." This is the first appearance of the term "television" in English. Also, Annexes, Congrès Internationale d'Electricité (Aug. 18–25, 1900): 54–6.

289 Poulsen, V. "Der Telegraphon." ANN. PHYS. 3 (Nov. 12, 1900): 754–60. See also ELECT. 46 (Nov. 30, 1900): 208–10; C.R. 130 (1900): 1754, 1755; SCI. AM. SUPP. 51 (Jan. 19, 1901): 20944. 6 illus. (287)

290 Sewall, Charles Henry. "The future of long-distance communication." HARPER'S WEEKLY 44 (Dec. 29, 1900): 1262, 1263. Illus. by W.D. Stevens. Among other predictions, the future development of a telectroscope, or "optograph," seems "thinkably possible," whereby time and distance would be overcome:

"With the instantaneous printing and development of photographic negative, the evolution from radiophone to optograph, and perfect control of conductors, all these things being thinkably possible, the child born today in New York City, when in middle age he shall visit China, may see reproduced upon a screen, with all its movement and color, light and shade, a procession at that moment passing along his own Broadway. A telephone line will bring to his ear music and the tramp of marching men. While the American pageant passes in the full glare of the morning sun its transmitted rays will scintillate upon the screen amid the darkness of an Asian night. Sight and sound will have unlimited reach through terrestrial space."

CHAPTER 4

DISTANT ELECTRIC VISION: 1901–1918

Advances in phototelegraphy during the first decade of the twentieth century brought experimental apparatus out of the laboratory into limited commercial use. The promising developments in transmitting graphic materials undoubtedly spurred those who were seeking answers to the problem of sending visual images over wires. Indeed, the younger sister art relied upon many components and techniques then beginning to serve practical ends in various expanding branches of electrotechnology. Because of this intermarriage of technical means, the difference between phototelegraphy (sometimes miscalled telephotography) and telectroscopy was not always clear to inventors and others; hence proposals range from graphic recording systems to hybrids with features of both graphic and visual reproduction to true television schemes.

Since the highlights of progress in physics have been included in previous pages, only a few major items are given in this chapter, mainly to provide background material and continuity. Electricity in gases, discharge tubes, and electron theory are largely represented by selected books; for instance, Stark (300), Lodge (302), Richardson (304, 441), Thomson (311, 340), Townsend (448), and Millikan (458). This elimination of many papers (excepting those directly related to television) leaves space for the literature on the more relevant subjects, particularly cathode-ray tubes, electron tubes, phototelegraphy, and television.

As the century began, there was little evidence of the epochal inventions and advances in cathode-ray tubes and electron tubes that were to become cornerstones of new technologies. The first sign of things to come in the television art appeared in 1906 when Dieckmann and Glage (336) applied Braun's indicator tube for visual display of graphic patterns. Another portent came the following year when Rosing (349) substituted a phototube for the selenium and also employed a cathode-ray-tube receiver.

Swinton's detailed plan (413) of 1911 for an electronic camera in an all-electric system is a particularly significant blueprint that later became a reality. Another strong hint of the future appears in Nicolson's patent (457) of 1917 which incorporates a phototube, cathode-ray tube, electron tubes, wave filters, and radio transmission. Continuing researches by Elster and Geitel (385) on phototubes, Einstein's theoretical paper (324), and Claude's work on neon tubes (393) were other precursors for the advances that came after World War I.

Two distinct lines of research—discharges in tubes with cold electrodes and electron emission from heated filaments—began to merge with Wehnelt's work on oxide-coated cathodes (306) for electron tubes in 1903, and for cathode-ray tubes (326) in 1905. Concurrent work on electron tubes is represented by Fleming's patent (319) for an oscillation valve in 1904, and de Forest's paper (339) on his experiments and the subsequent patent (346) of 1907 on the triode. The stimulus for developing these tubes as signal detectors came from contemporary advances in wireless telegraphy, already well established for maritime communications. The greater need, however, was for an amplifier or relay, for which the cathode-ray tube was first applied by von Lieben (329), and Dieckmann and Glage (337) in 1906, and later by von Lieben, Reisz, and Strauss (397).

The potential of the three-electrode tube to function as an amplifier was not realized for several years. This hidden capability, perceived by von Bronk (409) in 1911, was also discovered by de Forest during experiments in 1912. A sudden burst of activity by Arco and Meissner (419), Schloemilch and von Bronk (420), Franklin (422), Armstrong (427), de Forest (428), and Round (430) transformed this erstwhile laboratory novelty into a centerpiece among telecommunication components.

These developments included circuit arrangements for the related functions of the tube as an amplifier and, with the principle of regeneration (feedback or reaction), as an oscillator or generator, and as a modulator. Other contributions were the negative grid bias (415), filter circuits (446), and the theoretical works by Armstrong (436) and Latour (452). Experiments with thermionic emission in high vacua and the development of practical electron tubes for wire telephony and radio transmission were made possible by the improved vacuum pumps of Gaede (355), Langmuir (450), and others. Intensive efforts by large manufacturers in developing tubes and circuits to meet new wartime needs led to the rapid extension of radiotelephony and the rise of broadcast radio after the war.

This progress in electronics had no effect on developments in telectroscopy, which still depended on the older means and methods (except for innovations to be noted) until near the end of the period. Electrical components were in extensive use as operating and circuit devices, while optical and mechanical approaches grew in favor, largely reflecting the contemporary influences of electrical instrumentation, phototelegraphy, and cinematography.

A survey of the contributions to television (a term that was slowly adopted after 1907) reveals several characteristics of this period. The rising interest is indicated by the number of disclosures—2.4 per year—or twice that of previous years. Again, there were twenty-three patent applications, compared with only five from 1884 to 1900. Dealing with disclosures and reports of all kinds, there were twenty-seven up to 1900 and more than seventy in these years, which include the sparse period of World War I. Another aspect of this upsurge of inventive effort was the seemingly countless variations and combinations of devices and techniques, some old and some new, embodied in the diverse efforts to achieve potentially workable systems.

Established methods for scanning appear in some twenty-five proposals. With the frequency of use indicated, these are: vibrating or oscillating mirrors (8), perforated disks (7), mirror drums (5), slotted drums (4), slotted disks (2), and the lens disk. Scanning with perforated bands was employed by Ribbe (316) and adopted in five other schemes. The polyhedral mirror drum of Rosing appears to be an exclusive application, as is the lens drum of Hart (435) and the rotary mirror of Ekström (384). Scanning with a flying light spot, introduced by Rignoux (328), was also used by Ekström. The raster, inherent in some earlier schemes, appears in the demonstrations by Dieckmann and Glage. Interlaced linear scanning is seen for the first time in Hart's patent. Von Bronk's scheme (291), which combines Bakewell's distributor of 1848 with magnetic storage recently introduced by Poulsen, is a particularly novel proposal.

Notwithstanding the technical limitations, some bold suggestions were made for new transmission methods. These include two-way by von Bronk (295) and Hoglund (386), frequency-selective systems by Lux (342) and Ruhmer (372), and duplex-stereo and optical transmission with a light pipe by Sinding-Larsen (388). Though not a new idea, color transmission appears in the patents of von Bronk, von Jaworski, and Frankenstein (318), and the Andersens (369), and is mentioned also in the report on Fowler (334). Adoptions from the cinematograph are seen in the proposal using transparencies credited to Schneider (309), of Ekström, and in film transmission by Sellers (367) and others. An allied technique, that of graduated or shaded screens, appears in the proposals of Senlecq (354), Armengaud (361), and the Andersens.

A study of the descriptions and specifications reveals a bewildering array of components and techniques. This variety is summarized in Table 4, which gives the items in order of the frequency of use, as indicated by numbers in parentheses. Innovations are shown by asterisks. Though not complete, the list is sufficiently inclusive to show the diversity of means and methods and the items most in favor.

A dozen or so items of those starred in this list are technical preferences that represent the fashion of the times. Selenium cells, distributors, other rotary devices, and most of the electrical components continued to appear in plans beyond this era. Adoptions from the motion picture art include shaded screens, transparencies and film, viewing screens, cine projection, and rotary color filters. These features also represent a transition from phototelegraphy, with transmission via transparencies or film in mixed systems, toward true television intended for the instantaneous reproduction of images with either direct or reflected light. In addition to various disks or drums, legacies of this period that would endure through the mechanical era after the war include the flying light spot, raster, interlaced scan, and of course electronic methods and radio circuits.

TABLE 4 From Telectroscopy to Television: Components and Techniques (in order of frequency of use)

ELECTRICAL	OPTICAL	MECHANICAL
Selenium cell (10)	Viewing screen (9)	Perforated disk (7)
Selenium mosaic (9)	Vibrating mirror (8)	Perforated band (6)
Galvanometer (8)	Mirror drum (5)	Perforated drum (4)
Distributor (7)	*Graded screen (4)	Tuning fork (3)
Selenium group	Color filter (3)	Clockwork (2)
Battery (6)	Faraday cell (2)	Manometric flame
Transformer	*Light spot	*Vibrating reed
Arc lamp (5)	Light pipe	
Induction coil	*Raster	
Telephone	*Rotary mirror	
Spark gap (4)	Spiral scan	**ELECTRONIC**
Phonic wheel (3)	*Transparency	*Discharge tube (6)
A-C generator (2)	*Chopper (1)	*Cathode-ray tube (4)
Chopper	Cine projection	*Phototube
Dynamo	Color prism	*Camera tube (1)
Electromagnet	*Film	*Electron tube
Incandescent lamp	*Interlaced scan	X-ray tube
Motor	Lens disk	
Rotary contractor	*Lens drum	
Rotary resistor	Nicol prism	
*Magnetic storage (1)	Photo recording	**SYSTEMS**
Microphone relay	*Polyhedral drum	Color (4)
Oscillograph		*Two-way
Pulse sync		*Frequency selective (2)
*Resonant relay		Recording
*Rotary inductor		*Duplex-stereo (1)
Slip ring		*Optical transmission
Tesla coil		Radio transmission
Wave filter		*Velocity modulation

Innovations

The technical quality of the proposals ranges from the best of the times through degrees of credibility to suggestions that seem astonishing, to say the least. While the basic factors were understood by most inventors, the magnitude of the challenge was not, as is evident in the majority of the contrivances and in many patent claims. Errors or omissions in most of the plans impair the quality of perceptive thought given to their creation but do not greatly diminish either versatility or the ingenuity of the inventors. As time would prove, certain problems were not soluble with the means at hand, particularly those concerning inertia and rapidity of response, isochronous operation, amplification of weak signals, and the behavior of transient currents in components and along wires.

Despite the technical limitations, a high level of optimism concerning feasibility is found in most reports and patents. That things would function with the desired effect is assumed in the specifications. Apart from the apparatus of Dieckmann and Glage, Rosing, Ruhmer, also Rignoux and Fournier (378), however, it is doubtful that any claims were founded on experimental results. The faith that an inventor must have in his creation is implicit in any patent specification, but some dared to include potential applications as if they were realities. The Andersens, for instance, believed their apparatus to be capable of transmitting images with movement and color "altogether similar to the natural objects," for stage shows as well as utilitarian purposes. Sinding-Larsen, like them, included military applications with the addition of stereoscopic reproduction. Hoglund declared that his apparatus was cheap and simple to construct. Hart described how his camera could be remotely controlled from a receiving station, and how images could be recorded to permit moving pictures to be reproduced whenever desired.

Contemporary viewpoints in this rich period can be glimpsed in some of the entries. Continuing devotion to the art is evident in Senlecq's return with a revised system, in Sutton's reprint (391), and in the item by Jenkins (425). One echo from the recent past is the sad news of the end of Szczepanik's plans reported (330) in 1906. The belief that a solution was close at hand appears in the report on Armengaud (362). Bidwell's critical view of this news and his analysis of the problems (365) led to Swinton's initial suggestion (366) that cathode rays could be used to eliminate mechanical difficulties.

The clearest view of the future is given by Grimshaw (405), who describes how the electric eye could be applied for ocean exploration, geological research, airborne military surveillance, and closed-circuit industrial supervision. In 1915 Martin (444) was able to accept the possibility of television by wire but not by wireless. Three years later Burrows (459) pessimistically shut the door on any immediate prospects for television. The era ends with a brighter outlook presented by Gernsback (460), who, with his perennial optimism about anything electrical, believed that his imagined Telephot (a video-telephone) or something like it was indeed a coming invention of the first importance.

TABLE 5   CHRONOLOGY: 1901–1918

1901	von Bronk	Magnetic distributor, storage and scanning
1902	Korn	Phototelegraph
	von Bronk	Two-way and color, discharge tubes
	Coblyn	Perforated scanning drum, vibrating mirror, oscillograph
1903	Wehnelt	Concentrating cylinder in Braun tube
	Richardson	Electron emission
	Belin	Facsimile system, moving mirror, commutator, relay
	Wehnelt	Oxide-coated cathode
	Nisco	Distributor, microphone relay, spark-gap receiver
	Re	Nipkow disk, manometric flame receiver
	Schneider	Vibrating mirror, transparency, modulated arc
1904	Wehnelt	Electric valve patent
	Ribbe	Perforated scanning band
	Jaworski, Frankenstein	Mirrors on drums, color filter disks, spark-gap receiver
	Fleming	Oscillation valve (diode) patent
	Ribbe	Telephone-mirror modulator, photo recording

Year	Person	Contribution
1905	Einstein	Unitary theory of light
	Wehnelt	Improved Braun tube
1906	Rignoux	Double-mirror and light-spot scanning, arc modulator
	von Lieben	Cathode-ray relay
	Stephan	Nipkow disk, Faraday cell, two-way
	Fowler	Televue system
	Rothschild	Telautophote, slotted drum and belt, discharge tube
	Dieckmann, Glage	Telautograph with Braun tube, continuous scan, raster display
	Lux	Multifrequency system, vibrating reed receiver
1907	de Forest	Oscillation detector (triode) patent
	Korn	Improved phototelegraph
	Rosing	Polyhedral mirror drums, phototube, Braun tube receiver, inductor sync
	Korn	Picture transmission
	Kruh	Phototelegraph receiver, discharge tubes
	Senlecq	Modified Nipkow disk, shaded transparency and galvanometer modulator
	Gaede	Rotary mercury air pump
1908	Stephan	Two-way electric telescope
	Adamian	Two-color Geissler tube receiver
	Armengaud	Slotted belt scanner, shaded screen modulator
	Knudsen	Wireless phototelegraph
	Lux	Telautograph
	Bidwell	Critical letter on electric vision
	Swinton	Suggestion on cathode rays for scanning
	Sellers	Distributor, mirror galvanometer, mirror drum
	Andersens	Perforated ribbon, graded transparency, rotary color filter, screen projection, voice transmission
1909	Ruhmer	Frequency-selective system, resonant relays, matrix display
	Knothe	Multicircuit system, X-ray tube receiver
	Gernsback	Mosaics, electromagnets, shutters, lamps
	Rignoux, Fournier	Telephote, relays, distributor, Faraday cell, mirror wheel
	Baker	Phototelegraph
1910	Ekström	Transparency, light-spot scanning, double-motion rotary mirror scanner
	Elster, Geitel	Improved phototube
	Hoglund	Spirally slotted disks, modulated arc, two-way

Table continued on next page.

TABLE 5 (continued)

	Schmierer	Matrix system with distributors
	Sinding-Larsen	Optical/electrical system, stereo (duplicate)
	De Vendenil	Nipkow disk, manometric flame modulator
	Saint-René	Mosaics, galvanometers, light pipes
	Claude	Luminescent neon tubes
	von Lieben, Reisz, Strauss	Cathode-ray gas relay amplifier
1911	Rosing	Improved system with optical chopper, velocity modulation
	Elster, Geitel	Potassium phototube
	von Bronk	High-frequency triode amplifier
	Swinton	All-electric system, camera and picture tubes, a-c sync
1912	Lowenstein	Telephone relay, grid bias circuit
	Marino	Color phototelegraph, perforated ribbon scanning
	Gaede	Molecular air pump
1913	Arco, Meissner	Gaseous triode, radio-frequency amplifier
	Schloemilch, von Bronk	Regenerative circuit
	Franklin	Regenerative circuit
	Elster, Geitel	Improved potassium phototube
	Jenkins	Motion pictures by wireless
	Armstrong	Regenerative circuit
	de Forest	Audio telephone amplifier
	Langmuir	Electron discharge in high vacua
	Round	Regenerative circuit
1914	Hart	Lens drum scanner, interlaced scanning, discharge tube receiver, remote control, recording
	Armstrong	Triode operating theory
1915	Martin	Radiophotography
	Campbell	Wave filters
	Voulgré	Transparency, slotted band scanner, mercury-vapor lamp receiver, image projection
1916	Langmuir	Condensation vacuum pump
	Latour	Triode theory
1917	Low	Facsimile system
	Nicolson	Oscillating mirror, spiral scan, cathode-ray-tube receiver, electron tube circuits, radio transmission
1918	Gernsback	Telephot proposal

BIBLIOGRAPHY: 1901–1918

291 Bronk, Otto von (1872–1951). "Ueber ältere und neuere Fernseher-Konstruktionen mit besonderer Berücksichtigung des Selen-Bilder Phototelegraphen von O. von Bronk" [About older and newer television constructions with particular consideration of the selenium picture phototelegraph by O. von Bronk]. DER MECH. 9 (Jan. 20, 1901): 13–51(16). 10 illus. Signals from a bank of selenium cells are stored in a steel ring with a rotating pickup coil for readout. Based on Poulsen's Telegraphone (281), this arrangement was intended to minimize the sluggish response of selenium. Noteworthy features are the introduction of magnetic recording, which embodies the principle of intermediate signal storage, of an electromagnetic distributor, and the conversion of simultaneous signals from the camera mosaic into sequential signals for single-line transmission. The inventor was active in television developments into the 1930s. (295).

292 Woodruffe, H. "Seeing by electricity." ENG. MECH. 73 (July 26, 1901): 523; 74 (Aug. 23, 1901): 39. Letters on the Ayrton and Perry schemes. (127)

293 Korn, Arthur (1870–1945). "Uber einen Apparat zur Herstellung von elektrischen Fernphotographien" [About an apparatus for producing electric phototelegraphy]. E.T.Z. 23 (May 22, 1902): 454, 455. Korn was a leading exponent of phototelegraphy for many years. (303)

294 Fleming, J.A. "The electronic theory of electricity." POP. SCI. MON. 61 (May 1902): 5–23. Lecture at the Royal Institution, May 30. (265, 319)

295 Bronk, O. von. "Verfahren und Vorrichtung zum Fernsichtbarmachen von Bilden bzw. Gegenständen unter vorübergehender Auflösung der Bilder in parallele Punktriehen" [Method and apparatus for optically transmitting pictures or objects under temporary dissolution of pictures in parallel rows of points]. Ger. 155,528, June 12, 1902, Oct. 22, 1904. This ambitious scheme for two-way and color transmission includes mirror drums, distributors, slip rings, selenium cells, transformers, discharge tubes, prisms, and red, yellow, and blue filters. Light from a mirror drum is projected through prisms and three color filters onto three narrow rows of selenium cells. The cells are connected sequentially via a distributor and a transformer to the transmission lines. Another distributor in the receiver feeds the line currents to the corresponding contacts of three narrow multiple-electrode Geissler tubes, each equivalent to the row of selenium cells, that is, the length of a picture line. (291, 409)

296 Coblyn, J.H. "La vision à distance par l'électricité." C.R. 135 (Oct. 27, 1902): 684, 685. "Electric vision at a distance." ELECT. 50 (Nov. 14, 1902): 150. Preliminary details. ECL. ELECT. 33 (Dec. 27, 1902): 433–40. Proposal incorporates a scanning drum with skewed slots and a vibrating mirror for scanning, an oscillograph for modulating a constant light source, and synchronous control with tuning forks and contacts to the drum.

297 Dussaud, F. "Nouvelles expériences sur la résistance électrique du sélénium et ses application à la transmission des images et des impressions lumineuses" [New experiments on the electrical resistance of selenium and their application to the transmission of images and luminous impressions]. C.R. 135 (1902): 790, 791. (271)

298 Ruhmer, Ernest Walter (1878–1913). "Uber Teleautographen, mit besonderer Berücksichtigung des Gruhn'schen Kopiertelegraphen und des Korn'schen Fernphotographen" [On the teleautograph, with special consideration of the Gruhn copying telegraph and the Korn phototelegraph]. DER MECH. 10 (1902): 158, 171, 172, 185–7. (372)

299 Wehnelt, Artur Rudolph Barthold (1871–1944). "Über die Vertailung des Stromes an der Oberfläche von Kathoden in Entladungsröhren" [About the distribution of current at the surface of cathodes in discharge tubes]. ANN. PHYS. 7 (1902): 237–55. (301)

300 Stark, Johannes, (1874–1957). DIE ELEKTRIZITAT IN GASEN. Leipzig: J.A. Barth,

1902. xxviii + 509 pp., 144 illus. A basic work on electricity in gases. Stark was awarded the Nobel Prize for 1919. (471)

301 Wehnelt, A. "Eine Braunsche Röhre für elektrostatische Ablenkung" [Braun tube for electrostatic deflection]. D. PHYS. GES. 5 (Jan. 15, 1903): 29–34. The introduction of a negatively charged cylinder surrounding the cathode to concentrate the electron emission was an important improvement of the Braun tube. Variations of negative bias on the Wehnelt cylinder (control grid) vary the intensity of the electron beam and the screen brightness in display tubes such as oscilloscopes. Intensity modulation of the beam, which provides variations of light and shade on the screen of a picture tube, is similarly effected by the video signal applied to the grid. (299, 306)

302 Lodge, O.J. "On electrons." J. IEE. 32 (Feb. 1903): 45–116. These lectures were later published in a book. (243, 344)

303 Korn, A. "Sur la transmission de photographies à l'aide d'un fil télégraphique" [Transmission of photographs by telegraph wire]. C.R. (May 18, 1903): 1190–2. Selenium cell inside rotating glass cylinder carrying photo film. Galvanometer-operated spark gap in series with Tesla coil and discharge tube focused onto film on receiver cylinder. Sync control by start-stop method. (293, 314)

304 Richardson, (Sir) Owen Willans (1879–1959). "The electrical conductivity imparted to a vacuum by hot conductors." PHIL. TRANS. 201 (July 20, 1903): 497–549. This foundation paper fully explains the Edison effect and theory of electron emission. Richardson was awarded the Nobel Prize in 1928. (441)

305 Belin, Claude Joseph Edouard, and François Xavier Edouard Marcel Belin. "An improved method for the transmission to a distance of real optical images and apparatus therefor." Br. 26,586, Dec. 6, 1904, Feb. 16, 1905. Fr. 339,212, Dec. 8, 1903. A single-circuit facsimile system with a moving mirror that scans a cylindrical surface containing selenium cells connected to a commutator and relay. Electromagnets in the receiver operate a mechanism for perforating or printing reproductions on paper or metal sheets. Sync by electric clockwork. Cinematographic projection is also proposed. Belin turned his attention toward television in the 1920s. (348)

306 Wehnelt, A. "Uber die Phosphoreszenz-erregung durch langsame Kathodenstrahlen" [About phosphorescence excited by slow cathode rays]. D. PHYS. GES. 5 (Dec. 15, 1903): 423–6. Experiments with heated platinum wire coated with calcium oxide. The increase in the emission of negative ions (electrons) from heated filaments coated with lime (CaO) or other oxides of the rare earth elements, particularly barium (Ba) and strontium (Sr), was of considerable theoretical interest during succeeding years and of great practical value in the development of efficient electron tubes. (301, 312)

307 Nisco, Adriano. "La visione a distanza per mezzo dell'elettricità" [Vision at a distance by means of electricity]. BOLL. COLL. ING. ARCH. NAPOLI 21 (1905): 213–23. A screen of selenium is embedded in an insulated metal net with conducting wires connected to a distributor in the form of an ebonite cylinder with protruding contacts that are scanned by a rotating steel blade. From a telephone and battery circuit containing a microphone relay signals are conveyed to a similar circuit at the receiver which operates a spark gap inside a rotating slotted cylinder. Light from the slots of this cylinder is cast upon a viewing screen. One line carries the visual signals, the other is used for maintaining synchronism. (338, 412)

308 Re, Filippo. "La vision à distance par l'électricité." ECL. ELECT. 35 (1903): 215–8. Proposal employing Nipkow disks, selenium cell, and manometric flame receiver. (412)

309 Schneider, R. (System for transmitting pictures.) WEST. ELECT. 32 (1903): 188. Light from a carbon arc is reflected from a mirror vibrating on two axes through a transparency onto a selenium cell. Signals

via a line transformer control a modulated arc circuit at the receiver where the light from the arc is projected by a similar vibrating mirror onto a viewing screen. Coils of the telephone diaphragms that operate the mirrors are connected in series via four wire lines containing separate batteries and two rotary resistances which maintain synchronism. (412)

310 Lux, Friedrich. ELEKTRISCHER FERNSEHER. Ludwigshafen: J.A. Schönsiegel, 1903. (412)

311 Thomson. J.J. CONDUCTION OF ELECTRICITY THROUGH GASES. Cambridge: Cambridge University Press, 1903. viii + 566 pp. A classic work on fundamental research. 2nd ed. (1906), viii + 678 pp. 3rd ed. in two vols. (1928, 1933), reprinted, New York: Dover, 1969. (280, 315)

312 Wehnelt, A. "Elektrische Ventil" [Electric valve]. Ger. 157, 845, Jan. 15, 1904, Jan. 13, 1905. A vacuum tube with a central oxide-coated cathode and three anodes intended for rectifying single-phase or three-phase alternating current. (306, 313)

313 Wehnelt, A. "Uber ein elektrisches Ventilrohr" [About an electric valve-tube]. PHYS. Z. 5 (1904): 680. On the valve in the patent (312). (317)

314 Korn, A. "Uber Gebe- und Empfangsapparate zur elektrischen Fernübertrangung" [About sending and receiving apparatus for electric transmission]. PHYS. Z. 5 (Feb. 15, 1904): 113–8; (Mar. 15, 1904): 164–8. Cylinders at transmitter and receiver. High-voltage relay consisting of Tesla coil and galvanometer contacts controls light from a discharge tube for photo recording. Improved version of earlier system (303). See Also E.T.Z. 26 (Dec. 14, 1905): 1131–4. (322)

315 Thomson, J.J. ELECTRICITY AND MATTER. New York: Scribner's, 1904. vi + 162 pp. Silliman Memorial lectures given at Yale University, May 1903, published in March. (311, 340)

316 Ribbe, Paul. "Schirm mit spiralig angeordneten Öffnungen zum Zerlegen von Lichtstrahlen die in elektrische Wellen und dann wieder in Lichtstrahlen umgesetzt werden" [Screen with spirally arranged apertures for splitting light rays which are transformed into electric waves and then transformed back again into light rays]. Ger. 160,813, Apr. 19, 1904, May 19, 1905. Perforated disks or endless film with staggered apertures for line-by-line scanning. A more detailed specification covering a complete system is given in a later British patent. (321)

317 Wehnelt, A. "Uber den austritt Negativer Ionen aus glühenden Metallverbindungen und damit zusammenhängenden Erscheinungen" [On the emission of negative ions by glowing metallic oxides and related phenomena]. ANN. PHYS. 14 (July 12, 1904): 425–68. Also PHIL. MAG. 10 (July 1905): 80–90. (313, 325)

318 Jaworski, Werner von, and A. Frankenstein. "Verfahren und Vorrichtung zur Fernsichtbarmachung von Bildern und Gegenständen mittels Selenzellen, Dreifarbenfilter und Zerlegung des Bildes in Punktgruppen durch Spiegel" [Method and apparatus to optically transmit pictures and objects via selenium cells, three color filters, and splitting of the picture into groups of points by means of mirrors]. Ger. 172,376, Aug. 20, 1904, June 21, 1906. Scanning by three sets of mirrors mounted on radial supports in staggered series on drums. Three-color filter disks rotate in front of the optical apertures in the instrument boxes. A telephone-operated spark gap furnished modulated light in the receiver.

319 Fleming, J.A. "Improvements in instruments for detecting and measuring alternating electric currents." Br. 24,850, Nov. 16, 1904, Sept. 21, 1905. Ger. 186,034, Apr. 12, 1905, May 6, 1907. U.S. 803,684, Apr. 19, Nov. 7, 1905. First patent on a two-electrode vacuum tube intended for detecting or rectifying radio-frequency signals.

320 Ramsay, W. "The rare gases of the atmosphere. Nobel lecture, Dec. 12, 1904." NOBEL LECTURES, CHEMISTRY: 1901–

1912. Amsterdam, London, New York: Elsevier, 1966. Presentation speech, pp. 65–7. Lecture, pp. 68–77. Biography, pp. 78, 70. (270)

321   Ribbe, P. "Improvements in automatic photographing telegraphs." Br. 29,428, Dec. 31, 1904, Feb. 2, 1905. Scanning by an endless perforated band or by a disk with the equivalent spiral of staggered holes. The heating action of light on a flexible wire gauze coated with soot provides make-and-break contacts in the camera, signals from which via a line transformer operate a telephone at the receiver. The telephone membrane in turn actuates linkages that swing a concave mirror which more or less reflects light from a local source through the scanning mechanism onto photographic film or paper. (316)

322   Korn, A. ELEKTRISCHE FERNPHOTOGRAPHIE UND AHNLICHES [Electric phototelegraphy and the like]. Leipzig: S. Hirzel, 1904. 66 pp., 13 illus. 2nd ed. (1907), 87 pp. (314, 345)

323   Fleming, J.A. "On the conversion of electric oscillations into continuous currents by means of a vacuum valve." PROC., ROY., SOC. 74 (Mar. 1905): 476–87. 4 illus., 2 tables. Paper read Feb. 9. Reprinted in George Shiers, ed. THE TELEPHONE: AN HISTORICAL ANTHOLOGY. New York: Arno Press, 1977. (319, 331)

324   Einstein, Albert (179–1955). "Uber einen die Erzengung un Verwandlung des Lichtes betreffenden heuristischen Geischtspunkt" [On a heuristic standpoint concerning the production and transformation of light]. ANN. PHYS. 17 (1905): 132–48. A unitary theory of light, based on the quantum theory of Max Planck (1858–1947), particularly relevant to the photoelectric effect, photoluminescence, and the ionization of gases by ultraviolet light. Einstein was awarded the Nobel Prize in 1921 for his theory of relativity.

325   Wehnelt, A. "Ein elektrisches Ventilrohr" [An electric valve-tube]. SITZUNGBER. PHYS. MED. SOZ. ERLANGEN 37 (Oct. 1905): 264–9. (312) Also ANN. PHYS. 19 (Jan. 18, 1906): 138–56. ECL. ELECT. 46 (Feb. 17, 1906): 260–4. (317, 326)

326   Wehnelt, A. "Empfindlichkeitssteigerung der Braunschen Röhre durch Benutzung von Kathodenstrahlen geringer Geschwindigkeit" [Raising the sensitivity of the Braun tube by use of low-velocity cathode rays]. PHYS. Z. 6 (Nov. 1, 1905): 732, 733. Hot cathode coated with calcium oxide furnished a copious flow of electrons at a lower anode voltage; hence increased beam deflection sensitivity. The introduction of the oxide-coated cathode (306) and the concentrating cylinder (301) were fundamental steps in the development of Braun's indicator tube. (325, 327)

327   Wehnelt, A. "Demonstrationversuche über den Austritt negativer Elektronen aus glühenden Metalloxyden" [Demonstrations on the emission of negative electrons from glowing metal oxides]. UNTERRICHTSBL. MATH. NATUR. 12 (1906): 135, 136. (326)

328   Rignoux, Georges M. Fr. 364,189, Feb. 2; 382, 535, Dec. 1, 1906; 390,435, 1908. Double-mirror scanning, modulation by a singing arc, and tuning fork control. Rignoux is credited with introducing the flying-light-spot method of scanning, with reflected light collected by a selenium cell via a lens. (328)

329   Lieben, Robert von (1878–1913). "Kathodenstrahlen-Relais" [Cathode-ray relay]. Ger. 179,807, Mar. 4, Nov. 19, 1906. High-vacuum cathode-ray tube with magnetic beam defocusing intended as an amplifier for voice signals. A heated oxide-coated cathode has a concave shape to focus the rays onto apertures in the ends of two concentric cylindrical anodes. Input signals to magnetic coils vary the focus of the rays and the current in the output circuit from the anode. (337, 397)

330   "The selenium cell." ELECT. 56 (Mar. 16, 1906): 869. This brief "Note" announced the dismal end of Jan Szczepanik's once notorious plans. According to the correspondent of the STANDARD in Vienna, Szczepanik's patents, including the one on the telectro-

scope (262), were recently put up for sale by auction, but no bids were offered. (284)

331 Fleming, J.A. "The construction and use of oscillation valves for rectifying high frequency electric currents." PROC. PHYS. SOC. 20 (1906): 177–85; PHIL. MAG. 11 (1906): 656–65. Paper read Mar. 23. (323, 393)

332 Lenard, P. "On the cathode rays. Nobel lecture, May 28, 1906." NOBEL LECTURES, PHYSICS: 1901–1921. Amsterdam, London, New York: Elsevier, 1967. Presentation speech, pp. 101–4. Lecture, pp. 105–30, 11 illus. Chronological list of publications, pp. 131–4, 55 entries from 1860 to 1906. Biography, pp. 135–8. Prize awarded for 1905. (241)

333 Stephan, W. "Konstruktion eines elektrischen Fernsehers" [Construction of an electric television]. DER MECH. 14: (July 20, 1906): 159–62, 173–5. General discussion is followed by a proposal containing Nipkow disks and a Faraday cell modulator. A two-way system with duplicate scanners and modulators and switches for alternate functions is suggested. (217, 358)

334 "Seeing through the telephone." ELECT. 57 (Aug. 17, 1906): 685. Preliminary patents have been granted to J.B. Fowler, of San Diego, on a Televue system. Six-inch glass disk and selenium ribbon at the transmitter. Apparatus includes two batteries, induction coil, and a telephone. Color pictures reproduced on a disk 1 3/4 in. diameter. Tests reported over 1 mile. (338)

335 Rothschild, Sidney. "Telautophote." U.S. 874,868, Sept. 6, 1906, Dec. 24, 1907. Slotted drum and slotted belt serve for scanning; a vacuum tube or discharge lamp is a modulated light source. The single-wire circuit includes line transformers, batteries and generators, tuning forks, and an interrupter for sync control, and electric motors.

336 Dieckmann, Max (1882–1960), and Gustav Glage. "Verfahren zur Ubertragung von Schriftzeichen und Strichzeichnungen unter Benutzung der Kathodenstrahlenröhre" [Method for the transmission of letters and line drawings using a cathode-ray tube]. Ger. 190,103, Sept. 12, 1906, Sept. 9, 1907. This invention marks the half-way step between the telautograph and television (see Figs. 14 and 15). A writing pen is so arranged on slides that the coordinate positions of the pen vary two linear resistances, as in the Cowper (110) and similar telautographic systems. The novel part is the introduction of a Braun tube for visual display. Currents from the resistances vary the magnetic fields of two pairs of deflection coils and cause the beam to trace the corresponding pattern on the screen. Other methods were introduced by the inventors at this time. In one model, a modified Nipkow disk, fitted with a spiral of protruding contact pins, was used to transmit simple geometrical outlines by the on-off contact method. A more important innovation was a system that produced a continuous scan or raster in which the scanning coils were energized by periodic currents supplied from a rotating resistance and commutator, with the beam controlled by deflection coils and a diaphragm. Contemporary photographs of various screen displays generated by this method are probably the first pictures of script and graphic figures produced on a raster. (337)

337 Dieckmann, M., and G. Glage. (Cathode-ray relay.) Ger. 184,710, Oct. 10, 1906, Apr. 2, 1907. A cathode-ray tube with transverse magnetic coils to deflect the beam toward or away from collector plates and thereby provide a linear output proportional to the input signal. Similar function as von Lieben's relay. (336, 373)

338 Maver, William Jr. "Seeing by electricity." CASSIRER'S MAG. 30 (Oct, 1906): 519, 520; ENG. MECH. 84 (Oct. 19, 1906): 256; SCI.: AM. SUPP. 62 (Nov. 17, 1906): 25809. Mentions the Televue apparatus of J.B. Fowler (334) and a system with the same name by William H. Thompson, another U.S. inventor, and gives some details of Nisco's plan of "not long ago." (307, 560)

339 de Forest, Lee (1873–1961). "The Audion, a new receiver for wireless telegraphy."

PROC. AIEE 25 (Oct. 1906): 735–79. Reprinted, George Shiers, ed. THE TELEPHONE. New York: Arno Press, 1977. Also ELECT. 58 (Nov. 23, 1906): 216–8; SCI. AM. SUPP. 64 (Nov. 30, 1907): 348–50; (Dec. 7, 1907): 354–6. In this verbose paper on the two-electrode vacuum tube (read Oct. 26), the inventor recounts his earlier work on the flame detector and refers to the experiments of Elster and Geitel and others, including Fleming. He claims his device operates as a relay, quite different from Fleming's oscillation valve (319). He gives a long explanation of the theory of operation, even though he finds the phenomena "exceeding puzzling to explain." The long-standing feud between Fleming and de Forest and the eventual litigation over the radio tube patents began at this time. See letters by both men: ELECT. 58 (Nov. 30, 1906): 263; (Dec. 28, 1906): 425; (Jan. 4, 1907): 464. (346)

340 Thomson, J.J. "Carriers of negative electricity. Nobel lecture, Dec. 11, 1906." NOBEL LECTURES, PHYSICS: 1901–1921. Amsterdam, London, New York: Elsevier, 1967. Presentation speech, pp. 141–4. Lecture, pp. 145–53. Biography, pp. 154, 155. (315, 357)

341 Berndt, Georg. "Fernphotographie und Fernsehen" [Telephotography and television]. WELTALL 6 (1906): 355–61, 378–82.

342 Lux, F. "Bildübertragung" [Picture transmission]. BAYR. IND. GEWER. 38 (1906): 13. This proposal is based on the multiplex telegraph, with signals of different frequencies superimposed on a two-wire line. Each cell in a bank is supplied by alternating current of a specific frequency. A panel array in the receiver has 100 electromagnets and vibrating reeds with flags, each tuned to a particular frequency. Operating frequencies are supplied by small a-c generators or by d-c interrupters or choppers. The plan includes tuning forks, contactor wheels, and phonic wheels. This application of multiplex techniques, under development for many years, provides a more elegant alternative to selection by distributors; both convert multicircuit signals for distribution, one simultaneously the other sequentially. (412)

343 Fournier d'Albe, Edmund Edward (1868–1933). THE ELECTRON THEORY. A POPULAR INTRODUCTION TO THE NEW THEORY OF ELECTRICITY AND MAGNETISM. London: Longmans, Green, 1906. xxiii + 311 pp. Preface by G.J. Stoney, and his portrait. Other editions: (1907) xxv + 325 pp; (1909) xxvi + 327 pp., illus. (621)

344 Lodge, O.J. ELECTRONS, OR THE NATURE AND PROPERTIES OF NEGATIVE ELECTRICITY. London: George Bell, 1906. xvi + 230 pp., 24 illus. Based on lectures given at the Institution of Electrical Engineers in 1903. (302, 1172)

345 Korn, A. "On an apparatus for compensating the inertia of selenium." ELECT. 58 (Jan. 25, 1907): 577; C.R. (Dec. 3, 1906). Bridge circuit incorporating two selenium cells, two batteries, and galvanometer. (322, 347)

346 de Forest, L. "Improvements in oscillation detectors." U.S. 879,532, Jan. 29, 1907, Feb. 18, 1908. Br. 1427, Jan. 21, Apr. 30, 1908. Prime patent on the grid tube, or triode. (339, 428)

347 Korn, A. "Uber neue Methoden der elektrischen Fernphotographie" [About a new method for electrical phototelegraphy]. PHYS. Z. 8 (Feb. 15, 1907): 118–20. Photographic transmission. ELECT. 58 (Mar. 1, 1907): 765, 766. 2 diags. A Nernst lamp is focused on film wrapped around a cylinder with a selenium cell and reflector mounted inside. Start-stop sync with relay and cam. Includes circuit for compensating the inertia of selenium (345). Also PHYS. Z. 8 (Apr. 1, 1907): 198–200. (351)

348 "The problem of television." SCI. AM. SUPP. 63 (June 15, 1907): 26292. Early use of the word "television," though the article deals with Belin's telestereograph, a facsimile system. Camera has a reflective mirror and a bank of 80 selenium cells connected in circuit by a distributor. Other parts include an induction coil and a galvanometer oscillograph receiver. (305, 473)

349 Rosing, Boris (L'vovich) (1869–1933). (A method for the electrical transmission of images.) Russ. 18,076, July 25, 1907. "Verfahren zur elektrischen Fernübertragung von Bildern." Ger. 209,320, Nov. 26, 1907. "New or improved method of electrically transmitting to a distance real optical images and apparatus therefor." Br. 27,570, Dec. 13, 1907, June 25, 1908. In this patent the inventor, a lecturer at the Technological Institute in St. Petersburg, introduced a new method for optical scanning and several important innovations: use of a phototube as an alternative to the selenium cell, a Braun tube with deflection modulation for picture display, and a method for automatic synchronous control. Two polyhedral mirror drums rotating at right angles at very different speeds shift the image across a photocell; from this signals are impressed on a pair of modulating plates in a Braun tube, thereby deflecting the electron beam (from a cold cathode) more or less away from a pinhole aperture in a diaphragm. Currents to operate a pair of beam deflection coils on a picture tube are obtained from rheostats or from inductors mounted with the scanning mirrors. Rosing is said to have built experimental models and he later patented a modified system. (400)

350 Bidwell, S. "Practical telephotography." NATURE 76 (Aug. 29, 1907): 444, 445. On Korn's system (347) with facsimile reproductions and mention of the recent edition of his book. (188, 365)

351 (Korn, A.) "Electrical transmission of pictures." ELECT. 60 (Nov. 8, 1907): 133, 134. 2 diags. About Korn's system (347) and the new edition of his book (322). See also E.T.Z. 28 (Aug. 15, 1907): 808–10. Very satisfactory results were obtained during transmissions between Berlin and Munich. (352)

352 (Korn, A.) "Photo transmission." ELECT. (Nov. 15, 1907): 165. Photo of King Edward VII transmitted from L'ILLUSTRATION in Paris to the DAILY MIRROR in London. An excellent picture. British rights in Korn's apparatus acquired by the DAILY MIRROR. (351, 370)

353 Kruh, Osias Otto. "Telephotography." U.S. 968,484, Nov. 19, 1907, Aug. 23, 1910. Assigned G.E. This specification refers to a facsimile receiver employing a luminous tube and a photographic plate. Various types of discharge tubes and mercury vapor tubes have opaque coatings with small openings. The intensity of light emitted is varied according to the incoming signal by transverse electromagnets. There is no mention of any scanning means.

354 (Senlecq, C.) "The Senlecq telectroscope, an apparatus for electrical vision." SCI. AM. SUPP. 64 (Dec. 14, 1907): 372, 373. 6 diags. From Fr. 375,745. In this adaptation of Nipkow's disk the inventor employs separate cells or plugs of selenium instead of holes in a copper disk. Signals from each cell in turn are sent via an induction coil to a solenoid-type galvanometer which operates a shaded transparency to modulate light from a lamp in a receiver. The modulated beam is then passed through the holes in a scanning disk and projected onto a viewing screen. No specific method for synchronism is mentioned, but a screw is provided to adjust the disk speed at the receiver. (165)

355 Gaede, Wolfgang. "Demonstration einer neuen Verbesserung an der rotierenden Quecksilber-Luftpumpe" [Demonstration of a new improvement on the rotating mercury air pump]. DEUT. PHYS. GES. 8 (1907): 639–41; PHYS. Z. 8 (1907): 852, 853. (379)

356 "Fernsehen mittels Elektrizität" [Television by means of electricity]. Z. SCHWACH. 1 (1907): 253, 254.

357 Thomson, J.J. THE CORPUSCULAR THEORY OF MATTER. London: A. Constable, 1907. vii + 172 pp. An extension of lectures given at the Royal Institution the previous year. (340)

358 Stephan, W. "Einrichtung zur elektrischen Ubertragung reeler optischer Bilder in photographischer oder unmittelbar sichtbarer Wiedergabe unter Verwendung synchron rotierender, die Gesichts-felder in Elemente zerlegenden Scheiben und einer licht-

empfindlichen Selenzelle, welche im Okularteil eines Fernrohres fest angeordnet ist" [Arrangement for the electrical transmission of real optical images for telegraphic or instant visual reproduction using synchronously rotating disks, which dissolve view fields into elements, and a light-sensitive selenium cell which is permanently mounted in the ocular portion of a telescope]. Ger. 214,473, Feb. 27, 1908, Sept. 28, 1909. (333)

359 Adamian, Johannes. "Electrically controlled apparatus for seeing at a distance." Br. 7219, Apr. 1, May 28, 1908. This specification covers a receiver with a mirror galvanometer that directs light onto selenium cells arranged in two groups connected to Geissler tubes. One tube provides white light for the brighter tones, the other a red light for the darker tones. A transformer and Tesla coil in the cell-tube circuit furnish high-voltage, high-frequency currents to operate the discharge tubes which are viewed through a Nipkow disk. (470)

360 Armagnat, Henri. "Phototelegraphy." SMITH. INST. ANN. REP. for 1908 (1909): 197–207. 9 diags. From REV. SCI. 9 (Apr. 18, 1908). Survey of current systems: Korn, Berjonneau, Carbonnelle, Senlecq-Tival.

361 Armengaud, Jules. "La vision à distance par l'électricité; l'appa-reil" [Vision at a distance by electricity; the apparatus]. LA NATURE 36 (Apr. 1908): 390–2. (362)

362 "Long distance vision by electricity." TIMES (Apr. 28, 1908): 5d. Report on Armengaud's plan (361). From Paris newspapers: "Thanks to electricity it will before long be possible to see in Paris what is going on in the entire world." (368)

363 (Knudson, Hans.) "Knudson's system of wireless transmission of photographs." ELECT. 61 (May 1, 1908): 89, 90. 3 diags. Report of a demonstration to the press at Hotel Cecil, London, Apr. 28. (398)

364 Lux, H. "Telautograph." V.D.I.Z. 52 (May 9, 1908): 756. Revival of insulated tin foil on cylinder, with dotted reproduction.

365 Bidwell, S. "Telegraphic photography and electric vision." NATURE 78 (June 4, 1908): 105, 106. After referring to his article on Korn (350), to the work of Belin, Carbonnelle, Berjonneau, and the report of Armengaud's system (362), he critically analyzes the problems of seeing by electricity. With a mosaic system in mind, he estimates the technical requirements and the high cost, about 1,250,000 pounds. (350, 366)

366 Swinton, A.A.C. "Distant electric vision." NATURE 78 (June 18, 1908): 151. In this response to Bidwell's letter (365), and the problem of obtaining synchronism by mechanical means, Swinton suggests a solution and pinpoints the "real difficulties":

"...may I point out that though, as stated by Mr. Bidwell, it is wildly impracticable to effect even 160,000 synchronized operations per second by ordinary mechanical means, this part of the problem of obtaining distant electric vision can probably be solved by the employment of two beams of kathode rays (one at the transmitting and one at the receiving station) synchronously deflected by the varying fields of two electromagnets placed at right angles to one another and energized by two alternating electric currents of widely different frequencies, so that the moving extremities of the two beams are caused to sweep synchronously over the whole of the required surfaces within the one-tenth of a second necessary to take advantage of visual persistence.

"Indeed, so far as the receiving apparatus is concerned, the moving kathode beam has only to be arranged to impinge on a sufficiently sensitive fluorescent screen and given suitable variations in its intensity, to obtain the desired result.

"The real difficulties lie in devising an efficient transmitter which under the influence of light and shade, shall sufficiently vary the transmitted electric current so as to produce the necessary alterations in the intensity of the kathode beam of the receiver, and further in making this transmitter sufficiently rapid in its action to respond to the 160,000 variations per second that are necessary as a minimum.

"Possibly no photoelectric phenomenon at present known will provide what is required in this respect, but should something suitable be discovered, distant electric vision will, I think, come within the region of possibility.

"Swinton developed this idea and put forward details of a complete electrical system with an electronic camera tube in 1911. (286, 410)"

367 Sellers, Gilbert. "Electrical transmission of graphic messages." U.S. 939,338, July 18, 1908, Nov. 9. 1909. This specification covers the reproduction of visible, stationary, or movable images "direct from life or nature," as well as film transmission and graphic recording. The camera has a disk with lenses and selenium cells connected via a distributor to an oscillating mirror galvanometer in the receiver. Light from a local source, modulated by reflection from the moving mirror through a lens, is projected onto a series of mirrors on a revolving drum, upon which surfaces the image is viewed through an opening in the receiver case. Electric motors are assumed to provide synchronous operation.

368 Troller, A. "Electrical vision at a distance." SCI. AM. SUPP. 66 (Sept. 19, 1908): 180. 4 illus. This description of Armengaud's apparatus is from LA NATURE (361). The novel feature is the use of crossed slotted belts for scanning, one moving intermittently and the other continuously. A mirror galvanometer and a shaded screen provide modulation in the receiver, where the image is viewed on a ground glass screen. (362)

369 Andersen, Anders Christian, and Lauritz Sophus Andersen. "Apparatus for electrically transmitting images of natural objects to a distance." Br. 30,188, Dec. 24, 1909, Sept. 22, 1910. In Denmark Dec. 24, 1908. Ger. 233,688, Dec. 19, 1909. A single-circuit system with perforated ribbon or a perforated disk, selenium cell, graded transparency modulator, color filters on a disk, prism, screen projection, and clockwork sync control. A line switch permits alternate vision and voice along one wire. "This apparatus can be employed for verifying documents, for exhibiting samples, machines in movement, objects and various merchandise and for making all kinds of reports. It can also be very well employed in the army, not to mention passing events and theatrical representations." (396)

370 Dubois, Louis. "Korn's apparatus for photographic transmission." ELECT. 62 (Jan. 22, 1909): 570–3; (Feb. 5, 1909): 644–7. 13 illus., including photos of apparatus and reproductions of facsimiles. On tests from Paris to London and to Berlin. (352, 412)

371 Pictet, August Oswald. "Improvements in telegraphic receivers." Br. 10,450, May 3, July 22, 1909. Manometric flame operates in conjunction with a selenium cell. With several units connected in series via interstage transformers, this specification is an interesting example of the attempt at cascade amplification in the "pre-electronic" age.

372 Ruhmer, E.W. "Der elektrische Fernseher." DER MECH. 17 (June 1909): 145, 146. "Das elektrische Fernseher." Z. SCHWAB. 3 (1909): 393–5. Frequency-selective system with resonant relays and single-wire transmission. Matrix with 25 cells, and lamps. Apparatus said to have displayed simple geometric figures to show principles. (298, 396)

373 Dieckmann, M. "The problem of television, a partial solution." SCI. AM. SUPP. 68 (July 24, 1909): 61, 62. 8 illus., including photo of the word BRAUN in script as received on a cathode-ray tube. From an article in PROMETHEUS, this account describes the Dieckmann and Glage system (336), modified to provide a continuous scan or raster upon which the signals are impressed. (337, 374)

374 "Partial solution of the problem of television." SCI. AM. 101 (Aug. 7, 1909): 94. The Dieckman and Glage system. (373, 404)

375 Knothe, A. "Lösung des Problems des elektrischen Fernsehens" [Solution of the problem of electric television]. ELEKT. ANZ. 26

(1909): 263. This startling "solution" is a multicircuit system with many selenium cells, batteries, spark coils, and parabolic mirrors, with a special X-ray tube and fluorescent screen at the receiver.

376 Gernsback, Hugo (1884–1967). "Television and the telephot." MOD. ELECT. (Dec. 1909). Gernsback gives details of an idea which he proposed "some eight years ago," based on the electrical harmonica. Selenium cells in a mosaic are connected to the coils of electromagnets furnished with flexible reeds, which induce currents in the main coil of the assembly. This coil is connected via two wires to the corresponding coil in a similar receiving arrangement whereby individual variable-aperture galva-nometers, or light relays, modulate light from incandescent lamps. The Knothe proposal (375) and Ruhmer's system (372) are also described. Gernsback later claimed to have introduced the term "television" in this article, but he was preceded by the editors of SCIENTIFIC AMERICAN (348). The word "telephot" was also used earlier in a slightly different form (126). (460)

377 Braun, K.F. "Electrical oscillations and wireless telegraphy. Nobel lecture, Dec. 11, 1909." NOBEL LECTURES, PHYSICS: 1901–1921. Amsterdam, London, New York: Elsevier, 1967. Presentation speech, pp. 193–5. Lecture, pp. 226–45, 19 illus., cathode-ray work, pp. 236, 237 (263). Biography, pp. 246, 247. Braun shared this award with Marconi (258).

378 De Varigny, Henry. "La vision à distance." L'ILLUSTRATION 134 (Dec. 11, 1909): 451. 6 illus. On the Rignoux and Fournier téléphote. Selenium matrix with multiple relays connected to a distributor for single-line transmission. Faraday cell with Nicol prisms and mirror wheel for screen display. Original pattern (letter E) and reproduction are shown. See also Fr. 390,435, 1908. (328, 382)

379 Gaede, W. "Method and apparatus for producing high vacuums." U.S 1,069,408, Dec. 22, 1909, Aug. 5, 1913. (355, 417)

380 Czudnochowski, W. Biegon. "Das Problem des Fernsehens" [The problem of television]. Z. PHYS. CHEM. UNT. 27 (1909): 261–5.

381 Schewe, E. "Telautographie, Bildtelegraphie, Fernphotographieren und Fernsehen über Telegraphonleitungen" [Telautography, picture telegraphy, telephotography, and television via telegraph wires]. ARCH. POST TELEGR. 37 (1909): 161–73.

382 Honoré, Fernand. "The Rignoux-Fournier system of television." SCI. AM. 102 (Jan. 1, 1910): 13. (378, 443)

383 Baker, Thomas Thorne. "Recent work in the telegraphic transmission of pictures." NATURE 82 (Jan. 13, 1910): 309–11. Also, the Physical Society's exhibition (Dec. 23, 1909): 234. Note on Baker's apparatus, shown by the DAILY MIRROR. (390)

384 Ekström, Alfred. "Anordning för äfverförande af bilder pa afstand." Swedish 32220, Jan. 24, 1910, Feb. 3, 1912. Intended for transmitting pictures from transparencies, this system employs spotlight scanning, proposed earlier by Rignoux (328). A rotating mirror with a cam-operated oblique motion provides a spiral scan at each instrument. Light from a carbon arc is modulated by a variable-aperture galvanometer and projected onto a viewing screen.

385 Elster, J., and H. Geitel. "Uber gefärbte Hydride der Alkalimetalle und ihre photoelektrische Empfindlichkeit" [On colored hydrides of alkali metals and their photoelectric sensitivity]. PHYS. Z. 11 (Apr. 11, 1910): 257–62. Also 12 (Nov. 1910): 1082, 1083. (268, 408)

386 Hoglund, Gustav E. "Mechanism for electrically transmitting and reproducing images." U.S. 1,030,240, Apr. 18, 1910, June 18, 1912. Two scanning disks rotate in opposite directions; one has a spiral series of arcuate slots, the other a series of stepped openings that extend radially over the same area. A selenium cell, or an equivalent device "known to science," is connected to a transformer in the receiver, where the secondary output

modulates a light source, preferably a speaking arc. After passing through a similar pair of disks the image is reconstituted on a ground glass screen, or projected onto a viewing screen. Drive is by synchronous motors, but handles are provided on the disks for manual adjustment to bring the images into "proper relation." With a duplicate set of photocells and lamps, arranged diametrically opposite behind the scanning disks, it is possible to obtain two-way operation with simultaneous transmission.

387 Schmierer, M. "Kommutierungsverfahren für Bilderfernübertragung, bei welchem auf einer Tafel die einzelnen lichtempfindlichen oder lichterzeugenden Elemente zweckmässig in parallelen und senkrechten Reihen eingelassen sind" [Commutating process of long-distance transmission of pictures in which the particular light-sensitive or light-producing elements are assembled on a board in parallel and vertical rows]. Ger. 229,916, Apr. 30, 1910. Matrix arrangement of photocells and glow lamps interconnected with distributors. Also Ger. 234,853, Apr. 10; 235,601, July 8, 1910; 264,275, Nov. 3, 1912. (1108)

388 Sinding-Larsen, Alf. "Transmission of pictures of moving objects." U.S. 1,175,313, June 10, 1911, Mar. 14, 1916. Part assigned to Johan Henrik L'Abée Lund. Ger. 260,901, June 14, 1911. Br. 14,503, June 19, 1911, Mar. 21, 1912. Fr. 434,378, 1911. In Norway June 20, 1910. Light-tight boxes, one with a lens and the other with an eyepiece, contain resonant oscillating mirrors for analyzing and reconstituting the image. The mirrors are operated by electromagnets controlled by tuning forks, or by an interrupter and a motor-driven commutator. In a radical departure from the usual methods, the inventor utilizes optical transmission by means of a small silver pipe (inside diam. 2 mm), which may be evacuated or filled with gas such as hydrogen. This pipe also serves as an electrical connection between the stations. Three reflecting prisms suitably arranged in the instruments "make it possible to send pictures in both directions simultaneously."

For electrical transmission, where distances are greater, a liquid alloy regenerative photocell in a labyrinth form, like a set of interleaved plates, is specified. Signals at the receiver operate a "very small electric lamp or a powerful fluorescent body...." With duplicate apparatus "the pictures may be obtained in stereoscopic form, a method which may be of use for military purposes." (463)

389 Marlowe, A.C. "The De Vendenil system." MOD. ELECT. (July 1910). This simple arrangement has Nipkow disks and a selenium cell. A telephone-actuated pressure chamber in the receiver modulates an acetylene flame, fluctuations of which are projected through two lenses and a disk onto a viewing screen at the end of the box, as in the Le Pontois scheme (234).

390 Baker, T.T. "The telegraphy of photographs, wireless and by wire." NATURE 84 (Aug. 18, 1910): 220–6. 12 illus. Lecture before the Royal Institution, Apr. 22. SMITH. INST. ANN. REP. for 1910 (1911): 257–74. (383, 398)

391 Sutton, H. "Telephotography. A system of transmitting optical images electrically." SCI. AM. SUPP. 70 (Sept. 3, 1910): 151. Virtual reprint of the 1890 article (213).

392 Saint-René, H.C. "Sur une solution du problème de la vision à distance" [On a solution of the problem of vision at a distance]. C.R. 150 (1910): 446, 467. A mosaic system with selenium cells, lamps, and galvanometers for light modulation. To solve the spatial problems, the author suggests flexible glass tubes or light pipes with one set of ends at the modulators and the other set clustered to form a compact viewing surface.

393 Claude, Georges (1870–1960). "Sur les tubes luminescents au néon" [On luminescent neon tubes]. C.R. 151 (1910): 1122–4. This beginning of neon-tube technology arose from Claude's interest in the inert gases and the work of Ramsay (270). Geissler tubes and other discharge tubes had been proposed as modulated light sources by Vol'fke (276), Kruh (353), and Adamian

(359). Neon lamps became essential components as modulated light sources and for timing circuits in television systems during the 1920s. Earlier, J.A. Fleming had used a vacuum tube filled with rarefied neon as a detector of high-frequency radiations. See "Improvements in apparatus suitable for detecting electrical oscillations." Br. 13,762A, June 17, 1904. Claude also applied for a patent on a neon-tube detector, Br. 7997, July 11, 1914, which was not accepted. (331, 428)

394   Eichhorn, Gustav. "Elektrisches Fernsehen." WELTALL 10 (1910): 117, 118.

395   Gripenberg, William Sebastian. "Zum Problem des elektrischen Fernsehens" [On the problem of electrical television]. PHYS. Z. 11 (1910): 420.

396   Ruhmer, E.W. "Der Fernseher der Gebrüder Andersen" [The television apparatus of the Andersen brothers]. DER MECH. 18 (1910): 160. Also E.T.Z. 32 (1911): 1038. (372, 406)

397   Lieben, R. v., Eugen Reisz, and Siegmund Strauss (1875–1942). "An improved relay for undulatory currents." Br. 1482, Jan. 19, Sept. 28, 1911. Ger. 249,142, Dec. 20, 1910, July 12, 1912; U.S. 1,038,901, Jan. 30, 1911, Sept. 17, 1912. Supplement to Ger. 236,716, Sept. 4, 1910, July 11, 1911. Developed from the tube in the patent of 1906 (329). See also Ger. 264,554; U.S. 1,059,763. (434)

398   Baker, T.T. THE TELEGRAPHIC TRANSMISSION OF PHOTOGRAPHS. London: Constable; New York: Van Nostrand, 1910. xi + 146 pp., 66 illus. This pioneer book in English on facsimile considers theoretical aspects as well as practical matters, such as details of construction, operation, and circuit arrangements. Various systems are surveyed, particularly Korn's telautograph and the author's Telectrograph. Knudson's work (363) and the author's experiments on wireless transmission of photographs are covered in Ch. 7, pp. 127–41. (390, 524)

399   Pohl, Robert Wichard. DIE ELEKTRISCHE FERNUBERTRAGUNG VON BILDERN [The electric transmission of pictures]. Braunschweig: Vieweg, 1910. viii + 45 pp. (440)

400   Rosing, B.L. "Transmission of light pictures in electrical telescopic and similar apparatus." Br. 5486, Mar. 4, 1911, Feb. 29, 1912. Ger. 244,746, Mar. 2, 1911. U.S. 1,135,624, Apr. 5, 1911, Apr. 13, 1915; 1,161,734, Apr. 5, 1911, Nov. 23, 1915. In Russia Apr. 5, 1911. Like the previous patent (349), this employs two polyhedral mirror drums and a Braun tube, similar but without the apertured diaphragms. Problems of transmitting rapidly changing signals free from distortion, as caused by inductive and capacitive effects, and similar theoretical factors such as waveforms are discussed in detail. This new system specifies pulsations or interruptions in the optical path of the phototube, carried out by a chopper disk or by gratings, or by equivalent interruptions in the phototube circuit by means of a commutator. Alternative phototube arrangements are considered, with one or two tubes connected in series, in parallel, or in a bridge circuit. The chief innovation is the introduction of the principle of velocity modulation in the receiver whereby the scanning rate of the beam changes according to the signal strength: "with the result that the signalling point travels at relatively low speed over the lighter points of the picture field and at relatively high speed over its darker points." This use of velocity modulation was technically ineffective, however, since means to vary the scanning rate in the same manner at the transmitter were not specified. The light chopper disk was used by Baird in 1924 and by others. Velocity modulation was adopted in some experimental systems during the early 1930s. (491)

401   Rosing, B. (An electric telescope system with pulsating and alternating current.) ELEKTRICHESTVO 32 (1911): 349–59. Description of the new system (403).

402   Dosai, M. "Eine neuer Vorschlag zur Lösung des Fernseher-Problems" [A new proposal for the solution of the television problem]. DER MECH. 19 (1911): 54, 55, 137.

403 Rosing, B.L. "Uber elektrische Teleskopie und die einzige Möglichkeit ihrer Verwirklichung" [On electric telescopy and the unique possibility of its realization]. DER MECH. 19 (1911): 99, 110, 111–3, 124–6, 137, 138. (401, 405)

404 "Cathode rays in telephotography." SCI. AM. SUPP. 71 (Mar. 18, 1911): 163. Account of the improved Dieckmann and Glage system (373), from LA NATURE. (505)

405 Grimshaw, Robert. "The 'telegraphic eye.'" SCI. AM. 104 (Apr. 1, 1911): 335, 336. 3 illus. In this description of Rosing's earlier system (349) the author looks to the future and visualizes uses for the electric eye in scientific research, in military operations, and in industry. (403, 406, 426)

"It is not necessary to emphasize in great detail the importance of electric telescopy. Apart from the fact that it allows us to see through obstacles and to span any distance, as though we viewed things with our own eyes, new possibilities are opened to seeing that which no human eye has yet perceived. By fitting this electric eye with a strong electric lamp and sinking both together to the depths of the sea, we shall be able to systematically explore the ocean bed. It is difficult to say what innumerable scientific and material treasures are hidden in the unknown portions of our globe. Such an apparatus can also be employed for researches concerning the crust of the earth by letting it down into a volcanic crater, into chasms and crevices of mountains, or to the bottom of deep artesian wells.

"Electric eyes will most probably be employed on lighthouses and at military posts. With the help of this eye the commander of an army or of a fleet, working with the aid of an airship, will be able to observe the movements of an army or fleet. And finally, this invention can be of great service in the industries by enabling the engineer or superintendent to inspect his plants, shops, or other installations from his desk or office. In fact the possibilities presented to our minds are apparently inexhaustible."

406 Ruhmer, E.W. "Rosing's system of telephoty." ELECT. REV. 68 (June 16, 1911): 981, 982. (396, 405, 407, 411)

407 Boyer, J. "Prof. Rosing's electric eye, a new apparatus for television." SCI. AM. SUPP. 71 (June 17, 1911): 384. Description of Rosing's earlier system (349) with circuit diagram. From the author's article in COSMOS, derived from information in the BULLETIN OF THE INTERNATIONAL TECHNICAL SOCIETY of St. Petersburg. (273, 406, 411, 438)

408 Elster, J., and H. Geitel. "Weitere Untersuchungen an Photoelektrischen Zellen mit Gefärbten Kaliumkathoden" [Further investigations on photoelectric cells with colored potassium cathodes]. PHYS. Z. 12 (Aug. 1, 1911): 609–14. Also 13 (Aug. 15, 1912): 739–44. (385, 424)

409 Bronk, O. von. "Hochfrequenzverstärkung" [High-frequency amplifier]. Ger. 271,059, Sept. 11, 1911. Mar. 3, 1914. Br. 8821, Apr. 15, Oct. 2, 1914. Fr. 456,788, Apr. 17, Sept. 4, 1913. Aust. 63,593, Feb. 25, 1914. U.S. 1,087,892, July 21, 1914. Use of de Forest triode as a radio-frequency amplifier. (295, 420)

410 "Distant electric vision." TIMES (Nov. 15, 1911): 24b, c. Detailed report of part of Swinton's address to the Röntgen Society on Nov. 7, in which he describes a scheme for an all-electric television system. (366, 413)

411 Ruhmer, E.W. "Ein bedeutsamer Fortschritt im Fernsehproblem; der Rosingsche Fernseher" [Significant progress in the television problem; Rosing's televisor]. DIE UMSCHAU 15 (1911): 508–10. On Rosing's earlier system (349). An important step in the problem of television. SCI. AM. 105 (Dec. 23, 1911): 574. One illustration shows a cut-away view of the transmitter assembly, another shows the Braun tube mounted on a stand. (406, 407, 649)

412 Korn, A., and Bruno Glatzel (1878–1914). HANDBUCH FUR PHOTOTELEGRAPHIE UND TELAUTOGRAPHIE. Leipzig: Otto Nemnich, 1911. 488 pp., 292 illus. This

classic work thoroughly documents the history and progress of copying and writing telegraph systems. The last chapter, "Fernsehen und Fernseher," pp. 417–84, covers television and related systems, with 45 illus., and 68 footnote refs. Proposals or patents by the following are mentioned or described: the Andersens, Armengaud, Ayrton and Perry, Brillouin, von Bronk, Carey, Coblyn, de Paiva, Dieckmann and Glage, Dussaud, Jaworski and Frankenstein, Jenkins, Le-blanc, Le Pontois, Liesegang, Lux, Majorana, Nipkow, Nisco, Perosino, Re, Rignoux and Fournier, Rosing, Saint-René, Sawyer, Schmierer, Schneider, Senlecq, Simon, Sutton, Szczepanik, Weiller. (370, 423, 431)

413 Swinton, A.A.C. "Presidential address." J. RONTGEN SOC. 8 (Jan. 1912): 1–15. In this cardinal paper some philosophical views on physical science are followed by a full description of his plan for an electrical method for distant electric vision (366). Explanations in the text are supported by a circuit diagram which shows details of the camera and picture tubes coupled by a line wire and ground for the image signals. Two alternators supply currents to the series-connected deflection coils via two line wires and ground. The image screen in the camera tube is a mosaic of insulated cubes of rubidium faced by a metal gauze screen with a space between filled with a conductive gas, such as sodium vapor. The scanning beam charges the photoelectric elements negatively; those that are brightly illuminated release charges through the ionized gas to the gauze screen, or signal plate. This screen is connected to deflector plates in the picture tube which, being fitted with an apertured diaphragm, provides deflection modulation of the beam. Swinton made it clear that this arrangement was not a "really worked-out scheme for distant electric vision," but merely a record of "certain ideas that have occurred to my imagination in the hope that they may lead others to the invention of a more practicable method of arriving at what is wanted."

414 Swinton, A.A.C. "Fernsehen." Z. SCHWACH. 6 (1912): 149–53. (413, 586)

415 Lowenstein, Fritz. "Telephone relay." U.S. 1,231,764, Apr. 24. 1912, renewed Apr. 26, 1917, July 3, 1917. Triode circuit with negative bias on grid.

416 Marino, A. "Transmission des photographies et des images à distance, système Marino." LUM. ELECT. 19 (Aug. 31, 1912): 261–5. The Marino system of color phototelegraphy. SCI. AM. 108 (Mar. 22, 1913): 272. Scanning by ribbons with staggered holes. Seven selenium cells connected in parallel, with a prism, at the transmitter. Arc lamp and photographic plate at the receiver. An early example of color facsimile.

417 Gaede, W. "Die äussere Reibung der Gase und ein neues Prinzip für Luftpumpen: die Molekularluftpumpe" [The exterior friction of gases and a new principle for air pumps: the molecular air pump]. PHYS. Z. 13 (Sept. 15, 1912): 864–70. ELECT. 70 (Oct. 18, 1912): 48–50. D. PHYS. GES. 14 (Aug. 15, 1912): 775–87. See also ANN. PHYS. 41 (June 3, 1913): 337–80. (379, 437)

418 Wilson, Harold Albert (1874–1964). THE ELECTRICAL PROPERTY OF FLAMES AND INCANDESCENT SOLIDS. London: London University Press, 1912. vii + 118 pp.

419 Arco, Georg Wilhelm Alexander Hans Graf von (1869–1940), and Alexander Meissner (1883–1958). "Relay arrangements for alternating currents." Br. 252, Jan. 5, 1914, Aug. 19, 1915. Ger. 291,604, Apr. 10, 1913. Lieben-Reisz gaseous triode in feedback circuits, with applications for signal amplification, heterodyne reception, and generation of radio frequencies in wireless transmitters. (329, 397, 434)

420 Schloemilch, Wilhelm, and O. von Bronk. "Means for receiving electrical oscillations." U.S. 1,087,892, Mar. 14, 1913, Feb. 17, 1914. Br. 8821, Apr. 15, Oct. 2, 1913, Ger. 293,300. Assigned: Telefunken. Regenerative circuit for high and low frequencies. (409, 694)

421 Stille, Curt. "Image transformer for distant photography." U.S. 1,141,850, Apr. 22, 1913, June 1, 1915.

422 Franklin, Charles Samuel (1879–1964). "Wireless telegraphy and telephony receivers." Br. 13,636, June 12, 1913, June 11, 1914. Reactive or feedback circuits with triode for amplifying signals. Co-patentee, Marconi's Wireless Telegraph Co., Ltd. (804)

423 Korn, A. "The transmission of photographs and drawings by wireless telegraphy." W.W. 1 (Sept. 1913): 353–7. Erratum (Oct. 1913): 426. (412, 426)

424 Elster, J., and H. Geitel. "Die Proportionalität von Lichtstärke und Photostrom an Alkalimetallzellen" [The proportionality of light intensity and photoelectric current in alkali metal cells]. PHYS. Z. 14 (Sept. 1, 1913): 741–52. The potassium hydride phototube, with sensitivity greatly increased by processing the cathode with a glow discharge in hydrogen. (408)

425 Jenkins, C.F. "Motion pictures by wireless." MOTION PICT. NEWS (Oct. 4, 1913). Also Sept. 27 issue. (245, 464)

426 Grimshaw, R. "Rapid telephotography." SCI. AM. 109 (Oct. 11, 1913): 286. On Korn's work on phototelegraphy and kinematographic film pictures. "These experiments also throw light upon the question of whether or not the problem of television or seeing by telegraph can be solved in the near future." (405, 423, 506)

427 Armstrong, Edwin Howard (1890–1954). "Wireless receiving system." U.S. 1,113,149, Oct. 29, 1913, Oct. 6, 1914. Triode feedback circuits. Armstrong claimed Jan. 3 as the date of invention. (436)

428 de Forest, L. "The Audion; detector and amplifier." ELECT. 72 (Nov. 21, 1913): 285–8. Also W. AGE 1 (Jan. 1914): 273; PROC. IRE 2 (Mar. 1914): 24–30. First press notice, N.Y. HERALD (Nov. 7, 1913): 12. On the first public demonstration of the Audion as a telephone amplifier, with two- and three-stage circuits. Letters by de Forest and Fleming. ELECT. 72 (Jan. 23, 1914): 659–61. (346, 393, 791, 1241)

429 Langmuir, Irving (1881–1957). "The effect of space charge and residual gases on thermionic currents in high vacuum." PHYS. REV. 2 (Dec. 1913): 450–86. See also PHYS. Z. 15 (1914): 348–53, 516–26. Langmuir was awarded the Nobel Prize for Chemistry in 1932. (433)

430 Round, Henry Joseph (1881–1966). "Receivers for use in wireless telegraphy." Br. 28,413, Dec. 9, 1913, Dec, 9, 1914. Feedback circuits with triode. Also Br. 13,248, May 29, 1914. Co-patentee, Marconi's Wireless Telegraph Co., Ltd. (765)

431 Glatzel, B. "Die elektrische Bildübertragung" [The electric transmission of pictures]. NATUR 10 (1913): 172–82. (412)

432 Allen, Herbert Stanley (1873–1954). PHOTO-ELECTRICITY, THE LIBERATION OF ELECTRONS BY LIGHT. With chapters on fluorescence and phosphorescence, photochemical actions and photography. London: Longmans, Green, 1913. xii + 221 pp., 35 illus. Full survey with extensive historical background; over 400 footnote refs.

433 Langmuir, I. "Controlling electric currents or potential." U.S. 1,273,627, Feb. 5, 1914, July 23, 1918. Assigned: G.E. Output from a phototube is amplified in a triode circuit. This is an early application of an electron tube as a photoelectric amplifier. (429, 450)

434 Reisz, E. "A new method of magnifying electric currents." ELECT. 72 (Feb. 6, 1914): 726–9. Editorial note: 721. Also 73 (July 3, 1914): 538, 539. Description of the Lieben-Reisz-Strauss gaseous triode as an amplifier for telegraphy and telephony. See also de Forest letter 72 (Mar. 13, 1914): 956. (397, 419)

435 Hart, Samuel Lavington. "Transmitting pictures of moving objects and the like to a distance electrically." Br. 15,720, June 25, 1914, June 25, 1915. Lens drum scanners, discharge tube with deflection control, on-off sync. The most significant feature is the introduction of interlaced scanning, with alternate lines arranged singly or in groups.

Remote control of the viewing position of the transmitter, recording on punched tape or on a phonograph disk, and cinematographic projection are also mentioned.

436 Armstrong, E.H. "Operating features of the audion." ELECT. W. 64 (Dec. 12, 1914): 1149–52. 15 illus. First correct description of the theory of the triode and its operation as a detector and as a high-frequency amplifier. (427, 452)

437 Gaede, W. "Die Entwicklung der Luftpumpe" [The development of the air pump]. NATUR 10 (1914): 225–37. (417)

438 Bozer, J. LA TRANSMISSION TELEGRAPHIQUE DES IMAGES ET DES PHOTOGRAPHIES [The telegraphic transmission of images and photographs]. Paris: Charles-Mendel, 1914. 86 pp. (407, 492)

439 Hughes, Arthur Llewelyn. PHOTO-ELECTRICITY. Cambridge: Cambridge University Press, 1914. viii + 144 pp.

440 Pohl, R.W., and Peter Pringsheim. DIE LICHTELEKTRISCHEN ERSCHEINUNGEN [Photoelectric phenomena]. Braunschweig: Vieweg, 1914. 174 pp., 36 illus. (399)

441 Richardson, O.W. THE ELECTRON THEORY OF MATTER. Cambridge: Cambridge University Press, 1914. vi + 612 pp. 2nd ed. (1916), vi + 631 pp. (304, 454)

442 Martin, Marcus J. "Radiophotography." W.W. 2 (Jan.–July 1915): 656–8; 727–31; 755–9; 3:57–60, 102–6, 162–5, 228–32. Practical hints, on the author's work and apparatus, with photos and diags. (444)

443 Arapu, R. "The telephotographic apparatus of Georges Rignoux." SCI. AM. SUPP. 79 (May 22, 1915): 331. (382)

444 Martin, M.J. "Television." W.W. 3 (June 1915): 193. Subtitled "When shall we see as well as hear by wireless?" these notes refer to the "fascinating problem of television." (422, 453)

"There is no doubt that in the near future we may have some practical system of television to work over ordinary conductors; the idea of wireless television is, from a really practical point of view, absurdly improbable. To construct wireless apparatus capable of transmitting and receiving 40,000 signals in one-tenth of a second, and arrange them in their correct order, would surely tax to the utmost the powers of our cleverest inventors, and prove the limit of even human ingenuity."

445 "Facsimile telegraphy and phototelegraphy." SCI. AM. 112 (June 5, 1915): 571–3. A summary of progress from 1843, with about 70 names, dates, and brief descriptions.

446 Campbell, George Ashley. "Electric wave-filter." U.S. 1,227,113, July 15, 1915, May 22, 1917. Assigned: AT&T.

447 Voulgré, Andre Denis Joseph Antoine. "Television and telephotographic apparatus." U.S. 1,329,688, Apr. 1, 1916, Feb. 3, 1920. Fr. 478,361, Sept. 16, 1915. Slotted disks and slotted bands, mercury vapor lamp, transparency or photographic film. Proposals include variable focusing, variable scanning rate, manual framing control, and cinematographic projection.

448 Townsend, (Sir) John Sealy Edward (1868–1957). ELECTRICITY IN GASES. Oxford: Clarendon Press, 1915. xv + 496 pp.

449 Cooper, William Ranson. "Selenium cells." ELECT. 76 (Feb. 11, 1916): 676–9; (Feb. 18, 1916): 705–7; (Feb. 25, 1916): 735–8. From a new edition of the author's PRIMARY BATTERIES.

450 Langmuir, I. "A high vacuum mercury vapor pump of extreme speed." PHYS. REV. 8 (July 1916): 48–51. (433, 451)

451 Langmuir, I. "The condensation pump: an improved form of high vacuum pump." G.E. REV. 19 (Dec. 1916): 1060–71. Abstract, ELECT. 79 (July 13, 1917): 579, 580. (450, 2387)

452 Latour, Marius. "Theoretical discussion of the Audion." ELECT. 78 (Dec. 1, 1916): 280–2. 3 illus. LUM. ELECT. 35 (Dec. 30, 1916): 289–92. (436, 747)

453 Martin. M.J. THE WIRELESS TRANSMISSION OF PHOTOGRAPHS. London: Wireless Press, 1916. xi + 117 pp., 62 illus. Extended version of earlier articles (442). 2nd ed. 1919. (444, 467). Facsimile.

454 Richardson, O.W. THE EMISSION OF ELECTRICITY FROM HOT BODIES. London: Longmans, Green, 1916. vii + 304 pp, 35 diags., many tables. 2nd ed. 1921. (441, 2152)

455 Low, Archibald Montgomery (1888–1956). "Electrical transmission of optical images." Br. 191,405, Oct. 4, 1917, Feb. 8, 1923. Facsimile system with a selenium mosaic scanned by a roller, with spark discharges between the roller and cells, and bimetallic strip modulators at the receiver. The specification was accepted Jan. 28, 1918, but not published until long after the war, presumably "for military reasons." (542)

456 Moore, Daniel McFarlan (1869–1936). "Gaseous-conduction lamp." U.S. 1,316,967, Nov. 30, 1917, Sept. 23, 1919. Moore's corona glow lamp was used by Jenkins in his early radio movie apparatus. (730)

457 Nicolson, Alexander McLean (1880–1950). "Television." U.S. 1,470,696, Dec. 7, 1917, Oct. 16, 1923. Assigned: W.E. A single oscillating mirror provides a spiral scan; otherwise this system, with a cathode-ray-tube receiver, is all electronic. Innovative features include newly developed radio circuits, such as high-frequency generators, signal modulators, wave filters, amplifiers, and detectors, with carrier-wave transmission of both picture and synchronizing signals. (552)

458 Millikan, Robert Andrews (1868–1953). THE ELECTRON, ITS ISOLATION AND MEASUREMENT AND THE DETERMINATION OF SOME OF ITS PROPERTIES. Chicago: Chicago University Press, 1917. xii + 268 pp. Millikan was awarded the Nobel Prize in 1923. (595)

459 Burrows, Arthur Richard. "Wireless possibilities." YEAR BOOK OF WIRELESS TELEGRAPHY AND TELEPHONY. London: Wireless Press, 1918, pp. 952–62. The writer foresees radio broadcasting and the use of radio for various public services, including commercial support by advertisers, but has little faith in the demand for television or its arrival in the near future:

"The wireless transmission of photographs is by no means outside the realm of possibility, and some day, not very far distant, it may be possible to provide not merely wirelessly operated tape-machines in mid-Atlantic but pictures illustrative of the days' events. The nightmare of wireless television is unlikely to become a reality for some time. Mechanical and electrical difficulties exist which require for their solution a much more complete knowledge of the nature of light, electricity, and ether. Some day the solution may be forthcoming, but as such an invention would be of questionable popularity and its commercial application limited, the inventive faculties in most countries are likely for the present to be turned in other directions."

460 Gernsback, H. "Television and the telephot." ELECT. EXPER. 6 (May 1918): 12, 13, 51; (June 1918): 95, 96, 124, 125. 7 illus. A general discussion about this "Coming Invention, No. 1." Descriptions are given of systems by Dussaud, the Andersens, Hoglund, Rosing, Rothschild, and Sinding-Larsen. The writer proposes a hand-held looking-glass instrument attached to a telephone. A well-known prophet in the fields of science and electricity, Gernsback feels sure that something better than selenium is needed as a pickup element, that the future telephot must be as simple as the telephone without cumbersome machinery or a multiplicity of wires, and that to be successful the telephot must work in conjunction with the telephone. (376, 472)

"The future instrument on which the name 'Telephot' has been settled, is supposedly an apparatus attachable to our present telephone system, so that when we speak to our distant friend, we may see his likeness not only as an immovable picture, but we will see his image exactly as we see our image when looking into a mirror. In other words, the apparatus must faithfully follow every movement of our distant friend whether he is only five blocks away or one thousand miles. That such an invention is urgently required is needless to say. Everybody would wish to have such an instrument, and it is safe to say that such a device would revolutionize our present mode of living, just as much as the telephone revolutionized our former standard of living."

461 Reis, Christoph. DAS SELEN. Munich: J.C. Huber, 1918. 379 pp., 261 illus.

CHAPTER 5

BROADCASTING AND PICTURES: 1919–1924

A rising popular interest in science and technology and a renewed faith in their joint powers to benefit mankind in peacetime were among the legacies of the Great War. Some of the increasingly tangible signs of the everyday world to come were automobiles, commercial road transport, passenger aircraft, the cinema, and radio communications. The advent of broadcast radio at the popular level in 1920 and its rapid spread during the next five years heralded a revolution not only in telecommunications but in the domestic and cultural environment of almost everyone in the industrial countries. The radio boom of these postwar years brought science and technology into the home as amateurs of all ages built their simple receivers and followed accounts of new developments as well as techniques in newspapers and technical journals.

Public demand for topics related to radio prompted the birth of new periodicals, examples being POPULAR RADIO, POPULAR WIRELESS, PRACTICAL ELECTRICS, RADIO BROADCAST, and RADIO NEWS, to name a few. Articles and news on the new hobby were also offered by older publications such as NATURE, POPULAR MECHANICS, POPULAR SCIENCE, SCIENTIFIC AMERICAN, and WIRELESS WORLD. Their pages and those of many daily papers presented a wealth of material on construction, theory, operation, programs, new stations, and component parts, all supported by a barrage of advertisements to capture the attention and the pocket money of home constructors, amateur experimenters, and buyers of ready-made receivers. Though on the fringe of general interest in radio, the public was also made aware of progress in phototelegraphy and television, one an emerging practicality of commercial value especially to newspapers, the other still a matter of hope, skepticism, and debate.

The unprecedented commercial success of broadcast radio offered similar prizes to those who could produce workable methods for sending graphic messages and photographs over wires or by radio. New electronic techniques, married to most of the methods and devices that had been developed since Bakewell's invention of the cylinder machine, pointed the way to the future. Korn, Belin, and Dieckmann, each with some twenty years of experience, along with Jenkins, were the leaders in phototelegraphy. Experimental transmissions of graphic materials across the Atlantic were made by Belin (487, 495) and Korn (506) in 1922. Jenkins demonstrated his radio system (534) in Washington, D.C., in 1923. The following year saw the more impressive experiments with picture transmissions (594) over telephone wires by the American Telephone & Telegraph Company, and of photoradiograms (626) from London to New York by the Marconi Wireless Telegraph Company and the newly formed Radio Corporation of America.

This progress in picture transmission along with contemporary developments in radio provided a stimulus for those who were intent on devising television systems. The growing interest in television (the term became more general after 1922) is evident in the number of newcomers and in the increase of patent applications, especially after 1921. Of the seventy-four patent entries, twenty-nine were filed by men who entered the field during these years. Most of them were one-time contributors to the art, but several continued their work in later years, notably Baird, Clark, Ives, Karolus, von Mihály, and Zworkykin. Oldtimers who were still active include Belin, Dieckmann, Gernsback, Nipkow, Nisco, and Sinding-Larsen. Swinton revived his original plan (413) of 1911 updated with radio circuits (586), and Jenkins applied his extensive experience with motion pictures to the development of radio movies.

The full extent of this increasing activity was not recognized at the time since the emphasis was on patent protection with its attendant secrecy in preference to news releases or articles which were more common features of the prewar years. Items by Gernsback (502), Langer (521), and Swinton, along with material by or about Baird, Belin, Jenkins, and von Mihály, comprised the main fare for readers interested in television. Of forty-three patents related to television systems, twenty-eight were filed during the last two years of the period. The countries of origin and the totals are: Britain, nine; France, eight; Russia, four; United States, nineteen; and one each from Germany, Hungary, and Italy. The average rate of disclosures amounts to seven per year, compared with 2.4 per year during the period from 1901.

On the whole, a more refined approach toward the general problems and their solutions appears in the patents of the times, though classical methods still prevailed in most proposals, as can be seen in Table 5. The components and methods listed were all well established in the art with the exception of the unique prismatic disk (464) and the prism-lens combination (513) introduced by Jenkins. Other techniques with some degree of novelty include the disk with lamps and distributor described by Baird (593), which reflects the notion of a "rapidly-whirled stick" mentioned by Redmond (108), the rotating shutter with a stepped spiral slot specified by Ramsey (561), the one with a plain spiral slot by Baird (580), and quadrant scanning by Jenkins (516). The trend toward electronic solutions is apparent in the increasing preference for phototubes, picture tubes, electron tube circuits, and radio transmission, chiefly applied as auxiliaries to mechanical

TABLE 6   THE POSTWAR ART

ELECTRICAL	OPTICAL	MECHANICAL
Selenium cell (13)	Vibrating mirror (11)	Perforated disk (11)
Galvanometer (5)	Kerr cell (5)	Nipkow disk (7)
A-c sync (3)	Chopper (4)	Tuning fork
Oscillograph	Faraday cell	Manometric flame (1)
Relay	Lens disk (3)	Perforated drum
Transformer	Polyhedral drum	Perforated film
Distributor (2)	Transparency	
Phonic wheel	Graded screen (2)	**ELECTRONIC**
Selenium mosaic	Lens drum	Electron tube (19)
Arc lamp (1)	Zigzag scan	Cathode-ray tube (14)
Lamp bank	Cross scan (1)	Photocells (13)
*Rotary lamps	Interlaced scan	Phototube (9)
Telephone	Light spot	Camera tube (5)
	Mirror drum	Discharge tube (4)
	*Prismatic disk	
	*Prism-lens disk	**SYSTEMS**
	*Quadrant-scan	Radio transmission (10)
	Screen projection	Color (3)
	Spiral scan	Frequency selective
		Film recording (2)
		*Motion picture
		*Magnetic recording (1)
		Stereo
		Two-way
		Vision and sound

*Innovations

systems, and particularly in the proposals for camera tubes. The introduction of the cathode-ray tube developed by Johnson (485) at Western Electric and Rtcheouloff's magnetic recording for television (501) are other landmark events.

The limitations of electrical components and methods seem to have been recognized, since fewer proposals contain the old favorites such as batteries, electromagnets, induction coils and transformers, rotary contactors, spark gaps, and telephone assemblies. Selenium cells and mosaics were still specified but were beginning to be supplanted by phototubes. Galvanometers, oscillographs, and arc lamps lost favor as modulators or modulated light sources, with preference given to light valves based on the Faraday and Kerr effects. The utility of discharge tubes was appreciated by Jenkins with his use (558) of Moore's corona glow lamp (456), and by Baird (580) when he turned to the neon lamp. Then becoming commercially available (504), the neon lamp in a modified form was a staple component in disk receivers later in the decade.

For analyzing and synthesizing images the most common devices were perforated disks with a variety of aperture geometries and combinations, and the basic Nipkow disk soon to become dominant in working systems. Despite the inherent limitations on high-speed response and the actuating and timing problems, vibrating mirrors in a variety of forms appear in numerous schemes. Disks and drums with lenses and the polyhedral mirror drum were specified more often than before, whereas perforated drums and film and the mirror drum were virtually neglected.

No single technique for ensuring synchronism was strongly in favor during this period, though a-c circuits appear more often than any other means. In at least eight specifications for complete systems the fact that synchronous motions were requisite is merely assumed. Tuning forks operated by alternating or intermittent current, with or without phonic wheels, appear in seven patents. Common a-c supply lines or combinations of alternators and synchronous motors were equal choices in a total of twelve patents. Electron tube circuits for maintaining synchronism, in addition to the other functions served by the relatively new devices, appear in four patents. Miscellaneous methods include spot registration and a mechanical brake, both with photocells, speed control with rheostats, a centrifugal governor, an air jet with a musical tone, and a stroboscope. Of the four main methods, a-c drives from public power supplies with manual adjustment for phasing later became popular in mechanical receivers.

The technical range of the proposals extends from the primitive to the complex and (to use a modern term) sophisticated when compared with one another and the history of the art. Such a variety is to be expected since most inventors were working alone with no resources other than the meager literature scattered in various periodicals, few of which were at a technical level, and current books on selenium cells (466) and phototelegraphy (467), and the later ones by Korn (569), von Mihály (570), Bohringer (635), and Fournier d'Albe (636).

Though prominent independent inventors captured the news on television and its progress, several manufacturing companies were involved, especially in the United States. Phototubes and television were the concern of the General Electric Company, who obtained coverage overseas through the British Thomson-Houston Company. In addition to phototelegraphy and the cathode-ray tube, the Western Electric Company was engaged with television, with coverage abroad through their British group and in France through Le Matériel Téléphonique. Television developments were also undertaken by the Westinghouse Electric and Manufacturing Company. Other concerns were the Mills Novelty Company and Associated Electric Laboratories, both in Chicago, and the General Electric Company and the General Radio Company in Britain.

The emergence of camera tubes—unpublicized at the time and scarcely recognized ever since—is a major feature of the early 1920s. It is interesting that the notion of applying a modified cathode-ray tube containing a photoelectric element for image pickup (along the lines suggested by Swinton) came from five different sources: one in Britain, two in France, and two in the United States. The proposals fall into three types: plain image plate, image dissector, and image mosaic. Selenium image plates appear in the patent of the Seguin brothers (575) and in one by Blake and Spooner (577). The Schoultz patent (488) concerns an image dissecting arrangement not unlike the one by Dieckmann and Hell (665) of April 1925 and the one of January 1927 by Farnsworth (850), who already had the concept in mind. The most important design, however, is the mosaic image plate specified in Zworykin's premier patent

(566) and, in a different form, in the patent by McCreary (587). These specifications represent the conceptual beginnings of all-electronic methods and are, besides, good examples of almost coincidental inventions directed toward the same objective.

Examples of the more complex specifications are those of Clark (532), Hammond (550), and Hoxie (615). Whiston (486) incorporated some older electrical methods, a complex distributor is specified by Dauvillier (557), and the multifrequency approach is found in the proposals by Mills (497), Gernsback (502), and Sardina (598). Some surprising, even baffling, solutions appear in the patents of Rtcheouloff (500), Nisco (560), Sensicle (571), the Seguin brothers (575), and Skala (619). Three-color transmission is specified by Stephenson and Walton (537), Hammond, and McCreary, the latter being the first with camera tubes. The influence of the cinema industry is reflected in the specifications of Gardner and Hineline (556) which combine motion pictures with sound, of Hoxie, and Belin (633), besides those of Jenkins. The oldest idea of all—the Telephonoscope envisioned by Dumaurier (100) in 1878—appears in Zworykin's disclosure (581) for a two-way telephone subscriber system with simultaneous sight and sound.

Two other events to be noted are the beginning of Baird's work and the electronic system of Zworykin, both to be of major importance in the years to come. A greater contrast in the technical quality and potential of their ideas and their circumstances cannot be found. Baird, initially a lonely, impoverished inventor, started with primitive ideas (548), early sought publicity (583, 585, 592), and soon led the way with successes and a host of innovations from 1926. Zworykin, at the other extreme, with the resources of the Westinghouse Company available to him, developed the electronic system which remained secret for many years through extensive research until the early 1930s. Their concern with patent coverage also was quite different. Baird protected every idea he had (579, 580) from this time on, even including the forty-year-old Nipkow disk (656), whereas Zworykin's coverage concerned relatively few but important inventions.

Intimations that television was near at hand began to appear in print late in 1922, derived in part from optimistic comments by inventors and partly from journalistic insight, though few inventors or writers dared to offer firm predictions. A notable exception was Gernsback who, with a long history of technical forecasting, was undeniably delighted with the demonstration by Jenkins (559) of his radio vision apparatus, "the most marvelous invention of the age." With such an instrument in the home one would be able to "witness a baseball game...or see an opera" with sight and sound carried by radio over thousands of miles. The future roles of television in naval battles and in the control of aircraft (623) were also visible inside Gernsback's crystal globe.

The report on a demonstration of "long-distance sight" by Belin in December 1922 (523) was rather premature. Nearly one year later the inventor was still expecting a solution in the near future (555), which was extended another year at the beginning of 1924 (572). In March that year Baird followed Jenkins with a similar demonstration of shadowgraphs (585), little more than one year after he began what was to be a lifelong occupation. Simple image transmissions were also obtained experimentally by Zworykin, Karolus, and von Mihály during 1924. In his lecture in March, Swinton expressed mixed feelings about a speedy solution and whether or not the problem was worth solving unless a large company undertook development. Meanwhile, views on seeing around the world (591) and looking to the ends of the earth (629) reiterated the predictions so clearly expressed thirty years before by Munro (236). The more optimistic viewpoints, however, were soon to be justified by events of the two next two years.

TABLE 7 CHRONOLOGY: 1919–1924

1919	Feb.	18	von Mihály	Phase control with spot registration
	Oct.	23	Jenkins	Prismatic disks
	Nov.	28	Skaupy	Picture tube
1920	Jan.	19	Baden-Powell	Mirror drum, galvanometer
	Apr.	14	Adamian	Nipkow disk, transparencies, discharge tube
	Aug.	18	Kakourin	Nipkow disk, shutter modulator, radio transmission
		24	Egerton	Oscillating mirror, cross scanning
	Nov.		Belin	Facsimile, oscillating mirror, film recording
1921	Feb.	5	Jenkins	Patents with prismatic disks
	Mar.		Johnson	Low-voltage, gas-focused cathode-ray tube
	May	4	Whiston	Perforated film, arc lamp, screen projection
	Aug.	23	Schoultz	Camera tube, image plate, spiral scan
1922	Mar.	13	Jenkins	Prismatic disks, Kerr cell
	May		Belin	Transatlantic facsimile transmission
		16	Mills	Multifrequency, polyhedral mirror drums
		29	Dallugge	Perforated disks, Faraday cell, picture tube
	June		Korn	Transatlantic facsimile transmission
		27	Rtcheouloff	Camera and picture tubes with moving photoelements, magnetic recording
	July		Gernsback	Radiophot, multifrequency, selenium mosaic, vibrating mirror bank
	Aug.		Dieckmann	Radio facsimile system
			Korn	Radio facsimile system
		21	Fessenden	Picture transmission, shutter modulator
	Sept.	11	Jenkins	Various: lens drum, prism-lens disk, picture receivers, moving mirrors
	Dec.	27	Belin	Oscillating mirrors, oscillograph, graded screen
		29	Valensi	Overlapping disks, zigzag scan, discharge tube or cathode-ray tube modulator
		30	Stephenson, Walton	Sync with low-frequency a-c, radio transmission, filter circuits, relays
1923	Jan.	2	von Mihály	Galvanometer, phonic wheel, tuning fork
	Feb.	22	Allen	Graded screen, oscillograph
	Mar.		Jenkins	Photo transmission by radio
		26	Clark	Polyhedral mirror drum, slotted disk
	Apr.	18	Stephenson, Walton	Overlapping disks, interlaced scan, prisms, lenses, photocells, galvanometer, color
	June	27	Baird	Personal advertisement
	July	2	Hart	Photo modulator, amplifier
		12	Robb, Martin	Tuning fork and mirror, zigzag scan, oscillograph, slide and film transmission
		26	Baird	Nipkow disk, distributor, lamp bank
	Aug.	1	Clark	Rotating and reciprocating disks
		15	Hammond	Vibrating mirrors, galvanometers, rotating color disks, Faraday cell, radio transmission, stereo in color
	Sept.		Jenkins	Shadowgraph demonstration

Table continued on next page.

TABLE 7 (continued)

	Date		Name	Description
	Nov.	14	Belin	Lecture on long-distance vision
		28	Gardner, Hineline	Cathode-ray-tube pickup and display, motion picture and sound transmission, dual radio-frequency modulation
		29	Dauvillier	Nipkow disk, distributor, tuning forks, phonic wheel, picture tube
	Dec.	4	Nisco	Perforated drum, ultraviolet or X rays
		5	Ramsey	Coaxial disks, Faraday cell, common a-c supply, radio transmission, spot registration
		29	Baird	Nipkow disk with lenses
			Zworykin	Camera tube, mosaic image plate, picture tube, light-spot scanning of slides, radio transmission
		31	Ives	Picture transmission, light valve, magnetic modulator, slotted disk
1924	Jan.	8	Sensicle	Polyhedral mirror drums, selenium cell, light valve, telephone-manometric flame modulator, tuning fork, air jet and musical tone sync
		26	Tschernyschev	Cathode-ray-tube receiver
	Feb.	8	Seguin, Seguin	Cathode-ray tubes with selenium and fluorescent image plates
		21	Evans	Disks, moving mirrors, galvanometers
		28	Blake, Spooner	Camera tube, selenium image plate, picture tube, three-channel radio transmission
	Mar.		Baird	Shadowgraph demonstration
		12	Baird	Light-chopper disks
		17	Baird	Nipkow disk, slotted disk, selenium cells, a-c sync
			Zworykin	Two-way sight and sound for telephone circuits, carrier-current transmission
		26	Allouard-Carny	Tuning fork with mirror, perforated disk, radio circuits
	Apr.	9	Swinton	Lecture on revised system
		10	McCreary	Camera tube, mosaic image plate, picture tube, triple assembly for color, radio circuits
		23	Jenkins	Prismatic disk and lens disk receiver
	May	20	AT&T	Facsimile by wire
		23	Clark	Photo-telescopic receiver
		28	Sardina	Multifrequency, multicell assemblies, light-chopper disk
	June	21	Karolus	Kerr cell modulator
	Aug.	22	Ives	Receiver, slotted disk, graded screen
		29	Dieckmann	Single mirror, picture tube, three-channel radio transmission
	Sept.	23	Hoxie	Disks, bands, drums, light chopper, discharge lamp, film and direct view pickup, carrier-wave transmission
	Oct.	1	Skala	Light chopper, electro-optical assemblies with transformers, film recording
	Nov.	30	RCA, Marconi	Transatlantic facsimile tests, London-New York, RCA-Ranger system
	Dec.	9	Nipkow	Common a-c sync
		16	Belin	Vibrating mirrors

BIBLIOGRAPHY: 1919–1924

462 Mihály, Denes von. "Improvements in phototelegraphy." Br. 174,606, Jan. 25, 1922, May 25, 1923. Fr. 546,714, Jan. 25, 1922. In Hungary Feb. 18, 1919. Sync control by registration employing dark spots on the periphery of the field of view. Auxiliary circuits for phase control contain selenium cells, centrifugal governors, and variable resistors. (528)

463 Sinding-Larsen, A. "Picture transmission." U.S. 1,473,882, Sept. 16, 1919, Nov. 13, 1923. Assigned: A/S Telocle. Photoelectric circuit with interrupted current. (388)

464 Jenkins, C.F. "Motion picture machine." U.S. 1,385,325, Oct. 23, 1919, July 19, 1921. Claims refer to the annular refracting prism (prismatic disk) later used for radio movies. (425, 481)

465 Skaupy, Franz. "Braun'sche Röhre mit Glükathode, insbesondere für die Zwecke der elektrischen Bildübertragung" [Braun's tube with glow cathode, in particular for the purpose of electric picture transmission]. Ger. 349,838, Nov. 28, 1919, Mar. 10, 1922. Hot-cathode picture tube with built-in fluorescent screen, deflection plates, and control grid circuit. (1923)

466 Benson, Thomas William. SELENIUM CELLS: THE CONSTRUCTION, CARE AND USE OF SELENIUM CELLS, WITH SPECIAL REFERENCE TO THE FRITTS CELL. New York: Spon & Chamberlain, 1919. 63 pp.

467 Martin, M.J. THE WIRELESS TRANSMISSION OF PHOTOGRAPHS. London: Wireless Press, 1919. xv + 143 pp., 77 illus. 2nd ed. (453, 491)

468 Baden-Powell, Baden Fletcher Smyth (1860–1937). "An electrical method of reproducing distant scenes visually." Br. 161,706, Jan. 19, 1920, Apr. 19, 1921. Mirror drum with curved mirrors, and reflecting galvanometer for light modulation. Natural colors may be reproduced by colored reflectors or transparent colored screens. Sync not specified.

469 Case, Theodore Willard. "'Thalofide cell,' a new photo-electric substance." PHYS. REV. 15 (Apr. 1920): 289–92. (484)

470 Adamian, J.A. (Image transmitting system) Russ. 170 and 171, Apr. 14; 172, Apr. 26, 1920. Nipkow disk, transparencies, Geissler tube. (359)

471 Stark, J. "Structural and spectral changes of chemical atoms. Nobel lecture, June 3, 1920." NOBEL LECTURES, PHYSICS: 1901–1921. Amsterdam, London, New York: Elsevier, 1967. Presentation speech, pp. 423–6. Lecture, pp. 426–35. Bibliography, pp. 436, 437. (Award for 1919.) (300)

472 Gernsback, H. "Radio in 1945." RADIO N. 2 (July 1920): 5. This editorial includes forecasts on television: "One of the coming wonders without doubt is radio movies." (460, 502)

473 "Picture is sent over telephone." N.Y.T. 15 (July 29, 1920): 7. Belin transmits photo by wire from Lyons to Paris. (348, 477)

474 Kakourin, S.N. (Image transmission by radio.) Russ. 144, Aug. 18, 1920. A two-channel system employing Nipkow disks, phototube, shutter modulator, and electron tube circuits.

475 Egerton, Henry Clifford. "Television system." U.S. 1,605,930, Aug. 24, 1920, Nov. 9. 1926. Assigned: W.E. Cross scanning (Lissajous figures) with a compound vibrating mirror based on a patent for an electric (telephone) amplifier and motor, U.S. 1,232,514, Nov. 15, 1915, July 10, 1917. Includes electron tube circuits. Sync with common a-c supplies and filters. (719)

476 Coursey, Philip R. "The electrical transmission of pictures." NATURE 106 (Sept. 23, 1920): 115, 116. General discussion of the cylinder method, with diagram.

477 "The Belin system of telephotography." SCI. & INV. 8 (Nov. 1920): 717, 805, 812. 6 illus. Cylinders, microphone and stylus pickup line transformer, oscillating mirror, film recording. (473, 479)

478 Nakken, Theodorus Hendrik. "Means for transforming light impulses into electric-current impulses." U.S. 1,522,070, Nov. 3, 1920, Jan. 5, 1925, reissued Feb. 7, 1928. Photoelectric plate and filament in a vacuum tube. (1223)

479 Lescarboura, Austin C. "Sending photographs over wires." SCI. AM. 123 (Nov. 6, 1920): 474, 483, 484, 3 illus. Belin's facsimile system. (477, 480, 2413)

480 "Photographs sent 1,000 miles by wire." N.Y.T. 17:3, Nov. 15, 1920. Four pictures transmitted between New York and St. Louis by Belin's telesterograph. (479, 487)

481 Jenkins, C.F. "Sleevelike refracting prism." U.S. 1,440,466, Feb. 5, 1921, Jan. 2, 1923. Assigned: Discrola Inc. (464, 482)

482 Jenkins, C.F. "Objective lens." U.S. 1,544,155, Feb. 5, 1921, June 30, 1925. Assigned: Discrola Inc. Includes prismatic disk. (481, 483)

483 Jenkins, C.F. "High-speed motion-picture machine." U.S. 1,618,090, Feb. 5, 1921, Feb. 15, 1927. Assigned: Discrola Inc. Two overlapping prismatic disks arranged to compensate for optical errors in film transmission. (482, 493)

484 Case, T.W. "New strontium and barium photoelectric cells." PHYS. REV. 17 (Mar. 1921): 398, 399. (469, 490)

485 Johnson, John Bertrand (1887–1970). "A low voltage cathode ray oscillograph." PHYS. REV. 17 (Mar. 1921): 420, 421. Preliminary report on a cathode-ray tube developed at the Western Electric laboratory. (510)

486 Whiston, Ernest William. "Transmitting photographs, messages, views, and like devices by wire or wireless telegraphy." Br. 185,463, May 4, 1921, Sept. 4, 1922. Scanning with perforated film, selenium cell, battery in series with wire lines, transformer at receiver where the signals modulate an arc lamp for screen projection.

487 "Radio reproduces note across ocean." N.Y.T. 3 (Aug. 5, 1921): 4. Belin's test from New York to Paris. (480, 489)

488 Schoultz, Edvard Gustav. "Procédé et appareillage pour la transmission des images mobiles à distance" [Process and apparatus for the transmission of moving pictures at a distance]. Fr. 539,613, Aug. 23, 1921, Apr. 5, 1922. A camera tube in which light from the object is reflected from a curved plate in front of a hot cathode through a hole in the anode plate onto an auxiliary anode or photoelectric image plate. The electron beam from the cathode is made to explore the image plate in a spiral path by means of two pairs of deflection coils.

489 "Transmitting photographs and drawings by radio." SCI. AM. 125 (Sept. 3, 1921): 163, 173. Belin's apparatus, photo. (487, 492)

490 Case, T.W. "Photo-electric device." U.S. 1,628,822, Dec. 19, 1921, May 17, 1927. Assigned: Case Research Lab. Vacuum tube with filament, plate and photoelectric grid. (484, 702)

491 Martin, M.J. THE ELECTRICAL TRANSMISSION OF PHOTOGRAPHS. London: Pitman, 1921. xi + 136 pp. 3rd ed., with revised title. (453, 467)

492 Boyer, J. "La transmission électrique des images" [The electric transmission of images]. LA NATURE (Mar. 11, 1922): 151–7. 12 illus. On Belin's systems, wire and radio. (438, 489, 494)

493 Jenkins. C.F. "Transmitting pictures by wireless." U.S. 1,544,156, Mar. 13, 1922, June 30, 1925. Picture is scanned by two overlapping prismatic disks. A Kerr cell or Faraday cell modulates light from a lamp, and another pair of prismatic disks deflect the beam onto a view screen. (483, 496)

494 "Fingerprints are now transmitted by wire." N.Y.T. 7 (Mar. 19, 1922): 7. Belin's test between Paris and Lyons. (492, 495)

495 Belin, E. (Transatlantic radio-telephotography of written or printed characters and of drawings.) ONDE ELECT. 1 (May 1922):

271–83. Detailed report of successful experimental transmissions between Annapolis and Malmaison, and between Croix d'Hino and Bar Harbor. See also C.R. 174 (Mar. 5, 1922): 678–80 (June 19, 1922): 1623–5. (494, 498)

496 Jenkins, C.F. "Prismatic rings." TRANS. SMPE 14 (May 1922): 65–73. (493, 508)

497 Mills Novelty Co. "Apparatus for telegraphically reproducing pictures and the like." Br. 200,643, May 16, 1922, July 19, 1923. (British agent, Harold Wade.) A multifrequency system with separate electron tube circuits and antennas for each selenium cell in a bank. Scanning with polyhedral mirror drums, variable-aperture beam modulation. Resonant frequency receiver circuits operate a bank of electromagnetic mirrors. See also Henry K. Sandell, "Transmitting pictures and the like." U.S. 1,423,737, July 25, 1922. Assigned: H.S. Mills.

498 "Telegraphic transmission of photographs." NATURE 109 (May 27, 1922): 687, 688. Belin's apparatus, two photos. (495, 523)

499 Dallugge, Rudolph A. "Apparatus for television." U.S. 1,634,571, May 29, 1922, July 5, 1927. Scanning with pin-hole disks that swing and rotate, selenium cells for pickup and sync, Faraday cell modulator. An alternative receiver employs a cathode-ray tube with a built-in electromagnet that provides deflection modulation of the beam via diaphragms. The beam impacts a built-in fluorescent plate; the rays are then directed via a lens and reflecting mirror to the scanning disk for direct viewing or screen projection.

500 Rtcheouloff, Boris. "Television and telephotography." U.S. 1,745,029, Feb. 9, 1927, Jan. 28, 1930. Br. 287,643, Dec. 24, 1926, Mar. 26, 1928. Russ. 3803, June 27, 1922. Photoelement mounted on a compound vibrating spring in a vacuum tube for pickup, and a similar tube furnished in a like manner with a movable fluorescent point, both operated by magnetic deflection. (501)

501 Rtcheouloff, B. "Means of recording and reproducing pictures, images, and the like." U.S. 1,771,820, Mar. 9, 1927, July 29, 1930. Br. 288,680, Jan. 4, 1927, Apr. 1928. In Russia June 27, 1922. A moving strip, disk or cylinder of iron serves as the storage medium in a system for the linear recording and playback of sound along with picture signals. Provisions include d-c erasure and the simultaneous presentation of pictures and sound by a plurality of receivers. The remainder of the specification is the same as in the companion patent. (500)

502 Gernsback, H. "The radiophot. Television by radio." SCI. & INV. 10 (July 1922): 234, 235, 290. 2 illus. Proposal with selenium mosaic, multifrequency transmission by radio, tuned vibrating mirror bank with ground glass screen at receiver. The front cover of this issue portrays a futuristic television receiver with a square picture screen. (472, 559)

503 Isakson, D.W. "Developments in telephotography." TRANS. AIEE 41 (Aug. 1922): 794–801. 10 illus. Descriptions of the Leishman systems, one employing a halftone screen, the other based on a message code. Also SCI. & INV. 10 (Apr. 1923): 1158, 1241.

504 Pearson, S.O., and H. St. George Anson. "The neon tube as a means of producing intermittent currents." PROC. PHYS. SOC. 34 (Aug. 1922): 204–12. A neon lamp (Osglim lamp, General Electric Co.) and capacitor in parallel connected in series with a high resistance to a voltage source comprise a very simple and inexpensive means of producing intermittent currents. This pseudo-linear (top part of an exponential curve) sawtooth impulse generator is the simplest form of d-c time base for beam deflection. See also PROC. PHYS. SOC. 34 (June 1922): 175, 176; W.W. 10:284; 12:2–5, 34–7. (564)

505 Gradenwitz, Alfred. "Radio-telephotography. The Dieckmann process for the wireless transmission of drawings, etc., and its application in aviation." RADIO N. 4 (Aug. 1922): 236, 227. 11 illus. (404, 613, 770)

506 Benington, Arthur. "Transmission of photographs by radio." RADIO N. 4 (Aug. 1922): 230, 369–72. 2 illus. The Korn coded system. Photo of picture sent from Italy to America, and sample of letter code. (426, 569)

507 Fessenden, Reginald Aubrey (1866–1932). "Method and apparatus for the transmission of energy by high-frequency impulses." U.S. 1,617,241, Aug. 21, 1922, Feb. 8, 1927. Includes a strip-metal shutter modulator for image transmission. Subdivided Jan. 8, 14, 1927. (851) The inventor was a prominent radio pioneer from about 1900.

508 Jenkins, C.F. "Pneumatically controlled light valve." U.S. 1,525,548, Aug. 30, 1922, Feb. 10, 1925. Assigned: Radio Pictures Corp. (496, 509)

509 Jenkins, C.F. "Radio-picture-frequency chopper." U.S. 1,525,549, Aug. 30, 1922, Feb. 10, 1925. Assigned: Radio Pictures Corp. (508, 511)

510 Johnson, J.B. "A low voltage cathode ray oscillograph." J. OSA 6 (Sept. 1922): 701–12; B.S.T.J. 1 (Nov. 1922): 142–51. 7 illus. A hot-cathode, gas-focused tube with deflection plates, operable at 300–400 volts. Low in cost and portable, unlike the bulky pumped-down apparatus in use at the time, this tube remained the basic type for a decade. (485, 2478)

511 Jenkins, C.F. "Film reception of broadcasted pictures." U.S. 1,521,189, Sept. 11, 1922, Dec. 30, 1924. (509, 512)

512 Jenkins, C.F. "Drum lens carrier." U.S. 1,521,190, Sept. 11, 1922, Dec. 30, 1924. Assigned: Radio Pictures Corp. A spiral of lenses on a drum for broadcasting and receiving pictures by radio. (511, 513)

513 Jenkins, C.F. "Prism-lens disk." U.S. 1,521,191, Sept. 11, 1922, Dec. 30, 1924, reissued Dec. 29, 1926, Nov. 22, 1927. Assigned: Radio Pictures Corp. For transmitting pictures by radio. (512, 514)

514 Jenkins, C.F. "Electroscope picture reception." U.S. 1,521,192, Sept. 11, 1922, Dec. 30, 1924, reissued Dec. 29, 1926, Feb. 21, 1928. Assigned: Radio Pictures Corp. (513, 515)

515 Jenkins, C.F. "Radio receiving device." U.S. 1,544,157, Sept. 11, 1922, June 30, 1925. Assigned: Jenkins Labs. Radio receiver with a lamp in the output circuit. (514, 516)

516 Jenkins, C.F: "Wireless broadcasting of pictures." U.S. 1,544,158, Sept. 11, 1922, June 30, 1925. Assigned: Jenkins Labs. This system has multiple cells and lamps and simultaneous scanning of the quadrants of the screen. (515, 518)

517 "Say radio will carry pictures everywhere." N.Y.T. 36 (Oct. 2, 1922): 2. Report on experimental work by the General Radio Company, London.

518 Jenkins, C.F. "Two-way oscillating mirror." U.S. 1,537,087, Oct. 20, 1922, May 12, 1925. Assigned: Jenkins Labs. For broadcasting pictures. (516, 519)

519 Jenkins, C.F. "Flexing mirror." U.S. 1,525,550, Oct. 31, 1922, Feb. 10, 1925. Assigned: Radio Pictures Corp. (518, 520)

520 Claudy, C.H. "Motion pictures by radio. The promise of 'movie' broadcasts, with receiving stations in every home." SCI. AM. 127 (Nov. 1922): 320. Photo of Jenkins with ring-prism apparatus. (519, 529)

521 Langer, Nicholas. "A development in the problem of television." W.W. 11 (Nov. 11, 1922): 197–201. 9 illus. Description of the writer's experiments and analysis of the process at each stage. (531)

522 "Broadcasting photographs and motion pictures." POP. MECH. 38 (Dec. 1922): 824. Illus.

523 "Belin shows television." N.Y.T. 15 (Dec. 2, 1922): 3. Demonstration of long-distance sight at the Sorbonne, with flashes of light reproduced by a mirror. (498, 525)

524 "Picture is sent by wireless by London inventor's device." N.Y.T. 1 (Dec. 27, 1922): 2. A photo was transmitted by radio over 100

yards by T.T. Baker and published in the DAILY MAIL. (398, 616)

525 Belin, E. "Improvements in and relating to television." Br. 209,049, Nov. 16, 1923, Feb. 16, 1925. U.S. 1,670,795, Nov. 20, 1923, May 22, 1928. Fr. 571,785, Dec. 27, 1922. Oscillating scanning mirrors, oscillograph receiver with moving mirrors, and a graded transparent screen. A cathode-ray tube and a Kerr cell are suggested. (523, 536)

526 Valensi, Georges. "Receiving device for distant-vision installation." U.S. 1,664,798, Sept. 7, 1923, Apr. 3, 1928, Fr. 577,762, Dec. 29, 1922. This specification includes a transmitter in which the object is placed in an illuminated chamber. Two overlapping scanning disks have transparent tracks, one zigzag, the other spiral, which produce a zigzag scan. Other proposals include a discharge tube and a cathode-ray tube, both for light modulation. Color, stereo, and film recording are mentioned but not claimed. (822)

527 Stephenson, William Samuel, and George William Walton. "Means for synchronising the movements of two rotating bodies." Br. 213,654, Dec. 30, 1922, Mar. 31, 1924. U.S. 1,521,205, issued Dec. 30, 1924; Fr. 580,719, Apr. 15, 1924. Low-frequency signals from an a-c generator coupled to a rotating drum modulate the transmitted wave. These signals, separated from other signals by filter circuits, are applied to a synchronous motor similarly coupled to a drum. The patent includes electron tube circuits, a polarized relay, and a relay contactor with a lamp and battery for picture reproduction. This specification is incorporated in a later television patent (537).

528 Mihály, D.V. "Phototelegraphic apparatus." Br. 209,406, Dec. 18, 1923, Nov. 7, 1924. U.S. 1,625,967, Dec. 29, 1923, Apr. 26, 1927. Fr. 575,157, Dec. 9, 1923. Ger. 422,995, Dec. 25, 1923. In Hungary, Jan. 2, 1923. Oscillating mirror galvanometer operated by a phonic wheel and tuning fork for analyzing and recomposing a picture. (462, 551)

529 Jenkins, C.F. "Device for detecting synchronism." U.S. 1,537,088, Feb. 19, 1923, May 12, 1925. With prismatic rings for broadcasting pictures. Tuning forks, transformer, relay, lamp, and stroboscopic adjustment. See also U.S. 1,525,553, Apr. 21, 1923, Feb. 10, 1925. (520, 534)

530 Allen, John Gillespie. "Electric telescopy." U.S. 1,681,833, Feb. 22, 1923, Aug. 21, 1928. Graded screen and oscillograph.

531 Langer, N. "Television." PRACT. ELECT. 2 (Mar. 1923): 207. (521, 582)

532 Clark, Paul Loveridge. "Apparatus for the electrical transmission of visual images." U.S. 1,666,594, Mar. 26, 1923, Apr. 17, 1928. Polyhedral mirror drum and slotted disk with spiral segments. The specification includes a magnetically operated reflector and apertured plate for light modulation, and reflecting screens with specular or curved elements as in U.S. 1,222,192; 1,279,262; 1,535,985. Clark was active throughout the 1920s. (549)

533 "Une realisation experimentale de la télévision" [An experimental realization of television]. ANN. POSTES 12 (Apr. 1923): 517.

534 Davis, Watson, "Seeing by radio." POP. RADIO 3 (Apr. 1923): 266–75. 8 illus. On phototelegraphy. Said to be "the first detailed description of the remarkable invention of C. Francis Jenkins." Illustrations show Jenkins with his prismatic disk apparatus, a specimen photo of President Harding as received by the Jenkins system, a page from a patent (493), a view of Belin's apparatus, and pictures of Korn with his machine and a specimen picture. (529, 535, 558)

535 Winters, S.R. "The transmission of photographs by radio." RADIO N. 4 (Apr. 1923): 1772, 1773. 5 illus. Account of Jenkins' apparatus and demonstration transmission from the U.S. Navy Department at Anacostia to Jenkins' laboratory at 1519 Connecticut Avenue, Washington, D.C. (534, 540, 647)

536 Lacault, Robert E. "The Belin radio-television scheme." SCI. & INV. 10 (Apr. 1923):

1166, 1217. 3 illus. On a recent demonstration at the Sorbonne in Paris; perforated disk, phototube, radio transmission, vibrating mirror, and graded transparency at receiver. (525, 538)

537 Stephenson, W.S., and G.W. Walton. "Apparatus for transmitting electrically scenes or representations to a distance." Br. 218,776, Apr. 18, 1923, July 17, 1924. Interlaced scanning by overlapping disks with arcuate slots on polyhedral mirror drums. Color transmission by a prism to split the scanned ray through three lenses onto separate photocells. In the receiver, light is similarly divided into three paths, separately modulated by string galvanometers for red, blue, and green, then recombined to be cast through slotted scanning disks. Synchronism is by the method covered in a previous patent (527). Transmission details are not mentioned. (661)

538 Calfas, P. "Le téléstéréographe Belin, pour la transmission à distance des photographies" [The Belin telesterograph for the transmission of photographs at a distance]. GENIE CIVIL 82 (Apr. 21, 1923): 365–70. 11 illus. (536, 541)

539 "Photographs transmitted by radio." POP. MECH. 39 (May 1923): 678.

540 "To broadcast baseball by radio movies." POP. SCI. 102 (May 1923): 67. On Jenkins. (535, 558)

541 "Autograph telegrams now." N.Y.T. 14 (May 29, 1923): 7. Belin's invention is being installed in all French telegraph and post offices. (538, 543)

542 Low, A.M. "Wireless television." W. REV. 1 (June 2, 1923): 13. (455, 637)

543 "Telautogramme test wins." N.Y.T. 3 (June 17, 1923): 6. Belin's tests from Lyons to Malmaison near Paris. (541, 547)

544 Baird, John Logie (1888–1946). "Seeing by wireless. Inventor of apparatus wishes to hear from someone who will assist (not financially) in making working models. Write Box S686." TIMES (June 27, 1923): 1c. Notice in the "Personal" columns. (548)

545 Hart, Russell. "Telephotographic sending apparatus." U.S. 1,558,672, July 2, 1923, Oct. 27, 1925. Photo modulator and amplifier.

546 Robb, Frank Morse, and Robert Henry Martin. "Television." Br. 222,597, July 12, 1923, Oct, 9, 1924. The title is misleading since the patentees, students in Montreal, propose a system for the transmission of slides and moving film. Scanning is by pairs of mirrors mounted on tuning forks which produce a zigzag scan. Variable intensity modulation is effected by a moving coil oscillograph. The scheme includes a phototube and a viewing screen. (894)

547 Belin, E. "La télégraphie des images" [The telegraphy of images]. TECH. MOD. 15 (July 15, 1923): 417–26. 9 illus. On the phototelegraphic systems of Korn and the author, with comments on cinematography and television. (543, 555)

548 Baird, J.L., and Wilfred Ernest Lytton Day. "A system of transmitting views, portraits and scenes by telegraphy or wireless telegraphy." (544,554) Br. 222,604, July 26, 1923, Oct. 9, 1924. Nipkow scanning disk and light-sensitive cell, the output from which is connected at the receiver by a distributor to a bank of lamps. Baird suggests a disk with 18 holes and 18 rows of lamps. It is assumed that the disk and the distributor will revolve "in perfect synchronism." Wilfred Day gave Baird financial support. (544)

549 Clark, P.L. "Apparatus for the electrical transmission of visual images." U.S. 1,572,989, Aug. 1, 1923, Feb. 16, 1926. A companion to the earlier patent (532), this specification includes rotating and reciprocating apertured scanning disks. (596)

550 Hammond, John Hayes, Jr. (1888–1965). "System and method of television." U.S. 1,725,710, Aug. 15, 1923, Aug. 20, 1929. This extensive and highly detailed specification covers a mixed system with spiral scanning containing vibrating mirrors, galva-

nometers, phototubes and a cathode-ray tube, rotating disks, Nicol prisms and a Faraday-type light valve, and radio circuits. For full-color transmission, rotating disks carry alternate segments of orange-red and greenish blue filters. Detailed descriptions are given of the mechanical, electrical, and optical processes and of the electron tube circuits for amplification, frequency selection, filtering, and a-c synchronism. The claims also refer to stereoscopic projection in natural colors. Hammond was well known as a prolific inventor in the radio field from about 1910. (1055)

551 "The Telehor, a Hungarian invention." ELECT. W. 82 (Sept. 1, 1923): 454. Von Mihály's scheme. (528, 570)

552 Western Electric Co., Inc. "Electrical transmission of images." Br. 228,961, Sept. 7, 1923, Feb. 9, 1925. Nicolson's U.S. patent of 1917 (457). See also Br. 230,401; Le Matériel Téléphonique, Fr. 570,825, Sept. 14, 1923. (1044)

553 Poulsen, Arnold, and Axel Carl Georg Petersen. "A method for compensating the sluggishness of selenium cells." Br. 221, 817, Sept. 11, 1924, Dec. 11, 1925. In Denmark Sept. 13, 1923. Cell with inductive shunt in grid circuit of a triode, and cascade connections.

554 (Baird, J.L.) "Seeing by wireless." CHAMBERS J. 13 (Nov. 1923): 766,767. Brief description; perforated disk 20 in. diameter, selenium cell, multilamp receiver, and distributor. "At present the apparatus is complex and expensive...we may shortly be able to watch...a football match or the finish of the Derby." (548, 565)

555 "Long-distance vision." TIMES (Nov. 15, 1923): 9f. Lecture and demonstration by Belin to the Royal Society of Arts. "Vision at a distance, a problem long considered as chimerical, but today looked on as possible, and which tomorrow would be one of the realities...the expected solution was very near at hand." (547, 563)

556 Gardner, John Edward, and Harris Dale Hineline. "Television systems." Br. 225,553, Nov. 25, 1924, May 28, 1925. In U.S. Nov. 28, 1923. Assigned: Westinghouse. Transmission of motion pictures with music. Photoelectric cell, cathode-ray-tube pickup, electron-tube circuits, dual radio-frequency modulation, screen display from picture tube with lens.

557 Dauvillier, Alexandre. "Television process and means of realization." U.S. 1,661,603, Aug. 22, 1924, Mar. 6, 1928; Br. 225,516, Sept. 10, 1924, Dec. 10, 1925. Fr. 592,162; 592,164, Nov. 29, 1923. Also Fr. 572,716; 577,762, 1923. Nipkow disk with complex distributor and high-frequency alternator or "tuning fork operated chronometric motor." Phototube and tuning forks with slotted diaphragms, picture tube with magnetic focusing and electrostatic deflection. (780)

558 Davis, W. "The new radio movies." POP. RADIO 4 (Dec. 1923): 436–43. 6 illus. Jenkins' apparatus for facsimile and for pantomime transmission using disks with 48 compound lenses at a speed of 960 rpm, with corona glow lamp. Shadowgraphs demonstrated. Full-page photo of Jenkins and his 4-disk instrument. (534, 540, 559, 562)

559 Gernsback, H. "Radio vision." RADIO N. 5 (Dec. 1923): 681, 823. 5 illus. (502, 558, 568, 623)

"I have just left the laboratory of Mr. C. Francis Jenkins of Washington, D.C., and am still under the influence of what I consider to be the most marvelous invention of the age. I have seen an actual demonstration of seeing, not only around corners through thin wires, but through space as well. The demonstration—a private one—took place before a General of the Army, his staff and myself.

"Although the machine, the demonstration of which I have witnessed, is not yet perfected, I had been able to see my hand projected by radio and being received by radio. By placing...several small objects, such as a key, cross, clamp, etc....in the path of the light, the picture was transmitted by radio and was received again at the other side by a radio receiving apparatus. It was possible to wave these small objects in the path of the light ray of the transmitter and one could amuse oneself by seeing how these objects were actually being transmitted by radio.

"The day will come when you will be able to sit at home and witness a baseball game as it is being played five thousand miles away or you will be able to sit at home and not only listen to, but also actually see an opera as it is being sung and acted. In other words, not only the music, but the action will be broadcast simultaneously. In future wars, it will be possible for an Admiral to witness a naval battle and follow it with his own eyes, although his battleship squadron may be thousands of miles away."

560 Nisco, A. "Method to obtain television, telegraphy, telegraphotography, telephotography, telecinematography, teleradiography." Br. 225,860, Dec. 4, 1924. Complete not accepted. In Italy, Dec. 4, 1923. Also Fr. 589,425, Nov. 20, 1924. Apertured drums with a staggered series of square holes. Ultraviolet light source in transmitter, or X rays. The specification is so poorly written that the function of the parts cannot be determined. (338)

561 Ramsey, George. "Television." U.S. 1,602,121, Dec. 5, 1923, Oct. 5, 1926. Coaxial scanning disks, one with a double spiral of apertures, the other with a single stepped-spiral slot. Radio transmission with a common a-c power supply for motor drives. Faraday light valve with Nicol prisms, direct viewing or screen projection, with light-spot registration for framing. (3211)

562 Davis, W. "Seeing by wireless at last." W. REV. 2 (Dec. 15, 1923): 59. (558)

563 "French to open wire service for drawings and manuscript." N.Y.T. 1 (Dec. 22, 1923): 7. Belin's system. (555, 572)

564 Ryde, J.W. "Rare gas discharge lamps." NATURE 112 (Dec. 29, 1923): 944, 945. On neon lamps. (504, 600)

565 Baird, J.L., and W.E.L. Day. "A system of transmitting views by means of telegraphy or wireless telegraphy." Br. 230,576, Dec. 29, 1923, Mar. 19, 1925. The specification and single claim refer only to a disk with a spiral of lenses. (554,579)

566 Zworykin, Vladimir Kosma. (1889–1982) "Television system." U.S 2,141,059, Dec. 29, 1923, Dec. 20, 1938. Assigned: Westinghouse. An argon-filled camera tube has a mosaic of photoelectric globules deposited on aluminum oxide on aluminum foil, comprising a bank of insulated photosensitive elements capable of storing electrostatic charges proportional to the light intensities. The image is cast through a wire mesh grid onto the photosensitive mosaic, the back of which is scanned by an electron beam deflected by internal plates and external coils. A picture tube with a built-in fluorescent screen is also furnished with plates and coils for beam deflection. The specification includes complete electron tube circuits for radio transmission of visual and synchronizing signals and a method for light-spot scanning of photo negatives and slides. The excessive delay (15 years) before this cardinal patent was issued resulted from technical objections and various actions on interferences in the Patent Office. Swinton's plan (413) and other disclosures of prior art in foreign and U.S. patents delayed the proceedings for several years. Further delay was occasioned by conflicting claims and disclosures in applications by Case, Farnsworth, McCreary, Reynolds and Sabbah, and others. The original application was divided Nov. 21, 1931: U.S. 2,022,450. Meanwhile two other applications ensued: Mar. 17, 1924, and July 13, 1925. (581)

567 Ives, Herbert Eugene (1882–1953). "Transmission of pictures by electricity." U.S. 1,631,963, Dec. 31, 1923, June 14, 1927. Assigned: W.E. Light valve; variable-aperture magnetic modulator with slotted disk. See also U.S. 1,580,896, Dec. 27, 1923, Apr. 13, 1926. (611)

568 Jenkins, C.F. "Radio photographs, radio movies, and radio vision." TRANS. SMPE 16 (1923): 78, 79. (559, 590)

569 Korn, A. BILDTELEGRAPHIE [Phototelegraphy]. Berlin: W. de Gruyter, 1923. 146 pp. illus. (506, 625)

570 Mihály, D.v. DAS ELEKTRISCHE FERNSEHEN UND DAS TELEHOR [Electric television and the Telehor]. Berlin: M. Krayn, 1923. 114 pp., 70 illus. Foreword by Dr. Eugen Nesper. Some early schemes are surveyed, followed by the author's plans and developments of his Telehor. There are no references to original sources. (551, 582, 750)

571 Sensicle, Laurence Henry. "Continuous transmission of visual images by wire or wireless." Br. 236,464, Jan. 8, 1924, July 8, 1925. Polyhedral mirror drums, selenium cell, Nicol prisms with carbon disulfide and coil modulator for phosphorescent screen projection; also manometric flame and telephone modulator. Sync with tuning fork, air jet, and musical note.

572 "'Television' promised by French inventor." N.Y.T. 17 (Jan. 14, 1924): 4. Belin states "he would transmit animated surfaces and human faces within a year." (563, 574)

573 Tschernyschev, A.A. (Picture transmission system.) Russ. 769, Jan. 26, 1924. Cathode-ray-tube receiver. A description of his work appeared in April 1925 (660).

574 Belin, E. (Electrical transmission of photographs.) SOC. FR. ELECT. BULL. 4 (Feb. 1924): 185–202. Full technical report. (572, 578)

575 Seguin, Laurent, and Augustin Seguin. "Méthode et appareils pour la télévision" [Method and apparatus for television]. Fr. 577,530, Feb. 8, Sept. 6, 1924. Cathode-ray-tube assemblies with electrostatic beam deflection serve both instruments. The image is optically projected onto a selenium plate at the transmitter, and similarly projected from a fluorescent plate at the receiver.

576 Evans, Earl R. "Electrical system." U.S. 1,656,370, Feb. 21, 1924, Jan. 17, 1928. Disks, moving mirrors, and galvanometers.

577 Blake, George Joseph, and Henry John Spooner. "Apparatus for television." Br. 234,882, Feb. 28, 1924, May 28, 1925. Camera tube with a selenium anode and scanning coils. Picture tube with built-in fluorescent screen and deflection plates. Three-channel radio link, one for visual signals and the others for deflection controls.

578 Fournier, Lucien. "Television by the Belin system." PRACT. ELECT. 3 (Mar. 1924): 244. (574, 605, 771)

579 Baird, J.L., and W.E.L. Day. "Overcoming the time lag in a selenium or other light-sensitive cell used in a television or like system." (565, 580) Br. 235,619, Mar. 12, 1924, Jan. 12, 1925. A light-chopper consisting of two concentric disks with radial slots or serrations revolving in opposite directions to interrupt light at a high frequency. (593)

580 Baird, J.L, and W.E.L. Day. "Transmitting views portraits and scenes by telegraphy or wireless telegraphy." Br. 236,978, Mar. 17, 1924, July 17, 1925. Nipkow disk with holes and a concentric disk with radial slots and a selenium cell at the transmitter. Receiver has a disk with a spiral slot, a radially slotted disk, and a "varying source of light" (neon lamp). (Baird had used neon lamps in his earlier experiments, but they did not appear in his patents.) An a-c generator coupled to the shaft of the transmitter controls the speed of a synchronous motor at the receiver, with sync obtained by rotating the receiver disks. Transmission method and receiver modulation are not specified. (579, 583)

581 Zworykin, V.K. "Television system." U.S. 2,017,883, Mar. 17, 1924, renewed June 27, 1931, Oct. 22, 1935. The object of the invention is to provide simultaneous two-way communication of sight and sound between telephone subscribers via a central office or exchange. Camera tubes and picture tubes, similar to those described in the senior patent (566), are connected by electron tube circuits for carrier-current transmission along power lines. (695)

582 Langer, N. "Television." W.W. 13 (Mar. 19, 1924): 760–4; (Mar. 26, 1924): 94–6. 9 illus. Account of von Mihály's work. (531, 570, 592)

583 "Television experiments." POP. W. (Mar. 22, 1924): 121. Brief note on work by Baird, with mention of William Le Queux and Claude Frowde, "Can actually see moving objects." Brief references to Baird's work also appeared in the DAILY NEWS, Jan. 15, and in RADIO TIMES, Feb. 15. (580, 585)

584 Allouard-Carny, Paul. "Appareil sélecteur perfectionné pour dispositifs de transmission d'images à distance" [Perfected selection apparatus and devices for the transmission of images at a distance]. Fr. 579,254, Mar. 26, Oct. 13, 1924. Scanner consists of two mirrors mounted on a tuning fork and a disk with a circle of holes. Assembly includes a photocell and electron tube amplifiers.

585 Robinson, F.H. "The radio kinema." KINE. WKLY (Apr. 3, 1924). Report on a demonstration by Baird at Hastings. (See also RADIO TIMES, Apr. 25.) (583, 593)

"Not so very long ago I visited one John Logie Baird at his laboratory at Hastings, and saw a demonstration which proved that he has proceeded so far along the road to radio vision as to make it almost a commercial proposition.... I myself saw a cross, the letter "H," and the fingers of my own hand reproduced by this apparatus across the width of the laboratory. The images were quite sharp and clear, although perhaps a little unsteady. This, however, was mostly due to mechanical defects in the apparatus and not any fault of the system. Undoubtedly wonderful possibilities are opened up by this invention, its very simplicity and reliability placing it well to the front of many of the various complicated methods which have been employed to do the same work."

586 Swinton, A.A.C. "The possibilities of television with wire and wireless." W.W. 14 (Apr. 9, 1924): 51–6; (Apr. 16, 1924): 82–4; (Apr. 23, 1924): 114–8. 3 diags. In this paper, read at a meeting of the Radio Society of Great Britain on March 26, the author revives his original scheme of 1911 (413) and describes an expanded version with electron tube circuits for wire or wireless transmission, less sync methods. The discussion (pp. 114–8) includes comments by the president (William Henry Eccles), L.B. Atkinson, E.E. Fournier d'Albe, and others. Eccles observed that when television comes, "it will receive a warm reception from all around." Swinton was less optimistic over future progress: "I am not inclined to be too sanguine as regards a speedy solution of the problem. Indeed, I think I am fairly safe in prophesying that anyone who takes on the problem seriously, will be kept fairly busy for quite some time." He also thought that "it is probably scarcely worth anybody's while to pursue it," yet believed that the big research laboratories "would solve a thing like this in six months...." (414, 588)

587 McCreary, Harold J. "Television." U.S. 2,013,162, Apr. 10, 1924, Sept. 3, 1935. Assigned: Associated Electric Labs. This complete system has a camera tube and picture tube, both with deflection plates, each set supplied from two a-c generators, as in Swinton's scheme (413). The basic form of the image plate in the camera tube consists of an insulator with a large number of isolated conductors embedded therein, set between conductive grids, the faces coated with potassium hydride, selenium, etc. Transmission of images in natural colors is obtained with three tubes and conjunctive mirrors, with color filters at the transmitter and color fluorescent screens in the picture tubes, from which the combined images are viewed on a screen or reproduced on a photographic plate. Radio transmission on a single frequency, with amplifiers and filter circuits, is included. Conflict with Zworykin's prior patent (566) delayed the issuance for many years. (1105)

588 "Television: Mr. Campbell Swinton's system." ENGINEER 137 (Apr. 11, 1924): 384, 385. 3 illus. (586, 589)

589 "Mr. Swinton's views." POP. W. (Apr. 12, 1924): 245. Note on the lecture, March 26. (588, 805)

590 Jenkins, C.F. "Radio vision mechanism." U.S. 1,530,463, Apr. 23, 1924, Mar. 17, 1925. Reissued Feb. 14, 1928. Prismatic disk and lens disk receiver. Similar apparatus was used in the demonstration of September 1923 (559). (568, 602)

591 "Radio moving pictures of national wonders predicted." N.Y.T. 17 (Apr. 27, 1924): 1. "Scientists predict the day when television, or seeing by radio, will allow a person to sit at home and see around the world." See Munro's prediction (236).

592 Langer, N. "Radio television, the Mihály Telehor machine." RADIO N. 5 (May 1924): 1570, 1571, 1686–9. 9 illus. (582, 614, 617)

593 Baird, J.L. "An account of some experiments in television." W.W. 14 (May 7, 1924): 153–5. 4 illus. Baird describes his earlier experiments and apparatus; revolving disk with lamps and a distributor, and transmitter with Nipkow disk overlapped by a serrated disk (light chopper), with the object placed between a lamp and the lens in front of the scanning disks. See also AMATEUR W. May 10 and May 31. See Fig. 30. (585, 640)

594 "Pictures by wire sent with success for the first time." N.Y.T. 1 (May 20, 1924): 1, 9, ed. note 20:3. AT&T tests from Cleveland to New York. 4 photos. (604)

595 Millikan, R.A. "The electron and the light-quant from the experimental view. Nobel lecture, May 23, 1924." NOBEL LECTURES, PHYSICS: 1922–1941. Amsterdam, London, New York: Elsevier, 1965. Presentation speech, pp. 51–3, Lecture, pp. 54–66. Biography, pp. 67–9. (Award for 1923.) (458)

596 Clark, P.L. "Electrical photo-telescopic apparatus." U.S. 1,678,974, May 23, 1924, July 31, 1928. Receiver, image projected on screen. (549, 725)

597 "Pictures by radio restricted by interference and fading." N.Y.T. 9 (May 25, 1924): 15, 1.

598 Sardina, Camille Casimir Antoine. "Appareil de télévision" [Television apparatus]. Fr. 582,288, May 28, Dec. 15, 1924. A multifrequency system with a pierced light-chopper disk and vacuum tube assemblies, mosaic of photocells, and electroluminescent screen.

599 O'Connor, Sexton. "Experiments in television; progressing towards success." POP. W. (May 31, 1924): 504; (June 7, 1924): 539, 540, 552. 8 illus. Outline of systems by Belin, Korn, Dieckmann, Rosing, Jenkins, von Mihály, Baird. (1212)

600 Shaxby, J.H., and J.C. Evans. "Certain properties of the 'Osglim' neon-filled lamp." PROC. PHYS. SOC. 36 (June 1924): 253–61, 278–80. (564)

601 McLoud, M.C. "He sees by radio." POP. SCI. 104 (June 1924): 30.

602 Dastouet, P. "Radio vision." RADIOELECTRICITE 5 (June 10, 1924): 206–10. On Jenkins. (590, 618)

603 Strachan, James. "The early history of television." W.W. 14 (June 11, 1924): 305–7. Brief survey of items published from 1879 to 1882. An erroneous statement is made concerning the absence of any further developments for many years after 1882!

604 "Electrical transmission of pictures." ELECT. WORLD 83 (June 14, 1924): 1223, 1224. AT&T tests of May 20. (594, 608)

605 "First picture by radio is printed in France; Paris to New York transmission is planned." N.Y.T. 15 (June 21, 1924): 4. Belin system. (578, 633)

606 Karolus, August (1893–1972). "Verfahren zur trägheitsfreien Lichtsteuerung mittels Kerr-Effekt" [Method for inertialess light control via Kerr effect]. Ger. 471,720, June 21, 1924. A modified Kerr cell, later incorporated in a receiver patent (708).

607 Voss, August. "Das Problem des elektrischen Fernsehens" [The problem of electric television]. ELEKT. ANZ. 41 (June 28, 1924): 537,538; (July 1, 1924): 45, 46; (July 3, 1924): 53, 54; (July 5, 1924): 61–4. 25 illus. Selenium cells and their properties, details of proposed apparatus. (731)

608 "Photos sent over telephone wires are accurately reproduced." POP. MECH. 42 (Aug. 1924): 187, 188. (604, 610)

609 "Hearing light and seeing radio." POP. RADIO 6 (Aug. 1924): 160, 161. 4 photos with captions.

610 "Telephoning our press photographs." SCI. AM. 131 (Aug. 1924): 87, 139. AT&T demonstration, "ingenious and practical system of image transmission worked out by Bell System." (608, 612)

611 Ives, H.E. "Transmission of pictures by electricity." U.S. 1,656,915, Aug. 22, 1924, Jan. 24, 1928. Assigned: W.E. Receiver with variable-area lens, graded screen, and slotted disk. (567, 622)

612 "Colored photos by wire." N.Y.T. 11 (Aug. 29, 1924): 3. Experiments by AT&T in June with transmission of three separate pictures in black and white. Also editorial 8 (Aug. 30): 6. (610, 645)

613 Dieckmann, M. "Verfahren zur elektrischen Fernsichtbarmachung bewegter Bilder" [Electrical method for making moving pictures visible at a distance]. Ger. 420,567, Aug. 29, 1924, Oct. 26, 1925. A three-channel radio transmission system with a compound vibrating mirror and phototube at the transmitter and a picture tube with magnetic deflection and beam deflection control for display. (505, 665)

614 Mihály, D.v. "Das elektrische Fernsehen und das Telehor" [Electric television and the Telehor]. ELEKT. ANZ. 41 (Sept. 2, 1924): 763, 764; (Sept. 4, 1924): 69, 70; (Sept 6, 1924): 77, 78. 8 illus. Author describes his apparatus and comments on the work to be done. (592, 617)

615 Hoxie, Charles Alfred. "Electrical transmission of pictures." U.S. 1,648,687, Sept. 23, 1924, Nov. 8, 1927. Assigned: G.E. Br. 240,463, Sept. 23, 1925, Nov. 25, 1926. Assigned: B.T.-H. This hybrid system, intended for film transmission as well as direct viewing, includes perforated and slotted disks, bands and drums, phototube and discharge lamp, slotted light chopper, d-c and a-c machinery, electron tube circuits, and superimposed image and a-c sync signals for carrier wave transmission. (896)

616 Baker, T.T. "The telegraphy of photographs by wire and wireless." PHOTOGRAPHIC J. 64 (Oct. 1924): 469–73. (524, 840)

617 Langer, N. "The Telehor and television." PRACT. ELECT. 3 (Oct. 1924): 696. (592, 614, 720)

618 Jenkins, C.F. "The transmission of photographs by radio." ENG. NEWS 5 (Oct. 1924): 96, 110, 111. 4 illus. (602, 620)

619 Skala, Ljubomir William. "Art of television." U.S. 1,678,132, Oct. 1, 1924, July 24, 1928. Part assigned: Frank J. Schraeder Jr. It is claimed that this instrument, called a telectroscope, can transmit "an image in motion and natural colors to a distance." The object is focused through an apertured light-chopper disk along the axis of an electro-optical assembly consisting of Nicol prisms and a tube of carbon disulfide surrounded by the windings of a transformer. The receiver is virtually the same. The secondary coils of the transformers are connected by wires or by radio apparatus. Recording on motion picture film is incorporated. (1334)

620 Jenkins, C.F. "Resistor cell circuit." U.S. 1,693,509, Oct. 22, 1924, Nov. 27, 1928. Resistance-coupled radio-frequency amplifier or modulator circuits controlled by a light-sensitive cell. (618, 627)

621 Fournier d'Albe, E.E. "Apparatus for recording and reproducing sound." Br. 247,629, Oct. 23, 1924, Feb. 23, 1926. Sound impinges on a bank of hollow resonators with silvered reeds; light reflected therefrom affects a moving film. In reproduction, light is interrupted by a multi-apertured disk and passed through a transverse slot and the film onto a selenium cell, the output from which controls a telephone. This patent formed a basis for a later one on television (652). (343, 636)

622 Ives, H.E. "Photoelectric properties of thin films of alkali metals." ASTROPHYSICS J. 60 (Nov. 1924): 209–30. (611, 658)

623 Gernsback, H. "The radio controlled television plane." EXPERIMENTER 4 (Nov. 1924): 22, 23, 62. Full-page illus. Futuristic views of military applications. (559, 671)

624 Elwell, C.F. "Photo-electric cells." ELECT. 93 (Nov. 7, 1924): 520–2. 8 illus. Includes details of the Case high-vacuum type.

625 Korn, A. "Ubertragung von Zeichnungen und Photographien" [Transmission of designs and photographs]. E.N.T. 1 (Dec. 1924): 175–87. 9 illus. On selenium cells and television, with historical references from the work of Bakewell onward. (569, 1621)

626 "Pictures by radio sent from London here in 20 minutes." N.Y.T. 1 (Dec. 1, 1924): 6; 3:3–6. 6 photos. Test by RCA and the Marconi Co. with the Ranger facsimile (photoradiogram) system. (628)

627 "Pictures also sent by radio overland." N.Y.T. 1 (Dec. 1, 1924): 7. Demonstration by Jenkins of message transmission from the naval station at Anacostia, Washington, D.C. to Boston. Reception on film. Also 2 (Dec. 4, 1924): 3; 6:1, 2, and editorial 20 (Dec. 5, 1924): 6. Tests were cancelled Dec. 5 because static blurred the pictures. (620, 631)

628 "Photographs by wireless from London to New York, and reception in New York." TIMES (Dec. 1, 1924): 12f. (626, 631)

629 "Seeing under the whole heaven." N.Y.T. 24 (Dec. 2, 1924): 3. Editorial. "It can be only a question of time when man himself will not only be hearing around the globe but also looking to the ends of the earth and seeing everything under the sun almost at the moment of its happening."

630 "Will wireless next bring us radio sight?" N.Y.T. IX (Dec. 7, 1924): 1. Full-page feature article.

631 "How pictures are sent by radio." N.Y.T. IX (Dec. 7, 1924): 14. On the methods of Jenkins and Ranger. (627, 628, 634, 646)

632 Nipkow, P. "Einrichtung zur Erzielung des Synchronismus bei Apparaten zur elektrischen Bildübertragung" [Arrangement for achieving synchronism in apparatus for electric picture transmission]. Ger. 498,415, Dec. 9, 1924, May 22, 1930. Transmitting and receiving apparatus are to be connected to the same a-c power supply.

633 Belin, E. "Radiovision and telecinematography." Br. 261,195, Nov. 30, 1925, Nov. 18, 1926; U.S. 1,714,154, Dec. 11, 1925, May 21, 1929. In France Dec. 16, 1924. A system with vibrating mirrors, Kerr cell, and radio circuits, adaptable for direct viewing or film transmission and recording. (605, 723)

634 Jenkins, C.F. "Recent progress in the transmission of motion pictures by radio." TRANS. SMPE 17 (1924): 81–5. (631, 638)

635 Bohringer, Arthur John. THE A.B.C. OF WIRELESS TELEVISION. London: Taunton Bros., 1924, 33 pp., illus.

636 Fournier d'Albe, E.E. THE MOON-ELEMENT, AN INTRODUCTION TO THE WONDERS OF SELENIUM. London: T. Fisher Unwin, 1924. 166 pp., 33 illus. Extracts from Berzelius (2) and Smith (50). List of events from 1817 to 1921. Chapter 5, pp. 75–83, picture transmission and television. (621, 652)

637 Low, A.M. WIRELESS POSSIBILITIES. London: Kegan Paul, Trench, Trubner; New York: E.P. Dutton, 1924. Radio television, pp. 43–63, 2 diags. Popular treatment. "Now all over the world experiments are being conducted, many of them with success and some with the guarantee of reasonable success in twenty years of less." (542, 729)

CHAPTER 6
IMAGES AND PROMISES: 1925–1926

The end of the long road from 1878 was reached during 1925–1926 when the television art emerged from the laboratory into the public domain. Some half-dozen demonstrations by Baird and Jenkins showed steady progress ranging from the transmission of shadows and silhouettes to the ultimate success—true television with moving objects and faces reproduced in light and shade. Television became a subject in its own right, rather than an offshoot of phototelegraphy and radio, as a flow of articles and news reports brought inventors' progress to the public eye.

With the exception of a few reports on facsimile, mainly up to mid-1925, the emphasis in the following listings is solely on television. Jenkins continued his earlier work on facsimile (634) with development of a photorecorder (638, 647, 669). Experimental transmissions of color photos by wire and radio were conducted by the Bell System (645, 658). The transatlantic tests of radio facsimile by RCA-Marconi (626) were described in February 1925 (646), and a full technical report appeared in April the next year (756), when the service began on a commercial basis. Other reports on facsimile concern the Bartlane (668), Cooley (670), and Telefunken (810) systems. Books of the period are mainly on facsimile: Friedel (727) and Jenkins (728) of 1925; Baker (840), Eichhorn (842), Fuchs (843), and Lertes (844) of 1926. Dinsdale's book (841) and von Mihály's second edition (845), both on television, were published in 1926.

An indiction of the upsurge of interest in television is seen in the number of patents listed: thirty-seven for 1925, thirty-one for 1926, more than fourfold the annual rate of disclosures for the previous six years. Some twenty newcomers covered their ideas in patents, five of which concerned camera tubes, in addition to one by Zworykin. The countries of origin and the numbers are: Austria, one; Britain, twenty-two; France, three; Germany, six; Russia, six; United States, thirty. Baird led with seventeen applications, Jenkins followed with fourteen.

Some older electromechanical devices were still selected by inventors, examples being distributors, phonic wheels, and tuning forks; see Table 8. Scanning devices most in favor were Nipkow disks, slotted disks, lens disks, prismatic disks, and vibrating mirrors. Modulating methods included Kerr cells, neon lamps, galvanometers, and moving mirrors in addition to picture tubes. Peizoelectric crystals were adopted for scanning in two novel proposals: Whitten (677) and von Bronk (694). Selenium cells were still employed, though most inventors simply called for photocells without specifying the type.

More or less standard approaches appear in several patents by Baird, which were centered on Nipkow's disk, and by Jenkins, who relied upon various arrangements of prismatic and lens disks. Both men introduced a variety of modifications and alternatives in the search to improve and protect their basic ideas, which also built up their patent portfolios. Numerous types and combinations of disks were specified by others: Best (732), Clay (743), Brun (754), Hall (784), Ives (795), Kintner (801), and Valensi (822). Other common methods are found in the disclosures of Gouroff (752), Ives (763), and Schildenfeld (782), respectively employing lens drum, lamp bank, and perforated drum. Scanning patterns mentioned include spiral, cross, zigzag, double, and zone, though linear tracing of an image is assumed in some instances. Electron tube circuits and radio transmission also became more common elements in the proposals.

Some interesting and unusual suggestions appear in the number of specifications. Fournier d'Albe contrived a system employing acoustic resonators (652), the principle of which he demonstrated in April of 1925. The Blackwell and Herman apparatus (674) included provision for remotely controlling the scanning of a preferred area of a picture. The Parker plan (719) is an example of a complex arrangement employing a phosphorescent belt to carry an image, with infrared to enhance the image and a heater to erase it, combined with a mechanism that included moving shutters. The Voss proposal incorporates an X-ray tube (731). An optical transmission system is revealed in the Telefunken patent (734), which introduces relay stations. The notion of using a phosphorescent screen with double beams, one for producing and the other for obliterating an image, was covered in a Baird patent (814).

Baxter's proposal (751), unlike many others, deals with the problem of synchronism, albeit with unusual suggestions that include spark discharges and a revolution indicator. Clay's patent considers synchronous control with a neon lamp and capacitor time base and introduces the idea of triggering the receiver with pulses between picture lines. One am-

TABLE 8   TO SEE BY RADIO

ELECTRICAL	OPTICAL	MECHANICAL
Photocell (10)	Lens disk (10)	Nipkow disk (14)
Distributor (5)	Kerr cell (9)	Slotted disk (7)
Phonic wheel	Vibrating mirror	Tuning fork (6)
Lamp (4)	Fixed mirror (5)	Shutter (4)
Neon lamp	Light pipe (4)	Perforated drum (2)
Galvanometer (3)	Prismatic disk	Serrated disk (1)
Multicell	Spiral scan	Spiral slot
*Piezoelectric (2)	Light spot (3)	
Relay	Cross scan (2)	**ELECTRONIC**
Spark gap	Double scan	Electron tube (8)
*Pulse sync (1)	Lens drum	Camera tube (6)
Telephone	Mirror drum	Phototube (5)
	Phosphor screen	Picture tube (4)
	Photo film	Discharge tube (1)
	Polyhedral drum	Photomultiplier
	Color screen (1)	X-ray tube
	Mirror disk	
	Moving mirror	**SYSTEMS**
	Rotating mirror	Radio transmission (8)
	Zigzag scan	Color (4)
	*Zone scan	Multifrequency (3)
		Film (2)
		*Infrared scanning
		Ultraviolet scanning
		Vision and sound
		*Multibeam (1)
		Optical transmission
		Phono recording
		*Radio wave scanning
		Remote control
		Stereo
		Two-way

*Innovations

bitious scheme that made the headlines later in 1926 was Alexanderson's multichannel seven-spot system (803).

An interesting feature among optical methods is the use of light pipes, though the idea was old, having been proposed by Sawyer (134) in 1880, and by Sinding-Larsen (388) and Saint-René (392), both in 1910. Baird included a movable guide to channel light onto a photocell (640). A cluster of light pipes distributed on a rotating disk appears in a patent (758) by Jenkins. He revised this plan by employing guides of glass or quartz radiating from the axial part of a drum to the surface to distribute light impulses from a multielement neon lamp (767), an arrangement that was incorporated in a drum receiver in 1928. Round (765) specifies "light-tubes" clustered to form picture planes, with the other ends arranged in circles which are scanned by a rotating photocell and lamp, with suggestions incorporating distributors, multiple elements, and capacitors to store elemental image signals. These examples of the application of light-conducting elements to solve optical problems illuminate the inventive process and clearly show the step-by-step evolution of ideas.

Baird proposed a cellular structure of tubes (or rods of glass or quartz fibers) to serve as a lens assembly (797). This honeycomb lens, as it became known, was a newsworthy item for a while, as was the system of interleaved disks which Baird called an optical lever (699). Coincidentally, a similar notion of a honeycomb construction appeared in Reynolds' patent (821) for a camera tube less than two months after Baird's. Reynolds specified "relatively fine and long glass or quartz tubes . . . to divide the image into elements," and further stated that "a film of rubidium, potassium, or other photoactive material is deposited on the inner walls of these tubular photoelectric units." Perhaps, as in other instances of device applications or techniques, the notion of light pipes in optical systems during these years represents a fashion of the times.

As in the previous period, ideas on electronic methods for image pickup with various types of camera tubes occupied inventors, though none was publicized at the time. Dieckmann and Hell proposed a method of electrical dissection by sweeping an electron image across an apertured anode (665). Electron-beam scanning of a photosensitive image plate appears in two related patents of Sabbah, one intended for pickup from film (678, 679). Zworykin devised a color system (695) based on his earlier patent (566). Another beam scanning tube was covered by Case (702). An adaptation of Swinton's plan was reputedly conceived by Grabovsky and colleagues (718). As already mentioned, the Reynolds tube had a mosaic of light pipes. Three American manufacturers concerned with these patents were the American Telephone & Telegraph Company, General Electric, and Westinghouse. The electron multiplier by Jarvis and Blair (792) is a related device that was to be of great importance in the development of more sensitive camera tubes.

Among the advanced systems envisaged by inventors, color is predominant. Zworykin added mosaic color screens to his earlier camera and picture tubes. A duplicate system of disks, photocells, and colored screens was claimed by Baird to be applicable for color and stereo (704). In another scheme he employed selective amplification and double circuits for halftone or two-color effects (707). Ives also disclosed a method for full color transmission (764). As an alternative to visible light, ultraviolet was included in the specifications by Telefunken (734) and Hall (784). The infrared part of the spectrum, also mentioned by Hall, was specified (with ultraviolet) by Baird (798), demonstrations of which he gave in November and December of 1926 (827).

Baird's patents on phonograph recording and radio-frequency scanning reveal his versatility and his efforts to jump ahead in the art, even before he had achieved much more than the transmission of simple halftone images. The idea of phonograph recording had been put forward by Lardeur (275) in 1898, but Baird's plan (799) was specific and was demonstrated in 1927. Reflections of radio waves from distant objects was well known in 1926 when Baird specified that part of the spectrum adjacent to the infrared as a means for scanning (833), an idea that was clearly an extension of infrared. The Ives patent (795) for simultaneous two-way transmission of vision and sound was, like the earlier Zworykin patent (581), directed toward applications in telephone systems.

Public attention was focused on the work of Jenkins and Baird. Accounts of their progress in obtaining images were intermixed with predictions and promises, some fairly based on results and others far beyond the reach of immediate feasibility. Early in 1925, Jenkins looked forward to radio movies in the home and made the first suggestion for a television studio (642), which was the subject of a patent (654). In April he expanded his promise, forecasting all-inclusive applications for radio movies (666). Baird demonstrated shadowgraphs in public that month (664), an event that brought him some much-needed money and more publicity, revealed the crudity of his apparatus, and prompted some interesting comments (659). Two months later Jenkins also went public and demonstrated moving outline images transmitted by radio, hailed as the accomplishment of a "fantastic dream of science" (685).

The first demonstration of simultaneous sight and sound, given by Jenkins in August 1925 (700), was followed by the inventor's prediction that miniature screens for showing motion pictures would be part of radio sets in every household (709). During experiments early in October, success came to Baird, an event which he later said gave him "the one great thrill" of his researches. Unfortunately, he kept this initial achievement secret for several years and never revealed details of the apparatus or the changes that produced the first halftone images (for an account by the subject of his 1925 experiments, see 733). Belin came into the news again in December (723), declaring that television by radio was about to be realized. A few days later Jenkins looked toward the year to come, confident that radio pictures would soon be a reality (726).

Events moved fast early in 1926. Baird, now actively supported by his new partner Hutchinson, gave several demonstrations to the press during January, accompanied by some fantastic pronouncements on their plans. Largely inspired by Hutchinson's imagination, reports declared that television was now a commercial proposition, that television receivers were under production, and that the company had plans for establishing television stations (739). This promotional fanfare culminated in a public demonstration to members of the Royal Institution at Baird's laboratory on January 26, a milestone event that proved the validity of his claim to have achieved true television (740).

Further reports on Baird's work appeared in April (759) when he declared that "perfection is now only a matter of time and money," in July (772) and in August (776), when he expressed the hope (later fulfilled) of broadcasting the Derby (777). Television Limited (736) obtained the first licenses for television stations that month and images were transmitted across London (783), following earlier experimental transmissions in June (769). More reports on Baird appeared in September (788, 790), his early apparatus found a permanent home in the Science Museum that month (793), and further accounts were published in October (802), November (809), and December (816, 839).

In the meantime, news about Belin in February (742), July (771, 775), and December (817, 830); and of von Mihály in June (770) and December (819) revealed that they had not progressed beyond the stage of outline images. In contrast to the enthusiasm over Baird, de Forest expressed strong doubts about the prospects for television, believing that further developments depended on a radical discovery in physics (791). Because of the lack of progress with his radio movies and the pressure of other work on facsimile, Jenkins virtually dropped out of the news during 1926. The first reports on Alexanderson and his proposed apparatus appeared in December (826). At the end of the year Baird was, deservedly, the champion of television, a situation that would change in the coming months with the rise of criticism and competition.

Reports on the pictures displayed show progress from shadowgraphs to halftone images, with references in general terms but without such specifics as the size of the images or the definition. Baird could show letters in outline, a blurred resemblance of a hand in motion, and a dummy face during the early months of 1925 (643, 659, 675). In June, Jenkins' images of a model windmill in motion were easily distinguished but not clear-cut (685), and other witnesses saw the silhouette figure of a dancing girl on moving film (696). Baird's halftone images in January 1926 were faint, often blurred and unsteady, but objects in motion and the human face were recognizable. In April the image of Baird's features while he was talking "came through very clearly" (759).

In July a witness of Baird's apparatus reported that facial movements and even cigarette smoke were faithfully portrayed (772). In another account the image of a man's face flickered and appeared out of focus but was perfectly recognizable (788). Distortion affected the picture, producing a flattened or twisted effect (769), and a mass of whirling flakes or white flashes or a moving white band resulted from electrical interference. The term "white" refers to the highlights of a "sepia-colored light" on a ground-glass screen, or tones of neon-pink, not black and white.

Few of these reports mention the screen size, but photographs of mid-1926 indicate that screens some 3 or 4 inches in diameter were in experimental use (809). A model Baird receiver with a glass screen about 1 foot square was reported as being on display at the National Radio Exhibition in London in September (794). Near the end of the year a model of a proposed commercial Televisor (a registered trade name) was described as a handsome mahogany case about 24 by 20 by 18 inches with a ground-glass screen about 8 inches square. The "latest wonder" of the "miracle of radio" was now "an accomplished fact," though still very much experimental. The year had seen television become a reality indeed, if only with coarse images comparable with the earliest motion pictures, but Hutchinson's fantasy of mass-produced receivers was still in the future awaiting advances in technology and acceptance by the public.

TABLE 9   CHRONOLOGY: 1925–1926

Year	Month	Day	Name	Description
1925	Jan.	1	Baird	Extensive patent including Kerr cell, light pipe, zone scan
		2	Jenkins	Spiral-mounted lens disk
		16	Jenkins	Studio plans
	Mar.	12	Fournier d'Albe	Acoustic resonator system
	Apr.		Baird	Public demonstration of shadowgraphs
			Tschernyschev	Development of system
		5	Dieckmann, Hell	Image dissector camera tube
		18	Fournier d'Albe	Private demonstration
	May	7	Blackwell, Herman	Slotted disks, light valve, remote control
			Baird	Formation of Television Ltd.
		25	Whitten	Piezoelectric crystal scanner
		27	Sabbah	Camera tube
	June	13	Jenkins	Demonstration of radio vision
	July	6	von Bronk	Electrostatic scanner
		13	Zworykin	Electronic color system with mosaic screens
	Aug.	6	Baird	Optical lever, multiple-disk scanner
		11	Jenkins	Demonstration of image and sound
		25	Case	Camera tube
	Sept.	1	Baird	Two-color and stereo, high-intensity neon lamp
		5	Karolus	Nipkow disk, vibrating mirrors, Kerr cell
	Oct.	2	Baird	Successful experiment with halftone images
		21	Baird	Automatic sync, compensation circuits
	Nov.	6	Siemens & Halske	Sync with phonic wheels
		9	Grabovsky, et al.	Camera tube
		25	Parker	Vibrating mirrors, phosphorescent belt
		28	Tschernyschev	Mirror drum, Kerr cell
	Dec.	1	Reynolds	Optical system
		18	Belin	Public demonstration and lecture
		22	Clark	Polyhedral mirror drum, lens disk, vibrating mirror
1926	Jan.		Voss	Drums, X-ray tube, fluorescent screen
		7	Baird	Demonstration to the press

			Best	Rotating disks
		8	Telefunken	Optical system, relay stations
		20	Baird	Lens disk, Kerr cell, double scan
		26	Baird	Public demonstration of moving images with halftones
Feb.	9	Clay	Slotted disks, picture tube, pulse sync
Mar.	9	Latour	Multiple disks, multicell, interlaced scan
	23	Baxter	Perforated disks, serrated shutter, "telecamera"
		Gouroff	Lens drum, vibrating mirrors, galvanometer
	27	Brun	Coaxial disks
Apr.	22	Jenkins	Rotating disk with lamps, and with light pipes
May	1	RCA-Marconi	Commercial transatlantic facsimile service
	3	Baird	Spot registration and sync
	20	Ives	Lamp bank, distributor, tuning fork, phonic wheel, color
	21	Round	Light pipes, distributors, capacitive signal storage
June	2	Jenkins	Apertured drum, light pipes, multi-element neon lamp
Aug.	2	Dauvillier	Report on experiments
	9	Baird	First television station licenses, 2TV, 2TW
	10	Schildenfeld	Slotted drum, mirror, moving shutter
	17	Hall	Slotted disks, distributor, multiplex transmission
	19	Jenkins	Disk scanner, tuning fork, sync signals
Sept.	11	Baird	Early apparatus donated to the Science Museum
	15	Jarvis, Blair	Secondary emission electron multiplier
Oct.	1	Ives	Simultaneous two-way system
	15	Baird	Honeycomb lens with light pipes
	15		Infrared system, or Noctovision
	15		Disk recording, or Phonovision
	15		Cross-scanning
	15	Kintner	Mirror disk
	19	Alexanderson	Multichannel 7-spot system
		Franklin	Coaxial cable
Nov.	23	Baird	Private demonstration of Noctovision
	30	Baird	Phosphorescent screen with obliterating beam
Dec.		Belin, Holweck	Oscillating mirrors, cathode-ray oscillograph
		von Mihály	Oscillating mirror system
	3	Baird	Telephone actuator, grid shutter, Kerr cell
	4	Reynolds	Camera tube
	9	Valensi	Perforated disks, multiple light sources
	11	Busch	Cathode rays and magnetic fields
		Lorenz	Phonic wheels, eddy-current brakes, sync
	16	Alexanderson	Lecture on multiple beam system
	21	Baird	High-frequency radio-wave scanning
	30	Baird	Public demonstration of Noctovision

BIBLIOGRAPHY: 1925–1926

638 Herndon, Charles Allan. "1,000 printed words a minute by radio." POP. RADIO 7 (Jan. 1925): 11–5, 5 illus. Jenkins system with prismatic disks and recording film. (634, 639, 696)

639 "Projection of photos by radio." RADIO N. 6 (Jan. 1925): 1146. Photo of Jenkins. (638, 641)

640 Baird, J.L. "Apparatus for transmitting scenes or representations to a distance." Br. 253,957, Jan. 1, 1925, July 1, 1926. This extensive patent covers a reciprocating Nipkow disk with a circle of lenses, lens disk with slotted member, disk with spiral slot, vibrating or rocking mirrors, multiple photocells, Nicol prisms, Kerr cell modulator, light pipe of glass or silica or a polished tube, zone scan, and tuned-frequency amplifier. (593, 643)

641 Jenkins, C.F. "Spiral-mounted lens disk." U.S. 1,679,086, Jan. 2, 1925, July 31, 1928, reissued May 3, 1932. The lens disk covered in this patent was used by Jenkins for his demonstration of image transmission by radio in June 1925. (639, 642)

642 "Plans experiments on 'movies' by radio; inventor predicts cinemas in the home." N.Y.T. 1 (Jan. 16, 1925): 2, 3. Jenkins' plan to set up a small studio for dancing pantomines. (641, 647)

643 Baird, J.L. "Television. A description of the Baird system by its inventor." W.W. 15 (Jan. 21, 1925): 533–5. Diagram, 2 photos of the transmitter. Lens disks, serrated disk, fluid photocell, a-c sync, neon lamp. (640, 644)

644 "Mr. Baird and his apparatus." POP. W. (Jan. 24, 1925): 229. Photo and caption. (643, 650).

645 King, R.W. "Color pictures by radio." POP. RADIO 7 (Feb. 1925): 125–8. 3 illus. Bell System experiments. (612, 658, 960)

646 "The photoradiogram system in transatlantic tests." RADIO N. 6 (Feb. 1925): 1385, 1456, 1458, 1460. 5 illus. Tests between London and New York, Nov. 30, 1924. Description of apparatus and operation. (631, 756)

647 Winters, S.R. "The radio-photo letter." RADIO N. 6 (Feb. 1925): 1386, 1387. 3 photos. Jenkins facsimile system. (535, 642, 653, 672)

648 Aigner, Franz (1882–1945). "Ist nach dem gegenwärtigen Stand der Wissenschaft und Technik die Konstruktion eines elektrischen Fernsehers durchführbar?" [Is the construction of an electric television realizable at the present state of science and technology?] Z. HOCHFREQUENZTECH. 25 (Feb. 1925): 56–61.

649 Rosing, B.L. Russ. 3423, Feb. 25, 1925. (411, 688, 3407)

650 (Baird television apparatus.) GRAPHIC (Feb. 28, 1925). Full-page illustration with caption. (644, 651)

651 "The Baird system." POP. W. (Mar. 7, 1925): 61. Note on a demonstration to a POP. W. representative: "he has seen enough to convince him of the practicability of the Baird system." (650, 659)

652 Fournier d'Albe, E.E. "Telegraphic transmission of pictures and images." U.S. 1,571,897, Mar. 12, 1925, Feb. 2, 1926. Part assigned: Bernard Winfield. Reproduction of transparencies or of images of landscapes or solid objects by television. The system incorporates acoustic resonators as disclosed in the earlier patent (621). (636, 667)

653 Jenkins, C.F. "Radio vision illumination." U.S. 1,659,736, Mar. 14, 1925, Feb. 21, 1928. Two prismatic disks. (647, 654)

654 Jenkins, C.F. "Radio vision studio equipment." U.S. 1,684,736, Mar. 14, 1925, Sept. 18, 1928. (653, 655)

655 Jenkins, C.F. "Radio vision analysis." U.S. 1,747,173, Mar. 14, 1925, Feb. 18, 1930. Image of a picture is scanned and projected by a prismatic disk across the aperture of a photocell. (654, 656)

656 Jenkins, C.F. "Twin-light-cell transmitter." U.S. 1,642,733, Mar. 21, 1925, Sept. 20, 1927. Two photocells with triode amplifiers, selected by a rotating shutter. (655, 663)

657 "Radio vision is not an impossibility." N.Y.T. 12 (Mar. 21, 1925): 5. Editorial: "The capacity for feeling surprised at scientific, and especially at electrical, marvels has been pretty well exhausted for this generation."

658 Ives, H.E., Joseph W. Horton, Ralzemond D. Parker, and A.B. Clark. "The transmission of pictures over telephone lines." B.S.T.J. 4 (Apr. 1925): 187–214. 22 illus., 3-color plate of photo reproduction. (622, 645, 719, 763, 907, 909)

659 Baird, J.L. "Television, or seeing by wireless." DISCOVERY 6 (Apr. 1925): 142, 143. Photo of earlier apparatus and diagram. System is the same as described earlier (643) with radio link. The editor, Hugh B.C. Pollard, reports on a demonstration and comments on the future of television. (651, 662)

"I attended a demonstration of Mr. Baird's apparatus and was very favorably impressed with the results. His machinery is, however, astonishingly crude, and the apparatus in general is built out of derelict odds and ends. The optical system is composed of lenses out of bicycle lamps. The framework is an unimpressive erection of old sugar boxes, and the electrical wiring a nightmare cobweb of improvisations. The outstanding miracle is that he has been able to produce any result at all with the very indifferent material at his disposal.

"In the not too distant future we may expect not the wearying 'travel talk' from a broadcasting station, but direct wireless speech and vision transmitted from the ends of the earth and relayed to our firesides. We shall see on our screens the reproduction of distant events and hear them explained as they take place.

"It is a devastating outlook for eventually it will probably be applied to the ordinary telephone service and prevarication will be even more difficult than it is today. On the other hand, when it arrives, we shall find so many conveniences in it that we shall wonder how we ever got on without it in the past."

660 Tschernyschev, A.A. (Electric valves and some of their applications.) ELEK- TRICHESTVO (Apr. 1925): 234–8. Includes description of television apparatus under development by the author in the U.S.S.R. (573, 721, 3407)

661 Walton, G.W. "A new method of television." RADIO N. 6 (Apr. 1925): 1872, 1873, 2000. 3 illus. Description of the system developed by the author and W.S. Stephenson as disclosed in an earlier patent (537). (1542)

662 "Selfridge's present the first public demonstration of television." Pamphlet issued in connection with Baird's demonstrations at the store in Oxford Street, London, during April.

663 Jenkins, C.F. "Multiple light-cell transmitter." U.S. 1,641,633, Apr. 1, 1925, Sept. 6, 1927. Rotating mirror directs light onto a series of photocells in succession. (656, 666)

664 "Current topics and events." NATURE 115 (Apr. 4, 1925): 505, 506. Demonstration by Baird at Selfridge's, description of apparatus and results. (662, 675)

"A series of interesting demonstrations has been given at Messrs. Selfridge and Co., Ltd., London, W.1., by Mr. J.L. Baird, of an experimental apparatus of his own design for wireless 'television' (i.e. the simultaneous reproduction at a distance of an image of a fixed or moving object). The inventor does not claim any great perfection for his results, but we have seen the production in the receiver of a recognisable, if rather blurred image of simple forms, such as letters painted in white on a black card, held up before the transmitter. Mr. Baird has overcome many practical difficulties, but we are afraid that there are many more to be surmounted before ideal television is accomplished."

665 Dieckmann, M., and Rudolf Hell. "Lichtelektrische Bildzerlegerröhre für Fernseher" [Photoelectric picture dissection tube for television]. Ger. 450,187, Apr. 5, 1925, Oct. 3, 1927. Camera tube with photosensitive image plate (cathode) at one end and apertured anode with collector electrode at the other. Deflection coils at right angles sweep the electron image beam across the anode aperture. Farnsworth was occupied with

ideas for a similar type of image dissector tube at this time (850). (613, 1235)

666 "Jenkins predicts radio movies." N.Y.T. 23 (Apr. 8, 1925): 2. In a report to the American Chemical Society, Jenkins stated that the prismatic ring will enable radio fans to see the next Olympic games. He promised that stay-at-homes will see the presidential inaugural ceremonies, or a distant polo match, football or baseball game, the Mardi Gras, a flower festival, or a baby parade. Radio movies will also be of great value to teachers and students, especially those in rural areas, and to the military for surveys by airplanes with images sent to ground receivers. (663, 669)

667 "Current topics and events." NATURE 115 (Apr. 25, 1925): 613. Private demonstration by Fournier d'Albe of his acoustic television apparatus on April 18. No images were shown, only the production of a luminous patch on a ground-glass screen. (652, 753)

668 Hansen, Edmund H. "The new Bartlane system of radio transmission of pictures." POP. RADIO 7 (May 1925): 406–11. 4 illus. Facsimile system employing punched tape developed by H.G. Bartholomew and M.D. McFarlane.

669 Wilkerson, Dan C. "Visible radio communication." QST 9 (May 1925): 15–8. 8 illus. Jenkins' photorecorder and other work on facsimile. (666, 672)

670 Henry, Charles C. "A new method of transmitting pictures by wire or radio." RADIO BRD. 7 (May 1925): 18–28. Various current systems and the work of Austin C. Cooley.

671 Gernsback. H. "Radio in 1935." RADIO N. 6 (May 1925): 2050, 2051, 2086, 2087. 4 illus. One picture shows a receiver with a circular viewing screen mounted on top, as visualized for 1935. (623, 760)

672 Winters, S.R. "Television for amateurs." RADIO N. 6 (May 1925): 2091. Jenkins facsimile. 2 photos. (647, 669, 673, 715)

673 Jenkins, C.F. "Double-image radio picture." U.S. 1,559,437, May 5, Oct. 27, 1925. Separate scanning (linear and transverse) motions by prismatic disk and lens disk for objects, or by film and lens disk for motion pictures. (782, 681)

674 Blackwell, Otto B., and Joseph Herman. "Method and apparatus for television." U.S. 1,624,918, May 7, 1925, Apr. 19, 1927. Slotted disks provide a spiral scan which is adjustable to obtain a detailed view of a preferred part of a picture. Separate circuits for horizontal, vertical, and synchronizing controls and visual signals are connected via filters for wire transmission. Light valve modulator and a movable lens operated coordinately by moving coils at the receiver, which includes means for remotely controlling scanning of a preferred part of the picture. (2032)

675 Bird, P.R. "Wireless television, a review of the Baird system." POP. W. (May 23, 1925): 622, 623. Photo of Baird with his earlier apparatus. Full-page artist's diagram of the current system showing disk with a double spiral of lenses, serrated disk, colloidal photocell, radio receiver, ground-glass screen, viewing hood, and a dummy face. Description of a demonstration during the public exhibit at Selfridge's. (664, 676)

"The first public demonstration of Television ever given was by Mr. Baird, at Selfridge's in Oxford Street, and it was there I found him, amongst the mass of machinery with which he has proved the possibilities of wireless vision.

"Leaving me at the receiver, the inventor walked to the transmitter and started the machinery. On to the square screen in front of the transmitting disc, full in the light of the lamp, he placed a roughly-traced sketch. It represented a crude face like schoolboys draw—just two moony eyes and a large mouth. The instant Mr. Baird placed it in position it was wirelessed through to the receiving disk, which I was watching, where it leered away at me in the most disconcerting fashion.

"'I'll make it wink,' shouted the inventor, covering and uncovering one of its eyes. The uncanny, flickering image at my end promptly winked at me in unison, shutting and opening one eye in the most flagrant and uncommonly knowing fashion. A final talk with the inventor left me with the impression that Television has a long, long way to go before it reaches the perfection of present-day broadcasting, yet I think it may be said to be fairly started upon the road. [See also 659.]"

676   Roberts. J.H.T. "Television." POP. W. (May 23, 1925): 643. Note on the formation of Baird's new company 'Television Limited' with a nominal capital of 5,000 ordinary shares of 1 pound each. (675, 680, 744)

677   Whitten, William Henry. "Scanning devices for television systems." Br. 252,387, May 20, Dec. 2, 1926. In U.S. May 25, 1925. Assigned: Metropolitan-Vickers Electrical Co. A vessel filled with alcohol and glycerine contains a movable mirror actuated by two piezoelectric crystal assemblies energized from an a-c source. Light from the object, reflected between this mirror and a fixed mirror, is directed onto a separate vibrating mirror and thence to a photocell. (1000)

678   Sabbah, Camille A. "Transmission of pictures and views." U.S. 1,694,982, May 27, 1925, Dec. 11, 1928. Assigned: G.E. Camera with photoelectric film attached to a cathode-ray tube. Image formed on the film is scanned by an electron beam, the output goes to a radio transmitter via an electron tube amplifier. Similar to the companion patent (679).

679   Sabbah, C.A. "Transmission of pictures and views." U.S. 1,706,185, May 27, 1925, renewed Nov. 3, 1928, Mar. 19, 1929. Assigned: G.E. Camera tube with two perforated metal plates or gauze disks adjacent to the end face on which an optical image is cast from a camera. The tube contains a perforated diaphragm to limit the area of the cathode beam, which explores the image plane in a spiral or linear path controlled by deflection plates. Charges on the image plates at a scanned point, which depend on the degree of illumination at that point, are passed to a wire line or radio transmitter via an electron tube amplifier. These patents were in conflict with Zworykin's patent of Dec. 29, 1923 (566). (678)

680   "Wireless television, Baird apparatus." ENGINEERING 119 (May 29, 1925): 661, 662. 2 illus. (676, 683)

681   "The Jenkins television system." POP. W. (May 30, 1925): 657. Private demonstration of film transmission by radio between two rooms at the laboratory in Washington, D.C. The film, a continuous belt, depicted a Dutch windmill. The image seen on a small screen was a fairly good reproduction, but there was considerable flicker. A preview of the public demonstration of June 13 (685). (673, 684)

682   Burke, N. "One step nearer vision by radio." POP. SCI. 106 (June 1925): 36.

683   "Simplified radio television; new system uses colloidal photo-electric cell." SCI. & INV. 13 (June 1925): 160. Full-page diagram of Baird's system like the one in the Bird article (675). (680, 690)

684   Jenkins, C.F. "Light-converging-lens system." U.S. 1,695,980, June 5, 1925, Dec. 18, 1928. Combination of lens disk, spaced lens system, and photocell for scanning moving film. (681, 685)

685   "Radio shows far away objects in motion; Washington officials see test of invention." N.Y.T. 1 (June 14, 1925): 4. Receiver screen about 10 by 8 inches displayed a revolving Dutch windmill and motion picture film. Also, "Radio vision shown first time in history by Capital inventor." SUNDAY STAR (Washington, D.C.) (June 14, 1925). (684, 686)

"'Radio vision,' long the fantastic dream of science, became an accomplished fact yesterday afternoon, with Secretary of the Navy Wilbur and other high Government officials witnessing the feat. With the aid of a remarkable apparatus invented by the Washington scientist, C. Francis Jenkins, the Secretary of the Navy ...and others actually 'saw' by radio an object set in motion several miles distant in front of a 'radio eye' installed at the Naval Radio Station, NOF, at Bellevue, D.C. It was heralded as the first time in history that man has literally seen far-away objects in motion through the uncanny agency of wireless.

"What the officials saw yesterday afternoon was the image of a small cross revolving in a beam of light flashed across a light-sensitive cell at Station NOF. No other objects were used in the test. The image, while not clear-cut, was easily distinguishable."

686 Jenkins, C.F. "Plural lens-disk analyzer." U.S. 1,644,383, June 20, 1925, Oct. 4, 1927. Overlapping lens disks rotating at different speeds. (685, 687)

687 "Foresees colored radio pictures." N.Y.T. IX, 16 (June 21, 1925): 7. General discussion and comments by Jenkins on the problems and possibilities of color transmission. (686, 689)

688 Rosing, B.L. Russ. 3425, June 25, 1925. (649, 1032, 3407)

689 "Wireless movies." POP. W. (June 27, 1925): 832. On Jenkins' plans for a special studio "where miniature plays will be enacted before the transmitting camera." See patent, Mar. 14 (654). (687, 690)

690 "The prospect of television; recent experiments." TIMES (June 29, 1925): 7c. General discussion, with references to a special system of prismatic lenses (Jenkins) and a method of stroboscopic apparatus (Baird). (683, 689, 691, 699)

691 Bidwell, G.L. "Television arrives." QST 9 (July 1925): 9–14. 18 illus. On Jenkins' system and transmission of motion pictures in silhouette. An early account of the inventor's "radio movies." (692, 698)

"Motion pictures by radio are here! I saw them with my own eyes. The present motion pictures are silhouette. That is, they are just black and white pictures without half tones. But the half tones are coming just as sure as the sun will rise tomorrow morning. And then we will see as well as hear broadcasting.

"A very interesting thing about this apparatus of Jenkins is that he modulates his carrier wave with voice frequency also and so speech accompanies the picture with no interference. You see the picture. It is a Dutch windmill with vanes spinning. The loud speaker says: 'The mill will now slow down.' It slows down. Again: 'The mill will now stop.' It stops. 'The mill will turn backward.' It turns backward. After studying the process for two weeks it seemed almost uncanny since the motion picture film and the speaker are ten miles away."

692 Jenkins, C.F. "Prism-lens unit." U.S. 1,677,590, July 1, 1925, July 17, 1928. Lens disk. (691, 693)

693 "The Jenkins' method." POP. W. (July 4, 1925): 864. Note on Jenkins' facsimile instruments which are "quite small, very compact, and simple to operate." (692, 696)

694 Bronk, O.v. "Apparatus for the electrical transmission of pictures." U.S. 1,670,757, June 28, 1926, May 22, 1928. Br. 277,761, June 26, 1926, Sept. 26, 1927. In Germany July 6, 1925. Multiple crossed Kerr cells or an equivalent assembly of piezoelectric crystals between Nicol prisms comprise the picture dissecting and recomposing means. Differing voltages or frequencies control the "optical openings" with time displacement or phase change. Electron tube circuits, with rotating capacitors that provide the scanning controls, also furnish modulation for radio transmission. The optical elements in the receiver, coupled by series transformers to the output circuit, provide simultaneous cross scanning and light modulation. (420, 1750)

695 Zworykin, V.K. "Television system." U.S. 1,691,324, July 13, 1925, Nov. 13, 1928. Assigned: Westinghouse. Br. 255,057, July 3, 1926, Mar. 31, 1927. Essentially the same as the parent specification (566), this covers a color system employing mosaic screens with small squares of red, blue, and green. One screen is mounted between lenses at the optical end of the camera tube; the other is mounted between a lens and a ground-glass screen over the end face of the picture tube. (581, 947)

696 Herndon, C.A. "Motion pictures by ether waves." POP. RADIO 8 (Aug. 1925): 107–13. 6 photos. On Jenkins and his apparatus.

The writer saw the silhouette figure of a dancing girl on motion picture film transmitted by radio over 6 miles from Jenkins' laboratory. (638, 693, 697)

"I have just come from a shadow-show in the Washington suburban home of C. Francis Jenkins. The figure that produced the shadows was on a motion picture film being projected in the inventor's laboratory in Washington. It was separated from the screen by six miles of city and suburban streets and houses.

"While the little crowd of neighbors and friends watched a small screen which formed a panel in the receiving set, there suddenly appeared on it the silhouetted figure of a girl. There was no scenery. The details of the dancing figure were not shown. But the shadow-like figure moved—it danced. And those who were present seemed to realize that, simple silhouette though it was, it was really dancing at the wedding of the motion pictures with radio."

697 "Jenkins and his apparatus." RADIO N. 7 (Aug. 1925): 184. Photo and caption. (696, 698)

698 Jenkins, C.F. "Recent progress in transmissions of motion pictures by radio." TRANS. SMPE 21 (Aug. 1925): 7–11. (697, 700)

699 Baird, J.L. "Apparatus for transmitting views, scenes or images to a distance." Br. 265,640, Aug. 6, 1925, Feb. 7, 1927. U.S. 1,707,935, Aug. 4, 1926, Apr. 2, 1929. Lens disks are mounted on parallel shafts which rotate in opposite directions, with the disks interleaved along the optical axis, at the end of which is a disk with a spiral of lenses in front of a photocell. Described as an optical lever, this arrangement resulted in more rapid scanning without a corresponding increase in the rotational speed of the disks. (690, 704)

700 "Talking movies transmitted by radio." N.Y.T. 3 (Aug. 12, 1925): 2. Jenkins moved about before his transmitter and described his actions. Simultaneous images and sound were transmitted on a single wavelength to an audience in another room. Receiver apparatus designed as an attachment to the standard radio set. (698, 703)

701 "Boy reports success in movies by radio." N.Y.T. 26 (Aug. 23, 1925): 6. Douglas F.W. Coffey, age 18, student at the University of Wisconsin, successfully transmitted moving pictures by radio a distance of about seven miles. "Coffey has secrets he will not divulge."

702 Case, T.W. "Method and apparatus for transmitting pictures." U.S. 1,790,898, Aug. 25, 1925, Feb. 3, 1931. Assigned: Case Research Lab. The end face of a cathode-ray tube is coated internally with an opaque or semi-transparent photosensitive layer. The electron beam passes through an apertured diaphragm and a tubular anode. With two different frequencies supplied to the deflector plates, the beam explores the photosensitive screen with a linear trace. The visual signal is derived from the screen-cathode circuit. The image may be projected onto the end face via lens 10 or onto the inner surface via lens 11. A picture tube, similar to the camera tube but with a fluorescent screen, is also described. This patent was in conflict with Zworykin's patent of Dec. 29, 1923 (490).

703 Arvin, W.B. "See with your radio." RADIO N. 7 (Sept. 1925): 278, 384–7. 3 illus. Jenkins system and Moore glow lamp. (700, 709)

704 Television Ltd., and J.L. Baird. "Transmission and/or reproduction of views, scenes or images by wires or wirelessly." Br. 266,564, Sept. 1, 1925, Mar. 1, 1927. Nipkow disks with two spirals of holes or lenses. Two photocells and two stationary screens; orange-red, green-blue. Intended and claimed for stereoscopic and color transmission. (699, 705)

705 Baird, J.L. "Transmission and/or reproduction of views, scenes or images by wire or wirelessly." Br. 266,591, Sept. 1, 1925, Mar. 1, 1927. A multicell, multiple-frequency system. Scanning disk is concentric with an interrupter disk carrying two series of apertures, the outer set containing twice as many apertures as the inner set. Separate photo-

cells are connected to primary windings of an output transformer. The combined frequencies are separated by filters at the receiver. (704, 706)

706 Television Ltd., and J.L. Baird. "Electric glow-discharge lamps." Br. 267,056, Sept. 1, 1925, Mar. 1, 1927. A high intensity neon lamp with large electrodes and a screened emission area. (705,707)

707 Baird, J.L. "Transmission and/or reproduction of views, scenes or images by wires or wirelessly." Br. 267,378, Sept. 1, 1925, Mar. 1, 1927. Differential or selective amplification with branch circuits whereby lamps of different intensities provide halftone effects, or colored lamps or screens provide a two-color effect. (706, 711)

708 Karolus, A. "Receiver arrangement for electric television apparatus." U.S. 1,762,231, Aug. 31, 1926, June 10, 1930, reissued Sept. 23, 1930, July 19, 1932. Assigned: RCA. In Germany Sept. 5, 1925. Nipkow disk, or vibrating mirrors, and Kerr cell. (606, 755)

709 "Movies over the air expected as next step." N.Y.T. XI, 3 (Sept. 13, 1925): 6–8. "Washington inventor says miniature motion-picture screen will be attached to radio sets in every household." General discussion, with comments by Jenkins; "The idea of radio vision came to him about 12 years ago." (703, 716)

710 Kollatz, C.W. "Photo-telegraphy and television." ENG. PROG. 6 (Oct. 1925): 309–13. Survey of major systems.

711 Baird, J.L. "Television or like systems and apparatus." Br. 269,834, Oct. 21, 1925, Apr. 21, 1927. Automatic synchronous control with a special image (white or black band at one edge of the picture), in conjunction with flashing lights, photocells, slotted disk, or other means. (707, 712)

712 Baird, J.L. "Television systems and apparatus." Br. 270,222, Oct. 21, 1925, Apr. 21, 1927. To counter the time lag of response of selenium cells, circuits are arranged to introduce a current proportional to the rate of change of current from the cell, the composite output producing a sharp or near-square waveform. (711, 733)

713 Wood, A.B. "The cathode-ray oscillograph." J. IEE 63 (Nov. 1925): 1046–55. Includes description of instruments by Dufour, Western Electric, and the author.

714 MacGregor-Morris, John T., and R. Mines. "Measurements in electrical engineering by means of cathode rays." J. IEE 63 (Nov. 1925): 1056–1107. 54 illus., 8 tables. Bibliography, 125 articles and books referred to in the text. App., pp. 1096–1105, "The jet as a measuring device," by Mines. This "survey of the present state of knowledge" is a comprehensive review from the investigations of Plücker in 1858. Pages 1066–74 are largely historical up to 1900. Cold- and hot-cathode instruments, methods of focusing, indicating, recording, and time scales are treated in Part 2, pp. 1074–95. A basic historical paper. (3205)

715 Winters, S.R. "Radio vision of the future." POP. MECH. 44 (Nov. 1925): 705, 706. (672, 1695)

716 Jenkins, C.F. "Radio vision." PROC. U.S. NAVAL INST. 51 (Nov. 1925): 2150–5, 4 illus. (709, 726)

717 Siemens & Halske, A.-G. "An electric device for synchronising rotations." Br. 261,021, Nov. 5, 1926, Sept. 22, 1927. In Germany Nov. 6, 1925. Phonic wheels interconnected and coupled to driving motors. (1947)

718 Grabovsky, Popoff, and Piskounoff. Russ. 5592, Nov. 9, 1925. An elaboration of Swinton's scheme with a solid photosensitive image plate. (3407)

719 Parker, R.D. "Electrovision." U.S. 1,648,058, Nov.25, 1925, Nov. 8, 1927. Assigned: AT&T. Linear or spiral scan by compound vibrating mirrors of the type shown in the Egerton patent (475). The novel receiver consists of a light-proof chamber with two shuttered windows containing an endless belt with a phosphorescent surface. The belt moves intermittently with the shutters opened or closed synchronously via gearing with relay contactor and tuning fork control.

Light from a modulated spark gap or discharge tube is directed by a vibrating mirror onto the belt at the recording window; the belt then moves round pulleys to the viewing window where the image is enhanced by light from an infrared source. Images are erased by a heating coil inside the chamber. Radio transmission with electron tube and filter circuits, phototube pickup. (658, 2299)

720 Diner-Dines, P. "Der elektrische Fernseher, das Telehor" [Electric television, the Telehor]. V.D.I.Z. 69 (Nov. 28, 1925): 1507, 1508. 6 illus. Details of von Mihály's apparatus. (617, 770)

721 Tschernyschev, A.A. Russ. 3540, Nov. 28, 1925, also 3511. (660, 3407) See also ELEKTRICHESTVO (No. 4, 1925) for description of a mirror drum and Kerr cell system.

722 Reynolds, Frederick W. "Optical system." U.S. 1,593,639, Dec. 1, 1925, July 27, 1926. Assigned: AT&T. Vibrating mirrors, phototube. (821)

723 "Reports television an accomplished fact." N.Y.T. 10 (Dec. 19, 1925): 2. At a meeting in Paris of the Society of French Photography, Belin displays his latest invention and declares that "television by radio is on the point of being realized," since "his efforts to find a solution of the problem of television had finally succeeded." The report further states that "the announcement created a profound impression, since a veritable race is going on between inventors in France, America, Germany and England to reach the goal which M. Belin now claims to have achieved." See also ELECT. 96 (Jan. 1, 1926): 12. (633, 724)

724 "Marvelous but not miraculous." N.Y.T. 20 (Dec. 21, 1925): 5. Editorial comments on Belin's demonstration in Paris. (723, 739)

725 Clark, P.L. "Photo-electrical transmission apparatus." U.S. 1,648,042, Dec. 22, 1925, Nov. 8, 1927. Polyhedral mirror drum, lens disk, vibrating mirror, slotted diaphragms, incandescent lamp, electric motor drive, and mechanical assembly for sync control. (596, 859)

726 "Experts review radio growth and forecast new trends." N.Y.T. VIII, 14 (Dec. 27, 1925): 1, 2. Jenkins predicts radio pictures in 1926; "I hope to contribute to the general advance in this art, and expect vision by radio to have begun a useful service to mankind before the dawn of 1927." (716, 728)

727 Friedel, Walter. ELEKTRISCHES FERNSEHEN, FERNKINEMATOGRAPHIE UND BILDFERNÜBERTRAGUNG [Electric television, telecinematography and phototelegraphy]. Berlin: Hermann Meusser, 1925. xv + 176 pp., 153 illus. (779)

728 Jenkins, C.F. VISION BY RADIO, RADIO PHOTOGRAPHS, RADIO PHOTOGRAMS. Washington: Jenkins Laboratories, 1925. 140 pp., 65 illus. Portrait of Jenkins, photos of his apparatus, extracts from patents, numerous official testimonials, list of selected radio patents, general description of various facsimile systems and radio vision. See also his 1929 book (1823). (726, 757)

729 Low, A.M. THE FUTURE. London: George Routledge, 1925. vii + 203 pp., illus. Chapter 5 deals with wireless. The author visualizes walkie-talkies, radio tape recording, the rapid development of television, and the day "when it will play a big part in our existence." (637)

730 Sloane, Thomas O'Conor (1851–1940). "The Moore gaseous conductor lamp." EXPERIMENTER 5 (Jan. 1926): 136, 137. Two photos, diagrams of various lamps. General description of neon and corona glow lamps. (456, 1051)

731 "The Voss picture transmitter." QST 10 (Jan. 1926): 29, 30. 3 illus. Mirror drums, commutator for pulse sync, X-ray tube, perforated drum, and fluorescent screen. (607) Knothe proposed an X-ray tube in 1909 (375).

732 Best, Frank Ellison. "Device for transmitting vision electrically." U.S. 1,802,803, filed Jan. 7, 1926. This application Mar. 1, 1928, Apr. 28, 1931. Rotating disks. (1063)

733 British inventor sends pictures by wireless. DAILY EXPRESS 9 (Jan. 8, 1926): 4; also

EVENING STANDARD (Jan. 8, 1926). Two accounts of a demonstration to the press at 22 Frith Street, London, Jan. 7, by Baird and his partner, Oliver George Hutchinson. Reporters saw images of faces. Further reports of the inventor's achievement appeared during the next two weeks up to the historic demonstration of January 26. (712, 735, 736) Earlier, on Oct. 2, 1925, Baird first obtained a halftone image of a ventriloquist's dummy which he used in his experiments. He then "ran downstairs to obtain a living object"—William Taynton, a fifteen-year-old office boy, who in March 1929 gave the following account of this historic event:

"After I had sat down (in front of the transmitter) Mr. Baird went into the next room where the receiving machine was, and left me in front of the lights. Without realising that I was spoiling the experiment, I moved back a little way to avoid the glare and heat. After about five minutes Mr. Baird returned, and the moment he saw him he said: 'Ah! Why did you go back?—that explains it—you must keep exactly where I put you.'

"Knowing what was required I did not move this time, and held on as long as I could. I was just beginning to feel I could not keep still any longer, when I heard a shout from the next room, 'Open your mouth.' I did this, and was then told to turn sideways, and this was followed by Mr. Baird's sudden return to the transmitter saying: 'William, I saw you; would you like to see what television looks like?'

"Mr. Baird seemed very excited, and took me through into the other room where I looked through a little square opening at the face of a revolving plate. The square seemed covered with a reddish light. A minute or two later Mr. Baird went into the other room, and on a little screen his face immediately appeared. It was not very clear, but by looking closely I could see his eyes and I could see his mouth open and close, and recognise that it was Mr. Baird himself. Although I did not realise it at the time, I was the first man in the world whose face had been transmitted by television, and the second man to have seen a televised human face. (1781)"

734 Telefunken. "Television, picture transmission, telecinematography and the like." Br. 264,174, Jan. 7, Sept. 1, 1927. In Germany Jan. 8, 1926. An optical system incorporating a phototube, Kerr cell, Nicol prisms, mirror galvanometer, bolometer, and telescope assembly for visible light or ultraviolet transmission with relay stations. (949)

735 "Television." MAN. GUARD. 9 (Jan. 9, 1926): 5. Comments by Hutchinson, proposal for a station in Manchester, brief description of television. (733, 736)

736 "British Company formed to exploit television invention." ELECT. 96 (Jan. 15, 1926): 78. On Television Ltd., formed by Baird and his associates, J.Y.M. Broderip and O.G. Hutchinson. Photos of apparatus and images received taken by Lafayette Ltd. (733, 735, 737, 739)

737 Baird, J.L., and Television Ltd. "Transmission of views, scenes or images to a distance." Br. 269,658, Jan. 20, 1926, Apr. 20, 1927. U.S. 2,006,124, Dec. 31, 1926, renewed Apr. 4, 1929, June 25, 1935. Flying light spot, lens disk, double scanning, Kerr cell modulator. (736, 738)

738 "Television perfected, asserts London paper." N.Y.T. 10 (Jan. 23, 1926): 5. Report from MORNING POST, Jan. 22. "The international race for the perfection of television...has been won by Great Britain...." (737, 739)

739 Edwards, Norman. "Current topics." POP. W. (Jan. 23, 1926): 1208. Comments by the editor on reports about the work of Baird and Belin. "According to one daily newspaper," television has reached the "stage of a commercial proposition. Shortly a company (736), which has taken over Mr. Baird's invention, intends to place upon the market compact, home television sets. We understand that 500 television receivers are being made, and that they will cost anything from £30 to £50 each." Note: this was the begin-

ning of the commercial exploitation of Baird's work, largely due to Hutchinson, his business manager and director. (724, 736, 738, 740, 742, 769, 1483)

740 "The 'Televisor.'" TIMES (Jan. 28, 1926): 9c. Report on demonstration by Baird to members of the Royal Institution invited to his laboratory on Tuesday, Jan. 26. Recognizable images with movement and light and shade were shown in public for the first time on this historic occasion.

"Members of the Royal Institution and other visitors to a laboratory in an upper room in Frith Street, Soho, on Tuesday saw a demonstration of apparatus invented by Mr. J.L. Baird, who claims to have solved the problem of television. They were shown a transmitting machine, consisting of a large wooden revolving disc containing lenses, behind which was a revolving shutter and a light sensitive cell...."

"For the purpose of the demonstration the head of a ventriloquist's doll was manipulated as the image to be transmitted, though the human face was also reproduced. First on a receiver in the same room as the transmitter, and then on a portable receiver in another room, the visitors were shown recognisable reception of the movements of the dummy head and of a person speaking. The image as transmitted was faint and often blurred, but substantiated a claim that through the "Televisor," as Mr. Baird has named his apparatus, it is possible to transmit and reproduce instantly the details of movement, and such things as the play of expression on the face."

"The DAILY CHRONICLE also published an account on Jan. 27. William C. Fox, a Press Association journalist and friend of Baird, greeted the visitors, who signed a register of which, unfortunately, no trace remains. Baird had previously given Fox a personal demonstration: "The received image was admittedly crude, but it was recognisable as—whatever it might be—a face, a vase of flowers, a book opened and shut, or some simple article of every day life. The image received was pinkish in colour and tended to swing up and down." (739, 741, 1595)

"It was a cold January night and the members of the Royal Institution arrived in twos and threes. When they came out after the demonstration their remarks, such as I overhead, were much as one would expect. Some thought it was nothing worth consideration; others considered it the work of a young man who did not know what he was doing, while a few, a very few, thought there was something there capable of development. There was no realisation of the fact that they had been present at the birth of a new science." [W.C. Fox, February 27, 1975.]

741 "Seeing through walls by 'Televisor.'" TIMES (Feb. 2, 1926): 18a. Photo of Baird looking into a hooded receiver. (740, 742)

742 Delano, F.M., and K.D. Rogers. "Progress with television, the Baird and Belin claims." POP. W. (Feb. 6, 1926): 1293. "The apparatus which I demonstrated (723)," said Belin, "is merely one used in a study of such work. I cannot, with this machine, transmit pictures or scenes from a distance; but I have actually in existence such an apparatus, which lacks only at the moment a proper method of amplification to make it capable of transmitting pictures or images over long distances by wireless." Rogers interviewed Baird and saw the flickering image of a ventriloquist's doll. "It was undoubtedly a step forward from the results achieved last year, but whether the final solution will come by this method is still a matter of speculation." (739, 741, 744, 759, 2035)

743 Clay, Reginald Stanley. "Television and like apparatus." Br. 271,131, Feb. 9, 1926, May 9, 1927. Overlapping scanning disks with radial slots, or equivalent perforated steel ribbon. Cathode-ray-tube display with coils for deflection modulation. Synchronism with tuning fork or neon lamp and capacitor time base, with pulses between picture lines to trigger circuits in the receiver. The specification also mentions enclosing the disks in a vacuum chamber, a method that was incorporated later in more advanced disk sys-

tems. See also Br. 273,227, Feb. 9, 1926; U.S. 1,719,756, Feb. 3, 1927, July 2, 1929. (3054)

744 Roberts, J.H.T. "Television a close possibility." POP. W. (Feb. 13, 1926): 1354, 1378. Note on Belin's work. (676, 742, 749, 1042)

745 Dunlap, Orrin E., Jr. (1897–1970). "Seeing the world by radio." SCI. AM. 134 (Mar. 1926): 162, 163. 5 photos. By the radio editor of the NEW YORK TIMES. (748)

746 Kröncke, H. "Electric television, recent developments in Germany." W.W. 18 (Mar. 3, 1926): 353. (1463)

747 Latour, M. "Transmission of photographs or other images to a distance." Br. 267,513, Mar. 8, Nov. 24, 1927. In France Mar. 9, 1926. The proposal incorporates multiple scanning disks with individual photocells for interlaced transmission. (452)

748 "Says radio offers big opportunities." N.Y.T. 24 (Mar. 11, 1926): 1. General discussion by Dunlap, who "expects television soon." (745, 809)

749 "A television controversy." POP. W. (Mar. 13, 1926): 134. Note on the new Vienna radio station and plans for Belin's system. (744, 771)

750 Nesper, E. "Über das elektrische Fernsehen" [About electric television]. PHYS. BER. 7 (Mar. 15, 1926): 368. (570, 2409)

751 Baxter, Charles. "Television." Br. 263,005, Mar. 23, Dec. 23, 1926. Scanning by perforated disks or perforated bands with serrated disk or shutter in a "telecamera" for spotlight illumination. Synchronization with auxiliary disk and cell, or by spark discharges or contacts, with revolution indicator and speed control. (3155)

752 Gouroff, W.A. (System of television.) Russ. 30,723, Mar. 23, 1926. Lens drum, vibrating mirrors, prism, string galvanometer modulator. Apparatus was displayed but not demonstrated at Leningrad, Sept. 23, 1924.

753 Fournier de'Albe, E.E. "Problems of television." W.W. 18 (Mar. 24, 1926): 461, 462. Report of lecture at Oxford. (667, 985)

754 Brun, Etienne (Stephane) Julian. "Apparatus for selecting luminous points of an image for reproduction by television." U.S. 1,763,528, Mar. 24, 1927, June 10, 1930. Br. 293,093, Mar. 26, 1927. In France Mar. 27, 1926. Coaxial disks, one with radial slots and the other with slots at 45 degrees.

755 "The Karolus cell." ENG. PROG. 7 (Apr. 1926): 109. A Kerr cell with nitrobenzol dielectric and Nicol prisms. (708, 810)

756 Ranger, Richard Howland. "Transmission and reception of photoradiograms." PROC. IRE 14 (Apr. 1926): 161–80. 19 photos, diags. Brief history and details of the RCA equipment. (626, 646) Facsimile service between London and New York commenced at the end of the month.

757 Jenkins, C.F. "Converting electrical impulses into graphic representations." U.S. 1,650,361, Apr. 22, 1926, Nov. 22, 1927. Spiral of lamps on disk with distributor, translucent display screen. (728, 758)

758 Jenkins, C.F. "Converting light impulses into graphic representations." U.S. 1,683,136, Apr. 22, 1926, Sept. 4, 1928. Modulated light is directed via light pipes on a rotating disk, a modification of the companion patent (757) that eliminates the electrical distributor. (762) See Saint-René (392).

759 "Inventor describes his radio motion pictures." N.Y.T. IX (Apr. 25, 1926): 17:1, 2. Photo of Baird and apparatus.

"The set with which he gave a demonstration . . . is much larger than the ordinary receiving set. It is a box about 3 feet by 2 feet by 1 foot in size, with a hood projecting from one side. His voice and the picture of his face come through very clearly. The picture was in black and white, his lips could be seen enunciating each word, and the shadows changed with his changing expression. You have seen (said Baird) at what stage I have arrived in my efforts to put television on an efficient commercial basis. It is not yet as nearly perfect as I want it to be, but it is much better than a couple of months ago. Its perfection is now only a matter of time and money, and, for the first time since I began work on it in 1912, I have all the money at my disposal which I need."

See also DAILY TELEGRAPH (Apr. 28, 1926): 14. (742, 761)

760 Gernsback, H. "Radio television." RADIO N. 7 (May 1926): 1521. General comments. "Radio television, it must be said, is nearer at hand than most of us realize. The inventors of the entire world are racing frantically for the goal. But the individual application of television, to everyone's personal convenience, will not be practicable for many more years." Front cover of this issue shows a screen about 24-inches diameter mounted on a receiver. (671, 967)

761 Baird, J.L., and Television Ltd. "Apparatus for maintaining rotating bodies in synchronism for television and like purposes." Br. 275,318, May 3, 1926, Aug. 3, 1927. Spot registration via a perforated disk and photocell in conjunction with speed control by a synchronous motor and manual adjustment for correct framing at the receiver. (759, 768)

762 Dinsdale, Alfred. "Television apparatus." W.W. 18 (May 5, 1926): 642. Illus. On Jenkins. (758, 767, 788)

763 Ives, H.E. "Television." U.S. 1,673,828, May 20, 1926, June 19, 1928. Assigned: B.T.L. Lamp bank, distributor, tuning fork, and phonic wheel. (658, 764)

764 Ives, H.E. "Television." U.S. 1,738,007, May 20, 1926, Dec. 3, 1929. Assigned: B.T.L. Scanning disks, distributors, tuning forks, phonic wheels, and mirrors. Color transmission system; three phototubes, three color lamps. (763, 795)

765 Round, H.J. "Picture telegraphy." U.S. 1,759,594, May 11, 1927, May 20, 1930. Assigned: RCA. In Britain May 21, 1926. A number of "light-tubes" are clustered at one end to form a rectangular picture plane, the other ends form a circle around which a photocell rotates. In an identical receiver a lamp modulated by the signal similarly rotates in synchronism. Alternatives include multiple cells and lamps connected in sequence by distributors, and signal storage capacitors at the transmitter. (430)

766 Doty, Marion Foster. "Selenium 1817–1925: A list of references in the New York Public Library." N.Y.P.L. BULL. 30 (June–Oct. 1926): 440–8, 525–55, 599–629, 728–37, 793–824. Separate publication, 1927, 114 pp. An extensive collection of 1665 items arranged chronologically; bibliography and general works, constants, properties, chemistry, cells, industrial applications.

767 Jenkins, C.F. "Converting light impulses into enlarged graphic representations." U.S. 1,683,137, June 2, 1926, Sept. 4, 1928, reissued Nov. 29, 1929, Aug. 26, 1930. Perforated drum with axial light pipes of quartz or the like, multielement neon tube, commutator. (762, 785)

768 "Baird Televisor system." ENGINEER 141 (June 18, 1926): 641. Illus. (761, 769)

769 "Baird Televisor system." ELECT. 96 (June 25, 1926): 672. 3 photos. Objective report on a demonstration at Motograph House, Upper St. Martin's Lane, London. Image was clear but had considerable flicker. Experimental transmissions on 200 meters to a receiving station at Harrow have begun. Includes a picture of Hutchinson's face, the first living image to be photographed from a television screen. (739, 768, 772, 1075)

770 Gradenwitz, A. "The Mihály television scheme." POP. W. (June 26, 1926): 617, 619. 4 photos, including picture of the letters REX obtained on a receiver. (505, 720, 819, 1649)

771 Fournier, L. "The latest advance toward television." RADIO N. 8 (July 1926): 36, 37, 84. 3 photos, 3 diags. About Belin's work in his laboratory at Malmaison, near Paris. (578, 749, 775, 817)

772 Russell, Alexander. "Television." NATURE 118 (July 3, 1926): 18, 19. Comments on a

Baird demonstration at Motograph House. The results were far from perfect, but the likeness of an image was unmistakable, and all the motions were reproduced with absolute fidelity. Dr. Russell was principal of Faraday House and president of the Institution of Electrical Engineers in 1923. (769, 773, 874)

773 (Baird demonstration.) POP. W. (July 3, 1926): 648. Photo and caption. (772, 774)

774 (Baird apparatus.) POP. W. (July 10, 1926): 672. Photo and caption. (773, 776)

775 Belin's experiments in Paris. N.Y.T. 1 (July 29, 1926): 4. Editorial, 16 (Aug. 2, 1926): 5. (771, 813)

776 Donisthorpe, H. de A. "Some notes on television." RADIO 8 (Aug. 1926): 9, 10. 4 photos. Report on a demonstration by Baird. The effect of electrical interference is "a small snow storm with whirling white flakes passing across the screen." (774, 777, 802)

777 "Successful worker with television." RADIO N. 8 (Aug. 1926): 111. Photo of Baird with caption. "He hopes to broadcast before long the Derby, Great Britain's great sporting event." (776, 778)

778 "Television receivers for all listeners." RADIO N. 8 (Aug. 1926): 111. Photo and caption. "The inventor (Baird) is shown transmitting the image of the dummy head which he holds." (777, 783)

779 Friedel, W. "The broadcasting of pictures." RADIO N. 8 (Aug. 1926): 126, 184, 185. 4 diags., photo of ring lens invented by Mr. Büchner. Mainly on facsimile. (727, 819)

780 Dauvillier, A. "Sur le telephote, appareil de télévision par tubes à vide, resultats experimentaux preliminaires" [Preliminary experimental results on the telephote and television apparatus with vacuum tubes]. C.R. 183 (Aug. 2, 1926): 352. (557, 1089)

781 Maxwell, Herbert. "Television or teleoptics?" NATURE 118 (Aug. 7, 1926): 194. Letter on terminology. (933)

782 Schildenfeld, Rudolf. "Scanner for picture transmission." U.S. 1,715,517, Aug. 6, 1927, June 4, 1929. In Austria Aug. 10, 1926. Rotating drum with longitudinal slots, fixed mirror, moving shutter with a slot.

783 "Televisor now operating. Regular transmissions of scenes now taking place in England." N.Y.T. 20 (Aug. 10, 1926): 8. "It is not very clear just at present, but J.L. Baird...says that perfection will be attained." Baird obtained licenses from the Post Office for station 2TV at Motograph House and for 2TW at Harrow on Aug. 9. (778, 786)

784 Hall, Richard. "Transmitting and receiving apparatus for a television system." Br. 280,630, Aug. 17, 1926, Nov. 17, 1927. Slotted disks, one carrying photosensitive cells, with distributor and circuits for multiplex transmission of parts of an image. Infrared, ultraviolet, phono recording, and playback are mentioned.

785 Jenkins, C.F. "Picture transmission." U.S. 1,693,508, Aug. 19, 1926, Nov. 27, 1928. Disk scanner, low-frequency sync signals, tuning fork interrupter, and motor speed control. (767, 948)

786 "The latest wonder." POP. W. (Aug. 28, 1926): 872. Reference to newspaper reports on Baird receiving pictures at Harrow, nine miles from his laboratory in London. (783, 787)

787 "Sending pictures through the air." SPHERE (Aug. 28, 1926). Drawing of Baird's system. "How Mr. Baird's wonderful system of 'Television' transmits its wireless pictures." (786, 788)

788 Dinsdale, A. "Television an accomplished fact." RADIO N. 8 (Sept. 1926): 207, 280, 282, 283. 6 illus. "The image was flickering somewhat, and looked rather out of focus...in smooth gradations of light and shade, bright highlights, dark shadows, and half tones, and perfectly recognizable beyond all question or doubt." Report on Baird. (762, 787, 789, 811)

789 "Television and Osram valves." POP. W. (Sept. 4, 1926): 32. Full-page advertisement

by the General Electric Company announcing the Baird television apparatus will be on display at Stand No. 63 during the National Radio Exhibition, Olympia, Sept. 4–18. (788, 790)

790 "Television: A new radio 'miracle'—The transmission of pictures." ILLUS. LONDON NEWS 169 (Sept. 11, 1926): 445. Full-page drawing of Baird's apparatus: "The Televisor experimental transmitting station—2TV," with descriptive caption. (789, 793)

791 "Television awaits scientific genius. A radical discovery in physics is needed for development of movies through the air." N.Y.T. XI, 1 (Sept, 12, 1926): 7. Discussion and comments by de Forest: "So I repeat that while theoretically and technically television may be feasible, yet commercially and financially I consider it an impossibility; a development of which we need not waste little time in dreaming." (428, 1143)

792 Jarvis, Kenneth W., and Russell M. Blair. "Electron tube." U.S. 1,903,569, Sept. 15, 1926, Apr. 11, 1933. Phototube with a series of electrodes that provide electron multiplication by secondary emission.

793 "The Baird Televisor." ELECT. 97 (Sept. 17, 1926): 334. The original apparatus (donated Sept. 11) has been placed in the South Kensington Science Museum; that which Baird used to demonstrate true television in January 1926 is now on view at the National Radio Exhibition. (790, 794)

794 "The new Televisor." POP. W. (Sept. 18, 1926): 127. A model fitted with a glass screen about a foot square upon which the owner will be able to "look in" is on display by the Dubilier Condenser Company, Stand No. 154, National Radio Exhibition. (793, 796)

795 Ives, H.E. "Television system." U.S. 1,932,253, Oct. 1, 1926, Oct. 24, 1933. Assigned: B.T.L. Scanning disks with two spirals of apertures, phototubes, neon lamps, mirrors, light-spot illumination, and circuits for simultaneous two-way transmission by line or radio, particularly for telephone systems. (764, 890)

796 "Baird and his apparatus." POP. W. (Oct. 2, 1926): 258. Photo of Baird holding dummy beside the original apparatus presented to the South Kensington Science Museum. (794, 797)

797 Television Ltd., and J.L. Baird. "Producing optical images." Br. 285,738, Oct. 15, 1926, Feb. 15, 1928. A lens assembly of pipes, rods, or tubes of glass, or quartz fibers. In his experiments with this, Baird employed a cellular structure of tiny pipes, known as a honeycomb lens, in conjunction with two disks, one a shutter with a spiral slot and the other with radial slots, to eliminate the Nipkow scanning disk. A similar mosaic of light pipes was suggested by Reynolds. (796, 798)

798 Television Ltd., and J.L. Baird. "Television apparatus." Br. 288,882, Oct. 15, 1926, Apr. 16, 1928, divided from 289,104 (799). U.S. 1,781,799, Oct. 7, 1927, Nov. 18, 1930, reissued Sept. 9, 1931, May 16, 1934. Various arrangements of apertured and slotted disks, etc., for infrared or ultraviolet scanning of an object in darkness. Known as Noctovision, this use of "black light" was demonstrated in ensuing months. (797, 799)

799 Television Ltd., and J.L. Baird. "Recording of views of objects or scenes, or optical images." Br. 289,104, Oct. 15, 1926, Apr. 16, 1928. Visual signals are stored on, and reproduced from, phonograph disks by audio pickup via a loudspeaker and microphone, the output of which is applied to the recording stylus. Simultaneous recording and playback of sound is also specified. This system became known as Phonovision. Phonograph recording was proposed by Lardeur (275) in 1898. (798, 800)

800 Television Ltd., and J.L. Baird. "Television or like systems." Br. 289,307, Oct. 15, 1926, Apr. 16, 1928, divided from 289,104 (799). Disks with various apertures—holes, slots, lenses—arranged to scan in different directions with periodic changes of traversal, or cross-scanning. (802)

801 Kintner, Samuel Montgomery. "Television apparatus." U.S. 1,695,924, Oct. 15, 1926, Dec. 18, 1928. Assigned: Westinghouse. Br. 279,067, Oct. 4, 1927, Jan. 26, 1928. Disk with a series of concave mirrors and a concentric annular prism or prismatic disk.

802 Donisthorpe, H. de A. "Scotsman's television device sends images across London." N.Y.T. IX, 16 (Oct. 17, 1926): 1. Transmission from Motograph House, picture of Baird and Hutchinson on the roof showing 2TV antenna. Success is attributed to a sensitive photoelectric cell that responds instantly to the exceedingly high frequency vibrations. (776, 800, 805, 858)

803 Alexanderson, Ernst Fredrik Werner (1878–1975). "Electrical transmission of pictures." U.S. 1,694,301, Oct. 19, 1926, Dec. 4, 1928. Assigned: G.E. Br. 279,457, Oct. 19, 1927, Aug. 9, 1928. This multibeam system has a lens drum with internal mirrors and a corresponding number of photocells, lenses, amplifiers, and radio transmission channels, with mirror galvanometers for light modulation at the receiver. Modifications include a mirror drum and a multielectrode Kerr cell. (826)

804 Franklin, C.S. "Cables for transmitting high frequency electrical energy." Br. 284, 005, Oct. 19, 1926, Jan. 19, 1928. A concentric cable with the inner conductor air-insulated by spaced supports and the outer conductor grounded. An early coaxial cable. (422) See also Espenschied (1891).

805 Swinton, A.A.C. "Electric television." NATURE 118 (Oct. 23, 1926): 590. A reminder about the writer's proposal of 1908 and his papers of 1911 and 1924 on a system with camera and picture tubes. Some early "not very successful experiments" with a modified Braun tube are mentioned. (589, 1271)

806 "Baird with his original apparatus." POP. W. (Oct. 23, 1926): 406. Photo and caption. (802, 807)

807 "Television images recognized by sound." N.Y.T. IX, 19 (Oct. 24, 1926): 3. Report on Baird's lecture "Seeing by wireless" at a meeting of the Royal Institute of British Architects. The sounds of images vary; one man's face makes a humming "rip-rip-rip" and another "zur-zur-zur." Also SCI. AM. 136 (Jan. 1927): 66. (806, 808)

808 "Radio eye enables you to see stars in studio." POP. MECH. 46 (Nov. 1926): 777. Illustrated description of Baird's apparatus. (807, 809)

809 Dunlap, O.E. Jr. "The Televisor." POP. RADIO 10 (Nov. 1926): 649, 650, 668, 670. 4 illus. Baird apparatus and test transmissions between London and Harrow. (748, 808, 811, 870)

810 Fischel, Paul J.G. "Television en route; the 'Karolus Cell' betters reproduction." RADIO N. 8 (Nov. 1926): 466, 467. 7 photos, 2 diags. The Telefunken-Karolus facsimile system employing a potassium phototube developed by Fritz Schröter and a Kerr cell light valve due to A. Karolus. (755, 943, 1042)

811 Dinsdale, A. "Television; some particulars of the Baird apparatus." ELECT. REV. 99 (Nov. 5, 1926): 748. Illus. (788, 809, 812, 816)

812 "Television." ELECT. 97 (Nov. 5, 1926): 533. Note on a Baird paper read to the Radio Society of Great Britain on Oct. 26. "True television is quite a long way off, but the equipment has recently been much improved." (811, 814)

813 "E. Belin's laboratory." POP. W. (Nov. 6, 1926): 538, 542. Two photos with captions. (775, 817)

814 Television Ltd., and J.L. Baird. "Televison apparatus." Br. 291,121, Nov. 30, 1926, May 30, 1928. Two light sources project separate beams through adjacent holes spirally arranged on a disk onto a phosphorescent screen. One beam produces the image, the other obliterates it. A slot is also provided to obliterate the image at the end of each line. (812, 815)

815 Baird, J.L. "Television." EXP. W. 3 (Dec. 1926): 730–9. 9 illus. Read by Lt.-Col. J.R. Yelf before the Radio Society of Great Brit-

ain, Oct. 26. Historical background with mention of the schemes by Rignoux and Fournier, Ruhmer, Szczepanik, Rosing, Swinton, Belin and Holweck, and Jenkins. A very brief survey of the author's work is followed by comments and discussion. (814, 816)

816 Dinsdale, A. "And now, we see by radio!" RADIO BRD. 10 (Dec. 1926): 139–43. 7 illus. Background of Baird and the development of his system with details of operation and results. This longer version of an earlier article (788) mentions plans for a commercial Televisor with a screen about 8 inches square that will probably be priced around $250. Baird has "so far improved his apparatus that the light required is little more than is necessary in an ordinary photographic studio, and soon, probably, daylight alone will be found sufficient." (811, 815, 818, 841)

817 Fournier, L. "New television apparatus. Latest developments by Messrs. Belin and Holweck." RADIO N. 8 (Dec. 1926): 626, 627, 739, 740. 6 illus. Zigzag scanning of transparencies with oscillating mirrors, black-and-white (outline) reproduction with the Holweck pumped-down cathode-ray oscillograph fitted with a viewing prism. (771, 813, 830, 889)

818 "Television transmission licensed." RADIO N. 8 (Dec. 1926): 763, 764. Note on Baird transmission from 2TV on 200 meters. (816, 820)

819 Friedel, W. "The main problems of television." RADIO N. 8 (Dec. 1926): 767–70. 2 diags. Pictorial transmission with film on drum, von Mihály's system with oscillating mirror. (770, 779, 845, 2168)

820 Baird, J.L. "Apparatus for producing a varying light or illumination in television apparatus, photophones and the like." Br. 291,634, Dec. 3, 1926, June 5, 1928; U.S. 1,800,044, Oct. 7, 1927, Apr. 7, 1931. Telephone-actuated grid shutter and Kerr cell for light modulation. This specification is an interesting example of the revival of old ideas: Kerr cell, 1875 (62); telephone actuator and variable-aperture shutter, Leblanc, 1880 (145); grid shutter modulator, Dussaud, 1898 (271). (818, 827)

821 Reynolds, F.W. "Electro-optical transmission." U.S. 1,780,364, Dec. 4, 1926, Nov. 4, 1930. Assigned: AT&T. Camera tube has a mosaic of light pipes of glass or quartz behind a translucent conductive film or mesh of fine wires. Alternators of different frequencies provide voltages to deflection plates for either spiral or linear scan at the camera tube and picture tube, with phonic wheel, tuning fork, and relay control. Includes electron tubes and filters for radio transmission. This specification was in conflict with Zworykin's of December 1923 (566). A similar honeycomb assembly intended as a lens was disclosed earlier by Baird (797). (722, 2359)

822 Valensi, G. "Optical device for distant vision." U.S. 1,798,963, July 15, 1927, Mar. 31, 1931. In France Dec. 9, 1926. Perforated disks and a lens system with multiple light sources. (526, 983)

823 Busch, Hans. (Calculation of the paths of cathode rays in axial symmetric electromagnetic fields.) ANN. PHYS. 81 (Dec. 11, 1926): 974–93. Prime paper on the magnetic focusing of electron beams. (1048)

824 Perrin, J.B. "Discontinuous structure of matter." Nobel lecture, Dec. 11, 1926. NOBEL LECTURES, PHYSICS: 1922–1941. Amsterdam, London, New York: Elsevier, 1965. Presentation speech, pp. 135–7. Lecture, pp. 138–64. Biography, pp. 165, 166. (252)

825 C. Lorenz, A.-G. "Maintenance of constant frequency and phase relationship in periodic processes." Br. 282,098, Dec. 10, 1927, Aug. 23, 1928. In Germany Dec. 11, 1926. Synchronous control with phonic wheels, eddy-current brakes, and electron tube circuits, particularly for television. See also Br. 275, 594; 282,099; 302,901. (1362)

826 "Predicts vision across the ocean." N.Y.T. 1 (Dec. 16, 1926): 4. Address by Alexanderson at a meeting of the American Institute of Electrical Engineers in St. Louis. (803, 829)

827 "Sees in total darkness." N.Y.T. 2 (Dec. 16, 1926): 3, 4. Report on Baird's demonstration of infrared scanning (Noctovision), from the DAILY MAIL, London. Baird had demonstrated this privately on Nov. 23 (867). (820, 831)

828 "Television." N.Y.T. 22 (Dec. 17, 1926): 4. Editorial comments.

829 "Dr. Alexanderson explains his television projector." ELECT. W. 88 (Dec. 18, 1926): 1283. (826, 832)

830 "La télévision, par le procédé Edouard Belin" [Television by Edouard Belin's process]. GENIE CIVIL 89 (Dec. 18, 1926): 549–52. Illus. (817, 884)

831 "Television and twins." POP. W. (Dec. 18, 1926): 969. Note on a lecture by Baird at Newcastle-upon-Tyne, and his use of two ventriloquist's dolls as demonstration subjects. (827, 833)

832 "Cluster of seven lights basis of new television." N.Y.T. VIII (Dec. 19, 1926): 15:2–4; 20:2, 3. Alexanderson's system, photos of him and the apparatus. (829, 835)

833 Television Ltd., and J.L. Baird. "Transmitting views or images to distance." Br. 292,185, Dec. 21, 1926, June 21, 1928; U.S. 1,699,270, May 4, 1928, Jan. 15, 1929. Radio waves of short wavelength, adjacent to the infrared, are reflected from an object and scanned by a Nipkow disk, detected by a radio receiver, converted to modulated light, and reconstituted to form an image by another scanning disk. An extension of the scanning idea in the infrared patent (798). (831, 834)

834 "The invisible searchlight: seeing in the dark by 'black light.'" ILLUS. LONDON NEWS 169 (Dec. 25, 1926): 1271. Full-page diagram on Baird's infrared system, with descriptive caption. "Infrared rays and their uses in war: possible results of a remarkable invention." This is an artist's interpretation of a proposed system: "The inventor hopes to perfect a device similar to that illustrated," referring only to an infrared searchlight for observation with no mention of determining the range, or distance. (833, 836)

835 Kaempffert, Waldemar Bernhard. "Science now promises us radio sight across seas." N.Y.T. VIII (Dec. 26, 1926): 4. Illustrated feature article on generalities and Alexanderson's seven-spot scanning system. (832, 853, 892)

836 "A television experiment." W.W. 19 (Dec. 29, 1926): 867. Brief note about Baird's infrared system. (834, 839)

837 "New American television device." W.W. 19 (Dec. 29, 1926): 868.

838 "Television." ENGINEER 142 (Dec. 31, 1926): 705.

839 "Television in dark room." N.Y.T. 2 (Dec. 31, 1926): 4. Report from London on Baird's demonstration of infrared scanning to members of the Royal Institution, Dec. 30. See also reports on Noctovision, DAILY MAIL, and black light, DAILY TELEGRAPH, Dec. 31. (836, 846)

840 Baker, T.T. WIRELESS PICTURES AND TELEVISION: A PRACTICAL DESCRIPTION OF THE TELEGRAPHY OF PICTURES, PHOTOGRAPHS AND VISUAL IMAGES. London: Constable, 1926; New York: Van Nostrand, 1927. x + 188 pp., 99 illus. Chap. 12, "Television by wire and wireless," pp. 167–84, 9 illus. Historical background and references to the work of Swinton, Ruhmer, Mills, Ribbe, Andersen, Karolus, Schröter, Fournier d'Albe, Baird, and von Mihály. (616, 1353)

841 Dinsdale, A. TELEVISION. London: Pitman, 1926. 62 pp., 12 full-page illus. Some introductory and historical matter is followed by description of Baird's earlier apparatus and accounts of his accomplishments in popular and somewhat laudatory prose. First book in English devoted to television. An expanded edition appeared in 1928 (1682). (816, 839, 846, 926)

842 Eichhorn, G. WETTERFUNK, BILDFUNK, TELEVISION [Weather radio, pic-

ture radio, television]. Berlin: Teubner, 1926. v + 82 pp., illus. (394, 875)

843 Fuchs, Gerhard. DIE BILDTELEGRAPHIE [Phototelegraphy]. Berlin: Siemens, 1926. 134 pp., 35 illus. Enlarged 2nd ed., 1928, includes television.

844 Lertes, Peter. FERNBILDTECHNIK UND ELEKTRISCHES FERNSEHEN [Television technique and electric television]. Frankfurt: Bechhold, 1926. 160 pp., illus.

845 Mihály, D. v. DAS ELEKTRISCHE FERNSEHEN UND DAS TELEHOR [Electric television and the Telehor]. Berlin: Krayn, 1926. 196 pp., 112 illus. 2nd ed. (570). (819, 899)

CHAPTER 7

BY RADIO AND BY WIRE: 1927

Prospects for television as a viable art improved steadily during 1927 with an influx of inventors, writers, and commentators. A measure of the progress is shown by the number of articles, lectures, and demonstrations, each of which increased threefold over the average annual rate of the previous period (1925–1926). On the same basis, the number of patent applications more than doubled, with seventy-nine (excluding duplicates and others on auxiliaries) compared with thirty-four. Further evidence of the rising interest is shown in the number of newcomers attracted to the field; thirty-two compared with twenty for the two previous years. Of these, eighteen were independent, the others being allied with industrial concerns, primarily in the United States.

The highlight of the year was a public demonstration of long-distance transmission in April by Bell Telephone Laboratories, Inc. (B.T.L.), an organization that was jointly formed at the end of 1924 by the American Telephone & Telegraph Company (AT&T) and the Western Electric Company (W.E.). An associated group, Electrical Research Products, Inc. (E.R.P.), was organized late in 1926 as a subsidiary of Western Electric to promote and license nontelephonic by-products of research such as sound motion pictures, and to handle patent protection outside the United States. Other U.S. concerns with interest in television, in addition to the General Electric Company (G.E.) and Westinghouse Electric and Manufacturing Company, were the Federal Telegraph Company and Communication Patents, Inc. Other companies include Television Laboratories, Inc. of San Francisco (Farnsworth), Television Ltd. and Baird Television Development Company Ltd. of London, and Telefunken Gesellschaft für Drahtlose Telegraphie m.b.H. of Berlin.

Numerous inventors previously listed were active during the year. Jenkins dropped out of the news but continued his work on radio movies, as shown by five patent applications. Others still active though not necessarily in the news were Belin (with Holweck), Dauvillier and Valensi in France; Dieckmann, Karolus, von Mihály, and Schröter in Germany; Alexanderson, Clark, Fessenden, Ives (leading the Bell Labs team), Nicolson, Whitten, and Zworykin in the United States; Baird and Rosing. One newcomer of note is Farnsworth. His first patent (850) included a camera tube which he had conceived when a schoolboy in 1921. With financial aid and the establishment of a company in 1926, he developed an experimental hybrid system and is said to have obtained recognizable images at his San Francisco laboratory on September 7, 1927.

The joint demonstration by AT&T and Bell Labs on April 7 (909) marked the entrance of a large research team into the television field, although most of the planning and development had been done much earlier, being an extension of phototelegraphic systems developed commercially by the parent concerns. Based on Nipkow's disk, the system as a whole was a conglomerate of old and new ideas: rotating machinery, distributors, phototubes, discharge tubes, radio and wire transmission channels, special electrical networks, and electronic circuits working in conjunction with telephone apparatus. Apart from the circuit innovations, technical features of note include the increase in picture definition with 50 scanning lines and 18 pictures per second (compared with Baird's 30/12 1/2), and the large viewing screen, a special folded discharge tube with multiple electrodes connected to a massive distributor with 2,500 contacts. The system was demonstrated again in May to a large engineering audience (950), and a full technical description was presented at an engineering convention in June (990) and published that month. It was the subject of a movie (1052), apparently the first of its kind. More than thirty accounts of the system and its demonstrations appeared in various magazines up to September.

The largest share of patent applications during 1927 belonged to Bell Labs with at least thirty-four, half of them filed in Britain. Baird was equally active. With financial aid assured by the parent company, Television Ltd., and by the new concern, Baird Television Development Company Ltd. (914), the inventor added fourteen applications to his patent portfolio, compared with seventeen for the previous two years. Baird also attracted continuing publicity with some forty-five articles and news accounts about his activities, including phono recording and infrared systems. Meanwhile, he worked on variations of the disk system, designed a spherical selenium cell and a magnetic recording system (863), which was the most significant of his creations during the year.

The Bell Labs transmission by wire over more than 250 miles and the later transmission by radio (924) over more than 20 miles were outstanding achievements. Baird also had the conquest of distance in mind and succeeded in May (955) in transmitting images 438 miles by wire between London and Glasgow, a notable event that nevertheless received little publicity. Another long-distance transmission followed in September on the occasion of the British Association meeting at Leeds University (1043). Viewers in Baird's laboratory in London saw recognizable images sent over 170 miles by wire, though the sitters were in a darkened room. The high level of interest in Baird's work and in television in general at this meeting led to the proposal that a society be formed to further the progress of the new art. (1154)

The technical trend during 1927 followed a pattern similar to previous years, with proposals ranging from complex systems such as those of Bell Labs to the simplest arrangements from some independent inventors. Excepting Farnsworth's image

TABLE 10   For Transmitting Images

ELECTRICAL	OPTICAL	ELECTRONIC
Distributor (13)	Mirrors (7)	Electron tube (21)
Neon lamp (12)	Lens disk (6)	Phototube (14)
Photocell (9)	Prisms (5)	Discharge tube (5)
Spark (7)	Kerr cell (4)	Picture tube
Lamp (5)	Light valve	Camera tube (1)
Lamp bank	Color disk (3)	
Oscillograph	Light pipe	**SYSTEMS**
Multicell (3)	Mirror disk	Radio transmission (12)
Speed regulator	Polyhedral drum	Film transmission (7)
*Capacitor (2)	Mirror drum (2)	Multicircuit
*Compensating circuit	*Bubble (1)	Recording (6)
Piezoelectric	Chopper	Color (4)
Rotary lamp	Perforated screen	Two-way
Selenium	*Rotary prism	Vision and sound (3)
Transformer		Infrared scanning (2)
Contact disk (1)	**MECHANICAL**	Line transmission
Phonic wheel	Nipkow disk (16)	Multifrequency
Relay	Multispiral disk (7)	Stereo
	Slotted disk	*Intermediate film (1)
	Shutter (4)	*Monitor
	Perforated belt (2)	Radio wave scanning
	Tuning fork	*Secret
	Spiral slot (1)	Ultraviolet scanning

*Innovations

dissectors, some special cathode-ray tubes, and the more common usage of electron tubes and phototubes, opto-mechanical methods were still preferred. A fairly complete summary of the means and methods chosen for transmitting images is given in Table 10. Items most in favor were distributors, neon lamps, optical elements, and various forms of perforated disks. These selections, along with film transmission, multicircuit systems, and recording methods increased about threefold over the previous period (see Table 8).

Some ambitious schemes came from independent patentees, examples being Clark (859), Valensi (983), and Szenyovsky (1024), who collectively proposed means to achieve duplex transmission, color, stereo, and visual recording. Fessenden (856) disclosed a method for secret signaling, and Thurm (876) proposed a system incorporating magnetic storage which was almost coincidental with Baird's. Piezoelectric systems were conceived by Chilowsky and Guerbilsky (934) and Hough (1023). Novel applications for capacitive elements appear in the patents by Fessenden (851), Filica (897), and Mathes (1081). The luminous effects of spark discharges were incorporated in other novel proposals by Dawson and Milner (891), by Baird (893) in a Hertzian detector with high-frequency radio-wave scanning, and in four by Nicolson (1044, 1056, 1061, 1066).

Traditional optical elements such as mirrors, prisms, lenses, and rotating mirror devices appear in some two dozen proposals. Other opto-mechanical methods were specified by Zworykin (947, 1050) and by Farnsworth (1079). The patents by Hansell (1022) and Baird (1025) feature light pipes, one being for facsimile and the other an adaptation of an earlier idea (640). An intriguing but impracticable optical scanner is the moving-bubble aperture proposed by Baird (953) with the alternative suggestion involving luminous discharges. Baird also disclosed a luminous spot-position indicator (1018) and a special optical arrangement to increase the brilliance of an image (1082).

Film transmission appears in eight patents, an indication of the rising interest in the medium and a reflection of the current boom in the cinema industry. Those of particular interest are Ives and Gray (903), Jenkins (996), Thurm (1014), and Schröter (1090). Others are Aspden (977), Malm (979), and Valensi (983). With future applications in mind, the most notable one is the intermediate film system by Hartley and Ives (1047). Taken as an extension of the work being done at that time on sound recording and talking pictures, this specification well illustrates a combination of technical features and developments in allied fields being put to use for a new purpose. Like many others originating in the United States, this patent unfortunately suffered an extended delay of twelve years before acceptance in the U.S. Patent Office, a sharp contrast to the processing time common in other countries, such as two years or so in Britain.

Four specifications concern color. Clark and Szenyovsky relied on color disks, the latter with prisms; Baird (1083) called for color disks in a two-color system instead of color screens as in a previous scheme (704); and Ives covered a full-color multichannel system (1046), also as a follow-up from an earlier one (764). Two-way systems also had some attention. Television combined with the telephone—as envisaged by Dumaurier (100) fifty years before and later described by Amstutz (238)—which was the prime objective of AT&T—is the subject of two Bell Labs patents (890, 984). Baird employed disks for double scanning in a simple two-way proposal (1064), and Szenyovsky's arrangement also had two disks. None of these proposals was new, however, since others preceded them. For instance, motion pictures and sound were combined by Gardner and Hineline (556) in November 1923, Zworykin proposed a two-way system (581) in March 1924, Baird had a two-color and stereo system (704) in September 1925, and there was a two-way system (795) by Ives in October 1926.

Though mainly paper plans, these ambitious schemes exemplify the kind of advanced technology (as it is called today) that would someday vastly extend the range of telecommunications, less dramatically but just as surely as other contemporary achievements such as Charles A. Lindbergh's solo flight across the Atlantic in May. Like the intrepid aviator, Baird looked toward a similar conquest during the year, which he achieved early in 1928. His plans for color transmission and for stereo, which also came to fruition that year, were also underway in 1927. In jumping across frontiers, so to speak, even before satisfactory images in monochrome had been demonstrated, Baird was motivated by the desire to add more "firsts" to his list. Undoubtedly these efforts diluted his basic researches, which should have been directed to improving his apparatus. In contrast, the Bell Labs proposals and endeavors were based on the desire of AT&T to keep abreast of developments in the new art and the prospects for commercial applications in telephonic communications, producible from start to finish by a specialist team backed by vast resources that, it was expected, would surely overcome all technical obstacles.

Few of these trends were in the news, which was centered almost wholly on the demonstrations in Britain and the United States, with some peripheral reports on the Europeans. There was no question now, however, that television had arrived, at least experimentally. Observers saw a patchwork quilt of possibilities and difficulties in the new companion to radio and talking pictures. As the year began it seemed to one writer (848) that the promise of television already surpassed all the fairy tales of history. This was true, since the electric eye could see through obstacles, even in the dark, and its impressions could be stored on phonograph disks. Baird, always willing to link the future to the past, concluded one of his rare articles (940) thus: "The enormous possibilities of television stir the imagination, and open up long vistas crowded with marvelous speculative visions and achievements surpassing even those which the fabled Magic Carpet made possible." In September he foresaw the recording of images in the home (1049), a safe prophecy based on his own work but one that would not be realized for nearly fifty years.

Meanwhile, the question of what should be done with television was discussed by Elway (962), whose notions of the future partly echoed those of Munro (236) and Grimshaw (405). Vision combined with the telephone, especially for long-distance communications, would be the first successful application and the "chief permanent utility" of television. Uses in criminology and for medical purposes were next in importance, followed by scientific applications such as the study of volcanoes and of marine life far beneath the waves. The outlook for commercial uses was not so bright, however, while the prospects for television broadcasting seemed "much less likely to reach the first practical success."

In a careless moment, Gernsback (967) unhesitatingly declared that television "as applied to radio will not need an extra waveband," an assertion that followed the decision of the Federal Radio Commission (902) to allot the 1.5-to-2.0-megacycle band for experimental picture transmissions. The Commission's belief that television is "just around the corner" was to become an inspiration for devotees, a basis for sometimes acrimonious discussions, and a favorite theme of commentators and writers for the next few years.

Ives (990) naturally believed television would be an adjunct to the telephone and a service adaptable for public addresses and audience viewing, as well as a means for broadcasting scenic or other events of public interest. In July, one writer (1005) was of the opinion that images received in the home of artists performing in a studio would be a privilege of doubtful value, and that visual programs would depend largely upon motion pictures. Dreher (1015) expressed some thoughts that portray the pros and cons of possible television applications as they appeared to most observers, but in his view everyday television was some five to fifteen years in the future.

Most commentators either criticized the state of television and its prospects or supported the newcomer—now recognized as a potential rival to broadcast radio and the movies. Their viewpoints were futuristic; few looked backward at the long years of inventive efforts that had led to the recent realities. The Gernsback publication (1001), a magazine collection of prior articles, is an exception, though the history in its pages is incomplete and not entirely accurate. Before considering the dramatic events of 1928, therefore, this is an appropriate place to recognize the many contributors to the art that had begun fifty years before when seeing by electricity first became a topic for discussion.

As recorded in previous pages, television evolved through the slow accretion of ideas and techniques, some of them original solutions to unique problems and others borrowed mainly from electrical technology and physics. Those who contributed in one way or another to the mainstream of development are listed in Table 11 in the order of appearance. Jenkins, for instance, whose work on radio movies was done during the 1920s, is listed in 1894, the year when his first proposal was published. The list is limited to television; therefore those concerned with facsimile, such as Bidwell, Korn and others, and a miscellany of authors of numerous articles are not included, nor are the contributors prior to 1878, though the influence of their work must be acknowledged.

Among the 157 names there are several men who deserve special mention. Fundamental scanning elements were introduced by Leblanc, Nipkow, Weiller, Brillouin, and Majorana before 1900. System proposals came from Dieckmann, Rosing, and Swinton before the Great War. Postwar workers of note, in addition to Jenkins, include von Mihály, Belin, Baird, and Zworykin. Of the early inventors, Dieckmann, Rosing, and Belin were active in the 1920s, Jenkins continued up to 1931, and von Bronk remained in the field throughout the 1930s. Others who were active in 1927 and whose work continued well into the 1930s include Alexanderson, Farnsworth, Karolus, Schröter, and Zworykin, as well as Ives and his colleagues at Bell Labs. In contrast to this devotion, about a half-dozen of the newcomers during that year were one-time contributors.

TABLE 11   CONTRIBUTORS TO THE DEVELOPMENT OF TELEVISION: 1878–1927

1878	De Paiva		Allen
1879	Redmond		Clark
1880	Ayrton, Perry		Stephenson, Walton
	Carey		Robb, Martin
	Sawyer		Baird
	Leblanc		Hammond
1881	Senlecq		Gardner, Hineline
1882	Lucas		Dauvillier
1884	Nipkow		Ramsey
1885	Bakmet'yev		Zworykin
1889	Weiller	1924	Sensicle
1890	Sutton		Sequin, Sequin
1891	Brillouin		Evans
	Liesegang		Blake, Spooner
1893	Blondin		Allouard-Carney
	Le Pontois		McCreary
	Morse		Sardina
1894	Amstutz		Hozie
	Rabourdin		Skala
	Jenkins	1925	Fournier d'Albe
	Majorana		Tschernyschev
1895	Swedish		Hell
1897	Szczepanik		Blackwell, Herman
1898	Dussaud		Whitten
	Lardeur		Sabbah
	Vol'fke		Case
	Schöffler		Karolus
1899	Polumordvinov		Grabovsky, Popoff,
1901	Von Bronk		Piskounoff
1902	Coblyn		Parker
1903	Nisco	1926	Voss
	Re		Best
	Schneider		Clay
1904	Ribbe		Latour
	Jaworski, Frankenstein		Baxter

1906	Rignoux		Gouroff
	Stephan		Brun
	Fowler		Ives
	Rothschild		Round
	Dieckmann, Glage		Schildenfeld
	Lux		Hall
1907	Rosing		Kintner
1908	Adamian		Alexanderson
	Armengaud		Reynolds
	Sellers	1927	Farnsworth
	Anderson, Anderson		Torrabadella
1909	Ruhmer		Thrum
	Knothe		Dawson, Milner
	Gernsback		Filica
1910	Ekström		Gray
	Hoglund		Kishpaugh
	Schmierer		Mohr
	Sinding-Larsen		Horton
	De Vendenil		Morton
	Saint-rené		Legg
1911	Swinton		Chilowsky, Guerbilsky
1914	Hart		Wildhaber
1915	Voulgré		Schröter
1917	Nicolson		Konemann
1920	Baden-Powell		Centeno
	Kakourin		Mathes
	Egerton		Aspden
1921	Whiston		Malm
	Schoultz		Stoller
1922	Mills		Goldsborough
	Dallugge		Hough
	Rtcheouloff		Szenyovsky
	Fessenden		Termen
	Belin		Hartley
	Valensi		Rowe, Rowe
1923	Von Miláhy		Wagner

Although the 1920s witnessed a rapid rise in contributions to television in the form of letters, articles, and patents, progress was slow and sporadic during the preceding forty years. An initial burst of interest came in 1880, beginning with two schemes proposed by Ayrton and Perry and ending with the suggestions of Leblanc. During the next twenty years the topic remained chiefly a matter of academic interest, with the exception of Nipkow's prime patent of 1884 and four others near the end of the century. It is reasonable to assume that this shift toward patent coverage and the obvious realization of potential commercial applications by the patentees was prompted by contemporary developments in wireless telegraphy.

The worldwide spread of wireless communications and the increasing commercial value of electrical inventions in general after 1900 underlie the trend toward the protection of ideas in patents instead of their release in published accounts during the period up to 1910. Out of a total of thirty-two proposals during this decade, thirteen were covered in patents. Three of six proposals in 1906 were the subject of patents, and four out of five in 1908 appeared in specifications. This pattern is not consistent, however, since among the six proposals brought forward in 1910 only one is a patent application. During the next decade (which spanned the war years) only ten proposals appeared, nine of them in patents, the all-electric plan by Swinton in 1911 being the exception.

A repetition of history is seen in the accumulation of proposals from 1922, an upsurge prompted mainly by the phenomenal postwar growth of radio technology, particularly broadcasting. Prospects for success were enhanced by the availability of components and techniques previously limited to the laboratory. Many decades of research on cathode rays, phototelegraphy, photoelectricity, and allied subjects were the foundation for this advance. In many different ways inventors applied these resources in their plans for television methods and systems. Most of the specifications, however, are collections of old ideas with, in some cases, innovative variations; few are inventions in the true sense of the term.

Television, even though it was but a speculative idea, preceded the emergence of radio by nearly twenty years, despite the general belief that television is an offshoot of radio. This common misconception arose because television took longer to reach a demonstrable stage and did not appear in a practical form until after broadcast radio was well established. Again, attempts to devise a system of television became more numerous during the 1920s, a rise closely parallel to that of broadcast radio. Since almost all of the proposals were confined to patents, however, little was known at the time about these efforts. Technical publications and newspapers, meanwhile, paid attention to the newcomer, particularly with respect to demonstrations and similar newsworthy events. No longer a vehicle for displaying original ideas, journals and magazines nevertheless provided an essential service in disseminating news about the progress of television and in placing it before the public. Indeed, if all the printed pieces on television that appeared between 1922 and 1927 were included in a chart, it would reveal a similar burgeoning of interest.

As 1927 drew to a close, the technical pattern of television was well defined, but the mainstream of development along opto-mechanical lines would soon be challenged by the rival electronic approach, first on the receiving end and then in the camera. Dissatisfaction with apparatus containing moving parts was even then apparent, as was the possibility of the cathode-ray tube as a receiver. Dieckmann, Dauvillier, Karolus, and Holweck (with Belin) were experimenting with cathode-ray-tube receivers, and Farnsworth was progressing toward an all-electronic system.

In the meantime, mechanical methods were the most practicable. The vexing problems of keeping rotating parts in step had been solved, at a cost, by the Bell Labs team, and methods for speed regulation and synchronous control were proposed by others, particularly Jenkins, Baird, and Clark. Bell Labs also took forward steps in the analysis of the scanning process and in studying the image transmission characteristics of wire and radio channels. Finally, Baird and Belin had both begun the climb toward the more spacious region of short waves. Taken altogether, the efforts and events of 1927 can be perceived as a fitting climax to the first fifty years and the threshold to technical advances that would gain momentum in the year ahead.

TABLE 12   CHRONOLOGY: 1927

Jan. 6	Baird	Lecture, sounds of images demonstrated
7	Farnsworth	Camera tube system with electro-optical receiver
8	Fessenden	Opto-electric converter
14	Fessenden	Secret signaling device
20	Clark	Color, stereo, recording
21	Baird	Alternate scanning method
	Torrabadella	Multifrequency system
26	Baird	Magnetic recording
Feb. 5	Thurm	Magnetic recording
28	Belin, Holweck	Report on progress
Mar. 2	Ives	Two-way, simultaneous sight and sound
3	Dawson, Milner	Spark discharges, distributor
10	Baird	Radio wave scanning, spark detector screen
11	Robb	Mirror oscillographs
25	Filica	Two-circuit, double-disk system
Apr. 6	FRC	1.5–2.0 megacycle band allotted for television
	Ives, Gray	Film transmission
	Gray	Multielectrode neon lamp, distributor
	Kishpaugh	D-c, low-frequency suppression, image tone control
	Mohr	Scanning, analysis, compensating circuits
	Horton	Neon lamp and circuits
	Morton	Synchronizing system
7	Bell Labs	Demonstrations by wire between Washington, D.C., and New York, and by radio between Whippany, N.J., and New York
8	Baird	Baird Television Development Company Ltd.
9	Baird	Preliminary transatlantic experiments
11	Legg	Mirror oscillograph and moving prism
20	Bell Labs	Single channel transmission of sight and sound
26	Chilowsky, Guerbilsky	Piezoelectric system
27	Ives, Jewett	Demonstration to the FRC
May 6	Wildhaber	Disk, distributor, lamp bank
7	Baird	Special selenium photocell
11	Zworykin	Opto-mechanical system
21	Jenkins	Synchronous control
	Telefunken	Interlaced scan
23	Bell Labs	Demonstration in New York
24	Konemann	Recording system for pictures and sound
	Baird	London to Glasgow transmission by wire lines
25	Centeno	Photo oscillator
26	Baird	Moving-bubble scanner
	Wright	Kerr cell and control circuit
30	Thurm,	Polyhedral drum, shutter, neon

Table continued on next page.

TABLE 12 (continued)

		Gaisenband	lamp, and photocell arrays
	31	Mathes	Two-channel system
June	7	Baird	Synchronizing method
	8	Aspden	Multifrequency system, film transmission
		Jenkins	Scanning disk
	8	Malm	Motion picture transmission
	10	Telefunken	Rotary photocells and neon lamp
	11	Baird	Distributors and lamp bank
	16	Valensi	Multipurpose system
	17	Bell Labs	Two-way system with telephone stations
	20	Baird	Image strip transmission, facsimile
		Ives, et al.	Papers on Bell Labs system at AIEE Convention
	22	Ives, Horton	System with local monitor
		Jenkins	Film transmission
		Mertz	Television testing system
	23	Stoller, Morton	Synchronizing system
	25	Jenkins	Disk receiver, rotary lamps
		Whitten, Goldsborough	Television system
July	2	Ives	Four-channel system
	5	Baird	Variable area and zone scan
	21	Thurm	Film transmission
Aug.	9	Baird	Luminous spot-position indicator
	13	Hansell	Facsimile system with optical conductors
		Hough	Piezoelectric system
	16	Szenyovsky	Color and stereo
	17	Baird	Optical system with light pipes
	31	Rosing	Russian patents
Sep.		Termen	Report on apparatus, disk system
		Belin	Television experiments on short waves
	7	Baird	Lecture at Leeds, proposal for a Television Society
	9	Nicolson	Contact wheel, luminous discharges
	10	Ives	Three-channel color system
	14	Hartley, Ives	Intermediate film system
	21	Busch	Magnetic focusing of cathode rays
	23	Zworykin	Opto-mechanical system
		Bell Labs	Movie on system shown at Columbia University
	26	Rowe, Rowe	Slotted disks or bands, shutter modulator
	28	Nicolson	High-speed system, multianode cathode-ray tube
Oct.	11	Nicolson	Discharges with magnetic deflection
	17	Best	Disk and mirror drum
	19	Baird	Two-way system
	21	Gray	Disk-distributor system
	26	Nicolson	Movable electrodes and discharges
		Wagner	Helical scannerNov.

2	Horton	Disk and neon lamp
3	Telefunken	Karolus cell
7	Farnsworth	Electro-optical receiver
12	Ives, Mathes	Two-channel system
	Mathes	Disk-distributor system, capacitor storage
30	Baird	Optical system with special lenses
	Baird	Two-color system
Dec. 3	Thurm	Rotary neon lamp receiver
10	Dauvillier	Cathode-ray-tube receiver with mirrors
12	Schröter	Film and sound transmission
	Telefunken	Three-circuit Nipkow disk
28	Jenkins	Glow lamp receiver
31	Karolus	Cathode-ray-tube receiver with Kerr cell

BIBLIOGRAPHY: 1927

846 "Television by telephone." SCI. AM. 136 (Jan): 41. Photo of Baird and Televisor. (839, 847)

847 "Seeing by radio." SCI. AM. 136 (Jan): 66. Brief note on Baird's lecture at a meeting of the Royal Institute of British Architects (807). (846, 848)

848 "Baird expects sight across ocean soon." N.Y.T. 7 (Jan. 2): 1–6. Editorial by J.L. Garvin in the OBSERVER, London, on an interview with Baird, who states they will soon have a Televisor on the market priced about $150. "The facts of the moment and their promise for the future surpass all the fairy tales about wishing caps, invisible cloaks, magic carpets and seven league boots." (847, 849)

849 "Images recorded as sounds, a phenomenon of television." TIMES (Jan. 7): 6g. Report on Baird's lecture to members of the Physical and Optical Society at Imperial College of Science and Technology, Jan. 6. (848, 852)

850 Farnsworth, Philo Taylor (1906–1971). "Television system." U.S. 1,773,980, Jan. 7, 1927, Aug. 26, 1930. Assigned: Television Labs. Premier patent incorporating the nonstorage camera tube known as an image dissector. The specification discloses electronic circuits for transmitter and receiver, the latter being traditional with a light valve, Nicol prism, and magnetic coil, with mirror oscillographs for deflection. Farnsworth was involved with Zworykin (566) in Patent Office interference proceedings. (1079)

851 Fessenden, R.A. "Modulating electrical energy by light impulses." U.S. 1,899,026, Jan. 8, 1927, Feb. 28, 1933. Divided from U.S. 1,617,241 (507). A translucent capacitor is operated at high frequency as an opto-electric converter. (856)

852 "Faces and noises affect television." N.Y.T. II, 23 (Jan. 9): 6. Baird demonstration Jan. 8, reference to the lecture Jan. 6 (849) and sounds of faces and objects. (857)

853 "Radio movies in home forecast by expert to engineers here." N.Y.T. 1 and 17 (Jan. 11): 1 and 2, 3. Alexanderson's lecture at a meeting of the Institute of Radio Engineers. (835,867)

854 "Rescue for the home." N.Y.T. 24 (Jan. 12): 5. Editorial on television.

855 "Television in America." W.W. 20 (Jan. 12): 46.

856 Fessenden, R.A., and Helen M. Fessenden, executrix. "Television system." U.S. 2,059,221, Jan. 14, 1927, Nov. 3, 1936. Divided from U.S. 1,617,241 (507). Two polyhedral mirror drums with a reflecting mirror linking the light paths in a secret signaling system. (851, 1208)

857 "Television." NATURE 119 (Jan. 15): 73, 74. Critical comments by the editor on the

vagueness of Baird's statements during the lecture on Jan. 6 (849) and on his system: "From the information available...it appears highly probable that little further progress need be expected along the lines chosen by him." (852, 858)

858 Donisthorpe, H. de A. "Television's sensitive 'eye' can now see in the dark." N.Y.T. VII, 17 (Jan. 16): 5, 6. Feature article on Baird's infrared system. Infrared waves tend to distort the image. (802, 857, 860)

859 Clark, P.L "Radiographic apparatus." U.S. 1,745,528, Jan. 20, 1927, Feb. 4, 1930. This extensive specification refers to mirror drums, mirrors, prisms, photocells, disks with color segments, light choppers, light valve, oscillographs, special sync arrangements, and various electromechanical means said to be applicable for color or stereo transmission and recording of images, with sync signals interposed with visual signals. (725, 1233)

860 Baird, J.L., and Television Ltd. "Exploring devices for television apparatus." Br. 294,267, Jan. 21, 1927, July 23, 1928; U.S. 1,913,911, Jan. 6, 1928, June 13, 1933. Disk with two or more spiral sets of holes, angular mirrors, and reflecting rods or tubes for alternately exploring each part of an image. (858, 862)

861 Torrabadella, Pedro. "System of television." U.S. 1,764,232, Jan. 21, 1927, June 17, 1930. This plan from Argentina is a multifrequency system with multiple light cells, transformers, and tuning forks.

862 "Engineering: Television." MAN. GUARD. 14 (Jan. 25): 3. General discussion by a "scientific investigator," basic problems, and impressions of a "very crude picture" demonstrated by Baird. (860, 863)

863 Television Ltd., and J.L. Baird. "Transmission of signals for television." Br. 292,632, Jan. 26, 1927, June 26, 1928; U.S. 1,945,626, Jan. 6, 1928, Feb. 6, 1934. A recording system with rotating steel disks, recording and readout coils, and a-c erasure. Intended to provide variable-rate transmission with a plurality of signals, i.e., conversion of parallel recording to serial transmission. Earlier systems employing magnetic storage of visual signals were proposed by von Bronk (291) in 1901 and by Rtcheouloff (501) in 1922. See Thurm (876). (862, 864)

864 Baird, J.L. "Television." NATURE 119 (Jan. 29): 161, 162. Response to criticism in the Jan. 15 issue (857), with brief note by the editor. (863, 865)

865 "Records violet ray on the phonograph." N.Y.T. 5 (Jan. 29): 6. Baird's demonstration at Birmingham University; faces "were quite distinct." (864, 866)

866 "Progress in television." DISCOVERY 8 (Feb.): 64. Brief comments on Baird. (865, 869)

867 Alexanderson, E.F.W. "Radio photography and television." G.E. REV. 30 (Feb.): 78–84; RADIO 9 (Feb.): 18, 19, 48, 50–2; RADIO N. 8 (Feb.): 944, 945, 1030–4. Illus. General survey of both fields with remarks on the author's seven-spot multichannel system. (853, 868)

868 "A 'blackboard' demonstration that may some day be visible in the classrooms of all the world." POP. RADIO 11 (Feb.): 126. Photo of Alexanderson and his apparatus. (867, 870)

869 "Hearing faces by radio." RADIO N. 8 (Feb.): 957, 1050. On Baird and the sounds of images. (866, 871)

870 Dunlap, O.E. Jr. "Radio's silver screen." SCI. AM. 136 (Feb.): 106, 107. 6 photos. On phototelegraphy and Alexanderson's mirror drum apparatus. "Cluster of seven lights carries inventor toward the goal of wireless vision." (809, 868, 888, 900)

871 Baird, J.L. "Television." J. SCI. INSTR. 4 (Feb.): 138–43. 6 diags. Lecture to the Physical and Optical Society, Jan. 6 (849). General history and brief account of the progress made by the inventor, including infrared scanning and phono recording. Image

sounds demonstrated included the faces of three members, scissors, matchbox, bowler hat, and a cabbage. (869, 873)

872 Tiltman, Ronald Frank. "The conquest of television." WORLD TODAY 49 (Feb.): 273–8. Illus. (1059)

873 "Glasgow listens to sound of faces." N.Y.T. 6 (Feb. 4): 1. Baird's demonstration of sound recording at Glasgow, Feb. 3. "Television inventor shows how image of every substance emits distinctive refrain," including Scotch plaid and a derby hat. (871, 874)

874 Russell, A. "Television." NATURE 119 (Feb. 5): 198, 199. Reference to the demonstration by Baird in June 1926 (772), with comments on a private demonstration of infrared, Nov. 23. "The image on the screen was not quite so clearly defined as when visible rays were used...." (772, 873, 878, 1404)

875 Eichhorn, G. "La transmission des images par télégraphie sans fil et la télévision" [The transmission of images by wireless telegraphy and television]. REV. GEN. 21 (Feb. 5): 45. (842)

876 Thurm, Leon. "Electromagnetic apparatus for the transmission of images." U.S. 1,771,360, Jan. 23, 1928, July 22, 1930; Br. 284,717, Feb. 3, Oct. 18, 1928. In France Feb. 5, 1927. Magnetic recording with steel bands coiled into disks mounted on a common rotating shaft. A multicircuit system with photocells connected via separate amplifiers to the recording electromagnets at the transmitter; the same arrangements with neon lamps at the receiver. See Baird (863, 1292). (958)

877 "Television." ENGINEER 143 (Feb. 11): 147.

878 "Television by invisible rays." POP. W. (Feb. 12): 1417. (874, 880)

879 Kollatz, C.W. "Die neusten Fortschritte der elektrischen Bildübertragung" [The newest progress on electric picture transmission]. V.D.I.Z. 71 (Feb. 12): 227–32. Illus.

880 "Les essais de télévision d'après le système J.L. Baird" [Television experiments according to J.L. Baird's system]. GENIE CIVIL 90 (Feb. 19): 200, 201. (878,881)

881 "Baird is building new Televisor." N.Y.T. VIII, 21 (Feb. 20): 3. A single-wave 4-kw transmitter at Purley, Surrey. (880, 892).

882 "Engineer predicts television receivers." N.Y.T. VIII, 21 (Feb. 20): 6. Ralph H. Langley, Crosley Radio Corp., on combined radio and television receiving apparatus. (1009)

883 "Television." ELECT. REV. 100 (Feb. 25): 307.

884 "Sur la télévision. Premiers resultats dans la transmission des images animées, Belin et Holweck" [On television. The first results in the transmission of moving images, Belin and Holweck]. C.R. 184 (Feb. 28): 518. (830, 895)

885 "Hope of seeing by radio brought nearer fact." POP. MECH. 47 (Mar.): 359.

886 Free, E.E: "The possibilities of television." POP. RADIO 11 (Mar.): 267, 268. A critical view of the "newcomer" (television), mention of the Alexanderson scheme and of Baird's work, which is deprecated: "The announcements of Mr. Baird, in London, are of much less interest and importance than the suggestions of Dr. Alexanderson." (1003)

887 Armagnac, J.P. "We'll soon see by radio, too!" POP. SCI. 110 (Mar.): 37.

888 Felix, Edgar H. "Television: Europe or America first?" RADIO BRD. 10 (Mar.): 459–62. 5 illus. Alexanderson's system. (870, 920, 1370)

889 Fournier, L. "Television by new French system." SCI. & INV. 14 (Mar.): 988. (817, 1008)

890 Ives, H.E. "Television system." U.S. 2,082,339, Mar. 2, 1927, June 1, 1937. Assigned: B.T.L. Br. 286,262, Jan. 21, 1928, Apr. 22, 1929 (E.R.P.). Disk with two semispiral sets of apertures for image scanning and reconstitution. Two-way communica-

tion for simultaneous sight and sound, or video telephone, with infrared and ultraviolet scanning. (795, 903)

891 Dawson, Wilfred, and David Morton Milner. "Application of electric spark for television purposes." Br. 293,474, Mar. 3, 1927, July 3, 1928. A screen, placed between a source of light and the object to be viewed, contains a mosaic of holes with means for obscuring the holes by spark discharges, the sequence being controlled by a distributor.

892 Kaempffert, W.B. "How Baird sees through space by radio." N.Y.T. IX (Mar. 6): 5. Full-page feature article with diagram of system and illustrations of Baird and his apparatus. General description; disk with 16 lenses revolves at 800 rpm, slotted disk revolved at 4000 rpm. (835, 881, 893, 921)

893 Television Ltd., and J.L. Baird. "Apparatus for television by invisible radiation." Br. 297,014, Mar. 10, 1927, Sept. 10, 1928. This adaptation of a previous specification (833) based on high-frequency radio waves includes a scanning disk, suitable lenses, and a screen composed of insulated conducting particles such as powder whereon spark discharges reproduce an image of the object in a visible form. The screen, called a Hertzian detector, may be enclosed in an evacuated or gas-filled container and may also be employed to activate one or more photocells. (892, 898)

894 Robb, F.M. "Electrically transmitting imagery." U.S. 1,768,634, Mar. 11, 1927, July 1, 1930; Br. 292,659, Mar. 18, 1927. System with mirror oscillographs. (546, 1888)

895 "La télévision par le procédé Edouard Belin" [Television by Edouard Belin's process]. REV. GEN. 21 (Mar. 19): 494. (884, 901)

896 Hoxie, C.A. "Electrical transmission of pictures." U.S. 1,787,273, Mar. 23, 1927, Dec. 30, 1930. Assigned: G.E. Divided from U.S. 1,648,687 (615). Disks.

897 Filica, Enache. "Appareil de radio-télévision." Fr. 631,371, Mar. 25, Dec. 19, 1927. Two scanning disks, one having a double spiral slot and the other a series of holes in radial lines covering the same area. The first disk rotates at 10 rps, the other at 40 rps. Parallel transmission circuits with two selenium cells, radio transmitters, and receivers. Receiver outputs, connected to capacitor assemblies, actuate pivoted mirrors which reflect light from two separate lamps which is directed via separate lenses through the scanning disks to the viewing area.

898 Price, Clair. "A saga of the radio age—and its hero." N.Y.T. IV (Mar. 27): 6, 18. Large photo of Baird. Full-page feature article, popular narrative. (893, 899, 2344)

899 Mihály, D. v. "Television." EXP. W. 4 (Apr.): 239, 240. Discussion of Baird's paper in the Dec. issue (815). Comments on the problems of sync and on the need for increased picture definition; at least 90,000 picture elements rather than 10,000. (845, 898, 900, 1309)

900 Dunlap. O.E. Jr. "Televisor 'sees' in darkness." SCI. AM. 136 (Apr.): 282. On Baird. (870, 899, 913, 2331)

901 "Le problème de la télévision, une experience recente de MM. Belin et Holweck" [The problem of television, a recent experiment by Belin and Holweck]. REV. GEN. 21 (Apr. 2): 527. (895, 1037)

902 "Wave band taken to aid television." N.Y.T.; 23 (Apr. 6): 7; 2–4. Federal Radio Commission assigns frequency band (1500–2000 kc) for experimental television in General Order No. 4. C.F. Jenkins gave testimony on progress to the Commission, who believed that visual radio is "just around the corner." (Members were Rear Adm. W.H.G. Bullard, chairman, Henry A. Bellows, Orestes H. Caldwell, John F. Dillon, Eugene O. Sykes.) Col. Dillon: "The Commission recognizes the imminence of television by radio in the order we issued today (Apr. 5)." (936)

903 Ives, H.E., and Frank Gray. "Electro-optical system." U.S. 2,037,471, Apr. 6, 1927, Apr. 14, 1936. Assigned: B.T.L. Br. 288,234, Jan. 11, 1928, Apr. 11, 1929 (E.R.P.). Divided: Br. 302,239, Jan. 11, 1928, Apr. 11, 1929

(E.R.P.); Br. 302,240, Jan. 11, 1928, Apr. 11, 1929 (E.R.P.); addition Br. 291,370, Mar. 19, 1928 (E.R.P.). (959) Motion picture film scanning (telecine) with provisions for enlargement or close-up view. Includes d-c suppression at the transmitter and d-c compensation at the receiver, sync circuits, and two receivers, one with scanning disk and neon lamp and the other a large distributor controlling a folded neon lamp (904) suitable "for viewing by a number of persons at the same time." Apparatus covered in these and following patents (904–908) was employed in a public demonstration Apr. 7 (909). Technical description appeared in June (990). (890, 904, 938)

904 Gray, F. "Electro-optical transmission." U.S. 1,759,504, Apr. 6, 1927, May 20, 1930. Assigned B.T.L. Br. 288,238, Jan. 18, 1928, Apr. 18, 1929 (E.R.P.); Br. 288,239, Jan. 19, 1928, Apr. 11, 1929 (E.R.P.), divided Br. 301,474, Jan. 19, 1928 (E.R.P.). These specifications cover a receiver system employing a folded neon tube controlled by a distributor. The lamp consists of a number of parallel sections joined in series at alternate ends with an internal spiral electrode connected to a common line. External tinfoil electrodes are attached at intervals along the back of the tube and connected to pickup contacts on a distributor. In the apparatus demonstrated Apr. 7 (909) there were 50 contacts on 50 tube sections joined to 2,500 contacts on the distributor. A vessel attached to one end of the neon tube contains pure magnesium electrodes supplied with 150 vdc to purify the gas. (903, 991)

905 Kishpaugh, Arthur W. "Electro-optical transmission." U.S. 1,707,486, Apr. 6, 1927, Apr. 2, 1929. Assigned: B.T.L. Similar to U.S. 2,037,471 (903), and an improvement on U.S. 1,759,504 (904). Disk-distributor system with suppression of zero- and low-frequency currents and control of image tone values via a high-frequency circuit.

906 Mohr, Franklin. "System for converting light energy into electrical energy and vice versa." U.S. 1,768,288, Apr. 6, 1927, renewed May 25, 1929, June 24, 1930. Assigned: B.T.L. Br. 288,237, Jan. 16, 1928, Apr. 16, 1929 (E.R.P.). System with scanning disks, neon lamp, and electrical networks to compensate for aperture distortion, with analysis of the scanning problem. (903)

907 Horton, J.W. "Television system." U.S. 1,728,122, Apr. 6, 1927, Sept. 10, 1929. Assigned: B.T.L. Similar to the related patents; scanning disk, light-spot scan, phototube, and electron tubes, with a single neon lamp and potential-holding circuits. (658, 903, 991)

908 Morton, Edmund R. "Circuits for synchronous motors." U.S. 1,696,248, Apr. 6, 1927, Dec. 25, 1928. Assigned: B.T.L. Br. 288,236, Jan. 14, 1928, Apr. 16, 1929 (E.R.P.). Incorporated in related patents, this specification concerns tuned circuits in series with a motor armature to eliminate hunting. (903, 992)

909 "Far-off speakers seen as well as heard in a test of television." N.Y.T. 1 (Apr. 8): 1. Wire and radio demonstration of television by AT&T and Bell Laboratories on Apr. 7. Images (50 lines, 18 per sec.) and sound were transmitted by wire between Washington, D.C., and New York, a distance of more than 250 miles. Two receivers were used; a small one (scanning disk and neon lamp) with a screen 2 by 2 1/2 inches for personal viewing, and a large one consisting of a folded discharge tube with a multitude of elements connected to a distributor (904) for audience viewing. On the small screen "the likeness was excellent, reproduced with perfect fidelity." The results given by the large screen "were not so good." (903–908, 910–913, 966, 990–994) (658, 910)

910 "Television triumphs in its first demonstration between New York and Washington." N.Y.T. 20 (Apr. 8): 1–4. Two photos and diagram of transmission network, which consisted of two circuits (one spare) for pictures, two for speech, and one each for sync signals and operating orders. "The demonstration of combined telephone and television, in fact, is one that outruns the imagination of all the wizards of prophecy."

A vaudeville act by A. Dolan, the first ever, was staged in the Bell Labs studio (3XN) at Whippany, N.J., and transmitted by radio over 22 miles to New York. (909, 911)

911 "New conquest of nature." N.Y.T. 20 (Apr. 8): 4, 5. List of guests at the Bell Labs demonstration of television in New York; includes prominent engineers, scientists, business executives, educators, writers, and newspaper editors. (910, 912)

912 "Washington hails the test." N.Y.T. 20 (Apr. 8): 6. (911, 913)

913 "Astounding demonstration by Bell Labs, the first time in history." N.Y.T. 22 (Apr. 8): 2, 3. Editorial: "Only a research organization thoroughly versed in the complexities of telephone engineering can be expected to bring television to commercial perfection. The Bell Labs are far in the lead, with a young Scotsman, John L. Baird, a distant second." (900, 912, 914, 919)

914 "Baird Television Development Co. Ltd." ELECT. REV. 100 (Apr. 8): 568. Formation of Baird's new company with a capital of £125,000. (913, 915)

915 "Says his television has spanned ocean." N.Y.T. 5 (Apr. 9): 1. Experiments from Coulsdon to a station 25 miles outside New York. First news of Baird's transatlantic tests. (914, 928)

916 Legg, Joseph W. "Television system." U.S. 2,095,391, Apr. 11, 1927, Oct. 12, 1937. Assigned: Westinghouse. Mirror oscillograph and moving prism scanner.

917 "Television." ELECT. REV. 100 (Apr. 15): 594.

918 "Television, an engineering achievement." ELECT. W. 89 (Apr. 16): 795.

919 "Television becomes an actuality; demonstration of its practicability made by American Telephone and Telegraph Company." ELECT. W. 89 (Apr. 16): 824, 825. (913, 921)

920 "Tells how science proved television." N.Y.T. 5 (Apr. 16): 2. Lecture by Alexanderson at the New York Railroad Club, Schenectady. (888, 926)

921 Kaempffert, W.B. "Television knits the nations still closer. Seeing by wire and radio opens new highways in the field of communication. Practical uses of the invention described." N.Y.T. VIII, 5 (Apr. 17). 3 photos. Feature article on the Bell Labs demonstration and system. (892, 919, 923, 3100)

922 "Poets who were prophets." N.Y.T. IX, 18 (Apr. 17): 4. Stephen Phillips poem: Midnight—31st of December 1900. "And a maid in an English meadow have sight of her lover who wanders in far Cathay."

923 "Television. Experiments in America. Gestures by radio." TIMES (Apr. 18): 11f, 12a, 14. 3 illus. Bell Labs demonstration. (921, 924)

924 "Television by radio enters new phase." N.Y.T. 30 (Apr. 20): 2. Simultaneous transmission of sight and sound on one radio channel from the Bell Labs station, 3XN, Whippany, N.J., to New York. The test was reported a success. (923, 927)

925 "Television." W.W. 20 (Apr. 20): 475.

926 Dinsdale, A. "Phototelegraphy and television." W.W. 20 (Apr. 20): 476–80. Illus. Description of Alexanderson's multiple lightspot system and experimental drum. (841, 920, 929, 935)

927 "Television demonstration in New York." W.W. 20 (Apr. 20): 493. (924, 935)

928 "Faces across the sea." N.Y. DAILY HERALD, also DAILY NEWS and MORNING POST (Apr. 22). Baird's tests from Coulsdon to New York with 1 kw transmission on 45 meters. (915, 931)

929 Alexanderson, E.F.W. "Television." ELECT. WORLD 89 (Apr. 23): 878. (926, 956)

930 "A television triumph." POP. W. (Apr. 23): 339.

931 "The English experiments." POP. W. (Apr. 23): 339. (928, 932)

932 "New 'dark ray' will pierce fog and smoke, J.L. Baird, inventor of television, asserts." N.Y.T. 3 (Apr. 24): 2. Demonstration of Noctovision. "In the presence of Admiral Mark Kerr and others, Mr. Baird transmits a doll's features through an artificial fog produced by chemicals so dense as nearly to choke his assistants." (931, 939)

933 Cavanagh, D. Letter. N.Y.T. VIII, 16 (Apr 24.): 6. Suggests a name for television: "Poly-chromo-tele-panto-photo-phonograph." (781, 1013)

934 Chilowsky, C., and A. Guerbilsky. "Television apparatus." Br. 289,416, Apr. 26, 1928. In France Apr. 26, 1927. Piezoelectric system.

935 Dinsdale, A. "Television demonstrations in U.S.A." W.W. 20 (Apr. 27): 510. (926, 927, 939, 968)

936 "Radio Board tests television progress." N.Y.T. 17 (Apr. 28): 6. Demonstrations by H.E. Ives and Frank B. Jewett to the Federal Radio Commission; approval of radio band 1.5–2.0 megacycles. (902, 970)

937 "Sarnoff belittles Wells's radio ideas." N.Y.T. 14 (Apr. 29): 2. In this address at Syracuse University, David Sarnoff (1891–1971) rebuts the criticism of radio expressed by H.G. Wells and comments also on television which "would become an integral and successful part of the radio industry." (1669)

938 "A physicist whose study of the photo-electric cell played a large part in making television possible." ELECT. WORLD 89 (Apr. 30): 900. About H.E. Ives. (903, 990)

939 "News and views." NATURE 119 (Apr. 30): 647. Brief note on Baird's plans for transatlantic tests and the Bell Labs demonstration. (932, 935, 940, 941)

940 Baird, J.L. "The latest experiments with television and 'black light.'" POP. RADIO 11 (May): 447–51, 498. 4 photos. 2 diags. General discussion, some highlights of progress, outlines of apparatus, the honeycomb lens (797), phonograph recording (799), and infrared experiments (798). One photo shows a "Baird Televisor," a box with a rectangular screen, loudspeaker grille, and four control knobs. (932, 946)

941 "Advances in television." SCI. MON. 24 (May): 479, 480. On Bell Labs. (935, 950)

942 "Is television in sight?" W.W. 20 (May 4): 560.

943 Schröter, F. "Picture transmission." U.S. 2,056,301, May 1, 1928, Oct. 6, 1936. Assigned: Telefunken. In Germany May 5, 1927. Glow lamp array with distributors. (810, 949)

944 Wildhaber, Ernest. "Method of receiving pictures." U.S. 2,051,356, May 6, 1927, Aug. 18, 1936. Disk, lamp bank, and distributor.

945 "Recent television developments—an interesting American invention." POP. W. (May 7): 410.

946 Baird, J.L., and Baird Television Development Co. Ltd. "Light-sensitive electric devices." Br. 300,183, May 7, 1927, Nov. 7, 1928; U.S. 1,697,451, May 8, 1928, Jan 1, 1929. Intended to reduce the time lag of response to light, a spherical vessel with an optical opening is coated internally with selenium. Another design has double walls with provisions for cooling liquid and an electrical heating element for temperature regulation. (940, 953)

947 Zworykin, V.K. "Television system." U.S. 1,689,847, May 11, 1927. Oct. 30, 1928. Assigned: Westinghouse. Br. 290,245, May 2, Nov. 1, 1928. Camera assembly with rotary prisms, deflecting prisms, and spiral scan. (695, 1050)

948 Jenkins, C.F. "Synchronism in radio movies." U.S. 1,660,711, May 21, 1927, Feb. 28, 1928, renewed Dec. 8, 1928. Speed control of receiver motor via photocell, amplifier, and relay actuated by light through aperture in screen. (785, 978)

949 Telefunken. "Television apparatus." Br. 290,973, May 2, 1928. In Germany May 21, 1927. Interlaced scan in spaced groups to

eliminate dark lines. See also F. Schröter, Ger. 484,765, May 22, 1927. (734, 943, 980)

950 "600 at test of television." N.Y.T. 10 (May 24): 3. Bell Labs demonstration to a joint meeting of the American Institute of Electrical Engineers and the Institute of Radio Engineers at 55 Bethune Street, New York. (941, 957)

951 Konemann, H. "Recording sound, picture transmission." Br. 291,029, May 19, 1928. In Germany May 24, 1927. For television, picture transmission, and sound.

952 Centeno V, Melchor. "Photo-oscillator." U.S. 1,702,195, May 25, 1927, Feb. 12, 1929. Lamp, vibrating mirror, and screen for a television system. See also U.S. 1,637,293, Nov. 6, 1926, July 26, 1927. (1708)

953 Baird, J.L., and Baird Television Development Co. Ltd. "Exploring devices for use in television, photo-telegraphy and like systems." Br. 299,402, May 26, 1927, Oct. 26, 1928. A glass tube bent back and forth in parallel sections is filled with an opaque liquid which is circulated by a pump. A transparent bubble of gas moving through the liquid serves as a scanning aperture. Alternative constructions include multiple tube sections each with bubble, and tubes furnished with electrodes at close intervals connected to a distributor. Modulated discharges from the electrodes through the bubble to the liquid produce light at the receiver. (946, 955)

954 Wright, George Maurice. "Kerr cell and control means therefore." U.S. 1,834,117, May 18, 1928, Dec. 1, 1931. Assigned: RCA. Br. 296,124, May 26, 1927 (Marconi's). (1425)

955 "Bairds work London-to-Glasgow television as preliminary to transatlantic test soon." N.Y.T. 3 (May 27): 4, 5. Test arranged by the DAILY MAIL. "Images distinctly seen in Glasgow over 438 miles of telephone line. Next week some of Mr. Baird's experts will leave for America to arrange transatlantic test." (953, 968)

956 Bailey, F.G. "The new Alexanderson television scheme." POP. W. (May 28): 514. (929, 1110)

957 "The television reproducing screen used in the recent successful American demonstration." POP. W. (May 28): 524. (950, 960)

958 Thurm, L., and Palmyre Gaisenband. "Apparatus for use in television." Br. 291,365, May 30, Sept. 20, 1928. In France May 30, 1927. Spaced photocell and neon lamp arrays with cylindrical shutter and corresponding apertures. Scanning by polyhedral mirror drum. Transmission method and circuits not specified. (876, 1014)

959 Mathes, Robert C. "Electro-optical transmission." U.S. 1,671,302, May 31, 1927, May 29, 1928. Assigned: B.T.L. Br. 291,370, Mar. 19, 1928 (E.R.P.). An addition to Br. 288,234 (903). Two-channel system with phototubes, scanning disks, neon lamp, and electron tube circuits. Low-frequency circuit for average tone values, higher-frequency circuit for picture details. (991)

960 King, R.W. "The wonders of television." CURRENT HIST. 26 (June): 450–5. 6 diags. General account of the Bell Labs system by the editor of the B.S.T.L. (645, 957, 961)

961 "Another television system." DISCOVERY 8 (June): 193. Note on the Bell Labs demonstration. (960, 963)

962 Elway, Thomas. "What shall we do with television?" POP. RADIO 11 (June): 519–22, 579. 3 photos. General thoughts on applications for television. "Will television be a useful aid to mankind or an annoyance or merely a scientific toy?"

963 "The television demonstrations." QST 11 (June): 40, 41. 2 photos. Bell Labs. (961, 964)

964 "Les experiences Americaines de télévision." QSTF 8 (June): 44. (963, 965)

965 Hobart, Arthur. "Progress in television. A brief review of recent developments and future probabilities." RADIO 9 (June): 10. 3 illus. Bell Labs. (964, 966, 1036)

966 "Latest television developments." RADIO BRD. 11 (June): 81, 82. 2 photos. Comments on the Bell Labs demonstration. (965, 969)

"On April 7th, the American Telephone & Telegraph Company demonstrated an operative television system which brought the voice and face of speakers in Washington over telephone wires to New York in an astoundingly clear fashion. After the wire television method was shown to be workable, the immensely more difficult television by radio was undertaken between the Bell Laboratories in New York and experimental station 3XN at Whippany, New Jersey. Visual and audible reproduction was excellent in this medium as well.

"With the attainment of television, the Bell Telephone Laboratories have, in the space of but a few months, contributed to the perfection of three extraordinary scientific tools of modern life. First came the transatlantic radio telephone, then the Vitaphone, and now workable television. It is of course true that, in each of these accomplishments, the telephone engineers borrowed freely from all that had gone before, but all honor to the Telephone Company for actually accomplishing what others have attempted.

"The Telephone Company state that they have done nothing essentially new and shroud their accomplishment with no mystery. It became necessary to use a large photoelectric cell; forthwith Dr. Herbert Ives developed the largest ever built. An operative method of synchronism was required; H.M. Stoller and E.R. Morton developed a motor control synchronizing cleverly with 18 and 200 cycles, and the requirement is met; a score of specialist-engineers work unceasingly on the wire and radio problems involved. Under the synthesizing guidance of Doctor Ives, television is accomplished."

967 Gernsback, H. "Television to the front." RADIO N. 8 (June): 1419. General editorial comments. (760, 972)

968 Dinsdale, A. "Television sees in darkness and records its impressions." RADIO N. 8 (June): 1422, 1423, 1490–2. 3 photos, 2 diags. Baird apparatus, demonstration and progress. (935, 955, 975, 976)

969 Secor, Henry Winfield. "Radio vision demonstrated in America." RADIO N. 8 (June): 1424–6, 1480–2. 10 illus. Details of the Bell Labs system. (966, 973)

970 "Television's field." RADIO N. 8 (June): 1428. Federal Radio Commission's allotment of 1.5–2.0 megacycle band (150–200 meters) for experimental transmissions of "radio sight." (936, 1310)

971 "Televisionary." RADIO N. 8 (June): 1484. Also, "A to-be needed word," from WIRELESS MAG., London. Comments on terminology and suggested names: radioscape, teleopper, radiopper, teleopsis.

972 Gernsback, H. "After television—what?" SCI. & INV. 15 (June): 103. Editorial. (967, 1001)

973 Secor, H.W. "Television perfected at last." SCI. & INV. 15 (June): 108, 109, 177. 5 illus. Bell Labs. (969, 974, 1001)

974 Treadwell. Louis S. "Practical television demonstrated." SCI. AM. 136 (June): 385. 3 photos. Bell Labs. F. Gray, J.W. Horton, H.E. Ives, R.C. Mathes, and H.M. Stoller are shown in the photos. (973, 975)

975 Dinsdale, A. "Television demonstration in America." W.W. 20 (June 1): 680–6. Illus. (968, 974, 987, 1053)

976 Baird, J.L., and Baird Television Development Co. Ltd. "Driving television or other apparatus at a predetermined speed." Br. 301,847, June 7, 1927, Dec. 7, 1928; U.S. 1,816,106, May 14, 1928, July 28, 1931. A d-c motor and a constant-speed (phonic) motor with slip rings and an adjustable commutator. (968, 981)

977 Aspden, Ralph Leonard. "Television and like apparatus." Br. 298,255, June 8, 1927, Oct. 8, 1928. Intended for film transmission by radio, this is a multifrequency system with 3 spiral sets of apertures in the disks, 3 photocells, 3 neon lamps, and filter circuits. A rotary distributor for sequential signals is

an alternative. Another plan has mirrors on the disks which project a flying spot for direct scanning. (1719)

978 Jenkins, C.F. "Controlled-aperture scanning disk." U.S. 1,748,383, June 8, 1927, Feb. 25, 1930. (948, 996)

979 Malm, William. "Electrical transmission of motion pictures." U.S. 1,740,930, June 8, 1927, Dec. 24, 1929. Intermittent film motion and revolving shutter.

980 Telefunken. "Picture telegraph, television and the like receiving apparatus." Br. 291,786, Apr. 26, Aug. 9, 1928; F. Schröter, U.S. 1,751,606, May 25, 1928, Mar. 25, 1930. In Germany June 10, 1927. Single spiral of photocells or neon lamps on disks, with distributor. (949, 1090)

981 "News and views." NATURE 119 (June 11): 865. "On Tuesday, May 24, Mr. J.L. Baird gave a successful demonstration of television between Motograph House, London and the Central Hotel, Glasgow. The telephone lines connecting the two stations were 438 miles long." (976, 982)

982 Baird, J.L., and Television Ltd. "High-speed commutator switches in television apparatus." Br. 302,187, June 11, 1927, Dec. 11, 1928. Lamp-bank receiver with multiple distributors interconnected for sequential scanning. (981, 986)

983 Valensi, G. "Copying telegraphs and television apparatus." Br. 297,147, June 16, 1927, Sept. 17, 1928. Scanner with two oppositely rotating disks, each with star-shaped slots. Sync control by tuning fork, stroboscope, and synchronous motor. Other components are Kerr cell, phototube, gas discharge lamp, "ionic or electronic switch" (a multianode cathode-ray tube), batteries, resistors, and electron tubes. Said to be applicable for slides, cinematography, photo recording, and direct viewing with simultaneous transmission and reception. Three-color and stereo are mentioned but not claimed. (822, 1069)

984 Beatty, William Edward (Bell Telephone Laboratories, Inc.). "Television systems." Br. 297,152, June 17, 1927, Sept. 17, 1928. A simultaneous two-way system intended for vision and sound transmission between a plurality of telephone stations. Scanning disks with two sets of apertures, either semi-spirals or concentric spirals, with reflecting mirrors. Complete circuits for either wire line or radio station links. Similar to the Ives system (890). (938, 990, 1229)

985 Fournier d'Albe, E.E. "Our bookshelf." NATURE 119 (June 18): 887, 889. Review of books by T.T. Baker (840) and A. Dinsdale (841) with general comments. (753)

986 Jones, E. Taylor. "Television." NATURE 119 (June 18): 896. Report on the reception of images in Glasgow during Baird's tests from London. (982, 989)

"On May 24 and 26 I proceeded, at the invitation of Mr. John L. Baird, to the Central Station Hotel, Glasgow, to witness demonstrations of television between London and this city.

"The receiving apparatus was set up in a semi-darkened room, the lamp and shutter being enclosed in a case provided with an aperture. The observer looking into the apparatus saw at first a vertical band of light in which the luminosity appeared to travel rapidly sideways, disappearing at one side and then reappearing at the other. When any object having 'contrast' was placed in the light at the sending end, the band broke up into light and dark portions forming a number of 'images' of the object. The impression of sideway movement of the light was then almost entirely lost, and the whole of the image appeared to be formed simultaneously. The image was perfectly steady in position, was remarkably free from distortion, and showed no sign of the 'streakiness' which was, I believe, in evidence in the earlier experiments.

"The size of the image was small, not more than about two inches across when the 'object' was a person's face, and it could be seen by only a few people at a time...The amount of light and shade shown in the image was amply sufficient to secure recognisability of the person being 'televised,' and movements of the face or features were clearly seen. At the second demonstration some of those present had the experience of seeing the image of Mr. Baird transmitted from London while conversing with him (over a separate line) by telephone."

987 "At the transmitting end during the recent and striking television demonstration in America." POP. W. (June 18): 616. (975, 988)

988 "The receiving apparatus used in the recent television experiments carried out between New York and Washington." POP. W. (June 18): 626. (987, 990)

989 Baird, J.L., and Baird Television Development Co. Ltd. "Facsimile telegraphy." Br. 299,076, June 20, 1927, Oct. 22, 1928; U.S. 1,757,352, June 7, 1928, May 6, 1930. (986, 1011) In this departure from television the inventor uses a lens disk to scan moving strips of a drawing joined to form a continuous band. (1521)

990 Ives, H.E. "Television." TRANS. AIEE 46 (June): 913–7. Introduction to the following papers (991–994) on the Bell Labs system read at the summer convention, Detroit, June 20–4. Also B.S.T.J. 6 (Oct.): 551–9, reprinted by Arno Press, 1977. Particulars of the demonstration, Apr. 7 (909). Characteristic problems of television; pickup, light intensity, image frequency, picture elements, frequency band, transmission requirements, synchronization, signal level, and amplification. General account of the system, applications, and future developments. See also patents (903–8) and a reprint of the papers (1068).

991 Gray, F., J.W. Horton, and R.C. Mathes. "The production and utilisation of television signals." TRANS. AIEE 46 (June), 918–39. 30 illus. Also B.S.T.J. 6 (Oct.): 560–603. Light-spot scan with 50-hole disk, 18 rps, disk and neon lamp at receiver. Light pickup with 3 large phototubes about 15 in. long and 3 in. diameter. Large image screen with folded neon tube with multiple electrodes, distributor, and high-frequency excitation, for audience viewing. (904, 907, 995, 1065, 1080)

992 Stoller, H. M., and E.R. Morton. "Synchronisation of television." TRANS. AIEE 46 (June): 940–5. 10 illus. Also B.S.T.J. 6 (Oct.): 604–15. A d-c motor, with armature tappings at two points connected to slip rings, is coupled to a 240-pole sync motor. (908, 998)

993 Gannett, Danforth K., and Estil I. Green. "Wired transmission system for television." TRANS. AIEE 46 (June): 946–53. 10 illus., including map of circuits between Washington, New York, and Whippany, N.J. Also B.S.T.J. 6 (Oct): 616–32. Direct transmission along telephone lines with transformers, transpositions, and equalization with special distortion-correcting networks. General requirements, circuit details, measurements, and comparative image quality. (992, 994, 1220)

994 Nelson, Edward L. "Radio transmission system for television." TRANS. AIEE 46 (June): 954–62. 9 illus. Also B.S.T.J. 6 (Oct): 633–52. Details of installation at station 3XN, Whippany, N.J. Apparatus, circuits, tests, transmission characteristics. Multiple transmission from a single antenna; image 191 m, voice 207 m, sync 1600 m. (993, 1003, 1230)

995 Ives, H.E., and J.W. Horton. "Electro-optical transmission." U.S. 1,717,782, June 22, 1927, June 18, 1929. Assigned: B.T.L. Br. 292,546, Mar. 20, 1928 (E.R.P.). Disk scanner, light-spot scan, amplifiers, and local monitor via scanning disk and neon lamp. (990, 991, 1010, 1076)

996 Jenkins, C.F. "Transmitting motion pictures." 1,777,409, June 22, 1927, Oct. 7, 1930. Assigned: Jenkins Labs. Lens disk and moving film transmitter, lens disk with prismatic disk receiver. Includes references to other patents. (978, 999)

997 Mertz, Pierre. "Testing television and the like system." U.S. 1,706,538, June 22, 1927, Mar. 26, 1929. Assigned: AT&T. (1365)

998 Stoller, H.M., and E.R. Morton. "Speed regulator." U.S. 1,763,909, June 23, 1927, June

17, 1930. Assigned: B.T.L. Br. 292,597, June 13, 1928 (E.R.P.). Disk scanners with driving motors and synchronous motors interconnected with electron tube circuits and multiwound transformers to provide close sync control with very low- and high-frequency currents over separate lines. (992, 2298)

999 Jenkins, C.F. "Radio movie receiver." U.S. 1,697,527, June 25, 1927, Jan. 1, 1929. Lens disk and disk with a circle of lamps and distributor. (996, 1070)

1000 Whitten, W.H., and Thaddeus R. Goldsborough. "Television system." U.S. 1,768,874, June 25, 1927, July 1, 1930. Assigned: Westinghouse. (677, 3697)

1001 Secor, H.W., and John H. Kraus. ALL ABOUT TELEVISION INCLUDING EXPERIMENTS. New York: Experimenter Publishing Co., summer 1927. 112 pp. Preface by H. Gernsback. Called "a complete treatise," this is a collection of articles on phototelegraphy and television reprinted from RADIO NEWS and other Gernsback periodicals. Pages 7–13, 60–104 deal with television (much of the rest concerns facsimile). "In presenting this volume to those interested in the new art, we hope that you will realize that this is the first extensive work on television that has as yet appeared. It will probably become the forerunner of many others, once the art gets under way." A second issue appeared in 1928. (973, 1239, 1312)

1002 Abelli, A.A. "What next in television?" POP. MECH. 48 (July): 1–3. Illus.

1003 Free, E.E. "How the new television works." POP. RADIO 12 (July–Aug.): 62, 63. Bell Labs system. (886, 990, 1026)

1004 "Ships sighted in fogs, smoke pierced at a glance." POP. SCI. 111 (July): 12.

1005 "Probable progress of television." RADIO BRD. 11 (July): 141. Editorial comments.

1006 Dreher, Carl (1896–1976). "The place of television in the progress of science." RADIO BRD. 11 (July): 167, 168. Discussion of the telephone, telegraph, phonograph, motion pictures, talking pictures, and television. 3 tables of inventions and dates. (1015)

1007 Gernsback, H. "A prediction—and its fulfillment." RADIO N. 9 (July): 21. Editorial referring to the writer's statements in May 1926 (760) and the recent Bell Labs experiments with speech and image signals carried on one radio channel (924). (972, 1058)

1008 Fournier, L. "New European television scheme." SCI. & INV. 15 (July): 404. (889)

1009 "Engineer predicts television receivers." SCI. AM. 137 (July): 69. On comments by R.H. Langley. (882, 1346)

1010 Ives, H.E. "Electro-optical transmission." U.S. 1,796,931, July 2, 1927, Mar. 17, 1931. Assigned: B.T.L. Br. 293,308, June 30, 1928 (E.R.P.). Four-channel system with two phototubes per circuit, four amplifiers, etc., and scanning disks designed to simultaneously explore and reconstitute separate portions of an image. Also Br. 335,638, July 2, 1929, which is a similar three-channel system. (995, 1046)

1011 Baird, J.L. and Television Ltd. "Reproduction of pictures, views, scenes, images and the like." Br. 303,771, July 5, 1927, Jan. 7, 1929. Overlapping disks with arcuate slots for exploring different zones simultaneously with different widths of the scanned bands or areas to emphasize the center portion of the image. (1004, 1016)

1012 "How to hasten television." POP. W. (July 9): 711.

1013 Mandolf, H.I. "Defends the word 'television.'" ELECT. W. 99 (July 16): 117. (993, 1051)

1014 Thurm, L. "Optical device for radio cinematographic transmitters and receivers." U.S. 1,780,572, July 14, 1927, Nov. 4, 1930; Br. 294,257, July 20, 1928, Oct. 21, 1929. In France July 21, 1927. Disk with two offset semi-spiral sets of square holes, polyhedral mirror drum, slotted shutter moving transversely across moving film, apertured cylinder, neon lamps, and devices covered in an

1015 Dreher, C. "The future of television." RADIO BRD. 11 (Aug.): 235, 236. Further discussion of the communication arts with comments on possibilities. (1006, 1772)

"One thing should be noted before we embark on our self-appointed mission of prophecy. Practical television is not around the corner. Many moons will wax and wane before televisor screens in our homes show us distant events and people. Many sleepless nights are ahead of the engineers and scientists charged with the task of putting the new art on a production and commercial basis.... The everyday application of television is a remote possibility in five years, a fair possibility in ten, a probability in fifteen.

"But when the day arrives, and the engineers produce, for a reasonable expenditure, a television apparatus capable of reproducing distant events in a life-like manner on a sufficiently large screen, what then? Will the accomplishment be a blessing? Not always—take that from one who has seen many broadcast artists. For others, I wish we could have it tomorrow. Sometimes I have seen and heard some beautiful girl with an equally beautiful voice rehearsing her program in the afternoon, and, at the receiver in the evening, have had to be satisfied with hearing her only, and it has certainly been a deprivation.

"Television in conjunction with telephony might be employed to reproduce distant spectacles, not only in the home, but in theatres. For example, a movie house might interrupt its program for a short speech, reproduced visually and audibly, by the President—an appeal for aid, for example, in time of national disaster. If the visual component were added to broadcasting as we now know it, the motion picture theatres might find it a useful adjunct to their shows, probably in a form we do not foresee now."

1016 "Predicts sight machine. British television inventor forecasts combined phonograph." N.Y.T. 23 (Aug. 2): 4. Baird's address at Glasgow and his prediction of television recording with two needle tracks, one for voice and the other for sight. (1011, 1018)

1017 "Seeing not always believing." N.Y.T. 22 (Aug. 3): 6. Editorial.

1018 Television Ltd., and J.L. Baird. "Television." Br. 295,210, Aug. 9, 1927, Aug. 9, 1928, divided out of Br. 289,307 (800). Disks with slots and zigzag apertures. Position of luminous spot at transmitter indicated by the intersection of luminous lines at the receiver. (1016, 1025)

1019 "More television." W.W. 21 (Aug. 10): 178.

1020 Bower, D. "Television." W.W 21 (Aug. 10): 191.

1021 "Television news." POP. W. (Aug. 13): 843.

1022 Hansell, Clarence W. "Picture transmission." U.S 1,751,584, Aug. 13, 1927, Mar. 25, 1930. Assigned: RCA. Br. 295,601, Aug. 13, 1928 (Marconi's). A facsimile system employing a flexible quartz conductor or optical cable.

1023 Hough, Clinton W. "Television apparatus." U.S. 1,760,198, Aug. 13, 1927, May 27, 1930. Assigned: Federal Telegraph Co. Scanning by piezoelectric crystals with crossed vibrational axes. (1291)

1024 Szenyovsky, Ladislaus, and A. G. Schulz'sche "Televisual reproduction of stationary or moving pictures or objects by electrical means." Br. 295,653, Aug. 14, 1928, complete not accepted. In Austria Aug. 16, 1927. Concentric disks with straight and curved arcuate slots, overlapped belts with crossed angular slots, disk with blue, yellow, and red filters, and tricolor prisms. Said to be applicable for duplex operation, reproduction of pictures in their natural colors, and for stereo with separate viewing lenses.

1025 Baird, J.L., and Television Ltd. "Television apparatus." Br. 306,158, Aug. 17, 1927. Optical system including quartz-glass rods. Reference to Br. 269,658. (1018, 1028)

1026 "Television developments; symposium at A.I.E.E. summer meeting." ENGINEER-

ING 124 (Aug. 19, 26): 247–50, 281–3. Illus. Bell Labs (1003, 1036)

1027 Kasson, C.L. "Meaning of vision, sight and television still basis of discussion." ELECT. W. 90 (Aug. 20): 362.

1028 "The Leeds meeting of the British Association." NATURE 120 (Aug. 20): 276. Program schedule. Baird will demonstrate television between London and Leeds and will also demonstrate Noctovision and his Phonoscope. (1025, 1030)

1029 "Television demonstrated." W.W. 21 (Aug. 24): 245.

1030 "News in brief." ELECT. 99 (Aug. 26): 257. Note on a demonstration to be given by Baird at the tenth annual Model Engineers' Exhibition, Royal Horticultural Hall, Westminster, Sept. 17–24. (1028, 1038)

1031 "Television demonstration." W.W. 21 (Aug. 31): 276.

1032 Rosing, B.L. Russ. 3422 and 3424, Aug. 31. (688, 2145, 3407)

1033 Brittain, William J. "Television on the continent." DISCOVERY 8 (Sept.): 283–5. 5 illus. Interviews with von Mihály, Dieckmann, and Belin, with quotations and remarks. (1057)

"When I went through Europe visiting workers in television, I was given many surprises. I did not know they were so advanced, nor did I expect to find so many ways of applying the same principles.

"The first television worker I met on my tour gave me a great surprise, greeting with words to the effect that he was 'just going to give television to the world.' He was Denes von Mihály, a Hungarian, and young consulting engineer to the A.E.G., the great German electrical firm. He told me that he was ready to manufacture efficient television sets which could be sold at twenty pounds and, indeed, was coming to London in a few weeks to form a company to sell these sets. So efficient would the sets be, he said, that they would receive on their screen—seven inches by six—a boxing match or a horse race. 'You will be able to see the boxers' faces,' he told me, 'and the jockeys' caps.'

"Professor Max Dieckmann, whom I found in his ideal experimental station on the outskirts of Munich, made me no promise, but his work is full of promise. He has abandoned his old sending system and is working keenly on a new idea. He is trying to make electrons do the work of wheels, discs, and mirrors. With television's need for such extraordinary speeds, workers are hampered by the weightiness of their apparatus. Glass and steel and wood seem hardly the materials to attain this delicate speed. 'I came to the conclusion that mechanism could never achieve television,' Professor Dieckmann told me, 'and I scrapped my transmitting apparatus, which had mirrors to explore the object. I am now experimenting to make electrons do the work.... If I can make them explore the object and register the results I shall have mastered the problem.'

"M. Edouard Belin, at his station near Paris, is working in conjunction with M. Holweck of the Radium Institute. M. Belin showed me his transmitter. To achieve the rapid exploration he uses mirrors, but in a mechanical system his own. At present M. Belin is transmitting only silhouettes. His results are certainly important. On the screen at the top of the receiving apparatus the outline of the hand can be seen clearly. The hand can be seen to move, and the fingers to bend. A human profile and a simple photographic negative have also been transmitted with the same success. 'We are gradually improving,' M. Belin said to me, 'and the work of the next few months will show what value there is in our method.'"

1034 Everett, A. "Television." EXP. W. 4 (Sept.): 580.

1035 "A new Russian 'televisor' enters the field." POP. RADIO 12 (Sept.): 176. Diagram of receiver. Mirror disk scanner, moving coil mirror modulator, simultaneous radio transmission of image, and sync signals. Invention of L.C. Termen, Physical-Technical Institute, Leningrad. From an article in RA-

DIO LUBITEL [Radio Amateur], Moscow, 4 (1927): 13–6.

1036 Hobart, A. "Radio television. A simple explanation and description of the Bell Laboratories successful experiments." RADIO 9 (Sept.): 14, 15. 5 illus. (965, 1026, 1045)

1037 "Some of the Belin television apparatus." RADIO BRD. 11 (Sept.): 268. Photo and caption. (901, 1039)

1038 "New developments in radio." RADIO N. 9 (Sept.): 212. Photo of Baird and transmitter at Coulsdon. (1030, 1041)

1039 "Television developments of Edouard Belin." SCI. & INV. 15 (Sept.): 410. (1037, 1040)

1040 "The short-wave transmitter used by Edouard Belin in his television experiments conducted in France." SCI. AM. 137 (Sept.): 272. (1039, 1071)

1041 "Television pictures next. Inventor arranges with English to send them here." N.Y.T. 48 (Sept. 1): 2. Special commission of the British Post Office has been appointed to consider arrangements for Baird tests. (1038, 1043, 1532)

1042 Roberts, J.H.T. "The 'Karolus' cell." POP. W. (Sept. 3): 12. (744, 810, 1077, 1164)

1043 Baird, J.L. "Lecture on television." London: Television Society. Undated typescript, 3 pp. British Association meeting at Leeds University, Sept. 7. The proposal to form a society "to further the progress of Television" arose at this meeting, and the Television Society of Great Britain was founded at a subsequent special meeting. (1041, 1049, 1152)

"A vote of thanks was proposed by Mr. W.G.W. Mitchell, B.Sc. (a member of the British Association) who said: "I have listened with great interest to Mr. Baird's lecture and I have also witnessed a demonstration of Noctovision a few days ago which had the effect of stimulating my interest in an invention of which I had read quite a lot in the press and radio journals. Mr. Baird must have been placed at considerable inconvenience apart from the expense involved in placing his televisor and his own services at the disposal of the members of the British Association, and it is therefore with the greatest of pleasure and confidence that I propose a hearty vote of thanks to Mr. Baird for his Address tonight and I should also like to take this opportunity in view of the wide public interest in television to propose that a Society should be formed forthwith to further the progress of Television and give a stimulus to this new branch of Science."

"Lt. Col. J. Robert Yelf (a member of the British Association): 'I have much pleasure in associating myself with the remarks of Mr. Mitchell and to my mind it speaks well of the courage and confidence Mr. Baird has in his invention to submit it to the critical analysis of the scientific brains of this country. The queues outside the Demonstration Rooms last week speak for the enormous public interest in the subject of television and Mr. Baird's invention, and I feel with Mr. Mitchell that no time should be lost in establishing television as a new branch of science and in this connection the suggestion of forming a Society to deal with such a comprehensive subject will I am sure commend itself to all interested. I therefore have great pleasure in seconding the hearty vote of thanks to Mr. Baird for his interesting lecture tonight and further seconding the proposal that a Society should be formed forthwith to further the progress of television and give stimulus to this new branch of science.' The Chairman put the proposal to the meeting and it was carried unanimously."

1044 Nicolson, A.M. "Television." U.S. 1,779,747, Sept. 9, 1927, renewed Mar. 21, Oct. 28, 1930. Assigned: Communications Patents, Inc. Scanning apparatus comprises a wheel with spirally placed contacts that sweep across a screen to produce self-luminous discharges per unit area. The photocell output and an a-c sync supply common to the driving motor are transmitted by separate channels to a receiver. (552, 1056)

1045 "Les essais de télévision de l'American Telephone and Telegraph Co." GENIE CIVIL 91 (Sept. 10): 263. (1036, 1052)

1046 Ives, H.E. "Electro-optical transmission." U.S. 1,878,147, Sept. 10, 1927, renewed Apr. 28, 1930, Sept. 20, 1932. Assigned: B.T.L. Three-channel color system with components, connections, and arrangements similar to the patents of July 2 (1010). (1047)

1047 Hartley, Ralph Vinton Lyon, and H.E. Ives. "Electro-optical transmission system." U.S. 2,166,247, Sept. 14, 1927, renewed Aug. 27, 1930, July 18, 1939. Assigned: B.T.L. Br. 297,078, Mar. 19, 1928, June 19, 1929 (E.R.P.). An intermediate film system combining sight and sound. Sound recording on the film or separately. Disk scanners, phototubes, arc lamp projector or lamp bank, and distributor at receiver. Moving film is fully processed in equivalent apparatus at both stations, which are connected by three channels, one each for picture signals, sound, and sync. The intermediate film system was highly developed during the 1930s, particularly in Germany. (1046, 1080, 1422)

1048 Busch, H. "Uber die Wirkungsweise der Konzentrationsspule bei der Braunschen Röhre" [About the action of the concentration coil with the Braun tube]. ARCH. ELEKT. 18 (Sept. 21): 583–94. Theory of magnetic focusing of cathode rays; a short narrow coil acts the same as an optical lens. See earlier paper (823).

1049 "Television by gramophone. Mr. J.L. Baird's prophecy." TIMES (Sept. 22): 11c. Comments during a demonstration at the Model Engineers' Exhibition, Sept. 21. "When everybody who has a loud speaker has also a televisor attachment, it will be possible...to reproduce pictures of the performers from the extra spiral (groove) of the gramophone record on that attachment." (1043, 1064)

1050 Zworykin, V.K. "Television system." U.S. 1,715,732, Sept. 23, 1927, June 4, 1929. Assigned: Westinghouse. Opto-mechanical system. (947, 1757)

1051 Moore, D.M. "Why not 'Telerama'?" ELECT. W. 90 (Sept. 24): 624. A word coined by Moore. (739, 1013, 1308, 1332)

1052 "Movie at Columbia of television device." N.Y.T. 36 (Sept. 24): 3. Lecture by Prof. John H. Morecroft of the electrical engineering department at Columbia University and showing of a motion picture film made by AT&T about the Bell Labs system. (1045, 1053)

1053 Dinsdale, A. "Une demonstration officielle de la télévision en Amerique." REV. GEN. 22 (Sept. 24): 95. (975, 1052, 1062, 1068)

1054 Rowe, James Jesse, and Cyril Leslie Rowe. "Television and other signalling apparatus employing light sensitive devices." Br. 305,079, Sept. 26, 1927, Jan. 28, 1929. Concentric disks with arcuate slots, overlapped bands with equivalent slots, electromagnetic shutter modulator, and selenium or light cell.

1055 Hammond, J.H. "Television in 1925." W.W. 21 (Sept. 28): 464. (550, 1062, 1660)

1056 Nicolson, A.M. "High-speed television system." U.S. 1,779,748, Sept. 28, 1927, renewed Mar. 21, 1930, Oct. 28, 1930. Assigned: Communication Patents, Inc. (Comm. Pats.). Matrix of conductors provides visible discharges at predetermined points, with cross connections selected by a multianode cathode-ray-tube distributor and by a mechanical distributor. (1044, 1061)

1057 Brittain, W.J. "When we see by wireless." CHAMBER'S J. 14 (Oct.): 661, 662. (1033, 1086)

1058 Gernsback, H. "Seeing in the dark." SCI. & INV. 15 (Oct.): 489. (1007, 1223)

1059 Tiltman, R.F. "Seeing in darkness." WORLD TODAY 50 (Oct.): 462–6. Illus. (872, 1098)

1060 Bailey, L.W.A. "The Televisor." POP. W. (Oct. 1): 211.

1061 Nicolson, A.M. "Pilot television system." U.S. 1,953,817, Oct. 11, 1927, renewed Mar. 21, 1930, Apr. 3, 1934. Assigned: Comm. Pats. A periodic electrical discharge is magnetically deflected to scan the total area of a subject. (1056, 1066)

1062 Dinsdale, A. "Television in 1925." W.W. 21 (Oct. 12): 53. (1053, 1055, 1075, 1100)

1063 Best, F.E. "Television device." U.S. 1,802,802, Oct. 17, 1927, Apr. 28, 1931. Rotating disk, mirror drum, storage battery. (732)

1064 Baird, J.L., and Television Ltd. "Television apparatus." Br. 309,965, Oct. 19, 1927, Apr. 19, 1929. Disk with two spiral sets of apertures, lenses, or mirrors; two disks with single spiral sets of apertures on a common shaft. Intended for two-way transmission (1049, 1082)

1065 Gray, F. "Television system." U.S. 2,113,254, Oct. 21, 1927, Apr. 5, 1938. Assigned: B.T.L. Development of U.S. 1,759,504 (904). (991, 1148)

1066 Nicolson, A.M. "Scanning system for television." U.S. 1,799,749, Oct. 26, 1927, renewed Mar. 21, 1930, Oct. 28, 1930, reissued Dec. 19, 1930, Mar. 1, 1932. Assigned: Comm. Pats. Electric discharges between relatively movable linear electrodes. (1061, 1254)

1067 Wagner, Carl J. "Television sending and receiving apparatus." U.S. 1,765,292, Oct. 26, 1927, June 17, 1930. Scanner with a helix of openings, plurality of light sources.

1068 Bell Telephone Laboratories. SYMPOSIUM ON TELEVISION. New York, Nov. Reprint B-274, 20 pp., 59 illus. Articles from B.S.T.J., Oct. (990–994). (1052, 1074)

1069 Valensi, G. "L'etat actuel du problème de la télévision" [The present state of the television problem]. ANN. POSTES 16 (Nov.): 1046. (938, 1149)

1070 Jenkins, C.F. "Radio vision." PROC. IRE 15 (Nov.): 958–64. Reprinted by Arno Press, 1977. 6 illus. Survey of author's work, including facsimile. (999, 1095)

1071 "The new Belin Televisor." POP. RADIO 12 (Nov.) 347. 2 photos. (1040, 1085)

1072 "Television opera." POP. SCI. 111 (Nov.): 40.

1073 "New television idea." POP. SCI. 111 (Nov.): 58.

1074 "Radio delegates view plants here." N.Y.T. 31 (Nov. 1): 3, 4. Television and talking movies demonstrated by AT&T and Bell Labs at the International Radio Telegraph Conference in Washington, D.C. (1068, 1142)

1075 Hutchinson, O.G. "Television in 1925." W.W. 21 (Nov. 2): 628. (769, 1062, 1112)

1076 Horton, J.W. "Television system." U.S. 2,003,294, Nov. 2, 1927, renewed June 22, 1931, June 4, 1935. Assigned: B.T.L. Another variant of the Bell Labs system with scanning disks, neon lamp, and electron tube circuits. (995, 1141)

1077 Telefunken. "Light control devices, suitable for use in recording sounds or in picture telegraphy." Br. 299,884, Oct. 31, 1928, June 13, 1929. In Germany Nov. 3, 1927. The Karolus cell. A sandwich of thin glass plates interleaved with electrodes connected to a d-c bias supply and a signal circuit, with Nicol prisms and an optical assembly. (980, 1042, 1091, 1097)

1078 "A new television." POP. W. (Nov. 5): 525.

1079 Farnsworth, P.T. "Television receiving system." U.S. 1,773,981, Nov. 7, 1927, Aug. 26, 1930. Assigned: Television Labs. Divided from U.S. 1,773,980 (850). Optical assembly comprising a light valve (coil and carbon disulfide with Nicol prisms), a biaxial crystal with opposed gratings, and two mirror oscillographs for beam deflection. Also "Light valve." U.S. 1,806,935, Nov. 7, 1927, May 26, 1931. (1109)

1080 Ives, H.E., and R.C. Mathes. "Electro-optical image production." U.S. 2,058,882, Nov. 12, 1927, Oct. 27, 1936. Assigned: B.T.L. Br. 317,426, May 16, 1928 (W.E. Beatty). A two-channel (picture signals and sync) system with scanning disks, electron tube circuits, distributor, and bank of light-emitting elements. (991, 1047, 1081, 1182)

1081 Mathes, R.C. "Electro-optical image production." U.S. 2,058,898, Nov. 12, 1927,

Oct. 27, 1936. Assigned: B.T.L. This variant of the Bell Labs disk-distributor system incorporates storage of elemental image signals in a bank of capacitors connected to electron tube circuits. (1080, 1363)

1082 Baird, J.L., and Television Ltd. "Television apparatus." Br. 312,406, Nov. 30, 1927, May 30, 1929. Receiver scanning disk with cylindrical lenses of short focal length, or a stationary lens or equivalent optical system intended to limit the angular dispersion of the light rays and provide a brilliant image suitable for direct viewing. Divided: Br. 312,560 (1083). (1064)

1083 Baird, J.L., and Television Ltd. "Television apparatus." Br. 312,560, Nov. 30, 1927, May 30, 1929. Divided out of Br. 312,406 (1082). Two-color system with two separate scanning disks, colored filters, and photocells or lamps. In an alternative construction the disks overlap one another. The separate images are superposed upon a screen to reproduce a single image in natural colors. Reference is made to Br. 266,564 (704) and Br. 289,307 (800). (1100)

1084 "Limits seen for television." POP. SCI. 111 (Dec.): 39.

1085 "Television apparatus of a European scientist." RADIO BRD. 12 (Dec.): 102. Photo of Fernand Holweck's cathode-ray-tube receiver used in the Belin system. (1071, 1159)

1086 Brittain. W.J. "Television in Europe." RADIO BRD. 12 (Dec.): 103, 104. 3 photos. Von Mihály, Dieckmann, Belin and Holweck. (1057, 1101)

1087 Arnold, John P. "Photoelectricity, the means of television." RADIO N. 9 (Dec.): 640, 707, 708. 3 illus. (1488)

1088 Thurm, L. "Television apparatus." Br. 303,178, Dec. 29, 1928. In France Dec. 3, 1927. Receiver with neon lamps on a rotating frame. (1014, 1292)

1089 Dauvillier, A. "Television system." U.S. 1,766,885, Dec. 10, 1927, June 24, 1930. Divided from U.S. 1,661,603 (557). Cathode-ray-tube receiver, vibrating mirrors, electron tube circuits, automatic sync. (780, 1108)

1090 Schröter, F. "Combined television and audio broadcasting." U.S. 2,078,459, Dec. 5, 1928, Apr. 27, 1937. In Germany Dec. 12, 1927. Assigned: Telefunken. Scanning disk, transmission of motion picture film with sound track on one channel. (980, 1617)

1091 Telefunken. "Analysing or synthesizing apparatus for television." Br. 302,228, Nov. 28, 1928, Aug. 1, 1929. In Germany Dec. 12, 1927. Nipkow disk with a triple spiral set of holes, 3 photocells, 3-element neon lamp, and distributor. (1077, 1221)

1092 "Short-wave television." W.W. 21 (Dec. 14): 793.

1093 "Television in 1910." W.W. 21 (Dec. 21): 828.

1094 "Television abroad." POP. W. (Dec. 24): 897.

1095 Jenkins, C.F. "Persisting luminescent screen." U.S. 2,021,010. Dec. 28, 1927, Nov. 12, 1935. Assigned: E.T. Cunningham, Inc. Receiver with glow lamps. (1070, 1104)

1096 "Experiments in Holland." POP. W. (Dec. 31): 920.

1097 Karolus, A. "Television system." U.S. 1,889,990, Nov. 30, 1928, Dec. 6, 1932. In Germany Dec. 31, 1927. Assigned: RCA. Cathode-ray-tube receiver with Kerr cell. (1077, 1386)

1098 Tiltman, R.F. TELEVISION FOR THE HOME: THE WONDERS OF "SEEING BY WIRELESS." London: Hutchinson [1927]. xix + 106 pp. 8 plates. Introduction by Prof. A.M. Low. Nearly half the book is about the work of J.L. Baird. Other parts deal briefly with early history, mainly on selenium and phototelegraphy, with mention of von Mihály, Rosing, Belin and Holweck, Jenkins and Moore; radio apparatus and information for the amateur, television in America, and the future of television. (1059, 1160)

CHAPTER 8

A VERY GOOD YEAR: 1928

The rise of interest in television evident in the previous chapter grew perceptibly during the early months of 1928 and reached a crest before the end of the year. This expansion of the art on all fronts—repetitious of the radio boom of the early twenties—was linked with an increasingly optimistic commercial outlook and the rise of speculative business activities as well as the worldwide spread of telecommunications. Surface signs included a considerable growth in periodical literature and news reports, occasioned by a series of public demonstrations; transmission of images across the Atlantic and to a ship at sea, daylight pickup, pictures in full color, stereoscopic images, film transmissions, staged events, and exhibition displays. More than thirty companies were engaged in television ventures, a dozen radio stations began experimental transmission in the United States, and amateur construction of receivers became a new hobby. Judged by any standards, 1928 was indeed a very good year for television.

The growth of technical activities is shown by the number of patents listed: one hundred thirty-two compared with seventy-five for 1927. This increase was due in part to an influx of fifty newcomers; thirty-five of them, however, were one-time contributors. In contrast, Baird made a record for himself with thirty-two applications. Others who were still active one way or another include Alexanderson, Belin and Holweck, Clark, Dauvillier, Dieckmann, Fessenden, Ives and his colleagues, Jenkins, Karolus, von Mihály, Schröter, Thurm, and Valensi.

Appearing in some fifty patents, the Nipkow disk and its derivative forms and combinations was the favorite scanning device. Minor choices were mirror drums and wheels, apertured drums, lens disks, contact disks, and vibrating mirrors. The helical drum scanner was introduced by Jenkins (1196) in a receiver for radio movies. Other novel approaches to the scanning problem were Gardner's mirror screw (1472), one form of which became popular especially in Germany during the early 1930s, and Walton's echelon system (1542). Proposals for synchronizing included ball governors, brakes, electromagnets, tuning forks, and phonic wheels, with preference given to the use of common a-c power supplies and synchronous motors. Bell Labs applied a crystal oscillator with a tuning fork for frequency control (1142). Some form of hand control was generally used for phase adjustment or framing.

Mosaic methods with banks of lights or other matrix assemblies still had some appeal, despite the drawbacks of multiple wires and other complications. Jenkins revived his original multiwire idea (245) of 1894 adapted for radio transmission (1481) with a matrix of 2,304 elements controlled by a distributor, and Telefunken also had a matrix system (1221). Various forms of distributors and commutators were specified in a dozen schemes. Signal storage employing capacitors, previously disclosed by Round (765) in 1926, was applied by Phinney (1145), Johnston (1251), Jenkins (1348), and Mathes (1363). Applications for spark discharges had been suggested in 1927 by Dawson and Milner (891) and Nicolson (1061). The latter continued this technique (1254), a variant of which was proposed by Baird (1477), who also suggested a contact method intended to provide glowing points on platinum foil (1528).

A dozen or more patents reveal a diversity of ideas that seemed to offer possibilities. The following are some miscellaneous and unorthodox proposals: Bissiri (1107), electromagnetic mosaic; Adsit (1180), helical mirror drum; Fessenden (1208), message tape; Feingold (1211), multichannel piezoelectric system; Ruzicka (1228), special cell and scannerless system; Leeming (1269), phono recording for pictures and sound; Nyquist (1341), two-way and secret transmission; Peterson (1406), variable frequency modulation; Syphrit

(1465), spherical scanning assembly. Baird disclosed a message band system (1521) which was later used for displaying titles and other text in motion, along with an electrochemical reproducer (1522). Baird also covered an optical method for combining a prime scene with a ghost background (1530). Robinson applied television in a direction-finding system (1482), Donle suggested a method for interleaving sync and vision signals (1620), and Hammond had a plan (1660) incorporating distribution of magnetic recordings.

Developments at Bell Labs were covered in a dozen U.S. and British patents. Ives (1338) and Mathes (1364) disclosed multichannel systems, the former including film transmission. Hartley (1422, 1534) and Gray each covered two systems, the latter with a folded tube and distributors (1536) and one with light valves (1675). While the greatest activity occurred in Britain and the United States, work was continuing in Europe and elsewhere. After some absence from the scene, von Mihály (Telehor A.-G.) was engaged on a simplified disk system (1309)—having discarded oscillating mirrors (819)—and on sync methods (1357, 1664), discharge tube apparatus (1520), and a scanning disk (1673). Telefunken covered two systems, one with a disk-drum scanner (Schröter 1617). A sync method by C. Lorenz A.-G. (1362) was a follow-up from a previous patent (825).

In France there was Thuau (1146) with a disk, shutter, and film system; Belin and Holweck (1258), who still used vibrating mirrors; Thurm (1292) with a multifrequency system; Levy (1351) employing a disk, Kerr cell, and film; Besson (1405), who disclosed a double-disk system said to be applicable for use with aircraft and submarines. Société Indépendente de Télégraphie sans Fil revealed two proposals (1412). Other contributions came from Melbourne (Strange 1117), Vienna (Tschörner 1384), Cape Town (De Wet 1385), Budapest (Binder 1622); Tihanyi's patents were filed in Hungary or in Germany, Bruni's in Italy, while Rosing and others were active in Russia.

Electromechanical methods were soundly established by now, but electron beam techniques were being developed, notably and most devotedly by Farnsworth (1109). In addition to McCreary's improvement (1105), camera tube systems were proposed by Bruni (1226), Roberts (1304), Clarkson (1314), Sharma (1417), and Tihanyi (1289), who also incorporated an image intensifier in one application (1339). Picture tubes were specified by Farnsworth (1227) and McCreary (1606). This trend toward the future is apparent also in various proposals for color: Kell (1181), Joy (1367), De Wet (1385), Todd (1541), and Barnes (1615). Baird made six applications for color (1106), one of which included stereo (1335). McCreary also had a revised color system (1282) based on a previous camera tube patent (587).

In 1927 television was believed to be just around the corner (902). This imminence became a fact in 1928, with many demonstrations and a proliferation of reports and articles; newspaper items rose from 40 in 1927 to 120, and items of all kinds in periodicals increased from 125 to 325. This spread of printed matter was fostered by several monthlies, particularly RADIO NEWS and RADIO BROADCAST among others in the United States, and by the new magazine TELEVISION in Britain. The latter served also as the official journal of the Television Society, a combination which met the needs and interests of amateurs as well as professionals. Coverage in the NEW YORK TIMES increased threefold, while that in the TIMES and other British publications previously listed almost doubled. The biggest increase is accounted for by 100 listings from TELEVISION (this increase was even greater, since some 200 items that are repetitious, tutorial, or of marginal interest from a variety of sources are not listed).

As would be expected, this burgeoning of interest was accompanied by a range of opinions concerning the outlook for television as a viable art. Conflicting views on prospects in the United States varied according to the commentator's affiliation and depended also on whether or not television was regarded as a prime competitor to the radio broadcast industry, as a potential money maker, or as a will-o'-the-wisp to be avoided or derided. Ives and Alexanderson expressed cautionary views, a representative of RCA believed that television in the home was likely within a year (1185), but Richmond put such an event some five years in the future (1210). In April (1222) and in July (1315) various experts were pessimistic about any immediate prospects for a radio vision service.

One writer in June (1272) made some keen observations about the situation and concluded that radio vision was still a scientific curiosity. In August (1416), however, a Radiovisor was considered to be a suitable Christmas gift in view of the near prospects for regular vision transmissions. Other opinions were expressed again by experts in September (1466), Gernsback cautioned the public and pointed out that the art was still experimental (1498), and Raycroft discounted any close prospect for commercial development (1612).

These cautionary views were prompted in part by the enticing headlines about progress in the visual field and by the fact that television was threatening to invade the golden domain of radio, prospectively as a dilutant to the receiver industry and literally on the air. With more than 600 stations broadcasting radio programs in 1928, the Federal Radio Commission (Radio Board) found the regulation of television an additional and difficult task since the medium's requirements were largely unknown and naturally presented new problems. Close cooperation with experts and industry leaders provided the Commission some conflicting opinions, with the result that questions on station permits, frequency allocations, hours of transmission, and so forth remained indecisive or temporary matters until the end of the year.

According to an announcement in September (1452), the Commission's first report stated that equipment for the home was far from being ready. The board was reluctant to open the door for an expansion of stations, though the frequency band of 1500–2000 kc had been assigned for experimental purposes in April 1927 (902). Pressured by the impetus of developments and the growing commercial needs, however, authorizations were granted for experimental use of various frequencies and for licenses and construction permits (1310, 1355). An order issued by the Commission on November 2 set the bandwidth allowed to 10 kc on frequencies above 1.5 mc and limited the times of transmission (1597). Meanwhile, the adequacy of the broadcast band for visual transmissions was questioned by Felix (1546). The official report in December (1668) revealed that the Commission had not arrived at a firm policy on regulating television transmissions. The only clear point was the fact that television signals caused objectionable interference to radio programs, which led to the decision to end certain broadcasts and set up a special transmission band (1677).

The freedom given to experimental broadcasters in the United States was in sharp contrast to the stranglehold maintained in Britain by the Post Office and the British Broadcasting Corporation. To acquire broadcast facilities on the medium waves the Baird Company had to have permission from the Post Office, along with agreement by the BBC. Such facilities would violate the BBC monopoly or, if permitted through an existing station, would displace part of the regular programs. On one side Baird needed an official outlet to enter the market, on the other side the authorities were loath to grant facilities in the belief that their governmental mandate to provide and protect the public service would be jeopardized if they allowed visual experiments during the normal program hours.

This conflicting situation was exacerbated by undue publicity by the Baird people, whose advertisements and statements implied they could provide a satisfactory television service, and by running controversy and rumors in the press. Baird was supported by a dozen or so individuals, notably his business manager Hutchinson and a new and vocal aide in the person of Sidney Moseley. Hutchinson's persistent announcements on an increase of power and life-size images (1131), on tests from Newark, N.J., to London (1166), on a portable receiver (1173), on company activities in America (1358), and so forth harmed Baird's new British company (1328), and the American ventures (1325, 1366) were other points of criticism.

The Baird concern faced strong opposition from the BBC, represented in the main by their chief engineer, Capt. P.P. Eckersley, who rightly maintained that 30-line images were too poor to be acceptable for regular transmission which, if instituted, would imply some degree of official sanction. Eckersley also asserted, again correctly, that such transmissions would have to be on the shorter wavelengths, which alone could accommodate the wide bandwidth requisite for satisfactory picture quality. He was supported by Swinton (1354), who never had any faith in mechanical methods. Further opposition came from POPULAR WIRELESS with a challenge (1171) to Baird (which was wisely ignored), from some daily papers, and from the ELECTRICIAN, whose conservative viewpoint was flavored with criticism (1178) and impartiality concerning some demonstrations (1523). Other criticism came from America (1275, 1459).

The Baird Company's struggle with the authorities to obtain a broadcasting slot and the BBC's stand on the matter came into the open in July

(1347) with the BBC statement that they would be prepared to cooperate with Baird when his apparatus had reached a more developed stage. Some dickering had been going on behind the scenes about demonstrations, which were given to the Post Office on September 18 and to the BBC on October 9. These were followed by announcements on the official position (1535) and a rejoinder (1540) which clearly shut the door on Baird.

In attempts to counteract this unfavorable situation, Baird's supporters took every opportunity to air their views, with letters in the TIMES and articles in TELEVISION. The new periodical provided a natural and sympathetic forum for discussion in aid of television and the Baird interests, particularly by Robinson (1438, 1506), Fleming (1321, 1582), Tiltman (1587), Moseley (1509, 1645), and Gradenwitz (1649), who collectively pleaded the case for Baird while deploring the official restrictions on television developments in Britain. In contrast to this treatment of Baird, the BBC in a surprising move granted Wireless Pictures (1464) permission to broadcast facsimile pictures by the Fultograph system (1547). This service, of little interest or use to the public, added to the Baird-BBC conflict, which, however, was resolved later in 1929 in Baird's favor.

A series of demonstrations throughout the year gave ample proof that television had arrived on the public scene, beginning with Alexanderson's tests with a few home receivers (1110). The Atlantic transmission by Baird and his colleagues in February (1125) was followed by the reception of images from London aboard the liner *Berengaria* early in March (1167). To these "firsts" Baird added daylight pickup on June 11, a color demonstration on July 3 (1352), then a showing of stereo images on August 10 (1403). Bell Labs revealed an improved system in February (1142) and demonstrated daylight pickup in July (1340). Plans for television broadcasts through the RADIO NEWS stations WRNY and WXAL were continually promoted by Gernsback with preliminary notices in April and June, which began to materialize in August (1399). Demonstrations were given in New York that month (1411) and a program schedule appeared in the NEW YORK TIMES on August 21.

Jenkins, who had demonstrated silhouette figures (696) in 1925, came into the news again with a new radio movie system employing a helical drum scanner (1294), first patented (767) in 1927. The pantomime pictures which it produced were reported in May (1259) and broadcasts of these films began through station 3XK on July 2. Transmission of motion picture films over a short wire-radio circuit was demonstrated by Conrad (1395) in August at the Westinghouse laboratories in East Pittsburgh. Somewhat prematurely, the company promised regular programs on the short waves and also announced that they contemplated the commercial production of receivers (1568). A successful transmission of images and sound by the Sanabria system through station WCFL in Chicago was reported in June (1301). A demonstration of motion pictures through the same station was given by Schoenberg in December (1674).

Experimental broadcasts by the General Electric Company through station WGY in Schenectady were disappointing in May (1260) but more successful in June (1296) when a daily test schedule was announced (1302). A milestone was reached in August when New York Governor A.E. Smith accepted the nomination for U.S. President in Albany. With a portable camera on the stand and a wire link to WGY, this was the first outside broadcast of a topical news event (1559). Further success came the following month when G.E. presented a miniature play (1461). This demonstration marked the beginning of studio techniques: portable cameras, special lighting, a control panel for fading and mixing the views, a monitor receiver, and make-up for the performers' faces (1631).

During December a play was presented by the Baird Company. A complete stage scene with three performers and a cat was transmitted from a studio in Long Acre. About this time Baird demonstrated in-house transmission of a cyclist riding his machine in a circle and also a boxing match. A prelude to these staged events was a puppet show (1410) put on in August by the Daven Company at L. Bamberger's store in Newark, N.J. This two-minute symbolic drama, accompanied by music broadcast through station WOR, was the first experiment of its kind. A more noteworthy event, destined to cast a shadow over all the promising disk systems, was Farnsworth's demonstration of his electronic apparatus in San Francisco early in September (1453).

Public interest as well as industrial participation in the progress of television is evident in the trade exhibitions held during the latter half of the year. It was announced in August (1415) that demonstrations planned for the Radio World's Fair in New York would show the public how television works and clear away the "mystery and extravagant claims." According to a later report (1476), television was a major attraction that "thrilled the crowd." Actual displays were given by General Electric, A.J. Carter Company, and the Daven Company, and six kits were available for experimenters (1637). The Baird Company had sets for experimenters on display at Radiolympia in London (1475) and demonstration rooms nearby (1511). Presentations by several well-known performers during these demonstrations were described enthusiastically by Tiltman (1587). Baird also had a display in Rotterdam (1594). At the Radio Show in Berlin, von Mihály demonstrated his apparatus (1450) and Telefunken displayed the Karolus mirror drum system (1514).

Amateurs had contributed to the development and growth of radio earlier in the decade and there was a general belief that they would do the same for television. The potential market for components and for literature on the new hobby appealed to advertisers, publishers, and writers. Parts for assembling a simple shadowgraph machine were offered to the hobbyist by Baird in February (1137). Some twenty articles for the enthusiast appeared in the more popular periodicals throughout the year. These ranged from simple information about scanning disks to detailed instructions for assembling a complete receiver. There were also theoretical articles about neon lamps, photocells, electric motors, synchronizing methods, and scanning. One of the earliest constructional articles (1158) appeared in the first issue of TELEVISION, along with a warning to the reader that a sub-license to build a Baird receiver such as the one described would be required. Several manufacturers were prepared to cater to the needs of the hobbyist with stocks of disks, projection and neon lamps, selenium cells, mirrors, and motors, among them Philips Lamps Ltd., the Peto-Scott Company, and Television Supplies Ltd.

No such patent restrictions existed in America, where hobbyists were building disk receivers essentially the same as Baird's. Constructional articles gave information on components, assemblies, and their operation; often included photos of commercial and experimental equipment; and sometimes offered free blueprints. Details of different disks to be used to receive specific stations were usually given. The choice depended on the locality and the station, since there were variations in the number of scanning lines and number of pictures per second. These ranged from 24 through 45 and 48 to 60, with repetition rates of 7.5, 15, 18, and 21. A table published in October (1493) lists the schedules of eleven stations broadcasting experimental programs on the medium and short waves (448 to 22 m), along with figures for disk apertures and speeds. The first move toward standardizing this variety was taken by the Radio Manufacturers Association in October and reported in December (1665).

Test transmissions in America were on the air for short periods during the daytime and evening. Baird, however, was confined to transmissions after midnight from his experimental station 2TV, which began December 4. There are no reliable figures on amateur participation in any transmissions, but over 2,000 Baird licenses were issued by the end of the year and a similar level of response appeared in the United States. Experimental transmissions in Boston through station WLEX during April and May aroused great interest, which led to the sale of over 2,000 neon tubes and great quantities of sheet aluminum (1373); and another report (1308) mentioned large sales. Station WRNY was swamped by hundreds of enquiries about constructing receivers (1330) and about the availability of receivers (1633). Receivers and kits were advertised by the Daven Company in July; Baird advertised a receiver in June and had three "commercial" versions on display in September. The Pilot Company advertised components in October, and they were also available from the Insuline Company, Jenkins Laboratories, the National Company, and Raytheon Company.

Specifics about the quality of received images are tantalizingly absent in the reports about demonstrations and amateur receptions. In the early days of broadcast radio even the simplest homemade crystal receiver provided the listener with acceptable speech and music, but no equivalent for image reception existed in the case of Televisors in 1928. Many observers criticized the barely distinguishable, streaky, and wavering images displayed on small screens, generally limited to areas of 2 to 6 square inches or somewhat larger with magnifying lenses. Other responses ranged from cautious acceptance of crude pictures to unqualified support of a system or an inventor. Pertinent comments on low definition and its limitations and on the costs of a television service came from several observers.

Technical questions concerning such matters as synchronism, bandwidth, amplification, and radio transmission in the broadcast band and at higher frequencies were brought forward by those who were conversant with the radio art.

Behind these conflicts two important facts were evident: television had arrived, and it offered tremendous possibilities for the future. Independent inventors, industrial teams, financiers, and promoters were in a race for improvements and expansion, which were bound to come. Realization of these prospects is testified by the level of industrial activity and by the formation of new companies by Baird and Jenkins. The rapidity of growth, the broaching of frontiers such as daylight television, color, and stereo, and the inception of studio techniques, film transmissions, test programs, and trade exhibitions illustrate how vigorous the art had become in only three years after Baird first demonstrated visual images in light and shade.

TABLE 13 CHRONOLOGY: 1928

Jan.	13	Alexanderson	Tests with home receivers
Feb.	8	Baird	Transatlantic transmission
	11	Baird	Demonstrates infrared searchlight
	20	Baird	Shadowgraph components on sale
	25	Bell Labs	Improved system with crystal control
Mar.		Television Press	First issue of TELEVISION
	6	Baird	Transmission to ship at sea
Apr.		Jenkins	Drum receiver, pantomime pictures
May	1	Television Society	First general meeting
	11	G.E.	First scheduled service, station WGY
	18	Jenkins	Report on silhouette pictures
June	11	Baird	Daylight transmission
	12	Sanabria	Display at RMA Convention, Chicago
	13	Jenkins	Helical drum scanner
	20	Baird	Color system
		Sanabria	Transmission of sight and sound, station WCFL
	22	Baird Co.	Televisor advertised
		Roberts	Camera tube
	25	Baird	Baird International Television Ltd.
		FRC	Allocation of transmission bands
	26	von Mihály	Report on new system
July		Daven Corp.	Receiver and kits advertised
	2	Jenkins	Radio movies, station 3XK
	3	Baird	Demonstrates color images
	11	Baird	Stereo and color system
	12	Bell Labs	Daylight transmission
		Tihanyi	Electronic system with image intensifier
	16	BBC	Statement on television broadcasting
	22	Baird	Report on Phonovision for sight and sound
	28	Baird	Baird Television Corp.

Aug. 3	FRC	Authorizes experimental transmission bands
8	Conrad	Film transmission, station KDKA
10	Baird	Demonstrates stereo television
21	Daven Corp.	Puppet show, L. Bamberger Co., station WOR
	Gernsback	Demonstration at New York University: regular schedule of station WRNY
22	G.E.	Outdoor pickup, Albany to Schenectady, station WGY
24	Sharma	Camera tube
31	Karolus, von Mihály	Displays at Berlin Radio Show
Sept.	Baird Co.	Display at Industrial Exhibition, Rotterdam
3	Farnsworth	Demonstrates camera and picture tube system
11	G.E.	Broadcast of play "The Queen's Messenger"
17	Gardner	Mirror screw scanner
18	Baird	Demonstration to the Post Office
20	G.E., A.J. Carter, Daven Corp.	Exhibit at New York Radio Show
22	Baird Co.	Display at National Radio Exhibition
23	Jenkins	Matrix system
Oct.	Pilot Co.	Receiver kits advertised
3	Baird	Message band transmission system
9	Baird	Demonstration at the BBC
12	Baird	Optical system for double images
13	RMA	Engineering subcommittee considers standards
18	BBC	Refuses Baird's request for transmission facilities
22	Baird Co.	Reply to BBC statement
25	Walton	Echelon system
30	Fultograph	Facsimile transmission by BBC
Nov. 2	FRC	Regulations for television transmission
4	Baird	Midnight transmissions, station 2TV
Dec. 5	Jenkins	Jenkins Television Corp.
15	Baird	Transmission of play "Box and Cox"
16	FRC	Annual report, including television
17	Schoenberg	Film transmission, station WCFL
22	FRC	Plans to end transmissions in broadcast band

BIBLIOGRAPHY: 1928

1099 "Les appareils de télévision du service Vienne-Berlin" [Television apparatus of the Vienna-Berlin service]. QSTF 9 (Jan): 31.

1100 Dinsdale, A. "The problem of synchronism in television." RADIO N. 9 (Jan.): 750, 751. 2 photos, 2 diags. Baird's method with combined a-c and d-c motors. (1062, 1083, 1106, 1152)

1101 Brittain, W.J. "European progress in television." SCI. PROG. 22 (Jan.): 493, 494. Brief summary of various systems. (1086, 1119)

1102 "Television in the home." SCI. AM. 138 (Jan.): 66. Photo of G.E. phototube. Comments by a noted radio engineer: "I should say we still have a long way to go."

1103 Jones, P.C. "Television." TECH. ENG. NEWS 8 (Jan.): 336, 337, 358. 2 diags. Discussion of basics, methods, and apparatus, including sound.

1104 Jenkins, C.F. "Arc-lamp lens-disk transmitter." U.S. 1,763,357, Jan. 3, 1928, June 10, 1930. Assigned: Jenkins Labs. Film transmission. (1095, 1196)

1105 McCreary. H.J. "Television." U.S. 1,935,649, Jan. 3, 1928, renewed July 2, 1932, Nov. 21, 1933. Assigned: Associated Electric Labs. On an improved photoelectric plate in a camera tube, continuation of a previous patent (587). (1282)

1106 Baird, J.L., and Television Ltd. "Television." Br. 314,591, Jan. 4, 1928, July 4, 1929. Disk with three spiral sets of lenses, each set covered by red, blue, and green filters, for exploring and reconstituting an image by projection of colored light. (1100, 1112)

1107 Bissiri, Augusto. "Transmission of pictures." U.S. 1,713,213, Jan. 4, 1928, May 14, 1929. Assigned: G.E. Screen with a bank of electromagnetically operated pyramidal surfaces.

1108 Dauvillier, A. "La télévision électrique." REV. GEN. 23 (Jan. 7): 5–23; (Jan. 14): 61–73; (Jan. 21): 117–28. 47 illus. Early proposals are reviewed in the first part, with brief description or mention of 45 schemes and numerous references. Issued later as a pamphlet (1533). (1089, 1163)

1109 Farnsworth, P.T. "Photoelectric apparatus." U.S. 1,970,036, Jan. 9, 1928, Aug. 14, 1934. Assigned: Television Labs. In this image dissector tube the light path is normal to the axis. (1079, 1216)

1110 "Radio television to home receivers is shown in tests." N.Y.T. 1 (Jan. 14): 6; 2–5. Tests of Alexanderson's apparatus with receivers in three homes in Schenectady. Transmission from G.E. station WGY on 37.8 m. Scanning disk 24 in. diameter, 48 holes, 18 rps. Images 3 by 3 in. with magnifier, pictures unsteady. Sarnoff declared this "an epoch-making development...television would be an art and an industry in this country in five years." (956, 1111)

1111 "We catch a glimpse of tomorrow." N.Y.T. 20 (Jan. 16): 4. Editorial on the Alexanderson demonstration. (1110, 1113)

1112 "Television across Atlantic declared a fact; Baird's aide reports faces and hands seen." N.Y.T. 1 (Jan. 19): 4, 5. Report by Hutchinson in London on secret tests to New York. These tests had started in April 1927 (915). (1075, 1106, 1116, 1131)

1113 "Schenectady demonstration of improved form of television." ENGINEER 145 (Jan. 20): 75. (1111, 1114)

1114 "Television demonstrated by General Electric Company." ELECT. WORLD 91 (Jan. 21): 164. (1113, 1115)

1115 "Device for seeing by radio is easily attached to sets." N.Y.T. IX 14 (Jan. 22): 1, 2. Alexanderson's apparatus, photo. Brief mention of Baird. (1114, 1116)

1116 "Radio vision takes another step toward the home." N.Y.T. IX 14 (Jan. 22): 1. Alexanderson's demonstration, Baird's transatlantic test. (1112, 1115, 1120, 1150)

1117 Strange, Robert William. "Art of television." U.S. 1,776,298, Jan. 12, 1929, Sept. 23, 1930; Br. 304,730, Jan. 24, 1929, Apr. 3,

1930. In Australia Jan. 25, 1928. Receiver with a scanning drum carrying skewed tracks of apertures, adjustable viewing masks, and several neon lamps intended to furnish two or more different images or portions of one image.

1118 Weiss, E.H. "La télévision." REV. GEN. 23 (Jan. 28): 31.

1119 Brittain, W.J. "Television in America." DISCOVERY 9 (Feb. 2): 43, 44. 2 photos. Alexanderson, Ives, Jenkins. (1101, 1193)

1120 "Researches in Noctovision." DISCOVERY 9 (Feb. 2): 44, 45. Photo. Baird's experiments with infrared and his Phonovision. (1116, 1124)

1121 "Television systems." EXP. W. 5 (Feb.): 107.

1122 "Television is about to emerge from the laboratory." POP. RADIO 13 (Feb.): 106.

1123 De Lacy, B. "Now you can be a 'looker-in.'" POP. RADIO 13 (Feb.): 122–4, 168, 169. 4 illus. Home construction and operation of a receiver. (1158)

1124 "Persons in Britain seen here by television as they pose before Baird's electric eye." N.Y.T. 1 (Feb. 9): 3, 4. Baird transmission from London to Hartsdale, N.Y., Feb. 8–9. From station G2KZ (2 kw) to short-wave station 2CVJ owned by R.M. Hart. (1120, 1125)

1125 "Seeing across the Atlantic." MAN. GUARD. 11:7 (Feb. 10): 9, 10. "Another dream of science was realised in the early hours of yesterday morning when, by means of Mr. Baird's television apparatus, a group of people sitting in a darkened basement in a village outside New York saw the faces of other persons seated in an office in Long Acre, London." Transmission by land line from the Baird laboratory to a radio station (G2KZ) in Purley, thence by radio on 45 m to the short-wave receiving station (2CVJ) of R.M. Hart at Hartsdale, N.Y. Viewers saw the image of a ventriloquist's dummy, then the faces of Baird, of a Press Association reporter (W.C. Fox), and Mrs. Marie Howe, wife of an American reporter who was also present. The viewers, who saw poor but distinguishable moving images about 2 by 3 in., were O.G. Hutchinson, Benjamin Clapp (a Baird Co. engineer), R.M. Hart, and a Reuter's news representative. The latter's telegram, "What America saw," is in the same issue (12:1). (1124, 1126)

"Last night a man and a woman sat before an electric eye in a London laboratory and a group of people in a darkened basement in this village watched them turn their heads and move from side to side. The images were crude and broken, but they were images nevertheless.

"The transformed vision of a man and women in a London laboratory came through the air in the form of the drone of a bee, a musical buzz of irregular cadence representing in sound the lights and shadows of their faces. When the televisor, which looked like a compact black box, had done its work with this rhythmic hum from across the sea, the visions gradually built themselves up out of tiny oblongs of light suspended in a whirling rectangle of brilliance in the machine's mouth. These oblongs shifted and swirled almost unceasingly.

"The first figure to be put before the electric eye was a ventriloquist dummy. Because there was no motion to transmit, the picture of the dummy which appeared in the mouth of the television was much clearer than those of the living person who followed it. A British newspaper representative then went before the electric eye and his image was built up in a televisor in a form suggestive of a lighted 'Jack o'Lantern,' but one which could turn its head from side to side and open its mouth. After this a woman took her place before the transmitter in London and her image, although broken and scattered, was seen here. It was not so clear as that of the man but it was plain that the picture was of a woman and there was no question that she moved her head so that first her full face was visible and then her profile. It was impossible, however, to distinguish her features."

1126 "Inventor elated by Televisor test." N.Y.T. 11 (Feb. 10): 1, 2. Also, "Woman tells of experience," by Mrs. M. Howe, and "Sees television for public," a prediction by Hutchinson. (1125, 1127)

1127 "Transatlantic television. Images transmitted to New York. Mr. Baird's success." TIMES (Feb. 10): 14e. Also, "In London." (1126, 1128)

1128 "Eye taken from boy aided television." N.Y.T. 4 (Feb. 11): 2. Baird's attempt to experiment with a human eye. (1127, 1129)

1129 "Transatlantic television." N.Y.T. 16 (Feb. 11): 3, 4. Editorial on Baird's test transmission. "His success deserves to rank with Marconi's sending of the letter 'S' across the Atlantic. Whatever may be the future of television to Baird belongs the success of having been a leader in its early development." (1128, 1130)

1130 "Invisible ray films planes up in dark." N.Y.T. 21 (Feb. 12): 3, 4. Baird's demonstration in London with infrared searchlight. The British War Office had ended further information so that the secret might be kept for England alone. Baird to demonstrate his "electric eye" device when he visits New York. (1129, 1131)

1131 "Increase of power to aid television." N.Y.T. 23 (Feb. 13): 2. Publicity statement by Hutchinson on 10-kc transmission and life-size images. (1112, 1130, 1132, 1136)

1132 "Television to America." W.W. 22 (Feb. 15): 109. (1131, 1134)

1133 Arnaud, Joseph John. "Television apparatus." U.S. 1,756,232, Feb. 17, 1928, Apr. 29, 1930.

1134 "News and views." NATURE 121 (Feb. 18): 255. Baird's transmission to New York. (1132, 1136)

1135 "Experiences nouvelles concernant la télévision." REV. GEN. 23 (Feb. 18): 51.

1136 "Radio images are glimpsing across the Atlantic. Scotsman's road to television fraught with many obstacles." N.Y.T. IX, 14; 17 (Feb. 19): 1; 2, 3. 3 photos. Feature article on Baird by Hutchinson. (1131, 1134, 1137, 1166)

1137 "Baird puts television on sale, opening branch in Selfridge's; for shadowgraphs only." N.Y.T. 27 (Feb. 21): 2. Components on sale. (1136, 1138)

1138 "Transatlantic television." ELECT. REV. 102 (Feb. 24): 337. (1137, 1139)

1139 "Business items." ELECT. 100 (Feb. 24): 230. "A television section to their wireless department was opened by Selfridge, Ltd., on Monday." (1138, 1147)

1140 Manderfeld, Emanuel C. "Electro-optical image producing system." U.S. 1,874,200, Feb. 24, 1928, Aug. 30, 1932. Assigned: B.T.L. Br. 306,542, Feb. 18, 1929. Disks, neon lamp, a-c and d-c sync.

1141 Marrison, Warren A. and J.W. Horton. "Speed and position control for television apparatus." U.S. 1,860,935, Feb. 24, 1928, May 31, 1932. Assigned: B.T.L. Br. 306,535, Feb. 5, 1929 (E.R.P.). Disk, neon lamp, tuning fork with crystal control. (1076, 1894)

1142 "New device shows television strides." N.Y.T. 10 (Feb. 26): 1, 2. Bell Labs demonstration to members of the American Physical Society and American Optical Society. Quartz crystal oscillators for synchronous control, improved folded multielement display tube 24 by 36 in. (1074, 1170)

1143 "Radio experts doubt suits over television." N.Y.T. 16 (Feb. 28): 3–5. Views of Lee de Forest, Alfred North Goldsmith (1887–1975), and a Bell Labs engineer. "Principles probably too well known to be patentable." (791, 1467, 1470)

1144 "Television, where we stand today." W.W. 22 (Feb. 29): 209.

1145 Phinney, Edward D. "Reproducing optical images at a distance." U.S. 2,110,172, Feb. 29, 1928, Mar. 8, 1938. Assigned: RCA. Br. 306,962, Feb. 27, 1929 (Postal Telegraph-Cable Co.). Multielectrode discharge lamp, distributor, and capacitors for signal storage.

1146 Thuau, Urbain Jules, and Haig Antranikian. "Distant transmission and the reproduction of images." Br. 306,961, Feb. 27, 1929, Feb. 13, 1930. In U.S. Feb. 29, 1928. Lens disk and slotted shutter for film transmission and recording.

1147 Baird, J.S. "The Baird television system." MOD. W. 9 (Mar.): 259–62. (1139, 1160)

1148 Gray, F. "The use of a moving beam of light to scan a scene for television." J. OSA 16 (Mar.): 177–90. 6 illus. Scanning, illumination, optical system, requirements. (1065, 1536)

1149 Valensi, G. "L'Etat actuel du problème de la télévision" [Present state of the television problem]. PRAC. IND. MECH. 10 (Mar.): 485–93. 11 illus. (1069)

1150 "La télévision au foyer est realisée aux Etats-Unis" [Television in the home is realized in the United States]. QSTF 9 (Mar.): 37. (1116, 1151)

1151 Peck, A.P. "Television enters the home." SCI. AM. 138 (Mar.): 246, 247. 5 photos. Alexanderson's disk system. (1150, 1190, 1904)

1152 "Greetings to the world's first television journal." TELEV. 1 (Mar.): 8, 9. Ten letters, with portraits. Published by the Television Press and edited by A. Dinsdale, TELEVISION was the official organ of the Television Society until 1930. (1043, 1100, 1154, 1156)

1153 "Television 1873–1927." TELEV. 1 (Mar.): 10, 11, 23. 3 illus. Brief outline of television progress and photoelectric cells.

1154 "The birth of the Television Society." TELEV. 1 (Mar.): 16. Portraits of Dr. Clarence Tierney, chairman of the Executive Committee, Mr. W.G.W. Mitchell, Lt.-Col. J.R. Yelf. "The Society therefore came into existence to form a common meeting ground for the assistance of the amateur's needs, for lectures, and for professional research workers and others interested in the progress of television." The Society was incorporated July 12, 1930, and became the Royal Television Society in 1966. (1152, 1157)

1155 Rennie, J. Cameron. "Technical notes." TELEV. 1 (Mar.): 17, 23. Diag. (1200)

1156 Dinsdale, A. "Commercial television, when may we expect it?" TELEV. 1 (Mar.): 21. (1152, 1240)

1157 "Join the Television Society." TELEV. 1 (Mar.): 24, 44. Portraits of Viscount Haldane of Cloan (1856–1928), president, Sir James Percy, a vice-president, Miss Mary Proctor, member of council. "There is no shadow of doubt that the Television Society, which was formed on September 7th, 1927, will have very wide and far-reaching results upon the development of the new science." Letter from C. Tierney to the Baird Co. requesting release of their patents for use by amateur constructors and a favorable reply from T.W. Bartlett, secretary. Application form for a sub-license, p. 35; list of eight conditions governing the grant, p. 42, limited to two years. (1154, 1201)

1158 "How to make a simple televisor." TELEV. 1 (Mar.): 29, 30, 33, 34. 3 photos, 9 diags. Scanning disk 20 in. diam. with two semi-spiral sets of 10 holes. Light-chopper disk 10 in. diam. with 50 radial slots. Two 4-v d-c motors, 400-w projection lamp, selenium cell, Osglim neon lamp, and amplifiers. By the Technical Staff. Continued in April (1202). (1123, 1165)

1159 Dumont, M. "Television on the Continent." TELEV. 1 (Mar.): 36, 37. Photo of Belin, system diag. (1085, 1258)

1160 Tiltman, R.F. "Noctovision. Seeing in total darkness by television." TELEV. 1 (Mar.): 40–2. Spectrum diag. (1098, 1147, 1161, 1278)

1161 "Seeing across the Atlantic." TELEV. 1 (Mar.): Supp. Baird's transmission from London to Hartsdale, N.Y. (1160, 1166)

1162 "Television." ELECT. 100 (Mar. 2): 240. "It is certainly gratifying to learn that still another arm of electrical engineering will shortly come into public use."

1163 Dauvillier, A. "Television." ELECT. W. 91 (Mar.3): 468. (1108, 1533)

1164 Roberts, J.H.T. "Television, some authoritative facts." POP. W. (Mar. 3): 7. (1042)

1165 Kendall, G.P. "Building a home 'television' outfit." POP. W. (Mar. 3): 10. (1158, 1184, 1538)

1166 "To test television with more power." N.Y.T. 10 (Mar. 3): 4. On sailing for London, Hutchinson talks of proposed tests between Newark, N.J., and London. (1136, 1161, 1167)

1167 "Televisor on liner shows London picture." N.Y.T. 10 (Mar. 7): 6. Reception tests on board *S.S. Berengaria* by Hutchinson lasted for two hours. Images transmitted from London were remarkably clear at times. Stanley W. Brown, chief radio operator, recognized Miss Dora Selvey, his fiancée. (1166, 1168, 1173)

1168 "Television brings fiancée's living image to *Berengaria's* radio man." N.Y.T. 4 (Mar. 8): 4, 5. (1167, 1169)

1169 "Television at sea, successful experiments." TIMES (Mar. 8): 12d. (1168, 1171)

1170 "Advances in television." SCIENCE 67 (Mar. 9): Supp. 12. Bell Labs system with quartz crystal for sync control. (1142, 1229)

1171 "Wireless television." POP. W. (Mar. 10): 47. A challenge of £1000 to Baird to demonstrate transmission of images of simple objects over not less than 25 yards. The challenge was not accepted. (1169, 1174)

1172 Lodge, O.J. "The problem of television." POP. W. (Mar. 10): 51. (344)

1173 "Sees portable television." N.Y.T. 21 (Mar. 10): 5. Prediction by Hutchinson at Southampton. (1167, 1356)

1174 "Plans television to plane." N.Y.T. II, 2 (Mar. 11): 7. Report on Baird's plan from the DAILY MIRROR, London. (1171, 1175)

1175 "Sea voyagers for first time do not lose sight of land." N.Y.T. IX, 15 (Mar. 11): 7, 8. Tests aboard *S.S. Berengaria*. (1174, 1177)

1176 "Bath is bishop's only privacy, and now he fears television." N.Y.T. 1 (Mar. 13): 2. Remarks by the Bishop of St. Alban's (Dr. M.B. Furse) at Barnet.

1177 "Radio amateurs here catch London picture." N.Y.T. 19 (Mar. 14): 3, 4. Report that Boyd Phelps and Werner H. Olpe received pictures of Miss Selvey and made a record. (1175, 1178, 1630)

1178 "Television and the public; Seeing across the Atlantic; A final word." ELECT. 100 (Mar. 16): 296. Critical editorial comments on Baird publicity with particular reference to the transatlantic test (1125) and the test from *S.S. Berengaria* (1167). "We have nothing but admiration for the progress that has been made, so far, but we do not favour the publicity methods that are at present being employed. We do not think that commonplace home television can be expected for some considerable time to come." ELECTRICIAN and POPULAR WIRELESS criticized Baird's achievements and the dramatized reports in daily papers. (1177, 1183)

1179 Larner, Edgar Thomas. PRACTICAL TELEVISION. London: Ernest Benn; New York: Van Nostrand, (Mar. 16) 1928. 175 pp., 97 illus., including 13 plates. Foreword by J.L. Baird. Introductory and historical matter, selenium, photoelectricity and the photoelectric cell, Continental and American researches, cathode rays, image formation, the Baird Televisor, television technique, and recent developments. Appendix, p. 172, describes Baird's transatlantic test. (1125) 2nd ed., 1929 (2022). (1772)

1180 Adsit, Frank W. "Television device." U.S. 1,796,420, Mar. 19, 1928, Mar. 17, 1931, renewed Mar. 15, 1933, Feb. 24, 1936. Part assigned: James B. Skorstad. Helical mirror drum.

1181 Kell, Ray Davis. "Transmission of pictures." U.S. 1,748,883, Mar. 20, 1928, Feb. 25, 1930, Assigned: G.E. Br. 308,277, Mar. 20, Nov. 21, 1929 (B.T.H.). Disk with spiral segments, rotating shutter, for color. (1266)

1182 "Says costliness sets limits to television." N.Y.T. 40 (Mar. 22): 1. Views of H.E. Ives at

Yale University: "Where we now drop a nickel in the slot to hear a voice, we would have to pay a dollar to see a face." (1080, 1189)

1183 "A television challenge." ELECT. 100 (Mar. 23): 322. Editorial remarks on the POPULAR WIRELESS challenge to Baird (1171). "The fact that the challenge requires television to be conducted over twenty-five yards when Mr. Baird claims to have conquered the Atlantic seems almost absurd...." (1178, 1186)

1184 Harris, Percy W. "Television and the home constructor." POP. W. (Mar. 24): 131. (1165, 1202)

1185 "Television in home predicted in a year." N.Y.T. 25 (Mar. 26): 5. Views of RCA representative.

1186 Brown, S.W. "Seeing across the Atlantic." ELECT. 100 (Mar. 30): 362. Letter by the chief wireless operator, *S.S. Berengaria*. Reception at sea of images sent from London were witnessed by several ship's officers (1249) and passengers (1205). The writer recognized his fiancée Miss Selvey. (1183, 1205)

1187 Dantin, C. "La téléphotographie et la télévision." GENIE CIVIL 92 (Mar. 31): 301–6. 16 illus. On systems by Alexanderson, Belin and Holweck, Bell Labs, Dauvillier, Telefunken-Karolus, Valensi.

1188 Mills, John. THROUGH ELECTRICAL EYES: AN ELEMENTARY EXPOSITION OF THE PHYSICS AND CHEMISTRY INVOLVED IN TELEVISION. New York: Bell Telephone Laboratories, 1928. 40 pp.

1189 "Joint meeting with the Optical Society of America." PHYS. REV. 31 (Apr.): 703. Television demonstration by H.E. Ives at the Bell Telephone Laboratories in New York to members of the American Physical Society and the Optical Society of America. (1182, 1273)

1190 "Television for the home." POP. MECH. 49 (Apr.): 529–31. 4 illus. Alexanderson's system. (1151, 1194)

1191 Koller, Lewis R. "How the photo-electric cell is used for the 'eye' of television." POP. RADIO 13 (Apr.): 298–300, 348. 2 photos, 4 graphs, 2 diags. (1500)

1192 Armagnac, A.P. "Television brought into the home." POP. SCI. 112 (Apr.): 20. (2005)

1193 Brittain, W.J. "Beginnings of television." QUART. REV. 250 (Apr.): 276–82. (1119, 1398)

1194 Rowe, G.C.B: "Television comes to the home." RADIO N. 9 (Apr.): 1098, 1099, 1100, 1156. 8 illus. Alexanderson's disk system and tests in Schenectady. "How well did these faces cover over the air? It was possible to see every detail in the features, the individual teeth, for example; when the eyes were rolled, one could follow with ease the movement of the pupils." (1190, 1204)

1195 "Comments on television." SCI. AM. 138 (Apr): 364, 365.

1196 Jenkins, C.F. "Pantomime pictures by radio for home entertainment." J. SMPE 12 (Apr.): 110–6. 5 illus. Author's transmitter, drum receiver, pantomime pictures on film (Fig. 49). (1104, 1259)

1197 "'Seeing by electricity' in 1880." TELEV. 1 (Apr.): 8, 37. 9 diags. Carey's scheme, ENG. MECH. (June 18, 1880). (133)

1198 "Short waves and television." TELEV. 1 (Apr.): 9.

1199 Monteath, J. Darbyshire. "Invisible rays, the infra red." TELEV. 1 (Apr.): 11–3. 2 photos, 3 diags. Chart of radiant energy. Experiments and applications. (1248)

1200 Rennie, J.C. "The light spot." TELEV. 1 (Apr.): 14, 28. Continued from March. (1439)

1201 "The Television Society." TELEV. 1 (Apr.): 17. Report of founder's meeting. (1157, 1274)

1202 "How to make a simple Televisor." TELEV. 1 (Apr): 22, 23. Continued from March (1158). (1184, 1232)

1203 Ferguson, William A. "Light upon the receiving end." TELEV. 1 (Apr.): 29, 30. Neon tubes.

1204 "The General Electric Company's recent television experiments in America." TELEV. 1 (Apr): 31, 32, 37. 3 photos. (1194, 1260)

1205 Dennis, A.J. "Television in mid-Atlantic, a passenger's story." TELEV. 1 (Apr.): 38. (1186, 1206)

1206 "Transatlantic television." TELEV. 1 (Apr.): 38. Extracts from three American newspapers. (1205, 1207)

1207 "A television romance." TELEV. 1 (Apr.): 42. Photo of Miss Dora Selvey, with caption. (1206, 1313)

1208 Fessenden, R.A., and H.M. Fessenden, executrix. "Television apparatus." U.S. 2,059,222, Apr. 4, 1928, Nov. 3, 1936. Divided from U.S. 2,059,221 (856). Polyhedral mirror drum and message tape.

1209 "Television licences." ELECT. 100 (Apr. 6): 393. "Wireless licences covering experiments in television have been issued to a number of persons."

1210 "Public warned not to expect television within five years." N.Y.T. IX, 13 (Apr. 8): 7. Views of H.B. Richmond (RMA). (2076)

1211 Feingold, Samuel. "Television system." U.S. 1,789,521, Apr. 10, 1928, Jan. 20, 1931. Multichannel piezoelectric system.

1212 O'Connor, S. "Television by cathode rays." POP. W. (Apr. 14): 247. (599)

1213 Baird, J.L., and Television Ltd. "Television apparatus." Br. 320,639, Apr. 16, 1928, Oct. 16, 1929; U.S. 1,890,558, Apr. 2, 1929, Dec. 13, 1932. Various sync methods employing commutators, photocells, relays, flyball speed governor, and black or white line registration. Divided: Br. 320,627 (1214), Br. 320,628 (1215), Br. 320,909 (1225). References to Br. 269,834 (711), Br. 275,318 (761). (1207, 1214)

1214 Baird, J.L., and Television Ltd. "Television apparatus." Br. 320,627, Apr. 16, 1928; U.S. 1,781,800, Apr. 8, 1929, Nov. 18, 1930. Divided from Br. 320,639 (1213). Reflector arrangement allowing movement of subject. (1215)

1215 Baird, J.L., and Television Ltd. "Controlling speed of electric motors for television apparatus." Br. 320,628, Apr. 16, 1928. Divided from Br. 320,639 (1213). Centrifugal governor with two-way switch. (1214, 1217)

1216 Farnsworth, P.T. "Electrical discharge apparatus." U.S. 1,986,330, Apr. 17, 1928, Jan. 1, 1935. Assigned: Television Labs. Improved image dissector tube with magnetic coils, details of construction and mathematical formula. (1109, 1227)

1217 "Americans share Baird's invention." N.Y.T. 26 (Apr. 20): 6. Report from London about radio dealers buying shares in Baird's company; Nathan Felstern of Philadelphia, Herbert Pockress of New York, and Charles Izanstark of Chicago. Plans for publishing a magazine and for equipping steamers of the U.S. Lines with televisors, first on the Leviathan. Inventor says he has adapted moving pictures of singers to phonograph records. (1215, 1218)

1218 "The television challenge." POP. W. (Apr. 21): 282. (1217, 1225)

1219 "American views on television." POP. W. (Apr. 21): 286.

1220 Gannett, D.K., and E.I. Green. "Transmission par fil pour télévision" [Television transmission by wire]. REV. GEN. 23 (Apr. 21): 150. (993, 1396, 3418)

1221 Telefunken. "Television system." Br. 311,075, Apr. 21, 1928. Matrix system for halftone effects. Glow lamps with cathode, anode, and auxiliary electrode connected via two distributors. (1091, 1795)

1222 "Radio vision? Leaders tell when to expect it. Television is evolving at slow but sure pace." N.Y.T. X 15 (Apr. 22): 1–5. Portraits of Alexanderson, Baird, Jenkins; also photo of Jenkins and his "shadowgraph" machine. Feature article with views of experts: L.S. Baker, O.H. Caldwell, L. de Forest, C.F. Jenkins, F.B. Jewett, P.B. Klugh, J.H. Dellinger,

S. Pickard, M.I. Pupin, M.P. Rice, D. Sarnoff. Pessimistic as to early use of radio vision sets in the home. Much research remains to be done. Present apparatus is too complex.

1223 "Television for all planned for this fall." N.Y.T. 18 (Apr. 23): 3, 4. Plans of Joseph B. Ferguson, Newark, N.J., N. Felstern and C. Izanstark for complete receivers on the market in July or August. Plans for broadcast in the fall over 2XAL, the short-wave station of WRNY by the Nakken Television Corp., a new subsidiary of Pilot Electric Mfg. Co., Brooklyn, according to H. Gernsback, owner of the stations. (478, 1058, 1256, 1295)

1224 "Col. Green to test radio television." N.Y.T. 18 (Apr. 23): 7. Plans of E.H.R. Green for tests between South Dartmouth, Mass., and Miami Beach.

1225 Baird, J.L., and Television Ltd. "Television apparatus." Br. 320,909, Apr. 25, 1928. Common drive for scanning disk and phonograph. Divided from Br. 320,639 (1213). Reference to Br. 289,104 (799). (1218, 1236)

1226 Bruni, R. "Television system." Br. 310,424, Apr. 25, 1929. In Italy Apr. 25, 1928. Cathode-ray tube with selenium screen, heated filament and negative reflector, magnetic focusing and beam deflection. Receiver tube with fluorescent screen. Scanning coils operated from the same a-c supplies.

1227 Farnsworth, P.T. "Synchronizing system." U.S. 1,844,949, Apr. 25, 1928, Feb. 16, 1932. Assigned: Television Labs. Camera tube, picture tube, single-channel transmission for vision and sync signals, tuning fork control. (1216, 1453)

1228 Ruzicka, C. "Television system." Br. 316,340, Apr. 25, 1928. Flat-plate sandwich-type cell (Br. 314,834) in a scannerless system; similar cells in both stations. Polished surfaces flooded with light.

1229 Beatty, W.E. (Bell Telephone Laboratories, Inc.). "Television apparatus." Br. 318,160, Apr. 26, 1928. Scanning disk, neon lamp, electron tube circuits with d-c and very-low-frequency picture currents suppressed and reintroduced at the receiver. (1170, 1239)

1230 Nelson, E.L. "Installation radiotélégraphique pour télévision" [Radio transmission system for television]. REV. GEN. 23 (Apr. 28): 157. (994)

1231 "Television notes of the month." MOD. W. 9 (May): 531.

1232 Tait, Robert W. "Experimenting with television." POP. RADIO 13 (May): 363–5. 3 photos, diag. Technical staff's experiments with scanning disk, photocell, neon lamp. (1202, 1234)

1233 Clark, P.L. "Synchronizing television with light beams." POP. RADIO 13 (May): 381–3, 419. 3 illus., including full-page diag. of system showing mirror drums, photocells, and light choppers. (859, 1265)

1234 Harris, Irvin. "Scanning devices, what they do and how to make them." POP. RADIO 13 (May): 389, 390, 431. Photo, diag. Disk, belt. (1232, 1237)

1235 "Cathode-ray television." POP. RADIO 13 (May): 397, 406. 2 photos, diag. Dieckmann's cathode-ray tube. (665)

1236 Davis, H.C. "Attic inventor's magic eye sees across the ocean." POP. SCI. 112 (May): 41. (1225, 1238)

1237 Thomsen, Paul H. "Amateur television." QST 12 (May): 17, 18. 3 diags. Home construction. (1234, 1243)

1238 "Baird television apparatus on sale." RADIO BRD. 13 (May): 11. Baird outfits on sale for $32 at Selfridge's, consisting of the parts for building a shadowgraph transmitter. (1236, 1240)

1239 Secor, H.W. "Quartz crystals control television apparatus." RADIO N. 9 (May): 1230, 1231, 1281–3. 10 illus. Bell Labs modified system with single-channel image transmission and sync control employing crystal oscillators. An improved folded tube (904) with 72 sections and a total of 5,184 tinfoil electrodes is described. (1001, 1229, 1312, 1340)

1240 Dinsdale, A. "Seeing across the Atlantic ocean." RADIO N. 9 (May): 1232, 1233. 2 photos, diag. Account of Baird's tests (1125). (1156, 1238, 1249, 1380)

1241 Fleming, J.A. "Photo electric cells." TELEV. 1 (May): 9–12. 3 photos, 2 diags. (428, 1279)

1242 Crawley, C. "Visible speech across the Atlantic." TELEV. 1 (May): 20, 21. 3 photos. (1322)

1243 "Simple television between two rooms." TELEV. 1 (May): 22–5. 4 photos, diag. By the technical staff. (1237, 1253)

1244 "Methods of synchronism in television." TELEV. 1 (May): 26–9, 36. 3 photos, 2 diags. Isochronism and synchronism, problems, imperfect synchronism, practical details.

1245 "The protection of television inventions." TELEV. (May): 30.

1246 Maxwell, C.B. "Television problems and their solution." TELEV. 1 (May): 34–6. Photo of Baird, 2 diags. Basic problems, methods tried, apparatus, scanning mechanisms, synchronism.

1247 "The Television Society. Report on first formal meeting." TELEV. 1 (May): 37–9. 2 photos. (1201, 1277)

1248 Monteath, J.D. "Natural vision and television. Pt. 1. The rudiments of sight and colour vision." TELEV. 1 (May): 40–2. 5 diags. (1199, 1281)

1249 Sutcliffe, W. "Television in mid-Atlantic." TELEV. 1 (May): 43. Letter by the staff chief engineer written abroad S.S. Berengaria at Southampton, Apr. 9. "I saw rapidly moving dots and lines of orange light which gradually formed themselves into a definitely recognisable face." (1240, 1252)

1250 "Television chain to be formed here." N.Y.T. 16 (May 2): 6. An American syndicate has plans for a broadcasting chain in Canada, U.S., and Mexico. Statements by H. Pockress. (1217)

1251 Johnston, J. "Television apparatus." Br. 321,194, May 3, 1928. Neon lamps with distributor and capacitors to prolong the illumination.

1252 Baird, J.L., and Television Ltd. "Electric discharge lamp." Br. 321,196, May 4, 1928; U.S. 1,800,926, Apr. 5, 1929, Apr. 14, 1931. Neon lamp with ball cathode in front of a concave reflector. (1249, 1257)

1253 "'P.W.' builds the simple Televisor." POP. W. (May 5): 357. (1243, 1274)

1254 Nicolson, A.M. "Two-way television system." U.S. 2,197,005, May 7, 1928, Apr. 16, 1940. Assigned: Comm. Pats. Moving and fixed electrodes produce arc discharges; picture modulation and sync signals transmitted along a single channel. (1066, 2066)

1255 "Caldwell urges television study." N.Y.T. 30 (May 8): 2. Statement by O.H. Caldwell, member FRC. (1525)

1256 "Television by radio to be shown in June." N.Y.T. 24 (May 14): 1. T.H. Nakken on plans for transmissions from station WRNY. (1223, 1262, 1295)

1257 Baird, J.L., and Television Ltd. "Television." Br 317,143, May 15, 1928, U.S. 1,781,210, Apr. 8, 1929, Nov. 11, 1930. Two disks arranged to produce oblong pictures. (1252, 1261)

1258 Etablissements E. Belin et F. Holweck. "Television." Br. 311,743, May 15, 1929. In France May 15, 1928. Vibrating mirror system. (1159, 2404)

1259 "Radio movies." SCIENCE 67 (May 18): Supp. 10. Jenkins drum receiver. The picture is a silhouette and does not show gradations of light and shade. (1196, 1294)

1260 "Television waves pass unnoticed." N.Y.T. IX, 21 (May 20): 1, 2. No reports of images seen from broadcast by station WGY (G.E.). Sale of aluminum and neon lamps reveals great activity in Boston. (1204, 1264)

1261 "British are skeptical." N.Y.T. IX, 21 (May 20): 2. THE POPULAR WIRELESS challenge to Baird (1218). Objects to be recognized by a panel of judges are a series of three faces, five simple solid geometrical models in slow motion, four animal toys grouped and in slow motion, and a tray containing dice and marbles to a number not exceeding twelve. The challenge was later renewed (1333). (1257, 1267)

1262 "Picture broadcasts create interest in television." N.Y.T. IX, 12 (May 27): 1–3. 3 photos. Feature article, general discussion, comments by T.H. Nakken. (1256, 1295)

1263 "Warns Uncle Sam to annex waves." N.Y.T. IX, 13 (May 27): 1, 2. Statement by H.A. Lafount on frequency allocations. (1629)

1264 "Television schedule subject to change." N.Y.T. IX, 13 (May 27): 3. Statement by M.P. Rice on experimental broadcasts from G.E. station WGY. (1260, 1296)

1265 Clark, P.L. "Television apparatus." U.S. 1,776,148, May 29, 1928, Sept. 16, 1930. Mirror drum and slotted disk. (1233, 1731)

1266 Kell, R.D. "Apparatus for transmitting pictures." U.S. 1,778,674, May 29, 1928, Oct. 14, 1930. Assigned: G.E. Br. 312,651, May 29, 1929 (B.T.H.). Receiver disk and a-c motor with electromagnetic sync and manual framing adjustment. Also Br. 312,653, 312,654, May 29, 1929. (1181, 1361)

1267 Baird, J.L., and Television Ltd. "Television apparatus." Br. 318,278, May 31, 1928. Scanning disk serves as a loudspeaker diaphragm. (1261, 1268)

1268 Baird, J.L., and Television Ltd. "Television apparatus." Br. 321,138, May 31, 1928. Transmitter and receiver motor speeds with one a submultiple of the other. (1267, 1270)

1269 Leeming, Harry Toyne. "Recording electrical impulses for producing pictures and sound." U.S. 1,841,540, May 31, 1928, Jan. 19, 1932; Br. 320,900, July 23, 1928, Oct. 23, 1929. Phono recording.

1270 Baird, J.L. "Television." TRANS. INST. ENGRS. & SHIPBLDRS. IN SCOT. 71 (June): 608–14. (1268, 1273)

1271 Swinton, A.A.C. "Television by kathode rays." MOD. W. 9 (June): 595–8. Author's all-electric system, the Schoultz scheme, Zworykin's tube, patents, general discussion, historical notes, bibliography. (805, 1354)

1272 "Radio television." RADIO 10 (June): 9. Critical editorial discussion.

"Undue publicity is being given to the early advent of radio television in the home. It is being announced as 'just around the corner.' Television attachments for present radios are to be sold for $32.50. The full action of a football game may be seen instantaneously in any home during the next season. And so on, *ad nauseam* and *ad bunkum*.

"Such great developments follow a course of gradual evolution. First there came the wire transmission of still pictures, which is now in regular commercial use. Then there came the radio transmission of still pictures which, for limited applications, has also reached the commercial stage. Then there came the marvelous demonstration of wire and radio transmission of television by the Bell Laboratories. But these were of an experimental nature and exceedingly expensive. A single receiving set would cost $50,000 or more, which is hardly practical for general installation in homes. The transmitted images were scarcely recognizable and would never pass muster for a movie fan. But the demonstration, like the early experiments with radio telephony, proved that the feat could be done and verified the predictions of its ultimate practical accomplishment.

"Radio vision today is a scientific curiosity. After some years of research and development it will become a practical reality, not as a cheap attachment to a present day receiver, but as a relatively expensive piece of apparatus. Any tales to the contrary should be liberally salted before being swallowed."

1273 "British skeptical of Baird television accomplishments." RADIO BRD. 19 (June): 69. Critical comments on publicity statement about the transmission to *S.S. Berengaria* and on the POPULAR WIRELESS challenge. (1167, 1171) Reference to a recent statement by H.E. Ives: "bringing into the home by radio an actual spectacle like a great athletic event is unthinkable because its cost would be simply enormous. Television is most effectively accomplished through wire lines and displayed in theatres and auditoriums so that large numbers of people will divide the cost of the presentation." (1189, 1270, 1275, 1338)

1274 "Experimental television." RADIO LISTENERS' GUIDE 3 (June): 70–3, 151, 152. 5 photos, 5 diags. Discussion of disk system and constructional details of a combined transmitter and receiver. (1253, 1280)

1275 "England goes in for television." RADIO N. 9 (June): 1328, 1329. Television display at Selfridge's, with two photos of the store. List of components for a Baird system, with prices. "The Televisor described is a very crude piece of work; it serves as both transmitter and receiver; to avoid synchronizing, the two discs sit on the same spindle. I am afraid that the Baird system is hopeless, after all." (1273, 1276)

1276 "Baird Televisors for America first." TELEV. 1 (June): 7, 8. 3 photos. (1275, 1277)

1277 "The Television Society. Report of first general meeting." TELEV. 1 (June): 9–15. 5 photos, 5 diags. Meeting of May 1 and lecture by Baird, who demonstrated reception of images from the Baird laboratory in Long Acre by radio, despite trouble from interference in the signals. (1247, 1276, 1284, 1449)

1278 Tiltman, R.F. "America leaves us behind again. Television for the home—but not our home." TELEV. 1 (June): 16. (1160, 1503)

1279 Fleming, J.A. "Radiation—visible and invisible." TELEV. 1 (June): 17–20. 5 diags. Radiations, atomic structure, theories, Noctovision. (1241, 1321)

1280 "For the experimenter." TELEV. 1 (June): 21. 2 diags. Experiments with infrared and ultraviolet. By the technical staff. (1274, 1326)

1281 Monteath, J.D. "Natural vision and television. Pt. 2. Visual radiation and experiments." TELEV. 1 (June): 22–4, 33. 6 diags. (1248, 1327)

1282 Pollack, Justin Erwin. (Associated Telephone and Telegraph Co., Inc.). "Television." Br. 318,565, June 1, 1928, Sept. 2, 1929. McCreary color system with triple sets of camera and picture tubes and radio transmission on four frequencies, an improvement of an earlier proposal (587) of 1924. Divided: Br. 318,299 (1283). (1105)

1283 Pollack, J.E. (Associated Telephone and Telegraph Co., Inc.). "Television." Br. 318,299, June 1, 1928, divided from Br. 318,565 (1282). McCreary system. (1606)

1284 Baird, J.L., and Television Ltd. "Selenium cells." Br. 318,295, June 2, 1928. As shown in Br. 300,183 (946), modified with separate photo elements dispersed on the inner surface. (1277, 1285)

1285 Baird, J.L., and Television Ltd. "Television apparatus." Br. 321,389, June 5, 1928, Nov. 5, 1929; U.S. 1,925,554, May 18, 1929, Sept. 5, 1933. Scanning disk with a spiral set of holes in three sections, slip rings and three-section commutator, three color-sensitive (blue, red, green) photocells, and colored lights for illuminating the object. Three color lamps and corresponding components in the receiver, with image analysis and reconstitution in a series of overlapping bands. (1284, 1286)

1286 Baird, J.L., and Television Ltd. "Television apparatus." Br. 322,481, June 6, 1928, Dec. 6, 1929. Disks with rectangular holes. (1285, 1287)

1287 Baird, J.L., and Television Ltd. "Television apparatus." Br. 322,776, June 9, 1928. Multicell color system with multiturn spirals, three color lamps. (1286, 1288)

1288 "Plans television program. J.L. Baird expects to broadcast for first time in September." N.Y.T. 21 (June 11): 2. (1287, 1297)

1289 Tihanyi, Kalman (Koloman) (1898–1947). "Television apparatus." U.S. 2,158,259, June 10, 1929, divided Mar. 8, 1935, May 16, 1939. Assigned: RCA. Br. 313,456, June 11, 1929. In Germany June 11, 1928. V-shaped tube with photo mosaic scanned by electron beam. (1290)

1290 Tihanyi, K. "Television apparatus." U.S. 2,133,123, June 10, 1929, divided from U.S. 2,158,259 Mar. 8, 1935, Oct. 11, 1938. In Germany June 11, 1938. Image carrier with light-sensitive elements on a conductive mesh, and a fluorescent viewing screen. (1289, 1339)

1291 Hough, C.W. "Picture transmission and reception system." U.S. 1,996,963, June 12, 1928, Apr. 9, 1935. Assigned: Wired Radio. For transmitting motion picture film. (1023, 2500)

1292 Thurm, L. "Television system." Br. 313,504, June 12, 1929. In France June 12, 1928. Multifrequency with photocells, tuning forks, lamps in receiver. Reference to Br. 284,717 (876). (1088, 1313)

1293 "Television method shown in Chicago." N.Y.T. 32 (June 13): 2. Display by Ulysses (Ulises) A. Sanabria at the fourth annual Radio Manufacturers Association Convention, second annual Radio Trade Show. (1301)

1294 Jenkins, C.F. "Helical drum scanner." U.S. 1,730,976, June 13, 1928, Oct. 8, 1929. Assigned: Jenkins Labs. Receiver scanning drum with multiturn spiral of holes, multi-element neon lamp at the axis and light pipes from the lamp elements to the spiral tracks, with distributor. Reference to earlier patent (767). (1259, 1348)

1295 "Performers at WRNY to be seen over radio." N.Y.T. 10 (June 16): 2. Statements of H. Gernsback and T.H. Nakken at Hotel Roosevelt on plans for alternate transmissions of vision and sound. (1223, 1256, 1262, 1317, 1330)

1296 "Radio sends moving image. Experiments in television reported successful at Roselle Park, N.J." N.Y.T. 22 (June 20): 2. An image with a grotesque shape flitted across the screen at Roe Radio and Electric Shop, received from the G.E. station WGY. (1264, 1302). The only other station transmitting television signals is WLEX, Lexington, Mass. (1373)

1297 Baird, J.L., and Television Ltd. "Television apparatus." Br. 319,304, June 20, 1928, Sept. 20, 1929. Images of different areas are provided by disks with two or more concentric spiral sets of holes, lenses, or mirrors with different pitch and spacing of apertures. Divided: Br. 319,307 (1298), Br. 320,687 (1299), Br. 321,961 (1300). (1288, 1298)

1298 Baird, J.L., and Television Ltd. "Television apparatus." Br. 319,307, June, 20, 1928, Sept. 20, 1929. Divided from Br. 319,304 (1297). Scanning disk with spiral set of apertures in three sections, with color filters for the apertures in each section (blue, red, green). Three color lamps selectively connected by slip rings and segmented commutator, with a single-spiral disk for reception of colored images. (1287, 1335) Baird demonstrated color images with similar apparatus on July 3 (1352). (1297, 1299)

1299 Baird, J.L., and Television Ltd. "Television apparatus." Br. 320,687, June 20, 1928. Divided from Br. 319,304 (1297). Receiver combined with phonograph with two pick-ups and switches. Reference to Br. 289,104 (799). (1298, 1300)

1300 Baird, J.L. and Television Ltd. "Television apparatus." Br. 321,961, June 20, 1928. Divided from Br. 319,304 (1297). Adjustable photocell mounting. (1299, 1303)

1301 "Broadcast scene and sound." N.Y.T. 28 (June 21): 6. Successful reception several miles from station WCFL, Federation of Labor, Chicago. Simultaneous transmission of sight and sound by the system of U.A. Sanabria and M.L. Hayes. (1293, 1307, 1431)

1302 "Thinks television available in weeks." N.Y.T. 20 (June 22): 6. Report of images about 1-in. square clearly received in New Jersey from station WGY, Schenectady, on

380 m. Test schedule: 1.30–2.00 p.m., Tuesday, Thursday, Friday. (1296, 1308)

1303 "Television for all. A Baird 'seeing-in' set for £25." TIMES (June 22): 23f, g. Advertisement: "The Baird Televisor, which has been successfully demonstrated to radio and commercial experts, and will be on sale at the Radio Exhibition in September. To be shown at the Netherlands Industrial Exhibition, now being held." Portrait of Baird and a photo of a table set, a box with sloping top corners. (1300, 1311)

1304 Roberts, Coryton Ernest Carr. "Television and telephotographic apparatus." Br. 318,331, June 22, 1928, Sept. 5, 1929. A camera tube with a photoelectric image plate (cathode) and an anode plate with a central aperture behind which is a collector electrode. The electron stream from the cathode is swept across the anode by external deflection coils. Variations include a rotatable cathode and a gas-filled chamber behind the anode intended to increase the signal current by ionization. The structure of the photo-cathode is not specified.

1305 "Television developments." POP. W. (June 23): 558.

1306 Davis, Robert L. "Television." U.S. 1,797,259, June 23, 1928, Mar. 24, 1931. Assigned: Westinghouse. Br. 314,074, June 17, 1929. Receiver cabinet with scanning disk, motor, adjustable neon lamp, and viewing lens. (1788)

1307 "Chicago flier plans test of television in airplane." N.Y.T. II (June 24): 1, 2. Alva J. Carter, radio engineer of station WCFL. (1301, 1431)

1308 "'Sight' tubes aid image broadcasts." N.Y.T. IX, 13 (June 24): 1, 2. Neon tubes (Oramatrons), invented by D.M. Moore, engineer with G.E. at Harrison, N.J. Thousands have been sold within last few weeks, according to station WGY. (1051, 1302, 1316, 1414)

1309 "Hungarian develops simplified television." N.Y.T. 12 (June 26): 2. Von Mihály in Berlin uses a disk and a Wolfram point lamp. (899, 1357)

1310 "Radio Board lists television bands." N.Y.T. 28 (June 26): 2. Allocation by the FRC of 6000–23,000 kc. (970, 1355)

1311 "Television and photo-broadcasting." ELECT. 100 (June 29): 728. Editorial comments on publicity about Baird and on the picture broadcast (facsimile) system of Capt. Otto Fulton. (1303, 1320, 1464)

1312 Secor, H.W., and J.H. Kraus. ALL ABOUT TELEVISION. New York: Experimenter Publishing Co., Summer 1928. 32 pp., illus. Called Vol. I, No. 2, this is a supplement containing reprints of articles published after the 1927 issue. (1001, 1239, 2126)

1313 Thurm, L. "Un nouveau système de télévision et de télécinématographie." QSTF 8 (July): 55–7. Illus. (1292, 1554)

1314 Clarkson, R.P. "What hope for real television?" RADIO BRD. 13 (July): 125–8. 2 photos, 8 diags. Visual transmission, picture requirements, image size, scanning problems, and author's proposed version of Swinton's cathode-ray system. (1318)

1315 "No innovations or revolutions for 1928." RADIO BRD. 13 (July): 130. General discussion, views on progress and publicity, statements by F.B. Jewett, M.I. Pupin, J.H. Dellinger, L. de Forest, C.F. Jenkins, D. Sarnoff, P.W. Harris.

1316 "Progress in television." RADIO BRD. 13 (July): 130. Editorial on G.E. schedule of transmissions from station WGY. "It is probable that some other transmissions, made by Nakken, Jenkins, Baird and others will be on the air within a reasonable length of time." (1308, 1361, 1391)

1317 Nakken, T.H. "Practical demonstrations scheduled for WRNY." RADIO N. 10 (July): 20, 21, 84. 5 photos. General details of apparatus and proposed broadcasts. (1295, 1319)

1318 Clarkson, R.P. "Vacuum cameras to speed up television." RADIO N. 10 (July): 22, 23,

76, 77. 4 illus. Mainly on the author's plan reviving the Swinton system. (1314, 1369)

1319 "2XAL to broadcast television." SCI. AM. 139 (July): 77. Short-wave radio station of WRNY, work by Nakken Television Corp., subsidiary of Pilot Electric Mfg. Co. Plans for the fall and production of receivers. (1317, 1330, 1370)

1320 "The future of television." SCI. AM. 139 (July): 78. On comments by Baird. (1311, 1321)

1321 Fleming, J.A. "The inventor of the 'Fleming valve' visits the now world-famous Baird laboratory." TELEV. 1 (July): 5–7. 4 photos. Daylight television, Noctovision, Phonovision, light-spot system, sync, equipment operation. (1279, 1320, 1325, 1582)

1322 Crawley, C. "Wavelengths for television." TELEV. 1 (July): 8, 9, 19. 3 photos. Short waves essential for television. (1242, 1516)

1323 "Television today." TELEV. 1 (July): 10.

1324 Mitchell, W.G.W. "Lecture on light-sensitive cells." TELEV. 1 (July): 16, 31–6. 2 photos, 10 diags. (1515)

1325 "The Baird television system in America." TELEV. 1 (July): 20–2. 5 photos. Baird Television Development Corp., New York; B.W. Sangor, C. Izanstark, W.J. Jarrard, O.G. Hutchinson. (1321, 1328)

1326 "The marking out and construction of spiral discs." TELEV. 1 (July): 25, 26, 30. 3 diags. (1280, 1368)

1327 Monteath, J.D. "Natural vision and television. Pt. 3. Phenomena in vision." TELEV. 1(July): 27–9. 8 diags. (1281, 1382)

1328 "A new television company." TELEV. 1 (July): 30. Baird International Television Ltd. was founded on June 25 with a capital of £700,000. Particulars of shares, market value, subscriptions, and company directors; Rt. Hon. Lord Ampthill, Sir Edward Manville, Lt.-Col. George Bluett Winch, J.L. Baird, O.G. Hutchinson. (1325, 1329)

1329 "An office boy's part in television experiments." TELEV. 1 (July): 37. Portrait of W. Taynton, the 15-year-old boy whose face was the first living image seen in a television receiver by Baird in October 1925. (733, 1328, 1333, 1781)

1330 "Interest increasing in radio television. Station WRNY reports flood of inquiries on construction of receiving apparatus." N.Y.T. 8 (July 4): 6. Hugo Gernsback says over 2,000 letters received in two weeks. (1295, 1319, 1370, 1371)

1331 Chalfin, Philip, and Benjamin Chalfin. "Apparatus for reproducing images at a distance." U.S. 1,790,038, July 5, 1928, Jan. 27, 1931.

1332 Wiley, H.W. "Hybrid words." SCIENCE 68 (July 6): Supp. 15. "The word I have in view now is 'television.' Can anything worse be imagined?" Teloptiky, telopsis are proposed. (1051, 1570)

1333 "Television again!" POP. W. (July 7): 618. Repetition of challenge to Baird. (1329, 1335)

1334 Rogers, F.H. (Skala Research Laboratories.) "Television." Br. 322,504, July 9, 1928. Skala system (619).

1335 Baird, J.L., and Television Ltd. "Television apparatus." Br. 321,441, July 11,1928, Nov. 11, 1929. Disks with two or more spiral sets of apertures covered with colored light filters for stereoscopic and three-color transmission. Divided, Br. 322,822 (1336), Br. 322,823 (1337). (1333, 1336)

1336 Baird, J.L., and Television Ltd. "Television apparatus." Br. 322,822, July 11, 1928, Dec. 11, 1929. Divided from Br. 321,441 (1335). Spirals of neon lamps or circular discharge tubes with multiple electrodes mounted on disks with slip rings and distributors to obtain large receiver images. (1337)

1337 Baird, J.L., and Baird Television Ltd. "Television apparatus." Br. 322,823, July 11, 1928. Divided from Br. 321,441 (1335). Three-color receiver with discharge lamps: helium, mercury vapor, neon. (1336, 1352)

1338 Ives, H.E. "Electro-optical transmission." U.S. 1,989,618, July 11, 1928, Jan. 29,

1935. Assigned: B.T.L. Br. 315,308, July 3, 1929 (E.R.P.). Multichannel system with scanning disks and neon lamp; alternative large neon lamp (1010) and film scanning. (1273, 1624)

1339 Tihanyi, K. "Television apparatus." Br. 315,362, July 10, 1929. Complete not accepted. In Hungary July 12, 1928. This extensive specification concerns an electronic system with many variations of the proposed constructions for a camera tube, an image intensifier, picture tube, and circuits as shown in 68 diagrams and covered by 127 claims. Various substances are specified for the image carrier or photo matrix: selenium layers, alkali metal, zinc sulfide and copper, or crystalline particles. For color applications, three different photo-ohmic or crystalline spots, each sensitive to a primary color, are deposited next to one another in groups on the image carrier. (1290)

1340 "Television shows panoramic scene carried by sunlight." N.Y.T. 1 (July 13): 4;10:3, 4. Demonstration of daylight television by Bell Labs. Picture about 2 1/2 in. square. (1239, 1344)

1341 Nyquist, Harry. "Electro-optical system." U.S. 1,773,785, July 13, 1928, Aug. 26, 1930. Assigned: AT&T. Br. 315,417, July 9, 1929, Oct. 9, 1930 (E.R.P.). Apertured disks, one with the usual spiral of holes and the other with holes in arcuate sections arranged to scan nonadjacent lines. Intended to reduce ghost images due to mutual interference, to provide secret transmissions, and to form a complete two-way system. See also Br. 336,267.

1342 Corbett, Lawrence W. "B.B.C. and television." POP. W. (July 14): 655. 2 photos. Interview with Capt. Peter Pendleton Eckersley (1892–1963), chief engineer (1923–1929), British Broadcasting Corp. Eckersley had doubts about a sufficient demand existing for a television service and also believed that "a radical discovery is necessary before television will be practicable, just as the valve made broadcasting possible." (1347, 1479, 1556)

1343 "Television—the position today." POP. W. (July 14): 668.

1344 "Progress of television. New device demonstrated in New York." TIMES (July 14): 13b. Bell Labs daylight demonstration. (1340, 1345)

1345 "Radio and sunlight join for television." N.Y.T. IX, 16 (July 15): 7. Bell Labs. (1344, 1359)

1346 "Television explained by R.H. Langley, Director, Engineering, Crosley Radio Corp." N.Y.T.: IX, 16 (July 15): 8. (1009)

1347 "Television." MAN. GUARD. 10 (July 16): 6. A response to publicity and rumors on the development of television in which the BBC discounts any suggestion that it will take part in television transmissions. (1342, 1349)

1348 Jenkins, C.F. "Cell persistence transmitter." U.S. 1,756,291, July 16, 1928, Apr. 29, 1930, reissue Apr. 16, 1932, Apr. 2, 1940. Assigned: Jenkins Labs, RCA. Photocell matrix with image signals stored in capacitors which are connected sequentially to the transmission channel by distributors. (1294, 1372)

1349 "B.B.C. and television." W.W. 23 (July 18): 69. (1374, 1439)

1350 Donle, Harold P. "Television apparatus." U.S. 1,826,305, July 18, 1928, Oct. 6, 1931. Receiver with scanning disk, friction disk, brake and ball governor. (1471)

1351 Levy, L. "Television system." Br. 315,795, July 17, 1929. In France July 18, 1929. Photocell, slotted disk, arc light, Kerr cell, and neon lamp. Includes film transmission.

1352 Tierney, C. "Television by daylight." TIMES (July 19): 12e. Letter referring to news of the Bell Labs demonstration (1344). "Television by daylight was demonstrated in this country over a month ago. I was myself present on two occasions when the image of a person illuminated only by dull daylight was transmitted from the roof of the Baird Laboratories in Long Acre to the laboratory four floors beneath. Several demonstrations have since been witnessed not only of daylight television, but of the still more notable achievement of Baird, the transmission and reception of objects in natural colour." Baird demonstrated daylight pickup on June 11 and color on July 3. (1337, 1356, 1379) Bell Labs demonstrated images in color June 27, 1929 (1933).

1353 Baker, T.T. "Television; review of the present stage of development." ELECT. REV. 103 (July 20): 96–8. 4 illus. Overview, mechanical scanning, Baird and Bell Labs systems. (840, 2732)

1354 Swinton, A.A.C: "Television. Methods of reproducing pictures." TIMES (July 20): 10a. Comments on correspondence and mechanical methods. (1271, 1390)

1355 "Stations licensed for television." N.Y.T. 16 (July 21): 2. Issued for Jenkins (3XK), J.S. Dodge (1XAY); construction permits for seven others. (1310, 1435)

1356 "Soon to demonstrate Baird television here." N.Y.T. 16 (July 21): 4, 5. Statement by Hutchinson on demonstrations by Baird Television Development Corp. and American rights. (1173, 1352, 1358)

1357 Telehor A.-G., and D. v. Mihály. "Electric synchronous movements." Br. 315,859, June 21, 1929. In Germany July 21, 1928. Disk, phonic wheel, manual phase adjustment. (1309, 1450)

1358 "Record reproduces scenes with music." N.Y.T. 10 (July 22): 1, 2. Hutchinson describes Phonovision with double-grooved records. "The entire world will be 'televised.'" Plans for manufacturing plants in New York and Chicago. (1356, 1366, 1697)

1359 "Television's radio camera takes panoramic scenes. Radio 'eye' made sensitive, television works outdoors." N.Y.T. VIII, 12 (July 22): 1–3. 4 photos. Bell Labs demonstration. (1345, 1434)

1360 Robinson, J. "Television." TIMES (July 24): 12c. Reply to Swinton's letter (1354), with comment on dot versus strip (line) theory. Saw color images with 15 strips and monochrome images with 30 strips at Baird's laboratory. (1402)

1361 Alexanderson, E.F.W., and R.D. Kell. "Transmission of pictures." U.S. 1,783,031, July 24, 1928, Nov. 25, 1930. Assigned: G.E. Br. 316,179, July 1, 1929 (B.T.H.). Two disks with Kerr cell. (1266, 1316, 1429, 1849)

1362 C. Lorenz A.-G. "Electric synchronous movements." Br. 316,178, June 18, 1929. In Germany July 24, 1928. Receiver with sync lamp, stroboscopic disk, and eddy-current brake. Sync signals separated from visual signals by filter circuits. (825, 1820)

1363 Mathes, R.C. "Electro-optical image production." U.S. 1,760,159, July 24, 1928, May 27, 1930. Assigned: B.T.L. A charge-storage system (with Nipkow disk) whereby the photocell output is stored in capacitor groups which are selectively connected via distributors and commutators to a transmission channel. A similar arrangement at the receiver has a bank of lamps which are illuminated in interlaced or intermixed sequences. (1081, 1364)

1364 Mathes, R.C. "Signaling system and method." U.S. 2,103,481, July 24, 1928, Dec. 28, 1937. Assigned: B.T.L. Scanning disk and distributor for multichannel transmission, with distributor and amplifiers for a multipoint display. (1363)

1365 Mertz, P. "Television." U.S. 1,806,638, July 24, 1928, May 26, 1931, reissue May 17, 1932, Jan. 12, 1937. Assigned: AT&T. Br. 316,185, July 19, 1929, June 26, 1930 (E.R.P.). Perforated disks with a spiral of holes or spiral segments arranged to provide overlapped scanning paths. (997)

1366 "Launch television here. Delaware men incorporate to push production of Baird devices." N.Y.T. 5 (July 29): 6. Charters for Baird Television Corp., and Baird Parent, Inc. Engineers are C.I. Bingley and B. Clapp. (1358, 1378)

1367 Joy, Henry William. "Electrical transmission of colored pictures." U.S. 1,929,589, July 30, 1928, Oct. 10, 1933. Disks with a spiral set of apertures in groups of two or three covered by red-orange and blue-green, or red, green, and blue filters. Kerr cell light valve, drive by synchronous motors.

1368 Westman, Harold P. "Some more about amateur television." QST 12 (Aug.): 30, 32. Practical details on disks. (1326, 1548)

1369 Clarkson, R.P. "What can we see by radio?" RADIO BRD. 13 (Aug.): 185–7. 3 photos, 2 diags. Nipkow disk, image size (1 1/4 in. square with Raytheon neon lamp), frequency bandwidth, objects, images, and magnifiers, disk layout for reception from station WGY, synchronism. (1318)

1370 Felix, E.H. "Station WRNY will send television images under the supervision of Theodore Nakken." RADIO BRD. 13 (Aug.): 198. Brief note; 10 images per sec. on 380 meters. (888, 1319, 1330, 1399, 1546, 2651)

1371 Gernsback, H. "What to expect of television." RADIO N. 10 (Aug.): 103. "The ideal television receiver of the future will have no moving parts at all. What we probably will have is some sort of a cathode tube...there is no doubt that the built-up picture...will be far superior to what we have today." (1330, 1399)

1372 "Radio movies and television for the home." RADIO N. 10 (Aug.): 116–8, 173. 6 illus. Jenkins' radio movie transmitter with lens disk and motion picture film, receiver drum with quartz rods, multielement neon tube, four-segment commutator, angular mirrors, and magnifying viewing lens. (1348, 1428)

"Early in May of this year, C. Francis Jenkins, the noted radio inventor, demonstrated in Washington, D.C., his latest system of radio photography, or rather 'radio movies,' as he prefers to describe it. Using a wavelength of 300 meters, in the regular broadcast band, he transmitted a number of reels of specially-prepared standard-size motion-picture film, while members of the Federal Radio Commission and a number of nationally prominent individuals looked on.

"A private demonstration was arranged for a member of the staff of RADIO NEWS, who was very favorably impressed by what he saw. The original film showed, in black and white silhouette, a little girl bouncing a ball, dancing and kicking into the air. It was reeled off in front of the radio-movie transmitter at the rate of 15 pictures per second, the pictures at the receiving end being reproduced at the same rate. The image seen through the observing lens at the receiver was, apparently, about six inches square, and remarkably clean cut. In most of the systems of television and picture-transmission shown up to this time, it has been usually difficult for the observer to determine whether he is seeing the image of a rolled newspaper or that of a man scratching his nose; but with the Jenkins apparatus the definition is so good that the images are instantly recognizable. The illusion of motion is excellent; almost as good, in fact, as that produced by a regular motion picture thrown on a screen.

"It is the present plan of the inventor to produce the complete radio-movies instrument on a commercial basis and to sell it as an accessory to the regular broadcast receiver, as a device for home amusement.... The apparatus does work well, and its possibilities are numerous. There is no reason why it cannot be extended eventually to operate as a true television machine; that is, to transmit (and receive) the images of people as the latter stand in front of the televisor in the studio."

1373 "Television experiments in Boston create great interest." RADIO N. 10 (Aug.) 118. Experimental broadcasts sponsored by the BOSTON POST from short-wave transmitter of station WLEX, Lexington, Mass. (1296)

1374 "Scanning disc made for television." RADIO N. 10 (Aug.): 124, 125. Daven Radio Corp. disks, 12 and 18 in. diam., 24 and 36 holes, for receiving signals from stations WGY and WRNY. (1410)

1375 "Large neon tube now made for television." RADIO N. 10 (Aug.): 125. 3 diags. Raytheon Mfg. Co. (1377)

1376 Marcotte, E. "Téléphotographie et télévision." REV. IND. 58 (Aug.): 477–9. Description of various systems.

1377 "For television experimenters." SCI. AM. 139 (Aug.): 169, 170. Raytheon Kino lamp (neon tube) and Foto-Cell. Statement by Delbert E. Replogle on research program; C.G. Smith, inventor of the Raytheon tube. (1375, 1420, 1430)

1378 Church, Archibald. "Do we encourage genius?" TELEV. 1 (Aug.): 5, 6, 8. Baird's demonstrations, problems, and critical opposition in Britain. (1366, 1379, 1707)

1379 Tierney, C. "My impressions of daylight and colour television." TELEV. 1 (Aug.): 7, 8. (1352, 1378, 1389, 1733)

1380 Dinsdale, A. "Recent advances in television; television by daylight and television in colours." TELEV. 1 (Aug.): 9, 10, 26. 3 photos, diag. (1240, 1682)

1381 Desmond, Shaw. "Seeing round the world." TELEV. 1 (Aug.): 11–4. Prospects, possibilities, usages. (1445)

1382 Monteath, J.D. "Natural vision and television. Pt. 4." TELEV. 1 (Aug.): 15–8. Photo, 9 diags. Color vision, experiments, color images, color television. (1327, 1448)

1383 Byrne, Louis. "Some thoughts on the invention of daylight television." TELEV. 1 (Aug.): 19, 20.

1384 Tschörner, Ludwig. "Television apparatus." Br. 319,115, Aug. 15, 1928; U.S. 1,779,863, Sept. 19, 1928, Oct. 28, 1930. In Austria Aug. 1, 1928. Multiple spiral apertures and moving ruled screen. (2106)

1385 De Wet, Pieter Justinus. "Apparatus for television." Br. 319,454, Aug. 2, 1928, Sept. 26, 1929. This specification from South Africa covers the mechanical assembly of a camera-projector employing disks with various radial slots, with or without a fine mesh screen, a light-chopper disk, a sliding shutter and V-shaped aperture, centrifugal speed governor, friction clutch, and brake and projection lamp in the receiver. Color analysis is included in the claims, along with photo registration, turret lenses, and screen projection. (3723)

1386 "Perfection of television nearer as result of new light cell that speeds transmission." N.Y.T. 19 (Aug. 3): 4, 5. Karolus cell. (1097, 1388)

1387 Morrison, Frederick C. "Reproducing sound waves and light waves." U.S. 1,842,420, Aug. 3, 1928, Jan. 26, 1932. Combined optical and audio receiver on a movable stand.

1388 "High cost forecast for new television." N.Y.T. 6 (Aug. 4): 5, 6. On the Karolus mirror drum system; Bell Labs engineers refuse comment. (1386, 1424)

1389 "Daylight television, a new Baird system." POP. W. (Aug. 4): 746. (1379, 1392)

1390 Swinton, A.A.C. "Television." TIMES (Aug. 4): 8a. Reply to Robinson's letter (1360). Decries any possibility of success by mechanical means. (1354, 1391)

1391 "Television. Broadcast service difficulties." TIMES (Aug. 8): 6e. Comments on Swinton's letter and on the General Electric Company's progress in the United States. (1316, 1390, 1408, 1461)

1392 "Baird Television Corporation of Delaware." N.Y.T. 22 (Aug. 9): 4. Note about acquisition of the Baird Television Development Corp. of New York. (1389, 1394)

1393 Sharma, Devendra Nath. "Television, picture transmission, telecinematography." Br. 321,935, Aug. 9. 1928, Nov. 11, 1929. Images are recorded on fluorescent film which is scanned by cathode or Lenard rays; the light variations are then projected onto a photocell. The transmitter assembly includes facilities for processing the film from developing to drying and storage. Sound recording by a "talking strip" alongside the image strip is also specified. (1417)

1394 "Radio Exhibition." ELECT. 101 (Aug. 10): 164. List of exhibitors includes Baird Television Development Co., stands 11, 13, 14 (1392, 1403)

1395 "Transmission of film by wireless. Demonstration in U.S." TIMES (Aug. 10): 126. Demonstration by Frank Conrad (1874–

1941) of the Westinghouse system at East Pittsburgh, Aug. 8. Signals transmitted 2 miles by wire and 2 miles by radio. Images (60/16) received on a 10-by-12-in. ground-glass screen. (1397)

1396 Gannett, D.K. "Electro-optical system." U.S. 1,730,416, Aug. 10, 1928, Oct, 8, 1929, Assigned: AT&T. (1220)

1397 "'Radio movies' are demonstrated at East Pittsburgh." ELECT. W. 92 (Aug. 11): 276. (1395, 1407)

1398 Brittain, W.J. "A new television development." POP. W. (Aug. 11): 770. (1193, 1589)

1399 "WRNY to start daily television broadcasts. Radio audiences will see studio artists." N.Y.T. 19 (Aug. 13): 4, 5. "The first regular broadcasting of images by television over the radio for New York will begin tomorrow." Experimental transmissions were made Aug. 12. H. Gernsback estimates there are about 2,500 sets in the metropolitan area. (1370, 1371, 1411)

1400 Ballard, Harry W., and Jack F. Ballard. "Scanning device for television." U.S. 1,773,161, Aug. 13, 1928, Aug. 19, 1930. Cylinder with a helical series of apertures.

1401 "Public must wait for television." N.Y.T. 27 (Aug. 14): 2–3. RMA plans to provide public information. (1459)

1402 Robinson, J. "Television; means of transmission." TIMES (Aug. 15): 8c. Reply to Swinton's letter. (1360, 1438)

1403 "News in brief." ELECT. 101 (Aug. 17): 179. Baird's demonstration of stereoscopic television to the press on Aug. 10. Photo, p. 189. (1394, 1404)

1404 Russell, A. "Television." NATURE 122 (Aug. 18): 232–4. Review of Larner's book (1179), historical notes, outline of Baird's progress, and description of Baird's recent demonstration of color. "The coloured images we saw which were obtained in this way were quite vivid. Delphiniums and carnations appeared in their natural colours, and a basket of strawberries showed the red fruit very clearly." (874, 1403, 1409)

1405 Besson, M. "Television apparatus." Br. 317,709, Aug. 19, 1929. In France Aug. 18, 1928. Disk with a spiral of holes, another with a spiral slot. Visual signals supplied to a loudspeaker, thence to a microphone and radio transmitter. Electromagnetic shutter receiver. In addition to phono recording, applications include transmission from an aircraft or a submarine.

1406 Peterson, E.L. "Transmitting system." U.S. 1,747,791, Aug. 18, 1928, Feb. 18, 1930. Assigned: Ray-O-Vision Corp. of America. Br. 317,475, July 29, 1929. Two mirror drums and a special light cell produce changes in the wavelength and intensity of the transmitted signal. The receiver contains a mirror drum, a composite neon tube with actuating inductance, a light cell, and a luminescent tube.

1407 "Motion picture transmitter." N.Y.T. VIII, 17 (Aug. 19): 3–5. Photo of Conrad and apparatus demonstrated at the Westinghouse Co., East Pittsburgh. (1397, 1488)

1408 Swinton, A.A.C. "Television. Prolonged research needed." TIMES (Aug. 21): 8a, b. (1391, 1474)

1409 Baird, J.L., and Television Ltd. "Television." Br. 325,524, Aug. 21, 1928. Battery circuit with electron tube and neon lamp. (1404, 1444)

1410 "Television drama shown with music." N.Y.T. 1; 10 (Aug. 22): 2; 5. Puppet show at Bamberger's store, Newark N.J., with music transmitted from station WOR. Apparatus developed by Paul H. Kober, director of engineering, Daven Co. (1374, 1573)

1411 "Television on WRNY wave. Demonstration at Philosophy Hall, New York University." N.Y.T 10 (Aug. 22): 5. Gernsback demonstration, picture 1.5 in. square (1399, 1432, 1498)

1412 Société Indépendante de Télégraphie sans Fil. "Television." Br. 317,791, Aug. 19,

1929. In France Aug 22, 1928. Optical system with reflecting prisms, Nicol prisms, photocells, and split beams intended to reduce blurring. (1413)

1413 Société Indépendante de Télégraphie sans Fil. "Modulating a beam of light." Br. 317,792, Aug. 19, 1929. In France, Aug. 22, 1928. Piezoelectric Kerr cell. (1412)

1414 Moore, D.M. "Television." Br. 317,831, Aug. 23, 1929. Assigned: B.T.H. In U.S. Aug. 23, 1928 (G.E.). Receiver disk with a spiral of 24 lenses. (1308, 1956)

1415 "Radio Fair to give television facts." N.Y.T. 12 (Aug. 24): 5, 6. Plans for television, comments by G.C. Irwin. Demonstrations to clear away "needless mystery and extravagant claims." Complete studio and battery of receivers to show public how it works. System of A.J. Carter, screen 5 in. square. (1307, 1431, 1455)

1416 "Radiovision." SCIENCE 68 (Aug. 24): Supp. 12–4. "Radiovision and radiomovies will be received in thousands of homes during the coming winter. Radiovisors will be the novel and really smart Christmas gift this year."

1417 Sharma, D.N. "Television system incorporating transmitting and receiving apparatus with cathode rays." Br. 320,993, Aug. 24, 1928. Oct. 31, 1929. A normally semi-transparent composite plate is scanned by a beam of cathode rays. The point of impact becomes momentarily opaque and reflects light from the image onto a phototube. In the receiver, modulated light from a neon lamp is similarly reflected point by point onto the viewing screen. The composite plate consists of a thin sheet of glass or mica, a very thin metal foil, a mixture of fluorescent substances covered by a layer of fluorescent salts, and a final layer of mica or thin nickel foil. (1393)

1418 Jevons, J.C. "Television in colour." POP. W. (Aug. 25): 829. (1485)

1419 "Tomorrow's television." N.Y.T. II, 6 (Aug. 26): 4. General comments.

1420 "How to tune in on a Televisor." N.Y.T. VII, 16 (Aug. 26): 1, 2. Information compiled by Raytheon Mfg. Co. (1377, 1458)

1421 Cosens, C.R. "Television." TIMES (Aug. 27): 8a. Frequencies and bandwidth. (1408, 1460)

1422 Hartley, R.V.L. "Electro-optical system." U.S. 1,808,137, Aug. 28, 1928, June 2, 1931. Assigned: B.T.L (1047, 1534)

1423 Shinton, Joseph Sidney. "Television." Br. 320,999, Aug. 28, 1928. Oct. 31, 1929. Mirror wheel, slotted disk, slotted aperture, photocell. Receiver with two mirror wheels and Kerr cell.

1424 Karolus, A. "Mirror disk for television systems." U.S. 1,830,231, Dec. 9, 1929, Nov. 3, 1931. Assigned: RCA. In Germany Aug. 30, 1928. (1388, 1485)

1425 Wright, G.M., and S.B. Smith. "Television apparatus." Br. 322,225, Aug. 31, 1928. Photocell and commutator for intermittent output. (954)

1426 Lane, A.P. "The real facts about television." POP. SCI. 113 (Sept.): 43.

1427 Dewhirst, Thornton P. "Radiovision." QST 12 (Sept.): 15–8. 3 diags. General comments.

1428 Jenkins, C.F. "Synchronism." QST 12 (Sept.): 38. Disk drive, diag. (1372, 1437)

1429 "Dr. Alexanderson to demonstrate new television equipment." RADIO ENG. 8 (Sept.): 27. (1361, 1455)

1430 Replogle, E. "The elements of television reception." RADIO ENG. 8 (Sept.): 38. (1377, 1574)

1431 "Successful television accomplished on broadcast band." RADIO N. 10 (Sept.): 219, 220, 227. 4 photos. Demonstration of the Sanabria disk system and transmissions in June from station WCFL, Chicago. Disk 24 in. diam., 48 holes. "The images visible in the check receiver...were really very good...the televised faces are distinctly recognizable. The images are streaked with the fine lines characteristic of television disc systems; but they are distinct enough to show the reflections of eyeglasses on the subject's face and the shadow of smoke from a cigar in his mouth." (1301, 1307, 1565)

1432 "Giant photoelectric cells from WRNY's television transmitter." RADIO N. 10 (Sept): 221, 256, 258. 4 photos. Alkaline metal type made by Lloyd Preston Garner, 12 in. diam. and 22 in. long on the stem. Experimental television apparatus constructed by the Pilot Electric Mfg. Co. (1411, 1502)

1433 Mason, C.P. "The scanning disc, television's canvas." RADIO N. 10 (Sept.): 222, 223. (1693)

1434 "Television out of doors." RADIO N. 10 (Sept.): 258, 259. 2 photos. Demonstration at Bell Labs of a portable camera with focusing lens utilizing a large scanning disk 3 feet diam. with 50 holes. (1359, 1436)

1435 "Short-wave television broadcasting." RADIO N. 10 (Sept.): 259. Note on the issuance of 8 experimental licenses by the FRC. (1355, 1452)

1436 "Out-of-doors television, the latest advance." SCI. AM. 139 (Sept.): 255, 256. Photo. Bell Labs demonstration to representative. (1434, 1490)

1437 Jenkins, C.F. "The transmission of movies by radio." J. SMPE 12 (Sept.): 915. (1428, 1447)

1438 Robinson, J. "Reflections on television and its critics." TELEV. 1 (Sept): 5–7. Diag. Comments in support of Baird's system. (1402, 1460)

1439 Rennie, J.C. "Television and broadcasting." TELEV. 1 (Sept.): 8. Comments on television in the United States versus the BBC attitude toward British work. (1200, 1349, 1486, 1583)

1440 Cheshire, F.J. "Stereoscopic vision." TELEV. 1 (Sept.): 9–11. 6 diags. Experiments. (1704)

1441 Wolfson, H. "The influence of polarisation and frequency on the photoelectric effect." TELEV. 1 (Sept.): 12–4, 39. Technicalities, problems involved in color systems. (1513)

1442 Sylvester, Cyril. "Light; the essential of television." TELEV. 1 (Sept.): 15, 16. 2 photos, 3 diags. (1508)

1443 Mullard, Stanley Robert. "When electric sight comes into business." TELEV. 1 (Sept.): 17–9. Applications and possibilities.

1444 Verne, Denison A. "The stereoscopic Televisor." TELEV. 1 (Sept.): 20, 21. Photo, 3 diags. Description and explanation of Baird's apparatus. (1409, 1475)

1445 Desmond, S. "Television and the films." TELEV. 1 (Sept.): 23–5. Discussion with leading film producers. (1381, 1510)

1446 "How colour television images are obtained." TELEV. 1 (Sept.): 25. Diag.

1447 "Moving shadowgraph experiments in America." TELEV. 1 (Sept): 26–8. Photo, 2 diags. On Jenkins. (1437, 1456)

1448 Monteath, J.D. "Stereoscopic television and natural vision." TELEV. 1 (Sept): 31–3. 7 diags. (1382)

1449 Ling. F.W. "The Television Society." TELEV. 1 (Sept.): 38, 39. 2 photos. History and current events. (1277, 1515)

1450 "Berlin radio show proves big success." N.Y.T. 6 (Sept. 1): 8. Von Mihály's apparatus on display, shadowy images. (5th Annual Radio Exhibition, Aug. 31 to Sept. 9.) (1357, 1694, 2055)

1451 Tanimoto, Frank Ryozo. "Television device." U.S. 1,769,608. Sept. 1, 1928, July 1, 1930. Cylinder and lens.

1452 "Ethereal images present puzzle." N.Y.T. VIII, 19 (Sept. 2): 1, 2. First official report of the FRC, "to enlighten bewildered public...equipment for homes far from ready." (1435, 1473)

1453 "S.F. man's invention." S.F. CHRON. (Sept.3): II. Announcement by Farnsworth of his electronic system, developed at the Crocker Research Laboratories, 202 Green

Street, San Francisco, financed by W.W. Crocker and Roy N. Bishop. Photo of Farnsworth with his camera and picture tubes. Also N.Y.T. 20 (Sept. 4): 1. No revolving disk, receiver to retail at $100 or less. Cigar smoke plainly visible with man smoking. (1227, 1619)

1454 "Will direct music by television plan." N.Y.T. 21 (Sept, 4): 1. Cincinnati Symphony Orchestra. (1576)

1455 "Television devices to be shown here." N.Y.T. 22 (Sept. 6): 2. New York Radio Show, Madison Square Garden; Alexanderson 48-line disk apparatus. (1415, 1429, 1476, 2278)

1456 Jenkins, C.F. "Duplex scanning disk." U.S. 1,785,262, Sept. 6, 1928, Dec. 16, 1930. Assigned: Jenkins Labs. (1447, 1481)

1457 "News and views." NATURE 122 (Sept. 8): 377. Note on radiovision service in the U.S.; mention of Jenkins, G.E., and Westinghouse stations.

1458 "Neon lamp blinks at radio image." N.Y.T. IX, 13 (Sept. 9): 1–5. Raytheon's Kino lamp, technical details and hints. (1420, 1497)

1459 "Radio vision is subject of survey." N.Y.T. IX, 13 (Sept. 9): 6–8. Survey by the RMA. "We have in the foreign situation, particularly England, a pertinent example of the effect of premature ballyhoo on television." (1401, 1545)

1460 Robinson, J. "Television." TIMES (Sept. 10): 8c. Comments on correspondence. (1438, 1482)

1461 "Play is broadcast by voice and acting in radio-television." N.Y.T. 1; 10 (Sept. 12): 3, 4; 3, 4. Photo. Broadcast by station WGY, General Electric Co., Schenectady, of J. Hartley Manners' play "The Queen's Messenger," with two actors, Miss Izetta Jewel and Maurice Randall, directed by Mortimer Stuart. 24-line images. about 3 in. square, showed the heads and shoulders of the actors and props handled by two other performers. Three disk cameras were used, one for the effects, and two for the actors, with mixes and fades introduced from a control panel. Transmissions were 21.4 and 370.5 m for vision, and 31.96 m for sound. (1391, 1462)

1462 "Broadcasting a play. Actors seen and heard. Promising test." TIMES (Sept. 13): 12g. G.E. broadcast of Sept. 11. Audience, in the same building in Schenectady, saw images that often wavered, transmitted from station WGY 4 miles away. (1461, 1478)

1463 "Television in Germany." ELECT. REV. 103 (Sept. 14): 446. (746, 1922)

1464 "Pictures to be broadcast." TIMES (Sept. 14): 17f, g. Advertisement for the Fultograph facsimile system by Wireless Pictures (1928) Ltd. (1311, 1486)

1465 Syphrit, Samuel Thomas. "Television apparatus." U.S. 1,735,553, Sept. 14, 1928, Nov. 12, 1929. Assigned: A.J. Carter. Spherical members, one within the other, with slots at right angles.

1466 "Leaders survey future of radio." N.Y.T. XII, 1; 4 (Sept. 16): 7; 3–7. Views on television by O.H. Caldwell, H.A. Lafount, S. Pickard, M.P. Rice, Judge I.E. Robinson, D. Sarnoff, W.D. Terrell.

1467 "Inventor looks ahead ten years." N.Y.T. XII, 2 (Sept. 16): 7, 8. Predictions by L. de Forest. (1143, 1642)

1468 "Television hopes are over-played." N.Y.T. XII, 8 (Sept. 16): 2–4. H.P. Davis, vice-president, Westinghouse, warns against purchase of premature vision apparatus, but radio movies are in sight. (1579)

1469 "New goal is set for experimenters." N.Y.T. XII, 8 (Sept. 16): 5, 6. Views of M.P. Rice, General Electric Co., on possibilities. (1264)

1470 "Vital problems involved in radio-vision research." N.Y.T. XII, 11 (Sept. 16): 2–6. Discussion by A.N. Goldsmith, RCA, on picture detail, transmission, synchronism, bandwidth. (1143, 1495)

1471 Donle, H.P. "Television reception." U.S. 1,903,986, Sept. 17, 1928, Apr. 18, 1933.

Assigned: Radio Inventions. Sync method. (1350, 1620)

1472 Gardner, Delamere B. "Reflecting and scanning apparatus." U.S. 1,753,697, Sept. 17, 1928, Apr. 8, 1930. Metal plates with mirror surfaces on the edges assembled stepwise on a shaft form a composite helical mirror, or mirror screw. Note: Franz von Okolicsányi reputedly had the same idea for a scanner in mind in October 1927. (2305, 2436)

1473 "Radio Board to set limit on television." N.Y.T. 32 (Sept. 19): 6. Views of Caldwell and Lafount, FRC. (1452, 1487)

1474 Swinton, A.A.C. "Television. The right lines of research." TIMES (Sept. 20): 8c. (1408, 1483)

1475 "Radio Exhibition." ELECT. 101 (Sept. 21): 324. Sets for television experimenters on Stand 11, Baird Co. (1444, 1477, 1587)

1476 "Television thrills radio show crowd." N.Y.T. 24 (Sept. 21): 1–4. New York Radio Show, exhibits by G.E., A.J. Carter Co., and Daven Corp. the main attraction. 40,000 in a day see them. No longer a sideshow but a major attraction. (1455, 1637)

1477 Baird, J.L., and Television Ltd. "Television." Br. 325,527, Sept. 21, 1928. Image produced by discharges from a spiral of points on a disk. (1475, 1486)

1478 "General Electric broadcasts drama by television." ELECT. W. 92 (Sept. 22): 580. (1462, 1557)

1479 Eckersley, P.P. "Television." POP. W. (Sept. 22): 89. (1342, 1661)

1480 Moseley, Sydney Alexander (1881–1961). "What I saw by television." POP. W. (Sept. 22): 93. (1509)

1481 (Jenkins, C.F.) Photo. N.Y.T. IX, 12 (Sept. 23): 6. "C.F. Jenkins, Washington, D.C., inventor and his television board of 2304 tiny photoelectric cells for use in the broadcast of outdoor scenes by radio." This matrix system, with distributors and radio transmission, is an updated version of Jenkins' proposal of 1894 (245). (1456, 1484)

1482 Robinson, J. "Wireless signalling." Br. 327,112, Sept. 26, 1928. Application of television in a direction-finding system to show the direction of a pointer on a screen. (1460, 1506)

1483 Edwards, N. "Television." TIMES (Sept. 28): 10d. Favorable comments on Swinton's letters. Television in present form of little interest except to students. (739, 1474, 1550, 1556)

1484 "Radiovision in the United States." NATURE 122 (Sept. 29): 494. General comments on Jenkins' apparatus. Pictures from 3XK "appear in black silhouette on a pink ground." (1481, 1548)

1485 Jevons, J.C. "The Karolus television system." POP. W. (Sept. 29): 174. (1418, 1424, 1491)

1486 Benn, John A. "Editorial notes." DISCOVERY 9 (Oct.): 303. On the BBC, the Fultograph facsimile system, and Baird. Comments on a BBC statement of Sept. 8, "current rumours," and Baird's press statement. (1439, 1464, 1477, 1496, 1532, 1547, 1549)

1487 "Amateur television waves." QST 12 (Oct): 8. On Aug. 3 the FRC authorized amateur use of 1715–2000 kc (150–175 m) and 56–60 mc (5 m band) for television and picture transmissions. (1473, 1492)

1488 Arnold, J.P. "Radio picture transmission and reception." RADIO 10 (Oct.): 27, 28. 2 photos. System developed by Conrad at Westinghouse. (1087, 1407, 1505, 1555)

1489 "Premature publicity." RADIO 10 (Oct.): 28. Flippant remarks on news about television. "In the case of television, it is profitable to howl about something you haven't got or to exaggerate the value of what you have."

1490 "Television in the open." RADIO 10 (Oct.): 29. Photo. Bell Labs daylight demonstration. (1436, 1929)

1491 "Picture receiving methods." RADIO 10 (Oct.): 29, 30. 3 diags. Neon lamps, Kerr cell, Karolus cell, cathode-ray tube. (1485, 1514)

1492 (Federal Radio Commission.) RADIO 10 (Oct.): 30. Note on approval for construction and operation of experimental television stations, with list of 7 authorizations. (1487, 1494)

1493 Rhodes, Howard E. "Television—its progress today." RADIO BRD. 13 (Oct.): 331–3. 4 illus. A careful survey of the current status based largely on visits to various stations. One table lists 11 stations, with call signs, wavelengths, number of holes in disks, disk speeds, number of pictures per second, and schedule times of transmissions. Another table lists manufacturers of television apparatus, with details and prices: Daven Co., Insuline Corp., National Co., Raytheon Co., Interstate Electric Co.

1494 "Regulations for television and picture transmission." RADIO BRD. 13 (Oct.): 338, 339. (1492, 1495)

1495 (RCA request for television channels.) RADIO BRD. 13 (Oct.): 339, 340. Quotes from A.N. Goldsmith, in a brief before the FRC on May 14: "In the interest of saving both the vision and the television of the public, only an experienced and responsible organization, such as the Radio Corporation of America, should be granted license to broadcast television material, for only such organizations can be depended upon to uphold high ideals of service." (1470, 1494, 1546, 1668)

1496 (Baird Television, Ltd.) RADIO BRD. 13 (Oct.): 340. Report on Baird shares in the English company and on the formation of the Baird Television Corp. (1486, 1503)

1497 "A neon lamp for television." RADIO BRD. 13 (Oct.): 373. Photo, 3 diags. Raytheon's Kino lamp; 2 in. diam., 6 1/2 in. long, plate 1 1/2 in. square, priced at $12.50. (1458)

1498 Gernsback, H. "What is coming in television." RADIO N. 10 (Oct): 299. Cautionary editorial comments. "The public at large should know that television is purely an experimental art at the present time." (1411, 1504)

1499 "Television is here!" RADIO N. (Oct.) Full-page advertisement by Pilot Electric Mfg. Co. "In those three words, Pilot proclaims to a waiting world the miracle of practical, workable television." Premature publicity on assembling a "Pilot television outfit." (1640)

1500 Koller, L.R. "The photoelectric cell—radio's 'eye.'" RADIO N. 10 (Oct.): 305–7, 372. 4 photos, 2 diags. Explanation of basic principles, actions, characteristics, applications. (1191, 2673)

1501 "Efficiency of television increased by new disc." RADIO N. 10 (Oct): 312. Photo. National Co's. scanning disk, 24 in. diam., 48 square holes. Image 1 1/2 by 1 1/2 in.

1502 "Seeing music with a television receiver." RADIO N. 10 (Oct.): 314, 315, 385, 386. 6 illus. RADIO NEWS apparatus: disk, lamp, neon tube, circuit. (1432, 1539)

1503 Tiltman, R.F. "Television in natural colors demonstrated." RADIO N. 10 (Oct): 320, 374. Photo, diag. Baird's demonstration of daylight television June 11 and of color July 3, with description of the color apparatus, demonstration, and results. (1278, 1496, 1507, 1511)

"With his system Baird has been able to give demonstrations of television in natural colors. I was present at one of the demonstrations recently, and the vivid reality of the colorings was most remarkable, and adds very greatly indeed to the effect. A bunch of flowers, blue delphiniums, was placed in front of the transmitter, and appeared on the receiving screen in a most vivid blue. This was replaced by red carnations, and the red blossoms appeared very clearly.

"A human face was then transmitted, and when the tongue was put out, the pink color showed clearly, the face appearing in a different shade of pink. A policeman's helmet was then placed before the transmitter, and the blue shone up most strongly. By far the most impressive part of the demonstration was a basket of ripe strawberries, the red fruit showing in an amazingly vivid fashion against the white basket. I also clearly saw the living moving images of a man tying a red and blue handkerchief alternately around his head."

1504 Gernsback, H. "Facts on television." SCI. & INV. 16 (Oct.): 489. "Television has actually arrived, although, for the present time, it is only for the experimenter." (1498, 1566)

1505 "Movies by radio." SCI. AM. 139 (Oct.): 1358, 360. 3 photos. Transmission of motion pictures by Westinghouse, details of the Conrad apparatus. (1488, 1558)

1506 Robinson, J. "Television—an appeal for broadcasting facilities." TELEV. 1 (Oct.): 5, 7, 8, 10. 3 photos. (1482, 1584)

1507 Tiltman, R.F. "Television in America. Many experimental transmissions in progress." TELEV. 1 (Oct.): 9, 10. 3 photos. (1503, 1517)

1508 Sylvester, C. "Light; the essential of television. Pt. 2." TELEV. 1 (Oct.): 11, 12. 3 diags. (1442, 1588)

1509 Moseley, S.A. "Views on television." TELEV. 1 (Oct.): 13, 14. (1480, 1645)

1510 Desmond, S. "Television as 'booster.'" TELEV. 1 (Oct.): 15–7, 20. "The coming revolution in advertising. Give wireless a chance!" (1445, 2013)

1511 Baird Television Development Co. Ltd. Advertisement. TELEV. 1 (Oct.): 24, 25. "Inspect the Televisor and Super Radio Receiver and other Exhibits of Baird Television Development Company, Limited, Stands 13 and 14 at the Radio Exhibition, Olympia, September 22–29 and see an actual demonstration of Television at the Company's commodious premises adjoining." (1503, 1512)

1512 "The television demonstration given by Mr. J.L. Baird before the British Association at Glasgow." TELEV. 1 (Oct.): 31. Color television and stereoscopic images. (1511, 1518)

1513 Wolfson, H. "Photo-electric fatigue." TELEV. 1 (Oct.): 32–4, 37, 40. 3 diags. (1441, 1591)

1514 Newberger, Albert. "The Karolus system of television." TELEV. 1 (Oct): 35–7, 40. 6 photos. Kerr cell, picture elements, signal transmission, details of the Karolus (Telefunken) apparatus displayed at the Berlin Wireless Exhibition. (1491, 1760, 2209)

1515 Mitchell, W.G.W. "The Television Society." TELEV. 1 (Oct.): 41–4. 3 photos, 2 diags. Lecture at Glasgow University. (1324, 1449, 1585, 1647).

1516 Crawley, C. "Navigation by invisible rays." TELEV. 1 (Oct.): 45, 46. 2 photos. Infrared rays, Noctovision, short-wave beacons, direction-finding stations. (1322)

1517 Tiltman, R.F. "Progress in seeing by electricity." WINDSOR MAG. 68 (Oct.): 561–70. (1507, 1569)

1518 "Baird's television apparatus, some recent developments." W. CONSTRUCTOR 6 (Oct.): 407, 408, 450, 451. Scanning disk, double light source, optical lever, stereoscopic television. (1512, 1521)

1519 "Chicago to see television." N.Y.T. 23 (Oct. 2): 1. Statement by Herbert H. Frost, president, RMA.

1520 Mihály, D. v. "Television apparatus." Br. 326,729, June 12, 1929. In Germany Oct. 2, 1928. Assigned: Telehor A.-G. Linear discharge tube and cylindrical lens. (1450, 1688)

1521 Baird, J.L., and Television Ltd. "Television and like apparatus." Br. 324,029, Oct. 3, 1928, Jan. 3, 1930. Spirally apertured scanning disk, and moving message band transmitter. (1518, 1522)

1522 Baird, J.L., and Television Ltd. "Television and like apparatus." Br. 324,904, Oct. 4, 1928, Feb. 4, 1930. Electrochemical receiver for recording message bands. A prepared strip of "pole-finding" paper passes over a rotating metal drum beneath a row of contacts connected by a distributor to the signal lines. (1521, 1523)

1523 "The progress of television." ELECT. 101 (Oct. 5): 379. Demonstration of commercial Baird apparatus on Sept. 28 near Olympia. Description of model A (portable receiver), model B (Televisor and loudspeaker), model C (combined Televisor and radio set) with picture about 3 1/2 by 2 1/2 in. wide. Various subjects transmitted (by wire) are described and the results criticized. The model C console is illustrated. (1522, 1527)

"The progress so far made with television was demonstrated to a special representative of the ELECTRICIAN on Friday, September 28th, by the Baird Television Development Co., Ltd. The company is offering for public sale three types of "televisor" wherewith to receive by radio moving pictures of artistes and such other performers as it may care to transmit.

"The first figure subjected to projection was a doll's head, the received picture of which measured about 3 1/2 in. by 2 1/2 in. wide. The detail of the picture was not good, the flicker was unpleasant, and a number of black lines were transmitted by the analysing disc. The next subject was a human face which was less satisfactory than that of the doll. Below the eyes and chin the projection was darkened to such a degree that any detail which might have been there was to some extent blackened out, and while the movement of the eyes, the mouth, etc., could be easily distinguished, the picture on the whole was lacking in detail. A lady vocalist was next transmitted, her voice and the piano accompaniment being reproduced by a loud speaker. Here again the darkness under the chin and eyes was prominent, and while we would not describe the picture as being in any way distorted, it was a long way from being perfect. The movements of the singer, however, could be followed without difficulty, the illumination being good.

"The impression given by the demonstration was that, though television is possible, the progress so far made in this country still leaves much to be accomplished. The projection was not so good as were those of the first public performances of the cinematograph and the size of the picture is, in our opinion, on the small side. From the fact that the Baird Television Development Co. had developed receivers for public sale and that a television service is predicted, it is obvious that the company holds views other than those expressed by ourselves."

1524 "Television rights are questioned." N.Y.T. IX, 23 (Oct. 7): 1–3. On television in the broadcast band.

1525 "Playlet seen by television suggests chain of theatres." N.Y.T. IX, 23 (Oct. 7): 2, 3. Views of O.H. Caldwell. (1255)

1526 Tate, Alfred Orde. "Scanning disk." U.S. 1,904,566, Oct. 8, 1928, Apr. 18, 1933. See also U.S. 1,860,824; 1,866,915. (1663)

1527 Baird, J.L., and Television Ltd. "Television." Br. 324,049, Oct. 10, 1928. Divided: Br. 323,817 (1528). U.S. 1,869,735, Oct. 7, 1929, Aug. 2, 1932. Portable receiver and phonograph. (1523)

1528 Baird, J.L., and Television Ltd. "Television." Br. 323,817, Oct. 10, 1928. Divided from Br. 324,049 (1527). Platinum foil with contacts on a scanning disk produces a glowing picture. (1529)

1529 Baird, J.L., and Television Ltd., and Baird Television Development Co. Ltd. "Television." Br. 326,251, Oct. 10, 1928, Mar. 10, 1930. Divided from Br. 324,049 (1527), addition to Br. 253,957 (640). U.S. 1,807,464, Oct. 7, 1929, May 26, 1931. Disks with arcuate slots, several photocells and shutter to provide zone scan. (1528, 1530)

1530 Baird, J.L., and Television Ltd. "Television." Br. 323,818, Oct. 12, 1928. U.S. 1,807,465, Oct. 7, 1929, May 26, 1931. An auxiliary picture seen by reflection from an inclined sheet of glass, employing "Pepper's ghost" effect, provides a stationary background. (1529, 1532)

1531 Warren, S.F. "Television apparatus." Br 321,043, Oct. 12, 1928. Combination of scanning disk and lamp.

1532 "Wireless notes; television and the B.B.C." ELECT. 101 (Oct. 12): 418. Quote from

DAILY TELEGRAPH (important announcement): Baird Television Co. applied to the Postmaster General for a transmitting license. "The B.B.C. with the approval of the PMG has required a special demonstration of the Baird television apparatus before considering experimental transmissions from its stations." (1041, 1486, 1530, 1535, 1787)

1533 "Television and radiovision." NATURE 122 (Oct. 13): 589. General comments on inventive progress with reference to the pamphlet LA TELEVISION ELECTRIQUE by A. Dauvillier (1108). (1163, 2556)

1534 Hartley, R.V.L. "Electro-optical system." U.S. 1,786,652. Oct. 16, 1928, Dec. 30, 1930. Assigned: B.T.L. Split-image system with disk scanners, light valves, and single-channel transmission. (1422)

1535 "B.B.C. and television. No transmission at present." TIMES (Oct. 18): 13f. Demonstration by Baird on Oct. 9. "While the demonstration was interesting as an experiment, it failed to fulfill the conditions which would justify trial through a B.B.C. station." (1532, 1538, 1540)

1536 Gray, F. "Switch or commutating means." U.S. 1,812,828, Oct. 18, 1928, June 30, 1931. Assigned: B.T.L. Receiver with multielectrode folded tube controlled by two distributors. (1148, 1624)

1537 "Television." ENGINEER 146 (Oct. 19): 421.

1538 Kendall, G.P. "The Baird Televisors." POP. W. (Oct. 20): 323. (1165, 1535, 1540)

1539 "Electric industry displays its wares." N.Y.T. 8 (Oct. 20): 1. Station WRNY has television exhibit on view at the annual Electrical and Industrial Exposition, New York. (1502, 1560)

1540 "B.B.C. and television. Statement by the Baird Company." TIMES (Oct. 22): 16b. Official reply to the BBC statement refusing to furnish broadcasting facilities. "The company is taking steps with a view to securing independent broadcasting facilities for television." (1535, 1538, 1543)

1541 Todd, Leonard Pierce. "Telegraphic transmission of visual representations." Br. 325,790, Oct. 24, 1928, Feb. 24, 1930. Overlapping disks, one with radial slots the other with a circle of lenses, a vertical slot in an opaque screen, and a light chopper of parallel wires vibrated by an electromagnet. Colored lenses are specified in the claims. (2745)

1542 Walton, G.W. "Apparatus for television and for recording and reproducing pictures." Br. 328,286, Oct. 25, 1928, Apr. 25, 1930; U.S. 2,089,155, Oct. 19, 1929, Aug. 3, 1937. Assigned: Scophony. An echelon device of mirrors, prisms, or lenses forms a line image in successive staggered sections or steps which is then reflected from a vibrating mirror onto a photocell. Applicable for television, facsimile, and photo recording. (661, 1748)

1543 "Wireless notes." ELECT. 101 (Oct. 26): 479. Statements by the BBC and Baird Television Development Co. on demonstration of Oct. 9. The text of both statements (BBC Oct. 18, Baird Oct. 20) are given. (1540, 1544, 1547)

1544 Baird, J.L., and Television Ltd. "Television." Br 324,399, Oct. 26, 1928. Receiver for selective or simultaneous reception from two or more stations. (1543, 1549)

1545 "Definition of television." N.Y.T: X, 17 (Oct. 28): 8. "Television is officially defined by the Radio Manufacturers Association as vision by radio." (1459, 1656)

1546 "Radio picture rule protested by Felix." N.Y.T. 40 (Oct. 31): 1. Critical remarks by E.H. Felix on the FRC's ruling. Pictures cannot be satisfactorily broadcast on the broadcast band. (1370, 1495, 1561, 1597)

1547 "Broadcasting pictures. Transmission from Daventry." TIMES (Oct. 31): 14f. On facsimile transmission by the Fultograph system from BBC station 5XX to the Savoy Hotel, London. These transmissions were continued until November 1929. (1486, 1543, 1556)

1548 "Practical television." CIT. RAD. CALL BOOK 9 (Nov.): 80–5. 6 photos, 6 silhouettes, 10 diags. Instructions for building the "scanoscope," with circuit diagrams and parts list, based on the Jenkins system of radio movies. The silhouettes, which show children at play, are from Jenkins' films. (1368, 1484, 1562, 1571)

1549 Benn, J.A. "Editorial notes." DISCOVERY 9 (Nov.): 335. On a special demonstration by Baird Television Co. "The mere shadows which preceded the blurred facial image of a year ago have now given way to a fairly distinct picture, and the gold-rimmed spectacles of the sitter were clearly seen on the receiver as the head moved from side to side." (1486, 1544, 1551)

1550 Swinton, A.A.C. "Television; past and future." DISCOVERY 9 (Nov.): 337–9. Early ideas, basic principles, comparison with halftone photographs, mechanical factors, and the possibilities for the cathode-ray system proposed by the author "some twenty years ago." As for mechanical methods, "it is scarcely open to much doubt that the promised televising of extensive scenes, such as a cricket match at Lord's, or the race for the Derby, will remain impossible of achievement." Also EXP. W. 6 (Jan. 1929): 46. (1483, 1556)

1551 "Pictures in colors are sent by television." POP. MECH. 50 (Nov.): 750, 751. 2 photos, diag. Baird's color and daylight demonstrations. (1549, 1556)

1552 "What television offers you." POP. MECH: 50 (Nov.): 820–4. 4 photos, diag. Reproduction of received image shows a golfer. Various quotes.

1553 "Newest radio motion picture machine." POP. SCI. 113 (Nov.): 19.

1554 Thurm, L. "Un nouveau système de télévision et de télécinématographie." QSTF 9 (Nov.): 40–2. Continued from July (1313, 1689).

1555 Arnold, J.P. "Synchronous motors for visual communication." RADIO 10 (Nov.): 28. Photo, diag. Disk sizes, speeds, and driving motors. (1488, 1627)

1556 Corbett, L.W. "What prospects of television abroad?" RADIO BRD. 14 (Nov.): 11–3. 2 photos, 3 diags. Baird's apparatus and demonstrations in monochrome and color. The Baird versus BBC controversy. Campbell Swinton's cathode-ray plan, with extracts, also quotes from Swinton's critical letters. Includes: "The British Situation," by N. Edwards, managing editor of POPULAR WIRELESS and MODERN WIRELESS, which summarizes the Baird-BBC position. (1342, 1483, 1547, 1550, 1551, 1569, 1596, 1652, 1666, 1724)

1557 "The stage of a television drama." RADIO BRD. 14 (Nov.): 17. Photo and caption (G.E.). (1478, 1559)

1558 "The race for television publicity." RADIO BRD. 14 (Nov.): 17. Comments on the Westinghouse (Conrad) system. (1505, 1568)

1559 "A milestone in television." RADIO BRD. 14 (Nov.): 17. General Electric television broadcast via wire and radio from station WGY of the acceptance speech of Gov. Alfred E. Smith on Aug. 22 at the State House in Albany. (1557, 1599)

1560 "WRNY television transmission." RADIO BRD. 14 (Nov.): 17. Brief note. (1539, 1567)

1561 Felix, E.H. "Need for defining television practices." RADIO BRD. 14 (Nov.): 18. "Television is altogether too crude to be standardized." But temporary agreement should be reached on disk speed, direction of motion, and common multiple for number of holes. (1546, 1874)

1562 Bouck, Zeh, and James Millen. "Building receivers for television." RADIO BRD. 14 (Nov.): 35–7. 8 illus. Description of experimental receivers made by each author. List of parts, circuits, assembly, and operating instructions. (1548, 1565, 1811)

1563 "Television; frequency band required." RADIO BRD. 14 (Nov.): 58. Information sheet with table showing frequencies for number of lines (25 to 100) and number of pictures per second (10, 15, 20).

1564 "The I.C.A. television kit." RADIO ENG. 8 (Nov.): 50. Insuline Corporation of America. (3276)

1565 "Television for the experimenter." RADIO LISTENERS' GUIDE 3 (Nov.): 72–81. 11 photos, 8 diags. General discussion centered on the apparatus designed by U.A. Sanabria and the experimental equipment at station WCFL, Chicago, with details of construction and operation. (1431, 1634) The WRNY apparatus is also described. (1562, 1571)

1566 Gernsback, H. "Future progress in television." RADIO N. 10 (Nov.): 411. Editorial discussion of various aspects of mechanical systems, current situation, advertising possibilities, experiences at station WRNY, problems and remedies. (1504, 1632)

1567 Hertzberg, Robert. "Successful television programs broadcast by Radio News Station WRNY." RADIO N. 10 (Nov.): 412–5 490–2. 5 photos and newspaper clippings. Includes program schedule for Aug. 21 in the NEW YORK TIMES, claimed as "The first regular, daily, television broadcast service the world has known." Details of the equipment designed by John Geloso, chief engineer of the Pilot Electric Mfg. Co., and of the preparations and schedule. (1560, 1631, 1640)

1568 "Radio 'movies' from KDKA." RADIO N. 10 (Nov.): 416, 417. 3 photos. "Regular programs on the short waves promised." Details of the Conrad system. "The Westinghouse company is definitely contemplating the manufacture of commercial 'radio-movie' receivers." (1558, 1579)

1569 Tiltman, R.F. "How 'stereoscopic' television is shown." RADIO N. 10 (Nov.): 418, 419. 2 photos, diag. "Television images in, apparently, three dimensions were demonstrated for the first time on August 10 in the Baird laboratories in Long Acre, before an audience of scientists and representatives of the press. Professor Cheshire...stated that a man sitting at the transmitter was very clearly seen in perfect relief." (1517, 1556, 1578, 1587)

1570 "Televentures, telewitticisms and the televocabulary." RADIO N. 10 (Nov.): 419, 466, 468. Light-hearted discussion on terminology. (1332, 1618)

1571 "The Jenkins 'radio-movie' reception methods." RADIO N. 10 (Nov.): 420, 492, 493. A composite drawing shows the assembly of an "excellent television or 'radio-movie' receiver." Building and operating instructions for a disk receiver. (1548, 1565, 1572, 1602)

1572 "How to make your own television receiver." RADIO N. 10 (Nov.): 422–5, 466. 5 photos, 6 diags. Detailed assembly and operating instructions with layout for a 24-in., 48-hole disk, including amplifier. Free blueprint offered. (1571, 1575)

1573 "Synchronized broadcast joins images and music." RADIO N. 10 (Nov.): 426, 476. Demonstration of a puppet show at Bamberger and Co., Newark, N.J. Photo of apparatus; 24-in., 48-hole disk, flying spot scan, 900-w tungsten lamp, four 7-in. photocells, with wire link to receiver. Music transmitted from station WOR. (1410, 1896)

1574 Replogle, D.E. "The neon tube—television's 'loud speaker.'" RADIO N. 10 (Nov.): 427, 428. Photo, 4 diags. Basic theory, construction, operation. (1430, 1808)

1575 "How to adjust the television receiver for operation." RADIO N. 10 (Nov.): 428, 429. Positive and negative images, disk rotation, interference, and noise level. (1572, 1577)

1576 "Television directs two orchestras." SCI. & INV. 16 (Nov.): 587. (1454)

1577 "How to build the S & I television receiver." SCI. & INV. 16 (Nov.): 618–20, 632, 634, 636. 11 illus. Front cover has an illustration of the receiver. (1585, 1580)

1578 "Stereoscopic television." SCI. & INV. 16 (Nov.): 621. 4 illus. Baird's system. (1569, 1582)

1579 "Radio movies demonstrated." SCI. & INV. 16 (Nov.): 622, 623, 666. 3 illus. Westinghouse system (F. Conrad and H.P. Davis). Disk with 60 square holes. Mercury vapor tube. Sync control with tuning fork and sync receiver motor. Two-channel radio transmission for vision and sync. (1468, 1568, 1712, 2642)

1580 "Controlling the television scanning disk." SCI. AM. 139 (Nov.): 458. (1577, 1614)

1581 Laufer, Berthold. "The prehistory of television." SCI. MON. 27 (Nov.) 455–9. Oriental folklore, mythology, and literary allusions, with some extracts concerning magic mirrors, divining cups, wonderful ivory tubes, and far-off events said to have been witnessed by their aid.

1582 Fleming, J.A. "Criticisms and critics of television." TELEV. 1 (Nov.): 5–7, 46. 3 photos. Sir Ambrose Fleming, president of the Television Society (1928–1945), was an active supporter of Baird. "We find, therefore, in connection with every such cardinal invention, some persons who deprecate and underrate its utility in its initial stages. Television is, and will be, no exception to this rule. That recognisable images of moving and living objects such as human faces have been transmitted even to large distances by wire and wireless by Mr. Baird's methods, admits of no manner of doubt." (1321, 1578, 1586, 1905)

1583 Rennie, J.C. "Some figures." TELEV. 1 (Nov.): 8. Graph. Scanning, picture elements, frequency. (1439, 1705)

1584 Robinson, J. "Principles of image scanning." TELEV. 1 (Nov): 9–11, 26. 6 diags. (1506, 1644)

1585 "The Television Society." TELEV. 1 (Nov.): 12. News. (1515, 1651)

1586 "Conditions of sales of Televisors." TELEV. 1 (Nov.): 12. Details of Baird Co's. facilities, negotiations for licensing, order information. (1582, 1587)

1587 Tiltman, R.F. "The entertainment value of television today!" TELEV. 1 (Nov.): 13–6. 4 photos, 2 extracts. Baird demonstrations during the National Radio Exhibition, Olympia, with particulars of events and performers; Miss Peggy O'Neil, Harry Tate, Miss Lilian Davies and others. Comments on the current criticism and statements in support of Baird. "There is a real, definite entertainment value in television as it is today—allied with telephony, of course." (1475, 1569, 1586, 1589, 2640)

1588 Sylvester, C. "Light: the essential of television. Pt. 3." TELEV. 1 (Nov.): 17, 18. 5 diags. (1508, 1650)

1589 Brittain, W.J. "What I think now of Baird television." TELEV. 1 (Nov.): 21, 27. Supportive comments. (1398, 1587, 1594, 1618)

1590 Warschauer, Frank. "My impressions of television." TELEV. 1 (Nov.): 22, 44. Comments on von Mihály, Karolus, and Baird.

1591 Wolfson, H. "The influence of temperature and light intensity on the photo-electric effect." TELEV. 1 (Nov.): 23–6. 2 photos, 2 diags. (1513, 1653)

1592 Shrewsbury, John B. "Is the travelling spot essential to television?" TELEV. 1 (Nov.): 28, 48.

1593 "Television in America." TELEV. 1 (Nov.): 31. Current status.

1594 "Television demonstrations in Rotterdam." TELEV. 1 (Nov.): 32. Baird display at the International Industrial Exhibition. (1589, 1595)

1595 Fox, W.C. "Another scientific adventure." TELEV. 1 (Nov.): 43, 44. Baird demonstration in Rotterdam. (740, 1594, 1596, 1941)

1596 "News and views." NATURE 122 (Nov. 3): 704. Note on the BBC and Baird and the Corporation's decision not to broadcast television. "We see no reason, however, why preliminary experiments should not be permitted." (1556, 1595, 1598, 1600)

1597 "Board authorizes television band." N.Y.T. 24 (Nov. 3): 1. FRC Order issued Nov. 2 limits bandwidth to 10 kc on frequencies above 1.5 mc. Transmission time limited to one hour a day, except 6 to 11 p.m., until Jan. 1, 1929. (1546, 1629)

1598 "The B.B.C. and television." POP. W. (Nov. 3): 432. (1596, 1608)

1599 "Television actors 'framed' at WGY." N.Y.T. X, 19 (Nov. 4): 3. Positions limited in front of white screen, make-up techniques. (1559, 1631)

1600 Baird, J.L., and Television Ltd. "Television." Br. 324,949, Nov. 5. 1928. Disk scanner with a plurality of photocells or lamps at different locations. Reference to Br. 317,143. (1596, 1601)

1601 Baird, J.L., and Television Ltd. "Television." Br. 326,192, Nov. 5, 1928. Lamp bank and lens for screen projection. References to Br. 222,604 (548), 291,121 (814). (1600, 1608)

1602 Jenkins, C.F. "Contact scanning disk." U.S. 1,740,654, Nov. 5, 1928, Dec. 24, 1929. Assigned: Jenkins Labs. (1571, 1628)

1603 Bush, Vannevar. "Signaling system." U.S. 1,897,236, Nov. 6, 1928, renewed Nov. 22, 1930, Feb. 14, 1933. Assigned: Raytheon. Scanning disks, optical system, and phototube.

1604 Oskow, Louis. "Television apparatus." U.S 1,814,181, Nov. 8, 1928, July 14, 1931. Part assigned: Morris Kirschstein. Apertured stationary screen and a reciprocating shutter, with one line for picture signals and one to synchronize the operating electromagnets.

1605 "Outdoor television." SCIENCE 68 (Nov. 9): Supp. 10.

1606 McCreary, H.J. "Television." U.S. 1,978,684. Nov. 9, 1928, Oct. 30, 1934. Assigned: Associated Electric Labs. Divided, U.S. 1,849,679, Dec. 18, 1930. Br. 341,049, Oct. 9, 1929. Cathode-ray tube receiver. (1283, 2288)

1607 Walker, Jack L. "Television and telephoto device." U.S. 1,826,970, Nov. 9, 1928, Oct. 13, 1931. Receiver with two modulated light sources and two scanning disks, with lenses arranged to project the image onto both sides of a photographic plate or viewing screen.

1608 "The Baird Co. reply to the B.B.C." POP. W. (Nov. 10): 480. (1598, 1601, 1643, 1645)

1609 "Two-way television." POP. W. (Nov. 10): 493.

1610 "Television without mechanism." POP. W. (Nov. 10): 526.

1611 Cristesco, G. "Dispositif pour la transmission des images animées à distance à l'aide de l'electricité" [Arrangement for the transmission of moving images at a distance by means of electricity]. REV. GEN. 24 (Nov. 10): 167.

1612 "Public must wait for television." N.Y.T. XI, 18 (Nov. 11): 5–7. Views of L.B.F. Raycroft, vice-president, National Electrical Manufacturers Association. Industry is not prepared for commercial development. (1838)

1613 "Dutch television." ELECT. REV. 103 (Nov. 16): 856.

1614 "Radiovision." SCIENCE 68 (Nov. 16): Supp. 12. "The amateur radiovision enthusiast will soon have at least twenty-one stations broadcasting such programs, located all the way from Lexington, Mass., to Los Angeles, Calif. These are operated by eleven different broadcasters." (1580, 1625)

1615 Barnes, Allen C. "Television transmission and receiving apparatus." U.S. 1,774,348, Nov. 16, 1928, Aug. 26, 1930. For reproduction in natural color.

1616 "Forging an electric eye to scan the world." N.Y.T. X, 3 (Nov. 18): 1–8. Feature article, illus. RCA, Alexanderson and Kell, new projection (disk) apparatus, general discussion. (1599, 1631)

1617 Schröter, F. "Receiving television pictures." U.S. 1,884,287, Nov. 12, 1929, Oct. 25, 1932. In Germany Nov. 22, 1928. Assigned: Telefunken. Disk with a double spiral of apertures coacts with a drum with linear lenses, modulated light source inside the drum. (1090, 2080)

1618 Brittain, W.J. "Radiovision." NATURE 122 (Nov. 24): 809, 810. Comment on terminology and editorial reply. (1570, 1589, 1700, 1727)

1619 Farnsworth, P.T. "Method and apparatus for television." U.S. 2,037,711, Nov. 26, 1928, renewed Sept. 21, 1931, Apr. 21, 1936. Assigned: Television Labs. Improved image dissector tube with large and small apertures of wire mesh screen with a hole over the target aperture. (1453, 1694)

1620 Donle, H.P. "Television." U.S. 1,980,155, Nov. 28, 1928, Nov. 6, 1934. Assigned: Radio Inventions. Disk system with sync signals interposed between groups of visual signals comprising parts of a complete image. (1471, 1679)

1621 Korn, A. "Zur frage des Bildrunfunks" [Problem of television broadcasting]. E.T.Z. 49 (Nov. 29): 1747, 1748. On recent developments and the need for organization of broadcasts. (625, 1815)

1622 Binder, V. "Copying telegraphy." Br. 342,054, Nov. 29, 1929. Convention date Nov. 29, 1928. Nipkow disk system with phonic wheels, signal frequency proportional to changes in line images.

1623 Pullin, V.E. "Television past and future." DISCOVERY 9 (Dec.): 388. Letter commenting on Swinton's article in November. (1550)

1624 Gray, F., and H.E. Ives. "Optical conditions for direct scanning in television." J. OSA 17 (Dec.): 428–34. 2 illus. Study of the conditions applicable to television, light distribution to photocell. (1338, 1536, 1675, 1865)

1625 Brittin, Frank L. "Here is your television receiver!" POP. MECH. 50 (Dec.): 1004–7. 7 illus. Dimensioned assembly views and schematic. (1614, 1626)

1626 Carr, J. "Making a television disk." POP. SCI. 113 (Dec.): 53. (1625, 1630, 1687)

1627 Arnold, J.P. "Radio picture transmission and reception." RADIO 10 (Dec.): 17, 18. Photo, diag. General information. List of 11 television stations, with tentative schedule. (1555, 1726)

1628 Jenkins, C.F. "The Jenkins Radiovisor." RADIO 10 (Dec.): 18. 2 photos. Discussion of disk and drum methods of scanning. (1602, 1636)

1629 Lafount, H.A. "In the visual broadcasting field." RADIO BRD. 14 (Dec.): 94. The Commissioner's views on proposed FRC regulation of visual broadcasting (pictures and television) and advice to experimenters not to invest in equipment. (1263, 1597, 1668, 2100)

1630 Phelps, B. "Problems in synchronizing television receiving discs." RADIO BRD. 14 (Dec.) 123–5. 3 photos, map of the United States, diag. Table of power line frequencies. Synchronous motors, speed regulation, power frequencies. List of new U.S. television licenses shows 10 stations with powers from 100 to 20,000 w and wavelengths from 19 to 125 m, each band 100 kc. (1177, 1626, 1633, 1690)

1631 Hertzberg, R. "Television makes the radio drama possible." RADIO N. 10 (Dec.): 524–7, 587, 588. 6 photos, 2 diags. Details of the General Electric apparatus at station WGY, techniques of the performance for the play "The Queen's Messenger," extracts from Alexanderson's statement about the demonstration. (1567, 1599, 1634, 1638)

1632 "'Multiple television'—a forecast." RADIO N. 10 (Dec.): 528, 529, 589, 590. 2 photos, 2 diags. Picture from the EXPERIMENTER, Nov. 1924, shows six panels with different images to illustrate potential military applications. Gernsback revives his earlier proposal (623) and discusses its operation. "Why the possibility of receiving more than one television image at once is of practical importance." (1566, 3606)

1633 Bayer, H.M. "Equipment for television experiments." RADIO N. 10 (Dec.): 531–3, 570, 572. 10 photos. Survey of commercial components available from Pilot Electric Mfg. Co., Insuline Corp. of America, Clarostat Mfg. Co., Daven Radio Corp., Jenkins Labs, the National Co. (1630, 1641)

1634 Hertzberg, R. "New disc keeps down image-frequency." RADIO N. 10 (Dec.): 534, 535. 3 diags. Sanabria system. Details of disk and other apparatus, broadcasts from Chicago stations WIBO and WMAQ. (1565, 1631, 1691, 1917)

1635 "Several wavelengths used for high-frequency radio movies and television." RADIO N. 10 (Dec.): 535. Stations W1XAY, Lexington, Boston; W3XK, Washington, D.C.

1636 Green, Herndon. "Complex televisors to give large images." RADIO N. 10 (Dec.): 536, 537. Photo, diag. Jenkins' matrix system of 2,304 photocells with capacitors for signal storage and similar bank of flashlight lamps with distributors at both stations. "Mr. Jenkins predicts that within a year he will be able to transmit views of baseball games, inaugural ceremonies and other outdoor events, and to reproduce them before large audiences in theatres." (1628, 1658)

1637 "The fifth annual Radio World's Fair." RADIO N. 10 (Dec.): 542, 577. "Television the Big Hit." Six television kits offered. Demonstrations by Carter Electric Co., General Electric Co., and Daven Co. (1476, 1985)

1638 "Drama via television." SCI. & INV. 16 (Dec.): 694, 762. 4 illus. General Electric demonstration. (1631, 1785)

1639 "Television drama of tomorrow." SCI. & INV. 16 (Dec.): 695. 2 illus. with captions.

1640 "Television is here." SCI. & INV. 16 (Dec.): 726, 727. 4 illus. Description of the Pilot Co. apparatus and the transmission from RADIO NEWS station WRNY. (1499, 1567)

1641 Townsend, Henry. "Television receiver hints." SCI. & INV. 16 (Dec.): 728, 729, 753–6. 9 illus. Constructional details for a disk machine. (1633, 1690)

1642 De Forest, L. "Future radio receivers." SCI. & INV. 16 (Dec.): 732. 3 illus., including two television consoles. (1467, 1851)

1643 Ingalls, Albert G. "Television abroad." SCI. AM. 139 (Dec.): 550, 551. 3 photos, 3 diags. Brief survey of Baird's systems. (1608, 1648)

1644 Robinson, J. "Amount of the ether required by television." TELEV. 1 (Dec.): 5–8. Photo, 4 diags. Bandwidth, use of broadcasting band, modulation, television requirements. (1584, 1699)

1645 Moseley, S.A. "On the B.B.C. decision—and after." TELEV. 1 (Dec.): 9–11. (1509, 1608, 1652, 1699)

1646 Sanders, A.W. " Impressions and opinions of a layman." TELEV. 1 (Dec.): 12.

1647 Mitchell, W.G.W., and C.H. Westcott. "Neon lamps and the last stage of L.F. amplification." TELEV. 1 (Dec.): 13–5. 11 graphs and diags. Characteristic curves, impedance, lag. (1515, 1651)

1648 Lester, Mark. "What it feels like to be televised." TELEV. 1 (Dec.): 16. Comedian's comments on demonstration by Baird at Selfridge's in September. (1643, 1649)

1649 Gradenwitz, A. "Now, this is television!" TELEV. 1 (Dec.): 25, 26. 2 photos. Favorable comments on Baird. "Unquestionably the Baird system is immensely in advance of any system on the Continent. It seems to be extraordinary that a British invention should be unable to obtain facilities for its development in the country of its birth." (770, 1648, 1659, 1826)

1650 Sylvester, C. "Light: the essential of television. Pt. 4." TELEV. 1 (Dec.): 27, 28. 6 diags. (1588, 1703)

1651 Denton, John J., and W.G.W. Mitchell. "The Television Society." TELEV. 1 (Dec.): 29–32, 35. 4 photos, picture of the Society's badge. Report of Opening Meeting 1928–29 Session, Engineers' Club, Nov. 6. (1585, 1647, 1704)

1652 Moseley, S.A. "Another television critic exposed." TELEV. 1 (Dec.): 39. Discussion with N. Edwards, editor of POPULAR WIRELESS. (1645, 1697)

1653 Wolfson, H. "The neon lamp in theory and practice." TELEV. 1 (Dec.): 40–3. 5 diags. (1591, 1701)

1654 "American television developments." TELEV. 1 (Dec.) 44, 45.

1655 Anderson, Wilfred. "Television at home—when?" TELEV. 1 (Dec.): 55. Views of a "man in the street."

1656 "News and views." NATURE 122 (Dec. 1): 853. On the U.S. (RMA) standard for television scanning: 48 lines with 15 pictures per second. (1561, 1665)

1657 Gutafson, Victor G. "Television receiving apparatus." U.S. 1,814,382, Dec. 3, 1928, July 14, 1931. Two mirror wheels.

1658 "$10,000,000 concern to push television. Home radio movies promised as bankers float company to build Jenkins devices." N.Y.T. 3 (Dec. 5): 2. Formation of Jenkins Television Corp., holding company for capital stock of Jenkins Labs. Inc., formed in 1921. James W. Garside, president; A.J. Drexel Biddle Jr., chairman; C.F. Jenkins, vice-president, research; Donald S. Rogers, secretary; Phillip H. Diehl, treasurer. (1636, 1711)

1659 Baird, J.L., and Television Ltd. "Television." Br. 326,230, Dec. 5, 1928. Prism system. Reference to Br. 289,307 (800). (1649, 1666)

1660 Hammond, J.H. "System of television." U.S. 1,867,542, Dec. 6, 1928, July 12, 1932. Includes recording of picture signals on magnetic tape and subsequent transmission and reproduction of the original scene. (1055, 1949)

1661 Eckersley, P.P. "Invention and service." POP. W. (Dec. 8): 699. (1479, 2046)

1662 Tervo, Oscar. "Television scanning device." U.S. 1,791,481, Dec. 10, 1928, Feb. 3, 1931. Two mirror drums.

1663 Tate, A.O. "Scanning disk." U.S. 1,779,518, Dec. 13, 1928, Oct. 28, 1930. Nipkow disk. (1526, 1680)

1664 Telehor A.-G. "Television." Br. 350,987, Dec. 13, 1929. In Germany Dec. 13, 1928. Sync system. (1673)

1665 "Items." SCIENCE 68 (Dec. 14): Supp. 14. A subcommittee of the Radio Manufacturers Association's Committee on Engineering recently met in Chicago with representatives of the leading manufacturers and others interested in radiovision. This subcommittee of the RMA (founded 1924) met on Oct. 9. D.E. Replogle was chairman. Other members of present interest were C.F. Jenkins, H.J. McCreary, Capt. W.J. Jarrard of the Baird Co. and R. Hertzberg of RADIO NEWS. Jenkins' system was accepted as a standard: 48 lines per frame, 15 frames per second with scanning from top to bottom and left to right. (1656, 1999)

1666 Corbett, L.W. "A television demonstration and an interview with Mr. Baird." POP W. (Dec. 15): 789. (1556, 1659, 1698)

1667 Takayanagi, Kenjiro. "Experience de télévision [Television experiments]. REV. GEN. 24 (Dec. 15): 209. (3376)

1668 Federal Radio Commission. SECOND ANNUAL REPORT TO CONGRESS. Washington: G.P.O., Dec. 16. Television is dealt with in various parts and in Appendixes. "The recent advances in radio television threatens to create serious problems." App. M. (2), Television, or seeing at a distance, brief filed May 14 by A.N. Goldsmith, chief broadcast engineer, RCA. A survey in general terms is followed by descriptions of the probable services: urban, suburban and rural, international. In a one-sided dogmatic fashion, Goldsmith urged the commission to grant experimental licenses to RCA. "Permanent television broadcasting of high quality appears more likely upon the shorter wave lengths. The Radio Corporation of America has had wide experience in the handling of these short waves. The Radio Corporation can be depended upon...to develop television broadcasting along constructive and satisfactory lines...." Bandwidths for single side-band transmissions are listed: 24 lines, 5 kc; 48 lines, 20 kc; 96 lines, 80 kc. The allocation of bands 100 kc wide are advocated. "Television, so called, from irresponsible sources will benefit only the oculists of the United States in proportion as it ruins the eyesight of the public 'lookers-in.'" (1495, 1629, 1670, 1813)

1669 "Leaders dispel television fears." N.Y.T. X, 18 (Dec. 16.): 1, 2. Comments by D. Sarnoff: "Buy a radio now instead of waiting for television." (937, 1720)

1670 "Television puzzles Radio Commission." N.Y.T. X, 21 (Dec. 16): 7, 8. Policy not yet settled. (1668, 1672)

1671 "Television feat hailed." N.Y.T. 2 (Dec. 17): 6. Reception of fairly clear images in Johannesburg, South Africa, broadcast from station 2XAL, New York.

1672 "Problems increase, says Radio Board. Television at the front." N.Y.T. 29 (Dec. 17): 1–3. FRC's Annual Report. Television signals on broadcast band will create noises. (1670, 1677)

1673 Telehor A.-G. "Picture-scanning and picture-reconstituting discs for television apparatus." Br. 327,912, June 18, 1929, Apr. 17, 1930. In Germany, Dec. 17, 1928. Nipkow disk with rectangular holes provided with serrated, curved, or angular edges to reduce visibility of scanning strips. (1664, 1814)

1674 "Radio standard movie. Chicago Labor Station's engineer tells of television test." N.Y.T. 38 (Dec. 18): 4, 5. Virgil A. Schoenberg, chief engineer, station WCFL, succeeded in taking motion pictures. Representatives of the Television Corp. of America saw demonstrations of standard film. Mr. Schoenberg spent more than $100,000 of his own money in experiments.

1675 Gray, F. (E.R.P.). "Television." Br. 340,612, Oct. 4, 1929. In U.S. Dec. 21, 1928. Receiver with a plurality of light valves. (1624, 1742)

1676 Western Electric Co., Ltd. (Bell Telephone Laboratories). "Television." Br. 326,836, Dec. 21, 1928. 50-hole disk, light cell, and lens system.

1677 "To stop television in broadcast band." N.Y.T. 15 (Dec. 23): 3. Radio Board (FRC) plans to end broadcasts of stations WGY and WIBO. Complaints of interference, special transmission band will be set up. (1672, 1709)

1678 Geloso, J. "Television device." U.S. 1,811,465, Dec. 24, 1928, June 23, 1931. Assigned: Pilot Radio & Tube Corp. Single-spiral apertured disk with adjustable friction drive in a receiver cabinet.

1679 Donle, H.P. "Television." U.S. 1,800,057, Dec. 26, 1928, Apr. 7, 1931. Disk with a spiral of holes. Receiver with two concentric disks, one with radial sets of four holes per set, the other with three spiral-arc slots which acts as a shutter. Sync obtained by armature bars attached to the receiver disk with field coils actuated by impulses from an amplifier, per previous specifications. (1620, 2230)

1680 Tate, A.O. " Scanning disk." U.S. 1,825,486, Dec. 29, 1928, Sept. 29, 1931. Apertures arranged in reverse spirals. (1663, 1889)

1681 "Television is prominent in predictions for 1929." N.Y.T. VIII, 15 (Dec. 30): 1–6. Speculations by experts.

1682 Dinsdale, A. TELEVISION. London: Television Press, 1928, xx + 180 pp., 33 plates, 38 diags. Foreword by Dr. J.A. Fleming. 2nd ed., a much enlarged version of the 1926 book (841), more technical, with emphasis on the work of J.L. Baird. (1380, 1734)

1683 Gudden, Bernhard. LICHTELEKTRISCHE ERSCHEINUNGEN [Photoelectric phenomena]. Berlin: J. Springer, 1928. ix + 325 pp., illus.

1684 Lane, Henry M. THE BOSTON POST BOOK ON TELEVISION. Boston: Post Publishing Co., 1928. 35 pp., illus. (3384)

1685 Richards, Vyvyan. FROM CRYSTAL TO TELEVISION. "THE ELECTRON BRIDGE." A SIMPLE ACCOUNT OF WIRELESS AND TELEVISION. London: A. & C. Black, 1928. x + 116 pp., plate, 10 diags. Foreword by J.L. Baird. Chapter V, "Television," pp. 73–89.

CHAPTER 9

DESIGNS FOR TOMORROW: 1929

The vigorous growth of television during 1928 was not sustained in 1929. An increase in patent applications was offset by a decline in reportorial accounts and popular literature, a lessening that was in sympathy with reduced public interest. The drums announcing the arrival of real television in the home had been banged too hard and too long, while the dramatic events of 1928 had not led to demonstrable progress of the kind that would serve the public. Experimental services were still limited to amateurs who had no real visual equivalent of regular aural broadcasts to support or broaden their activities. Industrial participation in the United States similarly did not expand the home market as had been expected. Apart from inventive enthusiasm, the bright optimism that generally prevailed during 1928 now appeared somewhat streaked with doubt, despite a continued series of demonstrations and transmissions.

The year is noticeable more for a thrust toward the future than for acceptance of television as radio's new companion. After all, the art was still experimental, a fact that was evident in the demonstrations and transmissions, many of which relied on film for program material. Daily broadcasts began in Britain, Germany, and the United States, but without commercial support. With announcements near the end of the year that receivers would shortly be available in those countries, the possibility of television in the home began to creep into view. The picture tube also held promise as an alternative to the conventional mechanical receivers. Meanwhile, such innovative ideas as radio relays, beam transmissions, the coaxial cable, and networks at the higher frequencies, along with higher definition images, collectively formed a preview of the years to come.

Although the commercial market was less enthusiastic, industrial activity did increase, with an influx of fourteen companies: seven American, two each British, French, and German, and one Dutch. Major concerns in the United States were Bell Labs, General Electric, and Westinghouse, followed by Jenkins and RCA. New corporate entries of note included Compagnie pour la Fabrication des Compteurs et Matériel d'Usines à Gaz (Comp. Gaz) in France, Naamlooze Vennootschap Philips' Gloeilampenfabrieken (N.V. Philips) in Holland, and the Gramophone Company in Britain. This rise in corporate activities contrasts with the reduced personal contributions by inventors such as Baird, with six applications, and Jenkins with two, a change that indicates a trend as research and development became more and more the province of the larger industrial groups.

On the technical front, the increase in patent listings (from 132 in 1928 to 158 in 1929) is largely accounted for by the rise of activity in Germany, as shown by twenty-nine entries compared with ten for the previous year. Telehor A.-G. and the Telefunken Company each have six entries. C. Lorenz and Siemens & Halske are each represented by two entries; there are two by Karolus and seven by other individuals. Three entries are in the name of Fernseh A.-G., a company that was founded in July by Baird International Television Company, Loewe Radio G.m.b.H., Robert Bosch A.-G., and Zeiss-Ikon A.-G., which included the Paul Goerz optical firm. This growth, which was actively supported by the Reichs-postzentralamt (RPZ), or German Post Office, became apparent at the annual radio exhibition in Berlin.

Featured in more than seventy specifications, the disk in various forms and combinations was the prime scanning device. Apertured belts or drums appear in a dozen patents. Jenkins combined a shutter disk with an apertured drum in a compact receiver (2119) and covered another arrangement with coaxial drums (2155). Special types of scanning assemblies were specified by Watson (1791) and Fahrney (1800). Multicell or matrix arrangements appear in eight systems. The mirror drum, then coming into favor, is specified in seven entries. Kerr cells, neon lamps, phonic wheels, vibrating mirrors, and distributors are other standard components that were still in use. Various methods for obtaining synchronous control appear in a dozen patents, among which is Baird's toothed wheel (1961) that became well known in a commercial receiver. Picture tubes are specified in at least six entries, and there are three items dealing with cathode-ray tubes. This increasing awareness of the possibilities for an electronic receiver came into headlines in November when Zworykin released information about a film scanning system (1819) that incorporated a picture tube.

Most of the proposals are along conventional lines, but a dozen or so include unusual ideas. Examples of these are the scannerless methods of Kassner (1840) and Spindler (1858), Silberstein's vibrating photoelement (1756), which is reminiscent of Rtcheouloff's earlier scheme (500), Skaupy's Kerr cell apparatus (1923), Loiseau's stressed optical bodies (1946), the electrostatic system by Kendall (1993), and Birch-Field's electro-optical arrangement (2028). The hybrid system by Henroteau (1884) has a special phototube and optomechanical components, Wald's gas tube contains a matrix of crossed elements (1810), and Baird proposed a method with beam obliteration (1772). Others are the Morse (1836) and Nicolson (2066) arc methods, Walton's echelon system (1748), the three-channel system by Blackwell and Herman (2032), and the Buecker proposal (2161) with magnetic storage.

Selective or variable-area scanning methods were disclosed by Harries (1713), Baird (1759), Codelli (1898), and Bentley (1989). Suggestions to improve the optical performance of scanning disks came from Telehor A.-G. (1850), N.V. Philips (1854), Jenkins (1876), Smith (1931), and Huffman (1998). A secret transmission method applicable to all the major scanning systems was conceived by Hammond (1949), who also suggested the use of visual transmissions as a navigational aid for aircraft (1990). Other proposals of interest are Baird's double-drum arrangement with a light pipe (1721), Thun's velocity modulation in a film system (1886), Sanabria's interleaved group scan (1917), and light-beam pickup covered by Friebus (2042).

Further attempts to invade the future appear in several entries on stereo and color. Gleason's color proposal (1692) turned out to be similar to that which Baird had demonstrated previously in July. Mather's plan (1880) with perforated belts and the double-disk systems by Aspden (1719) and Lewis (1945) were intended for two-way or stereo. Loiseau's patents (1946) included colored screens, and a claim for a color system (later revealed) was put forward by Ahronheim (2037). The greatest efforts concerning the more advanced systems were made at Bell Labs, which resulted in several duplex or color patents: Ives (2072), four channels for color; Ives and Gray (1930), three channels for color; Gray (1860), a narrowed-band system for stereo or color; and two by Gray and Hefele (1742, 1859) also applicable for stereo or color.

In most respects these Bell patents were extensions of the earlier systems devised in 1927 for monochrome with the addition of newly developed photocells, color filters, neon and argon tubes, and a special semi-transparent mirror assembly in the disk receiver. With these modifications, a successful showing of color was given in June (1933). One of the highlights of the year, this demonstrated once again what could be achieved by a large organization, although the technical efforts did not bring practical television service any closer to reality. Another demonstration of a different order was that of picture transmission by a light beam (1896), staged at the Bamberger Company store in Newark in May.

Limitations of the broadcast band and the adjacent region, along with the move toward higher transmission frequencies, raised problems of bandwidth and spectrum use. Gleason (1692) discussed the need for high frequencies for color, Dinsdale (1734) covered modulation and bandwidth, Sleeper (1770) felt that adequate picture detail would require higher frequencies, Harries (1866) presented a theoretical analysis, including bandwidths, and Horton (2001) treated the subject of image transmission in general. Patents related to picture transmission include the use of composite signals by Goldsmith and Weinberger (1817), which were also covered in a companion RCA patent (1818), a method for interleaving signals by Gray (1860), a coaxial cable for the higher frequencies by Espenschied and Affel (1891), and a radio relay system by C. Lorenz A.-G. (1820). Farnsworth and Lubcke (2123) looked to the future with higher-definition images transmitted by beam relays operating in the 6-meter region. The last three items in particular represent benchmarks in the progress of the art. An allied subject, that of amplification in receivers, was discussed by Arnold (1726), Schröter (2080), and Langford-Smith (2139).

During the year the cinema industry was occupied with adding sound to motion pictures in the rush to convert to the "talkies." This innovation, coupled with the enormous popularity of the cinema, directed more attention to the use of film in television, known as telecinematography, or telecine. Since no type of camera tube was available, a film transmitter offered a way to provide program material relatively easily without the complications and limitations of live optomechanical scanning. Jenkins, who had spent most of the decade on radio movies, demonstrated his drum receiver in April (1837), still limited to silhouette pictures. Von Mihály's cinematographic method (1786), publicized in March as a "television machine" and described in April (1826), was reported to be successful during tests in Berlin (1843). Other film systems are those of Thun (1886), Hogan (1984), and John (2069).

This trend was most apparent in the United States. Film systems were developed at Bell Labs (Horton 1894) and General Electric (Hartley 2108). Patents by Smith (1962) were assigned to RCA. Those of Westinghouse include Davis (1788) with interlaced scanning, Batchelor and Vance (2104) with a picture tube, and Zworykin's (1819). Two systems were covered in British patents, one by Bowman-Manifold (2101) of the Gramophone Company, and the other by Kolster-Brandes (2151) representing the Federal Telegraph Company. Though not true television, despite the terminology sometimes used, these applications of film were further developed for mechanical and cathode-ray systems in the early 1930s.

Publicity throughout the year was more effective in promoting corporate images than in building up public demand for visual services. Baird and his associates were in the forefront with demonstrations in London, Berlin, New York, and South Africa, some of which were intended to display the Company's activities and progress and others to persuade the authorities to sanction experimental broadcasts in Britain. Bureaucratic forces were arranged two-to-one against Baird, but with some division between the BBC and the Post Office the struggle became a three-cornered affair. In response to political pressure early in the year, the Post Office considered arranging a "secret test" of the Baird system, but rumors about it quickly brought the conflict into the news again. A report (one of several) that a proposed broadcast service would commence in February (1710) was incorrect, as was the statement that plenty of receivers were available, having been "tested and approved." Such reports were evidently due to Baird's lieutenants, chiefly Hutchinson and Moseley, whose efforts at overpromotion seem to have equalled those devoted to technical developments in the laboratory.

The Baird Company's attempts to obtain broadcasting time entered a new phase with an official demonstration in March (1787), following which the Postmaster-General cautiously agreed that facilities should be made available for experimental broadcasts through the BBC's London station outside normal hours (1821). Repeated requests by the Baird people for action by the BBC eventually led in June to a paltry offer allowing morning transmissions of 15 minutes three times a week, which was refused. Further negotiations produced a more satisfactory allocation in August of 30-minute periods each weekday morning which, after formal agreement in September, started at the end of the month (2062). The opening ceremony—a victory for Baird—began a national service which the BBC later took over and continued up to September 1935.

While these proceedings were under way the Baird people continued their publicity efforts. Demonstrations to the press earlier in the year were favorably reported in NATURE (1805) and in the ELECTRICIAN (1812). But grand ideas were already being formed for expansion abroad (1762), where the official climate seemed to offer better commercial prospects for the Baird system. As more than one observer pointed out, Baird obtained greater recognition in Germany than he ever had in Britain. In a visit to Berlin he was well received by his peers and by the authorities who, unlike the British, were fostering television developments by encouraging and assisting the engineers.

Demonstrations in Berlin and the founding of the Fernseh group began a busy summer for Baird and his colleagues. In July they demonstrated their apparatus in South Africa. The following month Baird displayed an improved Noctovisor intended for navigational purposes (1988), as well as film transmission with sound called Teletalkies (1992). Plans for further international activities were revealed in New York during September (2023) and November (2102). Baird's contributions to the progress of television were recognized in November (2136) with a civic ceremony in Hastings commemorating his early experiments there in 1924.

Circumstances in Britain and Germany, where broadcasting facilities were unified under state control, were quite different from those in the United States, where the Federal Radio Commission faced growing demands for individual licenses utilizing different frequency bands. Baird's system was based on 30 lines at 12.5 pictures per second, the German standard (RPZ and Fernseh) was the same (exceptions were 12 and 48 lines), whereas the Americans were working with 24 to 60 lines up to 20 pictures (frames) per second. These higher picture rates clearly placed a burden on spectrum use, and the commissioners recognized that they would be confronted with "very serious problems if frequency bands are to be made available for regular television service." With more technical information at hand it now appeared that television broadcasting would have to be on the higher frequencies and that channel widths of 100 kilocycles were needed to transmit satisfactory picture detail. After a public hearing in February (1755), frequencies of 2000 to 2300 and 2750 to 2950 kc were allocated for experimental use for six months (later for one year), and licenses were granted to a growing number of applicants (1761).

This flurry of activity by broadcasters to provide visual services seems at variance with a more reserved public response, but promoters apparently were optimistic, since some two dozen U.S. stations were in various stages of readiness for television broadcasting by early summer (1920). Station W2XBS (RCA) began a daily schedule in March (1813). Daily programs by station W2XBU (H.E. Smith) were announced in July (1959). Westinghouse (W8XAY) began daily film broadcasts in August (1995). The Jenkins Corporation announced plans for a station (W2XCR) in Jersey City (1711) and for one (W3XK) near Washington (1715) in January, about which reports appeared from time to time up to the end of the year (2131). Other active stations were listed in September: W1XAY, Lexington, W2XCW, General Electric, Schenectady, and W9XAA, Chicago Federation of Labor. Alexanderson, Conrad, Farnsworth, Sanabria, and others who had made news in 1928 were, for the time being, no longer in the public eye.

Parallel questions on the provision of transmission services and receivers (an egg-and-chicken quandary) appeared to be insoluble except at increased cost to the broadcasters. Financial resources of concerns such as Baird's and Jenkins' had to provide for the development and construction of transmitting equipment, for demonstrations and publicity, and for the production of home receivers as well, since no other manufacturer had entered the domestic market. The Westinghouse plans of 1928 (1568) for producing receivers were not carried out, nor were those of other companies who had announced that their receivers or kits would be on sale—presumably because of the small demand. Some interest in amateur construction still existed, catered to by a few articles such as those in RADIO NEWS (1824) and TELEVISION (1912). Early in the year an improved receiver by von Mihály was reported in glowing terms (1763). An unnamed inventor demonstrated a receiver in Berlin in May (1882). The Jenkins Television Corporation proclaimed in November that receivers would soon be available (2081), and Fernseh also intended to market a standard receiver. Although there had been little response to the Baird range of receivers (1523) demonstrated in September 1928, a new table model (2147) was nevertheless ready for release to the market early in 1930.

Still much of a novelty, television was featured again at the national radio exhibitions in Berlin, New York, and London. The Television Society began a tradition with their first annual exhibition in March (1804). A highlight of the one-day event was a surprise display by L.B. Atkinson of apparatus which he had devised for experiments in 1882 (169). A full report of the exhibits appeared in April (1832). Television was said to have lured the crowds at the New York Radio Show in September (2043), where demonstrations excited great interest but did not present any threat to the radio dealers. The exhibition in Berlin, however, was particularly significant, since it revealed the beginning of intensive developments evolving through cooperation between government and industry. Displays were put on by the Post Office, which also ran regular film transmissions for the other exhibitors: Telefunken, von Mihály, Fernseh, and Baird.

Telefunken (Karolus) displayed a 48-line transmitter, an arc projection receiver with a Kerr cell, and a small neon-tube receiver, all with mirror drums. Following the tentative German standard (30/12.5), the Post Office and Fernseh systems employed disks with horizontal scanning and a picture ratio (height-to-width) of 3 to 4. Baird's was similar but with vertical scanning and a tall picture, about 2 to 1. Von Mihály showed a small 12-hole disk receiver, a larger one with a 30-hole disk and two transmitters, one for slides and the other for film. Fernseh and von Mihály were then transmitting experimental programs daily from Witzleben, and the Post Office had plans for daily film transmissions with a new transmitter later in the year. According to reports, the Fernseh display was most popular, as was a two-way telephone-television booth set up by the Post Office, an innovation ascribed to G. Krawinkel. Other accounts (2085, 2118) confirm the vitality of work in progress and a promising outlook for television in Germany.

Differences in various systems in the United States prompted further consideration of standards. These included number of lines, number of frames per second, and the picture proportions, the latter being expressed by a number equivalent to the scanning lines. The Jenkins stations and those in Chicago and Lexington operated with 48 lines and 15 frames per second (48/15) with square (48/48) pictures. Those of General Electric and Smith operated with fewer lines and a higher repetition rate (24/20), also with square pictures. The Bell Labs system in the color demonstration employed 50 lines at 18 frames per second. The RCA and Westinghouse systems provided greater detail with more lines (60/20) and a picture somewhat wider (60/72), or a ratio of 5 to 6. During the summer, the Television Standardization Committee of the RMA recommended the latter elements for commercial standards (1999) and others for amateurs (2051). These and other aspects of standards were treated in a technical paper (2003) by RCA engineers.

Comments by spokesmen and would-be prophets in America indicate a lowered level of enthusiasm over progress and more doubt about the future. According to Sarnoff and Raycroft, television for the home was not yet "around the corner." The evident fact that the infant art was still experimental was stressed by Sarnoff and Replogle. Richmond, believing that no important change was in sight, asserted that television could be "dismissed" for the present. Commissioner Lafount, however, could see rapid expansion toward more general use. De Forest thought otherwise, placing the advent of real television as being likely within five years, while radio men did not expect any commercial expansion for another two years. Opinions in Britain were mostly related to the national scene, with side glances at events abroad; views supporting Baird were chiefly expressed in TELEVISION, while the critics had their say elsewhere. Swinton's adamant opposition to mechanical methods, aimed primarily at Baird, finally gave way to recognition that his disk system could provide small but acceptable pictures. This gracious letter (2154), Swinton's last on the subject written shortly before his death, happily ended the long debate.

An overview of events shows continued technical progress in both the quantity of patents and their diversity. A move toward picture tubes was tentatively under way, the adoption of which awaited development of high-vacuum types that would be more efficient and dependable, longer lasting, and producible at reasonable cost. Camera tubes also awaited similar but more intensive developments in the laboratory. Since progress in technical matters was not general knowledge, the public and most industry leaders, at least in America, were inclined to suppose that the problems facing television would prevent any expansion into the commercial field for some time to come. Unlike the widespread acceptance enjoyed by radio some seven years earlier, the intruder was still a curiosity from the general point of view. Television, it seemed, was not yet ready for the living room. This apparent pause in progress, however, was no deterrent to the engineers and promoters, who already had designs for tomorrow as well as plans for a surge of activity with more impressive demonstrations in the year to come.

TABLE 14   CHRONOLOGY: 1929

Jan. 7	FRC	Limits transmission times
9	Baird Co., BBC	Premature reports on broadcasts
Feb. 18	FRC	Grants experimental licenses
21	Baird Co.	Report on progress
22	von Mihály	Report on new system
Mar. 2	FRC	Allocates high-frequency bands
5	Baird Co.	Demonstration to GPO and BBC
	Television Society	First exhibition
Mar. 15	Baird Co.	Demonstration to reporters
21	RCA	Broadcasts from station W2XBS
26	Zworykin	Film system with picture tube
27	C. Lorenz A.-G.	Radio relay system for television
28	GPO	Report on Baird demonstration, Mar. 5
Apr. 7	Jenkins	Report on silhouette film apparatus
11	FRC	Limits channel width
12	Jenkins	Plans test of airborne television
13	von Mihály	Report on reception in Berlin
14	Goldsmith	Report on demonstration
30	Gray	Interleaved-frequency system
May 14	IRE	Convention, papers on television
18	Thun	Film system with velocity modulation
23	Espenschied, Affel	Coaxial cable
28	U.S. Radio and Television Corp.	Demonstration with light beam at Bamberger & Co.
June	Baird Co.	Demonstrations in Berlin
7	Sanabria	Interleaved group scan
26	Ives, Gray	Color system
27	Bell Labs	Color demonstration
July	Fernseh A.-G.	New German television company
3	Hammond	System for secret television
7	von Mihály	Report on portable daylight apparatus
14	Smith	Broadcasts from station W2XBU
17	Baird	Toothed-wheel synchronizer
22	Baird Co.	Demonstrations in South Africa
Aug. 9	Baird	Demonstrates Noctovisor
17	Hammond	Navigational system for aircraft
19	Baird	Demonstrates Teletalkies
24	Westinghouse	Broadcasts from station W8XAY

Sept.	Various	Displays at Berlin Radio Show
2	Baird Corp.	Demonstration in New York
12	Baird Co.,	BBC statement on proposed broadcasts
22	Ahronheim	Report on claim for a color system
23	Baird Co.	Display at the British Radio Show
	Various	Displays at the Radio World's Fair, N.Y.
25	Friebus	Light-beam pickup for record disk
30	Baird Co.,	BBC first official transmission
Oct.	Dinsdale	Report on Berlin Radio Show
Nov.	Fernseh A.-G.	Plans for marketing receivers
	Jenkins Corp.	Plans for marketing receivers
7	Baird	Civic recognition at Hastings
15	Hutchinson	Publicity for Baird Co. in New York
16	Zworykin	Picture tube (Kinescope)
18	Zworykin	Lecture on film system with picture tube
Dec.	Farnsworth,	Article on higher-definition images,
	Lubcke	beam transmitters, and network broadcasting
	Zworykin	Report on film system with picture tube
6	Baird Co.	Plans for marketing receivers
16	Swinton	Favorable letter on Baird transmission
20	Baird Corp.	Demonstration in New York

BIBLIOGRAPHY: 1929

1686 "New television system minus disk." POP. SCI. 114 (Jan): 61.

1687 Carr, J. "Your first television set." POP. SCI. 114 (Jan.): 65. (1626)

1688 Vinogradow, C.N. "Télévision et téléviseurs." QSTF 10 (Jan.): 50–3. 11 illus. Methods, apparatus, modulation, sync, von Mihály's system. (1520, 1694)

1689 Thurm, L. "Un nouveau système de télévision et de télécinématographie." QSTF 10 (Jan.): 58,59. 6 illus. (1554)

1690 Phelps, B. "Unscrambling television." RADIO BRD. 14 (Jan.): 157, 158. 2 photos, diag. Experiments with sound to determine the scan frequency of signals. (1630, 1641, 1693, 1729)

1691 Hertzberg, R. "Television, the latest developments in the field." RADIO N. 10 (Jan.): 630, 631, 666, 668. 3 photos. Standards and definitions (1665). New disk system announced by Kodel Electric and Mfg. Co. List of television broadcasting schedules, 10 stations with wavelengths, and details of disks. (1634, 3275)

1692 Gleason, C. Sterling. "High frequencies for color television." RADIO N. 10 (Jan.): 632, 633, 678–80. Illus. Discussion of problems, mechanism, and bandwidth. System proposed is like Baird's. (Editorial note: Identical scheme to Baird's described in our October issue, not published when this manuscript was received.) "Mechanism required to produce images in true colors will present few difficulties, but great width of frequency bands will create some problems of transmission."

1693 Mason, C.P. "Giving television the 'last touches.'" RADIO N. 10 (Jan.): 634–6, 681, 682. 5 diags. Practical problems, frequency, light intensity, scanning apertures, picture detail, speed adjustment, sync, distortion. (1433, 1690, 1696)

1694 "New television systems." RADIO N. 10 (Jan.): 637. Two photos of Farnsworth and his apparatus, 3 photos of von Mihály apparatus. (1619, 1688, 1763, 2123)

1695 Winters, S.R. "Radiovision." SCI. & INV. 16 (Jan.): 840. 4 photos, diag. Karolus liquid light cell, Farnsworth apparatus, Jenkins mosaic and distributor assembly, and outdoor Radiovisor. (715)

1696 "Complete television receiver." SCI. & INV. 16 (Jan.): 841. Photo and text, disk machine. (1693, 1707)

1697 Moseley, S.A. "The power behind television." TELEV. 1 (Jan.): 5. On O.G. Hutchinson. (1358, 1652, 1706, 2102)

1698 "The world-wide influence of the Baird system." TELEV. 1 (Jan.): 6–8. 5 photos. New companies being formed abroad, great interest displayed, activities in Europe, South Africa, and New Zealand. (1666, 1699)

1699 Robinson, J. "Review of the present position in television." TELEV. 1 (Jan.): 9–11. 2 illus. Criticism of the BBC, discussion of Baird's system and response to criticism about it, amateur's part in television, technical points. (1644, 1645, 1698, 1710, 2053)

1700 Brittain, W.J. "Television—first with the news." TELEV. 1 (Jan.): 14. (1618, 1775)

1701 Wolfson, H. "Cathode rays." TELEV. 1 (Jan.): 17–21. Photo, 8 diags. Possibilities for application in television instead of mechanical methods, historical background, X rays, oscillographs, argon-filled cathode-ray tube, Swinton's proposal, Belin and Holweck system. (1653, 1736)

1702 "Who's who in television." TELEV. 1 (Jan.): 22. Sir Edward Manville, Lord Ampthill.

1703 Sylvester, C. "Light; the essential of television. Pt. 5." TELEV. 1 (Jan.): 23, 24, 29. Photo, 5 diags. (1650, 1740)

1704 Mitchell, W.G.W., and J.J. Denton. "The Television Society." TELEV. 1 (Jan.): 25–9. 5 photos, diag. Report of December meeting, lecture by F.J. Cheshire on tuning forks, other demonstrations. (1651, 1738)

1705 Rennie, J.C. "Vision in television." TELEV. 1 (Jan.): 30, 34. Comments on British and American attitudes. (1583, 1872)

1706 "S.A. Moseley tells the world!" TELEV. 1 (Jan.): 32, 37. On the British controversy and on Baird's critics, N. Edwards and P.P. Eckersley. (1697, 1735)

1707 Church, A. "Television and the amateur." TELEV. 1 (Jan): 33, 34. (1378, 1696, 1729)

1708 Centeno V, M. "Television." U.S. 1,800,601, Jan. 7, 1929, Apr. 14, 1931. Compound vibrating mirror assembly. (952, 1977)

1709 "Television limited to after midnight." N.Y.T. 40 (Jan. 8): 4. FRC order limiting transmission from midnight to 6 a.m. (1677, 1728)

1710 "Television next month. B.B.C. experimental broadcasts. Public reception." MAN. GUARD. 9 (Jan. 9): 4. "The B.B.C. have now apparently changed their attitude, and next month listeners-in will have the opportunity of looking-in as well." Baird television experts "have plans ready for musical and dramatic entertainments...if the experiment succeeds and the thing becomes regularised television sets will be available for the looker-in. Two thousand of these sets have been tested and approved." (1699, 1721, 1774)

1711 "Television due here soon." N.Y.T. 16 (Jan. 11): 3. Jenkins Television Corp., Clarement Avenue, N.J., to establish broadcasting station soon. (1658, 1715)

1712 Conrad, F. "Television." U.S. 1,991,082, Jan. 18, 1929, Feb. 12, 1935. Assigned: Westinghouse. Sync motor with scanning disk mounted on the rotor shaft. (1579, 1718)

1713 Harries, John Henry Owen. "Television." Br. 326,603, Jan. 19, 1929. Fine scan of selected parts of the field of view. (1866)

1714 Meenam, W.T. "Strange 'tongue' greets listeners." N.Y.T. IX, 18 (Jan. 20): 1. "Peculiar drones and squeals that indicate television images are in the air."

1715 "Jenkins to build television station." N.Y.T. IX, 19 (Jan. 20): 7, 8. Station now being erected about 5 miles north of the national capital, said to be the first strictly for television. Jenkins Corporation will distribute motion picture stories for use by television stations. (1711, 1746)

1716 Fries, G., and P. Sommer. "Television." Br. 347,251, Jan. 21, 1930. In Germany Jan. 21, 1929. Mirror disk and cam coacting with mirrors. Also photo recording. (1967)

1717 Naamlooze Vennootschap Philips' Gloeilampenfabrieken (N.V. Philips). (By S.G.S. Dicker). "Television." Br. 328,227, Jan. 21, 1929. Discharge tube circuit. (1743)

1718 Conrad, F. "Television system." U.S. 1,853,661, Jan. 23, 1929, Apr. 12, 1932. Assigned: Westinghouse. Scanning disk with belt drive and damper to eliminate speed variations. (1712, 1995)

1719 Aspden, R.L. "Television." Br. 325,362, Jan. 24, 1929. Disk with two semi-spiral sets of apertures and a selector disk with opposed outer and inner semi-spiral curved slots for stereoscopic television or telecinematography. (977, 2611)

1720 "Calls television infant." N.Y.T. 18 (Jan. 27): 1. Views of D. Sarnoff. (1669, 1744)

1721 Baird, J.L., and Television Ltd. "Television." Br. 328,616, Jan. 31, 1929, Apr. 30, 1930. Concave mirrors on two side-by-side drums. Specifies a neon lamp or a bent quartz rod (light pipe). Divided: Br. 330,220 (1722); Br. 328,691 (1747). Baird included a light pipe in a patent (640) in 1925. (1710)

1722 Baird, J.L., Television Ltd., and Baird Television Development Co. Ltd. "Television." Br. 330,220, Jan. 31, 1929, June 2, 1930. Divided from Br. 328,616 (1721); addition to Br. 291,121 (814). Image is obliterated at the end of each scan by light on an optically sensitive substance, such as gum guaiacum, or by current of opposite polarity through brush contacts on a disk acting on chemically prepared paper. (1733)

1723 Hughes, C.E. Letter. DISCOVERY 10 (Feb.): 49. A photo of a television image should not be used in judging the detail of a moving image.

1724 Swinton, A.A.C. "Television." DISCOVERY 10 (Feb.): 49. Letter reiterating his belief that "the present workers at the subject are engaged in a hopeless quest which can never lead to real success." Swinton also agrees with the BBC's decision "to leave the matter alone," and has some strong views on "Stock Exchange speculators." Reference to the editorial note (1549) and Pullin's letter (1623). (1556, 1815)

1725 "Radio pictures made lifelike." POP. SCI. 114 (Feb.): 58.

1726 Arnold, J.P. "Amplification of photoelectric currents." RADIO 11 (Feb.): 17, 18. Photo, 3 diags. Amplifiers in television circuits. Bibliography, 4 items. (1627, 1862)

1727 "'Televisualization' as it was." RADIO 11 (Feb.): 20. Newspaper quotations. N.Y. WORLD, June 10, 1909: devices are now almost as numerous as catarrh cures and just about as effective; Dec. 12, 1909: Alberto Sanchez, Mexico City, on the term "teleradiopticon." N.Y. HERALD, Apr. 8, 1910: on William Vincent Pruscino, Italian of Rochester, N.Y., object seen at thousands of miles in color, 3-D, etc. (1618, 2836)

1728 "Schedule of broadcast television transmission." RADIO BRD. 14 (Feb.): 234. Details of 12 stations, with note on the FRC limitations (1709). (1752)

1729 Phelps, B. "Transmitting amateur television." RADIO BRD. 14 (Feb.): 247–9. 4 photos, diag. Amateur construction, scanning disk, amplifier circuit. (1690, 1707, 1769)

1730 "What is happening in the television field?" RADIO N. 10 (Feb.): 719, 762. Review of activities.

1731 Clark, P.L. "Television light modulator." SCI. & INV. 16 (Feb.): 950, 951, 998. 3 illus. Light split through gratings, modulated by mirror oscillograph. (1265, 2175)

1732 "Television in the schools." SCI. & INV. 16 (Feb.): 951. Photo, with caption, of a group at the Lane Technical High School in Chicago.

1733 Tierney, C. "The future of television." TELEV. 1 (Feb.): 5–7. 3 photos. In support of Baird, with references to various demonstrations: exhibition boxing, a cyclist riding round a ring, and projection of an image onto "a screen some four feet in diameter." The cast of the play "Box and Cox" is shown in two photos. (1379, 1722, 1738, 2087)

1734 Dinsdale, A. "More room in the ether." TELEV. 1 (Feb): 8–10. 6 diags. Carrier wave, modulation, bandwidth, frequency modulation. (1682, 1796)

1735 Moseley, S.A. "Now then, Capt. Eckersley!" TELEV. 1 (Feb.): 11, 12. (1706, 1777)

1736 Wolfson, H. "The carbon arc." TELEV. 1 (Feb.): 15–8. 7 diags. Characteristics and construction, application in television. (1701, 1782)

1737 Lupton, Bertha. "A woman's view of television." TELEV. 1 (Feb.): 21, 22.

1738 Denton, J.J., and W.G.W. Mitchell. "The Television Society." TELEV. 1 (Feb.): 28–33. Photo, 5 diags. Report of January meeting and lecture by Denton, "On television research." Ionization, selenium cells, Baird's spotlight system, Phonovision recordings and reproduction, infrared and Noctovision, color television, stereoscopic television, invention, and team work. (1704, 1733, 1739, 1747, 1780)

1739 Mitchell, W.G.W. "The cathode-ray tube in practical television." TELEV. 1 (Feb.): 38–41. 6 photos, 5 diags. The cathode-ray oscillograph, effect of magnetic fields, principles, Lissajous figures, Swinton's plan (413), Zworykin's system (695). (1738, 1780)

1740 Sylvester, C. "Light; the essential of television. Pt. 6." TELEV. 1 (Feb.): 42, 43, 45. 5 diags. (1703, 1776)

1741 Reeve, A.S. "De Quincey foresaw television." TELEV. 1 (Feb.): 48. Letter, with quotation from Thomas De Quincey's "Travelling in England in the Old Days." (2599)

1742 Gray, F., and John R. Hefele. "Electro-optical transmission system." U.S. 1,769,918, Feb. 2, 1929, July 8, 1930. Assigned: B.T.L. Single spiral disk for duplex or stereo, with interposed image and nonimage signals. Also Br. 332,284. (1675, 1859)

1743 N.V. Philips (by S.G.S. Dicker): "Electric synchronous movements." Br. 325,979, Feb. 2, 1929. Receiver scanning disk has a wheel with magnetic teeth and coil actuated by relaxation oscillators and an electromagnetic brake. (1717, 1854)

1744 "Radio vision forges ahead but slowly." N.Y.T. IX, 19 (Feb. 3): 8. Views of D. Sarnoff: television for home use is not around the corner. (1720, 2247)

1745 "Television broadcast over WGY tonight." N.Y.T. IX, 20 (Feb. 3): 3. Transmission of picture of D.W. Griffith from station 2XAD and voice from WGY. Reception was reported in Los Angeles. (1638, 1779)

1746 "Jenkins broadcasting station in Jersey City." N.Y.T. IX, 20 (Feb. 3): 7. (1715, 1769)

1747 Baird, J.L., and Television Ltd. "Television." Br. 328,691, Feb. 4, 1929. Electrodeless discharge tube and circuit. Divided from Br. 328,616 (1721). (1738, 1753)

1748 Walton, G.W. "Scanning device." U.S. 2,088,626, Feb. 6, 1930, renewed Oct. 27, 1936, Aug. 3, 1937. In Britain Feb. 4, 1929. Cylindrical lens and echelon assembly in an optical system. (1542, 2612)

1749 Trouant, Virgil E. "Television." U.S. 1,832,672, Feb. 5, 1929, Nov. 17, 1931. Assigned: Westinghouse. Br. 354,294, Feb. 3, 1930. Void. Receiver with scanning disk and modulated discharge tube.

1750 Bronk, O.v. "Electric picture transmission." U.S. 1,976,377, Jan. 28, 1930, Oct. 9, 1934. In Germany Feb. 7, 1929. Assigned: Telefunken. Receiver with a bank of glow lamps and control circuits. (694, 2198)

1751 Schneider et Cie. "Television." Br. 353,851, Jan. 24, 1930. Void. In France Feb. 9, 1929. Apertured disks, sync by interrupted wavetrains.

1752 "A public hearing for television." N.Y.T. X, 21 (Feb. 10): 8. FRC hearing on allocations, Feb. 14. (1728, 1755)

1753 "Baird Television Development." TIMES (Feb. 12): 24g. Company report to June 30. Development and exploitation expenditure at £24,950, patent rights, trademarks, etc. at £21,092. Cash figures at £61,572. (1747, 1759)

1754 Gramophone Co. and R.B. Morgan. "Sound recording, television." Br. 326,306, Feb. 12, 1929. Discharge tube with magnetic control. (2228)

1755 "Oppose television on broadcast band." N.Y.T. 16 (Feb. 15): 1. Views of experts at FRC hearing, including de Forest, who said he had done practically nothing on television, and Jenkins, who wanted picture transmissions kept in the bands allocated. (1752, 1758)

1756 Silberstein, Ludwik. "Electrotelescopy." U.S. 1,839,706, Feb. 15, 1929, Jan. 5, 1932. Assigned: United Research. Photo-element on the free end of a compound vibrating rod. (1893)

1757 Zworykin, V.K. "Television." U.S. 1,817,502, Feb. 15, 1929, Aug. 4, 1931. Assigned: Westinghouse. Br. 332,886, Feb. 15, 1930. Spiral of opaque spots on a transparent scanning disk, glow lamp. (1050, 1819)

1758 "Radio aide backs nominees to Board." N.Y.T. 32 (Feb. 19): 6. Experimental licenses granted by FRC for use on short waves to Jenkins, Pilot Electric Co. of Brooklyn, station WAAM, Newark, N.J., and station WLEX, Lexington, Mass. (1755, 1761)

1759 Baird, J.L., and Television Ltd. "Television." Br. 329,664, Feb. 19, 1929. Different arrangements of scanning apertures with varying radial depths and sizes, improved disk construction, and optical features to give a finer grain in the center of an image and to eliminate the parallax effect. (1753, 1762)

1760 Karolus, A. "Photoelectric amplifying system." U.S. 2,042,602, Jan. 27, 1930, June 2, 1936. Assigned: RCA. In Germany Feb. 19, 1929. Disk system with two photocells in series. (1514, 1875)

1761 "Board licenses visual broadcasts." N.Y.T. 28 (Feb. 20): 6. FRC grants permits to 17 stations. (1758, 1765)

1762 "Baird Television Development Co. Remarkable progress reported. Installations in France and Germany." TIMES (Feb. 21): 23b-d. First ordinary general meeting, Sir Edward Manville's speech. A thorough overview of developments, with plans for expansion. (1759, 1773)

1763 "German announces improved television." N.Y.T. 16 (Feb. 22): 4. Von Mihály's new receiver. One type provides an image 4 by 6 inches, costs $25; a larger size costs $100. System considered to be superior to the English or U.S. versions, with larger pictures, perfect sync that needs no adjustments, pictures that keep sharp, low price. (1694, 1786)

1764 Tambert, Elmer A. "Scanning device." U.S. 1,767,718, Feb. 23, 1929, June 24, 1930. Aperture plate on a rotating carrier moves at right angles to the direction of motion.

1765 "Ripples of radio news eddying in the ether. Television licenses are granted several stations." N.Y.T. X, 17 (Feb. 24): 4–8. To RCA for stations W2XBW, New York, W2XBY, New Jersey; to Jenkins for W3XK, and others. (1761, 1785)

1766 Compagnie pour la Fabrication des Compteurs et Matériel d'Usines à Gaz (Comp. Gaz). "Synchronous movements." Br. 350,506, Feb. 4, 1930. In France Feb. 25, 1929. Speed control of disk with eddy-current brake, toothed wheel, commutator, and rotary magnet. See Telehor A.-G. (1835), Baird (1961). (1842)

1767 Cummings, Byron R. "Scanning disk." U.S. 1,810,598, Feb. 26, 1929, June 16, 1931. Assigned: G.E. Lens disk.

1768 "Problems of television." CIT. RAD. CALL BOOK 10 (Mar.): 97, 98. Picture detail, scanning and image composition, bandwidth, frequencies, luminosity, sync, film pickup, radio movies.

1769 "Jenkins broadcast suggestions." CIT. RAD. CALL BOOK 10 (Mar.): 98, 131, 132. Tips on driving motor assembly, sync, receiver adjustments. (1729, 1746, 1778, 1799)

1770 Sleeper, M.B. "What price television?" QST 13 (Mar.): 48, 49, 90. Critical comments: disk must be eliminated, high frequencies about 3 megacycles are needed for transmission of adequate details.

1771 d'Ailly, G.H. "L'amplification dans la télévision." QSTF 10 (Mar.): 45.

1772 Dreher, C. Book review. RADIO BRD. 14 (Mar.): 354. On Larner's PRACTICAL TELEVISION (1179). Quotes Hutchinson's "irresponsible ballyhoo" of the Baird system, and surveys the book's contents. (1015, 2022)

1773 "Prominent Continentals enthusiastic over British television." TELEV. 2 (Mar.): 5, 6. 3 illus. Favorable views on Baird's system. (1762, 1774)

1774 "How the 'war' ended." TELEV. 2 (Mar.): 9, 10. 2 photos. Comments on the BBC versus Baird. (1710, 1773, 1777)

1775 Brittain, W.J. "Television is the latest of the 'impossibilities.'" TELEV. 2 (Mar.): 16. General comments. (1700)

1776 Sylvester, C. "Light; the essential of television. Pt. 7." TELEV. 2 (Mar.): 19, 20, 22. 5 illus. (1740, 1830)

1777 Moseley, S.A. "On 'at last!'" TELEV. 2 (Mar.): 21, 22. BBC and Baird. (1735, 1774, 1781, 1787, 1827)

1778 Martin, E.V.R. "A simple shadowgraph transmitter." TELEV. 2 (Mar.): 23–6. 4 photos, diag. Description of homemade televisor demonstrated at Midland Institute, Derby, Jan. 15. (1769, 1824)

1779 "American instrument developments in 1928." TELEV. 2 (Mar): 27, 30. Photo. Review of G.E. apparatus. (1745, 2178)

1780 Denton, J.J., and W.G.W. Mitchell. "The Television Society." TELEV. 2 (Mar.): 31–8. 2 photos, 5 graphs, 5 diags. Report of Feb. 5 meeting and lecture by Ronald R. Poole on "Methods of light modulation in television receivers." Notes on early selenium systems, Korn light valve, Duddell oscillograph, von Mihály's vibrating mirror Telehor, cathode-ray oscillographs, neon tubes, Moore's tubes, characteristics of neon and limits on illumination, Kerr cell, measurements. (1738, 1739, 1792, 1832)

1781 Taynton, W. "The first television subject." TELEV. 2 (Mar.): 38. Portrait. Account of his participation in Baird's experiment. Oct. 2, 1925. (1329, 1777, 1787)

1782 Wolfson, H. "Luminescence." TELEV. 2 (Mar): 39–41. 2 photos. (1736, 1828)

1783 Belus, M. "La télévision ou transmission à distance des images animées" [Television or transmission of moving images at a distance]. TECH. MOD. 21 (Mar. 1): 129–33. 12 illus. General survey.

1784 Schmidling, Gilbert T. "Television." U.S. 1,765,453, Mar. 1, 1929, June 24, 1930. Assigned: A.J. Carter. Scanning disk and mirror. (2614)

1785 "Commission adopts television policy." N.Y.T. IX, 21 (Mar. 3): 6. Allocation of high frequencies for 6 months: 2000–2300 kc and 2750–2950 kc. (1765, 1794)

1786 Mihály, D. v. "Cinematographic television." U.S. 2,113,487, Mar. 3, 1930, Apr. 5, 1938. Assigned: Telehor A.-G. Br. 335, 518, June 18, 1929. In Germany Mar. 5, 1929. Nipkow disk and film transmission. (1763, 1806)

1787 "Baird television system." TIMES (Mar. 6): 8d, 8e. Demonstration witnessed by the Postmaster-General (Sir William Mitchell-Thompson, PMG 1924–1929, later Lord Selsdon, 1877–1938), a few MPs, BBC representatives, and Prof. Fleming. There was "widespread opinion that the whole system will not stand examination," also reports of "great speculation on the Stock Exchange." (1532, 1781, 1790, 1805)

1788 Davis, R.L. "Television system." U.S. 2,128,078, Mar. 6, 1929, Aug. 23, 1938. Assigned: Westinghouse. Film transmission with interlaced scanning. (1306)

1789 Watson, Arthur H. "Apparatus for producing speaking and sound pictures." U.S. 1,787,919, Mar. 6, 1929, Jan. 6, 1931. Receiver cabinet with record player, viewing screen, and loudspeaker. Record carries impressions for vision, sound, and sync. (1791)

1790 "The progress of television. More detailed images." TIMES (Mar. 7): 27c. Mainly on bandwidth. At a recent demonstration at Baird's laboratory the time on a watch could be seen. (1787, 1805)

1791 Watson, A.H. "Television." U.S. 1,787,920, Mar. 7, 1929, Jan. 6, 1931. Scanning wheel with spokelike concave reflectors and variants such as angular segmented reflectors placed inside or outside a cone-shaped carrier with constructional and assembly details. (1789, 1855)

1792 "Television progress." ELECT. 102 (Mar. 8): 286. Brief report on the Television Society's first exhibition held at the Engineers' Club, Mar. 5. (1780, 1803)

1793 "Columbia system selects new home." N.Y.T. 28 (Mar. 8): 5. New building at Madison Avenue and 52nd Street will have one studio equipped for television broadcasting. (2607)

1794 "Television broadcasters." SCIENCE 69 (Mar. 8): Supp. 12. On recent FRC hearings and permits for 11 experimental stations. (1785, 1841)

1795 Telefunken. "Television." Br. 350,959, Mar. 10, 1930. In Germany Mar. 8, 1929. Bank of photocells or lamps with mechanical distributor and an electronic distributor consisting of a multiple-anode tube and solenoids to control the discharge. (1221, 1890)

1796 "Our bookshelf." NATURE 123 (Mar. 9): 373. Review of Dinsdale's TELEVISION, 2nd ed. (1734, 2055)

1797 "Television developments." POP. W. (Mar. 9): 1336.

1798 "Will television be ready for the next inaugural?" N.Y.T. XI, 17 (Mar. 10): 1–3.

1799 "Television movies to start in month." N.Y.T. 30 (Mar. 11): 5, 6. Jenkins program for broadcasting silhouette films from station 2XCR, 5 kw, 140 m, images 48/15. Halftone images are to be broadcast later with a 50-kc bandwidth. Receiver provides images 6 in. sq. with magnifier. (1769, 1807)

1800 Fahrney, Callo D. "Television." U.S. 1,862,743, Mar. 11, 1929, June 14, 1932. Concentric cone-shaped drums, one slotted and one with spirals of apertures, mounted in a receiver cabinet with motor, gearing, lamp, and viewing mirror. (1801)

1801 Fahrney, C.D. "Television." U.S. 1,777,556, Mar. 13, 1929, Oct. 7, 1930. Scanning disk receiver with magnifying mirror. (1800, 2355)

1802 Lux, Heinz. "Picture scanning system." U.S. 1,852,784, Apr. 16, 1930, Apr. 5, 1932. Assigned: Telefunken. Br. 348,260, Mar. 1, 1930. In Germany Mar. 13, 1929. Disk with chordal slots and a rotary mirror. (2787)

1803 "Television exhibition." ELECT. REV. 104 (Mar. 15): 494. (1792, 1804)

1804 "Television exhibition." ELECT. 102 (Mar. 15): 331. 6 photos. Television Society's exhibition, Mar. 5. Description and pictures of L.B. Atkinson's apparatus of 1882 (169). Mention of other exhibitors. (1803, 1832)

1805 "News and views." NATURE 123 (Mar. 16): 422. On the Post Office considering the Baird system for a broadcasting service, with favorable comments on images transmitted by wire: "the time, for example, on the performer's watch can be easily read." (1787, 1790, 1812, 1821)

1806 "A television machine developed by Denes von Mihály in Berlin." N.Y.T. X, 18 (Mar. 17): 3. Photo of von Mihály with disk and film apparatus. (1786, 1826)

1807 "Television broadcasts planned for New York area within a few weeks." N.Y.T. X, 23 (Mar. 17): 2, 3. Jenkins. (1799, 1823)

1808 "Television needs three waves to be successful, says Replogle." N.Y.T. X, 23 (Mar. 17): 6. Separate channels for different services, at least 100 kc. (1574, 1925)

1809 Thilo, Hans Georg. "Diaphragm for apparatus for picture telegraphy." U.S. 1,924,700, Apr. 5, 1930, Aug. 29, 1933. Assigned: Siemens & Halske A.-G. In Germany Mar. 18, 1929. Variable width semi-spiral slotted disk and transverse aperture.

1810 Wald, George. "Transmission and reception of television." U.S. 1,754,491, Mar. 18, 1929, Apr. 15, 1930. Matrix of crossed elements in a gas-filled tube controlled by selectors for rows and columns in a receiver. (1792, 1804)

1811 "WNYC gets extension on building permit." N.Y.T. 35 (Mar. 19): 6. Permit granted to Z. Bouck, note on station W2XCL. (1562)

1812 "Television demonstrated." ELECT. 102 (Mar. 22): 339, 340. Demonstration of Baird apparatus over a wire circuit on Mar. 15. Favorable comments on the images and other remarks concerning future developments. (1805, 1821)

"Most of the deep shadows so prominent in the last demonstration attended by us appear now to have developed into shadows of a type that one might reasonably hope to overcome by suitably 'making-up' the 'televisee.' The picture, as it can at present be received by the Baird system is not perfect, but the results are, nevertheless, a distinct improvement on previous reception, and very encouraging. During the demonstration a group of four people was transmitted, and, considering the difficulties attaching to such a transmission, the results were remarkably good. Apart from the general movements of the subject, the main details of the picture, such as the teeth, whites of the eyes, etc., could be observed. Further, having seen a face by television one could recognize its owner in the flesh; this point is one of some importance, for it indicates that the distortion brought about by the transmission is not so serious as one might expect at this stage of development.

"In conclusion, we would express the opinion that the ultimate success and perfection of television is dependent upon the close co-operation of those interested in the subject. Mr. Baird has done his share, and, as present results show, is still doing useful work; nevertheless, if the past is any indication of the future, such a subject can never be fully developed by a single mind. As in the early days of radio, new thought brought new ideas, and so must it be with television. Mr. Baird has made considerable progress so far, and one may ask the question: Is he to carry on, or will someone else show the way?"

1813 "Television placed on daily schedule." N.Y.T. 20 (Mar. 22): 2. Station W2XBS now broadcasting images regularly from 7 to 9 p.m. Experimental work by A.N. Goldsmith, RCA. (1668, 1817, 1822, 1902)

1814 Telehor A.-G. "Combined picture and sound transmitter." Br. 334,967, June 18, 1929. In Germany Mar. 22, 1929. Nipkow disk, signals alternated at a high frequency. (1673, 1835)

1815 Swinton, A.A.C. "Practical television and its problems." NATURE 123 (Mar. 23): 449, 450. Reference to book review, Mar. 9 (1796). Comments on the inadequacies of mechanical methods, chiefly poor detail and the need for a broad transmission band. Includes a quote from a letter by Prof. Korn showing his agreement with these views. (1621, 1724, 1918)

1816 Crowe, Frederic C. "Picture transmission system." U.S. 1,762,470, Mar. 25, 1929, June 10, 1930. Part assigned: S.H. and C.L. Cauley. Multicell system with selectors and movable slotted aperture for line-by-line scan.

1817 Goldsmith, A.N., and Julius Weinberger. "Television." U.S. 1,770,205, Mar. 25, 1929, July 8, 1930. Assigned: RCA. Composite signal transmission whereby vision, speech, and sync occupy relatively large, small, and minute portions of a predetermined waveband. (1813, 1818, 1847)

1818 Weinberger, J., Theodore A. Smith, and George Rodwin. "Television." U.S. 1,975,055,

Mar. 25, 1929, Sept. 25, 1934. Assigned: RCA. Composite signals are received, amplified, converted to an intermediate frequency, amplified, and filtered to obtain separate signals for vision, sound, and sync in a disk system. (1817, 1834, 2003)

1819 Zworykin, V.K. "Facsimile transmission." U.S. 1,786,812, Mar. 26, 1929, Dec. 30, 1930, reissued Dec. 23, 1932, Sept. 11, 1934. Assigned: Westinghouse. Film transmission with vibrating mirror and picture tube receiver, with deflection plates connected to the a-c source driving the mirror and to a contact on the film drive. (1757, 1951)

1820 C. Lorenz A.-G. "Short-wave wireless transmitting arrangements." Br. 331,667, June 7, 1929, July 10, 1930. In Germany Mar. 27, 1929. A radio relay system employing intermediate stations, either reflective or with amplifiers, within the optical range for long-distance transmission of television signals and messages. An optical relay system was covered by Telefunken (734) in 1926. (1362, 1958)

1821 "Television. Facilities for the Baird system." TIMES (Mar. 28): 16d. Letter by G.E.P. Murray, General Post Office, giving the official views on the recent Baird demonstration. "In the Postmaster-General's opinion the system represents a noteworthy scientific achievement; but he does not consider that at the present stage of development television could be included in the broadcasting programmes within the broadcasting hours." This decision was based on the limited scope of the images, not upon their quality. (1805, 1812, 1825, 1827)

1822 "Television in its latest form." N.Y.T. IX, 18 (Mar. 31): 3–5. Photo of RCA apparatus. (1668,1847)

1823 Jenkins, C.F. RADIOMOVIES, RADIOVISION, TELEVISION. Washington: Jenkins Labs, 1929. 143 pp., 57 illus. Second Jenkins book (728). Sections on how to make a Radiovisor, lens-disc scanner, drum scanner, plate receiver, sensitive plate transmitter, weather maps by radio, and others on miscellaneous topics and inventions. List of visual radio patents, p. 129, 72 items, and 2 pages of silhouettes from frames of movies broadcast early in 1928 from station W3XK. (1807, 1837)

1824 "Successful television experiments in the home and workshop." RADIO N. 10 (Apr.): 923, 942, 944. 2 photos, 4 diags. Amateur equipment and results. (1778, 1912)

1825 "An amateur looks in." TELEV. 2 (Apr.): 57, 58. Dress rehearsals for Baird demonstration, Feb. 23, Mar. 2, 3, 4, in the mornings and at 11:30 p.m. to midnight; and report on the demonstration of Mar. 5. (1821, 1831)

1826 Gradenwitz, A. "Mihaly's tele-cinema." TELEV. 2 (Apr.): 59–62. 6 photos. Early apparatus, latest work, Berlin radio show, demonstrations in London, technical questions on picture elements, detail, persistence of vision, new super-frequency lamp. (1649, 1806, 1843, 1906)

1827 Moseley, S.A. "The test—and the result." TELEV. 2 (Apr.): 63, 64. Photo. "What was clear to friend and critic alike was that television is here." This was written before the PMG's report was published. (1777, 1821, 1846, 1867)

1828 Wolfson, H. "Panchromatism." TELEV. 2 (Apr.): 65–7. Graph, 2 diags. Light, color photography, color sensitivity, and photoelectric cells for television. (1782, 1942)

1829 Williams, Robert. "Television—positively marvellous.'" TELEV. 2 (Apr.): 68. Comments by a noted trade unionist.

1830 Sylvester, C. "Light; the essential of television. Pt. 8." TELEV. 2 (Apr.): 71, 72. 4 diags. (1776, 1907)

1831 "The progress of television. More detailed images." TELEV. 2 (Apr.): 76. From THE TIMES, Mar. 7. (1825, 1867)

1832 Denton, J.J., and W.G.W. Mitchell. "The Television Society. Report of exhibition held during March meeting." TELEV. 2 (Apr.): 83–90. 8 photos, 3 diags. Discussion of exhibits, details of Atkinson's early apparatus (169). (1780, 1804, 1871, 1872, 1910)

1833 Cioffari, Bernard. "Television." U.S. 2,011,271, Apr. 1, 1929, Aug. 13, 1935. Assigned: RCA. Br. 351,972, Apr, 1, 1930 (Marconi's). Light reflected from mirror drum or lens disk onto a number of spaced mirrors for interlaced scan.

1834 Smith, T.A. "Television scanning system." U.S. 1,790,491, Apr. 1, 1929, Jan. 27, 1931. Assigned: RCA. Br. 347,435, Mar. 29, 1930 (Marconi's). Mirror drum or disk with separate fixed mirrors for divided scan; one-half vertical, one-half horizontal. (1818, 1921)

1835 Telehor A.-G. "Synchronisation of television." Br. 345,610, Sept. 20, 1929, Mar. 20, 1931. In Germany Apr. 5, 1929. Nipkow disk, phonic wheel, tuning fork interrupter and series connected neon lamp. (1814, 1850)

1836 Morse, G.H. "Television." U.S. 1,802,441, Apr. 6, 1929, Apr. 28, 1931. Electromagnet and arc assembly with a coil for deflecting the arc. (235, 2390)

1837 "C. Francis Jenkins with his latest machine that broadcasts motion pictures in the form of silhouettes." N.Y.T. XI, 19 (Apr. 7): 1–3, 7, 8. 2 photos, including drum receiver with magnifying lens. (1823, 1845)

1838 "Popular television called still far off." N.Y.T. 23 (Apr. 8): 2. Statement by L.B.F. Raycroft to National Electrical Manufacturers Association on standard receiver parts: television is not "just around the corner." (1612)

1839 Felshin, Judah B. "Television." U.S. 1,814,137, Apr. 8, 1929, July 14, 1931. Part assigned: M. Kirschstein and L. Oskow. Disk with radial slots.

1840 Elektro-Physikalische Ges. (E. Kassner). "Television, discharge apparatus." Br. 340,964, June 29, 1929. Void. In Germany Apr. 10, 1929. Simultaneous transmission of all parts of an image by "electro-optical light image microphones." Photoelectric plate, capacitor, and tuned circuit.

1841 "Radio Board grants split short waves." N.Y.T. 32 (Apr. 12): 2. New FRC general order No. 62 issued for mid-channel operation of frequencies above 1500 kc. A visual broadcasting channel shall not be more than 100 kc wide. (1794, 1844)

1842 Comp. Gaz. "Synchronous movements." Br. 351,137, Apr. 11, 1930. In France Apr. 12, 1929. Moving aperture with sync drive. (1766, 2336)

1843 Bourquin, H. "Das Fernkino von Dénes von Mihály" [The telecinema of Dénes von Mihály]. ELEKT. ANZ. 46 (Apr. 13): 89, 90. 3 illus. Research at the Central Bureau of German Postal Service. Clean and undistorted pictures broadcast from Witzleben received in various parts of Berlin. (1826, 1948)

1844 "2 television waves asked by Freshman. Stations intended as an aid to home experimenters, five years of tests ahead." N.Y.T. 14 (Apr. 13): 5–7. Request by Charles Freshman Co., Cliften, N.J. (1841, 1863)

1845 "Jenkins to test an aerial television 'eye'; would give army pictures of enemy from air." N.Y.T. 19 (Apr. 13): 4. Airborne television. (1837, 1853)

1846 "The P.M.G. and television." POP. W. (Apr. 13): 156. (1827, 1869)

1847 "Images dance in space, heralding new radio era." N.Y.T. XI, 17 (Apr. 14): 1–3. Feature article on demonstration by A.N. Goldsmith. Pictures on a screen about 5 in. sq. as distinct as newspaper pictures. (1817, 1822, 1883, 1902)

1848 "Trade notes and comments." N.Y.T. XI, 21 (Apr. 14): 1. Remarks by A.J. Carter: introduction of television should stimulate sale of parts.

1849 Kell, R.D. "Transmission and reception of pictures." U.S. 1,992,009, Apr. 15, 1929, Feb. 19, 1935. Assigned: G.E. Br. 341,353, Apr. 10, 1930 (B.T.H.). Disk with a spiral of lenses, receiver with three lamps and delay circuits. (1361, 1856)

1850 Telehor A.-G. "Television." Br. 331,765, Sept. 20, 1929, July 10, 1930. In Germany

Apr. 16, 1929. Holes in a Nipkow disk are smaller in the transmitter than in the receiver; those in the latter may be square, rectangular, or sector-shaped to eliminate overlapping lines or streaks in the image. (1835, 1987)

1851 "De Forest gets Scott Medal." N.Y.T. 16 (Apr. 18): 4. The inventor gives his views on the popularity of television in 1939. (1642, 2070)

1852 Grutzmacher, M. "Television." Br. 359,475, Apr. 17, 1930. Void. In Germany Apr. 19, 1929.

1853 "Hopes to apply television to aerial use as war aid." N.Y.T. X, 18 (Apr. 21): 1, 2. C.F. Jenkins working on airborne apparatus. (1845, 1857)

1854 N.V. Philips (by S.G.S. Dicker). "Telegraphic transmission of pictures." Br. 332,559, Apr. 22, 1929, July 22, 1930. To reduce the visibility of image strips, a Nipkow disk is mounted off-center or is moved periodically at right angles to the shaft, or the spiral of apertures is split into two arcuate groups. (1743, 2346)

1855 Watson, A.H. "Television." U.S. 1,787,921, Apr. 22, 1929, Jan. 6, 1931. Rotary drum (1791) mounted in a cabinet with motor, lamp, and screen. (2262)

1856 Kell, R.D. "Transmission and reception of pictures." U.S. 1,796,030, Apr. 25, 1929, Mar. 10, 1931. Assigned: G.E. Br. 341,811, Apr. 25, 1930 (B.T.H.). Disk with a spiral of apertures, delay circuits, and distributor. Cone shutters, coils, and lamp in receiver. See also Br. 341,818, Apr. 25, 1930 (B.T.H.). (1849, 1955)

1857 "Our bookshelf." NATURE 123 (Apr. 27): 637. Brief notice of Jenkins' book (1823). (1853, 1864)

1858 Spindler, H. "Television." Br. 353,884, Apr. 28, 1930. In France Apr. 29, 1929. Two photoelectric plates in low-pressure gas; induction coil connected to receiver electrodes makes the gas luminous.

1859 Gray, F., and J.R. Hefele. "Electro-optical transmission." U.S. 1,769,919, Apr. 30, 1929, July 8, 1930. Assigned: B.T.L. Br. 350,454, Mar. 10, 1930; addition to Br. 332,284 (1742). Two or more disk scanners and circuits connected to one channel for simultaneous transmission of composite signals representing two images at same or different stations, applicable for color or stereo. (1742, 1860)

1860 Gray, F. "Electro-optical transmission." U.S. 1,769,920, Apr. 30, 1920, July 8, 1930. Assigned: B.T.L. Br. 350,455, Mar. 10, 1930; addition to Br. 332,284 (1742). Disk system for one-way or two-way operation over a single channel applicable for stereo or color or transmission of two or more scenes or combined telephone and television signals. Incorporates the principle of frequency interleaving whereby some signals are shifted in frequency so as to occupy open parts of the spectrum, or valleys, between other parts, or peaks. Such interleaving, by means of suitable carrier currents, filter circuits, etc., enables the frequency band to be compressed so that all the composite signals occupy a comparatively narrow frequency band. (1859, 1930)

1861 Gray, J.A. "Television, the history of its development." QUEEN'S QUART. 36 (Spring): 285–93.

1862 Arnold, J.P. "Radio picture transmission and reception. Scanning methods." RADIO 11 (May): 19, 20. 5 diags. Direct and spiral scan, multiple light beams. (1726, 2050)

1863 "Commission permits limited picture broadcasting." RADIO BRD. 15 (May): 9. FRC permits. (1844, 1920)

1864 "An improved scanning system." SCI. & INV. 17 (May): 55. 2 diags. Westinghouse patent recently issued, a disk with concave reflectors (801), and a Jenkins-type prismatic disk. (1857, 1876)

1865 Ives, H.E. "Television demonstration." J. SMPE 13 (May): 308. (1624, 1895)

1866 Harries, J.H.O. "A quantitative analysis of television." TELEV. 2 (May): 105–12. 2 photos, 6 diags. Quantitative problems, definition of picture size and optimum size, resolving power of the eyes, picture analysis, forms of modulation, scanning strips, continuous scan, bandwidths, area of maximum definition, measure of efficiency, maximum frequency, scanning ratio and standard, latitude in definition. (1713, 1943)

1867 Moseley, S.A. "The first television broadcast." TELEV. 2 (May): 113, 114. (1777, 1827, 1831, 1869, 1908, 1969)

1868 Malone, Cecil. "The future developments of television." TELEV. 2 (May): 115.

1869 "Television proves itself. News of the Post Office demonstration." TELEV. 2 (May): 116. By "Engineer" on the reception at St. Martins-le-Grand. (1846, 1867, 1870)

1870 Murray, G.E.P. "The Postmaster-General's decision." TELEV. 2 (May): 124. Reprint of letter in the TIMES, Mar. 28 (1821). (1869, 1892)

1871 Mitchell, W.G.W. "The cathode-ray tube in practical television. Pt. 2." TELEV. 2 (May): 129–31, 134. Photo, 4 diags. Cathode rays, unreliability of present-day tubes, Swinton's scheme (413), modulation of the beam, R.S. Clay's suggested tube with four pairs of modulating coils (743), effects of magnetic fields, patent of E.G. Schoultz on spiral scanning (488). Continued from Feb. (1832, 1910)

1872 Rennie, J.C. "The Television Society. Some notes on exploring." TELEV. 2 (May): 137–43, 147. 4 photos, full-page diag. of scheme for automatic sync omitted from the Apr. issue. Lecture at the meeting Apr. 9. The Baird Co., older methods of scanning, range of senses, the eye and peculiarities of human vision, questions of detail, continuous scanning. References to Robinson's papers, Nov., Dec. (1584, 1644). (1705, 1832, 1910)

1873 MacPherson, E.R. "Broadcasting and television." TELEV. 2 (May): 151–4. 5 photos. Reprint from REVIEW OF REVIEWS.

1874 Felix, E.H. "A Swedish seeker after television." WORLD TODAY 53 (May): 561–4. (1561, 2511)

1875 Karolus, A. "Mirror wheel for television." U.S. 1,850,629, Apr. 19, 1930, Mar. 22, 1932. In Germany May 1, 1929. (1760, 2249)

1876 Jenkins, C.F. "Scanning device." U.S. 1,828,867, May 2, 1929, Oct. 27, 1931. Assigned: Jenkins Labs. Scanning disk with a spiral of square holes for film transmission with a lens arrangement that magnifies the image frame, which allows a clear space between the film and disk, and minimizes aperture distortion. (1864, 1881)

1877 Universal and General Radio Co. Ltd., and Leonard Morris Myers. "Television." Br. 331,325, May 8, 1929. Receiver. Reference to Br. 331,633 (1878). (1885)

1878 Universal and General Radio Co. Ltd., L.M. Myers, and D.S.F. Adams. "Television." Br. 331,633, May 8, 1929. Reference to Br. 331,325 (1877).

1879 Deutsch, Ernest. "Television." U.S. 1,768,893, May 9, 1929, July 1, 1930. Two perforated endless belts.

1880 Mather, Frederick William. "Television." Br. 332,971, May 9, 1929, Aug. 7, 1930. An endless belt system with round, square, or oblong holes in one or two tracks in parallel staggered or zigzag formation. Applicable for dual use, or two-way with a telephone, or stereo; for transmitting large outdoor scenes and for reception on a small screen or on a cinema screen.

1881 "Movies by television to be broadcast soon. Films being made for use by Jenkins station." N.Y.T. 34 (May 10): 3. A series of short motion pictures being made by Visugraphic Pictures, Inc., for broadcast through station W2XCR. (1876, 1887)

1882 "Television apparatus." N.Y.T. IX, 4 (May 12): 5. Receiver demonstrated in Berlin by an unnamed inventor.

1883 "Television's speed the big problem. Dr. A.N. Goldsmith tells radio engineers that progress rests on meeting this requirement." N.Y.T. 34 (May 15): 5, 6. Remarks at IRE meeting May 14. (1847, 1902)

1884 Henroteau, François Charles Pierre. "Television." U.S. 1,903,112, May 29, 1929, renewed Aug. 13, 1931, Mar. 28, 1933. Br. 335,958, June 4, 1929, Oct. 6, 1930. See also Br. 335,995, June 4, 1929. In Canada May 16, 1929. Divided Sept. 8, 1930. A hybrid system with a special high-vacuum phototube which has a plate cathode consisting of tiny insulated photosensitive globules deposited on an insulating layer on a metal backing, an open-mesh grid of fine wires between the cathode and a ring anode, and an internal coating of photoelectric material. Auxiliary components include commutators, four light-chopper disks with segmental apertures, two overlapping lens disks, prisms, lenses, and optical screens. Applications suggested but not claimed include color with three phototubes and attachment to an astronomical telescope and a microscope. (2570)

1885 Universal and General Radio Co. Ltd. and L.M. Myers. "Television." Br. 333,623, May 17, 1929. Sync method with phonic wheel and Kerr cell in receiver. References to Br. 331,325 (1877), 334,505 (2235).

1886 Thun, Rudolph. "Picture transmission." U.S. 2,011,737, May 12, 1930, Aug. 20, 1935; Br. 355,319, May 15, 1930. In Germany May 18, 1929. Film transmission system employing oscillograph mirror, rotary lenses, a lens and mirrors with a constant light intensity and variable scanning rate, or velocity modulation. (2244)

1887 "C.F. Jenkins develops new television scanner." N.Y.T. X, 18 (May 19): 8. Jenkins report on drum scanner at IRE meeting May 14. (1881, 1904)

1888 Robb, F.M. "Television." U.S. 1,801,756, May 22, 1929, Apr. 21, 1931. Concentric disks, one with a single spiral slot, the other with radial slots. (894)

1889 Tate, A.O. "Scanning device." U.S. 1,825,487, May 22, 1929, Sept. 29, 1931. Disk with apertures arranged in reverse spirals. (1680, 2111)

1890 "Der Fernseher Telefunken-Karolus" [The Telefunken-Karolus television]. E.T.Z. 50 (May 23): 761. (1795, 1916)

1891 Espenschied, Lloyd, and Herman A. Affel. "Concentric conducting system." U.S. 1,835,031, May 23, 1929, Dec. 8, 1931. Assigned: AT&T. Br. 353,020, Apr. 17, 1930 (S.T.C.). Center conductor air-insulated by dielectric supports inside a tubular conductor, capable of transmitting signals from the low frequencies up to an order of megacycles. See Franklin's patent of 1926 (804).

1892 Baird, J.L., and Television Ltd. "Television." Br. 333,942, May 24, 1929. Lighting arrangement with scanning disk and photocell. Reference to Br. 303,771 (1011). (1870, 1900)

1893 Silberstein, L. "Television." U.S. 1,839,777, May 24, 1929, Jan. 5, 1932. Assigned: United Research. Two vibrating mirrors and modulator for reception. (1756)

1894 Horton, J.W. "Electro-optical transmission." U.S. 1,775,241, May 25, 1929, Sept. 9, 1930. Assigned: B.T.L. Br. 353,471, Apr. 24, 1930 (E.R.P.). Multichannel intermediate film system with three pictures transmitted simultaneously over separate channels. (1141, 2001)

1895 Ives, H.E. "Electro-optical transmission." U.S. 1,812,405, May 25, 1929, June 30, 1931. Assigned: B.T.L. (1865, 1930)

1896 "Ultra-violet rays used in television." N.Y.T. 28 (May 29): 5. Demonstration by United States Radio and Television Corp. at Bamberger and Co. store, Newark, N.J. Transmission by light and ultraviolet between apparatus about 50 feet apart. (1573, 2084)

1897 Baird, Hollis Semple. "Television." U.S. 2,050,149, May 29, 1929, Aug. 4, 1936. Assigned: Shortwave and Television. Endless belt with pulleys, drive, lens, and adjustment assembled in a cabinet. (2103)

1898 Codelli, Anton (Baron). "Electrical television." Br. 334,234, May 29, 1929, Aug. 20, 1930. Two electromagnets actuated by a two-phase current impart a swash-plate motion to a concave mirror from which the light beam passes through a variable-area diaphragm onto a photocell or lamp. A spiral-scanning method intended to provide finer detail in the center of vision. (2256)

1899 Sheldon, H. Horton, and Edgar Norman Grisewood. TELEVISION: PRESENT METHODS OF PICTURE TRANSMISSION. New York: Van Nostrand, 1929. x + 194 pp., 129 illus., including color plate. This first American book on the subject (not counting Jenkins' two volumes; 728, 1823) presents a comprehensive view of the art with technical explanations and examples of fairly recent advances. Essential elements, historical background, optical systems, electromagnetic waves, photoelectric cells, glow lamps, oscillographs, scanning, sync, telephotography; Baird, Bell, Jenkins and Alexanderson systems, relays, amateur equipment, the future of television. Also, London: Library Press, Jan. 1930.

1900 De la Forge, L. "L'état actuel des procédés Baird" [The present state of Baird's process]. QSTF 10 (June): 35–7. Reprint of article on the Baird Company in the TIMES, Feb. 21 (1762). (1892, 1908, 2258)

1901 "Cooley television system." RADIO 11 (June): 23, 42. 3 diags. Conversion of the Rayphoto facsimile receiver with a high-frequency oscillator and corona discharge to pins on scanning disk. (670)

1902 "Large television images broadcast by R.C.A." RADIO N. 10 (June): 1121. 3 photos. Statement by A.N. Goldsmith and details of station W2XBS, New York. Regular daily schedule, 7 to 9 p.m. on 2000–21000 kc, 250 w. Images 60/20, and 72 elements wide, no actual size given. (1813, 1847, 1883, 1974, 2000)

1903 "Latest radiovision news." SCI. & INV. 17 (June): 151. 3 photos. Von Mihály apparatus, Jenkins mosaic apparatus, and another inventor of a crater-type neon tube.

1904 Peck, A.P. "Television advances." SCI. AM. 140 (June): 526, 527. 7 photos. "With powerful transmitting stations furnishing radio vision broadcasts on schedule, receivers are being developed and tested by thousands of 'lookers-in'." On Jenkins' film system and drum scanner, with comments on amateur participation. (1151, 1887, 1936, 2131)

1905 Fleming, J.A. "Comparative tests of television apparatus." TELEV. 2 (June): 161–4. 2 illus. (1582, 2009)

1906 Gradenwitz, A. "Television progress in Germany." TELEV. 2 (June): 165, 166. 3 photos. Work of Karolus, demonstrations of Baird apparatus in London and in Berlin, comparison of results, transmitter, Kerr cell, and sync. (1826, 2143)

1907 Sylvester, C. "Talkies versus television." TELEV. 2 (June): 169, 170. 2 photos. General discussion; television has greater appeal for entertainment. (1830, 1909)

1908 Moseley, S.A. "Writes from Berlin." TELEV. 2 (June): 175, 176. (1867, 1900, 1940)

1909 Sylvester, C. "Light; the essential of television. Pt. 9." TELEV. 2 (June): 177, 178. 5 diags. (1907, 1938)

1910 Denton, J.J. and W.G.W. Mitchell. "The Television Society." TELEV. 2 (June): 189–90. 9 photos. Report of May 7 meeting. Paper by R.G. Wilson and A.A. Waters on construction of apparatus and demonstration of the authors' transmitter and receiver, and one by R.R. Poole on disks and synchronism, with model (1937). (1832, 1871, 1872, 1980)

1911 Buckley, Annette. "As one woman to another—about television." TELEV. 2 (June): 191, 192.

1912 Waters, A.A. "The construction of experimental television apparatus." TELEV. 2 (June): 193, 194. 2 diags. Shadowgraph apparatus. (1824, 1939)

1913 Nicolson, Norman J. "The spotlight principle in television." TELEV. 2 (June): 205–7. Photo, 5 diags. Arrangement of transmitter, details, square vs round holes, ideal perforations, photocell, distortion, problems of signal amplification, television in daylight. (1979)

1914 Garside, Colin. "Some notes on photo-electric cells." TELEV. 2 (June): 208, 209. Graph. Light-sensitive elements, color sensitivity, gas-filled and vacuum cells, emission, response, research.

1915 "Book on television." N.Y.T. IX, 15 (June 2): 8. Brief notice of book by Sheldon and Grisewood. (1899)

1916 Telefunken. "Television." Br. 344,736, June 4, 1930. In Germany June 5, 1929. Drum scanner with light filters. See also Br. 342,857, Jan. 2, 1930, in Germany June 16, 1929. Copying telegraph with three drums. (1890, 1919)

1917 Sanabria, U.A. "Scanning." U.S. 1,805,848, June 7, 1929, May 19, 1931. Assigned: Western Television. Disk with several partial spirals of holes arranged to scan sequential groups of lines alternately, or interleaved group scan. (1634, 2959)

1918 Swinton, A.A.C. "Television inventions." NATURE 123 (June 8): 874. References to Jenkins' book (1823) and his Phantoscope plan of 1894 (245), Dauvillier's article of Jan. 1928 (1108), the Carey scheme (133), and Dinsdale's book (1682) in a manner disparaging Baird's use of the Nipkow disk. (1815, 2155)

1919 Telefunken. "Television." Br. 348,414, May 30, 1930. In Germany June 8, 1929. Mirror drum and two or more light sources for scanning different parts of a scene. Receiver with Kerr cells and switch. See also Br. 344,738, June 5, 1930. In Germany June 9, 1929.

1920 "Roster of television stations." N.Y.T. IX, 21 (June 9): 6. List of 26 transmitters that "are now sending images into space." Compiled by the Radio Division, Department of Commerce. A note in an adjacent column mentions that the FRC will grant licenses for one year. (1863, 1928)

1921 Smith, T.A. "Television." U.S. 2,029,395, June 11, 1929, Feb. 4, 1936. Assigned: RCA. Br. 354,863, May 21, 1930 (Marconi's). Disk with a spiral of apertures and two or more glow lamps and lens system. Reference to Br. 341,353 (1849). (1834, 1931)

1922 Gulliland, A.A: "Television in Germany." POP. W. (June 15): 445. (1463, 1932, 1983)

1923 Skaupy, F. "Apparatus for refracting light rays." U.S. 1,923,891, June 16, 1930, Aug. 22 1933; Br. 352,693, June 19, 1930. In Germany June 19, 1929. Scanning by two vessels with electrodes in nitrobenzine excited by separate a-c sources, Kerr cell modulator. (465, 2485)

1924 Middelraad, Franciscus Leonardus. "Picture transmission system." U.S. 2,024,051, June 20, 1929, renewed Apr. 19, 1934, Dec. 10, 1935. Endless belt with angled series of holes and another screen with two sets of holes.

1925 Replogle, D.E. "Modulating system." U.S. 1,967,041, June 21, 1929, July 17, 1934. Assigned: Raytheon. Scanning disk, light source, phototube, and an additional light source varying from extinction to full brilliance directed onto the object. (1808, 2006)

1926 MacLulich, J.M. "Television receivers." Br. 356,201, June 4, 1930. In Australia June 24, 1929. Apertured disk and diaphragm.

1927 Wald, G. "Receiving apparatus for television." U.S. 1,810,692, June 24, 1929, June 16, 1931. A vacuum tube contains an array of intersecting electrodes with choke coils actuated by a distributor. (1810, 1997)

1928 "Broadcasters get 90 days' extension. Television license sought." N.Y.T. 34 (June 25): 4. Permits applied for by RCA Communications, Bound Brook, N.J., and Shortwave and Television Laboratories, Boston. (1920, 2038)

1929 "To exhibit latest in radio images." N.Y.T. 34 (June 25): 6. A demonstration of the marked advance in television made by the

Bell Laboratories is scheduled to be given within the next two weeks. (1490, 1933)

1930 Ives, H.E., and F. Gray. "Television." U.S. 1,873,411, June 26, 1929, renewed Oct. 6, 1931, Aug. 23, 1932. Assigned: B.T.L. Br. 354,853, May 20, 1930 (E.R.P.). A three-channel color system. Disk transmitter with photocells in cabinet. Receiver with three glow discharge lamps and color filters. Reference to Br. 286,262 (890). (1860, 1895, 1968, 1986)

1931 Smith, T.A. "Scanning element." U.S. 1,895,087, June 27, 1929. Jan. 24, 1933. Assigned: RCA. Br. 349,773, May 27, 1930 (Marconi's). Disk with apertures or lenses staggered to reduce flicker. References to Br. 315,417; Br. 336,267 (1341). (1921, 1962)

1932 "Television in Germany." ELECT. REV. 104 (June 28): 1150. (1922, 2065)

1933 "Television in color shown first time. American flag, watermelon and bunch of roses flashed on tiny screen in test." N.Y.T. 25 (June 28): 1, 2. Bell Labs transmission by wire over 100 feet; image about the size of a postage stamp. Other objects shown were the Union Jack, pot of geraniums, large colored ball, pineapple, and a young woman in a colored dress, all viewed through a peephole in a darkened room. See Baird's demonstration (1352). (1929, 1934)

1934 "Distance's new enchantments." N.Y.T. 16 (June 29): 3. Editorial on the Bell Labs color demonstration (1933). (1950)

"Such academic applications will be the least of the varied uses, esthetic and practical, to which this new miracle of television may be put. One's imagination thinks of flowers held in the hand of the lover, yet displayed in view of the loved one far away; of the splendors of the sunrise and the gorgeous hues of the sunset shared by those in mountain valleys or out upon the sea with those who are shut up in cities, of an afternoon in the Louvre spent at the end of a telephone receiver in a sick room. Distance has new enchantments to add to those which are visible to the naked eye or the telescope. And such practical uses may be suggested as picking out garments by telephone or flashing color telephone orders for paints and stains.

"In this new invention making possible and practicable the transmission of color is a promise that it may in time travel as widely as sound and so multiply the beauty of the earth by making it appear in more places than one at the same moment. This is said in confident belief which the lay world has come to hold that science will once more accomplish the impossible and again perform a miracle."

1935 "Television emerging from the laboratory." RADIO N. 11 (July): 10, 11. Photo of Jenkins with a new radio movie transmitter, and one of a German receiver, with comments on these and RCA's experimental broadcasts.

1936 "Aerial 'eyes' for future wars." SCI. & INV. 17 (July): 247. 3 illus. Jenkins' transmitter and receiver. (1904, 1954)

1937 Poole, R.R: "Some notes on scanning." TELEV. 2 (July): 221–4. 5 diags. Demonstration and lecture at the May meeting (1910). General arrangements, experiments, practical applications, transmission of picture detail, sidebands, linear distortion, secrecy of transmission.

1938 Sylvester, C. "Light; the essential of television. Pt. 10." TELEV. 2 (July): 239, 240. 4 diags. (1909, 2269)

1939 Waters, A.A. "The construction of experimental television apparatus. Pt. 2." TELEV. 2 (July): 241–3. 5 diags. On scanning disks. (1912, 1941, 1982)

1940 Moseley, S.A. "Writes from Berlin." TELEV. 2 (July): 244–6. 3 photos. Experiments with Baird apparatus, televising to London. (1908, 1961, 1978)

1941 Fox, W.C. "Some notes on exploring discs and their construction." TELEV. 2 (July): 247–9. 5 diags. Making disks, balancing, hints on sheet metal thickness and weight. (1595, 1939, 1975, 2015)

1942 Wolfson, H. "Photo-electric currents in a vacuum." TELEV. 2 (July): 254–8. 2 graphs,

5 diags. General survey, work of Hertz, Stolëtov, Hallwachs, Righi, Thomson, Lenard, Compton. (1828, 2020)

1943 Harries, J.H.O. "A quantitative analysis of television." TELEV. 2 (July): 259, 260, 272. 2 diags. Completion of article in May, with discussion (1866). (1981)

1944 "A review of commercial types of photoelectric cells." TELEV. 2 (July): 261–5. Graph, 5 photos, 5 diags. Osram (G.E.) photoelectric cells, types, characteristics, applications, and circuits.

1945 Lewis, William Turnor. "Television." U.S. 1,841,487, July 1, 1929, Jan. 19, 1932. Double-disk system, two-channel transmission, stereo effect.

1946 Loiseau, Louis Marie Jean. "Picture transmitting device." U.S. 1,997,371, June 25, 1930, Apr. 9, 1935; Br. 358,087, July 1, 1930, Oct. 1, 1931. Assigned: Comp. Gaz. In France July 1, 1930. Scanning with optic slots produced by the elastic deformation (by compression or shock waves) of transparent bodies such as quartz, tourmaline, glycerine, carbon sulfide, nitrobenzine, or a piezoelectric substance, including the dielectric of capacitors, with numerous variants and electron tube circuits. Claims include "grated screens" or strips of violet, green, and orange-red filters in the light zones and transmission with three separate colored screens. (2116)

1947 Siemens & Halske A.-G. "Television." Br. 350,274, July 1, 1930. In Germany July 1, 1929. Disk with square holes. (717)

1948 Haynes, F.H. "Television by the Mihály system." W.W. 25 (July 3): 7. (1843, 1952, 2157)

1949 Hammond, J.H. "Secret television." U.S. 1,910,540, July 3, 1929, May 23, 1933. A special oscillating cam in a system of gears, or an equivalent electromechanical arrangement, cyclically varies the scanning rate. Receivers without an identical cam or equivalent means cannot reproduce a clear picture. Constructional features are given to show applicability in a wide range of systems: Alexanderson's disk, Bell Labs distributor/folded tube, lens disk, Jenkins' prismatic disk, mirror drum, polyhedral mirror drums, one or two moving perforated belts, two disks with curved slots, two vibrating mirrors, cathode-ray tubes including Swinton's camera tube. (1660, 1990)

1950 "Color television." SCIENCE 70 (July 5): Supp. 10. Bell Labs apparatus and demonstration. (1934, 1953)

1951 Zworykin, V.K. "Facsimile transmission." U.S. 2,361,255, July 5, 1929, renewed Aug. 13, 1931, Oct. 24, 1944. Assigned: Westinghouse. Br. 355,890, July 7, 1930, Sept. 3, 1931. The invention relates to the film transmission for television purposes. Continuously moving film is scanned transversely by light reflected from a source by a curved mirror which is vibrated magnetically at 750 cps. This scanning frequency and a framing frequency are interposed with the picture signals, the framing frequency being controlled by a contact which closes the circuit from a 1200-cps source during the blanks between picture frames. Filters in the receiver separate these frequencies, which are then applied to the control and deflection electrodes of a picture tube. (1819, 2092)

1952 "Hungarian claims invention of television for outdoors." N.Y.T. 3 (July 7): 2. Von Mihály's portable daylight apparatus. (1948, 2082)

1953 "Images dance in color on the television screen." N.Y.T. IX, 15 (July 7): 1–5. 3 photos. Feature article on Bell Labs system. "Radio's flickering 'eyes' now sensitive to color." (1950, 1957)

1954 "C. Francis Jenkins latest idea of a television receiver with a magnifying lens set in what is called the shadowbox." N.Y.T. IX, 15 (July 7): 5. Photo shows a cabinet with a recessed viewing lens. (1936, 1965)

1955 Kell, R.D. "Transmission of pictures." U.S. 1,828,667, July 8, 1929, Oct. 20, 1931. Assigned: G.E. Br. 343,416, July 8, 1930

(B.T.H.). Biased Kerr cell, lens disk, projection screen. (1856, 2049)

1956 Moore, D.M. "Picture transmitting system." U.S. 1,824,731, July 9, 1929, Sept. 22, 1931. Assigned: G.E. Br. 358,050, July 2, 1930 (B.T.H.). Rotating mirrors with oblique movement and a lens system for linear scanning. (1414, 2302)

1957 "Television in colour." W.W. 25 (July 10): 37. (1953, 1971)

1958 C. Lorenz A.-G. "Television." Br. 348,440, June 24, 1930. In Germany July 11, 1929. Receiver with modulation circuit. (1820)

1959 "WOKO broadcasting television programs." N.Y.T. 24 (July 15): 2. Daily programs, 2:00 to 3:00 p.m., from station W2XBU (H.E. Smith), Mount Beacon, N.Y. Images of persons, placards, lettering, and small objects said to be "not perfect."

1960 Tolson, William A. "Transmission of pictures." U.S. 1,792,259, July 16, 1929, Feb. 10, 1931. Assigned: G.E. Br. 345,595, July 3, 1930 (B.T.H.). Plurality of disks for different scenes. (2492)

1961 Baird, J.L., and Television, Ltd. "Synchronising means for television." Br. 336,655, July 17, 1929, Oct. 17, 1930. A laminated soft iron armature in the form of a toothed wheel, attached to the shaft of a scanning disk, rotates between two poles of an electromagnet which is energized via an amplifier by the picture signals. Framing is effected by rotating the assembly and by a pushbutton switch that momentarily bypasses the magnet coils. (1940, 1978)

1962 Smith, T.A. "Television." U.S. 1,797,378, July 19, 1929, Mar. 24, 1931. Assigned: RCA. Br. 356,880, July 21, 1930 (Marconi's). Film scanning with spirally apertured disk. (1931, 1963)

1963 Smith, T.A. "Television." U.S. 1,810,188, July 19, 1929, June 16, 1931. Assigned: RCA. Br. 357,687, July 21, 1930 (Marconi's). Film scanning in which the film moves at a constant rate. (1962, 2003)

1964 Cawley, Aloysius J. "Television." U.S. 1,925,039, July 22, 1929, Aug. 29, 1933. Multicell system with photocells and incandescent lamps carried on rotating arms connected by distributors for scanning in a series of concentric circles. With or without a fluorescent viewing screen. (2026)

1965 "Plane will attempt television broadcast." N.Y.T. 28 (July 23): 5. Experiments planned by Jenkins. (1954, 1973)

1966 Buol, C.J. "Television." Br. 366,453, July 31, 1930. Void. Convention date July 23, 1929. Drum with helix of lenses.

1967 Fries, G. "Television." Br. 366,045, July 24, 1930. Void. In Germany July 24, 1929. Disk system. (1716)

1968 Gray, F. "Electro-optical system." U.S. 1,803,700, July 25, 1929, May 5, 1931. Assigned: B.T.L. Double-spiral disk, parallel transmission circuits, two-lamp receiver. (1930, 2048)

1969 "Television and the B.B.C." ELECT. 103 (July 26): 100. (1867, 1867)

"Once again friction has been caused between the B.B.C. and the Baird Television Development Co. over the vexed question of demonstration facilities. It will be remembered that last March the late Postmaster-General gave consent to the B.B.C. using one of their stations for the purpose of transmitting television, and expressed himself as anxious that facilities should be afforded, so far as was practicable without impairing the broadcasting service, for continued experiment with Baird apparatus. According to the Baird Television Co. the B.B.C. then offered three morning broadcasts weekly, each of a quarter of an hour's duration. This the Baird Co. insists is inadequate. Whatever may be the opinion of the B.B.C. of the progress so far made with television, we fail to see why the Corporation cannot provide better facilities for experiments in a science which must eventually become as public a service as that of broadcasting."

1970 Dawson, Leo H. "Scanning device." U.S. 1,825,781, July 30, 1929, Oct. 6, 1931. Lens disk.

1971 "Color television." CURRENT HIST. 30 (Aug.): 897, 898. Bell Labs system. (1957, 2007)

1972 "List of visual broadcasting stations." RADIO 11 (Aug.): 42. Details of 26 stations, from 50 to 30,000 w. Frequencies, 2.0–4.9 mc in 100-kc bands. (1920)

1973 "Television prospects." RADIO 11 (Aug.): 78, 80. On Jenkins' estimate of 20,000 "lookers-in," believed to be unduly optimistic. (1965, 1976)

1974 "Television at W2XBS." RADIO 11 (Aug.): 94. 2 illus. RCA apparatus. Transmission of various images: signs, letters, pictures, persons, and objects. (1902, 2124)

1975 Benson, Thomas W. "Synchronization still is a television problem." RADIO N. 11 (Aug.): 115, 185. 4 diags. "A suggestion for a simple method of keeping receiver and transmitter discs in step." (1941, 1982, 2706)

1976 Lynch, Arthur H., and C.F. Jenkins. "What are the facts about television?" RADIO N. 11 (Aug.): 124–7, 170, 171. 9 photos. General comments on recent news, remarks by de Forest at the IRE meeting in May, and lecture by Jenkins about his apparatus. (1973, 2002, 2459)

1977 "Photo oscillator gives enlarged television images." SCI. & INV. 17 (Aug.): 343. 3 illus. Light from neon lamp is reflected from a circular mirror vibrating on two axes to scan a viewing screen. See Centeno V (952). (1708, 2246)

1978 Moseley, S.A. "And the hidden hand." TELEV. 2 (Aug.): 283, 284. On Baird and the BBC. (1940, 1961, 1969, 1988, 2009, 2016)

1979 Nicolson, N.J. "The spotlight principle in television. Pt. 2." TELEV. 2 (Aug.): 299, 300, 303. Photo, 2 diags. Frequency, sensitivity, neon voltage, negative images. (1913, 2021)

1980 Denton, J.J., and W.G.W. Mitchell. "The Television Society." TELEV. 2 (Aug): 305–9. 6 photos. Report on visit to the G.E. Co. laboratories and British Talking Pictures at Wembley, with comments on vacuum tubes, loudspeakers, automatic lighting control, sound pictures, amplifiers. (1910, 2019)

1981 Harries, J.H.O. "Can frequency and phase-change modulation reduce interference?" TELEV. 2 (Aug.): 310–4. 6 diags. Discussion of various methods of modulation and quantitative aspects: sidebands, frequency modulation, phase modulation, harmonic analysis, angular velocity modulation, graphical representation. (1943, 2014)

1982 Waters. A.A. "The construction of experimental television apparatus. Pt. 3." TELEV. 2 (Aug.): 315, 316, 318. 3 diags. Projection lamps, lenses, ventilation, simple lantern, interference fringes. (1939, 1941, 2012)

1983 Gulliland, A.A. "The race for television." POP. W. (Aug. 3): 659. (1922)

1984 Hogan, John Vincent Lawless (1890–1960). "Television transmission." U.S. 1,976,699, Aug. 3, 1929, Oct. 9, 1934. Assigned: Radio Inventions. Disk system with film scanning for reproduction of writing. (2399)

1985 "Radio show plans television's newest." N.Y.T. 28 (Aug. 7): 4. "Images on screen visible sixty feet away among novelties at exhibition in September." (1637, 2036)

1986 "News and views." NATURE 124 (Aug. 10): 241. Ives color experiments with three-color filters, recent improvements in photocells. (1930, 2008)

1987 Telehor A.-G. "Television receivers." Br. 366,036, July 23, 1930. Void. In Germany Aug. 10, 1929. Double-spiral disk, movable lamp, and viewing aperture. (1850, 2149)

1988 "New device can 'see' through 2-mile fog." N.Y.T. II, 19 (Aug. 11): 2. "Invention of John Baird, called 'Noctovisor,' shown in England—of great value to ships." Nighttime demonstration of improved apparatus by Baird at his home at Box Hill, Aug. 9. (1978, 1991)

1989 Bentley, Jetson O. "Transmission of pictures." U.S. 1,788,227, Aug. 16, 1929, Jan. 6, 1931. Assigned: G.E. Br. 347,969, July 10, 1930 (B.T.H.). Disks with radial slots and rotary slot to scan in a series of radial lines, each with increased width toward the circumference.

1990 Hammond, J.H. "Navigational guide system." U.S. 2,027,527, Aug. 17, 1929, renewed Dec. 7, 1934, Jan. 14, 1936. Br. 356,906, Aug. 15, 1930. Picture of a map is televised to an aircraft pilot as a landing aid in foggy weather. (1949, 2093)

1991 "Television transmits British talking film; actor's voice is clearer than in theatre." N.Y.T. 5 (Aug. 20): 2, 3. Baird demonstration of Teletalkies in London, Aug. 19. (1988, 1992)

1992 "Talking films by television. A new development." TIMES (Aug. 20): 10d. Baird's Teletalkies. "At a demonstration given in London yesterday a short 'talkie' made by Mr. George Robey was seen and heard through the television machine with a substantial measure of success." The short film was a monologue called "The Bride." (1991, 2010)

1993 Kendall, James M. "Transmission and reception of pictures." U.S. 1,848,888, Aug. 20, 1929, Mar. 8, 1932. Assigned: G.E. Br. 354,953, July 10, 1930 (B.T.H.). Electrostatically controlled shutters (fixed and movable capacitor plates) with distributor.

1994 "Rules on radio licenses." N.Y.T. 20 (Aug. 22): 2. Commerce Department permits operators to handle television.

1995 "Television film goes on the air. Reels whirl at KDKA revealing remarkable progress in radio's affiliation with the movies." N.Y.T. IX, 15 (Aug. 25): 7. Daily film broadcasts from Westinghouse station W8XAY. Pictures about 3 by 4 in. (1718)

1996 Wikkenhauser, Gustav. "Television." U.S. 1,920,119, Aug. 27, 1930, July 25, 1933; Br. 336,765, Sept. 27, 1929. In Germany Aug. 29, 1929. Assigned: Telehor A.-G. Sync control with a phonic wheel connected by an elastic belt to the shaft of a Nipkow disk. (2535)

1997 Wald, G. "Television." U.S. 1,790,736, Aug. 30, 1929, Feb. 3, 1931. Mosaic assembly of sensitive light cells in a grid with connections excited by currents of varying frequencies. (1927, 2443)

1998 Huffman, Charles Edgar. "Television." U.S. 1,907,113, Aug. 31, 1929, May 2, 1933. Assigned: Jenkins Television. Disk system with repetitious group scan in which two adjacent non-overlapping lines are overlapped by another line scan. (2096)

1999 "Practical television." CIT. RAD. CALL BOOK 10 (Sept.): 97. Summary of RMA standards, list of 8 stations on regular schedules, with times, and 8 others. (1665, 2051)

2000 Goldsmith, A.N. "Image transmission by radio waves." PROC. IRE 17 (Sept.): 1536–9. Introduction to following papers (2001–2003) presented at the 4th annual IRE convention in Washington, May 14. Comparison of facsimile and telegraph transmission, relation of facsimile to television, of television to telephony, future television standards. (1902, 2541)

2001 Horton, J.W. "The electrical transmission of pictures and images." PROC. IRE 17 (Sept.): 1540–63. 5 graphs. Discussion of principles, relation between original image and the signals, use of modulated waves, transmission characteristics, efficiency, amplitude, and time, phase shift and frequency, electrical interference. (1894)

2002 Jenkins, C.F. "The drum scanner in radio-movies receivers." PROC. IRE 17 (Sept.): 1576–83. 7 photos. Drum with quartz rods and multielement glow lamp, assembly with mirror and magnifier. (1976, 2004)

2003 Weinberger, J., T.A. Smith and G. Rodwin. "The selection of standards for commercial radio television." PROC. IRE 17 (Sept.): 1584–94. 3 photos, 5 diags. Picture proportions, number of scanning elements, number of pictures per second, scanning method and direction, phase of transmitted current, sync, framing. Picture proportions (aspect ratio) 5 to 6 (height-width) as film. Picture detail with 60 lines, 20 pictures per second (60/20) considered practical. Spectrum of 100-kc television band, with vision signals occupying 80 kc. (1818, 1963, 2194)

2004 Miller, James N. "The latest in television." POP. MECH. 52 (Sept.): 472–6. 8 photos. Jenkins' disks and shadowgraphs. (2002, 2081)

2005 Armagnac, J.P. "Now—television in natural colors." POP. SCI. 115 (Sept.): 25. (1192)

2006 Replogle, D.E. "The problems of television." RADIO-CRAFT 1 (Sept.): 108–10, 137. 6 photos, 2 diags. General matters, channels, fundamentals, image sizes and limitations, scanning, light sources, sync, broadcast service, use of films. (1925, 2094)

2007 "Vision in natural color." RADIO N. 11 (Sept.): 202. Photo, Bell Labs equipment. (1971, 2050)

2008 Ives, H.E. "Television in color." SCI. & INV. 17 (Sept.): 400. (1986, 2073)

2009 Fleming, J.A. "The B.B.C. and television." TELEV. 2 (Sept.): 325–7. Pertinent remarks by the president of the Television Society about the restrictions placed on developments—"Shall Great Britain be left behind?" (1905, 1978, 2016, 2132)

2010 "First television demonstration in South Africa." TELEV. 2 (Sept.): 328. Photo. Report from the SOUTH AFRICAN WIRELESS WEEKLY, July 24, on a demonstration of Baird apparatus by Lord Angus Kennedy, vice-president of the Television Society, at the University of Cape Town. Demonstrations were also given in Durban and Johannesburg. (1992, 2011)

2011 "An 'eye' for ships. Remarkable new invention renders fog transparent. New triumphs for Mr. J.L. Baird." TELEV. 2 (Sept.): 337, 338. 3 photos. (2010, 2016)

2012 Waters, A.A. "The construction of experimental television apparatus. Pt. 4." TELEV. 2 (Sept.): 339, 340, 344. Photo, 3 diags. Amplifier, baseboard and panel layouts, wiring diagram, list of components. (1982, 2059)

2013 Desmond, S. "How television will kill 'time.' New worlds for old." TELEV. 2 (Sept.): 341–4. 3 illus. Forecasts of various uses. (1510)

2014 Harries, J.H.O. "The literature of television." TELEV. 2 (Sept.): 345–8, 351. List of works of reference and where they may be found, 52 entries. Details of author's reference system. (1981, 2144)

2015 Fox, W.C. "Concerning neon tubes." TELEV. 2 (Sept.): 349–51. 3 photos. G.E. Co. tubes, types and methods of manufacture. (1941, 2056)

2016 Moseley, S.A. "The new offer to Baird." TELEV. 2 (Sept.): 352, 353. Photo. On the BBC offer to allow 5 broadcast periods of one-half hour per week. (1978, 2009, 2011, 2017, 2029, 2058)

2017 "Talking film by television." TELEV. 2 (Sept.): 353. Account of Baird's demonstration from the TIMES, Aug. 20. (2016, 2018)

2018 Van Schie, J.W.A. "Baird television as seen by a Dutchman." TELEV. 2 (Sept.): 354. (2017, 2021)

2019 Denton, J.J., and W.G.W Mitchell. "The Television Society." TELEV. 2 (Sept.): 355–7, 363. 3 photos. Progress abroad, negotiations with the BBC, winter program. (1980, 2061)

2020 Wolfson, H. "The practical evolution of the photo-electric cell." TELEV. 2 (Sept.): 358–60, 363. 7 diags. Construction and materials, vacuum and gas-filled, proportional response, types, operation, details of specific phototubes. (1942, 2765)

2021 Nicolson, N.J. "Tele-cinematography." TELEV. 2 (Sept.): 361–3. Photo, 3 diags. Talking films, Baird's early experiments, sound reproducer, sync. Television versus telecine, lighting, scanning, light spot. (1979, 2018, 2023, 2054)

2022 Larner, E.T. PRACTICAL TELEVISION. London: Ernest Benn, 1929. 224 pp., 127 illus. Foreword by John L. Baird. 2nd ed. Expanded with an additional chapter on the broadcasting of television, with diagrams and details of improved apparatus in "this rapidly growing new science." (1772)

2023 "Voice and image go together over wire." N.Y.T. 29 (Sept. 3): 8. Demonstration by W.J. Jarrard at studio of the Baird Television Corp. in New York. Comments on the accord reached between Baird, BBC, and GPO, Baird's Teletalkies, the company's activities in Belgium and Germany, and plans for Australia, France, South Africa, and Spain. (2021, 2025)

2024 Prisner, S. "Optical projection apparatus." Br. 339,644, Sept. 3, 1929. For television and film.

2025 "Radio's tele-talkies called scientific achievement. Baird's television film is demonstrated here." N.Y.T. X, 14 (Sept. 8): 1–5. 3 photos. Feature article. (2023, 2029)

2026 Cawley, A.J. "Scanning process." U.S. 2,138,089, Sept. 10, 1929, renewed Aug. 18, 1937, Nov. 29, 1938. Two endless perforated belts, one inside the other in the same plane, with several photoelectric and optical elements on each side of the belts, a reflector, and screen. (1964, 2227)

2027 Garner, L.P. "Scanning apparatus." U.S. 1,907,057, Sept. 10, 1929, May 2, 1933. Assigned: Western Television. Perforated disk, construction. (1432)

2028 Birch-Field, Charles A. "Television." U.S. 2,077,030, Sept. 11, 1929, Apr. 13, 1937. Assigned: Mildred S. Reisman. Optical scanning assembly includes electrical conductors disposed transversely across the light beam and associated with a birefringent medium. Pulsating currents of constant frequency applied to the conductors. (2974)

2029 "Television. Broadcasts next month." TIMES (Sept. 12): 12b. Joint statement by Baird Co. and BBC on 30-line transmissions to begin Sept. 30 through station 2LO, 11:00 to 11:30 a.m., Monday–Friday. "In granting facilities for these experimental demonstrations, in which the public can, if they so desire, take part, neither the Postmaster-General nor the B.B.C. accept any responsibility for the quality of the transmission or the results obtained." (2016, 2025, 2030, 2031)

2030 "Synchronising apparatus for television receivers." ENGINEERING 128 (Sept. 13): 321. Illus. Baird system. (2029, 2034)

2031 "Television from 2LO." W.W. 25 (Sept. 18): 282. (2029, 2034)

2032 Blackwell, O.B., and J. Herman. "Television." U.S. 2,101,976, Sept. 18, 1929, Dec. 14, 1937. Assigned: AT&T. Three-channel system with restricted frequency range, entire image scanned concurrently with delays in each channel. (674, 3662)

2033 "Television." ELECT. REV. 105 (Sept. 20): 477, 478.

2034 "News and views." NATURE 124 (Sept. 21): 456. Plans for Baird broadcasts through station 2LO. (2030, 2031, 2035, 2062)

2035 Rogers, K.D. "Mr. Baird explains." POP. W. (Sept. 21): 81. (742, 2034, 2045)

2036 "Radio World's Fair opens tomorrow." N.Y.T. 12 (Sept. 22): 1, 2. Television to be shown. Plans of G.E. (1985, 2043)

2037 "German engineer invents color pictures for the radio." N.Y.T.12 (Sept 22): 5. Claim by Albert Alexander Ahronheim. "The inventor refuses, however, to give the secret away yet." (2420)

2038 "Radio Board renews television licenses." N.Y.T. 12 (Sept. 22): 6. For stations W2XBA, W2XBJ, W2XBW. (1928, 2462)

2039 Paley, William S. "Theatre forces join with radio." N.Y.T. XII, 3 (Sept. 22): 7. General comments on the stage, movies, and broadcasting. "Does television carry a threat?"

2040 Kennedy, T.R., Jr. "Mists of science hide television. When will the public see by radio?" N.Y.T. XII, 12 (Sept. 22): 1. (2345)

2041 Barthélemy, René (1889–1954) and Jean Le Duc. "Scanning images in television." U.S, 1,928,553, Sept. 12, 1930, Sept. 26, 1933; Br. 354,572, Aug. 28, 1930. Assigned: Comp. Gaz. In France Sept. 25, 1929. Alternate scanning in opposite directions by a disk with two offset and contrary semi-spiral sets of holes (heart-shaped pattern). Applicable also for film transmission. (2237)

2042 Friebus, Reginald T. "Reproducing pictures or scenes from recorded impulses." U.S. 1,877,447, Sept. 25, 1929, Sept. 13, 1932. Assigned: Columbia Phonograph. Light-beam pickup from a record disk with scanning disk for reproducing images.

2043 "Television luring radio show crowds. Average of 350 attend every 5-minute performance." N.Y.T. 24 (Sept. 26): 2. (2036, 2047)

2044 "Television." ELECT. REV.: 105 (Sept. 27): 528.

2045 "News and views." NATURE 124 (Sept. 28): 492. On Baird's toothed-wheel synchronizer. "We have seen the device working well when simultaneous speech and television was being demonstrated between two rooms of Baird's laboratory at 133 Long Acre." Receiver will be available when regular broadcasting begins. Receivers of this pattern are being put on the market in Germany by the Fernseh A.-G., which is the Baird organization in that country. (2035, 2054)

2046 Eckersley, P.P. "Television today." POP. W. (Sept. 28): 125. (1661, 2153)

2047 "New York talks about the show." N.Y.T. X, 15 (Sept. 29): 1–3. Television surprises. "It looks as if television has stolen the crowd." (2043, 2090)

2048 Gray, F. "Electro-optical transmission." U.S. 1,812,402, Sept. 30, 1929, June 30, 1931. Assigned: B.T.L. Disk system. (1968, 2202)

2049 Kell, R.D. "Transmission of pictures or views." U.S. 1,793,406, Sept. 30, 1929, Feb. 17, 1931. Assigned: G.E. Br. 366,477, Sept. 29, 1930 (B.T.H.). Cathode-ray tube with disk transmitter, capacitors, commutator, sync motor. (1955, 2105)

2050 Arnold, J.P. "Television in natural colors." RADIO 11 (Oct.): 35, 36. 2 photos. 2 diags. Bell Labs system. (1862, 2007, 2052)

2051 "Special channel and new standards for television." RADIO 11 (Oct.): 36, 74. On changes from the first RMA standards evolved more than a year ago (1665). Disks with 15, 20, 24 holes recommended for amateurs. (1999, 3321)

2052 Lewer, S.K. "Television in color." SCI. PROG. 24 (Oct.): 315, 316. (2050, 2343)

2053 Robinson, J. "Television and photo-telegraphy." TELEV. 2 (Oct.): 373–5. 2 photos. Limitations of broadcast band and need for space for television. Strong views about the monopoly held by radio broadcast stations. (1699, 2506)

2054 Nicolson, N.J. "Noctovision and the Noctovisor." TELEV. 2 (Oct.): 376–8. Photo, 4 diags. Technical details. Disk, layout, apertures. Direction-finding applications. (2021, 2045, 2057)

2055 Dinsdale, A. "Television at the Berlin Radio Exhibition." TELEV. 2 (Oct.): 379–89. 17 photos, 5 diags. Comment on the "dot theory" of image construction, which "still prevails in Germany." Technical details of apparatus displayed by the German Post Office, Fernseh A.-G., von Mihály, and Telefunken-Karolus. The Post Office had two-way television-telephone booths on display. German standard established at 30/12.5, picture proportion 3 to 4, horizontal scan. "The commercial prospects of television in Germany look very promising indeed." (1450, 1796, 2172, 2506)

2056 Fox, W.C. "More about neon tubes." TELEV. 2 (Oct.): 393, 394. Photo, 7 diags. Circuits and applications, Philips tube. (2015, 2184)

2057 Roberts. T.S. "Synchronisation in television." TELEV. 2 (Oct): 395–8. 2 photos, 7 diags. Baird's automatic sync. (2054, 2062)

2058 Moseley, S.A. "The future of television." TELEV. 2 (Oct.): 407, 408. (2016, 2138)

2059 Waters, A.A. "The construction of experimental television apparatus. Pt. 5." TELEV. 2 (Oct.): 409, 410, 419. 2 photos, 2 diags. (2012, 2086)

2060 Chapple, Harry John Barton (1894–1978). "Television and your wireless receiver." TELEV. 2 (Oct.): 413–5. 2 graphs, 2 diags. (2180)

2061 Denton, J.J., and W.G.W. Mitchell. "The Television Society." TELEV. 2 (Oct.): 416, 419. Recent correspondence on broadcasting. (2019, 2089)

2062 "Television. First experimental broadcast." TIMES (Oct. 1): 26a. Inauguration of experimental service by the Baird Television Development Company through BBC station 2LO at 11:00 a.m., Sept. 30. Program originated in the Baird studio in Long Acre, which was connected by land line to Savoy Hill and thence to the transmitter in Oxford Street, with sound and vision transmitted alternately in 2-minute sequences. Moseley opened the proceedings, followed by short speeches and presentations by Sir Ambrose Fleming, Prof. E.N. da Costa Andrade, Major A.G. Church, Sydney Howard, comedian, Lulu Stanley and Miss C. King, singers. (2031, 2057, 2063)

2063 "Radio television." ELECT. 103 (Oct. 4): 392. Baird-BBC inaugural broadcast. (2062, 2067, 2079)

"A ceremony which may perhaps prove to be historical in the progress of television took place on Monday, when the first official tests of radio television were made through 2LO. For the time being similar tests will be made each day between 11.00 and 11.30 a.m., in order that the Baird Television Development Co. may improve and develop this system of transmission. The service is of a purely experimental nature, and at the moment is confined to one wavelength, so that speech and vision cannot be transmitted simultaneously; in the circumstances it is necessary for the speaker to speak first and then change over to television. On the completion of the Brookman's Park station two wavelengths will be allocated, when both television and speech will be transmitted simultaneously....

"On Monday, televisors were installed at Savoy Hill, the G.P.O., Boxhill and elsewhere, though no receivers for public use will be available until the experimental period is passed and a satisfactory service can be guaranteed. The studio from which the artists are 'televised' is at the offices of the Baird Company, in London. From there the image is passed over land lines to Savoy Hill, where there is a check receiver, and then over the usual land lines to the transmitter at Oxford Street."

2064 "Radio is now beginning expansion of its magic." N.Y.T. X, 14 (Oct. 6): 1–5. General comments on television and film broadcasts. "Talking movies for home linked with the future radio set."

2065 "Pictures by radio are flashed far." N.Y.T. X, 16 (Oct. 6): 1, 2. Includes comment on television in Germany, where interest is very keen. The Post Office is to start actual television transmission from motion picture film this fall, with 30-line images. (1932, 2085)

2066 Nicolson, A.M. "Electrical production of images." U.S. 1,863,278, Oct. 7, 1929, June 14, 1932. Assigned: Comm. Pats. Br. 360,470, Aug. 6, 1930. Arc system with illuminating screen and arc path in a magnetic field. (1254, 2383)

2067 "B.B.C. transmission." ELECT. REV. 105 (Oct. 11): 108. (2063, 2122)

2068 "News and views." NATURE 124 (Oct. 12): 593. Comments on radio bandwidth (9 kc), with support of Robinson's viewpoint in TELEVISION for October (2053), and on the radio exhibition in Berlin. "The stand of the Fernseh A.G., which showed the Baird system was very popular."

2069 John Wesley Ernest. "Electrical transmission of moving pictures." U.S. 1,954,052, Sept. 16, 1930. Apr. 10, 1934. Br. 337,931,

Oct. 12, 1929. Picture from a motion picture film, projected onto a screen, is scanned by a disk for transmission.

2070 "Trade notes and comments." N.Y.T. X, 19 (Oct. 13): 1, 2. De Forest expects television within five years. (1851, 2334)

2071 Weinhart, Howard W., and Howard Hall. "Electro-optical apparatus." U.S. 1,867,340, Oct. 23, 1929, July 12, 1932. Assigned: B.T.L. Folded multielement neon tube. See also Br. 357,590, June 25, 1930, Br. 358,060; 358,061, July 2, 1930. (2330)

2072 Chevallier, Pierre Emile Louis. "Kinescope." U.S. 2,021,252, Oct. 20, 1930, Nov. 19, 1935; Br. 360,654, Oct. 30, 1930. In France Oct. 25, 1929. Picture tube. (3600)

2073 Ives, H.E. "Electro-optical system." U.S. 2,007,651, Oct. 25, 1929, July 9, 1935. Assigned: B.T.L. Br. 365,166, Oct. 16, 1930 (E.R.P.). Four-channel disk system for color. (2008, 2148)

2074 Gramophone Co., and Michael Bowman-Manifold. "Television." Br. 338,330, Oct. 26, 1929. Disk system with phonic wheels, tuning forks, and contactor disks. (2075)

2075 Gramophone Co., and M. Bowman-Manifold. "Television." Br. 340,356, Oct. 26, 1929. Disk and adjustable drive. (2074, 2101)

2076 "No big changes are foreseen says Richmond, who believes television may be dismissed for the present—home radio-talkies are another complication." N.Y.T. X, 14 (Oct. 27): 1, 2. Views of H.B. Richmond. (1210)

2077 Zimber, Raymond M. "Scanning device." U.S. 1,963,255, Oct. 28, 1929, June 19, 1934. Assigned: RCA. Two concentric drums with slots at right angles arranged in several helical tracks.

2078 Fernseh A.-G. "Television." Br. 354,630, Oct. 28, 1930. In Germany Oct. 29, 1929. Disk and mirror drum at right angles. (2097)

2079 Baird. J.L. "Television enters public life." DISCOVERY 10 (Nov.): 362–4. 3 photos. Brief comments on the BBC experimental broadcast by the Baird system, with editorial report, a summary of Baird's work. (2063, 2082)

2080 Schröter, F. "Abbildung und Verstärkung bei Fernsehen" [Reproduction and amplification in television apparatus]. E.N.T. 6 (Nov.): 439–53. 18 illus. (1617, 2167)

2081 "Television is here." RADIO-CRAFT 1 (Nov.): 233. Advertisement by Jenkins Television Corp., Jersey City, N.J. "Home Televisors have reached so practical a stage that they will shortly be placed on general sale....The year 1930 will be a television year. Write for a copy of TELEVISION— THE EYE OF RADIO." (2004, 2119)

2082 Reisser, Walter. "Television abroad. A comparison of the Baird and the von Mihály systems." RADIO N. 11 (Nov.1): 416–8, 458. 6 photos. Description of apparatus based on interviews in London and Berlin. (1952, 2079, 2083, 2129)

2083 "How Baird sees through fog with dark rays." SCI. & INV. 17 (Nov.): 591. 2 illus. The Noctovisor. (2082, 2087)

2084 "Invisible ray transmits pictures." SCI. & INV. 17 (Nov.): 629. 4 illus. Demonstration of light-beam transmission at L. Bamberger & Co. in Newark. (1896)

2085 Loewe, Siegmund, and Paul Goerz. "Forward! The progress of television in Germany." TELEV. 2 (Nov.): 428–30. Apparatus at the Berlin Radio Show, activities of the Fernseh Co., plans for placing a receiver on sale in December. (2065, 2118, 2169, 2694)

2086 Waters, A.A. "The construction of experimental television apparatus. Pt. 6." TELEV. 2 (Nov.): 432, 433. 2 diags. Characteristics of neon, layout and construction of filter, with circuit. (2059, 2137)

2087 Tierney, C. "Television in South Africa." TELEV. 2 (Nov.): 437. Baird Co. demonstrations. (1733, 2083, 2102, 2140)

2088 Birch, A.F. "Photographing a television image." TELEV. 2 (Nov.): 448. By one of Baird's associates. (2225)

2089 "The Proceedings of the Television Society." TELEV. 2 (Nov.): 454. (2061, 2139)

2090 "Television across the water." TELEV. 2 (Nov.): 460–3. 3 illus. New York radio show, keen public interest, film transmitter of the Jenkins Television Corp., commercial status of television, waveband allocations. (2047, 2583)

2091 Abbott, W. Barrie. "The fight for British television." TELEV. 2 (Nov.): 468. (2271)

2092 Zworykin, V.K. "View transmission system." U.S. 1,863,363, Nov. 1, 1929, June 14, 1932. Assigned: Westinghouse. Light-chopper disk with radial slots and a similar fixed element. (1951, 2107)

2093 Hammond, J.H. "Navigational guide system." U.S. 2,062,003, Nov. 2, 1929, renewed Sept. 26, 1935, Nov. 24, 1936. Br. 356,970, Oct. 17, 1930. Aircraft pilot receives a picture showing his three-dimensional position with reference to a relief map. (1990, 2435)

2094 "Light is shed on television." N.Y.T. X, 15 (Nov. 3): 5–7. D.E. Replogle on a new type of receiver required for television. (2006, 2099)

2095 Haberle, Sumner Dudley. "Television." U.S. 1,840,446, Nov. 5, 1929, Jan. 12, 1932. Assigned: Jenkins Television. Disk-drum receiver assembly with lamp and recessed viewing lens in a cabinet.

2096 Huffman, C.E. "Optical system." U.S. 1,801,430, Nov. 7. 1929, Apr. 21, 1931. Assigned: Jenkins Television. Three disks with spirals of apertures arranged to rotate in succession and scan in mutually intersecting lines. (1998, 2193)

2097 Fernseh A.-G. "Television." Br. 356,565, Nov. 7, 1930. In Germany Nov. 8, 1929. Disk apertures. (2078, 2098)

2098 Fernseh A.-G. "Synchronous movements." Br. 366,598, Nov. 7, 1930. In Germany Nov. 8, 1929. Phonic wheel with electron tube circuits. (2097, 2205)

2099 Replogle, D.E. "Progress and future of television." ELECT. W. 94 (Nov. 9): 931. Comments on the experimental nature of current transmissions. (2094, 2177)

2100 "Predicts television will soon be general. Radio Commissioner La Fount says football and baseball games will be shown." N.Y.T. 18 (Nov. 10): 4. (1629, 2440)

2101 Gramophone Co., and M. Bowman-Manifold. "Transmission and reception of moving picture records." Br. 343,084, Nov. 13, 1929, Feb. 13, 1931. Disk with a circle of apertures scans a continuously moving picture film, receiver disk with a spiral of apertures. (2075, 3455)

2102 "Baird television to be shown here." N.Y.T. 34 (Nov. 15): 3, 4. Information by Hutchinson, who "displayed official documents from the radio authorities of France, Germany, Belgium, and the Irish Free State, virtually giving the right to begin a television service in those countries." (1697, 2087, 2121, 2878)

2103 Baird, H.S. "Scanning apparatus for television." U.S. 1,908,809, Nov. 15, 1929, May 16, 1933. Assigned: Shortwave and Television. Apertured drum with another apertured scanning member. (1897, 2294)

2104 Batchelor, John C., and Arthur W. Vance. "Television." U.S. 1,955,320, Nov. 16, 1929, Apr. 17, 1934. Assigned: Westinghouse. Film scanner, cathode-ray-tube receiver, sync. (2964, 2977)

2105 Kell, R.D. "Transmission of pictures." U.S. 1,849,839, Nov. 16, 1929, Mar. 15, 1932. Assigned: G.E. Br. 350,371, Nov. 17, 1930 (B.T.H.). Disk system with narrow band of picture signals removed and replaced by sync signal. Controller reference to Br. 332,284 (1742). (2049, 2326)

2106 Tschörner, L. "Picture reproducing device for television." U.S. 1,888,893, Feb. 26, 1931, Nov. 22, 1932. In Austria Nov. 16, 1929. Crossed perforated film. (1384)

2107 Zworykin, V.K. "Vacuum tube." U.S. 2,109,245, Nov. 16, 1929, Feb. 22, 1938. Assigned: Westinghouse. A picture tube (kinescope) with second anode consisting of a metallic coating inside the cone-shaped part of the bulb, and external plates and coils for beam deflection. (2092, 2112)

2108 Hartley, Lowell J. "Transmission of sound and pictures." U.S. 2,022,505, Nov. 22, 1929, Nov. 26, 1935. Assigned: G.E. Br. 368,262, Nov. 24, 1930 (B.T.H.). Continuously moving film and disk with a circle of apertures. Controller reference to Br. 357,687 (1963).

2109 Rogan, John J. "Electro-optical system." U.S. 1,918,827, Nov. 22, 1929, July 18, 1933. Assigned: Hygrade Sylvania. Receiver. (2110)

2110 Rogan, J.J. "Electro-optical system." U.S. 2,055,088, Nov. 22, 1929, Sept. 22, 1936. Assigned: Hygrade Sylvania. Receiver. (2109)

2111 Tate, A.O. "System of scanning." U.S. 1,880,294, Nov. 22, 1929, Oct. 4, 1932. Disk with two arcuate series of square holes, each extending over 180 degrees, to traverse and retraverse portions of an image in an undulating motion. (1889, 2493)

2112 "New cathode ray tube pushes television ahead. Whirling disks and neon tube are eliminated by latest device—machine is simplified and takes radio vision near the parlor." N.Y.T. XI, 12 (Nov. 24): 1–5. Zworykin's picture tube. (2107, 2113)

2113 "Radio images painted on screen by pencil beams." N.Y.T. XI, 12 (Nov. 24): 3, 4. Photo of Zworykin with picture tube. (2112, 2125)

2114 "Taylor warns against television enthusiasm." N.Y.T. XI, 16 (Nov. 24): 6, 7. Cautionary views of A. Hoyt Taylor, head of the Naval Research Laboratory.

2115 Hitchcock, William J. "Cathode ray device." U.S. 1,814,805, Nov. 26, 1929, July 14, 1931. Assigned: G.E. Br. 363,103, Nov. 25, 1930. (B.T.H.). Photoelectric control element scanned by an electron beam from one of two cathodes.

2116 Loiseau, L.M.J. "Television." Br. 360,699, Nov. 29, 1930. Assigned: Comp. Gaz. In France Nov. 29, 1929. Addition to Br. 358,087 (1946). For color.

2117 Pfeiffer, George S. "Television." U.S. 1,943,395, Nov. 29, 1929, Jan. 16, 1934. Assigned: Kellog Switchboard & Supply. Multielement photocell and distributor.

2118 Noack, Fritz. "Das Fernsehen in Deutschland" [Television in Germany]. V.D.I.Z. 73 (Nov. 30): 1703–5. 4 illus. Survey of recent progress, standards, problems of film transmission by short waves, devices and methods available, and prospects for the production of receivers. (2085, 2265, 2411)

2119 "Jenkins announces scanner." CIT. RAD. CALL BOOK 10 (Dec.): 102. 3 photos. Scanning drum combined with slotted selector shutter replaces the helical drum scanner (1294). (2081, 2120)

2120 "Cages for televisionists." CIT. RAD. CALL BOOK 10 (Dec.): 102. Copper mesh shielding encloses film pickup apparatus and operator in Jenkins' station W2XCR. (2119, 2128)

2121 "English tele-talkie transmitter." CIT. RAD. CALL BOOK 10 (Dec.): 112. Photo, Baird apparatus. (2102, 2122)

2122 "Television broadcasting in England." POP. MECH. 52 (Dec.): 1010, 1011. 2 photos. Baird-BBC broadcasts. (2067, 2121, 2126, 2138)

2123 Farnsworth, P.T., and Harry R. Lubcke. "Transmission of television images. Intimations of how it may be ultimately accomplished in practice." RADIO 11 (Dec.): 36, 85, 86. 2 photos. Discussion of picture elements, degree of detail, bandwidth required for adequate picture quality, transmission frequency, entertainment value. Looking to the future, the authors see higher definition images of 250 lines broadcast by a network operating on the ultra-short waves. "Chain broadcasting will be handled by beam transmitters operating in the six meter region which will connect various cities in a television network." (1694, 2279, 2381)

"A certain minimum amount of detail must be transmitted by a television system in order that the received image may be said to possess 'entertainment value.' The system must transmit a person's face, for example, with sufficient detail to make the features readily discernible and sufficiently clear to 'entertain' the viewer if the person should talk and attempt to convey meanings by facial expressions. This minimum has been specified by some workers in the field as an image consisting of 2500 elementary areas, or elements. The picture shown herewith is made from a photograph of a television image, consisting of 20,000 elements. This image of a lady with her eyes closed was transmitted by the Farnsworth system of electrical scanning and is perhaps the first published American photograph of an actual television image. The original image was approximately 3 1/2 in. square. It can well be considered as having entertainment value.

"It is felt that real entertainment in television will require an image 8 in. square of some 60,000 elements. An image of this size containing 250 lines per side contains 62,500 elements and can be defined as one of real entertainment value. Such an image would extend the quality of the image to include semi-closeups and small full length groups. Apparatus for producing an image of this size and one approaching this quality is under construction and will be available shortly.

"The problem of real entertainment value of television is unique and difficult. Fundamentally it requires a wide spectrum of frequencies for its accomplishment. It cannot be realized with present voice broadcasting frequencies, channels, or methods. Attempts at such practices can only hope to yield approximations to what is really wanted. Not by means of broadcasting facilities, broadcasting networks, or semi-short waves will anything lasting be achieved, but by the use of short waves and ultra-short waves will real television finally be accomplished."

2124 "R.C.A.'s television work on short waves." RADIO-CRAFT 1 (Dec.): 254, 274, 275. Experiments at station W2XBS on 100-kc band between 143 and 150 meters. (1974, 2130)

2125 Zworykin, V.K. "Television with cathode-ray tube for receiver." RADIO ENG. 9 (Dec.): 38–41. 5 photos, 6 diags., 6 refs. "Special tube, called the Kinescope, eliminates usual scanning and synchronizing apparatus and provides larger picture with better detail." Technical description of film transmitter (1951) and picture tube receiver with a screen about 7 in. diam. Sync method and operation are given. New York: Arno Press, 1977, reprint. (2113, 2214)

2126 Secor, H.W. "Baird's newest Televisor." SCI. & INV. 17 (Dec.): 691, 732, 734. 5 illus. "Designed to bring talking movies into your home." Demonstration in New York. (1312, 2122, 2136)

2127 "Sends movies by radio." SCI. & INV. 17 (Dec.): 725. 2 illus. J.F. Brott, a radio engineer of Seattle, and his apparatus.

2128 "Jenkins now broadcasting movies." SCI. & INV. 17 (Dec.): 725. Disk apparatus, photo, and caption. (2120, 2131)

2129 "Portable Televisor." SCI. & INV. 17 (Dec.): 725. Von Mihály's apparatus, photo, and caption. (2082, 2170)

2130 "Look in! RCA is televising." SCI. & INV. 17 (Dec.): 725. Experimental transmissions from station W2XBS, photo, and caption. (2124, 2433)

2131 Peck, A.P. "Television's progress." SCI. AM. 141 (Dec.): 487. 5 photos. Jenkins transmitter in Jersey City, disk-drum receiver assembly, receiver cabinet with shadow box. (1904, 2128, 2156, 3428)

2132 Fleming, J.A. "Educational uses for television." TELEV. 2 (Dec.): 477–80. 3 diags. (2009, 2216)

2133 "Educational aspects of television." TELEV. 2 (Dec.): 480.

2134 Verralls, J.M. "America and television progress." TELEV. 2 (Dec.): 483.

2135 Trenton, Leslie. "Television and the public. What shall we see?" TELEV. 2 (Dec.): 484, 485. 4 photos.

2136 "Hastings honours Baird. Details of a simple ceremony." TELEV. 2 (Dec.): 486–8. 4 photos. A bronze plaque on the wall of a shop in Queen's Arcade, inscribed: "Television. First demonstrated by Mr. J.L. Baird, from experiments started in 1924" was unveiled Nov. 7. (2126, 2138)

2137 Waters, A.A. "The construction of experimental television apparatus. Pt. 7." TELEV. 2 (Dec.): 493, 494, 498. 2 diags. (2086, 2142, 2186)

2138 Moseley, S.A. "A new Richmond." TELEV. 2 (Dec.): 500–2. General comments on Baird and the BBC. (2058, 2122, 2136, 2140, 2179, 2300)

2139 "The Proceedings of the Television Society." TELEV. 2 (Dec.): 506–13. 3 photos, 2 graphs, 4 diags. Lecture, "Amplification and television," by F. Langford-Smith. (2089, 2183)

2140 Tierney, C. "The origin and progress of television. A statement of facts." TELEV. 2 (Dec.): 514–7. 5 photos. Summary of Baird's work. (2087, 2138, 2147, 2181)

2141 "The lower frequencies in television." TELEV. 2 (Dec.): 518, 520. 4 diags. By "D.C."

2142 Cato, George C. "More light through the scanning disk." TELEV. 2 (Dec.): 519, 520. 5 diags. (2137, 2182, 2321)

2143 Gradenwitz, A. "Television in Czecho-Slovakia." TELEV. 2 (Dec.): 522, 523. 2 photos. Account of W. Faerber's demonstration at the Bodenbach-on-Elbe radio show. Apparatus similar to Baird's. (1906, 2420)

2144 Harries, J.H.O. "Television." Br. 346,021, Dec. 2, 1929, U.S. 1,921,464, Dec. 1, 1930, Aug. 8, 1933. Lens system designed to emphasize the center of an image, to provide higher definition in the center and, by compression or distortion along with conversion to normal composition in the receiver, to economize in transmission bandwidth. Applicable also to film transmission and recording. (2014, 2437)

2145 Rosing, B.L. Russ. 16,265, Dec. 2, 1929. (1032, 3407)

2146 Kannenberg, Walter F. "Electro-optical system." U.S. 2,072,455, Dec. 4, 1929, Mar. 2, 1937. Assigned: B.T.L. Two-channel (vision and sync) disk system, multielement, folded tube, auxiliary light projection at receiver.

2147 "Television development. Intention of making apparatus available to public in January." ELECT. 103 (Dec. 6): 714. Announcement by Baird Television Development Co.: "The transmissions that have been taking place during past months have been so successful that the night facilities have been granted to us." (2140, 2157)

2148 Ives, H.E. "Electro-optical system." U.S. 1,907,114, Dec. 6, 1929, May 2, 1933. Assigned: B.T.L. Disk system with resistive photocell and helium glow discharge lamp. (2073, 2174)

2149 Telehor A.-G. "Synchronous movements." Br. 348,526, Feb. 7, 1930. In Germany Dec. 7, 1929. Television receiver sync. (1987, 2429)

2150 Ilberg, Waldemar. "Televisor transmission system." U.S. 2,090,004, Dec. 6, 1930, Aug. 17, 1937; Br. 351,378, Nov. 22, 1930. Assigned: Telefunken. In Germany Dec. 11, 1929. Interruptions of a constant-intensity beam in a picture tube correspond to the light and shade of a picture. (2255)

2151 Kolster-Brandes (Federal Telegraph Co.). "Television." Br. 344,091, Dec. 11, 1929. Film transmission with scanning disk and retardation networks arranged to repeat film signals while the film moves to next position. (2238)

2152 Richardson, O.W. "Thermionic phenomena and the laws which govern them." Nobel lecture, Dec. 12. NOBEL LECTURES, PHYSICS: 1922–1941. Amsterdam, London, New York: Elsevier, 1965. Presentation speech, pp. 221–3. Lecture, pp. 224–36. Biography, pp. 237, 238. Prize awarded for 1928. (454)

2153 Eckersley, P.P. "This television business." POP. W. (Dec. 14): 781. (2046, 2524)

2154 "More television experiments." POP. W. (Dec. 14): 784.

2155 Swinton, A.A.C. "Television." TIMES (Dec. 16): 8c. In this letter the hitherto severe critic of Baird softens his stand. "I recently went to see an exhibition of Baird television at the offices of the British Broadcasting Corporation. The television was very successful, and I was able to recognize a moving picture of the Prince of Wales." The small size of the picture, was, however a matter of criticism. (1918, 2710)

2156 Jenkins, C.F. "Electro-optical system." U.S. 1,859,828, Dec. 17, 1929, May 24, 1932. Assigned: Jenkins Labs. Perforated drum coaxial with a spirally slotted drum. (2131, 2162)

2157 Haynes, F.H. "A television reception test." W.W. 25 (Dec. 18): 669–73. 8 illus. Report on a Baird receiver. (1948, 2147, 2159)

2158 Davis, Chester Leslie. "Television." U.S. 1,848,324, Dec. 18, 1929, Mar. 8, 1932. Assigned: Wired Radio. Disk transmitter and a luminous inductance screen responsive to signals of varying frequencies. See also U.S. 1,756,086, Aug. 21, 1928, Apr. 29, 1930. (2431)

2159 "Walker televised at demonstration. Astonished at clearness of voice and images reproduced by Baird device." N.Y.T. 22 (Dec. 21): 2. Mayor John (Jimmy) Walker at public demonstration in New York. (2157, 2181, 3017)

2160 "Radio industry plans for 1930. Television on commercial scales not expected for at least two years." N.Y.T. IX, 9 (Dec. 22): 7, 8.

2161 Buecker, Heinrich, and Hubert Buecker. "Television." U.S. 1,974,911, Dec. 27, 1930, Sept. 25, 1934. In Germany Dec. 27, 1929. Disk scanning with intermediate magnetic storage in transmitter and receiver.

2162 Jenkins, C.F. "The transmission of movies by radio." TRANS. SMPE 36 (1929): 915–20. (2156, 2177)

2163 Campbell, Norman Robert, and Dorothy Ritchie. PHOTOELECTRIC CELLS: THEIR PROPERTIES, USE, AND APPLICATIONS. London: Pitman, 1929. vii + 209 pp., plate, 41 diags. Fundamentals, theory, construction, principles of use, applications.

2164 Library of Congress. TELEVISION, A BIBLIOGRAPHICAL LIST. Washington, 1929. 7 pp., 110 items.

2165 Yates, Raymond Francis. ABC OF TELEVISION OR SEEING BY RADIO. New York: Norman W. Henley, 1929. viii + 210 pp., 21 plates, 78 diags. General survey, basic systems, telegraphing pictures, photoelectric cells, amplifiers, neon lamps, selenium cells, scanning methods, synchronizing, construction of home transmitters and receivers.

CHAPTER 10

ON STAGE: 1930

Television progress during 1930 can be gauged by increases in the number of patent applications and technical papers, by engineering developments, and by the staged events that kept television in the public eye. Demonstrations of a large theater screen by General Electric and the two-way visual telephone by Bell Labs were top events in America. The English Baird concern mounted the vaudeville stage to bring large-size images to the public view. While the Baird studio, in cooperation with the BBC, commenced a regular broadcast service in London, experimental broadcasts were also put on by others in Berlin and in Boston, Chicago, Jersey City, New York, Schenectady, Washington, and other American cities.

Although there were more demonstrations in 1930 than in 1929, nevertheless public interest slackened, judging by the drop in news reports and periodical accounts, particularly in America. Items in the NEW YORK TIMES dropped from seventy-five to fifty-seven, which is a fair bellwether of the declining state of television in the country. A reduction in the number of entries from periodicals previously listed is offset by fifty-seven items published in FERNSEHEN, an organ of the German Television Society (Allgemeiner Deutscher Fernsehverein), founded at the beginning of the year, an event of general and professional interest. Another innovation came on August 9 with the presentation of a talking film sent from the Baird studio and received on the big screen at the Coliseum as an alternative to the transmission of live images. Described as "big events," these demonstrations were acclaimed as major achievements by Moseley, who was by now not only Baird's protector and leading publicist but also the self-appointed defender of British television. There is little evidence, however, that these publicity efforts on the stage and elsewhere did much to expand the home receiver market.

Similar promotional moves were made in the United States. General Electric demonstrated reception on a 6-foot translucent screen installed on the stage of Proctor's RKO theater in Schenectady on May 22. An invited audience saw a program of variety acts transmitted by radio from the company's laboratory about a mile away. A portable arc-light projector, mounted at the rear of the stage, contained a Karolus-type Kerr cell, lens system, and a 48-hole disk that produced 20 pictures per second with horizontal scanning. Observers reported that the brilliancy was about half that of the usual motion picture; the range of halftones was good, although the picture appeared somewhat hazy; there was some distortion; and imperfect synchronous control allowed the image to swing slowly from side to side.

Bell Telephone Laboratories came into the news once more on April 9 by demonstrating a two-way system between the AT&T offices and their premises in New York. Telephone booths at each end contained two disk systems, one with an arc light for transmission and the other with a special neon tube for reception, along with photocells, microphone, and loudspeaker. This elaborate apparatus, which produced 72-line images with 18 frames per second, required eight wire circuits between the stations. In keeping with their custom, full technical reports appeared in the BELL SYSTEM TECHNICAL JOURNAL. Papers also were presented at a meeting of the AIEE in June, and a special booklet was produced. The apparatus remained in experimental service for more than a year.

Called the "first radio television theatre," a program was put on at Lincoln Park in Jersey City with the visual broadcasts by Jenkins on April 7. Receivers were installed in about fifty places in the city, including the radio stores. It was reported that images (48/15) on a 4-inch screen were received with considerable clarity. This event, which was a joint performance by the Jenkins and de Forest concerns, was repeated with a public showing in New York on August 25. While the demonstrations aroused some enthusiasm, the efforts were not rewarded by an increase in receiver sales.

Receivers were becoming more readily available, either as complete models or in kit form for home assembly. Baird had a commercial table model on the market early in the year at the price of 25 guineas (about $130) and a kit of parts was on sale. One of these receivers was installed at 10 Downing Street, the residence of Prime Minister Ramsay MacDonald, on March 31. In July the Jenkins Television Corporation advertised several complete models and a Radiovisor kit with prices ranging from $42.50 to $750. The Short Wave & Television Laboratory in Boston also advertised their new Baird Universal Televisor that month, named after their chief engineer and designer H.S. Baird. The term "universal" referred to the receiver being adaptable for different signals on the air, such as 48/15 or 60/24. The Western Television Corporation in Chicago also announced their new receiver in July, a table model with a 6-inch viewing lens. Three receivers, two disk models, and one with a mirror drum, as well as component parts, were displayed by the Fernseh Company at the radio show in Berlin, where the Telehor Company also showed two disk receivers and a kit of parts.

In other news there are glimpses of varied activities in America. The Baird Noctovisor was demonstrated in New York in January as a navigational aid for ships. In a long-distance transmission test by General Electric the following month a simple graphic design was sent from Schenectady to Australia and back. Farnsworth in California produced a new experimental picture-tube receiver. In December he announced further progress, claiming success with a system that could provide a 300-line picture. Moreover, image transmission for this higher definition could be accommodated, it was said, within a narrow frequency band, a claim that was later dropped. Standards were still discussed, also the question of transmission bands, which the FRC modified with station reassignments in December. In the future there were plans for television in the proposed Rockefeller Center in New York, while the Columbia Broadcasting Company also was preparing to enter the field.

These public displays and announcements gave prominence to the work of seven companies, in addition to Bell Labs and General Electric, out of twenty-seven who were active during the year, as shown in the list of corporate patents in Table 15. Changes in the number of applications can be seen by comparing the figures for 1929. The drop in numbers for G.E. and Westinghouse and the increase for RCA resulted partly from the transference of personnel and research work from the former two to the RCA laboratories, which began during the year. Another change concerns the Jenkins Corporation, which came under the control of the De Forest Company, and the later acquisition of their assets by RCA. One new company of note is Radioaktien-Gesellschaft D.S. Loewe, whose main contributor at the time was Manfred von Ardenne. A new competitor to the long-established Telefunken Company and the younger firms Fernseh and Telehor, the D.S. Loewe radio company pioneered cathode-ray systems and became a prominent member of the German television industry.

The rise of corporate activity was matched by the work of independent individuals who were equally busy with their schemes. Considering patents not assigned to companies, fifty-nine applications were filed by forty-seven persons; the corresponding numbers for 1929 were forty-eight and thirty-nine. Circumstances in the United States clearly favored the team approach, with ninety-six corporate patents compared with twenty-two by eighteen individuals. The situation in Britain and Germany was quite different. None of the larger firms in Britain was engaged in television except the Gramophone Company, soon to become Baird's first national competitor. Corporate British applications amount to twenty-two, individual filings are nineteen; the respective figures for the German listings are seventeen each. The total of 205 for the year is an increase of forty-seven over 1929.

A survey of the technical features reveals the collection for the year to be mainly a new montage of old ideas consisting of improvements on known methods and variations of previous schemes. The scanning disk at last was losing favor, being specified in 29 percent of the patents compared with 44 percent in 1929. In the total of sixty employing disks there is the usual wide variety of different geometries and combinations, such as spirals or circles of apertures or lenses, straight or curved radial slots or sets of holes and others with lamps, photocells, discharge tubes, prisms, and color filters. There are single disks, concentric disks, overlapping disks, and others coacting with rotary shutters, cylinders, or drums.

TABLE 15 CORPORATE PATENTS

Company	1929	1930
Bell Telephone Laboratories	12	22
RCA	10	17
Baird Companies	6	12
Communication Patents	1	11
Comp. Gaz	5	9
Telefunken	6	9
Farnsworth Companies		8
General Electric	12	8
Jenkins Companies	5	8
Gramophone Company	4	7
Wired Radio	1	7
Radio Inventions	1	5
*D.S. Loewe		4
AT&T	2	3
Westinghouse	10	3
Associated Electric Laboratories		2
Fernseh	3	2
Telehor	7	2
British Thomson-Houston		1
*Electronic Television Company		1
Kolster Radio Corporation	1	1
N.V. Philips	3	1
*Nakken Patent Corporation		1
Short Wave & Television Laboratory	2	0
Universal and General Radio Company	3	1
Western Television Corporation	2	0
	96	145

*New entries in 1930

Alternative scanners such as apertured drums and cylinders amount to seven; there is a mirror cylinder, a disk with reflecting studs, a chain scanner, a light-pipe assembly and a couple of lens drums. Mirror drums occur in nine proposals. J.L. Baird followed up an earlier plan in exploring the merits of mirrors on a drum in February (2233), a move that heralded his waning interest in Nipkow's disk. John Wilson, his new engineering colleague, contributed another design (2486) in July, and three more applications came from the Baird laboratory. A more complex arrangement was suggested by Rosenfelder (2284). Mirror drums were embodied in patents by Gray (2547), Comp. Gaz (2643), and the Gramophone Company (2656), all of which represent a trend away from the disk. The five proposals with mirror screws also reveal a trend as well as a new technical approach and are interesting examples which show how similar ideas arise independently. Two came from Germany, one by Hatzinger (2296) and the other by von Okolicsányi and Wikkenhauser (2535). There are two versions by Wotton (2618) in Britain and a second by Gardner (2436).

Among other optical elements in the specifications there are nine or more Kerr cells, eight with fixed or vibrating mirrors, two with electrostatic light valves and a galvanometer light valve. Representative of a minority are those employing rotary prisms, cells, or lamps, capacitive circuits, and others relying on less usual methods such as electrochemical, electrostatic, or piezoelectric actions. Eight proposals depend upon arc or spark discharges, ten specify matrix or honeycomb arrangements with filament lamps, discharge tubes or lamps, or light valves, while the indispensable distributor appears in ten or more schemes.

Film scanning was still popular, particularly in the United States, where fifteen applications were lodged out of nineteen. Thirteen specifications were added to corporate portfolios, with four by Bell Labs and three each assigned to Jenkins Television Corporation, Radio Inventions, Inc., and RCA. The Gramophone Company disclosed a multichannel film system. Of the five independents, there were two American, two German, and one British. Some were variations on the main theme; for instance, in von Bronk's (2287) film scanning was an alternative, Hogan's (2399) included sound, one by Gray (2295) specified processing of intermediate film, and another (2682) was adaptable for film. Most used disks, exceptions being the first by Gray, which had a drum, Ross (2679) specified vibrating mirrors, and Harries' method (2437) was adaptable for mirrors or cathode-ray tubes. Thun's system (2244) with velocity modulation and Baird's telecine apparatus were based on earlier patents. According to reports, film transmissions were an essential part of experimental broadcast programs in the United States, and films were also transmitted from the Witzleben station in Berlin.

Color appears in nine patents, either as the chief objective or as a supplemental feature. Ives was the most active with four applications, all using disks. The first (2229), a color receiver with discharge lamps and mirrors, was followed by a multichannel system with colored light sources (2582), one employing special film and mirrors (2603), and another with three channels (2608). Nicolson modified his system of guided arc discharges by incorporating coated electrodes to provide color (2385). A complex arrangement with a color disk and folded discharge tubes, dependent on varied frequencies, was disclosed by Davis (2431), and Rosenfelder also specified color (2284). Drawing on earlier ideas, Baird devised a disk transmitter with color filters and a large receiver screen matrix with clusters of colored lamps controlled by distributors (2509). Bowtell's arrangement (2204) also included a disk with color filters.

The two-way system by Bell Labs is covered in a patent by Parker (2299) and the related ones by Ives (2339) and others. Baird applied for a two-way system (2650) employing disks or mirror drums with infrared scanning. Four multipurpose systems are listed; Maloney had an all-encompassing one (2395) for duplex, stereo, color, or film, and another (2474) for duplex or stereo. Nicolson adapted his moving arc method for sound and picture recording and projection (2397), and in another proposal (2403) included duplex, stereo, or color.

Eight proposals concern multichannel transmission, including the Bell Labs two-way system with eight wire circuits. Gray's two-channel system (2682), adaptable for single-channel operation as well as for film, has disks and a drum, rotary strip lamps, and split scanning; and another (2699) includes a multielectrode discharge lamp with distributor. Alexanderson's three-channel system (2354) includes a scanning disk, lenses, prisms, and three light beams pulsating at different frequencies. Two three-channel proposals by Ives relate to color, as mentioned, and Rosenfelder's complex scheme (2284) is applicable for stereo or color. The Gramophone Company's film system (2656) required five wire transmission channels for picture signals, each connected to separate phototubes and Kerr cells, and two more for sync and sound. Since the disadvantages of multiple transmission circuits were well known, such ambitious and expensive schemes sponsored by companies can only be accounted for by granting the management need to project the corporate image and the team desire to climb a mountain, both regardless of cost or ultimate practicality. On the plus side, however, research on complex apparatus of the kind described produced useful laboratory data and engineering experience applicable to future developments.

Half a dozen miscellaneous proposals deserve mention. The Telefunken transmitter (2192) incorporates a four-coil inductance and circuits to apply frequency modulation representing picture signals to a carrier wave. A method for fading visual signals in and out appears in Goldsmith's patent (2542). Henroteau modified his hybrid system (2570) and Walton did the same with a previous recording method (2612). Aspden disclosed a complex multi-circuit, narrow-band, single-channel system (2611) incorporating multispiral lens drums and magnetic or wax recording which included sound, the whole being adaptable for live pickup, film scanning, stereo, or color. One of the most far-sighted proposals is von Ardenne's cable distribution system (2441) based on ultra-short-wave transmissions.

More attention than hitherto was paid to the long-standing and vexatious problem of high-speed synchronous control. Methods to achieve close and consistent regulation in mechanical systems appear in more than twenty patents and are implicit in others. The choice was wide, since a dozen different ways appear in eighteen proposals by companies and in four by individuals. A common method in the United States relied upon the stability of commercial power frequencies. Six or more specifications include a synchronous motor, and four employ phonic wheels. Two suggest a beat frequency method and two specify line pulses. Other methods proposed are amplitude control, simultaneous or interposed sync signals, delay circuits, auxiliary motors, eddy-current control, a rotary resistance, and a pendulum with a crystal oscillator.

Some two dozen patents relate to or include discharge lamps and tubes. They range from the two-electrode glow lamps to others with more electrodes and special types and combinations in a variety of shapes and sizes the Victorians never imagined. Six are typical assemblies and three have provisions for cooling by fins or a liquid. Special forms and combinations appear in five disclosures, four have three or more electrodes, two have special electrodes, and in two others folded tubes are specified. The more complex examples include four stacked assemblies or arrangements comprising a screen or matrix. Four specifications concern color applications. Six articles on the subject appeared, all published in FERNSEHEN.

A noticeable trend of the year is the growth of electron beam technology. The sealed cathode-ray tube was beginning to be applied experimentally for observing and measuring low-voltage waveforms. This use extended the technique formerly limited by the bulky and expensive pumped-down apparatus required to examine and study high-voltage transients and similar phenomena. Of forty-six items listed there are twenty-two patents concerning cathode-ray tubes and receiver circuits, twelve articles about them, and twelve patents related to camera tubes, circuits, and systems. It seems appropriate that the most work on picture tubes and receivers was done in Germany, the home of the Braun tube. The Telefunken Company has five patents in their name, while von Ardenne, who had started his researches in 1928, was most active with eight applications, four of them assigned to the D.S. Loewe Company. All of the items on camera tubes, however, originated in the United States, eight of them by Farnsworth and two by Zworykin.

Increasing attention was given to technical aspects, particularly signal amplifications and image quality. The most detailed studies were undertaken in Germany, where eighteen articles were published in FERNSEHEN out of a total of twenty-eight. Six others appeared in TELEVISION and four in American periodicals in addition to the comprehensive reports by Bell Labs. Taken as a whole, this literature reveals a firm engineering basis for future developments. Topics include general techniques, transmission characteristics, questions of frequency and the use of ultra-short waves, image analysis, luminosity, flicker, definition, diffraction and picture enlargement, as well as neon lamps, disks, film transmission, and picture tubes. A related subject, associated more with art than engineering, concerned studio lighting and techniques, which were becoming important in the British experience with regular broadcasting.

Other writers discussed economic factors, utilitarian and communication aspects, and possible applications for business conferences, fashion shows, theater presentations, and sporting events. Courses for home study and technical training were introduced. On the practical side, the novelty of television was seized upon to advertise the Eugène hairdressing method with Baird apparatus at a show in November. Politics entered the art at the same time with a graphic broadcast of election returns through the DAILY NEWS station in Chicago. The well-known actress Peggy O'Neil was interviewed by television during the Ideal Home Exhibition at Southampton in April. These three events can be considered more important signposts toward the future than the flamboyant stage shows. Another demonstration in Chicago by the Western Television Corporation was given to police in December.

At the second annual exhibition of the British Television Society held in April there were more exhibits and an encouraging increase in the number of visitors. During the larger radio show in Berlin there were displays and demonstrations by the German Post Office, Fernseh Company, and the Telehor Company. Though still modest in scope—the Telefunken concern was absent and Loewe was not ready to show their products—television progress was clearly a serious objective of the German technical community.

Public response to visual broadcasts, demonstrations, and advertisements was minimal in the United States, where the darkening economic situation was of greater concern than elsewhere. News about amateur activities and home construction was noticeably reduced, and there seems to have been little of television interest at the radio show in New York. Baird had a display at the radio show in London and put on transmissions nearby, as he had done the previous year. The British amateur was better catered to, however, with thirty-five articles of special interest in TELEVISION, chiefly the continuing series by Waters and another by Woodford. Articles about home constructors and their apparatus by Fox and others became regular features in the magazine. Reports about reception came from many parts of the country and from Europe, all showing a lively amateur interest made possible by the regular broadcasts from London.

On the general scene television was still largely unknown except by name. Those technically inclined and other interested parties supported it, a few critics expressed doubts about it, some people were curious, and a few enjoyed it, but most believed it to be a novelty and remained unimpressed. Small and imperfect pictures and limited programs could not compete with the silver screen or with the universal radio set. Besides, receivers cost too much, and the business outlook grew worse as the months went by.

Opinions on the immediate future of television in America were more restrained and less specific than before. Some of those who were commercially active sounded positive and mildly optimistic and naturally tried to excite more amateur participation and to lure the public into buying complete receivers. Alexanderson hesitated over his prediction and vaguely mentioned that three, five, or even ten years would pass before practical television would arrive. In February, Sarnoff gave the art five years or less to reach some level of maturity and public acceptance. Two months later he felt sure that cinema patrons would be largely replaced by viewers in the home, and in July he voiced opinions about the cultural changes, particularly the wider appreciation of works of art, this expansion would bring. The same month de Forest, following a change of heart after dipping into the Jenkins television pool, announced his intention to take the plunge and start his own researches at the end of the year. With his usual flair for prophecy he also looked to the future—cautiously jumping ahead fifty years—to the time when the public, served by wire connections, would enjoy theater programs displayed in color on large screens at home. As for the months ahead, there were some rather faint expectations at the end of the year that prospects for home television in America would improve in 1931.

TABLE 16   CHRONOLOGY: 1930

Jan.		Berlin	German Television Society founded
		Berlin	First issue of FERNSEHEN
	15	Baird Corp.	Demonstration of Noctovisor in New York
	29	Baird Co.	Demonstration in Glasgow
Feb.	18	G.E. Co.	Transmission to Australia and back
Mar.		Baird Co.	Advertises commercial receiver
	24	Baird Co.	Demonstration at the Ideal Home Exhibition, London
	25	Hatzinger	Mirror screw
	31	Baird Co., BBC	Dual transmissions from Brookmans Park
		Baird Co.	Receiver installed in 10 Downing Street
Apr.		Farnsworth	New experimental picture-tube receiver
	7	Baird	Two companies amalgamated
		Jenkins, de Forest	Public broadcast reception in Jersey City
	8	Baird Co.	Demonstrations in Sunderland and Newcastle
	9	Bell Labs	Demonstration of two-way vision with telephone
		Television Society	Second annual exhibition
	16	Baird Co.	Demonstration in Manchester
	29	Baird Co.	Demonstration in Southampton
May	1	Zworykin	Improved photoelectric mosaic
	8	Baird Co.	Demonstration in Bournemouth
	22	G.E. Co.	Demonstrates large screen in Schenectady
June	14	Farnsworth	Improved image dissector
		RCA-RKO	Plans for Rockefeller Center and theater television
	23	Ives, et al.	Papers on Bell Labs system at AIEE Convention

	25	von Ardenne	Cable distribution system
July		Jenkins Corp.	Advertises Radiovisors
		Short Wave & Television Lab	Advertises Televisor
	1	Baird	Demonstrates large screen in Long Acre
	12	Television Society	Incorporated
	13	Western Television Corp.	Announces a broadcast receiver
	14	BBC, Baird Co.	Broadcast of play "The Man with a Flower in His Mouth"
	28	Baird Co.	Large screen reception at the Coliseum
	30	Baird	Large screen color system
Aug.	5	von Okolicsányi, Wikkenhauser	Mirror screw
	9	Baird Co.	Teletalkies on the large screen at the Coliseum
	14	Goldsmith	Dual system with fading control
	22	Various	Displays at the Berlin Radio Show
	25	Jenkins, de Forest	Public broadcast reception in New York
Sept.	18	Baird Co.	Demonstrates large screen in Berlin
	22	Jenkins Corp.	Display at the Radio World's Fair in N.Y.
Oct.		Baird Co.	Demonstrates large screen in Paris and Stockholm
	31	Wotton	Spiral mirror scanner
Nov.		Coyne Electrical School	Training courses in television
	4	DAILY NEWS	Election returns, station W9XAP, Chicago
	5	Eugène, Baird Co.	First commercial use of television
	12	Baird Co.	Display at the Bachelor Girls' Exhibition
Dec.	3	Farnsworth	New 300-line narrow-band system
	6	Western Television Corp.	Demonstration to police in Chicago
	13	FRC	Revises station assignments

BIBLIOGRAPHY: 1930

2166 Bredow, Hans. "Das Fernsehen im Rundfunk" [Television in broadcasting]. FERN. 1 (Jan.): 2, 3. Publicity, false claims, reactions, and consequences.

2167 Schröter, F. "Die Braunsche Röhre als Fernseher" [The Braun tube as televisor]. FERN. 1 (Jan.): 4–8. 3 illus. (2080, 2316)

2168 Friedel, W. "Die geschichtliche Entwicklung des Fernsehens" [The historical development of television]. FERN. 1 (Jan.): 12–7. 5 illus. Historical notes from 1875. (819, 2303)

2169 Goerz, P. "Die wirtschaftliche Seite des Fernsehens" [The economic side of television]. FERN. 1 (Jan.): 17–9. Possible practical and industrial applications. (2085, 2222)

2170 Mihály, D. v. "Uber die Synchronisierung Elektrischer Fernsehapparate" [On the synchronization of electric television apparatus]. FERN. 1 (Jan): 19–22. (2129, 2207)

2171 Krawinkel, Günther. "Empfänger und Verstärker zur Aufnahme der Fernseh-Versuchssendungen" [Receiver and amplifier for the reception of television test broadcasts]. FERN. 1 (Jan.): 22–8. 15 illus. (2407)

2172 Kette, G. "Was hat uns die Fernseh-Abteilung der Berliner Funkausstellung gezeigt?" [What did the television department of the

Berlin Radio Fair show us?]. FERN. 1 (Jan.): 28–35. (2055, 2362, 2584)

2173 "Die Fernseh-Versuchssendungen des Reichsportzentralamtes und die vorläufige Normung dieser Sendungen" [The television test broadcasts of the German Central Post Office and their preliminary classification]. FERN. 1 (Jan.): 37. (2065, 2407)

2174 Ives, H.E., and A.L. Johnsrud. "Television in colors by a beam scanning method." J. OSA 20 (Jan.): 11–22. 7 photos, 2 graphs, 2 diags. Color-sensitive photocells, high-speed colored lights, analyzing and recording images, three-color photography. (2148, 2176)

2175 Clark, P.L. "A novel scanning disk for television." RADIO-CRAFT 1 (Jan.): 314, 344, 345. 5 photos. Spiral of square holes with built-in centrifugal spark pointer. (1731)

2176 Ives, H.E. "Television images in natural colors." RADIO-CRAFT 1 (Jan.): 316, 317, 345. 5 photos, 3 diags. (2174, 2229)

2177 Replogle, D.E. "Where television is to-day. The commercial television receiver begins to take form." RADIO N. 11 (Jan.): 629–31, 677. 5 photos. Early work of Jenkins, station W2XCR, present commercial receivers including shadowbox cabinet and disk-drum assembly. (2099, 2162, 2195, 2213)

"Television is pretty much the same story as the 'House that Jack Built.' Most of us recall that one feature of Jack's House led to another and still another, in an endless chain. In television development, the situation is much the same; the solution of one feature leads to a new problem, the solution of which uncovers still another problem, and so on. Nevertheless, with the application of intensive research and specialized engineering effort, many problems of practical television have already been solved, and we are now on the eve of commercialized sight broadcasting.

"While the enthusiastic novelist and the dreamy inventor may have sold the public the idea of viewing a Broadway revue or a football game in vivid form on the television screen, the fact remains that such achievements are still in the dim future. For the present, we are in the babyhood of the television art, and must be contented first of all to master our ABC pictures.

"Sound broadcasting—a far simpler technique—required a half dozen years for development into practical merchandise and almost a decade to become satisfactory merchandise. With sight broadcasting, we may well expect to take at least five years and most likely a decade to attain satisfactory equipment for general use. Meanwhile, however, there is plenty of thrill in television. There are many potential pioneers, ready to take part in the everyday development of the young art. And so, with all the cards on the table, we are now ready to welcome television into the home, without unreasonable expectations on the one hand or unwarranted promises on the other."

2178 "Radio star viewed at new Televisor." SCI. & INV. 17 (Jan.): 820. Photo. G.E. apparatus and Miss Florence Shea at the radio show, New York. (1779, 2243)

2179 Moseley, S.A. "More facilities." TELEV. 2 (Jan.): 534, 535. (2138, 2217)

2180 Chapple, H.J.B. "Television and your wireless receiver. Pt. 2." TELEV. 2 (Jan.): 536–8. 3 diags. (2060, 2323)

2181 Tierney, C. "The origin and progress of television. Pt. 2." TELEV. 2 (Jan.): 543–6. (2140, 2159, 2196, 2375)

2182 Knipe, A.R. "How to make an accurate scanning disk." TELEV. 2 (Jan.): 547–9. Photo, 3 diags. (2142, 2186, 3248)

2183 Denton, J.J., and W.G.W. Mitchell. "The Proceedings of the Television Society." TELEV. 2 (Jan.): 554–61. 6 diags. Report of Dec. 3 meeting. Lecture by E. George Lewin, "Television, some suggested schemes." Details of patents by Rtcheouloff (500), Whitten (677), von Bronk (694), Mohr (906), Zworykin (947). References to 7 patents. (2139, 2218, 2272)

2184 Fox, W.C. "Motors and discs." TELEV. 2 (Jan.): 562, 563. 2 photos. (2056, 2219)

2185 Richardson, William J. "Low frequency amplifiers for television. Pt. 1." TELEV. 2 (Jan.): 564, 565, 569. 6 diags. (2224)

2186 Waters, A.A. "The construction of experimental television apparatus. Pt. 8." TELEV. 2 (Jan.): 570, 571, 574. 4 diags. (2137, 2182, 2187, 2220)

2187 Woodford, John W. "Television for the beginner. Pt. 1." TELEV. 2 (Jan.): 572–4. Photo, 2 diags. (2186, 2219, 2221)

2188 Kennedy, (Lord) A. "South Africa has seen—and believes." TELEV. 2 (Jan.): 575. See Tierney (2087). (2275)

2189 Nason, Charles H.W. "Electro-optical apparatus and method." U.S. 1,859,597, Jan. 3, 1930, May 24, 1932. Assigned: Jenkins Television. Film scanner with radially slotted disk. (2234)

2190 Wallace, Richard Edgar. "Electro-optical system and method of transmission." U.S. 1,954,969, Jan. 3, 1930, Apr. 17, 1934. Assigned: RCA. Disk scanner for film with light beam divided by mirrors onto two phototubes with respective amplified outputs combined for single-channel transmission. (2191)

2191 Wallace, R.E. "Electro-optical system." U.S. 1,959,044, Jan. 3, 1930, May 15, 1934. Assigned: RCA. Concentric disks with radial slots, spring coupled and arranged to provide variable-area openings. (2190, 2569)

2192 Telefunken. "Television." Br. 370,263, Jan. 1, 1931. In Germany Jan. 4, 1930. Frequency-modulated transmitter and receivers. (1919, 2198)

2193 Huffman. C.E. "Synchronizing system." U.S. 1,920,015, Jan. 9, 1930, July 25, 1933. Assigned: Jenkins Television. For separate stations supplied with commercial power at different frequencies. (2096, 2609)

2194 Weinberger, J. "Glow lamp." U.S. 1,954,231, Jan. 13, 1930, Apr. 10, 1934. Assigned: RCA. Br. 366,247, Jan. 9, 1931 (Marconi's). For sound recording as well as television. (2003)

2195 Jenkins, C.F. "Scanning apparatus." U.S. 1,844,508, Jan. 14, 1930, Feb. 9, 1932. Assigned: Jenkins Labs. Light pipes arranged as spokes on a scanning wheel distribute light from an arc lamp. (2177, 2201)

2196 "Ship captains see Noctovisor test." N.Y.T. 28 (Jan. 16): 2. Demonstration of Baird apparatus at 145 West 45th Street, N.Y. (2181, 2197)

2197 Richards, Claude Langdon, J.L. Baird, and Television Ltd. "Television." Br. 346,834, Jan. 18, 1930. Addition to Br. 336,655 (1961). Receiver with phonic motor. (2196, 2199, 3373)

2198 Telefunken and O. v. Bronk. "Television." Br. 371,832, Jan. 20, 1931. In Germany Jan. 20, 1930. Matrix of discharge tubes with two layers criss-crossed or combined in one envelope and controlled in sequence by an inductive distributor. Successive extinction of one tube in each set produces a moving dark spot. References to Br. 277,761 (694), 356,760 (2287). (1750, 2192, 2200, 2236)

2199 Baird, J.L., and Television Ltd. "Television receivers." Br. 347,254, Jan. 21, 1930. U.S. 1,957,815, Jan. 15, 1931, May 8, 1934. Relates to a matrix screen of lamps or electromagnetic shutters controlled by a distributor with circuits to prolong operation of the lamps. Five references (548, 814, 1213, 1961, 2203). (2197)

2200 Telefunken. "Television." Br. 377,169, Jan. 14, 1931. Void. In Germany Jan. 21, 1930. A double-disk multifrequency system, with a receiver consisting of a quartz block arranged in columns, with variants. (2198, 2581)

2201 Jenkins, C.F. "Electro-optical device." U.S. 1,964,062, Jan. 24, 1930, June 26, 1934. Assigned: RCA. Matrix system with electrostatic light valves. (2195, 2211)

2202 Gray, F. "Electro-optical system." U.S. 1,869,194, Jan. 25, 1930, July 26, 1932. Assigned: B.T.L. Scanning disk, discharge lamp, phototubes, and circuits. (2048, 2280)

2203 Baird, J.L., and Television Ltd. "Television receivers." Br. 347,741, Jan. 29, 1930. Bank of lamps divided into groups with coordinate switching by distributor. Six references (548, 814, 982, 1213, 1961, 2199). Divided (2240). (2223)

2204 Bowtell, G.M. "Television." Br. 340,833, Jan. 31, 1930. Disk with color filters and a rotary shutter with electromagnets, relays, and sync control via a watch. (2812)

2205 Fernseh A.-G. "Synchronous movements." Br. 377,240, Jan. 24, 1931. In Germany Jan. 31, 1930. Includes a phonic wheel, rotating disks, contacts, relay, and a magnet. (2098, 2265)

2206 Kruckow, A. "Fernsehen und Rundfunk" [Television and broadcasting]. FERN. 1 (Feb.): 49–51. Influence of radio practice in television.

2207 Mihály, D. v. "Uber die Synchronisierung Elektrischer Fernseh-apparte." FERN. 1 (Feb.): 52–7. (2170, 2723)

2208 Ewest, H. "Die Gasentladungsröhren in der Fernsehtechnik" [Gas discharge tubes in television engineering]. FERN. 1 (Feb.): 59–62. 3 illus. Types of glow lamps and their suitability for television.

2209 Neuberger, A. "Farbiges Fernsehen" [Color television]. FERN. 1 (Feb.): 62–8. 7 illus. Color work by Baird and Ives. (1514, 2306)

2210 Kirschstein, F. "Uber die beim Fernsehen zu übertragenden Frequenzen" [On the frequencies to be transmitted in television]. FERN. 1 (Feb.): 76–83. 7 illus. (2450)

2211 "Television at low cost now possible." POP. MECH. 53 (Feb.): 300, 301. 3 photos. Jenkins disk receiver. (2201, 2212)

2212 "Television schedule." RADIO BRD. 16 (Feb.): 23, 28. Jenkins stations: W2XCD Passaic, W2XCR Jersey City. (2211, 2213)

2213 Replogle, D.E. "The new Jenkins Radiovisor." RADIO-CRAFT 1 (Feb): 382, 384, 409. 3 photos, 3 graphs, 5 diags. Light-pipe drum and more recent disk-drum receiver. (2177, 2212, 2226, 2252)

2214 Zworykin, V.K. "The cathode-ray television receiver." RADIO-CRAFT 1 (Feb.): 384, 385. 3 photos, 3 diags. (2125, 2215)

2215 Zworykin, V.K. "Cathode-ray television receiver developed." SCI. AM. 142 (Feb.): 147. 2 photos. (2214, 2253)

2216 Fleming, J.A. "Television; present and future." TELEV. 2 (Feb.): 581–7. Portrait, 9 illus. Lecture at the Imperial College of Science, Jan. 9. (2132, 2231)

2217 Moseley, S.A. "Is television in danger?" TELEV. 2 (Feb.): 588, 589. (2179, 2267)

2218 Mitchell, W.G.W. "The cathode-ray tube in practical television. Pt. 3." TELEV. 2 (Feb.): 590–3. Continued from May 1929 (1871). 2 photos, 3 diags. (2183, 2272)

2219 Fox, W.C. "How amateurs are receiving the television broadcast." TELEV. 2 (Feb.): 594, 595. Photo. (2184, 2187, 2220, 2273)

2220 Waters, A.A. "The construction of experimental television apparatus. Pt. 9." TELEV. 2 (Feb.): 596–9. 2 photos, 5 diags. (2186, 2219, 2221, 2242)

2221 Woodford, J.W. "Television for the beginner. Pt. 2." TELEV. 2 (Feb.): 602–4. Photo, 2 diags. (2187, 2220, 2257, 2274)

2222 Goerz, P. "The economic side of television." TELEV. 2 (Feb.): 607, 608, 617. Portrait. By the director of Fernseh A.-G. (2169)

2223 "Baird television in America." TELEV. 2 (Feb.): 618. Photo. (2203, 2233)

2224 Richardson, W.J. "Low frequency amplifiers for television. Pt. 2." TELEV. 2 (Feb.): 619, 620. 2 photos, 2 diags. (2185, 2264)

2225 Birch, A.F. "To what end?" TELEV. 2 (Feb.): 621–3. 2 photos. On inventors, inventions, future uses, and effects. (2088)

2226 Jenkins, C.F. "Television scanning device." U.S. 1,984,682, Feb. 1, 1930, Dec. 18, 1934. Assigned: RCA. Scanning wheel with spokelike conductor rods arranged to produce spark discharges in apertures in the rim of the wheel, with an electrical distributor. (2213, 2254)

2227 Cawley, A.J. "Television." U.S. 2,032,526, Feb. 3, 1930, Mar. 3, 1936. Three concentric cylinders, two of which have apertures which intersect to form transversely moving points of light. (2026, 2393)

2228 Gramophone Co., and R.B. Morgan. "Television." Br. 347,321, Feb. 3, 1930. Scanning disk of thermoplastic material with paper core. (1754, 2290)

2229 Ives, H.E. "Electro-optical system." U.S. 1,993,604, Feb. 3, 1930, Mar. 5, 1935. Assigned: B.T.L. Br. 372,299, Feb. 3, 1931 (E.R.P.). Disk, discharge lamps, and mirrors in a color receiver. (2176, 2328)

2230 Donle, H.P. "Television apparatus." U.S. 1,894,944, Feb. 4, 1930, Jan. 24, 1933. Assigned: Radio Inventions. Disk with radial slots coacting with a drum with longitudinal slots. (1679, 2283)

2231 Fleming, J.A. "Television transmitter." Br. 348,139, Feb. 5, 1930. Scanning disk with polished studs which reflect light onto two photocells connected alternately by a commutator. (2216, 2289)

2232 Möller, Hans Georg, and Rolf Möller. "Television." U.S. 1,993,564, Jan. 31, 1931, Mar. 5, 1935. Assigned: Fernseh A.-G. Br. 372,348, Feb. 2, 1931. In Germany Feb. 5, 1930. Sync motor, sync signal at end of each scanning line. (2408, 3030)

2233 Baird, J.L., and Television Ltd. "Television." Br. 348,638, Feb. 7, 1930. Scanning with bands of variable width by mirror drum and variants. Reference Br. 303,771 (1011). (2223, 2240)

2234 Nason, C.H.W. "Electro-optical translation system." U.S. 1,828,875, Feb. 10, 1930, Oct. 27, 1931. Assigned: Jenkins Television. Film scanning with disk and capacitive circuit. (2189, 2260)

2235 Universal and General Radio Co. and L.M. Myers. "Television." Br. 334,505, Feb. 10, 1930. Kerr cell. Reference Br. 331,325 (1877). (1885, 3713)

2236 Bronk, O. v. "Television." Br. 372,415, Feb. 12, 1931. Assigned: Telefunken. In Germany Feb. 12, 1930. Addition to Br. 371,832 (2198). Same with an additional lamp behind crossed array. (2287)

2237 Barthélemy, R. "Television device." U.S. 1,854,682, Feb. 5, 1931, Apr. 19, 1932. Assigned: Comp. Gaz. Br. 364,376, Feb. 5,1931. In France Feb. 13, 1930. Receiver with perforated disk, reflectors, and magnifying lens to furnish two or more images. Addition, Br. 372,168 (2617). (2041, 2389)

2238 Kolster-Brandes (Kolster Radio Corp., Newark, N.J.). "Television." Br. 350,926, Feb. 13, 1930. Two piezoelectric crystals and oscillating lens or prism. Reference Br. 252,387 (677). (2151)

2239 "Forecasts big future for television." N.Y.T. 6 (Feb. 14): 2. Remarks by the Earl of Clarendon, chairman of the BBC, who sees "staggering possibilities."

2240 Baird, J.L., and Television Ltd. "Television receivers." Br. 348,211, Feb. 14, 1930. Bank of lamps or shutters with lamps enclosed in partitions. Divided from Br. 347,741 (2203). (2233, 2267)

2241 Gardiner, Ernest L., and R.G. Wilson. "Television." Br. 350,512, Feb. 14, 1930. Disk with a spiral of small discharge tubes which are excited one at a time in the field of view by a high-frequency field. (1910, 2242, 2784)

2242 Wilson, R.G., and A.A. Waters. "Television." Br. 345,770, Feb. 17, 1930. Scanning with a disk and a pair of eccentrically mounted rotary cylinders. (2220, 2241, 2266, 2655)

2243 "Schenectady flashes picture to Australia; gets it back in one-eighth of a second." N.Y.T. 1 (Feb. 19): 6. Transmission of a black rectangle on a white card from shortwave station W2XAF to VK2ME in Sydney, and back, a distance of 20,000 miles. (2178, 2307)

2244 Thun, R. "Television." Br. 377,175, Feb. 19, 1931. In Germany Feb. 20, 1930. Addition to Br. 355,319 (1886). Film transmission with velocity modulation, including alternative use of a cathode-ray tube. (1886, 2410)

2245 "Directing of trade by television seen." N.Y.T. 24 (Feb. 21): 4. Prediction by Dr. Zay Jeffries, of Cleveland, that "business men of the future will use it for conferences."

2246 Centeno V, M. "Television." U.S. 1,873,926, Feb. 21, 1930, Aug. 23, 1932, reissued Jan. 4, Mar. 7, 1933. Compound vibrating mirror assembly with electromagnets for ordinary or stereoscopic television or film transmission. (1977, 2867)

2247 Poore, Charles G. "David Sarnoff grew up in radio's vast field. President of the R.C.A. at the age of 39, he foresees a great development in communications service and broadcasting—the future of television." N.Y.T. IX, 6 (Feb. 23): 1–3. "I am confident that in less than 5 years you will be able to receive images through space as well as you are able to receive sound through space at the present time." (1744, 2350)

2248 "Foresighted leaders plan for radio vision." N.Y.T. IX, 18 (Feb. 23): 1–6. General comments and speculations.

2249 Karolus, A. "Picture receiver." U.S. 1,962,447, Feb. 24, 1930, June 12, 1934. Assigned: RCA. Matrix light system with electron tube circuits and distributor. (1875, 2490)

2250 Keogan, Charles J. "Scanning method." U.S. 1,897,483, Feb. 24, 1930, Feb. 14, 1933. Assigned: Jenkins Television. Two semi-spiral disks for overlapping scan.

2251 "Television progress." ELECT. 104 (Feb. 28): 252.

2252 Replogle, D.E. "Details now available for practical radiovision reception." CIT. RAD. CALL BOOK 11 (Mar.): 62. (2213, 2259)

2253 Zworykin, V.K. "Cathode ray tube television." CIT. RAD. CALL BOOK 11 (Mar.): 90–3. 5 photos, 6 diags. (2215, 2309)

2254 Garside, J.W. "Television—1930." CIT. RAD. CALL BOOK 11 (Mar.): 123–5. "An analysis of recent television progress and general prospects for 1930" by the president of Jenkins Television Corp. On Jenkins apparatus, programs, and developments. (2226, 2263)

"What is the present status of television? That is a question paramount in the minds of radio fans today. Until a year ago, television was a subject of almost universal discussion. Today, one hears comparatively little about it, both in the press and in general conversation. Perhaps the best way to account for this reticence is to say that television is now looked upon in the cold light of a problem, rather than in the poetic vein of a glowing promise.

"A year or so ago, television workers fired with enthusiasm, were eager to expound the marvels that seemed practically within their grasp. They felt that the big job of achievement was done and that commercial application was the least of their worries—an afterthought to be speedily dispatched. But when they buckled down to real engineering development preparatory to actual production, they found that simple theory was easier than practice. Many became disillusioned and left the field entirely. Certain radio organizations, quickly convinced of the tremendous amount of pioneering still to be done, gave up all thought of immediate exploitation and assumed what may be termed a negative attitude. Those who remained in the field were thoroughly conversant with the multitude of technical problems yet to be overcome and, consequently, were those to overcome them first and talk later, which explains the lack of accurate information at the present time. Those organizations actively engaged in the development of television at present, are pushing ahead. They are making real progress. They prefer to talk of achievement rather than anticipation."

2255 Ilberg, W. "Die Verwendung trägheitsloser Lichtrelais beim Fernsehen" [The use of inertialess light relays in television]. FERN. 1 (Mar.): 97–102. 5 illus. Light modulation, Kerr cells, and characteristics. (2150, 2394)

2256 Codelli, A. "Ein neues Fernseh-System" [A new television system]. FERN. 1 (Mar.): 107–14. 7 illus. Author's spiral scanning system (1898).

2257 Hewel, Horst. "Aus der Praxis des Fernsehempfangs" [On the practice of television reception]. FERN. 1 (Mar.): 118–27. 12 illus. Receiver built from the description in RADIO NEWS, Oct. 1928 (1502), reception in Berlin and developments. (2221, 2266, 2566)

2258 De la Forge, L. "La télévision en Grande-Bretagne." QSTF 11 (Mar.): 29. (1900)

2259 Replogle, D.E. "Image reception with a Radiovisor. Pt.2." RADIO-CRAFT 1 (Mar.): 451, 475, 476. 2 illus. (2252, 2297)

2260 Nason, C.H.W. "Amplifying the television signal." RADIO-CRAFT 1 (Mar.): 452, 457. 2 tables, graph, 3 diags. (2234, 2308)

2261 "Improved engineering and standardization of reproducers and television equipment." RADIO ENG. 10 (Mar.): 43.

2262 Hathaway, Kenneth A. "Television forges ahead." RADIO N. 11 (Mar.): 816, 817. Photo, 3 diags. Watson's system (1855).

2263 Jenkins, C.F. "The development of television and radiomovies to date." J. SMPE 14 (Mar.): 344–8. (2254, 2310)

2264 Richardson, W.J. "Low frequency amplifiers for television. Pt. 3." TELEV. 3 (Mar.): 5–9, 29. 4 photos, 4 diags. (2224, 2371)

2265 Russell, A.V.F.V. "Television in Germany." TELEV. 3 (Mar.): 10, 11, 29. Portrait, 3 photos. General news, including formation of the German Television Society, the new journal FERNSEHEN, and the founding of Fernseh A.-G. (2368). (2118, 2205, 2518, 2598)

2266 Waters, A.A. "The construction of experimental television apparatus. Pt. 10." TELEV. 3 (Mar.): 12–4. 2 photos, 2 diags. (2242, 2257, 2273, 2313)

2267 Moseley, S.A. "Good news." TELEV. 3 (Mar.): 15, 41. Photo of Baird's commercial receiver (Fig. 61). (2217, 2240, 2268, 2317)

2268 Bradly, Harold. "Behind the scenes with the Baird studio director." TELEV. 3 (Mar.): 19. Portrait. (2267, 2271, 2470)

2269 Sylvester, C. "Shadows; their effect upon the appearance of objects." TELEV. 3 (Mar.): 20, 21. 5 diags. Illumination, reflection, light projection, problems with shadows, studio techniques. (1938)

2270 Cox, Howard Havelock. "Television and the Empire. The survival of the quickest!" TELEV. 3 (Mar.): 26, 27, 48. Lines of communication, bureaucratic control, speed and cost, newspaper reproductions.

2271 Abbot, W.B. "British television in 1930." TELEV. 3 (Mar.): 28, 29. Photo of Baird dual exhibition receiver. Discussion of writer's letter and editorial controversy in MODERN WIRELESS, enthusiastic response at the exhibition in Glasgow. (2091, 2268, 2275, 2999)

2272 Denton, J.J., and W.G.W. Mitchell. "The proceedings of the Television Society." TELEV. 3 (Mar.): 30–6, 38. Report of Feb. 4 meeting. Lecture by George P. Barnard: "The photo-conductivity of selenium and various other substances." 4 graphs, 17 references. (2183, 2218, 2740, 3695)

2273 Fox, W.C. "Further reports of amateur television reception." TELEV. 3 (Mar.): 37, 38. Photo. (2219, 2266, 2274, 2314)

2274 Woodford, J.W. "Television for the beginner. Pt. 3." TELEV. 3 (Mar.): 39–41. 2 photos, 3 diags. (2221, 2273, 2313, 2315)

2275 Kennedy, A. "Scotland sees television!" TELEV. 3 (Mar.): 42. Photo of group in Glasgow, where the first public demonstration in Scotland was given at Kelvin Hall during the Wireless and Electrical Engineering Exhibition, Jan. 29 to Feb. 8. (2188, 2271, 2277)

2276 Debenham, Nancy. "Feminine reflections. Television fashion lessons." TELEV. 3 (Mar.): 44.

2277 Weald, Geoffrey. "Television." TELEV. 3 (Mar.): 47, 48. Article from the NEW

STATESMAN, Jan. 25. General comments, BBC transmissions, Baird apparatus, quality of images, Baird Noctovisor. (2275, 2281)

2278 "Dr. E.F.W. Alexanderson's Televisor at Schenectady." N.Y.T. IX, 15 (Mar. 2): 1, 2. Photo. (1455, 2354)

2279 Farnsworth, P.T. "Electron multiplier." U.S. 1,969,399, Mar. 3, 1930, Aug. 7, 1934, reissued May 18, 1936, June 14, 1938. Assigned: Television Labs. Secondary emission multiplier. (2123, 2311)

2280 Gray, F. "Electro-optical system." U.S. 1,957,953, Mar. 4, 1930, May 8, 1934, Assigned: B.T.L. (2202, 2295)

2281 "Baird television receiver tested." W.W. 26 (Mar. 5): 277. (2277, 2300)

2282 Iams, Harley A. "View transmission system." U.S. 1,955,332, Mar. 5, 1930, Apr. 17, 1934. Assigned: Westinghouse. Picture tube and receiver circuit. (3416)

2283 Donle, H.P. "Television." U.S. 2,025,027, Mar. 6, 1930, Dec. 24, 1935. Assigned: Radio Inventions. Film scanner. (2230, 2538)

2284 Rosenfelder, R.I. "Television." Br. 368,069, Mar. 9, 1931. In Germany Mar. 8, 1930. Multitrack mirror drums, mirrors, color-sensitive phototubes, and Kerr cells in a multichannel system for stereo and color.

2285 Lofgren, Benjamin F. "Television." U.S. 2,022,248, Mar. 10, 1930, Nov. 26, 1935. Assigned: AT&T. Slotted drum with spiral track.

2286 "Adds television for home study." N.Y.T. 21 (Mar. 11): 6. "Home study of television is being offered in a new course announced this week by the department of engineering extension of (Pennsylvania) State College."

2287 Bronk, O. v. "Electrical reception and transmission of pictures." Br. 356,760, Mar. 11, 1930, Sept. 11, 1931. Screen of linear glow discharge lamps excited by induction coil and sequentially controlled by time lag circuits with radially slotted disk, vibrating or rotary mirror, with variants, and alternative use for film transmission. Reference to Br. 277,761 (694). (2236, 2291)

2288 McCreary, H.J. "Television." U.S. 1,935,650, Mar. 11, 1930, renewed July 2, 1932, Nov. 21, 1933. Assigned: Associated Electric Labs. Divided from U.S. 1,935,649 (1105). Construction of photoelectric plate as parent specification. (1606, 2689)

2289 Fleming, J.A. "Television, present and future." ENGINEERING 129 (Mar. 14): 343. Summary of lecture, Jan. 9 (2216). (2231, 2318)

2290 Gramophone Co., Cecil Oswald Browne, and R.B. Morgan. "Synchronous movements." Br. 348,773, Mar. 14, 1930. Receiver with auxiliary motor and commutator. (2228, 2342, 2476)

2291 Bronk, O. v. "Receiver arrangement for electric picture transmission." U.S. 2,072,658, Mar. 7, 1931, Mar. 2, 1937. Assigned: Telefunken. Br. 374,015, Feb. 25, 1931. In Germany Mar. 15, 1930. Picture tube contains a grid of electrically controlled interlaced electrodes placed near the fluorescent screen, a pair of deflection plates, two slotted diaphragms, and a pair of plates for deflection modulation of the beam. A double-beam tube is described as an alternative. (2287)

2292 "Theatre for Cincinnati. $1,000,000 television house said to be projected by B.H. Moss." N.Y.T. 32 (Mar. 20): 3. (3153)

2293 Egger, Paul R. "Television." U.S. 1,792,683, Mar. 22, 1930, Feb. 17, 1931. Narrow mirrors mounted transversely on a rotatable shaft twisted to form a single-turn helix.

2294 "Boston 'sees' television." N.Y.T. X, 12 (Mar. 23): 3. Daily programs at station WEEI. Note on Horace (Hollis) Baird of Short Wave and Television Laboratory and a scanner in which the apertures are photographed on film. (2103, 2460)

2295 Gray, F. "Electro-optical system." U.S. 1,990,544, Mar. 25, 1930, Feb. 12, 1935. Assigned: B.T.L. Intermediate film processing with multitrack apertured drum and photocells for each track. (2280, 2338)

2296 Hatzinger, Hans. "Transmitting and receiving stationary and animated images." Br. 358,411, Mar. 16, Oct. 8, 1931. In Germany Mar. 25, 1930. Mirror screw. In the receiver a linear glow discharge lamp, linear lens, and slotted aperture are arranged parallel with the shaft of the mirror screw scanner. See Gardner (1472).

2297 Replogle, D.E. "Transmitting visual representations in color." U.S. 2,055,557, Mar. 26, 1930, Sept. 29, 1936. Assigned: RCA. Film system with two currents corresponding with black and white for shade and color range, transmitted and recombined in a receiver. (2259, 2363)

2298 Stoller, H.M., and E.R. Morton. "Speed regulator." U.S. 1,866,275, Mar. 28, 1930, July 5, 1932. Assigned: B.T.L. Divided from U.S. 1,763,909 (998). (2341)

2299 Parker, R.D. "Communicating system." U.S. 1,805,594, Mar. 29, 1930, May 19, 1931. Assigned: AT&T. Br. 375,785, Mar. 28, 1931, (E.R.P.). Combined telephone and two-way television system. Reference to Br. 375,422 (2339). See related Bell Labs patents (2339). (719)

2300 "Sight and sound broadcast. B.B.C. developments. Two wave lengths." MAN. GUARD. 9 (Mar. 31): 3. On the dual transmissions from Brookmans Park. "The new television broadcasts follow the placing on the market within the last few weeks of the Baird televisor...." (2138, 2281, 2312, 2317)

2301 Juhász, Béla. "Transmission of pictures by electrical means." U.S. 1,911,900, Mar. 25, 1931, May 30, 1933. In Germany Mar. 31, 1930. Rotary lens drum.

2302 Moore, D.M. "Gaseous discharge device." U.S. 1,900,578, Mar. 31, 1930, Mar. 7, 1933. Assigned: G.E. Br. 377,726, Mar. 27, 1931 (B.T.H.). Specifies various gases and cathode materials for different colors. (1956)

2303 Friedel, W. "Die Lichtverhältnisse beim Fernseh-Empfänger mit Nipkowscheibe und Glimmlampe" [The light conditions in television receivers with Nipkow disk and a glow lamp]. FERN. 1 (Apr): 152–6. 5 illus. (2168, 2451)

2304 Rhein, E. "Der erste Fernsehfilm wird gedreht" [The first television film will be made]. FERN. 1 (Apr.): 157–9.

2305 Okolicsányi, F. v. "Fernsehen und Rundfunkfrequenzband" [Television and the broadcasting frequency band]. FERN. 1 (Apr.): 160–9. 4 illus. High definition transmission and radio frequencies. (1472, 2513)

2306 Neuburger, A. "Das 'Kinescop,' ein neuer Fernseher" [The "Kinescope," a new televisor]. FERN. 1 (Apr.): 175–9. (2209, 2322)

2307 "Television signals transmitted 20,000 miles." PROJ. ENG. 2 (Apr.): 29. G.E. experiment (2243). (2391)

2308 Nason, C.H.W. "Pertinent notes on characteristics of television signals." RADIO BRD. 16 (Apr.): 318, 319, 357, 358. 2 photos, 2 graphs, 8 diags. Frequency band, neon tube circuits, sync methods. (2260, 2664)

2309 Zworykin, V.K. "Television through a crystal globe." RADIO N. 11 (Apr.): 905, 949, 954. 2 photos, 2 diags. Picture tube receiver. (2253, 2379)

2310 "Home radio talkies." RADIO N. 11 (Apr.): 920, 921. Photo and brief text on Jenkins system with two receivers. (2263, 2327)

2311 "Mormon youth aims to simplify television." SCI. & INV. 17 (Apr.): 1081. Farnsworth apparatus, photo and caption. (2279, 2381)

2312 "Baird Televisor." TELEV. 3 (Apr.): 54. Full-page photo of commercial receiver now on sale for £26.5s. (2300, 2317)

2313 Waters, A.A. "The construction of experimental television apparatus. Pt. II." TELEV. 3 (Apr.): 62–4. 3 photos. (2266, 2274, 2314, 2655)

2314 Fox. W.C. "How the amateur is receiving television." TELEV. 3 (Apr.): 65, 66. 2 photos. (2273, 2313, 2315, 2320)

2315 Woodford, J.W. "Television for the beginner. Pt. 4." TELEV. 3 (Apr.): 67, 68. Photo, 2 diags. (2274, 2314, 2320, 2373)

2316 Schröter, F. "Reproduction and amplification in television receivers." TELEV. 3 (Apr.): 71–6. 3 photos, 7 graphs, 4 diags. Mathematical treatment of picture elements, contours, contrast, detail. Reprinted from E.N.T. (2080). (2167, 2406)

2317 Moseley, S.A. "The dual transmission." TELEV. 3 (Apr): 77, 81. On the Baird-BBC simultaneous transmission from the new Brookmans Park station inaugurated Mar. 31. (2267, 2300, 2312, 2319, 2323, 2324)

2318 Fleming, J.A. "The relation of government to invention." TELEV. 3 (Apr.): 82–8. 5 photos. Presidential address at the second annual general meeting of the Television Society, Mar. 18. (2289)

2319 "We test a Baird television receiver." TELEV. 3 (Apr): 91, 93. 2 photos. Receiver with a 20-in. disk. (2317, 2323)

2320 Fox, W.C. "Receiving a television image. What one sees when tuning-in." TELEV. 3 (Apr.): 92, 93. Photo, 2 diags. Speed control, phasing, framing. (2314, 2315, 2321, 2372)

2321 Cato, G.C. "About scanning discs." TELEV. 3 (Apr): 94–6. 5 diags. Construction, hole placement, sizes. (2142, 2320, 2371)

2322 Neuberger, A. "A new cathode-ray tube for television." TELEV. 3 (Apr.): 99. 2 photos. Manfred von Ardenne's low-pressure gas-filled tube. (2306, 2357, 2515)

2323 Moseley, S.A., and H.J.B. Chapple. TELEVISION TO-DAY AND TO-MORROW. London: Pitman, 1930. xxiii + 130 pp. Portrait, 47 plates, 38 diags. Foreword by J.L. Baird. Almost wholly about Baird and his apparatus. A brief history is followed by chapters on general details, Baird transmitters and receivers, synchronism, photocells and neon lamps, the wireless receiver, Telecine and Teletalkies, Noctovision, daylight television and Phonovision, color and stereoscopic television, with the last five pages on television in other countries. First of five editions, the last in 1940. (2180, 2317, 2319, 2324, 2374, 2464)

2324 "Sight-sound program broadcast in Britain. Dual wavelengths synchronized—reception on two sets reported as clear." N.Y.T. 17 (Apr. 1): 3. Baird-BBC transmission, Mar. 31. (2317, 2323, 2325)

2325 "Television broadcast with sound. Success of the Baird experiments." TIMES (Apr. 1): 28c. Inauguration of dual transmissions from the new London Regional Station at Brookmans Park. General comments, the program, limitations of television. Television sets are to be sold for 25 guineas; kits are being sold in stores for 16 guineas. Lord Ampthill's speech. Vision on 261 m, sound on 356 m. (2324, 2331)

"The B.B.C. twin wavelength station at Brookman's Park broadcast sound and vision simultaneously at 11 a.m. yesterday. It is the first station to do so. Speech and music were transmitted in the usual way by the London Regional transmitter on 356 metres, while the television images of those before the microphone were simultaneously sent out by the National transmitter working on the wavelength of 261 metres. The programme broadcast originated in the studio of the Baird Television Company in Long Acre, from which the television and sound signals were conducted by separate lines through the B.B.C. control room at Savoy Hill to Brookman's Park, where they were radiated on the separate wavelengths.

"The whole transmission was very successful, and at a receiving station in the centre of London the whole programme was followed with great interest. By means of a Baird 'Televisor' and a little adjustment of the two knobs which respectively control the synchronization and the 'framing' of the picture, the rapidly swirling pattern was resolved into a steady head and shoulders image of the speaker. Two wireless sets were used, one for receiving the television signals and the other for the reception of the sound signals. A particularly noteworthy feature of the dual transmission was that there was no lag between vision and sound such as often destroys the illusion of the 'talkies.'"

2326 Kell, R.D. "Television receiver." U.S. 1,857,154, Apr. 1, 1930, May 10, 1932. Assigned: G.E. Br. 375,856, Mar. 31, 1931 (B.T.H.). Kerr cell assembly energized by projecting radial electrodes on a rotating disk with light source, optical system, and projection screen. Controller reference to Br. 277,761 (694). (2105, 2356)

2327 "Asserts television will show sports." N.Y.T. 22 (Apr. 2): 4. Application for permit for station WLTH by Jenkins Laboratories and comments on sports programs by J.A. Burch. (2310, 2334)

2328 Ives, H.E. "Electro-optical system." U.S. 2,052,298, Apr. 2, 1930, Aug. 25, 1936. Assigned: B.T.L. Br. 374,974, Mar. 23, 1931 (E.R.P.). Disk with apertures extending beyond a single spiral direct light to an observer and, via mirrors, to another viewing point for monitoring purposes. References to Br. 292,546 (995), 358,060 (2071). (2229, 2339)

2329 Prinz, Dietrich. "Television." U.S. 1,854,274, Apr. 4, 1931, Apr. 19, 1932. Assigned: Telefunken. In Germany Apr. 3, 1930. Picture tube receiver and scanning circuits. (2686)

2330 Weinhart, H.W. "Glow discharge lamp." U.S. 1,918,309, Apr. 5, 1930, July 18, 1933. Assigned: B.T.L. Br. 375,407, Mar. 26, 1931 (E.R.P.). Water-cooled gas-filled lamp with hydrogen reservoir. References to Br. 357,590; 358,060 (2071).

2331 Dunlap, O.E. Jr. "England sees and hears radio vaudeville show. Radio images that talk thrill London audience." N.Y.T. X, 14 (Apr. 6): 1–3. BBC broadcast, with comments on U.S. progress. "Baird, the Scottish inventor, gives a television show—Americans call it a good start, but nothing new—they point to previous demonstrations here." Baird portrait. (900, 2325, 2332, 2344, 2380)

2332 "Baird television companies. Amalgamation agreed upon. Independent short-wave station." MAN. GUARD. 12 (Apr. 8): 1. New company to be known as Television Ltd. (2331, 2333)

2333 "Baird Television Development Co., Ltd., and Baird International Television, Ltd. Scheme of amalgamation approved. Sir Mark Jenkinson's difficult task. Sir Edward Manville on progress of television." MAN. GUARD. 20 (Apr. 8): 6, 7. Report on meeting and plan for combining the companies by Sir Mark Webster Jenkinson. Brief survey of prior events; founding of Fernseh A.-G., first BBC broadcast Sept. 30, 1929, dual transmission Mar. 31. Plan for constructing a short-wave station outside London. Televisor installed at 10 Downing Street, Mar. 31. (2332, 2335)

2334 "Get television broadcast. Jersey City radio shops hear and see Hague, Carroll and de Forest." N.Y.T. 24 (Apr. 8): 5. "The first radio television theatre was opened at Lincoln Park, Jersey City, last night under the auspices of the Jenkins Radiovisor and the Jersey City Chamber of Commerce. About fifty reception sets had been installed in radio shops and other places throughout the city." Vision transmitted from stations W2XCR and W2XCD, sound via WRNY and WHOM. (2070, 2327, 2352, 2459)

2335 "Baird Television Development Company and Baird International Television, Limited. Scheme of amalgamation approved. Sir Mark Jenkinson's difficult task. Successful vision-and-sound transmissions. Overseas activities. Sir Edward Manville on the progress of television." TIMES (Apr. 8): 23a-d. An in-depth report: a noteworthy scientific achievement, regular vision transmissions, world leadership, Televisors on sale, a short-wave station being constructed, developments overseas, a German company formed, scheme for fusion of interests, difficulty of fixing valuation basis, allocation of new shares, capitalization of Baird Television Ltd., position of International "A" shareholders, sales of patent rights, the "B" shareholders, thanks due to Sir Mark

Jenkinson, the "International" meetings. (2333, 2344)

2336 Comp. Gaz. "Synchronous movements." Br. 371,326, Oct. 16, 1930. Void. In France Apr. 8, 1930. Eddy-current brake applied to a scanning disk. (1842, 2337)

2337 Comp. Gaz. "Television." Br. 386,289, Apr. 7, 1931. Void. In France Apr. 8. 1930. Defines the dimensions of the scanning spot in relation to the width of the scanning lines using a disk with circular holes. (2336, 2617)

2338 Gray, F. "Electro-optical transmission." U.S. 1,871,266, Apr. 8, 1930, Aug. 9, 1932. Assigned: B.T.L. Br. 385,591, Mar. 24, 1931 (E.R.P.). Void. Discharge lamp with specified gases intended to improve performance as a modulated light source in disk receivers. (2295, 2445)

2339 Ives, H.E. "Communication system." U.S. 2,099,115, Apr. 8, 1930, renewed June 5, 1936, Nov. 16, 1937. Assigned: B.T.L. Br. 375,422, Mar. 27, 1931 (E.R.P.). Disk system for two-way vision and sound, with viewing booth. Apparatus covered in this group of patents was employed in a demonstration of two-way vision with telephones on Apr. 9 (2343). Technical descriptions appeared in July (2446). See demonstration on Apr. 7, 1927 (909), and related patents; also Parker (2299). (2328, 2340)

2340 Ives, H.E., and Victor Subrizi. "Electro-optical transmission." U.S. 2,058,883, Apr. 8, 1930, Oct. 27, 1936. Assigned: B.T.L. Br. 386,296, Apr. 8, 1931 (E.R.P.). Void. Equalizing networks to counteract frequency distortion. (2339, 2351)

2341 Stoller, H.M. "Speed and position regulating." U.S. 1,999,376, Apr. 8, 1930, Apr. 30, 1935. Assigned: B.T.L. Br. 376,309, Apr. 8, 1931 (E.R.P.). Special d-c motor drive with a-c generator, electron tube circuits, and hydraulic damping coupling applied to phasing and sync control in a disk system. (2298, 2447)

2342 Gramophone Co., and R.B. Morgan. "Television receivers." Br. 352,104, Apr. 9, 1930. Hot cathode mercury vapor discharge lamp inside a neon lamp. Reference to Br. 326,729 (1520). (2290)

2343 "2-way television in phoning tested. Persons at ends of line see each other distinctly as they talk. Booths like usual ones. Speaker faces screen which records foot-square image for transmission. Glaring light eliminated. And most apparatus is hidden from view—commercial use awaits further development." N.Y.T. 29 (Apr. 10): 1. Demonstration between AT&T building, 195 Broadway, and Bell Telephone Laboratories, 463 West Street, New York, by wire line, Apr. 9. Pickup by arc lamp with blue filter and numerous phototubes 20 in. by 4 in. diameter. Image displayed in black and pink from a special water-cooled neon lamp with hydrogen reservoir. Two disks with 72 holes, 18 frames per second. Wire transmission by eight underground circuits; two for vision equalized to 40 kc, two for speech, two for orders, one for sync, and one spare. (2050, 2345)

"Special television booths have been developed about the same size as an ordinary telephone booth. Upon entering the booth the person to be 'televised' sits in a swivel chair and faces a frame in which he will see the person at the other end of the line to whom he will speak. The face is illuminated by a mild glow of blue light which is reflected from the face to the photoelectric cells, known as 'radio eyes.' This causes the current to flow which transmits the image to a distant booth.

"When the speaker turns in the chair and faces the apparatus he sees on the glass screen the words 'Ikonophone—Watch this space for the television image.' Then this sign lifts like a magic curtain and in its place the animated picture appears of the person at the other terminal. The two converse in ordinary tones as over the telephone. The images are about a foot square and are very clear.

"The person being 'televised' little realizes that his face is being swept eighteen times each second by the beam of light that illuminates it. Both parties in the television-telephone conversation see each other with sufficient detail to recognize the facial expressions. It is like an instantaneous motion picture in black and white on a pinkish background caused by the color of the high-powered water-cooled Neon tube utilized in the receiving set. No part of the system is annoying to the eye."

2344 Price, C. "America and England bid for television honors. The televisor prefers blondes for broadcast. Brunettes in disfavor at London radio vision studio—minimum facial make-up is used—no spotlights allowed—entertainers perform in dark room." N.Y.T. X, 15 (Apr. 13): 1–3. BBC broadcast, Baird studio. "On the $125 Baird receiving sets as sold at present the image appears in a sepia brown." (898, 2331, 2335, 2347, 2372)

2345 Kennedy, T.R. Jr. "Speakers on phone see images of each other. New light-sound television system enables persons at both ends of telephone line or radio circuit to converse face to face." N.Y.T. X, 15 (Apr. 13): 6–8. Bell Labs demonstration (2343). (2040, 2349, 2497)

2346 N.V. Philips. "Discharge lamp." Br. 386,638, Apr. 15, 1931. In Holland Apr. 15, 1930. Gas-filled glow lamp with liquid-cooled cathode for television receivers. (1854)

2347 "Manchester television demonstration." MAN. GUARD. 12 (Apr. 17): 3, 4. Demonstration of Baird apparatus by A. Franks, Ltd., by land line between two shops. "Head and shoulders of up to four people can appear in the small aperture of the televisor with decided success in detail." (2344, 2367)

2348 "Television exhibition. Number of exhibits nearly four times greater than last year." ELECT. 104 (Apr. 18): 500. Second annual exhibition of the Television Society at University College, London, Apr. 9. C.E.C. Roberts showed a model transmitter consisting of his camera tube (1304), R.W. Corkling exhibited a compact drum receiver called a Televidascope, and a color receiver working on the Baird principle was shown by M. Woodroffe, among more than 20 exhibits. (2272, 2370)

2349 "A.T.& T. demonstrates two-way television." ELECT. W. 95 (Apr. 19): 772. (2345, 2351)

2350 "Sarnoff for radio deal." N.Y.T. 28 (Apr. 19): 2. Predicts spread of home television—20 million receivers instead of 20 thousand theaters. (2247, 2480)

2351 "Ethereal images baffle experts. Two-way television requires as much wire as thirty telephone talks—fifteen radio waves needed for a sound-sight program." N.Y.T. VIII, 15 (Apr. 20): 4, 5. Two large diagrams of the Bell Labs apparatus. Ives quote: "Television for the present, at least, should stick to wire lines." (2340, 2349, 2353, 2364)

2352 Jenkins, C.F. "Electro-optical system." U.S. 1,984,683, Apr. 22, 1930, Dec. 18, 1934. Assigned: RCA. Matrix of electrostatic light valves and distributors. (2334, 2459)

2353 "America two-way television." W.W. 26 (Apr. 23): 437. (2351, 2364)

2354 Alexanderson, E.F.W. "Picture transmission." U.S. 1,866,338, Apr. 23, 1930, July 5, 1932. Assigned: G.E. Br. 377,681, Apr. 23, 1931 (B.T.H.). Disk system with prisms and three different frequency generators operating pulsating light sources for three-channel radio transmission. Controller references to Br. 319,115 (1384) and 342,857 (Telefunken, copying telegraph). (2278, 3107)

2355 Fahrney, C.D. "Television receiver." U.S. 2,021,889, Apr. 23, 1930, Nov. 26, 1935. Cone-shaped drum with motor, light source, and reflecting screen. (1801, 3087)

2356 Kell, R.D. "Television receivers." Br. 356,093, Mar. 27, 1931 (B.T.H.). In U.S. Apr. 23, 1930 (G.E.). Disk with a spiral of lenses, Kerr cell and lens system for screen projection. (2326, 2428)

2357 Ardenne, M. v., and Kurt Schlesinger. "Television receivers." Br. 387,640, Apr. 25, 1931. Void. In Germany Apr. 25, 1930. Circuits for a picture tube receiver. (2322, 2360, 2361)

2358 Jones, William Martin, Jr. "Television." U.S. 1,810,610, Apr. 26, 1930, June 16, 1931.

Disk with radial sets of holes and an overlapping shutter with curved radial slots.

2359 Reynolds, F.W. "Electron discharge device." U.S. 2,055,593, Apr. 30, 1930, Sept. 29, 1936. Assigned: AT&T. Divided from original, Dec. 4, 1926 (821).

2360 Ardenne, M. v. "Die Braunsche Röhre als Fernsehempfänger" [The Braun tube as television receiver]. FERN. 1 (May): 193–202. 10 illus. (2357, 2441)

2361 Schlesinger, K. "Kompensation der Bildpunktverschiebung beim Fernsehen mit Braunschen Röhren" [Compensation of the picture point displacement in television with Braun tubes]. FERN. 1 (May): 202–9. 6 illus. (2357, 2921)

2362 Kette, G. "Die gebräuchlichsten Arbeitsverfahren beim Fernsehen" [The most common working procedures in television]. FERN. 1 (May): 220–6. 6 illus. Historical development, film transmission, the scanning disk, and the mirror drum. (2172, 2584)

2363 Replogle, D.E. "A practical television system." PROJ. ENG. 2 (May): 7–11. 14 illus. (2297, 2522)

2364 Ives, H.E. "Two-way television." PROJ. ENG. 2 (May): 23, 24, 26. 4 illus. (2351, 2353, 2366, 2446)

2365 Chaplin, William Watts. "Eyes across the sea." SCI. & INV. 17 (May): 17, 63. 2 photos. A.P. reporter on Baird's transatlantic test in 1928 (1125).

2366 "Two-way television." SCI. MON. 30 (May): 476–80. 5 photos, diag. (2364, 2401)

2367 "Television demonstrations." TELEV. 3 (May): 107. By Baird Co. at the DAILY MAIL Ideal Home Exhibition at Olympia, Mar. 24 to Apr. 17. By land line from the transmitter at the premises of Major W.H. Oates, 195 Hammersmith Road. "It is estimated that about 30,000 members of the public witnessed the demonstrations." Successful demonstrations were given at Sunderland from Apr. 8 to 10, and at Manchester Apr. 16, 17. Further demonstrations are planned at Southampton from Apr. 24 to May 3, and at Bournemouth from May 8 to 17, under the auspices of the SOUTHERN DAILY ECHO. (2347, 2372)

2368 "German Television Society." TELEV. 3 (May): 107. On the All-gemeiner Deutscher Fernsehverein, its members, aims, and activities.

"Recently, due to private initiative, a German Television Society was formed in Berlin with the title 'Allgemeiner Deutscher Fernsehverein.' Unlike the English Society, which is rather frowned on in official circles, the German Society has as members the German Postmaster-General; and Dr. Banneitz, Director of the P.O. Television Laboratory, Dr. Feyerabrend, Under Secretary of State, Dr. Magnus, who is Vice-President of the Society, and Professor Dr. Leithaeuser, Director Knoeptke of the Berlin Broadcasting Company, while the Broadcasting Companies of Berlin, Breslau, Koenigsberg, and Leipzig have joined as bodies.

"The Society aims at assisting in every way possible the development of television in Germany, and is receiving support from all sections of the wireless industry, whether government or trade.

"At a meeting of the Technical Committee of the Society there were present representatives of the wireless industry, wireless constructors, prominent members of the German P.O., the Technical Research Dept. of the P.O., the Broadcast Companies and Professors of wireless science. The immediate tasks of television were discussed at the meeting and it was generally agreed that caution would have to be used in putting the first televisors on the market lest a reaction likely to jeopardise the ultimate adoption of television be created. The official organ of the Society is the recently founded monthly magazine, FERNSEHEN."

2369 Turner, Norman. "Television in Scotland." TELEV. 3 (May): 108.

2370 "Amateurs' exhibition." TELEV. 3 (May): 111, 113, 114. 4 photos. Television Society's exhibition, Apr. 9, notes on the exhibits. (2348, 2733)

2371 Richardson, W.J. "Assembling and working a Baird kit of components." TELEV. 3 (May): 115–7. 4 photos, 2 diags. (2264, 2321, 2373)

2372 Fox, W.C. "Simultaneous sight and sound broadcast. Television makes a further advance." TELEV. 3 (May): 118, 119, 122. 3 photos. On reception at Hendon of the inaugural BBC broadcast of a program from the Baird studio in Long Acre via the Brookmans Park twin transmitters on Mar. 31 (2300). Quotes from opening speeches. The reception was technically uneventful, the sync did not require adjustment, and there was no trouble with interference or fading. (2320, 2344, 2367, 2374, 2376, 2432)

2373 Woodford, J.W. "Television for the beginner. Pt. 5." TELEV. 3 (May): 120–2. 3 photos. (2315, 2371, 2376, 2416)

2374 Moseley, S.A. "Enthusiasm in Newcastle." TELEV. 3 (May): 123, 124. 2 photos. Baird demonstration. (2323, 2372, 2419, 2421)

2375 Tierney, C. "'Television to-day and to-morrow.'" TELEV. 3 (May): 125. Review of book by Moseley and Chapple (2323). (2181)

2376 Fox, W.C. "How television is being received. Reports from Czechoslovakia, Birmingham, Manchester, Leeds, Glasgow and Sunderland." TELEV. 3 (May): 128, 129. 2 photos. News about amateur activities and reception with some technical details, names, dealers, and places. (2372, 2373, 2416)

2377 Harrison, T.H. "Photo-electric cells and their applications." TELEV. 3 (May): 136–46. 7 photos, 9 diags. Lecture at the Television Society meeting, University College, Apr. 8. A thorough coverage, including historical events, developments, experimental work, types of phototubes, methods of manufacture, construction, materials, and applications; 58 references from 1887 to 1929.

2378 Stacho, Michael. "Television scanning device." U.S. 1,826,836, May 1, 1930, Oct. 13, 1931. Two slotted disks, electromagnetic brake, viewing lens.

2379 Zworykin, V.K. "Photoelectric mosaic." U.S. 2,246,283, May 1, 1930, June 17, 1941. Assigned: Westinghouse. One of the basic patents pertaining to the storage-type camera tube. (2309, 2494)

2380 Dunlap, O.E. Jr. "Eclipse of sun inspires radio men to prophecy. Television looms as aid to astronomers—those far from path of shadow may view next celestial show here on radio screens." N.Y.T. XII, 16 (May 4): 6–8. (2331, 2391)

2381 Farnsworth, P.T., and H.R. Lubcke. "Slope wave generator." U.S. 2,059,219, May 5, 1930, Nov. 3, 1936. Assigned: Farnsworth Television. Deflection circuits for picture tube with magnetic coils. (2123, 2311, 2382, 2558)

2382 Farnsworth, P.T. "Television scanning and synchronizing system." U.S. 2,246,625, May 5, 1930, June 24, 1941. Assigned: Farnsworth Television and Radio. Circuits applied to image dissector for beam deflection at two rates, with blanking of beam at the faster rate. (2381, 2434)

2383 Nicolson, A.M. "Alternating current television." U.S. 1,839,696, May 5, 1930, Jan. 5, 1932. Assigned: Comm. Pats. Br. 360,941, Aug. 6, 1930. Zigzag arc moving along electrodes. Reference to Br. 360,470 (2066). (2385)

2384 "The crystal receiver for television is here!" W.W. 26 (May 7): 493.

2385 Nicolson, A.M. "Color television." U.S. 1,901,116, May 8, 1930, Mar. 14, 1933. Assigned: Comm. Pats. Br. 358,183, Aug. 7, 1930. Arc moving along electrode rails. Colors obtained by coating the electrode rails with various substances, such as calcium (red), sodium (yellow), cobalt (blue), potassium (violet). (2383, 2397)

2386 "Television 'eyes' blink at Walter Dill Scott, President of Northwestern University, at station W9XAO, Chicago." N.Y.T. X, 15 (May 11): 4, 5. Photo. (2863)

2387 Langmuir, I. "Picture transmission." U.S. 1,828,571, May 17, 1930, Oct. 20, 1931. Assigned: G.E. Br. 357,941, May 5, 1931 (B.T.H.). Grant opposed. Two spiral disks, lens system, arc receiver. (451)

2388 Dillenback, Garrett Vander Veer, Jr. "Television motor structure." U.S. 2,006,796, May 20, 1930, July 2, 1935. Assigned: RCA. Perforated disk driven by eddy currents.

2389 Barthélemy, R. "Synchronizing system." U.S. 1,940,161, Apr. 21, 1931, Dec. 19, 1933; Br. 363,605, May 14, 1931. Assigned: Comp. Gaz. In France May 21, 1930. Sync signals oppose picture signals. References to Br. 356,506, in France Oct. 12, 1929; 356,637, in France Feb. 3, 1930. (2237, 2672)

2390 Morse, G.H. "Television receiving device." U.S. 1,831,924, May 22, 1930, Nov. 17, 1931. Spiral of square holes in pivoted members attached to an endless chain. (1836)

2391 Dunlap. O.E., Jr. "Television images perform in theatre. General Electric experts give world premiere on life-size screen at Schenectady." N.Y.T. 1 (May 23): 5; 2–4. Photo of apparatus. Presented on the stage of Proctor's RKO theater, with head and shoulders images (48/20) displayed on a portable 6-foot screen. Light from an arc projected through a lens system, water cell, multiplate Karolus light valve (Kerr cell), disk, and further lenses onto the back of the screen. Transmissions from a studio in the G.E. laboratories through station W2XCW on 139.5 m. with sound on 92 m. (2307, 2380, 2392, 2435)

"Television images performed on a theatre screen here today. They danced, sang and talked. Last Autumn Dr. Alexanderson showed images on a screen 14 inches square. Today his screen is 6 feet square. Often he has asked if television ever would be practical, or if it is only a dream. He has always shrugged his shoulders and smiled, 'Oh, television is a long way off, three years, possibly five or ten.' But today, like a magician, Dr. Alexanderson waved aside the veil of secrecy and showed on the stage of Proctor's Theatre here television tricks that astounded the audience. He proved without a doubt that television entertainers are ready to be booked for the vaudeville circuit.

"Vaudeville teams bantered back and forth by television. One member performed and joked before the televisor while the others replied from the stage. Duets were sung by vocalists a mile apart. The theatre orchestra in the pit was directed by a conductor who waved his baton on the screen.

"Local newspapers advertised the first theatre television show today. A capacity audience attended. As in any motion picture playhouse, the lights were dimmed. The curtains parted. In the centre of the stage was a screen. At the side stood a man with a telephone. He called the television studio a mile away, and the audience heard him announce that all was ready for the performance to begin."

2392 "Television on the stage. Display at Schenectady." TIMES (May 23): 14b. (2391, 2400)

2393 Cawley, A.J. "Television." U.S. 2,026,610, May 23, 1930, renewed May 24, 1935, Jan. 7, 1936. Combined transmitter and receiver with rotary cells and lamps connected in sequence by distributors. (2227, 2425)

2394 Ilberg, W. "Cathode ray scanning device." U.S. 1,976,400, May 21, 1931, Oct. 9, 1934. Assigned: Telefunken. In Germany May 23, 1930. Picture tube and receiver circuits. (2255)

2395 Maloney, Patrick Edward. "Transmission and/or reproduction of views, scenes, and other objects by electrical means." Br. 355,795, May 24, 1930, Aug. 24, 1931. Two or more concentric disks each with apertures or slots arranged in one or more spirals, with numerous variants. This multipurpose system is intended and claimed for duplex, color, stereo, or film. Reference to Br. 302,228 (1091). (2474)

2396 Vorobieff, A. "Television." Br. 366,392, May 20, 1931. In France May 24, 1930. Rotary prisms and oscillating mirrors.

2397 Nicolson, A.M. "Multiple sound and picture recording and projection system." U.S. 2,072,527, May 27, 1390, renewed July 29, 1936, Mar. 2, 1937. Assigned: Comm. Pats. (2385, 2403)

2398 Armstrong, Ralph W. "Multiple cardioid scanning disk." U.S. 1,877,547, May 28, 1930, Sept. 13, 1932. Assigned: Westinghouse. Heart-shaped pattern of apertures.

2399 Hogan, J.V.L. "System for television and sound." U.S. 2,049,384, May 29, 1930, July 28, 1936. Assigned: Radio Inventions. Film transmission. (1984, 2473)

2400 "Life-sized images achieved in television." ELECT. W. 95 (May 31): 1066. (2392, 2402)

2401 "News and views." NATURE 125 (May 31): 829. Note on the Bell Labs two-way demonstration described in WIRELESS WORLD, May 14. (2366, 2412)

2402 "News and views." NATURE 125 (May 31): 829. Note on the G.E. presentation, May 22, reference to the TIMES, May 23 (2392). (2400, 2432)

2403 Nicolson, A.M. "Stereovision." U.S. 1,866,169, May 31, 1930, July 5, 1932. Assigned: Comm. Pats. Br. 360,850, Aug. 7, 1930. Moving arc and electrode system intended for duplex or stereo or color. References to Br. 360,470 (2066), 360,941 (2383), 358,183 (2385). (2397, 2442)

2404 Bonfante, J. "Phototélégraphie et télévision." ELECTRICIEN 46 (June): 247–9. 2 illus. Apparatus of Etablissements Belin. (1258)

2405 "Television in the theatre." ELECTRONICS 1 (June): 147.

2406 Schröter, F. "Aus der Entwicklungsgeschichte der Glimmlampe" [On the history and development of the glow-lamp]. FERN. 1 (June): 244–8. (2316, 2417)

2407 Krawinkel, G. "Die Gegenseh-Einrichtung des Reichspostzentralamts im Deutschen Museum in München" [The two-way equipment of the Central Post Office in the Deutsches Museum in Munich]. FERN. 1 (June): 249–55. Two-way television-telephone apparatus demonstrated at the radio exhibition in Berlin. (2171, 2173, 2552)

2408 Möller, R. "Tritt an Nipkowscheibenlöchern Beugung ein?" [Is there diffraction on the holes of a Nipkow disk?] FERN. 1 (June): 259–61. 4 illus. Analysis of refraction at apertures in a disk. (2232, 2512)

2409 Nesper, E. "Zur Nipkowscheibe" [The Nipkow disk]. FERN. 1 (June): 261–6. 7 illus. Fundamentals, developments, types. (750, 2556)

2410 Thun, R. "Grundsätzliche Systeme der elektrischen Ubertragung bewegter Bilder" [Basic system for electric transmission of moving pictures]. FERN. 1 (June): 267–73. 6 illus. Fundamentals, image analysis and synthesis, methods. (2244, 2587)

2411 Noack, F. "Ein Vorschlag für die Aufnahmen von Fernsehfilmen" [A proposal for the reception of television film]. FERN. 1 (June): 274–6. (2118, 2452)

2412 "Telephone users see each other as they talk." POP. MECH. 53 (June): 892. 2 photos. (2401, 2415)

2413 Lescarboura, A.C. "Radiovision bids for public favor." PROJ. ENG. 2 (June): 15–7. 2 illus. Progress in receivers and programs. (479, 2590)

2414 Fitch, Clyde, J. "Solving television's problems." RADIO-CRAFT 1 (June): 636, 637. 3 illus.

2415 "Two-way television demonstrated." SCI. AM. 142 (June): 467. 2 photos, diag. (2412, 2430)

2416 Woodford, J.W. "Television for the beginner. Pt. 6." TELEV. 3 (June): 157, 158, 176. 2 photos. (2373, 2376, 2418, 2468)

2417 Schröter, F. "Reproduction and amplification in television receivers." TELEV. 3 (June): 159, 160. Graph, 2 diags. (2406, 2466)

2418 "The amateur gets to work." TELEV. 3 (June): 168–71. 3 photos, diag. Editorial report with extracts from letters received from many places in Britain and from Holland. Details of apparatus and reception. (2416, 2457)

2419 Moseley, S.A. "On cabbages and kings." TELEV. 3 (June): 172–4. 2 photos, portrait. Miscellaneous news and comments. (2374, 2465)

2420 Gradenwitz, A. "Ahronheim's television in natural colours." TELEV. 3 (June): 177, 178. 2 photos. Experimental work by A.A. Ahronheim, Berlin. (2037, 2143, 2591, 2595)

2421 "Television on the south coast." TELEV. 3 (June): 179, 180. 3 photos. Demonstrations at Southampton and Bournemouth, extracts from press reports. (2374, 2432)

2422 "Notes of the month." TELEV. 3 (June): 183, 184. Photo. German transmissions, Jenkins broadcasts, AT&T plans.

2423 Campbell, Desmond Robert. "Shadows and television." TELEV. 3 (June): 185–7. 5 illus. Studio lighting, photocell position, light path, contrast. (2463)

2424 "Microphone is still king. Despite television triumphs, broadcasters do not expect to supplement sound programs for images just yet." N.Y.T. IX, 8 (June 1): 6–8. Observations on the advent of television, problems in development, prospects for 1931.

2425 Cawley, A.J. "Television." U.S. 2,122,337, June 3, 1930, June 28, 1938. Receiver with rotary lamps and distributor. (2393, 2537)

2426 Gramophone Co., and Alfred Whitaker. "Synchronous movements." Br. 356,247, June 4, 1930. A beat-frequency method. (2476)

2427 British Thomson-Houston Co., and Alan Julian Maddock. "Synchronous movements." Br. 356,258, June 5, 1930, U.S. 1,874,774, June 5, 1931, Aug. 20, 1932 (G.E.). Phonic wheel and circuit.

2428 Kell, R.D. "Electro-optical light valve." Br. 389,080, June 6, 1931 (B.T.H.). In U.S. June 6, 1930 (G.E.). Disk system with Kerr cell and circuits. (2356, 3121)

2429 Telehor A.-G. "Synchronous movements." Br. 380,115, June 8, 1931. In Germany June 7, 1930. In a receiver a sync motor, driven by sync signals, is coupled to an asynchronous motor which furnishes the main driving power. Controller reference to Br. 261,021 (717), 325,979 (1743), 333,623 (1885). (2149)

2430 "The magic of a vast laboratory." N.Y.T. X (June 8): 3. 3 photos. Story of research at Bell Labs, including television. (2415, 2449)

2431 Davis, C.L. "Television." U.S. 1,896,167, June 12, 1930, Feb. 7, 1933. Assigned: Wired Radio. Object is scanned by a disk with a spiral of holes and a coacting disk with four color filters. Transmission by a varied-frequency method in which different frequencies correspond to different portions of the picture. At the receiver, several folded discharge tubes containing gases having different color characteristics are stacked on behind another from which light is projected onto a viewing screen. (2158, 2444)

2432 "News and views." NATURE 125 (June 14): 903. References to the G.E. large screen demonstration (2391) and Baird's large screen of December 1928. "A note from the Baird International Television Ltd.,...reminds us that television was projected upon a large screen in England as far back as December 1928, when Mr. Baird showed images on a screen 4 ft. by 4 ft. At present sight and sound are being broadcast daily by the British Broadcasting Corporation, and Great Britain is the only country in the world which has an official and regular service of broadcast sight and sound, and where 'televisors' are available to anyone who cares to purchase them." (2372, 2402, 2421, 2455, 2464, 2467)

2433 "Rockefeller plans huge culture center." N.Y.T. 1 (June 14): 5. "Four theatres designed for vaudeville, legitimate shows and concerts, as well as television will be housed in the new buildings." RCA has affiliated with Radio-Keith Orpheum (RKO) and has plans to install television receivers in theaters throughout the country. (2130, 2498)

2434 Farnsworth, P.T. "Electron image amplifier." U.S. 2,085,742, June 14, 1930, July 6, 1937, reissued July 5, 1939, Jan. 20, 1942. Assigned: Farnsworth Television. Image dissector with intensification of successive partial images. (2382, 2472)

2435 Dunlap, O.E. Jr. "Hammond describes marvels of radio-eye. Looks forward to the day when television will bring distant spectacles into the American home." N.Y.T. IX (June 15): 1. Full-page feature article with a large diagram showing the layout of his aircraft landing system employing television, and portrait. General discussion. (2093, 2391, 2539)

2436 Gardner, D.B. "Controlling and directing light." U.S. 1,892,142, June 16, 1930, Dec. 27, 1932. Mirror screw and manometric flame. (1472)

2437 Harries, J.H.O. "Television." Br. 357,143, June 16, 1930; U.S. 2,037,577, Dec. 1, 1930, Apr. 14, 1936. A method of variable-rate scanning whereby the center of interest of a view is explored at a slower rate than the extremities. Adaptable to film scan with moving mirrors or cathode-ray systems. (2144, 2438)

2438 Harries, J.H.O. "Television." Br. 358,971, June 16, 1930. Folded multielectrode discharge tube arranged to emphasize the center of an image in greater detail than the remainder. Reference to Br. 348,211 (2240). (2437, 2439)

2439 Harries, J.H.O. "Synchronous movements." Br. 359,947, June 18, 1930. Rotary resistance and circuit. (2438, 2731)

2440 "Images need wide path." N.Y.T. IX, 9 (June 22): 1. Views of H.A. Lafount: "television calls for a channel ten times width required for wire broadcast." (2100, 2834)

2441 Ardenne, M. v. "Television." Br. 366,856, June 24, 1931. In Germany June 25, 1930. In this cable distribution system, picture signals from an ultra-short wave station are conducted via a common amplifier through separate wire channels, each containing an isolating amplifier, to a number of receivers. Sync signals from another central station are fed into the receiver channels. (2360, 2553)

2442 Nicolson, A.M. "Impulse television system." U.S. 2,072,528, June 25, 1930, renewed July 29, 1936, Mar. 2, 1937. Assigned: Comm. Pats. Br. 367,915, Nov. 29, 1930. Matrix system with spark gaps and neon lamps. (2403, 2479)

2443 "Shows new device for television. Lieut. George Wald, inventor, says it simplifies the present system." N.Y.T. 24 (June 27): 4. Shown in New York June 26, called Telephonovision, Wald's transmitter has a special vacuum tube with selenium cells, and is said to transmit sound as well as sight and avoids sync problems. (1997, 2630)

2444 Davis, C.L. "Television." U.S. 1,874,171, June 28, 1930, Aug. 30, 1932. Assigned: Wired Radio. Receiver cabinet with glow discharge screen, optical system and viewing screen. (2431, 2475)

2445 Gray, F. "Electro-optical system." U.S. 2,072,478, June 28, 1930, Mar. 2, 1937. Assigned: B.T.L. Br. 380,839, June 24, 1931 (E.R.P.). Double-spiral prism disk transmitter with two phototubes and separate circuits. (2338, 2446)

2446 Ives, H.E., F. Gray, and M.W. Baldwin. "Image transmission system for two-way television." B.S.T.J. 9 (July): 449–69. 14 illus. Technical details of the telephone-television system demonstrated Apr. 9 (2343). This paper and others (2447, 2448) were presented at the AIEE Convention in Toronto, June 23–27; TRANS. AIEE 49 (Oct.): 1563–76, reprinted by Arno Press, 1977. Introduction, physical arrangement and operation, optical problems, photoelectric cells and associated circuits, two-way image signal amplifiers, transmission circuits, neon lamps and circuits, optical monitoring systems, signaling system, conclusion. See related patents (2338–41). (2364, 2445, 2510, 2547)

2447 Stoller, H.M. "Synchronization system for two-way television." B.S.T.J. 9 (July): 470–7. 5 illus. (2446) General requirements, description of motor, control circuit, control oscillator, framing, conclusion. (2341)

2448 Blattner, D.G., and L.G. Bostwick. "Sound transmission system for two-way television." B.S.T.J. 9 (July): 478–82. 3 illus. (2446)

2449 TWO-WAY TELEVISION. New York: Bell Telephone Laboratories, 1930. Monograph B-504. 37 pp., illus. (2430, 2495)

2450 Kirschstein, F. "Uber die Verstärkung beim Fernsehen" [On amplification in television]. FERN. 1 (July): 289–96. 10 illus. Amplifiers, reproduction quality. (2210, 2514)

2451 Friedel, W. "Die Braunsche Röhre als Fernseh-Sender" [The Braun tube as television transmitter]. FERN. 1 (July): 296–302. 5 illus. (2303, 3382)

2452 Noack, F. "Ein Universalfernseher" [A universal television]. FERN. 1 (July): 302–6. 7 illus. Apparatus with two disks adaptable to transmission with different numbers of scanning lines. (2411, 2518)

2453 Peters, H. "Uber die Zeitdauer der Emissionserscheinungen bei Glimmlampen" [About the duration of emission phenomena in glow lamps]. FERN. 1 (July): 306–10. 2 illus. Dependence of picture quality on glow lamp design. (2554)

2454 Schadow, R. "Synchronisierung durch au tomatische Bremsvorrichtung" [Synchronization by automatic braking equipment]. FERN. 1 (July): 310–20. 25 illus.

2455 "Television on the theatre screen." PROJ. ENG. 2 (July): 23, 24. 2 illus. Alexanderson (G.E.) system, equipment details, experiments, possible uses in theaters. (2432, 2516)

2456 Cockaday, Laurence M. "The latest developments in television methods." RADIO-CRAFT 2 (July): 24. 7 photos, 2 diags. (2990)

2457 Heller, Alexander Gordon. "The amateur's television projector." RADIO-CRAFT 2 (July): 25, 26. 3 photos, 2 diags. Disk scanner and apparatus for 35-mm silhouette film transmission. (2418, 2468)

2458 "Practical television is now here!" RADIO N. 12 (July): 26–9. Pictorial essay with 21 photos. Baird, Bell Labs, Jenkins, Short Wave & Television Labs, Western Television Corp.

2459 Lynch, A.H. "Television and band-pass receivers." RADIO N. 12 (July): 30–31. On short-wave receivers for television. Also note about Allen Balcom Du Mont (1901–1965), chief engineer of the De Forest Radio Co., and their joining forces with the Jenkins Television Corp. for experimental work. De Forest seeks permission from the FRC to construct a 20,000-w station at Passaic, N.J., using 2000–2100-kc band. (1976, 2334, 2352, 2461, 2496)

2460 "Announcing a new, practical, inexpensive Televisor. Some interesting facts about the new Baird Televisor." RADIO N. 12 (July): between pp. 48 & 49. Two-page advertisement by the Short Wave & Television Laboratory, Inc., Boston, Mass. Photo of cabinet and of the motor and disk assembly. "No larger than a radio receiver—so simply constructed that anyone can operate it. Turn the dial and see instead of hear it!" (2294, 2886)

2461 "Jenkins first in television." RADIO N. 12 (July): 59. Advertisement for Radiovisors by Jenkins Television Corp., Jersey City, N.J. Photo of disk receiver assembly. Two models available, one large and one small, and a kit as well as a special short-wave receiver at prices from $42.50 to $570. Nightly programs from station W2XCR, Jersey City, W3XK, Washington, D.C., and others. "Bigger, better, more entertaining programs are coming!" (2459, 2545)

2462 "Television station schedules." RADIO N. 12 (July): 95. List of eight stations, number of scanning lines: 24, 45, 48, 60. (2038, 2602)

2463 Campbell, D.R. "Broadcasting television." TELEV. 3 (July): 201–3. Photo, 2 diags.

General layout of control room, amplifiers, circuit, apparatus, procedure. (2423, 2565)

2464 Chapple, H.J.B. "Possible television developments." TELEV. 3 (July): 204–6. Photo, 2 diags. Baird magnetic recording system with three disks, arrangement, and operation. (2323, 2432, 2470, 2528)

2465 Moseley, S.A. "To my readers." TELEV. 3 (July): 207–9, 225. 2 photos. Miscellaneous comments, quotes from correspondents. (2419, 2524)

2466 Schröter, F. "Reproduction and amplification in television receivers." TELEV. 3 (July): 210, 211. Photo, 2 diags. (2417, 2531)

2467 "The first B.B.C. play to be broadcast by television." TELEV. 3 (July): 212–4. 5 photos. Advance details of "The Man with the Flower in his Mouth," by Luigi Pirandello. (2432, 2471)

2468 Woodford, J.W. "Television for the beginner. Pt. 7." TELEV. 3 (July): 215–7. 4 photos, 2 diags. (2416, 2457, 2469, 2523)

2469 "The enthusiast sees it through." TELEV. 3 (July): 222–5. 3 photos, 2 diags. Extracts from correspondents on amateur equipment and results. (2468, 2523)

2470 Bradly, H. "Baird studio topics." TELEV. 3 (July): 226, 227. 3 photos. (2268, 2464, 2488)

2471 "The 'Radio Times' on the B.B.C.'s forthcoming television play." TELEV. 3 (July): 228, 229. From RADIO TIMES, June 27. (2467, 2487)

2472 "Mr. Philo Farnsworth, a twenty-three-year-old San Francisco experimenter, with a new television receiver which he has made." TELEV. 3 (July): 231. Photo (Fig. 62). (2434, 2477)

2473 Hogan, J.V.L. "Television synchronization." U.S. 1,998,812, July 1, 1930, Apr. 23, 1935. Assigned: Radio Inventions. Film system. (2399, 2773)

2474 Maloney, P.E. "Television." Br. 358,433, July 2, 1930. Apertured disk or drum, for duplex or stereo. (2395)

2475 Davis, C.L. "Television." U.S. 1,874,172, July 3, 1930, Aug. 30, 1932. Assigned: Wired Radio. Zigzag glow discharge screen with receiver and modulator circuits. (2444, 2501)

2476 Gramophone Co., A. Whitaker, and C.O. Browne. "Television." Br. 356,363, July 3, 1930. U.S. 2,059,159, July 2, 1931, Oct. 27, 1936 (EMI). Vibrating mirror and electromagnetic assembly. Pair used for scanning, or singly for optical sound recording. (2290, 2426, 2571, 2656)

2477 Farnsworth, P.T. "Dissector target." U.S. 1,941,344, July 7, 1930, Dec. 26, 1933. Assigned: Television Labs. Shielded target with aperture, wire loop anode, and a secondary electron emission surface in an image dissector tube. (2472, 2548)

2478 Johnson, J.B. "Signaling." U.S. 2,155,192, July 7, 1930, Apr. 18, 1939. Assigned: B.T.L. Br. 380,859, June 29, 1931 (E.R.P.). Picture tube with two perforated curved disks or control electrodes placed between the deflection plates and the screen. (510, 3197)

2479 Nicolson, A.M. "Television scanning system." U.S. 2,108,827, July 7, 1930, Feb. 22, 1938. Assigned: Comm. Pats. Br. 368,705, Nov. 29, 1930. Special phototube scanned by a moving arc. Divided, U.S. 2,220,115, Jan. 29, 1938. Five references (2066, 2383, 2385, 2403, 2484). (2442)

2480 "In television Sarnoff sees a new culture." N.Y.T. IX, 1 (July 13): 1–8. A separate theater in every home will open a new era of art appreciation. (2350, 2911)

2481 "The latest in television broadcast receivers." N.Y.T. IX, 11 (July 13): 1. Photo of Western Television Corp. receiver. (2482)

2482 "The mid-west to look in." N.Y.T. IX, 11 (July 13): 1–5. On plans for television in Chicago. Photo of transmitter, station WMAQ. (2481, 2551)

2483 Banks, George Baldwin, and Baird Television. "Television." Br. 355,896, July 14, 1930. Electrolytic system. Changing opacity of a circulating liquid modulates light from a source to a mirror drum scanner. (2638)

2484 Triggs, W.W. (Communication Patents). "Television." Br. 358,920, July 14, 1930. Nicolson system with scanning by arc moving along electrodes. Reference to Br. 360,470 (2066). (2479, 2503)

2485 Skaupy, F. "Discharge lamp." Br. 373,817, June 19, 1931. In Germany July 14, 1930. Applications include television, with a three-electrode type for receivers. (1923)

2486 Wilson, John Charles (1909–1942), and Baird Television. "Television." Br. 358,916, July 14, 1930. Mirror drum with internal reflectors. References to Br. 230,576 (565), 328,616 (1721). (3010)

2487 "Television play is broadcast in Britain; dramatic critic sees perfection far off." N.Y.T. 1 (July 15): 2, 3. On the BBC broadcast of July 14, with comments from THE TIMES. (2471, 2488)

2488 "The first play in television. B.B.C. and Baird experiment." TIMES (July 15): 12b. "The Man with the Flower in his Mouth," a critical review. "The time for interest and curiosity is come, but the time for the serious criticism of television plays, as plays, is not yet." (2470, 2487, 2489)

2489 "First television play." TIMES (July 15): 14d. On the BBC broadcast, with note on a demonstration by Baird at the Coliseum. (2488, 2491, 2497)

2490 Karolus, A. "Television." U.S. 2,043,800, June 22, 1931, June 9, 1936. Assigned: RCA. In Germany July 15, 1930. Light-chopper disk with a circle of triangular holes and a spiral-shaped periphery, phototubes, light sources, and picture tube. (2249, 3271)

2491 "Television in the cinema, public demonstration." TIMES (July 16): 12c. Baird Co. plans for a stage demonstration at the Coliseum. A good general description of the large screen with 2,100 filament lamps and a "gigantic commutator," or distributor. A recent demonstration (July 1) of the large screen on the roof of the Baird laboratories in Long Acre is mentioned. (2489, 2497)

"Arrangements have been made for a demonstration of television in the cinema to form part of the programme of the Coliseum in the week beginning July 28th and onwards, as was announced in THE TIMES yesterday. The demonstration will consist of the recent developments of Baird's system of television, whereby an image can be seen by a large number of persons simultaneously.

"In Mr. Baird's new apparatus the receiving screen is broken up into as many as 2,100 elements, each of which consists of a cubicle in which is situated a small metal filament lamp such as is used in pocket electric torches. The front of the cells is covered with a sheet of ground glass. Each of these little lamps is connected to a separate bar of a gigantic commutator, which switches on only one lamp at a time, and, as the contact of the commutator revolves, each of the little lamps is switched on in succession. The contact switches on and off the whole of the 2,100 lamps in one-twelfth of a second.

"In operation the incoming television signal is first of all amplified, and this powerful current is then fed to the revolving commutator, which switches it to every lamp in turn. The current is strong at a bright part of the picture and weak at a dim part, so that the little lamps are bright or dark accordingly, and the picture is built up of a mosaic of bright and dark lamps. This device differs from any other television device previously shown, in that the lamps are not instantaneous in their action; they remain alight for quite a considerable time, and it is on this fact that, to a great extent, the success of the new device depends, great brilliancy and reduced flickering being easily attained."

2492 Tolson, W.A. "Television." U.S. 1,998,644, July 16, 1930, Apr. 23, 1935. Assigned: RCA. Includes a lens turret in a scanning system. (1960, 2973)

2493 Tate, A.O. "Scanning disk." U.S. 1,880,295, July 17, 1930, Oct. 4, 1932. Shutter assembly with sliding members operated by levers and electromagnets. (2111, 2508)

2494 Zworykin, V.K. "Television." U.S. 2,157,048, July 17, 1930, renewed Jan. 30, 1937, May 2, 1939. Assigned: RCA. Br. 369,832, July 9, 1931 (Marconi's). Camera tube with beam current converted to an electrostatic image which is then scanned to produce image signals, with variants. (2379, 2543)

2495 "Two-way television." ELECT. 105 (July 18): 74. Brief note on the Bell Labs system requiring eight circuits. (2449, 2510)

2496 "De Forest, moving to Hollywood, will give his time to film and television research." N.Y.T. 1 (July 19): 2, 3. Plans for January 1931. (2459, 2507)

2497 Kennedy, T.R., Jr. "A Scotsman's television hopes. Baird is building shortwave image transmitter for overseas experiments. England has 1,000 vision receivers." N.Y.T. IX, 11 (July 20): 6–9. Two photos of Baird 30-line receiver and one showing C.I. Bingley, chief engineer, Baird Television Corp., tuning a receiver. Also, radio-photo of actors in the BBC play "The Man with the Flower in his Mouth." (2345, 2489, 2491, 2505, 2525)

2498 "Television patents released by R.C.A." N.Y.T. 20 (July 21): 1. Licenses offered to 32 manufacturers, including television. (2433, 2502)

2499 Deisch, Noel. "Formation of images." U.S. 2,000,379, July 22, 1930, May 7, 1935. Part assigned: Thomas E. Stone, Jr. Kerr cell, prism, and mirror. (2578)

2500 Hough, C.W. "Motion picture television system." U.S. 1,869,424, July 22, 1930, Aug. 2, 1932. Assigned: Wired Radio. Receiver with light source, lenses, scanning disk, oscillating mirror, and viewing screen. (1291)

2501 Davis, C.L. "Television." U.S. 1,884,593, July 23, 1930, Oct. 25, 1932. Assigned: Wired Radio. Glow discharge tube with two electrodes, one an inductive screen and the other a variably adjustable concave reflector. (2475, 2504)

2502 "New equipment for WJZ. TV tests are planned by Radio Corporation." N.Y.T. 24 (July 24): 6. (2498, 2911)

2503 Nicolson, A.M. "Electro-optical control system." U.S. 1,951,523, July 24, 1930, Mar. 20, 1934. Assigned: Comm. Pats. Br. 372,521, Apr. 15, 1931. Phototube, piezoelectric crystal and oscillator, thermostatic control, optical system, and circuits. (2484, 2533)

2504 Davis. C.L. "Television." U.S. 1,889,852, July 25, 1930, Dec. 6, 1932. Assigned: Wired Radio. Optical arrangement of gas discharge chambers with signal electrodes. (2501, 2633)

2505 "News and views." NATURE 126 (July 26): 142. Comments on theater television and the proposed large screen demonstration by Baird at the Coliseum. "It seems quite feasible to broadcast these pictures to distant cinemas by means of land lines." (2497, 2509)

2506 "Briton here to scan television progress." N.Y.T. 16 (July 26): 2. Account of James Robinson's stenode radiostat. "A worldwide survey of television development is being made by A. Dinsdale of London." (2053, 2055, 2634)

2507 "De Forest looks far ahead." N.Y.T. IX, 11 (July 27): 1–3. Predictions for 1980 include cable television and theater television in the home in color on a 6-foot screen. (2496, 2545)

2508 Tate, A.O. "Television." Br. 359,591, July 29, 1930. Scanning disk, antidazzle screens. (2493)

2509 Baird, J.L., and Television Ltd. "Television." Br. 359,981, July 30, 1930, Oct. 31, 1931. Large-screen color system. Scanning disk has three contiguous partial spirals of apertures, each spiral covered with a translucent filter for separate colors: red, green, blue. Mosaic screen has elements of three lamps clustered in compartments, each lamp differently colored, with an overall translucent diffusing screen. Lamps are connected sequentially in columns and rows by distributors. This specification is a composite of earlier ones, to which references are made: lamp bank (548), (814); switching (2197),

(2201); sync (1213), (1961); lamp compartments (2240), and (640). (2505, 2519)

2510 Ives, H.E., and others. "Two-way television." J. AIEE 49 (Aug.): 682–4. Abridgment. (2446, 2495, 2515, 2582)

2511 Felix, E.H. "Requirements of television." ELECTRONICS 1 (Aug.): 235, 236, 266. Survey of progress, sync, picture elements, frequency, detail, terms. (1874, 2559)

2512 Möller, R. "Die optische Vergrösserung von Nipkowscheiben-Bildern" [The optical enlargement of Nipkow disk pictures]. FERN. 1 (Aug.): 342–9. 11 illus. Design of magnifying lenses. (2408, 2813)

2513 Okolicsányi, F. v. "Fernsehen und Bildgrammofon" [Television and picture gramophone]. FERN. 1 (Aug.): 349–58. 8 illus. Picture reproduction system like the phonograph. (2305, 2535)

2514 Kirschstein, F. "Fernsehfilm und Fotozellenverstärker" [Television film and photocell amplifier]. FERN. 1 (Aug.): 358–61. 4 illus. (2450, 2622)

2515 Neuburger, A. "Eine Americanische Gegenfernseh und Sprechanlage" [An American two-way television and sound installation]. FERN. 1 (Aug.): 361–4. 2 illus. Bell Labs apparatus, and the German equipment. (2322, 2510, 2588, 2818)

2516 "The first television show." POP. MECH. 54 (Aug.): 177–9. 2 photos. G.E. apparatus. (2455, 2517)

2517 "Television in the theatre takes its bow." RADIO-CRAFT 2 (Aug.): 84, 85. 5 photos, 4 diags. G.E. demonstration and apparatus. (2516, 2520)

2518 Noack, F. "Latest developments of German television methods." RADIO-CRAFT 2 (Aug.): 86, 87, 112. 6 photos. (2265, 2452, 2589)

2519 "Automatic television recorder." RADIO-CRAFT 2 (Aug.): 113. Note on Baird Co. development based on a report in AMATEUR WIRELESS. (2509, 2525)

2520 "Television in the theatre." RADIO N. 12 (Aug.): 100. Photo and caption, G.E. large screen. (2517, 2559)

2521 Bliss, H.N. "Building a simple stroboscope for synchronizing television discs." RADIO N. 12 (Aug.): 107. Diag. 6-inch disk for 48-line signals.

2522 Replogle, D.E. "How to synchronize for television." RADIO N. 12 (Aug.): 134, 135, 184. 5 photos, 3 diags. Manual, semi-automatic, automatic methods, special motors, adjustable drives, phonic wheel, sync signal. (2363, 2647)

2523 Woodford, J.W. "Television for the beginner. Pt. 8." TELEV. 3 (Aug.): 240–2. 4 photos, 2 diags. (2468, 2469, 2528, 2564)

2524 Moseley, S.A. "Enemies—and friends—of British television." TELEV. 3 (Aug): 245–7. Photo of the London Marionettes on stage for a television program. Mainly about Eckersley's opposition to Baird television, with quotes from letters about reception as far away as Newcastle. (2153, 2465, 2530)

2525 Sieveking, Lance. "The fourteenth of July, 1930." TELEV. 3 (Aug.): 252–4. 4 illus., portrait. "The first Television Play was transmitted on 14th July from the Baird Studio at 133 Long Acre. 'The Man with the Flower in his Mouth,' by Luigi Pirandello. The Man—Earle Grey, A Customer—Lionel Millard, The Woman—Gladys Young. Scenery by C.R.W. Nevinson. Adapted and produced by Lance Sieveking (B.B.C) and Sydney A. Moseley (Baird Television)." (2497, 2519, 2526, 2530)

2526 "A startling development in screen television." TELEV. 3 (Aug.): 255, 256. 3 photos, diag. Demonstration of Baird's large screen (2 by 5 feet) at 133 Long Acre, July 1. Brief details of the apparatus and the program, which lasted about 30 minutes. (2525, 2527)

2527 "Television in the cinema, public demonstration." TELEV. 3 (Aug.): 257. From THE TIMES, July 16 (2491). (2526, 2529)

2528 Chapple, H.J.B. "Positive and negative images." TELEV. 3 (Aug.): 258, 259. 2 photos.

Direction of current, detector stage, low-frequency coupling, operation of neon lamp, defects in receiver. (2464, 2523, 2532, 2593)

2529 Robinson, E.H. "Extracts from the wireless notes." TELEV. 3 (Aug.): 260. Comments on the operation of a Baird receiver and the results. "Everyone who sees the 'Televisor' at work is amazed at the definition and clarity of the image." (2527, 2536)

2530 Moseley, S.A. "How the first television play was received." TELEV. 3 (Aug.): 261, 262. Photo of the three performers. Selection of letters. (2524, 2525, 2561, 2631)

2531 Schröter, F. "Reproduction and amplification in television receivers." TELEV. 3 (Aug.): 264, 265, 272. 2 photos. (2466, 2581)

2532 "The enthusiast sees it through." TELEV. 3 (Aug.): 266, 267. Photo. (2528, 2562)

2533 Communication Patents. "Television." Br. 385,314, Apr. 15, 1931. In U.S. Aug. 2, 1930. Frequency control with crystal oscillator and pendulum carrying reflector and shaded film, including optical system and circuits. References to Br. 360,470 (2066), 372,521 (2503). (2601)

2534 Rathbun, John B. "Television." U.S. 1,870,465, Aug. 4, 1930, Aug. 9, 1932. Part assigned: Fred C. Wellman. Split polarized light beam with vibrating mirrors.

2535 Okolicsányi, F. v., and G. Wikkenhauser. "Television receivers." Br. 364,003, Aug. 21, 1930. Assigned: Telehor A.-G. U.S. 1,887,472, Sept. 17, 1930, Nov. 8, 1932. In Germany Aug. 5, 1930. Mirror cylinder or mirror screw, linear light source, phonic wheel. Reference to Br. 358,411, Hatzinger (2296). (1996, 2513, 2586)

2536 Baird, J.L., and Television Ltd. "Television transmitters." Br. 360,942, Aug. 6, 1930. Mirror drum with lenses. Reference to Br. 348,638. (2529, 2561)

2537 Cawley, A.J. "Scanning apparatus." U.S. 2,176,847, Aug. 7, 1930, Oct. 17, 1939; Br. 375,589, July 29, 1931. Scanning by several means such as a disk with one or more sets of radial slots coacting with a slotted cylinder and an optical system of prisms and lenses, along with neon lamps, a distributor, and a cabinet assembly. (2425, 2770)

2538 Donle, H.P. "Television scanning system." U.S. 1,969,456, Aug. 9, 1930, Aug. 7, 1934. Assigned: Radio Inventions. Radially slotted disk produces a distorted image which is optically corrected for viewing. (2283, 2963)

2539 Dunlap, O.E. Jr. "Who will see the images?" N.Y.T. IX, 9 (Aug. 10): 1–3. Hammond's system requiring a key or ticket to view scrambled signals. (2435, 2583, 3709)

2540 "Columbia projects television station." N.Y.T. 12 (Aug. 14): 3, 4. Application by the Atlantic Broadcasting Co. for a license, station WABC, New York, and for a portable station. (2691)

2541 Goldsmith, A.N. "Television." U.S. 1,924,277, Aug. 14, 1930, Aug. 29, 1933. Assigned: RCA. Br. 369,856, Aug. 14, 1931 (Marconi's). Complete disk and optical system assembly on a movable carriage. (2000, 2542)

2542 Goldsmith, A.N. "Television." U.S. 2,043,997, Aug. 14, 1930, June 16, 1936. Assigned: RCA. Br. 368,653, Aug. 14, 1931 (Marconi's). Dual system with two disks, phototubes, and amplifiers connected to a two-section potentiometer thence to the line for fading out one image and fading in another. (2541, 2641)

2543 Zworykin, V.K. "Reception by television." U.S. 2,025,143, Aug. 15, 1930, Dec. 24, 1935. Assigned: RCA. Br. 376,498, July 9, 1931 (Marconi's). A cathode-ray tube has an oblique control screen consisting of apertures covered by movable plates which serves as a light valve. Signals actuate the screen which modulates light from a constant source for projection onto an external viewing screen. (2494, 2580)

2544 Williams, W.E. "Television." Br. 361,355, Aug. 19, 1930. Matrix of three-electrode glow discharge lamps controlled by distributors. Reference to Br. 302,187 (982)

2545 "Television program in Times Square area. Noted entertainers and others enlisted for outdoor sound-and-sight shows." N.Y.T. 19 (Aug. 24): 2. Jenkins and de Forest plans for broadcast. (2461, 2507, 2546)

2546 "City crowds see 'radio-vision' show. First television performance in public here is given in Eighth Avenue store. Homes get broadcast, too. Clear images four inches square reproduce acts presented in Jersey City studio." N.Y.T. 26 (Aug. 26): 2. Reception at 57th Street and 8th Avenue from Jenkins station W2XCR (2800 kc), with sound from de Forest station W2XCD (187 m). Images of figures above the waistline only distinguished with considerable clarity. (2545, 2560, 2769)

2547 Gray, F. "Electro-optical system." U.S. 1,990,182, Aug. 26, 1930, Feb. 5, 1935. Assigned: B.T.L. Br. 388,422, Aug. 25, 1931 (E.R.P.). Mirror drum with apertured disk, including film recording. (2446, 2654)

2548 Triggs, W.W. (Television Laboratories). "Television." Br. 368,309, Aug. 27, 1930, Feb. 29, 1932. Complete Farnsworth system with image dissector and picture tubes and circuits. Divided (2549). (2477)

2549 Triggs, W.W. (Television Laboratories). "Television." Br. 368,721, Aug. 27, 1930, Feb. 29, 1932. Divided from Br. 368,309 (2548). Essentially the same as the companion patent, but with emphasis on the camera tube, which is covered explicitly in nine claims. Reference to Br. 318,331 (1304). (2558)

2550 De Amicis, Domenic Sicari. "Television." U.S. 1,945,968, Aug. 30, 1930, Feb. 6, 1934. Divided from U.S. 1,999,686, June 27, 1929. Perforated drum with lamps and reflectors inside drum and other reflectors outside to produce converging rays on the object or scene.

2551 "Broadcasting by television began at WMAQ during the past week." N.Y.T. IX, 8 (Aug. 31): 2. Photo. Call sign W9XAP (2800 kc). (2482, 2645)

2552 Krawinkel, G., and E. Perchermeir. "Der Fernsehsender des Reichspostzentralamtes in Berlin-Witzleben" [The television transmitter of the German State Central Post Office in Berlin, Witzleben]. FERN. 1 (Sept.): 385–90. 9 illus. Details of equipment. (2407, 2598, 2624, 2626)

2553 Ardenne, M. v. "Zur Anwendung ultrakurzer Wellen für das Fernsehen" [On the application of ultra-short waves for television]. FERN. 1 (Sept.): 390–2. Selection of frequencies, sync problems. See Busse (2585). (2441, 2653)

2554 Peters, H. "Naturkonstaten und Experimentalkonstanten" [Natural and experimental constants]. FERN. 1 (Sept.): 392–8. 5 illus. Theoretical study of inertia in television techniques. (2453, 3133)

2555 Aretz, E. "Glimmlampen." FERN. 1 (Sept): 398–409. 13 illus. Study of glow lamps.

2556 Nesper, E. "Die Röntgenfernseheinrichtung von Deauvellier" [The Röntgen television equipment of Dauvillier]. FERN. 1 (Sept.): 409–11. Application of television in X-ray equipment. (2409)

2557 Andersen, E. "Drehbare Glimmlampe für Berlin-London" [Revolving glow lamp for Berlin-London]. FERN. 1 (Sept.): 411, 412. 3 illus. Reception from both stations with two different disks or with a revolving glow lamp and one disk.

2558 Farnsworth, P.T., and H.R. Lubcke. "The transmission of television images." PROJ. ENG. 2 (Sept): 21–3. (2381, 2549, 2662, 2837)

2559 Felix, E.H. "Television advances from peephole to screen." RADIO N. 12 (Sept.): 228–30, 268, 269. 5 photos, 3 diags. General Electric's equipment demonstration May 22 (2391). Quality of reproduction, scanning, the light valve, limitations of the neon tube, Kerr effect, polarized light, distortion; when is television coming? (2511, 2520, 2588, 3237)

2560 Jenkins, C.F. "A silhouette studio." J. SMPE 15 (Sept.): 381–4. (2546, 2592)

2561 Moseley, S.A. "The big events." TELEV. 3 (Sept.): 283–5, 295. 3 photos. Coliseum demonstration, G.E. demonstration, Eckersley's diatribe and Edwards' adverse comments, miscellaneous items, and terminology; scanner, gazer, observer, looker, and looker-in. (2530, 2536, 2563, 2636)

2562 "The enthusiast sees it through." TELEV. 3 (Sept.): 290, 291. 2 photos. (2532, 2564)

2563 "Baird screen television. The Coliseum triumph." TELEV. 3 (Sept.): 292–5. 3 photos. "Demonstrations form part of a public theatre programme for the first time in the world's history." (2561, 2565)

2564 Woodford, J.W. "Television for the beginner. Pt. 9." TELEV. 3 (Sept): 298–300. 4 photos, 3 diags. (2523, 2562, 2566, 2596)

2565 Campbell, D.R. "The first public tele-talkies demonstration at the Coliseum." TELEV. 3 (Sept): 304–6. 3 photos, 2 diags. Presentation of Aug. 9. Description of apparatus, how it works, transmitting film, changing from television to film, talking films in theaters by television. (2463, 2563, 2567, 2729)

2566 Hewel, H. "Receiving Baird television in Berlin." TELEV. 3 (Sept.): 307–9. Photo, 2 diags. Receiver details, reception from Brookmans Park, circuit modifications. (2257, 2564, 2593, 2845)

2567 "The world's first public performance of television in a theatre." TELEV. 3 (Sept.): 311. Photo of poster announcing Baird television at the London Coliseum, July 28 (2491). (2565, 2573)

2568 Collier, T.W., D.H. Byron, and Baird Television. "Television." Br. 359,639, Sept. 6, 1930. Mirror drum method of mirror adjustments. (3742)

2569 Wallace, R.E. "Electro-optical method and apparatus." U.S. 1,990,884, Sept. 6, 1930, Feb. 12, 1935. Assigned: RCA. Mirror disk and apertured disk for film scanning. (2191)

2570 Henroteau, F.C.P. "Television." U.S. 1,903,113, Sept. 8, 1930, Mar. 28, 1933, reissued Oct. 31, 1933, Dec. 1, 1936. Assigned: The Electronic Television Co. Ltd., Ottawa, Canada. Divided from U.S. 1,903,112 (1884). (2751)

2571 Gramophone Co., and A. Whitaker. "Carrier wave television system." Br. 362,030, Sept. 12, 1930; U.S. 1,962,417, Aug. 27, 1931, June 12, 1934 (2476). Scanning control by beat frequency between two carrier waves.

2572 Gretton, J.F., and F.H. Haskell. "Television." Br. 362,950, Sept. 12, 1930. Two slotted drums, for duplex or stereo. (3287)

2573 Baird, J.L., and Baird Television. "Discharge lamps." Br. 359,054, Sept. 13, 1930. One V-shaped electrode to increase light intensity. References to Br. 321,930 and 328,691 (1747). (2567, 2635)

2574 Batstone, L.F., and B.T. Hogben. "Television." Br. 361,470, Sept. 13, 1930. Disk with tapered slot and a disk with apertures in two or more spirals.

2575 "Transatlantic television." TIMES (Sept. 17): 9d. "Mr. Douglas Walters last night picked up a television transmission from New York and discerned the head and shoulders of a person." First transatlantic reception by an amateur. (2600)

2576 Bedford, Alda V. "Picture transmission." U.S. 1,849,818, Sept. 19, 1930, Mar. 15, 1932. Assigned: G.E. Br. 363,979, Sept. 18, 1931 (B.T.H.). Disk system with correcting pulse at the end of each scanning line. (3462)

2577 "What television must achieve before it reaches the home." N.Y.T. XII, 2 (Sept. 21): 7, 8. Views of Morris Metcalf, president RMA, on broadcast television.

2578 Deisch, N. "Formation of images." U.S. 2,000,380, Sept. 24, 1930, renewed Oct. 1, 1934, May 7, 1935. Part assigned: T.E. Stone, Jr. Kerr cell, cathode-ray distributor, mechanical distributor, and circuits. (2499)

2579 Doering, U.W. "Cathode ray tube." Br. 378,681, Sept. 22, 1931. In Germany Sept. 24, 1930. Mercury vapor filling, electric heater, surrounding magnetic shield and enclosure, said to be for television.

2580 Zworykin, V.K. "Communication by television." U.S. 1,955,899, Sept. 25, 1930, Apr. 24, 1934. Assigned: RCA. Br. 381,306, Sept. 8, 1931 (Marconi's). Picture tube with magnetic deflection coils, a post-deflection accelerating electrode near the fluorescent screen, and receiver circuit. (2543, 2698)

2581 Telefunken. "Television receivers." Br. 380,602, Sept. 22, 1931. In Germany Sept. 26, 1930. Duration of fluorescence in a picture tube screen corresponds to the time of a complete scan in order to reduce flicker. See also F. Schröter, Ger. 574,085. (2200, 2531, 2666, 3050)

2582 Ives, H.E. "Electro-optical image production." U.S. 2,034,760, Sept. 27, 1930, Mar. 24, 1936. Assigned: B.T.L. Br 373,888, Sept. 16, 1931 (E.R.P.). Multiple lamps, lens disk and optical system for simultaneous multichannel transmission of different areas or for reproduction in color. Reference to Br. 315,308 (1338). (2510, 2603)

2583 Dunlap, O.E., Jr. "Heard and seen at the show." N.Y.T. IX, 9 (Sept. 28): 1–3. Review of the Radio World's Fair, New York, Sept. 22–27. "There was less television at the show this year than a year ago." A Jenkins receiver was on display. (2090, 2539, 2700, 3108)

2584 Kette, G. "Fernsehen auf der Berliner Funkausstellung 1930" [Television at the Berlin Radio Exhibition 1930]. FERN. 1 (Oct.): 433–46. 20 illus. Apparatus of the German Postal Service, Fernseh A.-G., Telehor A.-G. and amateur equipment. (2172, 2362, 2595, 2982)

2585 Busse, Ernest. "Geht's mit Ultrakurzwellen?" [Does it work with ultra-short waves?]. FERN. 1 (Oct.): 446–8. Television transmission on the ultra-short waves. See Ardenne (2553 and 2717). (3132)

2586 Okolicsányi, F. v. "Die Spiegelschraube, ein neuer Bildzerleger" [The mirror screw, a new picture decomposer]. FERN. 1 (Oct.): 448–52. 12 illus. Development of mirror screw scanning equipment. (2535, 2625)

2587 Thun, R. "Die physikalischen Grenzen der Bildgüte beim Fernsehen" [The physical limits of picture quality]. FERN. 1 (Oct.): 452–7. (2410, 2621)

2588 Neuburger, A. "Fernsehen in Lebensgrösse auf der Leinwand" [Television in life size on the screen]. FERN. 1 (Oct): 460–3. 3 illus. Alexanderson's system (G.E.) with large screen. (2515, 2559, 2628, 2723)

2589 Noack, F. "Die Bedeutung der Wellenlänge für das Fernsehen" [The importance of wavelength for television]. FERN. 1 (Oct): 463–7. (2518, 2591)

2590 Lescarboura, A.C. "Television crawls ahead." PROJ. ENG. 2 (Oct.): 15, 16, 19. 2 illus. General comments on progress, attitude of the radio industry, commercial television, picture size and quality. (2413, 2722)

2591 Noack, F. "Television in twelve colors." RADIO-CRAFT 2 (Oct.): 212, 213, 238, 239. 3 photos, 3 diags. Systems by Ahronheim and Fries. (2420, 2589, 3303, 3495)

2592 Jenkins, C.F. "Television systems." J. SMPE 15 (Oct): 445–50. Persistence of vision, motion pictures, television, radio movies. (2560, 2754)

2593 Chapple, H.J.B. "My first television image." TELEV. 3 (Oct.): 316, 317. 2 photos. Apparatus, experiments, results, and comments. (2528, 2566, 2596, 2762)

2594 Garside, C. P. "The Kerr cell." TELEV. 3 (Oct.): 391–21. Photo, 2 graphs. Light source, light valve requirements, cell and neon lamp, principles of operation, applications in television.

2595 Gradenwitz, A. "Television at the Berlin Radio Exhibition." TELEV. 3 (Oct.): 327, 328. 2 photos. Films were transmitted from Witzleben on 115 m during the show (Aug. 22–31) for display on receivers. The Post Office exhibited a light-spot transmitter constructed by Fernseh A.-G. A universal receiver by Telehor A.-G.. with replaceable disks to suit German and British transmission was on show, as was a kit of parts. The company also exhibited a small lens-disk projection receiver that produced images about 15 by 20 cm. Fernseh A.-G. displayed a variety of apparatus including a 67-hole disk transmitter and a receiver to suit, disk receivers with pictures about 6 by 9 cm, a compact mirror drum receiver with a screen about 9 by 12 cm, a sound film transmitter designed for 25 frames per second, receiver kits and Baird receivers. Telefunken did not exhibit their apparatus. (2420, 2584, 2598, 2727)

2596 Woodford, J.W. "Television for the beginner. Pt. 10." TELEV. 3 (Oct.): 329–31. 3 photos, 2 diags. (2564, 2593, 2597, 2639)

2597 "The enthusiast sees it through." TELEV. 3 (Oct.): 332–5. 3 photos, 4 diags. (2596, 2637)

2598 "The exhibit of the Fernseh A.G. as shown at the Berlin Radio Exhibition." TELEV. 3 (Oct.): 338–40. 5 photos. Special transmitter for the German Post Office, sound film transmitter, disk, and mirror drum receivers. (2265, 2552, 2595, 2623, 2727, 3039)

2599 Reeve, A.S. "The utilitarian aspects of television." TELEV. 3 (Oct.): 352. (1741)

2600 "Television from New York." TIMES (Oct. 1): 13e. Letter by Douglas Walters confirming reception of recognizable images. (2575)

2601 Nicolson, A.M. "Television mirror system." U.S. 2,006,812, Oct. 1, 1930, July 2, 1935. Assigned: Comm. Pats. Br. 371,612, May 1, 1931. Zigzag electrode matrix, arc discharges, electron tube circuits. References to Br. 360,470 (2066), 360,941 (2383). (2533, 2702)

2602 "Foresees television held to small areas." N.Y.T. 13 (Oct. 4): 8. Views of Merril A. Trainer (1905–1978) (G.E.) before the FRC. (2462, 2610, 3510)

2603 Ives, H.E. "Electro-optical system." U.S. 1,874,191, Oct. 4, 1930, Aug. 30, 1932. Assigned: B.T.L. Br. 390,158, Sept. 28, 1931 (E.R.P.). Color system with ridged film, slotted disk, spiral disk, and half-silvered mirrors. Reference to Br. 335,638 (1010). (2582, 2606)

2604 "Seeing by radio is inevitable. Says Shumaker, who calls combination sound-sight receivers logical and certain to come, but not tomorrow." N.Y.T. X, 11 (Oct. 5): 6–8. Comments by E.E. Shumaker, president of RCA-Victor. (2627)

2605 Vermillion, Charles O. "Television." U.S. 1,826,332, Oct. 8, 1930, Oct, 6, 1931. Assigned: Wired Radio. Single spiral disk and gears.

2606 Ives, H.E. "Electro-optical system." U.S. 2,001,730, Oct. 11, 1930, May 21, 1935. Assigned: B.T.L. Film transmission with disk, slotted mask, optical screen, and phototubes sensitive to different colors. (2603, 2608)

2607 "Columbia looks ahead to television progress." N.Y.T. IX, 11 (Oct. 12): 6. Columbia Broadcasting Co. (1793, 2866)

2608 Ives, H.E. "Electro-optical system." U.S. 2,017,659, Oct. 13, 1930, renewed Mar. 22, Oct. 15, 1935. Assigned: B.T.L. Three-channel disk system with separate phototubes, amplifiers, and glow discharge lamps to provide images in color for projection onto a screen or for direct viewing. References to allied U.S. patents: 1,878,147 (1046), 2,007,651 (2703), 1,918,309 (2330), 1,999,376 (2341), 1,874,191 (2603), 2,001,730 (2606). (2616)

2609 Huffman, C.E. "Electro-optical system." U.S. 2,017,901, Oct. 18, 1930, Oct. 22, 1935. Scanning disk, film scan, and screen to produce intermittent light. (2193, 3035)

2610 "Television undefined." N.Y.T. X, 11 (Oct. 19): 8. FRC to give a definition. (2602, 2658)

2611 Aspden, R.L. "Television." Br. 365,632, Oct. 20, 1930. Five-circuit system for direct pickup or film with multiple-track scanning drums, magnetic or wax storage of image signals and sound arranged for serial transmission to conserve bandwidth, and a rotating screen for color, with variations. (1719, 2915)

2612 Walton, G.W. "Television." Br. 369,644, Oct. 20, 1930. Recording system including multiple receivers which may be color selective. Reference to Br. 328,786 (1542). (1748, 2652)

2613 Stocker, Arthur C. "Synchronization in television and facsimile transmission system." U.S. 1,824,635, Oct. 21, 1930, Sept. 22, 1931. Assigned: G.E. Network with delay circuit.

2614 Schmidling, G.T. "Television transmitting system." U.S. 1,933,392, Oct. 25, 1930, Oct. 31, 1933. Two disks, each with a spiral of apertures, are spaced apart and driven via a chain by a sync motor. One disk scans the object with a projected light spot, the other picks up the reflected light. Two or more sets of double-disk scanners may be connected via a distributor to a final amplifier. (1784)

2615 "Radio City is no dream, but a practical scheme." N.Y.T. IX, 11 (Oct. 26): 4, 5. Comments on radio and television by Merlin Hall Aylesworth, president of NBC. (2779)

2616 Ives, H.E. "Television from a color movie." SCIENCE 72 (Oct. 31): Supp. 10, 11. On a speech at a meeting of the Optical Society of America, University of Virginia. (2608, 2646)

2617 Comp. Gaz. "Television receivers." Br. 372,168, July 21, 1931. In France Oct. 31, 1930. Disk and mirrors. Addition to Br. 364,376 (2237). (2337, 2643)

2618 Wotton, E. "Television." Br. 364,231, Oct. 31, 1930. A ring-shaped spirally twisted lens scanner. (2619)

2619 Wotton, E. "Television." Br. 364,232, Oct. 31, 1930. Spiral mirror scanner. (2618)

2620 Wiedemann, F. "Der Einfluss der Bildpunktzahl auf die Güte von Fernsehbildern" [The influence of the number of picture points on the quality of television pictures]. FERN. 1 (Nov.–Dec): 481–7. 7 illus. Analysis of image points and quality. Note: Issues No. 11 and 12 combined. (2715)

2621 Thun, R. "Die technischen Grenzen der Bildgüte des Fernsehens" [The technical limits of picture quality in television]. FERN. 1 (Nov.): 488–95. (2587, 2978)

2622 Kirschstein, F. "Glimmlampe als Fernsehlichtrelais" [Glow lamp as television light-relay]. FERN. 1 (Nov.): 495–501. (2514, 2843)

2623 Schubert, Georg. "Schaltung und Aufbau des Nipkowscheibenempfängers der Fernseh A.G" [Circuit and arrangement of the Nipkow disk receiver of Fernseh A.G.]. FERN. 1 (Nov.): 502–7. 7 illus. (2598, 2813, 2831)

2624 Krawinkel, G. "Bild und Ton beim Fernsehen" [Picture and sound in television]. FERN. 1 (Nov.): 507–13. 13 illus. (2552, 3377)

2625 Okolicsányi, F. v. "Uber die Helligkeit der Fernsehbilder" [About the luminosity of television pictures]. FERN. 1 (Nov.): 513, 514. Illus. (2586, 2975)

2626 Perchermeier, E. "Betrachtungen und Versuche über das Flimmern beim Fernsehen" [Observations and experiments on flickering in television]. FERN. 1 (Nov.): 515–8. 3 illus. Flickering and luminosity. (2552, 3131)

2627 Shumaker, E.E. "Television." PROJ. ENG. 2 (Nov.): 11. President of RCA-Victor on current status. (2604)

2628 Manning, E.L. "Photoelectric cells, scanning discs, tiny motors and tube-current meters, new tools for research." PROJ. ENG. 2 (Nov.): 20, 24. On equipment used in the demonstration at Schenectady. (2588, 2752)

2629 "Television projected in three dimensions." RADIO-CRAFT 2 (Nov.): 277. Diag. Proposal of Leslie Gould. (3165)

2630 Wald, G. "A new self-contained television reproducer." RADIO-CRAFT 2 (Nov.): 277, 306. 3 diags. U.S. 1,754,491 (1810). (2443)

2631 "British television work." RADIO-CRAFT 2 (Nov.): 306, 307. The BBC play, July 14. (2530, 2900)

2632 "Television now taught in technical schools." RADIO N. 12 (Nov.): 417. 2 photos. Coyne Electrical School. (2663)

2633 "Invents multiplex television system." RADIO N. 12 (Nov.): 471. Note on C.L. Davis receiver, a glass screen with parallel wires in gases, no disk or moving parts. (2504)

2634 Dinsdale, A. "Television needs new ideas—and less ballyhoo." SCI. AM. 143 (Nov.): 366–8. (2506, 2665)

2635 "Television put to its first commercial use!" TELEV. 3 (Nov.): 354. Full-page advertisement by Eugène Ltd. on their exhibit at the Hairdressing Fair of Fashion at Olympia, Nov. 5–13. "Visitors will be able to see an actual demonstration of the famous Eugène Method transmitted and received by Baird Television." (2573, 2636, 2671)

2636 Moseley, S.A. "The big screen in Germany." TELEV. 3 (Nov.): 358–60. 3 photos, one a portrait of Dr. Paul Goerz, and another of a group including Paul Nipkow. Report on the Baird demonstration at the Scala music hall in Berlin. Apparatus, problems, performances, and extracts from correspondents. (2561, 2635, 2638, 2667)

2637 "The enthusiast sees it through." TELEV. 3 (Nov.): 365–7. Photo, 2 diags. (2597, 2639)

2638 Banks, G.B. "Working the large screen in Berlin." TELEV. 3 (Nov.): 370, 371. 3 photos. Technical set-up problems. (2483, 2636, 2640, 2797)

2639 Woodford, J.W. "Television for the beginner. Pt. 11." TELEV. 3 (Nov.): 380–2. 2 photos, 2 diags. (2596, 2637, 2668, 2669)

2640 "Baird television at the Olympia Radio Exhibition." TELEV. 3 (Nov.): 384. Photo of Baird Co. stand. A temporary studio was set up at the premises of W.H. Oates. "Some 14,000 interested people made the journey from Olympia (a distance of about half a mile)." (1587, 2638, 2650, 3116)

2641 Goldsmith, A.N. "Television for the home is possible by 1940." N.Y.T. IX, 9 (Nov. 2): 1–3. Various predictions on radio and electronics. (2542, 2821)

2642 "Broadcasting evolved from the chaos of war. Davis describes events that led to first program—he looks ahead to television—future is untapped." N.Y.T. IX, 9 (Nov. 2): 7, 8. Comments by H.P. Davis, vice president, Westinghouse Co. "Undoubtedly we will have television. Then sight will have been added to sound with all the vast possibilities that this field develops." (1579)

2643 Comp. Gaz. "Television." Br. 373,539, Nov.4, 1931. In France Nov. 4, 1930. Mirror drum with fixed mirrors and lenses. (2617, 2659)

2644 Short, Donald William. "Scanning method and apparatus." U.S. 1,941,628, Nov. 4, 1930, Jan. 2, 1934. Assigned: Jenkins Television. Disks and color floodlighting. (3031)

2645 "Television shows standing in Lewis-McCormick race." N.Y.T. 7 (Nov. 5): 5. "Television station W9XAP put on the air tonight what was believed to be the first televised returns in a political election. Images of charts showing the progress of the Senatorial race were sent out from the station, which is operated by The Daily News." Election in Chicago, Nov. 4. (2551, 2677)

2646 Ives, H.E. "Electro-optical system." U.S. 1,970,310, Nov. 7, 1930, Aug. 14, 1934. Assigned: B.T.L. Receiver disk with a double spiral of prisms at different angles, two lamps and commutator to energize the lamps in alternate sequence. (2616, 2713)

2647 Replogle, D.E. "Electrical image transmission." U.S. 1,915,385, Nov. 7, 1930, June 27, 1933. Assigned: Jenkins Television. Disk, double light pickup, mixer. Intended to control shadow effects and, with filters, to control color. (2522, 2688)

2648 Secrest, J.D. "Eager eyes focused on television films." N.Y.T. X, 12 (Nov. 9): 1–4. "Two industries are preparing to capitalize

2649 Hudec, Erich. "Television." Br. 395,373, Nov. 10, 1931. In Germany, Nov. 11, 1930. Sync circuits, including picture tube receiver. (2716)

2650 Baird, J.L., and Baird Television Ltd. "Television." Br. 365,241, Nov. 12, 1930, Jan. 21, 1932. U.S. 2,056,761, Nov. 10, 1931, Oct. 6, 1936. A two-way system with infrared scanning and simultaneous reproduction of the images at each station. Disk with a spiral of holes and a spiral of lenses; or a mirror drum, disk and lamp; or two side-by-side mirror drums with a disk, and variations, intended for single-channel transmission with different frequencies. Reference to Br. 288,882 (798). (2640, 2667)

2651 Nakken, T.H. "Television." U.S. 1,991,409, Nov.12, 1930, Feb. 19, 1935. Assigned: Nakken Pat. Corp. Single-spiral disk and interrupter circuit with sync signals interposed with the picture signals. (1370)

2652 Walton, G.W. "Television." U.S. 2,086,833, Oct. 30, 1931, July 13, 1937. In Germany Nov. 12, 1930. Control currents for sync, phasing, and framing transmitted with the picture signals. (2612, 2750)

2653 Ardenne, M. v. "Television receiver." Br. 381,750, Nov. 16, 1931. In Germany Nov. 17, 1930. Picture tube and circuits. (2553, 2657)

2654 Gray, F. "Electro-optical system." U.S. 1,873,387, Nov. 17, 1930, Aug. 23, 1932. Assigned: B.T.L. Film or strip scanner with disk. (2547, 2682)

2655 Wilson, R.G., and A.A. Waters. "Synchronous movements." Br. 366,622, Nov. 17, 1930. Sync motor with floating field system for television. (2242, 2313, 2743)

2656 Gramophone Co. and C.O. Browne. "Electrical transmission of images." Br. 362,144, Nov. 21, 1930, Dec. 3, 1931. (Rights relinquished.) A five-channel zone system for film transmission. Light from the image is projected via a reflecting prism through lenses arranged in a helical path on a drum, thence through fixed apertures onto 5 phototubes. Receiver has a mirror drum, arc lamp, 5 Kerr cells, and lenses for screen projection. Connections by 7 wire circuits, including sound and sync. The apparatus was demonstrated early in January 1931. (2476, 2934)

2657 Ardenne, M. v. "Preventing variation in the speed of the electrons in the case of Braun tubes." U.S. 1,993,468, Nov. 23, 1931, Mar. 5, 1935. Assigned: D.S. Loewe. Br. 379,923, Nov. 23, 1931. In Germany Nov. 22, 1930. Anode supply for a picture tube is arranged to vary in phase opposition to changes of beam intensity. (2653, 2692)

2658 "Commission calls for conference to deal with television problems." N.Y.T. IX, 16 (Nov. 23): 2, 3. Sixteen companies invited to attend FRC meeting, Dec. 13, to consider commercial television broadcasting and use of ultra-high frequencies beyond the present 23,000-kc band. (2610, 2680)

2659 Comp. Gaz. "Television." Br. 373,540, Nov. 10, 1931. In France Nov. 26, 1930. Scanning with a vibrating mirror and a series of fixed mirrors. Addition to Br. 373,539 (2643). (2807)

2660 Keith, C.R. "Television receiver." Br. 367,911, Nov. 29, 1930 (E.R.P.). Galvanometer light valve.

2661 "Television faces hit skyscrapers and call for electrical 'surgery.'" N.Y.T. X, 10 (Nov. 30): 1, 2. Effects on transmissions.

2662 Farnsworth, P.T. "An electrical scanning system for television. Another vacuum-tube development." RADIO-CRAFT 2 (Dec.): 346–9. 4 photos, 6 diags. See also RADIO INDUSTRIES 5 (Nov.): 386–9. (2558, 2674)

2663 Lewis, Harold C. "Actual television now taught in school." RADIO-CRAFT 2 (Dec.): 350, 351. 3 photos. Account by the president, Coyne Electrical School, Chicago. (2632)

2664 Nason, C.H.W. "A new synchronizer for a television receiver." RADIO-CRAFT 2 (Dec.): 351, 362. Diag. Phonic wheel. (2308, 2895)

2665 Dinsdale, A. "Why television images split." SCI. & INV. 18 (Dec.): 702, 761, 763. 6 illus. (2634, 2725)

2666 Schröter, F. "The history of the neon lamp's development." TELEV. 3 (Dec.): 396–8. 4 photos. Extracts from FERNSEHEN, June (2406). (2581, 2737)

2667 Moseley, S.A. "The big screen in Paris." TELEV. 3 (Dec.): 405–7. (2636, 2650, 2671, 2761)

2668 "The enthusiast sees it through." TELEV. 3 (Dec.): 408, 409. (2639, 2669)

2669 Woodford, J.W. "Television for the beginner. Pt. 12." TELEV. 3 (Dec.): 423–5. 3 photos. (2639, 2668, 2728)

2670 "Television experiments in Capetown." TELEV. 3 (Dec.): 430, 431. Photo. Account of apparatus by H.J.R. Rieder.

2671 "Television at recent exhibitions." TELEV. 3 (Dec.): 431. Notes on the Hairdressers' Exhibition and Fair of Fashion, Olympia, Nov. 5–13, and use of Baird equipment for the first commercial by Eugène Ltd. (2635), and on Baird demonstrations at the Bachelor Girls' Exhibition, New Horticultural Hall, Westminster, Nov. 12. (2635, 2667, 2681)

2672 Barthélemy, R. "Système de télévision comportant, en particulier, un dispositif de synchronisation et de mise en phase automatique" [Television system including, in particular, a device for automatic synchronisation and phasing]. C.R. 191 (Dec. 1): 1051–3. See also GENIE CIVIL 97 (Dec. 20): 681; EXP. W. 8 (Feb. 1931): 102. (2389, 2675)

2673 Koller, L.R. "Photoelectric emission from thin films of caesium." PHYS. REV. 36 (Dec. 1): 1639–47. 8 graphs, 2 diags., 8 refs. A highly photosensitive surface obtained by treating caesium with oxygen. (1500)

2674 "Declares new tube solves television." N.Y.T. 24 (Dec. 4): 2. Farnsworth claimed success in obtaining a 300-line picture on a new cathode-ray tube and said "the system would require frequency bands no wider than those used for broadcasting." (2662, 2676)

2675 Barthélemy, R. "Gaseous luminous lamp." U.S. 2,045,288, Nov. 30, 1931, June 23, 1936. Assigned: Comp. Gaz. Br. 384,086, Dec. 4, 1931. In France Dec. 4, 1930. Two-electrode gas tube inside a polished tube as a light source for a television receiver. References to Br. 236,915 (arc lamps), 373,539 (2643), 373,540 (2659). (2672, 2690)

2676 Farnsworth, P.T. "Pulse transmission." U.S. 2,026,379, Dec. 4, 1930, Dec. 31, 1935. Assigned: Television Labs. Br. 390,565, Nov. 30, 1931. Waveform generation. Modification of Br. 368,309 (2548), 368,721 (2549). (2674, 2685)

2677 "Television images flash in Chicago as police watch the performance." N.Y.T. X, 12 (Dec. 7): 7. Demonstration by Western Television Corp. from station W9XAP to show application for police work. (2645, 2825)

2678 Cunningham, Henry. "Production of television images." U.S. 2,012,270, Dec. 8, 1931, Aug. 27, 1935. In Germany Dec. 8, 1930. Electrochemical method with scanning disk.

2679 Ross, Oscar A. "Method of scanning." U.S. 2,002,678, Dec. 9, 1930, May 28, 1935. Film scanning with vibrating mirrors, mask, two light sources, and optical paths.

2680 "Television and sound broadcasting." SCIENCE 72 (Dec. 12): Supp. 12. Recommendations by leading television engineers to the FRC. (2658, 2684)

2681 "Baird Television." TIMES (Dec. 13): 19b. Company notice for year ended June 30. (2671, 2735)

2682 Gray, F. "Electro-optical system." U.S. 2,063,998, Dec. 13, 1930, Dec. 15, 1936. Assigned: B.T.L. Br. 393,657, Dec. 12, 1931 (E.R.P.). Two-channel transmission, split scanning, disks with lenses and holes, drums, distributor, multiple phototubes, rotating strip lamps. Adaptable for single-channel working and for transmitting motion picture film. Sync according to Br. 376,309 (2341). Addition, Br. 393,950 (2699). (2654)

2683 Pajes, Wolf S. "Electro-optical system." U.S. 1,961,706, Dec. 13, 1930, June 5, 1934. Assigned: RCA. Scanning disk, Kerr cell with multiple reflecting prism of crystalline copper oxide, optical system, electromagnetic control. (2805)

2684 "Television broadcasters get new wave lengths." N.Y.T. X, 17 (Dec. 14): 3. List of 19 stations showing frequencies assigned by the FRC. (2680, 2758)

2685 "A radio idea from the West. Farnsworth television inventor from California, explains his image receiver—he believes scenic broadcasts are possible." N.Y.T. X, 24 (Dec. 14): 6–8. General description of the improved cathode-ray system and possibilities for transmitting outside scenes. (2676, 2800)

2686 Prinz, D. "Cathode ray intensity control system." U.S. 2,011,260, Dec. 15, 1931, Aug. 13, 1935. Assigned: Telefunken. In Germany Dec. 15, 1930. Picture tube and circuit. (2329, 2803)

2687 Bayer, Joseph Verne. "Fog penetrating televisor." U.S. 1,876,272, Dec. 16, 1930, Sept. 6, 1932.

2688 Replogle, D.E. "Electro-optical system." U.S. 1,914,580, Dec. 16, 1930, June 20, 1933. Assigned: Jenkins Television. Disk and film scan. (2647, 2864)

2689 McCreary, H.J. "Television." U.S. 1,849,679, Dec. 18, 1930, Mar. 15, 1932. Assigned: Associated Electric Labs. Divided from U.S. 1,978,684 (1606). Cathode-ray tube and neon tube oscillators. (2288)

2690 Barthélemy, R. "Receiving apparatus for television." U.S. 2,050,411, Dec. 16, 1931, Aug. 11, 1936. Assigned: Comp. Gaz. Br. 394,341, Dec. 21, 1931. In France Dec. 20, 1930. Glow discharge tube with ring anode inside a cathode-ray tube separated by a semi-conductive partition. (2675, 2720)

2691 "Experimental vision broadcaster ready for WABC early in 1931." N.Y.T. IX, 10 (Dec. 21): 1, 2. (2540, 3296)

2692 Ardenne, M. v. "Television process." U.S. 2,112,684, Dec. 23, 1931, Mar. 29, 1938. Assigned: D.S. Loewe. Br. 387,087, Dec. 21, 1931. In Germany Dec. 22, 1930. Cathode-ray tube and method of displaced line scanning with the beginning of each frame shifted. (2657, 2693)

2693 Ardenne, M. v. "Television." Br. 391,531, Dec. 21, 1931. In Germany Dec. 22, 1930. Picture tube with image and line frequency scanning circuits and frequency multiplier. (2692, 2694)

2694 Loewe, S., and M. v. Ardenne. "Television reception device." U.S. 2,053,526, Dec. 23, 1931, Sept. 8, 1936. Assigned: D.S. Loewe by von Ardenne. Br. 391,905, Dec. 21, 1931. In Germany Dec. 22, 1930. Picture tube assembly with enclosure that masks the edges of the picture to hide marginal distortion. (2085, 2693, 2695, 2913)

2695 Ardenne, M. v. "Television." Br. 388,524, Dec. 21, 1931. In Germany Dec. 23, 1930. Scanning signals derived from transmitter. Reference to Br. 387,640 (2357). (2694, 2696)

2696 Ardenne, M. v. "Television reception arrangement with Braun tubes." U.S. 2,100,704, Dec. 23, 1931, Nov. 30, 1937. Assigned: D.S. Loewe. Br. 396,051, Dec. 21, 1931. In Germany Dec. 23, 1930. Relates to a picture tube with beam concentrating, intensity control, and deflection electrodes, with circuit. (2695, 2697)

2697 Ardenne, M. v. "Television receivers." Br. 399,160, Dec. 21, 1931. In Germany Dec. 23, 1930. Similar to Br. 396,051 (2696). (2717)

2698 Zworykin, V.K. "Television." U.S. 2,084,364, Dec. 24, 1930, June 22, 1937. Assigned: RCA. Br. 384,094, Dec. 16, 1931 (Marconi's). Picture tube receiver with scanning coils, details of electrode assembly, and circuit operation. (2580, 2712)

2699 Gray, F. "Electro-optical system." U.S. 2,031,598, Dec. 27, 1930, Feb. 25, 1936. Assigned: B.T.L. Br. 393,950, Dec. 14, 1931 (E.R.P.). Addition to Br. 393,657 (2682). Two-channel system, disk transmitter and receiver with disk, multielectrode glow lamp, and distributors for the simultaneous reproduction of different areas. References to Br. 376,309 (2341), 385,591 (2338). (2742)

2700 Dunlap, O.E. Jr. "Radio's destiny in 1931 points toward television. Some expect new year will see more of television." N.Y.T. IX 8 (Dec. 28): 1–3. "It is expected that 1931 will see television move close to the home, if not into it." (2583, 3108)

2701 McGill, William J., and Edward L. Stalnecker. "Radio and television cabinet." U.S. 1,831,817, Dec. 30, 1930, Nov. 17, 1931. Recessed viewing screen.

2702 Nicolson, A.M. "Panoramic television system." U.S. 1,985,684, Dec. 30, 1930, Dec. 25, 1934. Assigned: Comm. Pats. Br. 388,071, Aug. 19, 1931. A honeycombed cylinder surrounds a circular assembly of zigzag rail electrodes. References to Br. 360,470 (2066) for sync and control of the moving arc, and to 360,941 (2383). (2601, 2774)

2703 Aisberg, Eugène. LA TRANSMISSION DES IMAGES: PRINCIPES FONDAMENTAUX DE LA PHOTOTELEGRAPHE ET DE LA TELEVISION [The transmission of images: fundamental principles of the phototelegraph and television]. Paris: Etienne Chiron, 1930. 172 pp., 82 illus. Preface by E. Belin. Popular explanation of principles and practices with an appendix on Belin's system. (2882)

2704 Anderson, John Spence (ed.). PHOTOELECTRIC CELLS AND THEIR APPLICATIONS. London: Physical and Optical Societies, 1930. 236 pp., illus.

2705 Barnard, G.P. THE SELENIUM CELL: ITS PROPERTIES AND APPLICATIONS. London: Constable; New York: Richard R. Smith, 1930. xxix + 331 pp., 258 illus. Preface by J.W.T. Walsh. Portrait, Willoughby Smith. This classic work thoroughly covers all aspects and provides full documentation with extensive references in all chapters. Applications for selenium cells in talking films, telephotography, and television are treated in Chap. 9, pp. 260–91. List of books and reviews, pp. 293–5, and 4 other appendixes. (2272)

2706 Benson, T.W. FUNDAMENTALS OF TELEVISION. New York: Mancell, 1930. xvii + 145 pp., illus. (1975)

2707 Hutchinson, Robert William. EASY LESSONS IN TELEVISION. London: W.B. Clive, University Tutorial Press, 1930. vii + 175 pp., 129 illus.

2708 Philip, Charles C. TELEVISION FOR ALL: A SIMPLE EXPLANATION OF TELEVISION FOR THE GENERAL PUBLIC. London: Percival Marshall, 1930. 82 pp., 8 diags. Basics, systems, Noctovision, television in color, and stereoscopic television.

2709 Stranger, Ralph (Ralph Judson). SEEING BY WIRELESS. London: Newnes, 1930, 63 pp.

2710 Swinton, A.A.C. AUTOBIOGRAPHICAL AND OTHER WRITINGS. London: Longmans, Green, 1930. ix + 181 pp., 18 plates. (2155)

2711 Winckel, Fritz Wilhelm. TECHNIK UND AUFGABEN DES FERNSEHENS, ETC. [Technique and tasks of television, etc.]. Berlin: Rothgiesser & Diesing, 1930. 74 pp., 65 illus. (3522)

2712 Zworykin, V.K., and Earl De Witt Wilson. PHOTOCELLS AND THEIR APPLICATION. New York: John Wiley; London: Chapman & Hall, 1930. xi + 209 pp., illus. Technical and practical aspects of the modern "electric eye," including applications in sound movies, facsimile, and television. 2nd ed. 1932. (2698, 2847)

CHAPTER 11

BIG PICTURES AND TINY BEAMS: 1931

The events of 1931 present a kaleidoscopic pattern of progress and change. Despite the numbing effects of commercial decline in the continued slide toward economic depression, together with fading hopes of a stronger public market, television displayed a remarkable tenacity and a vitality that stemmed more from technological drive than anything else. Visible signs were the increase of regular broadcasts and numerous instances where the screen was applied for publicity, to arouse human interest, or to show potential commercial value. Most of these events occurred in the United States where domestic receivers and big-screen displays were brought to public view. The continued rise of interest and accomplishment in Germany was, however, of more significance, especially with the introduction of picture tubes and other technical improvements that would take the lead in the immediate future.

Publishing activities remained at the same overall level with some noticeable changes in particular sources. The total entries for news items and periodicals amount to 317, essentially the same as for 1930. The increase in American items from 131 to 171 is mainly due to the larger number of entries from the NEW YORK TIMES, up at 108 from 57. There is one entry from the bimonthly TELEVISION NEWS. Other articles in this short-lived periodical have been omitted since they are, in the main, reprints or variations of other material that is listed. The British total of 119 is down from 133, with 70 entries from TELEVISION compared with 110, a drop that is compensated in part by 15 items from the new JOURNAL OF THE TELEVISION SOCIETY and increases in the entries from the ELECTRICIAN and WIRELESS WORLD. German entries are also down at 24, a drop of 33 largely because FERNSEHEN changed from a monthly to a quarterly publication. Entries from French sources (3) are the same as for 1930.

As in previous years, Baird and his company enjoyed the largest share of the news, both at home and in the United States. Early in January he demonstrated a multichannel zone system employing 30-line mirror drums in which three images were projected side by side onto a small ground-glass screen. He also showed a much more brilliant picture obtained from a directly modulated arc. On May 8 a street scene in Long Acre was picked up by a transmitter in a van parked outside the laboratory and transmitted to the studio. The most newsworthy event was the transmission of scenes from the Derby racecourse at Epsom Downs via the BBC station on June 3, an achievement that fulfilled Baird's promise made five years before. In mid-August Moseley, then in New York, said the company had plans to mass-produce receivers in the United States, a grandiose scheme similar to and just as premature as the one announced by Hutchinson early in 1926. At the same time it was declared that Baird transmissions would be made through station WMCA, a plan that was pursued but which eventually came to naught.

The lack of a commercial basis for television services in the United States did not deter most of the participants in their plans for development. The Jenkins Television Corporation began weekday broadcasts from station W2XCR at the end of January. De Forest's intentions to start independent work, which he had revealed the previous summer, culminated in the formation of his new company, American Television Laboratories, and the beginning of regular broadcasts through station W2XCD on February 23. At that time there was said to be a nation-wide audience of more than 10,000 television receivers. Two months later station W2XCR began daily broadcasts, which were called New York City's first on a regular schedule. This statement was misleading, since de Forest was earlier; besides, Gernsback's station WRNY had started regular (but short-term) visual broadcasts in August 1928. Early in July the National Broadcasting Company made public their plans for an experimental station in the Empire State Building, a feature of which was the erection of an antenna on the mooring mast. The Columbia Broadcasting System formally opened their station W2XAB later that month, which brought New York's total of visual transmitters to six.

A succession of other events kept television in the news, some intended to show the possibilities of the medium and others for publicity, which was constantly required to promote the sale of domestic receivers. A display of stock market prices on the screen in Chicago was reported at the end of January. The Bell Labs two-way system was demonstrated as an aid for bank personnel in February, and again for a clothing sale on April 24. Station W2XCR included some enterprising features in their broadcasts, beginning with a wedding ceremony in the studio early in May. This was followed by a fashion show later that month and by piano lessons which were given on August 1. In a million-dollar display, Columbia presented a broadcast view of the prestigious Cartier gems on September 8.

A long-distance test by General Electric was reported during February, with reception by the BBC in Britain and by Telefunken in Germany. On a more modest scale, images were received aboard the steamship Leviathan at sea on July 23, with signals from Boston and Washington of varying quality. This was said to be the first such test to a vessel, although Baird had demonstrated reception aboard the S.S. Berengaria at a much greater distance in March 1928. Similar transmissions were made to the S.S. Vulcania in September from stations in Boston, New York, and Passaic, New Jersey, with reception of clear images up to 50 miles.

The most surprising demonstrations were put on by Sanabria, who, having been out of the news for a couple of years, was now working independently on big-screen displays. He demonstrated a 6-foot screen at the radio trade show in Chicago during June, with the expectation of increasing the size at least fourfold. During the radio show at Madison Square Garden in September his giant 10-foot screen—a 350-pound ground-glass panel hanging above the booths—became a startling focal point as well as a key attraction for the crowds. The following month Sanabria again put the giant screen on display, this time in the Broadway Theatre in New York. If television was not yet in the home on any noticeable scale, it certainly was in public view.

A brief look at other events further illustrates current developments. At the beginning of the year the Gramophone Company demonstrated their five-zone apparatus. Early in March a telecine program was put on the air by Baird through the BBC. A portable camera developed by the Baird Company was installed in a BBC studio in April but was not put in service until later. A portable camera was also developed by the de Forest and Jenkins concerns and was demonstrated September 8. Moseley conducted an interview by landline for the DAILY HERALD in May. The closer cooperation between Baird and the BBC led to the first broadcast direct from a BBC studio on August 19. The use of three cameras in a CBS studio in October was another innovation. At the end of the month NBC began experimental field tests from the new station in New York. The Don Lee organization in Los Angeles also commenced experimental broadcasts through station W6XAO in November.

During the summer the German Post Office (RPZ) conducted experimental short-wave transmissions with telecine apparatus. Station MOSPS in Moscow began test broadcasts October 1, and in mid-December the First All-Union Conference on Television was held in Leningrad. Disk transmitters and receivers, mirror drum scanners, Kerr cell modulators, photocells, telecine apparatus, and cathode-ray tubes were all being developed in the U.S.S.R. at that time, with transmission standards similar to those in Germany. Television apparatus and systems were also being developed and tested in Japan. Alexanderson demonstrated his light-beam system in Schenectady on December 22. Near the end of the month, plans for improving the service were discussed by Baird and the BBC, which was anxious for more active participation in programming and in technical developments.

Corporate patent activities and the changes that occurred can be seen in Table 17. Restrictions on research expenditures in the United States are particularly evident in the reduction of applications by Bell Labs, down seventeen from 1930. The widespread effects of the economic plunge are also apparent in the lower entries by other concerns (except RCA): Communication Patents down eight, Jenkins down seven, Farnsworth and Wired Radio both down six, and General Electric down five. On the plus side, applications by Radio Inventions rose by three, while de Forest's assignments to the American Television Laboratories brought this increase to seven. There is also one patent assigned to the Philadelphia Storage Battery Company (later known as Philco Radio and Television Corporation), and one to the National Television Corporation, both new entries. The recession did not hinder the independents, however, whose twenty-nine applications are ten more than in 1930. Altogether, the U.S. total is seventy-five, which represents a severe drop of 33 percent for the year.

Although the fall-off in trade had spread to Europe, the commercial situation in Germany had little immediate effect on technical and corporate activities. The Fernseh Company, a small concern with few employees and a limited financial base, was nevertheless the most active with twenty patent applications. Telefunken increased their filings by four. Applications by the D.S. Loewe concern amount to five, but this figure may not show the total since there are related entries, such as some by von Ardenne, for which assignments to the company are not indicated. A new corporate entry, the Nuremberg firm Suddeutsche Telefon-Apparate Kabel- und Drahtwerke A.-G., Tekade, filed three patents, and two more were filed in Britain by the IMK Syndicate. Including twenty-three individual entries, the German total is seventy-one, or twice the number for 1930. This figure is probably conservative, however, because there were undoubtedly others by individuals who did not lodge applications outside Germany.

A smaller rise occurred in Britain. Marconi's Wireless Telegraph Company, Ltd., which had started research on television in the summer of 1930, was concerned with equipment for communication purposes and not, initially, for the domestic market. Their fifteen applications boosted the British total, while the Baird Company's filings remained the same at twelve. Work on television by the Gramophone Company dwindled, partly for economic reasons and partly because of changes in the company structure. During March this concern, one of the biggest in the British radio industry, was joined by the Columbia Gramophone Company. This amalgamation formed Electric and Musical Industries, Ltd. (EMI), which was incorporated April 20. During the next few years the firm established a leading role in the development of television. With the corporate applications and twenty-three individuals the British total is fifty-three, up from forty-two in 1930.

Continued participation by the independents is shown by seventy-five applications, which constitute 37 percent of the year's total, up from 29 percent. This rise is a contrast with the reduction of 4 percent in corporate contributions. The drop in American patents is offset by the British and German increases. Including others listed, the total is 206, essentially the same as for 1930. If the average yearly increase since 1927 had been maintained, the total would have been around 245. This "loss," which appears to be a pause in technological growth, is clearly due more to adverse economic factors than to a decline of ingenuity. But the art was by now so well established that nothing but technical barriers could impede its progress.

TABLE 17   CORPORATE PATENTS

Company	1930	1931
Fernseh	2	20
RCA	17	16
*Marconi's		15
Telefunken	9	14
Baird Television	12	12
Radio Inventions	5	8
Bell Telephone Laboratories	22	5
D.S. Loewe	4	5
*American Television Laboratories		4
Comp. Gaz	9	4
Communication Patents	11	3
General Electric	8	3
Gramophone Company	7	3
*Tekade		3
*AEG		2
*IMK Syndicate		2
Farnsworth Companies	8	2
*Comp. Générale de Télévision		1
Electronic Television Company	1	1
Jenkins Companies	8	1
*National Television Corporation		1
*Philadelphia Storage Battery Company		1
Short Wave & Television Laboratory		1
Siemens & Halske		1
Siemens-Schuckertwerke		1
Westinghouse	3	1
Wired Radio	7	1
	133	131

*New entries in 1931

A survey of the patents shows a decisive change in the technology, which is particularly noticeable in the continued decline of the scanning disk and the emphasis on the mirror drum as an alternative, and in the ascendancy of cathode-ray tubes. Disks of all kinds and combinations appear in thirty-nine entries, or 19 percent, down 10 percent from 1930. Mirror drums are specified in twenty-six entries, up seventeen from the year before. Applications with mirror screws remain the same at five, two of which are from Bell Labs where Gray (2923) and Ives (2927) were apparently attracted to this new scanner. There is little change also in the use of apertured drums, cylinders, and rings, with eight entries. Optical methods of all kinds show an increase from twenty to twenty-five. This figure includes Alexanderson's proposal for light-beam transmission (3221), which, however, was preceded by others such as Sinding-Larsen's (388) with a pipe, and the Telefunken relay scheme (734). Synchronous control is implicit in most of the systems, but the entries directly related to this are down at seven from twenty.

The development and application of cathode-ray tubes had become a major objective, particularly in Germany. Of fifty-eight patents concerned with the construction and improvement of these tubes and systems employing them, there are thirty-eight of German origin. In continuing work von Ardenne was the most active with seventeen applications, including two with Loewe, some of which were assigned to the D.S. Loewe Company. There are three by Schlesinger, who was associated with von Ardenne and the Loewe concern. In a master patent (2827), von Ardenne introduced a complete cathode-ray system in which film or a subject was scanned by a flying spot from the tube face in the transmitter. A similar photo scanning method, however, had been specified earlier (566) by Zworykin. Contributions by Telefunken engineers are listed in twelve patents. There are two assigned to Allgemeine Elektricitäts Gesellschaft (A.E.G.), two to the Fernseh Company, and one each filed by Siemens & Halske and Siemens-Schuckertwerke. The latter, by Rüdenberg (2929), concerns a picture tube with lines of colored phosphors. Von Ardenne also disclosed a color picture tube (2965).

Similar work in progress in the United States is represented by eighteen entries; twelve by RCA, two by Farnsworth, and two by individuals. Another by Zworykin (3190), assigned to Westinghouse, deals with an improved photo mosaic for a camera tube, and one by Sukumlyn (2922) refers to another type of image tube. One Farnsworth patent (3008) concerns a picture tube and circuits, and the other (3009) a projection tube. Von Ardenne also covered a tube for image projection (2966). Other U.S. filings are those by Lubcke (2837) and Kwartin (2914), and there is one by Henroteau (2751) which originated in Canada. A cabinet receiver assembly with a vertical tube and a reflecting mirror in the lid, which was described earlier by Zworykin (2125), appears in two RCA entries (2865, 3096). British applications that include cathode-ray tubes are Marconi's (2877, 3004), both by Dowsett and Cadzow, and Clay's (3054).

A good deal of engineering effort was devoted to the associated circuits for controlling electron beams. In addition to the usual radio techniques, the special requirements concerned wide-band (video) amplifiers, sweep generators (also known as sawtooth, tilting, relaxation, or deflection oscillators, impulse or scanning generators), synchronizing circuits and others for controlling beam focus and brightness as well as high-voltage and bias supplies. German examples of these circuit developments are those by von Ardenne (2830, 3151, 3152, 3161), Loewe and von Ardenne (2913), Schlesinger (2921), Fernseh (3029), and Schröter (2861, 3013, 3216). Comparable American entries (all RCA) are those by Vance (2964), Tolson (2973), Ballard (3057), George and Heim (3086), Kell (3121, 3127), and Carlson (3232).

Thirteen German applications disclose features of electrode construction and tube assemblies. Three entries are by von Ardenne (2829, 2838, 2967), and there is another one (2926) in conjunction with Loewe; one is by Schlesinger (3053). Fernseh is represented by the Möllers (3030) and Schiff (3051). Five entries are by Telefunken, including one by Schröter and Michelssen (3074). The Siemens and Halske entry is by Lübcke (2910). American entries, other than those mentioned, include one by Zworykin and Batchelor (2977) and another by Batchelor (3058), both RCA. Screen materials and methods for processing them appear in four German patents: von Ardenne (2828, 3012), Schlesinger (3228), and Telefunken (3050). There is one by RCA Victor (3188) assigned to EMI. Brief as they are, these capsule references to the entries show that a solid foundation for the new cathode-ray technology was established during 1931.

Articles on cathode-ray tubes show a similar rise from twelve in 1930 to twenty-one; eight in Britain, seven in Germany, and six in the United States. There are four items by von Ardenne, one fully describing his system (2841) and two others about his work. Farnsworth also gave a full description of his system (2801) and there are four by other writers on his work. One entry by Zworykin was published in November, and a paper by Johnson on the cathode-ray oscillograph appeared in December. That month a series of papers on cathode-ray television was published by the Television Society. Developments by the RPZ are described in two entries (3131). Except for the most general references, there is no mention of the developments under way by RCA who, unlike Bell Labs and the Germans, were now intent on maintaining secrecy about their program and progress.

Film techniques were still prominent in the art, both for scanning and storage, with eight American entries, six German, and one each British and French, or three less than the previous year. The one by Schubert and Möller (3183) describes the intermediate process in a system which was highly developed by the Fernseh Company and later adopted by Baird. Again, this approach was foreshadowed by Hartley and Ives (1047). In addition to his general use of film, one von Ardenne application (3120) covers another system of this class intended for outside pickup in which intermediate film is rapidly processed ready for the transmission of images and sound on a radio link to a broadcasting station. A curious etched-film method for screen projection by de Forest (2880) was intensively developed, but it did not prove satisfactory for commercial use.

Interest in color was maintained with seven British applications and four American, in addition to the color tubes by Rüdenberg and von Ardenne. All the British filings are by independents, notably Walton with three, one of which (2782) is said to be applicable for stereo. Pattinson suggested that his complicated multifrequency arrangement (2744) could be triplicated for color. Bowtell followed up an earlier scheme (2204) in another opto-mechanical system (2812) which included color. Todd's disk and mirror drum method (2745), applicable for color, also followed a previous scheme (1541). Baker, who had a long-time interest in phototelegraphy, television, and color photography, surveyed the problems of color television in a lecture (2732) and its use in the studio (3176) and also lodged a patent on a color disk system (3180) in November. Color patents filed in the United States include one by Nicolson (2774), Leishman's (2955), Gould's lamp/drum system (3165), and a film scanning method by Colgate (3233).

Technical features under discussion chiefly concerned photoelectricity and picture quality. Six entries on photocells appeared in TELEVISION, two by Wolfson (2765) and four by Schröter (2849). Another item on photocells is by Zworykin (2984). Seven entries related to the characteristics of images and elements of picture quality are German: Wiedemann (2715), Kinne (2719), Hudec (2933, 3196), Thun (2978), Schubert (2981), and Peters (3133). General aspects are treated in three entries by Barthélemy (2720) and in one by Browne (3134). Other topics include the Kerr cell (2903), standards (3034), and design (3035).

Transmission techniques were tending toward the higher frequencies, but there is little material directly related to television in the listings. Von Ardenne discussed the matter in January (2717), a note on the Federal Radio Commission's plans concerning ultra-short waves appeared in February, and the subject was mentioned by an FRC engineer in October (3164). Experiments in Germany were carried out by Telefunken (2980) and the Post Office (3039). RCA had plans for test transmissions on the shorter waves in New York, while Baird began to contemplate similar tests for the coming year. In the meantime, the FRC still regarded television to be purely experimental and not ready for commercial expansion. In spite of this official restriction, however, there were many new applications for licenses, according to a report in August (3060). By the end of the year, about two dozen stations were licensed for experimental transmissions.

The tiny screens hitherto seen, which had grown from the size of a postage stamp up to postcard dimensions, had long been a severe point of criticism. During the year, however, screens expanded to respectable sizes for ordinary receivers and on up the scale to giant dimensions suitable for audience displays, covering a range from 4 square inches to 100 square feet. Baird's box-type receiver (3116) at the Olympia show had a small screen, only 3 by 4 inches. The Western Television Corporation's console receiver (2976) had an 8-inch screen, and a similar receiver (2993) by the Short Wave and

Television Laboratories had a screen 8 by 10 inches, which was rightly called a "fair-sized picture." Barthélemy reportedly demonstrated (2891) reception with a bigger screen, 30 by 40 cm (12 by 16 inches), and another report (3170) mentioned a larger one, 15 by 18 inches. The Gramophone Company's five-zone screen was 20 by 24 inches. In addition to Sanabria's big screens, de Forest also contemplated a big screen for theaters in his film projection system.

Before the Coliseum display the previous July, Baird had begun to favor large screens for public viewing. Commercial applications in cinemas were a distinct possibility at the time; besides, if people would not purchase home receivers, then the alternative was to attract them to a big screen in the cinema. In a lecture in February, Mitchell indicated the line of development toward large screens which, it was believed, would lead to domestic receivers with larger and more satisfactory screens. Baird had earlier demonstrated a 3 by 6 foot screen, which was shown in September, and Moseley (2939) referred to another screen twice as big as the one in the Coliseum, or about 4 by 10 feet. He also suggested that big screens could be set up in suitable street locations for advertising purposes. At a meeting in May (3134), Dowsett mentioned that work on apparatus with a 3 by 6 foot projection screen was going on in the Marconi laboratory.

Although the receivers at the radio show in Berlin (3129, 3210) had more modest screens, they were indicative of future trends, especially those with cathode-ray tubes. Three exhibitors had picture tubes on display. The screen of the Tekade tube was 4 square inches, the RPZ tube was 6 square inches, the Loewe (von Ardenne) tube had twice that area, and another RPZ disk receiver also had a screen that size. Other apparatus with larger screens (area in square inches) were a Tekade mirror screw (14), RPZ mirror wheel (16), Fernseh disk scanner (16), and a lens disk with Kerr cell (27), also RPZ.

Amateur interest appears to have lessened, since articles on home construction total twenty-three compared with thirty-five in 1930, all in TELEVISION. There are thirteen items from this periodical and ten from American monthlies, chiefly POPULAR SCIENCE and RADIO NEWS. At least six firms had kits or components available for home assembly. The Baird Company advertised a "Junior" kit in April and in October again attempted to stimulate domestic sales with price reductions for their range of products: complete Televisor, kit of parts, experimental kit, and separate components. The Short Wave and Television Laboratories advertised a kit in June, and the Jenkins Television Corporation followed suit in August. In December a Telescanner kit by Freed Television and Radio Corporation was reported, and an advertisement by the Television Manufacturing Company of American for a See-All Television kit also appeared that month. The Tekade concern displayed components at the show in Berlin; otherwise the level of participation by amateurs in Germany is not known.

Opinions on the state of the industry and its prospects in America can be seen in the entries, which include eleven surveys, ten forecasts, and eight others with mixed comments. The NEW YORK TIMES was the chief forum for these views, where criticism was expressed by Dill (2752), Lafount (2835), and Holland (3124). Lafount (2834) and King (2909) brought up the question of censorship. Expectations by leaders of the industry rose during the year from indecision in June to the possibility of improvements in September and a brighter view in December. A critical and objective review of the situation at the beginning of the year came from Dinsdale. The only consensus among these views appears to be that improvements all around were needed before television would be ready for, and be accepted by, the public.

The more hopeful pronouncements came from officials of RCA-NBC, whose opinions were based on the corporation's research program and on plans for Radio City at the Rockefeller Center in midtown New York. In February, Aylesworth declared that the RCA system would be ready for service when the new complex opened in 1934. Sarnoff spoke of the dawn of a television era, in May, and in September he predicted the theater of the home would be a fact in 1932. All this was near at hand, but Goldsmith (2821) focused his crystal lens far ahead to 1981. This spokesman for the future pictured an "electrical entertainer" in the home which would have three large screens, a keyboard for self-created music, and a color organ as well—a technical fantasy that complements de Forest's prediction (2507) of the previous year. On a more realistic scale, however, engineers were pushing the art forward toward bigger and brighter pictures with higher definition and with transmissions in the upper region of the radio-frequency spectrum.

TABLE 18   CHRONOLOGY: 1931

Jan. 2	Baird Co.	Demonstrates three-zone system and modulated arc
6	Gramophone Co.	Demonstrates five-channel film system
31	Chicago	Stock market quotations displayed
	Jenkins Corp.	Weekday broadcasts, station W2XCR
Feb. 6	Marconi's	Drum scanner
13	G.E. Co.	Report of transmissions to Berlin, Leipzig, London
23	De Forest Co.	Regular broadcasts, station W2XCD
Mar.	Farnsworth	Details of complete electronic system
9	Baird Co.	Telecine broadcast
27	von Ardenne	Complete cathode-ray system
Apr.	Baird Co.	Advertises receiver kit
13	Baird Co.	Portable disk scanner in BBC studio
15	Television Society	Third annual exhibition
20	EMI	New company incorporated
24	Bell Labs	Clothing sale by two-way system
	de Forest	Etched film system
26	Jenkins Corp.	Regular broadcasts, stations W2XCR, WGBS
	Short Wave & Television Labs.	Receiver with 8-by-10-inch screen
May 1	Jenkins Corp.	Broadcast of a wedding, station W2XCR
8	Baird Co.	Outside pickup of a street scene
13	Moseley	Interview by landline for the DAILY HERALD
19	Jenkins Corp.	Fashion show, stations W2XCR, WGBS
21	Gray	Mirror screw
29	Ives	Mirror screw
30	Rüdenberg	Color picture tube
June	Short Wave & Television Corp.	Advertises receiver and kit
3	BBC, Baird Co.	Transmits scenes from the Derby, Epsom Downs
8	Various	Displays at radio trade show, Chicago
10	Sanabria	Demonstrates 6-foot screen in Chicago
19	von Ardenne	Color picture tube
27	von Okolicsányi	Multiturn mirror screw
	Western Television Corp.	Receiver with 8-inch screen
July 9	NBC	Plans for station in the Empire State Building
21	CBS	Open station W2XAB
23	S.S. *Leviathan*	Reception at sea from Boston and Washington
Aug.	Jenkins Corp.	Advertises receivers and kits
1	Jenkins Corp.	Piano lessons, station W2XCR
19	Baird Co.	Plans for receiver production in the U.S.
	BBC, Baird Co.	Broadcast from studio at Waterloo Bridge

24	Various	Displays at Berlin Radio Show
26	Baird Co.	Plans for broadcasts through station WMCA
Sept. 8	CBS	Display of Cartier jewels, station W2XAB
	Jenkins Corp.	Portable camera for daylight pickup
	S.S. *Vulcania*	Reception at sea from Boston, New York, Passaic, N.J.
12	FRC	Considers television still experimental
18	Baird Co.	Display at the National Radio Exhibition
21	Various	Displays at the New York Radio Show
23	Baird Co.	Display at the British Association meeting, London
	Sanabria	Demonstrates 10-foot screen at Madison Square Garden
25	von Ardenne	Intermediate film system for outside broadcasts
Oct.	Baird Co.	Advertises receiver, kit, and parts
1	Moscow	Test broadcasts from station MOSPS
6	von Ardenne	Film scan with velocity modulation
15	BBC, Baird Co.	Regular transmissions during broadcasting hours
18	Baird	Broadcast talk from stations WMCA, WPCH
22	Sanabria	Demonstrates 10-foot screen at the Broadway Theater
24	CBS	Three cameras in use at station W2XAB
30	Gould	Color receiver
	RCA, NBC	Experimental field tests
Nov. 2	Baker	Color system
5	Schubert, Möller	Intermediate film system
11	Television Society	Papers on cathode-ray television
23	Don Lee	Experimental broadcasts, station W6XAO, Los Angeles
Dec.	Television Mfg. Co. of America	Advertises receiver kit
12	FRC	Annual report
18	Leningrad	First All-Union Conference on Television
19	Alexanderson	Light-beam transmission system
24	Schlesinger	Metal-backed fluorescent screen
26	Colgate	Color system for film scan
28	BBC, Baird Co.	Discussion on plans for improving the service

BIBLIOGRAPHY: 1931

2713 Ives, H.E. "A multi-channel television apparatus." B.S.T.J. 10 (Jan.) 33–45. 5 illus. Also J. OSA 21 (Jan.): 8–19. Three-channel disk system. (2646, 2721)

2714 Leithäuser, G., and K. Sohnemann. "Synchronisierung des Fernsehempfängers" [Synchronization of television receivers]. FERN. 2 (Jan.): 5–8. 4 illus.

2715 Wiedemann, F. "Uber die Beziehung zwischen Bildpunktzahl, Bildgrösse und Helligkeit bei Fernsehbildern" [On the relationship between the number of picture points, picture size and intensity in television pictures]. FERN. 2 (Jan.): 8–13. 5 illus. (2620)

2716 Hudec, E. "Die Synchronisierung von Fernsehempfangsapparaten, insbesondere bei Verwendung der Braunschen Röhre" [The synchronization of apparatus for television reception, in particular by employing the Braun tube]. FERN. 2 (Jan.): 14–28. 15 illus. (2649, 2933)

2717 Ardenne, M. v. "Geht's mit Ultrakurzwellen?" [Does it work with ultra-short waves?] FERN. 2 (Jan.): 28–31. Discussion of article by Busse (2585) and the author's article (2553). (2697, 2793)

2718 Nentwig, K. "Gleichzeitiges Fernsehen und hören" [Simultaneous television and listening]. FERN. 2 (Jan.): 31–6. 8 illus. Television and radio reception from London.

2719 Kinne, Erich, "Zur Erzielung grösserer Bildpunktzahlen beim Fernsehen" [Increasing the number of picture points in television]. FERN. 2 (Jan.): 36–8. 2 illus. On increase in lines and decrease in repetition rate with image projected on a high-persistence screen.

2720 Barthélemy, R. "L'émission en télévision" [Television transmission]. ONDE ELECT. 10 (Jan.): 5–35. 15 illus. Scanning systems, photocells, modulation, and transmission of images. (2690, 2891)

2721 Ives, H.E. "Television in color from motion picture film." J. OSA 21 (Jan.): 2–7. 4 illus. Also J. SMPE 16 (May): 535–40. Disk system with ridged film (2603). (2713, 2755)

2722 Lescarboura, A.C. "Radio television is really here." PROJ. ENG. 3 (Jan.): 16–8. Survey deals with picture detail, entertainment value, programs, films, transmission channels, and commercial promotion. (2590, 2756)

2723 Neuburger, A. "The progress of television technique." RADIO-CRAFT 2 (Jan.): 414, 415. 2 photos, 2 diags. Von Mihály's system with large scanning disk and phonic wheel sync. (2207, 2588, 2869)

2724 "British synchronizing system." RADIO-CRAFT 4 (Jan.): 414, 415. 3 diags.

2725 Dinsdale, A. "De-bunking television." RADIO N. 12 (Jan.): 592–4, 660. 5 illus. Survey of early experiments, current work with mechanical systems, basic problems and limitations, advocacy of cathode-ray method. A critical view of the state of the art. (2665, 2817)

"All the indications point inexorably towards the development of some means whereby we can achieve television by purely electronic methods. The cathode ray tube appears to offer the desired solution. But the disadvantages of the cathode ray tube, as at present manufactured, are that its first cost is high, its life is short, it requires expensive auxiliary equipment which involves rather heavy upkeep and running expense, it is difficult to focus the pencil or stream or rays to a sufficiently fine point, and make it 'stay put' at that during scanning, and the degree of illumination produced on the fluorescent screen is low.

"However, I feel confident that the ultimate solution of the television problem will be found through the medium of the cathode ray tube, but I am equally confident that by the time a complete solution is reached the cathode ray tube, as we know it today, will have been altered out of all recognition."

2726 "Television in Europe." RADIO N. 12 (Jan.): 655, 659. Brief note on Baird, Telefunken, and display in the Deutsches Museum, Munich.

2727 Gradenwitz, A. "Television in Germany today." SCI. & INV. 18 (Jan.): 807, 857. 5 photos. Fernseh and Telehor apparatus at the Berlin radio show in 1930. (2595, 2598, 2902, 3095)

2728 "The enthusiast sees it through." TELEV. 3 (Jan.): 448–50. 6 photos. (2669, 2763)

2729 Campbell, D.R. "A use for the stroboscopic effect in television." TELEV. 3 (Jan.): 459, 460, 467. Photo, 3 diags. (2565, 3084)

2730 "Aberdeen experiments in television." TELEV. 3 (Jan.): 463, 467. Photo. Reprint from the PEOPLE'S JOURNAL, Nov. 29.

2731 Harries, J.H.O. "Some developments in television based on quantitative analysis." J. TELEV. SOC. 1 (Jan.): 1–12. 4 photos, 10 diags. Lecture Oct. 8; see earlier articles (1866, 1943). (2439, 2826)

2732 Baker, T.T. "Television in natural colours and the fundamental problems involved." J. TELEV. SOC. 1 (Jan.): 22–8. 3 diags. Lecture Dec. 10. Basics, color, luminosity, two- and three-color film processes, early work by Ruhmer, Belin and Anderson, Baird's demonstration in July 1928, Bell Labs (Ives) system, color sensitivity of modern photoelectric cells, and general discussion. (1353, 3176)

2733 "Proceedings of the Society." J. TELEV. SOC. 1 (Jan.): 29–31. (2370, 2859)

2734 "Standard definitions." J. TELEV. SOC. 1 (Jan.): 32. Committee recommendations, list of 11 terms.

2735 "Zone television. Use of telephone lines." TIMES (Jan. 5): 20c. Demonstration by the Baird Company, Jan. 2. Three-channel transmission, 30-line mirror drum, three phototubes, image projected from three neon lamps in three side-by-side sections onto a small ground-glass screen. A modulated arc was substituted for the neon lamps: "This scheme produced a picture of great brilliancy." (2681, 2741)

2736 "Physical Society exhibition. Display of television." TIMES (Jan. 6): 6e. Outline description of the Gramophone Company's five-channel apparatus demonstrated at the Imperial College of Science, South Kensington. (2738)

2737 Schröter, F. "Television." U.S. 1,996,492, Jan. 5, 1932, Apr. 2, 1935. Assigned: Telefunken. In Germany Jan. 5, 1931. An oscillating mirror directs invisible light onto the face of a cathode-ray tube to eradicate the original illumination. (2666, 2777)

2738 "Report television gains. British engineers say new system differs from others." N.Y.T. 12 (Jan. 7): 2. Gramophone Company's demonstration with motion picture film; small details said to be visible. The company is affiliated with RCA. (2736, 2739)

2739 "Instruments for science." TIMES (Jan. 7): 7c. Gramophone Company's exhibit. (2738, 2747)

2740 Mitchell, W.G.W. "Television." ELECT. 106 (Jan. 9): 45, 46. Photo. Brief survey of progress during 1930. "The progress made during last year was slight and has (for the most part) been confined to the actual details of improvement in methods already known and demonstrated." (2272, 2810)

2741 "News and views." NATURE 126 (Jan. 10): 67, 68. Mirror drum and "speaking arc" system which Baird demonstrated Jan. 2. Brilliance of the image called remarkable. "The television arc would therefore appear to have a useful future." (2735, 2760)

2742 Gray, F. "Electro-optical system." U.S. 2,010,543, Jan. 10, 1931, Aug. 6, 1935. Assigned: B.T.L. Scanning disk with a spiral of apertures and two sets of photocells, each arranged as a matrix. (2699, 2923)

2743 Wilson, R.G., and H.E. Dall. "Television." Br. 362,308, Jan. 10, 1931. Light from a neon lamp reflected from a prism to a mirror drum and reflected again before projection to a screen. (2655, 2775)

2744 Pattinson, R.J. "Television." Br. 369,311, Jan. 13, 1931. Multifrequency system with multiple photocells and neon lamps, tuned circuits, and aperture disk or band for simultaneous scanning of sections of the image. Triplicate sets are specified for color.

2745 Todd, L.P. "Telegraphic transmission of visual representations." Br. 377,187, Jan. 13, 1931, July 13, 1932. Lens disk coacts with a mirror drum, adaptable for color. (1541)

2746 Wainwright, Lawrence. "Television." U.S. 1,968,977, Jan. 13, 1931, Aug. 7, 1934. Mirror drum and optical assembly.

2747 "New television demonstration." W.W. 28 (Jan. 14): 29. Editorial on the Gramophone Company's system. Favorable comments on the improved definition are discounted by objections to the number of channels required, the use of wire links and of film. (2739, 2748)

2748 "A new television system." W.W. 28 (Jan. 14): 38, 39. 3 photos, diag. Technical description of the Gramophone Company's system. Image projected in five vertical sections onto a 20 by 24 inch ground-glass screen. (2747, 2749)

2749 "Twenty-first annual exhibition of the Physical and Optical Societies." NATURE 127 (Jan. 17): 110, 111. Brief details of the Gramophone Company's apparatus. (2748, 2824)

2750 Walton, G.W. "Light valve." Br. 369,698, Jan. 19, 1931. Refers to a special vacuum tube with two or more electrodes applicable for television. (2652, 2782)

2751 Henroteau, F.C.P. "Television." U.S. 2,083,995, Jan. 23, 1931, June 15, 1937. Assigned: The Electronic Television Co., Ltd., Ottawa. In Canada Jan. 20, 1931. Hybrid system with special photocell, contact disks, cathode-ray tube and circuits. (2570, 3739)

2752 "A Senator watches television perform in the house of magic." N.Y.T. IX, 8 (Jan. 25): 3. Views of Senator C.C. Dill after a demonstration by General Electric. "They are making great strides, but they convinced me that television is not ready for the public at large." (2628, 2776)

2753 Leishman, Leroy J. "Television." U.S. 2,005,344, Jan. 27, 1931, June 18, 1935. Scanning disk with multispiral apertures and two movable members. (2955)

2754 Jenkins, C.F. "Radiomovie lantern slide." U.S. 1,899,334, Jan. 29, 1931, Feb. 28, 1933. Assigned: C.F. Jenkins, Inc. Scanning disk and liquid slide in which bubbles are formed. (2592, 2769)

2755 Ives, H.E. "Some optical features in two-way television." J. OSA 21 (Feb.): 101–8. Also B.S.T.J. 10 (Apr.): 265–72. 5 illus. Deals with changes and improvements in the two-way system installed Apr. 9, 1930 (2343). (2721, 2767)

2756 Lescarboura, A.C. "Radiovision programs in making." PROJ. ENG. 3 (Feb.): 15, 16, 24. 3 illus. Programs and public acceptance. (2722)

2757 "New operating ideas for television." RADIO-CRAFT 2 (Feb.): 477, 503, 504. 3 diags. Crystal detector, an idea of W.J. Richardson; Dauvillier's X-ray system by E. Nesper (2556); and bypassing audio-frequencies, by P.L. Clark.

2758 "Television proposed on ultra-high waves." RADIO N. 12 (Feb.): 713, 749. Brief note on FRC plans. (2684, 2759)

2759 "Visual broadcasting still an experiment." RADIO N. 12 (Feb.): 761. Comments on FRC conference and order of Dec. 15. List of 19 licensed stations. (2758, 3060)

2760 "Zone television. Development of great importance to theatres & cinemas." TELEV. 3 (Feb.): 476, 477. 2 photos, diag. Baird's three-zone mirror drum system demonstrated Jan. 2. (2741, 2761)

2761 Moseley, S.A. "Television in 1930–1931." TELEV. 3 (Feb.): 479, 480. 2 photos. Brief mention of Baird Company developments. (2667, 2760, 2764, 2795)

2762 Chapple, H.J.B. "From my notebook." TELEV. 3 (Feb.): 489–91. 2 photos. German transmissions, television and sidebands, color proposals, how old is television? (2593, 3044)

2763 "The enthusiast sees it through." TELEV. 3 (Feb.): 492–6. 4 photos, 4 diags. (2728, 2796)

2764 "Demonstration of the Baird system of television at the 'Daily Mail' Schoolboys' Exhibition—January, 1931." TELEV. 3 (Feb.): 501. About 2,500 persons saw images in the reception booths each day. (2761, 2766)

2765 Wolfson, H. "Recent developments in photo-electricity." TELEV. 3 (Feb.): 502–5. Photo, 4 diags. Dry cuprous oxide cell, wet-type cell, lead sulfide-silver cell, construction and characteristics. (2020, 2799)

2766 "The Baird television arc." TELEV. 3 (Feb.): 511. (2764, 2780)

2767 "Ives takes images off tight rope and puts them on a 'bridge'." N.Y.T. IX, 9 (Feb. 1): 1,

2. Discussion of recent experiments and development of a triple-beam method for scanning film at Bell Labs. (2755, 2794)

2768 "Television reveals the action of the bulls and bears." N.Y.T. IX 9 (Feb. 1): 2, 3. Photo of Lloyd S. Tenny, Chicago, looking at a screen displaying market quotations.

2769 "Images on 147-meter wave." N.Y.T. IX, 9 (Feb.1): 8. Station W2XCR, Passaic, N.J., broadcasts weekdays from 2 to 3:30 and 7 to 9 p.m. with synchronized sound (8 to 9 p.m.) on 187 meters through de Forest station W2XCD. (2546, 2754, 2789, 2862)

2770 Cawley, A.J. "Reflex optical lever." U.S. 1,950,482, Feb. 4, 1931, Mar. 13, 1934. Similar to Baird's (699). (2537, 2916)

2771 Marconi's, and Harry Melville Dowsett. "Television." Br. 372,370, Feb. 6, 1931. Nipkow disk and mirror wheel. (2772)

2772 Marconi's, and H.M. Dowsett. "Television." Br. 370,094, Feb. 6, 1931. Apertured drum and mirror drum. (See Fig. 64.) (2771, 2791)

2773 Hogan, J.V.L. "Scanning system." U.S. 2,010,764, Feb. 10, 1931, Aug. 6, 1935. Assigned: Radio Inventions. Film scanner with a circle of lenses. (2473, 3056)

2774 Nicolson, A.M. "Color television." U.S. 1,985,685, Feb. 11, 1931, Dec. 25, 1934. Assigned: Comm. Pats. Three-lamp system with the field of view flooded with colored light corresponding to the unit area scanned. (2702, 2952)

2775 Wilson, R.G. "Television." Br. 369,355, Feb. 11, 1931. Special optical system. (2743)

2776 "Schenectady-to-Leipzig television a success; movie also made of images sent by radio." N.Y.T. 15 (Feb. 13): 3, 4. General Electric test transmissions to Berlin, Leipzig, and London. Reception by Telefunken and the BBC. (2752, 2778)

2777 "Doubts television is nearing success. German expert says tests show no ground for optimism as yet." N.Y.T. 7 (Feb. 14): 2. Comments by F. Schröter, Telefunken, with reference to transatlantic tests last autumn. (2737, 2787)

2778 "First motion picture of television made by Dr. E.F.W. Alexanderson in his laboratory at Schenectady." N.Y.T. VIII, 16 (Feb. 15): 6. Photo shows two frames. (2776, 2788)

2779 "Plans television for the Radio City. Aylesworth predicts process will be perfected for opening of center in three years." N.Y.T. 21 (Feb. 18): 2. (2615, 2961)

2780 Baird, J.L., and Baird Television. "Television." Br. 371,520, Feb. 18, 1931. Lens system with variable focal length. (2766, 2781)

2781 Baird, J.L., and Baird Television. "Television." Br. 373,196, Feb. 18, 1931. Two-channel stereo system with double scanning at right angles. Two banks of photocells, one on each side of the object, activate relays that provide "depth signals." Picture signals operate multielectrode lamps on a disk via a distributor while the depth signals are fed to the respective lamp sections via a relay-operated distributor. Other variants are mentioned. Reference to Br. 266,564 (704), 269,658 (737), and 292,365 (optical system). (2780, 2797)

2782 Walton, G.W. "Television." Br. 378,902, Feb. 19, 1931. Receiver with double lenses and echelon scanner (1542) adaptable for stereo or color. Reference also to Br. 369,644 (2612). (2750, 2783)

2783 Walton, G.W. "Television." Br. 378,922, Feb. 19, 1931; U.S. 1,918,358, Mar. 10, 1932, July 18, 1933. Vibrating mirror scanner and sync motor in a rotor and stator assembly including phase adjustment. (2782, 2785)

2784 "Inaudible television. Application of the Stenode Radiostat to reduce interference." ELECT. 106 (Feb. 20): 294. Report on lecture by E.L. Gardiner to the Television Society. (2241, 2945)

2785 Walton, G.W. "Television." Br. 379,303, Feb. 20, 1931; U.S. 1,914,314, Mar. 16, 1932, June 13, 1933. Modification of echelon system (1542), including vibrating mirror (2783), adaptable for color. Reference also to Br. 218,766 (537). (2783, 2786)

2786 Walton, G.W. "Television." Br. 379,317, Feb. 20, 1931. Comprises echelon system (1542), lenses, vibrating mirror (2783) or mirror drum, with colored disk varying continuously through the spectrum or a disk with seven equivalent color sections, and modifications, applicable for direct pickup or film scanning. Reference also to Br. 369,644 (2612). (2785, 2792)

2787 Schröter, F., and H. Lux. "Der heutige Stand des Fernsehens" [The present state of television]. V.D.I.Z. 75 (Feb. 21): 237–9. Illus. (2777, 2815)

2788 "Radio images and 'ghosts' are dancing in space. Television experts atop New York theatre roof are observing some strange effects." N.Y.T. IX, 17 (Feb. 22): 7, 8. Tests by G.E. engineers studying problems of static and reflections from tall buildings. (2778, 2925)

2789 "Television programs to be given daily." N.Y.T. 32 (Feb. 24): 8. Regular broadcasts began last night at station W2XCD by the De Forest Radio Co. after research indicated a nation-wide audience of more than 10,000 receivers. (2769, 2880)

2790 Gramophone Co. and W.D. Wright. "Electro-optical light valves." Br. 373,294, Feb. 26, 1931. Relates to optical modification of a Kerr cell, or combination of two cells, to reduce range of operating voltage and thus increase the sensitivity. (3191)

2791 Marconi's and H.M. Dowsett. "Television." Br. 373,288, Feb. 26, 1931. Message band scanned by a drum with apertures or lenses, receiver with apertured drum or mirror wheel, discharge lamp or Kerr cell, and sensitized tape. See Baird (1521). (2772, 2823)

2792 Walton, G.W. "Television." U.S. 2,100,044, Mar. 16, 1932, Nov. 23, 1937. In Britain Feb. 27, 1931. Optical scanning system (2786, 3160)

2793 Ardenne, M. v. "Further advances in the technique of the Braun tube." EXP. W. 8 (Mar. 4): 127–9. Illus. (2717, 2806)

2794 Ives, H.E. "Two-way television." J. SMPE 16 (Mar.): 293–301. (2767, 2927)

2795 Moseley, S.A. "What is America's game?" TELEV. 4 (Mar.): 4–6. 3 photos. On British television (Baird Company) and potential American competition, with extracts from AMERICA CONQUERS BRITAIN by Ludwell Denny. (2761, 2848)

2796 "The enthusiast sees it through." TELEV. 4 (Mar.): 10–3. 3 photos, 2 diags. (2763, 2850)

2797 Banks, G.B. "With the television lamp screen in Stockholm." TELEV. 4 (Mar.): 14, 31. Photo. (2638, 2781, 2798, 2951)

2798 "Television in France." TELEV. 4 (Mar.): 22. Formation of 'Television-Baird-Natan' to develop the Baird system in France, Belgium, Luxembourg, and in the French and Belgian colonies. Plans for broadcasts from the Radio-Vitus station in Paris. (2797, 2804, 3447)

2799 Wolfson, H. "Recent developments in photo-electricity." TELEV. 4 (Mar): 29–31. 3 diags. Glow discharge lamps, screen-grid photocells, circuits. (2765, 3391)

2800 "The Farnsworth claim." TELEV. 4 (Mar.): 40. Brief note expressing skepticism about news reports of Farnsworth and his cathode-ray system. "Until Mr. Farnsworth gives a demonstration his claims cannot be taken seriously." (2685, 2801)

2801 Farnsworth, P.T. "Scanning with an electric pencil." TELEV. NEWS 1 (Mar.–Apr.): 48–51, 74. 4 photos, 6 diags. In this first account of his system the inventor deals with the technical problems and describes the functioning of the parts. The discussion includes scanning and number of picture elements, radio and wire transmission, sync, details of the image dissector tube and the "Oscillite" picture tube, magnetic focusing, types of dissector tubes and targets, photoelectric substances and processing methods, wideband amplification, and the receiving system. (2800, 2817)

2802 "Television eyes the National Broadcasting Company's experimental studio." N.Y.T. IX, 8 (Mar. 1): 3–6. Photo of turntable on which toy images and animals are revolved in front of a disk camera. (2957)

2803 Prinz, D. "Cathode ray television system." U.S. 2,050,628, Feb. 29, 1932, Aug. 11, 1936. Assigned: Telefunken. Br. 374,400, Mar. 2, 1932. In Germany Mar. 2, 1931. Picture tube with electrostatic deflection. (2686, 3236)

2804 Baird, J.L., and Baird Television. "Television." Br. 374,114, Mar. 4, 1931; U.S. 1,980,150, Mar. 2, 1932, Nov. 6, 1934. Relates to a duplex system employing disks with two sets of apertures, arc lamp, and neon lamp, in which a sync correcting signal is derived from the two series of picture signals when they depart from phase opposition. Reference to Br. 321,930 (arc lamp) and six others (704, 737, 798, 1064, 1961, 2650). (2798, 2848)

2805 Pajes, W.S. "Electro-optical method." U.S. 1,954,947, Mar. 4, 1931, Apr. 17, 1934. Assigned: RCA. Light valve. (2683)

2806 Ardenne, M. v. "Cathode ray tubes." Br. 399,192, Feb. 25, 1932. In Germany Mar. 6, 1931. Addition to Br. 396,051 (2696). (2793, 2827)

2807 Comp. Gaz. "Gaseous luminous lamp." Br. 398,860, Dec. 17, 1931. In France Mar. 6, 1931. Addition to Br. 384,086 (2674). (2659, 3073)

2808 La Via, Joseph. "Light regulating means." U.S. 2,042,344, Mar. 6, 1931, May 26, 1936. Projection screen composed of a translucent plate and a transparent plate, with arc lamp and a light valve which rotates the plan of polarization.

2809 Pooler, Louis G. "Television." U.S. 1,985,690, Mar. 6. 1931, Dec. 25, 1934. Assigned: Comm. Pats. Discharge system with multiangled mirror wheel.

2810 "News and views." NATURE 127 (Mar. 7): 347, 348. Note on lecture by W.G.W. Mitchell to the Royal Society of Arts, Feb. 25. (2740, 2814)

2811 Barnecut, William John. "Television scanning device." U.S. 1,862,455, Mar. 11, 1931, June 7, 1932. Cylinder with a spiral of apertures and internal illumination coacts with an outer cylinder which has a spiral slot.

2812 Bowtell, G.M. "Television." Br. 368,071, Mar. 11, 1931. One or more rotary drums, each carrying three mirrors arranged at 120°, are mounted on a threaded shaft and moved linearly back and forth by levers and a spring. Alternative arrangements are suggested for color. (2204, 2822)

2813 Möller, R., and G. Schubert. "Automatic regulation of the amplification in telecine transmitting amplifiers." U.S. 2,063,694, Mar. 12, 1932, Dec. 8, 1936. Assigned: Fernseh A.-G. Br. 398,242, Mar. 11, 1932. In Germany Mar. 12, 1931. Picture currents derived from motion picture film are controlled according to the degree of contrast. (2512, 2623, 2842, 2844)

2814 "Television. Some views on future developments—the home televisor." ELECT. 106 (Mar. 13): 416. On Mitchell's lecture, Feb. 25. Big screens for the home cinema should be possible within a year or two. "The home televisor, possessing real entertainment value, would probably only come some years after this and as a development of it." (2810, 2898)

2815 Schröter, F. "Picture reproducing system." U.S. 2,058,636, Mar. 23, 1932, Oct. 27, 1936. Assigned: Telefunken. In Germany Mar. 14, 1931. Relates to the varying brightness which occurs during a line scan and a method of addition to provide a constant average brightness. (2787, 2849)

2816 Horny, F. "Television receivers." Br. 371,549, Mar. 16, 1931. Matrix screen formed by crossed sets of perforated strips actuated by separate electromagnets and springs.

2817 Dinsdale, A. "Television by cathode ray; the new Farnsworth system." W.W. 28 (Mar. 18): 286–8. 3 photos, 2 diags. General coverage with technical details but briefer than Farnsworth's (2801). (2725, 2801, 2845, 2899)

2818 "Banker and aides talk by television." N.Y.T. 14 (Mar. 21): 8. Conversation with vision by the Bell two-way Iconophone in New York, first demonstrated Apr. 9, 1930 (2343). (2515, 2875)

2819 Brown, Reynolds D., Jr. "Image transmission system." U.S. 2,054,893, Mar. 21, 1931, Sept. 22, 1936. Assigned: Philadelphia Storage Battery Co. Spirally arranged scanning elements on a rotating disk with the axis moved in a circular orbit.

2820 "Radio dealers foresee harvest in television." N.Y.T. VIII, 16 (Mar. 22): 7, 8. Optimistic comments by J.W. Griffin: "Development will be rapid when people become interested in the hobby of seeing by radio."

2821 "Electrical entertainment; a glimpse into the future. Dr. Goldsmith of the Radio Corporation predicts an instrument which at a touch of the fingers will bring to the home scenes and sounds, color symphonies, or a keyboard for self-created music." N.Y.T. IX (Mar. 22): 4. Feature article. Large illustration shows the home "electrical entertainer" of 1981. A color-organ casts "weird images" on the center screen, the side screens are for viewing motion pictures or television images. (2641, 3697)

2822 Bowtell, G.M. "Television." Br. 371,564, Mar. 23, 1931. A line of pivoted levers, like piano keys, have mirrors mounted on the free ends. A drum with projecting pins moves the levers to cause each mirror to scan one line. (2812)

2823 Marconi's and H.M. Dowsett. "Television." Br. 375,385, Mar. 23, 1931; U.S. 1,939,805, Mar. 18, 1932, Dec. 19, 1933 (RCA). Light is passed through apertures in a drum and reflected from sets of mirrors mounted on side-by-side drums onto a mirror from which three displaced beams scan the object. Light reflected from the object is directed by a similar set of mirror drums onto three photocells. Alternatives are mentioned. (2791, 2877)

2824 "The Gramophone merger." W.W. 28 (Mar. 25): 317. Amalgamation of the Gramophone Company and the Columbia Graphophone Company is called the "outstanding event of the past week." The new company, Electric & Musical Industries Ltd. (EMI), was incorporated Apr. 20. (2749, 3681)

2825 "First television play in U.S." W.W. 28 (Mar. 25): 317. Brief note. America's first television play, "The Maker of Dreams," has just been given from the Chicago broadcasting stations W9XAP and WMAQ. (2677, 2863)

2826 Harries, J.H.O. "Television." Br. 375, 408, Mar. 26, 1931. Method of scanning two fields of view, one within the other, by a disk with two semi-spiral sets of apertures. Alternatives are two mirrors, cathode-ray tube, or optical systems. Reference to Br. 326,603 (1712). (2731, 3209)

2827 Ardenne, M. v. "Television." Br. 387,536, Mar. 29, 1932, Feb. 9, 1933. In Germany Mar. 27, 1931. This extensive patent covers film or direct pickup by a cathode-ray tube with a similar tube for reception. Complete circuits are given, with descriptions of the scanning generators, or "tilting oscillators" for beam deflection, amplifiers, tube connections, and their operation. Screen phosphors, photocells, scanning frequencies, and general aspects of the system are also discussed. (2806, 2828)

2828 Ardenne, M. v. "Cathode ray tubes." Br. 402,411, Mar. 21, 1932. In Germany Mar. 27, 1931. Relates to fluorescent screens. See also Br. 402,418. (2827, 2829)

2829 Ardenne, M. v. "Braun tube." U.S. 2,083,209, Apr. 17, 1933, June 8, 1937. In Germany Mar. 27, 1931. Tube with deflection plates, apertured diaphragm, and other electrodes. (2828, 2830)

2830 Ardenne, M. v. "Television." U.S. 2,131,203, May 16, 1932, Sept. 26, 1938. Assigned: D.S. Loewe. In Germany Mar. 27, 1931. Picture tube circuit with safety relay in the high-voltage supply controlled by the line and frame scanning circuits. (2829, 2838)

2831 Fernseh A.-G. "Television." Br. 373,093, Mar. 21, 1932. In Germany Mar. 27, 1931. Mirror drum and lens system for even line placement. (2623, 2832)

2832 Fernseh A.-G. "Television." Br. 398,870, Mar. 21, 1932. In Germany Mar. 27, 1931. Addition to Br. 256,565 (2097). Modification with moving mirrors. (2831, 2833)

2833 Fernseh A.-G. "Television." Br. 398,871, Mar. 21, 1932. In Germany Mar. 27, 1931. Concerns the phase or voltage control of motors in transmitters and receivers supplied from a common power line or other separate network. (2832, 2839)

2834 "Would censor television. La Fount urges step in advance of its commercial development." N.Y.T. 26 (Mar. 28): 7. Abuses might arise through excess advertising or objectionable pictures. (2440, 2835)

2835 "Lifting ban on radio vision depends on public demand. Says La Fount, who reports Commission is mindful of progress in broadcasting images." N.Y.T. IX, 10 (Mar. 29): 1, 2. Improvements needed include more light and more detail in the images, and better make-up for the artists. (2834, 3251)

2836 "Television seeks a new name for its audience. Who has the word for it?" N.Y.T. IX, 10 (Mar. 29): 1–3. Names suggested by 13 industry leaders include radio spectator, spectauditor, televist, televiewer, telviewer, teleseer, lookers, lookstener, observer, viewer, viseur, televiseur, radioviseur. (1727, 2874)

2837 Lubcke, H.R. "Television." U.S. 2,075,818, Mar. 30, 1931, Apr. 6, 1937. Cathode-ray tube scanner, deflection circuits, double photocell pickup. (2558, 3337)

2838 Ardenne, M. v. "Cathode ray tubes." Br. 398,804, Mar. 11, 1932. In Germany Mar. 31, 1931. Addition to Br. 396,051 (2696). Modified spacing or screening of deflection electrodes. (2830, 2841)

2839 Fernseh A.-G. "Television." Br. 382,206. Mar. 30, 1932. In Germany Mar. 31, 1931. Mirror drum construction. (2833, 2855)

2840 "Movie television screen." ELECTRONICS 2 (Apr.): 602.

2841 Ardenne, M. v. "Uber neue Fernsehsender und Fernsehempfänger mit Kathodenstrahlröhren" [About a new television transmitter and receiver with cathode-ray tubes]. FERN. 2 (Apr.): 65–80. 23 illus., including second part (2979). Developments in cathode-ray tubes, scanning generators, operating voltages, sync methods, film transmission, amplifiers, experimental results. System as described in the patent (2827). (2838, 2879)

2842 Möller, R. "Das Weiller'sche Spiegelrad" [The Weiller mirror wheel]. FERN. 2 (Apr.): 80–97. 18 illus. Mirror drum introduced by Weiller (204), principles of operation, methods of construction, and characteristics. (2813, 3030)

2843 Kirschstein, F. "Nipkowscheibe oder Spiegelrad?" [Nipkow disk or mirror wheel?] FERN. 2 (Apr.): 98–104. 4 illus, (2622, 3378)

2844 Schubert, G. "Zur Netzsynchronisierung von Fernseh-Empfängern" [On the network synchronization of television receivers]. FERN. 2 (Apr.): 105–20. 15 illus. (2813, 2860)

2845 Hewel, H. "Einzelheiten amerikan Kathodenstrahl Fernsehsysteme" [Details of American cathode-ray television system]. FERN. 2 (Apr.): 123–8. Farnsworth's system. (2566, 2817, 2897, 3328)

2846 Vipond, L.C. "Romance of television." PROJ. ENG. 3 (Apr.): 17, 18. Review of progress and current status.

2847 Wright, H.R. "Cathode rays in television." RADIO ENG. 11 (Apr.): 29, 30. 3 illus. Description of the Westinghouse (Zworykin) system. (2712, 2865)

2848 Moseley, S.A. "The first tele-cine broadcast." TELEV. 4 (Apr.): 48, 49. Photo. A test film from the Baird studio was broadcast through the BBC station at midnight, Mar. 6, and another more formal transmission at 11:00 a.m. on Mar. 9. Quotes from letters about the reception. (2795, 2804, 2853, 2900)

2849 Schröter, F., and Günther Lubszynski. "Inertia in gas filled photo-electric cells." TELEV. 4 (Apr.): 51–4. 6 graphs, diag. Reprint from PHYS. Z. No. 20 (1930). Continued in May (2905). (2815, 2861)

2850 Dumert, V. "Useful hints for the experimenter." TELEV. 4 (Apr.): 57–9. 3 diags. (2796, 2851)

2851 "The enthusiast sees it through." TELEV. 4 (Apr.): 60–5. 5 photos, diag. (2850, 2895)

2852 Bocchi, R. "Reception of Baird television in Rome." TELEV. 4 (Apr.): 66, 67. 2 photos. (2944)

2853 Baird Television Ltd. "The Baird 'Junior' kit." TELEV. 4 (Apr.): 72. Full-page advertisement. Kit includes motor, sync gear, disk, neon lamp, holder, and two blueprints. Price 10 guineas. (2848, 2857)

2854 Bingley, Frank James (1906–1976), and Baird Television. "Amplifying circuits." Br. 375,825, Apr. 1, 1931. Concerns a wideband high-frequency amplifier for operating a Kerr cell. (3226)

2855 Fernseh A.-G. "Synchronous movements." Br. 378,826, Mar. 30, 1932. In Germany Apr. 4, 1931. Addition to Br. 366,598 (2098). Electron tube oscillator circuit. See also Br. 378,827 and 385,492, other additions of the same dates. (2839, 2871)

2856 Godefroy, Alexandre F. "Television." U.S. 1,859,824, Apr. 6, 1931, May 24, 1932. Receiver arrangement comprising a cylinder with colored glass areas, internal illumination, a multiplicity of solenoids, and projection lens.

2857 Baird, J.L., and Baird Television. "Television." Br. 374,564, Apr. 9, 1931. Various motor-driven reflector arrangements including mirror drum or wheel and variants. References to earlier patents (548, 1659, 2240). (2853, 2858)

2858 Baird, J.L., and Baird Television. "Television." Br. 375,900, Apr. 9, 1931. Mirror drum scanner with arc lamp, lenses, reflecting mirror, and modifications. References to other patents: Rosing (349), Baden-Powell (468), and Baird's (711, 737, 2536, 2650). (2857, 2900)

2859 "Television exhibition." ELECT. 106 (Apr. 10): 559. Note on the Television Society's exhibition to be held Apr. 15. (2733, 2870)

2860 Banneitz, Fritz (1885–1940), and G. Schubert. "Television." U.S. 1,930,071, Apr. 8, 1932, Oct. 10, 1933. Assigned: Fernseh A.-G. Br. 379,646, Apr. 4, 1932. In Germany Apr. 10, 1931. Nipkow disk with two supporting disks and air spaces between.

2861 Schröter, F. "Television." U.S. 2,076,674, Apr. 6, 1932, Apr. 13, 1937. Assigned: Telefunken. In Germany Apr. 10, 1931. Picture tube and circuits. (2849, 2905)

2862 "To test television transmitter. Tentative date for transmission April 19." N.Y.T. 17 (Apr. 11): 5. Station W2XCR. (2769, 2864)

2863 "Ninety-niners on the lookout. Each member of television club is watching for images—they reside in ninety-nine cities—Chicago sees larger pictures." N.Y.T. IX, 14 (Apr. 12): 6–8. Statement by Clem F. Wade, president, Western Television Corp. Also photo showing 16-inch photoelectric cell in studio of stations W9XAO and W9XAP, Chicago. (2625, 2976)

2864 "Radio images to talk when they go on the air. New York television studio to open this month—engineers seek to end 'blind' broadcasting." N.Y.T. IX, 15 (Apr. 13): 1–5. Comments by D.E. Replogle about the Jenkins station W2XCR and station WGBS. (2688, 2862, 2887, 2991)

2865 Zworykin, V.K. "Television." U.S. 1,870,702, Apr. 13, 1931, Aug. 9, 1932. Assigned: RCA. Br. 377,622, Mar. 30, July 28, 1932 (Marconi's). Cabinet assembly with picture tube mounted vertically and a reflecting mirror inside a hinged lid. In one modification a pickup tube is similarly mounted in the cabinet for two-way working. A receiver, amplifier, loudspeaker, microphone, frame antenna, and other component assemblies and parts are also specified. See also Br. 392,801 (3096). (2847, 2931)

2866 "Television studio nearing completion. The Columbia Company's picture broadcaster will begin sending programs about June 1." N.Y.T. 29 (Apr. 14): 7. "The picture broadcaster will be the fifth operating in the New York area. W2XAB, as it will be known, is to be opened about June 1." (2607, 2873)

2867 Centeno V, M. "Television." U.S. 1,873,696, Apr. 14, 1931, Aug. 23, 1932. Vibrating mirror apparatus. (2246, 3581)

2868 Laczay, T. von. "Television." Br. 394,446, Mar. 18, 1932. Assigned: IMK. In Germany Apr. 14, 1931. Drum with a spiral of apertures and a triangular prism rotating on the axis, with variants. (2869)

2869 Mihály, D. v. "Television." U.S. 1,998,347, Apr. 4, 1932, Apr. 16, 1935. Assigned: IMK. In Germany Apr. 14, 1931. Same as above. (2723, 3448)

2870 Television Society. "Third annual exhibition at University College." ELECT. 105 (Apr. 17): 585. Report on the displays, Apr. 15. (2859, 2883)

2871 Fernseh A.-G. "Television." Br. 387,543, Apr. 13, 1932. In Germany Apr. 17, 1931. Image signals transmitted over power lines for modulating short-wave transmitters. (2855, 3029)

2872 Becker, Carl W. "Television receivers." U.S. 1,981,942, Apr. 18, 1931, Nov. 27, 1934. Scanning ring with a spiral of apertures and driving motor assembly.

2873 "Fifth television transmitter planned for New York area. Columbia system expects to begin image tests June 1. Four rooms devoted to the installation." N.Y.T. IX, 10 (Apr. 19): 1, 2. On station W2XAB. (2866, 2957)

2874 "New words uncovered in hunt for television name. Search continues for the right word. Variety of strange names are suggested as listeners join the quest." N.Y.T. IX, 10 (Apr. 19): 1, 2. Samples: visual listeners, eyearer or earyer, tellser, sightener, audivise, audiviser, audiovision, hear-seer, noisivision, noisivisioners, teleceiver, televiewing rather than televisioning, radiospects (spectacle), radue, raduoner, raduolist, perceiver, lookhear, lookhearer, lookhearing, radioview, scanner, scanners, (radio scanner), radio spectator, spectauditor, televist, televiewer, teleseer, lookstener, observer, viewer, viseur, visuence, televisioner, looker-in. (2836)

2875 "The quality of television scenes." N.Y.T. IX, 10 (Apr. 19): 2, 7. Five photos by Bell Labs showing varying quality from 1 to 20 channels. (2818, 2884)

2876 Du Mont, A.B. "Television." U.S. 1,984,673, Apr. 21, 1931, Dec. 18, 1934. Assigned: RCA. Optical transmission system. (2459, 2988)

2877 Marconi's, H.M. Dowsett, and Robert Cadzow. "Television." Br. 377,277, Apr. 22, 1931. Mirror-wheel scanner and bank of Kerr cells, each connected in turn via contacts inside a cathode-ray tube with magnetic beam deflection. (2823, 2912, 3004)

2878 Bowman, G., and O.G. Hutchinson. "Television." Br. 377,283, Apr. 23, 1931. Matrix system for receivers with filament lamps controlled by distributors and alternative display screen consisting of crossed metal strips on glass plates, one set of strips being electron-emitting, the other coated with phosphorescent material, with interspaces evacuated or gas filled. (2102)

2879 Ardenne, M. v. "Cathode ray tubes." Br. 394,460, Apr. 21, 1932. In Germany Apr. 24, 1931. Addition to Br. 387,536 (2827). (2841, 2892)

2880 De Forest, L. "Television receiving method." U.S. 2,026,872, Apr. 24, 1931, Jan. 7, 1936. Assigned: American Television Labs. Br. 386,183, Apr. 14, 1932, Jan. 12, 1933. Film with a blackened surface (or silver coating) is passed under a scanning disk which has points connected sequentially by a distributor to a receiver output. Electrical discharges from the points through the film to a conducting strip below etch a pattern in the film which is then passed through a projector for display on a screen. (2789, 2987)

2881 Schubert, G. "Television." U.S. 2,049,629, Apr. 20, 1932, Aug. 4, 1936. Assigned: Fernseh A.-G. Br. 386,492, Apr. 19, 1932. In Germany Apr. 24, 1931. Receiver with a folded or zigzag discharge tube connected to a signal amplifier, and oscillator supplying high-frequency excitation to the tube. (2860, 2981)

2882 Aisberg, E. "L'appareil 'Televisor' pour la réception des images à distance" [Televisor apparatus for the reception of images at a distance]. GENIE CIVIL 98 (Apr. 25): 433. Illus. (2703, 3751)

2883 "News and views." NATURE 127 (Apr. 25): 638. Brief notes on the Television Society's exhibition. (2870, 2901)

2884 "Clothing displayed, sold by television. $5,000 order placed as salesman and buyer, two miles apart, close deal by new method." N.Y.T. 17 (Apr. 25): 8. Experimental commercial use of the Bell Labs two-way system in New York. (2875)

2885 Kerr, Alexander. "Television." U.S. 2,009,498, Apr. 23, 1932, July 30, 1935; Br. 402,397, Apr. 25, 1932. In Germany Apr. 25, 1931. X-ray tube with external perforated shutter and fluorescent screen for television and sound films.

2886 "New television set for home produces fair-sized picture. Baird introduces a receiver featuring screen eight by ten inches on front of cabinet." N.Y.T. IX, 9 (Apr. 26): 7, 8. New receiver by Short Wave & Television Labs (H.S. Baird), photo of console cabinet. (2460, 2896)

2887 "Stage stars parade in television show. Radio camera and electric eyes trained on a gala performance tonight." N.Y.T. IX, 9 (Apr. 26): 7, 8. Jenkins station W2XCR begins daily television broadcast tonight. (2864, 2888)

2888 "Radio talkies put on program basis. Actors and dancers do turns in City's first broadcast on regular schedule. Images marred by static." N.Y.T. 24 (Apr. 27): 1. Images broadcast by station W2XCR, Aeolian Hall, 5th Avenue and 54th Street, sound from station WGBS. (2887, 2889)

2889 "Report good results of sound-television. Receivers of radio talkies send encouraging messages on Sunday's program." N.Y.T. 30 (Apr. 28): 3. Favorable reports on the broadcasts from stations W2XCR and WGBS. (2888, 2906)

2890 Liacos, Stavros J. "Television." U.S. 1,866,413, Apr. 28, 1931, July 5, 1932. Three discharge lamps with the beams concentrated or focused on two scanning drums.

2891 "Barthelmy's television demonstrated." W.W. 28 (Apr. 29): 457. Brief note from Paris correspondent on Barthélemy's experimental radio transmission from studio at Montrouge over 1 1/4 miles to the Electrical High School at Malakoff. The picture, 30 by 40 cm, was described as "jerky and uncertain" but plainly discernible. (2720, 2985)

2892 Ardenne, M. v. "Television." U.S. 2,096,985, Apr. 27, 1932, Oct. 26, 1937. Assigned: D.S. Loewe. Br. 383,880, Apr. 28, 1932. In Germany Apr. 29, 1931. Cathode-ray-tube system (2827) incorporating film scan with the rate varied according to the shading. (2879, 2893)

2893 Ardenne, M. v. "Television." Br. 392,729, Apr. 28, 1932. In Germany Apr. 29, 1931. Line and image frequencies, superposed on an intermediate carrier, modulate a short-wave carrier on which wide-band picture signals are also superposed. Reference to Br. 387,536 (2827). (2892, 2913)

2894 "Two-way television improvements are sought." POP. MECH. 55 (May): 785.

2895 Nason, C.H.W. "Makeup of experimental television unit." RADIO ENG. 11 (May): 37, 38, 52. 4 illus. (2664, 2851, 2904, 3034)

2896 Calcaterra, Joseph. "The Boston television party." RADIO N. 12 (May): 986–8, 1028, 1029. 5 photos, list of 11 stations. General discussion of current status and description of the Short Wave & Television Corp. station W1XAV, their receiver and kit. The station list includes technical details and program schedules. (2886, 2935, 2936)

2897 Halloran, Arthur H. "Scanning without a disc." RADIO N. 12 (May): 998, 999, 1015. 4 photos, 5 diags. Farnsworth system. (2845, 2899)

2898 Mitchell, W.G.W. "London looks in at new television departure." SCI. & INV. 19 (May): 12, 78, 79. 3 photos, 2 diags. Gramophone Company's 5-zone system (2748). (2814, 2924)

2899 Dinsdale, A. "Television takes the next step." SCI. & INV. 19 (May): 46, 47, 72, 73. 11 illus. Farnsworth system. (2817, 2897, 3008, 3078)

2900 Moseley, S.A. "Important to readers of Television." TELEV. 4 (May): 84, 85. 2 photos. Admonition to readers to order TELEVISION, discussion of an article criticizing television, and announcement of Baird's portable transmitter installed in a BBC studio on Apr. 13. (2631, 2848, 2858, 2937, 2953)

2901 "The Television Society's third annual exhibition." TELEV. 4 (May): 92, 93. Report on the show at University College, Apr. 15, with brief details of the exhibits. (2883, 2946)

2902 "Origin of the word 'television'." TELEV. 4 (May): 93. Quote from the ATHENAEUM, Sept. 25, 1909, referring to an account of Ruhmer's experiment on "television" by Dr. Alfred Gradenwitz, who is credited with coining the word. See Perskyi (288). (2727, 2940, 3578)

2903 "The Kerr cell and how it works." TELEV. 4 (May): 94–6. Photo, 2 diags. Natural light, elliptical polarization, Verdet's constant, double polarization, change of shape, the Kerr effect.

2904 "The enthusiast sees it through." TELEV. 4 (May): 100–5. 7 photos, 2 diags. (2895, 2936)

2905 Schröter, F., and G. Lubszynski. "Inertia in gas filled photo-electric cells." TELEV. 4 (May): 115–7. 2 tables, graph, diag. Continued from April (2849). (2861, 2997)

2906 "First television wedding. Views of couple and preachers, with their words, are broadcast." N.Y.T. 22 (May 2): 3. Ceremony in station W2XCR, sound through WGBS. (2889, 2908)

2907 "Faces in television show survive lightning flashes. Radio images win battle with storm." N.Y.T. IX, 10 (May 3): 1, 2.

"It is estimated that there may be about 500 television receiving outfits in the New York area. Many of them are home-made, and are owned by amateur experimenters, as were the early broadcast receivers in 1920. Chicago is believed to have from 500 to 1000 vision sets, chiefly because there has been greater activity in visual broadcasts in that area.

"The images broadcast by stations W9XAO and W9XAP, Chicago, have been seen as they sped across the corn fields of Iowa, across the wheat fields of Minnesota and Kansas. They have found aerial wires in Michigan, Ohio and Missouri. One observer in Arizona reported that he caught a fleeting glimpse of them after they had traveled through the desert air. These television spectators say that they enjoy boxing bouts and performances that feature plenty of action."

2908 "Radio camera known as the television scanner used at station W2XCR." N.Y.T. IX,

10 (May 3): 2, 3. Photo of scanner and of WGBS studio. (2906, 2918)

2909 "Revision of the radio law needed to cover television. Senator King wonders about censorship of the visual broadcasts—he studies the problem." N.Y.T. IX, 10 (May 3): 7, 8. "Television is so new and so important in its public aspects as to stagger the imagination."

2910 Lübcke, Ernst. "Cathode ray tube." U.S. 1,979,392, Apr. 21, 1932, Nov. 6, 1934. Assigned: Siemens & Halske. In Germany May 4, 1931. Picture tube with magnetic focus.

2911 "Sarnoff predicts era of television. Tells stockholders of R.C.A. several stations will be in operation here next year. Expects sight element will complement broadcasting as invention is perfected." N.Y.T. 27 (May 6): 1. (2480, 2502, 2930, 3096)

2912 Marconi's, H.M. Dowsett, and Nyman Levin. "Television." Br. 378,079, May 6, 1931. Multibeam scanning with mirror wheel, bank of reflecting mirrors, and variants. Transmission over three channels with three light sources and mirror wheel at the receiver. (2877, 2919)

2913 Loewe, S., and M. v. Ardenne. "Television." Br. 386,849, May 9, 1932. In Germany May 9, 1931. A two-channel system with line scanning and picture signals transmitted on ultra-short waves and picture repetition signals conveyed along a wire channel. Includes receiver, picture tube, and sound. Reference to Br. 383,880 (2892). (2694, 2893, 2926)

2914 Kwartin, Bernard. "Electronic receiver for disk transmitters." U.S. 1,987,686, May 12, 1931, Jan. 15, 1935. Cathode-ray tube with two cathodes and auxiliary circuits. See also U.S. 2,055,174, May 12, 1931, Sept. 22, 1936.

2915 Aspden, R.L. "Television." Br. 378,111, May 14, 1931. Relates to view-finding apparatus containing a Nipkow disk with a pick-up at the edge for recording signals directly on the disk. Signals from a radio receiver are applied to a wire recording drum coupled to the shaft of a Nipkow disk scanner. Reference to Br. 365,632 (2611).

2916 Cawley, A.J. "Television." U.S. 1,999,867, May 14, 1931, Apr. 30, 1935. Slotted disk coacts with helically arranged lenses on a cylinder and an optical system. (2770, 3025)

2917 "A survey of television." NATURE 127 (May 16): 734, 735. Review of books by Moseley and Chapple (2323), Yates (2165), Sheldon and Grisewood (1899).

2918 "Television fashion show. Manikins in costume parade before 'electric eye' here." N.Y.T. 23 (May 20): 3. Six manikins from Saks Fifth Avenue store displayed 17 costumes and other apparel at station W2XCR-WGBS studio. (2908, 2988)

2919 Marconi's, H.M. Dowsett, Louis Edward Quintrell Walker, and N. Levin. "Television." Br. 378,948, May 20, 1931; U.S. 1,986,187, May 9, 1932, Jan. 1, 1935 (RCA). Lens drum with internal reflecting prism and a mirror drum, alternatively an apertured drum rotating inside a lens drum. Reference to Br. 374,094 (2772). (2912, 2920, 2928, 3002)

2920 Marconi's, H.M. Dowsett, and Donald Leopold Plaistowe. "Television." Br. 378,949, May 20, 1931; U.S. 1,971,372, May 4, 1932, Aug. 28, 1934 (RCA). Nipkow disk with two spirals of apertures, one for transmission and the other for monitoring, selectable by transverse movement of the disk assembly. (2919, 3002)

2921 Schlesinger, K. "Tilting oscillator and modulator." U.S. 2,075,140, May 21, 1932, Mar. 30, 1937; Br. 394,476, May 19, 1932. In Germany May 20, 1931. Sawtooth deflection oscillator and amplifier with phototube and cathode-ray tube in a film transmission system. (2361, 3053)

2922 Sukumlyn, Thomas W. "Control system for electron emission." U.S. 2,061,113, May 20, 1931, Nov. 17, 1936. A type of image dissector tube has a series of plates with alternately opposite polarities for dividing the electron beam between the photoelectric cathodes and the anode.

2923 Gray, F. "Scanning apparatus." U.S. 2,017,092, May 21, 1931, Oct. 15, 1935. Assigned: B.T.L. Br. 400,626, Apr. 27, 1932 (E.R.P.). Mirror screw with point light source. (2742, 2972)

2924 Mitchell, W.G.W. "Developments in television." J. ROY. SOC. ARTS 79 (May 22): 616–42. 9 photos, graph, 5 diags. Lecture Feb. 25 (2814). Review of present practice, phototubes, scanning, transmission channels, reception, two-way television by the Bell system, large screens (Bell Labs, Baird), Gramophone Company's 5-zone film system, electrical methods with cathode-ray tubes, Swinton's scheme, Farnsworth's system, trend of developments, discussion (pp. 639–42). Referring to a demonstration within the last fortnight in the Baird Laboratories, Mitchell notes that "very good brilliancy was obtained by optical projection on to a screen measuring approximately 6 ft. by 3 ft. at 10 ft. distance." (2898, 3269)

2925 "Exchange repartee by television device. Speakers at distance answer audience's questions in Schenectady demonstration." N.Y.T. 28 (May 22): 2. G.E. demonstration. (2788, 3227)

2926 Ardenne, M. v., and S. Loewe. "Cathode ray tubes." U.S. 2,077,288, May 20, 1932, Apr. 13, 1937. Assigned: D.S. Loewe by von Ardenne. Br. 401,727, May 19, 1932. In Germany May 23, 1931. Gas-filled tube with additional ionizing electrodes. (2913, 2940, 3556)

2927 Ives, H.E. "Scanning apparatus." U.S. 1,964,580, May 29, 1931, June 26, 1934. Assigned: B.T.L. Br. 402,401, May 28, 1932 (E.R.P.). Mirror screw with linear light source. References to Br. 358,411 (2296), 400,626 (2923). (2794, 3301)

2928 Marconi's, and L.E.Q. Walker. "Television." Br. 379,363, May 29, 1931; U.S. 2,048,761, May 11, 1932, July 28, 1936 (RCA). In this sync method the scanning line frequency component of a picture signal is selected, amplified, and applied to the windings of the receiver motor. (2919, 3003)

2929 Rüdenberg, Reinhold (1883–1961). "Device for producing colored pictures." U.S. 1,934,821, May 28, 1932, Nov. 14, 1933. Assigned: Siemens-Schuckertwerke A.-G. Br. 387,207, May 26, 1932. In Germany May 30, 1931. A cathode-ray tube for television receivers has an inserted screen carrying lines of phosphors recurring in groups of three different colors. See von Ardenne's color tube. (2965)

2930 "Sarnoff discloses plans for nation-wide TV. Radio-vision era is dawning. TV looms as mighty force, says Sarnoff—he predicts influence it will have on home, stage and screen." N.Y.T. IX, 9 (May 31): 1–5. (2911, 3111)

2931 "Vladimir Zworykin's television set." N.Y.T. IX, 9 (May 31): 2. Portrait. (2865, 2977)

2932 "Where television stands today." ELECTRONICS 2 (June): 671.

2933 Hudec, E. "Die Abbildung beim Fernsehen" [Image processing in television]. E.N.T. 8 (June): 229–45. 22 illus. Detail consideration and mathematical treatment of image make-up, qualities, comparison with halftone photos, scanning, and reproduction. (2716, 3131)

2934 Browne, C.O. "Technical problems in connection with television." EXP. W. 8 (June): 310, 311. Report on IEE lecture, May 6. (2656, 3134)

2935 "Short Wave & Television Corp. Baird television." RADIO N. 12 (June): Inside front cover. Full-page advertisement. "The most simple and efficient shortwave and television kit possible." Kit $60, receiver $75. "Our Television Station W1XAV was the first station in the world to televise regular broadcast programs." (2896, 2936)

2936 Calcaterra, J. "How to build a practical home Televisor." RADIO N. 12 (June):

1059–61, 1094, 1119. 10 illus. Hollis Baird kit. (2896, 2904, 2935, 2941, 2992, 2993)

2937 Moseley, S.A. "Zone television and the television arc." SCI. AM. 144 (June): 379. Photo, diag. Baird's system (2735). (2900, 2938, 2939)

2938 "Daylight television demonstrated. A street scene shown." TELEV. 4 (June): 124. Diag. Demonstration of outdoor pickup near the Baird laboratory, 133 Long Acre, May 8. Mirror drum transmitter. (2937, 2939)

"We were present at the demonstration on May 8th, and were vividly impressed with all we saw. Drawn up outside the Baird offices in Long Acre was a grey van housing the transmitting apparatus. From the van's open door the 'scene' was picked up and sent along a short length of land-line to 'Televisors' in the demonstration room. In these receiving instruments could be easily identified the people who were passing along and, during the course of the transmission, we had presented to our gaze business people, Covent Garden porters, a policeman who obviously had come along to see what was happening and why the crowd had congregated, etc.

"As was to be expected in fickle May the weather was not particularly good; the sun shone only on one or two rare occasions, and the sky was overcast. This was responsible for an alternation in signal strength, so that the quality of the images varied somewhat. However, the street scene was there, and with normal conditions the images are distinct and clear with a background clearly recognisable. The ramifications of this new development can well be left to the imagination of our readers."

2939 Moseley, S.A. "Latest developments in television." TELEV. 4 (June): 130, 131, 159. 2 photos. Reference to the televising of a street scene and to a demonstration by Baird of a large screen at least twice as big as the one installed at the Coliseum the previous July (2491). The commercial use of such big screens for street advertising is suggested. (2937, 2938, 2942, 2943)

2940 Gradenwitz, A. "Cathode ray television. Manfred von Ardenne's recent work." TELEV. 4 (June): 132, 133. 3 photos. (2902, 2926, 2965, 3146)

2941 "The enthusiast sees it through." TELEV. 4 (June): 138–43. 7 photos, 3 diags. (2936, 2992)

2942 "The first newspaper interview by television." TELEV. 4 (June): 147, 148. 3 photos. Report from the DAILY HERALD, May 14. By landlines between Moseley in the newspaper office and Mrs. Philip Snowden at 11 Downing Street. (2939, 2996)

2943 "The Baird portable television transmitter." TELEV. 4 (June): 149–51. 4 photos. A tubular tripod on rubber wheels carries an enclosed scanning disk with two movable lenses, one for close-up views, driving motor and arc lamp (2900). (2939, 2953)

2944 Bocchi, R. "Television reception abroad." TELEV. 4 (June): 155–7. 3 photos. Report on equipment and results obtained in Rome during April. (2852, 3140)

2945 Gardiner, E.L. "The Stenode Radiostat system of wireless reception and its application to television." J. TELEV. SOC. 1 (June): 33–42. Illus. (2784)

2946 "Third annual exhibition." J. TELEV. SOC. 1 (June): 55–60. Illus. Full report of exhibitors and exhibits at the show held Apr. 15 (2870). (2901, 2948)

2947 "Note on Physical and Optical Societies' exhibition." J. TELEV. SOC. 1 (June): 61, 62. (2736)

2948 "Report of the third annual business meeting." J. TELEV. SOC. 1 (June): 63–7. (2946, 3334)

2949 "Definitions and notices." J. TELEV. SOC. 1 (June): 68.

2950 Joers, Carl F. "Television." U.S. 2,080,942, June 1, 1931, May 18, 1937. Light valve in the form of a tank and a multiplicity of light tubes with individual control windings.

2951 Banks, G.B., and Baird Television. "Television." Br. 380,109, June 2, 1931. Concerns the construction of electrodes for a water-cooled arc lamp and modulating circuit which includes an amplifier coupled by a transformer to a tuned circuit containing the arc and a d-c generator. (2797, 3070)

2952 Nicolson, A.M. "Arc screen projection system." U.S. 1,893,504, June 2, 1931, Jan. 10, 1933. Assigned: Comm. Pats. Moving arc and zigzag electrodes. (2774, 3268)

2953 "Television transmission." TIMES (June 4): 16b. "Yesterday afternoon the Baird Television Company, in co-operation with the B.B.C., broadcast a television transmission of scenes from the Derby, including the parade of horses before the start and the scene at the winning-post during the race. This broadcast is important in that it is the first attempt which has been made, in this or any other country, to secure a television transmission of a topical event held in the open air, where artificial lighting is impossible." Transmission by Post Office lines to Long Acre, thence to the BBC transmitter at Brookmans Park. "On the whole the transmission was considered to be successful." (2900, 2943, 2960, 2996)

2954 Müller, C. "Television." Br. 380,473, June 4, 1931. A reflecting membrane controlled electrostatically or electromagnetically serves as a light valve.

2955 Leishman, L.J. "Coloring light formed images." U.S. 2,010,307, June 6, 1931, Aug. 6, 1935. A prism produces color bands which coact with a mirror scanner. (2753)

2956 "Leaders answer—how near are we to television? So near and yet so far. Survey reveals that more problems must be solved before the American home can see far by radio." N.Y.T. IX, 9 (June 7): 1–5. Views of nine leading radio men on prospects.

2957 (Television girls.) N.Y.T. IX, 9 (June 7): 3–6. Photo of Natalie Towers, CBS, and one of Dorothy Knapp, NBC. (2802, 2873, 3000, 3014)

2958 "Tiny sets feature radio trade show. Five makers display television devices." N.Y.T. 32 (June 9): 1, 2. Report on the radio trade show in Chicago. (2959)

2959 "Electric eyes give television at show. Demonstration is made on six-foot screen at radio trade meeting in Chicago. Images emerge from blur." N.Y.T. 34 (June 11): 2. Sanabria's display of a large screen. (1917, 2958, 2970)

2960 "News and views." NATURE 127 (June 13): 902. Note on Baird's transmission of the Derby and reference to the TIMES, June 4 (2953). (2995)

2961 "Television in home held likely soon. Aylesworth predicts use of sight apparatus in radio broadcasting programs." N.Y.T. 8 (June 13): 1. Views of M.H. Aylesworth, president of NBC, in speech to the National Electric Light Association. (2779, 3005)

2962 Compagnie Générale de Télévision (Procédés H. de France). "Television." Br. 384,207, June 10, 1932. In France June 13, 1931. Relates to a method for reducing transmission bandwidth by interrupting the signal for each elemental area. Overlapping disks, one with adjoining arcuate slots and the other with spaced slots, both in a single spiral, the latter serving as a shutter. Alternatives are Nipkow disk or Weiller mirror drum. Includes discharge lamp, electromagnetic sync, and electron tube circuits.

2963 Donle, H.P. "Television." U.S. 1,984,336, June 16, 1931, Dec. 11, 1934. Assigned: Radio Inventions. Mirror drum and optical assembly for scanning two motion picture films in opposite directions. (2538, 3007)

2964 Vance, A.W. "Television." U.S. 2,137,039, June 17, 1931, Nov. 15, 1938. Assigned: RCA. Br. 395,499, June 8, 1932 (Marconi's). Nipkow disk with outer circle of holes for generating sync signals in conjunction with lamp, photocell, and aperture mask. Receiver has a picture tube with deflection coils and sawtooth oscillators. Includes complete circuits and alternatives. (2104, 3394)

2965 Ardenne, M. v. "Television." Br. 388,623, June 8, 1932, Mar. 2, 1933. In Germany June 19, 1931. Addition to Br. 387,536 (2827). Concerns a cathode-ray-tube screen with three narrow strips of different phosphors for red, blue, green, each group representing one ordinary scanning line, or with the three phosphors superimposed. Applicable to the parent film transmission system, for black and white or color, and for velocity modulation. See Rüdenberg's color tube (2929). (2940, 2966)

2966 Ardenne, M. v. "Braun tube." U.S. 2,039,132, June 14, 1932, Apr. 28, 1936. Assigned: D.S. Loewe. Br. 405,977, June 16, 1932. In Germany June 19, 1931. A gaseous cathode-ray tube with an inwardly curved end-face and fluorescent screen projects via a lens an enlarged image onto a separate viewing screen. (2965, 2967)

2967 Ardenne, M. v. "Braun tube." Br. 407,377, June 16, 1932. In Germany June 19, 1931. A metallic screen outside the Wehnelt cylinder protects the cathode of a gaseous tube from ionic bombardment. (2966, 2979)

2968 "Building cathode ray tubes for television." N.Y.T. IX, 9 (June 21): 2, 3. Photo.

2969 Jacomb, William Wykeham (1897–1979), and Baird Television. "Television receiver." Br. 384,346, June 22, 1931. The line frequency component of picture signals provides sync control of a driving motor via an oscillator. References to previous patents (711, 761, 1213, 1961). (3299)

2970 "Enlarged television here. Inventor demonstrates use of screen six feet square." N.Y.T. 34 (June 23): 3. Sanabria's test in New York at the Short Wave & Television Labs. "Nearly 100 spectators sat at a distance of sixty to seventy feet from the screen of translucent glass to view the show. Mr. Sanabria said he hoped to increase the size of the images on the screen to about ten by sixteen feet." (2959, 3115)

2971 "Radio television on ship. Programs to be broadcast to the Leviathan on Halifax cruise." N.Y.T. 51 (June 25): 4. Will sail from New York on July 23. (3016)

2972 Gray, F. "Electro-optical system." U.S. 1,990,183, June 25, 1931, Feb. 5, 1935. Assigned: B.T.L. Double-sided mirror wheel with two light sources and two phototubes. (2923, 3105)

2973 Tolson, W.A. "Television." U.S. 2,062,198, June 25, 1931, Nov. 24, 1936. Assigned: RCA. Br. 387,915, June 27, 1932. Picture tube has external coils and plates connected to scanning oscillators which are controlled by separate framing pulses generated at the transmitter with timing by a switch actuated by a projection on a Nipkow disk. (2492, 3312)

2974 Birch-Field, C.A. "Television." U.S. 2,072,419, June 26, 1931, Mar. 2, 1937. Assigned: M.S. Reisman. Optical assembly with light valve and multiple magnetic controls. (2028, 3020)

2975 Okolicsányi, F. v. "Picture assembling apparatus for television receivers." U.S. 1,923,520, July 7, 1932, Aug. 22, 1933, reissued Aug. 10, 1935, Mar. 23, 1937. Br. 380,419, June 21, 1932 (Tekade). In Germany June 27, 1931. A multiturn mirror screw consists of a triplicate set of mirrors surrounded by a rotary cylinder screen with a helical slot that reveals only one spiral set of mirrors at one time. (2625, 3047)

2976 "Latest television receiver which produces the image on an eight-inch screen." N.Y.T. IX, 11 (June 28): 5, 6. Photo of console model by Western Television Corp. (2863, 3219)

2977 Zworykin, V.K., and J.C. Batchelor. "Cathode ray apparatus." U.S. 1,988,469, June 30, 1931, Jan. 22, 1935. Assigned: RCA. Br. 383,889, May 11, 1932 (Marconi's). Silver coating (focusing anode) on the conical part of a picture tube is treated to be nonreflective to improve contrast of the image on the fluorescent screen. (2104, 2931, 2984, 3058)

2978 Thun, R. "Helligkeitssteuerung und Liniensteuerung" [Brightness and line control]. FERN. 2 (July): 161–7. 5 illus. (2621, 3239)

2979 Ardenne, M. v. "Uber neue Fernsehsender und Fernsehempfänger mit Kathodenstrahlröhren." FERN. 2 (July): 173–8. Continued from April (2841). Experiments and results with picture tube receiver in the D.S. Loewe lab. (2967, 3012)

2980 Federmann, Wolfgang. "Fernsehempfang auf Kurzwelle" [Television reception on short waves]. FERN. 2 (July): 179–82. 4 illus. Short-wave experiments by Telefunken between Nauen and Geltow. (3596)

2981 Schubert, G. "Kinosende- und Empfangsanlage für höhere Bildpunktzahlen" [Cinema broadcast and receiving equipment for higher picture point numbers]. FERN. 2 (July): 182–7. 7 illus. High-definition equipment for transmitting and receiving motion pictures. (2881, 3028)

2982 Kette, G. "Der Empfang der Englischen Fernseh-Sendungen in Berlin" [The reception of the English television transmissions in Berlin]. FERN. 2 (July): 189–92. (2584, 3085)

2983 Kiepenheuer, K.O. "Der Spiegeloszillograf in der Fernsehtechnik" [The mirror oscillograph in television technique]. FERN. 2 (July): 192–8. 15 illus.

2984 Zworykin, V.K. "Photocell theory and practice." J. FRANKLIN INST. 212 (July): 1–41. 33 illus., 32 references. Thorough study dealing with types and applications including facsimile and television with some early history. (2977, 3166)

2985 Barthélemy, R. "La réception en télévision." ONDE ELECT. 10 (July): 281–302. 48 illus., including second part (3032). Principles, theory, amplification, receiving circuits, scanning, photocells. (2891, 3001)

2986 Waltz, G.H. "Get in on television." POP. SCI. 119 (July): 16, 17. (3033)

2987 "Television projector for screen pictures." PROJ. ENG. 3 (July): 13. 2 illus. De Forest apparatus intended for small theater audiences. (2880, 3052)

2988 Du Mont, A.B. "Practical operation of a complete television system." RADIO ENG. 11 (July): 33–6. 8 illus. Technical features of the Jenkins system. (2876, 2918, 2991, 3720)

2989 Dalpayrat, H.F. "New modulation tube for television." RADIO ENG. 11 (July): 37. (3199)

2990 Cockaday, L.M. "Future trends in radio—an authoritative forecast." RADIO N. 13 (July): 12–8, 74. 38 views by industry leaders, with portraits. Comments on television prospects by Alexanderson, H.S. Baird, Donle, Du Mont, Hogan, Jenkins, Replogle, and others. (2456, 3472)

2991 Replogle, D.E. "New York looks in." RADIO N. 13 (July): 30, 31, 89, 90. 5 photos, diagram showing layout of station W2XCR and its link with WGBS. Description of the Jenkins Television Corp. equipment, and studios at 655 Fifth Avenue, New York. "Television stepped out of the purely experimental stage early in April when television station W2XCR opened its special television studios in New York City for the synchronized broadcasting of radio talking movies on a regular daily program basis." (2864, 2988, 2994, 3038)

2992 Calcaterra, J. "How to build a home television receiver." RADIO N. 13 (July): 37–40, 72, 87. 5 photos, 3 diags., list of parts. (2936, 2941, 2998, 3037)

2993 "Standard television receiver." RADIO N. 13 (July): 56. Photo and brief description of cabinet set with short-wave receiver and 8-by-10 inch screen, Short Wave & Television Corp. (2936, 3011)

2994 Replogle, D.E. "Television now on schedule." SCI. AM. 145 (July): 33. (2991, 3036)

2995 "Seeing the Derby at a distance. A promise fulfilled to the confusion of the sceptics." TELEV. 4 (July): 164, 165. Photo, diag.

Broadcast from Epsom Downs race track on June 3 (2953). (2960, 2996)

"At 2:45 p.m. on Derby Day the first scenes came through and were built up in the 'Televisors' in use at the Baird offices. These varied, sometimes showing clearly and at other times appearing somewhat indistinct. Occasionally interference from the telegraph and telephone lines wiped out the picture, but, in spite of this unavoidable fact the parade of the horses and the jockeys was seen by all present, while, now and then, the close-up of a man or woman passing across the line of vision showed on the screen.

"A short pause and then we heard the announcer telling us that the horses were rounding Tatterham Corner. We held our breath and, before we realised it, the first three horses flashed by the winning post to the frenzied roar of the crowd. The rest of the field followed in close pursuit.

"And so we were able to see what was happening at fifteen miles distance. The experiment proved beyond doubt to the most sceptical die-hards that television had come out of the studio into the sphere of topical events. The restrictions of four walls and artificial light had been put aside, and Mr. Baird had fulfilled that promise which had once called down such a storm of disbelieving contempt on his head."

2996 Moseley, S.A. "Televising the Derby." TELEV. 4 (July): 172, 173. Photo. Brief personal account with quotes from five letters about the reception (2953). (2942, 2995, 2999, 3041, 3044)

2997 Schröter, F. "Latest forms of photo-electric cells." TELEV. 4 (July): 177–9. 3 graphs, table, diag. Photo effect in gases, selenium cells, alkali metal cells, surface treatment, monatomic cells, frequency sensitivity. (2905, 3013)

2998 "The enthusiast sees it through." TELEV. 4 (July): 184–8. 7 photos. (2992, 3040)

2999 Abbott, W.B. "The press, the B.B.C., and British television." TELEV. 4 (July): 189. Quotes from letters sent to the SCOTSMAN and the DAILY HERALD with reference to the Derby broadcast. (2271, 2996, 3041, 3064, 3147)

3000 "Asks television license. N.B.C. waits permit for its fourth experimental station." N.Y.T. 25 (July 2): 5. (2957, 3005)

3001 Barthélemy, R. "La réception en télévision." REV. GEN. 30 (July 4, 11): 3–12, 52–9. 29 illus. High-frequency amplification, detection, modulated light sources, sync. (2985, 3006)

3002 Marconi's, H.M. Dowsett, D.L. Plaistowe, and N. Levin. "Television." Br. 381,544, July 4, 1931. Disk with rectangular apertures and compensating lenses, including image enlargement. (2919, 2920, 3003, 3246, 3358)

3003 Marconi's, H.M. Dowsett, and L.E.Q. Walker. "Television." Br. 381,545, July 4, 1931. Double spiral disk and concentric disk with two semicircular slots on corresponding radii. Reference to Br. 302,228 (1091). (2928, 3002, 3004, 3187)

3004 Marconi's, H.M. Dowsett, and R. Cadzow. "Cathode ray tubes." Br. 381,573, July 4, 1931. Special form of cathode-ray tube with hot cathode and anode, other anodes and a photoelectric cathode, deflection plates, and coils, with lenses for film pickup. (2877, 3003, 3026, 3293)

3005 "Television studio for Empire State. National Company to use mooring mast to test broadcasting of pictures. World's highest station. Aylesworth predicts public use of radio pictures after a year's experiments." N.Y.T. 24 (July 10): 5, 6. Announcement of plans for the NBC station. (2961, 3000, 3021, 3306)

3006 Barthélemy, R. "Synchronizing system." U.S. 1,983,432, July 5, 1932, Dec. 4, 1934; Br. 385,546, July 11, 1932. Assigned: Comp. Gaz. In France July 11, 1931. Phase control of a receiver by a hysteresis motor and partially slotted disk. (3001, 3032)

3007 Donle, H.P. "Television." U.S. 1,957,101, July 11, 1931, May 1, 1934. Assigned: Radio Inventions. Rotary slotted disk and second scanner with intermediate diffusing screen. (2963, 3055)

3008 Farnsworth, P.T. "Scanning and synchronizing system." U.S. 2,051,372, July 14, 1931, renewed Feb. 11, 1935, Aug. 18, 1936. Assigned: Television Labs. Picture tube receiver circuits. (2899, 3009)

3009 Farnsworth, P.T. "Projecting oscillight." U.S. 2,140,284, July 14, 1931, Dec. 13, 1938. Assigned: Farnsworth Television. Picture tube with oblique screen. (3008, 3225)

3010 Wilson, John Charles, and Baird Television. "Television." Br. 381,254, July 14, 1931. Relates to a frequency changing system with parallel filters and frequency changing circuits, each set passing one of the predominant components of the picture signal, intended to condense the transmission band. (2486, 3216)

3011 Baird, H.S. "Scanning device for television." U.S. 1,962,474, July 16, 1931, June 12, 1934. Assigned: Short Wave & Television. Lens drum and zone plates. (2993)

3012 Ardenne, M. v. "Television." Br. 394,496, July 18, 1932. In Germany July 18, 1931. Addition to Br. 387,536 (2827). Modifications to the screen phosphor and to the transmitter amplifier in the parent specification. (2979, 3061)

3013 Schröter, F. "Television." U.S. 1,951,533, July 11, 1932, Mar. 20, 1934. Assigned: Telefunken. Br. 387,240, July 18, 1932. In Germany July 18, 1931. Picture tube and circuits with a multipole switch for selection of operation by either intensity or velocity modulation. (2997, 3042)

3014 "The newest television station W2XAB of the Columbia Broadcasting System." N.Y.T. IX, 13 (July 19): 4–6. Photo. (2957, 3015)

3015 "Six visual stations on the New York air. Peak of skyscraper selected as aerial site—new image broadcaster in debut this week." N.Y.T. IX, 13 (July 19): 7, 8. (3014, 3017)

3016 "Ship to pick up television. Broadcasts expected to be seen and heard on Leviathan cruises." N.Y.T. 20 (July 22): 3. (1971, 3019)

3017 "Television studio opened by Walker. Before 100 guests he draws curtain from radio 'eyes' at new station W2XAB. A program sent overseas. Transmitter is sixth of the Columbia Company in the Metropolitan area." N.Y.T. 21 (July 22): 4. Station W2XAB. Edwin K. Cohan, technical director, spoke on "What to expect of television." (2159, 3015, 3022)

"Television of today is perhaps comparable to the phonograph of 1910 and the moving picture of 1905, but upon this pioneering must rest the solid foundation of future progress. Television will advance from now on just as surely as sound broadcasting has, and I believe at no less a pace. It will progressively bring to spectators the individual and small groups and complete symphonic and stage presentations, the outdoor sporting events, the spot news events. It will eventually bring these things in natural color.

"In the future there will be television networks similar to our sound networks of today and functioning in much the same manner. To accomplish this, considerable progress will have to be made, particularly with regard to the transmission band. In addition, pickup flexibility and future program demands call for a suitable method of scanning whose illumination limitations are no greater than those of the present moving picture camera.

"We have but one purpose in opening television station W2XAB; our interest being solely that of a progressive broadcasting organization intent upon carrying on television experiments of its own to determine the scope and limitations of this new art and to build a well co-ordinated and efficient organization in advance of the day when television no longer remains the crude marvel that it now is."

3018 "Television license given. R.C.A. Victor may have unlimited time on air for new plant." N.Y.T. 38 (July 22): 2. Station W3XAD.

3019 "Leviathan at sea in television test. Reported to be first time reception by vessel has been successful." N.Y.T. 20 (July 24): 4. Reception from station W1XAV in Boston satisfactory, but signals from Columbia station W2XAV in Washington marred by an electrical storm. (3016, 3172)

3020 Birch-Field, C.A. "Television." U.S. 2,077,031, July 24, 1931, Apr. 13, 1937. Assigned: M.S. Reisman. Optical system employing polarizers and electromagnet control to produce sequential signals representing small portions of a scene. (2974, 3559)

3021 "Television station for Empire State. Radio Board gives the N.B.C. a permit for transmitter on 84th floor of building. Antenna on mooring mast." N.Y.T. 10 (July 25): 5. (3005, 3024)

3022 "Mayor on television picks up mustache somewhere in space. Electric storm paints freak effects on the images—engineer discusses present problems." N.Y.T. IX, 8 (July 26): 1, 2. Photo of Mayor Walker. Quotes from discussion by E. K. Cohan, technical director. (3017, 3068)

3023 "Television needs experts in radio and photography. Other arts give assistance. Seeing by radio is aided by the motion picture film, the camera and its lenses, and by broadcasting apparatus." N.Y.T. IX, 8 (July 26): 1–5.

3024 "Manhattan's steel fingers that 'steal' television images." N.Y.T. IX, 8 (July 26): 3–6. Photo of Manhattan and inset showing the NBC transmitter. (3021, 3192)

3025 Cawley, A.J. "Scanning apparatus." U.S. 2,247,348, July 27, 1931, July 1, 1941. Lens disk and plurality of photocells for multiple pickup. (2916, 3076)

3026 Marconi's, and H.M. Dowsett. "Television." Br. 382,326, July 27, 1931; U.S. 2,002,937, July 25, 1932, May 28, 1935 (RCA). Lamp bank receiver has auxiliary lighting superposed to reduce flicker and improve definition. Variants include smaller lamps placed between the image lamps in a matrix assembly, projection screen with back lighting, and other arrangements. (3004, 3187)

3027 "Television institute opens in fall." N.Y.T. 19 (July 28): 5. Plans for training television technicians at the new YMCA building in New York.

3028 Schubert, G. "Television." U.S. 2,026,915, July 28, 1932, Jan. 7, 1936. Assigned: Fernseh A.-G. Br. 386,563, July 12, 1932. In Germany July 30, 1931. Addition to Br. 386,492 (2881). Circuit modification. (2981, 3098)

3029 Fernseh A.-G. "Television receivers." Br. 389,709, July 12, 1932. In Germany July 30, 1931. Circuit arrangement to avoid loss of signal strength at higher frequencies. (2871, 3049)

3030 Möller, H.G., and R. Möller. "Braun tube." U.S. 1,993,565, July 28, 1932, Mar. 5, 1935. Assigned: Fernseh A.-G. Br. 406,009, July 13, 1932. In Germany July 31, 1931. Concerns a transparent metallic coating of zigzag electrodes deposited on the inner wall with separate parts connected to the anode and the screen. See also Br. 409,269. (2232, 2842, 3098)

3031 Short, D.W. "Television direct pickup camera." ELECTRONICS 3 (Aug.): 69. Spiral scanning disk. (2644, 3408)

3032 Barthélemy, R. "La réception en télévision." ONDE ELECT. 10 (Aug.): 338–54. Receiver apparatus including sync. Continued from July (2985). (3006, 3509)

3033 Waltz, G.H. "Buying the parts for your television receiver." POP. SCI. 119 (Aug.): 45, 46. (2986, 3077)

3034 Nason, C.H.W. "Standards of performance for commercial television receivers." RADIO ENG. 11 (Aug.): 30, 45. 2 illus. Technical aspects including selectivity, sensitivity, and fidelity in design. (2895)

3035 Huffman, C.E. "Design of a complete television system." RADIO ENG. 11 (Aug.): 36, 38. 10 illus. Engineering aspects and fundamentals. (2609)

3036 Replogle, D.E. "Television receiver kit easily assembled at home." RADIO N. 13 (Aug.): 110, 111, 176. 2 photos, diag. List of parts for short-wave receiver. (2994, 3079)

3037 Calcaterra, J. "Bringing in pictures with the home televisor." RADIO N. 13 (Aug.): 126, 127, 167. 2 photos. Operation of equipment described in June and July. Editorial note: "We have 'looked-in' on the Jenkins transmissions, the N.B.C.'s card announcements, and J.V.L. Hogan's radio 'movies' with great interest." (2992)

3038 "See the artist you hear." RADIO N. 13 (Aug.): 154. Advertisement by the Jenkins Television Corp. Radiovisor kit at $42.50, with lens $50. Ready-to-use models up to $350 in walnut cabinet. (2991, 3046)

3039 Rosen, Herbert. "Television on short waves at Döberitz." TELEV. 4 (Aug.): 214, 215. 4 photos. Experimental transmissions of the German Post Office at 142.9 m midway between Berlin and Nauen, with telecine apparatus. (2598, 3131)

3040 "The enthusiast sees it through." TELEV. 4 (Aug.): 216-9. 2 photos, 2 graphs, diag. (2998, 3077)

3041 "Television as an entertainment." TELEV. 4 (Aug.): 220, 221. 4 photos. Production methods at Baird studios. (2999, 3044)

3042 Schröter, F. "Latest forms of photo-electric cells." TELEV. 4 (Aug.): 225-8. 3 photos, 4 graphs, 4 diags. Alkali-metal cells, auxiliary grid, combined photo and amplifying effect, insulating coating, semiconductor surface. (3013, 3074)

3043 Bray, T. "Atmospherics and television." TELEV. 4 (Aug.): 232, 233. Photo, diag. Types, charges, pulses, television images.

3044 Moseley, S.A., and H.J.B. Chapple. TELEVISION TO-DAY AND TO-MORROW. London: Pitman, 1931. xxvii + 163 pp. Portrait, 62 plates, 44 diags. Foreword by J.L. Baird. Expanded from first edition (2323) with an additional chapter on new developments which covers the big screen at the Coliseum (2491) and elsewhere, teletalkies (2565), zone television, and the modulated arc (2735). (2762, 2996, 3041, 3063, 3138)

3045 "Plans television station. Rhines Hotel of Portland, Me., asks permit—to use new device." N.Y.T. 24 (Aug. 2): 3. Equipment for station WCSH by RCA Victor Co.

3046 "Seeing a radio teacher." N.Y.T. IX, 9 (Aug. 2): 2. Stations W1XAV, Boston, W2XCR, New York, piano teacher in New York. (3038, 3093)

3047 Okolicsányi, F. v. "Television receiver." U.S. 2,063,643, July 7, 1932, Dec. 8, 1936; Br. 384, 948, July 30, 1932 (Tekade). In Germany Aug. 5, 1931. Mirror screw, linear light source, optical system. (2975, 3103)

3048 Tekade. "Television receiver." Br. 384,947, July 30, 1932. In Germany Aug. 5, 1931. Mirror screw. See above.

3049 Fernseh A.-G. "Television." Br. 393,119, Aug. 2, 1932. In Germany Aug. 6, 1931. Nipkow disk with two or more spirals of apertures coacting with a mask, such as another apertured disk, moving mirror, or prism which obscures all but one of the spirals. Alternatives include a commutator to energize one of a plurality of light sources, and a mirror wheel. (3029, 3097)

3050 Telefunken. "Cathode ray tubes." Br. 405,964, Aug. 8, 1932. In Germany Aug. 6, 1931. Concerns screen materials. Reference to Br. 402,411 (2828). (2581, 3059)

3051 Schiff, Ludwig. "Electron ray tube." U.S. 2,159,712, Apr. 20, 1934, May 23, 1939. Assigned: Fernseh A.-G. In Germany Aug. 8, 1931. Cathode-ray tube with deflection plates between two focusing coils.

3052 De Forest, L. "Television sign." U.S. 2,049,763, Aug. 10, 1931. Aug. 4, 1936. Assigned: American Television Labs. Bank of glow tubes with distributors and receiver circuit arranged to provide zero-current connections. (2987, 3088)

3053 Schlesinger, K. "Braun tube." U.S. 2,038,061, Aug. 4, 1932, Apr. 21, 1936; Br.

408,297, Aug. 5, 1932. In Germany Aug. 10, 1931. Gaseous tube with deflection plates and annular electrode between the plates and the screen to neutralize ion oscillations and prevent "fringing" of the lines on the screen. (2921, 3189)

3054 Clay, R.S. "Television receiver." Br. 388,370, Aug. 14, 1931. Picture tube with vertical and horizontal conductive strips at two edges of the screen whereby the beam is returned by timing pulses at the end of each line and frame, with circuits and modifications. Reference to Br. 271,131 (743).

3055 Donle, H.P. "Television." U.S. 1,988,303, Aug, 14. 1931, Jan. 15, 1935. Assigned: Radio Inventions. Slotted disk and slotted drum with optical elements. (3007, 3067)

3056 Hogan, J.V.L. "Television scanning system." U.S. 1,994,708, Aug. 14, 1931, Mar. 19, 1935. Assigned: Radio Inventions. Receiver with pivoted mirrors on a drum which are tilted parallel to the axis of the drum. (2773, 3089)

3057 Ballard, Randall Clarence. "Television." U.S. 2,215,285, Aug. 15, 1931, Sept. 17, 1940. Assigned: RCA. Br. 392,383, July 23, 1932 (Marconi's). Picture tube with deflection coils and circuits to blank the return beam at the end of each line and frame. (3253)

3058 Batchelor, J.C. "Cathode ray tube." Br. 399,961, Aug. 15, 1932 (Marconi's). In U.S. Aug. 15, 1931 (RCA). Refers to the electrode assembly in a picture tube. (2977, 3254)

3059 Telefunken. "Cathode ray tubes." Br. 392,781, Aug. 15, 1932. In Germany Aug. 15, 1931. Specifies dimensional relationship between a small cathode, concentrating cylinder, and accelerating anode. See also Br. 395,882, Aug. 18, 1932, in Germany Aug. 18, 1931. (3050, 3195)

3060 "Requests for stations wane as cost of operation mounts. Television licenses increase." N.Y.T. IX, 8 (Aug. 16): 1, 2. "While applications for broadcasting facilities have decreased...the requests for television permits are mounting. Nearly a score of applications for such stations have been received in the last few weeks." (2759, 3072)

3061 "Cathode radio television sender on which Baron Manfred von Ardenne of Germany has been experimenting since 1928." N.Y.T. IX, 8 (Aug. 16): 4–6. Photo of cathode-ray transmitter. (3012, 3065)

3062 Gramophone Co., and George Edward Condliffe. "Television." Br. 388,404, Aug. 18, 1931. Mirror drum, bank of masking apertures and reflectors for film transmission, receiver with three light sources and a masking screen, and variants.

3063 "Here to push television. S.A. Moseley arrives from London to plan manufacture of sets." N.Y.T. 15 (Aug. 20): 6. Plans for producing one million receivers per year. (3044, 3064, 3071)

3064 "Television broadcast from B.B.C. studio." TIMES (Aug. 20): 8d. First broadcast by the BBC from Studio 10 near Waterloo Bridge with Baird mirror drum transmitter, Aug. 19. (2999, 3063, 3071, 3080)

3065 Ardenne, M. v. "Amplifier." Br. 410,147, Aug. 8, 1932. In Germany Aug. 20, 1931. Electron tube amplifier with correcting circuit for transmitter or receiver. (3061, 3095)

3066 "Early television system. Details of a picture transmission and television scheme of 1902." ELECT. 107 (Aug. 21): 249. Dark chamber with a lens contains a pin-hole scanner behind a ground-glass screen with selenium at the focal point. Receiver is similar with a source of light, a prism, electromagnet, and moving mirror. Quoted from the July issue of ELECTRICAL COMMUNICATION, the scheme is ascribed to J.L. McQuarrie and W.W. Cook, associated with the Western Electric Co.

3067 Donle, H.P. "Television." U.S. 1,961,632, Aug. 21, 1931, June 5, 1934. Assigned: Radio Inventions. Mirror drum with other scanning and light diffusing components. (3055, 3089)

3068 "Television make-up is an art. Hair of prize fighters is powdered white—blondes need dark background—Chicago sees New York images." N.Y.T. VIII, 9 (Aug. 23): 6–8. Images from CBS station W2XAB received clearly in Chicago. (3022, 3090)

3069 Michelssen, Fritz. "Electron tube." U.S. 2,151,789, Aug. 8, 1932, Mar. 28, 1939. Assigned: Telefunken. In Germany Aug. 25, 1931. Cathode-ray tube. (3074)

3070 Banks, G.B., and Baird Television. Br. 380,234, Aug. 25, 1931. Arc lamp, masking aperture with adjustments, mirror drum, and optical system for transmitter or receiver. References to prior patents (565, 2536, 2568, 2780, 2951). (3363)

3071 "Television ready for use in homes. Baird Company plans to begin regular programs here within a few weeks. Awaits federal permit. Arranging for manufacture of receiving sets to sell at moderate price. New device is perfected. S.A. Moseley says small portable apparatus will send pictures of news events." N.Y.T. 7 (Aug. 27): 1, 2. Plans for broadcasting through station WMCA and for producing sets to sell at $100. (3063, 3064, 3080, 3081, 3154)

3072 "Plans television station. Knickerbocker Broadcasting Company asks building permit." N.Y.T. 18 (Aug. 28): 7. Other applications to the Radio Commission by RCA-Victor Co. for W2XAJ, by RCA for W2XBB; and for W2XB, Long Island City, WXBZ, Saranac Lake. (3060, 3102)

3073 Comp. Gaz. "Television." Br. 387,592, July 14, 1932. In France Aug. 28, 1931. Film transmission with monitor and mechanical arrangement for frame adjustments. (2807, 3126)

3074 Schröter, F., and F. Michelssen. "Electron tube." U.S. 2,072,651, Aug. 8, 1932, Mar. 2, 1937. Assigned: Telefunken. Br. 391,360, Aug. 29, 1932. In Germany Aug. 29, 1931. Concerns the structures of the cathode, grid, and anodes in a cathode-ray tube which may have an argon filling to assist focusing. (3042, 3069, 3194, 3218)

3075 "Engineers to test television at sea. Three stations to broadcast programs to Vulcania on voyage September 4 to 8." N.Y.T. 33 (Aug. 31): 1. New York to Bermuda reception tests. (3090)

3076 Cawley, A.J. "Television." U.S. 2,116,425, Aug. 31, 1931, May 3, 1938. Light sources and light transmitting elements arranged alternately on a scanning disk with distributor. (3025, 3504)

3077 Waltz, G.H. "Easy way to make an accurate scanning disk, the heart of your television receiver." POP. SCI. 119 (Sept.): 71–3. (3033, 3040, 3082, 3135)

3078 Dinsdale, A. "Television turns to projection." RADIO ENG. 11 (Sept.): 19,20. 3 illus. Present status and possibilities, Baird and Sanabria apparatus. (2899, 3181)

3079 Replogle, D.E. "Building a Radiovisor." RADIO N. 13 (Sept.): 208,233, 235, 241. 9 illus. Jenkins disk receiver to operate with radio set described in August (3036). (3137)

3080 "A television broadcast from a B.B.C. studio. A happy augury." TELEV. 4 (Sept.): 244, 246. 2 photos. Morning program (one half hour) from studio 10 instead of from the Baird studio, Aug. 19. "From various reports the transmission was one of the best yet experienced, and marked a definite step forward." (3064, 3071, 3083, 3147)

3081 Moseley, S.A. "My television trip to America." TELEV. 4 (Sept.): 245, 246. 2 photos. "The claims from New York, Washington, and elsewhere with regard to discoveries in television have been so persistent of late that I am going over myself to discover what is being done." (3071, 3173)

3082 "The enthusiast sees it through." TELEV. 4 (Sept.): 250–3. 5 photos, 3 diags. (3077, 3135)

3083 Walker, R. "Baird television at Scarborough." TELEV. 4 (Sept.): 254, 255, 259. 2 photos. (3080, 3099)

3084 Campbell, D.R. "Scanned images with simple apparatus." TELEV. 4 (Sept.): 256–9. 4 photos, 2 diags. Experiments with a light source, photographic slide, lenses, ground-glass screen, and scanning disks. (2729, 3175)

3085 Kette, G. "The reception of the English television transmissions in Berlin." TELEV. 4 (Sept.): 268, 269. Photo, diag. Extracts from FERNSEHEN, July (2982). (3129)

3086 George, Roscoe Henry, and Howard John Heim. "Television." U.S. 2,100,279, Sept. 2, 1931, Nov. 23, 1937. Assigned: RCA. Picture tube receiver with scanning and sync circuits.

3087 Fahrney, C.D. "Television receiver." U.S. 1,889,727, Sept. 3, 1931, Nov. 29, 1932. Lens drum. (2355)

3088 De Forest, L. "Television." U.S. 2,052,133, Sept. 5, 1931, Aug. 25, 1936. Assigned: American Television Labs. Divided from U.S. 2,026,872 (2880). Series of Kerr cells in a spiral on a receiver disk with distributor. (3052, 3114)

3089 Hogan, J.V.L., and H.P. Donle. "Television." U.S. 1,943,238, Sept. 5, 1931, Jan. 9, 1934. Assigned: Radio Inventions. Mirror drum and mirrors. (3056)

3090 "Liner's music heard far. Singer from Roma entertains Vulcania, 4,500 miles away, by radio." N.Y.T. 6 (Sept. 6): 4. Swimming lessons by television from the Columbia station in New York were also received. (3068, 3075, 3092, 3094)

3091 "WLWL seeks television permit." N.Y.T. 14 (Sept. 6): 2.

3092 "Sees gems by television. Set owners get view of $1,000,000 Cartier display." N.Y.T. 29 (Sept. 9): 6. Experimental broadcast by Columbia Broadcasting Corp. (3090, 3163)

3093 "New camera widens range of television. Daylight apparatus publicly tested, more flexible than 'flying spot pick-up.'" N.Y.T. 36 (Sept. 9): 36. Portable camera demonstrated by the Jenkins Television Corp. at Park Central Hotel, New York. (3046, 3169)

3094 "Television on liner works 50 miles out. Vulcania reports clear reception from several shore stations—signals blur at 100 miles." N.Y.T. 55 (Sept. 9): 3. Clearest signals were from the CBS station W2XAB at 485 Madison Avenue, N.Y. Good reception also from the Jenkins station W2XCD in Passaic, N.J., and the Short Wave & Television Corp. station W1XAV in Boston. Apparatus on board was installed by the Short Wave & Television Corp. (3090, 3104)

3095 "Berlin radio show." W.W. 29 (Sept. 9): 253–7. Includes von Ardenne's cathode-ray system, with two photos of the apparatus and one of a received image taken in April. See also von Ardenne (3206). (2727, 3065, 3120, 3129)

3096 RCA. "Television receiver." Br. 392,801, Sept. 10, 1932. In U.S. Sept. 11, 1931. A picture tube with deflection coils in a screening enclosure mounted vertically in a cabinet with a viewing mirror attached to a hinged lid. See also Br. 377,622 (2865). (2502, 3436)

3097 Fernseh A.-G. "Television." Br. 383,946, Sept. 6, 1932. In Germany Sept. 12, 1931. Stationary enclosure for a Nipkow disk. (3049, 3139)

3098 Möller, R., and G. Schubert. "Television." U.S. 1,973,385, Sept. 7, 1932, Sept. 11, 1934. Assigned: Fernseh A.-G. Br. 384,965, Sept. 6, 1932. In Germany Sept. 12, 1931. Receiver has a Nipkow disk and discharge tube with a screen between them. The tube is enclosed in a box provided with heaters. (3028, 3030, 3183)

3099 "The outstanding inventions of the past eighty years." N.Y.T. X, 3 (Sept. 13): 3–6. Entry for 1926: "J.L. Baird sends recognizable television images over a wire." (740, 3083, 3101)

3100 Kaempffert, W. "From telegraph to television—and beyond." N.Y.T. X, 4 (Sept. 13). Full-page feature article on historical development. (921)

3101 "Television turns the air into vast kaleidoscope. A magic 'gypsy caravan.' Strange wagon appears at sports events to perform new wonders in radio science—Baird's latest achievements." N.Y.T. X, 14 (Sept. 13): 1–3. Photo of Baird at Epsom, cols. 4–7. Feature article by M. Marsland Gander, London (2953). (3099, 3116)

3102 "Commission sees television still confined to laboratory. Engineers advise that seeing by radio in the home must wait at least another year." N.Y.T. X, 16 (Sept. 13): 1, 2. Views of the FRC. (3072, 3164)

3103 "Spiral mirrors in new system minimize the flickering of images." N.Y.T. X, 16 (Sept. 13): 4–7. Mirror screw receiver exhibited at the radio show in Berlin by Tekade, designed by von Okolicsányi, Hungarian engineer. (3047, 3130)

3104 Palmer, Eric. "Opera on the high seas." N.Y.T. 16 (Sept. 14): 8. Letter correcting the report concerning reception aboard the Vulcania, Sept. 6 (3090). Radio transmission was from Rome, not from the vessel Roma. "The television experiments attracted large audiences." (3094)

3105 Gray, F. "Electro-optical system." U.S. 2,274,686, Sept. 16, 1931, Mar. 3, 1942. Assigned: B.T.L. Br. 406,672, Aug. 31, 1932 (E.R.P.). Disk system incorporating d-c suppression in the picture signals and restoration controlled by fluctuations produced in the received signals. (2972, 3255)

3106 Konkle, P.J. "Television." Br. 407,322, Sept. 8, 1932 (Marconi's). In U.S. Sept. 18, 1931. Film transmission with disk scanner incorporating circuits to limit the peak amplitude of picture signals and prevent interference with sync signals. Reference to Br. 398,242 (2813).

3107 Alexanderson, E.F.W. "Television receiver." U.S. 1,889,587, Sept. 19, 1931, Nov. 29, 1932. Assigned: G.E. Br. 382,939, Sept. 19, 1932 (B.T.H.). Refers to the Kell system (1849) modified by a multiplate Kerr cell modulator and apertured masks to produce three scanning beams projected from an arc lamp by a disk onto a screen. (2354, 3156)

3108 Dunlap, O.E., Jr. "Radio and television show comes to town this week. Images will perform. Radio Fair opens tomorrow with television on big screen and new sets on display." N.Y.T. IX, 8 (Sept. 20): 16. Photo of Sanabria and apparatus. (2583, 2700, 3109, 3123)

3109 "Leaders look ahead. Television expected to give impetus to industry in 1932—signs of improvement seen." N.Y.T. IX, 8; 9 (Sept. 20): 7, 8; 1, 2. Photo of Sanabria and apparatus. Views expressed by 14 persons. (3108, 3111)

3110 Worlitz, Daniel E. "Television." U.S. 1,978,288, Sept. 21, 1931, Oct. 23, 1934. Two vibrating armatures, photocells, amplifiers, and radio transmitting circuits.

3111 "Radio show opens, television to fore. Innovation attracts all eyes as Sarnoff at the Garden starts 'World's Fair.' New broadcast era seen. Visual transmissions hailed by R.C.A. official as 'lifting veil' from wireless." N.Y.T. 32 (Sept. 22): 1, 2. "At one end of the arena hangs a 350-pound ground glass televiewing screen in a silver frame, inside of which is a mat of crimson. The televisor is installed in the basement, on a platform in full view of the public. That is where the stage, screen and radio entertainers will appear before the electric 'eyes' to be seen on the big screen as soon as the machine is in operation." There were other exhibitors: "Four manufacturers have home television sets in their booths. They are equipped with small screens on the panel of the receiver." (2930, 3109, 3112, 3115)

3112 "Text of Sarnoff's address on radio's growth." N.Y.T. 32 (Sept. 22): 2–6. "I feel that next year, if one is privileged to indulge in a bit of prophecy, the theatre of the home will be established, and on the way to become an outstanding institution. Nor is the day distant when sight will be transmitted through the air to large numbers. We are on the threshold of television, and just as the shackles of silence were struck from the screen, so will the veil be lifted from our daily broadcasts." (3111, 3125)

3113 "Gimbel to install television." N.Y.T. 32 (Sept. 22): 2. Gimbel Brothers to install a transmitter in Philadelphia, announced by Richard Gimbel. (3296)

3114 De Forest, L. "Television receiving and projecting means and method." U.S. 2,003,680. Sept. 22, 1931, June 4, 1935. Assigned: American Television Labs. Etched film system. (3088, 3169)

3115 "Television draws big crowd at fair. Long line waits to see images flash on screen, the chief attraction at the show." N.Y.T. 18 (Sept. 23): 4, 5. Sanabria's demonstration of the smaller screens in the basement studio. (2970, 3111, 3117, 3119)

3116 "Baird television." W.W. 29 (Sept. 23): 330. Display by Baird Television at the National Radio Exhibition, Olympia, Sept. 18–26. The complete instrument (vision only), housed in a brown metal case, gives a 3-by-4-inch picture. Price 18 guineas, kit of parts 12 guineas. (2640, 3101, 3143, 3148)

3117 "First 10-foot television. Images in ghost story float over ground-glass plate set up in Garden's darkened arena." N.Y.T. 32 (Sept. 24): 2–4. Sanabria got the large screen working late in the afternoon of Sept. 23. "A group of actors presented a microphone and television version of a ghost story. Onlookers shuddered as weird visions floated over the plate, to the accompaniment of shrieks emitted by the actors to make the effect realistic." (3115, 3119)

3118 Nyman, Alexander. "Television." U.S. 2,066,048, Sept. 24, 1931, Dec. 29, 1936. Assigned: RCA. Multifrequency system with all subdivisions of the image scanned simultaneously.

3119 "Television stages a talking picture. Thousands at radio show see screen images converse over loud-speaker hook-up." N.Y.T. 30 (Sept. 25): 3. Demonstration of Sanabria's big screen. "Thousands of visitors at the radio show yesterday stood about the darkened arena of Madison Square Garden and gazed at ten-foot television images projected on a large screen." See also Dinsdale (3181). (3115, 3117, 3122)

3120 Ardenne, M. v. "Television." Br. 397,681, Sept. 19, 1932. In Germany Sept. 25, 1931. Refers to outside broadcast of topical events with images and sound recorded on film which is processed within a few seconds and transmitted on a wavelength of 1 meter or less to a central station for broadcasting on 7 meters. (3095, 3146)

3121 Kell, R.D. "Television." U.S. 2,289,914, Sept. 26, 1931, July 14, 1942. Assigned: RCA. Br. 408,656, Sept. 8, 1932 (Marconi's). Picture tube receiver circuits. Reference to Br. 395,499 (2964). (2428, 3127)

3122 "Radio show closes, had record crowds. Appeal of television led." N.Y.T. 23 (Sept. 27): 5–7. "Hundreds tried television. Throughout the week hundreds posed and spoke before the electrical eye of the Sanabria television transmitter." (3119, 3123, 3150)

3123 Dunlap, O.E. Jr. "Crowds applaud television and cheer radio industry. Sidelights of the show. Public displays keen interest in improved television images." N.Y.T. IX, 8 (Sept. 27): 1, 2. (3108, 3122, 3192)

3124 "Engineer sees much to be done before television is revolutionary." N.Y.T. IX, 8 (Sept. 27): 7, 8. Views of Walter E. Holland, chief engineer of Philco.

3125 "Television's future." N.Y.T. 18 (Sept. 28): 4, 5. Editorial on Sarnoff's speech with comments on the problems of television and its possibilities. (3112)

3126 Comp. Gaz. "Television." Br. 385,920, Sept. 28, 1932. In France Sept. 28, 1931. Sync method with impulses in line groups, edge reflectors at one side of the image area, sync motor, and circuit. Reference to Br. 363,605 (2389). (3073, 3266)

3127 Kell, R.F. "Television." U.S. 2,178,758, Sept. 30, 1931, renewed Nov. 19, 1937, Nov. 7, 1939. Assigned: RCA. Br. 407,409, Sept. 22, 1932 (Marconi's). Disk with a spiral of apertures for image scanning and an inner ring of apertures coacting with a photocell for producing line sync pulses. An arcuate slot closer to the axis provides framing pulses and is specially shaped to blank the return trace at the end of each picture. Includes picture tubes with deflection coils and circuits. Reference to Br. 392,383 (3057). (3121)

3128 Murray, A.F. "Measurement of fidelity in television systems." ELECTRONICS 3 (Oct.): 137, 138. 2 illus.

3129 Kette, G. "Das Fernsehen auf der Berliner Funkausstellung 1931" [Television at the Berlin radio fair 1931]. FERN. 2 (Oct): 225–40. (3085, 3095, 3146, 3641)

3130 Okolicsányi, F. v. "Bildpunktzahl, Bildgrösse und Helligkeit bei den Spiegelschraube" [Number of picture points, picture size, and brightness at the mirror screw]. FERN. 2 (Oct): 240–4. 6 illus. (3103)

3131 Hudec, E., and E. Perchermeier. "Die Fernsehanordnung des Reichspostzentralamtes mit Braunscher Röhre" [Television arrangement of the German Central Post Office with Braun tubes]. FERN. 2 (Oct.): 244–51. 13 illus. Details of the transmitting and receiving equipment employing cathode-ray tubes. See also Traub (3205). (2626, 2933, 3039, 3146, 3196, 3380)

3132 Busse, E. "Uber Fernempfangsversuche mit der Braun'schen Röhre" [On television reception experiments with the Braun tube]. FERN. 2 (Oct.): 252, 253. (2585, 3379)

3133 Peters, H. "Uber die Grenzen der Abbildungsfähigkeit der Kathodenstrahl-Oscillografen bei Fernsehübertragungen" [About the limits of capability for reproduction of the cathode-ray oscillograph in television transmission]. FERN. 2 (Oct.): 261–7. 2 illus. Characteristics, analysis, tests, and results. (2554, 3521)

3134 Browne, C.O. "Technical problems in connection with television." J. IEE 69 (Oct.): 1232–8. Meeting of the Wireless Section, May 6. Overview of the main problems: large number of picture elements and large band of frequencies required in transmission, and providing sufficient illumination at the receiver screen. Discussion by 8 persons. (2934, 3256) Referring to screen sizes, H.M. Dowsett said: "In our laboratories we are at present working on a projection picture area of 6 ft. x 3 ft., employing a special form of multiplex Kerr cell and mirror wheel." Dowsett also commented:

"The cathode ray television receiver appears to be extremely promising, but it is becoming more and more complicated every day. It is still a laboratory apparatus, and in my opinion is likely to remain so for a considerable time. I think the possibility that it will shortly be introduced as a home set is retiring into the distance. Every internal modification which has recently been suggested would tend to increase its price and reduce its life, so that not only would the equipment be expensive but it would also employ a high-voltage control and would have a limited life. The technique of making cathode ray tubes has to show a considerable advance before they need be seriously considered for home use."

R.W. Conkling:
"I do not think that the cathode ray has much to offer, as in whatever way it is developed it can only be used on a small screen and even then gives but a poor intensity of illumination."

J.H.O. Harries:
"The cathode ray system is, I think, the most promising if not the only one for home working, and the possibilities are that it will eliminate the synchronizing trouble."

3135 Waltz, G.H. "We assemble our television receiver and amplifier." POP. SCI. 119 (Oct.): 82, 83. (3077, 3082, 3144, 3168)

3136 Tanner, R.W. "Television reception with superheterodyne." RADIO ENG. 11 (Oct.): 23–5. 4 illus. (3170)

3137 Replogle, D.E. "Useful hints on tuning in television programs." RADIO N. 13 (Oct.): 291, 292, 331. 2 photos. (3079, 3523)

3138 Chapple, H.J.B. "Introducing the new Tele-Radio receiver." TELEV. 4 (Oct.): 284–7. 3 photos, 2 diags. (3044, 3174)

3139 "The Fernseh A.G. television exhibit." TELEV. 4 (Oct.): 288. 2 photos. Improvements concern the production of perfect spiral-holed disks with 90 or more holes and a new lamp that gives brighter images. A "Fern-Tonkinosender" (distant-sound film transmitter) or Telecine was demonstrated with a Zeiss Ikon sound film projector, which produced 90/25 images about 9 by 12 cm (about 16 sq. in.) on a disk receiver. A light-spot transmitter for live pickup and a receiver were also on display, which provided 80/16.6 images about 12 by 16 cm. Another disk receiver had a frosted glass screen on which bright images were projected. (3097, 3336)

3140 Bocchi, R. "Looking-in to London." TELEV. 4 (Oct.): 289–91. 2 photos. Report from Rome with details of images, reception conditions, and receiving equipment. (2944)

3141 "Neon lamps for television purposes." TELEV. 4 (Oct.): 294. Photo.

3142 Richardson, W.J. "Facing the facts." TELEV. 4 (Oct.): 295–7, 308. 3 photos. General comments on television, programs, sponsorship, and advertising. (2371, 3246)

3143 "Baird and apparatus at Selfridges." TELEV. 4 (Oct.): 296. Photo, with inset view of dummy's image (675). (3116, 3145)

3144 "The enthusiast sees it through." TELEV. 4 (Oct): 300–3. 3 photos, 4 diags. (3135, 3167)

3145 "Television at prices within reach of all." TELEV. 4 (Oct.): 309. Full-page advertisement by Baird Television Ltd. Photo shows a "happy family group enjoying television reception in the comfort of the home." Big price reductions: Televisor complete, 18 guineas; complete kit of parts, 12 guineas; experimenter's kit, £7 12s 6d. Also list of 13 components with prices. (3143, 3148)

3146 Gradenwitz, A. "Television at the Berlin Radio Exhibition." TELEV. 4 (Oct.): 310, 311, 318. 5 photos. The Post Office exhibited a cathode-ray receiver and opto-mechanical apparatus similar to that of Fernseh A.-G. The Tekade Company of Nuremberg showed an "interesting novelty"—a helical mirror receiver (Telehor system) designed to produce 84/25 images about 10 by 10 cm. "Manfred von Ardenne, in conjunction with the D.S. Loewe Radio Company, for the first time showed his cathode ray television." The work of von Mihály and of Karolus was not represented. (2940, 3120, 3129, 3131, 3151, 3210, 3328)

"Cathode ray television, though an interesting alternative system, does not possess any superiority over the mechanical-optical types. In fact, at its present stage of development, it is still inferior to the latter in the quality of performance, and although further developments may be anticipated in the near future, there does not seem to be any reason why the mechanical systems should not in turn be developed to the highest standards of perfection."

3147 Abbott, W.B. "Scottish notes." TELEV. 4 (Oct.): 313. Critical comments on the BBC's attitude to television. (2999, 3080, 3157, 3389)

3148 "The National Radio Exhibition." ELECT. 107 (Oct. 2): 463, 464. Includes a brief reference to the Baird exhibit, the reduction in selling price and an increase in the trade discount. (3116, 3145, 3149, 3610)

3149 "Television progress." ELECT. 107 (Oct. 2): 472. Refers to the Baird mirror drum and modulated arc system shown at the Mechanical Aids to Learning Exhibition, British Association meeting, London, Sept. 23–30. (3148, 3154)

3150 "Sanabria back in laboratory to build new television lamp. He was taught several lessons by demonstrating his machine at the radio show." N.Y.T. IX, 9 (Oct. 4): 4, 7. (3122, 3153)

3151 Ardenne, M. v. "Television." U.S. 2,047,533, Sept. 29, 1932, July 14, 1936. Assigned: D.S. Loewe. Br. 392,810, Oct. 3,

1932. In Germany Oct. 6, 1931. Cathode-ray system in which a constant-intensity beam scans a field of view with varying speed controlled by two oscillations, one producing a linear movement and the other a transverse movement. Reference to Br. 355,319 (1886). (3146, 3152)

3152 Ardenne, M. v. "Television." Br. 397,688, Oct. 5, 1932. In Germany Oct. 6, 1931. Film scanner with cathode-ray tube, constant-intensity beam, and variable speed scan. Includes transmitter and receiver circuits. (3151, 3161)

3153 "Television to link theatres in test. Electrical-sight demonstration planned by Moss as prophecy of wide use on stage. Also to be a variety act. Sanabria to conduct experiment in projection of performance as proof of possibilities." N.Y.T. 26 (Oct. 14): 2. Demonstration of 10-foot screen at the B.V. Moss Broadway Theatre. (2292, 3150, 3159)

3154 "Baird here to make $25 sets. Scottish inventor expects to produce 1,000,000 a year within a few months. Tells of work in Europe. Reports telephone experiments successful—WMCA to get his American contract." N.Y.T. 28 (Oct. 14): 5–8. (3071, 3149, 3157, 3203)

3155 Baxter, C.E. "Television." ELECT. 107 (Oct. 16): 528. Letter referring to a modulated arc in his patent of 1926 (751). Critical remarks on revolving drums and similar mechanical methods.

3156 Alexanderson, E.F.W. "Television." U.S. 1,935,427, Oct. 16, 1931, Nov. 14, 1933. Assigned: G.E. Disk with a spiral of apertures, overlapping disk with radial slots, separate photocells, and two-channel radio transmission. (3107, 3223)

3157 "News and views." NATURE 128 (Oct. 17): 670. Note on portable transmitter in a BBC studio, and on the BBC and Baird to investigate a wire link to carry signals to the North Regional Station at Slaithwaite. Reference to October TELEVISION, on BBC broadcast one evening per week. (3147, 3154, 3162, 3202)

3158 Sweeney, William H. "Television." U.S. 1,979,296, Oct. 19, 1931. Nov. 6, 1934. Vibrating mirrors and reflectors.

3159 "Television draws 1,700 to theatre. Audience absorbed by showing of scene from current play as transmitted to screen. Images generally clear. Demonstration intended as mark of Broadway's recognition of the possibilities in new art." N.Y.T. 26 (Oct. 23): 1. Sanabria's 10-foot screen at the Broadway Theatre, connected by wire lines from the Theatre Guild Playhouse a few hundred feet distant. "For the most part, the images were clear enough to afford recognition of a well-known face." (3153, 3275)

3160 Walton, G.W. "Television." Br. 379,552, Oct. 23, 1931. Relates to sync methods with shaded optical filters, including a Nipkow disk with radial shade intensities that change with the angle, other methods for sync, circuits, filters, light values, and variants applicable to mechanical, optical, and cathode-ray systems. Reference to Br. 218,766 (537). (2792, 3351)

3161 Ardenne, M. v. "Television." Br. 396,580, Oct. 17, 1932. In Germany Oct. 24, 1931. For a cathode-ray-tube system employing a constant-intensity beam and variable-rate scanning, mixing and separation circuits are incorporated to enable the two deflection potentials to be transmitted over a single channel. Reference to other patents (1886, 3151, 3152). (3206)

3162 "New York entrances a Scottish television expert. Baird discusses his magic. He deserts his laboratory to recuperate in New York—future of television as he sees it—skyscrapers fascinate him." N.Y.T. IX, 10 (Oct. 25): 1–5. Photo. (3157, 3174)

3163 "Scenery for television." N.Y.T. IX, 10 (Oct. 25): 8. Use of three cameras at CBS station W2XAB, one for the artist, one for the scenic effect, and another for the artist's shadows. (3092, 3171)

3164 "Tiny waves show promise." N.Y.T. IX, 10 (Oct. 25): 8. Views of Gerald C. Gross, FRC engineer, on high-frequency experiments. (3102, 3220)

3165 Gould, Leslie A. "Television." U.S. 2,086,382, Oct. 30, 1931, July 6, 1937. Assigned: Radio Inventions. Color receiver with linear discharge tubes spaced apart around a drum, alternate tubes of different colors, and a separate scanning element. (2629, 3267)

3166 Zworykin, V.K. "Improvements in cathode ray tube design." ELECTRONICS 3 (Nov.): 188–90. 7 illus. Hot cathode, high vacuum type with electrostatic focusing electrodes and special electrode to control beam intensity. (2984, 3186)

3167 Briggs, C.A. "Home made television receiver of advanced design." POP. MECH. 56 (Nov.): 824–6. (3144, 3168)

3168 Waltz, G.H. "How to complete your television receiver." POP. SCI. 119 (Nov.): 86. (3135, 3167, 3177, 3198)

3169 "Camera and cameraman enter television." RADIO CALL BOOK 12 (Nov.): 45. 3 photos. New camera designed by engineers of the Jenkins Television Corp. and the De Forest Radio Co. Mounted on a battery-driven truck, the camera comprises a scanning disk, lens, photocell, amplifier, motor, batteries, monitor, and accessories connected to the control panel by a flexible shielded cable. (3093, 3114, 3238, 3258)

3170 Tanner, R.W. "New television system." RADIO ENG. 11 (Nov.): 27, 28. 5 illus. Mirror drum and mercury arc tube, picture 15 by 18 inches. (3136)

3171 Kaufman, S. "Television progress. New York forges ahead." RADIO N. 13 (Nov.): 375, 376, 436. 3 photos, diag. Survey of experimental stations in New York City, particularly W2XAB, the first television station of CBS, with details of equipment programs, and the inaugural broadcast of July 21 (3017). The NBC station W2XBS, their reception tests, and plans for the new Empire State studios are discussed. Jenkins stations W2XCR, W2XCD, and W2XR operated by Radio Pictures Inc. (J.V.L. Hogan) are also mentioned. (3163, 3224, 3689)

3172 Hodgson, Violet. "Television goes to sea." RADIO N. 13 (Nov.): 386, 387, 439, 440. 5 photos. Reception tests on S.S. Leviathan from stations in New York. (3019)

3173 Moseley, S.A. "America, finance and the future." TELEV. 4 (Nov.) 324–6, 356. Portrait. Reprint of list from the NEW YORK TIMES, Sept. 13 (3099). Comments on the attitude to television in America after his visits to New York, Washington, Boston, and Montreal. "Baird shares...were the only thing in America that was selling." (3081)

3174 Chapple, H.J.B. "Recent developments in television." TELEV. 4 (Nov.): 334–7, 362–5. 4 photos, 3 diags. Address to the Television Society, Oct. 14. A survey of Baird's activities from 1929 with reference to the apparatus, experiments, demonstrations, and broadcasts. "I feel it only right to add that a debt of gratitude is due to the Baird Company for having provided a television service free of charge for such a long period of time." (3138, 3162, 3178, 3179)

3175 Campbell, D.R. "Recognising faults in television images." TELEV. 4 (Nov.): 338–41. 4 photos, 2 diags. Mechanical faults, circuits and constants, atmospherics, and other effects. (3084)

3176 Baker, T.T. "Studio television." TELEV. 4 (Nov.): 342–343. Photo, diag. Scanning methods, illumination, color television. (2732, 3180)

3177 "The enthusiast sees it through." TELEV. 4 (Nov.): 344–8. 5 photos, 6 diags. (3168, 3198)

3178 "Letter to Mr. Baird." TELEV. 4 (Nov.): 351. Letter of thanks, Apr. 5, 1930, from the Prime Minister, Hon. J. Ramsay MacDonald, for the installation of a receiver in 10 Downing Street, Mar. 31. "When I look at the transmission I feel that the most wonderful miracle is being done under my eye." (3174, 3203,)

3179 Chapple, H.J.B. "Introducing the new Tele-Radio receiver. Pt. 2." TELEV. 4 (Nov.): 352–6. 4 photos, 2 diags. Construction of vision apparatus. (3174, 3286)

3180 Baker, T.T. "Television." Br. 391,781, Nov. 2, 1931. Color system employing a Nipkow disk and a concentric disk with three transparent sections of different colors. (3176, 3327)

3181 Dinsdale, A. "New York radio show." W.W. 29 (Nov. 4): 519–22. Includes an account of the Sanabria display (3119). (3078, 3411)

"Unquestionably the biggest draw of all was television. It was well advertised in the newspapers, and drew enormous crowds. There seems little doubt that television saved the radio show, from the attendance point of view. The system exhibited was that of U.A. Sanabria, of Chicago. At the opposite end of the basement to the crystal studios he had his transmitting equipment on a raised platform, and thousands of people posed before the transmitter during the week. A few yards away, in a small theatre built in a corner of the basement, images were shown on a screen measuring about four feet square. Between three and four hundred people at a time saw these images, and each showing had to be curtailed to about ten minutes in order to cope with the mob.

"Most spectacular of all, however, were Sanabria's demonstrations on a ten-foot screen which was hung higher over the main auditorium of Madison Square Garden. This screen was of plate glass, frosted on one side, and weighed 350 lb. The images were projected on to it from behind. Twice a day, for fifteen minutes, at 4 p.m. and 10 p.m., all the lights were extinguished while as many as 50,000 people gathered in the aisles to watch the images of the artists in the basement, and hear them over the public address system.

"Sanabria uses a triple spiral disc, 15 holes per spiral, and transmits only 15 frames per second. The spirals are so arranged that succeeding light spots half overlap their predecessors. With these refinements the net result is an image which is almost devoid of both 'strip effect' and flicker. In my opinion the illumination of the screen is about half that of a cinema screen, and the image detail can bear comparison with similar close-up shots on the screen at the average cinematograph theatre."

3182 Adams, Harold A. "Television transmitter." U.S. 1,968,979, Nov. 4, 1931, Aug. 7, 1934. Film scanner.

3183 Schubert, G., and R. Möller. "Television." U.S. 2,075,360, Nov. 3, 1932, Mar. 30, 1937. Assigned: Fernseh A.-G. Br. 409,400, Nov. 3, 1932. In Germany Nov. 5, 1931. Refers to an intermediate film system in which the exposed film is passed through a developing tank, stored on rollers, and then scanned by a disk with a circle of apertures. See Hartley and Ives (1047), and Gray (2295). (3098, 3217, 3242)

3184 Harding, Robert Jr. "Sound and picture system." U.S. 2,112,527, Nov. 7, 1931, Mar. 29, 1938. Assigned: National Television Corp. Film scanner with disk, translucent screen, and loudspeaker.

3185 Hartman, Hans. "Submarine television." U.S. 2,060,670, Nov. 13, 1931, Nov. 10, 1936. Concerns an electrical transmitter with illumination sealed in a watertight casing.

3186 Zworykin, V.K. "Producing images of objects." U.S. 2,021,907, Nov. 13, 1931, Nov. 26, 1935. Assigned: RCA. (3166, 3190)

3187 Marconi's, H.M. Dowsett, and L.E.Q. Walker. "Television amplifier." Br. 392,229, Nov. 18, 1931. Tuned circuit with maximum response at the line-scanning frequency. (3003, 3026, 3249, 3358)

3188 RCA Victor. "Cathode ray tubes." Br. 391,887, Nov. 19, 1931 (EMI). Screen materials and method of deposition for picture tubes.

3189 Schlesinger, K. "Tilting oscillation generator." U.S. 2,039,118, Nov. 18, 1932, Apr. 28, 1936; Br. 393,865, Nov. 16, 1932. In Germany Nov. 19, 1931. Sweep generator. (3053, 3230)

3190 Zworykin, V.K. "Television." U.S. 2,022,450, Nov. 21, 1931, Nov. 26, 1935. Assigned: Westinghouse. Divided from U.S. 2,141,059 (566). Relates to modification of the photo mosaic in the camera tube. (3186, 3313)

3191 Gramophone Co., and W.D. Wright. "Light valve." Br. 377,871, Nov. 25, 1931. Kerr cell with shaped electrodes. (2790, 3516)

3192 Dunlap, O.E. Jr. "Tiny radio waves to spray New York with television. A skyscraper station. Images to leap from Empire State tower soon after New Year arrives—extensive tests planned." N.Y.T. IX, 7 (Nov. 29): 1, 2. NBC station. Map showing 50-mile coverage and views of antenna, columns 3–6. (3024, 3123, 3306, 3505)

3193 Guibiansky, J. "Television." Br. 374,966, Nov. 30, 1931. Concentric slotted disks, phototube or lamp, angled mirror, driving motor, and mechanical assembly in a box.

3194 Michelssen, F., and Johann Richter. "Electron tube." U.S. 2,003,301. Sept. 17, 1932, June 4, 1935; Br. 394,580 and 411,120, Nov. 30, 1932. Assigned: Telefunken. In Germany Nov. 30, 1931. Picture tube with deflection plates, cathode, and grid assembly. References to Br. 392,781; 395,882 (3059). (3074, 3596, 3598)

3195 Telefunken. "Cathode ray tube." Br. 411,120, Nov. 30, 1932. In Germany Nov. 30, 1931. Cathode and electrode assembly similar to previous patents, which are referred to. (3059, 3231)

3196 Hudec, E. "Zur Physiologie des Fernsehens" [Physiology of television]. E.N.T. 8 (Dec.): 544–54. Study with Nipkow disk and spiral apertures arranged to provide line overlap. (3131, 3308)

3197 Johnson, J.B. "The cathode ray oscillograph." J. FRANKLIN INST. 212 (Dec.): 687–717. 36 illus. 28 refs. Presented at the Franklin Institute Dec. 4. A good historical survey is followed by discussion of theory and operation, structural development of commercial tubes, practical operation of the hot-cathode low-voltage gaseous tube, with details of sweep circuits, waveform patterns, and practical uses in science and engineering. "Originally an intractable and little used device, the cathode ray oscillograph has become an almost universal scientific and industrial tool." Also B.S.T.J. 11 (Jan. 1932): 1–27. (2478)

3198 Waltz, G.H. "Operating a television set." POP. SCI. 119 (Dec.): 83, 84. (3168, 3177, 3204, 3244)

3199 Dalpayrat, H.F. "New system of color television." PROJ. ENG. 3 (Dec.): 13, 14. (2989)

3200 "Television kit." RADIO N. 13 (Dec.): 507. Brief note on "Telescanner" kit by Freed Television & Radio Corp.

3201 "Proven television now." RADIO N. 13 (Dec.): 528. Advertisement by the Television Manufacturing Company of America for a "See-All" Televisor kit, $19.75. "Less than 20 minutes required to assemble it." (3319)

3202 Allighan, Garry. "Fair play for television." TELEV. 4 (Dec.): 373, 404. Extract from the YORKSHIRE WEEKLY POST ILLUSTRATED, Nov. 7. "B.B.C. should support British inventors first." News about American plans to broadcast television programs for Great Britain from Radio City, New York. (3157, 3235)

3203 "A broadcast talk by John Logie Baird." TELEV. 4 (Dec.): 380–3. 6 photos. Given Sunday, Oct. 18, 1931, from stations WMCA and WPCH, New York. Recollections of early work from 1925. Plans for television broadcasts from station WMCA. "The problem of television is solved. What remains to be done is entirely a matter of technical and commercial development." (3154, 3178, 3235, 3280)

3204 "The enthusiast sees it through." TELEV. 4 (Dec.): 398–401. 3 diags. (3198, 3247)

3205 MacGregor-Morris, J.T. "Cathode ray television." J. TELEV. SOC. 1 (Dec.): 69, 70. Introductory remarks at a Society meeting, Nov. 11, when the following papers (3206, 3207) were read. (714)

3206 Ardenne, M. v. "The cathode ray tube method of television." J. TELEV. SOC. 1 (Dec.): 71–4. 5 photos. General discussion of the author's system: his work on cathode-ray tubes for television since 1928, the life of gas-filled tubes, quality of pictures, the question of using a cathode ray or mechanical transmitter, description of the experimental apparatus, reception from a mechanical transmitter, including tube voltages, amplifiers, special tubes, and picture detail. Images with 10,000 to 12,000 picture points at 20 frames per second were produced in May 1931. Pictures 8 by 9 cm were obtained sufficiently brilliant that they could be seen in an undarkened room; it was also possible to project the image onto a big screen (40 sq. cm) in a darkened room. (3161, 3241)

"It may nevertheless be doubted whether, at the present time, the introduction of the cathode ray tube television set can be thought of as a practical proposition. There are still questions to be considered and some period of concerted working between the laboratory and the factory will be necessary before a simple, serviceable and cheap cathode ray television receiver is available for general use."

3207 Traub, Ernest H. "The German Post Office cathode ray television system." J. TELEV. SOC. 1 (Dec.): 75–81. Photo, 12 diags. Thorough discussion of the RPZ system, based mainly on the paper by Hudec and Perchermeir (3131), particularly control of the cathode ray, scanning, saw-tooth wave generators and sync. A prototype developed by the Telehor Company (Tekade) is also described. (3210)

"It is significant of the trend of modern development that at the Berlin Show every one of the four television exhibitors showed a cathode ray tube of their own design, two of which were shown working. In conclusion, I should like to add that the cathode ray tube has now definitely emerged from the laboratory into the public's hands. Its application for television is no longer the scientist's dream, but a reality."

3208 Roberts, C.E.C. "A vacuum photo cell type of transmitter." J. TELEV. SOC. 1 (Dec.): 82, 83. 2 diags. Description of tubes disclosed in the earlier patent (1304).

3209 Harries, J.H.O. "Some notes on television in the U.S.A." J. TELEV. SOC. 1 (Dec.): 98, 99. (2826)

3210 Traub, E.H. "Television at the 1931 Berlin Radio Exhibition." J. TELEV. SOC. 1 (Dec.): 100–3. 5 photos, table, diag. General description of exhibits by R.P.Z., Fernseh, Tekade, and Loewe. "The trend of progress indicates that we may by next year expect pictures about 1 foot square in size and of detail up to 150 strips (30,000 elements). We shall then have as good as perfect television images." (3146, 3207, 3612, 3617)

3211 Ramsey, G. "Television receiver." U.S. 2,050,463, Dec. 4, 1931, Aug. 11, 1936. Light-transmitting points arranged on a disk in a series, each representing a single scanning line. (561, 3406)

3212 Hehlgans, Fredrich W. "Electron discharge tube." U.S. 2,067,840, Nov. 28, 1932, Jan. 12, 1937 (G.E.). In Germany Dec. 5, 1931 (A.E.G.). Cathode-ray tube. (3422)

3213 Peck, William Hoyt. "Television." U.S. 2,045,921, Dec. 7, 1931, June 30, 1936. Optical arrangement. (3375)

3214 Rosenberg, H. "Television." Br. 411,819, Dec. 7, 1932. In Germany Dec. 8, 1931. Film picture reproduced on a bank of incandescent lamps controlled by photocells and relays, with variants. See also Br. 408,128. (3677)

3215 Drewanz, Irwin, and Ernst Brüche. "Cathode ray tube." U.S. 2,089,692, Nov. 28, 1932, Aug. 10, 1937 (G.E.). In Germany Dec. 9, 1931 (A.E.G.).

3216 Wilson, J.C., E.E. Wright, and Baird Television. "Television." Br. 393,960, Dec. 9,

1931. Relates to the multichannel transmission of picture signals in which the frequency spectrum is divided into several bands and the signals are combined at a disk receiver. Reference to Br. 381,254 (3010). (3363)

3217 Schubert, G. "Discharge tube." U.S. 1,993,569, Dec. 6, 1932, Mar. 5, 1935; Br. 392,472, Dec. 9, 1932. In Germany Dec. 12, 1931 (Fernseh A.-G.). A positive-column discharge tube with a heated cathode provides increased luminosity and an almost white light in a television receiver. (3183, 3240)

3218 Schröter, F. "Synchronizing system." U.S. 2,098,598, Nov. 21, 1932, Nov. 9, 1937. Assigned: Telefunken. Br. 394,883, Dec. 12, 1932. In Germany Dec. 12, 1931. Concerns a picture tube with deflection plates, beam deflection circuits, and sync. (3074, 3483)

3219 "Uses film in television. Chicago company reports perfecting of a new broadcasting device." N.Y.T. II, 2 (Dec. 13): 4. Armando Conto, research engineer of the Western Television Corp., has devised means to scan duplicate film for transmission. (2976, 3257)

3220 "The commission reports. Television called experimental." N.Y.T. IX, 12 (Dec. 13): 7, 8. Overview of radio regulations in the fifth annual report of the FRC. (3164, 3342)

3221 Marconi's, and Ronald John Kemp. "Television." Br. 393,978, Dec. 16, 1931. Mirror wheel construction, mountings for mirrors. (3454)

3222 Herdman, William J. "Television receiver." U.S. 1,945,607, Dec. 17, 1931, Feb. 6, 1934. Assigned: Wired Radio. Conical mirror drum with mechanical movement that provides one scanning axis, with light source, motor, and screen in a cabinet.

3223 Alexanderson, E.F.W. "Signalling by light." Br. 395,242, Nov. 29, 1932 (B.T.H.). In U.S. Dec. 19, 1931 (G.E.). Light-beam transmission of picture signals. Photocell currents modulate a radio-frequency oscillator which in turn modulates an arc lamp. Light from the arc is picked up by a photocell, the amplified output from which operates a television receiver. A similar light-beam system is included for sound. (See 3227) (3156, 3634)

3224 "Santa Claus at station W2XAB, New York, looks across the country by television for the first time." N.Y.T. IX, 10 (Dec. 20): 3–6. Photo. (3171, 3335)

3225 "Philadelphia to look-in." N.Y.T. IX, 10 (Dec. 20): 8. Application for license by the Philadelphia Storage Battery Co. Farnsworth equipment will be used. (3009, 3405)

3226 Bingley, F.J., and Baird Television. "Television." Br. 387,771, Dec. 22, 1931. Machine for making mirror drums. Reference to Br. 359,639 (2568). (2854)

3227 "Light beam casts television images." N.Y.T. 26 (Dec. 23): 1. Demonstration of Alexanderson's light-beam transmission system (3223) at Schenectady. (2925, 3320)

3228 Papst, Hermann. "Television." Br. 405,783, Dec. 23, 1932. In Germany Dec. 23, 1931. Machine and method for mass production of mirror wheels in which the reflecting surfaces are given an optical polish by diamond tools. (3431)

3229 Gordon, George. "Scanning for television purposes." U.S. 2,013,559, Dec. 24, 1931, Sept. 3, 1935. Assigned: M.S. Reisman. Refers to a magneto-optic assembly.

3230 Schlesinger, K. "Braun tube." U.S. 2,029,639. Dec. 23, 1932, Feb. 4, 1936; Br. 413,720, Dec. 21, 1932. In Germany Dec. 24, 1931. A thin metal coating on a fluorescent screen reflects light and improves the brightness of the picture. (3189, 3262)

3231 Telefunken. "Cathode ray tubes." Br. 400,453, Dec. 24, 1932. In Germany Dec. 24, 1931. Cathode and cylinder assembly similar to an earlier specification (3059) with an extra diaphragm around the cathode. Reference to Br. 391,360 (3074). (3195, 3292)

3232 Carlson, Wendell L. "Television." U.S. 1,975,056, Dec. 26, 1931, Sept. 25, 1934, reissue Sept. 10, 1936, Apr. 19, 1938. Assigned: RCA., Br., 392,456, Nov. 15, 1932 (Marconi's). Vision and sound are transmitted on two adjacent carrier frequencies. The receiver comprises a picture tube with deflection coils and circuits for tuning, amplification, signal separation, modulation, scanning, and sync.

3233 Colgate, Samuel Bayard. "Television in color." U.S. 2,065,887, Dec. 26, 1931, Dec. 29, 1936. Film scanner; disk with three rings of apertures, optical system and phototube.

3234 "Radio in 1932 points to television and tiny waves. Radio vision expected to lead industry out of slump—stations foresee greater demand for time." N.Y.T. IX, 7 (Dec. 27): 1–6. Views of eight radio experts.

3235 "Television plans. B.B.C. to discuss development." TIMES (Dec. 29): 5e. On discussions between the BBC and the Baird Company with a view toward improving the entertainment value of the programs and program times and toward greater participation by BBC engineers. (3202, 3203, 3272, 3283)

"The immediate future of television is very difficult to foresee. The technical problems yet awaiting solution are difficult and intricate, but their magnitude should not blind us to the extent of the progress that has been made. We have in the ultra-short wavelengths of five to ten metres transmission media admirably adapted for local television broadcasts, and it is now generally agreed that the television of the future will be accomplished by means of ultra-short wave transmitters elevated on a tower or on a hill...."

3236 Prinz, D., and Waldemar Wehnert. "Generation of relaxation waves." U.S. 2,036,719, Dec. 30, 1932, Apr. 7, 1936. Assigned: Telefunken. In Germany Dec. 30, 1931. (2803)

3237 Felix, E.H. TELEVISION. ITS METHODS AND USES. New York: McGraw-Hill, 1931. x + 272 pp. 74 photos and diags., 4 tables. General discussion of technical aspects, processes, methods, components, and systems, referring almost wholly to American work. The last seven chapters (pp. 165–266) are concerned with broader subjects not hitherto treated in books, such as the relationship between the eye and the image, analysis of visual detail, programming possibilities, commercial prospects, establishing an entertainment service, industrial and commercial applications, and the future progress of television. This objective treatment presents a panoramic view of the state of the art in America. (2559, 3364)

3238 Jenkins, C.F. THE BOYHOOD OF AN INVENTOR. Washington, D.C.: published by the author, 1931. xix + 273 pp. 252 illus. This autobiography, the third and final book by the author, goes much further than the title indicates, with coverage of Jenkins' early work on motion pictures, development of facsimile and radio movies, and of other inventions as well as personal activities up to 1930. Eight broadcast subjects, pp. 205–72. Numerous illustrations, extracts, and parts of the text dealing with radio movies are from earlier books and articles. There is a list of text subjects but no index. (3169, 3340)

CHAPTER 12

THE DERBY AND ALL THAT: 1932

TABLE 19   CHRONOLOGY: 1932

Feb.		Insuline Corp.	Advertises receiver kit
		Ostrer	Acquires control of Baird Television
		Pioneer Television Co.	Advertises receiver
	1	Baird Co.	Reception on LNER express train
	5	CBS	Transmission to Gimbel Bros. store from station WABC
		Knoll, Ruska	Paper on electron lenses
	24	Essig	Photoelectric mosaic for a camera tube
	27	Bullimore, Bedford	Cathode-ray film system with velocity modulation
Mar.	6	Jenkins	Describes new projection system
		RMA	Report on survey of the industry
	14	BBC	Plans for late-evening transmissions
	20	Takayanagi	Demonstrates system at station JOAK, Tokyo
Apr.	6	Canadian	Formation of company Television Ltd.
		F.R.C.	Refuses permit for Baird system at station WMCA
	29	Baird Co.	Demonstrates ultra-short wave transmission
May	16	RCA, NBC	Demonstrates experimental system
	19	Baird Co.	Demonstrates two-way vision and sound in Paris
	21	Don Lee System	Transmissions to airplane, station W6XAD, Los Angeles
		RCA, NBC	Field tests of 120-line system
	23	Various	Displays at Radio Trade Show, Chicago
June	1	Baird Co.	Displays Derby on large screen, Metropole Cinema
	27	Baird Co.	Demonstrates new mirror drum receiver
July		Marconi's	Test transmissions from Chelmsford to Australia
	21	CBS	Vision and sound on one channel, station W2XAB
	29	Marconi's	Report on message tape system
Aug.		Baird Co.	Advertises new receiver
	15	Baird Co.	Demonstrates large screen at Selfridge's
	19	Various	Displays at the Berlin Radio Show
	22	BBC	Inaugural broadcast of late evening series
	25	Tedham, McGee	Photoelectric mosaic in a camera tube
	31	Marconi's	Demonstrates apparatus and reception at York

Sept.	W.C. Rawls & Co.	Advertises complete receiver
9	Baird Co.	Report on tape apparatus
23	Various	Report on Radio Show, Paris
Oct. 1	Schlesinger	Double-beam and color picture tube
11	CBS	Political broadcast from station W2XAB
Nov. 8	BBC, Baird	Transmission from London to Copenhagen
11	EMI	Report on company activities
25	Myers	Report on improved light-valve
Dec. 16	Baird Co.	Report on ultra-short wave transmissions

BIBLIOGRAPHY: 1932

3239 Thun, R. "Tonfilm und Fernsehen" [Sound film and television]. FERN U. TON. 3 (Jan.): 1–7. (2978, 3383)

3240 Schubert, G. "Die Entwicklung der Natrium-Dampflampen für Fernsehzwecke" [The development of sodium vapor lamps for television purposes]. FERN. U. TON. (Jan.): 9–18. Sodium vapor lamps (3217) and the Fernseh A.-G. receiver. (3217, 3515)

3241 Ardenne, M. v. "Uber Helligkeitsteuerung bei Kathodenstrahlröhren unter besonderer Berücksichtigung einer neuen Methode" [On the brightness control of cathode-ray tubes, with particular consideration of a new method].FERN. U. TON. 3 (Jan.): 18–29 Beam-intensity control with Wehnelt cylinder. (3206, 3338)

3242 Möller, R. "Helligkeitsfragen bei Fernsehsendern" [The question of brightness in television transmitters]. FERN. U. TON. 3 (Jan.): 29–41. Light sources and intensity, photocells, disk and mirror scanners. (3183, 3300)

3243 Angwin, (Sir) Arthur Stanley (1883–1959). "Radio telegraphy and telephony." J.IEE 70 (Jan.): 145–52. A review of progress, including television.

3244 Waltz, G.H. "Your television motor." POP. SCI. 120 (Jan.): 83, 84. (3198, 3272)

3245 Theile, Richard. "Television reception in Marburg." TELEV. 4 (Jan.): 412, 413. 4 photos, diag.

3246 Richardson, W.J. "Definitions and misnomers." TELEV. 4 (Jan.): 414–6. Photo, 3 diags. Television terms. (3142, 3281)

3247 "The enthusiast sees it through." TELEV. 4 (Jan.): 420–3, 442–5. 7 photos, 8 diags. (3204, 3248)

3248 Knipe, A.R. "A simple magnetic corrector." TELEV. 4 (Jan.): 434–6. 3 photos, diag. How to construct a toothed-wheel synchronizer. (2182, 3247, 3282)

3249 Marconi's, H.M. Dowsett, and D.L. Plaistowe. "Television receivers." Br. 394,710, Jan. 1, 1932. Double-disk system with neon lamps and monitor with provisions for receiving either horizontal or vertical scanning. (3002, 3187, 3250, 3415)

3250 Marconi's and D.L. Plaistowe. "Television." Br. 394,711, Jan 1, 1932. Sync with tuning fork, neon tubes, and electron tubes. (3249, 3442)

3251 "Television to profit by radio's mistakes." N.Y.T. (Jan. 3): IX, 10:8. Comments by Lafount: "The whole visual broadcasting situation will be regulated and controlled in an orderly manner." (2835, 3463)

3252 Gillespie, Henderson C. "Television synchronizing and monitoring system." U.S. 1,985,723, Jan. 5, 1932, Dec. 25, 1934. Assigned: Comm. Pats.

3253 Ballard, R.C. "Television." U.S. 2,093,395, Jan. 6, 1932, Sept. 14, 1937. Assigned: RCA. Br. 394,597, Dec. 30, 1932 (Marconi's). Camera tube and deflection circuits for film transmission. (3057, 3553)

3254 Batchelor, J.C. "Cathode-ray tubes." U.S. 2,114,136, Jan. 6, 1932, Apr. 12, 1938. Assigned: RCA. Br. 402,607, Jan. 3, 1933 (Marconi's). Receiver tube for projection. Reference to Br. 395,499 (2964). (3058, 3259)

3255 Gray, F. "Television." U.S. 2,041,127, Jan. 7, 1932, May 19, 1936. Assigned: B.T.L. Br. 409,367, Oct. 31, 1932 (E.R.P.). Movable transmitter assembly with pivoted mirrors, pantographic linkages and gearing. (3105)

3256 "Television. Five picture channel system giving an image 24 x 16 in." ELECT. 108 (Jan. 8): 37. Paper by C.O. Browne on the Gramophone Company's "Multi-channel television" read at the IEE meeting Jan. 6. Brief outline of technical details on the system, which was demonstrated in Jan. 1931 (2736). (3134, 3316)

3257 "Television offered by Chicago if democrats will go there." N.Y.T. 10 (Jan. 9): 2. Offer by THE CHICAGO DAILY NEWS, operator of station W9XAP, with equipment by the Western Television Corp. (3219, 3318)

3258 "W2XCD to test engineering band." N.Y.T. 20 (Jan. 9): 3. DeForest Radio Co. allocated a new frequency band (1600–1700 kc) to test suitability. (3169, 3302)

3259 Batchelor, J.C. "Television receiving system." U.S. 2,051,632, Jan. 15, 1932, Aug. 18, 1936. Assigned: RCA. Br. 392,869, Jan. 16, 1933 (Marconi's). Light of a complementary color is projected onto the image screen to compensate the original color, applicable to neon tubes or picture tubes. (3254)

3260 Briggs, Joseph A. "Scanning system for television apparatus." U.S. 2,008,272, Jan. 16, 1932. July 16, 1935. Assigned: RCA. Disk with two sets of apertures for scanning film and generating sync signals. (3261)

3261 Briggs, J.A. "Television." U.S. 2,056,247, Jan. 16, 1932, Oct. 6, 1936. Assigned: RCA. Br. 406,845, Dec. 16, 1932. (Marconi's). Sound film transmission. Apertured disk has an outer ring of apertures for generating sync signals. Reference to Br. 395,499 (2964) for picture tube receiver. (3260)

3262 Schlesinger, K. "Braun tube." U.S. 2,114,609, Jan. 5, 1933, Apr. 19, 1938; Br. 411,955, Jan. 16, 1933. In Germany Jan. 16, 1932. (3230, 3346)

3263 "Radio industry begins campaign for universal business in 1932." N.Y.T. 14 (Jan. 17): VIII, 7, 8. Television is not expected to be a sales factor during the year.

3264 Koeppe, L. "Television." Br. 384,463, Jan. 18, 1932. Three-color system with scanning by multiple apertures arranged zigzag fashion in zones and groups on a rotary annulus or in a continuous band.

3265 Mavis, Harry B. "Television scanning disk." U.S. 1,893,676, Jan. 21, 1932, Jan. 10, 1933. Reflecting prisms set on the angled edge of a disk.

3266 Comp. Gaz. "Television." Br. 394,904, Jan. 23, 1933. In France Jan. 22, 1932, Scanning with grouped mirrors and a mirror drum. (3126, 3290)

3267 Gould, L.A. "Television." U.S. 2,176,856, Jan. 23, 1932, Oct. 17, 1939. Assigned: Radio Inventions. Helical glow tube on a rotating drum and two scanning members. (3165, 3501)

3268 Nicolson, A.M. "Television." U.S. 2,010,240, Jan. 27, 1932, Aug. 6, 1935. Assigned: Comm. Pats. Receiver with moving electric discharges on electrode rails. (2952, 3531)

3269 Mitchell, W.A.W. "Television." ELECT. 108 (Jan. 29): 132. 3 photos. Review of progress in 1931; Baird, von Ardenne, Tekade. "It may be said that the flat disc (Nipkow disc) used with the flat plate type neon receiving lamp is now entirely out of fashion." (2924)

3270 Bullimore, William Richard (1887–1937), and Leslie Herbert Bedford. "Cathode-ray tube." Br. 396,422, Jan. 29, 1932. U.S.

1,973,606, Dec. 29, 1932, Sept. 11, 1934. Assigned: A.C. Cossor. Electrode structure and assembly in a picture tube. (3311)

3271 Karolus, A. "Television." Br. 374,391, Jan. 30, 1932. Side-by-side mirror drums and co-acting shutter with semicircular slots. (2490, 3547)

3272 Waltz, A.H. "Television scanning and synchronizing; interview with J.L. Baird." POP. SCI. 120 (Feb.): 84, 85. (3235, 3244, 3280, 3317)

3273 "When will television be reality?" CIT. RAD. CALL BOOK 13 (Feb.): 38, 42. General survey of problems in image transmission.

3274 "What about television?" RADIO N. 13 (Feb.): 644. General editorial comments and criticism of present service. "We think practical television is on the way, but we ask, who is going to do it and how soon?"

3275 Hertzberg, R. "Television hits Broadway." RADIO N. 13 (Feb.): 654, 655, 712, 713. 4 photos, 3 diags., reproduction of theatre program page. On the demonstration by Sanabria at the Moss Broadway Theatre, New York, Oct. 1931 (3159). (1691, 3277)

3276 Cisin, H.A. "New television receiver offers novel design features." RADIO N. 13 (Feb.): 683, 684, 729. 3 photos, 3 diags. The "Visionette" kit of the Insuline Corporation of America, designed by A.G. Heller, chief engineer. A 60-hole disk with magnifying lens and a tilting mirror screen provides images five inches square. List of parts. (1564, 3278)

3277 "Television on the stage." RADIO N. 13 (Feb.): 706. Sanabria's demonstration at the Broadway Theatre, views of B. Moss on the future or television linked with the theatre. (3275)

3278 "New Visionette." RADIO N. 13 (Feb.): 717. Advertisement by the Insuline Corporation of America (subsidiary of Standard Television and Electric Corp). "The first practical televisor for the home." Kit priced at $37.50. Short-wave radio television set at $39.50, kit of parts less tubes. (3276)

3279 "Pioneer television scanner." RADIO N. 13 (Feb.): 719. Advertisement by the Pioneer Television Company. 120-hole disk provides a picture over four inches wide. Price assembled $23.50, neon lamp $3.50, lens and holder $7.50.

3280 "Mr. Baird discusses television in 1932." TELEV. 4 (Feb.): 456. Photo of building in New York housing station WMCA. Brief comments on past events and future plans, including a contract with the Knickerbocker Broadcasting Corporation for television transmission from station WMCA. (3203, 3272, 3288, 3400)

3281 Richardson, W.J. "Motors for television." TELEV. 4 (Feb.): 457–9. 3 photos, 3 diags. (3246)

3282 Taylor, G.R.R. "Redesign your baseboard." TELEV. 4 (Feb.): 460–2. 2 photos, 3 diags. Assembly for motor, disk, sync coils and neon lamp. (3248, 3284)

3283 "Television plans. B.B.C. to discuss development." TELEV. 4 (Feb.): 466, 467. 3 photos. Reprinted from THE TIMES (Dec. 29). (3235, 3285)

3284 "The enthusiast sees it through." TELEV. 4 (Feb.): 468–71. Photo, 5 diags. (3282, 3326)

3285 "The television field." TELEV. 4 (Feb.): 472, 473. 3 photos. Comments on entertainment value and criticism of BBC. Reprinted from THE WIRELESS & GRAMOPHONE TRADER, Jan. 9. (3283, 3288)

3286 Chapple, H.J.B. "Television's magic power." TELEV. 4 (Feb.): 475–7, 487. 3 photos. Comments on critical remarks, bandwidth limitations, claims of Farnsworth, support for British efforts. (3179, 3325)

3287 Haskell, F.H. "Developing the slotted drum." TELEV. 4 (Feb.): 478–81. Photo, 5 diags. Description of apparatus designed and built with J.F. Gretton, model shown at the Television Society exhibition, 1931. See patent (2572).

3288 "Television on an express train." TIMES (Feb. 2): 14c. Reception from Brookmans Park station with a radio set and Baird televisor on the London & North Eastern Railway at speeds up to 70 mph between Sandy and Huntingdon. First experiment of its kind. The LNER had equipped a train with a wireless receiver and sterilized headphones. (3280, 3285, 3289, 3362)

3289 Baird, J.L., and Baird Television. "Television." Br. 381,924, Feb. 2, 1932. Disk with square and rectangular apertures in three partial spirals for scanning image areas with different degrees of fineness. Reference to Br 381,898 (3464). (3288, 3291)

3290 Comp. Gaz. "Television." Br. 395,627, Feb. 2, 1933. In France Feb. 2, 1932. Multiple sets of fixed mirrors. Addition to Br. 373,539 (2643). (3266)

3291 "Baird Television." W.W. 30 (Feb. 3): 120. News item about the control of Baird Television Ltd. being secured by Isidore Ostrer, president of the Graumont-British Picture Corp., by purchase of 800,000 deferred shares. (3289, 3298)

3292 Telefunken. "Cathode-ray tube." Br. 403,818, Jan. 19, 1933. In Germany Feb. 3, 1932. Construction of heated cathode and Wehnelt cylinders. References to Br. 391,360 (3074), 400,453 (3231). (3305)

3293 Marconi's and R. Cadzow. "Television receiver." Br. 396,442, Feb. 4, 1932. A linear or zigzag glow discharge tube with an extra photoelectric element is scanned with light of a different wavelength by an apertured disk. (3004, 3457)

3294 Knoll, Max H. (1897–1969), and Ernst August Friedrich Ruska. "Beitrag zur geometrischen Elektronenoptik" [Contribution to geometric electron optics]. ANN. PHYS. 12 (Feb. 5): 607–40; (Feb. 19): 641–61. Classic paper on the theory of electron lenses. See Busch (1048).

3295 "Sue for $25,000,000 over television's use. W.F. Cox interests allege that big corporations repudiated contract for inventions." N.Y.T. 3 (Feb. 6): 2. Suit filed by William F. Cox and Television, Inc. against ITT Corp. and Mackay Radio and Telegraph Corp. Other parties include Orange Securities Corp., Philadelphia Storage Battery Co., RCA, and Wired Radio, Inc.

3296 "Store shows television. 1,500 see demonstration at Gimbel's, including boxing match." N.Y.T. 13 (Feb. 6): 1. Transmission from station WABC. (2691, 3113)

3297 Koch, Earl L. "Scanning device for television." U.S. 2,034,583, Feb. 6, 1932, Mar. 17, 1936. Assigned: Earl L. Koch Holding Corp. Magnetically operated oscillating optical assembly.

3298 "British television broadcast received on speeding train." N.Y.T. III 3 (Feb. 7): 7. Brief report on experiment (3288). (3291, 3325)

3299 Jacomb, W.W., and Baird Television. "Light-value" Br. 391,931, Feb. 9, 1932. A Kerr cell with spaced electrode plates that match the angle of a divergent beam. Reference to Br. 253,957 (640). (2969, 3420)

3300 Möller, R. "Method of scanning films." U.S. 2,093,817, Feb. 2, 1933, Sept. 21, 1937; Br. 402,620, Feb. 7, 1933. In Germany Feb. 19, 1932 (Fernseh A.-G.). Relates to intermediate film immersed in a liquid and a Nipkow disk, applicable for transmission or reception. Reference to Br. 299,076 (989). (3242, 3381)

3301 Ives, H.E. "Electro-optical apparatus." U.S. 2,274,687. Feb. 10, 1932, Mar. 3, 1942. Assigned: B.T.L. Mirror drum and light-valve receiver. (2927, 3436)

3302 "De Forest changes his mind. Inventor is no longer doubtful about television—new developments surprise and convince him—he looks ahead." N.Y.T. VIII, 14 (Feb. 14): 6. "He predicts that 1934 will see television in full swing on a commercial basis." (3258, 3409)

3303 Ahronheim, A.A. "Transmitting colored moving pictures or scenes." U.S. 2,004,360, Feb. 17, 1832, June 11, 1935. Part assigned:

William Sparks. Divided from U.S. 2,004,359, Aug. 7, 1930 (facsimile system). Spirally apertured disk, prism, multiple photocells, and contact disk for sequential transmission. (2591, 3734)

3304 Tawil, E.P. "Piezoelectric light-valve." Br. 402,048, Feb. 20, 1932. In France Feb. 19, 1932. Void. Light beam is displaced by deformation of a cylindrical quartz assembly. May be applied for scanning in television.

3305 Telefunken. "Television." Br. 395,985, Feb. 20, 1933. In Germany Feb. 20, 1932. Motion picture film is scanned by light from a cathode-ray tube in which the fluorescent screen can be moved in its own plane to present other areas to the scanning beam. (3292, 3307)

3306 "Progress is observed. Television discussed by Aylesworth in annual report." N.Y.T. VII, 14 (Feb. 21): 7. NBC report: "Television is not ready for the general public." (3005, 3192)

3307 Telefunken. "Cathode-ray tube." Br. 400,062, Feb. 22, 1933. In Germany Feb. 22, 1932. (3305, 3402)

3308 Hudec, E. "Cathode-ray tube." Br. 420,067, Feb. 22, 1933. In Germany Feb. 23, 1932. Refers to electrode shapes and construction to provide beam modulation and concentration by electrostatic fields. Reference to Br. 271,131 (743). (3196, 3380)

3309 Schwartz, Erich. "High-vacuum cathode-ray tube." U.S. 2,123,636, Feb. 17, 1933, July 12, 1938; Br. 415,411, Feb. 22 1933. In Germany Feb. 23, 1932 (Fernseh A.-G.). Picture tube has conductive rings (or other variants) inside the cone to provide a continuous potential gradient between the electrodes and the screen. Reference to Br. 406,009 (3030).

3310 Essig, Sanford F. "Electrode structure." U.S. 2,065,570, Feb. 24, 1932, Dec. 29, 1936. Assigned: RCA. Br. 407,521, Feb. 24, 1933 (Marconi's). Describes methods for manufacturing mosaic electrodes for camera tubes. (3567)

3311 Bullimore, W.R., and L.H. Bedford. "Television." Br. 399,469, Feb. 27, 1932. Film scanning by cathode-ray tube. Incorporates velocity modulation and deflection circuits for transmitter and picture tubes. Developed at A.C. Cossor, Ltd. Reference to Br. 396,422 (3270).

3312 Tolson, W.A., and Justin R. Duncan. "Oscillator for use with kinescope deflecting circuits." U.S. 2,101,520, Feb. 27, 1932, Dec. 7, 1936. Assigned: RCA. Br. 402,629, Feb. 27, 1933 (Marconi's). Saw-tooth generators for picture tube. References to Br. 394,597 (3253), 395,499 (2964). (2373, 3423)

3313 Zworykin, V.K. "Electrical communication system." U.S. 2,028,857, Feb. 27, 1932, Jan. 88, 1936. Assigned: RCA. Concerns the distribution of television signals from a master directional beam to distant relay stations. (3190, 3355)

3314 "Television is awhirl. Lone singer can be televised, but there is no room on the radio screen for quartets." N.Y.T. VIII, 14 (Feb. 28): 7, 8. Discussion of problems, comparison with the state of the radio art in 1920. General opinion seems to be slightly in favor of the cathode-ray tube instead of the rotating disk for receivers.

3315 Richards, Amyle P. "Translating means for television impulses." U.S. 2,080,927, Feb. 29, 1932, May 18, 1937. Includes a magnetic assembly and pivoted mirror.

3316 Browne, C.O. "Multichannel television." J. IEE 70 (Mar.): 340–53. 15 photos and diags. Technical details of the Gramophone Company's five-channel system (2736), with discussion pp. 349–53. (3256, 3349)

3317 Waltz, G.H. "Television scanning with the cathode-ray tube." POP. SCI. 120 (Mar.): 82, 83. (3272, 3386)

3318 "Sound films and television broadcast." CIT. RAD. CALL BOOK 13 (Mar.): 17, 38. 3 diags. Double-film system developed by Conto, Western Television Corp. (3219). (3257)

3319 "Television note." CIT. RAD. CALL BOOK 13 (Mar.): 38. On demonstrations of "See-All" receivers by A. Pollak, president of the Television Manufacturing Company of America, in New York. "The wide range of models and prices of this line to be announced very shortly will place television within the means of everybody." (3201)

3320 "Television on a beam of light." CIT. RAD. CALL BOOK 13 (Mar.): 40. Alexanderson's demonstration. (3227). (3634)

3321 "RMA television notes." CIT. RAD. CALL BOOK 13 (Mar.): 53. Summary of proposals prepared by the RMA Engineering Divisions relating to transmission frequencies. (2051, 3322)

3322 Dunsheath, J. "Progress in television." RADIO ENG. 12 (Mar.): 11–3. General survey and RMA recommendations for the FRC. (3321, 3342)

3323 Weiller, P.A. "Television progress from an engineering viewpoint." RADIO ENG. 12 (Mar.): 16, 17, 37.

3324 Wenstrom, William H. "The march of television. Pt. 1." RADIO N. 13 (Mar.): 752, 753, 810. 2 photos, 4 diags. Survey of early ideas from Bakewell to Swinton. (3387)

3325 Chapple, H.J.B. "Televising a horse race." RADIO N. 13 (Mar.): 757, 812. Photo, diag. Derby transmission, June 1931 (2953). (3286, 3298, 3330)

3326 Holmes, E.J., and J.W. Holmes. "Two enthusiasts make progress." TELEV. 5 (Mar.): 8, 9. 3 photos, diag. Shadowgraph transmitter and receiver. (3284, 3329)

3327 Baker, T.T. "Television's new outlook." TELEV. 5 (Mar.): 10. Photo. Brief comments on television in America, British progress, studio technique. (3180)

3328 Gradenwitz, A. "Amateur television work in Berlin." TELEV. 5 (Mar.): 21. 2 photos. On the work of Horst Hewel. (2845, 3146)

3329 "The enthusiast sees it through." TELEV. 5 (Mar.): 22–5. 5 photos, 3 diags. (3326, 3385)

3330 Chapple, H.J.B. "Television on an express train." TELEV. 5 (Mar.): 26. Photo. Experiment on the LNER (3288). (3325, 3331)

3331 Chapple, H.J.B. "Recent advances in television." J. TELEV. SOC. 1 (Mar.): 106–12. 4 photos. On British progress and Baird Company's innovations. (3330, 3362, 3429)

3332 "Round the exhibitions." J. TELEV. SOC. 1 (Mar.): 125, 135. 4 diags.

3333 Shmakov, Paul. "Television in the U.S.S.R." J. TELEV. SOC. 1 (Mar.): 126–30. 9 photos, diag. A report on progress during 1931. Details of developments in various laboratories: The All-Union Electrotechnical Institute, Electrophysical Institute, the Komintern Wireless Factory, Central Laboratory for Communication by Wire.

3334 "Fourth annual report of the Council and balance sheet." J. TELEV. SOC. 1 (Mar.): 131–5. (2948)

3335 "Television used in search. Lindbergh baby's picture kept on air four hours continuously." N.Y.T. 9 (Mar. 4): 7. Broadcast from CBS station W2XAB, New York, from 2 to 6 p.m., and during the evening. (3224, 3399)

3336 Fernseh A.-G. "Television." Br. 402,631, Mar. 1, 1933. In Germany Mar. 4, 1932. Film for intermediate storage. (3139, 3365)

3337 Lubcke, H.R. "Television synchronization." U.S. 2,037,035, Mar. 4, 1932, Apr. 14, 1936. Picture tube and circuits. Two sets of pulses transmitted via an image-signal channel trigger scanning generators in the receiver. (2837, 3449)

3338 Ardenne, M. v. "Television receiver." Br. 417,590, Mar, 2, 1933. In Germany Mar. 5, 1932. Picture tube and blanking circuit. Reference to Br. 392,383 (3057). (3241, 3344)

3339 Mobsby, E.G.H. "Television." Br. 380,522, Mar. 5, 1932. Moving coil shutter, lens system, and apertured disk.

3340 "Jenkins describes a new radiovision." N.Y.T. II, 1 (Mar. 6): 3; 2: 2, 3. (3238, 3359)

3341 "Radio finds new tonic. All-wave outfits, automatic clock tuners and television show promise for 1932–33." N.Y.T. VIII, 14 (Mar. 6): 7, 8.

3342 "Industry wonders if public will be taxed for television. Complicated problems are seen—an increased cost of television might drive commercial sponsors away." N.Y.T. VIII, 14 (Mar. 6): 7, 8. Survey by members of the RMA. FRC will not grant commercial rights. (3320, 3343, 3425) [129]

3343 "New television outfits for WJR and WGAR." N.Y.T. VIII, 16 (Mar. 6): 6. Applications granted by the FRC (3342).

3344 Ardenne, M. v. "Valve circuits." Br. 395,297. Mar. 1, 1933. In Germany Mar. 7, 1932, Saw-tooth generator. (3338, 3345)

3345 Ardenne, M.v. "Braun tube." U.S. 2,097003, Mar. 6, 1933, Oct. 26, 1937. Assigned: D.S. Loewe. Br. 407,823, Mar. 2, 1933. In Germany Mar. 7, 1932. Concerns a picture tube designed for rectangular images. (3344, 3452)

3346 D.S. Loewe and K. Schlesinger. "Valve generator." Br. 399,398, Mar. 6, 1933. In Germany Mar. 7, 1932. Relaxation oscillator for high frequencies (120 kc or more). (3262, 3347)

3347 D.S. Loewe and K. Schlesinger. "Television." Br. 402,291, Mar. 6, 1933. In Germany Mar. 7, 1932. On sync circuits with frequency multipliers and dividers. (3346, 3350)

3348 Varian, Russell H., and Bernard C. Gardner. "Cathode-ray tube." U.S. 2,093,699, Mar. 8, 1932, Sept. 21, 1937. Assigned: Farnsworth Television. Picture tube.

3349 EMI and C.O. Browne. "Television." Br. 398,228, Mar. 9, 1932. Relates to film scanning by a mirror drum with provisions for changeover from one film to another, and optomechanical means for producing sync signals. (3316, 3535)

3350 D.S. Loewe and K. Schlesinger. "Valve generator." Br. 402,636, Mar. 8, 1933. In Germany Mar. 9, 1932. Relaxation oscillator with neon tube and tuned circuit applicable for a television receiver with a local sync generator. (3347, 3352)

3351 Walton, G.W. "Television." Br. 403,395, Mar. 9, 1932. Optical system with image splitter, echelon assembly (1542), vibrating mirror or mirror drum, with receiver circuit. Reference to Br. 379,552. (3160, 3368)

3352 D.S. Loewe and K. Schlesinger. "Cathode-ray tube." Br. 417,713, Mar. 9, 1933. In Germany Mar 10, 1932. Picture tube with electron-optical system to provide a light spot of constant shape and size. May be filled with argon or hydrogen. Divided from Br. 417,850. (3350, 3353)

3353 D.S. Loewe and K. Schlesinger. "Cathode-ray tube." Br. 417,850, Mar. 9, 1933. In Germany Mar. 10, 1932. Refers to an indirectly-heated cathode and control grid assembly. References to Br. 417,713 and 420,667 (3397). (3352, 3354)

3354 Schlesinger, K. "Braun tube for television." U.S. 2,049,781, Mar. 9, 1933, Aug. 4, 1936; Br. 420,876, Mar. 9, 1933. In Germany Mar. 10, 1932 (D.S. Loewe). Divided from Br. 417,850. (3353, 3366)

3355 Zworykin, V.K., and Gregory N. Ogloblinsky. "Television." U.S. 2,178,093, Mar. 10, 1932, Oct. 31, 1933. Assigned: RCA. Image dissector tube. (3313, 3583, 3640)

3356 Hazell, H.F., and R.H. Dent. "Television." Br. 402,069, Mar. 11, 1932. Endless bond with square apertures or movable lamps, tubular neon lamps, distributor and variants applicable for stereo or color. (3357)

3357 Hazell, H.F., and R.H. Dent. "Television." Br. 402,076, Mar. 11, 1932. Disk with a spiral of neon tubes or photocells and commutator, applicable for stereo or color. Divided from Br. 402,069 (3356).

3358 Marconi's, N. Levin, and L.E.Q. Walker. "Television." Br. 398,247, Mar. 11, 1932. Receiver arrangement incorporating double reflection with angled mirrors or prisms on a mirror wheel. (3002, 3187, 3415)

3359 "Jenkins and television." N.Y.T. III, 1 (Mar. 13): 4, 5. Editorial on Jenkins system. (3340, 3360)

3360 "Curious effects observed in Washington television." N.Y.T. VIII, 16 (Mar. 13): 6. On a demonstration with a Jenkins portable transmitter at station W2XAP: "All men televised looked as if they needed a shave and appeared to have sideburn whiskers." (3359, 3367)

3361 Robert, M. (Television transmission.) C.R. 194 (Mar. 14): 965–7. Analysis of transmission frequencies.

3362 "B.B.C. and television. Transmission four nights a week." TIMES (Mar. 14): 8g. Studio in Broadcasting House is to be equipped with Baird apparatus, and the program will be extended to four evening transmissions at 11 p.m. These arrangements will continue up to Mar. 31, 1934. (3288, 3331, 3371)

3363 Banks, G.B., J.C. Wilson, and Baird Television. "Television." Br. 398,512, Mar. 15, 1932. Two-channel system with sound and sync combined on one channel. (3070, 3216, 3395, 3421)

3364 Felix, E.H. "Television." U.S. 2,000,694, Mar. 16, 1932, May 7, 1935. Assigned: Radio Inventions. Film scanning system with two disks, two phototubes, and radio transmission with variable rate in which moving portions only are transmitted. (3237)

3365 Fernseh A.-G. "Cathode-ray tube." Br. 413,812, Mar. 16, 1933. In Germany Mar. 16, 1932. Picture tube with special modulating electrode. (3336, 3372)

3366 D.S. Loewe and K. Schlesinger. "Oscillation generator." Br. 399,408, Mar. 16, 1933. In Germany Mar 17, 1932. (3354, 3374)

3367 Jenkins, C.F. "Advances in television." SCIENCE 75 (Mar. 18): Supp. 10. Projection system with contacts on a disk from which sparks pass to a thin film of acid on a glass plate, which causes bubbles and a dark spot on the screen. (3360, 3410)

3368 Walton, A.W. "Television." Br. 403,397, Mar. 19, 1932. Concerns the transmission of sound in combined sound and picture transmissions. Sound is converted to an optical image wherein position and brightness are represented by frequency and intensity, respectively. References to echelon assembly. Br. 328,286 (1542), and discharge device, Br. 397,880. (3351, 3598)

3369 Allgemeine Elektrizitäts Gesellschaft (A.E.G.). "Cathode-ray tube." Br. 395,660, Mar. 22, 1933. Assigned: Int. G.E. In Germany Mar. 22, 1932. (3638)

3370 Beverage, Harold H. "Television." U.S. 2,081,730, Mar. 22, 1932, May 25, 1936. Assigned: RCA. Br. 401,563, Mar 10, 1933 (Marconi's). Disk system for film transmission with modulation and sync circuits.

3371 "Television at Broadcasting House." W.W. 30 (Mar. 23): 307. News item on a special studio for joint use by the BBC and the Baird Company for late evening transmissions. (3362, 3392, 3400)

3372 Fernseh A.-G. "Television." Br. 398,858, Mar. 24, 1933. In Germany Mar 24, 1932. Signals are generated by light reflected from a special photosensitive film in a film transmission system. Reference to Br. 306,158 (1025). (3365, 3517)

3373 Richards, C.L. and Baird Television. "Television." Br. 399,154, Mar. 24, 1932. Disk and drive assembly. (2197)

3374 Schlesinger, K. "Cathode-ray tube system." U.S. 2,075,141, Mar. 23, 1933, Mar. 30, 1937. In Germany Mar 24, 1932. For television. (3366, 3397)

3375 Peck, W.H. "Television." U.S. 1,979,840, Mar. 28, 1932, Nov. 6, 1934; Br. 399,108, Mar. 28, 1933. Lens disk and motor with a lens and screen in a cabinet. (3213, 3471)

3376 Nakashima, Tomomasa, and K. Takayanagi. "Television receiving system." U.S. 2,034,704, Nov. 8, 1932, Mar. 24, 1936. In

Japan Mar. 30, 1932. Picture tube and circuits. (1667, 3440, 3472)

3377 Krawinkel, G., and K. Ziebig. "Fernsehensuche mit Ultrakurzwellen" [Television experiments with ultra-short waves]. FERN U. TON 3 (Apr.): 65–9. Tests with R.P.Z. transmitter on 7 m. (2624, 3645)

3378 Kirschstein, F. "Auf dem Weg zum Projektionsfernsehen" [On the way to projection television]. FERN. U. TON. 3 (Apr.): 75–8. About Sanabria, American developments, and film systems. (2843, 3643)

3379 Busse, E. "Die Linsenscheibe" [The lens disk]. FERN. U. TON. 3 (Apr.): 78–87. Design for lens disks. (3132, 3529)

3380 Hudec, E., and E. Perchermeier. "Die Braunsche Röhre für Fernsehzwecke" [The Braun tube for television]. FERN. U. TON. 3 (Apr.): 87–94. Development of cathode-ray tubes, including types, details, and makes. (3131, 3308, 3467)

3381 Möller, R. "Helligkeitsfragen bei Fernsehsendern" FERN. U. TON. 3 (Apr.): 95–104. Continued from Jan. (3242). (3300, 3519)

3382 Friedel, W. "Lichtspeicherung bei Fernsehgeräten" [Light storage in television sets]. FERN. U. TON. 3 (Apr.): 104–6. (2451)

3383 Thun, R. "Die Lichttechnische Grundgleichung für Fernsehapparate" [Basic equation for light technique in television apparatus]. FERN. U. TON. 3 (Apr.): 106–8. (3239, 3518)

3384 Lane, H.M. "Resistance-capacitance coupled amplifier in television." PROC. IRE 20 (Apr.): 722–33. 10 illus. Mathematical treatment of amplifier performance. (1684)

3385 "Television disks you can make." POP. MECH. 57 (Apr.): 647, 648. Illus. On 48-hole and 45-hole 3-spiral disks. (3329, 3390)

3386 Waltz, G.H. "Enlarging television pictures." POP. SCI. 120 (Apr.): 85, 86. (3317)

3387 Wenstrom, W.H. "The march of television. Pt. 2." RADIO N. 13 (Apr.): 852, 853, 876–8. 14 photos. General discussion of increased definition and repetition rate, mechanical scanning, cathode-ray methods, transmission frequencies, and current progress in America. (3324)

3388 Firmin, L., and A. Rump. "Television at England's most easterly point." TELEV. 5 (Apr.): 48, 49. 3 photos, diag. On experiments at Lowestoft.

3389 Abbott, W.B. "Is British television still being impeded?" TELEV. 5 (Apr.): 50. Critical comments on the tardy attitude of British radio manufacturers and on British experiments abroad. (3147)

3390 "The enthusiast sees it through." TELEV. 5 (Apr.): 54, 58. 2 photos, 5 diags. (3385, 3481)

3391 Wolfson, H. "Further developments in photoelectricity." TELEV. 5 (Apr.): 64–6, 73. Photo, 5 diags. (2799)

3392 "B.B.C. and television." TELEV. 5 (Apr.): 71. Extract from THE TIMES, Mar. 14 (3362). (3371, 3477)

3393 Donle, H.P. "Television." US. 2,002,992, Apr 1,1932, May 25, 1935. Assigned: Radio Inventions. Receiver with two drums and concave mirrors for direct viewing. (3089, 3498)

3394 Vance, A.W. "Television." U.S. 2,102,139, Apr. 2, 1932, Dec. 14, 1937. Assigned: RCA. System with cathode-ray tubes and two channels for deflection signals. (2964, 3670)

3395 Banks, G.B., and Baird Television. "Television." Br. 401,311, Apr. 4, 1932. Mirror drum arranged to scan five adjacent lines simultaneously, five-element phototubes, two-channel transmission with phantom circuit, sound and sync on two side circuits, and five-element Kerr cell receiver. Also for film transmission. References (640, 2536, 3363, 3546). (3363)

3396 EMI and Alan Dower Blumlein (1904–42). "Sweep circuit." Br. 400,976, Apr. 4, 1932; U.S. 2,063,025, Apr. 1, 1933. Dec. 8, 1936, reissue Nov. 26, 1938, Mar. 19, 1940. Electromagnetic saw-tooth oscillator with deflection coils.

3397 Schlesinger, K. "Cathode-ray tube." Br. 420,667, Apr. 3, 1933 (D.S. Loewe); U.S. 2,227,032, Mar. 30, 1938, Dec. 31, 1940 (Loewe Radio). In Germany Apr.4, 1932. Picture tube with deflection plates and electron-optical focusing assembly. (3374, 3398)

3398 Schlesinger, K. "Electron optical system." U.S. 2,227,033, Mar. 30, 1938, Dec. 31, 1940 (Loewe Radio). In Germany Apr. 4, 1932. (3397, 3412)

3399 "Paintings are televised. Four works from independent show produced for first time." N.Y.T. 24 (Apr. 6): 2. Broadcast from station W2XAB. (3335, 3375)

3400 "America bars Baird television." W.W. 30 (Apr. 6): 350. Report that the FRC would not grant a license to station WMCA since the radio law prohibits alien ownership or directorates in the U.S. (3280, 3371, 3403, 3475)

3401 Kitroser, Isaac. "Television transmitter." U.S. 1,965,103, Apr. 6, 1932, July 3, 1934. Assigned: Keller-Dorian Colorfilm Corp. Disk scanner for color film, radio transmission.

3402 Telefunken. "Television." Br. 417,932, Apr. 6, 1933. In Germany Apr. 6, 1932. Refers to frequency multipliers for deriving the line scanning frequency from the picture scanning frequency. (3307, 3532)

3403 Baird, J.L., and Baird Television. "Television." Br. 399,552, Apr. 7, 1932. Scanning by an endless band of canted mirrors. (3400, 3419)

3404 Baker, Donald Jerome. "Television." U.S. 2,026,725, Apr. 11, 1932, Jan. 7, 1936. Two-channel system with superimposed back-and-forth scanning.

3405 Farnsworth, P.T. "Television." U.S. 2,168,768, Apr. 15, 1932, Aug. 8, 1939. Assigned: Farnsworth television and Radio. Divided from U.S. 1,970,036 (1109). Concerns a modified image dissector tube. (3225)

3406 Ramsey, A. "Television." U.S. 2,018,873, Apr. 15, 1932, Oct. 29, 1935. Slotted disk, commutator and multiple circuits containing time-delay elements. (3211)

3407 Rosing, B.L. "La participation des savants russes au développement de la télévision électrique" [The participation of Russian scientists in the development of electric television]. REV. GEN. 31 (Apr. 16): 507–15. 18 diags. Translation of an article in ELECTRITCHESTVO, May 1930, on work in the U.S.S.R. 24 references. (2145)

3408 Short, D.W. "Television." U.S. 1,970,632, Apr. 16, 1932, Aug. 21, 1934. Assigned: RCA. A portable scanning assembly has a disk with two spirals on opposite pitch, a photocell for one set, and a lamp for the other for monitoring. (3031)

3409 De Forest, L. "Receiving an projecting televised images in synchronism with sound." U.S. 2,045,570, Apr. 19, 1932, June 30, 1936. Assigned: American Television Labs. Divided from U.S. 2,026,872 (2880). Concerns a receiver with etched film, projection system and loudspeaker. (3302)

3410 "New television company. Canadian manufacturing concern to exhibit Jenkins invention." N.Y.T. 36 (Apr. 21): 4. On the formation of Canadian Television, Ltd. (3367, 3424)

3411 "Television in America." ELECT. 108 (Apr. 22): 572. Reviews of a paper by Dinsdale given before the Television Society, Apr. 13. (3181, 3482)

3412 D.S. Loewe and K. Schlesinger. "Cathode-ray tube." Br. 419,727, Apr. 18, 1933. In Germany Apr. 22, 1932. Includes electron-optical focusing system described in Br. 420,667 (3397). (3398, 3413)

3413 D.S. Loewe and K. Schlesinger. "Cathode-ray tube." Br. 421,521, Apr. 18, 1933; U.S. 2,111,940, Apr. 19, 1933, Mar. 22, 1938. In Germany Apr. 22, 19342. Divided from Br. 419,727 (3412). (3432)

3414 Bowen, J.P., and Marconi's. "Directive wireless signalling." Br. 400,273, Apr. 23,

1932. Rotating antenna and compass card, a portion of which is scanned by a disk, provides a picture giving a station name and direction of the transmission.

3415 Marconi's, H.M. Dowsett, and L.E.Q. Walker. "Synchronous movements." Br. 400,610, Apr. 23, 1932, Motor control via a variable resistance and automatic clutch. (3249, 3358, 3^453, 3457)

3416 Iams, H.A. "Unidirectional scanning." U.S. 2,246,918, Apr. 27, 1932, June 24, 1941. Assigned: Westinghouse. Magnetic coils and circuit provide beam deflection in one direction only. (2282)

3417 Fitch, William A. "Resistance-capacitance coupled amplifier." U.S. 1,990,781, Apr. 28, 1932, Feb. 12, 1935. Assigned: G.E. Br. 397,076, Apr. 25, 1933 (B.T.H.).

3418 Green, E.I. "Television." U.S. 2,095,360, Apr. 28, 1932, Oct. 12, 1937. Assigned: AT&T. Refers to a distribution system for sound and vision with multiple subscriber stations. (1220)

3419 Baird, J.L., and Baird Television. "Television." Br. 392,730, Apr. 29, 1932. Scanner with mirror drum, reflecting mirrors, and slotted masks. Addition to Br. 322,481 (1286). (3403, 3433)

3420 Jacomb, W.W., and Baird Television. "Television." Br. 387,881, Apr. 29, 1932. On construction of mirror wheels. (3299, 3546)

3421 Wilson, J.C., and Baird Television. "Television." Br. 381,882, Apr. 29, 1932. Disk with two semi-spiral sets of apertures arranged to trace partially overlapping paths as well as interlocking paths, with equivalent mirror drum as an alternative. References to Br. 374,564 (2857), 380,234 (3070). (3363, 3537)

3422 Hehlgans, F.W. "Electron tube." U.S. 2,078,797, Apr. 10, 1933, Apr. 27, 1937. Assigned: G.E. In Germany Apr. 30, 1932 (A.E.G.) Cathode-ray tube. (3212, 3460)

3423 Tolson, W.A. "Television." U.S. 1,999,378, Apr. 30, 1932, Apr. 30, 1935, reissue June 24, 1936, Apr. 20, 1937. Assigned: RCA. Br. 403,283, May 1, 1933 (Marconi's). Picture tube with deflection coils, saw-tooth, oscillators and sync circuits. Reference to Br. 395,499 (2964), 402,629)3312).

3424 "Radiovision to bring world to you." POP. MECH. 57 (May): 749. Illus. Jenkins large-screen projection system employing sparks through thin film of acid (3367). (3410)

3425 "Status of television." CIT. RAD. CALL BOOK 13 (May): 39, 40. RMA statement includes historical references from 1884 and lists current problems; method of scanning, transmission frequencies, amplification, light-modulators, financing, and reception methods. (3342)

3426 Lyle, A.E. "Sources of light for television." RADIO ENG. 12 (May): 16, 24.

3427 Batcher, Ralph R. "Lens design for scanning discs." RADIO N. 13 (May): 914, 915, 612. Photo, 2 charts. 5 diags.

3428 Peck, A.P. "Where is television?" SCI. AM. 146 (May): 284, 285. (2131, 3609)

3429 Chapple, H.J.B. "Progress in cathode-ray tube design." TELEV. 5 (May): 88, 89. (3331, 3624)

3430 Bowen, E.A. "The frequencies in television signals." TELEV. 5 (May): 104–6.

3431 Papst, H. "Scanning device." U.S. 2,010,411, May 2, 1933, Aug. 6, 1935; Br. 410,966, May 2, 1933. In Germany May 2, 1932. Assembly comprises two mirror drums at right angles with interposed reflecting mirror or prism. Reference to Br. 354,630 (2078). (3228)

3432 D.S. Loewe and K. Schlesinger. "Generating tilting oscillations." U.S. 2,083,202, May 2, 1933, June 8, 1937; Br 423,583, May 1, 1933. In Germany May 2, 1932. Sawtooth generator. (3413, 3443)

3433 "Ultra-short wave television. Mr. J.L. Baird's demonstration." TIMES (May 4): 9f. Test of Apr. 29 from studio and transmitter at Long Acre on 6.1 m to receiver at Selfridge's. Mr. Baird had some interesting remarks on future developments. "Although he had made experiments with both cathode-ray and mechanical methods of picture scanning and picture reproduction he was of opinion that, in the present stage of television technique, the mechanical methods gave the better results. But since he was by no means sure that this would always remain the case, he would be continuing work on both types of methods." (3419, 3438)

3434 "Pupin predicts far vision. Inventor says broadcasts soon will unite sight with sound." N.Y.T. 21 (May 5): 6. Remarks of Prof. Michael Idvorsky Pupin (1858–1935) of Columbia University. (3435)

3435 "International communication." N.Y.T. 20 (May 6): 3. Editorial on Pupin's comments (3434).

3436 Ives, W.E. "Electro-optical scanning system." U.S. 2,064,475, May 6, 1932, Dec. 15, 1936. Assigned: B.T.L. Disk scanner coacts with a spiral slot in a second disk. (3301)

3437 J. Pintsch A.-G. "Discharge lamps." Br. 417,855, Mar. 14, 1933. In Germany May 6, 1932. Matrix assembly.

3438 "Ultra-short wave television." NATURE 129 (May 7): 682. On Baird's demonstration Apr. 29. (3433, 3439)

3439 "Ultra-short waves over London." W.W. 30 (May 11): 481. Photo of antenna on the roof of the Baird Company's office in Long Acre. (3438, 3447)

3440 "Television in Japan." W.W. 30 (May 11): 491. 2 photos, including picture of received image. Takayanagi's apparatus at the Exhibition of Inventions, Tokyo. (3376, 3472)

3441 Goshaw, Iol R. "Television." U.S. 1,979,463, May 11, 1932, Nov. 6, 1934. Assigned: Wired Radio.

3442 Marconi's, W.A. Appleton, and D.L. Plaistowe. "Television receiver." Br. 401,355, May 12, 1932. Circuits include a spark gap or arc and tube oscillator. (3250, 3453)

3443 D.S. Loewe and K. Schlesinger. "Cathode-ray tube." Br. 417,714, Mar. 9, 1933. In Germany May 14, 1932. Divided from Br. 417,850 (3353). (3432, 3444)

3444 D.S. Loewe and K. Schlesinger. "Cathode-ray tube." Br. 421,050, May 12, 1933; U.S. 2,003,775, May 13, 1933, June 4, 1935. In Germany May 14 1932. (3443, 3445)

3445 D.S. Loewe and K. Schlesinger. "Cathode-ray tube." U.S. 1,993,457, May 13, 1933, Mar. 5, 1935; Br. 421,051, May 13, 1933. In Germany May 14, 1932. (3444, 3485)

3446 "Test television progress. Images sent from the top of Empire State Building in experiments." N.Y.T. 24 (May 18): 3. Report of a private demonstration by RCA, May 16. Pictures about five inches square on a cathode-ray tube were described as being "quite clear." (3096, 3450)

3447 "Disk system with infrared scanning. Screen 10 inches long by 5 inches wide. Television. Success of two-way experiment." TIMES (May 20): 14f. Demonstration of two-way transmission of images and sound over one mile of telephone lines between the Galeries Lafayette and offices of LE MATIN in Paris with Baird equipment supervised by Chapple. System to be exploited by the Baird-Nathan Company with commercial use to start between Paris and Lyons and later between Paris and London. (2798, 3439, 3459)

3448 Mihály, D. v. "Television." U.S. 1,969,633, Aug. 6, 1933, Aug. 7, 1934. Assigned: IMK. Br. 412,926, May 8, 1933. In Germany May 21, 1932. Helical apertures in a drum, spiral glow discharge lamp, reflecting mirror and lens. Addition to Br. 394,446 (2868). (2869, 3717)

3449 "Movie sent to plane in flight by television. Passengers in coast air liner view film flashed from radio station ten miles off." N.Y.T. II (May 22): 8. Images of a recent motion picture starring Loretta Young, transmitted from the Columbia-Don Lee station KHJ (W6XAO) in Los Angeles were received aboard a Western Air Express transport plane at 3,000 feet. Cathode-ray receiver tube developed by H.R. Lubcke, director of television for the Don Lee Broadcasting System. (3337, 3565, 3690)

3450 "Television images are leaping from a skyscraper pinnacle. Engineers see demonstration of new receiver that picks up Empire State Building broadcasts." N.Y.T. VIII 10 (May 22): 7, 8. RCA demonstration: "The engineers assert that by the winter of 1933 a new industry may come into being." (3446)

3451 Smith, John Paul. "Television." U.S. 2,045,315, May 23, 1932, June 23, 1936. Assigned: RCA. Amplifier.

3452 "New television system. Modified cathode-ray and 'variable speed' principle." W.W. 30 (May 25): 539. 2 photos. On von Ardenne's cathode-ray film system with velocity modulations. (3345, 3541)

3453 Marconi's, H.M. Dowsett, and D.L. Plaistowe. "Television." Br. 402,121, May 25, 1932. Refers to disk and neon tube apparatus in a direction-finding or navigational system. (3415, 3442, 3454)

3454 Marconi's, H.M. Dowsett, and R.J. Kemp. "Radio direction-finding system." Br. 402,122, May 25, 1932; U.S. 2,076,710, May 18, 1933, renewed June 14, 1935, Apr. 13, 1937. Television receiver for navigation. References to Br. 402,121 (3453), 402,443 (3457). (3221, 3668)

3455 EMI and M. Bowman-Manifold. "Control circuits for cathode-ray devices." Br. 401.634, May 26, 1932; U.S. 2,097,334, May 13, 1933, Oct. 26, 1937. Saw-tooth generator. (2101, 3456)

3456 EMI and M. Bowman-Manifold. "Television." Br. 402,134, May 26, 1932. Saw-tooth generator. Divided from Br. 401,634 (3455). (3511)

3457 Marconi's, H.M. Dowsett, L.E.Q. Walker, and R. Cadzow. "Wireless direction-finding system." Br. 402,443, May 26, 1932; U.S. 2,070,651, May 24, 1933, Feb. 16, 1937.

Disk scans a rotating compass card. (3293, 3415, 3454, 3524, 3604, 3622)

3458 "Television. Seven years of research and investigation." ELECT. 108 (May 27): 727. Abstract of paper by R.W. Cooking read at meeting of the Television Society, May 11.

3459 "Two-way television." ELECT. 108 (May 27): 740. Baird demonstration in Paris, May 19. (3447, 3461)

3460 Hehlgans, F.W. "Electric discharge device." U.S. 2,004,790, May 11, 1933, June 11, 1935. Assigned: G.E. Br. 402,876, May 25, 1933. In Germany May 27, 1932 (A.E.G.). Picture tube and circuit. (3422, 3484)

3461 "Two-way television." NATURE 129 (May 28): 788. Baird demonstration in Paris, May 19. (3459, 3464)

3462 Bedford, A.V. "Television." U.S. 2,085,409, May 28, 1932, renewed Oct. 22, 1936, June 29, 1937. Assigned: RCA. Br. 401,990, May 29, 1933 (Marconi's). Picture tube with deflection coils and sweep circuits. (2576, 3670)

3463 "Missing link in television is awaited by Commission. Cautious policy in licensing stations is explained—larger and clearer images are desired." N.Y.T. VIII 10 (May 29): 1, 2. Remarks by Lafount to the RMA. (3251)

3464 Baird, J.L., and Baird Television. "Television." Br. 381,898, May 30, 1932. A mirror drum coacts with a spirally slotted disk and a rocking mirror to produce interlaced groups of scanning lines. References to other patents (640, 800, 1285, 1529) and to Br. 322,841 (Gearing). (3461, 3475)

3465 Heinmann, Walter. "Cathode-ray tube." U.S. 2,124,401, May 11, 1933, July 19, 1938. Assigned: G.E. Br. 403,018, May 30, 1933 (Int. G.E.). In Germany May 30, 1932 (Lorenz).

3466 Hollmann, Hans Erich. "Braun tube." U.S. 2,046,513, Feb. 23, 1933, July 7, 1936. Assigned: Radio Patents. Br. 397,785, Mar. 10, 1933. In Germany May 30, 1932 (Telefunken). Concerns split deflection plates to neutralize time displacement of the beam.

3467 Hudec, E. "Die Helligkeitssteürung von Braunschen Röhren" [The brightness control in Braun tubes]. E.N.T. 6 (June): 213–25. Cathode-ray tube receiver, light control, sync. (3380, 3492)

3468 "Globe about cathode-ray television." CIT. RAD. CALL BOOK 13 (June): 37, 55. Comparison of mechanical methods and cathode-ray tube receivers. "In conclusion, the cathode-ray is certain to be the ultimate choice for television scanning." (3469)

3469 "Globe television receiver." RADIO-CRAFT 3 (June): 720. 2 photos. A disk with 60 lenses provides an image 4 by 5.5 inches. Globe Television and Phone Company receiver on display at the Radio Trade Show, Chicago, May 23–26. (3468)

3470 Block, I. "Design of lens scanning system for television." RADIO ENG. 12 (June): 9–12.

3471 "Peck television system." RADIO ENG. 12 (June): 22. (3375)

3472 Cockaday, L.M. "The editor—to you." RADIO N. 13 (June): 979. 3 photos. Extract from letter by Prof. Nakashima on the Takayanagi system demonstrated at station JOAK in the Fourth Exhibition of Inventions, Tokyo, Mar. 20–May 10, 1932. (2990, 3376, 3440, 3710)

3473 "Coming developments forecast a brilliant radio future." RADIO N. 13 (June): 987–93, 1046, 1047. Views by 56 radio men with portraits. Comments on television by Alexanderson, H.S. Baird, Jenkins, Replogle, and Sanabria.

3474 "Combined television and broadcast receiver." RADIO N. 13 (June): 1028. Photo. Brief description of tall cabinet with 7-by-8-inch screen, lens disk, sync motor, and Taylor neon arc projection lamp. Made by the Trav-Ler Manufacturing Corp., St. Louis, Mo. Displayed at the Radio Trade Show, Chicago.

3475 "U.S. bars Baird television because of alien identity." RADIO N. 13 (June): 1045. News item on the FRC denying application by station WMCA, New York, for visual broadcasting license. (3400, 3464, 3476)

3476 "Derby thrills by television. An historic transmission." TELEV. 5 (June): 127–30. 2 photos, diag. Images sent from the race course at Epsom Downs over 25 miles of telephone lines to the Metropole Cinema, London, June 1. Baird three-channel three-zone system with 30-line mirror drums, three phototubes, amplifiers, and light-valves. Cinema screen about 10 feet high and 8 feet wide viewed by about 2,000 people Extracts from seven newspapers and report on other transmissions from the studio to the cinema. (3475, 3478)

3477 "B.B.C. and television. Official statement of policy." TELEV. 5 (June): 131. An exclusive article with portrait of Sir John Charles Walsham Reith (1889–1971), Director-General of the BBC, and letter from him to the publisher, Benn Brothers, Ltd. Editorial comment by John A. Benn, p. 126. (3392, 3508)

3478 "Television by ultra-short waves." TELEV. 5 (June): 132, 133. Photo, Report on test transmissions of Apr. 29. (3476, 3480)

3479 "News from abroad." TELEV. 5 (June): 138, 139. 3 photos. Baird demonstration in Paris (3447), station W6XAO (3449). (3526)

3480 "Only seven years ago! An editor's foresight." TELEV. 5 (June): 140, 141. Photo, diag. Baird's article, Apr. 1925 (659). (3478, 3486)

3481 "The enthusiast sees it through." TELEV. 5 (June): 144–9. 3 photos, 8 diags. (3390, 3528)

3482 Dinsdale, A. FIRST PRINCIPLES OF TELEVISION. London: Chapman & Hall; New York: John Wiley, 1932. Reprint, New York: Arno Press, 1971. xv + 241 pp., 38 plates, 130 diags. Earlier chapters are concerned with elementary technical aspects, some history, at the Baird, Jenkins, and Bell Lab systems. Others deal with sync, image structure, and transmission channels. Two chapters are on the present state in Germany and England, and two other describe mechanical and cathode-ray systems in America. Opinions, possibilities, and applications are surveyed in the last chapter. Not documented except for a few references. (3411, 3616)

3483 Schröter, F. (ed.). HANDBUCH DER BILDTELEGRAPHIE UND DES FERNSEHENS [Handbook of photography and television]. Berlin: J. Springer, 1932. xvi + 487 pp., 365 illus. Introduction by A. Karolus. A comprehensive work by specialists, with some historical matter. Contributors are F. Banneitz, F. Biedermann, W. Ilberg, H. Lux, F. Michelssen, H. Muth, O. Schriever, F. Tuczek, and Schröter. Eleven chapters deal with methods of scanning pictures, scanning in television, modulation frequencies produced in scanning, photocells, receiving methods, sync, amplifiers, radio and wire transmission, latest developments. The work and apparatus of major concerns in Germany, Britain, and the United States are fully covered with many detailed references to articles and patents. Name and subject indexes. (3218, 3543)

3484 Hehlgans, F.W. "Cathode-ray tubes." U.S. 1,985,093, May 23, 1933, Dec. 18, 1934. Assigned: G.E. In Germany, June 1, 1932 (A.E.G.). (3460, 3491)

3485 D.S. Loewe and K. Schlesinger. "Valve generator." Br. 423,394, May 1, 1933. In Germany June 1, 1932. Sweep circuit. Reference to Br. 423,583 (3432). (3445, 3493)

3486 "4,000 see the Derby sent by television. Images thrown on London screen are hailed as 'marvelous' and Baird is cheered." N.Y.T. 2 (June): 5. "It was the first demonstration of television on such a scale." (3480, 3487)

3487 "Derby televised in London cinema. Successful public experiment." TIMES (June 2): 16c. The parade of horses before the race was televised, as well as the actual finish. (The Oaks Race, June 3, was also televised.) (3486, 3489)

3488 EMI and James Dwyer McGee. "Cathode-ray tube." Br. 402,460, June 2, 1932; U.S. 2,072,957, May 26, 1933, Mar. 9, 1937. (3602)

3489 "The Derby by television." ELECT. 108 (June 3): 750. Brief report on the reception at the Metropole Cinema, Victoria. There was noticeable flicker and also white bands dividing the three panels of the screen. (3487, 3490)

3490 "London sees a television Derby." N.Y.T. 18 (June 3): 5. Editorial comments. (3489, 3494)

3491 Hehlgans, F.W. "Cathode-ray tube." U.S. 2,075,717, May 23, 1933, Mar. 30, 1937. Assigned: G.E. In Germany June 4, 1932 (A.E.G.). (3484)

3492 Hudec, E. "Cathode-ray tube." Br. 420,752, June 6, 1933. In Germany June 6, 1932. Picture tube. (3467, 3545)

3493 D.S. Loewe and K. Schlesinger. "Television." U.S. 2,224,113, June 3, 1933, Dec. 3, 1940; Br. 420,679, June 6, 1933. In Germany June 7, 1932. Refers to sync circuits in a screened assembly. (3485, 3512)

3494 "Televising the Derby." W.W. 30 (June 8): 598. Photo. (3490, 3497)

3495 "Special film for television purposes)" W.W. 30 (June 8): 604. Communication from Dr. F. Noack, Berlin, on the suggestion to use two-films, one bright and one dark, to provide suitable contrast. (2591)

3496 Wienecke, Bruno. "Braun tube." U.S. 2,096,988, June 3, 1933, Oct. 26, 1936; Br. 420,538, June 6, 1933. In Germany June 8, 1932 (D.S. Loewe).

3497 "The Derby by television." ELECT. 108 (June 10): 786. Brief details of apparatus. (3494, 3508)

3498 Donle, H.P. "Television." U.S. 2,049,897, June 11, 1932. Aug. 4, 1936. Assigned: Radio Inventions. Concerns a film scanner with a mirror drum. (3393)

3499 Craig, T.J.D. "Multiplex system." Br. 402,855, June 16, 1932. A multicarrier acoustical proposal with multiple photocells, oscillators, modulators, filters, and resonators to operate a receiver with vibrating reeds.

3500 Gettinger, Joseph. "Television." U.S. 1,998,231, June 16, 1932, Apr. 16, 1935. Receiver includes a discharge system acting on film.

3501 Gould, L.A. "Television." U.S. 2,058,681, June 16, 1932, Oct. 27, 1936. Assigned: Radio Inventions. Photocell on a rotating arm coacts with a moving shutter. (3267)

3502 "Sues television interests. Agent seeks to stop 'unauthorized' deal for German patents." N.Y.T. 2 (June 17): 1. Injunction sought in Superior Court, Brooklyn, by Henry Goldman to restrain Harriman International Corp., Television Corp. of America, Frank Alexander, and Henry Rosenthal from using patents of the Zeitlin brothers (Appolinar and Gladislaw) and Rudolph Levy. (3534)

3503 Buckley, A.H. "Television." Br. 407,951, June 18, 1932. Refers to a multi-element, single-channel system wherein scanning is by oscillating mirrors controlled by a tuning fork, with multiple neon lamps and electron tube circuits in the receiver, Adaptable for film transmission or color with filters.

3504 Cawley, A.J. "Automatic television synchronizing apparatus." U.S. 2,125,991, June 18, 1932, Aug. 9, 1938. Concerns a rotating element with conductive segments. (3076)

3505 Dunlap, O.E. Jr. THE OUTLOOK FOR TELEVISION. New York: Harper & Bros., 1932. Reprint, New York: Arno Press, 1971. xiv + 297 pp., 5 plates. Introduction by J.H. Hammond, Jr. Foreword by W.S. Paley. Overview of historical events with observations and comments for general readers based mainly upon news reports in the NEW YORK TIMES, with extracts, quotes, and dates. Calendar of wireless-radio-television, pp. 266–88, from 640 B.C. to April 7, 1932. List of U.S. and Canadian television stations, pp. 288, 289. (3192, 3506)

3506 "Paint new world in television era." N.Y.T. 12 (June 20): 6. Comments on Dunlap's book, "published today." (3505, 3587)

3507 Applebaum, David. "Television receiver." U.S. 2,048,094, June 21, 1932, July 21, 1936. Cathode-ray tube, X-ray tube, scanning disk, and projection screen.

3508 "B.B.C. television." W.W. 30 (June 22): 654. Baird apparatus is being installed in studio BA, Broadcasting House. (3477, 3497, 3514, 3574)

3509 Barthélemy, R. "Telecinematographic emitter." U.S. 2,050,412, June 23, 1933, Aug. 11, 1936. Assigned: Comp. Gaz. Br. 407,230, June 26, 1933. In France June 25, 1932. Film transmitter. (3032, 3631)

3510 Trainer, M.A. "Television." U.S. 2,017,136, June 25, 1932, Oct. 15, 1935. Assigned: RCA. Disk system for film transmission. (2602, 3587)

3511 EMI and M. Bowman-Manifold. "Cathode-ray tubes." Br. 403,671, June 27, 1932. Deflection yoke assembly for picture tubes. (3456, 3536)

3512 D.S. Loewe and K. Schlesinger. "Television." Br. 421,603, June 26, 1933. In Germany June 27, 1932. Picture tube construction to eliminate distortion due to current between the beam and deflection plates. (3493, 3513)

3513 D.S. Loewe and K. Schlesinger. "Deflecting system." U.S. 2,154,386, June 24, 1933, Apr. 11, 1939; Br. 423,427, June 26, 1933. In Germany June 27, 1932. Divided from Br. 421,603. Deflection amplifiers to eliminate distortion due to current between the beam and deflection plates. (3512, 3542)

3514 "New home televisor. A nine-inch screen." TIMES (June 28): 16d. A new Baird receiver was exhibited yesterday at the laboratories in Long Acre. Table model with mirror drum and Kerr cell operated from the supply mains. "The most important advantage of the new instrument is that the image is reproduced on a screen 9 in. high by 4 in. broad so that it can be seen by a room full of people." (3508, 3516)

3515 Schubert, A. "Television." U.S. 2,079,880, June 27, 1933, May 11, 1937; Br. 410,338, June 29, 1933. In Germany June 30, 1932 (Fernseh A.-G.). Concerns duplicate film apparatus and controls to provide continuous operation involving more than one reel of film. Addition to Br. 409,400 (3183). (3240, 3517)

3516 "The Derby by television." DISCOVERY 13 (July): 233–5. 2 photos, diag. (3514, 3527)

3517 Schubert, G. "Der Fernseh-Zwischenfilmsender der Fernseh-Akr-Ges" [The intermediate film television transmitter of Fernseh A.-G.]. FERN. U. TON. 3 (July): 129–34. (3372, 3515, 3513)

3518 Thun, R. "Die Bedeutung des Programms für einen Erfolg des Fernsehens" [The importance of the program for successful television]. FERN. U. TON. 3 (July): 134–9. Picture transmission with sound, film transmission, program values. (3383, 3520)

3519 Möller, R. "Der Fernsehsender Rom" [The television transmitter, Rome]. FERN. U. TON. 3 (July): 153–6. Details of Fernseh equipment installed for Ente Italiano per le Audizioni Radiofoniche. (3381, 3517, 3544)

3520 Thun, R. "Ein Beitrag zur Berechnung von Fernsehapparaten" [A contribution to the design of television apparatus]. FERN. U. TON. 3 (July): 157–9. Analysis of image quantities. (3518, 3644)

3521 Peters, H. "Uber die Brauchbarkeit verschiedener Kathodenstrahloszillografen für Fernsehübertragungen" [On the utility of different cathode-ray oscillographs for television transmission]. FERN. U. TON. 3 (July): 159–68. Study of receiver tubes. (3133)

3522 Winckel, F.W. "Musikalische Forderungen für tonmodulierte Bildabtastung" [Musical requirements for sound modulated picture scanning]. FERN. U. TON. 3 (July) 170–3. Nipkow disk scanner and acoustical-optical reproduction. (2711)

3523 Replogle, D.E. "What television needs." RADIO N. 14 (July): 15, 55. Photos. (3137)

3524 Dowsett, H.M. "News by television. A Marconi development." TELEV. 5 (July): 164–6. 2 diags. Details of tape scanner with apertured drum (2791). (3457, 3564, 3578)

3525 "The press welcomes television. Widespread interest in new progress." TELEV. 5 (July): 167–70. Quotations from various newspapers and comments on the adverse views expressed by POPULAR WIRELESS.

3526 "News from abroad." TELEV. 5 (July): 174–7. 5 photos, diag. Reports on progress and apparatus in the United States, Canada, France, Germany, and Russia. (3479, 3576)

3527 "A new home 'Televisor'." TELEV. 5 (July): 183. 2 photos. Details of the Baird model revealed June 30. (3516, 3538)

3528 "The enthusiast sees it through." TELEV. 5 (July): 184–9. Photo, 7 diags. (3481, 3581)

3529 Busse, E. "Der Einfluss von Bildenhalt und Zerlegungssystem bein Fernsehen" [Influence of picture content and analyzing system in television]. Z. TECH. PHYS. 13 (July): 312–6. (3379)

3530 Flaherty, Mark. "Television." U.S. 2,047,020, July 1, 1932, July 7, 1936. Assigned: RCA. Br. 407,587, July 3, 1933 (Marconi's). Shield enclosure and mounting assembly for a vertical picture tube. Two references (2865, 2964)

3531 Nicolson, A.M. "Elastic wave television system." U.S. 1,972,492, July 1, 1932, Sept. 4, 1934. Assigned: Comm. Pats. Relates to a mosaic of elements on elastic supports. Output signals from an oscillator and receiver loosen the elements and thereby modulate light from a local source. (3268)

3532 Telefunken. "Cathode-ray tube." Br. 422,060, July 4, 1933. In Germany July 4,

1932. Contains an apertured diaphragm, modulating and deflecting plates and a magnetic coil for correcting undesired deflections. (3402, 3686)

3533 Cooper, H.J. "Television." Br. 397,648, July 5, 1932. An opaque disk has elongated slots at different angles. An alternative is a drum with mirrors at tangentially different angles.

3534 "Television writ denied. Court refuses to enjoin marketing of German patents here." N.Y.T. 22 (July 6): 3. Goldman suit (3502).

3535 EMI and C.O. Browne. "Television." Br. 404,020, July 6, 1932; U.S. 2,007,594, July 11, 1933, July 9, 1935. Film scanning by a mirror drum in which the size of an aperture is controlled by a shutter operated by a galvanometer to compensate for differences in the mean diversity of the film. (3349)

3536 EMI and M. Bowman-Manifold. "Television." Br. 402,181, July 7, 1932; U.S. 2,210,702. July 3, 1933, renewed Feb. 12, 1938, Aug. 6, 1940. On saw-tooth generator circuits for picture tubes with safety provisions to protect the screen from damage by a stationary beam. (3511)

3537 Wilson, J.C., and Baird Television. "Television transmitter." Br. 404,281, July 7, 1932. Mirror drum, arc lamp, and optical assembly mounted in a movable and adjustable carriage. Reference to Br. 269,658 (737) (3421, 3729)

3538 "Large television screens." ELECT. 109 (July 8): 30. On Baird's new mirror drum receiver. "The images produced are brilliant and clear, and the red colour of the neon tube has been eliminated." (3527, 3533)

3539 "New Baird televisor." W.W. 31 (July 8): 11. Photo. On the demonstration by the Baird Company, June 30. "The images were thrown on a screen 4 in. wide by 9–1/3 in. high and could be seen all over a large room with sufficient brilliancy to make the picture plainly visible even when the room was normally illuminated." (3538, 3540)

3540 Lyon, R., A.T. Stoyanowsky, and Emile Lubin. "Le problème de la transmission en télévision système Baird" [The transmission problem in Baird's television system]. GENE CIVIL 101 (July 9,): 29–32. About the apparatus employed in the Paris demonstration of May 19 (3447). (3539, 3573)

3541 Ardenne, M. v. "Braun tube." U.S. 2,081,344, July 8, 1933, May 25, 1937; Br. 423,793, July 8, 1933. In Germany, July 11, 1932. Concerns intensity control by magnetic coils mounted inside an anode tube with apertured end disks. (3452, 3563)

3542 D.S. Loewe and K. Schlesinger. "Television." Br. 407,857, July 10, 1933. In Germany July 11, 1932. Heater and control grid circuit of a cathode-ray tube are screened and filtered to eliminate ripple from the power supply. (3513, 3548)

3543 Schröter, F. "Television receiver." U.S. 1,977,409, July 25, 1933. Oct. 16, 1934. In Germany July 11, 1932 (Telefunken). Disk with a spiral of apertures and a spiral gas discharge tube with constrictions that enhance the glow at the apertures. (3483, 3597)

3544 Fernseh A.-G. "Cathode-ray tube." Br. 409,769, July 13, 1932. Void. Divided, see Br. 406,009 (3030). Screen coated with a thin metal layer connected to the anode. (3519, 3596)

3545 Hudec, E. "Cathode-ray tube." Br. 427,090, July 13, 1933. In Germany July 13, 1932. Deflection plates formed to keep beam deflection proportional to applied voltage. (3492)

3546 Jacomb, W.W., and Baird Television. "Light-valve." Br. 403,155, July 13, 1932. Concerns a multielement Kerr cell mounted in a vacuum tube filed with nitrobenzene, etc. Applicable to the cells described in Br. 401,311 (3395). Reference also to Br. 391,931 (3299). (3420, 3550)

3547 Karolus, A. "Light relay." U.S. 2,084,201, July 5, 1933, June 15, 1937. In Germany July 13, 1932. (3271)

3548 Schlesinger, K. "Tilting apparatus." U.S. 2,053,536, July 11, 1933, Sept. 8, 1936; Br. 424,490, July 14, 1933. In Germany July 15,

1932 (D.S. Loewe). Relaxation oscillator. Addition to Br. 394,476 (2921). (3542, 3549)

3549 D.S. Loewe and K. Schlesinger. "Valve Generator." Br. 427,168, July 14, 1933. In Germany July 15, 1932. Relaxation oscillator. Divided from Br. 424,490 (3548). (3552)

3550 Jacomb, W.W., and Baird Television. "Television." Br. 404,642, July 16, 1932. Sync motor and mirror drum. References to Br. 336,655 (1961), 384,346 (2963). (3546, 3744)

3551 Snow, Harold A. "Cathode-ray tube." U.S. 2,148,588, July 16, 1932, Feb. 28, 1939. Assigned: RCA.

3552 D.S. Loewe and K. Schlesinger. "Cathode-ray tube." Br. 422,708, July 17, 1933. In Germany July 18, 1932. Electrode assembly with deflection plates and apertured metal diaphragms. (3549, 3554)

3553 Ballard, R.C. "Television." U.S. 2,152,234, July 19, 1932, Mar. 28, 1933. Assigned: RCA. Br. 420,391, July 19, 1933 (Marconi's). Refers to a film system employing a disk with apertures in two circles, one for sync impulses, a picture tube with deflection coils, and a method of intermeshed line scan intended to reduce or eliminate flicker. (3253)

3554 Schlesinger, K. "Cathode-ray tube." U.S. 2,053,537, July 15, 1933, Sept. 8, 1936; Br. 427,703, July 19, 1933. In Germany July 19, 1932 (D.S. Loewe). Picture tube. (3552, 3555)

3555 Schlesinger, K. "Braun tube." U.S. 2,077,270, July 15, 1933, Apr. 13, 1937; Br. 423,036, July 19, 1933. In Germany July 19, 1932 (D.S. Loewe). A picture tube with deflection plates and a conductive coating on the screen and wall, the later connected to the anode, and a focusing assembly (3397). (3554, 3561)

3556 Loewe, S., and Peter Paul Fries. "Braun tube." U.S. 2,031,722, July 15, 1933, Feb. 25, 1936; Br. 427,718, July 20, 1933. In Germany July 20, 1932. References (2579, 2682), (2926, 3594)

3557 Winckel, F.W. "Am Wendepunkte des Fernsehens" [Turning point in television]. Z. FERN. 13 (July 20): 105–8. Summary of recent devices.

3558 Pye Radio and Peter Carl Goldmark (1906–77). "Television." Br. 405,006, July 20, 1932. Assembly with phonic wheel and mirror drum employed with a light source, optical system, and modulator for projecting the light beam onto a coated glass screen. (3559)

3559 Pye Radio and P.C. Goldmark. "Valve circuit." Br. 406,288, July 10, 1932. Capacitive-discharge tube circuit for driving a phonic motor. (3558)

3560 Birch-Field, C.A. "Television." U.S. 1,958,606, July 22, 1932, May 15, 1934. Faraday cell modulator with a quartz crystal. (3020)

3561 D.S. Loewe and K. Schlesinger. "Television." Br. 422,064, July 22, 1933. In Germany July 23, 1932. Refers to screened deflection electrodes and leads. Reference to Br. 398,804 (2838). (3555, 3562)

3562 Schlesinger, K. "Television tube." U.S. 2,114,610, July 21, 1933, Apr. 19, 1938; Br. 427,546, July 24, 1933. In Germany July 25, 1932 (D.S. Loewe). Addition to Br. 420,667 (3397). (3561, 3568)

3563 Ardenne, M. v. "Cathode-ray tube." Br. 405,892, July 27, 1933. In Germany July 28, 1932. Includes a compensating electrode between the deflection plates and screen. (3541, 3572)

3564 "News by television. Development of commercial apparatus by British engineers." ELECT. 109 (July 29): 151; ENGINEER 154 (July 29): 118. Lens drum scanner with tuning fork control for transmitting characters on a message tape, developed by Marconi's (2791). (3524, 3578)

3565 Lubcke, H.R. "Television." U.S. 2,055,748, July 29, 1932, Sept. 29, 1936. Picture tube receiver. (3449, 3690)

3566 Wotten, E. "Television." Br. 394,824, July 29, 1932. Construction of a mirror drum applicable to Br. 364,232 (2619)

3567 Essig, S.F. "Discharge apparatus." U.S. 2,020,305, July 30, 1932, Nov. 12, 1935. Assigned: RCA. Br. 421,201, July 31, 1933 (Marconi's). Silver globules on a photoelectric mosaic plate in a camera tube are oxidized by a hand-held electrode supplied from a high-frequency source, oxygen is then evacuated from the tube, and the screen is sensitized with caesium. (3310)

3568 Schlesinger, K. "Tilting apparatus." U.S. 2,039,119, July 27, 1933, Apr. 28, 1936; Br. 422,963, July 29, 1933. In Germany July 30, 1932 (D.S. Loewe). Sweep circuit. (3562, 3586)

3569 Zillger, Arno. "Television." U.S. 2,213,061, July 30, 1932, Aug. 27, 1940. Assigned: National Television Receiver with mirror screw and linear light source. (3590)

3570 Brown, Bradner. "Series modulation for television transmitters." ELECTRONICS 5 (Aug.): 263. Illus.

3571 Harder, E. "Bibliography on television." ELECTRONICS 5 (Aug.): 265.

3572 Ardenne, M. v. "Investigations on gas-filled cathode-ray tubes." PROC. IRE 20 (Aug.): 1310–23. 15 illus. Technical study including circuits, primarily for oscillography with mention of television applications. (3563, 3644)

3573 "Praised by the press." TELEV. 5 (Aug.): 200. Full-page advertisement of the new Baird receiver. Photo. Extracts from 11 publications. (3540, 3577)

3574 "B.B.C. and television." TELEV. 5 (Aug.): 203. Statement from the BBC on the transmissions to commence Aug. 22. (3508, 3580)

3575 "Visions and sound on one wave." TELEV. 5 (Aug.): 204. Report from New York on the CBS station W2XAB published in THE BROADCASTER. (3399, 3580)

3576 "News from abroad." TELEV. 5 (Aug.): 211–4. 5 photos, diag. Fernseh Company's positive column discharge lamp (3217), extracts from Peck's article (3428), and brief note on the Radio City, New York. (3526, 3613)

3577 "The new 'Televisor.'" TELEV. 5 (Aug.): 223. Photo, diag. Baird's mirror drum and Kerr cell receiver (3514). (3573, 3578)

3578 "'News' by television." TELEV. 5 (Aug.): 224, 225. Letter by R.E. Layzell (Secretary, Baird Television Ltd.) about the July article (3524) concerning the Marconi tube apparatus, with mention of the Baird system and patent (1521). Reply by Dowsett on the Marconi tube system and patent (2791), with photo of transmitter. (3524, 3564, 3577, 3583, 3595, 3604)

3579 "Origin of the word television." TELEV. 5 (Aug.): 225, 226. Letter by Federico S. Bassoli, Modena, Italy, about the statement in the May 1931 issue (2902). The writer correctly points out the use of the word by C. Pevskyi in his report of 1900 (288). (2902)

3580 "Points from the press. 'A real advance.'" TELEV. 5 (Aug.): 227, 228. Extracts from seven publications with comments on opinions about British television and the BBC. (3574, 3595)

3581 "The enthusiast sees it through." TELEV. 5 (Aug.): 229–31. 4 photos, diag. (3528, 3619)

3582 Centeno V, M. "Television." U.S. 2,066,715, Aug. 4, 1932, Jan. 5, 1937. Assigned: International Television Radio. Camera assembly with compound vibrating mirror and phototube. (2867)

3583 "News by television. A new Marconi system." W.W. 31 (Aug. 5): 101. Photo. Brief description of the message tape apparatus. (3578, 3615)

3584 Zworykin, V.K. "Television." U.S. 2,104,066, Aug. 5, 1932, Jan. 4, 1938. Assigned: RCA. Refers to a cathode-ray tube with deflection coils and plates, fluorescent screen with a lens system between the back of the screen, and a phototube, for transmission. (3355, 3585)

3585 Zworykin, V.K. "Television." U.S. 2,107,464, Aug. 5, 1932, renewed Sept. 12, 1936, Feb. 8, 1938. Assigned: RCA. Concerns a 3-D system with a plurality of scanners, picture tube with an optical grating in front of the screen, and a cabinet assembly with a vertical tube. (3584)

3586 Schlesinger, K. "Electric relay, particularly for purposes of television." U.S. 2,224,114, Aug. 5, 1933, Dec. 3, 1940; Br. 423,599, Aug. 5, 1933 (D.S. Loewe). In Germany Aug. 6, 1932. Receiver circuit with relaxation oscillator. Reference to Br. 420,679 (3493). (3568, 3606)

3587 Trainer, M.A. "Television." U.S. 2,085,556, Aug. 6, 1932, June 29, 1937. Assigned: RCA. Arc discharge control circuits for a disk scanner. (3510)

3588 Dunlap, O.E. Jr. "Television's mail. Nebraska observer tries to identify bald-headed men—ring on violinist's finger is seen in Tennessee." N.Y.T. IX 7 (Aug. 7): 1, 2. On reports of reception of images at far-off places transmitted from station W2XAB. Photo of boxing scene at the studio, columns 3–6. (3506, 3575, 3609, 3612)

3589 Worrall, Robert H. "Producing color in television." U.S. 2,002,515, Aug. 9, 1932, May 28, 1935. Receiver with light source, lens, prisms, and photo-active cell.

3590 Zillger, A. "Television." U.S. 2,077,866, Aug. 10, 1932, Apr. 20, 1937. Assigned: National Television. Mirror screw with a linear light source. (3569)

3591 Koch, Winfield R. "Television." U.S. 2,014,532, Aug. 11, 1932, Sept. 17, 1935. Assigned: RCA. Br. 412,435, Aug. 11, 1933 (Marconi's). Vertical picture tube and receiver assembly mounted on a metal chassis with balanced connections for tube filaments supplied from a center-tapped line transformer.

3592 McKay, John W. "Television lamp." U.S. 2,089,806, Aug. 11, 1932, Aug. 10, 1937. Assigned: National Television. Mercury vapor lamp with linear center stem.

3593 D.S. Loewe. "Electro-optical light-valve." Br. 427,092, Aug. 12, 1933. In Germany Aug. 12, 1932. Quartz crystals assembled at right angles with interleaved electrodes and Nicol prisms.

3594 Loewe, S. "Braun tube." Br. 427,093, Aug. 12, 1933; U.S. 2,083,198, Aug. 24, 1933, June 8, 1937. In Germany Aug. 13, 1932. Protective enclosure to minimize injury due to implosion. Reference to Br. 378,681 (2579). (3557, 3605)

3595 "Television broadcasts." TIMES (Aug. 17): 6g. Announcement by the BBC on transmissions with the Baird process to begin from Broadcasting House next Monday. Program times 11:00 to 11:30 p.m. on weekdays except Thursday. Vision from London National (261.3 m), sound form Midland Regional (398.9 m). (3578, 3580, 3600)

3596 "New film devised to aid television. German invention reduces time for developing and putting pictures on the air. Great improvement seen. Better reproduction than through direct transmission is held possible by photography." N.Y.T. 20 (Aug. 19): 8. Television with Zeiss Ikon intermediate film to be shown at the radio exhibition in Berlin. System developed by Fernseh A.-G. (3544, 3621)

3597 Richter, Otto Schriever, F. Schröter, and W. Federmann. "Electron tube." U.S. 2,079,085, Aug. 19, 1933, May 24, 1937. Assigned: Telefunken. In Germany Aug. 19, 1932. Gaseous cathode-ray tube with magnetic focusing and electrostatic deflection. (2980, 3194, 3543, 3701)

3598 Walton, G.W. "Light-valve." Br. 407,385, Aug. 19, 1932. Three-element Kerr cell between two double-image prisms. (3368, 3694)

3599 Michelssen, F. "Electron tube." U.S. 2,058,482, Apr. 6, 1934, Oct. 27, 1936. In Germany Aug. 22, 1932 (Telefunken). Cathode-ray tube with focusing electrode assembly. (3194, 3634)

3600 "Television. Broadcasts begun by the B.B.C." TIMES (Aug. 23): 12d. First of a new series of broadcasts with Baird equipment from studio BB, Broadcasting House. An introduction by Baird was followed by a variety program, 11:00 to 11:30 p.m. "Last night marked a new phase in television, and it should encourage a wider interest in the new science." (3595, 3610)

3601 Chevallier, P.E.L. "Kinescope." U.S. 2,021,253, Aug. 25, 1932, Nov. 19, 1935. Divided from U.S. 2,021,252 (2072).

3602 EMI, William Francis Tedham, and J.D. McGee. "Cathode-ray tube." Br. 406,353, Aug. 25, 1932; U.S. 2,077,442, Aug. 9, 1933, Apr. 20, 1937. Refers to a camera tube with a photoelectric mosaic mounted at a 45-degree angle to the axis, and to a method of oxidizing the silver layer and depositing caesium through a wire mesh of 300 lines per inch. (3488, 3705, 3708)

3603 Lippincott, Donald K. "Picture transmission." U.S. 2,226,436, Aug. 26, 1932, Dec. 24, 1940. Assigned: Farnsworth Television and Radio. Image dissector tube and method of scanning.

3604 Marconi's, H.M. Dowsett, and R. Cadzow. "Television." Br. 406,368, Aug. 26, 1932. Concerns a scannerless system in which all image points are transmitted simultaneously as different modulated frequencies. The transmitter tube contains two electrodes angularly placed in front of a photoelectric cathode on which the image is cast through a lens system. The receiver tube is similar but has a heated cathode and an internal fluorescent screen. (3457, 3578, 3615, 3661)

3605 Loewe, S. "Braun tube." U.S. 2,100,697, Aug. 24, 1933, Nov. 30, 1937. In Germany Aug. 29, 1932. (3594)

3606 D.S. Loewe and K. Schlesinger. "Deflecting voltage generator, more particularly for television receivers." U.S. 2,096,982, Aug. 24, 1933, Oct. 26, 1937; Br. 424,429, Aug. 21, 1933. In Germany Aug. 30, 1932. (3586, 3632)

3607 Gernsback, H. "What is wrong with television." RADIO-CRAFT 4 (Sept.): 137. Editorial. (1632)

3608 "The ultimate in television." RADIO N. 14 (Sept.): inside front cover. Advertisement by W.C. Rawls & Co., Norfolk, Va. Receiver with 16-inch 60-lens disk, sync motor, and lamp, including short-wave and broadcast receiver. List price $295.

3609 Peck, A.P. "Sight and sound on one wave." TELEV. 5 (Sept.): 240–2. 2 photos, 2 diags. (3428, 3588, 3613, 3628)

3610 "The B.B.C: 'First night.'" TELEV. 5 (Sept.): 243–6. 4 photos. Report on the initial broadcast, Aug. 22. Details of the program from Broadcasting House, of reception in London, and from Leeds, Newcastle-on-Tyne, and Crieff, Perthshire. (3600, 3614, 3650)

3611 "Television at Radiolympia." TELEV. 5 (Sept.): 247, 248. 4 photos. (3148)

3612 Dunlap. O.E. Jr. "Advertising by television." TELEV. 5 (Sept.): 257–9. 2 photos. (3588, 3672)

3613 "News from abroad." TELEV. 5 (Sept.): 260–2. 5 photos. On apparatus shown at the Berlin Radio Exhibition, and reports on reception of station W2XAB from various places in the United States. (3210, 3576, 3609, 3618, 3628, 3655)

3614 "Demonstration at Selfridge's." TELEV. 5 (Sept.): 264. Nine 15-minute performances were given daily from Aug 15 to Sept. 3 in a theatre seating about 200. Baird apparatus consisted of a mirror drum, grid cell, and arc lamp, which projected images onto a 3-by-7-foot screen. (3610, 3615)

3615 "'News' by television." TELEV. 5 (Sept.): 270. Letter by R.E. Layzell referring to the Dowsett letter in the August issue (3578). Photo of disk in the Baird tape apparatus. (3583, 3604, 3614, 3620, 3622, 3624)

3616 Dinsdale, A. "Television in America today." J. TELEV. SOC. 1 (Sept.): 137–49. 10 photos, 6 diags. List of 24 stations and CBS program for Dec. 23, 1931. Paper read Apr. 13 (3411). Reprinted by Arno Press, 1977. Bell Labs two-way system, NBC test transmissions and plans, Jenkins receiver, details of the Farnsworth system, Sanabria's projection apparatus, FRC functions, frequency bands, licenses, public interest, personalities in the television field. (3482)

3617 Wright, W.D. "The eye: a link in the television chain." J. TELEV. SOC. 1 (Sept.): 150–4. Photo, diag. (3191, 3668)

3618 Traub, E.H. "Television at the 1932 Berlin Radio Exhibition." J. TELEV. SOC. 1 (Sept.): 155–66. 17 photos, 2 diags, table showing manufacturers of transmitters and receivers, and the technical features. Report on equipment by Telefunken, Tekade, R.P.Z., Heinrich Hertz Institute, Fernseh, and Loewe Radio with particulars of components, systems, technicalities and the sizes and qualities of the images. (3210, 3612, 3630, 3730)

3619 Witsenberg, H.E. "Television in Holland." J. TELEV. SOC. 1 (Sept): 167, 168. Overview of the current situation and amateur activity. (3581, 3649)

3620 "Television demonstrated by Marconi's." J. TELEV. SOC. 1 (Sept.): 169. Photo, two others pp. 140, 151. (3615, 3623)

3621 Fernseh A.-G. "Cathode-ray tube." Br. 424,690, Aug. 25, 1933. In Germany Sep. 1, 1932. (3536, 3709)

3622 Marconi's, H.M. Dowsett, and L.E.Q. Walker. "Television." Br. 406,709, Sept. 2, 1932. Mirror drum with reflectors. (3457, 3615, 3661, 3668)

3623 "Television by wireless." TIMES (Sept. 2): 10e. See also ELECT. 109 (Sept. 9): 311, 312. and ENGINEER 154 (Sept. 9): 264. Demonstration by the Marconi Co., Sept. 1 during the British Association meeting at York, Aug. 31, to Sept. 7. Details of 15-line tape scan receiver with 3-by-25-inch screen, 50-line flying-spot transmitter with monitor, 50-line broadcast receiver with 8-inch screen and 50-line projection receiver with 4-foot screen. Images were sent 180 miles by radio from the Marconi works at Chelmsford (station G2BS) to St. Peter's School in York. (3620, 3629)

3624 Chapple, H.J.B. "Reading by television. Equipment for transmitting and recording script or type." ELECT. 109 (Sept. 9): 312. Diag. Baird tape apparatus. (3429, 3615, 3639, 3641)

3625 Robinson, James Michael. "Television scanning device." U.S. 1,927,754, Sept. 10, 1932, Sept. 19, 1933. Part assigned: Thomas Andrew Gosman. Two overlapping disks, one with angular radial slots and the other with apertures and movable plates.

3626 Cummings, Bryan Y. "Scanning system." U.S. 1,976,926, Sept. 15, 1932, Oct, 16, 1934. Two semicircular plates with spirals of rectangular holes overlap and rotate in opposite directions.

3627 Goldberg, Emmanuel. "Nipkow disk." U.S. 1,973,203, Sept. 15, 1932, Sept. 11, 1934. Assigned: Zeiss Ikon A.-G. Molded disk with lenses.

3628 Peck, A.P. "Television—broadcasting. Sight and sound on one wave—Columbia Broadcasting Company's new system—combination receiving sets." ELECT. 109 (Sept. 16): 344, 345. Photo, 2 diags. from TELEVISION (Sept.). (3609, 3613, 3664)

3629 "Television tests." W.W. 31 (Sept. 16): 277. Note on the Marconi Company's demonstration at York, and photo of the transmitters at Chelmsford. (3623, 3651)

3630 "Berlin radio show." W.W. 31 (Sept. 16): 280–3. 5 photos. Includes mention of apparatus by the Post Office, Telefunken, Tekade, Fernseh, and Loewe-von Ardenne. (3618, 3642)

3631 "Paris radio shows. Few technical advances—the Oscillophone." ELECT. 109 (Sept. 23): 375. Photo, diag. Some television was to be seen. Mention of the Barthélemy system and of the Bonovision firm, who showed a small apparatus that throws the picture onto a screen by means of a series of small mirrors. (3509)

3632 D.S. Loewe and K. Schlesinger. "Valve generator." Br. 425,686, Sept. 20, 1933. In Germany Sept. 24, 1932. Relaxation oscillator. (3006, 3633)

3633 Schlesinger, K. "Relaxation oscillation generator." U.S. 2,054,882, Sept. 16, 1933, Sept. 22, 1936; Br. 425,687, Sept. 20, 1933. In Germany Sept. 24, 1932 (D.S. Loewe). Scanning generator with blanking circuit. (3632, 3637)

3634 Michelssen. F. "Electron tube." U.S. 2,076,662, Sept. 13, 1933, Apr. 13, 1937. In Germany Sept. 24, 1932 (Telefunken). Cathode-ray tube with two magnetic focusing coils. (3599)

3635 Alexanderson, E.F.W. "Viewing invisible objects." Br. 412,905, Sept. 26, 1932 (B.T.H.). Void. Disk with two spiral sets of apertures and lenses, operating with a phototube and a lamp via an amplifier. (3223, 3675)

3636 Jackson, H. "Television." Br. 389,751, Sept. 27, 1932. Multichannel system with slotted cylinders for scanning intermediate film.

3637 Schlesinger, K. "Relaxation oscillation generator." U.S. 2,090,951, Sept. 16, 1933, Aug. 24, 1937; Br. 425,685, Sept. 20, 1933. In Germany Sept. 27, 1932 (D.S. Loewe.). Scanning generator with blanking circuit. (3633, 3658)

3638 A.E.G. "Valve generator." Br. 426,002, Sept. 28, 1933 (B.T.H.). In Germany Sept. 28, 1932. Relaxation oscillator. (3369)

3639 "Television—broadcasting." ELECT. 109 (Sept. 30): 420. Letter from R.E. Layzell of Baird Television commenting on the C.B. Co. item in the Sept. 16 issue (3628). (3624, 3641)

3640 Ogloblinsky, G.N. "Television." U.S. 2,040,813, Sept. 30, 1932, May 12, 1936. Assigned: RCA. Br. 412,813, Oct. 2, 1933 (Marconi's). Camera tube for film transmission with circuits for correcting distortion due to the obliquity of the scanning beams. (3355)

3641 Chapple, H.J.B. "Ultra-short waves and television." DISCOVERY 13 (Oct.): 330, 331. 2 photos. General discussion and some details of the Baird test transmission Apr. 29 (3433). (3624, 3639, 3648, 3653)

3642 Kette, A. "Das Fernsehen auf der Berliner Funkausstellung 1932" [Television at the Berlin radio fair 1932]. FERN. U. TON. 3 (Oct.): 193–205. Details of exhibits. (3129, 3630, 3643)

3643 Kirschstein, F. "Die Fernsehübertragungen mit dem Ultra-Kurzweller-Sender Witzleben auf der Funkausstellung 1932" [Television transmissions with the ultra-short wave transmitter Witzleben at the radio fair 1932]. FERN. U. TON. 3 (Oct.): 205–10. Motion picture transmitter supplied by Fernseh A.-G. (3378, 3642)

3644 Ardenne, M. v. "Die Praktische Durchführung der Thun'schen Liniensteuerung unter Anwendung neu entwickelter Methoden" [The practical design of Thun's line control and use of newly developed methods]. FERN. U. TON. 3 (Oct.): 210–21. Constant-intensity cathode ray with variable scanning speed, or velocity modulation. (3520, 3572, 3684)

3645 Krawinkel, G., and K. Ziebig. "Uber Hochfrequenzverstärkung beim Fernsehen" [On high-frequency amplification in television]. FERN. U. TON. 3 (Oct.): 221–7. Mathematical analysis and circuits. (3377)

3646 Scholz, Werner. "Fernsehempfang mit Spiegelschraube und Hochfrequenzgespeister Quecksilber-Argon-Lampe" [Television reception with mirror screw and high-frequency mercury-argon lamp]. FERN. U. TON. 3 (Oct.): 227–30. Experiments, circuits, results.

3647 Rohde, L. "Die Bedeutung der Hochfrequenzgasentladung für das Fernsehen" [The importance of the high-frequency gas discharge for television]. FERN. U. TON. 3 (Oct.): 230–4. Investigation of the characteristics of glow discharge lamps at high frequencies as light sources.

3648 "Thrilling race finish sent by television to theatre audience fourteen miles away." POP. MECH. 58 (Oct.): 608, 609. 2 illus. Baird transmission of the Derby (3486). (3641, 3656)

3649 "Experimental television in England." RADIO N. 14 (Oct.): 236. Photo, Extract of letter from experimenter in Cambridge on the British system and on reception from Königs Wusterhausen and Witzleben. (3619, 3654)

3650 "Last month's programmes." TELEV. 5 (Oct.): 280–3. 4 photos. Survey of the first month of television broadcasting by the BBC. (3610, 3691)

3651 "British Association at York. Demonstration of Marconi apparatus." TELEV. 5 (Oct.): 285, 286. Photo of 50-line scanner. Description of Marconi equipment issued by the Company. (3629, 3742)

3652 "Points from the press. Critics look to the future." TELEV. 5 (Oct.): 287–9. 2 cartoons.

3653 Chapple, H.J.B. "Is the scanning disc obsolete?" TELEV. 5 (Oct.): 290, 291. 2 photos. (3641, 3654)

3654 Chapple, H.J.B. "Constructing a mirror drum. The first stage." TELEV. 5 (Oct.): 292, 293. Photo, 4 diags. (3649, 3653, 3657, 3693)

3655 "News from abroad." TELEV. 5 (Oct.): 294, 295. 2 photos. Reports on the Don Lee transmission to an airplane (3449), the CBS transmission and reception reports, Berlin radio show (3642), Tekade mirror screw, and daily film transmission of 90/25 images on 7 m in Berlin. (3613, 3696)

3656 "'News' by television. The Baird process." TELEV. 5 (Oct.): 298, 299. Photo, diag. Details of apparatus. (3648, 3662)

3657 "The enthusiast sees it through." TELEV. 5 (Oct.): 302–5. 3 photos, 3 diags. (3654, 3695)

3658 Schlesinger, K. "Braun tube." U.S. 2,083,203, Sept. 29, 1933, June 8, 1937; Br. 426,138, Sept. 29, 1933. In Germany Oct. 1, 1932 (D.S. Loewe). Refers to a double-beam tube with one set of deflection plates common to both beams to produce two independent [?] for oscillography. Television images in two or three colors can be obtained with different color phosphors on the screen and an external reflecting system to project the images in optical alignment onto a viewing surface. (See 3789.) (3637, 3659)

3659 D.S. Loewe and K. Schlesinger. "Cathode-ray tube." Br. 427,765, Sept. 29, 1933. In Germany Oct. 1, 1932. Divided from Br. 426,138 (3658). (3660)

3660 Schlesinger, K. "Relaxation oscillation generator." U.S. 2,100,700, Sept. 29, 1933, Nov. 30, 1937; Br. 426,055, Sept. 27, 1933. In Germany Oct 1, 1932 (D.S. Loewe). (3659, 3676)

3661 Marconi's, H.M. Dowsett, and R. Cadzow. "Wireless direction finding system." Br. 408,015, Oct. 5, 1932; U.S. 2,081,530, Sept. 28, 1933, May 25, 1937. Includes visual indication at a receiver of the names of several transmitting stations by a disk with a stepped spiral slot coacting with a similarly apertured mask and a neon lamp. (3604, 3622, 3669)

3662 Baird, J.L., and Baird Television. "Television." Br. 408,596, Oct. 6, 1932. Scanning with two side-by-side mirror drums and light modulation by two neon tubes or arc lamps or Kerr cells. Reference to Br. 312,560 (1083). (3656, 3665)

3663 Herman, J. "Automatic line level regulation of multiple channel television systems." U.S. 2,064,540, Oct. 11, 1932, Dec. 15, 1936. Assigned: AT&T. (2032)

3664 "Television makes debut in political campaign; Democrats stage group broadcasts a show." N.Y.T. 48 (Oct. 12): 3. Half-hour program broadcast from station W2XAB and received at the Myers Laboratory in the Chrysler Building. Said to be the first use of television in a political campaign. (3628, 3691)

3665 Baird, J.L., and Baird Television. "Television." Br. 408,332, Oct. 12, 1932. Assembly with mirror drum driving motor, phonic wheel, automatic sync control and framing. (3662, 3702)

3666 EMI and W.D. Wright. "Television." Br. 399,654, Oct. 12, 1932. Refers to a cathode-ray tube with an oblique photoelectric plate or fluorescent screen and an optical system. (3617)

3667 "Create 'cold-light' in new radio tube. Engineers demonstrate bulb hailed as forward step in practical television." N.Y.T. 24 (Oct. 13): 6. High-frequency mercury vapor tube demonstrated at the Myers Electrical Research Laboratory, New York. (3674)

3668 Marconi's, R.J. Kemp, L.E.Q. Walker, and Ernest Frederick Goodenough. "Amplifier." Br. 408,678, Oct. 14, 1932. For television and news bulletin receivers. Reference to Br. 373,288 (2791). (3454, 3622, 3669, 3737)

3669 Marconi's, H.M. Dowsett, and L.E.Q. Walker "Television." Br. 408,679, Oct. 14, 1932. Concerns the formation of characters on a moving message band to minimize blurring. Reference to Br. 373,288 (2791). (3661, 3668, 3737)

3670 Bedford, A.V. "Cathode-ray apparatus." U.S. 2,004,099, Oct. 15, 1932, June 11, 1935. Assigned: RCA. Br. 427,112, Oct. 16, 1933 (Marconi's). Addition to Br. 427,113 (3671). Deflection yoke has two iron cores of unequal dimensions to provide a non-uniform magnetic field. (3462)

3671 Vance, A.W. "Cathode-ray apparatus." U.S. 2,006,063, Oct. 15, 1932, June 25, 1935. Assigned: RCA. Br. 427,113, Oct. 16, 1933 (Marconi's). Deflection yoke with four cores, two having coils with unequal numbers of turns and the other two displaced below the axis to provide even scanning (keystone scan) of a plate or screen disposed obliquely in a tube. (3394)

3672 Dunlap, O.E. Jr. "Television magic challenges youthful experimenters. Up against a stone wall. Baffling problems confront experts in quest of television—will an amateur find key to success as did Marconi?" N.Y.T. VIII (Oct. 16): 1–3. This speculative piece includes a comment by Eckersley. "They are on the wrong track in London"; one by Charles W. Horn, chief engineer of NBC, "We are up against a stone wall in television"; and an all-in wrap-up by the writer. "The trick today is to enlarge the picture, clarify the images, throw more light on the screens, simplify a receiver for home use, and invent a method of sending the scenes through space on narrow channels." (3612, 3673)

3673 Dunlap, O.E. Jr. "Are political rallies doomed?" N.Y.T. VIII 10 (Oct. 16): 2. "What will happen to large political mass meetings...when television handles the scene and speeches?" (3672)

3674 "A new 'cold' tube invented by Elman B. Myers gives 250,000 candlepower to television." N.Y.T. VIII, 10 (Oct. 16): 4–6. 2 photos. (3667)

3675 Alexanderson, E.F.W. "Television." Br. 414,022, Oct. 17, 1932 (B.T.H.). Void. Two adjacent lines are scanned simultaneously by a disk with a spiral of double-section prisms coacting with a radically slotted light-chopper. Adaptable for transmission or reception with two radio channels. (3635)

3676 Schlesinger, K. "Braun tube." U.S. 2,090,952, Oct. 12, 1933, Aug. 24, 1937; Br. 431,775, Oct. 16, 1933. In Germany Oct. 17, 1932 (D.S. Loewe). Picture tube. (3660, 3677)

3677 Schlesinger, K. "Cathode-ray apparatus." U.S. 2,114,611, Oct. 12, 1933, Apr. 19, 1938; Br. 431,773, Oct. 16, 1933. In Germany Oct. 17, 1932 (D.S. Loewe). Picture tube. Reference to Br. 420,752 (3492). (3676, 3680)

3678 Rosenberg, H. "Television." Br. 411,835, Dec. 7, 1932. In Germany Oct. 18, 1932.

Thyratron control for each lamp in a bank, as in Br. 411,819 (3214). (3736)

3679 Adams, Clayton Loftin. "Television." U.S. 2,024,790, Oct. 21, 1932, Dec. 17, 1935. Part assigned: J.S. and B.A. Francis. A perforated drum is outside another drum which has a band carrying light-sensitive elements and contacts.

3680 Schlesinger, K. "Braun tube." U.S. 2,075,142, Oct. 18, 1933. Mar. 30, 1937; Br. 430.650, Oct. 19, 1933. In Germany Oct. 21, 1932 (D.S. Loewe). Picture tube. Reference to Br. 398,804 (2838). (3677, 3681)

3681 Schlesinger, K. "Braun tube." U.S. 2,100,701, Oct. 28, 1933, Nov. 30, 1937; Br. 431,774, Oct. 16, 1933. In Germany Oct. 31, 1932 (D.S. Loewe). Electrode assembly in a picture tube. Reference to Br. 420,667 (3397). (3680, 3685)

3682 "Electric and Musical's first report." TIMES (Oct. 25): 20c. First company accounts from Apr. 20, 1931 (date of incorporation) to Sept. 30, 1932. (2824, 3683)

3683 "Electric and Musical Industries." TIMES (Oct. 25): 20f. A meeting is to be held Nov. 10. (3682, 3703)

3684 Ardenne, M. v. "Intensity control system for cathode-ray beams." U.S. 2,103,652, Oct. 24, 1933, Dec. 28, 1937. In Germany Oct. 25, 1932. Picture tube. (3644, 3706)

3685 Schlesinger, K. "Braun tube." U.S. 2,083,204, Oct. 23, 1933, June 8, 1937; Br. 432,209, Oct. 23, 1933. In Germany Oct. 25, 1932 (D.S. Loewe). (3681, 3687)

3686 Telefunken. "Cathode-ray tube." Br. 409,221, Oct. 26, 1933. In Germany Oct. 26, 1932. Concerns multiple deflection platen. (3532)

3687 D.S. Loewe and K. Schlesinger. "Television." Br. 414,249, Oct. 26, 1933. In Germany Oct. 27, 1932. Picture tube circuit in which the cathode takes longer to heat up than the deflection oscillator to obviate a stationary spot on the screen. Controller reference to Br. 402,181 (3536), (3685, 3700)

3688 Campbell, Richard L. "Television." U.S. 1,995,376, Oct. 29, 1932, Mar. 26, 1935. Assigned: RCA. Br. 412,092, Oct. 30, 1933 (Marconi's). Deflection yoke assembly with extra permanent magnets applied to a camera tube with an oblique photoelectric plate.

3689 Haefer, R., and H.G. Möller. "Uber das Pendeln von Nipkowscheiben" [Oscillation of Nipkow disks]. HOCH. ELEKT. 40 (Nov.): 170–75.

3690 Lubcke, H.R. "Television image reception in an airplane." PROC. IRE 20 (Nov.): 1732–40. 3 illus. Description of tests on May 21 (3449) from the Don Lee Broadcasting System station W6XAO in Los Angeles. Signals on 44.5 mc (6.75 m) produced 80/15 images on a picture tube receiver in a plane moving at 120 mph. (3449, 3565)

3691 Kaufman, S. "Television and sound on one wave!" RADIO N. 14 (Nov.): 270, 271, 314, 315. 4 photos, 2 diags. General discussion of the CBS system. (3171, 3664)

3692 "Last month's programmes." TELEV. 5 (Nov.): 320–3. 3 photos. (3650, 3693)

3693 "Reports from readers." TELEV. 5 (Nov.): 323, 324. On BBC transmissions. "Letters have already arrived from sixty different towns and cities in England, Wales, Scotland, Ireland, the Channel Isles, Holland, France, and Germany." (3692, 3702)

3694 Walton, A.W. "The problems of television. Limitations of scanning." TELEV. 5 (Nov.): 325–7. Extracts from a lecture to the British Kinematograph Society. General survey of scanning methods, light sources, and light modulators. (3598, 3727)

3695 Chapple, H.J.B. "Constructing a mirror drum." TELEV. 5 (Nov.): 328, 329. Photo, diag. (3654, 3657, 3698)

3696 "News from abroad." TELEV. 5 (Nov.): 330–2. 2 photos. Table of American stations and a European television timetable. New disk camera will monitor for outdoor pickup by the de Forest Radio Co., cathode-ray tubes by Globe Television and Phone Corp.,

the German Television Society and personalities, German broadcasts, activities and plans of various companies, developments, and prospects in France. (3655, 3728)

3697 Denton, J.J. "Talks on television." TELEV. 5 (Nov.): 338–40. 2 diags. Chronology from 1564 (Galileo) to 1927 (Bell Labs). (2272)

3698 "The enthusiast sees it through." TELEV. 5 (Nov.): 342–5. 2 photos, 2 diags. (3695)

3699 Goldsmith, A.N., and T.R. Goldsborough. "Television." U.S. 2,073,370, Nov. 1, 1932, Mar. 4, 1937. Assigned: RCA. Br. 417,282, Oct. 23, 1933 (Marconi's). Concerns the separate pickup of foreground and background with two camera tubes, prevention or production of ghost effects, monitor tube recording camera, and circuits. Three references (3232, 3253, 3423). (1000, 2821)

3700 Schlesinger, K. "Producing relaxation oscillations." U.S. 100,702, Oct. 31, 1933, Nov. 30, 1937; Br. 429,427, Oct. 30, 1933. In Germany Nov. 4, 1932 (D.S. Loewe). (3687, 3718)

3701 Schriever, O., and W. Federmann. "Relaxation oscillator." U.S. 2,146,769, Oct. 23, 1933, Feb. 14, 1939; Br. 412,833, Nov. 8, 1933. In Germany Nov, 8, 1932 (Telefunken). 3597, 3733)

3702 "Danish items in television programme." TIMES (Nov. 9): 106. BBC transmission Nov. 8. Baird spoke a few words of greeting; Carol Brisson sang. Reception on a large screen in the Arena Theatre, Copenhagen. (3665, 3693, 3723, 3743)

3703 "The E.M.I. meeting." TIMES (Nov. 11): 20d–e. Alfred Clark, the chairman, analyzed the "causes of the poor results of this important company." At the time of the merger (2824) there were 50 factories in 19 countries, and "last week the workpeople on the payroll number over 12,800." (3683, 3704)

3704 "Electric and Musical Industries. Review of past year's operations. Advantages of the merger. Mr. Alfred Clark's address." TIMES (Nov. 11): 21c–f This full report includes a brief mention of television research. (3703)

3705 EMI and W.E. Tedham. "Light-sensitive apparatus." Br. 410,142, Nov. 11, 1932; U.S. 2,005,059, Oct. 27, 1933, June 18, 1935. Multiplier phototube employing secondary emission. (3602)

3706 Ardenne, M.v. "System for energizing a cathode-ray tube." U.S. 2,096,987, Nov. 13, 1933, Oct. 26, 1937. In Germany Nov. 15, 1932. Refers to a power supply in which the anode potential to the tube is delayed until the cathode is heated. (3684, 3707)

3707 Ardenne, M.v. "Protective device in television receiver." U.S. 2,188,290, Oct. 14, 1936, Jan. 23, 1940. In Germany Nov. 15, 1932. Anode supply to a picture tube contains a thermostatic switch. Divided from U.S. 2,096,987. (3706, 3714)

3708 EMI and J.D. McGee. "Cathode-ray tube circuit." Br. 410,478, Nov. 15, 1932. Potential divider with capacitors. (3602, 3748)

3709 Fernseh, A.-G. "Television." Br. 413,178, Nov. 15, 1933. In Germany Nov. 15, 1932. Concerns the processing of film for intermediate storage. Reference to Br. 402,631 (3336). (3621, 3710)

3710 Fernseh A.-G. "Television." Br. 428,227, Nov. 9, 1933. In Germany Nov. 15, 1932. Intermediate film system. (3709, 3713)

3711 Hammond, J.H. "Navigational guide system." U.S. 2,027,530, Nov. 15, 1932, Jan. 14, 1936. Assigned: RCA. Includes television. (2539)

3712 Nakashima, T., and K. Takayanagi. "Cathode-ray tube." U.S. 1,981,322, Nov. 16, 1932, Nov. 20, 1934. (3472, 3739)

3713 Fernseh A.-G. "Television." Br. 410,023, Nov. 15, 1933. In Germany Nov. 18, 1932. Construction of rotary scanners. (3710, 3719)

3714 Ardenne, M.v. "Braun tube for producing television images rich in contrast." U.S. 2,090,922, Oct. 18, 1933, Aug. 24, 1937. In

Germany Nov. 21, 1932. Concerns tube structure and the fluorescent screen. (3707, 3730)

3715 Myers, L.M. "Light modulation. Improved method for use in television—brighter images." ELECT. 109 (Nov. 25): 665. Photo. Development at the Wilson Laboratory of a new prism which eliminates Nicol prisms, reduces optical losses, and increases picture brightness. (2235)

3716 Bronson, Harry. "Amplifier." U.S. 2,093,496, Nov. 26, 1932. Sept. 7, 1937. Assigned: RCA. Br. 415,619, Nov. 27, 1933 (Marconi's). For television.

3717 Mihály, D.v. "Television." U.S. 2,089,588, Nov. 23, 1933, Aug. 10, 1937; Br. 419,120, Nov. 27, 1933 (IMK). In Germany Nov. 26, 1932. Internal mirror drum with reflectors. Addition to Br. 394,446 (2868). Reference to Br. 412,026 (3448).

3718 D.S. Loewe and K. Schlesinger. "Cathode-ray tube." Br. 442,041, Apr. 23, 1933. In Germany Nov. 26, 1932. Divided from Br. 420,667 (3397). (3700, 3745)

3719 Fernseh A.-G. "Television." Br. 429,354, Nov. 29, 1933. In Germany Nov. 29, 1932. In an intermediate film system the film is exposed to the electron beam inside a cathode-ray tube. (3713, 3735)

3720 Morlock, William J. "Cathode-ray apparatus." U.S. 2,007,380, Nov. 30, 1932. July 9, 1935. Assigned: RCA. Br. 418,940, Nov. 30, 1933 (Marconi's). Deflection yoke and circuits.

3721 "A year of progress in television." DISCOVERY 13 (Dec.): 398–400. 2 photos. General review, chiefly British events.

3722 Du Mont, A.B. "An investigation of various electrode structures of cathode-ray tubes suitable for television reception." PROC. IRE 20 (Dec.): 863–77. 16 illus. Descriptions and analyses of different structures and electrode voltages with reference to beam modulation, spot size, and intensity. (2988)

3723 "Last month's programmes." TELEV. 5 (Dec.): 362–5. 3 photos. (3702, 3724)

3724 "Reports from readers." TELEV. 5 (Dec.): 365, 366. (3723, 3743)

3725 De Wet, P.J. "'Self-centered' television." TELEV. 5 (Dec.): 367, 368. 2 photos. (1385)

3726 "Big events in 1932. A year of progress." TELEV. 5 (Dec.): 369–72, 378. 5 photos. Survey, mainly British.

3727 Walton, G.W. "The problems of television. Transmission and reception." TELEV. 5 (Dec.): 376–8. Radio and wire channels, photocells, amplifiers, light sources and modulators, overview, television and the cinema industry. (3694)

3728 "News from abroad." TELEV. 5 (Dec.): 383. Photo. "Make-up" in the United States, amateur experiments and reception problems in Switzerland, note on Telehor film transmitter in Brussels by Viro-Radio, S.A., of Borgerhont, Anvers, Belgium. (3696)

3729 Wilson, J.C. "Mirror drum scanning. An elementary analysis." TELEV. 5 (Dec.): 384–6. 2 diags. Mathematical treatment. (3537)

3730 Traub, E.H. "New television systems. Thun's principle of variable speed applied to cathode ray by von Ardenne." J. TELEV. SOC. 1 (Dec.): 177–82. 4 photos, 7 diags. Thorough discussion of apparatus developed by von Ardenne in conjunction with Loewe Radio, laboratory tests and results. (3618, 3714)

3731 Bridgewater, Thornton H. "Some aspects of television reception." J. TELEV. SOC. 1 (Dec.): 183–200. 2 photos, 27 diags. This study of amplifiers, phase distortion, and receiver circuits was reprinted with additions by the Society as Publication No. 1.

3732 "Developments in television." ELECT. 309 (Dec. 2): 708. Report on IEE lecture by T.M.C. Lance, Nov. 25. Telefunken system, the mirror screw, 7 m transmission.

3733 Schriever, O. "Television." U.S. 2,114,688, Dec. 1, 1933, Apr. 19, 1938; Br. 413, 561, Dec. 4, 1933. In Germany Dec. 2, 1932

(Telefunken). Sync circuits for transmitter and receiver. (3701)

3734 "Sees television near for use in the home. Returning inventor reports only one obstacle." N.Y.T. 12 (Dec. 4): 6. Views of Ahronheim. Everything in television is ready for success except the handling of high-frequency waves. (3303)

3735 Fernseh A.-G. "Television." Br. 420,727, Dec. 6, 1933. In Germany Dec. 6, 1932. Amplifier with automatic control of the mean level of brightness. (3719, 3740)

3736 Rosenberg, H. "Television." Br. 408,128, Dec. 7, 1932. Film system in which pictures are reproduced on a screen of incandescent lamps controlled by relays. (3678)

3737 Marconi's, H.M. Dowsett, and R.J. Kemp. "Television." Br. 411,489, Dec. 8, 1932. Simultaneous scanning with two sets of parallel lens or mirror drums at right angles to one another. (3668, 3669)

3738 Marconi's, and George Fairburn Brett. "Light-valve." Br. 411,490, Dec. 8, 1932. A multielement Kerr cell.

3739 Nakashima, T., and K. Takayanagi. "Television receiving system." U.S. 2,093,157, Aug. 1, 1933. Sept. 14, 1937; Br. 409,970, Aug. 31, 1933. In Japan Dec. 12, 1932. Additional deflection coils on a picture tube produce an image with a dot structure instead of continuous lines. (3712, 3751)

3740 Fernseh A.-G. "Television." Br. 411,540, Dec. 13, 1933. In Germany Dec. 13, 1932. Scene is scanned through an aperture in the studio wall while on separate photocell, screened from an object in the room, is actuated by reflection from the inner walls. Reference to Br. 320,627 (1214). (3735, 3749)

3741 Henroteau, F.C.P. "Television." U.S. 2,146,822, Dec. 15, 1932, Feb. 14, 1939. Assigned: RCA. Br. 413,954, Dec. 13, 1933. In Canada, Dec. 15, 1932. Concerns a special linear phototube with a cathode-ray tube at right angles to the axis, two perforated scanning disks, optical filter, commutators,. and circuit. Reference to Br. 335,958, 335,995 (1884). (2751)

3742 "Television research. Development of transmitters and amplifiers—the scanning of groups." ELECT. 109 (Dec. 16): 790. Brief note on work by the Marconi Company from the current issue of THE MARCONI REVIEW. Items mentioned include high-gain amplifiers, light-beam scanner with Nipkow disk for producing a full-length picture in 30 lines, 50-line lens drum and mirror drum scanner, the news-tape apparatus, and a 100-line lens drum and mirror scanner for 75 kc transmission. (3651)

3743 "Television on B.B.C.'s 7-metre transmitter." W.W. 31 (Dec. 16): 535. Special transmissions by the Baird system sent out on 7.3 m from 3:00 to 5:00 p.m. on Wednesdays and Fridays. "Images with ninety lines up to as many as 240 lines in place of the present thirty-line pictures have been transmitted experimentally in the Baird laboratories." (3702, 3724, 3747)

3744 Jacomb, W.W., T.W. Collier, and Baird Television. "Electro-optical light-valve." Br. 410,546, Dec. 16, 1932. Assembly with Kerr cell, lamp, focusing lens, and polarizing prisms. References to the cell (640, 3299, 3546). (2568, 3551)

3745 D.S. Loewe and K. Schlesinger. "Cathode-ray tube." Br. 435,382, Dec. 19, 1933. In Germany Dec. 17, 1932. (3718, 3746)

3746 Schlesinger, K. "Braun tube." U.S. 2,013,645, Dec. 14, 1933, Dec. 28, 1937; Br. 434,111, Dec. 18, 1933. In Germany Dec. 20, 1932 (D.S. Loewe). Picture tube and circuits. Reference to Br. 432,209 (3685). Controller reference to Br. 423,427 (3513). (3745, 3750)

3747 "Ultra short-wave television." ELECT. 109 (Dec. 23): 804. Note on BBC's 7 m transmissions. (3741, 3753)

3748 EMI and J.D. McGee. "Cathode-ray tube." Br. 412,264, Dec. 23, 1932. Electrode assembly. (3708)

3749 Fernseh A.-G. "Amplifying circuit." Br. 412,126, Dec. 21, 1933. In Germany Dec. 23, 1932. Modulation control for a television transmitter. (3740)

3750 D.S. Loewe and K. Schlesinger. "Television receiver." Br. 435,682, Dec. 22, 1933; U.S. 2,054,883, Dec. 21, 1933, Sept. 22, 1936. In Germany Dec. 24, 1932. Voltage stabilizer with glow lamps. (3746)

3751 Nakashima, T. and K. Takayanagi. "Sawtooth wave from current and voltage generating device." U.S. 2,055,611, Aug. 1, 1933, Sept. 29, 1936. In Japan Dec. 29, 1932. (3739)

3752 Nobbs, W.J. "Television." Br. 412,285, Dec. 30, 1932. Concerns the construction of a mirror drum.

3753 Aisberg, E., and Robert Aschen. THEORIE ET PRATIQUE DE LA TELEVISION. Paris: Etienne Chiron, 1932. 236 pp., 216 illus. (2882)

3754 Alberti, Egon. BRAUNSCHE KATHODENSTRAHLROHREN UND IHRE ANWENDUNG [Braun cathode-ray tubes and their applications]. Berlin: J. Springer, 1932. vii + 214 pp., 158 illus. Thorough coverage from 1897; history, theory, construction, applications, and circuits, with 292 references.

3755 THE B.B.C. YEAR BOOK 1933. London: B.B.C., 1932. "Television in 1932," pp. 441–5, 447, by J.L. Baird. 2 photos, diag. Review of Baird-BBC collaboration; description of television processes; Baird receiver with mirror drum and Kerr cell; progress in France, Germany, and the United States; television in the cinema. (3747)

3756 Collins, Archie Frederick. EXPERIMENTAL TELEVISION. Boston: Lothrop, Lee & Shepard, 1932. xv + 313 pp., 185 illus. "A series of simple experiments with television apparatus, also how to make a complete television transmitter and television receiver.

3757 Dyck, Joseph Géréberne Regina van. LA TELEVISION EXPERIMENTALE. Paris: Dunod, 1932. 191 pp., illus. Preface by A. Henroteau. (3758)

3758 Dyck, J.G.R. van. RADIOVISIE—ZYN WEZEN EN MOGELIJKHEDEN [Radiovision—its being and possibilities]. Antwerp: N.V. Viro, 1932. 105 pp. (3757)

3759 Fleisher, Richard, and Horst Teichmann. DIE LICHTELEKTRISCHEN ZELLER UND IHRE HERSTELLUNG [The photoelectric cell and its manufacture]. Dresden and Leipzig: Theodor Steinkopff, 1932. xii + 175 pp.

3760 Hughes, A., and Lee Alvin DuBridge. PHOTOELECTRIC PHENOMENA. New York: McGraw-Hill, 1932. xii + 531 pp., 481 illus., 41 tables. About 1,350 footnotes and others with some tables. (439)

3761 Martin, Thomas (ed.). FARADAY'S DIARY: BEING THE VARIOUS PHILOSOPHICAL NOTES OF EXPERIMENTAL INVESTIGATIONS MADE BY MICHAEL FARADAY D.C.L., F.R.S. DURING THE YEARS 1820–1862. London: G. Bell & Sons, 1932–36. 7 vols., plus index vol. Foreword by Sir William H. Bragg. These laboratory notes are a detailed record of apparatus, experiments, effects. results, and related suppositions and conclusions, supported by extensive sketches. Vol 7, pp. 412–61, concern experiments on the discharge of electricity in rarefied gases. (6, 13, 24)

3762 Simon, H., and R. Suhomann. LICHTELEKTRISCHE ZELLEN UND IHRE ANWENDUNG [Photoelectric cells and their application]. Berlin: J. Springer, 1932. vii + 373 pp., 295 illus.

3763 Zworykin, V.K., and E.D.W. Wilson. PHOTOCELLS AND THEIR APPLICATIONS. New York: John Wiley; London: Chapman & Hall, 1932. xv + 331 pp., illus. Second edition with five new chapters.

CHAPTER 13

A MATTER FOR BIG BUSINESS: 1933

TABLE 20 CHRONOLOGY: 1933

Date		Entity	Event
Feb.		Baird Co.	Report on experiments with picture tubes
Mar.	6	Fernseh A.-G.	Single-gun color tube
Apr.		Sofar	Displays 90-line apparatus in Milan
	5	Television	Displays at exhibition Society
	6	Baird Co.	Demonstrates 120/25 reception on a picture tube
	18	Baird Co.	Demonstrates to BBC and G.P.O. representatives at Long Acre
	19	EMI	Demonstrates to BBC and G.P.O. representatives at Hayes
May	25	Baird Co.	Color system
June	26	Zworykin	Lecture in Chicago on 240/24 system
July		Bush Radio	Announces Baird console receiver
	7	Baird Co.	Report on Crystal Palace installation
	10	Sanabria	Demonstrates at Macy's in New York
Aug.		Germany	Standard of 180/25 considered for regular service
		Germany	Post Office wanted high-definition test transmission
		Scophony	Statement of developments and plans
	6	Dunlap	Article on the reminiscences of Paul Nipkow
	11	Farnsworth Co.	McCarger comments on system and plans
	15	Various	Displays at the National Radio Exhibition
	18	Various	Displays at the Berlin Radio Show
	22	BBC	Broadcasts a boxing match
Sept.	6	Baird, Marconi	Displays at the British Association meeting, Leicester
Oct.		Sofar	Displays at the National Radio Show, Milan
		Zworykin	Paper on the RCA all-electric system
	7	Farnsworth Co.	Image with electron multiplier
	13	BBC	Announcement on testing by Baird Co. and EMI
	16	Germany	Post Office plans for 180/25 transmissions
Dec.		RCA	Papers on experimental system

TABLE 21 CORPORATE PATENTS

Company	1932	1933
D.S. Loewe	50	60
Baird Companies	16	33
EMI	13	33
Telefunken	13	31
RCA	32	22
Fernseh A.-G.	15	16
Marconi's	17	10
*Tekade	0	9
A.C. Cossor	2	8
Farnsworth Companies	3	8
Bell Telephone Laboratories	3	5
*General Electric (U.K.)	0	4
National Television Corporation	3	4
A.E.G.	6	3
Communication Patents	3	3
General Electric (U.S.)	3	3
AT&T	2	1
Comp. Gaz	3	1
*I.G. Farben	0	1
C. Lorenz	1	1
*Radio Patents	0	1
*Schneider	0	1
	185	258

*New entries in 1930

BIBLIOGRAPHY: 1933

3764 Kleen, W. "Intensitätssteuerung gaskonzentrierter Elektronenstrahlen mittels Wehnalt-Zylinder" [Intensity control of gas concentrated electron rays by means of Wehnelt cylinders]. HOCH. ELEKT. 41 (Jan): 28–30. Study includes television tubes.

3765 White, Edwin Lee. "Modulation frequencies in visual transmissions." PROC. IRE 21 (Jan.): 51–5. Mathematical treatment of maximum frequencies.

3766 Fayard, G. "Sur la détermination des fréquences les plus élevées ã transmettre et l'influence de la distortion de phase en télévision" [On the determination of the highest frequencies for transmitting and the influence of phase distortion in television]. ONDE ELECT. 12 (Jan.): 53–60. Theoretical analysis.

3767 "Last month's programmes." TELEV. 6 (Jan.): 8–11.

3768 "News from abroad." TELEV. 6 (Jan.): 12. Germany; Post Office standards; Loewe Laboratories; double-beam tube.

3769 "The Baird screen in Copenhagen." TELEV. 6 (Jan.): 13, 14. 2 photos. On the display in the Arena Theatre in Nov.

3770 Peck, A.P. "White light for television." TELEV. 6 (Jan.): 15, 16. 2 photos. The mercury lamp of E.B. Myers. (3674)

3771 "Television and the Post Office. An official reply." TELEV. 6 (Jan.): 17. Photo of the Postmaster General, Sir (Howard) Kingsley Wood (1881–1943). On the rental of telephone lines for television experiments.

3772 "Design for projection apparatus." TELEV. 6 (Jan.): 22–4. Photo, 2 diags. Equipment by Mervyn Sound and Vision Co., Ltd.

3773 Denton, J.J. "Talks on television, II. Images and the retina." TELEV. 6 (Jan.): 26–8. Photo.

3774 "The enthusiast sees it through." TELEV. 6 (Jan.): 32–5. 4 photos, 5 diags.

3775 Schröter, F. (Picture telegraphy and television.) Z. PHYSIK. 1 (Jan.): 41–8.

3776 Dunlap, O.E. Jr. "Radio industry surveys the outlook for New Year. Opportunities for 1933. Television lurks behind the economic curtain—secrecy makes research mysteries." N.Y.T. VIII 5 (Jan. 1): 1–3. General survey, question of commercial expansion and economic restraints.

3777 Bowman-Manifold, M. "Television." U.S. 2,090,801, Jan. 11, 1934, Aug. 24, 1937, In Britain Jan. 2, 1933 (EMI). Cathode-ray scanning of film for velocity modulated signals.

3778 Kell, R.D. "Television." U.S. 2,166,214, Jan. 3, 1933, renewed Apr. 8, 1937, July 18, 1939. Assigned: RCA. Br. 431,207, Jan. 3, 1934 (Marconi's). Film projection via a disk onto a camera tube.

3779 Kell, R.D. "Television." Br. 431,258, Jan. 3, 1934 (Marconi's). In U.S. Jan. 3, 1933. Modification of and divided from, Br. 431,207 (3778).

3780 Ogloblinsky, G.N. "Television." U.S. 2,084,700, Jan. 3, 1933, June 22, 1937. Assigned: RCA. Br. 426,672, Jan. 3, 1934 (Marconi's). Concerns film transmission with a camera tube, and outdoor pickup.

3781 D.S. Loewe and Hans-Heinz Wolff. "Television." Br. 433,295, Jan 5, 1934. In Germany Jan. 6, 1933. Film scanning by cathode-ray in a velocity-modulated system.

3782 "Baird television." TIMES (Jan. 7): 15a. Company report.

3783 Schlesinger, K. "Producing correcting impulses." U.S. 2,137,351, Jan. 5, 1934, Nov. 22, 1938; Br. 431,521, Jan. 10, 1934 (D.S. Loewe). In Germany Jan. 10, 1933. Sync impulses are provided by a phonic wheel coupled to a gas triode and an oscillatory circuit.

3784 D.S. Loewe and K. Schlesinger. "Cathode-ray tube." Br. 420,881, Apr. 3, 1933. In Germany Jan. 12, 1933. Divided from Br. 420,667 (3397).

3785 EMI, W.F. Tedham, and J.D. McGee. "Cathode-ray tube." Br. 415,071, Jan. 16, 1933. vacuum tube with fluorescent screen, deflection plates, and coils. Details of construction include an electron lens and a silver coating on the inside of the tube.

3786 Marconi's, H.M. Dowsett, and E.F. Goodenough. "Television." Br. 413,645, Jan. 17, 1933. Construction and adjustment of a mirror wheel.

3787 "Television set makers plan output of 1,000 a day here." N.Y.T. (Jan. 23): 27:4. Plans of the Ray-O-Television Manufacturing Co. (subsidiary of the Ray-O-Vision Corporation of America) for plant in Long Island City.

3788 Mitchell, W.G.W. "Television." ELECT. 110 (Jan. 27): 115. 2 photos. Brief survey of progress in 1932.

3789 "Events of 1932." ELECT. 110 (Jan. 27): 118.

3790 "Colored television." W.W. 32 (Jan. 27): 68. Photo of Loewe Company's picture tube with two independent beams (3568).

3791 Holzer, Philip P. "Television." U.S. 1,980,406, Jan. 27, 1933, Nov. 13, 1934. Scanning disk with three 120-degree spirals.

3792 Bedford, A.V. "Television." U.S. 2,082,093, Jan. 28, 1933, June 1, 1937. Assigned: RCA. Film transmission in a scanning disk and camera tube.

3793 Campbell, R.L. "Television." U.S. 2,092,875, Jan. 28, 1933, renewed Oct. 16, 1936, Sept. 14, 1937. Assigned: RCA. Br. 422,658, Jan. 29, 1934 (Marconi's). Concerns a complete transmitting system employing a camera tube with magnetic deflection and circuits to blank the beam on the return traces.

3794 Gardner, B.C. "Cathode-ray tube." U.S. 2,020,025, Jan. 28, 1933, Nov. 5, 1935. Assigned: Television Labs. Includes a luminescent screen of flexible metal foil.

3795 Dunlap, O.E. Jr. "Secrecy of research adds to television mystery. Hopes of an industry. Research experts are harnessing tiny waves to carry television images—picture quality is being improved." N.Y.T. IX, 10 (Jan. 29): 1–3. Includes views of E.K. Cohan of station W2XAB.

3796 D.S. Loewe. "Thermionic valve circuits." Br. 434,274, Jan. 27, 1934. In Germany Jan. 31, 1933. Amplifiers and selector switches correct the relative contrast of tonal values (black, gray, white) in a film transmission system.

3797 "Television stations in the United States." RADIO N. 14 (Feb.): 478. List of 35 stations with call letters, power, company affiliation, and location.

3798 "Television in England." SCI. AM. 148 (Feb.): 76, 77. 3 photos. "A brief summary of events of 1932 that are indicative of the general trend." A report provided by TELEVISION.

3799 Chapple, H.J.B. "Picture shape in television." TELEV. 6 (Feb.): 44–6. 3 diags. Dimensions given for disks and drum. Baird image ratio (H-W) is 7:3 with vertical scanning, counter-clockwise; German ratio is 4:3 with horizontal scanning, clockwise, both 30 lines.

3800 "New research on cathode rays." TELEV. 6 (Feb.): 47, 48. Photo, diag. Laboratory experiments with picture tubes by the Baird Company.

3801 Benn, J. "A controversy and its outcome." TELEV. 6 (Feb.): 49–52. 2 photos. Recollections of reports by the author and of contemporary events from 1926.

3802 "Last month's programmes." TELEV. 6 (Feb.): 54–7. 3 photos.

3803 "News from abroad." TELEV. 6 (Feb.): 59, 60. Photos, European timetable. Comments from U.S. and on demonstrations in Paris, particularly by Barthélemy.

3804 Denton, J.J. "Talks on television, III. Photoelectric cells." TELEV. 6 (Feb.): 68, 69.

3805 "The enthusiast sees it through." TELEV. 6 (Feb.): 70–3. 2 photos, 3 diags.

3806 Rosenberg, K., and H. Rosenberg. "Electric reproduction of kinema films." Br. 432,501, Jan. 27, 1934. In Germany Feb. 3, 1933. Lamp screen and selector relays.

3807 Ardenne, M. v. "Television receiver." Br. 434,950, Feb. 5, 1934. In Germany Feb. 6, 1933. Picture tube circuits.

3808 McKay, J.W. "Transmitting images." U.S. 2,056,974, Feb. 6, 1933, Oct. 13, 1936. Assigned: National Television. Includes multiple reflecting plates on a rotary scanner.

3809 Telefunken. "Television." Br. 423,765, Feb. 6, 1934. In Germany Feb. 6, 1933. Modulation and sync circuits.

3810 Telefunken. "Cathode-ray tube." Br. 426,087, Feb. 6, 1934. In Germany Feb. 6, 1933. Refers to an electron lens structure and a silver coating inside the tube.

3811 Bullimore, W.R., and L.H. Bedford. "Television." Br. 413,401, Feb. 7, 1933 (A.C. Cossor). Receiver circuits in a velocity modulated system. References to prior patents (3270, 3311)

3812 Farnsworth, P.T. "Luminescent screen." U.S. 2,104,253, Feb. 8, 1933, Jan. 4, 1938. Assigned: Farnsworth Television.

3813 EMI and C.O. Browne. "Television transmitter." Br. 414,730, Feb. 9, 1933. Film scanning with mirror drum, lenses, apertured screen, and photocell.

3814 EMI, C.O. Browne, and John Hardwick. "Television." Br. 419,441, Feb. 10, 1933; U.S. 2,176,663, Feb. 9, 1934, Oct. 17, 1939. Sync circuits for receivers.

3815 EMI and C.O. Browne. "Television." Br. 419,523, Feb. 10, 1933. Mirror drum construction and adjustment.

3816 Fernseh A-G. "Cathode-ray tube." Br. 432,970, Feb. 7, 1934. In Germany Feb. 10, 1933. Addition to Br. 424,690 (3621).

3817 EMI, M. Bowman-Manifold, and Edward Cecil Cook. "Television." Br. 416,720, Feb. 13, 1933; U.S. 2,140,102, Feb. 12, 1934, Dec. 13, 1938. Sync circuit and saw-tooth generator.

3818 EMI, Frank Blythen, and J. Hardwick. "Receiving device." Br. 420,065, Feb. 13, 1933; U.S. 2,133,075, Feb. 12, 1934, Oct. 11, 1938. Picture tube and compensating circuit.

3819 Baird, J.L., and Baird Television. "Television." Br, 415,036, Feb. 14, 1933. Scanning with three fixed lenses, slotted disk, and a lens disk.

3820 EMI and C.O. Browne. "Television." Br. 415,118, Feb. 15, 1933; U.S. 2,133,422, Feb. 14, 1934, Oct. 18, 1938. Relates to circuits for processing sync and picture signals.

3821 Ardenne. M. v. "Cathode-ray tube." Br. 413,995, Feb. 19, 1934, Assigned: A.C. Cossor. In Germany Feb. 17, 1933.

3822 Schlesinger, K. "Photoamplifier." U.S. 2,063,195, Feb. 19, 1934, Dec. 8, 1936; Br. 435,387, Feb. 19, 1934. In Germany Feb. 20, 1933 (D.S. Loewe). Phototube and amplifier in a vacuum tube.

3823 "Commends the Times on Geneva broadcast, Evening Post foresees use of television by newspapers in the next 'surge forward.'" N.Y.T. 3 (Feb. 21): 6. Comments on an editorial in the NEW YORK EVENING POST.

3824 Ardenne, M. v. "Cathode-ray tube." Br. 421,507, Feb. 22, 1934. Assigned: A.C. Cossor. In Germany Feb. 22, 1933. A thin metal layer is deposited between a fluorescent screen and the glass face of a high-vacuum tube.

3825 Ardenne, M. v. "Television." Br. 432,225, Feb. 22, 1934. Assigned: A.C. Cossor. In Germany Feb. 22, 1933. Concerns filtering arrangements for cathode-ray tubes used for film scanning.

3826 Byron, D.H. "Television." Br. 415,404, Feb. 22, 1933. Construction and adjustment of mirror drums.

3827 Tekade. "Light valve." Br. 422,370, Feb. 22, 1934. In Germany Feb. 22, 1933. Solid zinc blend crystals and electrode assembly, developed by von Okolicsányi.

3828 EMI and J.D. McGee. "Cathode-ray tubes." Br. 415,143, Feb. 23, 1933. In tubes with oblique screens, for either pickup or display, the deflection plates are arranged to compensate for keystone distortion.

3829 Marconi's, H.M. Dowsett, and R. Cadzow. "Television transmitter." Br. 416,848, Feb. 23, 1933. Camera tube with a fine gauge screen in front of a photoelectric mosaic. Reference to Br. 395,597 (3253).

3830 D.S. Loewe. "Television." Br. 434,278, Feb. 26, 1934. In Germany Feb. 25, 1933. Film scanning by a disk with sync signals produced optically from a margin on the film.

3831 D.S. Loewe. "Amplifier." Br. 437,641, Feb. 26, 1934. In Germany Feb. 25, 1933. Divided from Br. 439,164 (3832), addition to Br. 410,147 (3065). For transmitters.

3832 D.S. Loewe. "Amplifier." Br. 439,164, Feb. 26, 1934. In Germany Feb. 25, 1933. Circuits intended to provide images with correct average intensity. Reference to Br. 434,274 (3796).

3833 Baird, J.L., and Baird Television. "Television transmitter." Br. 415,744, Feb. 27, 1933. Double-beam scanning with mirror drum, arc lamp, and two phototubes. References (565, 640, 1721, 2536).

3834 Holmes, Ralph S. "Television." U.S. 2,251,677, Feb. 28, 1933, Aug. 5, 1941. Assigned: RCA. Br. 434,496, Feb. 28, 1934 (Marconi's). Picture tube receiver with circuits for sync and control of average brilliancy.

3835 "Five years. The development of the programmes." TELEV. 6 (Mar.): 96–9. 4 photos. Retrospective view of transmissions from studios of the Baird Company and the BBC.

3836 "Last month's programmes." TELEV. 6 (Mar.): 102–5. 3 photos.

3837 "News from abroad." TELEV. 6 (Mar.): 107. Short-wave research in Germany.

3838 "The T.T.S. television transmitter. New Marconi equipment." TELEV. 6 (Mar.): 108–13. 2 photos, 11 diags. Description from the MARCONI REVIEW.

3839 "Television research." TELEV. 6 (Mar.): 116. Note on Baird Company's report (3782). Delay in making receiver, fresh capital needed to equip the factory.

3840 "The enthusiast sees it through." TELEV. 6 (Mar.): 120–3, Photo, 4 diags.

3841 "1933 television exhibition." J. TELEV. SOC. 1 (Mar.): 209–16. 2 photos, diag. Held

Apr. 5, 6 at the Imperial College of Science, South Kensington. Prof. Fleming's opening speech. Description of displays by Baird Television, Marconi's, General Electric, Edison Swan Electric, Radio Reconstruction, Westinghouse, Brake and Saxby Signal, British Thomson-Houston, G.E.C. Research Laboratories, the General Post Office, and 17 members of the Society.

3842 Harris, Norman L. "Gas discharge tubes and their application to television." J. TELEV. SOC. 1 (Mar.): 217–26. 10 photos, 5 diags. Some historical background is followed by technical description of various types and discussions.

3843 Kurtz, Edwin Bernard. "Television station W9XK at University of Iowa, U.S.A." J. TELEV. SOC. 1 (Mar.): 227, 228. 5 photos.

3844 "Fifth annual report of the council." J. TELEV. SOC. 1 (Mar.): 232, 233.

3845 "Practical television." J. TELEV. SOC. 1 (Mar.): 123–36. Summary of meeting, Dec. 14, 1932.

3846 Dome, Robert B. "Amplifier." Br. 419,914, Mar. 1, 1934 (B.T.H.). In U.S. Mar. 1, 1933 (G.E.). For television.

3847 D.S. Loewe. "Valve circuits." Br. 437,643, Mar. 2, 1934. In Germany Mar. 2, 1933. Television detector.

3848 Reveley, P.V., and Baird Television. "Valve circuits." Br. 415,155, Mar. 2, 1933. Amplifier and light-valve.

3849 Wilson, J.C., and Baird Television. "Amplifier." Br. 415,796, Mar. 3, 1933. Circuits for correcting amplitude and phase distortion at television frequencies. Reference to Br. 381,254 (3010).

3850 Fernseh A.-G. "Cathode-ray tubes." Br. 423,696, Mar. 5, 1934. In Germany Mar. 4, 1933. Fluorescent screen on flexible material that can be inserted through the neck of the tube.

3851 Dunlap, O.E. Jr. "Pioneers in television survey the road ahead. Faces that lurk in space: Television observers in Indiana and Maine look in on New York—but a cat looks like a Scotty." N.Y.T. IX, 10 (Mar. 5): 1–3. Quotes on reception from letters received from various parts of the country.

3852 "New 'electrical lens' an aid to television." N.Y.T. IX, 10 (Mar. 5): 3. On Zworykin's announcement concerning an electromagnetic lens at a meeting of the American Physical Society at Columbia University.

3853 Fernseh A.-G. "Television." Br. 432,989, Mar. 6, 1934. In Germany Mar. 6, 1933. Concerns reproduction in color from one or several screens in a single-beam tube.

3854 Fernseh A.-G. "Television." Br. 434,868. Mar. 6, 1934. In Germany Mar 6, 1933. Strips of different phosphors on a screen, scanned in various ways by a single beam, produce images in color. Divided from above. Reference to Br. 425,267.

3855 D.S. Loewe. "Television." Br. 436,142, Mar. 5, 1934. In Germany Mar. 6, 1933. Refers to ultra-short wave transmission of picture and screening signals on two adjacent channels with reception by two receivers.

3856 EMI and C.O. Browne, "Television transmitter." Br. 419,811, Mar. 7, 1933; U.S. 2,122,974, Mar. 5, 1934, July 5, 1938. Film scanning by a shutter disk mirror drum, and apertured screen with impulses for line and frame sync generated optically via a light source, phototube, and the disk.

3857 Schröter, F. "Television scanning system." U.S. 2,124,404, Mar. 8, 1934, July 19, 1938. In Germany Mar. 8, 1933 (Telefunken). Refers to a transmitter employing a cathode-ray tube and two phototubes.

3858 Tekade. "Television." Br. 428,721, Mar. 8, 19324. In Germany Mar. 8, 1933. Multispiral disk or multispiral mirror screw with obturator to expose one active scanning surface at a time.

3859 Maguire, Irwin Leonard. "Television." Br. 421,247, Mar. 10, 1933. Void. This Australian plan comprises an apertured disk, rotating reflectors and slotted mask applicable for transmission or reception.

3860 Knoll, M. "Braun cathode-ray tube." U.S. 2,078,449, Mar. 6, 1934, Apr. 27, 1936. In Germany Mar. 11, 1933 (Telefunken).

3861 D.S. Loewe. "Television." Br. 439,734, Mar. 12, 1934. In Germany Mar. 11, 1933. Refers to the transmission of deflection potentials on separate carrier waves to provide interlaced scanning in a picture tube receiver. Addition to, and modification of, Br. 436,142 (3855), divided from Br. 439,866.

3862 Schlesinger, K. "Wireless transmission of sound-films." U.S. 2,086,961, Mar. 6, 1934, July 13, 1937. In Germany Mar. 11, 1933.

3863 Knoll, M. "Braun tube for television receiver." U.S. 2,064,981, Mar. 6, 1934. Dec. 22, 1936. In Germany Mar. 13, 1933 (Telefunken).

3864 Rosenberg, K. and H. Rosenberg. "Television." Br. 433,969, Mar. 14, 1934. In Germany Mar. 14, 1933. Reproduction of pictures form film by means of banks of lamps, light-sensitive cells and relays. Reference to Br. 411,819 (3214).

3865 EMI and. C.O. Browne. "Television." Br. 416,723, Mar. 15, 1933. Film scanning with mirror drum and shutter disk similar to Br. 419,811. Reference to Br. 398,228 (3349).

3866 Peck, W.H. "Television." Br. 405,821, Mar. 18, 1933. Mirror drums and lenses.

3867 Martin, L.C. "Television." Br. 417,052, Mar. 21, 1933. A low-speed scanning system with disk transmitter, mirror drum, and Kerr cell receiver, for film reproduction.

3868 A.E.G. "Valve generator." Br. 435,486, Mar. 23, 1934. In Germany Mar. 23, 1933. Relaxation oscillator. Reference to Br. 394,476 (2921).

3869 Dobke, Günther. "Electron tube." U.S. 2,177,350, Mar. 15, 1934, Oct. 24, 1939. In Germany Mar. 23, 1933 (A.E.G.). Cathode-ray tube.

3870 Fernseh A.-G. "Television." Br. 432,992, Mar. 24, 1934. In Germany Mar. 25, 1933. Refers to the exposure of an intermediate film at less than normal rate, with signals transmitted a plurality of times to obtain pictures at a normal rate of 25 per second.

3871 EMI and C.O. Browne. "Television transmitters." Br. 417,181, Mar. 28, 1933. Concerns alternate transmission of two films with separate shutter disks, a common mirror drum, dual sync circuits, and means to control the film system in use.

3872 Schlesinger, K. "Cathode-ray tube for television." U.S. 2,118,865, Mar. 26, 1934. May 31, 1938; Br. 435,203, Mar. 24, 1934. In Germany Mar. 29, 1933 (D.S. Loewe). Reference to Br. 432,209 (3685).

3873 Schlesinger, K. "Braun tube." U.S. 2,077,271, Mar. 26, 1934, Apr. 13, 1937; Br. 438,882, Mar. 24, 1934. In Germany Mar. 29, 1933 (D.S. Loewe). Refers to a three-plate deflection arrangement and circuits. Addition to Br. 432,209 (3685). Reference to Br. 423,427 (3513).

3874 Schlesinger, K. "Detector for ultra-short waves." U.S. 2,068,768, Mar. 26, 1934, Jan. 26, 1937; Br. 435,417, Mar. 24, 1934. In Germany Mar. 29, 1933 (D.S. Loewe). Television receiver for modulation frequencies up to at least 100 kc, with push-pull circuit.

3875 Schlesinger, K. "Transmission and modulating arrangement. U.S. 2,063,196, Mar. 26, 1934, Dec. 8, 1936; Br. 435,561, Mar. 24, 1934. In Germany Mar. 29, 1933 (D.S. Loewe).

3876 Standard Telephone & Cables, W.T. Gibson, and D.H. Black. "Cathode-ray tube." Br. 417,182, Mar. 29, 1933. Electron tube structure with plug-in base and a metallic fluorescent screen nearly parallel with the axis of the tube.

3877 "Danes build a television set from discarded Ford motor." N.Y.T. 11 (Mar. 30): 5. "Poul Larsen and Axel Neilsen ... have constructed a television receiver which they say will reproduce a London vaudeville performance."

3878 Iams, H.A. "Television transmission." U.S. 2,099,980, Mar. 30, 1933, Nov. 23, 1937.

Assigned: RCA. Br. 420,479, Apr. 3, 1934 (Marconi's). Call letters of the transmitter are superimposed onto the photosensitive mosaic of a camera tube by a mask or other means.

3879 Iams, H.A. "Mosaic screen." U.S. 2,120,099, Mar. 30, 1933, renewed Aug. 21, 1936, June 7, 1938. Assigned: RCA. Br. 422,158, Apr. 3, 1934 (Marconi's). A thin mica sheet is coated on one side with platinum and with silver on the other. The latter is ruled with grooves to form tiny isolated squares that are photosensitized.

3880 Marconi's, H.M. Dowsett, and L.E.Q. Walker. "Wireless direction finding system." Br. 417,196, Mar. 31, 1933; U.S. 2,098,281, Mar. 20, 1934, Nov. 9, 1937 (RCA). A transmitter, such as the one described in Br. 400,279 (3414), has two rotating antennas for radiating television signals.

3881 "Last month's programmes." TELEV. 6 (Apr.): 132–5. 2 photos.

3882 Clarke, B.R. "Television in the ideal home." TELEV. 6 (Apr.): 141–2. Display at the Ideal Home Exhibition.

3883 Friedman, L.B. "Television and home talkies." TELEV. 6 (Apr.): 142.

3884 "Sixty-line scanning. Demonstration at University College." TELEV. 6 (Apr.): 143, 144. 2 photos. Portable apparatus displayed by Capt. R. Wilson and E.L. Gardiner, talk by J.J. Denton.

3885 Benn, J.A. "Seeing is believing. A word to the radio critics." TELEV. 6 (Apr.): 145, 146. Photo.

3886 "News from abroad." TELEV. 6 (Apr.): 147, 148. Comments on events in Germany and the United States. Photo of cathode-ray tube exhibited by M.A.E. Pressler at the Leipzig Fair.

3887 "A critic challenged. Is real television here?" TELEV. 6 (Apr.): 149–51. On comments in the radio press critical of the BBC transmissions by the Baird system.

3888 Chapple, H.J.B. "From my notebook." TELEV. 6 (Apr.): 152, 153. Photo of Televisor similar to the one installed in a BBC listening room. Screen is about 16 inches high and seven inches wide; images are black and white and "remarkably bright."

3889 Farnsworth, P.T. "Scanning oscillator." U.S. 2,059,683, Apr. 3, 1933, Nov. 3, 1936. Assigned: Farnsworth Television. Scanning generator for magnetic deflection.

3890 "Television exhibition. Reception demonstrations on 7.75 metres at South Kensington." ELECT. 110 (Apr. 7): 472. Review with details of exhibits.

3891 C. Lorenz A.-G. "Television receiver." Br. 436,160, Apr. 6, 1934. In Germany Apr 7, 1933. Cathode-ray tube, mirror drum, and fixed mirrors.

3892 Bedford, A.V. "Intelligence transmission." U.S. 2,089,639, Apr. 8, 1933, Aug. 10, 1937. Assigned: RCA. Br. 434,882, Mar. 12, 1934 (Marconi's). Concerns delay networks for sound and sync. Reference (2869).

3893 Branson, Harry "Television." Br. 434,891, Apr. 9, 1934 (Marconi's). In U.S. Apr. 8, 1933 (RCA). Refers to cathode-ray tubes and circuits for compressing storing, and processing picture, sound, and sync signals. References (2964, 3127, 3716, 3892).

3894 Hudec, E. "Braun tube." U.S. 2,129,005, Mar. 26, 1934, Sept. 6, 1938; Br. 438,117, Apr. 7, 1934. In Germany Apr. 8, 1933. Electrode assembly in a picture tube.

3895 Zworykin, V.K. "Television." Br. 434,890, Apr. 6, 1934 (Marconi's). In U.S. Apr. 8, 1933 (RCA). A television-telephone system in which sound is transmitted during the return trace of the scanning beam, with a special cathode-ray tube for storing and distributing the sound signals. Reference (3127).

3896 EMI and Peter William Willans. "Television." Br. 422,906, Apr. 13, 1933; U.S. 2,252,746 renewed June 6, 1940, Aug. 19, 1941. A triode circuit for reinserting the direct-current components of a picture signal.

3897 EMI, P.W. Willans, William Spencer Percival, Eric Lawrence Casling White, and Charles Percy Osborne. "Television." Br. 422,824, Apr. 13, 1933; U.S. 2,194,514, Apr. 12, 1934, Mar. 26, 1940. Relates to the separation of line and framing impulses, d-c reinsertion, and saw-tooth generator. Divided from Br., 422,906 (3896). References to Br. 400,976 (3396), 413,561 (3733).

3898 "Television." ELECT. 110 (Apr. 14): 480. Comments on the demonstrations given at the Television Society's exhibition.

3899 "Television exhibition. Greater participation by manufacturing interests—short-wave demonstration." ELECT. 110 (Apr. 14): 499. Summary of displays.

3900 "New opportunities. Television beckons to youth as wireless did to Marconi—Goldsmith looks ahead." N.Y.T. VIII, 12 (Apr. 16): 7, 8. Views of A.N. Goldsmith.

3901 Ardenne, M. v. "Braun tube." U.S. 2,096,986, Apr. 17, 1933, Oct. 26, 1937. Assigned: D.S. Loewe. Divided from U.S. 2,131,203 (2830).

3902 Ardenne, M. v. "Television receiver." Br. 416,834, Apr. 23, 1934. Assigned: A.C. Cossor. In Germany Apr. 21, 1933. Light from the screen of a cathode-ray tube is projected via lenses onto a viewing screen, with corrections for spherical and chromatic aberrations.

3903 Marconi's, H.M. Dowsett, and E.F. Goodenough. "Thermionic valve circuit." Br. 420,074, Apr. 24, 1933; U.S. 2,074,831, May 25, 1934, Mar. 23, 1937 (RCA). Amplifier for matching a neon tube.

3904 Tekade. "Television receiver." Br. 422,752, Mar. 29, 1934. In Germany Apr. 24, 1933. Linear light source, Kerr cell, ground-glass screen, and mirror screw.

3905 Farnsworth, P.T. "Image dissector." U.S. 2,087,683, Apr. 26, 1933, July 20, 1937 reissued Dec. 29, 1939, July 9, 1940. Assigned: Farnsworth Television and Radio.

3906 Ogloblinsky, G.N. "Television." U.S. 2,093,288, Apr. 29, 1933, Sept. 14, 1937. Assigned: RCA. Br. 417,435, Apr. 30, 1934 (Marconi's). Receiver tube with an oil-filled chamber or lens and an external projection lens.

3907 Watt, Robert A. Watson, J.F. Herd, and L.H. Bainbridge-Bell. APPLICATIONS OF THE CATHODE-RAY OSCILLOGRAPH IN RADIO RESEARCH. London: H.M.S.O., 1933. xvi + 290 pp., 17 plates, 113 diags. Primarily on work done at the Radio Research Station on wave propagation and direction-finding, with full description of cathode-ray tubes, additional features, and circuits, potentially time-bases and sync methods. A list of references gives 50 items. No index.

3908 Hudec, E. "Die Verzerrungen durch die Raumladung in der Braunschen Röhre" [Distortion produced by space charges in the Braun tubes]. E.N.T. 10 (May): 215–20. Illus. Effects in gas-filled tubes at the center of the screen with high brightness; improved form with off-center screens.

3909 Zworykin, V.K. "On electron optics." J.F.I. 215 (May): 535–55. 16 illus., 7 references. Description of experimental work with mathematical treatment.

3910 Stoyanowsky, A.T. "A new process of television out of doors." J. SMPE 20 (May): 437–43. Fernseh intermediate film system.

3911 "Last month's programmes." TELEV. 6 (May): 168–71. 2 photos.

3912 "The television exhibition. Fine display of apparatus at the Imperial College." TELEV. 6 (May): 179–82.

3913 "News from abroad." TELEV. 6 (May): 183. Germany, United States.

3914 Wilson, J.C. "Mirror drum scanning. The optical efficiency." TELEV. 6 (May): 184–6. 3 diags.

3915 Benn, J.A. "Time is running out." TELEV. 6 (May): 187, 188. Views on the comparative quality of reproduction by the disk and mirror drum, on BBC programs and times, and the lack of commercial receivers by the Baird Company. The number of lookers is variously estimated to be between 15,000 and 20,000.

3916 Swift, F.G. "Holding the image steady." TELEV. 6 (May): 189, 190.

3917 Chapple, H.J.B. "From my notebook." TELEV. 6 (May): 193–5. Various topics, including comments on the Baird demonstration of a cathode-ray tube receiver on Apr. 6, showing 120/25 images.

3918 Alexanderson, E.F.W. "Colored television." U.S. 1,988,931, May 2, 1933, Jan. 22, 1935. Assigned: G.E. Br. 424,743, May 2, 1934 (B.T.-H.). Images in color obtained from two cathode-ray tubes with red and green phosphors, or via color filters, which are observed through a partially silvered mirror. Scanning of alternate lines by a single sawtooth generator is specified.

3919 A.C. Cossor and Owen Standige Puckle. "Condenser relaxation circuit." Br. 419,298, May 5, 1933; U.S. 2,114,938, Apr. 17, 1934, Apr. 19, 1938. Scanning generator with triode and two pentodes.

3920 EMI and J.D. McGee. "Television." Br. 419,452, May 5, 1933; U.S. 2,100,259, May 3, 1934, Nov. 23, 1937. Camera tube with a double-sided mosaic screen consisting of short aluminum wires coated with silver. Photoelectric emissions from the front face are collected by a grounded grid, while the secondary electrons emitted from the back face are collected by a ring, or signal, electrode connected to an output amplifier.

3921 Marconi's, H.M. Dowsett, and L.E.Q. Walker. "Wireless direction finding system." Br. 420,662, May 6, 1933; U.S. 2,018,349, June 22, 1934, Oct. 22, 1935 (RCA). Visual indication of the position of a rotating antenna by a compass scale, and station identity, is provided by a disk scanner.

3922 Marconi's and E.G. Herriott. "Light-valve." Br. 419,072, May 6, 1933. Multiplate Kerr cell.

3923 Benford, Frank A. "Television scanning apparatus." U.S. 2,023,217, May 11, 1933, Dec. 3, 1935. Assigned: G.E.

3924 Fernseh A.-G. "Cathode-ray tube." Br. 422,614, May 11, 1934. In Germany May 11, 1933. Electrode structures.

3825 Fernseh A.-G. "Cathode-ray tube." Br. 436,314, May 11, 1934. In Germany May 11, 1933. Deflection plates.

3926 Herbst, Philip, J. "Television distribution." U.S. 2,135,577, May 11, 1933, Nov. 8, 1938. Assigned: RCA. Switching system for sound and vision with a plurality of receivers.

3927 Fernseh, A.-G. "Television." Br. 419,419, May 15, 1934. In Germany May 15, 1933. Intermediate film in which the picture size is reduced and sound is recorded in the margin.

3928 D.S. Loewe. "Television." Br. 441,761, May 22, 1934. In Germany May 19, 1933. Refers to modulation, deflection and sync circuits for transmission and reception.

3929 Ives, H.E. "Television." Br. 437,656, May 3, 1934 (E.R.P.). In U.S. May 24, 1933 (B.T.L.). Scanning disks, one with radial slots, the other with a circular or spiral slot.

3930 Baird, J.L., and Baird Television. "Television." Br. 418,527, May 25, 1933. Color system with mirror drum, apertured, mask and filters in a slotted disk. References to Br. 321,389 (1285), 381,898 (3464).

3931 Banks, G.B., and Baird Television. "Television." Br. 420,091, May 25, 1933. Scanning oscillator and picture tube circuit. References to Br. 320,639 (1213), 336,655 (1961).

3932 Campbell, R.L. "Television." U.S. 102,256, May 26, 1933, renewed Oct. 16, 1936, Dec. 14, 1937. Assigned: RCA. Br. 428,168, May 28, 1934 (Marconi's). Camera tube and circuits for magnetic deflection, beam blanking, sync generators, and amplifiers in a single-channel system.

3933 Schlesinger, K. "Container and arrangement for Braun tubes." U.S. 2,114,612, May 19, 1934, Apr. 19, 1938; Br. 443,484, May 28, 1934. In Germany May 27, 1933 (D.S. Loewe). Picture tube permanently enclosed by a metallic container.

3934 Schlesinger, K. "Cathode-ray tube for television." U.S. 2,188,579, May 19, 1934, Jan. 30, 1940; Br. 440,560, May 19, 1934. In Germany May 27, 1933 (D.S. Loewe). Relates to a high-vacuum picture tube with pole-shoes fitted inside the envelope excited by external coils, adaptable for concentrating, deflection, or controlling the intensity of the beam, including the use of the pole-shoes for electrostatic control.

3935 Tekade. "Television." Br. 418,566, Mar. 29, 1934. In Germany May 27, 1933. Telescopic method of adjusting mirrors on a mirror screw.

3936 "Television awaits its cue." N.Y.T. VIII, 4 (May 28): 4, 5. Views of J.V.L. Hogan.

3937 Fernseh A.-G. "Television transmitter." Br. 416,298, May 29, 1934. In Germany May 29, 1933. Adaptation of intermediate film equipment for transmitting normal film along with sound.

3938 Headrick, Lewis Barnard. "Electron tube." U.S. 2,069,441, May 30, 1933, Feb. 2, 1937. Assigned: RCA. Cathode-ray tube with secondary emission screen.

3939 Orth, Richard Tempel. "Electron tube." U.S. 2,099,749, May 30, 1933, Nov. 23, 1937. Assigned: RCA. Br. 439,492, May 30, 1934 (Marconi's). Cathode-ray tube.

3940 Orth, R.T. "Cathode-ray tube." Br. 440,390, May 30, 1934 (Marconi's). In U.S. May 30, 1933 (RCA). Divided from above.

3941 Knudsen, H. "Television." Br. 424,763, May 31, 1933; U.S. 2,054,202, Feb. 25, 1935, Sept. 15, 1936. Scanning with endless apertured metallic band at transversely moving photocells for transmission, or with lamps for reception. Dual sets of apertures for two-way operation.

3942 Chapple, H.J.B. TELEVISION FOR THE AMATEUR CONSTRUCTOR. London: Pitman, 1933. xx + 233 pp., 48 plates, 102 diags. Foreword by J.L. Baird. General theory, the home workshop, construction and operation of Baird-type receivers.

3943 Walker, Ronald Claude, and T.M.C. Lance. PHOTOELECTRIC CELL PUBLICATIONS. London: Pitman, 1933. vii + 193 pp., 111 photos and diags. A practical book describing the uses of photoelectric cells in television, talking pictures, electrical alarms, counting devices, etc.

3944 Robinson, Gordon D. "Theoretical notes on certain features of television receiving circuits." PROC IRE 21 (June): 833–43. 2 graphs. Mathematical study concerned with amplifiers and detectors.

3945 Chapple, H.J.B. "A useful disc marker." TELEV. 6 (June): 202–5. Photo, 6 diags.

3946 "Last month's programmes." TELEV. 6 (June): 206–8. 2 photos.

3947 "News from abroad." TELEV. 6 (June): 216–8. United States, France, Australia.

3948 Byron, D.H. "Mirror drums without tools" TELEV. 6 (June): 219, 220. 2 diags.

3949 "The next step in America. Hollywood's television challenge." TELEV. 6 (June): 224. On news about a studio being constructed by RKO, and comments on other American views.

3950 Baird, J.L., and Baird Television. "Television." Br. 423,854, June 1, 1933. Combination of mirror wheels or drums, including a triple-mirror drum, and lens disks for interlaced scanning. Divided from Br. 418,759 (3953).

3951 Campbell, R.L. "Television." U.S. 2,110,982, June 1, 1933, renewed Aug. 6, 1937, Mar. 15, 1938. Assigned: RCA. Br. 443,699, June 1, 1934 (Marconi's). Camera tube and circuits similar to previous entry (3950), applicable to interlaced scanning (3553), with frame sync signals suppressed during transmission of line-sync signals to prevent interference.

3952 "Cathode-ray television. Special tubes introduced." W.W. 32 (June 2): 392. "Edison Company have now introduced a special tube for television purposes." The Edison Swan Electric Company demonstrated a cathode-ray tube showing a 30-line raster at the Television Society's exhibition in April (3841). A full-page announcement appeared in TELEVISION (May), p. 164.

3953 Baird, J.L., and Baird Television. "Television." Br. 418,759, June 2, 1933. Scanning by a triple-mirror-drum and a separate mirror drum, with alternative lenses and deflecting prisms.

3954 Schlesinger, K. "Television." U.S. 2,107,392, June 1, 1934, Feb. 8, 1938; Br. 443,558, June 2, 1934. In Germany June 3, 1933 (D.S. Loewe). Picture tube and deflection circuits. Addition to Br. 435,203 (3872).

3955 Golay, Marcel J.E. "Television transmission." U.S. 2,098,236, June 6, 1933, Nov. 9, 1937. Photocells arranged in columns and connected serially with time-delay circuits.

3956 Ardenne, M. v. "Cathode-ray tube." U.S. 2,115,093, May 24, 1934, Apr. 26, 1938. Assigned: RCA. In Germany June 10, 1933. Contains an oblique screen for indirect viewing.

3957 Fernseh A.-G. "Cathode-ray tube." Br. 425,267, June 11, 1934. In Germany June 10, 1933. Brightness of the light spot is modulated electrostatically by conductive strips spaced parallel to the line scan on a picture tube screen.

3958 Schlesinger, K. "Braun tube." U.S. 2,136,286, June 11, 1934, Aug. 9, 1938; Br. 442,511, June 9, 1934. In Germany June 10, 1933 (D.S. Loewe). This detailed specification for a picture tube includes an electron-optical system and other electrodes, dimensions, assembly, and numerous variants.

3959 D.S. Loewe. "Cathode-ray tube." Br. 442,427, June 9, 1934. In Germany June 10, 1933. Addition to Br. 421,050 (3444), divided from above.

3960 Ardenne, M. v. "Cathode-ray tube." U.S. 2,080,449, May 24, 1934, May 18, 1937. Assigned: RCA. Br. 419,872, June 11, 1934. Assigned: A.C. Cossor. In Germany June 12, 1933 Contains accelerating and decelerating electrodes and an oblique screen.

3961 Ardenne, M. V. "Cathode-ray tube." Br. 439,636, June 11, 1934. Assigned: A.C. Cossor. In Germany June 12, 1933.

3962 Bray, T.E., and Baird Television. "Cathode-ray tube." Br. 421,065, June 13, 1933. Concerns the mounting of a picture tube in a receiver cabinet whereby the tube can be rotated so that the screen matches a mask or can be changed from vertical to horizontal scan.

3963 Nobbs, W.J. "Television." Br. 417,477, June 13, 1933. Scanning disk or drum with lenses or mirrors.

3964 Fernseh, A.-G. "Television." Br. 431,959, June 14, 1934. In Germany June 15, 1933. Light-sensitive emulsion is stored in a Dewar flask in an intermediate film system.

3965 EMI and A.D. Blumlein. "Supply of electrical energy to varying loads." Br. 421,546, June 16, 1933; U.S. 2,035,457, June 13, 1934, Mar. 31, 1936. Relates to impedance networks and valve circuits applicable for amplifying television signals.

3966 Lubcke, H.R. "Cathode-ray tube." U.S. 2,081,942, June 16, 1933, June 1, 1937.

3967 Gillespie, H.C. "Electrical discharge control and television system." U.S. 2,063,804, June 21, 1933, Dec. 8, 1936. Assigned: Comm. Pat. Br. 437,602, Apr. 27, 1934. A modulated arc moves along a zigzag path of parallel corrugated electrodes controlled by a surrounding magnetic field. References (2066, 2383)

3968 Maguire, I.L. "Television." Br. 425,971, June 21, 1933. Void. Scanning by a stationary apertured disk, a rotating set of reflecting prisms, and optical system.

3969 Dunlap, O.E. Jr. "Television expert to reveal new electrical eye. Novel radio optic 'sees.' Dr. Zworykin to describe his Iconoscope 'eye,' called fully adequate for television—speed equals movie camera." N.Y.T. IX, 7 (June 25): 1–3. Photo of Zworykin, columns 4, 5. On a lecture at the IRE meeting in Chicago, June 26. Reference to earlier patent (695).

3970 Walton, G.W. "Television." Br. 425,984, June 26, 1933; U.S. 2,110,945, Aug. 30, 1933, Mar. 15, 1938. Refers to an optical scanning system employing rotating refracting laminae in a spiral or echelon formation with lenses, apertured mask, and photocell. Reference to Br. 328,286 (1542).

3971 Lawrence, William L. "Human-like eye made by engineers to televise images. 'Iconoscope' converts scenes into electrical energy for radio transmission. Fast as a movie camera. Three million tiny photo cells 'memorize,' then pass out pictures. Step to home television. Developed in ten years' work by Dr. V.K. Zworykin, who describes it at Chicago." N.Y.T. I (June 27): 1; 15, 1–3. Announcement of the camera tube developed by RCA, and report of IRE lecture June 26.

3972 Schlesinger, K. "Braun tube for projecting images of large size." U.S. 2,111,941, June 11, 1934, Mar. 22, 1938; Br., 440,106, June 10, 1934. In Germany June 27, 1930 (D.S. Loewe). Includes magnetic and electrostatic deflection and a metallic wall coating. The electrodes are spaced up to 30 cm or more from the screen, giving images larger than 10 by 15 cm.

3973 Tekade. "Television receiver." Br. 416,286, Mar. 29, 1934. In Germany June 27, 1933. Light from a modulated source is swept saw-tooth fashion by piezoelectric deflection through an assembly of thin crystal plates.

3974 Rosenberg, H. "Television." Br. 438,219, June 29, 1934. In Germany June 29, 1933. Addition to Br. 411,835.

3975 Hardy, René. "Reception of television. How the cathode-ray oscillograph can be utilized." ELECT. 110 (June 30): 854–56. 3 photos, 8 diags. Translated from article in the May issue of LA TECHNIQUE CINEMATOGRAPHIIQUE. General description of principles, circuits, and operation.

3977 "Zworykin's Iconoscope." ELECTRONICS 6 (July): 188. Diag.

3978 Gardiner, E.L. "A complete mirror drum receiver." TELEV. 6 (July): 234–40. 2 photos, 3 diags. Full details for the home constructor, including circuit and cabinet assembly. List of components; mirror drum, optical parts, viewing screen, and crater lamp by Mervyn Sound and Vision Co. are specified.

3979 "Manufacture of new 'Televisors.' Bush Radio Ltd., announce plans." TELEV. 6 (July): 241, 242. 2 photos, Brief description of the console assembly with comments by the company, who "will act as sole manufacturers and distributors of the new mirror-drum "Televisor" for Baird Television.

3980 "Television. The Baird Televisor—its newest form and performance." TELEV. 6 (July): insert. Pamphlet by Bush Radio, Ltd. Walnut cabinet, approximately 4 feet high, 15 inches wide, and 20 inches deep, contains a pull-out screen 9 by 4 inches and a loudspeaker for connecting to a separate radio receiver. The vision receivers comprises a 30-line mirror drum, Baird grid cell unit, 100 w lamp, optical system, and four-stage amplifier. Priced at 75 guineas.

3981 "A new lensed disc." TELEV. 6 (July): 242. Brief details, with illustration, of an experimental assembly by the Mervyn Sound and Vision Co.

3982 "News from abroad." TELEV. 6 (July): 247. U.S., Germany.

3983 Parr, Geoffrey. "Cathode-rays and the amateur." TELEV. 6 (July): 248, 249, 254. Photo, 2 diags. Deals with the tube manufactured by the Edison Swan Electric Co., and scanning circuits.

3984 "Last month's programmes." TELEV. 6 (July): 250–2. 2 photos.

3985 "The enthusiast sees it through." TELEV. 6 (July): 256–9. 2 photos, 3 diags.

3986 Schlesinger, K. "Radio receiving system." U.S. 2,107,393, June 29, 1934, Feb. 8, 1938; Br. 444, 881, June 30, 1934. In Germany

July 1, 1933 (D.S. Loewe). Circuits for reception in a two-channel, ultra-short wave television-telephone system.

3987 Dunlap, O.E. Jr. "Interest is focused on television for the home. Outlook for radio sight television not expected to disturb broadcasting system or receivers—images to travel on tiny waves." N.Y.T. IX, 6 (July 2): 1–3. Zworykin's iconoscope, its inventor, prospects for television in the home.

3988 "Pertinent facts about electrical eye invented by Zworykin for television." N.Y.T. IX, 6 (July 2): 2, 3.

3989 Telefunken. "Cathode-ray tube." Br. 426,706, July 4, 1933. Void.

3990 Tekade. "Light-valve." Br. 426,233, Mar. 29, 1934. In Germany July 5, 1933. An assembly of crystals with deposited electrodes in a cell with crystal prisms and a color filter. Reference to Br. 422,370 (3827).

3991 "Television from the Crystal Palace." W.W. 33 (July 7): 13. Exclusive news item on the Baird Company installing ultra-short wave apparatus on the top of one of the towers.

3992 Schlesinger, K. "Braun tube." U.S. 2,077,272, July 6, 1934, Apr. 13, 1937; Br. 442,724, July 7, 1934. In Germany July 8, 1933 (D.S. Loewe). Refers to an arrangement comprising two electron-optical lenses in series assembled with other electrodes. Addition to Br. 442,511 (3958). Reference to Br. 435,382 (3745).

3993 Wolff, H.H. "Cathode-ray tube." U.S. 2,185,138, July 6, 1934, Dec. 26, 1939; Br. 440,810, July 7, 1934. In Germany July 8, 1933 (D.S. Loewe). With internal magnetic poles and coils outside. Reference to Br. 271,131 (743).

3994 "Hudson's television theatre." N.Y.T. IX, 12 (July 9): 5. Opened by Hudson-Essex in the Electrical Building, Chicago's World Fair. Demonstrations every half-hour.

3995 D.S. Loewe. "Television." Br. 441,133, July 9, 1934. In Germany July 10, 1933. Braun tube designed to produce large images 15 by 15 cm or more.

3996 Schlesinger, K. "Braun tube." U.S. 2,100,703, July 6, 1934, Nov. 30, 1937; Br. 442,519, July 9, 1934. In Germany July 10, 1933 (D.S. Loewe). Concerns the method for mounting an image screen inside a tube.

3997 "Television device shown. Demonstration given at Macy's by Chicago inventor." N.Y.T. (July 11): 3. Demonstration by Sanabria in New York.

3998 EMI, C.O. Browne, J. Hardwick, and A.D. Blumlein. "Television." Br. 422,914, July 11, 1933. Sync and d-c insertion circuits for transmitter and receiver. Reference to Br. 422,906 (3896).

3999 Ardenne, M. v. "Television." Br. 422,034, June 26, 1934. Assigned: A.C. Cossor. In Germany July 12, 1933. Picture tube with switches to reverse direction of scanning for either direct viewing or optical projection.

4000 EMI, E.C. Cook, and M. Bowman-Manifold. "Television." Br. 422,481, July 12, 1933. Refers to sync generators in a film system with mirror drum. The line frequency is obtained optically by light from the drum passing through a sinusoidal opening in a mask onto a separate phototube, while the frame frequency is derived from a generator driven by the film mechanism.

4001 Marconi's, H.M. Dowsett, and N. Levin. "Light-valve." Br. 424,196, July 12, 1933. Kerr cell with optical assembly equivalent to Nicol prisms.

4002 "The 'eye' gains prestige. Sanabria displays images whirled by a disk—he praises the electrical optic." N.Y.T. IX 7 (July 16): 5, 6. On Sanabria's disk system with arc lamp and large screen, and his favorable comments on Zworykin's camera tube.

4003 Bodroux, D., and R. Rivault. "Sur quelques réceptions lointaines des émissions de radio-vision de Londres" [On several long-distance receptions of television broadcasts from London]. C.R. 197 (July 17): 231, 232.

4004 A.E.G. "Cathode-ray tube." Br. 427,393, July 17, 1933. Void. Assigned: Int. G.E.

4005 EMI, M. Bowman-Manifold, and W.S. Percival. "Television." Br. 422,710, July 19, 1933; U.S. 2,137,798, July 14, 1934, Nov. 22, 1938. Picture tube receiver circuits including saw-tooth generator, sync, and protection of the latter from atmospherics by a voltage limiter. Reference to Br. 419,441 (3814).

4006 Schlesinger, K. "Audion arrangement for short-wave television." U.S. 2,029,640, July 17, 1934, Feb. 4, 1936; Br. 441,285, July 19, 1934. In Germany July 19, 1933 (D.S. Loewe). Push-pull detector for receiver. Addition to Br 435,417 (3874).

4007 Schlesinger, K. "Connecting Braun tubes." U.S. 2,094,676, July 17, 1934, Oct. 5, 1936; Br. 441,762, July 19, 1934. In Germany July 19, 1933 (D.S. Loewe). Switching circuits for protecting a picture tube from high-voltage transients.

4008 D.S. Loewe and K. Schlesinger. "Cathode-ray tube." Br. 427,703, July 19, 1933. Void. Picture tube with predeflection electrodes.

4009 Baird, J.L., and Baird Television. "Television." Br. 423,101, July 21, 1933. Scanning generators applied to picture tubes in various ways, including oscillators in Br. 420,091 (3931), and an obliterating beam described in Br. 291,121 (814). Reference to Br. 381,8908 (3464).

4010 Baird, J.L., and Baird Television. "Cathode-ray tube." Br. 424,632, July 21, 1933. Concerns a picture tube screen of platinum black which is rendered incandescent by the beam, for direct viewing or optical projection.

4011 Baird, J.L., and Baird Television. "Television." Br. 424,633, July 21, 1933. Photo record on a disk or drum is exposed, developed, scanned, cleaned, and re-emulsified for continuous operation. Motion picture projection at the receiver.

4012 D.S. Loewe. "Television." Br. 443,286, July 20, 1934. In Germany July 21, 1933. Relates to a portable receiver operated by a buzzer-rectifier supply for military or police use. Includes a rotating commutator and a rotating capacitor with means provided to handle signals in cipher for secret transmissions.

4013 Schlesinger, K. "Deflecting device." U.S. 2,226,990, July 17, 1934. Dec. 31, 1940; Br., 444,474, July 20, 1934. In Germany July 21, 1933 (D.S. Loewe). Deflection electrodes and circuits for a picture tube. Modification of and addition to Br. 435,561 (3875). Reference to Br. 441,761 (3928).

4014 Ardenne, M. v. "Cathode-ray device." U.S. 2,108,091, June 4, 1934, Feb. 15, 1938. Assigned: RCA. Br. 442,512, July 3, 1934. Assigned A.C. Cossor. In Germany July 22, 1933. Picture tube with split deflector plates and circuits arranged to prevent origin distortion.

4015 Schlesinger, K. "Electronic tube." U.S. 2,123,159, June 24, 1934, July 5, 1938; Br. 443,364, July 26, 1934. In Germany July 26, 1933 (D.S. Loewe). Cathode-ray tube with electron-optical assembly and special electrode arrangements applicable for various functions including television reception.

4016 Schröter, F., and Arthur Schleede. "Television." U.S. 2,121,990, Aug. 4, 1934, June 28, 1938; Br. 426,173, July 27, 1934. In Germany July 27, 1933 (Telefunken). Picture tube and circuits.

4017 "Televisor with cinema film quality." W.W. 33 (July 28): 61. News item on a 180-line cathode-ray receiver by D.S. Loewe and Dr. Schlesinger to be displayed at the German radio exhibition.

4018 Federmann, W., and J. Richter. "Electron tube." U.S. 2,137,202, July 20, 1934, Nov. 15 1938. In Germany July 28, 1933 (Telefunken). Cathode-ray tube and luminescent screen.

4019 Schröter, F. "Electron tube." U.S. 2,108,617, July 14, 1934, Feb. 15, 1938. In Germany July 28, 1933 (Telefunken). Cathode-ray tube.

4020 Schröter, F. "Television." U.S. 2,189,351, June 14, 1934, Feb. 6, 1940. In Germany

July 29, 1933 (Telefunken). Concerns transmission system with a cathode-ray tube, spot projection, and moving film.

4021 Dunlap, O.E. Jr. "Television now faces social and economic problems. Lifting the blindfold. New social era foreseen when radio optics look afar—educators expect television blackboard." N.Y.T. IX, 7 (July 30): 1, 2. Discussion of financing, methods of transmission, use of local stations and networks, educational prospects.

4022 Hensel, Bernhard, Kurt Hess, and J. Richter. "Cathode-ray tube." U.S. 2,114,346, July 26, 1934. Apr. 19, 1938. In Germany July 31, 1933 (Telefunken).

4023 Knoll, M. "Cathode-ray tube." U.S. 2,094,606, July 26, 1934, Oct. 5, 1937. In Germany July 31, 1933 (Telefunken).

4024 Knoll, M. "Television receiver tube." U.S. 2,106,250, July 14, 1934, Jan. 25, 1938. In Germany July 31, 1933 (Telefunken).

4025 Knoll, M. "Cathode-ray tube." U.S. 2,139,683, July 26, 1934, Dec. 13, 1938. In Germany July 31, 1933 (Telefunken).

4026 Knoll, M. "Cathode-ray tube." U.S. 2,139,684, July 26, 1934, Dec. 13, 1938. In Germany July 31, 1933 (Telefunken).

4027 Knoll, M. "Electrical lens." U.S. 2,172,735, July 26, 1934, Sept. 12, 1939. In Germany July 31, 1933 (Telefunken). Cathode-ray tube, electrode assembly.

4028 Knoll, M., and Ernest Sommerfeld. "Electron tube." U.S. 2,110,911, July 27, 1934, Mar. 15, 1938. In Germany July 31, 1933 (Telefunken). Electron lens with magnetic coil.

4029 Richter, J., B. Hensel, and K. Hess. "Electron tube." U.S. 2,128,759, July 1, 1934, Aug. 30, 1938. In Germany July 31, 1933 (Telefunken). Cathode-ray tube.

4030 Telefunken. "Cathode-ray tube." Br. 441,693, July 20, 1934. In Germany July 31, 1933. Picture tube with accelerating electrodes deposited inside the glass.

4031 Schriever, O. "Die technischen Einrichtungen für einen Fernsehrundfunk" [Technical equipment for television transmission]. FERN. UND TON. 4 (Aug.): 31–35.

4032 "A new Baird branded component for house constructors." TELEV. 6 (Aug.): 272. Full-page advertisement by Baird Television Ltd., announcing the Baird Grid Cell consisting of the sealed Kerr cell, Nicol prisms, lens, and light source in one assembly. Price £5.

4033 "Scophony: an official statement correcting unauthorized announcements." TELEV. 6 (Aug.): 274. While developing their apparatus for 100-line pictures, the company plans to make available a receiver for the present 30-line BBC transmissions.

4034 "Television at Radiolympia. What to see at the exhibition." TELEV. 6 (Aug.): 275.

4035 Gardiner, E.L. "A complete mirror drum receiver." TELEV. 6 (Aug.): 276–82. 2 photos, 2 diags. List of components.

4036 Peck, A.P. "A new cathode-ray tube." TELEV. 6 (Aug.): 283, 284. Description of Zworykin's iconoscope, with photo.

4037 "News from abroad." TELEV. 6 (Aug.): 284. Brief note on the German radio exhibition and exhibitors. All will demonstrate reception of 180-line pictures.

4038 "New optical assembly. Marconi method for television projection receiver." TELEV. 6 (Aug.): 285, 286. Photo, diag. From MARCONI REVIEW, article by N. Levin, referring to a 7-by-1.5-foot screen.

4039 "Last month's programmes." TELEV. 6 (Aug.): 287–9. 2 photos.

4040 Banks, G.B., T.W. Collier, and Baird Television. "Television." Br. 423,508, Aug. 1, 1933. A rotary enclosure with transparent windows excludes dirt from the apertures in a scanning disk or drum.

4041 Jacomb, W.W., and Baird Television. "Television." Br. 423,863, Aug. 1, 1933. Glass covers protect a scanning disk from dirt.

4042 Knoll, M. "Cathode-ray tube." U.S. 2,131,563, Aug. 4, 1934, Sept. 27, 1938. In Germany Aug. 1, 1933 (Telefunken).

4043 Knoll, M. "Electron tube." U.S. 2,110,553, Aug. 4, 1934, Mar. 8, 1938. In Germany Aug. 2, 1933 (Telefunken). Cathode-ray tube.

4044 Knoll, M. "Cathode-ray tube." U.S. 2,139,829, Aug. 4, 1934, Dec. 13, 1938. In Germany Aug. 2, 1933 (Telefunken).

4045 Knoll, M., and F. Schröter. "Cathode-ray tube." U.S. 2,088,419, Aug. 4 1934, July 27, 1937; Br. 439,990, Aug. 2, 1934. In Germany Aug. 2, 1933 (Telefunken).

4046 EMI and G.E. Condliffe. "Valve generator." Br. 425,035, Aug. 3, 1933. Saw-tooth oscillator.

4047 West, A.G.D., and Baird Television. "Television." Br. 423,247, Aug. 4, 1933. Cathode-ray tube projection with lens for film scanning.

4048 West. A.G.D., and Baird Television. "Television receiver." Br. 424,961, Aug, 4, 1933. Adjustable lens in front of a picture tube.

4049 Schröter, R. "Relaxation circuit." U.S. 2,089,038, Aug. 4, 1934, Aug. 3, 1937. In Germany Aug. 5, 1933 (Telefunken). Scanning generator.

4050 Dunlap, O.E. Jr. "A fifty-year riddle. Inventor of television disk in 1884 tells how he thought of the idea—he applauds latest marvels." N.Y.T. X, 7 (Aug. 6): 1, 2. Reminiscences of Paul Nipkow. After experimenting with a telephone and microphone, he turned to the idea of an electric telescope employing a rotating apertured disk as a scanner on Christmas Eve 1883 (181).

4051 Percival, W.S., C.O. Browne, E.L.C. White, and EMI. "Television." Br. 425,220, Aug, 8, 1933; U.S. 2,147,266, Aug. 3, 1934, Feb. 14, 1939. Concerns a film transmission system with mirror drum, shutters, slotted apertures, photocells, and circuits including sync and scanning signals, black-out impulses, and a picture tube. References to Br. 395,499 (2964), 423,685 (4184).

4052 D.S. Loewe. "Cathode-ray tube." Br. 447,039, Aug. 9, 1934. In Germany Aug. 9, 1933. Modification of the tube described in Br. 443,364 (4015) to serve as oscillator and amplifier. References to Br 435,382 (3745), 438,117 (3894).

4053 "Television declared ready to broadcast, starting sectionally, with relays later." N.Y.T. 18 (Aug. 11): 2, 3. View of Jesse B. McCarger, president of Television Laboratories on the Farnsworth system, its development, costs, and possibilities.

4054 Fernseh A.-G. "Valve generators." Br. 426,537, Aug. 13, 1934. In Germany Aug. 12, 1933. Deflection voltages from a picture tube provided by two oppositely connected relaxation oscillators.

4055 Fernseh A.-G. "Cathode-ray tube." Br. 437,216, Aug. 13, 1934. In Germany Aug. 12, 1933. Cooling projections on electrodes in a picture tue.

4056 Wilkins and Wright, and J.H. Hewitt. "Television." Br. 419,634, Aug. 12, 1933. Mirror drum construction.

4057 Wilson, J.C., and Baird Television. "Television." Br. 424,199, Aug. 12, 1933. Relates to photocell pickup of changing light intensities from a cathode-ray tube on the screen of which an image to be transmitted is projected.

4058 EMI, C.O. Browne, and J. Hardwick. "Picture and sound transmission." Br. 428,852, Aug. 14, 1933; U.S. 2,124,394, Aug. 10, 1934, July 19, 1938. Concerns intensity contrast of the images in a film system employing a mirror drum and either a neon tube or picture tube receiver. Reference to Br. 422,906 (3896).

4059 Schlesinger, K. "Relaxation oscillator generator. "U.S. 2,163,211, Aug. 10, 1934, June 20, 1939; Br. 442,740, Aug. 14, 1934. In Germany Aug. 14, 1933 (D.S. Loewe).

4060 Byron, D.H., and Radio Reconstruction. "Television." Br. 423,050, Aug. 15, 1933. Apparatus for simulating a television signal optically or electrically by scanning film strip.

4061 Wilson, J.C., T.E. Bray, and Baird Television. "Television." Br. 423,748, Aug. 15, 1933. Motor, toothed disk, magnetic coils, commutator, saw-tooth oscillator, and electron tube circuits for sync and deflection signals in a picture tube receiver. Reference to Br. 420,091 (3931).

4062 "The National Radio Exhibition." ELECT. 111 (Aug. 18): 195, 196. Mention of displays of Baird Television, Ferranti, Bush Radio, Grafton Radio, and description of complete receiver by E.L. Gardiner.

4063 "Radio Exhibition, Olympia." TIMES (Aug. 18): 8a. Review of radio displays and brief mention of Baird's exhibits. "The B.B.C. on several occasions this week have invited the public who 'look-in' at the television programmes to communicate with them. This will enable the officials to get an idea of the number of people in possession of television apparatus and to what extent the programmes are enjoyed. Correspondents are asked to address their post-cards, marked 'Z,' to the B.B.C., Portland Place, W."

4064 Ives, H.E. "Television." U.S. 2,099,889, Aug. 18, 1933, Nov. 23, 1937. Assigned: B.T.L. Three-channel disk system for color.

4065 "Stride in television is shown in Germany. Reproduction called nearly perfect is exhibited at annual radio display in Berlin." N.Y.T. 4 (Aug. 19): 7. Show opened Aug. 18 by Dr. Paul Joseph Goebbels, Minister of Propaganda. The unnamed exhibit referred to displayed a 180/25 picture on a 15-by-15cm screen.

4066 Loewe, S. "Cathode-ray tubes." Br. 429,251, Aug. 31, 1933. Void. Method of de-degassing electrodes.

4067 Banfield, A.C., and Baird Television. "Television." Br. 424,887, Aug. 22, 1933. Concerns an intermediate film system. Reference to Fernseh A.-G. patents (3300, 3372).

4068 Nakashima, T., and K. Takayanagi. "Television." Br. 424,773, Aug. 22, 1933. On sync methods in a two-channel system, one for picture signals and the other for sound and sync, with disk scanner and picture tube receiver with magnetic deflection.

4069 National Television Corp. "Discharge lamp." Br. 424,211, Aug. 22, 1933. Elongated double-bulb gas-filled lamp for television.

4070 Nyquist, H. "Electro-optical system." U.S. 2,031,728, Aug. 22, 1933. Feb. 25, 1936. Assigned: AT&T. Disk receiver with discharge lamp and amplifier.

4071 "Boxing by television. Successful experiment by B.B.C." TIMES (Aug. 23): 10a. First time in this country and in the world. Considered highly satisfactory by the experts.

4072 "Progress of television." ELECT. 111 (Aug. 25): 225, 226. Editorial comments on Baird's picture tube receiver at Radiolympia, the use of ultra-short waves for television, and a favorable view of the intermediate film system.

4073 "Olympia's story." W.W. 33 (Aug. 25): 157–82. This "stand-to-stand" review mentions receivers by Baird Television, Bush Radio, Grafton Radio, the Baird grid cell (price now £2), and cathode-ray tubes by Edison Swan Electric Co.

4074 "New television system uses auto light bulb." N.Y.T. X, 7 (Aug. 27): 6. Note on W.H. Peck and his apparatus with special reflectors surrounding a 6-volt bulb.

4075 Bullimore, W.R., and L.H. Bedford. "Television." Br. 412,794, Aug. 28, 1933 (A.C. Cossor). Refers to compensation for the movement of continuously moving film scanned by a cathode-ray tube. Details similar to Br. 399,469 (3311).

4076 Banca, Maggio C. "Cathode-ray device." U.S. 2,103,312, Aug. 29, 1933, Dec. 28, 1937. Assigned: RCA. Film scanning by a camera tube.

4077 D.S. Loewe. "Television." Br. 446,263, Aug. 27, 1934. In Germany Aug. 31, 1933.

Cathode-ray tube with rotating mirror and light-valve. Reference to Br. 444,881 (3986).

4078 Schubert, G. "Treating continuous film." U.S. 2,124,085, Aug. 31, 1934, July 19, 1938; Br. 441,151, Aug. 31, 1934, In Germany Aug. 31, 1933 (Fernseh A.-G.). Addition to Br. 428,227 (3710). Reference to Br. 419,419 (3927).

4079 Arnold, Frank Atkinson. BROADCAST ADVERTISING, THE FOURTH DIMENSION. TELEVISION EDITION. New York: J. Wiley; London: Chapman and Hall, 1933. xix + 284 pp., illus. Foreword by the late Harry P. Davis. Television introduction by Dr. Alfred N. Goldsmith. An account of advertising methods employed in sponsored programs in the United States. Note: Commercial television broadcasting is not permitted by the F.R.C.

4080 Wenstrom, W.H. "Notes on television definition." PROC. IRE 21 (Sept.): 1317–27. 16 photos. A qualitative study of images with 60, 120, 200, and 400 lines, based on photographs.

4081 "Mosaic television for the home." POP. MECH. 60 (Sept.): 321–4. Illus. Zworykin's camera tube.

4082 Peck, A.P. "A real electric eye; the iconoscope." SCI. AM. 149 (Sept.): 117.

4083 "B.B.C. television policy. Rumours and facts." TELEV. 6 (Sept.): 306. Comments on the BBC request for postcards from viewers, misleading reports in the press on the BBC attitude toward television, and the continuance of the broadcasts until Mar. 1934, and about research on 120-line transmissions on the ultra-short waves.

4084 "Progress of Radiolympia. Mirror drums and cathode rays." TELEV. 6 (Sept.): 308, 309. 2 photos. Mention of the two classes of receivers and comments on cathode-ray tubes.

4085 "News from abroad." TELEV. 6 (Sept.): 310, 311. Reports from the United States, the radio exhibitions in Berlin and Argentina.

4086 "Last month's programmes." TELEV. 6 (Sept.): 318, 319. 2 photos.

4087 Gardiner, E.L. "A complete mirror drum receiver." TELEV. 6 (Sept.): 320–5. 2 photos, 2 diags. List of components.

4088 Walker, L.E.Q. "Problems of synchronisation." TELEV. 6 (Sept.): 326–9. 5 diags. Extracts from the MARCONI REVIEW.

4089 Wilson, J.C. "The design of television transmission equipment." J.TELEV. SOC. 1 (Sept.): 237–71. 5 photos, 21 diags., 8 tables.

4090 "Television." ELECT. 111 (Sept. 1): 263. Note on boxing match broadcast by the BBC, review of the National Radio Exhibition and the radio show in Berlin.

4091 "The Iconoscope, America's latest television favourite." W.W. 33 (Sept.): 197. 8 photos, diag. Clear description of the tube structure and important features.

4092 Nicolson, A.M. "Elastic wave television system." U.S. 2,042,859, Sept. 2, 1933, June 2, 1936. Assigned: Comm. Pats. Divided from U.S. 1,972,492 (3531).

4093 A.C. Cossor, L.H. Bedford, and O.S. Puckle. "Television." Br. 427,625, Sept. 4, 1933. Transmitter and receiver circuits, particularly for scanning and sync, in a system employing velocity and intensity modulation with cathode-ray tubes. References (3311, 3811, 3919, 4075, 4266).

4094 A.C. Cossor, L.H. Bedford, and O.S. Puckle. "Television." Br. 428,602, Sept. 4, 1933. Divided from and similar to previous entry. Same references.

4095 Lora, Luis A. "Television." U.S. 2,108,132, Sept. 5, 1933, Feb. 15, 1938. Assigned: Radio Patents. A receiving tube containing a metallic grid and conductive mosaic.

4096 "Television. Transmissions over light beam at British Association meeting." ELECT. 111 (Sept. 8): 299. Description of apparatus with 4-foot receiver screen and optical link demonstrated by the Marconi Company at Leicester.

4097 C. Lorenz A.-G., and M. v. Ardenne. "Cathode-ray tube." Br. 443,844, Sept. 7, 1934. In Germany Sept. 8, 1933. Electrode arrangements in a gas-filled tube.

4098 Telefunken. "Television." Br. 444,065, Sept. 10, 1934. In Germany Sept. 9, 1933. Concerns sync signals with reference to Br. 431,561.

4099 EMI, C.O. Browne, and J. Hardwick. "Television." Br. 425,177, Sept. 11, 1933. Circuits for compensating reinserted low-frequency signal components. Reference to Br. 422,906 (3896).

4100 EMI and W.F. Tedham. "Cathode-ray tube." Br. 425,234, Sept. 11, 1933. Electrode structures and alignment.

4101 EMI and J.D. McGee. "Cathode-ray tube." Br. 422,429, Sept. 12, 1933. Electrode structure including a conical part which screens the beam from charges on the wall of the tube.

4102 RCA. "Television." Br. 413,894, Sept. 13, 1933 (Marconi's). Relates to a stereoscopic system employing two camera tubes and two side-by-side picture tubes, with variants including a camera tube with a split mosaic plate, mirrors, and scanning disk. Right- and left-eye picture lines are scanned alternately, while the two images are viewed on a single screen via a grating. Three references (2865, 2964, 3127)

4103 "Television at the Berlin show. A review of the year's progress in Germany." W.W. 33 (Sept. 15): 234, 235. 7 photos, diag. "With a regular television transmission on ultrashort waves, Germany is at present taking a lead in television development in Europe. Apparatus for the reception of these transmissions is being developed by a number of manufacturers." Descriptive report on apparatus by von Ardenne, Fernseh, D.S. Loewe, von Mihály, Tekade, Telefunken, and the Post Office.

4104 "Bush Radio Baird television receiver. An efficient mirror drum Televisor." W.W. 33 (Sept. 15): 327, 328. 3 photos. Thorough review, including the mirror drum and optical assembly, adjustment, operation, and performance. Priced at 50 guineas.

4105 West, A.G.D., and Baird Television. "Television." Br. 425,615, Sept. 15, 1933. Refers to a glass or celluloid scanning disk and photographic method for producing apertures.

4106 Traub, E. "Scanning device." Br. 425,552, Sept. 18, 1933; U.S. 2,070,460, Sept. 13, 1934, Feb. 9, 1937. Receiver with light source, Kerr cell, two mirror drums, double reflection, and lenses. References to Br. 394,446 (2868), 419,170 (3717).

4107 Jacomb, W.W., and Baird Television. "Television." Br. 424,657, Sept. 19, 1933. Film transmitter with optical system, scanning disk, and phototube.

4108 Fernseh A.-G. "Television receiver." Br. 429,463, Sept. 21, 1934. In Germany Sept. 22, 1933. Film support in an intermediate film receiver.

4109 Telefunken. "Cathode-ray tube." Br. 430,739, Sept. 22, 1933. Void. Beam concentrations and deflections by electrostatic or electromagnetic means.

4110 Baird, J.L., and Baird Television. "Television receivers." Br. 430,900, Sept. 25, 1933. Simultaneous recording of identical images on film via lenses and apertured disk.

4111 Nicolson, A.M. "Television." U.S. 2,011,947, Sept. 28, 1933, Aug. 20, 1935; Br. 432,455, Apr. 21, 1934. Assigned: Comm. Pats. Arc discharge system. References to Br. 360,470 (2066), 360,941 (2383).

4112 D.S. Loewe and K. Schlesinger. "Cathode.ray tube." Br. 427,765, Sept. 29, 1933. Divided from Br. 426,138 (3658).

4113 Church, A. "Recent developments in television." NATURE 132 (Sept. 30): 502–5. 3 diags. Retrospective on Baird's work is followed by an impartial overview of other developments in Germany and the United States, along with technical trends and problems. Paper presented at the British Association meeting in Leicester on Sept. 13.

4114 Ogloblinsky, G.N. (deceased) by V.K. Zworykin. "Cathode-ray tube." U.S. 2,069,460. Sept. 30, 1933, Feb. 2, 1937. Assigned: RCA. Camera tube and film transmission.

4115 Hémardinquer, Pierre. LA TELEVISION ET SES PROGRES. [Television and its progress]. Paris: Dunod, 1933. xiv + 243 pp., 150 illus. History and progress, general principles, typical apparatus, and a look at future developments in England, France, Germany, Belgium, and the United States.

4116 Tiltman, R.F. BAIRD OF TELEVISION: THE LIFE STORY OF JOHN LOGIE BAIRD. London: Seeley Service, 1933. Reprint, New York: Arno Press, 1974. 220 pp., 8 plates, 10 facsimiles, 4 diags. Foreword by Lord Angus Kennedy. An excellent and favorable account in general terms by a long-time friend of Baird.

4117 Kette, G. "Das Fernsehen und der Jubiläums-Funkausstellung in Berlin 1933" [Television and the anniversary radio fair in Berlin 1933]. FERN. U. TON. 4 (Oct): 53–61. Report on exhibitions and displays.

4118 Schubert, G. "Kontinuierlich arbeitender Zwischenfilm-Grossprojektionsempfänger" [Continually working intermediate film large projection receiver]. FERN. U. TON. 4 (Oct.): 62.

4119 Zworykin, V.K. "Television with cathode-ray tubes." J. IEE 73 (Oct.): 437–51. 2 photos, 8 graphs, 12 diags. Full description of the theory, characteristics, and operation of a system incorporating a camera tube with a single-sided mosaic, picture tube, and complete circuits for transmitter and receivers. A brief historical introduction is followed by sections on the iconoscope, the Kinescope, scanning, synchronization, and reproducing equipment. Discussion: J. IEE 74 (Mar. 1934): 276, 277.

4120 Washburne, R.D. "The new cathode-ray television tube." RADIO-CRAFT 5 (Oct): 207, 233. 3 photos, 2 diags. RCA-Victor, Zworykin.

4121 Cummings, Merle S. "Television advances!" RADIO N. 15 (Oct.): 214, 215, 245–7. 9 photos. Description and general explanation of Zworykin's camera and picture tube and of Sanabria's disk system and the display at Macy's in New York.

4122 "New Baird projector components for home constructors." TELEV. 6 (Oct,): 336. Full-page advertisement of the parts for a complete mirror drum assembly by Baird Television.

4123 "New-light source for television." TELEV. 6 (Oct.): 337, 361. 2 photos. On the use of zinc sulphide crystal by von Okolicsányi. To be marketed by Tekade Company.

4124 Chapple, H.J.B. "Ultra-short waves and the amateur." TELEV. 6 (Oct): 338–40. 2 photos, 3 diags.

4125 "Demonstrations at the 'B.A.'" TELEV. 6 (Oct.): 341–3. 3 photos, diag. Marconi's 50-line large screen apparatus and Baird's 120-line disk-picture-tube equipment demonstrated at the British Association meeting in Leicester, with comments on Major Church's paper.

4126 "Last month's programmes." TELEV. 6 (Oct.): 344–6. 2 photos.

4127 "The Grafton receiver." TELEV. 6 (Oct.): 346. Brief report on a demonstration of the Grafton "Ethovisor," a table model receiver for combined sight and sound. "The demonstration was a further proof that television is now 'a commercial proposition' in every sense."

4128 Gardiner, E.L. "The mirror drum receiver." TELEV. 6 (Oct.): 347–50. Diag.

4129 "News from abroad." TELEV. 6 (Oct.): 351. Photo. France, Madeira.

4130 Walker, L.E.Q. "Problems of synchronisation. Pt. II." TELEV. 6 (Oct.): 353–5. 6 diags.

4131 "Our constructor's circle." TELEV. 6 (Oct.): 358–60. 2 diags. List of members: 151 from 18 counties and London.

4132 "Putting over television. Do the programmes cost too much?" TELEV. 6 (Oct.): 362. Comments on correspondence in THE YORK-

SHIRE OBSERVER. How many people looking in? Our estimate is 14,000; Garry Allingham puts the figure at 5,000. Quote from Leslie Bailey in the ERA: "Those who take part now are, at any rate, in at the birth of an art which may grow to out-proportion all other forms of public entertainment."

4133 "Quest of television extends across sea." N.Y.T. IX, 9 (Oct. 1): 4. Quotes by a noted radio engineer on television developments in England, France, Germany, and Russia.

4134 Schlesinger, K. "Braun Tube." U.S. 2,152,820, Sept. 28, 1934, Apr. 4, 1939; Br. 446,635, Oct. 1, 1934. In Germany Oct. 2, 1933 (D.S. Loewe). Picture tube with a cylindrical stem and flattened spherical bulb with electrode arrangements including an electron-optical system. Reference to Br. 440,560 (3934).

4135 EMI, M. Bowman-Manifold, and W.S. Percival. "Valve generator." Br. 424,221, Oct. 3, 1933. Saw-tooth oscillator. Addition to Br. 401,990 (3462).

4136 EMI, G.E. Condliffe, Sir Isaac Shoenberg (1880–1963), and W.F. Tedham. "Cathode-ray tube." Br. 431,327, Oct. 3, 1933; U.S. 2,119,119, Sept. 29, 1934, May 31, 1938. High-vacuum picture tube and electrode structure, including accelerating and decelerating electrodes, apertured diaphragm, with electrostatic or electromagnetic focusing.

4137 "This television." W.W. 33 (Oct. 6): 287. News item referring to BBC and television, and the Baird tests on ultra-short waves at the Crystal Palace. "For one week the 30-line television will go out on 6.25 meters; then, for a week, 60-line images will be transmitted, followed by a week on 120-lines."

4138 "Television progress. The present stage of development." W.W. 33 (Oct. 6): 288–90. 3 photos, 2 diags. General discussion overview of principles, synchronizing, methods of coding or scanning transmission frequencies.

4139 Farnsworth, P.T. "Electron multiplying device." U.S. 2,071,515, Oct. 7, 1933, Feb. 23, 1937; Br. 450,138, Oct. 5, 1934. Assigned: Farnsworth Television. Refers to an image dissector with a central fine-mesh screen which emits secondary electrons, along with electromagnetic coils and operating circuits.

4140 "Gain in television amazes Marconi. Wireless inventor foresees early availability of sets for household use. Visits plant in Camden." N.Y.T. 25 (Oct. 11): 5. Comments by Marching during a tour of the RCA-Victor Co, in New Jersey.

4141 D.S. Loewe. "Television." Br. 445,428, Oct. 11, 1934. In Germany Oct. 11, 1933. Amplitude filter with gas-filled diode for separating sync and picture signals.

4142 D.S. Loewe. "Valve modulating circuits." Br. 447,046, Oct. 11, 1934. In Germany Oct. 11, 1933. Transmitter circuit for preventing high frequencies from reaching the low-frequency side has a pentode modulator that serves as a frequency multiplier.

4143 D.S. Loewe. "Valve circuits." Br. 447,401, Oct. 11, 1934. In Germany Oct. 11, 1933. Push-pull detector. Addition to Br. 435,417 (3874) and 441,285 (4006).

4144 Schlesinger, K. "Safety means for television tubes." U.S. 2,083,205, Oct. 5, 1934, June 8, 1937; Br. 446,171, Oct. 11, 1934. In Germany Oct. 11, 1933 (D.S. Loewe). Glow-lamp circuit connected between cathode and control electrode in a picture tube safeguards against excess potentials.

4145 Browne, C.O. "Television transmitter." Br. 426,735, Oct. 12, 1933; U.S. 2,152,464, Oct. 10, 1934, Mar. 28, 1939 (EMI). Film transmission system with galvanometer, illuminated gate, mirror drum, apertured screen, phototubes, and sync circuits in which picture signals and auxiliary signals are fed into the transmission channel on opposite side of the "black" level.

4146 Schröter, F. "Television." U.S. 2,118,115, Oct. 27, 1934, May 24, 1938; Br. 428,661, Sept. 14, 1934. In Germany Oct. 12, 1933 (Telefunken). Film system with Nipkow disk scanner, picture tube receiver, and two transmission channels, one for picture signals and the auxiliary one for sound and sync signals.

4147 "High-definition television. B.B.C. experiments." TIMES (Oct. 13): 12c. Tests on the ultra-short waves; first by Baird Television up to the end of the year, second by EMI beginning in Jan.

4148 "Television in Germany. New types of transmitter and receiver." TIMES (Oct. 23): 12c. Brief review of E.H. Traub's lecture to the Television Society, Oct. 11.

4149 "Television progress. Problems of the next step." W.W. 33 (Oct. 13): 302–4. 4 photos, Discussion of transmission on the ultra-short waves, services in Germany, synchronizing on the British "Grid System," standard of detail, the question of one system or many.

4150 A.C. Cossor and L.H. Bedford. "Television." Br. 427,630, Oct. 13, 1933. Circuits for accenting the higher frequencies in a velocity-intensity modulated system. Four references (3311, 3811, 3919, 4093).

4151 "New magic is expected. Marconi views television—Sykes optimistic on the outlook." N.Y.T. IX, 9 (Oct. 15): 6. Comments by Judge E.O. Sykes, chairman of the FRC.

4152 Brolly, Archibald West. "Generating a pulse in a cathode-ray tube." U.S. 2,107,778, Oct. 16, 1933, Feb. 8, 1938. Assigned: Farnsworth Television. Picture tube with pulse circuit triggered by the electron beam.

4153 Telefunken. "Television." Br. 430,463, Sept. 20, 1934. In Germany Oct. 18, 1933. Refers to deflection, sync, and line frequency control in a two-channel system with picture tube receiver.

4154 Wilson, J.C., and Baird Television. "Television." Br. 410,678, Oct. 18, 1933. Concerns framing control and sync in a mixed system with scanning disk, picture tube, commutator relay, toothed wheel assembly, and electron tube circuits. References to Br. 320,639 (1213), and 336,655 (1961).

4155 Walton, G.W. "Television." Br. 432,017, Oct. 19, 1933. Multichannel system employing an echelon device (1542) with mirror drum, multiple apertures, and phototubes, and one or more electromagnetic or electrostatic distributors. Reference to Br. 379,303 (2785), and 403,395 (3351).

4156 Traub, E.H. "The crystal cell. A new light modulator for television." W.W. 33 (Oct. 20): 323, 324. 4 photos, diag. Description of the zinc sulphide light-valve developed by von Okolicsányi.

4157 "High definition tests." W.W. 33 (Oct. 20): 325. News item on tests by Baird Television and EMI. First by Baird will start soon and continue until the end of the year. EMI, who demonstrated their apparatus to the BBC in December 1932, will start tests in Jan. on 120 and 180 lines.

4158 Schlesinger, K. "Rectifier for wireless television reception." U.S, 2,068,769, Oct. 17, 1934, Jan. 26, 1937; Br. 449,466, Oct. 22, 1934. In Germany Oct. 21, 1933 (D.S. Loewe). Push-pull detector.

4159 G.E.C. and C.R. Dunham. "Valve generator." Br. 422,809, Oct, 23, 1933. Sweep generator with gas discharge tube.

4160 Schlesinger, K. "Detector." U.S. 2,188,866, Oct. 20, 1934, May 31, 1938; Br. 449,316, Oct. 22, 1934. In Germany Oct. 23, 1933 (D.S. Loewe). Receiver circuit with glow lamp to prevent loss of high frequencies. Reference to Br. 447,401 (4143)

4161 Schlesinger, K. "Cathode-ray tube." U.S. 2,129,033, Oct. 20, 1934, Sept. 6, 1938; Br. 449,245, Oct. 22, 1934. In Germany Oct. 23, 1933 (D.S. Loewe). Auxiliary electrodes arranged close to the deflection plates in a picture tube prevent distortion of the beam by marginal fields.

4162 Banks, G.B., J.C. Wilson, and Baird Television. "Television." Br. 426,356, Oct. 24, 1933. Transmission of sync on sound channel. Addition to Br. 398,512 (3363). Reference to Br. 420,091 (3931).

4163 Gabrilovitch, L., V. Isnard, and R. Berthon. "Television." Br. 441,896, Oct. 24, 1934. In France Oct. 25, 1933. A multichannel system employing different radio and audio frequencies, banks of photocells and lamps divided into groups, tuned circuits, microphones, telephones, and simultaneous transmission of the picture points.

4164 Telefunken. "Cathode-ray tube." Br. 426,254, Oct. 25, 1934. In Germany Oct. 25, 1933. Gas-filled picture tube with two sets of deflection plates arranged to eliminate the ion cross on the screen.

4165 "Television explained. Pt. 1. The principles of scanning." W.W. 33 (Oct. 27): 334, 335. 3 photos, 2 diags.

4166 "German Post Office and television." W.W. 33 (Oct. 27): 342. News item referring to an official statement released at a conference held Oct. 16. Plans to push research for transmission of 180/25 images on ultra-short waves. Germany must retain the "advantage which it has at present gained in television technique over developments in other countries."

4167 Schlesinger, K. "Higher-frequency coupling system." U.S. 2,225,085, Oct. 23, 1934, Dec. 17, 1940; Br. 446,346, Oct. 27, 1934. In Germany Oct. 27, 1933 (D.S. Loewe). Wide-band transfer-coupled amplifier for television.

4168 "Electric and Musical Industries." TIMES (Oct. 31): 21b. Company news and financial statement. Loss of £374,482 for the year ended June 30.

4169 Zworykin, K. "Système de télévision par tubes à rayons cathodiques" [Television system with cathode rays]. ONDE ELECT. 12 (Nov.): 500–39.

4170 Gernsback, H. "The radio set of 1950." RADIO-CRAFT 5 (Nov.): 263. Will include a picture tube receiver with an image size of at least 9 by 12 inches, and the pictures will be better and steadier than those seen in the motion-picture house. Sets will swivel for ease of viewing, and the better ones will provide images in full color.

4171 Hollywood, John M. and Marshall P. Wilder. "The how and why of cathode-ray tubes for television and other uses." RADIO N. 15 (Nov.): 268–70, 313. 3 photos, 6 diags. Principles, tube construction, sweep circuits.

4172 Kroker, A., and S. Felgenstreu. "Das Verhalten des Widerstands-Kapazitäts-gekoppelten Verstärkers bei Schallvorgängen" [The behavior of resistance-capacity coupled amplifiers]. T.F.T. 22 (Nov.): 277–87. On circuits and signals in television transmitters.

4173 "Last month's programmes." TELEV. 6 (Nov.): 370–2. 2 photos.

4174 "Future of B.B.C. transmissions. An official statement." TELEV. 6 (Nov.): 373, 374. On the statement in WORLD RADIO, Oct. 13, about experimental tests on the ultra-short waves and the continuance of the present 30-line service The limited range of transmissions on the higher frequency, the unavailability of suitable receivers, and the question of how many "lookers" there are the country are also discussed.

4175 "News from abroad." TELEV. 6 (Nov.): 380–2. 3 photos. Germany, Italy, the United States. Plans of the German Post Office for ultra-short wave transmissions of 120/25, a second transmitter to operate on 7 m, and cable transmission. Exhibits at the National Radio Show in Milan during October included a disk scanner for film and life scenes giving 90-line images, and receivers using disks, mirror screws, and picture tubes. "Reception was of a very high order and there was a constant stream of 'lookers' throughout the exhibition. In Bakersfield, Calif., the Pioneer Mercantile Company's station W6XAH transmits a vaudeville program (90/20) twice daily, with sound from station W6XE.

4176 Wilson, J.C. "The theory of the Kerr cell." TELEV. 6 (Nov.): 383–5.

4177 "The Television Society. Progress in Germany." TELEV. 6 (Nov.): 386. Review of German work by E. Traub given at the Society's meeting. Oct. 11.

4178 "A rival to the cinema? Some points of view." TELEV. 6 (Nov.): 387, 388.

4179 Hall, C.P. "Filters for mirror drums." TELEV. 6 (Nov.): 389, 391. 4 diags. Mechanical couplings.

4180 "Our constructor's circle." TELEV. 6 (Nov.): 392–5. 2 diags. Account of activities from 118 members in 22 counties and London, 15 in Scotland, 8 in Wales, 3 in Ireland and 6 overseas.

4181 Kroker, G. and S. Felgenstreu. "Das Verhalten des Widerstands-Kapazitäts-gekoppelten Verstärkers bei Schallvorgängen" [Study of resistance-capacity amplifiers, concerned with signals in television transmitter circuits]. T.F.T. 22 (Nov.): 277–87.

4182 Ardenne, M. v. "High efficiency cathode-ray tube." W. ENG. 10 (Nov.): 592–5.

4183 "Television explained, Pt. 2. The transmitter and receiver." W.W. 33 (Nov.): 355. 2 diags. Disk scanner, photocell, neon tube.

4184 Bowman-Manifold, M., and W.S. Percival. "Television." Br. 423,685, Nov. 3, 1933; U.S. 2,096,877, Nov. 2, 1934, Oct. 26, 1937 (EMI). Sync separation with oscillators for line and frame frequencies in a picture tube receiver.

4185 EMI and W.S. Percival. "Thermionic valve circuit." Br. 427,901, Nov. 3, 1933. Sawtooth oscillator for magnetic deflection. Addition to Br. 401,990 (3462). Reference to Br. 424,221 (4135).

4186 D.S. Loewe. "Valve circuit." Br. 443,046, Nov. 5, 1934. In Germany Nov. 4, 1933. Ultra-short wave television receiver.

4187 G.E.C. and Leslie Connock Jesty. "Cathode-ray tube." Br. 422,728, Nov. 6, 1933. Method of depositing a conductive coating on the inner wall of a picture tube.

4188 G.E.C. and L.C. Jesty. "Cathode-ray tube." Br. 425,493, Nov. 6, 1933. A picture tube enclosed in a metal shield with external pole pieces for a magnetic lens and centering adjustment. Reference to Br. 407,587 (3530).

4189 Pugh, David W., and Baird Television. "Valve circuit." Br. 428,371, Nov. 6, 1933. Supernet receiver for television. Reference to Br. 393,960 (3214).

4190 Tekade. "Television." Br. 421,937, Apr. 7, 1934. In Germany Nov. 6, 1933. Scanning signals and sound for a picture tube receiver are combined on one radio channel; another carries the picture signals.

4191 Rutherford, Robert E. "Image dissector and method of electron beam analysis." U.S. 2,135,149, Nov. 7, 1933, Nov. 1, 1938. Assigned: Farnsworth Television. Image dissector tube.

4192 G.E.C. and C.R. Dunham. "Television." Br. 423,963, Nov. 8, 1933. Sweep circuit with an inductor arranged to deflect the beam in a picture tube off the screen during the return strokes. Reference to Br. 400,976 (3339), 422,809 (4159).

4193 Schlesinger, K. "Television tube." U.S. 2,170,251, Nov. 2, 1934, Aug. 22, 1939; Br. 451,574, Nov. 5, 1934. In Germany Nov. 8, 1933 (D.S. Loewe). Concerns a high-vacuum picture tube with metallic coatings on the inner wall to serve for focusing, a magnetic shield on the conical part, complete assembly of other electrodes, and external connections. Reference to Br. 393,826 (A.E.G., Oct. 9, 1931), 427,090 (3532).

4194 Kette, A. "Die Behörden-Sonderausstellungen auf der 10. Deutschen Jubiläums-Funkausstellung" [The official special exhibition at the 10th German Jubilee radio show]. E.T.Z. 54 (Nov. 9): 1085–8. Description of the Post Office exhibits.

4195 Richardson, H.A. "Television." Br. 428,459, Nov. 9, 1933. The number of lines in a scanning system is multiplied by various means, including a mirror drum with mirrors at different angles, reflecting mirrors, plane mirrors, lenses, and prisms. Controller references: (2643, 2659, 2857).

4196 Tekade. "Television receiver." Br. 423,546, Mar. 10, 1934. In Germany Nov. 9, 1933. Method of forming the reflecting surfaces of a mirror screw and its assembly with a Kerr cell or crystal light-valve (3827).

4197 "Television explained. Pt. 3. The problem of synchronisation." W.W. 33 (Nov. 10): 375. Diag. Discussion of the Baird system with phonic wheel and disk scanner for 30/12.5 images with a black strip along the top of the picture, and explanation of the difference between isochronism and synchronism.

4198 Schlesinger, K. "Television tube." U.S. 2,226,991, Nov. 21, 1934, Dec. 31. 1940. Assigned: Loewe Radio. In Germany Nov. 10. 1933. External circuits to deflection plates include a pair of discharge tubes.

4199 D.S. Loewe. "Cathode-ray tube circuit." Br. 447,070, Nov. 10, 1934. In Germany Nov. 10, 1933. Push-pull amplifier for deflection plates. Addition to Br. 423,427 (3513).

4200 Schlesinger, K. "Push-pull detector." U.S. 2,072,315, Nov. 7, 1934. Mar. 2, 1937; Br. 450,241, Nov. 10, 1934. In Germany Nov. 10, 1933 (D.S. Loewe). References to Br. 447,401 (4143), 449,466 (4158).

4201 D.S. Loewe. "Thermionic valve circuit." Br. 450,351, Nov. 10, 1934. In Germany Nov. 10, 1933. Push-pull detector. Divided from Br. 450,241 (4200). Three references (3873, 4143, 4158).

4202 Lance, T.M.C., D.M. Johnstone, and Baird Television. "Television." Br. 429,832, Nov. 11, 1933. Refers to a two-channel system with one carrying sync and sound. References to Br. 398,512 (3363, 426,356 (4162).

4203 I.G. Farben. "Television." Br. 428,382, Nov. 13, 1933. Rapid film processing of intermediate film and its handling for transmission and reception.

4204 Barthélemy, R. "Picture reproducer." U.S. 2,155,033, Nov. 8, 1938, Apr. 18, 1939; Br. 431,827, Nov. 13, 1934. In France Nov. 14, 1933 (Comp. Gaz). Scanning system with cathode-ray tube projection, polyhedral mirror drum, sync motor, and phonic wheel.

4205 "Television explained. Pt. 4. The requirements for a good image." W.W. 33 (Nov. 17): 395, 396. Photo, diag. Discussion of number of lines, picture frequency, flicker, modulation frequency, and bandwidths of the carrier at the higher frequencies.

4206 Marconi's and Wilson Stuart Leader Tringham. "Transmitter." Br. 428,700, Nov. 17, 1933; U.S. 2,076,685, Nov. 16, 1934, Apr. 13, 1937 (RCA). Refers to a cathode-ray tube and switching circuit for monitoring the carrier wave modulation applicable to television transmission.

4207 "Electric & Musical Industries. End of adverse trading in sight. Progress of radio business. Mr. Alfred Clark's review." TIMES (Nov. 18): 18a, b. On television: "Active and I may say, very successful work has been carried on throughout the year..." Apparatus is to be installed in Broadcasting House early next year. "Television broadcasting, however, is not expected to count as an early profit earner."

4208 Baird, J.L., and Baird Television. "Television." Br. 430,569, Nov. 18, 1933. Method of scanning with arc light projected via lenses out a mirror drum.

4209 Baird, J.L., and Baird Television. "Television." Br. 430,570, Nov. 18, 1933. Scanning system with lenses fixed aperture, and lens disk.

4210 Walton, G.W. "Light-valve." Br. 431,958, Nov. 20, 1933. Liquid cell with interleaved control plates, details of construction. Reference to Br. 407,385 (3598).

4211 Baird, J.L., and Baird Television. "Television." Br. 433,853, Nov. 21, 1933. Film scanning by a cathode-ray tube.

4212 Fernseh A.-G. "Synchronous movements." Br. 434,102, Nov. 22, 1933. Void. Concerns the damping of a sync motor for television. Reference to Br. 366,598 (2098).

4213 Kette, G. "Die Fernseh-Schau auf der Jubiläums-Funkausstellung in Berlin 1933"

[The television show at the Jubilee radio in Berlin 1933]. E.T.Z. 54 (Nov. 23): 1141–3. Survey of apparatus by von Ardenne, Fernseh, von Mihály, the Post Office and Telefunken.

4214 "Television. Generation at high frequency." ELECT. 111 (Nov. 24): 666. Comment on talk by R.W. Corkling about television on the ultra-short waves at the meeting of the Television Society on Nov. 8.

4215 "Television explained. Pt. 5. Mechanical scanning systems." W.W. 33 (Nov. 24): 411–2. 2 photos, 2 diags. Mirror drum, vibrating mirrors, mirror screw.

4216 Schlesinger, K. "Radio receiving system." U.S. 2,107,394, Nov. 21, 1934. Feb. 8, 1938; Br. 449,470, Nov. 24, 1934. In Germany Nov. 24, 1933 (D.S. Loewe). Highly selective superhet circuit for television. Reference to Br. 443,046 (4186).

4217 King, J.B. "Television." Br. 426,792, Nov. 27, 1933. Optical system with a diffusing wire gauze, prisms and lenses, slotted rotating drum, and photocell. Filters may be added in the optical path for color reproduction.

4219 D.S. Loewe. "Amplifier." Br. 451,021, Nov. 26, 1934. In Germany Nov. 27, 1933. Divided from Br. 450,962 (4218). Reference to Br. 443,364 (4015).

4220 D.S. Loewe. "Cathode-ray tube." Br. 452,650, Nov. 26, 1934. In Germany Nov. 27, 1933. Electrode dimensions, spacing, and assembly in a high-vacuum tube. Reference to Br. 447,070 (4199).

4221 D.S. Loewe. "Cathode-ray tube." Br. 452,844, Nov. 26, 1934. In Germany Nov. 27, 1933. Divided from Br. 452,650 (4220). Reference to Br. 442,511 (3958). Controller reference)3030, 3074, 3353, 3397) and to Br. 380,381, Mar. 27, 1931 (M. Kroll).

4222 Baird, J.L., and Baird Television. "Television." Br. 434,527, Nov. 28, 1933. Refers to a mirror drum system with scanning of tow or four lines interleaved at the transmitter and receiver to avoid interline flicker. Five references (640, 1285, 1529, 3266, 3464).

4223 Ardenne, M. v. "Braun tube." U.S. 2,093,876, Nov. 17, 1934, Sept. 21, 1937; Br. 431,246, Oct. 19, 1934. In Germany Nov. 30, 1933.

4224 Pulvari-Pulvermacher, K. "Light-valve." Br. 442,381, Sept. 26, 1934. Convention date Nov. 30, 1933 (Budapest). Concerns various tube constructions containing a crystal or a similar electro-optically sensitive plate or screen, which coacts with scanning electron beams to produce a bright projected image in conjunction with a light source, Nicol prisms, and lenses.

4225 Banfi, A. "I recenti progressi della radiotelevisione" [Recent developments in television]. ALTA FREQUENZA 2 (Dec.): 629–44.

4226 "The balance sheet of television." ELECTRONICS 6 (Dec.): 323. Editorial. "Is television ready for the public? Some say Yes. Others insist No." List of seven discouraging aspects and seven encouraging aspects.

4227 Engstrom, Elmer William. "A study of television image characteristics." PROC. IRE 21 (Dec.): 1631–51. 8 graphs, 2 diags., 15 photos, table. This paper discusses general considerations, properties of vision, scanning lines, picture size, viewing distance, optical system for motion picture film, and special films for the study. A list classifies the number of scanning lines as follows: 180 minimum acceptable, 240 satisfactory, 360 excellent, 480 equivalent for practical auditions. Part 2 appeared in Apr. 1935.

4228 Engstrom, E.W. "An experimental television system." PROC. IRE 21 (Dec.): 1652–4. Introduction to the following three papers describing the apparatus developed by RCA-Victor Company from 1931 and the subsequent tests of the 120/24 image transmissions in New York on 40 to 80 megacycles.

4229 Zworykin, V.K. "Description of an experimental television system and the kinescope." PROC. IRE 21 (Dec.): 1655–63. 4 photos, 7 graphs, 7 diags. General discussion of a two-channel system with disk transmitter and picture tube receiver, including saw-tooth generators, deflection circuits, sync, and details of the cathode-ray tube.

4230 Kell, R.D. "Description of experimental television transmitting apparatus." PROC. IRE 21 (Dec.): 1674–91. 8 photos, 4 graphs, 6 diags. Theoretical design, scanning, sync, frequencies, mechanical design of the film and studio scanners, the production of television signals, amplifiers, and radio circuits.

4231 Beers, G.L. "Descriptions of experimental television receivers." PROC. IRE 21 (Dec.): 1692–1706. 5 photos, 7 graphs, 4 diags. Discussion covers types of receivers and details of circuit for picture and sound, receiver assembly, antennas, and observations on interference and fading.

4232 Kwal, B. "Note sur une solution provisoine du problème de la télévision: La transmission ralenti" [Television by retarded transmission: Film reading with transmission at reduced speed]. ONDE ELECT. 12 (Dec.): 577–9.

4233 "Movie-film pictures broadcast by radio." POP. SCI. 123 (Dec.): 51.

4234 "Recent radio developments." RADIO-CRAFT. 5 (Dec.): 332. 11 photos. Brief notes on display in Berlin and London including those by von Mihály, mirror screw by von Okolicsányi, Telefunken, and mention of the Peck Television Corp.

4235 "Television and aircraft stations in the U.S." RADIO N. 15 (Dec.): 351.

4326 "Elusive television." SCI. AM. 149 (Dec.): 257.

4237 Peck, W.H. "What constitutes perfect detail in television?" SCI. AM. 149 (Dec.): 273.

4238 "News from abroad." TELEV. 6 (Dec.): 406, 407. U.S., Greece.

4239 Davies, K.S., and E.L.C. White. "Positive synchronising." TELEV. 6 (Dec.): 411–3, 416. 2 diags.

4240 "Last month's programmes." TELEV. 6 (Dec.): 414–6. 2 photos.

4241 "Milestones." TELEV. 6 (Dec.): 417. 5 photos and caption on developments during 1933.

4242 Chapple, H.J.B. "A Cheap television receiver." TELEV. 6 (Dec.): 418–20. 2 photos, diag. Disk assembly.

4243 Wilson, J.C. "The theory of the Kerr cell." TELEV. 6 (Dec.): 422. 3 diags.

4244 "Our constructor's circle." TELEV. 6 (Dec.): 425, 426. Reports of 40 amateurs in 14 counties and London, and 3 in Scotland.

4245 Traub, E.H. "Television of the 1933 Berlin Radio Exhibition." J. TELEV. SOC. 1 (Dec.): 273–85. 21 photos, 9 diags. table of transmitters, receivers, and manufacturers showing technical features. Report on equipment by Fernseh, Tekade, Telefunken, Loewe Radio, von Mihály (International Television Corporation), RPZ, Heinrich Hertz Institute, and von Ardenne. The zinc sulphide crystal light-valve by von Okolicsányi and the mirror ring by von Mihály are also described. The following summarizes the methods employed. Transmitters: 8 disks, 1 mirror drum, 1 cathode-ray tube. Receivers: 8 cathode-ray tubes, 4 mirror screws, 1 disk, 1 mirror drum, 1 mirror ring. Scanning lines: 1 at 80, 6 at 90, 1 at 96, 1 at 120, 5 at 180, all with 25 pictures per second. Transmissions were chiefly by wire, with others by radio on 7 m. Image sizes ranged from 3 by 4 inches up to 12 by 16 inches on small receivers, with large-screen display up to 6 by 8 feet. The writer considered the Loewe receiver with picture tube to be "far in advance" of the others, provided "the nearest approach to a perfect television image." that he had seen. He also extended congratulations to Dr. Schlesinger "on having achieved such wonderful results in the short time of only 16 months that he has been with Loewe."

4246 Corkling, R.S. "Ultra-short waves and their application to television." J.TELEV. SOC. 1 (Dec.): 286, 287. Diag.

4247 Kurtz, E.G., and R.R. Whipple. "Optimum colour combination for the television stage." J. TELEV. SOC. 1 (Dec.): 291–3. 8 photos, 2 diags.

4248 Myers, L.M. "Electro-optics and television." J. TELEV. SOC. 1 (Dec.): 294–310. 7 photos, 18 diags. Theoretical treatment.

4249 "Television explained. Pt. 6. The cathode-ray tube." W.W. 33 (Dec. 1): 429, 430. 2 photos, diag. Principles of operation, sync.

4250 Holmes, R.S. "Television." U.S. 2,109,618, Dec. 1, 1933, Mar. 1, 1938. Assigned: RCA. Picture tube receiver and circuits.

4251 Ives, H.E. "Scanning device." U.S. 2,075,523, Dec. 1, 1933, Mar. 30, 1937. Assigned: B.T.L. Br. 429,570, Nov. 30, 1934 (E.R.P.). Nipkow disk for motion-picture film.

4252 Marconi's, H.M. Dowsett, and L.E.Q. Walker. "Television." Br. 429,690, Dec. 5, 1933. Scanning by rotating reflectors, fixed mirror ring, and other reflectors.

4253 Marconi's, H.M. Dowsett, and L.E.Q. Walker. "Television." Br. 430,161, Dec. 6, 1933; U.S. 2,146,804, Dec. 6, 1934, Feb. 14, 1939 (RCA). Concerns a heterodyning method to reduce the bandwidth required for picture transmission.

4254 D.S. Loewe. "Television." Br. 451,578, Dec. 5, 1934. In Germany Dec. 6, 1933. Sync separation circuit with gas-filled tubes for a picture tube receiver. Addition to Br. 445,428 (4141). References to Br. 441,761 (3928), 447,401 (4143).

4255 D.S. Loewe. "Television." Br. 453,463, Dec. 5, 1934, In Germany Dec. 6, 1933. Divided from above. Reference to Br. 447,401 (4143).

4256 Schlesinger, K. "Picture receiving system." U.S. 2,226,992, Dec. 5, 1934, Dec. 31, 1940; Br. 444,149, Dec. 5, 1934. In Germany Dec. 6, 1933 (D.S. Loewe). Sync separation with gas-filled tubes. Reference to Br. 441,761 (3928).

4257 Tedham, W.F. "Television transmitting system." Br. 426,505, Dec. 6, 1933; U.S. 2,153,163, Nov. 23, 1934, Apr. 4, 1939 (EMI). An image is continuously projected via a lens and oblique mirror onto a photosensitive mosaic which is scanned by a light beam from the fluorescent screen of a cathode-ray tube.

4258 Urtel, Rudolf. "Cathode-ray apparatus." U.S. 2,100,618, Dec. 14, 1934, Nov. 30, 1937; Br. 433,996, Dec. 7, 1934. In Germany Dec. 7, 1933 (Telefunken). Air-core deflection coils with magnetic yoke for picture tube.

4259 "The B.B.C. and television." ELECT. 111 (Dec. 8): 719. The BBC notified Baird Television in Sept. that the 30-line transmissions would be ended Mar. 31, 1934.

4260 Schlesinger, K. "Braun tube for television." U.S. 2,226,107, Dec. 5, 1934, Dec. 24, 1940; Br, 453,223, Dec. 8, 1934. In Germany Dec. 9, 1933 (D.S. Loewe). Electrode structures and arrangements. Three references (3723, 3958, 4261)

4261 D.S. Loewe. "Cathode-ray tube." Br. 453,270, Dec. 8, 1934. In Germany Dec. 9, 1933. Divided from above. References to Br. 435,382 (3721), 442,511 (3958).

4262 Schröter, F. "Television." Br. 431,904, Dec. 12, 1934; U.S. 2,109,321, Jan. 5, 1935, Feb. 22, 1938. In Germany Dec. 12, 1933 (Telefunken). A mirror drum projects the image onto a linear multicell phototube, the elements being connected to a circle of corresponding electrodes in a cathode-ray tube which are scanned by a rotary beam.

4263 Gardner, B.C. "Cathode-ray oscillator." U.S. 2,104,834, Dec. 13, 1933, Jan. 11, 1938. Assigned: Farnsworth Television. Cathode-ray tube.

4264 "Television explained, Pt. 7. Variable speed scanning." W.W. 33 (Dec. 15): 461, 462. Photo, diag. Description of von Ardenne's velocity-modulated system.

4265 Baird, J.L., and Baird Television. "Television." Br. 435,103, Dec. 15, 1933. Linear scanning of motion-picture film by a mirror drum with other moving mirrors or prisms to provide an interlaced scan.

4266 A.C. Cossor. L.H. Bedford, and O.S. Puckle. "Television." Br. 423,098, Dec. 15, 1933. Concerns a sync circuit in a picture tube receiver in which the absence of the line-sync pulse at the end of a complete scan returns the spot to the first scanning line. References to Br. 399,459 (3311), 419,298 (3919).

4267 Nightingale, Harry C. "Scanning device." U.S. 1,997,307, Dec. 15, 1933, Apr. 9, 1935. A rotary member has slots inclined at different angles and an internal linear light source.

4268 G.E.C., Bernard Phineas Dudding, and L.C. Jesty. "Cathode-ray tubes." Br. 429,045, Dec. 19, 1933; U.S. 2,089,546, Nov. 30, 1934, Aug. 10, 1937. Relates to the proportions of the conical envelope of a picture tube.

4269 Harding, R. Jr. "Television transmitting apparatus." U.S. 2,043,245, Dec. 19, 1933, June 9, 1936. Assigned: National Television. Single-spiral disk, photocells, and amplifiers.

4270 Schleede, A., and F. Schröter. "Fluorescent screens." U.S. 2,137,118, Dec. 6, 1934. Nov. 15, 1938. In Germany Dec. 19, 1933 (Telefunken). Cathode-ray tube.

4271 Schlesinger, K. "Television amplifier." U.S. 2,141,411, Dec. 17, 1934, Dec. 27, 1938; Br. 453,886, Dec. 20, 1934. In Germany Dec. 20, 1933 (D.S. Loewe). Wide-band amplifier, Reference to Br. 450,247, Dec. 13, 1933 (D.S. Loewe, radio receiver circuits).

4272 Lenier, H.R. "Television." Br. 435,534, July 30, 1934. Void. In France Dec. 21, 1933. Disk, phototube, glow lamp, and filter for infrared pickup.

4273 Bridgewater, T.H. "Image reception. Significance of 180° phase changes—design of a complete receiver." ELECT. 111 (Dec. 22): 780. Review of paper read at a meeting of the Students' Section of the IEE, Dec. 19. Preservation of very low and very high frequencies, effects of phase distortion, comparison of detectors, amplifier design, theoretical analysis, and practical features.

4274 Hankly, H.A. "Television. New optical devices—piezo-electric modulator." ELECT. 111 (Dec. 22): 780. Report on paper by L.M. Myers dealing with his researches on electro-optics, given to the Television Society, Dec. 14.

4275 Zillger, A. "Television." U.S. 2,209,439, Dec. 22, 1933, renewed Dec. 19, 1939, July 30, 1940. Assigned: National Television. Complete assembly for film scanning with sound.

4276 Johnson, J.B., and H.W. Weinhart. "Electron discharge device." U.S. 2,063,314, Dec. 27, 1933, Dec. 8, 1936. Assigned: B.T.L. Picture tube with magnetic focusing and electrostatic deflection.

4277 Weinhart, H.W. "Electron discharge device." U.S. 2,096,415, Dec. 27, 1933, Oct. 19, 1937. Assigned: B.T.L. Cathode-ray tube with conductive coating between the emitter and electron-optical lens.

4278 "Television explained. Pt. 8. A survey of development." W.W. 33 (Dec. 29): 498. Discussion of the advantages and drawbacks of ultra-short waves, intensity modulation versus velocity modulation, disks, drums, and cathode-ray tubes. "The chief problems lie in the television apparatus, and while there is no doubt that a solution will eventually be found, perhaps by methods now unknown, it will be a long time before anything approaching finality is reached."

4279 Blumlein, A.D. "Television." Br. 432,485, Dec. 29, 1933; U.S. 2,165,028, Mar. 15, 1935, July 4, 1939 (EMI). Multispot scanning in a picture tube is obtained by a grid of wires across a linear cathode. Control impulses applied to the wires through a phase-retarding network result in a series of modulated spots close together along each scanning line.

4280 Lance, T.M.C., D.M. Johnstone and Baird Television. "Valve generating circuit." Br. 428,557, Dec. 30, 1933. The wave-form of a relaxation oscillator is modified by a correcting wave transmitted with the sync signals. Reference to Br. 420,091 (3931).

4281 Schröter, F. "Electron tube." U.S. 2,143,390, Jan. 5, 1935, Jan. 10, 1939. In Germany Dec. 30, 1933 (Telefunken). Cathode-ray tube with internal voltage divider.

4282 Wilson, J.C., and Baird Television. "Television." Br. 428,805, Dec. 30, 1933. Holes in a multispiral disk are exposed in sequence by a rotating shutter with ace-shaped radial slots. Three references (860,1530,2486).

4283 Ardenne, M. v. DIE KATHODENSTRAHLROHRE UND IHRE ANWENDUNG IN DER SCHWACH-STROM-TECHNIK [The cathode-ray tube and its applications in weak current techniques]. Berlin: J. Springer, 1933. viii + 398 pp. 432 photos, graphs, diags. With the collaboration of Dr.-Ing. Henning Knoblauch. A thorough coverage of the theory, construction, and applications of cathode-ray tubes and auxiliary equipment for electrical measurements in light-current engineering, including radio circuits and high frequencies. The last section (pp. 342–84) deals with sound films and television transmitters and receivers. List of chapter notes (pp. 385–92) and numerous footnotes. A modified version in English appeared in 1939 (8618).

4284 Cameron, James Ross. RADIO AND TELEVISION. Woodmont, Conn.: Cameron Publishing Co., 1933. 541 pp., 348 illus. Television detailed on pp. 62–82; 270–311; 417–532.

4285 Camm, Frederick James. FIFTY TESTED WIRELESS CIRCUITS. London: G. Newnes, 1933. 144 pp. 99 illus. With instructions for building a television receiver.

4286 Hathaway, Kenneth A. TELEVISION: A PRACTICAL TREATISE ON THE PRINCIPLES UPON WHICH THE DEVELOPMENT OF TELEVISION IS BASED. Chicago: American Technical Society, 1933. 174 pp., illus. An elementary treatment chiefly on mechanical systems.

4287 Mesney, René. TELEVISION ET TRANSMISSION DES IMAGES [Phototelegraphy and television]. Paris: A. Colin, 1933. 220 pp., 97 illus.

CHAPTER 14

HIGH NOON OF LOW DEFINITION: 1934

TABLE 22　CHRONOLOGY: 1934

Jan.		Zworykin	Paper on the iconoscope
Feb.	7	A.C. Cossor	Lecture on system by Bedford and Puckle
Mar.	20	Baird Co.	Demonstrates 180/25 transmission at company meeting
Apr.		Sofar	Displays 180-line telecine at the 15th Milan Fair
	1	Germany	Post Office establishes 180/25 system as standard
	18	Germany	Experimental film transmissions from Berlin-Witzleben
	30	U.K.	Plans announced for a television committee
May	12	EMI	Safer Emitron by Lubszynski and Rodda
	14	U.K.	Announcement on the Television Committee
	22	Marconi-EMI	New combined registered
	29	RCA-Victor	Tests from New York to Camden, N.J.
	29	U.K.	First meeting of the Television Committee
July	1	U.S.	Federal Communication Commission established
Aug.		Farnsworth	Report on demonstration of 220/30 images
	3	EMI	C.P.S. Emitron by Blumlein and McGee
	16	London	Cathode-ray tubes on show at Olympia
		London	Bush and Plew display 30-line receivers at Olympia
	17	Berlin	Display by seven manufacturers at the radio show
	24	Farnsworth	Demonstrates system at the Franklin Institute
Oct.		Sofar	Displays 180/25 apparatus at the radio show in Milan
		Japan	Report on 100/20 system at Hamamatsu
	24	U.K.	Members of the Television Committee start visit to U.S.
Nov.	5	U.K.	Members of the Television Committee visit Germany
	6	A.E.C.	Color tube by Jesty

TABLE 23   CORPORATE PATENTS

Company	1933	1934
D.S. Loewe	60	62
RCA	22	43
EMI	33	41
Baird	33	38
Marconi's	10	18
Telefunken	31	18
Fernseh A.-G.	16	13
General Electric (U.K.)	4	9
Bell Telephone Laboratories	5	8
Communication Patents	3	7
Comp. Gaz	1	6
C. Lorenz	1	5
National Television Corporation	4	5
* Scophony	0	5
A.E.G.	3	3
A.C. Cossor	8	3
Farnsworth	8	3
* N.V. Philips	0	3
* Ferranti	0	2
* Hazeltine	0	2
* Automatic Electric	0	1
* Du Mont	0	1
* Electric Television	0	1
I.G. Farben	1	1
* International Television Radio Corp.	0	1
* Radio Inventions	0	1
Schneider	1	1
* Television and Electric	0	1
	244	302

New entries in 1934.

BIBLIOGRAPHY: 1934

4288   Knoll, M. "Elektrische Elektronenlinsen für Kathodenstrahlröhren" [Electric electron lens for cathode-ray tubes]. ARCH. ELEKT. 28 (Jan. 17): 1-8.

4289   Maloff, Loury Gregory. "Problems of cathode-ray television." ELECTRONICS 7 (Jan.): 10, 12, 19. 10 diags. Focusing of electron beams, scanning, frequency band.

4290   Zworykin, V.K. "Television." J.F.I. 217 (Jan.): 1-37. 12 photos, 9 graphs, 10 diags. Reprint, New York: Arno Press, 1977. This paper describing the all-electronic system developed by RCA was presented at a meeting of the Franklin Society on Oct. 18, 1933.

4291   Zworykin, V.K. "The iconoscope, a modern version of the electric eye." PROC. IRE 22 (Jan.): 16-32. 2 photos, 4 graphs, 8 diags. Theory, construction, characteristics, mode of operation, and application in television.

4292   "New television system." POP. SCI. 124 (Jan.): 25.

4293   Baird, J.L., and Baird Television. "Television." Br. 431,339, Jan. 3, 1934. Refers to an unorthodox method of interlaced scanning called "skipping-line," intended to reduce flicker, in a system employing a picture tube and a mechanical transmitter with mirror drum, auxiliary apertured disks, and phototubes. References (1213, 3363, 3464, 4339)

4294   Baird, J.L., and Baird Television. "Television." Br. 431,458, Jan. 3, 1934. Divided from above, same references.

4295   Wilson, J.C., and Baird Television. "Television." Br. 431,340, Jan. 3, 1934. Optical methods for generating sync signals by the film to be transmitted.

4296   Bullimore, W.R., L.H. Bedford, and A.C. Cossor. "Television." Br. 430,179, Jan. 4, 1934. Addition to Br. 399,469 (3311). Deflection circuit for velocity modulation.

4297   Henroteau, F.C.P. "Television." U.S. 2,104,862, Jan. 4, 1934, Jan. 11, 1938. Assigned: Electronic Television. An evacuated vessel contains a scanning plate close to a screen of photocells.

4298   Plew, F., and E.H. Wright. "Television." Br. 429,516, Jan. 4, 1934. Producing apertured disks or strips photographically.

4299   Lance, T.M.C., and Baird Television. "Valve generator." Br. 431,567, Jan. 5, 1934. Scanning oscillator. Reference to Br. 420,091 (3931).

4300 Karolus, A. "Picture transmission." U.S. 2,129,738, Jan. 5, 1935, Sept. 13, 1938. Assigned: RCA. In Germany Jan 10, 1934 (Telefunken). Modulating arrangement with filament lamp.

4301 Karolus, A. "Picture transmission." U.S. 2,185,302, Jan. 5, 1935, Jan. 1940. Assigned: RCA. In Germany Jan. 10, 1934 (Telefunken). Similar to above.

4302 Schlesinger, K. "Cathode-ray tube." U.S. 2,137,352, Jan. 7, 1935, Nov. 22, 1938; Br. 455,084, Jan. 12, 1935. In Germany Jan. 12, 1934 (D.S.Loewe). Electrode structures and assembly in a high-vacuum picture tube. References: (3353, 3397, 3958, 3992).

4303 Fernseh A.-G. "Cathode-ray tubes." Br. 430,803, Jan. 17, 1935. In Germany Jan. 17, 1934. A screen of metal gauze treated with fluorescent material is connected to a conductive coating on the inner wall of a tube. References to Br. 423,696 (3850).

4304 Automatic Electric and L.M. Simpson. "Television." Br. 432,199, Jan. 18, 1934. Concerns a method of transmitting signals in an intermediate film system at a lower than normal rate so that the signals occupy a standard broadcasting band of 9 kc.

4305 A.C. Cossor and O.S. Puckle. "Amplifier." Br. 432,268, Jan. 19, 1934. Paraphrase circuit with voltage stabilizer for photocell input.

4306 Baird, J.L., and Baird Television. "Television." Br. 433,935, Jan. 22, 1934. Divided from Br. 432,635 (Group XX). An intermediate film is scanned by a pair of lenses. Reference to Br. 381,898 (3464). See also U.S. 2,032,164, Jan. 23, 1934, Feb. 25, 1936.

4307 G.E.C. and L.C. Jesty. "Television." Br. 424,093, Jan. 22, 1934. Three-phase deflection equivalent to linear scanning applied to three cathode-ray tubes with masked screens, optical projection to combine the images, with color suggested.

4308 Scophony and John Henry Jeffree. "Scanning device." Br. 433,945, Jan. 23, 1934; U.S. 2,140,584, Jan. 23, 1935, Dec. 20 1938. Light from a linear source, reflected by a rotary scanner of polished metal rods, passes through a line of reversing prisms and a cylindrical lens onto a mirror drum and thence to a viewing screen. A beam converter employing this principle was shown at the Science Museum exhibition in 1937.

4309 Wilson, J.C., and Baird Television. "Television." Br. 437,021, Jan. 23, 1934. Concerns a method of simultaneous double-scanning an intermediate film for low and high definition.

4310 Barthélemy, R. "Synchronizing cathode beams." U.S. 2,143,932, Jan. 16, 1935, Jan. 16, 1939; Br. 432,783. In France Jan. 25, 1934 (Comp. Gaz). In a receiver the frame sync circuit is triggered by the absence of a line-sync signal once per image. Reference to Br. 423,098 (4266).

4311 D.S. Loewe. "Television." Br. 452,715, Jan. 24, 1935. In Germany Jan. 25, 1935. Addition to Br.. 445,428 (4141).

4312 Schlesinger, K. "Television receiver." U.S. 2,173,495, Jan. 21, 1935, Sept. 19, 1939; Br. 454,319, Jan. 24, 1934. In Germany Jan. 25, 1934. Superhet circuit.

4313 "Cathode-ray television." ELECT. 112 (Jan. 26): 90. Report of lecture by G. Parr and T.W. Price on Jan. 17 at a meeting of the Television Society.

4314 Mitchell, W.G.W. "Television progress." ELECT. 112 (Jan. 26): 114. Brief review of developments in America, Britain, and Germany during 1933, with mention of the increased activity with cathode-ray tubes and the trend toward higher definition images comprising from 120 to 240 lines at 25 pictures per second requiring band-widths of 150 kc up to 1000 kc.

4315 D.S. Loewe. "Light valve." Br. 450,859, Jan. 24, 1935. In Germany Jan. 26, 1934. A multicellular diaphragm of two sets of thin intersecting plates making up square tubes or an equivalent honeycomb used with a Kerr cell or combined with a piezoelectric crystal.

4316 Ruska, E. "Braun tube." U.S. 2,178,458, Jan. 24, 1935, Oct. 31, 1939; Br. 450,973,

Jan. 25, 1935. In Germany Jan. 26, 1934 (Fernseh A.-G.). Refers to the electrode arrangements in a picture tube including two electrostatic lenses.

4317 Knoll, M. "Electron tube." U.S. 2,086,718, Feb. 9, 1935, July 13, 1937. In Germany Jan. 27, 1934 (Telefunken). Cathode-ray tube with a rotating fluorescent disk.

4318 Harding, R. Jr. "Television." U.S. 2,094,983, Jan. 29, 1934, Oct. 5, 1937. Assigned: National Television. Drum with stacked plates.

4319 Telefunken. "Television." Br. 436,622, Jan. 17, 1935. In Germany Jan. 30, 1934. Magnetic deflection circuit in a picture tube receiver.

4320 "Television is ready but curbed by cost." N.Y.T. 15 (Jan. 31): 4. On a lecture by Charles A. Wall of NBC.

4321 Barthélemy, R. "Television receiver." U.S. 2,143,933, Jan. 16, 1935, Jan. 17, 1939; Br. 428,926, Jan. 30, 1935. In France Jan. 31, 1934 (Comp. Gaz). A constant line width on a picture tube screen is obtained by high-frequency oscillations of small amplitude superimposed on the frame-scanning frequency.

4322 Carlson, W.L. "Television." U.S. 2,041,456, Jan. 31, 1934, May 19, 1936. Assigned: RCA. Refers to modulated picture carriers transmitted simultaneously for pictures and sound on adjacent carrier frequencies in the range of 49 to 55 mc.

4323 I.G. Farben. "Light valve." Br. 450,686, Jan. 22, 1935 In Germany, Jan. 31, 1934. Piezoelectric crystal assembly with electrode gratings for numerous applications, including television.

4324 Kirschstein, F., and J. Lamb. "Fernsehübertragungen mittels Drahtleitungen" [Television transmission by means of wire]. FERN. U. TON. 5 (Feb.): 1-4.

4325 Holst, Gilles, Jan Hendrick de Boer, Marten Cornelis Teves, and Cornelis Frederik Veernemans. "An apparatus for the transformation of light of long wavelength into light of short wavelength." PHYSICA 1 (Feb.): 297-305. Plate, 4 diags. Experiments with photocathodes sensitive to red and infrared, and fluorescent screen emitting visible light. See also Ger. 535,208.

4326 Gernsback, H. "What about television?" RADIO-CRAFT 5 (Feb.): 453.

4327 "Cathode-ray television. After-glow in relation to traversing speed—double time-base circuit—mains unit for supplying potentials to anodes." ELECT. 112 (Feb. 2): 168, 169. 2 diags. Lecture and demonstration by A. Parr and T.W. Price on Jan. 17.

4328 Knoll, M. "Electron tube." U.S. 2,121,356, Feb. 21, 1935, June 21, 1938; Br. 451,590, Feb. 4, 1935. In Germany Feb. 2, 1934 (Telefunken). Vaporized coating of metal on a fluorescent screen.

4329 Blumlein, A.D. "Television." Br. 434,876, Feb. 5, 1934; U.S. 2,134,851, Feb. 16, 1935, Nov. 1, 1938 (EMI). Refers to an auxiliary circuit with phototube to compensate for sudden changes in the general brightness in a camera-tube transmitter for direct pickup or film scanning.

4330 Nicolson, A.M. "Variable speed television." U.S. 2,109,339, Feb. 8, 1934, Feb. 22, 1938. Assigned: Comm. Pats. Includes folded lamp controlled by surrounding magnetic fields for transmitter and receiver.

4331 "Television system operating on velocity modulation principle." ELECT. 112 (Feb. 9): 86. Report on IEE lecture of Feb. 7 by L.H. Bedford and O.S. Puckle.

4332 "New television system. Velocity and intensity modulation combined." W.W. 34 (Feb. 9): 88-91. 5 photos, 6 diags. Full description of the Bedford and Puckle system developed at A.C. Cossor Company's works in North London.

4333 Schlesinger, K. "Wireless television receiver for talking television pictures." U.S. 2,129,034, Feb. 8, 1935, Sept. 6, 1938; Br. 451,670, Feb. 9, 1935. In Germany Feb. 9, 1934 (D.S. Loewe). Intermediate-frequency circuits in a receiver adapted for double-carrier transmissions of sound and vision. Reference to Br. 391,456 (3230).

4334 Schlesinger, K. "Magnetic distortion correcting means for cathode-ray tubes." U.S. 2,224,933, Feb. 8, 1935, Dec. 17, 1940; Br. 451,604, Feb. 9, 1935. In Germany Feb. 9, 1934 (D.S. Loewe). Magnetic or electromagnets mounted around the neck of a tube for neutralizing the earth's field.

4335 Schlesinger, K. "Connection system for television tubes." U.S. 2,144,775, Feb. 9, 1935, Jan. 24, 1939. In Germany Feb. 12, 1934 (D.S. Loewe). Refers to common grounded connections for receiver circuits and picture tube.

4336 Schlesinger, K. "Relaxation oscillator." U.S. 2,152,821, Feb. 9, 1935, Apr. 4, 1939; Br. 446,547, Feb. 11, 1935. In Germany Feb. 12, 1934 (D.S. Loewe). Circuit includes gas tubes and a safety relay to prevent burning of a picture tube screen.

4337 Schlesinger, K. "Television receiver." U.S. 2,226,993, Feb. 9, 1935, Dec. 31, 1940; Br. 451,042, Feb. 11, 1935. In Germany Feb. 12, 1934 (D.S. Loewe). Circuit for selectively amplifying sync signals.

4338 "Cathode-ray television." ELECT. 112 (Feb. 16): 212. Note on the Bedford and Puckle lecture about the A.C. Cossor system.

4339 Baird, J.L., and Baird Television. "Television." Br. 433,552, Feb. 16, 1934. Concerns methods for interlacing sync impulses between successive picture lines, with line sync in the "black" or zero-carrier direction and the picture sync in the "white" direction. References: (711, 3930, 4293).

4340 Denham, Alfred M. "Multiple photo television." U.S. 1,984,466, Feb. 16, Dec. 18, 1934. Scanning disks with multiple slots.

4341 Schlesinger, K. "Detector for television." U.S. 2,141,412, Feb. 13, 1935, Dec. 27, 1938; Br. 452,118, Feb. 15, 1935. In Germany Feb. 16, 1934 (D.S. Loewe). Addition to Br. 435,417 (3874).

4342 Schlesinger, K. "Generating tilting oscillators." U.S. 2,188,288, divided Feb. 16, 1934, Jan. 23, 1940. Assigned: Loewe Radio. Sawtooth generator. Divided from U.S. 2,083,202 (3432).

4343 Baird, J.L., and Baird Television. "Television." Br. 433,720, Feb. 20, 1934. Relates to a variety of means such as disks with spiral slots, mirror disk or prism, oscillating mirror, and mirror drum allied with interlaced scanning and previous specifications. (640, 1529, 2486, 3464)

4344 Henroteau, F.C.P. "Television transmitter." Br. 413,996, Feb. 23, 1934. Concerns a hybrid system with a special multi-electrode phototube revolving shutter, commutator, cathode-ray oscillograph, and a source of ultraviolet light. Features are similar to those in earlier specifications (1884); mention is made of three similar units and that strong images of faint views as in telescopes and microscopes can be obtained.

4345 Marconi's and Arthur James Young. "Circuits for cathode-ray tubes." Br. 434,199, Feb. 23, 1934; U.S. 2,179,11, Feb. 23, 1935, Nov. 7, 1939. Refers to anode modulation of beam intensity with compensating variations in the deflection circuits.

4346 Zworykin, V.K. "Cathode-ray tube." U.S. 2,139,296, Feb. 23, 1934, Dec. 6, 1938. Assigned: RCA. Concave photo-mosaic in a camera tube.

4347 Banks, G.B., and Baird Television. "Cathode-ray tubes." Br. 428,525, Feb. 26, 1934. Electrode structures in high-vacuum and gas-filled tubes.

4348 Stern, Milton M. "Scanning device." U.S. 2,099,872, Feb. 26, 1934. renewed Oct. 19, 1936, Nov. 23, 1937. Mirror drum with combined rotary and transverse motion.

4349 Flory, Leslie E. "Photoelectric device." U.S. 2,045,984, Feb. 28, 1934, renewed Aug. 28, 1935. June 30, 1936. Assigned: RCA. Br. 454,422, Feb. 28, 1935 (Marconi's). Refers to a double-sided mosaic screen with a grid pattern formed of insulated fine-mesh gauze for a camera tube. The apertures (22,500 or 40,000 per square inch) are filled with metal which is then photosensitized on one side. The screen is mounted in the tube with an open-mesh, positive electrode on the optical side, which collects secondary electrons emitted from the photosensitive surface, while the screen is scanned on the other side by the cathode beam.

4350 Holmes, R.S. "Television." U.S. 2,178,234, Feb. 28, 1934, Oct. 31, 1939. Assigned: RCA. Picture tube and circuits.

4351 Hudec, E. "Uber die Plastik von Fernsehbildern bei Trägerfrequenzverstärkung" [On the double image of television pictures at carrier frequency amplification]. E.N.T. 11 (Mar.): 99-109. On the causes of double images.

4352 Hollywood, J.M. and M.P. Wilder. "Television applications of cathode-ray tubes." RADIO N. 15 (Mar.): 538, 539, 566, 567. 2 photos, 3 diags, 2 parts lists. Photocell amplifier.

4353 Fleming, J.A. "Invention in relation to national welfare and legislative control." J. TELEV. SOC. 1 (Mar.): 313-9. Presidential address on Mar. 14. Historical survey of legislation concerned with the telegraph, telephone, and electric lighting in the 19th century, and with the early years of radio. Critical remarks on governmental control of scientific and engineering enterprises, unwise legislation, the role of the General Post and British Broadcasting Corporation, with views on television and its prospects, particularly for educational uses.

4354 "Sixth Annual Report of the Council and Balance Sheet." J. TELEV. SOC. 1 (Mar.): 320-2.

4355 Parr, G., and T.W. Price. "The application of the cathode-ray tube to television." J. TELEV. SOC. 1 (Mar.): 323-8. 3 graphs, 6 diags. Focusing, modulation, characteristics of screen materials, deflection and time-base circuits, power supplies, origin distortion in gaseous tubes, sync methods, advantages of cathode-ray tube receivers. Lecture on Jan. 17.

4356 Windred, G. "Review of the theory and applications of photo-electric effects." J. TELEV. SOC. 1 (Mar.): 329-38. 7 photos, graph. Historical survey from 1817, with many references to contemporary papers and a bibliography of 24 items.

4357 Iams, H.A. "Television receiver." Br. 439,547, Mar. 1, 1934 (Marconi's). Void. Circuits for automatic reinsertion of d-c components in a picture tube receiver. Reference to Br. 395,499 (2964).

4358 "Broadcast television. The case of continuing 30-line transmissions." W.W. 34 (Mar. 2): 1467, 1470. 2 illus. Discussion of the pros and cons of narrow-band (30-line) and wide-band transmissions (yet to come). Picture content, contrast, screen size and aspect ratio, horizontal pictures preferred over the vertical (7:3) in use, program content, subject matter, and transmission times.

4359 "Television: 30-line tests are wanted." W.W. 34 (Mar. 2): 151, 152. 2 photos. Selections from 28 letters among very many received from all over the country.

4360 Scophony and J.H. Jeffree. "Electro-optical light-valves." Br. 439,236, Mar. 3, 1934; U.S. 2,155,659 and 2,155,660, Feb. 27, 1935, Apr. 25, 1939, both divided Mar. 2, 1937. Ultrasonic vibrations set up in a medium contained in a trough produce interference-fringe modulation of light passed through or projected onto the surface of the medium. Various structures, assemblies, and applications are described, particularly scanning and projection with mirror drums for television transmission and reception.

4361 Schlesinger, K. "Television tube." U.S. 2,137,353, Feb. 28, 1935, Nov. 22, 1938; Br. 457,757, Mar. 4, 1935. In Germany Mar. 3, 1934 (D.S. Loewe). Refers to electrode structures in a high-vacuum tube. References (4161, 4218, 4362, 4363).

4362 D.S. Loewe. "Cathode-ray tube." Br. 457,846, Mar. 4, 1935. In Germany Mar. 3, 1934. Divided from above. References to Br. 431,327 (4136), 457,848 (4363).

4363 D.S. Loewe. "Cathode-ray tube." Br. 457,848, Mar. 4, 1935. In Germany Mar. 3, 1934. Divided from Br. 457,757 (4361).

4364 Banfi, A. "I recenti progressi della radiotelevisione" [Recent developments in television]. ELETTROTECNICA 21 (Mar. 5): 144-8. Review, particularly in Germany.

4365 Dowd, Andrew D. "Electro-optical system." U.S. 2,041,822, Mar. 6, 1934, May 26, 1936. Assigned: B.T.L.

4366 Maguire, I.L. "Controlling the signal frequencies in television systems." U.S. 2,169,654, Apr. 26, 1938, Aug. 15, 1939; Br. 451,610, Mar. 5, 1935. In Australia Mar. 6, 1934. Refers to a modulating signal in a receiver obtained from the differential of two signals derived from the simultaneous scanning of two similar areas. Radially slotted disks, a mirror drum, and a cathode-ray tube are mentioned.

4367 Roosenstein, Hans Otto. "Relaxation circuit." U.S. 2,153,158, Mar. 5, 1935, Apr. 4, 1939. In Germany Mar. 6, 1934 (Telefunken).

4368 "Television prospects. Some thoughts on the present position and tendencies." W.W. 34 (Mar. 9): 174, 175. 3 photos, diag. Discussion of the cathode-ray oscillograph, Cossor system, tests of 120-line transmission on 7 m by the Baird Company and by the H.M.V. Company (EMI) at Broadcasting House, use of film and the intermediate film system with mention of the Zworykin iconoscope.

4369 Communication Patents (by W.W. Triggs). "Television transmitter." Br. 425,723, Mar. 10, 1934. Moving arc system. References to Br. 360,941 (2383), 371,612 (2601).

4370 Fernseh A.-G. "Television." Br. 434,873, Mar. 11, 1935. In Germany Mar. 10, 1934. Concerns the emulsion of film and its exposure.

4371 "Baird Television." TIMES (Mar. 12): 23d. Company report to June 30, 1933, financial statement.

4372 Ardenne, M. v. "Discharge apparatus." Br. 439,868, Mar. 12, 1934. Assigned: A.C. Cossor. Void. Concerns the structure of electron tubes, cathode-ray tubes, and circuits, including oscillation generators.

4373 Hardie, K.F., and L.H. Soundy. "Cathode-ray tube." Br. 435,191, Mar. 12, 1934. An electrode behind a cathode modulates the beam intensity without affecting the focus.

4374 D.S. Loewe. "Television." Br. 439,866, Mar. 12, 1934. Void. Receiver circuits for sound and vision transmitted on two adjacent short-wave carriers.

4375 Harding, R. Jr. "Television receiver." U.S. 2,112,528, Mar. 12, 1934. Mar. 29, 1938. Assigned: National Television. Mirror screw, linear light source, optical system.

4376 Harding, R. Jr. "Multiple scanning system." U.S. 2,202,795, Mar. 12, 1934, May 28, 1940. Assigned: National Television. Mirror screw with 1.5 turns.

4377 Banks, G.B., and Baird Television. "Television." Br. 436,650, Mar. 13, 1934. Sync circuit. References to Br. 269,834 (711), 320,639 (1213).

4378 Penning, Frans Michel. "Photoelectric tube." U.S. 2,031,331, Mar. 13, 1935, Feb. 18, 1936 (RCA). In Germany Mar. 14, 1934 (N.V. Philips). With auxiliary secondary emitting electrode.

4379 Schütz, W. "Kathoden-Oszillograph mit kalter Kathode als Fernsehempfänger" [Cathode oscillograph with cold cathode for television receiver]. ARCH. ELEKT. 28 (Mar. 15): 183-94.

4380 "The control of invention. Restricted development of television." TIMES (Mar. 15): 12d. Annual general meeting of the Television Society, Mar. 14, and Prof. Fleming's lecture.

4381 Comp. Gaz. "Television." Br. 439,146, Mar. 9, 1935. In France Mar. 17, 1934. Sync circuit controlled by a periodic voltage derived from the transmitter scanner, such as an apertured disk.

4382 Johnstone, D.M., and Baird Television. "Valve generator." Br. 435,196, Mar. 19, 1934. Saw-tooth oscillator applicable for magnetic or electrostatic deflection.

4383 McGee, J.D., and G.E. Condliffe. "Cathode-ray tubes." Br. 429,854, Mar. 19, 1934; U.S. 2,176,974, Mar. 15, 1935, Oct. 24, 1939 (EMI). Concerns the electrode structures including electron lens in a high-vacuum picture tube with electrostatic or magnetic deflection.

4384 Nicolson, A.M. "Radiating, transformation, and reinforcement system." U.S. 2,153,586, Mar. 20, 1934, Apr. 11, 1939. Assigned: Comm. Pats. Cathode-ray tube and lens adapted for increased velocity in the mid-portions of the scanning paths.

4385 "Televised film. Demonstration to Baird's stockholders." MAN. GUARD. 14 (Mar. 21): 5. Report on address by the Chairman, Sir Harry Greer (1876-1947), transmitted on the new 180/25 ultra-short wave system from the south tower of the Crystal Palace to the company meeting in Film House, Wardour Street. "It is claimed by the company that they are now in a position to supply televisual entertainment from the south tower of the Crystal Palace to ten million people living in and around Greater London. They have been working so far on an experimental license, and now need to obtain a license from the Postmaster-General to give a public service. Receivers can be manufactured at once for the public if a service is inaugurated."

4386 "New television test succeeds in London. Greer is heard and seen by the Baird stockholders in speech he makes 7 miles away." N.Y.T. 12 (Mar. 21): 6.

4387 "Baird Television. A year of progress. Remarkable strides in the invention. Chairman's practical demonstration. Sir Harry Greer on the outlook." TIMES (Mar. 21): 23a, b. Full report of the company meeting. "The Prime Minister and television, Company ready to transmit programmes, the Postmaster-General's visit. A new scheme of development, the accounts, the outlook."

4388 Maloff, I.G. "Electron tube." U.S. 2,104,566, Mar. 21, 1934, Jan. 4, 1938. Assigned: RCA. Cathode-ray tube.

4389 "B.B.C.'s television experiments." MAN. GUARD. 10 (Mar. 23): 6, 7. The Corporation had no statement on Baird's new system, but 30-line transmissions will continue.

4390 Selényi, Paul. "Production of images." U.S. 2,143,214, Mar. 20, 1935, Jan. 10, 1939; Br. 449,824, Mar. 22, 1935. Assigned: Egyesült Izzólámpa és Villamosági Reszveny-Tarsasag. In Hungary Mar. 22, 1934. Pictures and sounds, recorded on an insulating band or film by electrostatic charges produced by a controlled beam of ions, are rendered visible by dusting the surface with powder, which may be fixed with heat or varnish. Applicable to an intermediate film receiver with a scanning disk and mirror drum, and for color with triple scanning and different powders.

4391 Telefunken. "Cathode-ray tubes." Br. 436,189, Mar. 22, 1935. In Germany Mar. 22, 1934. Picture tube with deflection plates and a metal coating on the inner wall.

4392 Tolson, W.A. "Impulse generator." U.S. 2,074,033, Mar. 22, 1934, Mar. 16, 1937. Assigned: RCA. Picture tube receiver circuits with saw-tooth generator.

4393 "Great advance in television." ELECT. 112 (Mar. 23): 390. Favorable comments on the Baird Company transmission from the Crystal Palace to Wardour Street on Mar. 20 and 21. "The company announces its readiness to accept any challenge and to 'deliver the goods' if the necessary facilities are accorded."

4394 "Television. Presidential address on invention in relation to national welfare." ELECT. 112 (Mar. 23): 406. Review of Fleming's address to the Television Society, Mar. 14.

4395 Marconi's and N. Levin. "Scanning device." Br. 435,478, Mar. 23, 1934; U.S. 2,149,449, Mar. 23, 1935, Mar. 6, 1939 (RCA). Application of telephoto lenses with a lens disk or drum.

4396 Marconi's, Wilfrid Earnshaw Benham, and A.J. Young. "Cathode-ray tubes." Br. 435,566, Mar. 24, 1934. Electrode structures and assembly.

4397 Broadway, L.F., and W.F. Tedham. "Cathode-ray tube." Br. 437,594, Mar. 26, 1934; U.S. 2,058,293, Mar. 29, 1935, Oct. 20, 1936 (EMI). Electrode structures and assembly comprising an electron gun.

4398 Broadway, L.F., and W.F. Tedham. "Cathode-ray tube." Br. 435,623, Mar. 26, 1934; U.S. 2,194,380, Mar. 21, 1935, Mar. 19, 1940 (EMI). Tube and modulation circuit. Reference to Br. 431,327 (4136).

4399 Broadway, L.F., W.F. Tedham, and Frederick Hermes Nicoll. "Cathode-ray tube." Br. 435,690, Mar. 26, 1934. Divided from Br. 437,594 (4397). Reference to Br. 417,182 (3876).

4400 Karolus, A "Television." U.S. 2,109,198, Mar. 23, 1935, Feb. 22, 1938. Assigned: RCA. In Germany Mar. 26, 1934. Matrix array of photocells, each with an amplifier in the columns, and a high-speed distributor connecting the rows.

4401 Karolus, A. "Television." U.S. 2,110,576, Mar. 23, 1935, Mar. 8, 1938. Assigned: RCA. In Germany Mar. 26, 1934. Similar to above with lamps.

4402 Bull, Cabot Seaton, and C.S. Agate. "Valve circuits." Br. 435,933, Mar. 27, 1934 (EMI). Receiver circuit for pictures and sound employing special twin-section electron tubes. Reference to Br. 423,932, Aug. 23, 1933 (special electron tube).

4403 Vierl, Hermann. "Scanning device." Br. 459,042, Mar. 27, 1935; U.S. 2,145,562, Mar. 29, 1935, Jan. 31, 1939. In Germany Mar. 27, 1934. A slotted tube containing a photocell or lamp rotates transversely inside a tube filled with a slotted diaphragm, which also rotates. Film scanning and a rotary three-color filter are mentioned.

4404 Kolozsy, Louis W. "Providing television pictures." U.S. 2,103,420, Mar. 28, 1934, Dec. 28, 1937. Assigned: Television and Electric Corp. of America. Mirror screw with transparent enclosure.

4405 Tolson, W.A. "Television." U.S. 2,178,766, Mar. 28, 1934, renewed Apr. 6, Nov. 7, 1939. Assigned: RCA. Picture tube and circuits.

4406 Barthélemy, R. "Controlling cathode beams." Br. 432,856, Mar. 8, 1935; U.S. 2,105,177, Mar. 14, 1935, Jan. 11, 1938. In France Mar. 29, 1934 (Comp. Gaz). Beam deflection circuit, particularly for frame scan.

4407 Marconi's and E.F. Goodenough. "Thermionic valve circuit." Br. 435,815, Mar. 29, 1934; U.S. 2,168,870, Mar. 29, 1935, Aug. 8, 1939 (RCA). Amplifier circuit with Kerr cell.

4408 Marconi's, L.E.Q. Walker, and W.E. Benham. "Television receiving system." Br. 435,814, Mar. 20, 1934; U.S. 2,173,347, Mar. 29, 1935, Sept. 19, 1939 (RCA). Circuit provides area modulation in a picture tube by varying the diameter of the spot while maintaining the beam intensity constant.

4409 Marconi's and A.J. Young. "Thermionic valve circuit." Br. 435,816, Mar. 29, 1934; U.S. 2,172,746, Mar. 29, 1935, Sept. 12, 1939 (RCA). Saw-tooth oscillator.

4410 "High definition television. Baird Company's tests with 180-line scanning." W.W. 34 (Mar. 30): 219. 3 illus. Brief details of apparatus at the Crystal Palace. Picture signals transmitted on 6 m with sound on 6.25 m. Favorable report on a demonstration in Wardour Street of reception on a picture tube 4 feet long with a 12-inch diameter screen, which gave images 8 by 10 inches in a pleasing sepia tone on a cream base.

4411 Schlesinger, K. "Synchronizing method for television." U.S. 2,144,776, Mar. 29, 1935, Jan. 24, 1939; Br. 442,333, Mar. 27, 1935. In Germany Mar. 31, 1934 (D.S. Loewe). Vision signals are transmitted on one ultrashort wave carrier with sound and line-sync on an adjacent carrier. The line-frequency signal, weakened or interrupted at the transmitter at each image change, serves to synchronize the frame scan oscillator in a picture tube receiver with common tuning circuits for vision and sync.

4412 D.S. Loewe. "Cathode-ray tube." Br. 456,331, Mar. 4, 1935. In Germany Mar. 31, 1934. Addition to Br. 423,427 (3513), divided from Br. 457,757 (4361). References to Br. 447,070 (4199), 452,650 (4220).

4413 D.S. Loewe. "Cathode-ray tube." Br. 456,717, Mar. 4, 1935. In Germany Mar. 31, 1934. Addition to Br. 423,427 (3513). Divided from Br. 457,757 (4361).

4414 Vance, A.W. "Electrical apparatus." U.S. 2,124,044, Mar. 31, 1934, July 19, 1938. Assigned: RCA. Film transmission system with disk d-c amplifier, and picture tube.

4415 Moseley, S.A., and H.J.B. Chapple. TELEVISION TO-DAY AND TOMORROW. London: Pitman, 1934. xxxi + 208 pp. Portrait, 70 plates, 56 diags. Foreword by J.L. Baird. Fourth edition, revised from the third (1933). A comprehensive but partisan review of Baird's work from the early days, with descriptions and technical explanations at the popular level. A fifth edition appeared in 1940.

4416 "Myriad dots of light give new television." POP. SCI. 124 (Apr.): 60.

4417 Hollywood, J.M., and M.P. Wilder. "Television with cathode-ray tube." RADIO N. 15 (Apr.): 584, 585, 637-9. 3 photos, 3 diags., parts list. Photo pickup with cathode-ray tube, 60/20 system, wire links in laboratory.

4418 Phinney, E.D. "Television." U.S. 2,146,912, Apr. 3, 1934, Feb. 7, 1939. A system for apartment houses with a scanner and bell at the entrance to each door with receivers.

4419 EMI and C.S. Agate. "Duplex wireless signalling." Br. 437,731, Apr. 5, 1934. Addition to Br. 392,456 (3230). Receiver circuit.

4420 Gray, F. "Electro-optical transmission." U.S. 2,138,577, Apr. 6, 1934, Nov. 29, 1938. Assigned: B.T.L. Disk system and circuits for transmission and reception.

4421 Schlesinger, K. "Television transmitter." U.S. 2,163,215, Apr. 5, 1935, June 20, 1939; Br. 457,879, Apr. 5, 1935. In Germany Apr. 6, 1934 (D.S. Loewe). Concerns a limiting amplifier in which the picture signals control amplification to avoid manual adjustments in transmitting "thin" and "dense" films.

4422 Agate, C.S. "Television receiver." Br. 436,301, Apr. 9, 1934. Cabinet with a mirror bid on which the picture is projected from a nearly-horizontal cathode-ray tube via a lens and mirror.

4423 Schiff, L. "Cathode-ray tube." Br. 439,737, Apr. 9, 1934. Refers to a two-stage focusing method to provide large images, with the focusing coils placed fore and aft of the deflection plates. For transmitting, the fluorescent screen is replaced by photocells on which the picture is focused by a lens.

4424 Schiff, L. "Television." Br. 438,716, Apr. 9, 1934. Divided from above. An image to be transmitted is focused through a side window in a cathode-ray tube onto a photoelectric cathode. The electron image projected from the cathode is then scanned over the end face of the tube containing a pickup electrode.

4425 Johnstone, D.M., and Baird Television. "Valve amplifier." Br. 435,574, Apr. 11, 1934. Relates to a super-regenerative circuit which interrupts the output from a phototube at a high rate to improve the signal-to-noise ratio. Reference to Br. 393,960 (3214).

4426 "Television developments." ELECT. 112 (Apr. 16): 464. Favorable comments on the Baird system.

4427 Blumlein, A.D., and C.O. Browne. "Valve amplifier." Br. 436,734, Apr. 17, 1934. Wideband direct-coupled circuit for phototube.

4428 Scophony, J.H. Jeffree, and G. Wikkenhauser. "Television." Br. 438,424, Apr. 18, 1934. A rotary set of cylindrical lenses and a stationary cylindrical lens provide for scanning in one direction, applicable to motion-picture film. Reference to Br. 328,286 (1542).

4429 Karolus, A. "Television." U.S. 2,136,442, Apr. 8, 1935, Nov. 15, 1938. Assigned: RCA. Br. 441,969, Apr. 11, 1935. In Germany Apr. 19, 1934. Matrix array of lamps with rows connected by a distributor, in which all the points of one line are transmitted simultaneously over separate channels.

4430 Schlesinger, K. "Braun tube for television." U.S. 2,123,160, Apr. 15, 1935, July 5, 1938; Br. 458,401, Apr. 18, 1935. In Germany Apr. 20, 1934 (D.S. Loewe). Addition to Br. 457,846 (4362). Concerns the operation of a gas-filled tube in relation to image size. Three references (3685, 4302, 4362).

4431 Schlesinger, K. "Television receiver." U.S. 2,137,354, Apr. 15, 1935, Nov. 22, 1938; Br. 446,707, Apr. 18, 1935. In Germany Apr. 20, 1934 (D.S. Loewe). Addition to Br. 435,417 (3874). Push-pull detector and sync. References to Br. 445,428 (4141), 446,396 (4167).

4432 Karolus, A. "Television." U.S. 2,136,441, Apr. 8, 1935, Nov. 15, 1938. Assigned: RCA. In Germany Apr. 21, 1934. Viewing panel with matrix of lamp similar to previous patents (4400).

4433 Maloff, I.G. "Television receiver." U.S. 2,077,574, Apr. 21, 1934, Apr. 20, 1937. Assigned: RCA. Picture tube with deflection coils and saw-tooth generator.

4434 G.E.C. and L.C. Jesty. "Television." Br. 429,221, Apr. 23, 1934. Deflection circuits to compensate keystone distortion. Reference to Br. 412,813 (3640).

4435 G.E.C. and L.C. Jesty. "Cathode-ray tubes." Br. 430,534, Apr. 23, 1934. Details of deflection plates.

4436 Urtel, R. "Electric wave generator." U.S. 2,124,719, Apr. 27, 1935, July 26, 1938. In Germany Apr. 23. 1934 (Telefunken).

4437 Ferranti, Maurice Kenyon Taylor, and Sidney Atkinson. "Synchronizing system." Br. 436,896, Apr. 24, 1934, U.S. 2,113,470, Apr. 18, 1935, Apr. 5, 1938. Receiving arrangement for framing an image includes a combined sync motor and wave generator, mixing stage for sync signals, galvanometer, tilting mirror, and optical scanner.

4438 Gettinger, J. "Television." U.S., 2,108,852, Apr. 27, 1934, Feb. 22, 1938. Receiver with scanning drum and recording on film by electric discharges.

4439 Vrabely, T. "Television transmitter." Br. 455,785, Apr. 27, 1935. In Hungary Apr. 27, 1934. Disk system and circuits with photocells and optical parts arranged to synchronously scan separate foreground and background views with supplementary illumination of the later. Reference to Br. 417,282 (3699).

4440 Communication Patents (by W.W. Triggs). "Television." Br. 430,940, Apr. 28, 1934. Refers to a mosaic structure of resonant elements on wires that act as shutters, surrounded by a magnetic coil energized by the picture signals, a lens mosaic, and oscillators. Reference to Br. 360,470 (2065).

4441 Pulvari-Pulvermacher, K. "Electro-optical light-valve." Br. 445,106, Oct. 1, 1934. Convention date Apr. 28, 1934 (Budapest). Addition to Br. 442,381 (4224).

4442 Schlesinger, K. "Amplitude filter." U.S. 2,226,994, Apr. 24, 1935, Dec. 31, 1940; Br. 444,049, Apr. 27, 1935. In Germany Apr. 28, 1934 (D.S. Loewe). Sync separation circuit for a picture tube receiver.

4443 D.S. Loewe. "Television." Br. 460,982, Apr. 27, 1935. In Germany Apr. 28, 1934. Void. Receiver assembly with a magnetic shield between the picture tube and loudspeaker.

4444 Tolson, W.A. "Electrical control apparatus." U.S. 2,165,770, Apr. 28, 1934, July 11, 1939. Assigned: RCA. Picture tube receiver with magnetic deflection and generator circuits.

4445 Vance, A.W. "Television transmitter." Br. 434,936, Apr. 29, 1935 (Marconi's). In U.S. Apr. 28, 1934. Refers to the scanning of motion picture film by the interrupted light spot from a cathode-ray tube.

4446 Zworykin, V.K. "Cathode-ray device." U.S. 2,168,892, Apr. 28, 1934, Aug. 8, 1939. Assigned: RCA. Br. 455,926, Apr. 29, 1935

(Marconi's). Construction and assembly of a picture tube.

4447 Reyner, John Hereward. TELEVISION: THEORY AND PRACTICE. London: Chapman & Hall, 1934. xi + 196 pp., 12 plates, 88 diags. A straightforward and up-to-date review of general principles with a minimum of mathematics. The main chapters cover photocells, the cathode-ray tube, deflection circuits, and receivers for television. Others deal with film and color television, special systems including velocity modulations, trends in Europe and America, and the short wave.

4448 Hollywood, J.M., and M.P. Wilder. "Television receiver design." RADIO N. 15 (May): 664, 665, 702. 3 graphs, 2 diags.

4449 Engstrom, E.W. "A study of television image characteristics." J. SMPE 22 (May): 290-313. See Dec. 1933 (4227).

4450 "Television inquiry." TIMES (May 1): 16g. Postmaster-General's announcement in the House of Commons yesterday that the committee will consist of representatives from the Post Office, BBC, and Department of Scientific and Industrial Research.

4451 Lance, T.M.C., and Baird Television. "Television." Br. 436,809, May 1, 1934. Concerns the generation of sync impulses by auxiliary slots in a scanning disk with a separate light source and phototube, the output from which is later mixed with picture signals. References (711, 2549, 4556).

4452 "Britain will study television system. Plans to adopt either the new Baird invention or 120-line 'higher definition' device." N.Y.T. 23 (May 2): 5. "Sir Kingsley Wood, the Postmaster-General, stated in the House of Commons last night that he hoped soon to announce the composition of the committee and the terms of reference." Mention of Baird's new invention and the 120-line system sponsored by EMI.

4453 "The government and television." ELECT. 112 (May 4): 596. Comment on the Postmaster-General's announcement to set up a committee on the development of television. During the past few months the BBC has been investigating two rival systems: Baird and EMI.

4454 Comp. Gaz. "Television." Br. 435,749, Apr. 29, 1935. In France May 5, 1934. Film scanning by cathode-ray tube with photocell pickup sync with saw-tooth oscillator triggered by an alternator or slotted disk, and feedback from the photocell amplifier to the grid of the cathode-ray tube to compensate for variations in transparency of the film.

4455 "Television as a teacher." N.Y.T. IX, 9 (May 6): 7, 8. On experiments by E.B. Kurtz at station W9Xk, University of Iowa.

4456 Ardenne, M. v. "Cathode-ray tube." Br. 442,500, May 7, 1934. Assigned: A.C. Cossor. Void. A metal image screen is mounted obliquely in the spherical bulb of a hydrogen-filled tube. Distortion due to the angular position of the screen is compensated by the formation and disposition of the deflection plates and by a cathode with an oval emissive surface.

4457 B.T.H. "Photo-electric apparatus." Br. 456,728, May 8, 1935. Convention date May 8, 1934. Relates to electron image tubes of the dissector type, one with a fluorescent screen and another with deflection plates mounted inside a screen for image pickup. Controller references to Farnsworth patents (2548, 2549).

4458 Schlesinger, K. "High-vacuum television tube." U.S. 2,131,192, May 4, 1935, Sept. 27, 1938; Br. 461,235, May 8, 1935. In Germany May 9, 1934 (D.S. Loewe). Electrode construction and arrangement, including electron-optical system, deflection plates, relaxation oscillator, and circuits described in related patents (3513, 4302, 4361, 4362, 4459).

4459 Schlesinger, K. "Television amplifier." U.S. 2,226,995, May 4, 1935, Dec. 31, 1940; Br. 461,177, May 7, 1935. In Germany May 9, 1934 (D.S. Loewe). Circuits to avoid shadow effects in receiver.

4460 D.S. Loewe. "Valve circuits." Br. 456,208, May 8, 1935. In Germany May 9, 1934. Addition to Br. 423,427 (3513).

4461 Wilson, J.C. "Colour television in practise." ELECT. REV. 114 (May 11): 667, 668. Lecture at the Royal Society of Arts.

4462 "Television in colour." ELECT. 112 (May 11): 623. Editorial on Wilson's lecture and problems involved in transmitting colored images with higher definition than 30 lines.

4463 Priess, W.H. "Radiant energy resonant vibrating system." U.S. 2,090,853, May 11, 1934, Aug. 24, 1937. Assigned: International Television Radio. Br. 461,128, May 10, 1935. Assembly details of a compound vibrating mirror for two-dimensional scanning in a transmitter or receiver.

4464 Lubszynski, Hans Gerhard, and Sidney Rodda. "Television." Br. 442,666, May 12, 1934; U.S. 2,244,466, May 4, 1935, June 3, 1941 (EMI). Relates to camera tubes in two forms, one with a single-sided mosaic and the other with a double-sided mosaic, incorporating secondary electron emission from the mosaic plate to increase sensitivity.

4465 "The Television Committee." TIMES (May 15): 8e. In reply to a question by Capt. Cunningham-Reid, Sir Kingsley Wood, Postmaster-General, announced the personnel and terms of reference of the Committee.

4466 "Development of television. The Advisory Committee." TIMES (May 15): 16f. Members: Lord Selsdon, chairman, Sir John Cadman (1877-1941), vice-chairman, Col. A.S. Angwin, N. Ashbridge (1889-1975), O.F. Brown, Sir Charles Douglas Carpendale (1874-1968), F.W. Phillips, J. Varley Roberts. Terms of reference: To consider the development of television, and to advise the Postmaster-General on the relative merits of the several systems and on the conditions under which any public service of television should be provided.

4467 Bedford, A.V. "Television." U.S. 2,178,218, May 18, 1934, Oct. 31, 1939. Assigned: RCA. Br. 434,469, May 20, 1935 (Marconi's). Saw-tooth oscillator circuits in a transmitter with a camera tube employing interlaced scanning, with reference to Ballard (3553).

4468 Hardwick, J., and F. Blythen. "Valve generating circuits." Br. 442,938, May 18, 1934. Describes a combination of impulse generators (blocking oscillators) and saw-tooth oscillators for magnetic deflection and sync in a camera tube and picture tube system. References to Br. 423,685 (4184), 443,012 (4469).

4469 Hardwick, J., and F. Blythen. "Television." Br. 443,012, May 18, 1934. Divided from above. References to Br. 423,685 (4184), 425,220 (4051).

4470 Gray, F. "Scanning system." U.S. 2,284,417, May 19, 1934, May 26, 1942. Assigned: B.T.L. Br. 439,225, May 17, 1935 (E.R.P.). Relaxation oscillators and sync signals in a picture tube receiver with displaced or interleaved line scanning.

4471 "Marconi Company in merger to promote television." N.Y.T. 10 (May 23): 4. Combined with EMI (registered May 22) on an equal-shares basis to develop high definition television. Lord Inverforth, chairman of Marconi's, is chairman; other board members are Marchese Marconi, Alfred Clark, chairman of EMI, Louis Sterling, managing director of EMI, H.A. White, managing director of Marconi's, Isaac Shoenberg (1880-1963), director of research at EMI, and H.R.C. Van de Velde, acting general manager of Marconi's.

4472 "New television company. Marconi-EMI merger." TIMES (May 23): 16g. On the formation of the Marconi-EMI Television Company Ltd. and agreement to develop high-definition television. The company is essentially British in both control and personnel.

4473 Vance, A.W. "Television." U.S. 2,105,870, May 23, 1934, June 18, 1938. Assigned: RCA. Br. 457,135, May 23, 1935 (Marconi's). On the production of deflection impulses from an a-c source with frequency multipliers and dividers applied to interlaced scanning as in Ballard's patent (3553).

4474 Fernseh A.-G. "Cathode-ray tube." Br. 440,087, May 24, 1935. In Germany May 24, 1934. High-vacuum picture tube with electron lenses and electrode structures intended for deflection modulation.

4475 Vance, A.W., and H. Branson. "Television." U.S. 2,147,760, May 24, 1934, Feb. 21, 1939. Assigned: RCA. Br. 434,942, May 24, 1935 (Marconi's). A camera tube with a single-sided mosaic plate has an auxiliary electron gun and anode, the potentials of the latter being adjusted so that the velocity of the auxiliary electrons sprayed onto the photomosaic result in a lowering of secondary electron emission.

4476 Gray, F. "Electro-optical scanning." U.S. 2,109,744, May 26, 1934. Mar. 1, 1938. Assigned: B.T.L. Linear light source, mirror screw, and image screen.

4477 Iams, H.A. "Television transmitting apparatus." U.S. 2,098,390, May 26, 1934, Nov. 9, 1937. Assigned: RCA. Br. 458,750, May 24, 1935 (Marconi's). Scanning voltages produced by saw-tooth generators are controlled in order to scan a selected part of a single-sided mosaic in a camera tube provided with auxiliary deflection coils.

4478 Poch, Waldemar J. "Television receiver." U.S. 2,122,990, May 26, 1934, July 5, 1938. Assigned: RCA. Picture-tube circuit with amplifier.

4479 Dunlap, O.E. Jr. "Television's rumble again echoes in the spring air. What surprises are ahead? Marconi promises one—leaders wonder if 1934 is opportune for television—Radio City to be equipped." N.Y.T. (May 27): 9, 1-3. General discussion.

4480 Marconi's and L.M. Myers. "Electro-optical device." Br. 439,050, May 28, 1934; U.S. 2,164,539, Apr. 25, 1935, July 4, 1939 (RCA). A light-valve for television receivers consisting of quartz laminae with interleaved electrodes.

4481 "Home television held 5 years off. Dr. Baker tells radio engineers at Philadelphia costs would be prohibitive. High power flows found. It creates cross-modulation in European receivers." N.Y.T. 21 (May 29): 8. Comments by Walter R.G. Baker, vice-president and general manager of RCA-Victor Company at IRE annual meeting, May 28-30.

4482 Bedford, A.V. "Television." U.S. 2,192,121, May 29, 1394, renewed June 17, 1938, Feb. 27, 1940. Assigned: RCA. Br. 448,065, May 29, 1935 (Marconi's). Concerns a system with a camera tube controlled by an apertured disk, line-sync generation by another apertured disk, with phototubes and circuits applied for interlaced scanning and d-c insertion. References to Br. 434,496 (3834), 443,699 (3951).

4483 Browne, C.O. "Television." Br. 439,121, May 29, 1934. Interlaced scanning is obtained by triple reflection of light from a rotating mirror to mirror on the inside periphery of a drum.

4484 "Television sent 90 miles in tests. Successful transmission of 'skills' made from radio studios here at Camden. Relay at half-way point. Engineers report result of tests to Institute in session in Philadelphia." N.Y.T. 15 (May 30): 6. Comments by E.W. Engstrom on television development by the RCA-Victor Co.

4485 "The Television Committee." TIMES (May 31): 20d. The Advisory Committee held first meeting on Tuesday, May 29. Notice inviting any society, firm or individual wishing to submit evidence to communicate with the secretary, Mr. J. Varley Roberts.

4486 D.S. Loewe. "Valve generators." Br. 457,101, May 20, 1935. In Germany May 31, 1934. Addition to Br. 423,427 (3513). Saw-tooth generators for line and frame deflection voltages, with amplifiers, and provision for deflecting a cathode ray to prevent damage to the screen during start-up. Includes manual controls for adjusting the picture size and the frequencies. Reference to Br. 426,055 (3660).

4487 Orvin, Lars Jörgen. "Infrared-ray viewing screen." U.S. 2,120,765, May 28, 1935, June 14, 1938; Br. 445,156, May 31, 1935. In Norway May 31, 1934. An image converter contains a photoelectric mosaic with the elements connected to a grid electrode. An infrared image projected onto the mosaic results in a discharge through another electrode in the chamber, which then produces a visible image on a fluorescent screen.

4488 "Television nears technical solution." ELECTRONICS 7 (June): 172, 173. 2 photos. Report by RCA-Victor engineers given at the IRE convention in Philadelphia.

4489 Scholz, W. "Fernsehempfang in Gross-Berlin" [Television reception in Greater Berlin]. FERN. U. TON. 5 (June): 25.

4490 Takayanagi, K., S. Suzuki, and K. Matsuyama. [Study of Ardenne cathode-ray television system.] J. IEE JAPAN 54 (June): 495-500. Experiments with von Ardenne's system employing cathode-ray tubes.

4491 D.S. Loewe. "Cathode-ray tubes." Br. 459,231, May 30, 1935. In Germany June 1, 1934. On the formation of photoelectric mosaic screens for camera tubes. Reference to Br. 407,521 (3310).

4492 Stumpf, F. "Stand des Fernsehens bei der Deutschen Reichpost" [Status of television in the German Post Office]. T.F.T. 23 (June): 133-7. Present situation, technical problems, public opinion, and attitude toward television.

4493 D.S. Loewe. "Television." Br. 444,163, June 2, 1934. Void. Addition to Br. 422,064 (3361). Arrangements to avoid interference between deflection circuits in a picture tube receiver.

4494 Orth, R.T. "Electron tube." U.S. 2,123,957, June 2, 1934, July 19, 1938. Assigned: RCA. Br. 451,451, May 23, 1935 (Marconi's). Methods for constructing cathode-ray tubes with a fluorescent screen or a photoelectric mosaic. Reference to Br. 402,607 (3254).

4495 Dunlap, O.E. Jr. "Television's road to the home is financial riddle. Radio's huge picture puzzle. Television is warned of million-dollar obstacles—some wonder if amateurs hold key to success." N.Y.T. IX 9 (June 3): 1. General discussion on costs and financing, with quotes from lecture by W.R.G. Baker.

4496 "Educators survey television. Advisory Council reports on seeing by radio in schools." N.Y.T. IX 9 (June 9): 1-3. Engineering report of the National Advisory Council on Radio in Education.

4497 "Dr. V.K. Zworykin and the Leibmann Memorial Prize." N.Y.T. IX 9 (June 3): 4, 5. Portrait, text on the Morris Leibmann award presented by the IRE for inventions.

4498 Schwartz, E. "Braun tube." U.S. 2,134,267, June 29, 1935, Oct. 25, 1938. In Germany June 3, 1934 (Fernseh A.-G.).

4499 Hewitt, W.S. "Television." Br. 439,494, June 5, 1934. A slotted band serves as a camera gate for strip exposure of sensitized film for recording, in conjunction with an optical system. Reference to Br. 328,286 (1542).

4500 Schlesinger, K. "Transformer coupling for television amplifiers." U.S. 2,131,193, June 4, 1935, Sept. 27, 1938; Br. 457,773, June 4, 1935. In Germany June 5, 1934 (D.S. Loewe). Interstage circuit. Reference to Br. 446,346 (4167).

4501 D.S. Loewe. "Television." Br. 457,853, June 4, 1935. In Germany June 6, 1934. Refers to the separation of sync and picture signals.

4502 Brüche, E. "Die Braunsche Röhre als Problem der geometrischen Elektronenoptik" [The Braun tube considered as a problem in geometrical electron optics]. ARCH. ELEKT. 28 (June 7): 384-90.

4503 Ardenne, M. v. "Phototube for translation of images." U.S. 2,258,436, June 1, 1935, Oct. 7, 1941. Assigned: Radio Patents. Br. 444,998, June 7, 1935. In Germany June 7, 1934. A straight tube assembly contains an electro-optical system, a photocathode set obliquely at one end, and a fluorescent screen set at the opposite oblique angle at the other end. Several tubes are arranged in cascade via lenses which couple the screen of one tube with the cathode of the next.

4504 D.S. Loewe. "Television." Br. 459,602, June 6, 1935. In Germany June 7, 1934. Addition to Br. 441,761 (3928).

4505 Bedford, A.V. "Television." U.S. 2,137,010, June 9, 1934, Nov. 15, 1938. Assigned: RCA. Br. 458,161, June 11, 1935 (Marconi's). Film transmission, camera tube, and apertured disk, interlaced scan, deflection and sync circuits.

4506 Richardson, H.A. "Television." Br. 425,660, June 9, 1934. The cathode surface of a phototube with a grid and anode is exposed to an optical image and scanned by a light-beam from a disk or mirror drum. Controller reference to Br. 368,705 (2479).

4507 Schlesinger, K. "Highly sensitive cascade amplifiers." U.S. 2,141,413, June 7, 1935, Dec. 27, 1938; Br. 457,803, June 5, 1935. In Germany June 9, 1934 (D.S. Loewe). Circuits and assembly features in a television receiver designed to suppress spurious oscillations and unwanted feedback.

4508 Stocker, A.C. "Electric discharge tube oscillator." U.S. 2,147,114, June 9, 1934, Feb. 14, 1939. Assigned: RCA. Deflection circuit for cathode-ray tube.

4509 "Television Committee." TIMES, (June 11): 14c. Has held several meetings and has made arrangements to hear further evidence.

4510 Krawinkel, G. "Modulator." U.S. 2,093,729, June 8, 1935, Sept. 21, 1937; Br. 440,474, June 11, 1935. In Germany June 11, 1934 (Fernseh A.-G.). Power television transmitter.

4511 Browne, C.O. "Television." Br. 442,668, June 12, 1934. Scanning by a mirror drum and mirror screw adaptable for interlaced scan with a slotted disk or alternative means.

4512 Comp. Gaz. "Cathode-ray tube." Br. 451,303, May 29, 1935. In France June 13, 1934.

4513 Fernseh A.-G. "Cathode-ray tube." Br. 439,414, June 13, 1935. In Germany June 13, 1934. Two electron lenses and deflection plates.

4514 Baird, J.L., and Baird Television. "Television." Br. 438,903, June 14, 1934. Scanning system with mirror drum, oscillating mirror, mirror disk, and lenses adaptable for interlaced scan. References to (1720, 3464, 4208, 4209, 4222, 4343).

4515 Marconi's and R.J. Kemp. "Sweep circuit." Br. 439,813, June 14, 1934; U.S. 2,143,379, June 11, 1935. Jan. 10, 1939 (RCA). Refers to a double-generator employing gaseous discharge tubes for line and frame deflection with sync control applied to magnetic coils around the tubes.

4516 Wilson, J.C., and Baird Television. "Television." Br. 438,533, June 18, 1934. Concerns various methods to obtain an inset view, ghost images, and fading out on colored portion of an object. References to Br. 323,818 (1530), 358,916 (2486).

4517 Starr, Arthur T., and Baird Television. "Receiving system circuits." Br. 439,977, June 19, 1934. Phase-correcting networks for television.

4518 Ives, H.E. "Multichannel television system." U.S. 2,177,256, June 23, 1934, Oct. 24, 1939. Assigned: B.T.L.

4519 Bowman-Manifold, M. "Television." Br. 441,847, June 25, 1934. Sync separation circuit in a picture tube receiver.

4520 Tolson, W.A. "Electrical control apparatus." U.S. 2,108,152, June 26, 1934, Feb. 15, 1938. Assigned: RCA. Saw-tooth oscillator for picture tube.

4521 Iams, H.A. "Cathode-ray apparatus." U.S. 2,146,017, June 27, 1934, Feb. 7, 1939. Assigned: RCA. Picture tube.

4522 Holmes, R.S. "Sound and television receiver." U.S. 2,056,607, June 28, 1934 Oct. 6, 1936. Assigned: RCA. Br. 458,798, June 28, 1935 (Marconi's).

4523 Vance, A.W. "Television." U.S. 2,136,810, June 28, 1934, Nov. 15, 1938. Assigned: RCA. Picture tube receiver circuits.

4524 Zworykin, V.K. "Picture transmitting tube." U.S. 2,201,215, June 28, 1934. May 21, 1940. Assigned: RCA. Camera tube with secondary electron collector.

4525 Wilson, J.C. "Trichromatic reproduction in television." J. ROY. SOC. ARTS 82 (June 29): 841-62. General discussion of principles and systems for color transmission, description of Baird's disk method with color filters, results of color experiments, and problems to be solved.

4526 Soller, Walter. "Television." U.S. 2,243,132, June 30, 1934, renewed Dec. 9, 1938, May 27, 1941. One-half assigned to William H. Woodin Jr. System includes a picture tube receiver.

4527 Jannes, H., and P. Marzin. "Recherches sur la construction des circuits pour courants de haute fréquence" [Researches on the construction of circuits for high frequency]. ANN. POSTES 23 (July): 605-30. Discussion includes television circuits and concentric transmission lines.

4528 Mertz, P., and F. Gray. "A theory of scanning and its relation to the characteristics of the transmitted signal in telephotography and television." B.S.T.J. 13 (July): 464-515. 30 graphs and diag. Mathematical treatment.

4529 Bedford, L.H., and O.S. Puckle. "A velocity modulation television system." J. IEE 75 (July): 63-82, discussion 83-92. Illus. Experimental equipment, circuits, theory, development and operation.

4530 Wright, E.E. "Velocity modulation in television." PROC. PHYS. SOC. 46 (July 1): 512-4.

4531 Ardenne, M. v. "Television." Br. 445,834, July 3, 1934. Assigned: A.C. Cossor. Void. Velocity-modulated system with cathode-ray tube scanning and phototube pickup with picture tube receiver circuits.

4532 Bowman-Manifold, M. "Cathode-ray apparatus." Br. 443,952, July 4, 1934; U.S. 2,176,973, June 1, 1935, Oct. 24, 1939 (EMI). Relaxation oscillators and correction circuits applied to a camera tube to correct distribution due to the angle of the scanning beam on an oblique mosaic screen. Reference to Br. 403,283 (3423).

4533 Browne, C.O. "Television." Br. 440,729, July 4, 1934. Refers to interlaced scanning of sound film by a mirror drum, with motor drives designed to preserve the correct speed relationship between the pictures and sound.

4534 "$200 television sets promised by de Forest." N.Y.T. 20 (July 5): 2. Prediction that receivers costing $200 to $250 will be available within a year.

4535 Farnsworth, P.T. "Oscillation generator." U.S. 2,071,516, July 5, 1934, Feb. 23, 1937; Br. 451,724, July 5, 1935 (Farnsworth Television). Electron multiplier with two facing cathodes, one of which emits secondary electrons, a central ring anode, a surrounding focusing solenoid, and associated tuned circuit. Reference to Br. 450,138 (4139).

4536 McGee, J.D. "Electron discharge apparatus." Br. 443,777, July 5, 1934; U.S. 2,176,221, June 28, 1935, Oct. 17, 1939 (EMI). A secondary emission multiplier tube with a zigzag series of electrodes, with or without magnetic concentrating coils.

4537 Nicolson, A.M. "Line television." U.S. 2,122,750, July 5, 1934, July 5, 1938. Assigned: Comm. Pats. A two-way system with multiple light channels.

4538 Percy, James D., and Baird Television. "Television." Br. 435,637, July 5, 1934. Short radial fins provided on a scanning disk reduce air pressure in an enclosing chamber.

4539 Hogan, J.V.L. "Cathode-ray system." U.S. 2,212,640, July 7, 1934, Aug. 27, 1940. Assigned: Radio Inventions. Cathode-ray tube.

4540 Nicolson, A.M. "Television communicator." U.S. 2,125,006, July 10, 1934, July 26,

1938. Assigned: Comm. Pats. Refers to a telephone and television assembly.

4541 West, A.G.D., and Baird Television. "Television." Br. 439,579, July 10, 1934. Method of processing film in an intermediate storage system. Reference to Br. 412,126, (3749).

4542 Marconi's, B. Levin, and N. Levin. "Electro-optical light-valve." Br. 441,274, July 13, 1934. Kerr cell with heated electrodes to maintain the birefringent element in the nematic phase. Suitable materials are specified.

4543 Schröter, F. "Television scanner." U.S. 2,153,646, July 23, 1935, Apr. 11, 1939; Br. 444,151, July 15, 1935. In Germany July 14, 1934 (Telefunken). A double-ended camera tube contains a photocathode at one end, an electron gun at the other, a signal-storage mosaic, and electron lens. The image, projected line by line onto the cathode, produces emissions which are directed by the lens electrodes onto a line of separate electrodes on the mosaic.

4544 G.E.C. and L.C. Jesty. "Cathode-ray tube." Br. 432,615, July 20, 1934. Picture tube container and mounting.

4545 Schlesinger, K. "Relaxation apparatus." U.S. 2,113,163, July 16, 1935, Apr. 5, 1938; Br. 453,011, July 10, 1935. In Germany July 20, 1934 (D.S. Loewe). Addition to Br. 423,394, (3485).

4546 Bodroux, D., and R. Rivalt. "Sur quelques réceptions lointaines des émissions de radiovision de Londres" [On several long-distance receptions of television broadcasts from London]. C.R. 199 (July 23): 269-71. Continued study from July 17, 1933 (4003).

4547 Ardenne, M. v. "Cathode-ray tube." Br. 446,252, July 23, 1934. Assigned: A.C. Cossor. Void. Addition to Br. 442,500 (4456).

4548 Barthélemy, R. "Photoelectric cell modulator." U.S. 2,155,034, July 17, 1935, Apr. 18, 1939. In France July 23, 1934 (Comp. Gaz).

4549 Telefunken. "Cathode-ray tube." Br. 446,254, July 23, 1934. Void. A tube has an inclined screen with optical characteristics that can be varied by the intensity of a scanning cathode ray. Phosphorescent and fluorescent materials, mica sheet heated by cathode rays, and ultraviolet rays are mentioned.

4550 G.E.C. and L.C. Jesty. "Television." Br. 438,386, July 24, 1934. Deflection circuit. Reference to Br. 421,603 (3512).

4551 Hall, C.P., and H. Flynn, "Television." Br. 441,558, July 25, 1934. Concerns the recording of vision and sound signals in parallel tracks on sensitized film by two beams of modulated light.

4552 "New television receiver without lenses and visible from 3 sides promised in fall." N.Y.T. 21 (July 26): 6, 7. National Television Corporation's mirror drum receiver with a special lamp and spiral reflector that provides an image visible on three sides. Will be ready for manufacturing, "provided suitable television broadcast programs are available on the air."

4553 Wilson, J.C., and Baird Television. "Television." Br. 441,410. July 26. 1934. Interlaced scanning by a mirror drum and another drum in the form of a truncated cone with mirrors in two or more spiral tracks. References (640, 1791, 3464).

4554 Tolson, W.A. "Cathode-ray-tube deflecting circuit." U.S. 2,173,239, July 27, 1934, Sept. 19, 1939. Assigned: RCA. Br. 459,535, July 10, 1935 (Marconi's). Saw-tooth oscillators, sync, and other circuits in a receiver.

4555 C. Lorenz A.-G. "Cathode-ray tube." Br. 445,665, July 19, 1935. In Germany July 20, 1934. Deflection coils, one air-cored and the other iron-cored, for a picture tube.

4556 West, A.G.D., and Baird Television. "Television." Br. 436,108, July 31, 1934. Relates to picture and sync circuits for alternately modulating a carrier wave above and below a datum line. References (711, 761, 1213).

4557 Brolly, A.H. "Television by electronic methods." ELECT. ENG. 53 (Aug.): 1153-60. 2 photos, 11 diags. Full technical description of the Farnsworth system with image dissector, picture tube, and circuits.

4558 "An electron multiplier." ELECTRONICS 7 (Aug.): 242, 243. 3 photos, 2 diags. Farnsworth's amplifier tube for television with two cathodes, central anode ring, and external focusing coil. In a demonstration to the editors of outdoor pickup with a camera using this amplifier, the received picture (270/30) was of considerable brightness. "It was possible to see, distinctly, moving automobiles, and passengers leaving their cars. The swaying leaves of nearby trees could easily be distinguished."

4559 Messner, Maximilian. "Television." U.S. 2,161,305, July 27, 1935, June 6, 1939; Br. 442,408, July 30, 1935. In Germany Aug. 1, 1934 (C. Lorenz A.-G.). Deflection circuits.

4560 "Financial aspects of television." W.W. 35 (Aug. 3): 74, 75. Reference to Baker's remarks in his IRE paper (4481) on probable costs of a television service in the United States and the comparable position and problems in Britain.

4561 Blumlein, A.D., and J.D. McGee. "Television transmitting system." Br. 446,661, Aug. 3, 1934; U.S. 2,182,578, Aug. 2, 1935, Dec. 5, 1939 (EMI). One form of a camera tube has a double-sided mosaic screen with insulated plugs photosensitized on the optical side, a facing ring anode, a fine mesh grid close to the screen on the other side, an electron gun, and magnetic deflection coils. Circuit arrangements are such that the scanning beam has a low velocity, the mosaic screen potential is lowered to that of the cathode, shading effects are reduced, and the efficiency is increased. A tube with a single-sided mosaic is also described. References to Br. 442,666 (4464), 446,664 (4616).

4562 Merdler, L.R., and Baird Television. "Television." Br. 439,652, Aug. 3, 1934. Circuit for maintaining sync signals at a constant level in a receiver.

4563 N.V. Philips. "Fluorescent screens." Br. 441,813, May 21, 1935. Convention date Aug. 4, 1934.

4564 Schlesinger, K. "Television transmitter." U.S. 2,248,548, Aug. 2, 1935, July 8, 1941; Br. 460,709, July 31, 1935. In Germany Aug. 4, 1934 (D.S. Loewe). Film scanning by an apertured disk with auxiliary illumination.

4565 G.E.C. and L.C. Jesty. "Television." Br. 434,905, Aug. 7, 1934. Photocells of a mosaic array on which an image is projected and discharged by a beam of light projected onto a similar set of photocells at the back, corresponding cells being connected in series. References (1884, 2479, 3741, 4344).

4566 Baird, J.L., and Baird Television. "Television." Br. 439,434, Aug. 8, 1934. Spot-light scanning with lenses and an apertured disk, with a spirally slotted disk coacting to produce interlaced scan. Reference (743, 2486, 3464).

4567 D.S. Loewe. "Valve modulating circuits." Br. 450,057, Aug. 2, 1935. In Germany Aug. 9, 1934. For transmitter. Reference to Br. 435,561 (3875).

4568 G.E.C. and D.C. Espley. "Television." Br. 435,639, Aug. 10, 1934. Circuit compensates non-linearity in a picture tube. Reference to Br. 420,065 (3818).

4569 Agate, C.S., and W.S. Percival. "Television." Br. 444,177, Aug. 15, 1934. Picture tube receiver with separate demodulators for picture and sync signals. Reference to Br. 422,824 (3897).

4570 G.E.C., L.C. Jesty, and G.W. Seager. "Cathode-ray tube." Br. 437,624, Aug. 17, 1934. Construction and electrode assembly of a picture tube. Reference to Br. 430,534 (4435).

4571 Brüche, E., and Walter Henneberg. "Deflection of electron beams." U.S. 2,101,669, Aug. 5, 1935, Dec. 7, 1937 (G.E.); Br. 454,460, Aug. 19, 1935 (B.T.-H.). In Germany Aug. 22, 1934 (A.E.G.). Deflection coils with auxiliary solenoid.

4572 Mattke, Charles F. "Electro-optical scanning apparatus." U.S. 2,107,759, Aug. 23, 1934, Feb. 8, 1938. Assigned: B.T.L. Lens disk, apertured screen, and multiple smaller lenses.

4573 "Scientific radio at Olympia. The cathode-ray tube in operation." W.W. 35 (Aug. 24): 156. 2 photos. Display by the Radio Research Board. Referring to higher-definition television (120 or 180 lines) with cathode-ray tubes, the comment is made: "Considerable interest therefore attaches to an exhibit in which the cathode-ray tube effectively makes its first bow to the great British public, and introduces itself in words, pictures, and demonstrations."

4574 "Olympia." W.W. 35 (Aug. 24): 157-80. This stand-to-stand review of the radio exhibits (Aug. 16 to 24) mentions a Baird mirror drum receiver by Bush Radio and three disk receivers by Plew Television, all for 30 lines.

4575 Bray, T.E., and Baird Television. "Television." Br. 439,994, Aug. 24, 1934. Refers to the spot-scanning of motion picture film by a cathode-ray tube and display from a film projector with circuits for beam deflection and speed control. References to Br. 269,834 (711), 320,639 (1213).

4576 Lance, T.M.C., D.W. Pugh, and Baird Television. "Television receiver." Br. 443,031, Aug. 24, 1934. Sync separation circuits. Reference to Br. 320,639 (1213), 436,108 (4556).

4577 Lance. T.M.C., D.W. Pugh, and Baird Television. "Television." Br. 443,032, Aug. 24, 1934. Sync shaping circuit.

4578 Vance. A.W. "Television deflecting circuits." U.S. 2,074,496, Aug. 24, 1934. Mar. 23, 1937. Assigned: RCA. Deflection coils.

4579 "Tennis stars act in new television. Instrument demonstrated at Franklin Institute said to be most sensitive built. Apparatus like a camera." N.Y.T. 14 (Aug. 25): 4, 5. "Principle of system discovered by P.T. Farnsworth, 28, laboratory head."

4580 Gray, F. "Electro-optical image producing device." U.S. 2,141,796, Aug. 25, 1934, Dec. 27, 1938. Assigned: B.T.L. Rotary screw with apertures and lenses, linear and lamp inside.

4581 Reveley, P.V., and Baird Television. "Light-valve." Br. 437,988, Aug. 28, 1934. Refracting prism with Kerr cell.

4582 Wright, E.E., and Baird Television. "Electro-optical light-valve." Br. 441,505, Aug. 28, 1934. Biased Kerr cell. Reference to Br. 375,825 (2854).

4583 Marconi's and A.J. Young. "Cathode-ray tube." Br. 443,730, Aug. 30, 1934; U.S. 2,153,223, Aug. 23, 1935, Apr. 4, 1939 (RCA). Construction of a picture tube.

4584 Bedford, A.V., and R.D. Kell. "Television transmitter." U.S. 2,108,097, Aug. 31, 1934, Feb. 15, 1938. Assigned: RCA. Br. 461,646, Aug. 21, 1935 (Marconi's). Camera tube has an additional cathode and control grid for spraying electrons onto the mosaic screen. External features include three shutter disks, photocells, and amplifiers for controlling the scanning sequence.

4585 Cork, E.C., M. Bowman-Manifold, and C.O. Browne. "Synchronizing means for television." Br. 448,031, Aug. 31, 1934; U.S. 2,192,122, Aug. 30, 1935, renewed Dec. 8, 1939, Feb. 27, 1940 (EMI). Concerns interlaced scanning by a mirror drum, with multiple photocells and circuits to generate suppression pulses and to interrupt the line and frame pulses. References (3951, 4468, 4483, 4644).

4586 Cork, E.C., and M. Bowman-Manifold. "Synchronizing means for television." Br. 448,066, Aug. 31, 1934. Divided from above. References (3951, 4051).

4587 Wilson, J.C., and Baird Television. "Valve generator." Br. 438,285, Aug. 31, 1934. Saw-tooth oscillator with amplitude control.

4588 Chapple, H.J.B. TELEVISION FOR THE AMATEUR CONSTRUCTOR. London: Pitman, 1934. xxiii + 266 pp. 58 photos, 125 diags. Foreword by J.L. Baird. Practical treatment, as in the first edition (3942). There are four chapters on the construction and operation of disk and mirror drum apparatus, and a brief discussion of high-definition television on the ultra-short waves in the final chapter.

4589 "Television progress. Mechanical and cathode ray systems share in television advance." ELECTRONICS 7 (Sept.): 272, 273. Photo. Notes on Zworykin, Farnsworth, Priess, Zillger, Peck, and German intermediate film.

4590 Michelssen, F. "Einige Geschichtspunkte über den Aufbau und Betrieb gasgefüllter Braunscher Röhren für Fernsehzwecke" [Construction and application of gas-filled cathode-ray tubes for television]. HOCH. F. ELEKT. 44 (Sept.): 95-100.

4591 Traub, E.H. "Television at the Berlin Radio Exhibition, 1934." J. TELEV. SOC. 1 (Sept.): 341-51. 32 photos, table of transmitters, receivers, and manufacturers, showing technical features. Report (Oct. 10) on equipment by Fernseh, Tekade, Telefunken, R.P.Z., Loewe, von Ardenne, and the German Broadcasting Co. (R.R.G.). The following summarizes the methods employed. Transmitters: 9 disks, 1 mirror drum, and the Berlin transmitter on 7 meters (von Ardenne). Receivers: 7 picture tubes, 3 mirror screws, 1 disk, 1 mirror drum. Scanning lines: 1 at 90, 1 at 96, 1 at 120, 7 at 180, all with 25 pictures per second. All transmission links were wire, except von Ardenne. Image sizes on picture tubes ranged from 10 by 12 cm to 25 by 30 cm, by mirror screws from 9 by 11 cm to 18 by 22 cm, by disks from 12 by 15 cm to a large-screen display (Fernseh) of 9 by 12 feet. Screen colors of picture tubes were 5 white, 3 sepia, 3 pink, and 1 pale yellow. A notable exhibit was the RRG intermediate film transmitting van for outside broadcasting, made by the Fernseh Company. The writer was impressed by "The enormous amount of money that seems to be available in Germany for television research."

4592 Ruff, H.R. "Recent developments in photoelectric cells and their applications." J. TELEV. SOC. 1 (Sept.): 352-66. 11 photos, 15 diags.

4593 Kurtz, E.G. "Teaching by television." J. TELEV. SOC. 1 (Sept.): 367-9. 6 photos.

4594 "Visit to Berlin." J. TELEV. SOC. 1 (Sept.): 374.

4595 "The Government Advisory Committee on Television." J. TELEV. SOC. 1 (Sept.): 375. Questionnaire sent to Society members in June and replies. The following are some selected responses. Interested in reception for experiments, 55%. 30-line transmissions should be continued, 92%. High-definition transmissions in addition to 30 lines, 84%. Prefer film transmissions with sound, 70%. High-definition transmissions practicable now for home constructors, 31%. The BBC should be solely responsible for transmissions, 38%. Desirable to license private concerns for transmissions, 62%.

4596 "New radios in England feature 'spectrum tuners' and tilted dials." N.Y.T. VIII 11 (Sept. 2): 1. On the exhibition at Olympia, with mention of an advertisement in THE RADIO TIMES by Plew Television Ltd.—"Television is here."

4597 "Germany to try television as a service to the public." N.Y.T. VIII 11 (Sept. 2): 6. Plans for an experimental service (180/25) to be broadcast on microwaves.

4598 "Sound-film is utilized in a television test." N.Y.T. VIII, 11 (Sept. 2): 6. On a 60-line system with a cable link of 10 feet between sets, demonstrated by W.H. Peck in New York.

4599 Blumlein, A.D. "Television." Br. 446,663, Sept. 4, 1934. Amplitude limiter in a picture tube receiver.

4600 Blumlein, A.D. "Amplifier." Br. 448,421, Sept. 4, 1934; U.S. 2,178,985, Aug. 30, 1935, Nov. 7. 1939 (EMI). Chiefly for television.

4601 Henroteau, F.C.P. "Electrical image transmission." U.S. 2,164,520, Sept. 3, 1935, July 4, 1939; Br. 445,413, Sept. 4, 1934. A side-by-side assembly of two tubes, one containing a mosaic screen and an adjacent grid on which an image is projected. the other containing an extension of the lines of the

4602 Schlesinger, K. "Television transmission." U.S. 2,186,931, Aug. 13, 1935, Jan. 9, 1940; Br. 463,863, Aug. 6, 1935. In Germany Sept. 4, 1934 (D.S. Loewe). Interlaced scanning of film with apertured disk and an oscillating glass plate with other lenses in the optical system, which includes an auxiliary light source for generating sync signals, and a phototube pickup.

4603 D.S. Loewe. "Television." Br. 465,184, Aug. 6, 1935. In Germany Sept. 4, 1934. Similar to above, with a double-spiral disk and shutters, one of which produces framing signals.

4604 Wilson, J.C., and Baird Television. "Cathode-ray tube." Br. 443,788, Sept. 5, 1934. Picture tube with a concave-like screen surface.

4605 Ferranti and M.K. Taylor. "Cathode-ray tube." Br. 445,464, Sept. 6, 1934. Refers to a double-sided fluorescent screen in a double-ended tube, with the screen normal to the axis for oblique viewing or inclined for round viewing. The spots produced by the two scanning rays may coincide for brighter images or be displaced for interlacing. Reference to Br. 423,696.

4606 C. Lorenz A.-G. "Television." Br. 446,618, Aug. 30, 1935. In Germany Sept. 7, 1934. Deflection coil circuits.

4607 Baird, J.L., and Baird Television. "Television." Br. 438,989, Sept. 8, 1934. Optical system for a picture tube or mirror drum receiver.

4608 Schlesinger, K. "Television receiver." U.S. 2,226,996, Sept. 6, 1935, Dec. 31, 1940; Br. 466,770, Sept. 5, 1935. In Germany Sept. 8, 1934 (D.S. Loewe). Ripple eliminator circuit connected to the grid of a picture tube.

4609 Browde, Hirsh. "Scanning images." U.S. 2,226,658, Dec. 28, 1936, Dec. 31, 1940; Br. 476,714, Dec. 18, 1936. In U.S.S.R. Sept. 9, 1934. Proposal refers to a tube with a linear grid, which is scanned by a cathode beam. The back of the mosaic is scanned along a transverse line by light from a moving rectilinear lamp.

photoelectric cathode, plates, and other electrodes. An image, either direct or with optical scanning or from moving film, is projected line-by-line onto the cathode. Reference to Br. 453,698 (4846).

4610 Browne, C.O., and EMI. "Television." Br. 444,074, Sept. 12, 1934. Addition to Br. 404,020 (3535). A method for counteracting variations of pickup signal amplitudes with reference to a camera tube and an iris diaphragm operated by a solenoid. References to Br. 442,666 (4464), 446,661 (4561).

4611 "Television in Germany. The progress reviewed from a survey of the apparatus exhibited at the Berlin Radio Show." W.W. 35 (Sept. 14): 235, 236. 5 photos. Brief mention of displays. "The picture brightness has been increased considerably by the use of high-power high-vacuum cathode-ray tubes. The cathode-ray tube is now practically universal, but Tekade still keeps to the mirror screw."

4612 Nicolson, A.M. "Television time system." U.S. 2,114,500, Sept. 15, 1934, Apr. 19, 1938. Assigned: Comm. Pats. A plurality of receivers with a common antenna and selection of one receiver for showing the face of a clock.

4613 Browne, C.O., F. Blythen, and A.D. Blumlein. "Amplifying electrical oscillations." Br. 449,242, Sept. 18, 1934; U.S. 2,190,753, Sept. 14, 1935, Feb. 20, 1949 (EMI). Concerns an improvement on the circuit pertaining to d-c reinsertion (3897), for stabilizing the operation periodically at a fixed datum level. This method referred to as a "clamp," improved transmitter efficiency and that of receivers since the "black-level" remained constant.

4614 Du Mont, A.B. "Cathode-ray tube." U.S. 2,163,256, Sept. 18, 1934, June 20, 1939.

4615 Vance, A.W. "Producing electrical waves." U.S. 2,085,402, Sept. 18, 1934, June 29, 1937. Assigned: RCA. Oscillator circuit for a receiver.

4616 McGee, J.D. "Cathode-ray tube." Br. 446,664, Sept. 20, 1934. A camera tube with a single-sided mosaic screen and adjacent grid, similar to one described in Br. 446,661 (4561). Reference also to Br. 442,666 (4464).

4617 McGee, J.D., and Leonard Klatzow. "Cathode-ray tube." Br. 447,819, Sept. 20, 1934. Divided from Br. 446,664 (above). Concerns a modified construction of a camera tube with a double-sided mosaic screen whereby low-speed secondary emissions restore the potentials of the mosaic elements to a datum level. References to Br. 442,666 (4464), 447,824 (4660).

4618 D.S. Loewe. "Amplifier." Br. 447,312, Sept. 13, 1935. In Germany Sept. 21, 1934. Method for varying the amplification ratio without causing distortion in a picture-frequency circuit.

4619 Schröter, F. "Der Stand des Fernsehens" [The state of television]. V.D.I.Z. 78 (Sept. 22): 1097-1102. Review of cathode-ray tube receivers.

4620 "Sarnoff sees television near." N.Y.T. 14 (Sept. 25): 2. Short piece concerning Sarnoff's views on the future of television.

4621 Baird, J.L., and Baird Television. "Television receiver." Br. 439,771, Sept. 25, 1934. Divided from Br. 430,900 (4110). Refers to various disk and other methods for presenting alternate images a plurality of times in a system employing intermediate film.

4622 Bedford, A.V. "Television transmitting device." U.S. 2,258,728, Sept. 29, 1934, Oct. 14, 1941. Assigned: RCA. In a camera tube with a mosaic screen, an additional photoelectric plate close to but offset from the cathode is illuminated from an external source.

4623 Marconi's and A.J. Young. "Television." Br. 442,582, Sept. 29, 1934. Power supply for a cathode-ray tube.

4624 Vance, A.W. "Circuits for cathode-ray tube." U.S. 2,074,495, Sept. 29, 1934, Mar. 23, 1937. Assigned: RCA. Br. 462,253, Sept. 24, 1935 (Marconi's). Circuit with saw-tooth generator and deflection coils provides a high voltage for the second anode of the tube.

4625 Espenschied, L., and M.E. Strieby. "Systems for wide-based transmissions over coaxial lines." B.S.T.J. 13 (Oct.): 654-79. 4 photos, 14 graphs and diags.

4626 "Television—the transmitter problem and Federal funds." ELECTRONICS 7 (Oct.): 299. Editorial on the cost of transmission, urging that government aid would be beneficial to promote the new industry.

4627 "Television: a survey of present-day systems." ELECTRONICS 7 (Oct.): 300-5. 8 photos, table of representative systems, with technical details, diag. Persons interviewed included W.R.G. Baker, P.T. Farnsworth, I.V.C. Hogan, W.E. Holland, A.F. Murray, W.H. Peck, W.H. Priess, and A. Zillger. Reviews of developments by RCA-Victor Television Laboratories, Philco, Peck Television, International Television, and Hogan.

4628 Farnsworth, P.T. "Television by electron image scanning." J.F.I. 218 (Oct.): 411-44. 5 photos, 4 graphs, 13 diags. Reprint, New York: Arno Press, 1977. Full technical description of image dissector, electron multiplier, picture tube, camera assemblies, and methods of operation.

4629 Nakashima, T., and K. Takayanagi. [Wireless transmission and reception of television.] J. IEE JAPAN 54 (Oct.): 1039, 1040. Experimental 100-line system at Hamamatsu Technical College.

4630 Takayanagi, K., T. Horii, A. Yamashita, and K. Yamaguchi. [Television transmitting apparatus.] J. IEE JAPAN 54 (Oct.): 1040-7. As above.

4631 Kette, A. "Fernsehvorführungen auf der 11. Grossen Deutschen Funkausstellung in Berlin" [Television broadcasts of the 11th Great German radio fair in Berlin]. T.F.T. 23 (Oct.): 251-8. On displays and demonstrations by exhibitors.

4632 Lewis, Harold M., and Madison Cawein. "Television." U.S. 2,052,183, Oct. 5, 1934,

Aug. 25, 1936; Br. 463,318, Sept. 24, 1935 (Hazeltine). Film and sound transmission, transmitter, and receiver circuits, including picture tube. Reference to Br. 468,057 (4635).

4633 Peck, W.H. "Television." U.S. 2,092,953, Oct. 5, 1934, Sept. 14, 1937. Sound-film scanning.

4634 G.E.C. and L.C. Jesty. "Television." Br. 443,896, Oct. 6, 1934. Cathode-ray tube screen with color strips, control electrodes, and circuits applicable for interlaced scanning and stereo reproduction. Reference to Br. 425,267 (3957).

4635 Lewis, H.M. "Television." U.S. 2,118,977, Oct. 8, 1934. May 31, 1938; Br. 468,057, Sept. 24, 1935 (Hazeltine). Void. Saw-tooth generators. Reference to Br. 463,318 (4632).

4636 Francis, Oliver T. "Television." U.S. 2,131,886, Oct. 9, 1934, Oct. 4, 1938. System with camera tube and picture tube.

4637 Schlesinger, K. "Television transmitter." U.S. 2,226,997, Oct. 8, 1935, Dec. 31, 1940; Br. 464,049, Oct. 7, 1935. In Germany Oct. 11, 1934 (D.S. Loewe). Film transmission, apertured disk, optical system, interlaced scan. Reference to Br. 465,184 (4603).

4638 Schlesinger, K. "Propagation of television images." U.S. 2,226,998, Oct. 8, 1935, Dec. 31, 1940; Br. 452,068, Oct. 7, 1935. In Germany Oct. 11, 1934 (D.S. Loewe). A five-wire cable connects extension picture tubes to a receiver.

4639 Baird, J.L., and Baird Television. "Cathode-ray tubes." Br. 440,386, Oct. 13, 1934. Specifies materials for screens to produce light by fluorescence, photophorescence, and incandescence. Reference to Br. 424,632 (4010).

4640 Merdler, L.R., and Baird Television. "Valve generators." Br. 442,686, Oct. 13, 1934. Scanning generators in series, with an amplifier, for supplying deflection plates or coils. Reference to Br. 435,196 (4382).

4641 EMI and M. Bowman-Manifold. "Television." Br. 447,403, Oct. 16, 1934; U.S. 2,137,262, Jan. 30, 1936, Nov. 22, 1938. Addition to Br. 392,383 (3057). Concerns a "black-out" circuit and deflection solenoid for blanking the return trace in a picture tube.

4642 N.V. Philips. "Cathode-ray tubes." Br. 442,411, Aug. 2, 1935. In Holland Oct. 17, 1934. Construction.

4643 Browne, C.O. "Television." Br. 445,912, Oct. 18, 1934. Mirror drum rotating shutter, lamp on disk, mirror, prism, and mask for interlaced scan. The system includes two motors and a motor-generator.

4644 Browne, C.O., E.C. Cork, and M. Bowman-Manifold. "Television." Br. 448,097, Oct. 18, 1934. Divided from Br. 448,031 (4585). Pulse control of sync circuits. Reference to Br. 442,938 (4468),

4645 Marconi's. "Valve generating circuits." Br. 463,255, Sept. 24, 1935. Convention date Oct. 18, 1934. Refers to pulse generators and frequency divides for scanning control and sync.

4646 "Television in Germany; preponderance of cathode-ray equipment at Berlin Radio Show." ELECT. 113 (Oct. 14): 506. Survey of E.H. Traub's paper to the Television Society, Oct. 10.

4647 Fernseh A.-G. "Cathode-ray tubes." Br. 464,637, Oct. 21, 1935. In Germany Oct. 19, 1934. Semicircular magnets compensate for undesired deflections due to external or internal fields. Reference to Br. 451,604 (4334).

4648 Marconi's, H.M. Dowsett, and L.E.Q. Walker. "Television." Br. 445,894, Oct. 19, 1934. Double-image projection and apertured scanning disk with two photocells or neon lamps operative alternatively via a commutator.

4649 Marconi's, H.M. Dowsett, and L.E.Q. Walker. "Television." Br. 445,938, Oct. 19, 1934. Lens drum.

4650 Eaton, Roland D. "Optically reproducing electric impulses." U.S. 2,128,631, Oct. 20,

1934, Aug. 30, 1938. Six assignees. Special tube with an oblique photoelectric cathode plate and resistive screen.

4651 Meyer, Eugene Carl. "Television." U.S. 2,147,452, Oct. 22, 1934, Feb. 14, 1939. Assigned: Richard W. Werner. Scanning with a pair of coacting mirrors.

4652 Stocker, A.C. "Television." U.S. 2,202,171, Oct. 23, 1934, May 28, 1940. Assigned: RCA. Picture tube and circuits for magnetic deflection.

4653 Bowman-Manifold, M., and A.D. Blumlein. "Coil for producing a magnetic field of approximate uniform flux density." Br. 449,533, Oct. 24, 1934; U.S. 2,148,398, Oct. 23, 1935, Feb. 21, 1939 (EMI). Two overlapping coils concentric with the neck of a cathode-ray tube.

4654 McGee, J.D., and George Stanley Percival Freeman. "Television transmitting apparatus." Br. 445,485, Oct. 24, 1934; U.S. 2,149,455, Oct. 23, 1935, Mar. 7, 1939 (EMI). Concerns the construction and processing of a signal plate and mosaic screen in a camera tube.

4655 Nicoll, Frederick Hermes. "Cathode-ray tube." Br. 446,180, Oct. 24, 1934. Construction and assembly of cathode, shield, and other electrodes.

4656 "Television inquiry." TIMES (Oct. 26): 12a. Lord Selsdon and three other members left England yesterday for New York. Members going to Germany next week include O.F. Brown, A.J. Gill, H.L. Kirke, and J.J. Roberts.

4657 Schlesinger, K. "Scanning device." U.S. 2,147,555, Oct. 22, 1935, Feb. 14, 1939; Br., 464,831, Oct. 24, 1935. In Germany Oct. 25, 1934 (D.S. Loewe). Film transmission with apertured disk, lenses, and mirrors.

4658 Schlesinger, K. "Television transmission." U.S. 2,163,216, Oct. 19, 1935, June 20, 1939; Br. 464,483, Oct. 19, 1935. In Germany Oct. 25, 1934 (D.S. Loewe). Double-spiral disk with sync slots, photocell, lenses, prisms, and film; picture tube with a special electrode for return-trace blanking.

4659 Bedford, A.V. "Television." U.S. 2,166,712, Oct. 26, 1934, July 18, 1939. Assigned: RCA. Br. 463,967, Oct. 8, 1935 (Marconi's). Details of a camera tube system with circuits to eliminate uneven shading of the image.

4660 Blumlein, A.D., and Herbert Edward Holman. "Photoelectric screen for cathode-ray tubes." Br. 447,824, Oct. 26, 1934; U.S. 2,143,907, Oct. 10, 1935, Jan. 17, 1939 (EMI). Method of making a screen of metal mesh insulated by a glass coating. Reference to Br. 447,754 (glass coating), 446,661 (4561).

4661 Marconi's, H.M. Dowsett, and R. Cadzow. "Cathode-ray oscillograph." Br. 447,828, Oct. 26, 1934; U.S. 2,116,671, Nov. 22, 1935, May 10, 1938 (RCA). A circuit for a picture tube receiver compensates variations of the spot size due to changes in the beam intensity and boosts picture signals of the higher frequencies.

4662 Traub, E. "Television." Br. 440,055, Oct. 26, 1934. Mirror drum and a set of fixed mirrors with multiple back-and-forth reflections between them, applicable for transmission or reception. References to Br. 419,120 (3717), 425,552 (4106).

4663 D.S. Loewe. "Television." Br. 464,140, Oct. 25, 1935. In Germany Oct. 27, 1934. Camera tube with oblique screen and built-in lens, and external inclined mirrors for trapezoidal projection of an image. Reference to Br. 399,654 (3666).

4664 Tolson, W.A. "Television." U.S. 2,124,478, Oct. 31, 1934, July 19, 1938. Assigned: RCA. Refers to a system with a camera tube and picture tube.

4665 Vance, A.W. "Deflecting circuit." U.S. 2,144,351, Oct. 31, 1934, Jan. 17, 1939. Assigned: RCA. Saw-tooth generator and pulse circuit

4666 Hudec, E. "Die durch die Ablenkfelder in der Braunschen Röhre verursachten Störungen" [Disturbances due to the deflecting fields in a Braun tube]. E.N.T. 11 (Nov.): 376-83. Theoretical study; disturbances in cathode-ray tubes as caused by sweeping fields.

4667 Ardenne, M. v. "Beitrag zur Konstruktion von Braunschen Röhren mit Hochvakuum für Fernseh- und Mesozwecke" [Construction of high-vacuum Braun tubes for television and measurement purposes]. HOCH. ELEKT. 44 (Nov.): 166-73.

4668 Takayanagi, K., A. Yamashita, and K. Yamaguchi. [Television receivers.] JIEE JAPAN 54 (Nov.): 1187-96. Description of experimental receivers including cathode-ray tubes and deflection circuits.

4669 Takayanagi, K., S. Takahashi, and I. Ochial. [Synchronizing system for television.] JIEE JAPAN 54 (Nov.): 1196-1202. Simultaneous transmission of sync and image signals in 100-line system.

4670 Engstrom, E.W. "An experimental television system." PROC. IRE 22 (Nov.): 1241-5. Table, 3 diags. Introduction to the following three papers on tests in Camden, N.J., during the early part of 1933.

4671 Kell, R.D., A.V. Bedford, and M.A.. Trainer. "An experimental television system. Pt. 2: The transmitter." PROC. IRE 22 (Nov.): 1246-65. 10 photos, 3 graphs, 9 diags. Camera tube, circuits, and installation for 180-24 transmissions, including remote pickup and radio relay. Subjects were motion-picture film in addition to studio and outdoor scenes.

4672 Holmes, R.S., W.L. Carlson, and W.A. Tolson. "An experimental television system. Pt. 3: The receivers." PROC. IRE 22 (Nov.): 1266-85. 5 photos, 3 graphs, 14 diags. Description of picture, sound, sync, and deflection circuits; apparatus, installation, and performance.

4673 Young, Charles J. "An experimental television system. Pt. 4: The radio relay link for television signals." PROC. IRE 22 (Nov.): 1286-94. 4 graphs, diag. Description of station and directive antennas used in tests over 86 miles from New York to Camden, N.J., with a relay at Arney's Mount, 23 miles from Camden.

4674 "The latest in television." POP. MECH. 62 (Nov.): 643, 644. 5 photos, German developments.

4675 "Television with telephone planned in Germany." RADIO-CRAFT 6 (Nov.): 263. Photo.

4676 Lippincott, D.K., and H.E. Metcalf. "Cold cathode tube." RADIO ENG. 14 (Nov.): 18, 19. Farnsworth electron multiplier and oscillator.

4677 "Sound movies by television." SCI. AM. 151 (Nov.): 257, 258.

4678 Schlesinger, K. "Television transmitter." U.S. 2,129,035, Nov. 1, 1935, Sept, 6 1938; Br. 465,185, Oct. 31, 1935. In Germany Nov. 2, 1934 (D.S. Loewe). Addition to Br. 465,184, (4603).

4679 Willans, P.W., and Baird Television. "Television." Br. 446,432, Nov. 2, 1934. Sync separator. Reference to Br. 436,108 (4556).

4680 Farnsworth, P.T. "Scanning means." U.S. 2,280,572, Nov. 5, 1934, Apr. 21, 1942. Assigned: Farnsworth Television & Radio. Br. 459,400, Nov. 2, 1935. Refers to oscillator circuits and combined outputs for interlaced scanning and film transmission. Reference to Br. 423,101 (4009).

4681 Farnsworth, P.T. "Projection apparatus." U.S. 2,091,705, Nov. 6, 1934, Aug. 31, 1937. Assigned: Farnsworth Television. Br. 470,092, Nov. 2 1935. Void. Intermittent-feed film projector and camera tube. Reference to U.S. 1,773,980 (850).

4682 Johnstone, D.M., and Baird Television. "Television." Br. 446,585, Nov. 6, 1934. A cylindrical pickup tube contains a photoelectric screen subject to an external scanning beam, an image plate of photosensitized transverse conductors, and an anode connected to an output circuit.

4683 Schlesinger, K. "Television receiving connection system." U.S. 2,196,364, Nov. 1, 1935, Apr. 9, 1940; Br. 465,141, Nov. 2,

1935. In Germany Nov. 6, 1934 (D.S. Loewe). Picture tube with auxiliary electrode, circuit for beam blanking at line frequency, and sync separator.

4684 D.S. Loewe. "Television receiver." Br. 465,094, Oct. 24, 1935. In Germany Nov. 6, 1934. Divided from Br. 464,831 (4657). Picture tube with an inclined fluorescent screen from which the image is projected via lenses and a mirror onto a large screen. Reference to Br. 399,654 (3666).

4685 Broadway, Leonard Francis. "Cathode-ray tube." Br. 451,766, Nov. 8, 1934; U.S. 2,124,270, Nov. 5, 1935, July 19, 1938 (EMI). Describes the formation and disposition of hyperbolic electrodes constituting electron lenses. Reference to Br. 431,327 (4136).

4686 Brüche, E., and Walter Schaffernicht. "Electronic image transmission." U.S. 2,172,726, Nov. 9, 1935, Sept. 12, 1939. In Germany Nov. 9, 1934 (A.E.G.). Image tube with photoelectric cathode, mosaic signal plate, and focusing coil.

4687 Brüche, E., and W. Schaffernicht. "Electronic image tube." U.S. 2,172,727, Nov. 12, 1935, Sept. 12, 1939; Br. 465,966, Nov. 22, 1935 (B.T.-H.). In Germany Nov. 9, 1934 (A.E.G.). Similar to above, with an auxiliary light beam scanning the photoelectric cathode. Reference to Br. 368,705 (2479).

4688 "British Committee here is studying television." N.Y.T. IX 15 (Nov. 11): 2.

4689 N.V. Philips. "Cathode-ray tube." Br. 445,676, Sept. 14, 1935. In Holland Nov. 12, 1934. Safety wire attached to the stem of a picture tube.

4690 D.S. Loewe. "Television." Br. 451,745, Nov. 15, 1935. In Germany Nov. 17, 1934. Concerns interlaced scanning with groups of lines simultaneously transmitted over multiple channels and a cathode-ray tube containing a diaphragm with four apertures and corresponding emissive cathodes.

4691 "England on the television brink, wonders whether to jump first." N.Y.T. IX 13 (Nov. 18): 1, 2. Report on a dinner in Washington, D.C., given by the FCC to honor the members of the Television Committee, which included Lord Selsdon, A.S. Angwin, N. Ashbridge, and F.W. Phillips.

4692 Browne, C.O., J. Hardwick, F. Blythen, and E.L.C. White. "Television transmitting system." Br. 450,675, Nov. 19, 1934; U.S. 2,212,199, Nov. 19, 1935, Aug. 20, 1940 (EMI). Relates to circuits for suppressing spurious signals and processing picture signals from a camera tube. References to Br. 422,658 (3793), 422,906 (3896).

4693 Nicoll, F.H., and EMI. "Modulating means for cathode-ray tubes." Br. 447,493, Nov. 19, 1934; U.S. 2,112,378, Nov. 16, 1935, Mar, 29, 1938. Addition to Br. 431,217 (4137). Arrangement of one or more modulating diaphragms.

4694 D.S. Loewe. "Cathode-ray tube." Br. 466,188, Nov. 15, 1935. In Germany Nov. 20, 1934. Addition to Br. 453,270 (4261). Reference to Br. 425,234 (4100).

4695 Schlesinger, K. "Television tube." U.S. 2,126,287, Nov. 15, 1935, Aug. 9, 1938; Br. 470,496, Nov. 15, 1935. In Germany Nov. 20, 1934 (D.S. Loewe). Electrode assembly in a picture tube comprising parts in other specifications (4302, 4360, 4694).

4696 Schlesinger, K. "Television receiving connection." U.S. 2,226,108, Nov. 20, 1935, Dec. 24, 1940; Br. 463,001, Nov. 18, 1935. In Germany Nov. 22, 1934 (D.S. Loewe). Special receiver tube and circuit operating in a system with blacker than black sync and zero carrier amplitude.

4697 Schlesinger, K. "Relaxation oscillator." U.S. 2,152,822, Nov. 20, 1935, Apr. 4, 1939; Br,. 454,471, Nov. 21, 1935. In Germany Nov. 23, 1934 (D.S. Loewe).

4698 Schlesinger, K. "Ultra-short-wave connection system." U.S. 2,137,355, Nov. 20, 1935, Nov. 22, 1938; Br. 466,124, Nov. 21, 1935. In Germany Nov. 24, 1934 (D.S. Loewe). Superhet circuit for a television receiver.

4699 Dunlap, O.E. Jr. "Science finds television allied with economics. Removing radio's blinders. Baker says new developments improve excellence of television—he justifies delay in giving 'pictures' to the public." N.Y.T. IX 13 (Nov. 25): 1-3. Feature article with comments by W.R.G. Baker.

4700 Rogowski, Walter, and Peter Deserno. "Cathode-ray tube." U.S. 2,196,838, Nov. 19, 1935, Apr. 9, 1940. In Germany Nov. 27, 1934. (C. Lorenz A.-G.).

4701 A.C. Cossor and L.H. Bedford. "Valve circuits." Br. 448,111, Nov. 28, 1934. Sweep generator for electrostatic deflection. References to Br. 423,427 (3513).

4702 Zillger, A. "Scanning drum construction." U.S. 2,112,390, Nov. 28, 1934, Mar. 29, 1938. Assigned: National Television. Mirror screw.

4703 Zillger, A. "Television receiver." U.S. 2,210,745, Nov. 28, 1934, renewed Dec. 19, 1939, Aug. 6, 1940. Assigned: National Television. Radio receiver with tubular discharge lamp and reflector.

4704 "Reproducing televised events. Film record of signals." TIMES (Nov. 29): 19c. Report on Edison Bell's film recording system employing the variable density method. "In the demonstration recently given the reproduced images were of such poor definition as to be almost unrecognizable." Baird's earlier gramophone record disk is mentioned.

4705 Rogowski, W., and P. Deserno. "Television." Br. 445,094, Nov. 15, 1935. In Germany Nov. 29, 1934 (C. Lorenz A.-G.). Focus control of a cathode ray with a solenoid and deflection circuit.

4706 Bedford, A.V. "Picture transmitting system." U.S. 2,173,466, Nov. 30, 1934, renewed Apr. 8, 1938, Sept. 19, 1939. Assigned: RCA. Saw-tooth generator and deflection circuits for camera tube.

4707 Diels, Kurt. "Electron device." U.S. 2,128,639, Jan. 9, 1936, Aug. 40, 1938. In Germany Nov. 30, 1934 (Telefunken). Cathode-ray tube.

4708 Knoll, M. "Mosaic electrode for television tubes." U.S. 2,116,901, Jan. 20, 1936, May 10, 1938. In Germany Nov. 30, 1934 (Telefunken). The mosaic plate, mounted on a flat end of a tube facing a stem through which the optical image is projected, is scanned at an angle from an electron gun in an offset stem.

4709 Schwartz, E. "Wall coating for Braun tubes." U.S. 2,151,992, Apr. 6, 1936, Mar. 28, 1939. In Germany Nov. 30, 1934 (Fernseh A.-G.).

4710 Shorney, A.B. "Discharge apparatus." Br. 445,372, Nov. 30, 1934. Refers to a cellular photoelectric screen for image pickup.

4711 "British Television Commission." ELECTRONICS 7 (Dec.): 392. Photo of group: A.S. Angwin, N. Ashbridge, F.W. Phillips, and Lord Selsdon, with officials of the Philco Radio and Television Corp.

4712 Maloff, I.G., and David William Epstein. "Theory of electron gun." PROC. IRE 22 (Dec.): 1386-1411. 23 graphs and diags. Mathematical and graphical treatment of the various parts and functions based on electron optics.

4713 "New television system uses magnetic lens." POP. MECH. 62 (Dec.): 838, 839. 3 photos. Farnsworth's system.

4714 Bernsley, J.T. "Latest in television." RADIO-CRAFT 6 (Dec.): 330, 331, 358. 8 photos. W.H. Peck's mirror-lens disk and apparatus recently demonstrated with a wire link.

4715 "Experimental television stations." RADIO N. 16 (Dec.): 359. List of 27 stations.

4716 Martin, Louis Claude. "The paraxial equations of electron optics." J. TELEV SOC. 1 (Dec.): 377-83. 10 diags. The refractive index, potential layer lens, axially symmetrical electric field, combined electric and magnets fields, the Smith-Helmholtz relation and others, a few deductions, restrictions, and limitations on the foregoing theory. Bibliography, 9 items.

4717 Hergenrother, Rudolph C. "The Farnsworth electronic television system." J. TELEV.

SOC. 1 (Dec.): 384-8. Photo, 6 diags. Brief technical description.

4718 "Retrospect on television in 1934." J. TELEV. SOC. 1 (Dec.): 388. This brief review mentions systems by Scophony, Cossor, Baird, Farnsworth, RCA; the experimental 180-line service in Germany, advances in cathode-ray tubes, mechanical scanners, and light-valves.

4719 Ives, H.E. "Multiple channel electro-optical image production using mirror helix." U.S. 2,107,153, Dec. 1, 1934. Feb. 1, 1938. Assigned: B.T.L. Mirror screw.

4720 Schlesinger, K. "Television transmitter." U.S. 2,227,000, Nov. 29, 1935, Dec. 31, 1940; Br. 466,508, Nov. 29, 1935. In Germany Dec. 1, 1934 (D.S. Loewe). Refers to an apertured disk and optical system for generating sync signals for film transmission.

4721 D.S. Loewe. "Television transmitter." Br. 466,571, Nov. 29, 1935. In Germany Dec. 1, 1934. Addition to Br. 441,761 (3928). Modification of sync circuit. Reference to Br. 464,049 (4637),

4722 Telefunken. "Cathode-ray tubes." Br. 471,501, Dec. 2, 1935. Void. In Germany Dec. 2, 1934. Focusing electrode and connections.

4723 Traub, E. "Television." Br. 448,238, Dec. 3, 1934. A cabinet assembly contains two mirror drums, stationary mirrors with multiple reflections between them, a light source, modulator, and controls. Modifications for interlaced scanning and color with filters are mentioned. References (3717, 4106, 4662).

4724 D.S. Loewe. "Television receiver." Br. 468,437, Dec. 3, 1935. In Germany Dec. 4, 1934. Arrangement of controls on the rear and front of a receiver cabinet. References to Br. 451,670 (4333), 463,001 (4696).

4725 Ruska, E. "Deflection system for Braun tubes." U.S. 2,139,854, Apr. 6, 1936, Dec. 13, 1938; Br. 466,790, Dec. 4, 1935. In Germany Dec. 4, 1934 (Fernseh A.-G.). Electrode assembly.

4726 Traub, E. "Light-valve." Br. 445,498, Dec. 4, 1934. A right-angled assembly with a prism between a Kerr cell and a Nicoll prism.

4727 Nicoll, F.H., and L.F. Broadway. "Cathode-ray tube." Br. 442,103, Dec. 7, 1934. Electron gun assembly. Reference to Br. 437,594 (4397).

4728 Schlesinger, K. "Regulation of television receivers." U.S. 2,227,001, Dec. 9, 1935, Dec. 31, 1940; Br. 464,492, Dec. 9, 1935. In Germany Dec. 10, 1934 (D.S. Loewe). Automatic gain control with a special rectifier tube. Reference to Br. 464,483 (4658).

4729 Schnabel, W. "Untersuchung von Fluoreszenzmaterialien für Fernseh und katodenoszillographische Zwecke" [Study of fluorescent materials for television and cathode-ray oscillograph purposes]. ARCH. ELEKT. 28 (Dec. 12): 789-97.

4730 Möller, R. "Recording television images." U.S. 2,160,888, Dec. 10, 1935, June 6, 1939. In Germany Dec. 12, 1934 (Fernseh A.-G.). Film recording from a cathode-ray tube.

4731 Ruska, E. "Deflecting device for Braun tubes." U.S. 2,152,363, Dec. 6, 1934, Mar. 28, 1939; Br. 466,826, Dec. 24, 1935. In Germany Dec. 12, 1934 (Fernseh A.-G.). Configuration of deflection plates. Reference to Br. 466,790 (4725).

4732 Batchelor, J.C. "Electron emitter." U.S. 2,146,364, Dec. 13, 1934, Feb. 7, 1939. Cathode-ray tube.

4733 Tolson, W.A. "Deflection device for cathode-ray tube." U.S. 2,074,764, Dec. 15, 1934, Mar. 23, 1937. Assigned: RCA. Magnetic assembly with coils.

4734 Baird, J.L., and Baird Television. "Television." Br. 440,917, Dec. 19, 1934. Disk with wedge-shaped slots to correct curvature and even the scanning gap, applicable to interlacing. Reference to Br. 381,898 (3464).

4735 Baird, J.L., and Baird Television. "Cathode-ray tube." Br. 442,963, Dec. 19, 1934. A screen in a picture tube contains a zigzag array of fine wires for electrically preheating the screen, which is raised to incandescence by the impact of the cathode beam. References (1528, 4011, 4639).

4736 Ruska, E. "Combined deflecting device for cathode-ray tubes." U.S. 2,143,579, Dec. 18, 1935, Jan. 10, 1939. In Germany Dec. 20, 1934. Electromagnetic and electrostatic arrangement.

4737 Urtel, R. "Serrated wave form generator." U.S. 2,135,740, Dec. 20, 1935, Nov. 8, 1938; Br. 470,752, Dec. 20, 1935. In Germany Dec. 20, 1934 (Telefunken). Saw-tooth oscillator for magnetic deflection.

4738 Urtel, R. "Television receiving apparatus." U.S. 2,182,326, Dec. 20, 1935, Dec. 5, 1939. In Germany Dec. 20, 1934 (Telefunken). Picture tube circuit.

4739 Batchelor, J.C. "Forming a fluorescent screen." U.S. 2,199,309, Dec. 21, 9134.

4740 Hickok, Willard H. "Photoelectric device." U.S. 2,047,369, Dec. 21, 1934. July 14, 1936. Assigned: RCA. Br. 467,838, Dec. 23, 1935 (Marconi's). Covers a process for making a mosaic screen of wire mesh and its assembly in a pickup tube.

4741 Marconi's, L.M. Myers, and R. Cadzow. "Television." Br. 449,177, Dec. 21, 1934. Relaxation oscillator circuit combined with a pair of deflecting plates in a cathode-ray tube.

4742 Marconi's, A.J. Young, and L.M. Myers. "Television receiver." Br. 449,176, Dec, 21, 1934. Picture tube with an open-mesh electrode interposed between a fluorescent screen and an electric gun.

4743 Schlesinger, K. "Television transmitter." U.S. 2,199,272, Jan. 22, 1936. Apr. 30, 1940; Br. 472,160, Dec. 17, 1934. In Germany Dec. 21, 1934 (D.S. Loewe). Addition to Br. 465,184 (4603). Adjustable film projector, lens system, and two spiralled disks. References to Br. 464,831 (4657), 465,185 (4678).

4744 Johnstone, D.M., and Baird Television. "Valve generator." Br. 444,133, Dec. 24, 1934. Dual-function circuit generates sawtooth oscillations at line and frame frequencies for magnetic deflection. Reference to Br. 435,196 (4382).

4745 "Television. A forecast of developments." W.W. 35 (Dec. 28): 543. Editorial guesses on the probable outcome of the Television Committee's work: a high-definition service, adoption of a British system under the authority of the BBC, and a patent pool for manufacturers of receivers.

4746 Bower, D. "Television and the cinema. Are the two arts compatible?" W.W. 35 (Dec. 28): 550-2. 3 photos. "Television programmes of the future will depend upon film records for the artistic completeness which would be lacking in direct or 'real life' television."

4747 Scophony and J.H. Jeffree. "Television." Br. 443,393, Dec. 28, 1934. Refers to film scanning by a rotary ring of lenses with an optical system. References to Br. 328,286 (1542), 438,424 (4428).

4748 Stocker, A.C. "Deflecting circuits." U.S. 2,086,926, Dec. 29, 1934, July 13, 1937. Assigned: RCA. Magnetic deflection for cathode-ray tube.

4749 Brüche, E., and O. Scherzer. GEOMETRISCHE ELEKTRONENOPTIK: GRUNDLAGEN UND ANWENDUNGEN [Geometrical electron optics: Fundamentals and applications]. Berlin: J. Springer, 1934. 332 pp., 403 illus. A full theoretical treatment in the first half is followed by practical applications, including the electron microscope and the mass spectrograph.

4750 Caccia, Giacomo. TELEVISIONE. Milan: Songogne, 1934. 351 pp., 304 illus.

4751 Camm, F.J. NEWNES TELEVISION AND SHORT-WAVE HANDBOOK. London: G. Newnes, 1934. 256 pp., 230 illus. A practical treatment intended for the amateur enthusiast and home constructors, with clear explanations of basic theory, excellent diagrams, and numerous photographs of parts, assemblies, and related equipment, primarily on disk and drum apparatus for low-definition reception. With a comprehensive dictionary of television terms, pp. 193-254.

4752 Campbell, N.R., and D. Ritchie. PHOTO-ELECTRIC CELLS: THEIR PROPERTIES, USE, AND APPLICATIONS. London: Pitman, 1934. vii + 219 pp., 69 illus. Third edition.

4753 Kwal, Bernard. LES BASES PHYSIQUES DE LA TELEVISION. [The physical basis of television]. Paris: E. Chiron, 1934. 169 pp., illus.

4754 Thun, R. FERNSEHEN UND BILDFUNK: DIE ALLGEMEINEN GRUNDLAGEN DER GEGENWARTIGE STAND. [Television and facsimile transmission: The general basis and present state]. Stuttgart: Franckh, 1934. 83 pp., 80 illus.

4755 Zworykin, V.K., and E.D.W. Wilson. PHOTOCELLS AND THEIR APPLICATION. New York: John Wiley; London: Chapman & Hall, 1934. xv + 348 pp., 180 illus. Second edition revised, with the chapter on the photocell in television revised and expanded.

CHAPTER 15

RACE FOR SUCCESS: 1935

TABLE 24   CHRONOLOGY: 1935

Date		Entity	Event
Jan.	31	Germany U.K.	Paper by Scholz on a proposed network Television Committee report published
Feb.	5	Baird Co.	Demonstrates 180-line transmission from Crystal Palace
Mar.	16 22	Germany Germany	Report on broadcasting plans Commences public tests with 180/25 images
May	 7 13 29	France RCA Plew Germany	Tests of 60–25 transmissions begun in Paris (WW 463) Sarnoff announces plans for field tests Demonstrates 30-line disk Television recording First television congress, plans for 1936 Olympics
June	6 8 20 20 16	U.K. Peck Farnsworth Baird Co. West	Alexandra Palace selected as site for London station Reports on developments in Montreal Announces contract with Baird Corporation Greer reports on company's activities and facilities Paper on cinema television and cable transmission
July	 30	Cruse Farnsworth	Report on European tour Demonstrates 240/24 images in Philadelphia
Aug.	12 16 25	U.K. Various Royal	Statement on Alexandra Palace and equipment Displays at the Berlin Radio Show Report on television in Germany
Sept.	6 10 11	West EMI BBC	Paper at the British Association meeting in Norwich Image tube with semiconductor elements Final broadcast by the 30-line system
Oct.	4 23	Baird, RCA	Release details of signal wave-Marconi-EMI forms Zworykin demonstrates electron multipliers
Nov.	 17	Telefunken France	Roosenstein describes FE IV receiver Eiffel Tower station (Barthélemy 180-25) opened

TABLE 25   CORPORATE PATENTS

Company	1935
Baird	69
D.S. Loewe	59
EMI	53
RCA	50
Telefunken	50
Marconi's	33
G.E.C.	28
Fernseh A.-G.	25
Farnsworth	23
N.V. Philips	14
Philco	9
C. Lorenz	8
Comp. Gaz	7
Ferranti	7
A.E.G.	6
Bell Telephone Laboratories	6
A.C. Cossor	5
Scophony	4
B.T.-H.	3
Hazeltine	3
Mat. Tel. Soc. Anon.	2
Comp. Thomson-Houston	1
Emyradio	1
Int. Carrier-Call	1
Kapella	1
Kolorama	1
Magnavox	1
Markia	1
Murphy	1
National Television Corporation	1
STC	1
Trutolife	1
Zeiss Ikon	1
	476

BIBLIOGRAPHY: 1935

4756   Du Mont, A.B. "Elimination of distortion in cathode-ray tubes." ELECTRONICS 8 (Jan.): 16, 17. Photo, 6 diags.

4757   "German government aids television." ELECTRONICS 8 (Jan.): 10, 11, 30. 2 photos. "Hitler and Goebbels aim to have Fatherland lead world in new television development."

4758   Scholz, W. "Die rundfunkmässige Verbreitung von Tonbildsendungen auf Ultrakurzen Wellen in Deutschland" [Broadcasting both sound and vision on ultra-short waves]. E.N.T. 12 (Jan.): 3–16. On a proposed method for covering Germany.

4759   Iams, H.A., and Bernard Solzberg. "The secondary emission phototube." PROC. IRE 23 (Jan.): 55–64. Photo, 5 graphs.

4760   "Hitler takes up television." RADIO-CRAFT 6 (Jan.): 392. German plans for a short-wave television network and inexpensive receivers for local reception.

4761   "What 1935 holds forth for television and facsimile." RADIO N. 16 (Jan.): 402, 443. 3 photos. Views of de Forest, Hergenrother, Hogan, Peck, Sarnoff, and Lord Selsdon.

4762   Castro, Cesar A. "Picture transmitter." U.S. 2,133,844, Jan. 2, 1935, Oct. 18, 1938. An electromagnetic assembly with a photocell mosaic.

4763   Schlesinger, K. "Television receiver circuit" U.S. 2,163,217, Dec. 30, 1935, June 20, 1939; Br. 467,916, Dec. 24, 1935. In Germany Jan. 2, 1935 (D.S. Loewe). References (4144, 4158, 4198).

4764   Weiss, G. "Electron multiplier." Br. 471,800, Jan. 8, 1936. In Germany Jan. 8, 1935. Cathode, anode, and intermediate secondary emitting electrodes with electrostatic or magnetic focusing.

4765   Weiss, G. "Electron multiplier." Br. 468,665, Jan. 8, 1936. In Germany Jan. 8, 1935. Divided from above.

4766 Wilson, J.C., and Baird Television. "Television." Br. 446,354, Jan. 8, 1935. Sync circuits for transmitter and receiver.

4767 Schlesinger, K. "Television transmission." U.S. 2,227,002, Jan. 7, 1936, Dec. 31, 1940; Br. 468,505, Jan. 6, 1936. In Germany Jan. 19, 1935 (D.S. Loewe). Picture tube receiver and sync circuits.

4768 Hudec, E. "Die Bildfehler beim Fernsehen mit Braunschen Röhren und ihre Behebung" [Picture defects in television with Braun tubes and their remedies]. E.T.Z. 56 (Jan. 10): 28–32.

4769 Batchelor, J.C. "Electro-optical method and apparatus." U.S. 2,113,973, Jan. 10, 1935, Apr. 5, 1938. Transmission employing three scanners and circuits for combined output.

4770 Cork, E.C., M. Bowman-Manifold, and Charles Leslie Faudell. "Television." Br. 455,375, Jan. 15, 1935; U.S. 2,227,066, Jan. 14, 1936, Dec. 31, 1940 (EMI). Sync separator.

4771 Marconi's and H.M. Dowsett. "Television transmitter." Br. 450,413, Jan. 16, 1935. Refers to a multicell arrangement in which one or more cells or bank of cells are effective in sequence with a spot-light scanner, adaptable for stereoscopic effect.

4772 Marconi's, H.M. Dowsett, and R. Cadzow. "Television receiver." Br. 452,148, Jan. 16, 1935; U.S. 2,166,399, Jan. 30, 1936, July 18, 1939 (RCA). The image on the screen of a picture tube, which fluoresces on the inside toward the cathode, is cast forward by a surrounding mirror onto a ground-glass viewing screen.

4773 Marconi's, R.J. Kemp, and J.J. Mason. "Light-valve." Br. 450,463, Jan. 13, 1935. Multiplate Kerr cell. Reference to Br. 419,072 (3922).

4774 A.C. Cossor and L.H. Bedford. "Cathode-ray tube." Br. 450,940, Jan. 24, 1935. Electrode structures including electron lenses and deflection plates in a high-vacuum tube.

4775 "Television prospects. How the British service may develop." W.W. 36 (Jan. 25): 86, 87. 3 diags. Speculations on the Television Committee's report, forecast of the recommendations, and resumé of current technical possibilities.

4776 Harman, M. "Discharge tube." Br.469,558, Jan. 27, 1936. Convention date Jan. 25, 1935. A scanning beam changes the transparency of smoke particles suspended in a chamber adjacent to a viewing screen. The device is said to be applicable for television.

4777 Marconi's and R.J. Kemp. "Direction finding system." Br. 450,975, Jan. 25, 1935; U.S. 2,150,551, Jan. 21, 1936, Mar. 4, 1939 (RCA). Disk scanner and transparency provide visual signals for assisting airplane landings.

4778 Nicoll, F.H. "Cathode-ray tube." Br. 443,864, Jan. 25, 1935. Electrode structures and circuits.

4779 Schlesinger, K. "Television." U.S. 2,227,004, Jan. 22, 1936, Dec. 31, 1940; Br. 465,775, Jan. 23, 1936. In Germany Jan. 26, 1935 (D.S. Loewe). Refers to an optical arrangement for producing a trapezoidal area from a rectangular area. Reference to Br. 464,831 (4657).

4780 A.C. Cossor and L.H. Bedford. "Valve generator." Br. 451,117, Jan. 29, 1935. Scanning oscillator. Reference to Br. 448,111 (4701).

4781 Koch, W.R. "Signalling system." U.S. 2,118,610, Jan. 29, 1935, May 24, 1938. Assigned: RCA. Simultaneous transmission of pictures and sound.

4782 Malter, Louis. "Electric discharge device." U.S. 2,073,599, Jan. 30, 1935, Mar. 9, 1937. Assigned: RCA. Br. 469,477, Jan. 27, 1936 (Marconi's). Electron multiplier with multiple targets, external magnetic field, electrode construction, processing, and circuits.

4783 Morton, George A. "Discharge apparatus." Br. 471,109, Jan. 27, 1936 (Marconi's). In U.S. Jan. 30, 1935 (RCA). Structure and processing of a double-sided photoelectric mosaic for a camera tube. Reference to Br. 471,137 (4784).

4784 Morton, G.A. "Television transmitting tube." U.S. 2,149,977, Jan. 30, 1935, Mar. 7, 1939. Assigned: RCA. Br. 471,137, Jan. 27, 1936 (Marconi's). Divided from above. Structure and method of forming a double-sided photoelectric mosaic, assembly, and circuits with a camera tube. Reference to Br. 447,819 (4617).

4785 Morton, G.A., and A.W. Vance. "Television transmitting tube." U.S. 2,180,946, Jan. 30, 1935, Nov. 21, 1939. Assigned: RCA. Br. 471,149, Jan. 27, 1936 (Marconi's). Divided from Br. 471,109 (4783). Double-sided mosaic, assembly with other electrodes and circuits.

4786 Schlesinger, K. "Photoamplifier." U.S. 2,054,884, Jan. 30, 1935, Sept. 22, 1936. Divided from U.S. 2,063,195 (3822).

4787 Telefunken. "Television receiver." Br. 453,043, Jan. 30, 1936. In Germany Jan. 30, 1935. Refers to a lens system adjacent to the fluorescent screen, or built in the end face, of a cathode-ray tube, for projecting the image onto a screen.

4788 REPORT OF THE TELEVISION COMMITTEE. London: H.M.S.O., Jan. 31. 27 pp. Appendix I, list of witnesses, names 38 persons and 13 organizations. Other Appendices not printed: II, Notes of evidence; III, Reports on visits to the United States and Germany; IV, Description of television systems examined in Great Britain; V, Details of estimated cost of providing and working the London station. Recommendations included the establishment of a station in London with installations by Baird Television and Marconi-EMI, operating on ultra-short waves with a definition not less than 240 lines and a minimum picture frequency of 25 per second, the appointment of an Advisory Committee, with the BBC as the operating authority. The cost of the service up to the end of 1936 estimated to be £180,000. Reprinted in 8837.

4789 Batchelor, J.C. "System of communication." U.S. 2,140,730, Jan. 31, 1935, Dec. 20, 1938. Television distribution with repeater stations.

4790 Bouwers, Albert. "Electron tube." U.S. 2,179,916, Jan. 11, 1936, Nov. 14, 1939; Br. 455,736, Oct. 22, 1935. In Holland Jan. 31, 1935 (N.V. Philips). Cathode-ray tube.

4791 Soller, W. "Television." U.S. 2,189,843, Jan. 31, 1935, Feb. 13, 1940. Part assigned: W.H. Woodin, Jr. Receiver with cathode-ray tube and vibrating wire control.

4792 Zworykin, V.K. "Electron multiplier." U.S. 2,144,239, Jan. 31, 1935, Jan. 17, 1939. Assigned: RCA. A ring electrode assembly with external magnetic coil.

4793 Walker, R.C., and T.M.C. Lance. PHOTOELECTRIC CELL APPLICATIONS. London: Pitman, 1935. x + 245 pp. 142 illus. Second edition, expanded from the first (3943). Chapter on television pp. 169–86.

4794 [Velocity-modulation television systems.] ANN. POSTES 24 (Feb.): 116–25. Review of history; Ardenne and Cossor.

4795 Heimann, W. "Elektronenoptische Abbildung von Photokathoden als Grundlage für Fernseh-Ubertragung" [Electro-optical images as the basis for reproduction of photocathodes as fundamentals for television transmission]. E.N.T. 12 (Feb.): 68–70.

4796 Angwin, A.S. "Radio telegraphy and radio telephony." J. IEE 76 (Feb.): 177–84. Includes television.

4797 Gernsback, H. "The radio set of 1950." RADIO-CRAFT 6 (Feb.): 458, 493, 494. Diagram. Composite receiver in console with rotatable cathode-ray screen on top and facsimile apparatus inside.

4798 Lyford, Elmore B. "The new Priess television scanner." RADIO N. 16 (Feb.): 467, 509. 2 photos. "Periodic scanner" or vibrating metal mirror by William H. Priess.

4799 "Television's development. Recommendations of Committee of Inquiry. Relations of the B.B.C. and the industry." MAN. GUARD. 6 (Feb.): 2–6. BBC versus private control; Advisory Committee; Waves and stations; Revenue for television; London service this year?; Developing outside broadcasts; Receiving sets; Looking to the future.

4800 "'Sponsored' programmes. Suggested revival of abandoned practice to obtain revenue." MAN. GUARD. 8 (Feb. 1): 1, 2.

4801 "The Television Report." MAN. GUARD. 8 (Feb. 1): 2, 3. Editorial.

4802 "First steps toward public television service. Planning Committee appointed. Station to be broadcasting within few months. B.B.C. and Treasury to bear cost." MAN. GUARD. 9 (Feb. 1): 1, 2.

4803 "British television." N.Y.T. 23 (Feb. 1): 8. On the Committee's Report and plans for regular broadcasts.

4804 "Television. Government action at once." TIMES (Feb. 1): 7c, d. Sir Kingsley Wood, Postmaster-General, comments on the Report of the Television Committee and the steps to be taken in setting up a television station in London later in the year.

4805 "Television. Advice on trial service. Selsdon Committee's Report." TIMES (Feb. 1): 8c e. Outline of the report: Experimental service; Scope of television; Operating authority; Advisory Committee; Choice of system; A patent pool?; Start of services; Extended trial of two systems in London; Programmes; Cost of London station; Reply to objections.

4806 "Television plans. Trial service this year. London test of two systems." TIMES (Feb. 1): 14d. Discussion of highlights of the Advisory Committee's report.

4807 "Television." TIMES (Feb. 1): 15c. Editorial on the Television Committee's report.

4808 "Stock Exchange. Television shares higher." TIMES (Feb. 1): 19c. Baird Television and Marconi-EMI shares rise in value due to news about the government report.

4809 "Scanning in television. An attempt to make better use of the medium waveband." W.W. 36 (Feb. 1): 117. "A proposal to transmit greater definition over important parts of the subject which are in motion and reduce definition over the practically stationary background."

4810 Batchelor, J.C. "Electron tube." U.S. 2,124,224, Feb. 1, 1935, July 19, 1938. Cathode-ray tube.

4811 Brown, William Stewart. "Television." Br. 454,486, Feb. 1, 1935. Assembly of a mosaic screen in a camera tube similar to that described in Br. 445,485 (4654), modified to minimize spurious signals. Reference also to Br. 431,206 (3778), 442,666 (4464).

4812 G.E.C. and L.C. Jesty. "Television." Br. 442,323, Feb. 1, 1935. Receiver cabinet with an inclined sheet of glass in front of the picture tube and a loudspeaker below.

4813 G.E.C. and L.C. Jesty. "Cathode-ray tube." Br. 442,695, Feb. 1, 1935. Mask assembly.

4814 "Television plans rushed in London. 280-foot tower of the Crystal Palace is expected to be used for broadcasts. 25-mile test is clear. Four pioneers in the work are expected to reap fortunes from new entertainments." N.Y.T. 15 (Feb. 2): 7. Isidore Ostrer, J.L. Baird, D. Sarnoff, and I. Shoenberg are mentioned.

4815 "British television speeds move here. Experts say the United States will not lag in race—find problems are different. Federal subsidy urged. Great cost in this country is seen as too burdensome for private capital." N.Y.T. 15 (Feb. 2): Comments by A.N. Goldsmith, E.K. Cohan, and F. Schröter.

4816 "British television." N.Y.T. IV, 8 (Feb. 3): 3, 4. Editorial comments on the size and cost of programs to satisfy so many stations that would be needed in the United States.

4817 Andrieu, Robert. "Oscillation producing system." U.S. 2,139,432, Jan. 30, 1936, Dec. 6, 1938. In Germany Feb. 5, 1935 (Telefunken). Saw-tooth wave generator.

4818 "Television Advisory Committee." TIMES (Feb. 6): 10e. First meeting at the GPO; Lord Selsdon, chairman.

4819 "Television." ELECT. 114 (Feb. 8): 173, 174. Editorial comments on the Selsdon report.

4820 "Future of television. Report of Lord Selsdon's Committee. High-definition London station to be established. Use of two systems." ELECT. 114 (Feb. 8): 177.

4821 "Demonstration of Baird system. Reception of direct and delayed television on 7-metres with 180-line scanning." ELECT. 114 (Feb. 8): 177. Brief report on "a very convincing demonstration" witnessed in the company's offices at 58 Victoria Street (Feb. 5) with transmissions from the Crystal Palace by direct pickup and by the intermediate film method. Two receivers available for immediate production; one with a 6-by-8-inch screen at £50, the other with a 9-by-12-inch screen at £80.

4822 "Report of the Television Committee. Technical recommendations summarized." W.W. 36 (Feb. 8): 142, 143. Photo.

4823 Batchelor, J.C: "Fluorescent structure." U.S. 2,125,599, Feb. 8, 1935, Aug. 2, 1938. Cathode-ray tube.

4824 Fernseh A.-G. "Cathode-ray tube." Br. 470,186, Feb. 10, 1936. In Germany Feb. 8, 1935. Focusing coil assembly inside a tube.

4825 Merdler, L.R., and Baird Television. "Wireless receiver." Br. 444,774, Feb. 8, 1935. Superhet circuit for composite television signals.

4826 Wilson, J.C., and Baird Television. "Television." Br. 451,663, Feb. 8, 1935. Circuits to provide automatic brightness control.

4827 "Television arrives: plans for a London service—Crystal Palace transmitters, and a home receiving set." ILLUS. LONDON NEWS (Feb. 9): 213. 5 photos and text.

4828 Lewis, H.M. "Electric wave generator." U.S. 2,052,184, Feb. 9, 1935, Aug. 25, 1936. Assigned: Hazeltine. Br. 449,743, Jan. 6, 1936. Saw-tooth oscillator, regenerative stage, and sync in a receiver circuit.

4829 Lubszynski, H.G., and J.D. McGee. "Electron discharge device." Br. 455,123, Feb. 9, 1935; U.S. 2,150,980, Apr. 17, 1936, Mar. 21, 1939 (EMI). Divided from Br. 455,085 (4830). Camera tube with a transparent mosaic, separate photoelectric cathode, and ring electrode for collecting secondary electrons from the mosaic screen. References to Br. 442,666 (4464), 444,485 (May 1934).

4830 Lubszynski, H.G., and S. Rodda. "Television." Br. 445,085, Feb. 9, 1935. Addition to Br. 442,666 (4464). Refers to camera tubes with single-sided or double-sided mosaic screens.

4831 "Dawn of television." N.Y.T. IV, 8 (Feb. 10): 6. Editorial in THE DAILY EXPRESS, London. "But do not expect much in your home for a long time yet. This is a miracle, but it is a miracle that will take years to perfect."

4832 Dunlap, O.E. Jr. "England's entry in television race stirs America. Uncle Sam may quicken pace. Britain's acceptance of television challenge finds American research experts equipped for scientific marathon." N.Y.T. VIII, 13 (Feb. 10): 1–3. 2 photos. Feature article on the effect of British plans on television and radio in the United States.

4833 Brüche, E. "Die Grundlagen der engewandten geometrischen Elektronenoptik" [Fundamentals of applied geometrical electron optics]. ARCH. F. ELEKT. 29 (Feb. 11): 79–109. Fundamentals, theory, applications to Braun tube. Extensive bibliography.

4834 Deserno, P. "Ablenkung des Elektronenstrahls und Fleckverzerrung bei der Braunschen Röhre" [Deviation of electron beam and spot distortion in Braun tube]. ARCH. F. ELEKT. 29 (Feb. 11): 139–48.

4835 Rogowski, W., and Franz August Becker. "Cathode-ray tube." U.S. 2,161,316, Feb. 12, 1936, June 6, 1939; Br. 460,477, Feb. 7, 1936. In Germany Feb. 11, 1935 (C. Lorenz A.-G.). Concentrating lens system and control circuit.

4836 Percival, W.S. "Electron multiplier." Br. 451,866, Feb. 12, 1935. Two-electrode tube and circuit.

4837 Nicoll, F.H. "Cathode-ray tube." Br. 452,012, Feb. 13, 1935. Picture tube and circuit for selecting two degrees of deflection sensitivity, and arrangement for camera tube.

4838 Nicoll, F.H. "Cathode-ray tube." Br. 452,125, Feb. 13, 1935. Divided from Br. 452,012. Camera tube. References to Br. 419,452 (3920), 431,327 (4136).

4839 Van den Bosch, François Joseph Gerard. "Cathode-ray tube." Br.444,775, Feb. 13, 1935; U.S. 2,062,538, Jan. 23, Dec. 1, 1936.

4840 Van den Bosch, F.J.G. "Cathode-ray tube." Br. 445,975, Feb. 13, 1935.

4841 Batchelor, J.C. "Luminescent screen." U.S. 2,124,225, Feb. 14, 1935, July 19, 1938. Cathode-ray tube.

4842 Marconi's and A.J. Young. "Oscillation generator." Br. 452,017, Feb. 14, 1935; U.S. 2,155,210, Feb. 3, 1936, Apr. 18, 1939 (RCA). Relaxation oscillator.

4843 Howe, George W.O. "Television: Its progress and present position." ELECT. REV. 116 (Feb. 15): 240.

4844 Batchelor, J.C. "Electro-optical method and apparatus." U.S. 2,203,347, Feb. 15, 1935, June 4, 1940. Camera tube and circuit.

4845 Lippincott, D.K. "Television transmitters." Br. 452,369, Feb. 15, 1935. Relates to a method of single-line scanning with the signal differentiated to correspond to scanning with an infinitely small aperture, applicable to a Farnsworth image dissector or to a scanning disk with auxiliary shutter.

4846 Lippincott, D.K. "Television." Br. 453,698, Feb. 15, 1935. Divided from, and similar to, the above.

4847 Turner, F.S. "Cathode-ray tube." Br. 445,316, Feb. 15, 1935. Picture tube with special luminescent screen and magnetic coils for projection of an enlarged image.

4848 Turner, F.S. "Television." Br. 448,648, Feb. 15, 1935. Picture tube with receiver and sound circuits.

4849 Turner, F.S. "Television." Br. 452,037. Feb. 15, 1935. Image dissector. References (1109, 2548, 2549).

4850 Turner, F.S. "Photoelectric tube." Br. 452,109, Feb. 15, 1935. Divided from above. Image dissector. References as above.

4851 Turner, F.S. "Cathode-ray tube." Br. 452,368, Feb. 15, 1935. Picture tube with incandescent screen for large-image projection. References to Br. 442,963 (4735), and the following.

4852 Turner, F.S. "Cathode-ray tube." Br. 452,406, Feb. 15, 1935. Divided from above. References to Br. 423,696 (3850), 430,809 (4303).

4853 Richardson, H.A. "Television transmitters." Br. 451,959, Feb. 16, 1935. Addition to Br. 425,660 (4506). Camera tube with a photoemissive plate which is scanned by the beam from a cathode-ray tube. Includes mention of an electron multiplier and use for color or stereo.

4854 "From Britain's television report." N.Y.T. VIII 13 (Feb. 17): 4,5. Excerpts.

4855 "No menace seen. William A. Brady welcomes television as a renaissance of the theatre." N.Y.T. VIII, 13 (Feb. 17): 7, 8.

4856 Busse, E. "Cathode-ray apparatus." U.S. 2,188,647, Feb. 15, 1936, Jan. 30. 1940; Br. 474,434, Jan. 24, 1936. In Germany Feb. 18, 1935 (N.V. Philips). Picture tube and circuits.

4857 Graham, George Edward Gordon, and Baird Television. "Television." Br. 444,360, Feb, 19, 1935. Line or picture frequencies automatically changed to correspond with transmitted signals in a picture tube receiver.

4858 Maguire, Irwin Leonard. "Television." U.S. 2,166,313, Feb. 15, 1936, July 18, 1939; Br. 464,366, Feb. 20, 1936. In Australia Feb. 20, 1935. Scanning system with multiple oscillating and rotating reflectors.

4859 Kinne, E. (by E. Michaelis). "Television." Br. 460,741, Feb. 21, 1936. In Germany Feb. 21, 1935. Deflection circuits in a velocity modulated system.

4860 "Cathode-ray television. Explanation of the general principles." W.W. 36 (Feb. 22): 182–4. 8 diags.

4861 "The television transmitter. Where will it be located?" W.W. 36 (Feb. 22): 186, 187. Drawings of a relief model of the London area covering 20 miles, map of field strength from the Baird 10 kw 7 m transmitter at the Crystal Palace.

4862 G.E.C. and B.P. Dudding. "Storage photoelectric device." Br. 445,843, Feb. 22, 1935; U.S. 2,092,206, Feb. 15, 1936, Sept. 7, 1937. Structure of a mosaic screen in a camera tube.

4863 Zeitline, V., A. Zeitline, and V. Kliatchko. "Cathode-ray tube." Br. 472,539, Feb. 21, 1936. In Germany Feb. 22, 1935. Electrode structures and assembly in a picture tube.

4864 "The technique of television: a new scientific 'miracle' enabling fireside 'telescanners' to see distant events." ILLUS. LONDON NEWS (Feb. 23): 306, 307. Diags. and text.

4865 "England looks-in. Television starts quest for a new word to replace 'listener.'" N.Y.T. VIII 13 (Feb. 24): 7, 8. On Baird demonstration from Crystal Palace and discussion of the term "lookers."

4866 Dowing, George Victor. "Multiplex wireless signalling." Br. 450,263, Feb. 25, 1935. Picture tube receiver with two-channel reception for broadcast sound, or pictures and sound with changeover switch.

4867 Nicoll, F.H., and EMI. "Cathode-ray tube." Br. 452,589, Feb. 25, 1935; U.S. 2,153,269, Feb. 25, 1936, Apr. 4, 1939. Addition to Br. 431,327 (4136). Reference to Br. 447,493 (4693).

4868 Schaffernicht, W. "Uber die Umwandlung von Lichtbilden in Elektronenbilder" [Conversion of light pictures into electron images]. Z. PHYS. 93 (Feb. 26): 762–68.

4869 "Television gains reported by RCA. Harbord and Sarnoff assert progress in Europe is not ahead of United States. Service soon unlikely. Future 'home theatre' seen as stimulus to art of stage — laboratories push tests." N.Y.T. 21 (Feb. 27): 5. Remarks by Maj. Gen James A. Harbord, chairman of the board, RCA, and D. Sarnoff.

4870 Schlesinger, K. "Coupling transformer." U.S. 2,152,823, Feb. 24, 1936, Apr. 4, 1939; Br. 465,915, Feb. 26, 1936. In Germany Feb. 26, 1935 (D.S. Loewe). Wide-band amplifier for television receiver. References to Br. 446,346 (4167), 457,773 (4500).

4871 Linder, Ernest G. "Electrical translating device." U.S. 2,228,895, Feb. 28 1935, Jan. 14, 1941. Assigned: RCA. Br. 472,896, Feb. 28, 1936 (Marconi's). Electron multiplier with a series of concentric mesh electrodes and surrounding magnetic coil.

4872 D.S. Loewe. "Television." Br. 462,929, Feb. 26, 1936. In Germany Feb. 28, 1935. Picture tube monitor circuit. References (3586, 3830, 4460).

4873 Morton, G.A., and L.E. Flory. "Electric discharge device." U.S. 2,165,805, Feb. 28, 1935, renewed May 12, 1936, July 11, 1939. Assigned: RCA. Br. 469,488, Feb. 28, 1936 (Marconi's). Electron multiplier. References to Br. 443,777 (4536), 469,477 (4782).

4874 Ogloblinsky, G.N., by V.K. Zworykin, administrator. "Cathode-ray device." U.S. 2,156,769, Feb. 28, 1935, May 2, 1939. Assigned: RCA. Mosaic structure in a camera tube.

4875 Smith, J.P. "Producing electric images." U.S. 2,132, 655, Feb. 28, 1935, Oct. 11, 1938. Assigned: RCA. Camera tube, sawtooth oscillators, frequency dividers, and deflection circuits.

4876 "Text of British television report." ELECTRONICS 8 (Mar.): 76, 77. 2 photos.

4877 "German television receivers." ELECTRONICS 8 (Mar.): 81. 5 photos, TKD and Telefunken, both 180 lines.

4878 Ardenne, M. v. "Zum Fernsehempfang mit Braunscher Röhre" [Television reception with cathode-ray tubes]. HOCH. ELEKT. 45 (Mar.): 73–80.

4879 Besson, P. "Le poste de télévision de Berlin" [The Berlin television station]. ONDE ELECT. 14 (Mar.): 131–9. Telefunken equipment.

4880 Bouwers, A. "The focusing of narrow electron beams in vacuo." PHYSICA 2 (Mar.): 145–54. 4 graphs.

4881 de Forest, L. "Miracles in television." POP. MECH. 63 (Mar.): 322–4, 130A. 7 photos.

4882 "Film television with mirrored lenses." POP. MECH. 63 (Mar.): 421. 5 photos. W.H. Peck apparatus.

4883 [Progress made by the German Post Office during 1934]. T.F.T. 24 (Mar.): 58–66. Includes description of the new 180-line transmissions.

4884 Parr, G., and T.W. Price. "Recent improvements in cathode-ray tubes for television." J. TELEV. SOC. 2 (Mar.): 15–8.

4885 "Television Society. Annual Report." J. TELEV. SOC. 2 (Mar.): 19–21.

4886 "The Selsdon Report." J. TELEV. SOC. 2 (Mar.): 22, 23.

4887 Fleming, J.A. "Short names for television." J. TELEV. SOC. 2 (Mar.): 24.

4888 "Television in Great Britain." SCIENCE 81 (Mar. 1): 220, 221. Report from THE TIMES on the Advisory Television Committee, Baird Television, and EMI.

4889 "Television scanning by cathode ray. Amplification by electron multiplication." W.W. 36 (Mar. 1): 208, 209. 3 photos, 2 diags. Description of Farnsworth's image dissector and electron multiplier.

4890 A.C. Cossor, L.H. Bedford, and Walter Henry Stevens. "Television." Br. 452,730, Mar. 1, 1935. Protective circuit reduces the beam current in the absence of deflection voltages to prevent burning of the fluorescent screen.

4891 Knoll, M. "Electro-optical device." U.S. 2,131,185, Feb. 24, 1936, Sept. 27, 1938; Br. 471,365, Mar. 2, 1936. In Germany Mar 1, 1935. Electron lens, and fluorescent screen which, with lenses and mirrors, serves as an image intensifier.

4892 Schaffernicht, W. "Photoelectric tube." U.S. 2,092,814, Feb. 14, 1936, Sept. 14, 1937; Br. 454,832, Mar. 2, 1936. In Germany Mar. 1, 1935 (A.E.G.). Tube with a concave photocathode magnetic lens, cylindrical anode, and fluorescent screen.

4893 Schlesinger, K. "Television receiving rectifier." U.S. 2,194,571, Feb. 24, 1936, Mar. 26, 1940; Br. 462,416, Feb. 28, 1936. In Germany, Mar. 1, 1935 (D.S. Loewe). Picture tube receiver circuit.

4894 Marconi's, H.M. Dowsett, and L.E.Q. Walker. "Kerr cell." Br. 453,136, Mar. 4, 1935; U.S. 2,147,693, Jan. 25, 1936, Feb. 21, 1939 (RCA). Multi-section assembly with plates connected in series and internal lenses.

4895 Marconi's and Alfred Aubyn Linsell. "Television." Br. 453,135, Mar. 4, 1935; U.S. 2,200,753, Feb. 21, 1936, May 14, 1940 (RCA). Picture tube receiver for vision and sound with super-regenerative circuit.

4896 B.T.-H. "Electron multipliers." Br. 454,133, Mar. 5, 1936. Convention date Mar. 7, 1935. Reference to Br. 381,306 (2580).

4897 A.C. Cossor, L.H. Bedford, and O.S. Puckle. "Multiple wireless signalling." Br. 453,484, Mar. 7, 1935. Two-channel receiver for images and sound.

4898 "Finding a home for London's television station." W.W. 36 (Mar. 8): 234. Photo of Alexandra Palace.

4899 "Components and accessories for television sets. Notes on apparatus at present available for low- and high-definition systems." W.W. 36 (Mar. 8): 243–5. 13 photos. Listing and description of parts available from more than 20 companies, including short-wave receiver components.

4900 G.E.C. and D.C. Espley. "Valve generator." Br. 450,986, Mar. 8, 1935. Saw-tooth oscillator. Reference to Br. 438,285 (4587).

4901 "England is urged to prepare for censorship in television." N.Y.T. VIII 11 (Mar. 10): 1, 2. Speculations by Basil Dean, motion picture producer, in THE DAILY TELEGRAPH (London).

4902 D.S. Loewe. "Light-valves." Br. 471,747, Mar. 9, 1936. In Germany Mar. 11, 1935.

4903 G.E.C. and D.C. Espley. "Multiplex wireless signalling." Br. 445,140, Mar. 11, 1935. Receiver with split circuits for images and sound.

4904 G.E.C. and G.W. Seager. "Cathode-ray tube." Br. 453,496, Mar. 11, 1935. References (3496, 4397, 4398, 4570).

4905 Marconi's and A.A. Linsell. "Television receiver." Br. 453,439, Mar. 11, 1935; U.S. 2,180,944, Jan. 22, 1936, Nov. 21, 1939 (RCA). Picture tube receiver with switch or special electrodes in the tube to provide tuning indication on the screen.

4906 Farnsworth, P.T. "Electron multipliers." U.S. 2,143,262, Mar. 12, 1935, Jan. 10, 1939; Br. 471,399, Mar. 2, 1936. Divided from 471,199.

4907 Farnsworth, P.T. "Image dissectors." U.S. Mar. 12, 1935; Br. 471,492, Mar. 2, 1936. Divided from 471,199.

4908 Schröter, F. "Electron beam converter." U.S. 2,175,573, Mar. 20, 1936, Oct. 10, 1939; Br. 471,913, Mar. 12, 1936. In Germany Mar. 12, 1935 (Telefunken). Refers to a double-ended multi-purpose storage tube with photomosaic screen and two electron guns for speech and television signals.

4909 Knoll, M. "Electron tube." U.S. 2,151,628, Mar. 17, 1936, Apr. 11, 1939. In Germany Mar. 13, 1935 (Telefunken). Cathode-ray tube with metallic wall coating.

4910 Farnsworth Television. "Photoelectric cells." Br. 468,333, Mar. 2, 1936. In U.S. Mar. 13, 1935. Divided from Br. 471,359 (4912). Manufacturing process for an image dissector tube.

4911 Farnsworth Television and R.H. Varian. "Cathode-ray tubes." Br. 463,829, Mar. 2, 1936; U.S. 2,075,378, Mar. 13, 1935, Mar. 30, 1937.

4912 Farnsworth Television and R.H. Varian. "Cathode-ray tubes." Br. 471,359, Mar. 2, 1936. In U.S. Mar. 13, 1935. Divided from Br. 468,333. Methods of processing a photoelectric mosaic in an image intensifier.

4913 Farnsworth Television and R.H. Varian. "Cathode-ray tubes." U.S. 2,056,545, Mar. 13, 1935, Oct. 6, 1936; Br. 471,480, Mar. 2, 1936. Picture tube.

4914 Varian, R.H., and Farnsworth Television. "Means and method of collecting secondary electrons in an image dissector tube." U.S. 2,075,378, Mar. 13, 1935, Mar. 30, 1937.

4915 Varian, R.H., and Farnsworth Television. "Means and method of forming discrete areas." U.S. 2,075,377, Mar. 13, 1935, Mar. 30, 1937.

4916 Varian, R.H., and Farnsworth Television. "Cathode-ray oscilloscope." U.S. 2,153,949, Mar. 13, 1935, Apr. 11, 1939.

4917 Varian, R.H., and Farnsworth Television. "Time-delay oscilloscope." U.S. 2,075,379, Mar. 13, 1935. Mar. 30, 1937.

4918 Knoll, M. "Cathode-ray tube." U.S. 2,147,372, Mar. 14, 1936, Feb. 14, 1939. In Germany Mar. 14, 1935 (Telefunken).

4919 Knoll, M., and J. Schoemilch. "Cathode-ray tube." U.S. 2,195,460, Mar. 14, 1935, Apr. 2, 1940.

4920 Scheppmann, Wilhelm. "Television." U.S. 2,151,942, Mar. 13, 1936, Mar. 28, 1939; Br. 454, 539, Mar. 10, 1936. In Germany Mar. 14, 1935 (C. Lorenz A.-G.). Refers to carrier wave amplitude and sync impulses.

4921 Ardenne, M. v. "The image in a television receiver. Effect of various typical disturbances and faults." W.W. 36 (Mar. 15): 254, 255. 12 photos. Photos show the images obtained from motion picture film received in the laboratory at Lichterfeld via ultra-short wave transmissions from Berlin.

4922 "Germany to offer television service. Broadcasts thrice a week to be available within thirty-mile radius of Berlin. Receiving sets too costly. Practical ones sell at 3500 Marks—programs to include news reels and old movies." N.Y.T. 9 (Mar.16): 5. Plans for two ultra-short wave stations with broadcasts for 2.5 hours beginning at 8 p.m. (1 Mark = 40.45 cents).

4923 Knoll, M. "Arrangement for reflecting of cathode rays." U.S. 2,156,915, Mar. 14, 1936, May 2, 1939. In Germany Mar. 16, 1935 (Telefunken).

4924 Bray, T.E., and Baird Television. "Television receiver." Br. 453,848, Mar. 18, 1935. Film reproduction by cathode-ray tube. Reference to Br. 425,267 (3957).

4925 G.E.C. and D.C. Espley. "Television receiver." Br. 449,822, Mar. 18, 1935. Corrective circuits to eliminate image distortion in a picture tube due to a-c fields.

4926 C. Lorenz A.-G. "Television receiver." Br. 459,260, Mar. 3, 1936. In Germany Mar. 18, 1935. Superhet receiver circuit with screened picture tube.

4927 Merdler, L.R., and Baird Television. "Impedance network." Br. 453,847, Mar. 18, 1935. Filter circuit for television receiver.

4928 Skinner, G.D., and Magnavox. "Television receiver." Br. 448,653, Mar. 18, 1935. Coaxial arrangement of a picture tube and loudspeaker. Reference to Br. 321,043 (1531).

4929 White, E.L.C. "Television." Br.456,650, Mar. 18, 1935; U.S. 2,186,742, Mar. 5, 1936, Jan. 9, 1940 (EMI). Relates to a switching system and network for image and sync signals in selecting two or more camera tubes. References to Br. 448,031 (4585), 450,675 (4692).

4930 G.E.C., D.C. Espley, and G.C. Morris. "Multiplex wireless signalling." Br. 449,205, Mar. 19, 1935. Dual frequency receiver circuit for sound and vision.

4931 Keyston, John Edgar, F.H. Nicoll, and Otto Klemperer. "Electron discharge apparatus." Br. 458,746, Mar. 19, 1935; U.S. 2,123,911, Mar. 31, 1936, July 5, 1938 (EMI). Refers to corrective means, such as special electrodes and circuits, that compensate for deflection distortion due to a sloping mosaic screen or to the effects of deflection plates in a picture tube, applicable also to image dissectors. Reference to Br. 445,094 (4705).

4932 Keyston, J.E., F.H. Nicoll, and O. Klemperer. "Electron discharge apparatus." Br. 458,744, Mar. 19, 1935. Divided from above, same reference.

4933 Batchelor, J.C. "Electro-optical apparatus." U.S. 2,196,691, Mar. 20, 1935, Apr. 9, 1940; Br. 472,173, Mar. 17, 1936. Concerns a type of image dissector employing secondary electron emission for converting and intensifying an infrared image with display on a fluorescent screen.

4934 Blumlein, A.D. "Transmission of electrical signals having a direct current component." Br. 458,585, Mar. 20, 1935; U.S. 2,224,134, Mar. 20, 1936, Dec. 10, 1940 (EMI). Covers a variety of corrective circuits handling picture and sync signals for inserting the last d-c component or to compensate for varying attenuation. References to Br. 422,906 (3896), 422,824 (3897).

4935 Guibiansky, J. "Television." Br. 434,544, Mar. 20, 1935. Assembly of two mirror drums, gearing, and phonic motor.

4936 Klatzow, L. "Photoelectric cathodes." Br. 458,586, Mar. 20, 1935. Method of processing a mosaic screen for a camera tube. Reference to Br. 426,505 (4257).

4937 White, E.L.C. "Generator of electrical oscillations." Br. 455,497, Mar. 21, 1935; U.S. 2,143,397, Mar. 21, 1936, Jan. 10, 1939 (EMI). Concerns various saw-tooth generator circuits.

4938 "High-definition television in Germany. Public tests begin at Berlin 'Funkterm.'" W.W. 36 (Mar. 22): 288, 289. 4 photos. Transmissions of 180/25 images on the ultra-short waves to begin this day. "The ultimate aim of those responsible for broadcasting in National-Socialist Germany is to make it technically possible for every German not only to listen to the speeches of the Führer but also to see him speaking."

4939 "Sound broadcasting and television. A misconception removed." TIMES (Mar. 23): 7d. Television a different service from radio.

4940 Urtel, R. "Television." U.S. 2,200,048, Mar. 17, 1936, May 7, 1940. In Germany Mar. 25, 1935 (Telefunken). Transmission circuit.

4941 G.E.C. and B.P. Dudding. "Television receiver." Br. 445,978, Mar. 26, 1935. A colored and illuminated screen surrounding a picture tube. Reference to Br. 392,869 (3259).

4942 Kell, R.D., and A.V. Bedford. "Television." U.S. 2,293,147, Mar. 26, 1935, Aug. 18, 1942. Assigned: RCA. Br. 456,564, Mar. 26, 1936 (Marconi's). Magnetic deflection circuits for a camera tube.

4943 Urtel, R. "Electron tube system." U.S. 2,153,216, Mar. 17, 1936, Apr. 4, 1939. In Germany Mar. 26, 1935 (Telefunken). Picture tube circuit.

4944 Urtel, R. "Television." U.S. 2,195,103, Mar. 26, 1936, Mar. 26, 1940; Br. 450,303, Mar. 26, 1936. In Germany Mar. 26, 1935 (Telefunken). Circuits for connecting a transmitter to camera equipment at a distant point.

4945 Marconi's, R.J. Kemp, and D.L. Plaistowe. "Radio direction finder." Br. 454,256, Mar. 27, 1935; U.S. 2,155,492, Mar. 27, 1936, Apr. 25, 1939 (RCA). Includes a disc scanning a compass card to provide visual indication to a navigator in a radio beacon system.

4946 Andrieu, R., and Rudolf Schienemann. "Magnetic coil for deviating cathode rays." U.S. 2,227,053, Mar. 26, 1936, Dec. 31, 1940. In Germany Mar. 28, 1935 (Telefunken).

4947 Federmann, W. "Deflection coil." U.S. 2,172,733, Mar. 2, 1936, Sept. 12, 1939.

4948 Schlesinger, K. "Television transmitter." U.S. 2,173,496, Mar. 23, 1936, Sept. 19, 1939; Br. 472,900, Mar. 28, 1936. In Germany Mar. 28, 1935 (D.S. Loewe). Modulation and sync circuits. References to Br. 457,879 (4421), 465,915 (4870).

4949 "Television in Germany." ELECT. 114 (Mar. 29): 398. Note on the high-definition service that began in Berlin Mar. 22. Video on 6.772 m, sound on 7.059 m.

4950 Comp. Gaz. "Television." Br. 462,782, Mar. 20, 1936. In France Mar. 29, 1935. Film transmission by cathode-ray tube scanning with each image framed twice in 1/25 second.

4951 Lance, T.M.C., and Baird Television. "Television." Br. 454,383, Mar. 29, 1935. Circuit for providing signals corresponding to the average brightness in conjunction with an image dissector. References to Br. 368,309 (2548), 368,721 (2549).

4952 Rust, N.M. "Band-pass filter." U.S. 2,161,593, Mar. 26, 1936, June 6, 1939; Br. 454,503, Mar. 29, 1935. Interstage coupling for television frequencies.

4953 Schlesinger, K. "Television receivers." U.S. 2,094,677, Mar. 23, 1936, Oct. 5, 1937; Br. 459,422, Mar. 27, 1936. In Germany Mar. 29, 1935 (D.S. Loewe). Saw-tooth generator and amplifier circuit.

4954 Flory, L.E., and G.A. Morton. "Electric discharge device." U.S. 2,156,625, Mar. 30, 1935, May 2, 1939. Assigned: RCA. Refers to a cathode-ray tube with electromagnetic lens employing a secondary emission.

4955 Painter, William H. "Electric discharge device." U.S. 2,170,663, Mar. 30, 1935, Aug. 22, 1939. Assigned: RCA. Cathode-ray tube.

4956 Traub, E. "Television." Br. 451,297, Mar. 30, 1935. Mirror drum with prisms. References to Br. 425,552 (4106). 440,055 (4662).

4957 Vance, A.W. "Cathode-ray tube deflection circuits." U.S. 2,093,177, Mar. 30, 1935, Sept. 14, 1936. Assigned: RCA.

4958 Zworykin, V.K. "Television." U.S. 2,133,882, Mar. 30, 1935, Oct. 18, 1938.

Assigned: RCA. Camera tube with shutter and d-c amplifier.

4959 Ardenne, M. v. FERNSEHEMPFANG, BAU UND BETRIEB EINER ANLAGE ZUR AUFNAHME DES ULTRA-KURZWELLEN-FERNSEHRUND-FUNKS MIT BRAUNSCHER ROHRE [Television reception. Construction and operation of a cathode-ray tube receiver for the reception of ultra-short wave television broadcasting.] Berlin: J. Springer, 1935. xv + 117 pp. 80 illus. Chapters survey the technical problems, the cathode-ray tube and its operation, power supplies, deflection circuits, sync separators, detectors, superhet receiver and construction, receiver for sound, all with references to the Berlin transmissions of 180/25 at Witzleben. For English translation, see 6570.

4960 Osborn, E.A. TELEVISION FOR YOU; BEING A PRACTICAL GUIDE FOR THE MAN-IN-THE-STREET: TO THE MYSTERIES OF TELEVISION UP-TO-DATE. London: Practical Press, 1935. viii + 78 pp. 13 photos, 14 diags. Includes a rather full summary of the Selsdon report (4788).

4961 Valensi, G. "Le problème de la télévision à grande distance" [The problem of long-distance television]. ANN. POSTES 24 (Apr.): 301–46.

4962 "Der Fernsehbetrieb in Berlin eröffnat" [The television operation in Berlin has opened]. FERN. U. TON. 6 (Apr.): 13–6. Inauguration speeches of Mar. 22.

4963 Möller, R. "Die Fernsehabtaster des Ultrakurzwellensenders Berlin-Witzleben" [The television scanner of the ultra-short wave station, Berlin-Witzleben]. FERN. U. TON. 6 (Apr.): 16–9. Details of the 180-line equipment made by Fernseh A.-G.

4964 "Die Fernsehen in England" [Television in England]. FERN. U. TON. 6 (Apr.): 21–4. Edited translation of the Television Committee's report.

4965 "Neues von Fernsehen. Unmittelbare Uebertragungen mittels Lichtstrahlabtaster" [Television news. Direct transmission by means of spot-light transmitter]. FERN. U. TON. 6 (Apr.): 29. Official communication on the inauguration of the 180-line spot-light transmitter in Berlin.

4966 Engstrom, E.W. "A study of television image characteristics. Pt. 2." PROC. IRE 23 (Apr.): 295–310. 9 graphs, 2 diags. Determination of frame frequency in terms of flicker characteristics. Also J. TELEV. SOC. 2 (June): 44–51.

4967 "New-type cable aids television." RADIO-CRAFT 6 (Apr.): 583. Photo. Bell Labs coaxial cable.

4968 Schrage, Wilhelm E. "A modern picture of television." RADIO-CRAFT 6 (Apr.): 589, 628. 3 photos. General discussion.

4969 Howe, G.W.O. "Broadcasting of sound and vision on ultra-short waves." W. ENG. 12 (Apr.): 177, 178.

4970 Vance, A.W. "Valve generator." Br. 442,334, Apr. 1 (Marconi's). Saw-tooth generator and magnetic deflection circuit.

4971 Vance, A.W. "Amplifier." Br. 454,511, Apr. 1 (Marconi's). Refers to a d-c amplifier and sync circuits with a disk scanner for film transmission.

4972 Blumlein, A.D., and Eric Arthur Nind., "Television." Br. 456,135, Apr. 3, 1935; U.S. 2,182,839, Apr. 17, 1936, Dec. 12, 1838 (EMI). Transmitter circuits for picture and sync signals.

4973 Urtel, R. "Electron beam control system." U.S. 2,202,612, May 21, 1936, May 28, 1940. In Germany Apr. 3, 1935 (Telefunken). Cathode-ray tube and circuits.

4974 Urtel, R. "Signalling circuit." U.S. 2,205,504, Oct. 27, 1936, June 25, 1940. In Germany Apr. 3, 1935 (Telefunken). Television transmitter.

4975 White, E.L.C. "Coupling means for thermionic valve circuits." Br. 456,450, Apr. 3, 1935; U.S 2,120,823, Apr. 8, 1936, June 14,

1938 (EMI). Wide-band direct-coupled amplifier.

4976 "Television." MAN. GUARD. 11 (Apr. 4): 3. About a rumor that Alexandra Palace will be selected as the site for a transmitting station, although the Television Committee has not yet reached a decision.

4977 "Alexandra Palace picked as British television site." N.Y.T. 1 (Apr. 4): 2.

4978 Baird, J.L., and Baird Television. "Television." Br. 454,588, Apr. 4, 1935. On sectional scanning by various means, with reference to generators of saw-tooth and square-topped waves, a cathode-ray tube, mirror drum, fixed reflectors, sectional Kerr cell, and photocells.

4979 Baird, J.L., and Baird Television. "Television." Br. 454,589, Apr. 4, 1935. A dual-purpose tube contains a matrix of multiple light-valve cells and an electron gun, the beam from which activates the cells. Applicable for transmission or reception.

4980 Wilson, J.C., and Baird Television. "Cathode-ray tubes." Br. 454,601, Apr. 5, 1935. Screen materials and tube construction to diminish afterglow of the scanning spot, particularly for film transmission.

4981 Wilson, J.C., and Baird "Television." "Television transmitters." Br. 454,602, Apr. 5, 1935. A photomatrix on the surface of a drum enclosed in a vacuum tube with an electron gun, coacts with a film camera and a scanning disk. Reference to Br. 433,945 (4308).

4982 Schlesinger, K. "Filter amplifier for television synchronizing." U.S. 2,152,824, Apr. 2, 1936, Apr. 4, 1939; Br. 472,992, Apr. 3, 1936. In Germany Apr. 6, 1935 (D.S. Loewe).

4983 Whilems, C.J. "Cathode-ray tubes." Br. 454,937, Apr. 8, 1935. Method of forming photomosaic screens for transmitting tubes.

4984 Bowman-Manifold, M. "Television." Br. 456,651, Apr. 9, 1935. Receiver circuits with deflection generator and sync for interlaced scan. References (4051, 4585, 4770).

4985 Percival, W.S., and M. Bowman-Manifold. "Television." Br. 456,709, Apr. 9, 1935; U.S. 2,181,572, Apr. 17, 1936, Nov. 28, 1939 (EMI). Divided from above. References (4051, 4770, 4942).

4986 Günther, Johannes. "Starting circuit for cathode-ray tubes." U.S. 2,155,486, Apr. 2, 1936, Apr. 25, 1939; Br. 455,479, Apr. 4, 1936. In Germany Apr. 9, 1935 (Fernseh A.-G.). Protective circuit to prevent burning of the screen in a receiver.

4987 Merdler, L.R., and Baird Television. "Amplifier." Br. 454,945, Apr. 9, 1935. For television receiver.

4988 Tingley, G.R., and Baird Television. "Valve circuits." Br. 454,048, Apr. 9, 1935. Receiver amplifier circuit for image and sync signals employing a magnetron.

4989 Andrieu, R. "Oscillograph device." U.S. 2,134,094, May 21, 1936, Oct. 25, 1938. In Germany Apr. 10, 1935 (Telefunken). Cathode-ray tube for television.

4990 Marconi's and W.S.L. Tringham. "Modulated carrier circuit." Br. 454,956, Apr. 10, 1935; U.S. 2,188,068, Apr. 9, 1936, Jan. 23, 1940 (RCA). Transmitter circuit for image and sync signals.

4991 Möller, R. "Synchronizing method." U.S. 2,204,427, Apr. 2, 1936, June 11, 1940; Br. 477,971, Apr. 4, 1936. Void. In Germany Apr. 10, 1935 (Fernseh A.-G.). Optical arrangement with disk, shutter, mirrors, and lenses applicable for a spot-light scanner, film scanner, or camera tube.

4992 Ives, H.E. "Multichannel television system." U.S. 2,139,233, abandoned June 30, 1930, refiled Apr. 11, 1935, Dec. 6, 1938. Assigned: B.T.L. Two-channel transmission for pictures and sound.

4993 "Newark group asks television license. 500-watt station would be used—application asserts home sets are ready." N.Y.T: 19 (Apr.

12): 3. Application by National Television Corp.

4994 Comp. Gaz. "Television." Br. 471,825, Apr. 14, 1936. In France Apr. 12, 1935. Perforated disk for intermeshed scanning.

4995 Holman, H.E. "Cathode-ray tubes." Br. 455,233, Apr. 15, 1935. Method for making a photomosaic screen. References to Br. 442,666 (4464), 447,824 (4660).

4996 Wilson, J.C., and Baird Television. "Cathode-ray tubes." Br. 455,237, Apr. 15, 1935. Refers to a television tube with a strip cathode, apertured electrode, and deflection coil.

4997 Wright, E.E., and Baird Television. "Electron multiplier." Br. 454,973, Apr. 15, 1936. Concerns the temperature control of photoelectric and secondary emitting surfaces.

4998 Zeitline, V., A. Zeitline, and V. Kliatchko. "Valve generators." Br. 473,650, Apr. 14, 1936. In Germany Apr. 15, 1935. Saw-tooth generators for picture tubes with deflection plates. References to Br. 423,427 (3513), 426,537 (4054).

4999 Ferranti and M.K. Taylor. "Cathode-ray tube." Br. 455,499, Apr. 16, 1935. Tube assembly with internal coating of colloidal graphite.

5000 Keyston, J.E., and L.F. Broadway. "Signalling system." Br. 455,555, Apr. 17, 1935; U.S. 2,241,204, Apr. 17, 1936, May 6, 1941 (EMI). Relates to a camera tube with two modulating electrodes in the gun assembly, one supplied with carrier frequency potentials and the other with sync signals.

5001 Schunack, Johannes. "Detector output circuit." U.S. 2,137,545, Apr. 13, 1936, Nov. 22, 1938. In Germany Apr. 17, 1935 (Fernseh A.-G.). For television.

5002 "The future of broadcasting. Inquiry set up. Television and Empire service. One woman member." MAN. GUARD. 9 (Apr. 18): 4. Postmaster-General Sir Kingsley Wood announced on Apr. 17 the formation and terms of the committee on broadcasting and the BBC. Lord Ullswater, chairman.

5003 "'Television.' New word approved by BBC. Committee's list of pronunciations." TIMES (Apr. 18): 9e.

5004 Busse, Ernst, Jan van der Mark, and Adolph Venis. "Sweep circuits." U.S. 2,126,243, May 2, 1936, Aug. 9, 1938; Br. 452,965, Feb. 8, 1936. In Holland Apr. 18, 1935 (N.V. Philips). Saw-tooth generators.

5005 Marconi's, H.M. Dowsett, and L.E.Q. Walker. "Television transmitter." Br. 455,356, Apr. 18, 1935; U.S. 2,145,295, Apr. 15, 1936, Jan. 31, 1939 (RCA). Refers to a transmitting tube containing a light-permeable partition screen. An image is projected onto a photoelectric layer from which electrons are collected by a ball anode. The opposite fluorescent layer of the screen is scanned by cathode rays.

5006 Batchelor, J.C. "Entertainment receiver." U.S. 2,068,002, Apr. 19, 1935, Jan. 19, 1937. Combined sound and image circuits.

5007 Zeitline, V., A. Zeitline, and V. Kliatchko. "Cathode-ray tube." Br. 473,893, Apr. 18, 1936. In Germany Apr. 19, 1935. Special construction of deflection electrodes.

5008 Zeitline, V., A. Zeitline, and V. Kliatchko. "Cathode-ray tube." Br. 473,673, Apr. 18, 1936 In Germany Apr. 19, 1935. Divided from Br. 473,893 (5007). Angular screen viewed from the scanned side. References to Br. 442,500 (4456).

5009 Zeitline, V., A. Zeitline, and V. Kliatchko. "Cathode-ray tube." Br. 473,674, Apr. 18, 1936. In Germany Apr. 19, 1935. Divided from Br. 473,893 (5007). Deflection plates with auxiliary electrodes to prevent distortion due to the edge-effect of the plates. Reference to Br. 449,245 (4161).

5010 Zeitline, V., A. Zeitline, and V. Kliatchko. "Cathode-ray tube." Br. 473,675, Apr. 18, 1936. In Germany Apr. 19, 1935. Divided from Br. 473,893 (5007). Auxiliary electrodes between the two sets of deflection plates and between the plates and the screen.

5011 "Broadcasting problems." TIMES (Apr. 20): 13c, d. Editorial.

5012 Bumstead, Ralph W. "Multiplex television systems." U.S. 2,207,716, Apr. 20, 1935, July 16, 1940. Refers to a projection system.

5013 Gander, L.M. "Television's bogy. England opens truth campaign to stop slump in sales of radio sets." N.Y.T. IX, 11 (Apr. 21): 7, 8.

5014 Batchelor, J.C. "Electronic apparatus." U.S. 2,146,366, Apr. 23, 1935, Feb. 7, 1939. Cathode-ray tube.

5015 Barthélemy, R. [Cathode-ray television with automatic synchronization.] C.R. 200 (Apr. 24): 1470–2.

5016 Blumlein, A.D. "Signalling system." Br. 455,858, Apr. 24, 1935; U.S. 2,212,558, Apr. 24, 1936, Aug. 27, 1940 (EMI). Refers to a switching system for line and frame impulses and sync. References to Br. 425,220 (4051), 448,097 (4644).

5017 Bedford, A.V. "Television transmitter." U.S. 2,151,072, Apr. 25, 1935, Mar. 21, 1939. Assigned: RCA. Wide-band amplifier in a camera tube system.

5018 Scophony and G.W. Walton. "Television scanning system." Br. 451,132, Apr. 25, 1935; U.S. 2,157,468, Apr. 15, 1936, May 9, 1939. A method employing two mirror drums rotating at different speeds, and lenses.

5019 Cocking, Walter Tusting. "LF amplification in television receivers. Designing intervalve couplings for high frequencies." W.W. 36 (Apr. 26): 417–9. Photo, 3 graphs, 3 diags.

5020 Parker, Louis W. (formerly L.W. Kolzosy). "Television." U.S. 2,144,379, Apr. 26, 1935, Jan. 17, 1939. Multiple mirrors and a projection system.

5021 Marconi's and A.A. Linsell. "Wireless receivers." Br. 455,649, Apr. 26, 1935. For broadcast sound with switch for short-wave television.

5022 Marconi's and L.M. Myers. "Electro-optical light-valve." Br. 451,876, Apr. 26, 1935. Kerr cell.

5023 Brüche, E. "Braun tube." U.S. 2,122,555, Apr. 27, 1936, July 5, 1938. In Germany Apr. 27, 1935 (A.E.G.).

5024 Stocker, A.C. "Deflecting circuit." U.S. 2,110,245, Apr. 27, 1935, Mar. 8, 1938. Assigned: RCA. Relaxation oscillator.

5025 Tolson, W.A. "Deflecting circuits." U.S. 2,183,340, Apr. 27, 1935, Dec. 12, 1939. Assigned: RCA. Saw-tooth generator and picture tube.

5026 Jarrard, W.J., J.C. Wilson, and Baird Television. "Cathode-ray tube." Br. 455,973, Apr. 30, 1935. Optical lens secured to the screen end.

5027 Schlesinger, K. "Short-wave television transmitter." U.S. 2,199,273, Apr. 30, 1936, Apr. 30, 1940; Br. 469,628, Apr. 27, 1936. In Germany Apr. 30, 1935 (D.S. Loewe). Refers to modulating and amplifying circuits.

5028 Wilson, J.C., and Baird Television. "Television." Br. 455,972, Apr. 30, 1935. Lines of successive pictures are displaced by glass plates oppositely inclined that reciprocate in front of the scanning area of a disk. Inclined glass spokes on a disk is one of several modifications.

5029 Valensi, G. "Le problème de la télévision à grande distance." ANN. POSTES 24 (May): 401–54.

5030 Ardenne, M. v. "Zur Frage der Zerlegsnormen beim Fernsehen" [The question of scanning standards in television]. FERN. U. TON. 6 (May): 30.

5031 Theile, R. "Eine Fernseh-Demonstrations-Apparatur." FERN. U. TON. 6 (May): 31–6.

5032 Schrage, W. "A modern picture of television." RADIO-CRAFT 6 (May): 673, 674.

5033 Puckle, O.S. "Transient aspect of wideband amplifiers; examination with cathode-ray oscillograph." W. ENG. 12 (May): 251–6.

5034 Bell, J., and W.S. Worthington. "Electro-optical light-valve." Br. 455,983, May 1, 1935. Interleaved assembly.

5035 Cocking, W.T. "LF amplification in television receivers. Designing an amplifier." W.W. 36 (May 3): 444–6. Photo, 6 graphs, diag.

5036 Andrieu, R. "Oscillation producing system." U.S. 2,147,229, May 4, 1936, Feb. 14, 1939. In Germany May 3, 1935 (Telefunken). Deflection circuit.

5037 Forman. J.R.H., and Baird Television. "Valve generator." Br. 456,138, May 3, 1935. Deflection coil with capacitive coupling to sweep generator.

5038 Schlesinger, K. "Circuit with gas-filled grid controlled glow discharge tubes." U.S. 2,114,614, May 1, 1936, Apr. 19, 1938; Br. 474,400, May 1, 1936. In Germany May 3, 1935 (D.S. Loewe). Relaxation oscillator and tube.

5039 Dunlap, O.E. Jr. "America takes a cue from England's television bogy. Unmasking a science of sight. Idea for a 'truth campaign' in television wins new followers—they would reveal outlook to the public." N.Y.T. IX (May 5): 1–3. Quotes from the Television Committee's report and from reports and remarks by industrialists.

5040 Farnsworth, P.T. "Multipactor phase control." U.S. 2,071,517, May 7, 1935, Feb. 23, 1937; Br. 463,514, May 1, 1936 (Farnsworth Television). Electron multiplier. References (2549, 4139, 4535).

5041 Farnsworth, P.T., and Harry S. Bamford. "Producing incandescent images." U.S. 2,155,478, May 6, 1935, Apr. 25, 1939; Br. 467,367, May 1, 1936 (Farnsworth Television). Tube with incandescent screen for a picture tube.

5042 "First field tests in television, costing $1,000,000, to begin here. RCA will take sight transmission out of laboratory. Empire State Building likely as centre—science will not interfere with radio, Sarnoff says." N.Y.T. 1 (May 8): 2, 3, 15: 4. Announcement by D. Sarnoff on May 7 at RCA stockholders meeting. "Mr. Sarnoff stressed the fact that the United States is further advanced in television than any other country."

5043 "Television." N.Y.T. 20 (May 9): 3, 4. Editorial on Sarnoff's report. "There never was a technical problem so difficult as television."

5044 "Television in U.S.A. $1,000,000 to be spent on experiments." TIMES (May 9): 18e.

5045 Zeitline, V., A. Zeitline, and V. Kliatchko. "Cathode-ray tubes." Br. 476,865, May 11, 1936. In Germany May 9, 1935. A type of camera tube adaptable for direct pickup, film transmission, and color.

5046 Zeitline, V., A. Zeitline, and V. Kliatchko. "Cathode-ray tubes." Br. 478,121, May 11, 1936. In Germany May 9, 1935. Divided from above. Tube modified for pickup or display.

5047 Lance, T.M.C., and Baird Television. "Television." Br. 455,146, May 10, 1935. A method of interlaced scanning with apertured disk for film transmission, and variants. References (3464, 3819, 4280).

5048 Chapter, C.F., and Baird Television. "Television." Br. 456,582, May 11, 1935. Refers to control circuits whereby views from one or another scanner may be mixed and changed with "rolling cuts" either vertically or horizontally.

5049 Herbst, P.J. "Television distribution." U.S. 2,135,577, May 11, 1935, Nov. 8, 1938. Assigned: RCA. A switching system for multiple receivers with pictures and sound.

5050 Marconi's and N.M. Rust. "Signalling system." Br. 456,584, May 11,1935; U.S. 2,200,725, May 5, 1936, May 14, 1940 (RCA). Transmission of television signals by coaxial cable with separation of low frequencies and recombination with high frequencies at the receiving end.

5051 Dunlap, O.E. Jr. "Million-dollar plan brightens television outlook. Sky to be the laboratory. Television waves will leap from aerial atop skyscraper—field tests expected to spur progress." N.Y.T. X (May 12), 1–3. D. Sarnoff's statements. Work at RCA and their plans for 343-line experiments. Photo of V.K. Zworykin, columns 4, 5.

5052 G.E.C. and D.C. Espley. "Valve generator." Br. 450,041, May 14, 1935. Saw-tooth oscillator. Reference to Br. 438,386 (4550).

5053 "Television in Germany." TIMES (May 15): 13b. "The German Post Office yesterday opened the first public televiewing post outside Berlin in the Post Office administration building at Potsdam."

5054 Baird, J.L., and Baird Television. "Television." Br. 437,339, May 15, 1935. Divided from Br. 431,339 (4293). Concerns a method of interleaved scanning by deflecting a cathode ray at the image and line frequencies. Reference to Br. 381,898 (3464).

5055 G.E.C. and L.C. Jesty. "Television receiver." Br. 451,980, May 15, 1935. Container for a cathode-ray tube has an eyepiece with magnifiers that produce coincident images. Two tubes with separate eyepieces provide stereoscopic viewing.

5056 Urtel, R. "Synchronizing system." U.S. 2,168,251, May 20, 1936, Aug. 1, 1939; Br. 475,189, May 15, 1936. In Germany May 15, 1935 (Telefunken).

5057 D.S. Loewe. "Valve generators." Br. 468,808, May 15, 1936. In Germany May 16, 1935. Picture tube receiver with relaxation oscillator, amplifier, and coupling circuits to improve the transmission of low frequencies. References (4059, 4602, 4697).

5058 G.E.C. and L.C. Jesty. "Cathode-ray tube." Br. 455,797, May 16, 1935. Picture tube with lens system and circuit controls to change the spot size to suit transmissions with differing numbers of lines while retaining true focus.

5059 "State of television technique." ELECT. 114 (May 17): 626. Comments on Sarnoff's talk of May 7.

5060 G.E.C. and L.C. Jesty. "Cathode-ray tube." Br. 448,146, May 17, 1935. Refers to the correction of keystone distortion due to an indirect screen. Reference to Br. 412,813 (3640).

5061 Tingley, George Richard, D.W. Pugh, and Baird Television. "Valve generator." Br. 456,666, May 17, 1935. Scanning oscillator for magnetic deflection. Reference to Br. 456,138 (5037).

5062 Tingley, G.R., D.W. Pugh, and Baird Television. "Valve generator." Br. 456,640, May 17, 1935. Divided from above. Saw-tooth oscillator. Reference to Br. 456,138 (5037).

5063 Schlesinger, K. "Television transmitter." U.S. 2,147,557, May 16, 1936, Feb. 14, 1939; Br. 468,809, May 18, 1936. In Germany May 18, 1935 (D.S. Loewe). Refers to film transmission with sync signals produced from the margin of the film, amplitude filter, and modulator stage.

5064 Zeitline, V., A. Zeitline, and V. Kliatchko. "Image intensifier." Br. 475,547, May 18, 1936. In Germany May 18, 1935. A spherical tube with a photoelectric screen and a fluorescent screen at right angles. Reference to Br. 444,998 (4503).

5065 Zeitline, V., A. Zeitline, and V. Kliatchko. "Discharge apparatus." Br. 477,326, May 18, 1936. In Germany May 18, 1935. An image transmitting tube with intermediate photoelectric and fluorescent screens for image amplification, with surrounding magnetic coil and a final photomosaic scanned by a light beam, and variants. Reference to Br. 442,666 (4464).

5066 Zeitline, V., A. Zeitline, and V. Kliatchko. "Cathode-ray tube." Br. 478,499, May 18, 1936. In Germany May 18, 1935. Divided from above. Image transmitting tube with a photoelectric screen, cylindrical collecting electrode, an opposite fluorescent screen that is scanned obliquely by an electron beam, and a surrounding focusing coil. References as above.

5067 Zeitline, V., A. Zeitline, and V. Kliatchko. "Image intensifier." Br. 478,641, May 18, 1396. In Germany May 18, 1935. A tubular arrangement with a photoelectric screen at one end and a fluorescent screen at the other, intermediate electrodes with photoelectric and fluorescent layers on opposite faces, focusing coil, and external optical systems.

5068 Torres, H.Z. "Germany's 'Mirror.'" N.Y.T. IX (May 19),11: 5, 6. On the regular 180-line service and the television program "Mirror of the Day."

5069 Heimann, W. "Photoelectric cells." Br. 455,899, May 16, 1936. In Germany May 20, 1935 (Fernseh A.-G.). Method of oxidizing the surface of a photoelectric plate as for an image pickup tube.

5070 Heimann, W. "Electron lenses." Br. 456,316, May 16, 1936. In Germany May 20, 1935 (Fernseh A.-G.). Arrangement for a photoelectric cathode and accelerating electrode in an image pickup tube.

5071 Henneberg, W. "Electron optics." U.S. 2,161,466, July 8, 1936, June 6, 1939; Br. 458,015, May 20, 1936 (B.T.-H.). In Germany May 20, 1935 (A.E.G.). Electrode structures in a display tube.

5072 Schlesinger, K. "Cathode-ray television apparatus with adjustable size of image point." U.S. 2,227,005, May 19, 1936, Dec. 31, 1940; Br. 480,521, May 22, 1936. In Germany May 22, 1935 (D.S. Loewe). Refers to a picture tube circuit with deflection oscillators and switching system to accommodate different numbers of scanning lines. References to Br. 455,797 (5058), 466,770 (4608).

5073 Tingley, G.R., and Baird Television. "Television." Br. 457,129, May 22, 1935. Separation circuit for signals at line and frame frequencies. References to Br. 443,031 (4576), 456,666 (5061).

5074 Holman, H.E. "Cathode-ray tubes." Br. 458,675, May 23, 1935; U.S. 2,115,855, Oct. 1, 1936, May 3, 1938 (EMI). Method of forming metal mesh screen for a camera tube mosaic. Reference to Br. 458,736.

5075 Holman, H.E. "Cathode-ray tubes." Br. 458,736, May 23, 1935. Divided from above. References to Br. 447,824 (4660), 455,233 (4995).

5076 C. Lorenz A.-G. "Television." Br. 461,105, May 22, 1936. In Germany May 23, 1935. Concerns a picture tube with an oblique screen, deflection plates, focusing coil, and circuit for trapezoidal scanning and constant focus. Reference to Br. 445,094 (4705).

5077 Ruska, E. "Cathode-ray deflection apparatus." U.S. 2,143,580, May 20, 1936, Jan. 10, 1939; Br. 475,527, May 22, 1936. In Germany May 23, 1935 (Fernseh A.-G.). Deflection coils on a ferromagnetic glass, or ceramic structure mounted inside the tube. Reference to Br. 449,533 (4653).

5078 Ruska, E. "Magnetic deflecting system for Braun tubes." U.S. 2,206,125, May 20, 1936, July 2, 1940. In Germany May 23, 1935 (Fernseh A.-G.). Similar to above.

5079 "Television from wax records." ELECT. 114 (May 24): 693. Demonstration of Gramovision by Plew Television, Ltd., at Selfridge's on May 13. 30-line images like Baird's phonovision.

5080 Dinsdale, A. "American television tests. 'Premature standardisation would freeze the art.'" W.W. 36 (May 24): 513. On RCA plans with quotes from Sarnoff's speech on May 7.

5081 "National television plans for Germany. Service of twenty-one stations proposed." W.W. 36 (May 24): 525, 526. Map of proposed stations and their service areas. Diagrams of frequency bands. Based on Scholz's article (4758).

5082 D.S. Loewe. "Valve generator." Br. 471,280, May 22, 1936. In Germany May 24, 1935. Relaxation oscillator and amplifier circuit for keeping the center of the scan in the center of the screen. Reference to Br. 425,687 (3633).

5083 Marconi's and E.W.B. Gill. "Electron multiplier." Br. 456,991, May 23, 1935. Parallel plates with tuned circuit and magnetic field.

5084 Marconi's and A.A. Linsell. "Television receiver." Br.457,274, May 24, 1935; U.S. 2,202,390, May 16, 1936, May 28, 1940 (RCA). Picture tube with a protective concave window.

5085 Tolson, W.A. "Television." U.S, 2,207,839, May 24, 1935, July 16, 1940. Assigned: RCA. Picture tube receiver, saw-tooth generators, and sync circuits.

5086 Baird Television, G.W. White, A.J. Brown, and P.W. Willans. "Valve circuits." Br.458,861, May 27, 1935. Three-stage transmitter amplifier and push-pull modulator. Reference to Br. 457,827.

5087 de Boer, J.H., and M.C. Teves. "Luminescent screen." U.S. 2,161,458, Sept. 22, 1936, June 6, 1939. In Germany May 29, 1935 (N.V. Philips).

5088 N.V. Philips. "Cathode-ray tubes." Br. 456,629, Feb. 24, 1936. In Holland May 29, 1935. Black conductive coating on the inside of the tube.

5089 "Olympic games television. German broadcast." MAN. GUARD. 9 (May 30): 3. Special television conference May 29 at German Broadcasting Co. headquarters in Berlin, it was announced that the Olympic games would be broadcast by television in 1936. Homage was paid to Nipkow, and a film of the Olympic team at practice was shown by low-frequency method. The film was also shown on the public band that evening.

5090 "Reich plans to televise events in 1936 Olympics." N.Y.T. 2 (May 30): 7. "This announcement was the crowning point of the first television congress, meeting in the Berlin Radio House to inspect the apparatus now available and to study recent developments in the new science."

5091 Bowman-Manifold, M., and Rolf Edmund Spencer. "Oscillation generator." Br. 457,661, May 30, 1935; U.S. 2,125,732, May 14, 1946, Aug. 2, 1938 (EMI). Relaxation oscillator.

5092 Lubszynski, H.A., and J.E. Keyston. "Electron tube apparatus." Br. 457,493, May 30, 1935; U.S. 2,227,097, May 28, 1936, Dec. 31, 1940 (EMI). A linear transmitting tube incorporating an electron multiplier with a transparent photoelectric screen, intermediate secondary-emitting grids, a mosaic electrode scanned by an electron beam, electrostatic shields, and focusing coils, with variants. References (4464, 4536, 4561, 4685).

5093 "Television developments." ELECT. 114 (May 31): 704. Comments on Lord Inverforth's speech about MWT Co. plans for television. The company is ready to supply complete transmitter system for 405 line, 50 pictures per-sec.

5094 Hefele, J.R. "Electro-optical system." U.S. 2,036,1663 May 31, 1935, Apr. 14, 1936. Assigned: B.T.L. Refers to multichannel transmission, disk scanning, number of light elements equal to number of lines, mirror screw receiver, for color.

5095 Ives, H.E. "Electro-optical system." U.S. 2,037,167, May 31, 1935, Apr. 14, 1936. Assigned: B.T.L. Similar to above.

5096 Hefele, J.R., and H.E. Ives. "Television." Br. 458,654, June 2, 1936 (S.T.C.). In U.S. May 31, 1935 (B.T.L.). Multichannel system for color, similar to above. Reference to Br. 402,401 (2927).

5097 Poch, W.J. "Television." U.S. 2,151,149, May 31, 1935, Mar. 21, 1939. Assigned: RCA. Picture tube receiver with magnetic deflection circuits.

5098 Poch, W.J. "Television." U.S. 2,236,066, May 31, 1935, Mar. 25, 1941. Assigned: RCA. Br. 477,765, June 2, 1936 (Marconi's). Similar to above. Reference to Br. 407,409 (3127).

5099 Valensi, G. "Le problème de la télévision à grande distance." ANN. POSTES. 24 (June): 501–33.

5100 "Million cycle co-axial cable for television?" ELECTRONICS 8 (June): 189. Photo. AT&T cable installation between New York and Philadelphia. Cost $580,000 for one television channel.

5101 Schwartz, E. "Uber Nachteschleunigung bei Braunsche Röhren" [About acceleration in cathode-ray tubes]. FERN. U. TON. 6 (June): 37–40.

5102 Barthélemy, R. "L'état actuel de la télévision" [Present state of television]. ONDE ELECT. 14 (June): 391–405. Survey of development, current status, equipment in use, and prospects. Continued in July.

5103 "Electron camera 'shoots' television images." POP. MECH. 63 (June): 878, 879. Full-page diags. and captions. London station to serve ten million people. Baird studios at Crystal Palace and intermediate film apparatus.

5104 Kaufman, S. "British television." RADIO N. 16 (June): 728, 772. 6 photos. On the Selsdon report.

5105 Wraight, W.L. "Reception of the B.B.C. 30-line television transmissions in Madeira." J. TELEV. SOC. 2 (June): 25 8. 4 photos, 2 diags. Description of receivers used with disk, mirror drum, and mirror screw.

5106 Myers, L.M. "Kerr cell design for high definition practice." J. TELEV. SOC. 2 (June): 29–31. 3 diags. Table of operating voltages.

5107 Wright, E.E. "Scanning aperture distortion." J. TELEV. SOC. 2 (June): 32. Graph. On phase distortion.

5108 "High definition television services in England. Views on the two standards of definition." J. TELEV. SOC. 2 (June): 34–43. Table, 3 graphs. Opinions contributed by M. von Ardenne, E.L. Gardiner, T.M.C. Lance, E.H. Traub, and E. Wikkenhauser, none of them favorable toward the 405–50 interlaced system proposed by EMI.

5109 "Television with colors is a reported discovery." N.Y.T. 1 (June 2): 4. An invention of Léon Damas employing a special screened lamp, according to the Belgian press.

5110 West, A.G.D., and Baird Television. "Television." Br. 457,800, June 5, 1935. Protective circuits limits the intensity of a cathode-ray beam. References to Br. 446,663 (4599), 455,237 (4996).

5111 McConnell, E.D., and Baird Television. "Television." Br. 457,812, June 6, 1935. Circuit for separating picture and sync signals. Reference to Br. 443,031 (4576).

5112 McGee, J.D., A.S.P. Freeman, and W.S. Brown. "Electronic image indicating device." Br. 457,531, June 6, 1935; U.S. 2,185,601, June 5, 1936, Jan. 2, 1940 (EMI). Refers to a single-camera tube. Reference to Br. 442,666 (4464).

5113 "Television for London. Alexandra Park. First station in Selsdon scheme." MAN. GUARD. 11 (June 7): 3. Announcement by the Postmaster-General (Sir Kingsley Wood), the previous evening. General news about the two systems; Baird at 240 lines and Marconi-EMI at 405 lines. Also a statement by the Baird Company that they are ready to deliver a complete transmitter to the BBC, and that two receivers are ready for production, with screens giving pictures 6 by 8 and 9 by 12 inches.

5114 "London television station. Alexandra Palace chosen." TIMES (June 7): 13d.

5115 Campbell, R.L. "Electrical system." U.S. 2,141,343, June 7, 1935, Dec. 27, 1938; Br. 477,038, May 20, 1936 (Philco). Saw-tooth generator and sync circuit for picture tube with deflection coils controlling line scan. Reference to Br. 468,505 (4767).

5116 Campbell, R.L. "Television receivers." Br. 477,433, May 20, 1936. In U.S. June 7, 1935 (Philco). Divided from above.

5117 Murphy Radio, K.S. Davies, and H.F.W.J. Freundlich. "Valve circuits." Br. 457,532, June 7, 1935. Circuit for separating picture and sync signals.

5118 Adam, M. "Les récents progrès de la télévision; le système Barthélemy et les émissions de Paris-P.T.T." [Recent progress of television; Barthélemy's system and the transmissions from Paris-Posts, Telegraphs and Telephones]. GENIE CIVIL 106 (June 8): 549–53.

5119 Barthélemy, R. "La synchronisation automatique dans la télévision cathodique" [Automatic synchronization in cathode-ray television]. GENIE CIVIL 106 (June 8): 553, 554.

5120 "W.M. Peck on developments in Montreal reports a television gain. Inventor, here, says images are almost as distinct as home film projections. City-wide service near. Broadcasting system uses no more current than ordinary 100-watt bulb." N.Y.T. 17 (June 8): 4. "We are now broadcasting pictures sixteen inches square on a wavelength of six meters. Three new 180-line transmitters are now under construction in Canada for installation in Montreal, New York, and London."

5121 B.T.-H. "Image intensifier." Br. 476,338, June 8, 1936. In Germany June 8, 1935 (A.E.G.).

5122 Marconi's and G.B. Banks. "Electron beam deflection circuits." Br. 457,529, June 8, 1935; U.S. 2,170,847, June 3, 1936, Aug. 29, 1939 (RCA). Deflection coils are short-circuited during the fly-back period.

5123 S.T.C. "Television." Br. 462,877, May 29, 1396. Convention date June 8, 1935. A multi-element, multifrequency piezoelectric system.

5124 Schlesinger, K. "Scanning device." U.S., 2,227,006, June 5, 1936, Dec. 31, 1940; Br. 476,181, June 9, 1936. In Germany June 11, 1935 (D.S. Loewe). Apertured disks and optical system for interlaced scanning of film and generation of sync signals. Reference to Br. 465,184 (4603).

5125 Mat. Tel. Soc. Anon. "Valve generator." Br. 459,998, June 5, 1936 (S.T.C.). In France June 12, 1935. Saw-tooth oscillator for electrostatic deflection. Reference to Br. 426,537 (4054).

5126 Van der Mark, Jan. "Oscillation generator." U.S. 2,153,217, June 12, 1936, Apr. 4, 1939. In Holland June 12, 1935.

5127 N.V. Philips. "Valve generator." Br. 451,204, Jan. 11, 1936. In Holland June 12, 1935. Saw-tooth oscillator.

5128 "Baird Television." TIMES (June 13): 20d. Company news and report for the 15 months ending Sept. 30, 1934.

5129 Zeitline, V., A. Zeitline, and V. Kliatchko. "Discharge apparatus." Br. 478,238, June 13, 1936. In Germany June 13, 1935. A right-angled tube contains a photosensitive screen and a fluorescent screen at the ends, with other electrodes at the bend serving as an electron mirror. Reference to Br. 475,547 (5064).

5130 Zeitline, V., A. Zeitline, and V. Kliatchko. "Cathode-ray tube." Br. 481,590, June 13, 1936. In Germany June 13, 1935. Picture tube.

5131 Zeitline, V., A. Zeitline, and V. Kliatchko. "Cathode-ray tube." Br. 481,659, June 13, 1936. In Germany June 13, 1935. Divided from above. Refers to a picture tube with a curved electron mirror centered on a ball cathode.

5132 Zeitline, V., A. Zeitline, and V. Kliatchko. "Cathode-ray tube." Br. 481,660, June 13, 1936. In Germany June 13, 1935. Divided from Br. 4581,590 (5130). Picture tube with three planar metallic grids, apertured diaphragm, lens, and magnetic coils.

5133 "News in brief. Television development." ELECT. 114 (June 14): 805. Short note on a system providing sound and vision in color by Léon Damas and Prof. Baethelmans.

5134 Cocking, W.T. "Television IF amplifiers. Designing wide-band intermediate frequency circuits." W.W. 36 (June 14): 586–8. 2 photos, 3 graphs, 2 diags.

5135 "Television. A Post Office statement." W.W: 36 (June 14): 592. On the adoption of Alexandra Palace as the site for the first television station in North London. Aerial photo of the Palace.

5136 N.V. Philips. "Cathode-ray tubes." Br. 472,240, Mar. 20, 1936. In Holland June 14, 1935. Construction of an incandescent picture screen. References to Br. 452,368 (4851), 452,406 (4852).

5137 Schwartz, E. "Image screen for Braun tubes." U.S. 2,163,918, June 6, 1936, June 27, 1939. In Germany June 14, 1935 (Fernseh A.-G.).

5138 Kinne, E. (by E. Michaelis). "Image intensifiers." Br. 472,073, June 15, 1936. In Germany June 15, 1935. For television.

5139 Campbell, R.L. "Composite signal device." U.S. 2,236,705, June 17, 1935, Apr. 1, 1941; Br. 477,329, May 21, 1936 (Philco). Refers to pulse combining and shaping circuits. References to Br. 443,699 (3951), 477,038 (5115).

5140 Campbell, R.L. "Television." Br. 477,377, May, 21, 1936. In U.S. June 17, 1935 (Philco). Divided from above.

5141 Ruska, E., and E. Schwartz. "Combined electric and magnetic deflecting system for cathode-ray tubes." U.S. 2,119,795, June 6, 1936, June 7, 1938; Br. 455,200, June 19, 1936. In Germany June 19, 1935 (Fernseh A.-G.). Assembly mounted inside the tube.

5142 "British get television. Empire rights to American invention are obtained." N.Y.T. 21 (June 20): 1. Announcement by J.B. McCarger that a contract to use Farnsworth equipment had been signed with Baird Television.

5143 Schlesinger, K. "Multiple cathode-ray tube." U.S. 2,141,415, June 16, 1936, Dec. 27, 1938; Br. 477,043, June 19, 1936. In Germany June 20, 1935 (D.S. Loewe). A high-vacuum tube containing three sets of electrodes in a common assembly provides separate spots on the screen, applicable for television and other purposes. References to Br. 432,485 (4279), 451,745 (4690).

5144 "Television and broadcasting." ELECT. 114 (June 21): 812, 820. Editorial comments about the selection of Alexandra Palace as the site of the high-definition station. German plans for a number of stations, the question of the range of ultra-short waves, and the effect of television on public demand for radio receivers.

5145 "Baird Television Ltd. Progress in transmission. Sir Harry Greer on Committee's report." MAN. GUARD. 18 (June 21): 6. Report on company activities, work at the Crystal Palace laboratories, development of the intermediate film system and co-operation with Fernseh Company, agreement with Farnsworth Company, development of the electron camera, electron multipliers, and large-screen high-definition apparatus for cinemas.

5146 "Baird Television Limited. Progress in the invention. Company's practical experiences. Television Committee's report. Further important developments. Sir Harry Greer's address." TIMES (June 21): 25a–c. Company has given 40 demonstrations of complete programs which were seen by over 2000 people in London on Baird televisors. Complete and self-contained facilities available for manufacturing apparatus including cathode-ray tubes and electron multipliers.

5147 Kinne, E. (by E. Michaelis). "Television." Br. 464,064, June 22, 1936. In Germany June 22, 1935. Cathode-ray tube circuit with feedback from the anode to the control grid. Reference to Br. 403,876 (3460).

5148 White, E.L.C. "Television transmission system." Br. 462,110, June 24, 1935; U.S. 2,143,398, June 9, 1936, Jan. 10, 1939 (EMI). Refers to integrating circuits to overcome uneven shading due to spurious signals from a camera tube. References to Br. 442,666 (4464), 463,967 (4659).

5149 Marconi's and L.M. Myers. "Electron multipliers." Br. 477,345, June 25, 1935.

5150 Reader, E., and L. Glass. "Television." Br. 456,288, June 25, 1935. Receiver circuit with deflection generators, push-pull input to deflection plates, and beam blanking during fly-back.

5151 Schlesinger, K. "Television tube." U.S. 2,123,161, June 22, 1936, July 5, 1938; Br. 480,672, June 25, 1936. In Germany June 25, 1935 (D.S. Loewe). Picture tube with two sets of electron lenses. References to Br. 442,511 (3958), 442,724 (3992).

5152 Thompson, Harry C. "Cascaded secondary electron emitter amplifier." U.S. 2,141,322, June 25, 1935, Dec. 27, 1938. Assigned: RCA. Br. 460,356 June 24, 1936 (Marconi's). Electron amplifier.

5153 B.T.-H., T.H. Kinman, and D.S. Watson. "Wireless receiver." Br. 459,070, June 26, 1935. Superhet circuit for vision and sound. References (3230, 3750, 3846), and by Controller (4333, 4897, 4930).

5154 Reveley, P.V., J.L. Baird, and Baird Television. "Television." Br. 437,340, June 26, 1935. Addition to Br. 431,458 (4294). Apertured disks for generating impulses in an interlaced scanning system.

5155 Baird Television, T.M.C. Lance, and E.H. Foden-Pattinson. "Television." Br. 458,791, June 27, 1935. Refers to an optical method with a lenticular grating, light filter in three color zones, lenses, and film for producing images in color or stereo, applicable for transmission or reception.

5156 N.V. Philips. "Discharge apparatus." Br. 457,253, Apr. 6, 1936. In Holland June 27, 1935. Concerns the electrode construction and assembly in a cathode-ray tube including an electron lens and a built-in potentiometer.

5157 Schlesinger, K. "Electron-optical arrangements." U.S. 2,147,558, June 26, 1936, Feb. 14, 1939; Br. 480,779, June 26, 1936. In Germany June 27, 1935 (D.S. Loewe). On electrode geometries and operating potentials in a picture tube. Reference to Br. 442,511 (3958).

5158 Gander, L.M. "Television race. England finds competition is keen—405 lines interlaced form images." N.Y.T. X, 11 (June 30): 7. "Experiments of EMI have been surrounded with a smoke screen of secrecy. It appears that the greatest enemy of television progress in Britain is needless secrecy all around." The article also mentions that EMI is using Zworykin's inventions and that they are co-operating with RCA in the development of television.

5159 Fielding, Thomas James. PHOTO-ELECTRIC AND SELENIUM CELLS: THEIR OPERATION, CONSTRUCTION, AND USES. London: Chapman & Hall; Pittsburgh: Instruments Publishing Company, 1935. vi + 140 pp. 74 illus. Practical and elementary treatment intended chiefly for the experimenter and general student.

5160 Scroggie, Marcus Graham. TELEVISION. London: Blackie, 1935. ix + 68 pp. 7 plates, 18 diags. A clear and basic explanation for the non-technical reader and the wireless amateur.

5161 "Television advances abroad." ELECTRONICS 8 (July): 229, 230. News on events in France, Italy, Germany, Czechoslovakia, Japan, Canada, and Australia.

5162 Nagashima, M. [Braun tubes.] J. IEE JAPAN 55 (July): 571–83. Study of low-voltage tubes and action of electron.

5163 Barthélemy, R. "L'état actuel de la télévision." ONDE ELECT. 14 (July): 455–69. Continued from June.

5164 "Exchange of patents speeds home television." POP. MECH. 64 (July): 24, 25. 3 photos. Farnsworth and Fernseh A.-G.

5165 "Television to the front!" RADIO N. 17 (July): 4. Editorial on RCA's plans for television development.

5166 Schrage, W.E. "German television." RADIO N. 7 (July): 9, 60. 7 photos.

5167 Goldsmith, A.N. "Television and motion pictures." J. SMPE 25 (July): 37–45.

5168 Lubcke, H.R. "Theatrical possibilities of television." J. SMPE 25 (July): 46–9.

5169 Farnsworth, P.T. "Projection means." U.S. 2,143,145, July 1, 1935, Jan. 10, 1939. Assigned: Farnsworth Television. Divided from U.S. 2,091,705 (4681).

5170 Farnsworth, P.T. "Electron image amplifier." U.S. 2,292,437, July 1, 1935, Aug. 11,

1942; Br. 472,859, June 23, 1936 (Farnsworth Television). Image dissector modified with a photoelectric grid exposed to an optical image and to the beam from an electron gun.

5171 Eisler, Paul. "Stereoscopic television." U.S. 2,209,747, July 1, 1936, July 30, 1940; Br. 472,562, July 2, 1936 (with F. Pevny). In Austria July 2, 1935. Refers to sectional pictures with each set of lines scanned sequentially and viewed through a grating which provides visual strips corresponding to the right and left eyes. Numerous variants, such as disks, lenses, film recording, other optical systems, and one or more iconoscopes are described.

5172 Bailey, W.C. "Television." Br. 439,229, July 3, 1935. A receiver comprises a mirror disk, series of moving reflector strips, a transparent screen with opaque strips to match, and a modulated light source.

5173 C. Lorenz A.-G. "Television." Br. 457,417, Nov. 15, 1935. In Germany July 3, 1935. Circuit isolates and reverses the phase of blacker than black sync signals.

5174 Heinmann, W. "Neuere Bildzerleger in der Fernsehtechnik" [New picture dissector in television technique]. T.T.Z. 56 (July 4): 761, 762. On mechanical scanners and electrical image dissector.

5175 Baird, J.L., and Baird Television. "Television." Br. 459,177, July 4, 1935. A method of scanning in groups of parallel lines in which the orientation of successive groups is changed; variants include reversing two deflection generators, a reversing relay, or rotation of a cathode-ray tube or deflection coils. Reference to Br. 289,307 (800).

5176 Wilson, J.C., and Baird Television. "Television." Br. 459,178, July 4, 1935. A method of diagonal scanning in groups of lines in which successive groups are oriented in the opposite sense. References (262, 800, 2857, 4282).

5177 "Cables for television." ELECT. 115 (July 5): 2. Comment on address by Capt. West at the Conference of the Cinematograph Exhibitors' Association at Cardiff on June 26. Concentric cables had been developed capable of carrying high-definition signals; these would be applied for distribution between centers of population.

5178 "Television Centre in Rome." ELECT. 115 (July 5): 2. Note on a proposal to establish an "international television centre" under the aegis of the International Institute of Educational Cinematography.

5179 "Television in the cinema. Conference of the Cinematograph Exhibitors' Association at Cardiff—The frequency problem and 400-line definition." ELECT. 115 (July 5): 24. Paper by A.G.D. West. Topics include transmission on ultra-short waves, definition ranges from 150 to 400 lines, reception tests around London from the Crystal Palace transmitter, methods for producing large-screen displays in cinemas, and the use of microwaves or cable links between a central program source and cinemas.

5180 G.E.C., N.R. Campbell, and L.C. Jesty. "Television receivers." Br. 457,510, July 5, 1935. Arrangement of a picture tube inclined in a cabinet at a suitable viewing angle.

5181 Marconi's and G.B. Banks. "Oscillation generator." Br. 459,302, July 5, 1935; U.S. 2,148,096, June 6, 1936, Feb. 21, 1939 (RCA). Saw-tooth oscillator.

5182 Farnsworth, P.T. "Charge storage dissector." U.S. 2,140,695, July 6, 1935, Dec. 20, 1938; Br. 472,861, June 23, 1936 (Farnsworth Television). Image dissector incorporating amplification by secondary emission. Reference to Br. 472,859 (5170).

5183 Farnsworth, P.T. "Image analysis." U.S. 2,216,264, July 6, 1935, Oct. 1, 1940; Br. 472,862, June 23, 1936 (Farnsworth Television). Image dissector. Reference to above.

5184 Farnsworth, P.T. "Cathode-ray amplifier." U.S. 2,228,388, July 6, 1935, renewed June 12, 1940, Jan. 14, 1941; Br. 472,860, June 23, 1936 (Farnsworth Television). Image amplifier with incandescent screen.

5185 Farnsworth, P.T. "Charge storage amplifier." U.S. 2,233,888, July 6, 1935, Mar. 4, 1941; Br. 471,448, June 23, 1936 (Farnsworth Television). Image tube with electron gun employing secondary emission.

5186 Schlesinger, K. "Television tube." U.S. 2,191,415, June 22, 1936, Feb. 20, 1940; Br. 481,430, July 6, 1936. In Germany July 6, 1935 (D.S. Loewe). Electrode structures, including a double-lens system, and operating potentials in a picture tube. References (4218, 4411, 4474, 4695).

5187 "Hollywood is becoming a radio centre—plans of artists." N.Y.T. IX, 11 (July 7): 4. NBC plans for a new studio. A coaxial cable will be necessary for transmission from California to the East Coast, but shipment by reels of film is more practical.

5188 Blumlein, A.D. "Amplifier circuits." Br. 462,530, July 8, 1935. Impedance networks to reduce the effect of stray capacitance in coupled circuits.

5189 Blumlein, A.D. "Amplifying circuits." Br. 462,583, July 8, 1935. Divided from above.

5190 Blumlein, A.D. "Amplifying circuits." Br.462,584, July 8, 1935; U.S. 2,149,331, July 8, 1936, Mar. 7, 1939 (EMI). Divided from Br. 462,530 (5188). Coupling circuits for reducing the effect of shunt capacitance or reactance introduced by circuit elements.

5191 Emyradis Soc. A.R.L. "Television." Br. 458,242, July 8, 1936. In France July 8, 1935. Mirror helix for producing two scanning lines per revolution.

5192 Knoll, M., and R. Urtel. "Electron optics." U.S. 2,151,777, July 8, 1936, Mar. 28, 1939. In Germany July 8, 1935 (Telefunken). Cathode-ray tube with electrostatic electron lens and deflection coils.

5193 Telefunken. "Television." Br. 455,598, July 7, 1936. In Germany July 8, 1935. Scanning with line and frame deflection fields at an angle other than a right-angle for trapezium-shaped areas.

5194 Urtel, R., and R. Andrieu. "Cathode-ray tube control circuits." U.S. 2,153,655, July 15, 1936, Apr. 11, 1939. In Germany July 8, 1935 (Telefunken). Deflection coil connections.

5195 Hardwick, J., and E.L.C. White. "Amplifier." Br. 459,526, July 9, 1935; U.S. 2,212,203, June 30, 1936, Aug. 20, 1940 (EMI). Discriminating network for correcting the lower response at high frequencies.

5196 Hardwick, J., and E.L.C. White. "Intervalve coupling." Br. 459,581, July 9, 1935; U.S. 2,161,959, July 8, 1936, June 13, 1939 (EMI).

5197 Toulon, Pierre Marie Gabriel. "Cathode-ray tube." U.S. 2,213,060, July 9, 1936, Aug. 27, 1940. In France July 9, 1935. Picture tube for image projections.

5198 Van Den Bosch, F.J.G. "Cathode-ray tube." Br. 445,820, July 10, 1935. Electrode assembly.

5199 Van Den Bosch, F.J.G. "Cathode-ray tube." Br. 445,523, July 10, 1935. Divided from above.

5200 Banneitz, F. "Uber Fernsehen." E.T.Z. 56 (July 11): 785–9. On latest developments in mechanical and cathode-ray scanning methods.

5201 D.S. Loewe. "Television." Br. 474,266, July 10, 1936. In Germany July 11, 1935. Receiver circuit with detector, amplifier, amplitude filter, and picture tube.

5202 D.S. Loewe. "Electron multiplier." Br. 477,916, July 10, 1936. In Germany July 11, 1935.

5203 C. Lorenz A.-G. "Valve generator." Br. 462,882, July 10, 1936. In Germany July 11, 1935. Saw-tooth oscillator.

5204 Codel, Martin. "America takes the plunge. 343-line television: 60 frames a second." W.W. 37 (July 12): 37. Photo. Note on RCA's plans. "So much publicity has been given to European television, notably in connection with the forthcoming tests of EMI and Baird in London, that the RCA has felt compelled to make a start."

5205 Messner, M. "Television receiver." U.S. 2,189,916, Feb. 29, 1936, Feb. 13, 1940; Br. 449,224, Nov. 15, 1935. In Germany July

12, 1935 (C. Lorenz A.-G.). Refers to intermediate frequency amplifiers and band-pass filters preceding a picture tube.

5206 White, E.L.C. "Television." Br. 459,853, July 12, 1935; U.S. 2,210,995, July 2, 1936, Aug. 13, 1940 (EMI). Compensating circuit in a receiver. References to Br. 442,906 (3896), 449,242 (4613).

5207 Lance, T.M.C., P.W. Willans, and Baird Television. "Valve amplifiers." Br. 459,723, July 13, 1935. Two amplifiers in parallel, one for higher and the other for lower frequencies, each with special coupling circuits.

5208 Priess, W.H. "Television." Br. 480,673, June 25, 1936; U.S. July 13, 1935.

5209 Priess, W.H. "Television." Br. 480,944, June 25, 1936; U.S. July 13, 1935. Divided from above.

5210 "What Europe sees. Broadcasters hear Mr. Cruse's television report on two month's survey." N.Y.T. IX, 11 (July 14): 7, 8. Comments by Andrew W. Cruse, chief of the Electrical Equipment Division, Department of Commerce, on television in Britain, Germany, and France.

5211 Farnsworth, P.T. "Image receiving tube." U.S. 2,118,186, July 15, 1935, May 14, 1938; Br. 482,357, June 23, 1936. Image dissector similar to U.S. 2,292,437 (5170). Reference to Br. 472,861 (5182).

5212 Szegho, C., and Baird Television. "Cathode-ray tubes." Br. 459,860, July 15, 1935. Concerns a permanent magnet structure for focusing the beam.

5213 Korshenewsky, Nicolai von. "Cathode-ray tube." U.S. 2,158,314, July 15, 1936, May 16, 1939. In Germany July 16, 1935. Cathode-ray tube with fluorescent screen.

5214 Ruska, E. "Magnetic deflection system for Braun tubes." U.S. 2,208,939, July 1, 1936, July 23, 1940; Br. 478,260, July 16, 1936. In Germany July 16, 1935 (Fernseh A.-G.).

5215 Kinne, E. (by E. Michaelis). "Television transmission." Br. 477,561, July 20, 1936. In Germany July 20, 1935. A photoelectric cathode is subjected to light from an object and is scanned by a light beam from another source (to produce saturation emission), which may be a cathode-ray tube. Reference to Br. 426,505 (4257).

5216 N.V. Philips. "Television." Br. 477,612, June 2, 1936. Convention date July 20, 1935. An image on an incandescent metal screen in a cathode-ray tube is enlarged by projection onto a separate screen. Applicable for color with several tubes and color filters.

5217 "Notes of interest in shipping world." N.Y.T. 25 (July 21): 1. Tests of television at sea with Reichpost on the Hamburg-American liner S.S. CARIBIA.

5218 Baird, J.L., and Baird Television. "Television." Br. 460,197, July 22, 1935. Mirror screw with linear displacement or oscillating mirror for producing an interlaced scan. Reference to Br. 442,668 (4511).

5219 Bray, T.E., and Baird Television. "Television." Br. 460,204, July 22, 1935. An intermediate film receiver with the film processed and projected before drying.

5220 Merdler, L.R., and Baird Television. "Wireless signalling." Br. 460,198, July 22, 1935. In a receiver for images and sound, the amplifier gain for both is controlled by the amplitude of the sound signals.

5221 Richardson, H.A. "Television." Br. 451,966, July 22, 1935. Addition to Br. 428,459 (4195). Concerns an optical system for separating the vertical and horizontal focal points.

5222 Brown, A.J., and Baird Television. "Television." Br. 460,222, July 23, 1935. Modulation by picture and sync signals.

5223 Busse, E. "Optical image intensifier." U.S. 2,177,360, July 3, 1936, Oct. 24, 1939. In Germany July 23, 1935 (N.V. Philips).

5224 Ruska, E. "Cathode-ray focusing system." U.S. 2,159,534, July 1, 1936, May 23, 1939; Br. 478,666, July 23, 1936. In Germany July 23, 1935 (Fernseh A.-G.). Coil provides a homogeneous field in image dissectors.

5225 Percival, W.S. "Electron discharge tubes." Br. 464,977, July 24, 1935; U.S. 2,211,859, July 9, 1936, Aug. 20, 1940 (EMI). Refers to special electrode construction, circuits, and applications, including electron multipliers.

5226 Percival, W.S. "Valve amplifiers." Br. 460,562, July 24, 1935. Series circuits for wide frequency bands.

5227 Bedford, A.V. "Cathode-ray-tue deflection circuits." U.S. 2,092,871, July 24, 1935, Sept. 14, 1937. Assigned: RCA. For electrostatic deflection in a camera tube.

5228 B.T.-H. "Cathode-ray tubes." Br. 477,216, June 24, 1936. In Germany July 25, 1935 (A.E.G.). Refers to a camera tube with a phosphorescent screen for intensifying the image formed on a photoelectric cathode, with supplemental scanning of the screen by infrared.

5229 D.S. Loewe. "Amplifier circuit." Br.464,553, July 24, 1936. In Germany July 25, 1935. Anti-flicker circuit comprises a preamplifier stage for a photocell followed by resistance-capacitance coupled stages.

5230 Schlesinger, K. "Stability of image amplifiers." U.S. 2,163,217, July 23, 1936, June 20, 1939; Br. 468,350, July 24, 1936. In Germany July 25, 1935. Divided from 464,553.

5231 Flory, L.E., and G.A. Morton. "Electric discharge device." U.S. 2,093,166, July 26, 1935, Sept. 14, 1937. Assigned: RCA. Br. 478,967, July 27, 1936 (Marconi's). Camera tube with attached electron multiplier. References (4349, 4464, 4873).

5232 Telefunken. "Television." Br. 477,363, June 26, 1936. In Germany July 26, 1935. A viewing screen on which an image is projected from a cathode-ray tube is curved to correct for distortion.

5233 Zeitline, V., A. Zeitline, and V. Kliatchko. "Cathode-ray tube." Br. 484,181, July 25, 1936. Void. In Germany July 26, 1935. A tube with a perforated disk and output electrode serves as an oscillation generator.

5234 Zworykin, V.K., and L. Malter. "Electron multiplying device." U.S. 2,147,825, July 26, 1935, Feb. 21, 1939. Assigned: RCA. Br. 478,970, July 27, 1936 (Marconi's). Reference to Br. 469,477 (4782).

5235 "Sarnoff off to Europe. Will seek to learn of developments in television." N.Y.T. 16 (July 27): 5. Sailed yesterday on the BERENGARIA, to visit England, France, and Germany.

5236 Baird Television and C. Szegho. "Cathode-ray tube." Br. 460,445, July 27, 1935. With built-in diode rectifier.

5237 Campbell, R.L. "Television." U.S. 2,178,736, July 27, 1935, Nov. 7, 1939. Assigned: RCA. Picture tube and receiver circuits.

5238 Schlesinger, K. "Frequency reduction device." U.S. 2,227,008, July 23, 1936, Dec. 31, 1940; Br. 475,595, July 24, 1936. In Germany July 27, 1935 (D.S. Loewe). Refers to an oscillator circuit producing unidirectional impulses of a subharmonic frequency, applicable for interlaced scanning.

5239 EMI and W.S. Percival. "Signalling system." Br. 462,228, July 29, 1935; U.S. 2,227,197, July 15, 1936, Dec. 31, 1940. Addition to Br. 446,663 (4599). Light intensity control in a picture tube receiver.

5240 Schlesinger, K. "Impulse generator." U.S. 2,185,131, July 23, 1936, Dec. 26, 1939; Br. 466,930, July 28, 1936. In Germany July 29, 1935 (D.S. Loewe). Sync generators applicable for interlaced scanning. References to Br. 423,394 (3485), 459,602 (4504).

5241 Szegho, C., T.M.C. Lance, and Baird Television. "Discharge apparatus." Br. 460,579, July 29, 1935. An optical image cast upon a photoelectric surface releases electrons which are accelerated and focused upon a fluorescent screen at the offsite end of the tube. Reference to Br. 444,998 (4503).

5242 Karolus, A., and F. Schröter. "Cathode-ray switch." U.S. 2,202,527, Sept. 10, 1936, May 28, 1940. In Germany July 30, 1935 (Telefunken). Cathode-ray tube with multiple photoelectric elements and conducting members in which the beam acts as a selector.

5243 Lippincott, D.K. "Cathode-ray tubes." Br. 460,773, July 30, 1935. Camera tube containing a photoelectric cathode plate at an angle of 45 degrees to the axis, a facing target with a mesh anode in front and a backing plate set at the same angle, an electron gun offset in an extension perpendicular to the target, with focusing coils at each end of the tube.

5244 Schlesinger, K. "Synchronization method." U.S. 2,227,007, July 23, 1936, Dec. 31, 1940; Br. 471,286, July 28, 1936. In Germany July 30, 1935 (D.S. Loewe). Refers to the generation of two sets of sync signals by means of a rotating slotted disk, coacting shutter, and amplifier.

5245 Zeitline, V., A. Zeitline, and V. Kliatchko. "Image intensifier." Br. 478,426, May 18, 1936. In Germany July 30, 1935. A tube contains a photoelectric screen, an adjacent accelerating electrode of wire mesh, a fluorescent screen at the opposite end, and, between the screens, a bundle of tubes coated inside with a secondary-emissive substance. Reference to Br. 457,493 (5092).

5246 "Gain in television is demonstrated. Philo T. Farnsworth shows clear images picked up by his system. A small screen is used. But he predicts at Philadelphia home sets soon with large-scale projection." N.Y.T. 15 (July 31): 4. Demonstration of 240/24 images at Television Laboratories, Chestnut Hill, by wire and by radio on 44 mc. Screen 5.5 by 7 inches.

5247 Massa, Ernest A., and L. Malter. "Electron multiplier." U.S. 2,113,378, July 31, 1935, Apr. 5, 1938. Assigned: RCA. Br. 477,347, June 25, 1936 (Marconi's).

5248 Poch, W.J. "Television." U.S. 2,219,579, July 31, 1935, Oct. 29, 1940. Assigned: RCA. Receiver circuits and picture tube.

5249 Chapple, H.J.B. POPULAR TELEVISION: UP-TO-DATE PRINCIPLES AND PRACTICES EXPLAINED IN SIMPLE LANGUAGE. London: Pitman, 1935. xiii + 112 pp. 46 illus. A clear explanation of basics with examples of apparatus and technologies in England in particular, and in Germany and the United States.

5250 Schubert, G. "Der erste Fernsehen Aufnahmewagen nach Zwischenfilmverfahren" [The first television reception by the intermediate film process]. FERN. U. TON. 6 (Aug.): 49.

5251 Weiss, G. "Gegensehen bei der Reichpost" [Two-way television at the German Post Office]. FERN. U. TON. 6 (Aug.): 53.

5252 Gernsback, H. "Presenting the multiple-image television receiver." RADIO-CRAFT 7 (Aug.): 74, 102. 4 diags. Console cabinet with three screens on top. Suggestions include electronically operated flat glass plates, translucent glass screens with three projection-tube scanners, and a three-way projection tube with separate screens.

5253 "Television present and future." RADIO-CRAFT 7 (Aug.): 75, 102. Statement by Lee de Forest includes: "In my opinion the inherent limitations of the cathode-beam tube will prevent its general acceptance by the public." Alfred N. Goldsmith states "Television development will proceed at a moderate pace in an orderly way during the next decade."

5254 Washburne, R.D., and W.E. Schrage. "World-wide television." RADIO-CRAFT 7 (Aug.): 76–80, 123–6. 43 illus. This broad survey presents "a working cross-section of television today throughout the world." Coverage includes companies, organizations, and systems in Canada, United States, Japan, England, France, Germany, Italy, Spain, Holland, Russia, South Africa and Czechoslovakia.

5255 Du Mont, A.B. "Cathode ray applications in television." RADIO-CRAFT 7 (Aug.): 81, 105. 6 illus. Discussion of types, and characteristics, problems, and advantages.

5256 Brolly, A.H., and R.C. Hergenrother. "Some facts about the Farnsworth system." RADIO-CRAFT 7 (Aug.): 82, 103. 3 illus. Brief technical details.

5257 Robinson, J.A. "Television in the school." RADIO-CRAFT 7 (Aug.): 90, 108. 3 photos.

5258 "Television sets may be rented!" RADIO N. 17 (Aug.): 70. Editorial.

5259 Kaufman, S. "Using cathode rays for high-definition television." RADIO N. 17 (Aug.): 76, 77. 5 photos. Barthélemy's system and plans for television in France.

5260 Babits, Victor A. "Latest television invention." RADIO N. 17 (Aug.): 77, 107. Diag. Description of the writer's cathode-ray tube with a photoelectric screen.

5261 Krawinkel, G. "Zur Frage des Fernsehens in natürlichen Farben" [On the question of television in natural colors]. E.T.Z. 56 (Aug.): 866.

5262 Brown, Jesse E. "Cathode-ray tube." U.S. 2,163,233, Aug. 2, 1935, June 20, 1939.

5263 Marconi's and G.B. Banks. "Electrical oscillation generator." Br. 463,625, Aug. 2, 1935; U.S. 2,160,052, July 24, 1936, May 30, 1939 (RCA). Blocking oscillator provides triangular wave forms and square-topped pulses applicable for suppressing a cathode beam during fly-back.

5264 Osawa, Juichi. "Electronic scanning device." U.S. 2,300,591, June 5, 1936, Nov. 3, 1942. Assigned: International Standard. Br. 468,483, Aug. 4, 1936 (S.T.C.). In Japan Aug. 3, 1935. Refers to an image pickup tube containing a thin metal plate which, when scanned by a cathode beam, emits secondary electrons towards an adjacent photomosaic plate, the latter being exposed is an optical image via a signal output electrode.

5265 Pratt, Harry P. "Television." U.S. 2,048,517, Aug, 5, 1935, July 21, 1936. Tube with a cathode, control electrode, anode, crystal, and screen.

5266 Schlesinger, K. "Level-maintenance for television amplifiers." U.S. 2,173,497, Aug. 4, 1936, renewed June 6, 1939, Sept. 19, 1939; Br. 468,905, Aug. 4, 1936. In Germany Aug. 5, 1935 (D.S. Loewe). Transmitter circuit. Reference to Br. 462,929 (4872).

5267 Schröter, F. "Cathode-ray tube." U.S. 2,210,987, Aug. 5, 1936, Aug. 13, 1940. In Germany Aug. 5, 1935 (Telefunken). Image pickup with double sided photomosaic, backing plate, electron gun, and focusing coils.

5268 Schlesinger, K. "Television scanning means." U.S. 2,227,010, Aug. 4, 1936, Dec. 31, 1940; Br. 470,500, Aug. 4, 1936. In Germany Aug. 6, 1935 (D.S. Loewe). Film transmission with apertured disk arranged for line sync signals and interlaced scan. References to Br. 465,184 (4603), 472,160 (4743).

5269 Ruska, E. "Braun tube." U.S. 2,128,597, Aug. 5, 1936, Aug. 30, 1938; Br. 479,471, Aug. 7, 1936. In Germany Aug. 7. 1935 (Fernseh A.-G.). Tube with internal resistive and conductive coatings, and coils for focusing and deflection.

5270 Walton, G.W. "Television." Br. 460,721, Aug. 7, 1935; U.S. 2,182,043, Aug. 1, 1936, Dec. 5, 1939. Concerns parallel circuits whereby signals proportional to the image frequency and the average light intensity are combined for transmission and separated at the receiver. Reference to Br. 379,552 (3160).

5271 Warren, H. "The television prospect. Some commercial and technical considerations." ELECT. 115 (Aug. 9): 161–3. General discussion of the art in England, Germany, and the United States, with views on the attitude of the entertainment industry, methods of scanning, levels of definition, RCA's camera tube, aspects of transmission, reception problems, and television in the home. See also editorial, p. 160.

5272 "The television position. Where we stand today." W.W. 37 (Aug. 9): 142, 143. 3 photos. Discussion of the Television Committee's recommendations, rumors about the systems favored by the Baird Company and EMI, the probable cost of receivers, and the future course of developments in Britain. "Although great secrecy is being observed concerning the technical side of television, especially as regards the design of suitable receivers, enough can be gleaned to assure us that striking progress has been made. Until essential technical details are divulged designers cannot attempt to produce receivers, nor can we estimate their cost with any accuracy."

5273 Farnsworth, P.T. "Cathode-ray amplifier tube." U.S. 2,251,124, Aug. 10, 1935, July 29, 1941; Br. 484,186, July 28, 1936 (Farnsworth Television). Tube contains a wire grid adjacent to a luminescent screen, and electron gun from which a high-velocity beam scans the grid, and two sources of low-velocity electrons between the primary electron gun and the grid-screen assembly.

5274 EMI and A.D. Blumlein. "Electrical network." Br. 462,823, Aug. 12, 1935; U.S. 2,138,996, Aug. 12, 1936, Dec. 6, 1938. Addition to Br. 421,546 (3965). Modified amplifier circuit.

5275 Bull, C.S., and W.S. Percival. "Electrical oscillation generator." U.S. 2,161,948, Aug. 7, 1936, June 13, 1939. In Britain Aug. 12, 1935.

5276 Bull, C.S., and W.S. Percival. "Valve generator." Br. 461,325, Aug. 12, 1935. Saw-tooth oscillator for magnetic deflection. Reference to Br. 451,204 (5127).

5277 Urtel, R. "Television transmission apparatus." U.S. 2,202,613, Aug. 11, 1936, May 28, 1940; Br. 479,302, Aug. 12, 1936. In Germany Aug. 12, 1935 (Telefunken). Relates to a variety of modular circuits.

5278 "Alexandra Palace television station." MAN. GUARD. 10 (Aug. 13): 3, 4.

5279 "Television next year. Public service from London." TIMES (Aug. 13): 12f. Baird Company and EMI to supply complete equipment for Alexandra Palace station. Postmaster-General's statement.

5280 Urtel, R., and R. Andrieu. "Saw-toothed wave form generator." U.S. 2,164,968, Aug. 11, 1936, July 4, 1939. In Germany Aug. 13, 1935 (Telefunken).

5281 Johnstone, D.M., and Baird Television. "Television." Br. 461,273, Aug. 14, 1935. Sync generator. Reference to Br. 437,339 (5054).

5282 Jones, V.A., and Baird Television. "Cathode-ray tube." Br. 461,197, Aug. 14, 1935. Refers to various constructions of a double-sided, multielement charge-storage electrode in a tube with an electron gun and a photoelectric cathode on the end face.

5283 Jones, V.A., and Baird Television. "Cathode-ray tube." Br. 461,312, Aug. 14, 1935. Divided from above. Construction of a mosaic screen.

5284 Schröter, F. "Television scanning apparatus." U.S. 2,176,190, Sept. 14, 1936, Oct. 17, 1939. In Germany Aug. 14, 1935 (Telefunken). Refers to a pickup tube with photosensitive electrodes and a gas-tight compartment exposed to an optical image on one side and scanned by a cathode beam on the other.

5285 "Television in six months." ELECT. 115 (Aug. 16): 202. Note on new transmissions from Alexandra Palace.

5286 "Television for air defence." ELECT. 115 (Aug. 16): 204. Note on German television being controlled by the Air Ministry with the exception of high-definition displays in public viewing rooms in Berlin.

5287 "Germany wireless show. Political radio. Dr. Goebbels on its role under Nazis." MAN. GUARD. 14 (Aug. 16): 1. Goebbels opened the Berlin radio show on Aug. 16.

5288 Johnstone, D.M., and Baird Television. "Photoelectric cells." Br. 461,434, Aug. 16, 1935. Refers to a tube with a fluorescent anode and oscillating circuit applicable to a camera tube.

5289 Gray, Robert C. "The Rev. John Kerr, F.R.S., inventor of the Kerr cell." NATURE 136 (Aug. 17): 245–57. 3 photos.

5290 A.C. Cossor and W.H. Stevens. "Cathode-ray tube." Br. 461,629, Aug. 19, 1935. Tube structure and operating potentials. Reference to Br. 450,940 (4774).

5291 Schlesinger, K. "Keystone correction." U.S. 2,227,009, Aug. 4, 1936, Dec. 31, 1940; Br. 479,305, Aug. 14, 1936. In Germany Aug. 19, 1935 (D.S. Loewe). Movable lenses in an imaging system applicable for film transmission with a scanning disk, camera tube, or picture tube.

5292 Telefunken. "Cathode-ray tube." Br. 485,453, Aug. 19, 1936. In Germany Aug. 19, 1935. A camera tube contains a photoelectric screen on the end for a single-sided mosaic screen of semiconducting material with a signal plate, and, in front, a grid or ring which collects secondary electrons emitted from the mosaic screen when it is scanned by a beam from an electron gun offset at an angle from the axis of the tube. Reference to Br. 315,362 (1339).

5293 "Fire at Berlin exhibition. Wireless halls destroyed. Escapes from tower restaurant." TIMES (Aug. 20): 12g.

5294 Andrieu, R. "Electromagnetic cathode-ray deflection apparatus." U.S. 2,164,891, Aug. 11, 1936, July 4, 1939. In Germany Aug. 20, 1935 (Telefunken). Deflection yoke.

5295 Comp. Gaz. "Valve generator." Br. 472,293, Aug. 21, 1936. In France Aug. 21, 1935. Saw-tooth oscillator for magnetic deflection.

5296 Kallman, Heinz Erwin, and O. Klemperer. "Electric discharge device." Br. 461,892, Aug. 21, 1935; U.S. 2,143,378, Aug. 13, 1936, Jan. 10, 1939 (EMI). Electron multiplier. Reference to Br. 450,138 (4139).

5297 Cawein, M. "Television receiving apparatus." U.S. 2,169,831, Aug. 22, 1935, Aug. 15, 1939. Assigned: Hazeltine. Circuit reduces the intensity of the cathode beam in the absence of negative bias.

5298 D.S. Loewe. "Television receivers." Br. 479,139, Aug. 14, 1936. In Germany Aug. 22, 1935. The frequencies of two relaxation oscillators can be changed to adapt the receiver for simple or interlaced picture signals. Reference to Br. 419,298 (3919), 423,394 (3485).

5299 D.S. Loewe. "Television." Br. 480,279, Aug. 21, 1936. In Germany Aug. 22, 1935. Relates to a system of film transmission with two separate scanners and transmitters, each handling different image and sync signals, along with separate sound pickup and transmission.

5300 Messner, M. "Television receiver." U.S. 2,285,043, Aug. 22, 1936, June 2, 1942; Br. 464,610, Aug. 11, 1936. In Germany Aug. 23, 1935 (C. Lorenz A.-G.). Relaxation oscillator circuit arranged to blank the beam during flyback. Reference to Br. 392,383 (3057).

5301 Wolff, H.-H. "Impulse generating arrangement." U.S. 2,191,185, Aug. 18, 1936, Feb. 20, 1940; Br. 485,904, Aug. 21, 1936. In Germany Aug. 23, 1935 (D.S. Loewe). In a cathode-ray tube the undeflected beam strikes a collecting electrode when the a-c deflection voltage passes through zero, thereby triggers a scanning oscillator. Applicable also for demodulating frequency-modulated television signals. Reference to Br. 433,295 (3781).

5302 "Home from Europe, Royal envisions expansion of broadcasting. Television as a pastime." N.Y.T. XI, 11 (Aug. 25): 3, 4. Report by John F. Royal, vice president NBC, on the popularity of German transmissions. "Television is rapidly becoming a national pastime in Germany." Local pickups by vans equipped with the intermediate film system are transmitted to a central station. Crowds around the public viewing booths at 10-to-20 minute intervals when 8-by-9-inch 180-line pictures are displayed.

5303 Roosenstein, H.O., and Max Geiger. "Signalling apparatus." U.S. 2,194,456, Nov. 27, 1936, Mar. 19, 1940. In Germany Aug. 27, 1935 (Telefunken). Picture tube receiver and control circuits.

5304 Ardenne, M. v. "Cathode-ray tubes." Br. 462,275, Aug. 18, 1936. In Germany Aug. 28, 1935. Deflection plates connected by sheets of highly-resistive material comprise a screen that surrounds the beam.

5305 Flory, L.E., and G.A. Morton. "Electro-optical device." U.S. 2,248,977, Aug. 29, 1935,

July 15, 1941. Assigned: RCA. Image intensifier.

5306 Poch, W.J. "Oscillator." U.S. 2,109,752, Aug. 29, 1935, Mar. 1, 1938. Assigned: RCA. Relaxation circuit.

5307 Szegho, C., W.P. Anderson, and Baird Television. "Cathode-ray tubes." Br. 461,999, Aug. 29, 1935. Conductive coatings inside and outside the tube serve as a smoothing capacitor in the high-voltage circuit.

5308 "Television progress." ELECT. 115 (Aug. 30): 244. Comment on the BBC decision to end 30-line transmissions on Sept. 15. (The last program was broadcast Sept. 11.)

5309 Marconi's and A.J. Young. "Cathode-ray tube." Br. 461,907, Aug. 31, 1935; U.S. 2,177,762, July 23, 1936, Oct. 31, 1939 (RCA). Construction of deflection plates and guard rings to reduce trapezium distortion.

5310 Warren, H. "Television and the future." DISCOVERY 16 (Sept.): 276–9. 2 illus. From THE ELECTRICIAN, Aug. 9.

5311 Cruse, A.W. "The status of television in Europe." ELECT. ENG. 54 (Sept.): 966–9. An address at the 13th annual convention of the National Association of Broadcasters, Colorado Springs, July 8.

5312 "Television transmitters planned." ELECTRONICS 8 (Sept.): 28, 29. 3 photos. "P.T. Farnsworth tells press at Philadelphia demonstration that three 7-meter transmitters are under way. 20 kw. stations to have 30-mile range." Brief report on a half-hour program of direct pickup and film transmitted over short distances by wire, and by radio on 40 mc, given July 30. Images (240/24 interlaced) were shown on 7-inch and 14-inch tubes. The film pickup was said to be "of a very high order of excellence, and was the equal to the average home movie in detail, brilliance, and contrast."

5313 Scholz, W. "Störungen des Ultrakurzwellen-Empfangs" [Interference in ultra-short-wave aerials]. FERN. U. TON. 6 (Sept.): 68.

5314 "Television for millions." POP. MECH. 64 (Sept.): 321–3, 142A. 7 photos, diag. On Baird's system and apparatus at the Crystal Palace.

5315 Oakville, Rupert. "Television in Canada." RADIO N. 17 (Sept.): 142, 143, 186, 187. 4 photos, diag. On the Peck Television Corporation. Daily broadcasts given by Station VE9AK, Dominion Square Building, Montreal. Receiver with light valve and car headlight bulb projects pictures 14 by 16 inches.

5316 "Television status in the United States." RADIO N. 17 (Sept.): 162. List of 27 stations.

5317 Brown, A.J., and Baird Television. "Amplifying circuit." Br. 462,247, Sept. 4, 1935. Compensation circuit for a cathode-ray tube.

5318 "German advance in television." ELECT. 115 (Sept.): 280. Note on the German radio exhibition. Twenty sets by five manufacturers with screens 7 by 9 inches up to 9 inches square, costing from £66 to £250. Programs by the Ministry of Propaganda transmitted by the Post Office.

5319 "The Berlin radio show. The twelfth great German wireless exhibition reviewed." W.W. 37 (Sept. 6): 266–9. Brief reference to television section, with mention of Telefunken, Fernseh A.-G., Lorenz (Ardenne), Loewe, Philips, and Tekade. Except the mirror screw by Tekade, all receivers used picture tubes.

5320 "A Briton in Berlin. The two radio shows compared." W.W. 37 (Sept. 6): 277, 278. 2 photos. "Undoubtedly a large section of the crowds in the Berlin exhibition had been attracted by the television exhibits."

5321 Bronk, O. v. "Television transmitting and receiving apparatus." U.S. 2,149,001, Feb. 17, 1937, Feb. 28, 1939. In Germany Sept. 6, 1935 (Telefunken).

5322 Marconi's. "Electric discharge device." Br. 481,170, Sept. 7. 1936. Convention date Sept. 6, 1935. Electron multiplier. References (4782, 5149).

5323 Walton, G.W. "Television." Br. 462,258, Sept. 6, 1935. Addition to Br. 432,017 (4155). Multicell array of light-sensitive surfaces, multiple apertures, subdivided optical path with a series of lenses, and multichannel transmission. References to Br. 379,303 (2785), 403,395 (3351).

5324 "Seeing 'news' in the making. Television progress. A service for cinemas." MAN. GUARD. 13 (Sept. 7): 3. On a paper read by A.G.D. West at the British Association meeting in Norwich.

5325 "Reveals television plans." N.Y.T. 8 (Sept. 7): 1, 2. On West's paper.

5326 "Television in the near future. A powerful influence." TIMES (Sept 7): 8a. On West's paper.

5327 Farnsworth, P.T. "Image analyzing tube." U.S. 2,100,841, Sept. 7, 1935, Nov. 30, 1937. Assigned: Farnsworth Television.

5328 Farnsworth, P.T. "Charge storage dissector tube." U.S. 2,141,836, Sept. 7, 1935, Dec. 27, 1938; Br. 485,646, Aug. 20, 1936 (Farnsworth Television). Void. An image dissector with an addition thermionic cathode in front of a photosensitive screen.

5329 Marconi's and R.J. Kemp. "Television picture reproducing apparatus." Br. 462,330, Sept. 7, 1935; U.S. 2,200,749, Sept. 8, 1936, May 14, 1940 (RCA). Concerns the optical projection of an image from a picture tube onto an intermediate multicell screen; connections from the elements of this screen control corresponding light sources, such as miniature cathode-ray tubes, grouped to form a large mosaic screen.

5330 Telefunken. "Television." Br. 481,132, Sept. 7, 1936. In Germany Sept. 7, 1935. Receiver with screen scanned by infrared via a Nipkow disk and flooded intermittently by infrared from another source.

5331 White, E.L.C. "Amplifier." Br. 462,536, Sept. 7, 1935. Wide-band direct-coupled circuit. Reference to Br. 448,421 (4600).

5332 "Television programmes. Regular service in October." TIMES (Sept. 8): 10c. Broadcasting from Alexandra Palace suspended until the end of Oct., when installation will be completed.

5333 B.T.-H. "Amplifier." Br. 486,941, Sept. 9, 1936. In Germany Sept. 9, 1935 (A.E.G.). Wide-band for high television frequencies.

5334 Brüche, E. "Elektronenoptische Untersuchungen zur Braunschen Hochvakuumröhre" [Electron-optical researches on high-vacuum Braun tubes]. ARCH. ELEKT. 29 (Sept. 10): 642–54.

5335 Miller, Harold. "Picture transmitter." Br. 462,550, Sept. 10, 1935; U.S. 2,212,923, Aug. 12, 1936, Aug. 27, 1940 (EMI). Refers to a mosaic screen with a semiconducting layer, signal plate, blocking layer, and photosensitive elements utilizing the photovoltaic effect. Details of preparation, construction, and operation are given. Reference to Br. 455,123 (4829).

5336 D.S. Loewe. "Television." Br. 481,444, Sept. 10, 1936. In Germany Sept. 11, 1935. Deflection oscillator circuit arrayed to deflect the cathode beam outside the image area during line flyback.

5337 Gilbert, A.H., L.R. Merdler, and Baird Television. "Cathode-ray tubes." Br. 462,684, Sept. 12, 1935. Deflection yoke.

5338 Gilbert, A.H., L.R. Merdler, G.R. Tingley, and Baird Television. "Cathode-ray tubes." Br. 462,683, Sept. 12, 1935. Magnetic shield assembly.

5339 McKay, J.W. "Transmitting images." U.S. 2,109,622, Sept. 12, 1935, Mar. 1, 1938. Assigned: National Television. Divided from U.S. 2,056,974 (3808). Disk with a double set of spiral apertures and shutter.

5340 Schröter, F. "Electronic device." U.S. 2,212,249, Sept. 10, 1936, Aug. 20, 1940. In Germany Sept. 12, 1935 (Telefunken). Cathode-ray tube.

5341 "British Association." ELECT. 115 (Sept. 13): 305. This report on the meetings at Norwich mentions Capt. West's paper and his demonstration of recent apparatus, with comments by others, including those of Major A. Church.

5342 Wilhelmy, H.J. "Through German eyes. English and German techniques compared." W.W. 37 (Sept. 13): 306, 307. Includes photo of large Telefunken-Karolus screen with 10,000 lamps, and photo of a projected image.

5343 Farnsworth, P.T. "Charge storage tube." U.S. 2,100,842, Sept. 14, 1935, Nov. 30, 1937; Br. 485,645, Aug. 19, 1936 (Farnsworth Television). Void. Image tube similar to U.S. 2,233,888 (5185). Reference to Br. 472,859 (5170).

5344 Mat. Tel. Soc. Anon. "Television." Br. 466,071, Sept. 3, 1936 (S.T.C.). In France Sept. 18, 1935. Refers to shifted portions of a wide frequency transmission band in relation to a network of coaxial cables in a television distribution system.

5345 "Eiffel Tower to be used for a television station." N.Y.T. 21 (Sept. 19): 2. A government station will begin operating in six months.

5346 Reyner, J.H. "Television experiments. A high-definition test transmitter." W.W. 37 (Sept. 20): 331. 3 photos. Film scanning with a cathode-ray tube and photocell for 120-line (or 180-line) demonstrations.

5347 Baird Television and J.R.H. Forman. "Light-sensitive multiplier." Br. 463,061, Sept. 20, 1935. Electron multiplier. Reference to Br. 450,138 (4139).

5348 Barthélemy, R. "La télévision à l'Exposition Universelle et Internationale de Bruxelles (1935)" [Television at the Universal and International Exhibition at Brussels]. REV. GEN. 38 (Sept. 21): 405–10. Description of the displays and apparatus, including the French Post Office 60/25 system with Nipkow disk and picture tube receiver.

5349 Urtel, R. "Television scanning apparatus." U.S. 2,210,992, Sept. 21, 1936, Aug. 13, 1940. In Germany Sept. 21, 1935 (Telefunken). Transmission system employing a plurality of carrier-wave generators, modulators, and cathode-ray tubes.

5350 Lubszynski, H.G. "Television transmitter." Br. 464,919, Sept. 24, 1935; U.S. 2,314,648, Sept. 10, 1936, Mar. 23, 1943 (EMI). Image tube with a double-sided mosaic, auxiliary light beam, and circuit. References (4464, 4660, 4829, 5092).

5351 Miller, H. "Picture transmitter." Br. 463,297, Sept. 24, 1935; U.S. 2,211,145, Sept. 17, 1936, Aug. 13, 1940 (EMI). Image tube with a photoconductive screen, electron gun, and electrode for collecting secondary electrons. Preparation of the screen with zinc selenide and other substances is given.

5352 Miller, H. "Picture transmitter." U.S. 2,211,146, Sept. 23, 1936, Aug. 13, 1940. In Britain Sept. 24, 1935 (EMI). Similar to above.

5353 Ruska, E. "Cathode-ray tube." U.S. 2,143,581, Sept. 26, 1936, Jan. 10, 1939. In Germany Sept. 24, 1935 (Fernseh A.-G.).

5354 Schröter, F. "Electro-optical signalling." U.S. 2,155,509, Sept. 29, 1936, Apr. 25, 1939; Br. 482,208, Sept. 24, 1936. In Germany Sept. 24, 1935 (Telefunken). Concerns a phototube with a phosphorus dielectric layer between a plate and a mesh electrode in a bridge circuit with a cathode-ray amplifier tube. An image, projected line by line onto the phototube via a mirror wheel, acts in conjunction with an oscillating cathode beam.

5355 Skaupy, F. "Image intensifier." Br. 479,617, Sept. 24, 1936, In Germany Sept. 24, 1935. Grouped phototubes, each with a light-sensitive cathode, grid anode, and fluorescent screen, form a mosaic screen.

5356 Geiger, M. "Saw-tooth wave generator." U.S. 2,168,403, Sept. 21, 1936, Aug. 8, 1939. In Germany Sept. 25, 1935 (Telefunken).

5357 Kinne, E. (by E. Michaelis). "Saw-tooth generator." Br. 966,396, Sept. 25, 1934. In Germany Sept. 25, 1935.

5358 Bridgewater, T.H. "Valve amplifier." Br. 460,673, Sept. 26, 1935. Circuit with a switch provides positive or negative images.

5359 Ferranti and M.K. Taylor. "Television." Br. 458,618, Sept. 26, 1935. Mirror disk.

5360 Kinne, E. (by E. Michaelis). "Valve detector circuit." Br. 466,545, Sept. 25, 1936. In Germany Sept. 26, 1935. Circuit favors high picture frequencies. References to Br. 425,417 (3874), 452,118 (4341).

5361 Kinne, E. (by E. Michaelis). "Valve generator." Br. 468,995, Sept. 25, 1936. In Germany Sept. 26, 1935. Saw-tooth oscillator.

5362 Scophony, J.D. Baynes, and G. Wikkenhauser. "Television." Br. 458,382, Sept. 27, 1935. Relates to a method for reducing the light intensity during a change of scene.

5363 Winckel, F.W. "Fernsehen auf der Berliner Funkausstellung" [Television at the Berlin radio exhibition]. Z. FERN. 16 (Sept. 28): 132, 133.

5364 Ogloblinsky, G.N. (by V.K. Zworykin). "Picture transmitting apparatus." U.S. 2,176,225, Sept. 28, 1935, Oct. 17, 1939. Assigned: RCA. Refers to an image tube for film transmission.

5365 George, R.H. "Television." U.S 2,194,278, Sept. 30, 1935, Mar. 19, 1940. Assigned: RCA. Picture tube circuit including control of amplification.

5366 George, R.H. "Cathode-ray tube." U.S. 2,222,942, Sept. 30, 1935, Nov. 26, 1940. Assigned: RCA.

5367 George, R.H., and H.J. Heim. "Amplifier." U.S. 2,137,278, Sept. 30, 1935, Nov. 22, 1938. Assigned: RCA. Multistage photoelectric amplifier, scanning disk, and film.

5368 Holmes, R.S. "Television." U.S. 2,165,794, Sept. 30, 1935, July 11, 1939. Assigned: RCA. Sound and picture receiver.

5369 Ruska, E. "Deflecting coil for cathode-ray tubes." U.S. 2,152,362, Sept. 16, 1936, Mar. 28, 1939; Br. 482,513, Sept. 30, 1936. In Germany Sept. 30, 1935 (Fernseh A.-G.).

5370 Sprague, Carlton S., and R.H. George. "Cathode-ray deflecting electrode." U.S. 2,161,437, Sept. 30, 1935, June 6, 1939. Assigned: RCA.

5371 Okolicsányi, F. "Die Zeilensprungmethode bei mechanischen Fernseh-Systemen" [The line interlacing method in mechanical television systems]. FERN. U. TON. 6 (Oct.): 69.

5372 "Television on trial." POP. MECH. 64 (Oct.): 524–6, 135A. 7 photos. BBC tests.

5373 "Television rumors from here and abroad." RADIO N. 17 (Oct.): 198, 252, 253. 4 photos. Editorial report on AT&T, Farnsworth, Philco, RCA, FCC, Automatic Electric Co., Baird, Marconi-EMI, Alexandra Palace, German test with the S.S. CARIBIA.

5374 Oakville, R. "Reporting television's programs in America." RADIO N. 17 (Oct.): 210, 211, 241. 5 photos.

5375 Hall, Victor. "New coaxial cable for television." RADIO N. 17 (Oct.): 211, 249. 2 photos, Bell Labs.

5376 Ferranti and S. Atkinson. "Valve circuits." Br. 465,108, Oct. 2, 1935. Photocell modulator and video amplifier. Reference to Br. 386,296 (2340).

5377 Ferranti and M.K. Taylor. "Valve circuits." Br. 465,405, Oct. 2, 1935. Demodulator for television.

5378 Ferranti, M.K. Taylor, and S. Atkinson. "Television transmitter." Br. 463,867, Oct. 2, 1935. Methods of scanning film by a disk, drum, image pickup tube, or cathode-ray tube.

5379 Ferranti and J.C. Wilson. "Cathode-ray tubes." Br. 465,266, Oct. 3, 1935. Cathode-rays from a side chamber are focused through the side of a Wehnelt cylinder onto a surface that emits secondary electrons.

5380 Schröter, F., and M. Knoll. "Cathode-ray tube." U.S. 2,156,435, Oct. 19, 1936, May 2, 1939. In Germany Oct. 3, 1935, (Telefunken).

5381 "High-definition television. Specifications of the Baird and Marconi-EMI wave-forms to be radiated from the Alexandra Palace." ELECT. 115 (Oct. 4): 409, 410. 3 diags. Technical description of both systems and of the Marconi-EMI method of interlaced scanning, reproduced in full as supplied by the companies.

5382 "Television transmissions. Details of the Baird and Marconi-EMI systems." W.W. 37 (Oct. 4). Photo, 3 diags. As above, with editorial comments and a table comparing the characteristics.

5383 Barthélemy, R. "Relaxation oscillation generator." U.S. 2,168,508, Sept. 24, 1936, Aug. 8, 1939; Br. 482,724, Oct. 3, 1936. In France Oct. 4, 1935 (Comp. Gaz).

5384 Comp. Gaz. "Valve generator." Br. 482,725, Oct. 3, 1936. In France Oct. 4, 1935. Divided from above. Saw-tooth oscillator. Reference to Br. 432,856 (4406).

5385 Lewis, H.M., and M. Cawein. "Television." U.S. 2,137,123, Oct. 4, 1935, Nov. 15 1938. Assigned: Hazeltine. Picture tube with magnetic and electrostatic deflection, full receiver circuit.

5386 Schlesinger, K. "Television scanning means." U.S. 2,227,011, Sept. 29, 1936, Dec. 31, 1940; Br. 488,419, Oct. 5, 1936. In Germany Oct. 4, 1935 (D.S. Loewe). Relates to film transmission with scanning by a rotating ring of lenses, a spiral of lenses, a spirally apertured disk and lens system, with provisions for the generation of sync signals and interlaced scan. References (4602, 4658, 4720).

5387 D.S. Loewe. "Television." Br. 488,486, Oct. 5, 1936. In Germany Oct. 4, 1935. Divided from above.

5388 Baird Television and L.R. Merdler. "Television." Br. 463,971, Oct. 8, 1935. Sync circuit. Reference to Br. 435,196 (4382).

5389 Baird Television and L.R. Merdler. "Television." Br. 463,973, Oct. 8, 1935. Signal amplifier and magnetic focusing circuit.

5390 Baird Television and G.R. Tingley. "Television." Br. 463,972, Oct. 8, 1935. Magnetic deflection assembly with four coils for different circuit functions. Reference to Br. 456,138 (5037).

5391 Rothe, Horst, and Warner Kleen. "Electron discharge device." U.S. 2,112,050, Sept. 18, 1936, Mar. 22, 1938. In Germany Oct. 8, 1935 (Telefunken). Cathode-ray tube.

5392 Henderson, S.T. "Discharge apparatus." Br. 464,105, Oct. 9, 1935. Relates to the preparation and application of a non-reflecting coating on an electrode on the inner surface of a cathode-ray tube.

5393 Bähring, Herbert. "Two-tube deflection circuit." U.S. 2,178,772, Sept. 16, 1936. Nov. 7, 1939. In Germany Oct. 10, 1935 (Fernseh A.-G.). Saw-tooth generator.

5394 Baird Television and L.R. Merdler. "Valve circuits." Br. 464,037, Oct. 10, 1935. Scanning generator circuit in a super-regenerative receiver.

5395 Zeiss Ikon A.-G. "Television." Br. 475,000, Sept. 8, 1936. In Germany Oct. 12, 1935. Optical system for film transmission with a transparent roller and disk scanner.

5396 N.V. Philips. "Cathode-ray tube." Br. 465,763, July 16, 1936. Convention date Oct. 14, 1935. Focus coil assembly mounted inside a tube.

5397 Bähring, H. "Coupling circuit independent of frequency." U.S. 2,172,150, Sept. 16, 1936, Sept. 5, 1939. In Germany Oct. 15, 1935 (Fernseh A.-G.).

5398 Ruska, E. "Braun tube." U.S. 2,151,530, Sept. 16, 1936, Mar. 21, 1939. In Germany Oct. 154, 1935 (Fernseh A.-G.).

5399 D.S. Loewe. "Electron discharge device." Br. 486,657, Oct. 8, 1936. In Germany Oct. 16, 1935. Refers to the increase of emissions from a secondary emissive target when heated. In an image pickup tube with a single-sided mosaic screen heated by a filament adjacent to the signal plate, the screen is scanned by the electron image emitted from a primary photoelectric screen and by the beam from an electron gun at right angles to the optical axis.

5400 D.S. Loewe. "Image intensifier." Br. 486,750, Oct. 8, 1936. In Germany Oct. 16, 1935. Divided from above. Modified form of tube with the electron gun replaced by a fluorescent screen.

5401 D.S. Loewe. "Cathode-ray tube." Br. 486,915, Oct. 8, 1936. In Germany Oct. 16, 1935. Divided from Br. 486,657 (5399). Picture tube containing a heated secondary emissive plate for intensifying the image and auxiliary deflecting and focusing coils.

5402 Klemperer, O. "Electric discharge device." Br. 464,413, Oct. 16, 1935; U.S. 2,138,928, Oct. 9, 1936, Dec. 6, 1938 (EMI). Electron multiplier with apertured screen for selectively stopping electrons according to velocity. Reference to Br. 443,777 (4536).

5403 S.T.C., D.H. Black, and W.W. Marsh. "Cathode-ray tube." Br. 464,430, Oct. 18, 1935. Electrode construction and assembly.

5404 Buschbeck, Werner. "Resistance-coupled amplifier." U.S. 2,143,540, Oct. 31, 1936, Jan. 10, 1939. In Germany Oct. 22, 1935 (Telefunken). Wide-band amplifier.

5405 Buschbeck, W. "Wide-band amplifier." U.S. 2,164,899, Oct. 8, 1936, July 8, 1939. In Germany Oct. 22, 1935 (Telefunken).

5406 G.E.C. and D.C. Espley. "Cathode-ray tube." Br. 459,963, Oct. 22, 1935. Picture tube with inner conductive coating and outer metal shield.

5407 Schlesinger, K. "Television receiver." U.S. 2,147,554, Oct. 22, 1935, Feb. 14, 1939 (D.S. Loewe). Divided from U.S. 2,173,495 (4312).

5408 Schlesinger, K. "Television receiver." U.S. 2,226,999, Oct. 22, 1935, Dec. 31, 1940 (D.S. Loewe).

5409 Shoenberg, I. "Television transmitters." Br. 464,692, Oct. 22, 1935. Refers to various optical and electrical means for compensating the uneven illumination on a mosaic screen due to the oblique optical angle. Reference to Br. 444,074 (4610).

5410 Baird Television and P.W. Willans. "Television." Br. 464,828, Oct. 23, 1935. Reinsertion of the d-c component.

5411 Baird Television and P.W. Willans. "Television." Br. 464,979, Oct. 23, 1935. Reinsertion of the d-c component. Reference to Br. 406,672 (3105).

5412 "New radio device spurs television. Dr. Zworykin shows engineers amplifier that converts light into electricity. Noises are eliminated." N.Y.T. 2 (Oct. 24): 5. Demonstration of electron multipliers at a meeting of the IRE Oct. 23, "This advantage over ordinary tubes held to be special aid in television field."

5413 G.E.C. and D.C. Espley. "Television." Br. 459,735, Oct. 24, 1935. Concerns the separate generation of picture signals and the d-c component, and their recombination in a film transmitter. References (959, 3364, 3830, 4482).

5414 Ruska, E. "Deflection coil." U.S. 2,186,595, Aug. 5, 1936, Jan. 9, 1940; Br. 475,539, Oct. 21, 1936. In Germany Oct. 24, 1935 (Fernseh A.-G.). Addition to Br. 475,527 (5077).

5415 Marconis and W.S.L. Tringham. "Modulated carrier wave transmitter." Br. 464,788, Oct. 24, 1935; U.S. 2,172,553, Oct. 10, 1936, Sept. 12, 1939 (RCA). Addition to Br. 428,700 (4206). Cathode-ray tube monitor applicable for television.

5416 West, A.G.D. "Present position of television." ENGINEERING 140 (Oct. 25): 457–9. (Nov. 1): 485, 486. Lecture at the British Association meeting Sept. 6.

5417 Cawley, A.J. "Television." U.S. 2,118,160, Oct. 25, 1935, May 24, 1938. Divided from U.S. 2,122,337 (2425). Receiver with polarized light beam split and recombined.

5418 D.S. Loewe. "Cathode-ray tubes." Br. 489,362, Oct. 23, 1936. In Germany Oct. 25, 1935. In an image pickup tube with the mosaic screen set at a right-angle to the optical axis, the screen is scanned by the beam from an electron gun parallel to the screen, the beam being deflected at a right angle to strike the screen normal to the surface. Other variants refer to a pickup tube and a picture tube.

5419 G.E.C., R.J. Dippy, and D.C. Espley. "Television receiver." Br. 458,878, Oct. 25, 1935. Switch and circuit for selecting either of two systems.

5420 Morton, G.A. "Electron multiplier." U.S. 2,174,162, Oct. 25, 1935, Sept. 26, 1939. Assigned: RCA. Br. 483,826, Oct. 26, 1936 (Marconi's). Reference (4873).

5421 Schlesinger, K. "Transformation of relaxation oscillations." U.S. 2,147,559, Oct. 16, 1936, Feb. 14, 1939; Br. 483,667, Oct. 23, 1936. In Germany, Oct. 25, 1935 (D.S. Loewe).

5422 Goldmark, P.C. "Television." U.S. 2,173,476, Oct. 26, 1935, Sept. 19, 1939. Assigned: Markia. Large-screen projection from a cathode-ray tube via lens and mirror drum.

5423 "Radio company applies for television permit." N.Y.T. IX 13 (Oct. 27): 6. Philco.

5424 Andrieu, R. "Energy generator for cathode-ray deflection." U.S. 2,227,480, Nov. 7. 1936, renewed May 10, 1939, Jan.7, 1941; Br. 483,999, Oct. 28, 1936. In Germany Oct. 28, 1935 (Telefunken). Saw-tooth generator. Reference to Br. 412.813 (3640).

5425 Baird Television and E.E. Wright. "Television." Br. 465,055, Oct. 29, 1935. Scanning oscillator for line and frame frequencies. Reference to Br. 444,133 (4744).

5426 B.T.-H., J. Moir, and R.G. Hibberd. "Amplifier." Br. 465,053, Oct. 29, 1935. Wide-band push-pull circuit.

5427 Ferranti and J.C. Wilson. "Valve generator." Br. 464,141, Oct. 29, 1935. Saw-tooth oscillator for deflection coils.

5428 Miller, H. "Television transmitting apparatus." Br. 465,060, Oct. 29, 1935; U.S. 2,177,736, Oct. 14, 1936, Oct. 31, 1939 (EMI). Refers to the construction of a single-sided image screen bearing a layer of photoconductive material coated with a substance, such as the borate of an alkali metal, that is an emitter of secondary electrons. Reference to Br. 463,297 (5351).

5429 B.T.-H. and D.J. Mynall. "Amplifier." Br. 465,118, Oct. 30, 1935. Deflection amplifier.

5430 Zworykin, V.K., and E.A. Massa. "Electric discharge device." U.S. 2,078,304, Oct. 30, 1935, Apr. 27, 1937. Assigned: RCA. Br. 484,099, Oct. 30, 1936 (Marconi's). Electron multiplier. Reference to Br. 477,347 (5247).

5431 Bedford, A.V. "Television." U.S. 2,173,467, Oct. 31, 1935, Sept. 19, 1939. Assigned: RCA. Image pickup tube, saw-tooth oscillator, amplifiers, and corrective network.

5432 Farnsworth, P.T. "Television." Br. 465,344, Oct. 31, 1935. Picture tube receiver circuits.

5433 Maloff, I.G. "Cathode-ray tube deflecting device." U.S. 2,164,931, Oct. 31, 1935, July 4, 1939. Assigned: RCA. Deflection yoke assembly.

5434 Poch, W.J. "Television." U.S. 2,151,526, Oct. 31, 1935, Mar. 21, 1939. Assigned: RCA. Picture tube receiver circuit.

5435 Risdon, P.J. TELEVISION REALLY EXPLAINED; POPULAR TELEVISION FOR ALL. London: W. Foulsham, 1935. 94 pp., illus. Elementary treatment centered on 30-line apparatus.

5436 "Secondary emission electron multipliers." ELECTRONICS 8 (Nov.): 10–3. 5 photos, 5 diags. Report on the Oct. meeting of the IRE when Dr. Zworykin and his associates demonstrated the tubes developed at the RCA Victor Research Laboratory. Technical features of various types are given, and there is a list of 18 U.S. and British patents.

5437 Davis, Robert F. "Television scanning—a survey." ELECTRONICS 8 (Nov.): 30–2. 6 diags. Chiefly on Thun's work with variable velocity scanning, with mention of von Ardenne (2892) and Sellers (367).

5438 Roosenstein, H.O. "Neuentwicklung im Fernsehenbau" [New development in television construction]. FERN. U. TON. 6 (Nov.): 77–9. Description of the Telefunken FE IV receiver with sound and vision circuits; screen 19 by 22 cm.

5439 Carnahan, Chalon W. "The steady-state response of a network to a periodic driving force of arbitrary shape, and applications to television circuits." PROC. IRE 23 (Nov.): 1393–1404. 9 diag.

5440 Goldsmith, A.N. "Television in the theatre." RADIO-CRAFT 7 (Nov.): 283, 316. 2 photos.

5441 Kaufman, S. "Demonstrates high-definition television." RADIO N. 17 (Nov.): 265, 308. 3 photos. Report on a demonstration to the editorial staff given at the laboratories of Farnsworth Television in Philadelphia.

5442 G.E.C., George William Edwards, and D.C. Espley. "Television receiver." Br. 458,879, Nov. 1, 1935. Amplifier and sync separation circuit.

5443 Fernseh A.-G. "Discharge apparatus." Br. 468,330, Nov. 2, 1936. In Germany Nov. 2, 1935. In an image pickup tube with a window at one end and a photoelectric mosaic at the other end, an electron gun is situated near the window on the optical axis. External coils focus and deflect the electron beam.

5444 Urtel, R., R. Andrieu, and Max Geiger. "Television receiver operating level control." U.S. 2,158,261, Oct. 28, 1936, May 16, 1939; Br. 480,275, Oct. 27, 1936. In Germany Nov. 2, 1935 (Telefunken). Picture and sync circuits.

5445 Knoblauch, Henning, and Werner Fluge. "Cathode-ray image scanner with magnetic deflection." U.S. 2,178,374, Nov. 28, 1936, Oct. 31, 1939. In Germany Nov. 3, 1935 (Telefunken).

5446 Baird Television and D.M. Johnstone. "Valve circuit." Br. 465,276, Nov. 4, 1935. Super-regenerative receiver with quenching during fly-back.

5447 Baird Television and D.M. Johnstone. "Valve generator." Br. 465,147, Nov. 5, 1935. Sync circuit with amplifier and switch for sequential or interlaced scanning. Reference to Br. 456,666 (5061).

5448 Gray, F. "Electro-optical system." U.S. 2,169,179, Nov. 5, 1935, Aug. 8, 1939. Assigned: B.T.L. Film scanning with cathode-ray tube.

5449 Eaton, R.D. "Electronic device." U.S. 2,128,632, Nov. 6, 1935, Aug. 30, 1938. 5 assignees. Divided from U.S. 2,128,631 (4650). Special tube with an oblique photoelectric plate, optical system, deflected light beam, and external screen.

5450 Toulon, P.M.G. "Television." Br. 473,166, Nov. 6, 1936. In France Nov. 5, 1935. Transmitting tube with two mesh grids between a photoelectric cathode and a ring anode. Light from a motion picture film is projected onto the cathode, the other scanning motion being provided by an oscillator connected to the grids.

5451 Toulon, P.M.G. "Television receiving set." U.S. 2,165,078, Nov. 6, 1936, July 4, 1939. Assigned: RCA. In France. Nov. 6, 1935. Cabinet assembly with receiver and picture tube.

5452 Guibiansky, J.A. "Television." Br. 464,700, Nov. 8, 1935. Scanner with two mirror drums and provision for varying the speed of transmission.

5453 Keystone, J.E. "Electron multiplier." Br. 468,623, Nov. 8, 1935; U.S. 2,210,034, Nov. 5, 1936, Aug. 6, 1940 (EMI).

5454 D.S. Loewe. "Cathode-ray tube." Br. 488,644, Nov. 9, 1936. In Germany Nov. 9, 1935. Conductive coating for an image pickup tube.

5455 Schwartz, Erich, and E. Ruska. "Television." U.S 2,191,590, Nov. 6, 1936, Feb. 27, 1940; Br. 484,598, Nov. 9, 1936. In Germany Nov. 9, 1935 (Fernseh A.-G.). Relates to an electron multiplier with input signals from an image pickup tube applied to a control grid. Light from an external source is projected by an oblique mirror onto the photocathode, from which electrons are focused by a coil to pass between two electrodes where secondary emission takes place, the multiplied stream being collected by a ring anode.

5456 Rinia, Herre. "High frequency amplifying arrangement for a very broad frequency band." U.S. 2,195,098, Oct. 28, 1936, Mar. 26, 1940; Br. 465,030, Nov. 9, 1936. In Germany Nov. 11, 1935 (N.V. Philips). Coupling circuits in a television amplifier.

5457 Schröter, F. "Television scanner." U.S 2,152,158, Nov. 21, 1936, Mar. 21, 1939. In Germany Nov. 11, 1935 (Telefunken). Gas-filled tube with photoelectric mosaic.

5458 Urtel, R. "Signalling system." U.S. 2,204,058, Nov. 10, 1936, June 11, 1940. In Germany Nov. 11, 1935 (Telefunken). Television transmission and reception circuits.

5459 Verbeek, Henri Petrus Johan, and Bernardus Dominicus Hubertus Tellegen. "Amplifier circuit." U.S. 2,202,361, Oct. 28, 1936, May 28, 1940. In Germany Nov. 11, 1935.

5460 G.E.C. and L.C. Jesty. "Cathode-ray tube." Br. 461,450, Nov. 13, 1935. Assembly with magnetic and electrostatic shields. Reference to Br. 425,493 (4188).

5461 Krawinkel, G. "Der 12 Grosse Deutschen Rundfunkausstellung" [The 12th Great German radio exhibition]. E.T.Z. 56 (Nov. 14): 1251–4. Review of apparatus, including television.

5462 Comp. Gaz. "Television receiver." Br. 479,151, Nov. 3, 1936. In France Nov. 14, 1935. Line and frame deflection circuits.

5463 G.E.C., H.W.B. Gardiner, and W.O. Russell. "Television." Br. 465,790, Nov. 14, 1935. Method for making scanning disks. Reference to U.S. 1,907,057 (2027).

5464 Möller, R., and E. Ruska. "Cathode-ray tube with photocell mosaic." U.S. 2,160,510, Nov. 6, 1936, May 30, 1939; Br. 484,913, Nov. 10, 1936. In Germany Nov. 14, 1935 (Fernseh A.-G.). Image pickup tube with a single-sided mosaic and facing grid electrode.

5465 Baird Television and G.W. White. "Amplifier." Br. 465,887, Nov. 15, 1935. Wide-band push-pull circuit.

5466 Baird Television and L.R. Merdler. "Television." Br. 465,892, Nov. 16, 1935. Deflection oscillator and picture tube circuit. Reference to Br. 435,196 (4382).

5467 Schlesinger, K. "Cathode-ray tube." U.S. 2,173,498, Nov. 10, 1936, Sept. 19, 1939; Br. 489,028, Nov. 16, 1936. In Germany Nov. 16, 1935 (D.S. Loewe). Refers to an electron lens system and a rectifier contained in the heater assembly.

5468 Clothier, Stewart L., and Harold C. Hogencamp. "Television." U.S. 2,163,537, Nov. 18, 1935, June 20, 1939; Br. 485,622, Nov. 18, 1936 (Kolorama). Refers to scanning with tangential mirrors on a disk and a vibrating mirror, Kerr cell, lens system, and screen.

5469 Schlesinger, K. "Synchronizing signal generation system." U.S. 2,227,012, Nov. 10, 1936, Dec. 31, 1940; Br. 485,119, Nov. 16, 1936. In Germany Nov. 18, 1935 (D.S. Loewe). Marginal electrodes on a mosaic screen.

5470 D.S. Loewe. "Television." Br. 485,132, Nov. 16, 1936. In Germany Nov. 18, 1935. Divided from above.

5471 G.E.C. and D.C. Espley. "Valve generator." Br. 459,610, Nov. 20, 1935. Saw-tooth oscillator and amplifier. Reference to Br. 423,427 (3513).

5472 Knoop, William A. "Electro-optical image producing system." U.S. 2,195,864, Nov. 20, 1935, Apr. 2, 1940. Assigned: B.T.L. Two-channel transmission and scanning disks.

5473 Marconi's and G.B. Banks. "Electron discharge device." Br. 465,963, Nov. 20, 1935; U.S. 2,161,272, Nov. 11, 1936, June 6, 1939 (RCA). Transmitting tube with a single-sided image plate, electron gun for scanning the plate, and coating on the inner surface of the bulb for collecting secondary electrons. Adaptable for infrared or ultraviolet as well as visible light.

5474 Marconi's, L.M. Myers, and E.F. Goodenough. "Light valve." Br. 466,031, Nov. 20, 1935; U.S. 2,185,379, Nov. 18, 1936, Jan. 2, 1940 (RCA). A reflecting prism with surface particles, between a light source and a screen, is scanned by a modulated electron beam that reduces the adhesive attraction and changes the reflectivity.

5475 Rigby, E.J., and W.N. Hurst. "Television." Br. 462,122, Nov. 21, 1935. Helically apertured drum combined with a mirror drum, one for scanning an object obscured by fog, the other for reconstituting the image.

5476 Scophony and J.H. Jeffree. "Light valve." Br. 466,212, Nov. 21, 1935. Refers to a piezoelectric crystal assembly for generating mechanical waves at supersonic frequency. Reference to Br. 439,236 (4360).

5477 "The secondary-emission multiplier. A step towards better television." W.W. 37 (Nov. 22): 539, 540. Photo, graph, 2 diags. On the RCA tubes demonstrated Oct. 23, by Zworykin and his associates.

5478 D.S. Loewe. "Cathode-ray tube." Br. 489,422, Nov. 20, 1936. In Germany Nov. 22, 1935. Divided from above, same reference.

5479 G.E.C. and D.C. Espley. "Television." Br. 458,883, Nov. 22, 1935. Refers to sync signals derived from a light siren.

5480 Schlesinger, K. "Electron discharge device for television transmission." U.S. 2,227,013, Nov. 20, 1936, Dec. 31, 1940; Br. 490,924, Nov. 20, 1936. In Germany Nov. 22, 1935 (D.S. Loewe). In one form of pickup tube, the image is projected via an internal mirror onto a photoelectric cathode on the inside of the tube, from which the electron image is focused by a coil onto a mosaic screen at the opposite end, which is scanned via another internal mirror by light from an external source. Reference to Br. 489,362 (5418).

5481 Baird Television and L.R. Merdler. "Television." Br. 466,419, Nov. 23, 1935. Sync separator and demodulator.

5482 Bingley, F.J. "Electrical system." U.S. 2,171,536, Nov. 23, 1935, Sept. 5, 1939; Br. 485,924, Nov. 23, 1936 (Philco). Television transmission and reception circuits.

5483 Bingley, F.J. "Valve circuit." Br. 485,989, Nov. 23, 1936. In U.S. Nov. 23, 1935 (Philco). Divided from above.

5484 Bingley, F.J. "Valve amplifier." Br. 485,990, Nov. 23, 1936. In U.S. Nov. 23, 1935 (Philco). Divided from Br. 485,924 (5482).

5485 Bingley, F.J. "Television." Br. 485,991, Nov. 23, 1936. In U.S. Nov. 23, 1935 (Philco). Divided from Br. 485,924 (5482). Reference to Br. 477,329 (5139).

5486 Bingley, F.J. "Valve circuits." Br. 485,999, Nov. 23, 1936. In U.S. Nov. 23, 1935 (Philco). Divided from Br. 485,924 (5482).

5487 "Television for 1936. New York television project is under way for tests within six months." N.Y.T. IX, 15 (Nov. 24): 7, 8. Old RCA equipment of the NBC in the Empire State Building being dismantled, new installation to be completed by Jan. 500 receivers in four different models to be used by observers.

5488 Scophony, G. Wikkenhauser, and J. Sieger. "Amplifier." Br. 444,058, Nov. 25, 1935. Wide-band direct-coupled stages for 30 mc.

5489 Trutolife and D.S.B. Shannon. "Cathode-ray tube." Br. 466,604, Nov. 25, 1935. Scanner consists of a cathode-ray tube with an oblique fluorescent screen coacting with a piezoelectric deflection system subject to line and frame frequencies in a separate assembly, from which the picture is displayed on a viewing screen.

5490 Wolff, H.-H. "Braun tube with synchronizing electrode." U.S. 2,196,375, Nov. 24, 1936, Apr. 9, 1940; Br. 485,598, Nov. 25, 1936. In Germany Nov. 25, 1935 (D.S. Loewe). Addition to Br. 485,119 (5469). Auxiliary electrode at the edge of a photoelectric screen in a transmitting tube.

5491 B.T.-H. "Television." Br. 489,426, Nov. 26, 1936. In France Nov. 26, 1935 (Compagnie française pour l'exploitation des Procédés Thomson-Houston). Picture tube circuit.

5492 "Skyscrapers and television." N.Y.T. 20 (Nov. 27): 4. Editorial on television in New York. The FCC "has been told that television, as a practical affair, is still a good ways off."

5493 Baird Television and A.H. Johnson. "Cathode-ray tube." Br. 466,426, Nov. 27, 1935. Bulb construction.

5494 Bowman-Manifold, M. "Cathode-ray tube." Br. 471,103, Nov. 27, 1935; U.S. 2,108,523, Nov. 10, 1936, Feb. 15, 1938 (EMI). Deflection coil assembly.

5495 G.E.C. and D.C. Espley. "Wireless signalling." Br. 460,675, Nov. 27, 1935. Receiver for sound and vision; automatic volume control circuit. References (3230, 4333, 4897).

5496 Toulon, P.M.G. "Television." Br. 477,864, Nov. 27, 1936. In France Nov. 27, 1935. Sync circuit. Reference to Br. 468,505 (4767).

5497 "Eiffel Tower television transmissions. Details of the latest French television broadcasting." W.W. 37 (Nov. 29): 558, 559. 4 photos. Station opened by George Mandel Nov. 17. Barthélemy mechanical system for 180/25 images.

5498 Adam, M. "Le nouvel émetteur de télévision Parisien installé sur la Tour Eiffel" [The new television transmitter in Paris installed in the Eiffel Tower]. GEN. CIV. 107 (Nov. 30): 521, 533.

5499 Andrieu, R. "Modulator circuit." U.S. 2,204,061, Dec. 2, 1936, June 11, 1940. In Germany Nov. 30, 1935 (Telefunken). Balanced bridge circuit for image transmission.

5500 Linder, E.A. "Electron multiplier." U.S. 2,156,264, Nov. 30, 1935, May 2, 1939. Assigned: RCA. Br. 485,672, Nov. 30, 1936 (Marconi's).

5501 Morton, G.A. "Electro-optical device." U.S. 2,189,319, Nov. 30, 1935, Feb. 6, 1940. Assigned: RCA. Br. 489,846, Nov. 30, 1936 (Marconi's). Image pickup tube with a photoelectric cathode, a ring-shaped electron lens system for varying the magnification of the image, and a fluorescent screen for direct viewing or a photomosaic. References to Br. 368,309 (2548), 484,099 (5430).

5502 Marconi's. "Discharge apparatus." Br. 488,920, Nov. 30, 1936. In U.S. Nov. 30, 1935 (RCA). Divided from above. Controller reference to Br. 454,832 (4892).

5503 Richardson, H.A. "Signalling system." Br. 450,444, Nov. 30, 1935. Refers to frequency modulation with a cathode-ray tube, a graduated transparent screen, photocell, and image pickup tube.

5504 Tolson, W.A., and I.G. Maloff. "Deflecting coil for cathode-ray tubes." U.S. 2,155,514, Nov. 30, 1935. Apr. 25, 1939. Assigned: RCA.

5505 Brüche, E., and W. Schaffernicht. "Bericht über elektronenoptische Fragen auf dem Fernsehgebiet" [Report on electron optical problems in the television field]. E.N.T. 12 (Dec.): 381–92.

5506 Banneitz, F. "Uber das Fernsehen in Deutschland" [On television in Germany]. FERN. U. TON. 6 (Dec.): 89.

5507 Besson, P. "Le récepteur de télévision FE IV." ONDE ELECT. 14 (Dec.): 783–93. Telefunken's FE IV receiver.

5508 Barthélemy, R. "La télévision cathodique à synchronisme automatique" [Cathode-ray television with automatic synchronization]. ONDE ELECT. 14 (Dec.): 794–803.

5509 "Oscillight television receiver." POP. MECH. 64 (Dec.): 901, 146A. 3 photos, diag. Farnsworth system.

5510 Goldsmith, A.N. "Television in the theatre." RADIO-CRAFT 7 (Dec.): 333, 362, 363. 2 photos.

5511 Kaufman, S. "Farnsworth television. How cathode rays are used in both transmission and reception." RADIO N. 17 (Dec.): 330,

331, 375. 6 photos, diag. This continuance of the Nov. article explains the mode of operation and gives some technical details.

5512 Ryftin, J. "Quality of television images." TECHNICAL PHYSICS OF THE U.S.S.R. 1 (Dec.): 449–68. In English.

5513 Traub, E.H. "Television at the Berlin Radio Exhibition." J. TELEV. SOC. 2 (Dec.): 53–61. 9 photos, table of transmitters, receivers, and manufacturers, showing technical features. Report on equipment by Fernseh, Telefunken, Tekade, Loewe, Lorenz, Müller (Philips), R.P.Z., Heinrich Hertz Institute, R.R., and von Ardenne. The following summarizes the methods employed. Transmitters: 6 disks, 1 lens disk, 1 mirror drum, and the Berlin station. Receivers: 12 picture tubes, 3 mirror screws with Kerr cells, 1 lamp screen. Scanning lines: 3 at 90, 1 at 100, 3 at 180, 1 at 320, all with 25 pictures per second, 4 interlaced (50). Image sizes on picture tubes ranged from 15 by 18 cm to 25 by 30 cm, the 18 by 22 cm being most popular by mirror screws from 15 by 18 cm to 25 by 30 cm, the large Karolus screen with 10,000 lamps 2 by 2 m, and the RRG intermediate film 3 by 4 m. Screen colors of picture tubes were 5 white, 3 sepia, 2 pale blue, 1 green, and 1 yellow. Outstanding features, according to the writer, were the Fernseh 320-line intermediate film transmitter, the high quality of the images on the accompanying receiver, the Loewe receiver and its black and white pictures with a bluish tinge.

5514 Reyner, J.H. "Experiences with a cathode-ray scanner on 120 lines." J. TELEV. SOC. 2 (Dec.): 62–7. 4 diags.

5515 Shmakov, P. "The secondary emission of electrons from caesium cathodes." J. TELEV. SOC. 2 (Dec.): 68–74. 13 graphs and diags. Mentions a secondary emission multiplier by Kubetsky, Russian patent 24,040, 1930.

5516 "Marconi's-EMI television." J. TELEV. SOC. 2 (Dec.): 75–81. 5 photos. Technical description of transmitting equipment.

5517 "High-definition television transmission from London." J. TELEV. SOC. 2 (Dec.): 82–84. 2 diags. Specification of radiated wave-form of the Marconi-EMI system.

5518 "Details of the signal radiated by the Baird Company's apparatus." J. TELEV. SOC. 2 (Dec.): 85. Diag.

5519 Wilson, J.C. "Twenty five years' change in television." J. TELEV. SOC. 2 (Dec.): 86–93. 3 photos, 37 references. Table of early disclosures. Reprinted New York: Arno Press, 1977.

5520 Kurtz, E.B. "Single versus multi-spiral discs." J. TELEV. SOC. 2 (Dec.): 94, 95. 3 diags.

5521 Diels, K., and M. Knoll. "Proof of the aberrations of an electron lens by point imagery." Z. TECH. PHYS. 16 (Dec.): 617–21.

5522 "New station aids study of television waves." N.Y.T. XI, 19 (Dec. 1): 2. On the 50-watt CBS station W2XDV at 485 Madison Ave., New York. Transmissions 5 to 10 p.m. daily on 8.43 m. and others on 9.5 m, 7.78 m, and 3.49 m.

5523 Gander, L.M. "More than pale shadows. Television experts in England rush work for tests in London with Alexandra Palace as the radio theatre." N.Y.T. XI, 19 (Dec. 1): 6–8. The new station, Baird and EMI equipment, BBC expenses.

5524 Baird Television and G.W. White. "Valve modulator." Br. 466,715, Dec. 2, 1935. For picture and sync signals. Reference to Br. 460,222 (5222).

5525 Fernseh A.-G. "Electron multiplier." Br. 486,437, Dec. 2, 1936. In Germany Dec. 2, 1935.

5526 Schlesinger, K. "Transmitter with spiral-aperture disks." U.S. 2,173,499, Nov. 28, 1936, Sept. 19, 1939; Br. 488,253, Dec. 1, 1936. In Germany Dec. 2, 1935 (D.S. Loewe). For interlaced scanning with holes spaced to correct for trapezium distortion. References to Br. 465,184 (4603), 472,160 (4743).

5527 Andrieu, R. "Serrated wave form generator." U.S. 2,143,366, Nov. 18, 1936, Jan. 10, 1939; Br. 486,528, Dec. 3, 1936. In Germany Dec. 3, 1935 (Telefunken). Saw-tooth deflection oscillator. References to Br. 400,976 (3396), 476,336 (May 1936).

5528 G.E.C. and G.W. Edwards. "Television." Br. 466,780, Dec. 3, 1935. Nipkow disk film scanner and optical system to correct trapezoidal distortion.

5529 Marconi's and A.A. Linsell. "Television receiver." Br. 466,756, Dec. 3, 1935; U.S. 2,226,229, Nov. 27, 1936, Dec. 24, 1940 (RCA). Automatic adjustment of the line frequency and spot size.

5530 Marconi's and A.A. Linsell. "Television receiver." Br. 466,866, Dec. 3, 1935; U.S. 2,226,230, Nov. 27, 1936, Dec. 24, 1940 (RCA). Divided from above.

5531 G.E.C. and L.C. Jesty. "Cathode-ray tube." Br. 461,374, Dec. 5, 1935. Safety switch to open the high-voltage supply to a picture tube in the event of tube breakage.

5532 "'Cathode Ray.' An unsung pioneer. A proposed television system of a quarter of a century ago." W.W. 37 (Dec. 6): 591, 592. Portrait, diag. Swinton's proposal of 1911 (413).

5533 Gardner, D.B. "Solid weave scanning apparatus." U.S. 2,131,504, Dec. 6, 1935, Sept. 27, 1938. Mirror screw rotatable in two directions.

5534 "Sarnoff predicts television in 1940. Problems too great for wide use in immediate future, head of R.C.A. asserts. But sees rapid strides. Lack of method of amplifying 'sight' bars progress like that of early radio." N.Y.T. II, 3 (Dec. 8): 8.

5535 G.E.C., G.W. Edwards, D.C. Espley, and D.O. Walter. "Television." Br. 464,810, Dec. 9, 1935. Sync signals generated in a circuit including a-c voltages and magnets on a disk coupled to a scanning disk, with an electromagnet pickup. References to Br. 425,220 (4051), 457,135 (4473).

5536 Wolff, H.-H. "Television transmission." U.S. 2,201,069, Dec. 4, 1936, May 14, 1940; Br. 470,551, Dec. 10, 1936. In Germany Dec. 10, 1935 (D.S. Loewe). Concerns a slotted shutter for interrupting light coacting with the photosensitive plate in an image pickup tube, adaptable for film transmission and interlaced scanning. Reference to Br. 465,184 (4603).

5537 Baird Television and T.M.C. Lance. "Television transmitter." Br. 467,188, Dec. 11, 1935. Sync generator. References to Br. 431,339 (4293), 431,458 (4294).

5538 Baird Television and J.L. Baird. "Television receiver." Br. 467,195, Dec. 12, 1935. An image is reconstituted on a screen in quarter zones by four picture tubes with masks and adjustable projection lenses.

5539 D.S. Loewe. "Television." Br. 486,896, Dec. 12, 1936. In Germany Dec. 12, 1935. Similar to Br. 479,551 (5536).

5540 Okolicsányi, F. v. "Television." Br. 468,191, Dec. 11, 1936. In Germany Dec. 12, 1935. In a system that avoids high-speed scanning, a receiver has a number of tuned circuits of different frequencies, and each operating a light-valve from which lines of light are projected over a screen by a mirror drum. Reference to Br. 439,236 (4360).

5541 Okolicsányi, F. v. "Television." U.S. 2,202,541, Dec. 8, 1936, May 28, 1940; Br. 472,009, Oct. 15, 1936. In Germany Dec. 12, 1935. A multifrequency system employing vibrating reeds.

5542 Okolicsányi, F. v. "Television." Br. 486,604, Dec. 11, 1936. In Germany Dec. 12, 1935. The field of view of a transmitter is changed by remote control from a receiver to correspond to the movement of a viewer. Reference to above.

5543 Okolicsányi, F. v. "Television." Br. 492,353, Dec. 11, 1936. Void. In Germany Dec. 12, 1935. Changes in a more finely scanned part of a picture at a receiver are controlled by corresponding signals from the transmitter.

5544 "Sees new science killing all noise. A.W. Cruse tells engineers television will make 'silent areas' possible. Predicts big aids in war. In address at Schenectady he points also to benefits to astronomers." N.Y.T. 27 (Dec. 13): 7.

5545 Diels, Kurt. "Cathode-ray tube." U.S. 2,153,616, Dec. 22, 1936, Apr. 11, 1939. In Germany Dec. 14, 1935 (Telefunken).

5546 "New year holds key to television. Cruse expects advances here and abroad in 1936–37." N.Y.T. XI, 17 (Dec. 15): 4–6. Comments by A.W. Cruse related to his overseas trip.

5547 D.S. Loewe. "Television transmitter." Br. 487,240, Dec. 16, 1936. In Germany Dec. 16, 1935. Light from a subject is projected onto an image pickup tube via a light-valve controlled by a photocell circuit to reduce the range of fluctuations in the mean light intensity. References to Br. 404,020 (3535), 486,896 (5539).

5548 International Carrier-Call & Television Corp. "Television." Br. 490,837, Nov. 17, 1936. Void. Convention date Dec. 16, 1935. Scanning system with vibrating mirrors for transmission and reception.

5549 Traub, E. "Television." Br. 465,970, Dec. 16, 1935; U.S. 2,149,198, Dec. 15, 1936, Feb. 28, 1939. Mirror drum and mirror scanning apparatus modified from Br. 425,552 (4106) and 448,238 (4723). References (2868, 3448, 3717, 4252, 4662).

5550 D.S. Loewe. "Cathode-ray tube." Br. 487,241, Dec. 16, 1936. In Germany Dec. 17, 1935. Picture tube with a small internal fluorescent screen from which the image is projected via a spherical or parabolic reflector. References (3397, 4361).

5551 Schlesinger. K. "Television amplifier." U.S. 2,227,014, Dec. 11, 1936, Dec. 31, 1940; Br. 487,242, Dec. 16, 1936 (D.S. Loewe). Resistance-capacity circuit with smoothing elements to eliminate ripple voltages from the anode supply.

5552 Telefunken. "Cathode-ray tube." Br. 485,298, Dec. 17, 1936. In Germany Dec. 17, 1935.

5553 Wolff, H.H., and Gerhard Leibman. "Television transmission." U.S. 2,227,413, Dec. 23, 1936, Dec. 31, 1940; Br. 487,243, Dec. 16, 1936. In Germany Dec. 18, 1935 (D.S. Loewe). Amplifier for increasing the contrast in the light and dark parts of an image derived from a pickup tube.

5554 "Seek television license. Counsel for local station tell FCC field tests are necessary." N.Y.T. 15 (Dec. 20): 3. Hearing application for a 500 w station by the National Television Corp.

5555 G.E.C. and L.C. Jesty. "Cathode-ray tube." Br. 467,611, Dec. 23, 1935.

5556 Schröter, F., M. Knoll, and Bernhard Bartels. "Television screen." U.S. 2,146,994, Jan. 9, 1937, Feb. 14, 1939. In Germany Dec. 23, 1935 (Telefunken). Construction of a mosaic screen with the photoelectric material on inserts in a metallic structure.

5557 Schunack, Johannes. "Intermediate modulation in television transmission." U.S. 2,206,130, Dec. 11, 1936, July 2, 1940; Br. 487,501, Dec. 21, 1936. In Germany Dec. 23, 1935 (Fernseh A.-G.). Amplifier between two successive transmission channels with sync separation, amplification, and reinsertion.

5558 Ruska, E., and Fernseh A.-G. "Cathode-ray tube." Br. 466,826, Dec. 24, 1935. Deflection plates. Reference to Br. 466,790 (4725).

5559 Marconi's and N. Levin. "Television." Br. 467,995, Dec. 27, 1935. Concerns a lens attached to a picture tube in front of the screen. Reference to Br. 417,435 (3906).

5560 Marconi's and G.M. Wright. "Television." Br. 467,918, Dec. 27, 1935. Picture tube with a totally reflecting prism on the end face, by which light from a local source is modulated and reflected onto a viewing screen.

5561 Warmisham, A., and Kapella. "Television transmitter." Br. 467,986, Dec. 27, 1935.

Lens system, scanning disk, and photocell for film transmission.

5562 Van Mierlo, Stanislas. "Electron multiplier." U.S. 2,346,952, Nov. 18, 1936, Apr. 18, 1944. Assigned: International Standard. Br. 486,020, Nov. 27, 1936 (S.T.C.). In France Dec. 28, 1935. Construction and circuit.

5563 Coeterier, Frederik, and M.C. Teves. "Optical image reproducer." U.S. 2,153,614, Dec. 24, 1936, Apr. 11, 1939; Br. 478,852, Dec. 28, 1936. In Germany Dec. 30, 1935 (N.V. Philips). Image intensifier.

5564 Bedford, A.V. "Television." U.S. 2,164,297, Dec. 31, 1935, June 27, 1939. Assigned: RCA. Br. 488,268, Dec. 31, 1936 (Marconi's). Several different pictures fed into a common signal channel via a separate program controller provided a variety of results, such as the insertion of descriptive matter, a spot-light effect, superposed views, ghost effects, and changeover of scenes. References to Br. 417,282 (3699), 458,161 (4505).

5565 Bedford, A.V. "Television." Br. 490,203, Dec. 31, 1936 (Marconi's). In U.S. Dec. 31, 1935 (RCA). Divided from above.

5566 Comp. Gaz. "Television transmitter." Br. 467,073, Dec. 29, 1936. In France Dec. 31, 1935. Photocell circuit.

5567 Farnsworth, P.T. "Dissector tube." U.S. 2,153,918, Dec. 31, 1935, Apr. 11, 1939; Br. 486,787, Dec. 11, 1936. Assigned: Farnsworth Television and Radio. Reference to Br. 471,199 (Mar. 1935), 471,492 (4907).

5568 G.E.C., N.R. Campbell, and L.C. Jesty. "Television receiver." Br. 462,281, Dec. 31, 1935. Divided from Br. 457,510 (5180). Picture tube inside a metal shield adjustable for viewing angle. Reference to Br. 377,622 (2865).

5569 Maloff, I.G. "Cathode-ray deflecting device." U.S. 2,157,182, Dec. 31, 1935, May 9, 1939. Assigned: RCA. Magnetic assembly.

5570 Morton, G.A. "Electro-optical device." U.S. 2,189,320, Dec. 31, 1935, Feb. 6, 1940. Assigned: RCA. Image pickup tube.

5571 Baker, W.R.G., and L. Malter. A SURVEY OF TELEVISION PROGRESS IN AMERICA. London: G. Newnes, 1935. Booklet.

5572 Dowding, G.V. (ed.). BOOK OF PRACTICAL TELEVISION. London: Amalgamated Press, 1935. 320 pp. 63 plates, 232 graphs and diags. 26 chapters by 12 contributors cover all aspects from elementary theory to the construction of receivers.

5573 Hathaway, K.A. TELEVISION. Chicago: American Technical Society, 1935. 170 pp. History, light and optics, photocells, glow lamps, mechanical scanning, cathode-ray tubes, receiving circuits, and accessories.

5574 Hutchinson, R.W. TELEVISION UP-TO-DATE. London: University Tutorial Press, 1935. xii + 184 pp. 15 photos, 125 diags. A simple and clear exposition intended primarily for the beginner.

5575 Molloy, Edward (gen. ed.). TELEVISION TODAY: PRACTICE AND PRINCIPLES CLEARLY EXPLAINED. London: G. Newnes, n.d. (1935). 2 vols. iv + iv + 776 pp. 300 photos, 82 graphs, 31 tables, 600 diags. A comprehensive and authoritative collection by 39 contributors, most of them associated with companies in the field. A Classified Key groups the contents of 121 chapters and parts as follows: Introductory, Theory of television, Low-definition television, Modern television systems, The transmission and reception of television, Television apparatus and components, The cathode-ray receiver and apparatus, Station work, Miscellaneous. The work, intended for men in the radio and cinema industries, home constructors, and servicemen, provides clear explanations of theory and practice that range from elementary topics to more advanced tutorial levels. Fifty chapters have short lists of basic questions and answers. Systems and equipment covered include: American — Bell Labs, Farnsworth, RCA; British — Baird, Cossor, EMI, International Television, Scophony; French — Barthélemy, Chauvierre, De France, Mardy; German — von Ardenne, Fernseh, Kinne,

Loewe, Lorenz, R.P.Z., Tekade, Telefunken; Italian — Sofar.

5576 Robinson, E.H. TELEVIEWING. London: Selwyn & Blount, 1935. 288 pp., 35 diags. Foreword by Gerald Cock. Revised edition 1936.

5577 TELEVISION FOR THE MILLION. London: British Television Supplies, 1935. Reprinted from typewriting.

5578 Zworykin, V.K., and G.A. Morton. POSSIBILITIES OF THE ICONOSCOPE IN TELEVISION. London: G. Newnes, 1935. Booklet.

CHAPTER 16

END OF AN ERA: 1936

5579 Bertolotti, S. "Il sincronismo nella televisione e gli amplificatori a resistenza e capacita [Synchronization in television and resistance capacity amplifiers]." ALTA FREQ. 5 (Jan.): 5–41.

5580 Fuchs, F. "Die 12. Grosse Deutsche Rundfunkausstellung [The 12th Great German Radio Fair]." HOCH ELEKT. 47 (Jan.): 1–8. Reviews apparatus, including television.

5581 van der Mark, J. "Experimental television transmitter and receiver." PHIL. TECH. REV. 1 (Jan.): 16–21. Tests with Philips image pickup tube and circuits for 180/25 pictures.

5582 Schrage, W.E. "Television and the ultrashort waves." RADIO-CRAFT 7 (Jan.): 398, 428, 429. 6 illus.

5583 Schiffenbauer, R.G. "Phase distortion in television." W. ENG. 13 (Jan.): 21–6. Discusses work in the U.S.S.R., 1933–34. Bibliography.

5584 Schnabel, W. "Significance of choice of suitable fluorescent material for television scanning with cathode-ray light scanner." Z. TECH. PHYS. 17 (Jan.): 25–7.

5585 Coeterier, Frederik, and M.C. Teves. "Optical image reproducer." U.S. 2,196,854, Apr. 9, 1940. In Germany Jan. 3, 1936.

5586 "AT&T loses fight for limit on hearing. Testimony on commercial use of coaxial cable to Philadelphia begun by FCC." NYT (Jan. 7): 7: 4.

5587 Schlesinger, K. "Cathode-ray tube." U.S. 2,227,003, Jan. 7, 1936, Dec. 31, 1940. Original in Germany Oct. 17, 1932; U.S. Oct. 12, 1933. Assigned: D.S. Loewe.

5588 Schlesinger, K. "Cathode-ray tube and method of operating this tube." U.S. 2,090,952, Jan 7, 1936, Aug. 24, 1937.

5589 N.V. Philips. "Discharge apparatus." Br. 469,588, Jan. 5, 1937. Convention date Jan. 8, 1936. Electron multiplier and picture tube.

5590 Schlesinger, K. "Optical arrangement for scanning machines." U.S. 2,191,182, Feb. 20, 1940; Br. 488,221, Jan. 6, 1937. In Germany Jan. 10, 1936, Jan. 6, 1937.

5591 Schlesinger, K. "Cathode-ray tube." U.S. 2,185,132, Jan. 6, 1937, Dec. 26, 1939; Br. 486,214, Jan. 8, 1937. In Germany Jan. 11, 1936. Photosensitive electrode scanned by cathode beam. Assigned: D.S. Loewe. References to Br. 458,187, 493,543 (5593).

5592 Murray, Albert F. "Television signal system." U.S. 2,181,064, Jan. 11, 1936, Nov. 21, 1939. Assigned: Philco Radio & Television Corp.

5593 D.S. Loewe. "Cathode-ray tube." Br. 493,543, Jan. 8, 1937. In Germany Jan. 11, 1936. Reference to Br. 489,362 (Oct. 25, 1935).

5594 "Television is foreseen as 'momentous happening.'" NYT (Jan. 12): IX, 15: 2. British television; BBC statements on importance of broadcasting stations and engineering problems.

5595 Baird Television and G.E.G. Graham. "Television." Br. 468,837, Jan. 13, 1936. Double-image scanning and frequency conversion with single-channel transmission and reverse process of receiver.

5596 Schlesinger, K. "Television apparatus." U.S. 2,129,036, Jan. 13, 1936, Sept. 6, 1938. In

Germany July 15, 1932. Divided from U.S. 2,053,536, July 11, 1933, Sept. 8, 1936. Saw-tooth generator.

5597 Farnsworth, P.T. "Television." Br. 465,631, Jan. 13, 1936. Camera tube with small and large target apertures and circuit to provide signals with small contrast and great detail, and great contrast and small detail, which are combined with low resultant noise.

5598 G.E.C. and D.C. Espley. "Valve generator." Br. 468,394, Jan. 14, 1936.

5599 Schunack, Johannes. "Method for producing rectangular shape synchronizing in pictures." U.S. 2,160,522, Dec. 11, 1936, May 30, 1939. In Germany Jan. 14, 1936.

5600 Scophony and J.H. Jeffree. "Light valve." Br. 469,018, Jan. 14, 1936. Supersonic piezoelectric crystal assembly for modulating light. References to Br. 439,236, 466,212.

5601 Lubszynski, H.G. "Cathode-ray tube." Br. 472,162, Jan. 14, 1936. Camera tube with photoelectric screen, mosaic screen, and two electron guns for amplification by secondary emission. References to Br. 456,728, 457,493.

5602 Lubszynski, H.G. "Electron discharge device." U.S. 2,199,438, Jan. 15, 1937, May 7, 1940; Br. 468,965, Jan. 15, 1936. Assigned: EMI. Camera tube. References to Br. 381,306, 409,221, 446,661.

5603 Lubszynski, H.G., and G.S.P. Freeman. "Cathode-ray tube." Br. 469,079, Jan. 15, 1936; U.S. 2,149,849, Jan. 15, 1937, Mar. 7, 1939. Assigned: EMI. Photo-sensitizing process in a camera tube. References to Br. 353,555, 406,507.

5604 Lubszynski, H.G. "Cathode-ray tube." Br. 469,033, Jan. 16, 1936; U.S. 2,280,922, Jan. 15, 1937, Apr. 28, 1942. Assigned: EMI. Camera tube with secondary electron emission and mosaic screen stabilized at the cathode potential.

5605 "Television progress." ELECT. 116 (Jan. 17): 79. Brief note on proposed television tests from Alexandra Palace in March.

5606 Schlesinger, K., and D.S. Loewe. "Control grid arrangement in cathode-ray tubes." U.S. 2,185,133, Jan. 20, 1936, Jan. 15, 1937; Br. 488,948, Jan. 18, 1937. References to Br. 447,493, 452,589.

5607 Williams, W.E. "Electron multiplier." Br. 469,111, Jan. 18, 1936.

5608 Comp. Gaz. "Electron multiplier." Br. 494,329, Jan. 20, 1937. In France Jan. 21, 1936.

5609 D.S. Loewe. "Cathode-ray tube." Br. 494,145, Jan. 18, 1937. In Germany Jan. 21, 1936. Picture tube.

5610 Roosenstein, H.O. "Cathode-ray deflector apparatus." U.S. 2,161,977, Feb. 10, 1937, June 13, 1939. In Germany Jan. 21, 1936.

5611 Williams, W.E. "Cathode-ray tube." Br. 469,404, Jan. 23, 1936. Camera tube with interleaved secondary emitting grids and electron lenses.

5612 G.E.C. and G.C. Morris. "Television." Br. 463,888, Jan. 23, 1936. Picture tube with a number of magnifying lenses, each providing a view of the complete image.

5613 "Germany's new television service." W.W. 38 (Jan. 24): 80. 2 photos.

5614 Baird Television and E.B. King. "Electron multiplier." Br. 469,409, Jan. 24, 1936.

5615 Marconi's and G.F. Brett. "Cathode-ray tube." Br. 469,455, Jan. 24, 1936. Reference to Br. 469,418 (Jan. 24, 1936).

5616 Brett, G.F. "Cathode-ray tube." U.S. 2,172,530, Jan. 15, 1937, Sept. 12, 1939; Br. 469,418, Jan. 24, 1936. Assigned: RCA.

5617 Brett, G.F., and G.B. Banks. "Cathode-ray tube." U.S. 2,171,970, Jan. 7, 1937, Sept. 5, 1939; Br. 469,419, Jan. 24, 1936. Picture tube.

5618 Marconi's and G.B. Banks. "Cathode-ray tube." Br. 469,420, Jan. 24, 1936; U.S. 2,203,483, Jan. 15, 1937, June 4, 1940. An electron beam is deflected magnetically from the gun at right angles onto a screen, which may be fluorescent or a photoelectric mosaic. Opposite the screen is an optical plate or lens for image projection.

5619 Schubert, G. "Modulation circuit using a multigrid photoelectric cell." U.S. 2,172,324, Dec. 11, Sept. 5, 1939. In Germany Jan. 24, 1936. Electron multiplier circuit.

5620 Roosenstein, H.O., and Horst Hewel. "Cathode-ray deflector apparatus." U.S. 2,153,643, Feb. 12, 1937, Apr. 11, 1939. In Germany Jan. 24, 1936.

5621 Telefunken. "Television." Br. 489,307, Jan. 25, 1937. In Germany Jan. 24, 1936.

5622 Bull, C.S., and F.H. Nicoll. "Cathode-ray tube." Br. 469,429, Jan. 25, 1936.

5623 Jeffree, J.H. "Television and the like system." Br. 469,426, Jan. 25, 1936; U.S. 2,161,299, Jan. 23, 1937, June 6, 1939. Assigned: Scophony.

5624 Jeffree, J.H. "Optical device." U.S. 2,193,422, Jan. 23, 1937, Mar. 12, 1940; Br. Jan. 25, 1936. Assigned: Scophony. For television.

5625 "Commercial television unlikely in '36, says Gubb." NYT (Jan. 26): IX, 13: 8. Lawrence E. Gubb, president of Philco.

5626 Farnsworth Television. "Multipactor oscillator." U.S. 2,137,528, Jan. 27, 1936, Nov. 22, 1938; Br. 485,620, Nov. 18, 1936. Electron multiplier.

5627 Brüche, Ernst. "Electronic device." U.S. 2,206,387, Jan. 23, 1937, July 2, 1940. In Germany Jan. 28, 1936. Cathode-ray tube with luminescent screen and electron lens.

5628 Schlesinger, K., and Gerhard Liebmann. "Picture transmitter." U.S. 2,227,015, Jan. 23, 1937, Dec. 31, 1940. In Germany Jan. 29, 1936. Assigned: D.S. Loewe. Mosaic tube. References to Br. 493,043 (Jan. 29, 1937), 489,362 (Oct. 25, 1935).

5629 B.T.-H. "Image converter." Br. 467,556, Jan. 28, 1937. Convention date Jan. 28, 1936.

5630 Baird Television and J.L. Baird. "Television." Br. 469,673, Jan. 30, 1936. Scanning disk with slots and a stationary slot. Reference to Br. 440,917.

5631 Michaelis, E., and E. Kinne. "Cathode-ray tube." Br. 469,127, Jan. 30, 1936.

5632 Toulon, Pierre Marie Gabriel. "Television receiving apparatus." U.S. 2,179,205, Jan. 25, 1937, Nov. 7, 1939. In France Jan. 30, 1936. Two-gun picture tube. Multi-cellular collecting grid between two guns and fluorescent screen.

5633 "Marconi-EMI television." ELECT. 116 (Jan. 31): 166. Note on Marconi-EMI publication of an illustrated booklet on their television equipment.

5634 Hughes, L.E.C. "Television: Progress towards a regular high-definition service." ELECT. 116 (Jan. 31): 141.

5635 "The London television transmitter. First description of the Marconi-EMI installation." W.W. 38 (Jan. 31): 103, 104. 4 photos, diagram.

5636 MARCONI-EMI TELEVISION. THE SYSTEM OF TO-DAY AND TO-MORROW. Pamphlet No. M.E.M.I.-1. 21 pp. 5 photos, 1 diag.

5637 Bedford, A.V. "Television system." U.S. 2,145,332, Jan. 31, 1936, Jan. 31, 1939. Assigned: RCA. Slotted wave generator.

5638 G.E.C. and D.C. Espley. "Television." Br. 466,966, Jan. 31, 1936. Disk with unequally spaced holes to correct keystone distortion. Reference to Br. 466,780.

5639 B.T.-H. and J. Moir. "Amplifier." Br. 469,813, Jan. 31, 1936. For television.

5640 Ives, H.E. "Optical scanning apparatus using mirror helix." U.S. 2,199,433, Jan. 31, 1936, May 7, 1940.

5641 Lubcke, H.R. "Television." Br. 473,059, Jan. 31, 1936.

5642 Möller, Rolf, and Fritz Below. "Electron multiplier." U.S. 2,204,428, Dec. 4, 1936, June 11, 1940. In Germany Jan. 31, 1936.

5643 Zworykin, V.K., and Louis Malter. "Electronic discharge device." U.S. 2,150,573, Jan. 31, 1936, Mar. 14, 1939. Div. from 2,189,305, Sept. 8, 1938. Oscillation multiplier.

5644 Roosenstein, H.O. "New developments in television receivers." ELECTRONICS 9 (Feb.): 46. Description of Telefunken FE IV receiver. Diagram. From FERN. U. TON. 6 (1935): 77–9.

5645 Holman, H.E. "New developments in television receivers." ELECTRONICS 9 (Feb.): 46, 48. Translation of a brochure from C. Lorenz A.-G. describing their receiver for sound and vision with a screen 19 x 23 cm. Photo.

5646 "Color pictures sent by television or wire." POP. MECH. 65 (Feb.): 253. 2 photos.

5647 "RCA secretly prepares television apparatus." RADIO-CRAFT 7 (Feb.): 455.

5648 Ardenne, M. von. "New German television receivers." RADIO-CRAFT 7 (Feb.): 470, 505. 3 photos. Receivers built by C. Lorenz A.-G. on display at the Berlin radio show.

5649 Zworykin, V.K. "A rival of the vacuum tube." SCI. AM. 154 (Feb.): 68, 69.

5650 Holman, H.E. "Mosaic screen structure for television and like purposes." U.S. 2,179,090, Jan. 26, 1937, Nov. 7, 1939. Br. Feb. 1, 1936.

5651 Marconi's and G.F. Brett. "Electron multiplier." Br. 469,899, Feb. 3, 1936.

5652 Marconi's and G.F. Brett. "Electron multiplier." Br. 469,900, Feb. 3, 1936.

5653 Marconi's and. Levin. "Cathode-ray tube." Br. 470,004, Feb. 3, 1936. U.S. 2,172,739, Feb. 2, 1937, Sept. 12, 1939.

5654 Marconi's and. Levin. "Cathode-ray tube." Br. 469,897, Feb. 3, 1936. U.S. 2,172,738, Jan. 30, 1937, Sept. 12, 1939.

5655 Faudell, C.L., and E.L.C. White. "Valve generator circuit." Br. 471,737, Feb. 4, 1936. See 479,275 (May 1, 1936).

5656 Faudell, C.L., and E.L.C. White. "Electronic oscillation generator." U.S. 2,188,653, Apr. 12, 1937, Jan. 30, 1940. Br. Feb. 4, 1936. Assigned: EMI.

5657 G.E.C. and L.C. Jesty. "Cathode-ray tube." Br. 463,891, Feb. 5, 1936. Spherical receiver tube with central curved luminescent screen, from which the image is reflected by a mirror onto an external screen. Reference to Br. 452,148.

5658 Scophony and F. von Okolicsányi. "Television." Br. 474,970, Feb. 5, 1936. Scanning and modulating system with Kerr cell, supersonic light-valve, and mirror drum applicable for direct or film transmissions. References to Br. 439,236, 433,945.

5659 Robinson, James Michael. "Scanning device." U.S. 2,136,926, Feb. 5, 1936, Nov. 15, 1938. Two scanning disks, one with radial slots, the other a lens with spiral tracks with three primary color filters.

5660 Okolicsányi, F. von. "Television system." Br. 474,970, Feb. 5, 1936. U.S. 2,158,990, Feb. 4, 1937, May 16, 1939. Liquid cell and wave generator.

5661 G.E.C. and D.C. Espley. "Television." Br. 464,946, Feb. 6, 1936.

5662 Michaelis, E. (by E. Kinne). "Television." Br. 467,286, Feb. 6, 1936.

5663 Michaelis, E., and by E. Kinne. "Valve generator circuit." Br. 470,010, Feb. 6, 1936. Saw-tooth generator.

5664 Michaelis, E., and E. Kinne. "Television" Br. 469,907, Feb. 6, 1936. The effects of afterglow in a picture tube are obviated by an electron tube relay or by a second cathode-ray tube with a duplicate phototube.

5665 Schröter, F. "Cathode-ray tube for television picture scanning." U.S. 2,185,609, Feb.18, 1937, Jan. 2, 1940. In Germany Feb. 7, 1936. Assigned: Telefunken. Camera tube.

5666 Banks, G.B. "Electron discharge device." Br. 471,672, Feb. 8, 1936. U.S. 2,245,174,

Mar. 16, 1937, June 10, 1940. Assigned: RCA.

5667 Brett, G.F. "Electron discharge device." Br. 470,026, Feb. 8, 1936. U.S. 2,227,062, Feb. 8, 1937, Dec. 31, 1940. Assigned: RCA. Electron multiplier.

5668 Marconi's and Leonard Morris Myers. "Electron multiplier." Br. 470,102, Feb. 8, 1936.

5669 Zeitline, V., A. Zeitline, and V. Kliatchko. "Electron multiplier." Br. 486,795, Dec. 16. In France Feb. 8, 1936.

5670 Farnsworth, P.T. "Scanning current generator." U.S. 2,214,077, Feb. 10, 1936, Sept. 10, 1940. Br. 482,007, Jan. 13, 1937. Assigned: Farnsworth Television.

5671 Fernseh A.-G. "Electron multiplier." Br. 490,229, Feb. 10, 1937. In Germany Feb. 10, 1936. Reference to Br. 490,230 (Feb. 10, 1937).

5672 Schwartz, E., and Heinrich Strübig. "Secondary electron amplifier." U.S. 2,216,282, Feb. 9, 1937, Oct. 1, 1940. In Germany Feb. 10, 1936.

5673 Farnsworth, P.T. "Multipactor." U.S. 2,135,615, Feb. 11, 1936, Nov. 8, 1938; Br. 487,610, Jan. 13, 1937. Electron multiplier.

5674 Schlesinger, K. "Television cathode-ray tube." U.S. 2,227,016, Feb. 5, 1937, Dec. 31, 1940; Br. 495,185, Feb. 9, 1937. In Germany Feb. 11, 1936. Assigned: D.S. Loewe. References to Br. 430,650, 452,650, 455,084.

5675 Lewis, H.M. "Valve generator." U.S. 2,118,352, Feb. 12, 1936, May 24, 1938. Television receiver circuit.

5676 Andrieu, R., and Telefunken. "Saw-tooth wave generator." U.S. 2,254,344, Feb. 10, 1937, Sept. 2, 1941; Br. 490,529, Feb. 15, 1937. In Germany Feb. 13, 1936. References to Br. 426,537 (Aug. 12, 1933), 459,998 (June 12, 1935), 473,650 (Apr. 15, 1935), 482,725 (Oct. 4, 1935).

5677 Baird Television and J.L. Baird. "Television." Br. 470,347, Feb. 13, 1936. Cathode-ray tube with a mosaic of photocells adaptable for transmission and reception. References to Br. 412,179, 433,455, 437,741, 454,589.

5678 Baird Television and J.L. Baird. "Cathode-ray tube." Br. 470,480, Feb. 13, 1936. Replaceable luminescent screen, consisting of pliable material on rollers, or a set of screens replaceable by tilting.

5679 Roosenstein, H.O. "Television receiver for high definition." W.W. 38 (Feb. 14): 160–2. 2 photos, 2 diagrams. Telefunken cathode-ray tube, 180 lines.

5680 Andrieu, R., and Telefunken. "Electrical-impulse segregation circuit." U.S. 2,265,988, Jan. 30, 1937, Dec. 16, 1941. In Germany Feb. 14, 1936.

5681 Hazeltine. "Valve generator circuit." Br. 489,625, Jan. 29, 1937. In U.S. Feb. 15, 1936.

5682 Fernseh A.-G. "Cathode-ray tube." Br. 490,391, Feb. 15, 1937. In Germany Feb. 14, 1936. Reference to Br. 442,666.

5683 Knudsen, H. "Television." Br. 475,407, Feb. 17, 1936.

5684 G.E.C. and D.C. Espley. "Television." Br. 466,050, Feb. 19, 1936.

5685 Schlesinger, K. "Cathode-ray tube apparatus." U.S. 2,185,134, Feb. 17, 1937, Dec. 26, 1939. In Germany Feb. 19, 1936. Assigned: D.S. Loewe.

5686 Brauer, Gerhard. "Secondary emitter tube." U.S. 2,159,519, Feb. 17, 1937, May 23, 1939. In Germany Feb. 20, 1936. Br. 490,761, Feb. 22, 1937.

5687 Andrieu, R. "Circuit arrangement in television receivers." U.S. 2,217,396, Feb. 15, 1937, Oct. 8, 1940. In Germany Feb. 20, 1936. Br. 490,760, Feb. 22, 1937. Assigned: Telefunken.

5688 Roosenstein, H.O. "Signalling system." U.S. 2,227,108, Feb. 19, 1937, Dec. 31, 1940. In Germany Feb. 20, 1936. Assigned: Telefunken. Vision and sound transmission.

5689 Hughes, L.E.C. "Telecommunication XXI: Basic requirements in television." ELECT. 116 (Feb. 21): 263, 264. General survey; entertainment aspects.

5690 "Television service links Berlin and Leipzig fair." NYT (Feb. 21): 9: 5. First commercial telephone-television line, Berlin to Leipzig, to be opened Mar. 1.

5691 Baird Television and V.A. Jones. "Television." Br. 470,785, Feb. 21, 1936. Flyback cut-off in an image dissector tube.

5692 G.E.C., G.W. Edwards, and D.C. Espley. "Television." Br. 466,051, Feb. 21, 1936. Scanning disk for a 405-line system with co-acting single-spiral slotted disk and fixed slot for generating sync signals. References to Br. 437,340 (June 26, 1935), 458,883 (Nov. 22, 1935), 466,050 (Feb. 19, 1936).

5693 Ives, H.E. "Electro-optical scanning apparatus." U.S. 2,184,525, Feb. 21, 1936, Dec. 26, 1939. Assigned: Baird Television. Scanning disk with two sets of engraved opaque film.

5694 Percival, W.S. "Electron wave filter." U.S. 2,156,656, Feb. 18, 1937, May 2, 1939. Br. 475,490, Feb. 21, 1936. For video-frequency amplification.

5695 Collard, John. "Electron cable." U.S. 2,153,174, Feb. 19, 1937, Apr. 4, 1939. Br. Feb. 22, 1936.

5696 Zeiss Ikon A.-G. "Cathode-ray tube." Br. 489,188, Feb. 22, 1937. In Germany Feb. 22, 1936. Mosaic screen.

5697 Baird Television and D.M. Johnstone. "Valve generator circuit." Br. 470,922, Feb. 24, 1936. Saw-tooth generator.

5698 Baird Television and L.R. Merdler. "Television receiver." Br. 470,920, Feb. 24, 1936. Control indicator.

5699 Brett, G.F. "Cathode-ray tube." U.S. 2,211,844, Jan. 7, 1937, Aug. 20, 1940. Br. Feb. 24, 1936. Assigned: RCA.

5700 Farnsworth, P.T. "Multipactor oscillator and amplifier." U.S. 2,091,439, Feb. 24, 1936, Aug. 31, 1937. Br. 488,661, Jan. 13, 1937. Electron multiplier.

5701 Farnsworth, P.T., and Donald K. Lippincott. "Radiation frequency converter." U.S. 2,107,782, Feb. 24, 1936, Feb. 8, 1838. Br. 486,048, Jan. 13, 1937. Electron multiplier.

5702 Faudell, C.L., and Noel Atkinson. "Television receiver." Br. 475,728, Feb. 24, 1936; U.S. 2,227,492, Feb. 20, 1937, Jan. 7, 1941. Assigned: EMI. References to Br. 422,906 (Apr. 13, 1933) 455,375 (Jan. 15, 1935).

5703 Reichel, Wilhelm, and Ernst Ruska. "Picture transmission." U.S. 2,228,402, Feb. 11, 1937, Jan. 14, 1941; Br. 491,020, Feb. 24, 1937. In Germany Feb. 24, 1936. Assigned: Fernseh A.-G. Image dissector.

5704 Geiger, Max. "Signalling system." U.S. 2,203,865, Feb. 20, 1937, June 11, 1940; Br. 492,753, Feb. 25, 1937. In Germany Feb. 25, 1936. Reference to Br. 489,307 (Jan. 24, 1936).

5705 Gray, F. "Cathode-ray sweep circuit." U.S. 2,209,199, Feb. 25, 1936, July 23, 1940. Br. 467,958, Dec. 18, 1936.

5706 Philco. "Cathode-ray tube." Br. 486,467, Feb. 12, 1937. In U.S. Feb. 25, 1936. Magnetic deflecting assembly; yoke.

5707 Orthuber, Richard, and Eberhard Steudel. "Amplifier." U.S. 2,212,948, Feb. 26, 1937, Aug. 27, 1940. In Germany Feb. 26, 1936. Electron multiplier.

5708 Baird Television. "Amplifier." Br. 494,757, Feb. 26, 1937. Convention date Feb. 26, 1936. Wide-band for television.

5709 Scophony and G. Wikkenhauser. "Television." Br. 471,066, Feb. 26, 1936. Supersonic light valve with variable frequency control to produce linear movement of the emergent light beam.

5710 Steudel, Eberhard, and Richard Orthuber. "Electron multiplier." U.S. 2,185,611, Feb. 15, 1937, Jan. 2, 1940. In Germany Feb. 26, 1936.

5711 Traub, E. "Television." Br. 465,642, Feb. 26, 1936. Optical correction for curvilinear distortion with scanners, as in 448,238.

5712 "Television cable approved by FCC. AT&T allowed to build test line between here and Philadelphia. Wire must be open to all." N.Y.T. (Feb. 27): 21: 8. Tentative plans call for "booster" stations at 10-mile intervals to retain full cycle band.

5713 Hughes, L.E.C. "Telecommunications XXII: Pictures and vision." ELECT. 116 (Feb. 28): 293, 294.

5714 Andrieu, R., and Telefunken. "Saw-tooth wave generator." U.S. 2,254,025, Feb. 27, 1937, Aug. 26, 1941. In Germany Feb. 28, 1936.

5715 Farnsworth, P.T. "Cathode-ray tube receiver." Br. 463,896, Feb. 28, 1936. Reference to Br. 445,094. Picture tube with deflection and focusing coils, oblique screen, and lens for projecting an enlarged image on an external screen.

5716 Tolson, William A. "Cathode-ray tube deflection device." U.S. 2,167,379, Feb. 28, 1936, July 25, 1939. Br. 495,016, Mar. 1, 1937 (Marconi's). Magnetic deflector.

5717 "Coaxial cable plan accepted." N.Y.T. (Feb. 29): 8: 5.

5718 Baird Television, T.M.C. Lance, V.A. Jones, and P.W. Williams. "Cathode-ray tube." Br. 471,191, Feb. 29, 1936. Construction of photoelectric mosaic in a charge-storage camera tube. Reference to Br. 461,197.

5719 Vance, A.W. "Electronic device." U.S. 2,237,896, Feb. 29, 1936, Apr. 8, 1941; Br. 491,448, Mar. 1, 1937 (Marconi's). References to Br. 315,362 (July 12, 1928), 407,521 (Feb. 24, 1932), 472,859 (July 1, 1935); 472,861 (July 6, 1935).

5720 "Scophony Television." ELECTRONICS 9 (Mar.): 30–3. 4 photos, 2 diagrams.

5721 "New Italian television." ELECTRONICS 9 (Mar.): 46. Photo, diagram.

5722 Zworykin, V.K., G.A. Morton, and Louis Malter. "The secondary emission multiplier, a new electronic device." PROC. IRE 24 (Mar.): 351–75. 18 illus.

5723 Ardenne, M. von. "Experimental television receiver using cathode-ray tube." PROC. IRE 24 (Mar.): 409–24.

5724 "Television's status." SCI. AM. 154 (Mar.): 121.

5725 Baird, J.L. "The Kerr cell and its use in television." J. TELEV. SOC. 2 (Mar.): 118–24. 2 photos, diagram.

5726 Shmakov, Paul. "The development of television in U.S.S.R." J. TELEV. SOC. 2 (Mar.): 97–105. 7 photos, diag., 3 graphs. Summary of recent laboratory work, theoretical and practical; electron-beam and photocathode tubes; screen television; television broadcasting; and high-quality television.

5727 "Television cable soon to be started. Dr. F.B. Jewett of AT&T thinks line to Philadelphia will be ready in 6 months. FCC permit accepted." N.Y.T. (Mar. 1): II, 1: 2. Installation of new "pipe" is expected to be a boon to television industry.

5728 "Radio 'eyes' for London. British television tests expected to begin soon." N.Y.T. (Mar. 1): X, 10: 2, 3. Start of tests in London; limitations on programs because of viewer fatigue.

5729 Roosenstein, H.O., and Georg Paffrath. "Cathode-ray tube deflection system." U.S. 2,195,470, Apr. 2, 1940. In Germany Mar. 2, 1936, Mar. 2, 1937.

5730 "Television phones operated in Germany. First long-distance service links Berlin to Leipzig spring fair 8-inch images seen." N.Y.T. (Mar. 3): 19: 3.

5731 "Public television in Germany. Seeing by telephone." TIMES (Mar. 3): 15b. 3 photos. Two-way telephone-television between Berlin and Leipzig opened Mar. 1; first such service in the world. Excellent quality (180/25). Apparatus in Berlin made by the German Post Office laboratory; that in Leipzig by Fernseh A.-G.

5732 Bowman-Manifold, M., and John Collard. "Impedance networks." Br. 476,799, Mar. 3, 1936. U.S. 2,158,978, Feb. 26, 1937, May 16, 1939. Electric signal transmitting system.

5733 Cawley, A.J. "Television." U.S. 2,274,039, Mar. 3, 1936, Feb. 24, 1942. Scanning band.

5734 D.S. Loewe. "Cathode-ray tube." Br. 492,961, Jan. 29, 1937. In Germany Mar. 3, 1936.

5735 Schlesinger, K. "Method of generating impulses." U.S. 2,190,504, Feb. 26, 1937, Feb. 13, 1940. In Germany Mar. 3, 1936. Br. 491,450, Mar. 1, 1937. Reference to Br. 475,525.

5736 Van den Bosch, F.J.G. "Valve generator." Br. 471,430, Mar. 3, 1936.

5737 "The 'television telephone.'" MAN. GUARD. (Mar. 4), 10:4.

5738 Baird Television and V.A. Jones. "Cathode-ray tube." Br. 471,526, Mar. 4, 1936. V-shaped camera tube with separate light-sensitive and signal-storage electrodes.

5739 Gray, F. "Electro-optical system." U.S. 2,150,160, Mar. 4, 1936, Mar. 14, 1939. Assigned: Baird Television. Cathode-ray tube scanner with photocell, cathode-ray tube receiver.

5740 Gray, F. "Electro-optical system." U.S. 2,195,486, Mar. 4, 1936, Apr. 2, 1940. Assigned: Baird Television. Disk scanner with photoelectric cell and lamp.

5741 Gray, F. "Electro-optical system." U.S. 2,236,172, Mar. 4, 1936, Mar. 25, 1941. Assigned: Baird Television. Disk and optical system.

5742 Gray, F. "Television system." U.S. 2,260,709, Mar. 4, 1936, Oct. 28, 1941. Assigned: Baird Television. Cathode-ray tube and special phototubes.

5743 Gray, F. "Electro-optical system." U.S. 2,303,930, Mar. 4, 1936, Dec. 1, 1942. Assigned: Baird Television. Light-spot scanner, disks, special phototube.

5744 Electrical Research Products. "Discharge tube, light-sensitive cells." Br. 473,464, Feb. 18, 1937. U.S. Mar. 4, 1936.

5745 Electrical Research Products. "Photoelectric cells, cathode-ray tube." Br. 480,996, Feb. 19, 1937. U.S. Mar. 4, 1936.

5746 Ives, H.E. "Electro-optical system." U.S. 2,150,168, Mar. 4, 1936, Mar. 14, 1939. Assigned: Baird Television.

5747 Ross, John King. "Television apparatus." U.S. 2,128,967, Mar. 4, 1936, Sept. 6, 1938. Disk scanner and optical system.

5748 Ruska, Ernst. "Secondary electron tube." U.S. 2,147,756, Feb. 11, 1937, Feb. 21, 1939. In Germany Mar. 4, 1936.

5749 "'Cold' tube yields more radio power. Farnsworth, inventor, shows new amplifying principle adds to efficiency." NYT (Mar. 5): 2: 1, 2. "Sees aid to television." Engineers view device, also hailed as key to lighter airplane equipment.

5750 Baird Television, C. Szegho, and D.M. Johnstone. "Cathode-ray tube." Br. 471,539, Mar. 5, 1936. Picture tube with fluorescent screen and an intermediate screen intended to reduce flicker.

5751 Headrick, L.B. "Electron tube." U.S. 2,169,046, Mar. 5, 1936. Cathode-ray tube with fluorescent screen.

5752 Rosenthal, Adolf Heinrich "Light-valve." Br. 473,061, Mar. 5, 1936. Light cell comprising a particulate medium controlled by electrostatic or electromagnetic fields, adaptable for black-and-white or color television.

5753 "Telephone-television." ELECT. 116 (Mar. 6): 310. Note on German service over 100 mi. between Berlin and Leipzig. Mechanical scanning, image of head and shoulders, 9 in. square.

5754 Hughes, L.E.C. "Telecommunication XXIII: Television scanning." ELECT. 116 (Mar. 6): 319, 320.

5755 "The German television-telephone." NATURE 137 (Mar. 7): 391.

5756 Ross, Albion. "Berlin plans television to aid visitors outside Olympic stadia. With 400,000 tourists and excursionists likely to jam city, committee considers tents in central locations. Reservations made by 45,000 foreigners." NYT (Mar. 8): V, 3: 4, 5.

5757 "'Eye' adds light to phone line. Berlin television wire recalls tests made here six years ago." NYT (Mar. 8): X, 10: 3.

5758 Farnsworth, P.T. "Incandescent light-source." U.S. 2,089.054, Mar. 9, 1936, Aug. 3, 1937. Cathode-ray tube with screen composed of a helix wire.

5759 Farnsworth Television. "Cathode-ray tube amplifier." Br. 496,747, Mar. 9, 1936, Mar. 2, 1937.

5760 Farnsworth, P.T. "Absorption oscillator." U.S. 2,159,521, Mar. 9, 1936, May 23, 1939. Br. 479,318, Mar. 2, 1937.

5761 Ferranti and M.K. Taylor. "Cathode-ray tube." Br. 472,165, Mar. 11, 1936. Magnetic lens.

5762 Murphy Radio, K.S. Davies, and G.F. Hawkins. "Receiver." Br. 471,762, Mar. 11, 1936. For television.

5763 Hughes, L.E.C. "Telecommunications XXIV: The Raster." ELECT. 116 (Mar. 13): 351, 352.

5764 D.S. Loewe. "Television." Br. 492,168, Mar. 11, 1937. In Germany Mar. 16, 1936. Receiver.

5765 Brüche, Ernst, and Eberhard Steudel. "Electron multiplier." U.S. 2,185,172, Mar. 26, 1937, Jan. 2, 1940. In Germany Mar. 17, 1936.

5766 Andrieu, R. "Saw-tooth wave generator." U.S. 2,182,608, Mar. 17, 1937, Dec. 5, 1939. In Germany Mar. 19, 1936.

5767 Telefunken. "Television." Br. 490,676, Feb. 15, 1937. In Germany Mar. 19, 1936.

5768 Knoll, M. "Electronic device." U.S. 2,188,661, Mar. 13, 1937, Jan. 30, 1940. In Germany Mar. 19, 1936. Cathode-ray tube with amplifier and screen.

5769 Knoll, M., Bernhard Bartels, Otto Spengler, and Telefunken. "Cathode-ray screen." U.S. 2,180,710, Apr. 19, 1937, Nov. 21, 1939. In Germany Mar. 19, 1936.

5770 Schlesinger, K. "Rectifier for television signals." U.S. 2,201,794, Mar. 13, 1937, May 21, 1940. In Germany Mar. 19, 1936.

5771 Hughes, L.E.C. "Telecommunication XXV: Mechanical scanning." ELECT. 116 (Mar. 20): 381.

5772 Baird Television and George Dovaston. "Television." Br. 472,274, Mar. 20, 1936.

5773 Baird Television, V.A. Jones, and P.W. Williams. "Valve circuit." Br. 472,401, Mar. 20, 1936.

5774 Nicoll, F.H. "Cathode-ray tube." Br. 472,284, Mar. 20, 1936.

5775 Barthélemy, R. "Television receiver." U.S. 2,181,720, Mar. 19, 1937, Nov. 28, 1939. In France Mar. 21, 1936.

5776 de Forest, Lee. "Radial scanning television system." U.S. 2,163,749, Mar. 21, 1936, June 27, 1939. Assigned: American Television Labs, Inc.

5777 Schlesinger, K. "Television." U.S. 2,194,572, Mar. 18, 1937, Mar. 26, 1940; Br. 492,276, Mar. 16, 1937. In Germany Mar. 21, 1936. Assigned: D.S. Loewe.

5778 Baird Television and T.M.C. Lance. "Electron multiplier." Br. 472,485, Mar. 23, 1936.

5779 Andrieu, R. "Synchronizing system." U.S. 2,176,948, Mar. 24, 1937, Oct. 24, 1939. In Germany Mar. 24, 1936. Assigned: Telefunken. Interlaced scanning with multiple impulses.

5780 Farnsworth, P.T. "Secondary emission electrode." U.S. 2,139,813, Mar. 24, 1936, Dec. 13, 1938. Br. 482,168, Mar. 2, 1937. Assigned: Farnsworth Television Inc. Image dissector tube.

5781 Roosenstein, H.O., and K. Diels. "Cathode for cathode-ray tube." U.S. 2,182,881, Mar. 24, 1939, Dec. 12, 1939. In Germany Mar. 24, 1936.

5782 Zeiss Ikon A.-G. "Image dissector." Br. 475,995, Dec. 31, 1936. In Germany Mar. 24, 1936. Camera tube with secondary emission multiplier.

5783 Guanella, Gustav. "Television and other signal-transmission systems." U.S. 2,225,741, Mar. 25, 1937, Dec. 24, 1940. In Germany Mar. 26, 1936. Assigned: Radio Patents Corp.

5784 Marconi's. "Television." Br. 483,372, Mar. 26, 1936.

5785 Baird Television and G.R. Tingley. "Valve generator circuit for television." Br. 472,645, Mar. 26, 1936.

5786 Hughes, L.E.C. "Telecommunication XXVI: The illumination problem in television." ELECT. 116 (Mar. 27): 421, 422.

5787 Andrieu, R. "Oscillation circuit." U.S. 2,196,845, Mar. 19, 1937, Apr. 9, 1940. In Germany Mar. 27, 1936.

5788 Baird Television, and V.A. Jones. "Television." Br. 472,762, Mar. 28, 1936. Method for mixing separate signals derived from two scenes. Reference to Br. 417,282.

5789 Holmes, Ralph S. "Cathode-ray tube apparatus." U.S. 2,223,990, Mar. 28, 1936, Dec. 3, 1940. Magnetic deflection circuit.

5790 Malter, Louis, Jan A. Rajchman, E. Goodrich, Robert Rhea, and RCA. "Electronic oscillator." U.S. 2,121,360, Mar. 28, 1936, June 21, 1938. Secondary emission oscillator.

5791 Poch, W.J. "High-frequency amplifier." U.S. 2,183,203, Mar. 28, 1936, Dec. 12, 1939. Receiver circuit.

5792 Schlesinger, K. "Transposition of relaxation oscillations." U.S. 2,173,500, Mar. 18, 1937, Sept. 19, 1939; Br. 491,270, Mar. 16, 1937. In Germany Mar. 28, 1936 (D.S. Loewe).

5793 "Talk-see line is being built. Engineers expect to test new television cable in six months." NYT (Mar. 29): X, 10: 3.

5794 "Television possibilities as seen in Europe." NYT (Mar. 29): X, 10: 5. New Berlin-Leipzig telephone-television cable.

5795 Ferranti and E. Anderson. "Valve generator circuit." Br. 473,836, Mar. 31, 1936.

5796 Massa, E.A. Jr. "Electric discharge device." U.S. 2,135,039, Mar. 31, 1936, Nov. 1, 1938.

5797 Orthuber, Richard, and Eberhard Steudel. "Electronic discharge device." U.S. 2,177,374, Mar. 26, 1937, Oct. 24, 1939. In Germany Mar. 31, 1936.

5798 Weiss, G. "Electron multiplier." Br. 492,698, Mar. 25, 1937. Convention date Mar. 31, 1936. Reference to Br. 464,413 (Oct. 16, 1935).

5799 (Barthélemy, R.) "Automatic synchronization of television images." ELECTRONICS 9 (Apr.): 42, 43.

5800 Scholz, W. "Der heutige Stand der drahtlosen Tonbildempfangstechnik [Present status of the wireless reception technique of sound pictures]." FERN U. TON. 7 (Apr.): 25.

5801 Kell, R.D., A.V. Bedford, and M.A. Trainer. "Scanning sequence nd repetition rate of television images." PROC. IRE 24 (Apr.): 559–76.

5802 "La troisième exposition de pièces detachées, accessoires et lampes de T.S.F. [Third exhibition of radio parts, accessories, and tubes]" ONDE ELECT. 15 (Apr.): 208–25. Review mentions television.

5803 Barthélemy, R. "Television synchronizing signals. Note sur le sens et la forme du signal de synchronisation en télévision." ONDE ELECT. 15 (Apr.): 240–44.

5804 Zworykin, V.K., and G.A. Morton. "Applied electronic optics." J. OSA 26 (Apr): 181–9.

5805 "Television in France." RADIO-CRAFT 7 (Apr.): 591. 5 photos. Six receivers in Paris for public demonstrations.

5806 "The electron image tube." RADIO-CRAFT 7 (Apr.): 594, 622. 7 photos, 1 diagram.

5807 Galle, J.B. "Les dispositifs modernes de télévision [The modern means of television]." TECH. MOD. 28 (Apr. 1): 233–8. Electron-beam equipment.

5808 Goldmark, Peter C. "Television." U.S. 2,261,848, Apr. 1, 1936, Nov. 4, 1941. Assigned: Markia Corp. Disk and cathode-ray tube for film scanning.

5809 Bähring, H. "Push-pull amplifier for relaxation oscillations." U.S. 2,197,751, Apr. 1, 1937, Apr. 16, 1940. In Germany Apr. 2, 1936.

5810 Baird Television and V.A. Jones. "Television." Br. 472,980, Apr. 2, 1936.

5811 Richardson, H.A. "Television." Br. 452,105, Apr. 2, 1936. Addition to Br. 428,459 (Nov. 9, 1933).

5812 Hughes, L.E.C. "Telecommunication XXVII: The cathode-ray tube." ELECT. 116 (Apr. 3): 451, 452.

5813 "New electron multipliers: High-power high-frequency generating demonstrated." W.W. 38 (Apr. 3): 336–8.

5814 Bell, J., and W.S. Worthington. "Electro-optical light-valve." Br. 456,112, Apr. 3, 1936. Reference to Br. 455,983 (May 1, 1935).

5815 Langenwalter, H.-W. "Secondary emitting tube." U.S. 2,225,786, Apr. 2, 1937, Dec. 24, 1940. In Germany Apr. 3, 1936. Electron multiplier.

5816 Fernseh A.-G. "Electron multiplier." Br. 493,296, Apr. 5, 1937. In Germany Apr. 3, 1936.

5817 Geiger, Max. "Wave-form modifying circuit." U.S. 2,178,340, Mar. 29, 1937, Oct. 31, 1939. In Germany Apr. 3, 1936.

5818 Baird Television, and V.A. Jones. "Cathode-ray tube." Br. 473,006, Apr. 4, 1936. Camera tube with combined storage electrode and collecting electrode situated between a photoelectric cathode and an electron gun.

5819 Knoll, M. "Electrode structure." U.S. 2,193,101, Apr. 27, 1937, Mar. 12, 1940. In Germany Apr. 4, 1936. Mosaic electrode for camera tube.

5820 "FCC urged to fix television rules. Staff expert says effect on radio, press, and movies should be studied. Hearing set for June 15. Announced on plea that new inventions be kept for present on experimental basis." NYT (Apr. 5): 7: 5.

5821 Hollmann, H.E. "Electronic device." U.S. 2,180,957, Apr. 14, 1937, Nov. 21, 1939. In Germany Apr. 6, 1936. Electron amplifier.

5822 Bell, J., and W.S. Worthington. "Television." Br. 458,923, Apr. 8, 1936.

5823 Baird Television and J.C. Wilson. "Amplifier." Br. 457,886, Apr. 8, 1936. Reference to Br. 450,138 (Oct. 7, 1933).

5824 Baird Television and J.L. Baird. "Television." Br. 473,303, Apr. 9, 1936. Color receiver electro-optical system with prisms and light valves, split rays, and two color filters. Divided from Br. 473,323. References to Br. 459,171, 470,347.

5825 Baird Television and J.L. Baird. "Television." Br. 473,323, Apr. 9, 1936, Mar. 16, 1937, Oct. 11, 1937. Picture tube viewed through revolving disk with three color filters.

5826 Baird Television and V.A. Jones. "Image dissectors." Br. 473,348, Apr. 9, 1936. Camera tube with secondary multiplier grids.

5827 Condliffe, G.E. "Television." Br. 475,032, Apr. 9, 1936; U.S. 2,225,033, Apr. 8, 1937, Dec. 17, 1940. Assigned: EMI. Cathode-ray tube via mirrors scans a continuously moving film displaced to produce interlaced lines.

5828 Percival, W.S. "Wireless receiving apparatus." Br. 473,427, Apr. 9, 1936. For television.

5829 Hughes, L.E.C. "Telecommunication XXVIII: The electron beam." ELECT. 116 (Apr. 10): 485, 486.

5830 Fernseh A.-G. "Electron multiplier." Br. 493,714, Apr. 12, 1937. In Germany Apr. 11, 1936.

5831 "Dodging that big, bad television. The film barons hire a man to sing 'Who's afraid?' for them, despite the British Jeffrey Bernerd's cries of 'Wolf!'" N.Y.T. (Apr. 12): IX, 4: 2–4.

5832 Dunlap, O.E. Jr. "A panoply of power. Radio men returning from Old World tell of big verbal 'guns' and television." NYT (Apr. 12): X, 8: 1, 2. European developments. Reports from C.W. Horn, C.B. Jolliffe, and E.K. Cohan.

5833 Addink, N.W.H., J.H. de Boer, and N.V. Philips. "Cathode-ray tube fluorescent screen." U.S. 2,182,860, Apr. 14, 1937, Dec. 12, 1939. In Netherlands Apr. 14, 1936. Mixture for luminescent screen.

5834 de Boer, J.H., and N.V. Philips. "Electron discharge device." U.S. 2,159,946, Apr. 8, 1937, May 23, 1939. In Netherlands Apr. 14, 1936. Cathode-ray tube with luminescent screen and fluorescent screen.

5835 Baird Television and C. Szegho. "Cathode-ray tube." Br. 473,554, Apr. 14, 1936. Camera tube with combined charge-storage screen and a fluorescent screen situated between a photoelectric cathode and an electron gun, with an external photocell. Reference to Br. 461,312.

5836 Hollmann, H.E. "Electronic device." U.S. 2,180,957, Apr. 19, 1937, Nov. 21, 1939. In Germany Apr. 14, 1936. Amplifier.

5837 Hollmann, H.E. "Electronic system." U.S. 2,180,958, Apr. 19, 1937, Nov. 21, 1939. In Germany Apr. 14, 1936. Cathode-ray tube oscillator.

5838 "Television in France on a daily schedule." NYT (Apr. 19): X, 10: 3. French television; daily programs in Paris.

5839 Fernseh A.-G. "Television." Br. 494,164, Apr. 20, 1937. In Germany Apr. 20, 1936.

5840 Telefunken. "Electron multiplier." Br. 494,230, Apr. 20, 1937. In Germany Apr. 20, 1936.

5841 Hollmann, H.E. "Electron discharge device." U.S. 2,171,212, Mar. 27, 1937; Br. 494,230, Aug. 29, 1939. In Germany Apr. 20, 1936. Secondary electron emitter.

5842 Schlesinger, K. "Cathode-ray tube." U.S. 2,188,581, Apr. 20, 1937, Jan. 30, 1940; Br. 494,298, Apr. 20, 1937. In Germany Apr. 22, 1936. Assigned: D.S. Loewe. Projection tube.

5843 Schlesinger, K. "Band-filter coupling circuit for television amplifiers." U.S. 2,224,115, Apr. 12, 1937, Dec. 3, 1940. In Germany Apr. 16, 1936. Assigned: D.S. Loewe.

5844 D.S. Loewe. "Valve amplifier." Br. 499,132, Apr. 16, 1937. In Germany Apr. 16, 1936. For television.

5845 Hughes, L.E.C. "Telecommunication XXIX: The fluorescent screen." ELECT. 116 (Apr. 17): 513, 514.

5846 "Marconi foreign contracts. Revival of business." TIMES (Apr. 18): 19c.

5847 Dunlap, O.E. Jr. "New York selected as proving ground for television. Turning a corner. In June television will come into the open for extensive field tests here." NYT (Apr. 19): X, 10: 1. RCA tests in New York City planned for June.

5848 Baird Television and J.L. Baird. "Television." Br. 473,980, Apr. 23, 1936. Camera tube with a mosaic of conductive elements is scanned by light controlled by a scanning disk. References to Br. 446,585, 454,589, 464,919, 473,006.

5849 Hughes, L.E.C. "Telecommunication XXX: The electron lens." ELECT. 116 (Apr. 24): 555, 556.

5850 Goldmark, Peter C. "Electron discharge device." U.S. 2,132,783, Apr. 24, 1936, Oct. 11, 1938. Assigned: Markia Corp. Picture tube.

5851 Roosenstein, H.O., and Max Geiger. "Sawtooth wave generator." U.S. 2,227,513, Mar. 26, 1937, Jan. 7, 1941. In Germany Apr. 24, 1936.

5852 Dunlap, O.E. Jr. "Outdoor scene is broadcast in successful television test. Staged 'fire' in Camden recorded clearly on apparatus mile away. Try-out is preliminary to $1,000,000 field survey to begin here in June." N.Y.T. (Apr. 25): 1: 4, 5; 15: 1, 2. Report on successful broadcast of outdoor scene in Camden, N.J.

5853 Henneberg, Walter, and Alfred Recknagel. "Electronic device." U.S. 2,163,787, Apr. 26, 1937, June 27, 1939. In Germany Apr. 25, 1936. Cathode-ray tube with indirect electron mirror.

5854 B.T.-H. "Cathode-ray tube." Br. 499,848, Apr. 23, 1937. Convention date Apr. 25, 1936. References to Br. 458,015 (May 20, 1935), 460,288 (Apr. 19. 1934). Divided from Br. 460,397 (Apr. 19, 1934).

5855 Krawinkel, Günther. "Electron discharge device system." U.S. 2,201,587, Apr. 21, 1937, May 21, 1940. In Germany Apr. 25, 1936.

5856 Krawinkel, Günther. "Cathode-ray tube." Br. 499,642, Apr. 21, 1937. In Germany Apr. 25, 1936. Divided from Br. 499,487, Apr. 25, 1936. References to Br. 434,890 (Apr. 8, 1933) 434,891 (Apr. 8, 1933). Includes electron multiplier.

5857 Krawinkel, Günther. "Electron multiplier." Br. 499,487, Apr. 21, 1937. In Germany Apr. 25, 1936. Divided from Br. 499,642 (Apr. 25, 1936).

5858 Maloff, I.G. "Cathode-ray deflecting device." U.S. 2,165,803, Apr. 25, 1936, July 11, 1939; Br. 494,672. RCA.

5859 Andrieu, R. "Black-spot compensation apparatus." U.S. 2,202,511, Apr. 28, 1937, May 28, 1940; Br. 475,473, Apr. 28, 1937. In Germany Apr. 28, 1936. Telefunken. For camera tubes.

5860 Avey, Albert Franklin. "Telescreen." U.S. 2,120,596, Apr. 28, 1936, June 14, 1938. Assembly of lens and projector with mirrors.

5861 Baird Television, T.M.C. Lance, and V.A. Jones. "Discharge apparatus." Br. 474,296, Apr. 28, 1936. Electron tube has a photoelectric cathode faced by a negatively charged electrode, with a signal-storage anode or fluorescent screen at the other end for either image pickup or display.

5862 Scophony and F. von Okolicsányi. "Television receiver." Br. 477,604, Apr. 28, 1936. Supersonic light valve, oscillating mirrors, apertured mask, and reflecting mirrors.

5863 Blumlein, A.D. "Thermionic valve circuit." Br. 479,223, Apr. 29, 1936; U.S. 2,241,762, Apr. 26, 1937, May 13, 1941. For use in television, amplifying saw-tooth scanning currents. Reference to Br. 401,990 (May 28, 1932).

5864 Marconi's, R.J. Kemp, and D.J. Fewings. "Television." Br. 472,923, Apr. 29, 1936; U.S. 2,177,723, Apr. 16, 1937, Oct. 31, 1939. RCA. Separating television signals.

5865 Marconi's and D.C. Plaistowe. "Television." Br. 474,386, Apr. 29, 1936; U.S. 2,211,860, Apr. 16, 1937, Aug. 20, 1940. RCA. Electrical wave segregation circuit, for television receivers.

5866 Baird Television and C. Szegho. "Cathode-ray tube." Br. 474,391, Apr. 30, 1936. Picture tube with intermediate luminescent-photoelectric screen, accelerating electrode, and large fluorescent viewing screen.

5867 Linder, Ernest G. "Secondary emissive electronic discharge device." U.S. 2,117,098, Apr. 30, 1936, May 10, 1938. RCA.

5868 Zworykin, V.K., and Louis Malter. "Electric discharge device." U.S. 2,205,055, Apr. 30, 1936, June 18, 1940. RCA. Method of preparing secondary emission electrode.

5869 Barthélemy, R. "La télévision." ANN. POSTES 25 (May): 409–37. Paris installations; developments by Compagnie des Compteurs.

5870 "Coaxial cable used on German television circuit." ELECTRONICS 9 (May): 54. Installed by Siemens & Halske between Berlin and Leipzig. 40,000 kc capacity; 500 kc for television; 180/25.

5871 Urtel, Rudolf. "Der Stand der Fernseh-Entwicklung." FERN. U. TON. 7 (May): 33.

5872 Gibos, H. "Television in Germany." PROC. IRE 24 (May): 741–50.

5873 Zworykin, V.K. "L'optique électronique et ses applications [Electronic optics and applications]." ONDE ELECT. 15 (May): 265–98.

5874 "That corner in television." RADIO N. 17 (May): 645+.

5875 "Short-wave station list: Police, fire, and television stations." RADIO N. 17 (May): 669+.

5876 "Motor synchronises with all television transmission." SCI. AM. 154 (May): 269.

5877 Zworykin, V.K. "Iconoscopes and kinescopes in television." J. SMPE 28 (May): 473–97.

5878 Wright, E.E., and G.E.G. Graham. "Measurement of amplification and phase shift in video amplifiers." W. ENG. 13 (May): 259–61.

5879 "High-definition television in Holland. The Philips Company demonstrate their 405-line system on ultra-short waves." W.W. 38 (May 1): 451, 452. 3 photos.

5880 Baird Television and L.R. Merdler. "Television receiver." Br. 474,399, May 1, 1936.

5881 Faudell, C.L., and E.C.L. White. "Valve generator circuit." Br. 479,275, May 1, 1936. Divided from Br. 471,737 (Feb. 4, 1936). References to Br. 400,976, 423,832, 471,737.

5882 Schlesinger, K. "Amplitude filter circuit for television receivers." U.S. 2,097,804, May 1, 1936, Nov. 2, 1937. Divided from original German patent Oct. 11, 1933.

5883 LeDuc, J., and R. Barthélemy. "Characteristiques techniques du poste émetteur de télévision de la Tour Eiffel" [Technical characteristics of the television transmitter at the Eiffel Tower]. REV. GEN. 39 (May 2): 651–61.

5884 Fernseh A.-G. "Television receiver." Br. 494,967, May 3, 1937. In Germany May 2, 1936. Reference to Br. 469,558.

5885 Dunlap, O.E. Jr. "Television cavalcade is forming around the corner. Seeing is believing. Television procession awaits the signal to march into the open air." N.Y.T. (May 3): XI, 14: 1. Description of camera, equipment, and laboratory tests. Illustrated.

5886 Baird Television and P.W. Willans. "Valve generator circuit." Br. 474,683, May 4, 1936.

5887 Cackett, F.W. "Valve generator." Br. 476,336, May 4, 1936. Saw-tooth wave generator.

5888 Andrieu, R. "Television synchronizing circuit." U.S. 2,175,335, May 6, 1937, Oct. 10, 1939. In Germany May 6, 1936.

5889 Farnsworth, P.T., and B.C. Gardner. "Luminescent screen." U.S. 2,098,000, May 6, 1936, Nov. 2, 1937. Farnsworth Television.

5890 Karolus, A. "Television receiver." U.S. 2,189,315, May 1, 1937, Feb. 6, 1940. In Germany May 6, 1936. Assigned: Telefunken. Cathode-ray projection tube.

5891 Ploke, Martin. "Picture-translating tube." U.S. 2,159,568, May 3, 1937, May 23, 1939; Br. 496,756, May 3, 1937. In Germany May 6, 1936. Assigned: Zeiss Ikon A.-G. Image dissector.

5892 Marconi's. "Amplifier." Br. 481,343, May 6, 1937. Convention date May 6, 1936.

5893 Baird Television and P.V. Reveley. "Television." Br. 474,776, May 7, 1936.

5894 Mildenstein, W.R., and J.F. Best. "Television." Br. 476,383, May 7, 1936. Compound vibrating mirror oscillograph for scanning.

5895 Clothier, S.L., and H.C. Hogencamp. "Method of and apparatus for interlaced scanning." U.S. 2,163,541, May 9, 1936, June 20, 1939; Br. 493,885, May 4, 1937. Assigned: Kolorama Labs.

5896 A.C. Cossor, A.V. Bedford, and S.T. Stevens. "Valve generator circuit." Br. 474,623, May 9, 1936.

5897 Goldmark, Peter C. "Method and apparatus for televising a picture film." U.S.

2,177,365, May 9, 1936, Oct. 24, 1939. Assigned: Markia Corp. Film transmission via cable.

5898 Strübig, Heinrich. "Television picture analyzer." U.S. 2,161,643, Apr. 21, 1937, June 6, 1939; Br. 495,330, May 10, 1937. In Germany May 9, 1936.

5899 Baird Television, V.A. Jones, and P.W. Willans. "Cathode-ray tube." Br. 475,047, May 11, 1936. Various forms of camera tubes with mosaic storage grid and adjacent equipotential grid, plane cathode, fluorescent screen, focusing, and beam accelerating means.

5900 Baird Television, L.R. Merdler, and A.H. Gilbert. "Television receiver." Br. 475,046, May 11, 1936.

5901 Fernseh A.-G. "Cathode-ray tube." Br. 495,406, May 13, 1937. In Germany May 12, 1936. Mosaic screen.

5902 Geiger, Max. "Oscillation generator." U.S. 2,207,511, May 8, 1937, July 9, 1940. In Germany May 12, 1936. Two-stage amplifier with feedback.

5903 Marconi's. "Cathode-ray tube." Br. 478,475, Apr. 23, 1937. Convention date May 12, 1936.

5904 Telefunken. "Television." Br. 495,394, May 11, 1937. In Germany May 12, 1936.

5905 Urtel, Rudolf. "Black-spot correcting means." U.S. 2,169,714, May 13, 1937, Jan. 6, 1939; Br. 477,253, May 13, 1937. In Germany May 13, 1936. Assigned: Telefunken.

5906 "Women television announcers." MAN. GUARD. (May 14): 1.

5907 "'Hostess-announcers' for BBC. Television work at the Alexandra Palace." TIMES (May 14): 12a. Miss Bligh and Cornell appointed. Will work alternately.

5908 Philco. "Amplifier." Br. 493,289, Apr. 2, 1937. Convention date May 14, 1936. For television. See Br. 493,341 (below).

5909 Philco. "Television." Br. 493,341, Apr. 2, 1937. Convention date May 14, 1936. Divided from Br. 493,289 (above).

5910 "Broadcasting and television." ELECT. 116 (May 15): 626. Comment on proposed date for trial television programs; may begin in July.

5911 Hughes, L.E.C. "Telecommunication XXXI: The iconoscope." ELECT. 116 (May 15): 637, 638.

5912 Blumlein, A.D. "Television system." Br. 476,935, May 15, 1936; U.S. 2,254,204, May 11, 1937, Sept. 2, 1941.

5913 Toulon, Pierre Marie Gabriel. "Television." Br. 481,592, July 9, 1936. In France May 15, 1936.

5914 "Television faces economic hurdles. Commission preparing for hearing, fears prohibitive cost for entertainment. Sport a promising field. But official questions if public would buy sets for service limited to contests." NYT (May 16): 17: 7. FCC report.

5915 Farnsworth, P.T. "Means and method of controlling electron multiplier." U.S. 2,140,832, May 16, 1936, Dec. 20, 1938.

5916 Farnsworth, P.T., and Farnsworth Television. "Means and method for producing electron multiplication." U.S. 2,204,479, May 16, 1936, June 11, 1940.

5917 Farnsworth Television. "Electon multiplier." Br. 494,351, May 16, 1936, Apr. 30, 1937.

5918 Farnsworth Television. "Electron multiplier." Br. 495,438, May 16, 1936, May 11, 1937.

5919 Farnsworth Television. "Electron multiplier." Br. 495,458, May 16, 1936, May 11, 1937.

5920 Headrick, L.B. "Electron tube." U.S. 2,173,165, May 16, 1936, Sept. 19, 1939. Picture tube and electrode assembly.

5921 Schlesinger, K. "Coupling transformer for television arrangements." U.S. 2,186,932,

May 12, 1937, Jan. 9, 1940. In Germany May 16, 1936. High frequency.

5922 S.T.C. "Amplifier." Br. 477,240, May 16, 1936, Feb. 19, 1937.

5923 "Where is television?" NYT (May 17): IV, 8: 3, 4. "Hence the proposal to photograph plays and games, to illuminate the resultant film brilliantly, and thus to overcome the faulty lighting of the scene itself. Possibly the Germans may be compelled to resort to this technical subterfuge. But this is like making a phonograph record of a symphony concert and broadcasting from that. The public will surely demand direct television. More formidable is the difficulty of high cost if entertainment is what we seek. The communications commission in Washington, now trying to forecast the social and economic effects of television, stresses the financial hopelessness of staging, rehearsing, and transmitting plays on the scale that Hollywood considers necessary, with vistas of a metropolis and hundreds of actors participating in some gorgeous Belshazzar's feast. Possible cost: $200,000."

5924 Urtel, Rudolf. "Television scanning apparatus." U.S. 2,239,748, Nov. 5, 1936, Apr. 29, 1941. In Germany May 17, 1936. Assigned: Telefunken. Disk scanner, photoelectric sync for disk, time-delay circuit for mixing vision and sync signals.

5925 Gardner, Bernard C. "Five beam electron gun." U.S. 2,128,581, May 18, 1936, Aug. 30, 1938; Br. 477,874, Apr. 30, 1937. Assigned: Farnsworth Television. Picture tube.

5926 Zeiss Ikon A.-G. "Electron multiplier." Br. 480,062, May 19, 1936. Film sound amplification.

5927 EMI and H.G. Lubszynski. "Cathode-ray tube." Br. 475,928, May 20, 1936. Mosaic screen characteristics and materials and electron-beam scanning in a camera tube. References to Br. 442,666 (May 12, 1934); U.S. 2,225,063 (May 14, 1937).

5928 Percival, W.S. "Thermionic valve circuit." U.S. 2,171,671, May 17, 1937, Sept. 5, 1939; Br. 478,734, May 20, 1936.

5929 Percival, W.S. "Amplifier." Br. 478,734, May 20, 1936. EMI.

5930 Baird Television and V.A. Jones. "Television." Br. 475,517, May 21, 1936. Relay system employing intermediate transient images. References to Br. 437,021, 471,539, 475,047.

5931 Painter, William H. "Cathode-ray tube." U.S. 2,096,466, May 21, 1936, Oct. 19, 1937. Assigned: RCA.

5932 Hughes, L.E.C. "Telecommunication XXXII: The image dissector." ELECT. 116 (May 22): 667, 668.

5933 Comp. Gaz. "Television." Br. 485,412, Mar. 20, 1937. In France May 23, 1936.

5934 Scophony and J.H. Jeffree. "Television." Br. 473,907, May 23, 1936. Film scanning with lenses and mirror drum.

5935 Hollmann, H.E. "Electronic device." U.S. 2,206,668, May 26, 1937, July 2, 1940. In Germany May 26, 1936.

5936 Poch, W.J. "Protective circuit." U.S. 2,178,864, May 26, 2936, Nov. 7, 1939. For cathode-ray tube.

5937 Baird Television and Dennis Gábor. "Electron multiplier." Br. 480,786, May 27, 1936. For television receiver.

5938 Schröter, F., M. Knoll, Werner Klüge, and Hellmuth Erzold. "Arrangement for receiving television images." U.S. 2,220,688, May 27, 1937, Nov. 5, 1940. In Germany May 27, 1936. Assigned: Telefunken. Cathode-ray tube with secondary emissions.

5939 Baird Television and Dennis Gábor. "Electron multiplier." Br. 481,012, May 27, 1936. Divided from Br. 480,786.

5940 Gábor, Dennis. "Electron multiplier." U.S. 2,254,422, May 20, 1937, Sept. 2, 1941; Br. May 27, 1936.

5941 Clothier, S.L., and H.C. Hogencamp. "Method of and apparatus for television scanning." U.S. 2,163,540, May 28, 1936,

June 20, 1939; Br. 492,065, May 25, 1937. Assigned: Kolorama Labs.

5942 Ploke, Martin, and Zeiss Ikon A.-G. "Cathode-ray tube." U.S. 2,149,101, May 3, 1937, Feb. 28, 1939; Br. 478,410, May 25, 1937. In Germany May 28, 1936. Electro-magnetic lens.

5943 Soc. Anon. and J. Loeb. "Cathode-ray tube." Br. 480,859, May 28, 1936.

5944 Marconi's. "Electron multiplier." Br. 496,556, May 31, 1937. Convention date May 29, 1936. References to Br. 373,867 (Dec. 6, 1930), 379,893 (Dec. 6, 1930), 393,967 (Sept. 15, 1931).

5945 Pione, Emanuel R., and Louis Malter. "Electrode for electronic discharge devices." U.S. 2,123,024, May 29, 1936, July 5, 1938.

5946 Hughes, L.E.C. "Telecommunication XXXIII: Television electron systems." ELECT. 116 (May 29): 695, 696. Diag.

5947 D.S. Loewe. "Television." Br. 499,744, May 25, 1937. In Germany May 30, 1936.

5948 Krenzien, Otto. "Electronic device." U.S. 2,190,914, May 27, 1937, Feb. 20, 1940. In Germany May 30, 1936. Secondary emission phototube.

5949 Fernseh A.-G. "Electron multiplier." Br. 496,564, May 31, 1937. In Germany May 30, 1936.

5950 "Pretty girls with beautiful voices to be London television announcers." N.Y.T. (May 31): X, 10: 1, 2. Selections of Jasmine Bligh and Elizabeth Cornell.

5951 Dunlap, O.E. Jr. "Radio parley planned to avert television tangle. At the crossroads. Doctrine of 'evolution and experiment' recommended to guide television." N.Y.T. (May 31): X, 10: 1, 2. FCC inquiry to guide growth of industry to begin June 15.

5952 "Television today the status quo." ELECTRONICS 9 (June): 27–30, 53, 54. Review of field since 1934.

5953 Bedford, L.H. "The comparative properties of soft and hard cathode-ray tubes." J. SCI. INSTR. 13 (June): 177–84.

5954 "Address given by Sir Noel Ashbridge, Chief Engineer, BBC, on the occasion of the eighth annual meeting." J. TELEV. SOC. 2 (June): 125–8. Participants: Noel Ashbridge, J.A. Fleming.

5955 "Discussion on the future of high-definition television." J. TELEV. SOC. 2 (June): 132–7. Remarks by E.H. Robinson (OBSERVER), J.C. Wilson (Ferranti, formerly Baird), M.K. Taylor (Ferranti).

5956 Johnstone, D.M. "Notes on design of line scanning transformer." J. TELEV. SOC. 2 (June): 138–46. 5 photos, 8 diags., table. Baird Television Ltd.

5957 Puckle, O.S. "A time base employing hard valves." J. TELEV. SOC. 2 (June): 147–55. 7 photos, 6 diags.

5958 "The London television station, Alexandra Palace." J. TELEV. SOC. 2 (June): 156–60. A brief technical description, issued by the BBC, of the premises, the aerials, and the sound transmitter.

5959 Farnsworth, P.T. "Cathode-ray tube." U.S. 2,158,279, June 1, 1936, May 16, 1939. Assigned: Farnsworth Television. Br. 480,073, May 26, 1937.

5960 Farnsworth, P.T. "Multistage multipactor." U.S. 2,141,837, June 1, 1936, Dec. 27, 1938. Electron multiplier.

5961 Farnsworth Television. "Electron multiplier." Br. 482,026, May 26, 1937. In U.S. June 1, 1936.

5962 Ressler, Hugh C. "Cathode-ray tube system." U.S. 2,114,572, June 1, 1936, Apr. 19, 1938.

5963 Geiger, Max. "Relaxation oscillation generator." U.S. 2,159,792, June 2, 1937, May 23, 1939. In Germany June 3, 1936. Saw-tooth generator.

5964 Traub, E. "Television." Br. 473,910, June 3, 1936. Scanning by mirror drum with a number of stationary reflectors. References to Br. 419,120, 425,552, 440,055, 448,238.

5965 Bailey, W.C. "Television." Br. 462,216, June 4, 1936. Two mirror drums, one octagonal, the other pentagonal.

5966 Johnstone, D.M. "Cathode-ray tube." Br. 476,233, June 4, 1936. References to Br. 446,585, 469,404 (Jan. 23, 1936), 471,539. Picture tube with intermediate mosaic screen.

5967 B.T.-H. and Dennis Gábor. "Cathode-ray tube." Br. 481,094, June 4, 1936; U.S. 2,122,095, July 13, 1937, June 28, 1938. Picture tube.

5968 Fischer, F., and M. Lattmann. "Cathode-ray tube." Br. 496,662, June 3, 1937. Convention date June 4, 1936. Cathode-ray tube with mosaic incandescent screen.

5969 Koempfner, R. "Cathode-ray tube." Br. 476,311, June 4, 1936. Camera tube with inclined photosensitive grid, electron gun, output electrode, and deflection means and variations.

5970 Williams, W.E. "Cathode-ray tube." Br. 476,237, June 4, 1936. Single-line scan of electron image in a camera tube passes through slit in a magnetic shield.

5971 "Television in Japan." ELECT. 116 (June 5): 720. Report that separate studies by different organizations are to be combined to develop television.

5972 Hughes, L.E.C. "Telecommunication XXXIV: The television signal." ELECT. 116 (June 5): 733, 734.

5973 Schlesinger, K. "Detector." U.S. 2,129,037, June 5, 1936, Sept. 6, 1938. Divided from German patent Nov. 10, 1933. Push-pull for television.

5974 Telefunken. "Television transmitter." Br. 479,413, June 8, 1937. In Germany June 8, 1936. Camera tube and film projector.

5975 I.M.K. Syndicate. "Television receiver." Br. 475,971, June 9, 1936. Reference to Br. 439,236.

5976 Urtel, Rudolf. "Cathode-ray picture scanner." U.S. 2,196,130, June 8, 1937, Apr. 2, 1940; Br. 478,939, June 4, 1937. In Germany June 9, 1936. Assigned: Telefunken. Camera tube with additional diffused illumination of the image plate.

5977 Hughes, L.E.C. "Telecommunication XXV: Time bases." ELECT. (June 12): 787, 788. Diag.

5978 Michaelis, E., and E. Kinne. "Television." Br. 477,814, June 12, 1937. Convention date June 12, 1936. Picture tube receiver with back projection onto a curved viewing screen.

5979 Gregory, (Sir) R. "Science in a changing world: Recollections and reflections." NATURE 137 (June 13): 981–8. Report on Royal Inst. lecture, May 15.

5980 N.V. Philips. "Valve circuits for television." Br. 472,956, June 10, 1937. In Holland June 13, 1936. Wide-band signal rectifier.

5981 Schlesinger, K. "Electrical synchronization generator." U.S. 2,185,136, June 11, 1937, Dec. 26, 1939. Assigned: Loewe Radio. Br. 497,071, June 11, 1937. In Germany June 13, 1936.

5982 "Television and movies." NYT (June 14): IV, 8: 4.

5983 N.V. Philips. "Cathode-ray tube." Br. 486,063, June 12, 1937. Convention date June 15, 1936.

5984 Lubcke, H.R. "Television." Br. 476,808, June 15, 1936.

5985 Geiger, Max. "Oscillator." U.S. 2,157,533, June 8, 1937, May 9, 1939. In Germany June 16, 1936 (Telefunken).

5986 Schlesinger, K. "Photoelectric storage device." U.S. 2,227,018, June 11, 1937, Dec. 31, 1940. Assigned: Loewe Radio. In Germany June 16, 1936. Camera tube with mosaic element. Reference to Br. 498,672 (June 1, 1937).

5987 D.S. Loewe. "Cathode-ray tube." Br. 499,860, May 25, 1937. In Germany June 16, 1936.

5988 "Places television many years ahead. Radio manufacturer says house sets will compare in price with autos. Asks for more channels. Paley urges caution by FCC in the public use of television now." NYT (June 17): 23: 1.

5989 Ferranti and J.C. Wilson. "Electron multiplier." Br. 476,815, June 17, 1936.

5990 Strübig, Heinrich. "Mosaic plate." U.S. 2,164,961, May 18, 1937, July 4, 1939; Br. 497,018, June 10, 1937. In Germany June 17, 1936. Double-sided mosaic.

5991 Baird Television, L.R. Merdler, and G.R. Tingley. "Cathode-ray tube." Br. 476,947, June 18, 1936.

5992 Baird Television and P.W. Willans. "Television receiver." Br. 476,948, June 18, 1936.

5993 G.E.C. and R.J. Dippy. "Valve generator circuits for cathode-ray tubes." Br. 470,300, June 18, 1936. Magnetic deflection system.

5994 "Schools here plan new television use. A.L. Colston tells FCC 'master teachers and blackboards' will be used when practicable." N.Y.T. (June 19): 17: 4.

5995 Toulon, Pierre Marie Gabriel. "Television." Br. 497,367, June 18, 1937. Convention date June 19, 1936.

5996 "A television plan. Radio manufacturers suggest policies as a guide for the evolution of new industry." NYT (June 21): IX, 10: 3, 4. Suggestions by James M. Skinner, chairman of special television committee, RMA.

5997 "Radio's outlook: Free development is urged at parley and no strait-jacket rules." NYT (June 21): IX, 10: 7, 8. Includes comments by Sarnoff to the FCC on television.

5998 Jonker, Johan Lodewijk Hendrik, Edmund Heinrich Löpp, Adrianus Johannes Wilhelms Marie van Overbeek, and Hendrik Filippo. "Secondary electron discharge tube." U.S. 2,146,580, June 22, 1937, Feb. 7, 1939 (N.V. Philips). In Holland June 22, 1936.

5999 Löpp, Edmund Heinrich, and Adrianus Johannes Wilhelms Marie van Overbeek. "Secondary electron discharge tube." U.S. 2,151,783, June 22, 1937, Mar. 28, 1939 (N.V. Philips). In Holland June 22, 1936. Electron multiplier.

6000 N.V. Philips. "Electron multiplier." Br. 497,589, June 19, 1937. Convention date June 22, 1936. References to 460,356 (June 25, 1935), 469,477 (Jan. 30, 1935), 470,026 (Feb. 8, 1936).

6001 N.V. Philips. "Electron multiplier." Br. 490,652, June 19, 1937. Convention date June 22, 1936.

6002 N.V. Philips. "Electron multiplier." Br. 489,923, June 19, 1937. Convention date June 22, 1936.

6003 Jonker, J.L.H., Edmund H. Löpp, and A.J.W.M. van Overbeek. "Secondary electron emitter screen tube." U.S. 2,171,214, June 22, 1937, Aug. 29, 1939. In Holland June 22, 1936 (N.V. Philips).

6004 D.S. Loewe. "Discharge apparatus." Br. 501,270, June 23, 1937. In Germany June 23, 1936. For mosaic screen in television transmission.

6005 "Backs amateur aid in television test. Philo T. Farnsworth appeals to FCC to permit free development of the sets. He predicts rapid gains. J.V.L. Hogan, at conference, urges early broadcast of only small subjects." NYT (June 24): 41: 6.

6006 Holman, Herbert Edward. "Means and method of producing flat surfaces." U.S. 2,194,551, June 11, 1937, Mar. 26, 1940. Br. 479,024, June 25, 1936 (EMI).

6007 Klatzow, Leonard. "Cathode-ray tube." Br. 480,946, June 25, 1936; U.S. 2,178,233 June 11, 1937, Oct. 31, 1939 (EMI). Reference to Br. 458,586.

6008 Marconi's and G.B. Banks. "Electron multiplier." Br. 478,813, June 25, 1936.

6009 Marconi's and Leonard Morris Myers. "Electron multiplier." Br. 477,345, June 25, 1936.

6010 Baird Television, V.A. Jones, and T.M.C. Lance. "Television receiver." Br. 477,355, June 26, 1936. Film recording, storage, and stationary viewing.

6011 Baird Television, C. Szegho, and G.A.R. Tomes. "Cathode-ray tube." Br. 477,406, June 26, 1936. Tube with internal luminescent screen and two-way projection.

6012 Banks, G.B. "Electron multiplier." U.S. 2,113,264, Aug. 31, 1937, Apr. 5, 1938 (RCA). In Britain June 26, 1936 (Marconi's).

6013 Steudel, Eberhard, and Jurg Johannessen. "Cathode-ray tube." U.S. 2,220,181, June 22, 1937, Nov. 5, 1940. In Germany June 26, 1936 (A.E.G.). With photoelectric cathode and deflector plates.

6014 Vance, Arthur W. "Cathode-ray deflecting system." U.S. 2,207,499, June 26, 1936, July 9, 1940. Assigned: RCA. Camera tube and deflector circuits.

6015 Zeitline, V., A. Zeitline, and V. Kliatchko. "Cathode-ray tube." Br. 474,797, Dec. 5, 1936. Convention date June 26, 1936.

6016 Lucas, William. "The scanning principle in television." NATURE 137 (June 27): 1076.

6017 Dunlap, O.E. Jr. "Television flutters its wings for a test flight. Faces in space. Images to leap from skyscraper in test which opens here tomorrow." NYT (June 28): XI, 10: 1, 2.

6018 "Costs of sight. Farnsworth, television expert, discusses the outlook for home reception." NYT (June 28): IX, 10: 7, 8.

6019 "Television 'show' starts here today. $1,000,000 tests expected to go a long way in deciding when homes will get sets. But they shun all prophecy or 'ballyhoo.' Transmitter atop Empire State Building." NYT (June 29): 17: 3.

6020 "Experimental television." NYT (June 30): 18: 2, 3.

6021 "Tests of television started in secret. Favorable debut indicated in ideal weather here for image broadcast. Wide interest reported. But public may be forced to wait six months to learn results of experiment." NYT (June 30): 21: 6.

6022 Wendt, Karl R. "Cathode-ray tube deflecting circuit." U.S. 2,207,389, June 30, 1936, July 9, 1940. Assigned: RCA. Magnetic deflector, sync generator, modulator with camera tube.

6023 "FCC plans future of UHF regime." ELECTRONICS 9 (July): 7–10. 2 diagrams. FCC hearings began June 15 and included discussion of television.

6024 Ardenne, M. v. "Cathode-ray scanner for televising film." ELECTRONICS 9 (July): 46. Quotes from FERN. U. TON. 7 (1936): 9–13, and Z. TECH. PHYS. 16 (1935): 61–7.

6025 "'Seeing-talking' in Berlin-Leipzig." ELECTRONICS 9 (July): 48. Photo. Telephone booth at Leipzig Fair; 380 miles of cable to Berlin; service inaugurated by German Post Office, Mar. 1, 1936; 180/25; cathode-ray tube receiver 18 by 20 cm.

6026 Ardenne, M. v. "Uber die Umwandlung von Lichtbildern aus einem Spektralgebiet in ein anderes durch elektronenoptische Abbildung von Photokathoden" [On the transformation of light pictures from one spectral window to another]. E.N.T. 13 (July): 230–5.

6027 Ring, F. "Fernsehübertragung auf Fernsprechleitungen" [Television transmission and telephone lines]. FERN. U. TON. 7 (July): 49.

6028 "Fernsehen bei der Olympic Speil 1936" [Television at the 1936 Olympic Games]. FERN. U. TON. 7 (July): 57.

6029 Kette, G. "Fernsehen auf der Rundfunkausstellung 1935" [Television at the 1935 Radio Fair]. FERN. U. TON. 7 (July): 61.

6030 Zworykin, V.K. "Electron optical systems and their applications." J. IEE 29 (July): 1–10. 3 plates.

6031 Levy, Leonard, and Donald W. West. "Fluorescent screens for cathode-ray tubes for television and other purposes." J. IEE 79 (July): 11–9.

6032 "Seeing's believing! A report on a television demonstration." RADIO N. 18 (July): 19, 55.

6033 Clement, L.M., and E.W. Engstrom. "RCA television field tests." RCA REV. 1 (July): 32–40.

6034 Zworykin, V.K. "Iconoscopes and kinescopes in television." RCA REV. 1 (July): 60–84. Also see J. SMPE (May 1937).

6035 "Two years to go." SCI. AM. 155 (July): 9.

6036 "Television from standpoint of motion picture production industry." J. SMPE 27 (July): 74–6. Report of Scientific Committee of Research Council.

6037 Baird Television and A.H. Gilbert. "Cathode-ray tube." Br. 477,539, July 2, 1936.

6038 Baird Television and P.W. Willans. "Television." Br. 477,540, July 2, 1936.

6039 Clothier, S.L., and H.C. Hogencamp. "Television scanning system." U.S. 2,163,547, July 2, 1936, June 20, 1939. Assigned: Kolorama Labs.

6040 Orthuber, R., and Mahl. "Cathode-ray tube." U.S. 2,222,955, June 17, 1937, Nov. 26, 1940. In Germany July 3, 1936 (A.E.G.).

6041 Orthuber, R., and E. Steudel. "Electron multiplier." U.S. 2,227,103, June 26, 1937, Dec. 31, 1940. In Germany July 3, 1936 (A.E.G.).

6042 Blumlein, A.D. "Thermionic valve amplifying circuit." Br. 482,740, July 4, 1936 (EMI); U.S. 2,185,367, Jan. 2, 1940. References to 443,589 (Aug. 31, 1934), 448,421 (Sept. 4, 1934), 456,450 (Apr. 3, 1935).

6043 Görlich, Paul. "Piezoelectric cathode." U.S. 2,172,164, June 30, 1937, Sept. 5, 1939. In Germany July 4, 1936 (Zeiss Ikon).

6044 Ploke, Martin, and Wilhelm Lang. "Secondary electron multiplier." U.S. 2,150,632, July 6, 1937, Mar. 14, 1939. In Germany July 4, 1936 (Zeiss Ikon).

6045 Ploke, Martin, and Wilhelm Lang. "Secondary electron multiplier." U.S. 2,163,700, Dec. 2, 1938, June 27, 1939. In Germany July 4, 1936 (Zeiss Ikon).

6046 Zeiss Ikon A.-G. "Electron multiplier." Br. 503,211, June 26, 1937. In Germany July 4, 1936. Void.

6047 "Britain rules out sponsors. For 'ethical integrity' advertising is banned for second decade." NYT (July 5): IX, 10: 3. Includes television.

6048 "Films' chance to repay radio." NYT (July 5): IX, 10: 6, 7. Mentions television.

6049 "Police radio order is postponed by FCC. Television protests on allocation of frequencies hold up action until July 20." NYT (July 7): 4: 5.

6050 "Television 'show' today." NYT (July 7): 22: 1. RCA demonstration.

6051 "Broadcasting: Major Tryon and the Ullswater Report." TIMES (July 7): 8e-g, 9a-c. Parliamentary discussion on renewing the BBC charter at the end of the year.

6052 Deserno, Peter, and Maximilian Messner. "Television apparatus." U.S. 2,164,906, July 7, 1937, July 4, 1939. In Germany July 7, 1936. Assigned: C. Lorenz A.-G. Cathode-ray tube with external magnetic coils arranged to compensate strong fields.

6053 Hollmann, Hans Erich. "Electro-mechanical oscillating device." U.S. 2,154,127, June 9, 1937, Apr. 11, 1939. In Germany July 7, 1936 (Telefunken). Cathode-ray tube with built-in vibrator.

6054 Orthuber, R., and E. Steudel. "Electron multiplier." U.S. 2,240,713, July 1, 1937, May 6, 1941. In Germany July 7, 1936 (A.E.G.).

6055 "Television stages first real show. Dancers, speakers, and various acts seen clearly by invited guests of the RCA. 'Outsiders' view it, too. As in sound programs, there is no way to keep them out Fine weather aids test." NYT (July 8): 21: 3.

6056 Baird Television and A.H. Gilbert. "Television." Br. 477,897, July 8, 1936.

6057 Heymann, Otto. "Electron discharge device." U.S. 2,200,745, Oct. 15, 1937, May 14, 1940. In Germany July 8, 1936 (Siemens).

6058 Schlesinger, K., and D.S. Loewe. "Multistage frequency reducer." U.S. 2,227,019, July 6, 1937, Dec. 31, 1940. In Germany July 8, 1936. Reference to Br. 475,595.

6059 Toulon, P.M.G. "Synchronization system for television." U.S. 2,227,815, July 3, 1937, Jan. 7, 1941. In France July 8, 1936. Reissued Apr. 24, 1941, Mar. 24, 1942 (Hazeltine). Television receiver.

6060 Baird Television and L.R. Merdler. "Valve circuits." Br. 477,906, July 9, 1936.

6061 Geiger, Max. "Signalling apparatus." U.S. 2,240,136, July 7, 1937, Apr. 29, 1941. In Germany July 9, 1936 (Telefunken). Cathode-ray tube.

6062 Toulon, P.M.G. "Screen television receiver." U.S. 2,201,066, July 1, 1937, May 14, 1940. In France July 9, 1936. Reference to Br. 497,404 (June 18, 1937).

6063 "Servicing of television sets." ELECT. 117 (July 10): 32. Comment on James Nelson's presidential address to the Institute of Wireless Technology and the need for informed engineers to maintain television receivers in working order.

6064 "Patent suit filed on RCA television. Westinghouse Company begins action in Delaware courts over radio inventions." N.Y.T. (July 10): 6: 7. Westinghouse suit against RCA to obtain issue of patents on Zworykin's inventions.

6065 Baird Television and P.W. Willans. "Cathode-ray tube." Br. 479,750, July 10, 1936.

6066 Schunack, Johannes, and Ernst Ruska. "Electron multiplier." U.S. 2,213,076, June 19, 1937, Aug. 27, 1940; Br. 498,304, July 5, 1937. In Germany July 10, 1936 (Fernseh A.-G.).

6067 Farnsworth, P.T., and Farnsworth Television. "Image source." U.S. 2,213,070, July 11, 1936, Aug. 27, 1940.

6068 "Radio leaders plan orderly evolution of television. The 'air' apparents. Broadcasters expect to inherit television so begin to study the new art." NYT (July 12): X, 14: 1, 2. 5 photos. FCC hearing; summary of findings.

6069 Bähring, Herbert. "Method of operating cathode-ray tubes." U.S. 2,224,587, July 16, 1937, Dec. 10, 1940. In Germany July 13, 1936 (Fernseh A.-G.).

6070 Baird Television, D.M. Johnstone, and V.A. Jones. "Valve generator." Br. 479,935, July 13, 1936.

6071 Marconi's and G.B. Banks. "Electron multiplier." Br. 478,001, July 13, 1936.

6072 Clothier, S.L., and H.C. Hogencamp. "System for television scanning." U.S. 2,163,548, July 16, 1936, June 20, 1939. Assigned: Kolorama Labs. With rotary mirror.

6073 G.E.C., W.H. Aldous, D.W. Fry, and C.H. Simms. "Electron multiplier." Br. 478,262, July 16, 1936.

6074 Schlesinger, K. "Transposition of relaxation oscillations." U.S. 2,170,252, July 10, 1937, Aug. 22, 1939. In Germany July 16, 1936 (D.S. Loewe). Addition to Br. 483,667. Reference to Br. 491,270 (Mar. 28, 1936).

6075 Farnsworth, P.T. "Means and method for transmitting synchronizing pulses in television." U.S. 2,155,479, July 11, 1936, Apr. 25, 1939; Br. 497,605, June 30, 1937. Assigned: Farnsworth Television and Radio Corp.

6076 Schlesinger, K. "Synchronization signal transmitter." U.S. 2,185,445, July 10, 1937, Jan. 2, 1940. Assigned: Loewe Radio. Br. 498,841, July 15, 1937. In Germany July 16, 1936. Film scanner.

6077 D.S. Loewe. "Cathode-ray tube." Br. 503,954, July 15, 1937. In Germany July 16, 1936.

6078 "Fight withdrawal of radio channels. Purdue University and television group accuse FCC of favoring big companies." NYT (July 17): 15: 4.

6079 Faudell, C.L. "Thermionic valve circuits." Br. 478,511, July 17, 1936 (EMI); U.S.

2,233,596, July 7, 1937, Mar. 4, 1941. Thermionic valve oscillation circuits.

6080 Harding, Robert Jr. "High-definition television apparatus." U.S. 2,192,376, July 17, 1936, Mar. 5, 1940. Assigned: National Television Corp. Helical mirror drum.

6081 Snyder, Richard L. "Concentric multipactor." U.S. 2,147,934, July 18, 1936, Feb. 21, 1939.

6082 Farnsworth Television. "Electron multiplier." Br. 493,801, June 30, 1937. In U.S. July 18, 1936.

6083 Farnsworth Television. "Television." Br. 494,365, June 30, 1937. In U.S. July 18, 1936.

6084 "Television here and abroad." NYT (July 19): X, 10: 1. Discusses Bell coaxial cable; new Eiffel Tower transmitter; NBC in New York exhibition; television station in Poland; German developments.

6085 G.E.C. and W.H. Aldous. "Electron multiplier." Br. 469,283, July 21, 1936.

6086 Marconi's and David John Fewings. "Valve generator circuits for television." Br. 483,545, July 21, 1936; U.S. 2,205,760, July 16, 1937, June 25, 1940 (RCA).

6087 Zeitline, V., A. Zeitline, and V. Kliatchko. "Television." Br. 478,653, July 21, 1936.

6088 Schnabel, W. "Kaltkathodenstrahl-Lichtabtaster für Fernsehzwecke" [Cold cathode-ray light scanner for television purposes]. ARCH. ELEKT. 30 (July 22): 461–75.

6089 Ballard, R.C. "Cathode-ray tube circuits." U.S. 2,173,221, July 22, 1936, Sept. 19, 1939 (RCA).

6090 G.E.C. and D.C. Espley. "Amplifier." Br. 476,067, July 22, 1936.

6091 Malter, L. "Electronic discharge device." U.S. 2,219,871, July 22, 1936, Oct. 29, 1940 (RCA). Electron multiplier.

6092 Marconi's. "Electron multiplier." Br. 499,649, July 22, 1937. Convention date July 22, 1936. Addition to Br. 469,477 (Jan. 30, 1935).

6093 Abrahamsohn, Max. "Cathode-ray transmitting tube." U.S. 2,202,614, July 10, 1937, May 28, 1940. Assigned: Telefunken. In Germany July 23, 1936. Camera tube.

6094 G.E.C. and D.C. Espley. "Television." Br. 471,285, July 23, 1936. Synchronizing circuits.

6095 Horton, Arthur W. Jr. "Electro-optical system." U.S. 2,184,743, July 23, 1936, Dec. 26, 1939. Assigned: B.T.L. Br. 480,483, Feb. 12, 1937 (S.T.C.).

6096 B.T.-H. and A.E.G. "Electron multiplier." Br. 477,757, July 7, 1937. In Germany July 24, 1936.

6097 G.E.C., D.C. Espley, and Edwards. "Television." Br. 478,815, July 24, 1936. Amplifier.

6098 Nicoll, F.H. "Cathode-ray tube." Br. 480,948, July 25, 1936 (EMI); U.S. 2,181,850, July 17, 1937, Nov. 28, 1939. References to Br. 431,327, 428,525, 458,270.

6099 Marconi's. "Electron multiplier." Br. 499,665, July 26, 1937. Convention date July 25, 1936. Reference to Br. 464,413 (Oct. 16, 1935).

6100 Zworykin, V.K., and L. Malter. "Electronic discharge device." U.S. 2,157,585, July 25, 1936, May 9, 1939 (RCA).

6101 Zworykin, V.K. "Television system." U.S. 2,206,654, July 25, 1936, July 2, 1940. Assigned: RCA. Br. 483,622, July 26, 1937 (Marconi's). Single-channel, interlaced, cathode-ray tube.

6102 Dunlap, O.E. Jr. "Television paths are being charted through space. Learning A-B-Sees. So man may look across the horizon, engineers formulate the standards." NYT (July 26): IX, 10: 1, 2. Review of U.S. and European progress and recommendations to FCC. 4 photos.

6103 "Television here and abroad." NYT (July 26): IX, 10: 1, 2. Discusses electrical interference in New York; new transmitters at German Post Office; Alexandra Palace; and protests to FCC by Purdue University and National Television Corp. of New York.

6104 Geiger, Max. "Saw-tooth wave generator." U.S. 2,182,555, July 24, 1937, Dec. 5, 1939. In Germany July 27, 1936 (Telefunken).

6105 Marconi's and G.F. Brett. "Cathode-ray tube." Br. 478,971, July 27, 1936; U.S. 2,195,444, July 17, 1937, Apr. 2, 1940 (RCA).

6106 Coeterier, F. "Electronic discharge device." U.S. 2,163,270, July 20, 1937, June 20, 1939. In Germany July 28, 1937 (N.V. Philips).

6107 N.V. Philips. "Electron multiplier." Br. 485,427, July 26, 1937. Convention date July 28, 1936.

6108 Fernseh A.-G. "Discharge apparatus." Br. 499,662, July 26, 1937. In Germany July 28, 1936. Reference to Br. 463,829.

6109 Ferranti, M.K. Taylor, and J.C. Wilson. "Television." Br. 478,599, July 28, 1936.

6110 Vestergren, Harry Einar Maurits. "Television plant." U.S. 2,215,365, July 24, 1937, Sept. 17, 1940. Assigned: Gustaf Sylven. Br. 482,835, Oct. 5, 1936. In Sweden July 28, 1936. Camera tube, picture tube with remote control for the receiver.

6111 "Television permits granted." NYT (July 29): 20: 3. The FCC grants permission to the National Television Corp. of New York to operate its station until Sept. 15.

6112 B.T.-H. "Electron multiplier." Br. 497,160, July 29, 1937. Convention date July 30, 1936.

6113 Fernseh A.-G. "Electron multiplier." Br. 499,661, July 26, 1937. Convention date July 30, 1936.

6114 Wright, W.D., and O. Klemperer. "Electron lenses." Br. 480,857, July 30, 1936 (EMI).

6115 "Television delays." ELECT. 117 (July 31): 132. Critical comparison with early radio broadcasting.

6116 B.T.-H. and Dennis Gábor. "Cathode-ray tube." Br. 479,064, July 31, 1936.

6117 G.E.C. and W.H. Aldous. "Electron multiplier." Br. 473,571, July 31, 1936.

6118 S.T.C. "Electron multiplier and circuit." Br. 491,773, May 21, 1937. Convention date July 31, 1936. Divided from Br. 493,217 (below).

6119 S.T.C. "Electron multiplier and circuit." Br. 493,217, May 21, 1937. Convention date July 31, 1936. Divided to Br. 491,773 (above).

6120 S.T.C. "Electron multiplier and circuit." Br. 495,839, May 21, 1937. Convention date July 31, 1936. Divided to Br. 495,843 (below).

6121 S.T.C. "Electron multiplier and circuit." Br. 495,843. May 21, 1937. Convention date July 31, 1936. Divided from Br. 495,839 (above).

6122 "Notes on the Paris International Radio Exposition." ELECTRONICS 9 (Aug.): 40. The exposition ran May 20–June 2, 1936. Television was broadcast every day from 4:00 to 5:00 p.m., 180 lines. The Loewe set provided good black-and-white images. In France, television receivers are not yet produced in quantity. Complications in Germany have interfered with D.S. Loewe's plans.

6123 "West Coast television." ELECTRONICS 9 (Aug.): 42. Photo of Don Lee receiver. Claimed to be the first public demonstration of high-definition television in the U.S. with daily transmissions of 330/24 on 45 MHz.

6124 Epstein, D.W. "Electron optical system of two cylinders as applied to cathode-ray tubes." PROC. IRE 24 (Aug.): 1095–1139.

6125 Gernsback, H. "Television problems." RADIO-CRAFT 8 (Aug.): 69. Editorial. This issue was a special television number.

6126 "Japan conducts television tests." RADIO-CRAFT 8 (Aug.): 70. Subsidy of 300,000 yen for development of system by K. Takayanagi.

6127 Schrage, W.E. "What about television?" RADIO-CRAFT 8 (Aug.): 72, 73, 102. 3 photos, 4 diags. Speculation about practical television: plans, costs, possibilities.

6128 Washburne, R.D. "New developments in television." RADIO-CRAFT 8 (Aug.): 74, 75, 120, 121. 2 photos, 2 diags., 2 facsimiles from newspapers, 2 tables of television stations in U.S. Discussion of technical problems and current plans.

6129 de Forest, Lee. "High-intensity illuminants in television." RADIO-CRAFT 8 (aug.): 76, 105. Photo of Westinghouse 85-watt mercury lamp (June 1, 1936).

6130 Lee, Don. "Television on the West Coast." RADIO-CRAFT 8 (Aug.): 76, 110. 2 photos, 1 diag. of receiver. Station W6XAO began Nov. 23, 1931. Airplane to Los Angeles, May 21, 1932.

6131 Sanabria, U.A. "The importance of interlaced scanning." RADIO-CRAFT 8 (Aug.): 79, 122, 123. 2 illus., 1 table.

6132 Priess, William H. "Mechanical vs. cathode television systems." RADIO-CRAFT 8 (Aug.): 79, 126, 127. 1 illus.

6133 Goldsmith, Alfred N. "Television as home entertainment." RADIO-CRAFT 8 (Aug.): 80, 102. 1 illus.

6134 Tetzner, Carl. "Television in Germany." RADIO-CRAFT 8 (Aug.): 83, 123. 5 illus.

6135 "Television progress in Italy." RADIO-CRAFT 8 (Aug.): 86.

6136 Peck, William Hoyt. "The opto-mechanical system of television." RADIO-CRAFT 8 (Aug.): 88, 124. 3 illus.

6137 Chauvièrre, Marc. "A French television system." RADIO-CRAFT 8 (Aug.): 91, 103. 2 illus. A 60-line system; scanning disk in transmitter, cathode-ray tube in receiver; 25 frames per second interlaced.

6138 Farnsworth, P.T. "An improved television camera." RADIO-CRAFT 8 (Aug.): 92, 113.

6139 Stager, A. "A cathode-ray film scanner." RADIO-CRAFT 8 (Aug.): 94, 115. 2 illus. M. von Ardenne's newest method.

6140 "How will television affect radio industry?" RADIO ENG. 16 (Aug.): 5–7.

6141 Strange, John William, and William Horace Connell. "Electron discharge device." Br. 479,356, Aug. 1, 1936 (EMI); U.S. 2,158,640, July 31, 1937, May 16, 1939. Cathode-ray tube, luminescent screen.

6142 "Television here and abroad." NYT (Aug. 2): X, 10: 1, 2. Progress in Europe and U.S.

6143 Gander, A. Marsland. "Britain's royal plan. New charter maps future policy for radio and provides for television decade." NYT (Aug. 2): X, 10: 7, 8. BBC charter.

6144 "Television of the games. Disappointing result." TIMES (Aug. 3): 12a. "Three 'electric eyes' and two intermediate film mobile television vans are being used by the German Post Office to televise the Olympic Games [in Berlin]." 180/25 from Witzleben. 18 extra viewing rooms added to existing 10. Very poor pictures.

6145 Boersch, Hans. "Electron device." U.S. 2,202,620, Aug. 13, 1937, May 28, 1940; Br. 479,420, Aug. 5, 1937 (B.T.-H.). In Germany Aug. 5, 1936 (A.E.G.). Electromagnetic lens.

6146 G.E.C. and D.W. Fry. "Electron multiplier." Br. 472,717, Aug. 5, 1936.

6147 Mead, John Edward, and Hector Gordon Merson Spratt. "Television receiving apparatus." Br. 479,751, Aug. 5, 1936; U.S. 2,164,537, July 30, 1937, July 4, 1939.

6148 "Olympics in television. But pictures are indistinct, like men floating in milk." N.Y.T. (Aug. 6): 24: 8. German television. Olympic events are broadcast to Berlin theatres.

6149 Baird Television, T.M.C. Lance, and. Austin. "Television." Br. 479,458, Aug. 6, 1936.

6150 D.S. Loewe. "Cathode-ray tube." Br. 503,520, Aug. 6, 1937. In Germany Aug. 7, 1936.

6151 Brüche, Ernst, and Walter Schaffernicht. "Electron image tube." U.S. 2,179,083, Aug. 13, 1937, Nov. 7, 1939. Assigned: A.E.G. In Germany Aug. 8, 1936. Luminescent screen at one end, layer of photosensitive material at other end, intermediate anode.

6152 Schlesinger, K. "Scanning device." U.S. 2,173,501, Aug. 6, 1937, Sept. 19, 1939; Br. 500,225, Aug. 6, 1937. In Germany Aug. 8, 1936. Assigned: D.S. Loewe.

6153 "The status of television." NYT (Aug. 9): IX, 10: 2.

6154 "Television here and abroad." NYT (Aug. 9): IX, 10: 7, 8. Discusses Baird Television; equipment for transmitting motion pictures; move toward use of broader bands.

6155 "Television shows relay. From 10-mile bleachers American team exhibited strain." NYT (Aug. 10): 12: 6. Relay race broadcast from Olympic Games.

6156 Baird Television and D.M. Johnstone. "Valve generator circuits." Br. 479,760, Aug. 10, 1936.

6157 Baird Television and C. Szegho. "Cathode-ray tube." Br. 479,761, Aug. 10, 1936. Camera tube.

6158 Holzer, Philip P. "Television apparatus." U.S. 2,172,845, Aug. 10, 1936, Sept. 12, 1939. Cathode-ray tube for receiver.

6159 Marconi's and Leonard Morris Myers. "Cathode-ray tube." Br. 481,434, Aug. 10, 1936; U.S. 2,264,708, Aug. 28, 1937, Dec. 2, 1941 (RCA). Picture tube for television and like reproducer.

6160 Zeiss, C. "Image converter." Br. 505,270, July 31, 1937. Convention date Aug. 10, 1936.

6161 G.E.C. and D.C. Espley. "Television." Br. 481,792, Aug. 11, 1936; U.S. 2,140,107, Aug. 10, 1937, Dec. 13, 1938. Synchronizing means.

6162 Schlesinger, K. "Cathode-ray deflecting means." U.S. 2,227,020, Aug. 10, 1937, Dec. 31, 1940; Br. 505,355, Aug. 6, 1937. Assigned: Loewe Radio. In Germany Aug. 12, 1936.

6163 Urtel, R. "Cathode-ray control apparatus." U.S. 2,235,053, July 24, 1937, Mar. 18, 1941. Assigned: Telefunken. In Germany Aug. 12, 1936.

6164 Lawrence E. Davies. "Ring fight shown in television test. Telephone talkers also seen and heard in experiment by Philco Corporation. Images appear distinct. But goal is not yet achieved, engineers say after Philadelphia demonstration." NYT (Aug. 12): 21: 8. Report on demonstration by Philco Radio and Television Corp. in Philadelphia.

6165 Heimann, W. "Cathode-ray tube." Br. 500,587, Aug. 13, 1937 (Fernseh A.-G.). Convention date Aug. 13, 1936. Camera tube.

6166 Plaistowe, D.L. "Radio apparatus for detecting aircraft." U.S. 2,207,267, July 8, 1938, July 9, 1940 (RCA). In Britain Aug. 13, 1936 (Marconi's). With cathode-ray tube.

6167 Bowie, Robert M. "Cathode-ray tube." U.S. 2,211,613, Aug. 14, 1936, Aug. 13, 1940.

6168 "Asks television permit. Concern here also plans to build two experimental stations." NYT (Aug. 15): 11: 7.

6169 Borries, B. von, and E. Ruska. "Angewandte Elektronenoptik" [Applied electron optics]. V.D.I.Z. 80 (Aug. 15): 989–94. Survey of applications.

6170 "Television here and abroad." NYT (Aug. 16): X, 10: 7, 8. Discusses Philco; Philips' 405-line interlaced and 180-line; pictures found to need 450 lines.

6171 Gardner, Bernard C. "Mosaic and translucent surface." U.S. 2,123,412, Aug. 18, 1936, July 12, 1938. Assigned: Farnsworth Television. Br. 487,921, Aug. 5, 1937.

6172 Gardner, Bernard C. "Photoelectric surface." U.S. 2,128,582, Aug. 18, 1936, Aug. 30, 1938. Assigned: Farnsworth Television. See Br. 499,891 (Aug. 5, 1937).

6173 Farnsworth, P.T. "Means and method of operating electron multipliers." U.S. 2,128,580,

Aug. 18, 1936, Aug. 30, 1938. Assigned: Farnsworth Television. See Br. 503,671 (Aug. 5, 1937).

6174 Farnsworth, P.T. "Image dissector." U.S. 2,216,265, Aug. 18, 1936, Oct. 1, 1940. Assigned: Farnsworth Television.

6175 Bamford, Harry S. "Incandescent screen." U.S. 2,097,994, Aug. 18, 1936, Nov. 2, 1937; Br. 486,373, Aug. 5, 1937 (Farnsworth Television).

6176 Murray, Howard J. "Magnetic decomposing and reassembling television system." U.S. 2,194,094, Aug. 18, 1936, Mar. 19, 1940. Light valve.

6177 Baird Television, V.A. Jones, and T.M.C. Lance. "Electron multiplier." Br. 480,263, Aug. 19, 1936.

6178 Baird Television, D.M. Johnstone, and C. Szegho. "Cathode-ray tube." Br. 480,275, Aug. 20, 1936.

6179 Fernseh A.-G. "Television." Br. 500,978, Aug. 20, 1937. In Germany Aug. 20, 1936.

6180 S.T.C. "Cathode-ray tube." Br. 481,549, Aug. 16, 1937. Convention date Aug. 20, 1936.

6181 "Television in France." ELECT. REV. 119 (Aug. 21): 240.

6182 "'Flicker' removed in television." NYT (Aug. 21): 13: 1. Report on FCC hearing on application by Farnsworth Television for an experimental station in Springfield, Pa.

6183 Ives, H.E. "Cathode-ray device." U.S. 2,179,243, Aug. 21, 1936, Nov. 7, 1939. Assigned: B.T.L.

6184 Schlesinger, K. "Self-synchronization of television scanning means." U.S. 2,173,502, Aug. 6, 1937, Sept. 19, 1939; Br. 495,902, Aug. 20, 1937. Assigned: D.S. Loewe. In Germany Aug. 21, 1936.

6185 Steudel, E. "Electrode mounting." U.S. 2,202,607, July 31, 1937, May 28, 1940. In Germany Aug. 21, 1936 (A.E.G.).

6186 B.T.-H. and S.R. Eade. "Television." Br. 480,532, Aug. 22, 1936.

6187 Gander, L. Marsland. "Images over London. Big television station is ready for action stores plan public viewing rooms." NYT (Aug. 23): IX, 10: 7, 8. Feature article on Alexandra Palace installations.

6188 "'Pipe' almost complete." NYT (Aug. 23): IX, 10: 8. B.T.L. report on progress of New York-Philadelphia coaxial cable.

6189 "Television arrives." MAN. GUARD. (Aug. 24): 8: 6. Brief note on press tour of London television station at Alexandra Palace on Aug. 23.

6190 "The new television. Images as clear as a film. First transmission this week. Range may be wider than expected." MAN. GUARD. (Aug. 24): 10: 1, 2.

6191 "The modern television. Clear as film. Marvels of new station. Hopes of wider range." MAN. GUARD. (Aug. 24): 9: 6. Brief report on tour of Alexandra Palace.

6192 "Television this week. Alexandra Palace equipment. The two systems." TIMES (Aug. 24): 10e. Report on press tour of London television station at Alexandra Palace on Aug. 23. The pictures shown by Baird's spotlight method "were excellent in every possible way." First public broadcast to take place on Aug. 26.

6193 Baird Television and V.A. Jones. "Cathode-ray tube." Br. 480,691, Aug. 25, 1936.

6194 C. Lorenz A.-G. "Cathode-ray tube." Br. 506,418, Aug. 25, 1937. In Germany Aug. 25, 1936. Receiver.

6195 "Baird Television shares active." MAN. GUARD. (Aug. 26): 14: 4. Stock market report. Baird Television deferred closed at 91 1/2 up 4 1/2d. EMI shares rose 9d to 24s 3d.

6196 "The wireless exhibition. Television exhibits prominent." TIMES (Aug. 26): 10b, c.

6197 "Broadcasting. Television test transmissions." TIMES (Aug. 26): 10d. Transmission times published for first broadcasts on

Baird system from Alexandra Palace: noon–1:30 p.m., 4:30–6:00 p.m.

6198 "First television broadcast. Demonstration at radio show. To-day's programme." TIMES (Aug. 26): 12g. Timetable of Baird transmissions from Alexandra Palace to the Olympia Radio Exhibition. 12:00 noon and 4:30 p.m.: Opening announcement by Leslie Mitchell. 1:20 and 5:50 p.m.: Closing announcement. "The public will be able to pass in a continuous stream by a variety of television receivers in action at the exhibition."

6199 "A newcomer at Olympia." TIMES (Aug. 26): 13c. Television transmissions at Olympia Radio Exhibition attended by Baird Co. and Marconi-EMI.

6200 Kautz, Robert J. "Electronic camera." U.S. 2,156,813, Aug. 26, 1936, May 2, 1939.

6201 "Radiolympia. Queues for television demonstration." MAN. GUARD. (Aug. 27): 10: 3.

6202 "The wireless exhibition. Experiments in television." TIMES (Aug. 27): 10b.

6203 "To-day's television transmissions. Orchestra of 22 players." TIMES (Aug. 27): 10b.

6204 "Wireless exhibition opened. Public demonstrations of television." TIMES (Aug. 27): 12e.

6205 Baldwin, Millard Warner Jr. "Cathode-ray sweep circuit." U.S. 2,178,464, Aug. 27, 1936, Oct. 31, 1939 (B.T.L.). Saw-tooth generator.

6206 Marconi's and. Levin. "Cathode-ray tube." Br. 480, 711, Aug. 27, 1936.

6207 S.T.C. "Cathode-ray tube." Br. 474,591, Br. June 25, 1937. Convention date Aug. 27, 1936.

6208 White, and A.D. Blumlein. "Valve generator circuits." Br. 482,370, Aug. 27, 1936 (EMI); U.S. 2,212,217, Aug. 21, 1937, Aug. 20, 1940. Oscillating electric circuits.

6209 "Television at Olympia." ELECT. 117 (Aug. 28): 242. Note that television items at the radio exhibition were of chief interest.

6210 "Alexandra Palace." ELECT. 117 (Aug. 28): 243, 244. "Visit to London Television Station. Three transmitters now working on short waves."

6211 "The National Radio Exhibition." ELECT. 117 (Aug. 28): 256.

6212 "Public television commences: Transmissions from Alexandra Palace." ELECT. REV. 119 (Aug. 28): 271, 272.

6213 "London Television-Broadcasting Station." ENGINEERING 142 (Aug. 28): 228, 232–4. Continued in 142 (Sept. 4): 258–260. Also in ENGINEER 162 (Aug. 28): 208, 211, 212.

6214 "Television in the home. Signing of the Anglo-Egyptian treaty." TIMES (Aug. 28): 14e. Reception of Marconi-EMI transmission in a house at St. John's Wood, London.

6215 Barthélemy, R. and Comp. Gaz. "Amplifier for electrons." U.S. 2,179,112, Aug. 10, 1937, Nov. 7, 1939. In France Aug. 28, 1936. Electron multiplier.

6216 Comp. Gaz. "Electron multiplier." Br. 493,968, July 22, 1937. In France Aug. 28, 1936.

6217 Ferranti and J.C. Wilson. "Valve generator circuits." Br. 480,754, Aug. 28, 1936.

6218 Michaelis, E., and E. Kinne. "Amplifier." Br. 479,421, Aug. 24, 1937. Convention date Aug. 28, 1936. Low-frequency amplifier for television.

6219 Michaelis, E. "Television." Br. 481,264, Aug. 24, 1937. Convention date Aug. 28, 1936.

6220 Michaelis, E. "Cathode-ray tube." Br. 500,533, Aug. 17, 1937. Convention date Aug. 28, 1936. For television. Divided from Br. 491,050 (below).

6221 Michaelis, E. "Cathode-ray tube." Br. 491,050, Aug. 17, 1937. Convention date Aug. 28, 1936. See above.

6222 Ver. Gluh. A.-G. "Electron multiplier." Br. 501,740, Aug. 30, 1937. Convention date Aug. 28, 1936.

6223 "Television: How sound and vision are transmitted from the Alexandra Palace to the Radio Exhibition at Olympia." ILLUS. LONDON NEWS (Aug. 29): 363. 4 photos.

6224 Borries, B. von, and E. Ruska. "Angewandte Elektronenoptik" [Applied electron optics]. V.D.I.Z. 80 (Aug. 29): 1075–83. Discusses cathode-ray tube in television.

6225 Ring, F. "Fernsehsprechdienst Berlin-Leipzig" [Television-telephone service between Berlin and Leipzig]. V.D.I.Z. 80 (Aug. 29): 1091.

6226 C. Lorenz A.-G. "Cathode-ray tube." Br. 501,802, Aug. 27, 1937. In Germany Aug. 29, 1936.

6227 Marconi's. "Amplifier." Br. 501,211, Aug. 30, 1937. Convention date Aug. 29, 1936. Wide-band amplifier for television.

6228 Marconi's. "Television amplifier." Br. 486,377, Aug. 30, 1937. Convention date Aug. 29, 1936.

6229 Schröter, F. "Television system." U.S. 2,202,605, Aug. 7, 1937, May 28, 1940; Br. 501,532, Aug. 30, 1937. Assigned: Telefunken. In Germany Aug. 29, 1936.

6230 Begrich, H. "Die Entwicklung des Fernsehens" [The development of television]. ARCH. POST TELEGR. 64 (Sept.): 241–58.

6231 Kette, G. "Die Fernsehschau der Deutschen Reichspost auf der Rundfunk-Ausstellung 1936" [The television show of the German Post Office at the 1936 Radio Fair]. FERN. U. TON. 7 (Sept.): 65.

6232 Ardenne, M. von. "Weit. Versuche mit Hochspannungs-Elektronenstrahl-Einrichtungen für hohe Zeilenzahl" [Long-range experiment with high-voltage electron-beam arrangements for television lines]. FERN. U. TON. 7 (Sept.): 68.

6233 Schröter, F. "Die Entwicklung und Bedeutung der Kathodenstrahlröhre für das Fernsehen" [The development and importance of the cathode-ray tube for television]. HOCH ELEKT. 48 (Sept.): 77–81.

6234 McLachlan, N.W. "Reproduction of transients by a television amplifier." PHIL. MAG. 22 (Sept.): 481–91.

6235 Teale, E. "Television and pocket radios promised by latest short-wave tests." POP. SCI. 129 (Sept.): 9–11+.

6236 "Philco Television." RADIO ENG. 16 (Sept.): 9, 10.

6237 "Farnsworth television receiver." RADIO ENG. 16 (Sept.): 14, 15. 19-tube receiver.

6238 Morton, G.A. "The electron-image tube, a means for making infra-red images visible." J. SMPE 27 (Sept.): 321–30.

6239 "Technical details of the television equipment supplied by Baird Television Ltd. to the British Broadcasting Corporation at Alexandra Palace." J. TELEV. SOC. 2 (Sept.): 161–8. 3 photos, diagram.

6240 "Marconi-EMI television equipment at the Alexandra Palace." J. TELEV. SOC. 2 (Sept.): 169–76. 3 photos, 3 diagrams. Report issued by Marconi-EMI Television Co. Ltd.

6241 Ardenne, M. von. "High-voltage cathode-ray tube for high-definition film-scanning." W. ENG. 13 (Sept.): 483–5.

6242 Langenwalter, Hans-Wolfgang, and Ernst Ruska. "Electron multiplier." U.S. 2,159,529, Aug. 19, 1937, May 23, 1939. In Germany Sept. 1, 1936 (Fernseh A.-G.).

6243 Overbeek, A.J.W.M. van, and E.H. Löpp. "Secondary electron discharge device." U.S. 2,167,097, Aug. 25, 1937, July 25, 1939. In Holland Sept. 1, 1936 (N.V. Philips).

6244 Hefele, J.R. "Electro-optical image production." U.S. 2,208,927, Sept. 2, 1936, July 23, 1940. Assigned: B.T.L.

6245 Knoop, W.A. "Electro-optical image production." U.S. 2,274,709, Sept. 2, 1936, Mar 3, 1942. Assigned: B.T.L.

6246 Bowman-Manifold, M., and A.D. Blumlein. "Cathode-ray tube apparatus." U.S. 2,132,933, Sept. 3, 1936, Oct. 11, 1938. Assigned: EMI. In Britain Oct. 24, 1934. Picture tube.

6247 "G.E.C. television reception. Demonstration at Wembley." TIMES (Sept. 4): 10e. Photo of G.E.C. picture tube receiver.

6248 Benjamin, Mark, and Ronald Osmond Jenkins. "Construction of electrodes for cathode-ray tubes and the like." Br. 476,830, Sept. 4, 1936 (G.E.C.); U.S. 2,125,418, Aug. 25, 1937, Aug. 2, 1938.

6249 "'All-wave' sets at Radiolympia. Varied designs and prices. Lessons of television." TIMES (Sept. 5): 15a.

6250 Schlesinger, K. "Television transmitter." U.S. 2,248,549, Aug. 31, 1937, July 8, 1941; Br. 487,560, Sept. 6, 1937. Assigned: D.S. Loewe. In Germany Sept. 5, 1936.

6251 "Testing 'eyes' of television. Experts seek a standard through experiments here and abroad." NYT (Sept. 6): IX, 10: 3. Comments by Oscar B. Hanson on experiments.

6252 "London views first telecast. Radiolympia visitors see television. Artists on the screen." NYT (Sept. 6): IX, 10: 6.

6253 "Radiolympia records." MAN. GUARD. (Sept. 7): 2: 2. 212,621 visitors attended Radiolympia; 123,683 saw television demonstrations.

6254 "Radiolympia closed." TIMES (Sept. 7): 10d. Television demonstrations seen by 123,683 persons.

6255 "French wireless exhibition. Television the feature." TIMES (Sept. 7): 10e. "Television is undoubtedly the main feature of the thirteenth French Wireless Exhibition, which opened 1st week at the Grand Palais."

6256 Colberg, Rolf. "Electron multiplier." U.S. 2,218,744, Aug. 24, 1937, Oct. 22, 1940. In GermanySept. 7, 1936 (Fernseh A.-G.).

6257 Ruska, Ernst. "Electron multiplier." U.S. 2,213,769, Aug. 19, 1937, Sept. 3, 1940. Assigned: Fernseh A.-G. In Germany Sept. 7, 1936.

6258 Andrieu, R. "Saw-tooth wave generator." U.S. 2,221,069, Sept. 15, 1937, Nov. 12, 1940. In Germany Sept. 9, 1936 (Telefunken).

6259 Schlesinger, K. "Scanning disk device." U.S. 2,192,244, Aug. 31, 1937, Mar. 5, 1940. In Germany Sept. 9, 1936 (D.S. Loewe).

6260 Schlesinger, K. "Scanning device with sync device." U.S. 2,241,964, Mar. 31, 1939, May 13, 1941. In Germany Sept. 9, 1936. Television transmitter. Double-spiral disk and shutter for selecting one spiral only.

6261 Heimann, Walter. "Television scanner cathode." U.S. 2,139,018, Sept. 21, 1937, Dec. 6, 1938; Br. 502,024, Sept. 9, 1937. Assigned: Fernseh A.-G. In Germany Sept. 10, 1936.

6262 Lubszynski, H.G. "Cathode-ray tube." Br. 481,563, Sept. 10, 1936; U.S. 2,264,540, Sept. 9, 1937, Dec. 2, 1941 (EMI).

6263 "Television receivers." ELECT. 117 (Sept. 11): 311–3. G.E.C. demonstration at Wembley, Sept. 3.

6264 "French wireless exhibition." ELECT. 117 (Sept. 11): 313.

6265 "Television receivers." ELECT. REV. 119 (Sept. 11): 340–1.

6266 B.T.-H. "Electron lenses." Br. 501,931, Sept. 10, 1937. In Germany Sept. 11, 1936 (A.E.G.).

6267 Baird Television and A.H. Gilbert. "Cathode-ray tube." Br. 481,516, Sept. 11, 1936.

6268 D.S. Loewe. "Cathode-ray tube." Br. 491,443, Jan. 29, 1937. In Germany Sept. 11, 1936.

6269 "Says television will halt drift of boys from farms." NYT (Sept. 12): 3: 3. Comment by T.S. Lyon.

6270 Fernseh A.-G. "Valve generator." Br. 502,356, Sept. 14, 1937. In Germany Sept. 14, 1936. Scanning generator.

6271 Percival, W.S. "Thermionic amplifier circuits." U.S. 2,200,519, Sept. 11, 1937, May

14, 1940; Br. 483,732, Sept. 15, 1936 (EMI). Wide-band video amplifier.

6272 Gloess, Paul François Marie. "Television system." U.S. 2,186,542, Aug. 12, 1937, Jan. 9, 1940. Assigned: International Standard Electrical Corp. Br. 480,646, July 30, 1937 (S.T.C.). In France Sept. 17, 1936. Camera tube and auxiliary photoelectric system.

6273 D.S. Loewe. "Cathode-ray tube." Br. 507,228, Sept. 6, 1937. Void. In Germany Sept. 17, 1936.

6274 Michaelis, E., and E. Kinne. "Television receiver." Br. 481,944, Sept. 18, 1936.

6275 Linsell, A.A. "Modulated carrier wave receiving installation." Br. 481,893, Sept. 18, 1936 (Marconi's); U.S. 2,183,718, Sept. 9, 1937, Dec. 19, 1939 (RCA). Cathode-ray tube receiver with luminescent screen, for television and sound.

6276 S.T.C. "Valve generator circuit." Br. 505,269, July 30, 1937. Void. Convention date Sept. 19, 1936. Sweep circuit.

6277 "Television postponed six weeks in London." NYT (Sept. 20): IX, 11: 6.

6278 Dunlap, O.E. Jr. "Telefilmed faces. Roosevelt and Landon seen in television newsreel tests across New York." NYT (Sept. 20): IX, 13: 1, 2.

6279 "Television called answer to song How to keep 'em down on the farm." NYT (Sept. 20): IX, 13: 1, 2.

6280 "A council reports. Television in education must equal home movie to serve in schools." NYT (Sept. 20): IX, 13: 7, 8. FCC decides that experiments must continue.

6281 Blumlein, A.D. "Cathode-ray tube." Br. 482,195, Sept. 21, 1936 (EMI); U.S. 2,243,893, Sept. 9, 1937, June 3, 1941. Electromagnetic coil; deflector coil.

6282 G.E.C. and N.R. Bligh. "Electron multiplier." Br. 481,750, Sept. 21, 1936. References to Br. 443,777 (July 5, 1934), 469,477 (Jan. 30, 1935), 469,488 (Feb. 28, 1935).

6283 Kessler, J. "Cathode-ray tube." Br. 481,948, Sept. 21, 1936.

6284 Schlesinger, K. "Cathode-ray tube." U.S. 2,152,825, Sept. 21, 1936, Apr. 4, 1939. Original in Germany July 8, 1933.

6285 "Scophony Ltd. The development of television. Scophony's lead in large-size pictures. Potentialities of the system. Sir M. Bonham-Carter's review." TIMES (Sept. 22): 20a, b. Sir Maurice Bonham-Carter, chairman of Scophony Ltd.

6286 Espley, Dennis Clark, and Derek Oscar Walter. "Apparatus kincluding a scanning disk for transmitting television." U.S. 2,206,546, Sept. 16, 1937, July 2, 1940. Assigned: General Electric Co. Br. 482,049, Sept. 22, 1936. References to Br. 464,831, 466,966.

6287 Flechsig, Werner. "Device for reproduction of instantaneous occurrences." U.S. 2,213,761, Aug. 14, 1937, Sept. 3, 1940. Assigned: Fernseh A.-G. In Germany Sept. 22, 1936.

6288 Michaelis, E. "Television." Br. 487,737, Sept. 22, 1937. Convention date Sept. 22, 1936.

6289 G.E.C. and F.R. Jones. "Cathode-ray tube." Br. 459,355, Sept. 23, 1936.

6290 Michaelis, E. "Television." Br. 479,149, Sept. 23, 1936.

6291 Percival, W.S. "Thermionic amplifier circuit." Br. 483,734, Sept. 24, 1936; U.S. 2,151,795, Sept. 14, 1937, Mar. 28, 1939. Wide-band amplifier.

6292 "Size of television pictures." ELECT. 117 (Sept. 25): 354. Report on the first ordinary meeting of Scophony Ltd., Sept. 21. Sir Maurice Bonham-Carter, chairman: " . . . it is in the direction of larger pictures that progress must be made before television will make a real advance in popular favour."

6293 "Electrical and Musical Industries." MAN. GUARD. (Sept. 25): 15: 2. Brief note on EMI company.

6294 "Electric and Musical Industries." TIMES (Sept. 25): 23a. Brief report on EMI company.

6295 Vance, A.W. "Deflecting circuits." U.S. 2,149,077, Sept. 26, 1936, Feb. 28, 1939. Saw-tooth generator for cathode-ray tube with magnetic coils.

6296 "London plans for television. Equipment being altered. Receivers for home expected for 1937." NYT (Sept. 27): X, 10: 6.

6297 Kallmann, Heinz Erwin, and Rolf Edmund Spencer. "Valve circuits, television system." Br. 484,202, Sept. 30, 1936; U.S. 2,241,553, Sept. 9, 1937, May 13, 1941 (EMI).

6298 Tolson, W.A. "Picture reproducing apparatus." U.S. 2,232,084, Sept. 30, 1936, Feb. 18, 1941 (RCA). Cathode-ray tube receiver circuit.

6299 Marconi's. "Television." Br. 503,087, Sept. 30, 1937. Convention date Sept. 30, 1936. References to Br. 407,409 (Sept. 30, 1931), 448,065 (May 29, 1934), 474,386.

6300 Kette, G. "Die Fernsehschau auf der Rundfunk-Ausstellung 1936" [The television show at the 1936 radio fair]. FERN. U. TON. 7 (Oct.): 73–80.

6301 Banneitz, F. "Uebersicht über Entwicklung und Stand die Fernsehens" [Survey of development and status of television]. FERN. U. TON. 7 (Oct.): 81.

6302 Schröter, F. "Physikalische Grundlagen, Möglichkeiten und Grenzen d. Fernsehübertragung" [The physical foundations, potentialities, and frontiers of television transmission]. FERN. U. TON. 7 (Oct.): 83–7.

6303 "Mad scramble for television privilege threatens amateurs." RADIO N. 18 (Oct.): 201, 202+.

6304 Trevor, B., and O.E. Dow. "Television radio relay." RCA REV. 1 (Oct.): 35–46. 177 Mc link between RCA Building and Empire State Building.

6305 "More television." SCI. AM. 155 (Oct.): 240.

6306 McLachlan, N.W. "Reproduction of transients by television amplifiers." W. ENG. 13 (Oct.): 519–23.

6307 "Olympia, 1936." W. ENG. 13 (Oct.): 524–33. Description of apparatus, including television.

6308 (Ardenne, M. von). "Conversion of optical images." W. ENG. 13 (Oct.): 536–8. Review of paper.

6309 Iams, H.A. "Electron discharge device." U.S. 2,131,892, Oct. 1, 1936, Oct. 4, 1938. Assigned: RCA.

6310 Muller, E.N. "Television receiver." Br. 503,025, Oct. 1, 1937. Convention date Oct. 1, 1936. Reference to Br. 467,195 (Dec. 12, 1935).

6311 "London television service. I: The Baird studio and scanning equipment of the Alexandra Palace BBC sound transmitter." ELECT. 117 (Oct. 2): 403–5. 7 photos.

6312 Gardner, Delamere B. "Solid-weave scanning device." U.S. 2,103,253, Oct. 2, 1936, Dec. 28, 1937. Mirror screw with rotating axis as a receiver.

6313 D.S. Loewe. "Valve circuit." Br. 503,207, Oct. 1, 1937. In Germany Oct. 2, 1936. For television. Addition to Br. 487,243 (Dec. 18, 1935).

6314 D.S. Loewe. "Cathode-ray tube." Br. 505,167, Oct. 1, 1937. In Germany Oct. 2, 1936. Divided from Br. 503,207 (above).

6315 Scophony, J. Sieger, and J.H. Jeffree. "Electro-optical light modulation device." Br. 482,665, Oct. 2, 1936.

6316 de Forest, Lee. "Television system and method." U.S. 2,122,456, Oct. 3, 1936, July 5, 1938. Assigned: American Television Labs Inc. Scanner with zigzag apertures.

6317 Ferranti and E. Anderson. "Cathode-ray tube." Br. 478,083, Oct. 5, 1936.

6318 Clothier, S.L., and H.C. Hogencamp. "Television." Br. 503,327, Sept. 29, 1937. In U.S. Oct. 6, 1936. Reference to Br. 503,391 (below).

6319 Clothier, S.L., and H.C. Hogencamp. "Television." Br. 503,391, Sept. 29, 1937. In U.S. Oct. 6, 1936. Divided from Br. 503,327 (above). Reference to Br. 475,000 (Oct. 12, 1935).

6320 Krawinkel, G. "Die 13. Grosse Deutsche Rundfunkausstellung, Berlin 1936" [The 13th Great German Radio Fair, Berlin 1936]. E.T.Z. 57 (Oct. 8): 1169–71.

6321 "New vacuum tube may aid television. Ultra-high-frequency unit described at Institute of Radio Engineers. Two sets of elements. Device developed in telephone laboratories may utilize now-neglected waves." NYT (Oct. 8): 25: 5.

6322 Bronk, Otto von. "Television." Br. 484,706, Oct. 8, 1936.

6323 Schlesinger, K. "Arrangement for magnetic deflection of a cathode ray." U.S. 2,227,021, Oct. 5, 1937, Dec. 31, 1940; Br. 497,620, Oct. 8, 1937 (D.S. Loewe). In Germany Oct. 8, 1936.

6324 Willans, Peter William, and Baird Television. "Electron discharge device." Br. 482,959, Oct. 8, 1936; U.S. 2,158,450, Oct. 5, 1937, May 16, 1939. Cathode-ray tubes. References to Br. 475,047 (May 11, 1936), 505,618 (Nov. 10, 1937).

6325 "Alexandra Palace television equipment." ELECT. 117 (Oct. 9): 426. Brief comments on recent visit. The "Baird intermediate film . . . is also a wonderful example of modern wizardry."

6326 "London television service. II: Marconi-EMI equipment, the Emitron camera, transmitter, vision and sound aerials." ELECT. 117 (Oct. 9): 431, 432. 2 diags.

6327 "Television demonstrations." ELECT. 117 (Oct. 9): 432.

6328 "Baird Television." MAN. GUARD. (Oct. 9): 15: 2. Company report up to June 30. The company has provided complete equipment for Alexandra Palace and has a "stock of receivers to meet the anticipated demand from the public on the opening of the public service."

6329 "Company results. Baird Television." TIMES (Oct. 9): 21f. Brief financial report on Baird Television Ltd.

6330 Schlesinger, K. "Voltage-controlled electron multiplier." U.S. 2,227,022, Oct. 5, 1937, Dec. 31, 1940. Assigned: D.S. Loewe. In Germany Oct. 9, 1936.

6331 Glass, Myron S. "Electron discharge device." U.S. 2,139,678, Oct. 10, 1936, Dec. 13, 1938 (B.T.L.).

6332 Michaelis, E. "Amplifier." Br. 494,536, Oct. 12, 1937. Convention date Oct. 12, 1936. Television receiver.

6333 D.S. Loewe. "Electron multiplier." Br. 505,557, Oct. 8, 1937. In Germany Oct. 14, 1936.

6334 Winckel, F.W. "Fernsehen 1936" [Television 1936]. Z.F. FERN. 17 (Oct. 15): 154, 155. Report on Berlin radio exhibition.

6335 Clothier, S.L., and H.C. Hogencamp. "Light-modulating cell and electrode therefor." U.S. 2,163,549, Oct. 15, 1936, June 20, 1939. Assigned: Kolorama Labs.

6336 Clothier, S.L., and H.C. Hogencamp. "Multiple-cell light modulator." U.S. 2,163,550, Oct. 15, 1936, June 20, 1939. Assigned: Kolorama Labs.

6337 Strübig, H., and Rolf Colberg. "Projectiong electrical recordings." U.S. 2,238,137, Oct. 8, 1937, Apr. 15, 1941 (Fernseh A.-G.); Br. 503,858, Oct. 15, 1937. In Germany Oct. 15, 1936.

6338 Ferranti, M.K. Taylor, and S. Jackson. "Electron multiplier." Br. 482,454, Oct. 16, 1936.

6339 Murray, Howard J. "Television system." U.S. 2,169,071, Oct. 16, 1936, Aug. 8, 1939.

6340 McGee, J.D. "Campbell Swinton and television." NATURE 138 (Oct. 17): 674–6.

6341 Paffrath, Georg. "Television and sound receiver." U.S. 2,169,883, Nov. 2, 1937, Aug. 15, 1939; Br. 504,029, Oct. 18, 1937 (Telefunken). In Germany Oct. 17, 1936.

6342 Traub, E. "Light valves." Br. 478,840, Oct. 17, 1936. Supersonic light valve with modifications.

6343 "Television pictures projected on screen." N.Y.T. (Oct. 18): X, 10: 7. Illus. of camera. German television; apparatus for large pictures on 3-foot-square screen.

6344 "A television experiment. Scenery to be used." MAN. GUARD. (Oct. 19): 12: 3. Beginning of BBC's tests of the Marconi-EMI studio at Alexandra Palace.

6345 "Baird Television Ltd. End of the experimental period. Receiving sets ready." MAN. GUARD. (Oct. 19): 17: 6. The company has more than 200 British patents and more than 200 more awaiting completion.

6346 "Range of television transmissions. Sir Harry Greer's statement." TIMES (Oct. 19): 23b. Report of company meeting on Oct. 16.

6347 Blumlein, A.D. "Cathode-ray tube." Br. 483,650, Oct. 20, 1936.

6348 Traub, E., and Marcus James Goddard. "Television." Br. 483,332, Oct. 20, 1936. Reference to Br. 439,434.

6349 Traub, E. "Television." Br. 483,385, Oct. 20, 1936. Receiver. Reference to Br. 439,236.

6350 Banks, G.B., and Marconi's. "Electron multiplier." Br. 483,575, Oct. 21, 1936; U.S. 2,115,155, Dec. 15, 1937, Apr. 26, 1938 (RCA).

6351 Benham, W.E. "Television." Br. 485,653, Oct. 21, 1936. Receiver circuits. Reference to Br. 395,373.

6352 Hurd, Volney D. "Television apparatus." U.S. 2,229,456, Oct. 21, 1936, Jan. 21, 1941. Disk and mirror assembly with motor and gears.

6353 I.M.K. Syndicate and M.J. Goddard. "Light valve." Br. 478,842, Oct. 21, 1936. Supersonic light valve.

6354 Zeitline, V., A. Zeitline, and V. Kliatchko. "Television." Br. 481,917, Oct. 21, 1936.

6355 Labin, Emile. "Electron discharge device." U.S. 2,203,334, July 7, 1937, June 4, 1940 (S.T.C.). In France Oct. 22, 1936. Cathode-ray tube.

6356 "Inventor of cathode-ray television." ELECT. 117 (Oct. 23): 484. Comments on article by J.D. McGee in NATURE (Oct. 17).

6357 Bouwers, Albert. "Cathode-ray tube." U.S. 2,211,843, Feb. 5, 1938, Aug. 20, 1940 (RCA). In Germany Oct. 23, 1936 (N.V. Philips).

6358 N.V. Philips. "Cathode-ray tube." Br. 481,556, Oct. 20, 1937. Convention date Oct. 23, 1936. Addition to Br. 472,240 (June 14, 1935).

6359 N.V. Philips. "Cathode-ray tube." Br. 482,704, Oct. 20, 1937. Convention date Oct. 23, 1936. Picture tube.

6360 Warnecke, Robert. "Secondary electron-emitting electrode." U.S. 2,189,971, Oct. 15, 1937, Feb. 13, 1940 (Comp. Sans Fil). In France Oct. 23, 1936. For electron multipliers.

6361 Bouwers, Albert. "Incandescent screen tube." U.S. 2,227,484, Oct. 9, 1937, Jan. 7, 1941 (RCA). In Germany Oct. 24, 1936 (N.V. Philips). Television receiver tube.

6362 Goldmark, P.C. "Sound and television receiving system." U.S. 2,186,455, Oct. 24, 1936, Jan. 9, 1940. Assigned: Markia Corp. Circuit for broad frequencies or ultra-short waves.

6363 Rabuteau, Guy, and Emile Labin. "Secondary emission device." U.S. 2,209,847, Oct. 20, 1937, July 30, 1940. Assigned: International Standard Electric Corp. In France Oct. 24, 1936.

6364 S.T.C. "Electron multiplier." Br. 501,726, Oct. 1, 1937. Convention date Oct. 24, 1936.

6365 S.T.C. "Electron multiplier." Br. 502,976, Oct. 1, 1937. Convention date Oct. 24, 1936.

6366 "Thirty 'long' years. Sarnoff reviews three radio decades he sees television wonders ahead." N.Y.T. (Oct. 25): X, 10: 4, 5.

6367 "Research in television is planned in Japan." N.Y.T. (Oct. 25): X, 10: 5. Plans for experiments by Japan Broadcasting Corp.

6368 "Helen McKay sings 'Here's looking at you' as she is televised in the London studio at Alexandra Palace." N.Y.T. (Oct. 25): X, 10: 6, 7. Illus. of London test.

6369 "American telecasting interferes with London." N.Y.T. (Oct. 25): X, 12: 6. "London television experts are planning to shift away from the 7-meter wave length because of interference from U.S. British conducting tests at Ally Pally, also plan to increase power of transmitter."

6370 "Picture Page is televised. First magazine of the air called brilliant success in London." N.Y.T. (Oct. 25): X, 12: 6. Description of the program "Picture Page."

6371 Linsell, A.A. (Marconi's). "Electron multiplier." Br. 483,586, Oct. 26, 1936; U.S. 2,188,410, Sept. 30, 1937, Jan. 30, 1940. Assigned: RCA.

6372 Ring, Friedrich, and Georg Weiss. "Fluorescent screen." U.S. 2,186,393, Dec. 15, 1937, Jan. 9, 1940. In Germany Oct. 26, 1936.

6373 Ring, Friedrich. "Cathode-ray tube." Br. 506,911, Oct. 25, 1937. Convention date Oct. 26, 1936. Reference to Br. 481,094 (June 4, 1936).

6374 Schlesinger, K. "Interlaced line method." U.S. 2,227,023, Oct. 5, 1937, Dec. 31, 1940; Br. 504,460, Oct. 25, 1937. Assigned: D.S. Loewe. In Germany Oct. 26, 1936.

6375 Geiger, Max, and Telefunken. "Valve generator circuits." Br. 484,157, Oct. 28, 1936. Saw-tooth wave generator.

6376 Castellani, A., and Sofar. "Television." Br. 484,003, Oct. 28, 1936.

6377 Castellani, A., and Sofar. "Cathode-ray tube." Br. 483,679, Oct. 28, 1936.

6378 Warnecke, Robert, and Comp. Sans Fil. "Secondary electron-emitting electrode." U.S. 2,189,971, Oct. 15, 1937, Feb. 13, 1940. In France Oct. 26, 1936.

6379 Morton, G.A. "Electro-optical device." U.S. 2,189,321, Mar. 4, 1937, Feb. 6, 1940. Assigned: RCA. Substitute for abandoned application Dec. 24, 1935. In France Oct. 28, 1936.

6380 Percival, W.S. "Amplifier." U.S. 2,240,715, Oct. 21, 1937, May 6, 1941. In Britain Oct. 28, 1936.

6381 Ramberg, E.J. "Electron multiplier." U.S. 2,147,173, Oct. 28, 1936, Feb. 14, 1939.

6382 Goldsmith, A.N. "Signalling system." U.S. 2,181,564, Oct. 19, 1936, Nov. 28, 1939.

6383 Hollmann, H.E. "Cathode-ray device." U.S. 2,182,382, Apr. 29, 1937, Dec. 5, 1939. In Germany Oct. 29, 1936 (Telefunken).

6384 B.T.-H. and Dennis Gábor. "Cathode-ray tube." Br. 488,188, Oct. 30, 1936; U.S. 2,197,523, Oct. 13, 1937, Apr. 16, 1940 (G.E.).

6385 Holst, Gilles, and Menno Wolf. "Electronic device." U.S. 2,212,206, Oct. 21, 1937, Aug. 20, 1940 (RCA). In Holland Oct. 30, 1936 (N.V. Philips).

6386 "FCC approves television station." N.Y.T. (Oct. 31): 24: 6. Farnsworth Television's experimental station is approved by FCC.

6387 Farnsworth Television, P.T. Farnsworth, and Richard L. Snyder. "Repeater." U.S. 2,143,146, Oct. 31, 1936, Jan. 10, 1939. Electron multiplier.

6388 Farnsworth, P.T., and Farnsworth Television. "Electron multiplier." Br. 504,629, Oct. 29, 1937. In U.S. Oct. 31, 1936.

6389 Farnsworth Television. "Discharge apparatus." Br. 503,106, Oct. 29, 1937. In U.S. Oct. 31, 1936. Reference to Br. 467,366 (May 7, 1935).

6390 Flaherty, Mark. "Television receiver." U.S. 2,119,102, Oct. 31, 1936, May 31, 1938. Assigned: RCA. Cathode-ray tube in cabinet with mirror at an angle.

6391 Urtel, R. "Die Wirkungsweise der Kathodenstrahlbildzerleger mit Speicherwirkung" [The operation of a cathode-ray picture dissector with storage effect]. HOCH ELEKT. 48 (Nov.): 150–5.

6392 Mark, J. van der. "Television." PHIL. TECH. REV. 1 (Nov.): 321–6.

6393 "Russian television." RADIO-CRAFT 8 (Nov.): 269. Photo. Transmitter with a tube similar to the Zworykin Iconoscope.

6394 Murray, A.F. "The new Philco system of television." RADIO-CRAFT 8 (Nov.): 270, 315.

6395 "Television as good as home movies. Demonstration staged in Philadelphia." RADIO N. 18 (Nov.): 265, 266+. Philco demonstration.

6396 "Amateurs can build television receivers." RADIO N. 18 (Nov.): 267.

6397 "Television test here is planned for Nov. 6." N.Y.T. (Nov. 1): X, 12: 2. NBC plans.

6398 "Auto show televised." N.Y.T. (Nov. 1): X, 12: 4. Recent auto show outside Alexandra Palace in London was televised.

6399 "Television in London on regular schedule." N.Y.T. (Nov. 1): X, 12: 4. Regular television service begins in London Nov. 2.

6400 Farnsworth, P.T. "Beam scanning dissector." U.S. 2, 124,057, Nov. 2, 1936, July 19, 1938. Assigned: Farnsworth Television. Camera tube.

6401 Farnsworth, P.T. "Cathode-ray tube." U.S. 2,135,814, Nov. 2, 1936, Dec. 13, 1938; Br. 498,867, Oct. 29, 1937. Assigned: Farnsworth Television. Image dissector tube.

6402 Farnsworth, P.T., and Frank J. Somers. "High-power projection oscillograph." U.S. 2,109,289, Nov. 2, 1936, Feb. 22, 1938. Assigned: Farnsworth Television. Cathode-ray tube with collecting electrode connected to an oscillator.

6403 Farnsworth Television. "Image dissector." Br. 494,620, Oct. 29, 1937. In U.S. Nov. 2, 1936.

6404 Percival, W.S. "Amplifying system." Br. 484,404, Nov. 2, 1936; U.S. 2,210,497, Oct. 29, 1937, Aug. 6, 1940. Television receiver circuit.

6405 "The BBC television service. A 'first performance' reminiscent of the cinema. Britain 'leading the world.'" MAN. GUARD. (Nov. 3): 5: 6, 7. Report on the first regular broadcasts from Alexandra Palace, Nov. 2.

6406 "Problems of television." MAN. GUARD. (Nov. 3): 10: 3, 4. Editorial on opening of Alexandra Palace television station. Limited range; cost of operation; cost of receivers.

6407 "The television era begins." MAN. GUARD. (Nov. 3): 10: 5, 6. Report on the crowd at Alexandra Palace for the formal opening of the new service.

6408 "Television in London. Opening of regular service. More stations promised." TIMES (Nov. 3): 9a, b. Report on beginning of regular television broadcasts from Alexandra Palace.

6409 "BBC television programme. Problem of intimacy." TIMES (Nov. 3): 9c. General criticisms of BBC staff before the camera, with some discussion of program contents.

6410 "Public demonstrations." TIMES (Nov. 3): 9c. First demonstration given Nov. 2 by G.E.C. at their offices in Kingsway, London. Demonstrations will be given at 3:00–4:00 p.m. and 9:00–10:00 p.m. until further notice. The company has already sold a number of sets. Advertisements on p. 9e-g show two receivers at 95 guineas and 120 guineas.

6411 "Television." TIMES (Nov. 3): 17c, d. Editorial on opening of Alexandra Palace station. "The moment long seen afar off by eyes of faith has come at last."

6412 Arathoon,. "Television." Br. 481,621, Nov. 3, 1936. Reference to Br. 468,294 (Jan. 21, 1936).

6413 Telefunken and Horst Hewel. "Receiver." U.S. 2,285,857, Nov. 11, 1937, June 9, 1942; Br. 505,031, Nov. 3, 1937. In Germany Nov. 3, 1936. Television receiver. Reference to Br. 458,798, 471,762 (Mar. 11, 1936).

6414 Schlesinger, K. "Cathode-ray deflecting circuit." U.S. 2,188,580, Nov. 3, 1936, Jan. 30, 1940. Assigned: D.S. Loewe. Divided from original U.S. 2,077,271, Mar. 26, 1934; in Germany Mar. 19, 1933.

6415 Farnsworth, P.T. "Cold cathode electron discharge tube." U.S. 2,184,910, Nov. 4, 1936, Dec. 26, 1939. Assigned: Farnsworth Television. Divided U.S. 2,263,032, Apr. 5, 1939, Nov. 18, 1941.

6416 Murphy Radio and H.A. Fairhurst. "Television receiver." Br. 484,412, Nov. 4, 1936.

6417 Baird Television and V.A. Jones. "Cathode-ray tube." Br. 484,574, Nov. 5, 1936. Reference to Br. 469,404 (Jan. 23, 1936).

6418 Baird Television and D.M. Johnstone. "Cathode-ray tube." Br. 484,575, Nov. 5, 1936. Mosaic screen.

6419 "Television to-day and to-morrow." ELECT. 117 (Nov. 6): 562. Comment on the opening of the BBC high-definition service on Nov. 2. "For the moment television receivers are luxury articles . . . "

6420 "BBC television service." ELECT. 117 (Nov. 6): 563.

6421 "'Viewers' see television." MAN. GUARD. (Nov. 6).

6422 "Television test today. 250 invited to demonstration at Rockefeller Center." N.Y.T. (Nov. 6): 28: 1. NBC test.

6423 G.E.C. and. Bloch. "Television receiver." Br. 483,841, Nov. 6, 1936.

6424 Mierlo, Stanislas van. "Device applicable mainly to television." U.S. 2,256,300, Oct. 15, 1937, Sept. 16, 1941. Assigned: International Standard Electric Corp. Br. 501,375, Oct. 15, 1937 (S.T.C.). In France Nov. 6, 1936.

6425 "Television show seen by 200 here. New York's first complete program is reproduced on 7 by 12 inch screens. Newsreels put on air. Radio singer also appears. Device held still too costly for large-scale use." N.Y.T. (Nov. 7): 19: 5. NBC tests.

6426 Hehlgans, F.W. "Cathode-ray tube." U.S. 2,183,398, Nov. 7, 1936, Dec. 12, 1939 (G.E.) Picture tube. Divided from original U.S. 2,075,717, May 23, 1933. In Germany June 4, 1932 (A.E.G.).

6427 "Slow-motion television features boxing lesson." N.Y.T. (Nov. 8): X, 12: 6. BBC broadcast.

6428 "Television's future. Mr. Cook, director of London's telecasts, discusses plans for the show." N.Y.T. (Nov. 8): X, 12: 7, 8. "Believes newsreels will play a big part in ethereal cinema. Mr. Cook confesses at the outset that many years will pass before an ideal television standard can be achieved, and he suspects that 'when it can, many of those responsible for the early efforts will be in their graves.'"

6429 Bouwers, Albert. "Television receiving system." U.S. 2,193,857, Oct. 9, 1937, Mar. 19, 1940. Assigned: RCA. Br. 492,132, Nov. 6, 1937 (N.V. Philips). In Holland Nov. 9, 1936.

6430 N.V. Philips. "Television." Br. 494,375, Nov. 6, 1937. Convention date Nov. 9, 1936. Reference to Br. 472,240 (June 14, 1935).

6431 EMI and W.S. Percival. "Thermionic valve circuit." Br. 484,218, Nov. 9, 1936; U.S. 2,226,255, Nov. 2, 1937, Dec. 24, 1940. Addition to Br. 448,421 (Sept. 4, 1934). Wideband amplifier.

6432 Farnsworth, P.T., and Richard L. Snyder. "Electron multiplier." U.S. 2,179,996, Nov. 9, 1936, Nov. 14, 1939. Assigned: Farnsworth Television. See Br. 504,630 (Oct. 29, 1937).

6433 "Radio's advances hailed at dinner." N.Y.T. (Nov. 10): 28: 4–6. NBC tenth anniversary dinner. Sarnoff predicts that within ten years the millions who now listen in their homes will be able to see as well as hear by radio.

6434 Blumlein, A.D., and C.O. Browne. "Television." Br. 490,205, Nov. 10, 1936; U.S. 2,243,079, Nov. 9, 1937, May 27, 1941 (EMI). Television transmitting apparatus.

6435 G.E.C. and W.H. Aldous. "Electron multiplier." Br. 477,648, Nov. 10, 1936.

6436 G.E.C. and W.H. Aldous. "Electron multiplier." Br. 478,613, Nov. 10, 1936.

6437 Goldmark, Peter C. "Television-facsimile system." U.S. 2,211,926, Nov. 10, 1936, Aug. 20, 1940. Assigned: Markia Corp. Sound and television on separate transmissions. Mixed transmitter circuits with switching for sound, vision, and facsimile signals.

6438 Knoblauch, Henning, and Werner Klüge. "Television transmitter tube." U.S. 2,220,964, June 21, 1938, Nov. 12, 1940. Assigned: Telefunken. In Germany Nov. 11, 1936.

6439 Schlesinger, K. "Electron scanning tube." U.S. 2,227,024, Nov. 6, 1937, Dec. 31, 1940; Br. 507,414, Nov. 11, 1937. Assigned: D.S. Loewe. In Germany Nov. 11, 1936. Addition to Br. 489,362 (Oct. 25, 1935).

6440 "The next ten years." N.Y.T. (Nov. 12): 26: 3. Editorial on Sarnoff and NBC. Prediction by Sarnoff and mention of BBC.

6441 "Trans-sea television forecast by Marconi. 'We will soon be able to see each other,' he telles Sarnoff in land-sea sky broadcast." N.Y.T. (Nov. 12): 29: 7.

6442 Bünger, Walter, and Erich Kosche. "Telecine system." U.S. 2,218,498, Nov. 11, 1937, Oct. 15, 1940; Br. 505,574, Nov. 12, 1937. Assigned: Fernseh A.-G. In Germany Nov. 12, 1936.

6443 Görlich, P. "Cathode-ray tube." U.S. 2,186,636, Nov. 10, 1937, Jan. 9, 1940. In Germany Nov. 12, 1936.

6444 D.S. Loewe. "Amplifier." Br. 505,448, Nov. 11, 1937. In Germany Nov. 12, 1936. For television.

6445 "Television and radio apparatus in flats." ELECT. REV. 119 (Nov. 13): 673.

6446 "Television in flats. Special aerial system to meet needs of big buildings, avoidance of interference." ELECT. 117 (Nov. 13): 614. Report on installation, the first of its kind, by EMI Service Ltd. at Carrington House, Hertford Street, Mayfair, London.

6447 "New Manchester cable. Official notice would serve for television." MAN. GUARD. (Nov. 13): 16: 5. Announcement by Postmaster General Maj. G.C. Tryon, in a speech at an RMA luncheon, Nov. 12, on the installation of coaxial cable from Birmingham to Manchester.

6448 "Post Office and the BBC. Major Tryon on future of television." TIMES (Nov. 13): 22b. At a meeting of the RMA on Nov. 12, Postmaster General G.C. Tryon announced that the installation of coaxial cable from London to Birmingham is completed.

6449 Bailey, W.C., and E.S. Ashdown. "Television." Br. 467,227, Nov. 13, 1936. Scanner for receivers with two mirror drums, one with rocking mirrors, and an intermediate fixed reflecting mirror.

6450 Ploke, Martin. "Image dissector tube." U.S. 2,160,672, Nov. 10, 1937, May 30, 1939; Br. 491,758, Oct. 7, 1937. Assigned: Zeiss Ikon A.-G. In Germany Nov. 13, 1936.

6451 Scophony and Lee. "Television." Br. 487,318, Nov. 13, 1936.

6452 "Electric and Musical Industries." MAN. GUARD. (Nov. 14): 19: 2. Brief report on EMI company meeting.

6453 "Electric and Musical Industries. Divided of 10 per cent. Further record sales of receiving sets. Growing demand for household appliances, Progress of television. Mr. Alfred Clark's address." TIMES (Nov. 14): 19a–c. Report on EMI company meeting. "Our television sets are now on sale."

6454 Schlesinger, K., and D.S. Loewe. "Low-frequency correction of image amplifiers." U.S. 2,248,550, Nov. 9, 1937, July 8, 1941; Br. 500,991, Nov. 15, 1937. In Germany Nov. 14, 1936.

6455 Dunlap, O.E. Jr. "Television flashes pictures through New York's air. Seeing a telecast. Television reveals amusement value new opportunity seen for artists." N.Y.T. (Nov. 15):

XI, 10: 1, 2. 4 photos. Feature article on 1936 broadcasts.

6456 "Hopes of the future. Freedom of speech and era of radio sight widely discussed at celebration." N.Y.T. (Nov. 15): XI, 10: 3. NBC anniversary celebration.

6457 "Television heads cited for inquiry. State moves against Oliver C. Harriman and Associates in stock flotation. Private deal is alleged. 2 salesmen held in Dutchess for selling shares bought at 50 cents for $5 to $10." N.Y.T. (Nov. 16): 1, 6. Television Corporation of America stock.

6458 Ferranti and J.C. Wilson. "Cathode-ray tube." Br. 485,111, Nov. 16, 1936.

6459 "Television inquiry published by Bennett. Aide will attend grand jury hearing of 2 stock salesmen in Poughkeepsie tomorrow. Company denies blame. O.C. Harriman admits shares were sold to Albany man, who was viewed as 'all right.'" N.Y.T. (Nov. 17): 9: 3, 4. Television Corporation of America stock.

6460 "See television by 1938. Speakers tell radio engineers it is unlikely next year." N.Y.T. (Nov. 17): 12: 5. IRE meeting, Nov. 16.

6461 Winckel, F.W. "Das Elektronenbild" [Electronic images]. Z.F. FERN. 17 (Nov. 17): 170, 171. Progress in television as demonstrated at the Berlin Radio Fair.

6462 Ruska, Ernst, Wilhelm Reichel, and Rolf Colberg. "Cathode-ray projection tube." U.S. 2,201,245, Oct. 22, 1937, May 21, 1940; Br. 505,850, Nov. 17, 1939. Assigned: Fernseh A.-G. In Germany Nov. 17, 1936.

6463 "Oppenheim is questioned. Officer of Television Corporation examined on stock sales." N.Y.T. (Nov. 18): 28: 4.

6464 Knoop, W.A. "Electron discharge apparatus." U.S. 2,134,718, Nov. 20, 1936, Nov. 1, 1938. Electron multiplier.

6465 Ploke, Martin. "Method of electro-optically enlarging images." U.S. 2,234,806, Feb. 28, 1938, Mar. 11, 1941. In Germany Nov. 20, 1936 (Zeiss Ikon A.-G.).

6466 Teal, G.K. "Electron discharge apparatus." U.S. 2,160,796, Nov. 20, 1936, May 30, 1939 (B.T.L.). Electron multiplier.

6467 Teal, G.K. "Electron discharge apparatus." U.S. 2,160,797, Nov. 20, 1936, May 30, 1939 (B.T.L.).

6468 Teal, G.K. "Electron discharge apparatus." U.S. 2,160,798, Nov. 20, 1936, May 30, 1939 (B.T.L.). Electron multiplier.

6469 E.R.P. "Electron multiplier." Br. 500,447, Nov. 12, 1937. Convention date Nov. 20, 1936.

6470 E.R.P. "Electron multiplier." Br. 500,448, Nov. 12, 1937. Convention date Nov. 20, 1936.

6471 E.R.P. "Electron multiplier." Br. 505,663, Nov. 19, 1937. Convention date Nov. 20, 1936.

6472 D.S. Loewe. "Electron multiplier." Br. 511,681, Nov. 20, 1937. In Germany Nov. 20, 1936.

6473 Zeiss Ikon A.-G. "Image dissector." Br. 505,380, Nov. 22, 1937. In Germany Nov. 20, 1936.

6474 D.S. Loewe. "Electron multiplier." Br. 494,459, Nov. 20, 1937. In Germany Nov. 21, 1936. Addition to Br. 472,900.

6475 Dunlap, O.E. Jr. "Broadcasters celebrate at gateway of television. November milestones. Ten years of coast-to-coast hook-ups finds broadcasters planning telecasts." N.Y.T. (Nov. 22): XI, 12: 1, 2. RMA television committee accepts 441 lines.

6476 "Television will draw 441 lines to 'etch' the pictures clearly." N.Y.T. (Nov. 22): XI, 12: 1, 2.

6477 "Who will televise? Cultivation of 'television personalities' urged Goldsmith would ban studio audience." N.Y.T. (Nov. 22): XI, 12: 3, 4, 5.

6478 "Television program as London sees it." N.Y.T. (Nov. 22): XI, 12: 6. Reports BBC schedule of television broadcasts as printed in the DAILY MAIL on opening day of London telecasts.

6479 Telefunken. "Television transmitter." Br. 482,812, Nov. 23, 1937. In Germany Nov. 23, 1936. Addition to Br. 479,413 (June 8, 1936).

6480 Weiss, G. "Cathode-ray tube." Br. 505,453, Nov. 23, 1937. Convention date Nov. 24, 1936. Camera tube.

6481 B.T.-H. and D.J. Mynall. "Valve generator." Br. 485,934, Nov. 26, 1936. Relaxation oscillations.

6482 Brüche, Ernst. "Electron discharge device." U.S. 2,172,728, Mar. 31, 1938, Sept. 12, 1939. Assigned: G.E. In Germany Nov. 26, 1936.

6483 Schlesinger, K., and D.S. Loewe. "Synchronization of scanning means." U.S. 2,248,551, Nov. 23, 1937, July 8, 1941; Br. 495,599, Nov. 20, 1937. In Germany Nov. 26, 1936. Television transmitter with slotted disk and two photoelectric cells for odd-line interlaced scan at two fields per frame.

6484 Baird Television and G.R. Tingley. "Valve generator." In Britain Nov. 27, 1936.

6485 "Natural color television forecast by new patent." SCI. N. LETTER 30 (Nov. 28): 345. Refers to U.S. 2,055,557 (2297).

6486 Bedford, A.V. "Television system." U.S. 2,232,044, Nov. 28, 1936, Feb. 18, 1941. Assigned: RCA. Camera tube with coils, deflector on sync circuit, transmitter circuits.

6487 Lewis, Harold M., and Rudolf C. Hergenrother. "Cathode-ray signal-generating tube." U.S. 2,169,840, Nov. 28, 1936, Aug. 15, 1939. Assigned: Hazeltine. Pickup tube with a photosensitive target electrode, and an anode that collects secondary electrons emitted from the target.

6488 "Radio receiver off tune aids clearer television." N.Y.T. (Nov. 29): XII, 10: 5. Single-sideband transmission; picture clarity improved. Report to IRE by W.J. Poch and D.W. Epstein of RCA Labs.

6489 "Television calls for make-up. Radio borrows Hollywood's art of painting faces for camera lips are shaded brown jewelry is ruled out." N.Y.T. (Nov. 29): XII, 10: 6–8.

6490 "Behind the scenes. Performers warned to prepare for air talkies Braddock to broadcast Jolson heads new show." N.Y.T. (Nov. 19): XII, 12: 1, 2.

6491 "Professor sees television calling for new tactics in radio speaking." N.Y.T. (Nov. 29): XII, 12: 6, 7. T.H. Pear on new radio methods in THE LISTENER.

6492 "For sightseers. London heralds advent of radiovision 1936 May televise Edward's coronation." N.Y.T. (Nov. 29): XII, 12: 7, 8. Comments on BBC service, dedication ceremony, prospects.

6493 Battig, R. "Cathode-ray tube." Br. 512,764, Nov. 29, 1937. Convention date Nov. 30, 1936. Void.

6494 G.E.C., L.I. Farren, and E.P. George. "Electron multiplier circuit." Br. 481,996, Nov. 30, 1936.

6495 Plaistowe, D.L., and D.W. Fewings. "Oscillograph." Br. 486,041, Nov. 30, 1936 (Marconi's); U.S. 2,159,818, Oct. 2, 1937, May 23, 1939 (RCA).

6496 Siebertz, Karl. "Electron multiplier." U.S. 2,187,184, Nov. 17, 1937, Jan. 17, 1940. In Germany Nov. 30, 1936 (Siemens & Halske).

6497 "Television at hand." ELECTRONICS 9 (Dec.): 14, 15. 6 photos. Discusses Farnsworth studio and control panels, Philadelphia; NBC transmitter, Empire State Building, New York City; Philco receivers and transmitters; station W3XE.

6498 Morton, G.A., and Eduard G. Ramberg. "Electron optics of an image tube." PHYSICS 7 (Dec.): 451–9. 14 illus.

6499 "Television shorts." RADIO-CRAFT 8 (Dec.): 326. Farnsworth demonstration to FCC; Don Lee television service from W6XAO; Olympic games; receivers at Radiolympia.

6500 "The television demonstration." SCI. MON. 43 (Dec.): 582–4. 3 photos: Zworykin and cathode-ray tube, Iconoscope, and NBC camera. Discusses NBC and RCA demonstration in New York, Nov. 6.

6501 Kette, G. "Fernsehen auf der 13. Grossen Deutschen Funkausstellung 1936" [Television at the 13th Great German Radio Fair]. T.F.T. 25 (Dec.): 332–9.

6502 Traub, E.H. "Television at the Berlin radio exhibition, 1936." J. TELEV. SOC. 2 (Dec.): 181–7. 11 photos.

6503 Taylor, M.K. "A summary of impressions of the Berlin television exhibition, 1936." J. TELEV. SOC. 2 (Dec.): 188–91. Diagram. Table of exhibits with details and comments.

6504 Lance, T.M.C. "The Baird 'Televisor' receiving set." J. TELEV. SOC. 2 (Dec.): 192–7. Photo, 2 diags. A demonstration took place on Nov. 11.

6505 Rodda, Sydney. "Electron optics." J. TELEV. SOC. 2 (Dec.): 198–212. 16 diagrams. Errata and addenda published Mar. 1937, pp. 253–4. Lecture given at University College, London, Dec. 9.

6506 Randall, J.T. "Luminescence and its applications." J. TELEV. SOC. 2 (Dec.): 213–6. 43 tables. Summary of lecture given at Royal Society of Arts, Jan. 27, 1937. Historical references given on pp. 215, 216.

6507 "Appeal to owners of television sets." J. TELEV. SOC. 2 (Dec.): 218. Request by BBC for postcard comments on programs and reception.

6508 "Director of television on forthcoming programmes." J. TELEV. SOC. 2 (Dec.): 219. Talk by Gerald Cook, Jan. 22, 1937.

6509 "Mr. J.L. Baird." J. TELEV. SOC. 2 (Dec.): 219. Note on the presentation of the medal of the International Faculty of Sciences to J.L. Baird.

6510 Busch, H. "Grundlagen und Entwicklung der Elektronenoptik" [Foundations and development of electron optics]. Z. TECH. PHYS. 17 (Dec.): 584–8.

6511 Brüche, E. "Übersicht über die experimentelle Elektronenoptik und ihre Anwendung" [Survey of experimental electron optics and its applications]. Z. TECH. PHYS. 17 (Dec.): 588–93. Review of recent theories and developments.

6512 Scherzer, O. "Die Aufgaben der theoritischen Elektronenoptik" [Problems of theoretical electron optics]. Z. TECH. PHYS. 17 (Dec.): 593–6. Review of theoretical problems and analysis.

6513 Schaffernicht, W. "Der elektronenoptische Bildwandler" [The electro-optical picture transformer]. Z. TECH. PHYS. 17 (Dec.): 596–604. Discusses work at A.E.G.

6514 Knoll, M. "Die Elektronenoptik in der Ferhsehtechnik" [Electron optics in television technology]. Z. TECH. PHYS. 17 (Dec.): 604–17.

6515 Weiss, G. "Uber Sekundärelektronen-Vervielfacher" (On secondary electron multiplication). Z. TECH. PHYS. 17 (Dec.): 623–9.

6516 Heimann, W. "Entwicklungsgang der Braunschen Röhre" [Development of the cathode-ray tube]. Z. TECH. PHYS. 17 (Dec.): 630–5. Development of cathode-ray tubes, with a historical survey from Braun's original tube.

6517 "'Television pipe' gets first test. Apparatus to bring 'talking pictures' to home can carry 240 conversations at once. Work still incomplete. Present trials between New York and Philadelphia may simplify phone system." N.Y.T. (Dec. 2): 33: 3.

6518 "Television station licensed." N.Y.T. (Dec. 2): 34: 4. Farnsworth Television.

6519 Blumlein, A.D. "Network for coupling electronic cable circuits." U.S. 2,204,721, Nov. 13, 1937, June 18, 1940. In Britain Dec. 2, 1936.

6520 Marris, J.C. "Television." ELECT. 117 (Dec. 4): 712. Address by J.C. Marris of

G.E.C. to joint meeting of the Association of Supervising Electrical Engineers at the Institute of Engineers-in-Charge at Magnet House, Nov. 24.

6521 "Television." ELECT. 117 (Dec. 4): 715. Edison Swan Electric Co. Also in ELECT. REV. 119 (Dec. 4): 781.

6522 Flechsig, W. "Multistage electron multiplier." U.S. 2,192,270, Dec. 15, 1937, Mar. 5, 1940. In Germany Dec. 5, 1936 (Fernseh A.-G.).

6523 "Television 'eye' looks across a sparkling panorama. Targets of sight. Blinking lights on horizon mark range for television men atop skyscraper." N.Y.T. (Dec. 6): XII, 16: 1, 2.

6524 Williams, W.E. "Cathode-ray tube." Br. 486,548, Dec. 7, 1936. Mosaic electrode.

6525 Walton, G.W. "Picture recording and reproducing system." U.S. 2,112,002, Dec. 9, 1936, Mar. 22, 1938 (Scophony). Divided from U.S. 2,089,155, Oct. 19, 1929; in Britain Oct. 25, 1928.

6526 "Television stock barred by court. O.C. Harriman enjoined in sale of Television Corporation of America securities. Fraud on widows seen. Affidavits say shares at $1 value, lacking assets, were sold for $5 to $10." N.Y.T. (Dec. 10): 2: 2.

6527 Bull, Eric William. "Cathode-ray tube." U.S. 2,246,291, Dec. 31, 1937, June 17, 1941 (EMI). In Britain Dec. 10, 1936.

6528 Gallup, John L. "Enameled mesh base electrode." U.S. 2,175,689, Dec. 10, 1936, Oct. 10, 1939 (RCA). Mosaic electrode.

6529 Krenzien, Otto. "Electron multiplier tube." U.S. 2,189,318, Dec. 9, 1937, Feb. 6, 1940. In Germany Dec. 10, 1936 (Siemens & Halske).

6530 Lewis, Harold M. "Television receiver." U.S. 2,173,173, Dec. 10, 1936, Sept. 19, 1939. Assigned: Hazeltine. Cathode-ray tube and circuits.

6531 Banks, G.B., and Marconi's. "Electron multiplier." Br. 486,888, Dec. 11, 1936.

6532 White, "Thermionic valve circuits." U.S. 2,185,363, Dec. 8, 1937, Jan. 2, 1940. In Britain Dec. 12, 1936 (EMI). Saw-tooth wave generator.

6533 "Radio in Japan to be extended." N.Y.T. (Dec. 13): XI, 12: 7. "Extension of television research and increased power for broadcasting stations are provided for in the Japan Broadcasting Corporation's plans for 1937."

6534 "New television station planned for Philadelphia." N.Y.T. (Dec. 13): XI, 14: 3. Farnsworth Television.

6535 "Images seen 70 miles away. New York's television reaches high mast at Riverhead." N.Y.T. (Dec. 13): XI, 14: 6. NBC.

6536 "London tele-theatres crowded to capacity." N.Y.T. (Dec. 13): XI, 14: 8. "So interested is the British public in television that the demonstration 'theatres' in London's large stores are reported to be filled to capacity during the hours the Alexandra Palace video transmitter is on the air. Phonograph audition rooms are being converted into television booths in numerous shops."

6537 Martin, Karl, Johannes Flügge, and Hans Georg Roll. "Projecting television image." U.S. 2,229,302, Dec. 8, 1937, Jan. 21, 1941. Assigned: Emil Busch A.-G. In Germany Dec. 14, 1936.

6538 Flaherty, Mark, and Ralph S. Holmes. "Television receiver." U.S. 2,207,510, Dec. 15, 1936, July 9, 1940. Assigned: RCA. Cabinet with reflecting mirror in lid.

6539 B.T.-H. "Cathode-ray tube." Br. 498,103, Dec. 16, 1937. Convention date Dec. 16, 1936. Mesh screen.

6540 Below, F., Paul Lindner, and E. Schwartz. "Projection receiver." U.S. 2,234,227, Dec. 15, 1937, Mar. 11, 1941 (Fernseh A.-G.); Br. 507,582, Dec. 16, 1937. In Germany Dec. 16, 1936.

6541 Schlesinger, K. "Amplifier for television purposes." U.S. 2,227,026, Dec. 16, 1937, Dec. 31, 1940; Br. 499,538, Dec. 15, 1937 (D.S. Loewe). In Germany Dec. 16, 1936.

6542 Steudel, Eberhard. "Cathode-ray tube." U.S. 2,215,199, Dec. 11, 1937, Sept. 17, 1940 (G.E.). In Germany Dec. 16, 1936.

6543 Johnstone, D.M. "Cathode-ray tube." Br. 487,329, Dec. 17, 1936. Reference to Br. 484,575 (Nov. 5, 1936).

6544 Baird Television, T.M.C. Lance, and G.E.G. Graham. "Electron multiplier." Br. 487,328, Dec. 17, 1936.

6545 Görlich, Paul, and Martin Ploke. "Cathode-ray tube." U.S. 2,209,159, Dec. 2, 1937, July 23, 1940 (Zeiss Ikon A.-G.); Br. 505,601, Nov. 15, 1937. In Germany Dec. 18, 1936. Rectifies chromatic error of electron lenses.

6546 N.V. Philips. "Image intensifier." Br. 481,865, Dec. 18, 1936. Addition to Br. 469,588 (Jan. 8, 1936).

6547 Adam, M. "Les réalisations du service national de la radio-diffusion" [Realizing a national broadcasting service]. GENIE CIVIL 109 (Dec. 19): 549–52. Review of progress in France, including television.

6548 Iams, H. "Electronic relay device." U.S. 2,259,507, Dec. 19, 1936, Oct. 21, 1941 (RCA).

6549 Eaglesfield, Charles Cecil. "Television receiver circuit." U.S. 2,203,722, Dec. 16, 1937, June 11, 1940. Assigned: RCA. In Britain Dec. 21, 1936.

6550 Schlesinger, K. "Modulation system." Br. 507,495, Dec. 15, 1937; U.S. 2,227,027, Dec. 31, 1940. In Germany Dec. 21, 1936.

6551 Görlich, Paul, and Martin Ploke. "Glow cathode for cathode-ray tubes." U.S. 2,216,942, Jan. 17, 1938, Oct. 8, 1940 (Zeiss Ikon A.-G.). In Germany Dec. 22, 1936.

6552 Miller, H., and John Edwin Islington Cairns. "Cathode-ray tube." Br. 487,833, Dec. 22, 1936 (EMI). Conductive support for a mosaic plate to eliminate microphonic effects.

6553 Cork, E.C., and J.L. Pawsey. "Impulse networks." Br. 488,254, Dec. 23, 1936; U.S. 2,270,416, Dec. 22, 1937, Jan. 20, 1942 (EMI). For television; electric wave system.

6554 Lubszynski, H.G. "Cathode-ray tube." Br. 487,787, Dec. 23, 1936 (EMI). Mosaic screen.

6555 Cawein, Madison. "Cathode-ray tube scanning system." U.S. 2,177,688, Dec. 24, 1936, Oct. 31, 1939. Assigned: Hazeltine. Br. 500,502, Nov. 29, 1937.

6556 Jarvis, K.W., and R.M. Blair. "Electronic device." U.S. 2,220,452, Dec. 24, 1936, Nov. 5, 1940 (RCA). Electron multiplier.

6557 Knoop, W.A. "Multiple channel electro-optical system." U.S. 2,203,870, Dec. 24, 1936, June 11, 1940. Assigned: B.T.L. Br. 484,286, Dec. 20, 1937 (E.R.P.).

6558 Nicoll, F.H. "Electron mirror." Br. 489,428, Dec. 24, 1936; U.S. 2,264,709, Dec. 23, 1937, Dec. 2, 1941 (EMI). Image converter.

6559 Schlesinger, K., and D.S. Loewe. "Inter-line scanning of film running async with the scanning means." U.S. 2,248,552, Dec. 23, 1937, July 8, 1941; Br. 508,373, Dec. 24, 1937. In Germany Dec. 24, 1936. Disk scanning for film.

6560 Schlesinger, K., and D.S. Loewe. "Modulation system." U.S. 2,248,553, Dec. 23, 1937, July 8, 1941; Br. 506,189, Dec. 24, 1937. In Germany Dec. 24, 1936.

6561 Lindemann, Frederick Alexander. "Cathode-ray tube." Br. 487,940, Dec. 28, 1936, June 28, 1938. Camera tube. Reference to Br. 482,959 (Oct. 8, 1936).

6562 Fernseh A.-G. "Valve generator." Br. 508,379, Dec. 29, 1937. In Germany Dec. 29, 1936. Deflector circuit.

6563 Wendt, Karl R. "Protective circuit." U.S. 2,119,372, Dec. 19, 1936, May 31, 1938 (RCA). Cathode-ray tube and circuit.

6564 Davisson, Clinton J. "Cathode-ray device." U.S. 2,217,197, Dec. 30, 1936, Oct. 8, 1940 (B.T.L.).

6565 E.R.P. "Cathode-ray tube." Br. 484,790, Dec. 23, 1937. Convention date Dec. 30, 1936.

6566 Iams, Harley A. "Television-transmitting apparatus." U.S. 2,156,392, Dec. 30, 1936, May 2, 1939. Assigned: RCA. Br. 505,686, Dec. 30, 1937 (Marconi's).

6567 Richards, Claude Langdon. "Television system." U.S. 2,203,634, Dec. 28, 1937, June 4, 1940. Assigned: RCA. Br. 497,116, Dec. 28, 1937 (N.V. Philips). In Holland Dec. 30, 1936.

6568 Flory, L.E. "Photoelectric cathode." U.S. 2,175,888, Dec. 31, 1936, Oct. 10, 1939 (RCA).

6569 Hickok, Willard. "Television transmitting tube." U.S. 2,156,391, Dec. 31, 1936, May 2, 1939. Assigned: RCA. Mosaic electrode.

6570 Ardenne, M. von. TELEVISION RECEPTION. Translated by O.S. Puckle. London: Chapman & Hall; New York: Van Nostrand, 1936. 121 pp., 43 plates and illus. Construction and operation of a cathode-ray tube receiver for the reception of ultra-short-wave television broadcasting. For German language original, see 4959.

6571 Cannell, John Clucas. ROMANCE OF TELEVISION. London: Harrap & Co., 1936.

6572 Chapman, Ernest Hall. WIRELESS TODAY. (The Pageant of Progress Series.) London: Oxford University Press, 1936. 158 pp., 24 plates.

6573 Eckhardt, George H. ELECTRONIC TELEVISION. Chicago: Goodhart-Wilcox Co., 1936. 162 pp., 82 illus. Reprinted New York: Arno Press, 1974. Details work of Farnsworth.

6574 Ford, D'Arcy. A NEW THEORY: INVENTIONS AND EXPERIMENTS IN WIRELESS AND TELEVISION. Exeter: Published by the author, 1936. 44 pp.

6575 Halloran, Arthur Hobart. TELEVISION WITH CATHODE-RAYS. San Francisco: Pacific Coast Radio Publishing Co., 1936. vi + 286 pp. Photos, diagrams, 2 folding charts. Lecture notes, university extension. Includes electron optics, radio theory, applications for Farnsworth and RCA systems. Reviews in RADIO-CRAFT (Sept. 1936) and ELECTRONICS (Sept. 1936).

6576 Lange, Bruno. DIE PHOTOELEMENTE UND IHRE ANWENDUNG. 2 vols. Leipzig: J.A. Barth, 1936. 297 pp. Translated by Ancel St. John as PHOTOELEMENTS AND THEIR APPLICATION. New York: Reinhold, 1938.

6577 Lewis, Edwin John Godfrey. TELEVISION: TECHNICAL TERMS AND DEFINITIONS. London: Pitman, 1936. 95 pp. Dictionary.

6578 MacGregor-Morris, J.T., and J.H. Henley. CATHODE-RAY OSCILLOGRAPHY. London: Chapman & Hall; Pittsburgh: Instruments Publishing Co., 1936. xiii + 249 pp., 151 photos and diagrams. Includes television applications.

6579 Moseley, S.A., and Herbert McKay. TELEVISION: A GUIDE FOR THE AMATEUR. London: Oxford University Press, 1936. 144 pp., 31 plates, 50 diagrams.

6580 Moyer, James Ambrose, and John F. Wostel. RADIO-RECEIVING AND TELEVISION TUBES. New York: McGraw-Hill, 1936. 635 pp. First edition published in 1929 as RADIO-RECEIVING TUBES.

6581 Myers, Leonard Morris. ELECTRON OPTICS: AN INTRODUCTION. London: Pitman, 1936. x + 338 pp., 214 photos and diagrams, 2 folding charts. Second edition published in 1938. Discusses theory of image projection, photometry, the Kerr effect, mechanical optical scanning systems, electron optical scanning systems.

6582 RCA. RCA TELEVISION. COLLECTED PAPERS. Vol. I. New York: RCA Institutes Technical Press, 1936. x + 452 pp. Vol. II published in 1937 (7373).

CHAPTER 17

BATTLE OF THE SYSTEMS: 1937

6583 Busch, H. "Electron optics of long magnet coils." ANN. PHYS. 28 (Jan.): 11–20.

6584 Fuchs, F. "Die 13. grosse Deutsche Rundfunkausstellung" [The 13th Great German Radio Fair]. ARCH. F. ELEKT. 49 (Jan.): 2–8.

6585 Mierlo, S. van, and P. Alvess. "An experimental television transmitter." ELECT. COMM. 15 (Jan.): 232–5. This article and the one below describe equipment of Les Laboratoires de Matériel Téléphonique, Paris. Definition ranging from 180 to 400 lines.

6586 Mierlo, S. van, and C.A. Pullas. "An experimental television receiver." ELECT. COMM. 15 (Jan.): 236–8.

6587 "RCA describes television system." ELECTRONICS 10 (Jan.): 8–11, 48. 6 photos, 1 diagram. Report of Ralph Beal's paper at the New York IRE, "The RCA television field test system," early Dec. 1936.

6588 Leverenz, Humboldt W. "Problems concerning the production of cathode-ray tube screens." J. OSA 27 (Jan.): 25–35. 9 graphs and diagrams.

6589 "Television system of advanced design." POP. MECH. 67 (Jan.): 97. 3 photos.

6590 "News in television." RADIO-CRAFT 8 (Jan.): 390. Photo. Plans for television in Moscow and Tokyo; Telefunken's cathode-ray tube projector.

6591 "New high-intensity cathode-ray tube effects television theatre." RADIO-CRAFT 8 (Jan.): 394. 3 photos. German plans; new projector tube by Telefunken.

6592 "How to make the Radio-Craft 1937 television receiver." RADIO-CRAFT 8 (Jan.): 398–9, 426–7. 3 photos, 3 diagrams. Table of RMA standards, list of parts. Continued in Feb. issue.

6593 Porter, B.H. "Notes on cathode-ray tubes." RADIO ENG. 17 (Jan.): 13, 14.

6594 "Britain inaugurates television for public use." RADIO N. 18 (Jan.): 391, 392, 446.

6595 Poch, W.J., and D.W. Epstein. "Partial suppression of one side band in television reception." RCA REV. 1 (Jan.): 19–35. Also in PROC. IRE 25 (Jan.): 15–31. 12 graphs and diagrams.

6596 Beal, R.R. "Equipment used in the current RCA television field tests." RCA REV. 1 (Jan.): 36–48. 9 photos, 2 diagrams.

6597 Engstrom, E.W., nd C.M. Burrill. "Frequency assignments for television." RCA REV. 1 (Jan.): 88–93. Summary of technical aspects.

6598 Schwartz, Erich. "Projection screen." U.S. 2,213,077, Aug. 27, 1940. In Germany Jan. 2, 1937.

6599 "Television in London. Ultra-short-wave test by BBC from Alexandra Palace, range 25 miles." N.Y.T. (Jan. 3): X, 10: 7.

6600 "1937 stirs new hopes. Ongoing field tests in New York." N.Y.T. (Jan. 3): X, 10: 8. Changing from 343 to 441 lines.

6601 Dunlap, O.E. Jr. "Signs of progress. Report on the state of television development and field tests." N.Y.T. (Jan. 3): X, 12: 7.

6602 Zworykin, V.K. "Intelligence transmission system." U.S. 2,146,876, Jan. 4, 1937, Feb. 14, 1939. Assigned: RCA. Electrostatic storage and scanning.

6603 "FCC: Television not yet ready for public service. Radio rise shown in federal report." N.Y.T. (Jan. 6): 9: 1.

6604 Bronk, O. von. "Color television." U.S. 2,191,515, Jan. 6, 1938, Feb. 27, 1940. In Germany Jan. 7, 1937 (Telefunken). Cyclical transmission of color images.

6605 "Present state of television." MAN. GUARD. (Jan. 8), 12.

6606 "Large screen television." ELECT. 118 (Jan. 8): 32. Report on demonstration at Dominion Theatre with 6-by-8-foot screen. 120 lines, multimesh, 17 fr. high-intensity arc. "Flicker, 'rain,' and a rather dim appearance make the demonstration noticeably inferior in quality to that obtained with the small-screen television receivers now in the market."

6607 Zeiss Ikon A.-G. "Light valve; cathode-ray tube." Br. 490,981, Jan. 9, Nov. 26, 1937. Light modulation with bimetallic strips, deformed by the heat of the beam.

6608 D.S. Loewe. "Television." Br. 492,495, Jan. 9, 1937, Jan. 10, 1938. Capacitance neutralization in synchronizing circuit.

6609 "Albert F. Murray, chief television engineer, Philco, expects television in six years. A tele-view of the future." N.Y.T. (Jan. 10): X, 10: 7.

6610 Dunlap, O.E. Jr. "News for Congress. Second annual report of FCC. Substantial increase of public interest in television." N.Y.T. (Jan. 10): X, 12: 1.

6611 "New transmitter by Farnsworth in Philadelphia. More television planned for Philadelphia area." N.Y.T. (Jan. 10): X, 12: 2.

6612 Behne, Rudolf, and Heinrich Hinderer. "Fluorescent screen for cathode-ray tubes." U.S. 2,155,465, Jan. 21, 1938, Apr. 12, 1939. Assigned: Fernseh A.-G. In Germany Jan. 12, 1937. Deposition of zinc silicate and cadmium silicate.

6613 Colberg, Rolf, and Heinrich Strübig. "Image-analyzing tube." U.S. 2,230,134, Jan. 12, 1938, Jan. 28, 1941. Assigned: Fernseh A.-G. In Germany Jan. 13, 1937. Camera tube with electron multiplier.

6614 Stoll, (Sir) Oswald. "Television." Br. 490,523, Jan. 13, 1937. Commutator switches for picture elements and sound.

6615 Percival, W.S. "Thermionic valve amplifier circuit." U.S. 2,173,914, Sept. 12, 1939. In Britain Jan. 14, 1937.

6616 Briza, J. "Television." Br. 483,935, Jan. 15, 1937. Vacuum tube circuitry for television receiver.

6617 "Irrational fear about television. 'Seeing things.'" N.Y.T. (Jan. 17): IV, 9: 1.

6618 "A tele-van for London. Mobile television camera." N.Y.T. (Jan. 17): X, 10: 7.

6619 Ploke, Martin. "Cathode-ray tube screen." U.S. 2,182,451, Jan. 21, 1938, Dec. 5, 1939. Assigned: Zeiss Ikon. In Germany Jan. 18, 1937. Mosaic structure in camera tube; screen with bimetallic reeds.

6620 "Injunction against Television Corp. of America." N.Y.T. (Jan. 19): 4: 5.

6621 Baird Television and P.W. Willans. "Television." Br. 489,102, Jan. 19, 1937. Separation of synchronizing signals.

6622 Flory, Leslie E. "Photoelectric cathode." U.S. 2,189,322, Jan. 19, 1937, Feb. 6, 1940. Assigned: RCA.

6623 Faudell, Charles L. "Television system." U.S. 2,212,933, Jan. 18, 1938, Aug. 27, 1940. Assigned: EMI. In Britain Jan. 20, 1937. Signal separator stage.

6624 Percival, W.S., C.O. Browne, L.R.J. Johnson, and Frank Blythen. "Cathode-ray tube." Br. 490,845, Jan. 20, 1937; U.S. 2,258,557, Jan. 18, 1938, Oct. 7, 1941. Assigned: EMI. Camera tube.

6625 Schlesinger, K., and Loewe Radio Inc. "Synchronizing method and means." Br. 509,831, Jan. 19, 1938 (RCA); U.S. 2,227,018, Jan. 18, 1938, Dec. 31, 1940. In Germany Jan. 20, 1937.

6626 M-O Valve Co. and W.H. Aldous. "Electron multiplier." Br. 479,978, Jan. 21, 1937. Treated silver electrode.

6627 "Prepares for television. Acquisitions of radio stations by movie company." N.Y.T. (Jan. 22): 37: 3.

6628 Baird Television, V.A. Jones, and Thomas Cayton Nuttall. "Cathode-ray tube." Br. 489,282, Jan. 22, 1937. Mosaic electrodes.

6629 "London see big images. Large-screen projection in London by unnamed company and by Alexanderson of GE in Schenectady." N.Y.T. (Jan. 24): X, 10: 8.

6630 "Tests of television's 441-line images begun. Empire State Building, N.Y." N.Y.T. (Jan. 24): X, 12: 8.

6631 Flory, Leslie E., and G.A. Morton. "Electronic discharge device." U.S. 2,173,229, Jan. 28, 1937, Sept. 19, 1939. Assigned: RCA. Electron multipliers.

6632 Marconi's. "Cathode-ray tube." Br. 491,425, Jan. 28, 1938. Convention date Jan. 28, 1937. Cathode-ray tube with electron multiplier.

6633 Hughes, L.E.C. "Television. Opening of London high-definition service — Great Britain's lead." ELECT. 118 (Jan. 29): 144. Photo.

6634 Pione, Emanuel R. "Secondary electron emitting electrode." U.S. 2,147,669, Jan. 30, 1937, Feb. 21, 1939. Assigned: RCA. Use of borate of an alkaline-earth metal.

6635 Marconi's. "Cathode-ray tube." Br. 510,266, Jan. 30, 1937, Jan. 31, 1938. Focusing mechanism.

6636 "Radio vision plans told. A.F. Murray outlines progress expected; lecture at Franklin Institute." N.Y.T. (Jan. 31): XI, 11: 5.

6637 Chappell, Alan. "The real future of television." DISCOVERY 18 (Feb.): 43–45.

6638 "Radio progress during 1936. Pt. IV. Report by the Technical Committee on Television and Facsimile." PROC. IRE 25 (Feb.): 199–210.

6639 Barthélemy, R. [Characteristics of television.] ONDE ELECT. 16 (Feb.): 85–8.

6640 Richards, C.L. "Television receiver." PHIL. TECH. REV. 2 (Feb.): 33–8.

6641 "Television news shorts." RADIO-CRAFT 8 (Feb.): 454.

6642 "European version of Farnsworth's television camera." RADIO-CRAFT 8 (Feb.): 455. Photo.

6643 "NBC-RCA television 'on the air.'" RADIO-CRAFT 8 (Feb.): 465, 485. 5 photos.

6644 "How to make the Radio-Craft 1937 television receiver." RADIO-CRAFT 8 (Feb.): 466, 467, 495. 4 photos, diagram, list of parts. Continued in Mar. issue.

6645 "Television abroad." RADIO-CRAFT 8 (Feb.): 472. 5 photos. Ekco-Scophony mirror drum, 12 by 16 inches. Pye 8-by-10-inch screen. Telefunken projector.

6646 "The next ten years will be 'television.'" RADIO N. 18 (Feb.): 457, 458, 498, 499.

6647 Gandtner, V. "Ueber Fernsehzwischenverstaerker" [On a television intermediate amplifier]. T.F.T. 26 (Feb.): 37–40. Equipment installed on the Berlin-Leipzig cable route.

6648 Parr, A. "The history of the cathode-ray tube." TELEV. & S.W.W. 10 (Feb.): 85–7.

6649 Andrieu, Robert. "Saw-tooth wave generator." U.S. 2,207,529, July 13, 1938, July 9, 1940. Assigned: Telefunken. In Germany Feb. 2, 1937.

6650 Baird Television and —. Brown. "Television." Br. 489,716, Feb. 2, 1937. Reference to Br. 460,222 (July 23, 1935).

6651 Baird Television, V.A. Jones, and T.C. Nuttall. "Television transmitter." Br. 489,717, Feb. 2, 1937. References to Br. 472,762 (Mar. 28, 1936), 456,582, 470,785 (Feb. 21, 1936), 472,401 (Mar. 20, 1936).

6652 G.E.C., C.H. Simms, and L.R.G. Treloar. "Electron multiplier." Br. 487,899, Feb. 2,

1937. Reference to Br. 478,262 (July 16, 1936).

6653 Wilson, R.G., and W.D. Silver. "Television." Br. 475,999, Feb. 3, 1937. Screen scanned in halves by a mirror drum, fixed reflecting mirror, and a rotating mirror.

6654 B.T.-H. and W.J. Scott. "Television receiver." Br. 490,029, Feb. 4, 1937.

6655 Schubert, Georg, Ulrich Knick, and Ernst Ruska. "Electric discharge tube." U.S. 2,143,582, Feb. 5, 1937, Jan. 10, 1939. Assigned: Fernseh A.-G. In Germany Feb. 4, 1937. Camera tube with electron multiplier.

6656 "British television bars Baird system. Decision in favor of Marconi-EMI." N.Y.T. (Feb. 5): 8: 6.

6657 Blumlein, A.D. "Thermionic valve and other electric circuits." U.S. 2,176,200, Feb. 3, 1938, Oct. 17, 1939. Assigned: Fernseh A.-G. Br. 489,950, Feb. 5, 1937 (EMI). Coupling circuit.

6658 Bünger, W., and Erich Kosche. "Prism arrangement for producing double images, particularly for television purposes." U.S. 2,265,264, Feb. 5, 1938, Dec. 9, 1941. Assigned: Fernseh A.-G. In Germany Feb. 6, 1937.

6659 Goldsmith, A.N. "Television system." U.S. 2,219,149, Feb. 6, 1937, Oct. 22, 1940. Scanning scheme.

6660 "Tiny waves 'see' afar. Exceeding expected range in London and New York." N.Y.T. (Feb. 7): X, 10: 8.

6661 "Seen in London. Description of television program." N.Y.T. (Feb. 7): X, 12: 2–3.

6662 Baird Television. "Electro-optical light valve." Br. 489,964, Feb. 8, 1937.

6663 Comp. Gaz. "Television." Br. 505,057, Feb. 7, 1938. In France Feb. 8, 1937.

6664 D.S. Loewe. "Cathode-ray tube." Br. 522,245, Feb. 7, 1938. In Germany Feb. 8, 1937.

6665 Knick, Ulrich. "Scanning device." U.S. 2,195,863, Feb. 8, 1938, Apr. 2, 1940. Assigned: Fernseh A.-G. In Germany Feb. 9, 1937. Flyback scanning scheme.

6666 D.S. Loewe. "Cathode-ray tube." Br. 490,278, Feb. 10, 1937. Divided from Br. 480,521.

6667 "Television." ELECT. 118 (Feb. 12): 205. Editorial commenting on Alexandra Palace service and the decision to drop Baird.

6668 "Television shows big gain in clarity. Observations of Philco trials." N.Y.T. (Feb. 12): 25: 8.

6669 Arni, Hans, and Hans Neugebauer. "Television receiving apparatus." U.S. 2,254,057, Feb. 12, 1938, Aug. 26, 1941. Assigned: Siemens & Halske. In Germany Feb. 12, 1937. Cathode-ray tube screen.

6670 "20 television stations are experimenting here. Roster of FCC licensed stations." N.Y.T. (Feb. 14): X, 10: 7.

6671 Dunlap, O.E. Jr. "Epochal televiews. General observations on the state and future of television." N.Y.T. (Feb. 14): X, 12: 1–6.

6672 McCarthy, James. "Television method and means." U.S. 2,195,676, Feb. 15, 1937, Apr. 2, 1940. Use of glow lamp for sound transmission.

6673 Baird Television and V.A. Jones. "Cathode-ray tube." Br. 490,533, Feb. 16, 1937.

6674 Schlesinger, K. "Electron amplifier." U.S. 2,227,030, Feb. 5, 1938, Dec. 31, 1940. Assigned: D.S. Loewe. In Germany Feb. 16, 1937. Electron multiplier.

6675 D.S. Loewe. "Electron multiplier." Br. 512,711, Feb. 14, 1938. In Germany Feb. 16, 1937.

6676 D.S. Loewe. "Electron multiplier." Br. 517,806, Feb. 14, 1938. In Germany Feb. 16, 1937.

6677 Ardenne, M. von. "Method of operating cathode-ray tubes." U.S. 2,249,066, Feb. 17, 1937, July 15, 1941. Assigned: RCA. In

Germany June 10, 1933. Cathode-ray tube with inclined screen.

6678 Dillenburger, Wolfgang, and K. Thöm. "Control voltage limiter." U.S. 2,240,289, Feb. 15, 1938, Apr. 29, 1941; Br. Feb. 16, 1938. Assigned: Fernseh A.-G. In Germany Feb. 17, 1937. Signal limiter for cathode-ray tube.

6679 Holman, H.E., and EMI. "Mosaic screen structure for cathode-ray tube." Br. 490,537, Feb. 17, 1937. See Br. 479,024 (June 25, 1936).

6680 Collard, John, et al. "Networks." Br. 495,815, Feb. 18, 1937. Divided from Br. 476,799.

6681 Kursemeijer, H.J. "Television." Br. 514,880, Feb. 15, 1938. Convention date Feb. 18, 1937.

6682 White, E.L., and Osbert L. Ratsey. "Television transmitting or receiving system." U.S. 2,227,050, Feb. 12, 1938, Dec. 31, 1940. In Britain Feb. 18, 1937. Assigned: EMI. Nonlinear stage.

6683 Hughes, L.E.C. "Television in practice: Some notes on the present position at Alexandra Palace." ELECT. 118 (Feb. 19): 247.

6684 Electrical Research Products, Inc. "Cathode-ray tube." Br. 517,756, Feb. 13, 1939. In U.S. Feb. 19, 1937.

6685 Low, A.M. "Television." Br. 491,011, Feb. 19, 1937. Photoelectric mosaic with connection to a disk.

6686 Geiger, Max. "Saw-tooth wave generator." U.S. 2,225,300, June 8, 1938, Dec. 17, 1940. Assigned: Telefunken. In Germany Feb. 20, 1937.

6687 Günther, J. "Deflecting device for cathode-ray tubes." U.S. 2,227,711, Feb. 16, 1938, Jan. 7, 1941. Assigned: Fernseh A.-G. In Germany Feb. 20, 1937. Deflection arrangement.

6688 Langenwalter, H.W. "Electron multiplier." U.S. 2,204,503, Feb. 22, 1938, June 11, 1940. Assigned: Fernseh A.-G. In Germany Feb. 20, 1937.

6689 Zeitline, V., A. Zeitline, and V. Kliatchko. "Cathode-ray tube." Br. 495,919, Jan. 6, 1938. Convention date Feb. 20, 1937.

6690 "Tele-see set, prices cut. Price reductions in British television receivers." N.Y.T. (Feb. 21): X, 10: 8.

6691 "Television show reveals current state of the art. What the audience thinks of television." N.Y.T. (Feb. 21): X, 12: 1–7.

6692 "Seeing radio 'ghosts.' Reflections of transmission by charged layers in atmosphere." N.Y.T. (Feb. 21): X, 12: 6.

6693 Baier, Otto. "Cathode-ray tube." U.S. 2,195,914, Feb. 23, 1938, Apr. 2, 1940. Assigned: C. Lorenz A.-G. In Germany Feb. 22, 1937. Electrode assembly.

6694 Schlesinger, K. "Production of an interlaced line screen with mechanical scanning means." U.S. 2,248,554, Feb. 19, 1938, July 8, 1941. Assigned: D.S. Loewe. In Britain Feb. 21, 1938. In Germany Feb. 22, 1937.

6695 Overbeek, A. van. "Secondary electron discharge device." U.S. 2,146,607, Feb. 15, 1938, Feb. 7, 1939. Assigned: N.V. Philips. In Holland Feb. 23, 1937. Electron multiplier.

6696 G.E.C., D.C. Espley, E.L. Gardiner, and —. Russell. "Television." Br. 480,997, Feb. 23, 1937.

6697 Schlesinger, K. "Phototube with electron multiplier." U.S. 2,227,031, Feb. 19, 1938, Dec. 31, 1940. Assigned: D.S. Loewe. In Germany Feb. 24, 1937.

6698 "Television will be used at coronation procession." N.Y.T. (Feb. 27): 7: 3.

6699 Beers, George L. "Television transmitter." U.S. 2,165,778, Feb. 27, 1937, July 11, 1939. Assigned: RCA.

6700 Comp. Gaz. "Television." In Britain Feb. 22, 1938. In France Feb. 27, 1937.

6701 Iams, H.A. "Electron discharge device." U.S. 2,244,365, Feb. 27, 1937, June 3, 1941. Assigned: RCA. Camera tube.

6702 Morton, G.A., and L.E. Flory. "Electron discharge device." U.S. 2,192,579, Feb. 27, 1937, Mar. 5, 1940. Assigned: RCA. Camera tube.

6703 Pione, Emanuel R. "Thin insulating film." U.S. 2,178,080, Feb. 27, 1937, Oct. 31, 1939. Assigned: RCA. For camera tube.

6704 Pione, Emanuel R. "Thin insulating film." U.S. 2,178,081, Feb. 27, 1937, Oct. 31, 1939. Assigned: RCA. Br. 508.391, Jan. 12, 1938 (Marconi's). Mosaic structure for camera tube. Reference to Br. 471,137 (Jan. 30, 1935).

6705 Marconi's. "Cathode-ray tube." Br. 507,511, Jan. 20, 1938. Convention date Feb. 27, 1937.

6706 "Philco shows 441-line television." ELECTRONICS 10 (Mar.): 8, 9. 4 photos. Technical difficulties encountered in shifting from 345 to 441 lines. Demonstration by Philco to newsmen in Philadelphia, Feb. 11, 1937. 12-inch picture tubes, 7.5-by-10-inch picture, interlaced scanning.

6707 "Television — European style." ELECTRONICS 10 (Mar.): 32. 3 photos. German and British equipment.

6708 Karolus, A. "The problem of large images in television." FERN. U. TON. 8 (Mar.).

6709 Rinia, H., and Cornelis Dorsman. "Television system with Nipkow disc." PHIL. TECH. REV. 2 (Mar.): 72–6. Transmitter for film, with electron multiplier.

6710 Bouwers, A. "Convergence of electrons by magnetic coils." PHYSICA 4 (Mar.): 200–6.

6711 "Television news shorts." RADIO-CRAFT 8 (Mar.): 518. Photo. Crystal Palace destroyed by fire; CBS center in New York; first test of coaxial cables; BBC's plans for the coronation; Farnsworth Television, Inc., expecting license for new station W3XPF in Philadelphia.

6712 "Marconi-EMI high-definition television at Alexandra Palace." RADIO-CRAFT 8 (Mar.): 526, 562. Photos.

6713 "A German television receiver." RADIO-CRAFT 8 (Mar.): 528, 555. D.S. Loewe. 12-inch picture tube; image about 9 inches square.

6714 "How to make the Radio-Craft 1937 television receiver, Pt. 3." RADIO-CRAFT 8 (Mar.): 530, 531, 563. 2 photos, 2 diagrams. List of parts.

6715 "Italy's progress in the video art." RADIO N. 18 (Mar.): 519 ff.

6716 Strafford, F.R.W. "Electrical interference with broadcast and television reception." J. TELEV. SOC. 2 (Mar.): 221–5. 5 diagrams.

6717 Bedford, L.H. "The Cossor television receiver." J. TELEV. SOC. 2 (Mar.): 226–9. Photo, 3 diagrams.

6718 Watson, G.H. "The EMI television receiver." J. TELEV. SOC. 2 (Mar.): 230–4. 4 photos, 5 diagrams.

6719 Goddard, M.J. "Some aspects of the design of the Mikaly-Traub television receiver." J. TELEV. SOC. 2 (Mar.): 235–50. 19 diagrams, table of optical data. Mirror drum. Home receiver, 405 lines, interlaces, 20 inches wide, big screen projects 405 lines, 10 feet wide.

6720 Nagy, Paul. "The design of vision-frequency amplifiers." TELEV. & S.W.W. (Mar.): 160.

6721 "Broad-band television cables." W. ENG. 14 (Mar.): 111, 112. Losses in cables using styroflex insulation.

6722 G.E.C. and —. Edwards. "Television receiver." Br. 438,348, Mar. 1, 1937.

6723 Jeffree, J.H. "Light modulating device." U.S. 2,155,661, Mar. 2, 1937, Apr. 25, 1939. In Britain Mar. 3, 1934. Assigned: Scophony.

6724 Blumlein, A.D. "Television system." Br. 490,150, Mar. 4, 1937; U.S. 2,210,523, Mar. 1, 1938, Aug. 6, 1940. Assigned: EMI. Addition to Br. 455,375, Jan. 15, 1935.

6725 Knick, Ulrich. "Scanning method for television." U.S. 2,246,631, Mar. 4, 1938, June 24, 1941. In Germany Mar. 4, 1937.

6726 Bandringa, Menge, and Marten Cornelis Teves. "Mosaic electrode structure." U.S. 2,198,327, Feb. 28, 1938, Apr. 23, 1940. Assigned: RCA. Br. 496,014, Mar. 2, 1938 (N.V. Philips). In Germany Mar. 5, 1937. For television transmitter tube.

6727 C. Lorenz A.-G.. "Valve generator." Br. 501,096, Mar. 5, 1938. In Germany Mar. 5, 1937.

6728 Below, Fritz. "Synchronizing impulse generator." U.S. 2,233,881, Mar. 4, 1938, Mar. 4, 1941. In Germany Mar. 6, 1937.

6729 Knick, Ulrich. "Scanning method for storage tubes." U.S. 2,242,034, Mar. 4, 1938, May 13, 1941; Br. 512,489, Mar. 7, 1938. In Germany Mar. 6, 1937.

6730 White, Hardwick. "Thermionic valve amplifier." Br. 496,872, Mar. 6, 1937. Assigned: EMI. U.S. 2,246,331, Mar. 4, 1938, June 17, 1941.

6731 "Albany broker convicted. Misrepresented stock value of Television Corp. of America." N.Y.T. (Mar.7): 34: 5.

6732 "Television for Chicago." N.Y.T. (Mar. 7): XI, 12: 3.

6733 "Television research expanded in Japan. Japan Broadcasting Corp." N.Y.T. (Mar. 7): XI, 12: 6.

6734 "BBC television director outlines program plans." N.Y.T. (Mar. 7): XI, 12: 7.

6735 RAG. "Television." Br. 515,679, Mar. 7, 1938. In Germany Mar. 7, 1937.

6736 Branson, H. "Intelligence transmission system." U.S. 2,257,562, Mar. 8, 1937, Sept. 30, 1941. RCA.

6737 Graefe, Kurt Heinz. "Television scanning disk." U.S. 2,173,478, Mar. 7, 1938, Sept. 19, 1939; Br. 506,691, Mar. 7, 1938. In Germany Mar. 8, 1937. Assigned: D.S. Loewe.

6738 van der Mark, Jan. "Television receiver." U.S. 2,265,090, Mar. 2, 1938, Dec. 2, 1941. In Germany Mar. 8, 1937. Assigned: RCA. Cathode-ray tube.

6739 N.V. Philips. "Television receiver." Br. 488,843, Mar. 5, 1938. Convention date Mar. 8, 1937.

6740 "Milne sentence is deferred." N.Y.T. (Mar. 10): 14: 6.

6741 Lubszynski, H.G. "Photoelectric cells." Br. 492,036, Mar. 10, 1937; U.S. 2,243,108, Mar. 10, 1938, May 27, 1941. Assigned: EMI. Light-sensitive electrode.

6742 Lubszynski, H.G., and Harold Miller. "Electro-optical image device." U.S. 2,185,857, Mar. 4, 1938, Jan. 2, 1940; Br. 492,167, Mar. 10, 1937. Assigned: EMI.

6743 Marconi's. "Amplifier." Br. 480,424, Aug. 9, 1937. Convention date Mar. 10, 1937.

6744 White, —. "Television." Br. 491,728, Mar. 10, 1937 (EMI); U.S. 2,212,941, Mar. 2, 1938, Aug. 20, 1940. Circuit arrangement for separating electrical signal pulses.

6745 B.T.-H. and D.S. Watson. "Television receiver." Br. 491,873, Mar. 11, 1937.

6746 Schlesinger, K. "Insuring the synchronization in television transmitters." U.S. 2,248,555, Mar. 8, 1938, July 8, 1941. In Germany Mar. 11, 1937. Assigned: D.S. Loewe.

6747 Scophony and J.H. Jeffree. "Amplifier." Br. 491,389, Mar. 11, 1937.

6748 Baird Television and A.H. Gilbert. "Television receiver." Br. 491,886, Mar. 12, 1937.

6749 Baird Television and V.A. Jones. "Circuit." Br. 491, 887, Mar. 12, 1937.

6750 Faudell, C.L., and E.L.C. White. "Valve generator circuit." Br. 491,934, Mar. 12, 1937 (EMI). References to Br. 400,976 (Apr. 4, 1932), 471,737 (Feb. 4, 1936).

6751 Schiller, Saul. "Scanning device." U.S. 2,113,411, Mar. 12, 1937, Apr. 5, 1938.

6752 Wald, George. "Picture transmitter." U.S. 2,217,326, Mar. 15, 1937, Oct. 8, 1940.

6753 Baird Television and V.A. Jones. " Circuit." Br. 492,284, Mar. 16, 1937. Camera tube. Reference to Br. 482,959.

6754 Fewings, D.J. "Valve generator circuit." U.S. 2,207,509; Br. 492,278, Mar. 16, 1937. Saw-tooth generator.

6755 Messner, Maximilian, and Peter Deserno. "Television receiver." U.S. 2,248,711, Aug. 5, 1938, July 8, 1941. In Germany Mar. 16, 1937. Assigned: C. Lorenz A.-G.

6756 Massa, E.A., and —. Martin. "Electronic discharge device." U.S. 2,178,238, Mar. 17, 1937, Oct. 31, 1939. RCA.

6757 "Paris television station to be the most powerful. Planned 30 kw transmitter on Eiffel Tower." N.Y.T. (Mar. 18): 12: 4.

6758 Percival, W.S., and —. White. "Television." Br. 497,637, Mar. 18, 1937 (EMI); U.S. 2,266,509, Mar. 8, 1938, Dec. 16, 1941. Electric signal pulse controlling circuit.

6759 Flechsig, Werner, and Rudolf Behne. "Electron multiplier." U.S. 2,183,309, Mar. 17, 1938, Dec. 12, 1939. In Germany Mar. 19, 1937.

6760 Geiger, Max. "Saw-tooth wave generator." U.S. 2,250,706, Sept. 29, 1938, July 29, 1941. In Germany Mar. 19, 1937 (Telefunken).

6761 Kessler, Jacob. "Photoelectric image converter." U.S. 2,142,609, Mar. 19, 1937, Jan. 3, 1939. Cathode-ray tube.

6762 Thomson, E.E., and H. Miller. "Circuit." Br. 492,442, Mar. 20, 1937 (EMI). Camera tube.

6763 Farnsworth, P.T. "Diode oscillating tube construction." U.S. 2,189,358, Mar. 22, 1937, Feb. 6, 1940. Assigned: Farnsworth Television. Electron multiplier.

6764 Farnsworth, P.T. "Multiplier coupling system." U.S. 2,140,285, Mar. 22, 1937, Dec. 13, 1938. Assigned: Farnsworth Television.

6765 Farnsworth, P.T. "Split cathode multiplier tube." U.S. 2,141,838, Mar. 22, 1937, Dec. 27, 1938. Assigned: Farnsworth Television.

6766 Farnsworth, P.T. "Self-energized alternating current multiplier." U.S. 2,174,487, Mar. 22, 1937, Sept. 26, 1939. Assigned: Farnsworth Television.

6767 Farnsworth, P.T. "Method of operating electron multipliers." U.S. 2,180,279, Mar. 22, 1937, Nov. 14, 1939. Assigned: Farnsworth Television.

6768 Farnsworth, P.T. "Two-stage oscillograph." U.S. 2,216,266, Mar. 22, 1937, Oct. 1, 1940. Assigned: Farnsworth Television.

6769 Farnsworth, P.T. "Split cathode multiplier." U.S. 2,217,860, Mar. 22, 1937, Oct. 15, 1940. Assigned: Farnsworth Television. See Br. 512,040 (Feb. 28, 1938).

6770 Farnsworth Television. "Electron multiplier." Br. 498,566, Mar. 22, 1937, Feb. 28, 1938.

6771 Farnsworth, P.T. "Electron oscillator." Br. 503,359, Mar. 22, 1937, Feb. 28, 1938.

6772 Farnsworth Television. "Electron multiplier." Br. 515,297, Mar. 22, 1937, Feb. 28, 1938.

6773 Baird Television and V.A. Jones. "Television transmitter." Br. 492,662, Mar. 23, 1937.

6774 Knick, Ulrich, and Hans-Wolfgang Langenwalter. "Television device." U.S. 2,260,911, Mar. 25, 1938, Oct. 28, 1941. In Germany Mar. 27, 1937. Assigned: Fernseh A.-G. Camera tube.

6775 "British spent $605,375 on television in 1936." N.Y.T. (Mar. 28): XI, 12: 4. BBC costs.

6776 "No scarcity of tele-shows. London television programming." N.Y.T. (Mar. 28): XI, 12: 4–5.

6777 Baird Television and T.C. Nuttall. "Electron multipliers." Br. 493,048, Mar. 30, 1937. Reference to Br. 492,662.

6778 Baird Television and P.W. Willans. "Amplifier." Br. 493,050, Mar. 30, 1937.

6779 Baird Television, P.W. Willans, and T.C. Nuttall. "Television." Br. 493,049, Mar. 30, 1937.

6780 Veenemann, C.F., E.H. Löpp, and Hajo Bruining. "Secondary electron emitter." U.S. 2,159,774, Mar. 15, 1938, May 23, 1939. In Holland Mar. 30, 1937.

6781 Bruining, Hajo, J.H. de Boer, and C.F. Veenemann. "Electronic discharge device." U.S. 2,228,945, Mar. 15, 1938, Jan. 14, 1941. In Holland Mar. 30, 1937.

6782 Hickok, Willard. "Cathode-ray tube." U.S. 2,178,232, Mar. 30, 1937, Oct. 31, 1939; Br. 491,292, Jan. 22, 1938. Assigned: RCA. Camera tube.

6783 Rose, Albert. "Cathode-ray tube." U.S. 2,171,224, Mar. 30, 1937, Aug. 29, 1939. Assigned: RCA. Camera tube.

6784 Vance, A.W. "Television transmitter." U.S. 2,232,190, Mar. 30, 1937, Feb. 18, 1941. Assigned: RCA. See Br. 513,021 below (6786).

6785 "Circuit." Br. 513,019, Mar. 30, 1938. Convention date Mar. 30, 1937.

6786 "Television transmitter." Br. 513,021, Mar. 30, 1938. Convention date Mar. 30, 1937.

6787 C. Lorenz A.-G. "Circuit." Br. 489,270, Mar. 30, 1938. In Germany Mar. 31, 1937.

6788 S.T.C. "Television." Br. 498,271, Feb. 18, 1938. Convention date Mar. 31, 1937.

6789 Skellett, Albert M. "Cathode-ray device." U.S. 2,165,308, Mar. 31, 1937, July 11, 1939.

6790 Eddy, William C. "Television studio considerations." COMM. & BCAST. ENG. 4 (Apr.): 12, 13. Continued in issues for May, June, and July.

6791 Stevens, S.T. "Modern developments in television." ROY. SOC. EE. 30 (Apr.): 37–45. Part 1. Part 2 published in 30 (July): 129–37.

6792 "Television news shorts." RADIO-CRAFT 8 (Apr.): 583. Report from Philco. "British television is highly unsatisfactory and primitive, and the received images are so distorted at times that arms and legs look like bags of sand." Farnsworth Television Inc. started field tests at 441 lines. BBC television van and coaxial cable. FCC report. British programs; 8 manufacturers in England.

6793 "How to make the Radio-Craft 1937 television receiver, Pt. 4." RADIO-CRAFT 8 (Apr.): 596, 597, 624. 3 photos, 7 diagrams. Continued in Aug.

6794 Hanson, O.B. "Experimental studio facilities for television." RCA REV. 1 (Apr.): 13–7. Radio City studio. 7 photos, 1 diagram.

6795 Miller, H. "Circuit." Br. 496,751, Apr. 1, 1937 (EMI). Camera tube.

6796 Strübig, Heinrich. "Electron discharge device." U.S. 2,239,022, Mar. 22, 1938, Apr. 22, 1941. In Germany Apr. 1, 1937.

6797 "Plans television station. Application by CBS for transmitter on Chrysler Building, N.Y." N.Y.T. (Apr. 2): 25: 5.

6798 Bruining, Hajo, J.H. de Boer, and M.C. Teves. "Secondary electron emitter." U.S. 2,190,695, Mar. 15, 1938, Feb. 20, 1940 (RCA). In Holland Apr. 2, 1937.

6799 "Television prices drop. Price reductions on British TV receivers." N.Y.T. (Apr. 4): X, 12: 8.

6800 Baird Television, E.D. McConnell, and —. Bruce. "Television transmitter." Br. 493,304, Apr. 6, 1937. Reference to Br. 493,279.

6801 G.E.C., W.H. Aldous, and L.R.G. Treloar. "Electron multiplier." Br. 492,055, Apr. 6, 1937. Reference to Br. 345,375 (Jan. 6, 1930).

6802 Telefunken. "Television." In Britain Apr. 6, 1938. In Germany Apr. 6, 1937.

6803 Cawley, A.J. "Diavision." U.S. 2,225,097, Apr. 8, 1937, Dec. 17, 1940.

6804 Fernseh A.-G. "Cathode-ray tube." Br. 493,751, Apr. 8, 1938. In Germany Apr. 8, 1937.

6805 Statz, Willi, F. Marlsch, and —. Beslin. "Electron tube." U.S. 2,197,652, Apr. 8, 1937, Apr. 16, 1940.

6806 Dunlap, O.E. Jr. "A spring tonic." N.Y.T. (Apr. 11): XI, 12: 1. On the start of CBS transmission.

6807 Brüche, Ernst. "Electronic device." U.S. 2,237,651, Apr. 1, 1938, Apr. 8, 1941. In Germany Apr. 12, 1937.

6808 G.E.C. and C.H. Simms. "Electron multiplier." Br. 492,059, Apr. 12, 1937. References to Br. 345,375 (Jan. 6, 1930), 469,477 (Jan. 30, 1935).

6809 Fernseh A.-G. "Cathode-ray tube." Br. 513,549, Apr. 13, 1938. In Germany Apr. 13, 1937.

6810 "Berlin sees television opera." N.Y.T. (Apr. 14): 31: 5.

6811 Banks, G.B., and Marconi's. "Electron multipliers." Br. 493,861, Apr. 15, 1937.

6812 Fernseh A.-G. "Cathode-ray tube." Br. 513,739, Apr. 19, 1938. In Germany Apr. 15, 1937.

6813 Ardenne, M. von. "Cathode-ray tube." U.S. 2,185,239, Apr. 16, 1937, Jan. 2, 1940. Assigned: RCA. Divided from original Germany June 12, 1933; U.S. 2,080,449, May 24, 1934, Jan. 2, 1940.

6814 Fernseh A.-G. "Cathode-ray tube." Br. Apr. 19, 1938. In Germany Apr. 16, 1937.

6815 Barthélemy, R. "Les derniers perfectionnements apportés à la télévision" [The latest improvements in television]. GENIE CIVIL 110 (Apr. 17): 361.

6816 Lubcke, H.R. "Cathode-ray tube." Br. 493,882, Apr. 17, 1937.

6817 Nicoll, F.H. "Electronic device." Br. 495,707, Apr. 17, 1937; U.S. 2,240,120, Apr. 6, 1938, Apr. 29, 1941. Cathode-ray tube. Electron lens arrangement.

6818 "Dionnes seen on tele-screen." N.Y.T. (Apr. 18): XI, 12: 3. The Dionne quintuplets were born in 1934.

6819 "Television 'pipe' extended in the British Isles. Coaxial cable between London and Birmingham." N.Y.T. (Apr. 18): XI, 12: 3.

6820 Möller, R., E. Schwartz, and George Jaeckel. "Means of projecting images." U.S. 2,260,228, Apr. 21, 1938, Oct. 21, 1941. In Germany Apr. 21, 1937.

6821 Cock, Gerald. "Television the coronation process." RADIO TIMES (Apr. 23).

6822 Andrieu, Robert, and Max Geiger. "Oscillation generator." U.S. 2,193,850, Aug. 9, 1938, Mar. 19, 1940. In Germany Apr. 23, 1937 (Telefunken). Saw-tooth generator.

6823 Flechsig, Werner. "Electron multiplier." U.S. 2,238,634, Apr. 2, 1938, Apr. 15, 1941. In Germany Apr. 23, 1937.

6824 Fernseh A.-G. "Electron multiplier." Br. 513,879, Apr. 22, 1938. In Germany Apr. 23, 1937.

6825 Kessler, J. "Cathode-ray tube." Br. 494,310, Apr. 23, 1937. Reference to Br. 481,948 (Sept. 21, 1936).

6826 Scophony and J.H. Jeffree. "Valve generator circuit." Br. 496,121, Apr. 23, 1937. Reference to Br. 474,970.

6827 White, E.L.C. "Television and like transmitting system." Br. 496,119, Apr. 23, 1937. Assigned: EMI. U.S. 2,212,967, Apr. 16, 1938, Aug. 27, 1940. Valve circuits, pulse generator for television.

6828 Fernseh A.-G. "Oscillator." Br. 513,878, Apr. 22, 1938. In Germany Apr. 24, 1937. For cathode-ray tube.

6829 Grundmann, Gustave L. "Band-pass amplifier." U.S. 2,207,796, Apr. 24, 1937, July 16, 1940. Assigned: RCA.

6830 Marconi's. "Networks." Br. 514,064, Apr. 25, 1938. Convention date Apr. 24, 1937.

6831 "When television comes." N.Y.T. (Apr. 26): 18: 3. Editorial on potential TV programming.

6832 Farnsworth, P.T. "Cathode-ray tube." U.S. 2,149,045, Apr. 26, 1947. Feb. 28, 1939. Assigned: Farnsworth Television. Original Mar. 12, 1935. Electron multiplier.

6833 Farnsworth, P.T. "Detector." U.S. 2,156,807, Apr. 26, 1937, May 2, 1939. Original Mar. 12, 1935. Assigned: Farnsworth Television.

6834 Farnsworth, P.T. "Two-stage electron multiplier." U.S. 2,151,620, Apr. 26, 1937, June 6, 1939. Assigned: Farnsworth Television.

6835 Farnsworth, P.T. "Oscillator." U.S. 2,174,488, Apr. 26, 1937, Sept. 26, 1939. Original Mar. 12, 1935; U.S. 2,143,262, Jan. 10, 1939. Div. Apr. 26, 1937. Assigned: Farnsworth Television.

6836 Farnsworth, P.T. "Amplifier." U.S. 2,221,473, Apr. 26, 1937, Nov. 12, 1940. Original U.S. 2,143,262, Mar. 12, 1935, Jan. 10, 1939. Assigned: Farnsworth Television. Electron multiplier.

6837 Hepp, Gerard. "Cathode-ray control apparatus." U.S. 2,217,409, Nov. 19, 1937, Oct. 8, 1940 (RCA). In Germany Apr. 26, 1937.

6838 D.S. Loewe. "Television cathode-ray tube." Br. 521,637, Apr. 25, 1938; U.S. 2,252,441, Apr. 22, 1938, Aug. 12, 1941. In Germany Apr. 26, 1937. Addition to Br. 423,427 (June 27, 1932). Sharp-edge deflection.

6839 Baird Television and G.R. Tingley. "Discharge apparatus." Br. 494,586, Apr. 27, 1937.

6840 Farnsworth Television. "Cathode-ray tube." Br. 506,454, Apr. 27, 1937, Apr. 20, 1938.

6841 Baird Television and A.H. Gilbert. "Television receiver." Br. 494,677, Apr. 28, 1937. Synchronizing circuits.

6842 Baird Television and G.R. Tingley. "Valve generator circuit." Br. 494,685, Apr. 29, 1937. References to Br. 456,138, 465,344, 472,686.

6843 B.T.-H. and Leonard Rushforth. "Cathode-ray tube." Br. 493,790, Apr. 30, 1937. Electron generator array.

6844 Gábor, Dennis, and Leonard Rushforth. "Cathode-ray tube." U.S. 2,185,807, Apr. 30, 1937, Apr. 8, 1938, Jan. 2, 1940.

6845 Scophony, J. Sieger, and —. Dodington. "Television receiver." Br. 491,611, Apr. 30, 1937.

6846 Scophony, J. Sieger, and —. Dodington. "Television." Br. 500,036, Apr. 30, 1937. References to Br. 439,236, 474,970.

6847 Snyder, R.L. "Divided stream electron multiplier." U.S. 2,208,938, Apr. 30, 1937; Br. 501,316, Apr. 20, 1938, July 23, 1940.

6848 Flanze, G., and A. Gehrts. "Die Fernsehvorfuhrungen der Deutschen Reichsport auf der Internationalen Ausstellung, Paris 1937" [Television broadcasts of the German Post Office at the International Fair, Paris, 1937]. FERN. U. TON. 8 (May): 33.

6849 Knoll, M. and F. Schröter. "Electron image transmission wth insulating and semi-conducting layers." PHIL. TECH. REV. 2 (May): 330–3.

6850 "Television this month." RADIO-CRAFT 8 (May): 646. EMI, Baird Television. Erection plans, report of the Electrical Division of the Bureau of Foreign and Domestic Commerce, Washington, D.C., on television in England and Italy.

6851 "The 'kiddie-car' television set." RADIO-CRAFT 8 (May): 658, 681. Photo. Fernseh receiver on trolley.

6852 "Build this Don Lee television receiving set." RADIO N. 18 (May): 649–51, 694, 695, 697, 704. 7 photos, list of parts, diagram. By the Don Lee staff.

6853 Taylor, S. Gordon. "Television now ready by kept 'under wraps.'" RADIO N. 18 (May): 652, 692, 693. 8 photos. Philco system.

6854 "New studios and a new transmitter employing 441 lines announced by Farnsworth

Television." RADIO N. 18 (May): 654, 655, 679, 688.

6855 Zworykin, V.K. "Iconoscopes and kinescopes in television." J. SMPE 28 (May): 473–97. See RCA REV. (July 1936).

6856 Denison, V. "Methods for two-way scanning in television." TECH. PHYS. OF U.S.S.R. 4.5 (May): 383–403.

6857 B.T.-H. and D.J. Mynall. "Cathode-ray tube." Br. 494,839, May 1, 1937. Picture tube magnetic focusing.

6858 Mynall, D.J. and B.T.-H. "Cathode-ray apparatus." U.S. 2,219,193, Apr. 21, 1938, Oct. 22, 1940. In Britain May 1, 1937 (G.E.C.).

6859 Klemperer, O. "Electron device." U.S. 2,243,102, Apr. 23, 1938, May 27, 1941. In Britain May 1, 1937 (EMI). References to Br. 420,752 (June 6, 1932), 444,471, 465,144 (Nov. 2, 1935), 469,419 (Jan., 24, 1936), 471,250 (Mar. 13, 1935).

6860 "Moscow television center to use American devices." N.Y.T. (May 2): XI, 12: 2.

6861 "Ban tele-eye from Abbey." N.Y.T. (May 2): XI, 12: 3. TV cameras not allowed during coronation in Westminster Abbey.

6862 Telefunken and R. Andrieu. "Cathode-ray tube." Br. 496,812, May 3, 1937. Addition to Br. 433,996. Deflection circuits.

6863 Flechsig, Werner. "Electron multiplier." U.S. 2,216,267, May 3, 1938, Oct. 1, 1940. In Germany May 3, 1937. Assigned: Fernseh A.-G.

6864 Fernseh A-G. and Baird Television. "Electron multiplier." Br. 514,335, May 3, 1937.

6865 C. Lorenz A.-G. "Cathode-ray tube." Br. 500,017, May 5, 1938. In Germany May 5, 1937.

6866 S.T.C. "Electron multiplier." Br. 501,701, Apr. 14, 1938. Convention date May 5, 1937.

6867 BBC. THE RADIO TIMES CORONATION NUMBER. 108 pp. plus 8-page television supplement. RADIO TIMES (May 7).

6868 Fernseh A.-G. "Television." Br. May 9, 1938. In Germany May 8, 1937.

6869 "Royalty on parade." N.Y.T. (May 9): XI, 12: 4–5. Plans for televising coronation procession in Britain.

6870 "Big tele-lens aid big screen." N.Y.T. (May 9): XI, 12: 7. Discusses Zworykin, projection of image from cathode-ray tube through lens onto wall.

6871 Baird Television and V.A. Jones. "Television." Br. 495,331, May 10, 1937.

6872 Gardner, B.C. "Method of depositing fluorescent materials." U.S. 2,221,474, May 10, 1937, Nov. 12, 1940. Farnsworth Television.

6873 Farnsworth, P.T. "Cathode-ray tube." Br. 489,199, May 11, 1937.

6874 Hazeltine. "Valve amplifier circuit." Br. 490,656, Apr. 22, 1938. Convention date May 11, 1937. Broad-balanced amplifier for video signals.

6875 Hermann, D. "Electrical wave generator." U.S. 2,181,328, June 24, 1938, Nov. 28, 1939. In Germany May 11, 1937. Saw-tooth generator.

6876 Law, Russell R. "Electronic device." U.S. 2,266,773, May 11, 1937, Dec. 23, 1941. RCA.

6877 Mynall, D.J., and B.T.-H. "Magnet for cathode-ray tubes." U.S. 2,219,194, Apr. 21, 1938, Oct. 22, 1940. In Britain May 11, 1937 (G.E.C.).

6878 Percival, W.S. "Amplifier." Br. 497,004, May 11, 1937 (EMI).

6879 "World listens in on coronation today." N.Y.T. (May 12): 17: 4. Television transmission of procession.

6880 Iams, H.A. "Photovoltaic target." U.S. 2,175,691, May 12, 1937, Oct. 10, 1939. Assigned: RCA.

6881 Fernseh A.-G. "Television." Br. 514,650, May 12, 1938. In Germany May 12, 1937.

6882 Urtel, Rudolf. "Television system." U.S. 2,227,045, May 12, 1937, Dec. 31, 1940. Assigned: Telefunken.

6883 "Television brings parade to 50,000." N.Y.T. (May 13): 16: 2. Television transmission of coronation.

6884 Farnsworth, P.T. "Television apparatus." Br. 487,719, May 13, 1937.

6885 McGee, J.D. "Image converters." Br. 495,338, May 13, 1937 (EMI); U.S. 2,237,445, Jan. 11, 1938, Apr. 8, 1941.

6886 "Televising the coronation procession." ELECT. REV. 120 (May 14): 730.

6887 Marconi's and L.M. Mayers. "Cathode-ray tube." Br. 495,646, May 14, 1937. References to Br. 486,657, 486,915.

6888 Morton, G.A. "Electronic tube." U.S. 2,251,573, May 15, 1937, May 16, 1938, Aug. 5, 1941 (RCA).

6889 Dunlap, O.E. Jr. "Tele-movies advance." N.Y.T. (May 16): X, 12: 1–2. Refers to Zworykin, RCA, projection kinescope.

6890 "What tele-viewers see." N.Y.T. (May 16): X, 12: 4–5. Programming in London.

6891 "Eiffel Tower station ready in July." N.Y.T. (May 16): X, 12: 5.

6892 Perkins, Theodore B. "Regulation of magnetic electron multipliers." U.S. 2,130,152, May 18, 1937, Sept. 13, 1938 (RCA).

6893 Lubszynski, Hans Gerhard. "Electron lens." U.S. 2,203,734, May 12, 1938, June 11, 1940; Br. 497,465, May 20, 1937. Assigned: EMI. Cathode-ray tube. Reference to Br. 442,666 (May 12, 1934).

6894 S.T.C. "Cathode-ray tube." Br. 503,455, May 20, 1938. Convention date May 22, 1937.

6895 "McDonald says television must surmount obstacles." N.Y.T. (May 23): X, 12: 5. Speech by president of Zenith.

6896 Fernseh A.-G. "Generator." Br. 515,115, May 24, 1938. In Germany May 24, 1937.

6897 Marconi's. "Cathode-ray tube." Br. 501,437, May 24, 1937. RCA.

6898 G.E.C. and C.H. Simms. "Electron multiplier." Br. 489,130, May 25, 1937. References to Br. 469,283 (July 31, 1936), 478,262 (July 16, 1936).

6899 Konkle, Philip J. "Amplifier for television system." U.S. 2,233,317, May 25, 1937, Feb. 25, 1941 (Philco); Br. 517,666, May 3, 1938. Video amplifier.

6900 Koller, Lewis R. "Photoelectric device." U.S. 2,121,636, May 26, 1937, June 21, 1938. Assigned: G.E.C.

6901 Ramberg, Edward J. "Electron multiplier." U.S. 2,125,750, May 26, 1937, Aug. 2, 1938. Reissued Nov. 1, 1939, Nov. 4, 1941.

6902 Clothier, S.L., and H.C. Hogencamp. "Kerr cell electrode." U.S. 2,163,551, May 27, 1937, June 20, 1939. Assigned: Kolorama Labs.

6903 Lewis, Harold M. "Signal-generating system." U.S. 2,247,511, May 27, 1937, July 1, 1941; Br. 500,842, Apr. 22, 1938. Assigned: Hazeltine. Camera tube and circuits.

6904 G.E.C. and D.C. Espley. "Television." Br. 487,175, May 28, 1937.

6905 Freeman, G.S.P. "Mosaic electrode structure." U.S. 2,222,940, May 19, 1938, Nov. 26, 1940; Br. 498,134, May 28, 1937 (EMI). Mosaic screen. References to Br. 407,521 (Feb. 24, 1932), 480,946 (June 25, 1936).

6906 Chouguet, C. "Le télécinéma, ou la télévision par film intermédiaire, système des Etablissements Grammont" [The telecinema, or television by Grammont's intermediate film system]. GENIE CIVIL 110 (May 29): 484, 487. 1 illus.

6907 Headrick, Lewis B. "Distortion correction for television systems." U.S. 2,210,078, May 29, 1937, Aug. 6, 1940. Assigned: RCA.

6907a Iams, H.A. "Television system." U.S. 2,177,366, May 29, 1937, Oct. 24, 1939. Assigned: RCA. Camera tube with multibeam scanning.

6908 Iams, H.A. "Distortion correction for television systems." U.S. 2,197,863, May 29, 1937, Apr. 23, 1940. Assigned: RCA.

6909 Morton, G.A. "Electron tube." U.S. 2,212,645, May 29, 1937, Aug. 27, 1940. Assigned: RCA.

6910 Riesz, Robert, and Hugh S. Wertz. "Cathode-ray device." U.S. 2,245,364, May 29, 1937, June 10, 1941 (B.T.L.).

6911 S.T.C. "Cathode-ray tube." Br. 500,005, Feb. 18, 1938. Convention date May 29, 1937.

6912 S.T.C. "Cathode-ray tube." Br. 501,179, May 29, 1937.

6913 van den Bosch, F.J.G. "Electron multiplier." Br. 496,939, May 29, 1937.

6914 Brüche, E. "Electron device." U.S. 2,225,901, May 21, 1938, Dec. 24, 1940 (G.E.C.). In Germany May 31, 1937. Cathode-ray tube with electron lens.

6915 Goldsmith, A.N. "Ultra-high-frequency domain." ELECT. ENG. 56 (June): 662–6. Mentions use of the 6-mc band for television.

6916 "IRE sees projection television." ELECTRONICS 10 (June): 7–13. On papers at 25th annual convention, New York, May 10–12. 5 photos, 5 diagrams.

6917 Fink, Donald G. "Television terminology." ELECTRONICS 10 (June): 14–7, 68. Photo, 4 diagrams. Technical jargon and studio slang.

6918 Weiss, Georg. "Zur Frage der Deutschen Fernseh-Rundfunknormung" [On the question of standardizing German television and radio]. FERN. U. TON. 8 (June): 45.

6919 Ashbridge, Noel. "Television in Great Britain." PROC. IRE 25 (June): 697–707.

6920 Barthélemy, R. "Progrès en télévision" [Progress in television]. ONDE ELECT. 16 (June): 341–59.

6921 "Broadcasting in television." RADIOCRAFT 8 (June): 710. Don Lee film premiere broadcast through TV station WGX-AO. Commercial station started in Paris to replace experimental transmitter.

6922 MacGregor-Morris, J.T. "The history and development of the cathode-ray tube." J. TELEV. SOC. 2 (June): 257–62. 4 photos, 4 diags.

6923 Mitchell, W.G.W. "Television exhibition, Science Museum, London, June–Sept. 1937." J. TELEV. SOC. 2 (June): 265–73. 6 photos of apparatus, including photo of a model of the television camera proposed by Swinton in 1911 (constructed by EMI).

6924 "Television for the deaf." J. TELEV. SOC. 2 (June): 273.

6925 "Field-strength measurements on ultra-short wavelengths." J. TELEV. SOC. 2 (June): 274–9. 4 diags.

6926 "Televising Wimbledon." J. TELEV. SOC. 2 (June): 278, 279. Photo. Reprinted from WORLD RADIO, June 25, 1937.

6927 "Radiolympia, 1937." J. TELEV. SOC. 2 (June): 280. Photos from TELEV. & S.W.W., 2-page table of 14 models, with data.

6928 Baird Television. "Use of the word 'televisor.'" J. TELEV. SOC. 2 (June): 288. Notice about abandoning the registration claim of this word, introduced by Baird in 1925.

6929 "Television seen 90 miles away." J. TELEV. SOC. 2 (June): 288. Comments on reception at the A.E.G. works in Coventry on June 28, 1937. Extract from letter by W.H. Peters, chief radio engineer. Images were recognizable, sync held steady, but the program did not have entertainment value.

6930 Reick, J. "Image brighteners in picture projection technique." V.D.I.Z. 81 (June), No. 6.

6931 "Special television cable." ELECT. REV. 120 (June 1): 889, 890.

6932 Baird Television, V.A. Jones, and T.C. Nuttall. "Electron multiplier circuit." Br. 496,398, June 1, 1937.

6933 Mahl, Hans. "Electron discharge device." U.S. 2,225,197, May 28, 1938, Dec. 24, 1940. In Germany June 2, 1937. Electron lens.

6934 "Television exhibition." ELECT. 118 (June 4): 763.

6935 Baird Television, C. Szegho, and G.A.R. Tomes. "Cathode-ray tube." Br. 496,778, June 4, 1937. Divided from Br. 477,406. Reference to Br. 469,420.

6936 Skellett, A.M. "Electro-optical system." U.S. 2,233,876, June 4, 1937, Mar. 4, 1941. Assigned: B.T.L.

6937 Banks, G.B. (Marconi's). "Electron device." U.S. 2,207,503, July 9, 1940 (RCA). In Britain June 5, 1937. Electron multiplier amplifier.

6938 Blumlein, A.D. "Thermionic valve amplifying circuit." Br. 496,883, June 5, 1937; U.S. 2,218,902, May 18, 1938, Oct. 22, 1940.

6939 Snyder, R.L. "Stabilized oscillating circuit." U.S. 2,168,052, June 5, 1937, Aug. 1, 1939 (Farnsworth Television). Electron multiplier.

6940 Snyder, R.L. "Electron multiplier." U.S. 2,233,878, June 5, 1937, Mar. 4, 1941. Assigned: Farnsworth Television.

6941 Snyder, R.L. "Electron multiplier." Br. 499,714, June 5, 1937, May 23, 1938. Assigned: Farnsworth Television.

6942 Farnsworth Television. "Electron multiplier." Br. 515,097, June 5, 1937, May 23, 1938.

6943 "'See' line in London." N.Y.T. (June 6): X, 8: 8. Coaxial cable.

6944 Blumlein, A.D. "Television receiver." Br. 495,724, June 7, 1937. Assigned: EMI.

6945 Blumlein, A.D., and R.E. Spencer. "Television system." U.S. 2,244,239, June 7, 1937, May 28, 1938, June 4, 1941; Br. 501,966. Assigned: EMI.

6946 de Boer, J.H. "Luminescent screen." U.S. 2,242,644, June 7, 1938, May 20, 1941 (RCA). In Germany June 7, 1937 (N.V. Philips). Secondary amplifier in cathode-ray tube.

6947 Thomas, Albert B. "Electron device." U.S. 2,143,095, June 7, 1937, Jan. 10, 1939. Cathode-ray tube with secondary emission electrodes.

6948 Blumlein, A.D. "Thermionic amplifier." U.S. 2,222,933, May 24, 1938, Nov. 26, 1940; Br. 497,060, June 9, 1937 (EMI). Reference to Br. 479,485 (Aug. 4, 1936).

6949 de Boer, J.H. (Netherlands). "Projection system." U.S. 2,227,070, June 8, 1938, Dec. 31, 1940. Assigned: RCA. In Germany June 9, 1937 (N.V. Philips).

6950 Toulon, P.M.G. "Television transmitter." Br. 512,508, Apr. 21, 1938. In France June 9, 1937.

6951 Diels, K. "Electron device." U.S. 2,197,033, June 16, 1938, Apr. 16, 1940. In Germany June 19, 1937 (Telefunken). Cathode-ray tube.

6952 Schlesinger, K. "Relaxation apparatus." U.S. 2,224,116, Dec. 3, 1940, June 7, 1938. In Germany June 10, 1937 (RAG).

6953 Scophony and J.H. Jeffree. "Light modulator." Br. 492,468, June 10, 1937. References to Br. 439,236, 492,469.

6954 Scophony and G.W. Walton. "Light modulator." Br. 497,069, June 10, 1937. References to Br. 439,236, 492,496.

6955 Scophony and J.H. Jeffree. "Television." Br. 496,964, June 10, 1937. References to Br. 439,236, 451,132.

6956 "Special television cable." ELECT. REV. 120 (June 11): 889.

6957 "Television to-day." TIMES (June 11): 17c, d. Editorial on television exhibition at Science Museum, London.

6958 Dunlap, O.E. Jr. "Radio faces a big riddle in nation-wide television." N.Y.T. (June 13): XI, 10: 1–2. Speculations on networks.

6959 Geiger, M. "Saw-tooth wave generator." U.S. 2,217,401, Sept. 17, 1938, Oct. 8, 1940; Br. 515,903, June 15, 1938. In Germany June 15, 1937 (Telefunken).

6960 Geiger, M., and R. Urtel. "Saw-tooth wave generator." U.S. 2,237,425, June 15, 1938, Apr. 8, 1941. In Germany June 15, 1937 (Telefunken).

6961 Toulon, P.M.G. "Television receiver." Br. 506,877, June 9, 1938. In France June 15, 1937. Addition to Br. 497,367, June 19, 1936. Reference to Br. 497,404 (July 9, 1936).

6962 Teves, M.V., Hajo Hubertus Kraak, and M. Bandringa. "Cathode-ray tube." U.S. 2,197,625, Aug. 9, 1938, Apr. 16, 1940. Assigned: RCA. In Holland June 17, 1937 (N.V. Philips).

6963 Urtel, R. "Saw-tooth wave oscillator." U.S. 2,250,686, Sept. 17, 1938, July 29, 1941. In Germany June 17, 1937 (Telefunken).

6964 "Television exhibition." ENGINEER 163 (June 18): 704, 705. Exhibition at Science Museum, London.

6965 Epstein, D.W. "Cathode-ray tube." U.S. 2,185,590, June 18, 1937, Jan. 2, 1940. Assigned: RCA.

6966 "Television exhibition at the Science Museum." NATURE 139 (June 19): 1077.

6967 Crowther, B.M. "Cathode-ray tube." Br. 497,406, June 19, 1937. Reference to Br. 457,493 (May 30, 1935).

6968 Rudkin, E.P. "Television receiver." Br. 497,371, June 19, 1937.

6969 Truell, John. "Cathode-ray tube." U.S. 2,164,555, June 19, 1937, July 4, 1939. Assigned: RCA.

6970 Geiger, M. "Saw-tooth wave generator." U.S. 2,220,712, Aug. 30, 1938, Nov. 5, 1940; Br. 516,357, June 21, 1938. In Germany June 21, 1937 (Telefunken).

6971 D.S. Loewe and K. Schlesinger. "Television." Br. 520,775, June 20, 1938; U.S. 2,248,556, July 8, 1941. In Germany June 21, 1937. Receiver circuit with cathode-ray tube. Interlaced line method.

6972 Zworykin, V.K. "Electron tube assembly." U.S. 2,249,552, June 22, 1937, July 15, 1941. Assigned: RCA. Divided from U.S. 2,084,364, Dec. 14, 1930. Cathode-ray tube for television.

6973 Snyder, R.L., and Farnsworth Television. "Box element multiplier." U.S. 2,163,966, June 22, 1937, June 27, 1939. Electron multiplier.

6974 Farnsworth Television. "Electron multiplier." Br. 507,448, June 22, 1937, May 23, 1938.

6975 Lorenzen, Rolf. "Television in natural color." U.S. 2,200,285, June 22, 1937, May 14, 1940. Part assigned: George H. Calloghan, Felix Spiegel. Cathode-ray tube with single electron gun and three-color fluorescent screen.

6976 Clavier, André Gabriel, P.F.M. Gloess, and Henri Jean Le Boiteux. "Electron discharge device." U.S. 2,226,696, June 22, 1938, Dec. 31, 1940. In France June 23, 1937 (International Standard Electrical Corp.). Secondary emission amplifier.

6977 Kniepkamp, Heinrich. "Electronic system for cathode-ray tubes." U.S. 2,202,588, June 22, 1938, May 28, 1940. In Germany June 23, 1937 (Siemens & Halske).

6978 Bowie, R.M. "Cathode-ray tube." U.S. 2,211,614, June 24, 1937, Aug. 13, 1940. Divided from U.S. 2,211,613, Aug. 14, 1936.

6979 Diels, K. "Electron device." U.S. 2,199,540, July 6, 1938, May 7, 1940; Br. 516,246, June 24, 1938. In Germany June 14, 1937 (Telefunken). Cathode-ray tube.

6980 Ferranti and M.K. Taylor. "Amplifier." Br. 498,037, June 24, 1937. Wide band for television.

6981 "Home television pictures shown to radio engineers." SCI. N. LETTER 31 (June 26): 405.

6982 Flechsig, W. "Electron multiplier." U.S. 2,221,447, June 17, 1938, Nov. 12, 1940. In Germany June 26, 1937 (Fernseh A.-G.).

6983 Kemp, R.J. "Electrical oscillator and time base circuits." Br. 497,760, June 26, 1937 (Marconi's); U.S. 2,266,047, June 26, 1938, Dec. 16, 1941 (RCA).

6984 Lubszynski, H.G., H. Miller, and J.E.I. Cairns. "Electron discharge device." U.S. 2,151,785, June 25, 1938, Mar. 28, 1939; Br. 499,869, June 26, 1937 (EMI). Reference to 480,946 (June 25, 1936). Cathode-ray tube.

6985 Maloff, I.G., D.W. Epstein, and K.R. Wendt. "Electron gun for cathode-ray tubes." U.S. 2,185,378, June 26, 1937, Jan. 2, 1940. Assigned: RCA.

6986 Prescott, Charles M., Jr. "Photoelectric tube." U.S. 2,151,797, June 26, 1937, Mar. 28, 1939. Assigned: B.T.L.

6987 Iams, H.A. "Electrode arrangement for cathode-ray tubes." U.S. 2,160,021, June 29, 1937, May 30, 1939.

6988 Rupp, H. "Photo-electric device." Br. 497,566, June 29, 1938. Convention date June 29, 1937. Mosaic.

6989 Schade, Otto H. "Electron discharge device." U.S. 2,219,117, June 29, 1937, Oct. 22, 1940. Assigned: RCA.

6990 Urtel, R., M. Geiger, and R. Andrieu. "Impulse segregation circuit." U.S. 2,265,825, Sept. 10, 1938, Dec. 9, 1941; Br. 516,581, June 29, 1938. In Germany June 29, 1937 (Telefunken).

6991 Blain, Albert. "Cathode-ray tube support." U.S. 2,165,779, June 30, 1937, July 11, 1939. Assigned: RCA.

6992 Hinsch, Wilhelm. "Cathode-ray tube." U.S. 2,227,087, June 24, 1938, Dec. 31, 1940. In Germany June 30, 1937 (Siemens & Halske).

6993 Mahl, H. "Electron discharge device." U.S. 2,223,040, June 25, 1938, Nov. 26, 1940 (G.E.). In Germany June 30, 1937 (A.E.G.). Divided U.S. 2,264,541, Dec. 14, 1938, Dec. 3, 1941. Cathode-ray tube.

6994 Lewis, H.M. "Standards in television." ELECTRONICS 10 (July): 10–3, 50, 51. 6 diagrams. See Dec. 1936.

6995 Pieplow, H. "Zur Verstaerkung seht weiter Frequenzbereiche" [On the amplification of very wide frequency bands]. E.N.T. 14 (July): 225–32.

6996 "News bulletin by television." POP. MECH. 68 (July): 97.

6997 "Television newspaper broadcasts words typed on tape." POP. SCI. 131 (July): 23.

6998 "Television pictures shown in color." POP. SCI. 131 (July): 53.

6999 "Television in the news." RADIO-CRAFT 9 (July): 7. News of CBS, RCA, the Marconi Co.

7000 "'Empire State' television shows marked advance." RADIO N. 19 (July): 7, 8, 60, 61.

7001 Gootee, T.E. "Television operators wanted: Requirements." RADIO N. 19 (July): 15, 59.

7002 (Don Lee). RADIO N. 19 (July): 51.

7003 Shelby, Robert Evart, and R.M. Morris. "Television studio design." RCA REV. 2 (July): 14–29. Describes Radio City.

7004 Conklin, J.W., and H.E. Gihring. "Television transmitters operating at high power and ultra-high frequencies." RCA REV. 2 (July): 30–44.

7005 Hudec, E. "Ein neues Zweitmodulationsverfahren für Bildubertragungen auf kurzen Wellen" [A new method of time modulation for television transmission on short waves]. T.F.T. 26 (July): 148–57.

7006 Hermann, D. "Impulse discriminating system." U.S. 2,199,202, July 1, 1938, Apr. 30, 1940. In Germany July 1, 1937 (Telefunken). Television synchronizing.

7007 G.E.C. and W.H. Aldous. "Electron multiplier circuit." Br. 490,265, July 2, 1937.

7008 Van den Bosch, F.J.G. "Electron multiplier." Br. 500,189, July 3, 1937.

7009 Van den Bosch, F.J.G. "Electron multiplier." Br. 503,314, July 3, 1937. Divided from above.

7010 "Televiews from London." N.Y.T. (July 4): X, 10: 8.

7011 A.C. Cossor, L.H. Bedford, and —. Pollock. "Feeder lines for television receivers." Br. 498,475, July 6, 1937.

7012 Ferseh A.-G. "Cathode-ray tube." Br. 516,737, July 6, 1938. In Germany July 6, 1937.

7013 Telefunken. "Cathode-ray tube." Br. 516,743, July 6, 1938. In Germany July 6, 1937.

7014 Brüche, E. "Electron lens for electron discharge tubes." U.S. 2,260,851, June 28, 1938 (G.E.). In Germany July 7, 1937 (A.E.G.). Cathode-ray tube.

7015 Hergenrother, R.C. "Cathode-ray tube system." U.S. 2,174,580, July 8, 1937, Oct. 3, 1939. Assigned: Hazeltine. Camera tube.

7016 Hergenrother, Rudolf C. "Electron multiplier." U.S. 2,246,172, July 8, 1937, June 17, 1941. Assigned: Hazeltine.

7017 A.C. Cossor, E.E. Shelton, and B.C. Fleming-Williams. "Cathode-ray tube." Br. 498,484, July 9, 1937.

7018 A.C. Cossor, E.E. Shelton, and B.C. Fleming-Williams. "Cathode-ray tube." Br. 498,491, July 9, 1937. Divided from above.

7019 Goldsmith, A.N. "Television control system." U.S. 2,172,936, July 9, 1937, Sept. 12, 1939.

7020 Goldsmith, A.N. "Television control." U.S. 2,193,869, July 9, 1937, Mar. 19, 1940.

7021 "Tennis games telecast." N.Y.T. (July 11): X, 8: 5. Tennis matches at Wimbledon.

7022 Baird Television and P.W. Willans. "Cathode-ray tube." Br. 498,824, July 13, 1937.

7023 de Forest, Lee. "Television radial scanning system employing cathode beam." U.S. 2,241,809, July 13, 1937, May 13, 1941. Assigned: Ruth C. Gilman.

7024 Banks, G.B. "Electron multiplier." Br. 498,843, July 15, 1937 (Marconi's); U.S. 2,264,269, July 13, 1938, Dec. 2, 1941 (RCA).

7025 Rudkin, E.P., and G.M. Hellings. "Television." Br. 504,268, July 15, 1937.

7026 Klemperer, O. "Cathode-ray tube." Br. 504,109, July 16, 1937; U.S. 2,227,092, July 9, 1938, Dec. 31, 1940. Assigned: EMI.

7027 Clothier, S.L., and H.C. Hogencamp. "Television apparatus." U.S. 2,163,538, July 17, 1937, June 20, 1930. Assigned: Kolorama Labs. Divided U.S. 2,260,559, June 16, 1939; Oct. 28, 1941.

7028 Clothier, S.L., and H.C. Hogencamp. "Method of and apparatus fo scanning motion-picture film." U.S. 2,163,543, July 17, 1937, June 20, 1939. Assigned: Kolorama Labs.

7029 Clothier, S.L., and H.C. Hogencamp. "Film-scanning apparatus and method." U.S. 2,163,544, July 17, 1937, June 20, 1939. Assigned: Kolorama Labs.

7030 Dunlap, O.E. Jr. "Television as seen at the end of a year's test." N.Y.T. (July 18): X, 10: 1. 2 photos, 1 drawing.

7031 Barthélemy, R. "Electronic television transmitter." U.S. 2,199,608, July 15, 1938, May 7, 1940; Br. 518,311, July 18, 1938. In France July 19, 1937. Assigned: Comp. Gaz. Film scanner.

7032 G.E.C., L.C. Jesty, and —. Sharpe. "Cathode-ray tube." Br. 491,748, July 19, 1937. For optical projection in television receivers.

7033 Takayanagi, K. "Television transmitter." Br. 491,266, July 19, 1937.

7034 Wolff, H.-H. "Television transmission device." U.S. 2,227,414, July 16, 1938, Dec. 31, 1940; Br. 499,454, July 18, 1938 (D.S.

Loewe). In Germany July 19, 1937. Assigned: Loewe Radio Inc.

7035 Banks, G.B. "Electron multiplier." Br. 499,218, July 20, 1937 (Marconi's); U.S. 2,232,158, Apr. 27, 1937, Feb. 18, 1941.

7036 Geiger, M. "Electronic impulse segregating circuits." U.S. 2,281,934, Aug. 9, 1938, May 5, 1942. In Germany July 21, 1937.

7037 Bünger, W. "Contrast cathode-ray tube for television systems." U.S. 2,250,293, July 23, 1938, July 22, 1941. In Germany July 23, 1937.

7038 C. Lorenz A.-G. "Receiver." Br. 501,891, July 8, 1938. In Germany July 23, 1937.

7039 Lemest, R.D. "Television." Br. 519,575, July 25, 1938. Convention date July 24, 1937.

7040 Schlesinger, K. "Cathode-ray tube system." U.S. 2,248,557, June 21, 1938, July 8, 1941; Br. 522,195, July 18, 1938. In Germany July 24, 1937. Assigned: D.S. Loewe.

7041 "Television hailed as aid in teaching." N.Y.T. (July 25): VI, 5: 1. Report of National Research Council.

7042 "New art is reviewed. Programming in London." N.Y.T. (July 25): X, 8: 8.

7043 "Television extensions planned for New York. Madison Square Garden." N.Y.T. (July 25): X, 10: 7.

7044 "Tomorrow's plan." N.Y.T. (July 25): X, 10: 7–8. Editorial on television.

7045 "Television deal signed." N.Y.T. (July 27): 8: 4. Licensing agreement between Farnsworth and A.T.&T.

7046 Baird Television, V.A. Jones, and T.C. Nuttall. "Television transmitter." Br. 499,755, July 27, 1937.

7047 Clay, R.S. "Television." Br. 497,691, July 27, 1937.

7048 Mullard, S.R., C.C. Eaglesfield, and — Archer. "Valve generator circuits." Br. 499,878, July 27, 1937. Saw-tooth generator.

7049 Baird Television and T.M.C. Lance. "Cathode-ray tube." Br. 499,828, July 28, 1937.

7050 Comp. Gaz. "Television transmitter." Br. 517,392, July 26, 1938. In France July 28, 1937. Reference to Br. 514,038 (Feb. 27, 1937).

7051 C. Lorenz A.-G. "Television receiver." Br. 507,809, July 8, 1938. In Germany July 28, 1937.

7052 Baird Television, V.A. Jones, and —. Samson. "Discharge apparatus." Br. 499,785, July 29, 1937.

7053 Ehrenberg, Werner. "Cathode-ray tube." U.S. 2,244,245, July 14, 1938, June 3, 1941. In Britain July 30, 1937 (EMI). Picture tube.

7054 Goldsmith, A.N. "Television system." U.S. 2,168,566, July 30, 1937, Aug. 8, 1939.

7055 Browne, C.O., and H.E. Holman. "Optical image-producing and viewing circuit." U.S. 2,279,555, July 30, 1938, Apr. 14, 1941. In Germany July 31, 1937. Projection screen for television.

7056 Iams, H.A. "Electron discharge apparatus." U.S. 2,213,547, July 31, 1937, Sept. 3, 1940. Assigned: RCA.

7057 Freeman, R.C., and J.D. Schantz. "Video amplifier design." ELECTRONICS 10 (Aug.): 22–5, 60, 62. 10 diagrams, table. Correction in 10 (Nov.): 52.

7058 Somers, F.J. (Farnsworth Television). "Television terms." ELECTRONICS 10 (Aug.): 34. Supplement to June 1937.

7059 Zworykin, V.K., and W.H. Painter. "Development of the projection kinescope." PROC. IRE 25 (Aug.): 937–53. Abstract in ELECTRONICS 10 (June): 7.

7060 Law, R.R. "High current electron gun for projection kinescope." PROC. IRE 25 (Aug.): 954–76. Abstract in ELECTRONICS 10 (June): 8.

7061 Langmuir, David B. "Theoretical limitations of cathode-ray tubes." PROC. IRE 25 (Aug.): 977–91.

7062 Burnett, Carlos E. "A circuit for studying kinescope resolution." PROC. IRE 25 (Aug.): 992–1011. Abstract in ELECTRONICS 10 (June): 8.

7063 Stocker, A.C. "An oscilloscope for television development." PROC. IRE 25 (Aug.): 1012–33.

7064 Iams, H.A., Robert B. Janes, and W.H. Hickok. "The brightness of outdoor scenes and its relation to television transmission." PROC. IRE 25 (Aug.): 1034–47.

7065 Iams, H.A., and A. Rose. "Television pickup tubes with cathode-ray beam scanning." PROC. IRE 25 (Aug.): 1048–70.

7066 Zworykin, V.K., G.A. Morton, and L.E. Flory. "Theory and performance of the iconoscope." PROC. IRE 25 (Aug.): 1071–92. Abstract in ELECTRONICS 10 (June): 9.

7067 Wolf, M. "The enlarged projections of television pictures." PHIL. TECH. REV. 2 (Aug.): 249–53. Small cathode-ray tube projection on ground-glass screen up to 1.0 x 1.20 m.

7068 Gernsback, H. "Television economics." RADIO-CRAFT 9 (Aug.): 69.

7069 "How to make the Radio-Craft 1937 television receiver. Pt. 5." RADIO-CRAFT 9 (Aug.): 72, 73, 101. 2 photos, 5 diags., additional data and corrections.

7070 "A television 'streamer' for spot news." RADIO-CRAFT 9 (Aug.): 76, 77, 101. 7 photos, 3 diags. News transmission and display; 25-line system.

7071 Schrage, W.E. "The balance sheet of television." RADIO-CRAFT 9 (Aug.): 80, 81, 102. 7 diags. Comparison of television and the cinema 1929–37 vs. 1897–1933. Bandwidth, lines, and definition of images 1929–37 (60 to 441 lines). Relative efficiencies of images 1929–37 (3 by 3 to 9 by 12 inches).

7072 "The projection kinescope makes its debut." RADIO-CRAFT 9 (Aug.): 83, 110. 2 photo, diag. Introduced at IRE convention in May 1937.

7073 Washburne, R.D. "Experimental high-fidelity television." RADIO-CRAFT 9 (Aug.): 86, 113. 4 photos. Philco 441-line tests at station WZXE in Philadelphia. Comments by A.F. Murray at the Franklin Institute, Philadelphia, in Jan.

7074 Priess, W. H. "The future status of television programs." RADIO-CRAFT 9 (Aug.): 87, 122. Analysis by the president of the International Television Radio Corp.

7075 "Radio and television in recent public addresses." RADIO-CRAFT 9 (Aug.): 87, 120, 121. Abstract of talks by David Sarnoff before the American Physical Society, and by Thomas F. Joyce of RCA before the Motion Picture Theatre Owners Assn.

7076 Barz, G. "The art of television make-up." RADIO-CRAFT 9 (Aug.): 90, 112.

7077 "Don Lee television inaugurates new sound channels." RADIO-CRAFT 9 (Aug.): 117.

7078 Beal, R.R. (RCA). "Development in television." J. SMPE 29 (Aug.): 121–43.

7079 "Television from standpoint of motion picture producing industry." J. SMPE 29 (Aug.): 144–8. Supplement to report of May 15, 1936.

7080 Babitz, V.A. "A novel scheme for television in colours." TELEV. & S.W.W. 10 (Aug.): 480.

7081 "Radio leaders reveal plans for the new season." N.Y.T. (Aug. 1): X, 10: 1. Brief forecasts for radio and television.

7082 Klemperer, O., and W.D. Wright. "Cathode-ray tube." Br. 496,603, Aug. 3, 1937 (EMI). Addition to Br. 480,857, July 30, 1936.

7083 Kessler, J. "Cathode-ray tube." Br. 500,430, Aug. 4, 1937. Camera tube. Reference to Br. 494,310.

7084 Klemperer, O. "Electron lens." U.S. 2,212,208, July 29, 1938, Aug. 20, 1940. In Britain Aug. 4, 1937 (EMI). Camera tube.

7085 Baird Television and D.M. Johnstone. "Amplifier." Br. 500,217, Aug. 5, 1937. Application for cathode-ray tube.

7086 Lubszynski, H.G., and W.S. Brown. "Cathode-ray tube." Br. 501, 919, Aug. 5, 1937; U.S. 2,256,523, July 29, 1938, Sept. 23, 1941. Assigned: EMI. Camera tube with electron multiplier.

7087 Neidhardt, Peter. "Television system." U.S. 2,244,794, Mar. 14, 1939, June 10, 1941. In Germany Aug. 5, 1937. Assigned: C. Lorenz A.-G.

7088 "German television." ELECT. 119 (Aug. 6): 156. Brief note on Berlin radio exhibition. Fernseh experimental system with 729 lines. Large screens: 3 by 4 feet, 6 by 8 feet. 15-by-21-inch home receivers were obtainable. High-definition service to be started on 441 lines, 50 frames, from three transmitters.

7089 Brett, G.F. "Electron discharge device." U.S. 2,213,540, July 13, 1938, Sept. 3, 1940. In Britain Aug. 7, 1937.

7090 Colberg, R. "Cathode-ray apparatus." U.S. 2,247,350, Aug. 10, 1938, July 1, 1941; Br. 517,839, Aug. 8, 1938. In Germany Aug. 7, 1937. Assigned: Fernseh A.-G.

7091 Plaistowe, D.L. "Television receiver." U.S. 2,268,671, July 16, 1938, Jan. 6, 1942 (RCA); Br. 500,358, Aug. 7, 1937 (Marconi's).

7092 Teves, M.C. "Electron discharge tube comprising a fluorescent screen." U.S. 2,237,123, Nov. 1, 1938, Apr. 1, 1941 (RCA). In Holland Aug. 7, 1937 (N.V. Philips).

7093 Van den Bosch, F.J.G. "Electron multiplier." Br. 500,356, Aug. 7, 1937.

7094 "Television in Los Angeles." N.Y.T. (Aug. 8): X, 10: 2. Schedule of station W6XAO.

7095 "London views the show." N.Y.T. (Aug. 8): X, 10: 5–6. Report by Allen B. Du Mont on a trip to London.

7096 Schunack, J., Rolf Maly, and Frithjof Rudert. "Synchronization system for television." U.S. 2,230,092, Aug. 9, 1938, Jan. 28, 1941. In Germany Aug. 9, 1937 (Fernseh A.-G.).

7097 Schlesinger, K. "Stabilization of television amplifiers." U.S. 2,186,933, Aug. 10, 1937, Jan. 9, 1940. Divided from U.S. 2,163,219, July 23, 1935. Assigned: Loewe Radio.

7098 Roosenstein, H.O. "Magnetic shielding." U.S. 2,292,161, Mar. 2, 1940, Aug. 4, 1941. In Germany Aug. 12, 1937. For cathode-ray tube.

7099 Wolff, H.-H. "Television." U.S. 2,376,645, Aug. 5, 1938, May 22, 1945. In Germany Aug. 12, 1937. Disk with fine spirals for film scanning. Reference to Br. 525,543.

7100 D.S. Loewe and H.-H. Wolff. "Television." Br. 525,542, Aug. 10, 1938. In Germany Aug. 12, 1937.

7101 Batchelor, J.C. "Television reproducer." U.S. 2,186,570, Aug. 13, 1937, Jan. 9, 1940.

7102 Batchelor, J.C. "Entertainment receiver." U.S. 2,205,461, Aug. 13, 1937, June 25, 1940. For use in television.

7103 Cackett, F.W. "Television." Br. 500,875, Aug. 13, 1937 (Telefunken). Receiver circuit.

7104 Zeiss Ikon A.-G. "Cathode-ray tube." Br. 487,372, Oct. 7, 1937. In Germany Aug. 13, 1937. Electron multiplier.

7105 Fernseh A.-G. "Television transmitter." Br. 518,090, Aug. 15, 1938. In Germany Aug. 14, 1937.

7106 "Wide interest in television." N.Y.T. (Aug. 15): X, 10: 3. Report on the meeting of the International Radio Consulting Committee.

7107 Below, F., and Johannes Gunther. "Television synchronization." U.S. 2,265,979, Aug. 10, 1938, Dec. 16, 1941. In Germany Aug. 17, 1937. Assigned: Fernseh A.-G.

7108 Gardner, B.C. "Image analyzing and dissector tube." U.S. 2,200,166, Aug. 17, 1937, May 7, 1940 (Farnsworth Television); Br. 504,526, July 20, 1938. Camera tube.

7109 Zworykin, V.K. "High-frequency oscillation." U.S. 2,271,193, Aug. 18, 1937, Sept. 19, 1939 (RCA).

7110 Batchelor, J.C. "Electro-optical reproducer." U.S. 2,239,769, Aug. 19, 1937, Apr. 29, 1941.

7111 Ehrenberg, W., and S.T. Henderson. "Cathode-ray tube." Br. 500,805, Aug. 19, 1937.

7112 Buschbeck, W. "Oscillation generator." U.S. 2,206,388, Aug. 30, 1938, July 2, 1940. In Germany Aug. 20, 1937 (Telefunken).

7113 Holmes, R.S. "Television receiver." U.S. 2,204,992, Aug. 20, 1937, June 18, 1940. Assigned: RCA.

7114 Marconi's. "Cathode-ray tube." Br. 518,574, Aug. 22, 1938. Convention date Aug. 20, 1937.

7115 Bull, C.S. "Cathode-ray tube." U.S. 2,223,908, Aug. 19, 1938, Dec. 3, 1940; Br. 501,058, Aug. 21, 1937. Assigned: EMI. For mosaic screen. Reference to Br. 434,111.

7116 Soller, W. "Television system and apparatus." U.S. 2,177,676, Aug. 21, 1937, Oct. 31, 1939. Part assigned: W.H. Woodin.

7117 "Television to be seen in miniature theatres." N.Y.T. (Aug. 22): X, 8: 7. Demonstration rooms at London exhibition.

7118 "Europe's race to see by radio spurs television." N.Y.T. (Aug. 22): X, 10: 1–2. Race between Germany and Britain.

7119 "Tele-movies zip on mesh screen." N.Y.T. (Aug. 22): X, 10: 6. Incandescent screen by Farnsworth (U.S. patent 2,089,054).

7120 "Grand Central is site of television studio." N.Y.T. (Aug. 22): X, 10: 6.

7121 McGee, J.D. "Cathode-ray tube." Br. 502,796, Aug. 23, 1937.

7122 Headrick, L.B. "Cathode-ray tube." U.S. 2,202,631, Aug. 24, 1937, May 28, 1940 (RCA).

7123 Marconi's, D.J. Fewings, and R.J. Kemp. "Television receiver." U.S. 2,268,811, Aug. 5, 1938, Jan. 6, 1942; Br. 501,349, Aug. 25, 1937. Automatic volume control.

7124 Hepp, G. "Saw-tooth current circuit." U.S. 2,215,177, June 30, 1938, Sept. 17, 1940 (RCA). In Holland Aug. 25, 1937 (N.V. Philips).

7125 N.V. Philips. "Valve generator." Br. 507,129, Aug. 22, 1938. In Holland Aug. 25, 1937. Saw-tooth generator.

7126 Pye, —., and G. Liebmann. "Cathode-ray tube." Br. 503,074, Aug. 25, 1937.

7127 Pye, —., and G. Liebmann. "Cathode-ray tube." Br. 503,125, Aug. 25, 1937. Divided from above. References to Br. 476,830 (Sept. 4, 1936), 503,126.

7128 Pye, —., and G. Liebmann. "Cathode-ray tube." Br. 503,126, Aug. 25, 1937. Divided from Br. 503,074 above.

7129 Bowie, R.M. "Electron gun structure and assembly." U.S. 2,174,853, Aug. 26, 1937, Oct. 3, 1939.

7130 (E.R.P.) Teal, G.K. "Electron multiplier." U.S. 2,236,041, Aug. 26, 1937, July 14, 1938, Mar. 25, 1941 (Baird Television). Electron discharge device; secondary electron emission assembly.

7131 (G.E.) "Television. Table model receiver with short-wave adaptor." ELECT. 119 (Aug. 27): 242. Photo. Sets by G.E. and other manufacturers.

7132 Lewis, H.M. "Television receiving system." U.S. 2,208,374, Aug. 28, 1937, July 16, 1940. Assigned: Hazeltine.

7133 "Tele-ballet wins applause." N.Y.T. (Aug. 29): X, 10: 8. London.

7134 Hergenrother, R.C. "Cathode-ray signal generating tube." U.S. 2,192,971, Aug. 30, 1937, Mar. 12, 1940; Br. 506,237, July 26, 1938. Assigned: Hazeltine. Camera tube.

7135 N.V. Philips. "Television receiver." Br. 503,179, Aug. 27, 1938. Convention date Aug. 30, 1937.

7136 Schlesinger, K. "Fading regulation in television receivers." U.S. 2,197,900, July 8, 1938, Apr. 23, 1940; Br. 518,740, Aug. 30, 1938. In Germany Aug. 30, 1937 (Loewe Radio). Addition to 464,492 (Dec. 10, 1934).

7137 Schlesinger, K. "Cathode-ray tube." U.S. 2,227,034, July 8, 1938, Dec. 31, 1940. In

Germany Aug. 30, 1937. Assigned: Loewe Radio.

7138 Baird Television and T.C. Nuttall. "Cathode-ray tube." Br. 501,535, Aug. 31, 1937.

7139 Clothier, S.L., and H.C. Hogencamp. "Apparatus and method for television transmission." U.S. 2,163,545, Aug. 31, 1937, June 20, 1939. Assigned: Kolorama Labs.

7140 Kaufmann, Henry W. "Screen for cathode-ray tubes." U.S. 2,160,022, Aug. 31, 1937, May 30, 1939 (RCA).

7141 Marconi's. "Cathode-ray tube." Br. 518,588, Aug. 31, 1938. Convention date Aug. 31, 1937. Incandescent screen.

7142 E.R.P. "Electron multiplier." Br. 502,005, July 13, 1938. Convention date Aug. 31, 1937.

7143 E.R.P. "Electron multiplier." Br. 502,528, July 18, 1938. Convention date Aug. 31, 1937.

7144 Teal, G.K. "Electron discharge apparatus." U.S. 2,196,278, Aug. 31, 1937, Apr. 9, 1940 (B.T.L.).

7145 Wilder, M.P. "Television in Europe." ELECTRONICS 10 (Sept.): 13–5. 4 photos. Report on developments in Germany (German Post Office, Telefunken, Fernseh A.-G.) and in Britain (A.C. Cossor, BBC at Alexandra Palace, Edison, Science Museum).

7146 Raeck, F. "Einheitliche Bezeichnungen in der deutschen Ferseh-technik" [Uniform terminology in German television technology]. FERN. U. TON. 8 (Sept.): 75.

7147 Barthélemy, R. "La teinte moyenne en télévision" [Color shading of television images]. ONDE ELECT. 16 (Sept.): 497–516.

7148 "Television?" RADIO N. 19 (Sept.): 138, 186, 187.

7149 "Big screen television pictures." RADIO N. 19 (Sept.): 143, 173. Law Kinescope cathode-ray system.

7150 Fernseh A.-G. "Television." Br. 518,643, Sept. 1, 1938. In Germany Sept. 1, 1937.

7151 "Television." ELECT. 119 (Sept. 3): 255. Editorial.

7152 "Radiolympia. A review of outstanding features." ELECT. 119 (Sept. 3): 259, 260.

7153 Miller, W.E. "Radio exhibition." ELECT. REV. 121 (Sept. 3): 303.

7154 Baird Television and L.R. Merdler. "Television." Br. 501,753, Sept. 3, 1937.

7155 Van den Bosch, F.J.G. "Cathode-ray tube." Br. 501,816, Sept. 3, 1937.

7156 "Asks television license." N.Y.T. (Sept. 4): 31: 8. NBC requests portable transmitter.

7157 "New camera is promised." N.Y.T. (Sept. 5): X, 10: 7. Report from Europe by Peter C. Goldmark of CBS.

7158 "Radio show features television." N.Y.T. (Sept. 5): X, 10: 8. Radiolympia, London.

7159 G.E.C. and F. Poperwell. "Television." Br. 500,809, Sept. 6, 1937.

7160 Batchelor, J.C. "Line reproducer." U.S. 2,247,112, Sept. 10, 1937, June 24, 1941. With luminescent screen of varying temperature according to invisible radiation.

7161 S.T.C. and V.J. Terry. "Television." Br. 502,098, Sept. 10, 1937.

7162 Kerber, K.H. "Television." Br. 514,021, Aug. 27, 1938. Convention date Sept. 11, 1937.

7163 Klemperer, O. "Cathode-ray tube." U.S. 2,173,257, July 30, 1938, Sept. 19, 1939; Br. 502,104, Sept. 11, 1937 (EMI).

7164 "New tricks in television." N.Y.T. (Sept. 12): XI, 8: 8. Miniature scenery.

7165 Nicoll, F.H., and Bernard Joseph Mayo. "Cathode-ray tube." Br. 505,751, Sept. 13, 1937 (EMI); U.S. 2,229,766, Sept. 13, 1938, June 28, 1941. References to 431,327 (Oct. 3, 1933), 470,004 (Feb. 3, 1936).

7166 Percival, W.S. "Television." Br. 504,021, Sept. 13, 1937 (EMI); U.S. 2,219,936, Sept. 8, 1938, Oct. 29, 1940. Signalling system.

7167 Tihanyi, K. "Cathode-ray tube." Br. 519,168, Sept. 12, 1938. Convention date Sept. 13, 1937.

7168 Baird Television and Denis V. Ridgeway. "Television receiver." Br. 502,351, Sept. 14, 1937.

7169 Van de Velde, H.R.C. (by A. Carpmael). "Television." Br. 502,358, Sept. 14, 1937.

7170 Hoyt, Karl Robert. "Image transmitting and receiving system." U.S. 2,176,136, Sept. 15, 1937, Oct. 17, 1939. Assigned: Radio-Vision Corp. of America.

7171 Marchant, E.W. "Electrical vibrations and their application in television." ENGINEERING 144 (Sept. 17): 330–1.

7172 "18 stations send image." N.Y.T. (Sept. 19): XI, 10: 8. List of licensed U.S. television stations.

7173 "Radio and television courses listed for N.Y.U." N.Y.T. (Sept. 19): XI, 10: 8.

7174 Winckel, F.W. "Fernsehen 1937" [Television in 1937]. Z. FERN. 18 (Sept. 20): 144–7.

7175 Farnsworth Television and B.C. Gardner. "Means for producing an incandescent image." U.S. 2,179,086, Sept. 20, 1937, Nov. 7, 1939. Image projecting system.

7176 Dehn, F.B. "Cathode-ray tube." Br. 493,232, Sept. 21, 1937 (Zeiss Ikon). Camera tube.

7177 Baird Television and E.G.O. Anderson. "Electron multiplier." Br. 502,686, Sept. 22, 1937.

7178 Cork, E.C., and J.L. Pawsey. "Impulse networks." Br. 502,722, Sept. 22, 1937 (EMI). Divided from Br. 488,254.

7179 Percival, W.S. "Electrode with filter for thermionic valve amplifiers." U.S. 2,226,739, Sept. 15, 1938, Dec. 31, 1940; Br. 502,615, Sept. 22, 1937. Addition to Br. 475,490, Feb. 21, 1936.

7180 D.S. Loewe. "Television transmitters." Br. 520,531, Sept. 20, 1938. In Germany Sept. 23, 1937.

7181 Rose, A. "Television transmitting tube." U.S. 2,213,173, Sept. 23, 1937, Aug. 27, 1940. Assigned: RCA.

7182 "Television tests planned outdoors." N.Y.T. (Sept. 24): 23: 1. Concerns NBC.

7183 Shoenberg, I., G.E. Condliffe, and W.F. Tedham. "Cathode-ray tube." U.S. 2,178,973, Sept. 24, 1937, Nov. 7, 1939 (EMI). Divided from patent of Sept. 28, 1934; in Britain Oct. 3, 1933.

7184 Zworykin, V.K. "Cathode-ray tube." U.S. 2,183,634, Sept. 24, 1937, Dec. 19, 1939 (RCA).

7185 S.T.C. "Television modulator." Br. 518,341, Sept. 9, 1938. Convention date Sept. 25, 1937.

7186 "'Grafting' on tele-eye." N.Y.T. (Sept. 26): XI, 10: 3. Discusses RCA patent 2,093,166; electron multiplier in iconoscope.

7187 Clothier, S.L., and H.C. Hogencamp. "Synchronizing method and apparatus." U.S. 2,163,542, Sept. 27, 1937, June 20, 1939. Assigned: Kolorama Labs.

7188 Brown, Charles H. "Electron device." U.S. 2,181,170, Sept. 28, 1937, Nov. 28, 1939 (RCA). Electron multiplier.

7189 Lester, Paul S. "Photoelectric device." U.S. 2,189,988, Sept. 28, 1937, Feb. 13, 1940. Assigned: RCA. Camera tube.

7190 Jones, —. "Electrode for television tubes." U.S. 2,204,251, Sept. 29, 1937, June 11, 1940 (RCA).

7191 Marconi's and Robert B. Jones. "Multiple wireless signal." Br. 519,727, Sept. 28, 1938; convention date Sept. 29, 1937. U.S. 2,204,251, June 11, 1940 (RCA). Television receiver; electrode for television tubes.

7192 Bedford, A.V. "Electrical transmission system." U.S. 2,200,073, Sept. 30, 1937, May 76, 1940 (RCA).

7193 Koch, W.R. "Frequency discharge network." U.S. 2,203,498, Sept. 30, 1937, June 4, 1940.

7194 Rose, A. "Mosaic electrodes." U.S. 2,175,701, Sept. 30, 1937, Oct. 10, 1939. Assigned: RCA. Method of manufacture.

7195 Ver. Gluh. A.-G. "Electron multiplier circuit." Br. 520,882, Sept. 30, 1938. In Germany Sept. 30, 1937.

7196 Zeiss, C. "Light modulator." Br. 509,376, Sept. 24, 1938. Convention date Sept. 30, 1937.

7197 Goldsmith, A.N. "Television economics." COMM. 17 (Oct.): 10, 50–52.

7198 Somers, F.J. "Scanning in television receivers." ELECTRONICS 10 (Oct.): 18–21. 13 diags.

7199 Lewis, H.M., and Arthur V. Loughren. "Television in Great Britain." ELECTRONICS 10 (Oct.): 32–5, 60, 62. 3 photos, 6 diags. Report on British system and results.

7200 Hudec, E. "Die bei der Ubertragung und Wiedergabe von Funkbilden auftretendedn Fehler und ihre Behebung" [Distortion and remedies in the transmission and reception of radio pictures]. E.N.T. 14 (Oct.): 311–25.

7201 Peterson, H.O., and D.R. Goddard. "Field strength observatons of transatlantic signals, 40 to 45 megacycles." PROC. IRE 25 (Oct.): 1291–9.

7202 Mumford, A.H.M. "London-Birmingham coaxial cable system." J. RO.E.E. 30 (Oct.): 206–14. Also see J. RO.E.E. 30 (Jan. 1938): 270–83; 31 (Apr. 1938): 51–56; 31 (July 1938): 132–6.

7203 Collard, J. "London's television twin cable links." J. RO.E.E. 30 (Oct.): 215–21.

7204 "Television range extended." RADIO N. 19 (Oct.): 203, 239. Photo, diagram. RCA field coverage tests at Riverhead, Long Island (NBC): 441 lines. Reception up to 69 miles. Daily transmissions to receivers in homes of engineers and executives.

7205 Sarnoff, David. "Television." RCA REV. 2 (Oct.).

7206 Rife, M.W. "A novel relay broadcast mobile-unit design." RCA REV. 2 (Oct.): 141.

7207 Seeley, Stuart W., and C.N. Kimball. "Analysis and design of video amplifiers." RCA REV. 2 (Oct.): 171–83.

7208 Zworykin, V.K. "Television and the electron." TELEV. 11 (Oct.): 194–8.

7209 Okolicsányi, F. v. "The wave-slot; an optical television system; Scophony supersonic light control." W. ENG. 14 (Oct.): 527–36.

7210 "Olympia 1937, a technical survey." W. ENG. 14 (Oct.): 541–51.

7211 Knoofs, William A. "Image producing system." U.S. 2,196,867, Oct. 1, 1937, Sept. 22, 1938, Feb. 24, 1941.

7212 "Football seen by television." N.Y.T. (Oct. 3): XI, 10: 3. BBC.

7213 "Outdoor tests for tele-eye." N.Y.T. (Oct. 3): XI, 10: 5–6. NBC.

7214 Soller, Walter. "Television modulator system and apparatus." U.S. 2,192,942, Oct. 4, 1937, Mar. 12, 1940. Part assigned: William H. Woodin.

7215 "Television broadcast set. 34th annual business show." N.Y.T. (Oct. 5): 23: 3.

7216 E.R.P. "Valve generator." Br. 509,658, Sept. 29, 1938. In U.S. Oct. 5, 1937.

7217 Marconi's and A.A. Linsell. "Television receiver." Br. 503,419, Oct. 5, 1937.

7218 N.V. Philips. "Electron multiplier." Br. 504,998, Oct. 3, 1938. Convention date Oct. 5, 1937.

7219 D.S. Loewe and K. Schlesinger. "Television transmitter." Br. 519,757, Oct. 3, 1938; U.S. 2,301,820, July 8, 1938, Nov. 10, 1942 (RCA). In Germany Oct. 5, 1937. Modulator for photo-current amplifiers, for television transmitter.

7220 S.T.C. "Television." Br. 504,887, Sept. 9, 1938. Convention date Oct. 5, 1937.

7221 Traub, E. "Television." Br. 502,696, Oct. 5, 1937.

7222 Traub, E. "Television." Br. 503,026, Oct. 5, 1937.

7223 Traub, E. "Television." Br. 503,493, Oct. 5, 1937.

7224 Traub, E. "Television." Br. 503,494, Oct. 5, 1937.

7225 "Television to depict state health activities." N.Y.T. (Oct. 6): 26: 2. Convention of the American Public Health Association in New York.

7226 Baird Television and A.H. Gilbert. "Television." Br. 503,539, Oct. 7, 1937.

7227 Baird Television and V.A. Jones. "Electron multiplier." Br. 503,762, Oct. 7, 1937.

7228 Cawein, M. "Periodic wave generator." U.S. 2,203,519, Oct. 7, 1937, June 4, 1940 (Hazeltine). Relaxation oscillation receiver circuit.

7229 Clothier, S.L., and H.C. Hogencamp. "Apparatus and method for television reception." U.S. 2,163,546, Oct. 8, 1937, June 20, 1939. Assigned: Kolorama Labs.

7230 G.E.C. and A.E. McLeod. "Electron multiplier." Br. 498,703, Oct. 9, 1937. Reference to Br. 478,262 (July 16, 1936).

7231 "Observers report on television here and abroad." N.Y.T. (Oct. 10): XI, 12: 1. Comments by Sarnoff and Paley.

7232 Scophony and F. von Okolicsányi. "Television." Br. 505,653, Oct. 11, 1937. Reference to Br. 439,236 (Mar. 3, 1934).

7233 White, E.L.C., and C.L. Faudell. "Cathode–ray tube television." Br. 505,490, Oct. 11, 1937 (EMI); U.S. 2,222,426, Oct. 8, 1938, Nov. 19, 1940.

7234 Teves, M.C., and M. Bandringa. "Electronic device." U.S. 2,264,488, Sept. 29, 1938, Dec. 2, 1941 (RCA). In Germany Oct. 12, 1937 (N.V. Philips). Camera tube.

7235 N.V. Philips. "Cathode-ray tube." Br. 506,143, Oct. 10, 1938. Convention date Oct. 12, 1937. Camera tube; mosaic.

7236 White, E.L.C. "Television." Br. 503,426, Oct. 12, 1937 (EMI); U.S. 2,235,659, Oct. 5, 1938, Mar. 18, 1941. Electronic apparatus; receiver circuit. Reference to Br. 418,940.

7237 Blumlein, A.D. "Television." Br. 503,555, Oct. 14, 1937; U.S. 2,222,934, Oct. 12, 1938, Nov. 26, 1940. Assigned: EMI. Television transmitting and receiving system.

7238 G.E.C., D.C. Espley, and D.O. Walter. "Television." Br. 505,760, Oct. 14, 1937. Addition to Br. 482,049. References to Br. 464,831 (Oct. 25, 1934), 465,184 (Sept. 4, 1934), 466,051 (Feb. 21, 1936).

7239 "Show of television uses larger screen." N.Y.T. (Oct. 15): 19: 5. Demonstration of 3-by-4-foot screen by RCA.

7240 E.R.P. "Television transmitter." Br. 504,898, Oct. 7, 1938. Convention date Oct. 15, 1937.

7241 White, E.L.C. "Television system." Br. 505,764, Oct. 15, 1937 (EMI); U.S. 2,209,436, Oct. 5, 1938, July 30, 1940. Television receiver.

7242 Davisson, C.J. "Cathode-ray device." U.S. 2,217,198, Oct. 16, 1937, Oct. 8, 1940 (B.T.L.). Cathode-ray tube.

7243 "Television as a celestial show offers Jerseyites front row seat." N.Y.T. (Oct. 17): XI, 12: 2. Speech by A.N. Goldsmith.

7244 Baird Television and E.B. King. "Cathode-ray tube." Br. 504,188, Oct. 20, 1937. Mosaic screen.

7245 Clothier, S.L., and H.C. Hogencamp. "Method and system for television transmission." U.S. 2,201,554, Oct. 20, 1937, May 21, 1940. Assigned: Kolorama Labs.

7246 D.S. Loewe. "Television cathode-ray tube." Br. 521,638, Oct. 17, 1938. In Germany Oct. 20, 1937. Addition to Br. 423,427, June 27, 1932.

7247 Schlesinger, K., and D.S. Loewe. "Electrostatic wide-angle deflector." U.S. 2,227,036, July 23, 1938, Dec. 31, 1940. In Germany Oct. 20, 1937. For television.

7248 Epstein, D.W. "Cathode-ray tube." U.S. 2,206,666, Oct. 22, 1937, July 2, 1940. Assigned: RCA.

7249 G.E.C. and L.C. Jesty. "Television receiver." Br. 496,835, Oct. 22, 1937.

7250 Schlesinger, K. "Television tube." U.S. 2,248,558, July 23, 1938, July 8, 1941. In Germany Oct. 22, 1937. Assigned: Loewe Radio.

7251 White, E.L.C., and Maurice Geoffrey Harker. "Thermionic valve amplifier." Br. 502,578, Oct. 22, 1937; U.S. 2,221,122, Oct. 21, 1938, Nov. 12, 1940.

7252 Fernseh A.-G. and H. Bähring. "Television." Br. 502,489, Oct. 24, 1938; U.S. 2,250,884, Oct. 22, 1938, July 29, 1941. In Germany Oct. 23, 1937. Centering arrangement for cathode-ray beams, in a scanning system.

7253 "A grotesque art." N.Y.T. (Oct. 24): XI, 12: 5–6. Make-up for television.

7254 "Television at the zoo." N.Y.T. (Oct. 24): XI, 12: 8. London.

7255 "Watching a radio shadow show." N.Y.T. (Oct. 24): XI, 14: 3. Parallel in quality between television and early movies.

7256 Farnsworth Television. "Electron control device." U.S. 2,286,076, Apr. 3, 1940, June 9, 1942. In Germany Oct. 25, 1937. Assigned: Farnsworth Television and Radio Corp.

7257 Iams, H.A. "Television transmitting tube." U.S. 2,195,489, Oct. 26, 1937, Apr. 2, 1940; Br. 520,106, Oct. 26, 1938.

7258 McGee, J.D. "Manufacture of grids for use in electron discharge device." Br. 504,200, Oct. 26, 1937; U.S. 2,254,616, Oct. 26, 1937, Sept. 2, 1941. Reference to Br. 457,497.

7259 McGee, J.D. "Electron multiplier." Br. 504,927, Oct. 28, 1937; U.S. 2,254,617, Oct. 27, 1938, Sept. 2, 1941. Assigned: EMI.

7260 Cawein, M. "Television system." U.S. 2,203,520, Oct. 29, 1937, June 4, 1940. Assigned: Hazeltine.

7261 Iams, H.A. "Television transmitting tube." U.S. 2,175,692, Oct. 29, 1937, Oct. 10, 1939. Assigned: RCA.

7262 Blain, A. "Radio apparatus." U.S. 2,203,811, Oct. 30, 1937, June 11, 1940. Assigned: RCA. Television receiver.

7263 Rajchman, J.A., and Eugene W. Pike. "Electron multiplier." U.S. 2,231,682, Oct. 30, 1937, Feb. 11, 1940. Assigned: RCA.

7264 "Coaxial cable television transmission." COMM. 17 (Nov.): 9–11. New York to Philadelphia.

7265 Murray, A.F. (RMA). "Television frequencies and standards." COMM. 17 (Nov.): 20–2.

7266 Hughes, L.E.C. "The practics of television." DISCOVERY 18 (Nov.): 329–31. 1 diag. Survey of Marconi-EMI system, studio practice, etc.

7267 Maloff, I.G., and D.W. Epstein. "Screens for television tubes." ELECTRONICS 10 (Nov.): 31–4. Correction 10 (Nov.): 54.

7268 Ardenne, M. v. "Distortion of saw-tooth wave forms." ELECTRONICS 10 (Nov.): 36–8.

7269 Maloff, I.G. "Direct viewing type cathode-ray tube for large television images." PROC. IRE 25 (Nov.). Summary of article in RCA REV. 2 (Jan. 1938): 289–96.

7270 Banneitz, F. "Die neue Fernsehnorm der deutschen Reichspost" [The new television standards of the German Post Office]. FERN. U. TON. 8 (Nov.): 85.

7271 "Television receiver for experimenters." POP. MECH. 68 (Nov.): 237. 3 photos.

7272 Du Mont, A.B. "Is television in America asleep?" RADIO-CRAFT 9 (Nov.): 268,306. 2 photos. Frank opinions about television in England, France, Belgium, and Holland, following visits there.

7273 "German 8 x 10 ft. television image." RADIO-CRAFT 9 (Nov.): 271, 318. 5 illus. Telefunken's combined audio and video public address system displayed at Berlin radio exhibition.

7274 Sanabria, U.A. "Television students learn by making cathode-ray tubes, pt. 1." RADIO-CRAFT 9 (Nov.): 284–309, 319. 2 photos. Data suppled by American Television Institute.

7275 Vogel, T. "La qualité des images dans les divers systèmes de télévision" [The quality of images in different television systems]. TECH. MOD. 29 (Nov.): 713–7. On picture quality in Farns-worth, PTT Française, Scophony, and Zworykin systems.

7276 Nicoll, F.H. "Electron lenses." Br. 504,802, Nov. 1, 1937. Assigned: EMI.

7277 Nicoll, F.H. "Permanent magnet device for producing axially symmetrical magnetic fields." U.S. 2,200,039, Oct. 28, 1938, May 7, 1940. In Britain Nov. 1, 1937. Cathode-ray-tube focusing.

7278 G.E.C. and D.C. Espley. "Television transmission." Br. 502,051, Nov. 2, 1937.

7279 Faudell, C.L. "Valve generator circuits." Br. 502,022, Nov. 3, 1937; U.S. 2,254,031, Nov. 1, 1938, Aug. 26, 1941. Assigned: EMI.

7280 Holman, H.E. "Method for producing thin strips of material on supporting surfaces." Br. 505,183, Nov. 3, 1937; U.S. 2,279,567, Oct. 26, 1938, Apr. 14, 1942. References to Br. 294,987, 381,306, 454,937, 455,123, 480,918, 500,805.

7281 Langmuir, I. "Image reproduction." U.S. 2,198,479, Nov. 3, 1937, Apr. 23, 1940.

7282 McGee, J.D., and H.G. Lubszynski. "Electron discharge device." Br. 510,696, Nov. 4, 1937; U.S. 2,277,246, Nov. 4, 1938, Mar. 24, 1942. Assigned: EMI. Cathode-ray tube.

7283 Percival, W.S. "Valve generator circuits." Br. 505,252, Nov. 4, 1937; U.S. 2,254,087, Oct. 27, 1938, Aug. 26, 1941. Assigned: EMI.

7284 Carnahan, C.W. "Television receiving system." U.S. 2,227,630, Nov. 5, 1937, Jan. 7, 1941.

7285 Dovraston, G., and G.E. Graham. "Compensation for local variations in the brightness of a scanning system." Br. 505.197, Nov. 5, 1937; U.S. 2,188,679, May 27, 1939, Jan. 30, 1940. Assigned: Baird Television.

7286 Blumlein, A.D., and E.L. White. "Background reinserter." Br. 505,480, Nov. 6, 1937; U.S. 2,227,056, Nov. 7, 1938, Dec. 31, 1940. Assigned: EMI. References to Br. 422,906 and item below.

7287 Blumlein, A.D., and E.L. White. "Thermionic valve amplifier." Br. 507,239, Nov. 6, 1937; U.S. 2,241,534, Nov. 7, 1938, May 13, 1941. Assigned: EMI. References to Br. 422,906, 449,242, 458,585, 497,637, and item above.

7288 Maloff, I.G. "Electron device." U.S. 2,206,413, Nov. 9, 1937, July 2, 1940. Assigned: RCA.

7289 Lubszynski, H.G., and J.D. McGee. "Image dissector." Br. 505,618, Nov. 10, 1937; U.S. 2,237,679, Nov. 10, 1938, Apr. 8, 1941. Assigned: EMI. Reference to Br. 482,959 (Oct. 8, 1936).

7290 G.E.C. and D.C. Espley. "Television transmission." Br. 498,625, Nov. 11, 1937. References to Br. 482,049, 472,160.

7291 Faudell, C.L., and N. Atkinson. "Television receiver." Br. 505,899, Nov. 13, 1937. Assigned: EMI.

7292 G.E.C. and D.C. Espley. "Television transmitter." Br. 498,945, Nov. 15, 1937.

7293 Blain, A. "Cathode-ray tube." U.S. 2,207,777, Nov. 16, 1937, July 16, 1940; Br. 521,356, Nov. 16, 1938. Addition to Br. 495,016, Feb. 28, 1936.

7294 "EMI super-emitron camera." W.W. 41 (Nov. 18): 497–8.

7295 EMI and —. Clark. "Technical advances in television." ELECT. (Nov. 19): 592.

7296 Ives, Ronald L. "Television and the coaxial cable." SCIENCE 86 (Nov. 19): supp. 11-12. Also SCI. N. LETTER 31 (Nov. 20): 326–7.

7297 Schlesinger, K. "Testing generator for image reproduction systems." U.S. 2,227, 037, Oct. 7, 1938, Dec. 31, 1940; Br. 523,050, Nov. 22, 1938. In Germany Nov. 24, 1937. Assigned: Loewe Radio.

7298 E.R.P. "Electron multiplier." Br. 521,077, Nov. 18, 1938. Convention date Nov. 26, 1937.

7299 Cawein, M. "Periodic wave generation system." U.S. 2,226,706, Nov. 29, 1937, Dec. 31, 1940. Assigned: Hazeltine. Television circuit; receiver diagram shows block with video amplifiers, modulators, limiters.

7300 Harnett, Daniel E. "Television scanning system." U.S. 2,203,528, Nov. 29, 1937, June 4, 1940; Br. 511,733, Nov. 4, 1938. Assigned: Hazeltine.

7301 Snyder, R.L. "Electron multiplier tube." U.S. 2,172,155, Nov. 29, 1937, Sept. 5, 1939. Assigned: Farnsworth Television and Radio Corp.

7302 Snyder, R.L. "Electron multiplier." U.S. 2,226,077, Nov. 29, 1937, Dec. 24, 1940; Br. 521,299, Nov. 14, 1938.

7303 Gallup, J.L. "Electrode structure for television transmitting tube." U.S. 2,162,808, Nov. 30, 1937, June 20, 1939. Assigned: RCA.

7304 Janes, R.B. "Television transmitting tube and electrode structure." U.S. 2,171,213, Nov. 30, 1937, Aug. 29, 1939. Assigned: RCA. Br. 521,992, Nov. 30, 1938. Assigned: Marconi's.

7305 Snyder, Richard L. Jr. "Electron multiplier." U.S. 2,231,691, Nov. 30, 1937, Feb. 11, 1941. Assigned: RCA.

7306 "Rochester, 1937." ELECTRONICS 10 (Dec.): 11–5, 67–71. Photo, 8 diags. Burnett (RCA) on the Monoscope; Bigley (Philco) on synchronizing pulses; G.A. Fink and R.M. Bowie on screen color of cathode-ray tube; A.V. Bedford (RCA) on figure of noise etc.; I.G. Maloff (RCA) on large (3 ft.) cathode-ray tube; W.N. Parker (Philco) on wideband modulator; A.F. Murray (RMA) on television standards; E.M. Bartelink (G.E.) on wide-band amplifiers; C.B.H. (RCA) on space-charge limitations on the focus of electron beams.

7307 "Bell Labs test coaxial cable." ELECTRONICS 10 (Dec.): 18–9. 3 photos. Video signal, produced by scanning film at 240 lines, 24 frames per second, is applied to coaxial system linking New York and Philadelphia.

7308 West, S. "See for yourself." ELECTRONICS 10 (Dec.): 32. 7 photos showing reception 70 miles from London at 40 MHz.

7309 Hudec, E. "Die Schwund- und Echoerscheinungen bei der Ubertragung von Funkbildern und ihre Behebung" [Fading and echo phenomena in the transmission of radio pictures and their remedies]. E.N.T. 14 (Dec.): 388–408.

7310 "Neue Fernseh-Aufnahmeraume in Berlin" [New television studios in Berlin]. FERN. U. TON. 8 (Dec.): 97.

7311 Agricola, A. "Ein Fernseh-Kabelverstärker für 1.3 MHz Trägerfrequenz" [A television cable amplifier for 1.3 MHz carrier frequency]. T.F.T. 26 (Dec.): 275.

7312 Denison, V. "Two-way scanning in television." TECH. PHYS. OF USSR 4, no. 5 (Dec.): 383–403.

7313 "Television in Germany." POP. MECH. 68 (Dec.): 894–5. 8 photos.

7314 "Trucks house mobile television studio." POP. SCI. 131 (Dec.): 20.

7315 Wilder, M.P. "Introduction to modern cathode-ray television reception." QST 21 (Dec.): 11.

7316 "Television now out on the corner." RADIO-CRAFT 9 (Dec.): 326. NBC mobile station; news from Britain, with comments by Baird and H.H. Beverage.

7317 Sanabria, U.A. "Television students earn by making cathode-ray tubes, pt. 2." RADIO-CRAFT 9 (Dec.): 335, 368. 2 photos.

7318 "How soon television?" RADIO N. 19 (Dec.): 327–8.

7319 "Television demonstration at fall convention." J. SMPE 29 (Dec.): 596–602.

7320 Traub, E.H. "Television at the Berlin radio exhibition, 1937." J. TELEV. SOC. 2 (Dec.): 289–97. 10 photos, 3 diags. Fernseh A.-G., Telefunken, D.S. Loewe, C. Lorenz A.-G., German Post Office, Tekade.

7321 Nield, J.H. "Television reception at 60 miles." J. TELEV. SOC. 2 (Dec.): 297. 4 photos. Report on reception at Herne Bay, Kent, Nov. 5.

7322 Davies, K.S. "Some considerations in the design of the Murphy television receiver." J. TELEV. SOC. 2 (Dec.): 299–305. 4 diags.

7323 "Cinema television." J. TELEV. SOC. 2 (Dec.): 310–2.

7324 Sanabria, U.A. "Interlaced scanning." J. TELEV. SOC. 2 (Dec.): 313–5. 2 diags.

7325 Jesty, L.C., and G.T. Winch. "Television images: An analysis of their essential qualities." J. TELEV. SOC. 2 (Dec.): 316–34. 3 photos, 20 graphs and diags, 4 tables. Also discussed Mar. 1938, pp. 395–96; correction p. 396.

7326 "Commercial television." J. TELEV. SOC. 2 (Dec.): 336. Report on annual meeting of Baird Television Ltd.

7327 "Tenth anniversary dinner." J. TELEV. SOC. 2 (Dec.): supplement. 4 pp. 5 photos. Television Society anniversary.

7328 Banks, G.B., and Marconi's. "Electron multipliers." Br. 506,661, Dec. 1, 1937; U.S. 2,221,070, Oct. 7, 1938, Nov. 12, 1940. Assigned: RCA.

7329 Myers, L.M. "Luminescent screen." Br. 506,798, Dec. 1, 1937; U.S. 2,241,215, Nov. 26, 1938, May 6, 1941. Assigned: RCA.

7330 Kemp, R.J. "Radio direction finder." Br. 506,743, Dec. 1, 1937; U.S. 2,293,739, Nov. 26, 1938, Aug. 25, 1942. Assigned: RCA.

7331 Cawein, M. "Television synchronizing system." U.S. 2,230,284, Dec. 2, 1937, Feb. 4, 1941; Br. 513,984, Nov. 10, 1938. Assigned: Hazeltine.

7332 Lewis, H.M. "Synchronizing and background control for television receivers." U.S. 2,249,532, Dec. 2, 1937, July 15, 1941. Assigned: Hazeltine.

7333 McGee, J.D. "Mosaic screen." Br. 506,800, Dec. 2, 1937. Assigned: EMI.

7334 Percival, W.S. "Oscillation generator." Br. 508,845, Dec. 2, 1937; U.S. 2,331,723, Dec. 1, 1938, Oct. 12, 1943. Assigned: EMI.

7335 Maguire, I.L. "Television system." U.S. 2,211,066, Nov. 16, 1938, Aug. 13, 1940; Br. 521,477, Nov. 21, 1938. In Australia Dec. 3, 1937.

7336 McGee, J.D. "Cathode-ray tube." Br. 507,059, Dec. 3, 1937; U.S. 2,237,681, Dec. 2, 1938, Apr. 8, 1941. Assigned: EMI. References to Br. 442,666, 475,928, 506,800.

7337 Strupf, F., and F. Ring. "Discharge apparatus." Br. 506,998, Dec. 4, 1937. Reference to Br. 506,911 (Oct. 26, 1936).

7338 Okolicsányi, F. v., and Scophony. "Television receiver." Br. 507,146, Dec. 7, 1937.

7339 Blumlein, A.D. "Radio receiver." U.S. 2,227,057, Dec. 7, 1938, Dec. 31, 1940. In Britain Dec. 8, 1937. Assigned: EMI.

7340 Iams, H.A. "Electronic device." U.S. 2,286,280, Dec. 14, 1937, June 16, 1942. Assigned: RCA.

7341 Iams, H.A. "Electronic device." U.S. 2,322,361, Dec. 14, 1937, June 22, 1943. Assigned: RCA.

7342 Bedford, A.V. "Television system." U.S. Dec. 18, 1937, June 2, 1942. Assigned: RCA.

7343 Kell, R.D. "Television apparatus." U.S. 2, 166,688, Dec. 18, 1937, July 18, 1939. Assigned: RCA.

7344 Murphy, —., and —. Hawkins. "Valve generator circuit." Br. 511,600, Dec. 20, 1937.

7345 Sieger, J., F. von Okolicsányi, and Scophony. "Light valve." Br. 508,065, Dec. 21, 1937. References to Br. 439,236, 482,665.

7346 Ballard, R.C. "View transmitter system." U.S. 2,217,831, Dec. 23, 1937, Oct. 15, 1940.

7347 Brolly, A.H. "Means for generating a pulse in a cathode-ray tube." U.S. 2,237,334, Dec. 23, 1937, Apr. 8, 1941. Original U.S. 2,107,778, Oct. 16, 1933.

7348 Hermann, D. "Oscillator circuit." U.S. 2,237,668, Dec. 22, 1938, Apr. 8., 1941. In Germany Dec. 23, 1937.

7349 Leonard, J. "Television receiver." Br. 508,076, Dec. 23, 1937.

7350 Roosenstein, H.O., and Ernst Reimann. "Television cabinet switch." U.S. 2,259,393, Dec. 14, 1938, Oct. 14, 1941. In Germany Dec. 23, 1937. Assigned: Telefunken.

7351 Schlesinger, K. "Television amplifier system." U.S. 2,248,560, Oct. 7, 1938, July 8, 1941. In Germany Dec. 23, 1937. Assigned: Loewe Radio.

7352 Urtel, R. "Cathode-ray deflecting circuit." U.S. 2,239,865, Feb. 1, 1939, Apr. 29, 1941. In Germany Dec. 23, 1937.

7353 Truefitt, E.V. "Television receiver." Br. 508,038, Dec. 24, 1937.

7354 Blumlein, A.D. "Television circuit." Br. 508,377, Dec. 24, 1937; U.S. 2,244,240, Dec. 22, 1938, June 3, 1941. Assigned: EMI. Divided to Br. 512,109 (below).

7355 Blumlein, A.D., and —. White. "Television circuit." Br. 512,109, Dec. 24, 1937; U.S. 2,258,732, Dec. 22, 1938, Oct. 14, 1941. Divided from Br. 508,377 (above).

7356 Linder, E.G. "Electron multiplier." U.S. 2,220,161, Dec. 24, 1937, Nov. 5, 1940; Br. 508,037, Dec. 24, 1937. Divided from U.S. 2,156,269, Nov. 30, 1935. Assigned: RCA.

7357 Goldsmith, A.N. "Television-telephone system." U.S. 2,236,501, Dec. 27, 1937, Apr. 1, 1941.

7358 Seeley, S.W. "Television system." U.S. 2,220,977, Dec. 27, 1937, Nov. 12, 1940. Assigned: RCA.

7359 Hollmann, H.E. "Oscillating generator." U.S. 2,245,669, Dec. 17, 1938, June 17, 1941. In Germany Dec. 29, 1937.

7360 Knick, U. "System of synchronizing television transmission." U.S. 2,265,290, Apr. 13, 1940, Dec. 9, 1941. In Germany Dec. 30, 1937. Assigned: Fernseh A.-G. Reference to Br. 523,457 (Dec. 30, 1938).

7361 "Television programmes." ELECT. 119 (Dec. 31): 800. Note on Baird Television Ltd. meeting of Dec. 29 and critical comments of Sir H. Green.

7362 Marcus, —. (G.E.). "Cathode-ray tube." Br. 508,552, Dec. 31, 1937.

7363 Skellett, A.M. "Electronic device." U.S. 2,244,318, Dec. 31, 1937, June 3, 1941.

7364 "Electron multiplier." Br. 523,281, Dec. 30, 1938. Convention date Dec. 31, 1937.

7365 THE ABC OF TELEVISION. New York: Short Wave and Television, 1937. 36 pp., illus.

7366 BBC. THE LONDON TELEVISION STATION: ALEXANDRA PALACE. Revised edition. London: BBC, 1937. 36 pp.

7367 Camm, F.J. NEWNES TELEVISION AND SHORT-WAVE HANDBOOK. Third edition. London: G. Newnes, 1937. 255 pp., illus.

7368 Garratt, Gerald R.M., and G. Parr (eds.). TELEVISION: AN ACCOUNT OF THE DEVELOPMENT AND GENERAL PRINCIPLES OF TELEVISION AS ILLUSTRATED BY A SPECIAL EXHIBITION HELD AT THE SCIENCE MUSEUM, JUNE–SEPT. 1937. Intro. by E.E.B. Mackintosh. London, 1937. 64 pp., 16 illus. Reprinted in 8837.

7369 Hutchinson, R.W. TELEVISION UP-TO-DATE. Second edition. London: University Tutorial Press, 1937. 211 pp., illus. First edition published in 1935.

7370 Memardinquer, P. LA TELEVISION ET SES PROGRES: RADIOVISION A BASSE

ET HAUTE DEFINITION, TELECINEMATOGRAPHE, TELEVISION CATHODIQUE [Television and its progress: Low- and high-definition radiovision, telecinematography, cathode-ray television]. Second edition. Preface by A. Dunod. xiv + 335 pp. Paris: Dunod, 1937. First edition Sept. 1933.

7371 Board of Education (City of London). TELEVISION. London: Board of Education (City of London), 1937.

7372 Parr, G. THE LOW-VOLTAGE CATHODE-RAY TUBE AND ITS APPLICATIONS. London: Chapman & Hall, 1937. x + 177 pp. 76 photos and diags.

7373 RCA TELEVISION (COLLECTED PAPERS), Vol. 2. New York: RCA Institutes Technical Presentation, 1937. vii + 435 pp. Volume 1 published in 1936 (6582).

7374 Reyner, J.H. TELEVISION: THEORY AND PRACTICE. Second edition. London: Chapman & Hall, 1937. First edition 1934. xi + 224 pp. 126 diags., 24 plates.

7375 Schröter, F., et al. FERNSEHEN. Berlin: J. Springer, 1937. 260 pp., 228 illus. Eight lectures given late in 1936 on television and electron optics.

7376 Tyers, Paul D. TELEVISION RECEPTION TECHNIQUE. London: Pitman, 1937. x + 144 pp., 85 illus. Electronic systems.

7377 Wilson, John C. TELEVISION ENGINEERING. Foreword by J.L. Baird. London: Sir Isaac Pitmann, 1937. xv + 492 pp., 276 illus. Comprehensive text devoted almost entirely to mechanical systems with full analyses of principles and techniques covering a wide range of proposals, inventions and methods. Appendices, refs.

7378 Witts, Alfred T. TELEVISION CYCLOPAEDIA. New York: Van Nostrand, 1937. 151 pp., diagrams. Technical dictionary.

CHAPTER 18

INTERNATIONAL SCENE: 1938

7379 Everest, F. Alton. "Amplification problems of television." COMM. 18 (Jan.): 15-9, 38.

7380 "Reviewing the video art." ELECTRONICS 11 (Jan.): 9-11. Abstract of Radio Manufacturers Association committee meeting at Rochester, Nov. 1937. Reports by Hazeltine, BTL, Philco, CBS on technical aspects, problems, and performances in U.S. and Britain. 3 photos.

7381 Everest, F. Alton. "Wide-band television amplifiers." ELECTRONICS 11 (Jan.): 16-9. Continued in May issue.

7382 Heimann, W., and K. Wemheuer. "Beitrag zur Wirkungsweise des Elektronenstrahl-Bildabtasters (Contributions to the operation of the electron beam picture scanner)." E.N.T. 15 (Jan.): 1-9.

7383 Zworykin, V.K., G.A. Morton, and L.E. Flory. "Theory and performance of the Iconoscope." J. IEE 82 (Jan.): 105-14. Continued in 82 (May): 561-2.

7384 van der Mark, J. "Transportable television installation." PHIL. TECH. REV. 3 (Jan.): 1-4.

7385 "Television looks for sponsors." RADIO-CRAFT 9 (Jan.): 390.

7386 "Flickerless film-television." RADIO-CRAFT 9 (Jan.): 395. Continually moving film, drum with oscillating mirrors, fixed mirrors, and Iconoscope for 441-line screen. European design; name not given.

7387 Sanabria, U.A. "Television students learn by making cathode-ray tubes. Pt. 3." RADIO-CRAFT 9 (Jan.): 403, 439-40. 2 photos.

7388 Sprayberry, F.L. "Practical lessons in television." RADIO N. 19 (Jan.): 394-6. Continued in (Feb.) 474-6, (Mar.) 526-8.

7389 Burnap, R.S. "Television cathode-ray tubes for the amateur." RCA REV. 2 (Jan.): 297.

7390 B.T.-H. and D. Gabor. "Cathode-ray tubes." Br. 508,520, Jan. 3, 1938; U.S. 2,212,396, Aug. 4, 1940, Aug. 20, 1940. Electronic deflector system.

7391 G.E.C. and D.C. Espley. "Television." Br. 503,692, Jan. 3, 1938.

7392 G.E.C. and D.C. Espley. "Television." Br. 502,509, Jan. 3, 1938.

7393 Hepp, Gerard. "Amplifier." U.S. 2,212,204, Jan. 4, 1939, Aug. 20, 1940. In Germany Jan. 4, 1938 (N.V. Philips). Wide band.

7394 Hepp, G. "Amplifier." U.S. 2,212,205, Jan. 4, 1939, Aug. 20, 1940. In Germany Jan. 4, 1938. Wide band.

7395 Klemperer, O. "Electron discharge device utilizing electron multiplication." U.S. 2,203,225, Jan. 4, 1939, June 4, 1940. Br. 508,852, Jan. 4, 1938. Assigned: EMI.

7396 Marconi's and G.B. Banks. "Television." Br. 508,695, Jan. 4, 1938. Interfilm.

7397 Nicoll, F.H., and B.J. Mayo. "Electron gun." Br. 510,702, Jan. 4, 1938; U.S. 2,226,439, Dec. 31, 1938, Dec. 24, 1940.

7398 Farnsworth, P.T. "Electron amplifier." U.S. 2,239,149, Jan. 5, 1938, Apr. 22, 1941. Br. 525,402, Dec. 22, 1938.

7399 Toulon, P.M.G. "Thermionic distributors for television." Br. 523,263, Dec. 29, 1938. In France Jan. 5, 1938.

7400 "Television troubles." ELECT. 120 (Jan. 7): 1-2. Editorial.

7401 Theile, R. "Television transmitting tube." U.S. 2,266,920, Jan. 9, 1939, Dec. 23, 1941. In Germany Jan. 8, 1938 (Telefunken). Camera tube.

7402 Du Mont, A.B. "Method and system for television communication." U.S. 2,157,749, Jan. 11, 1938, May 9, 1939. Assigned: A.B. Du Mont Labs, Inc.

7403 Kemp, Lloyd A.W.E. "Magnetic lens system." U.S. 2,240,700, Jan. 6, 1939, May 6, 1941. Br. Jan. 11, 1938 (G.E.C.).

7404 McGee, J.D., H.G. Lubszynski, and F. Blythen. "Television transmitting system." U.S. 2,215,186, Jan. 7, 1939, Sept. 17, 1940. Br. Jan. 11, 1938. Assigned: EMI.

7405 Shelby, R.E. "Television system." U.S. 2,222,957, Jan. 14, 1938, Nov. 26, 1940. Assigned: RCA.

7406 Weiss, G. "Electron multiplier." Br. 523,863, Jan. 17, 1939. Convention Jan. 17, 1938.

7407 B.T.-H. "Electron multiplier." Br. 523,982, Jan. 18, 1939. Convention Jan. 18, 1938.

7408 Scophony and A.H. Rosenthal. "Cathode-ray tube." Br. 508,712, Jan. 18, 1938.

7409 Scophony and A.H. Rosenthal. "Television receiving system." U.S. 2,270,232, Jan. 12, 1939, Jan. 20, 1942. Br. 509,766, Jan. 18, 1938.

7410 Tingley, G.R. "Continuing the deflection of cathode rays and like means." U.S. 2,260,546, May 18, 1939, Oct. 28, 1941. Br. 509,430, Jan. 17, 1938 (Baird Television). Assigned: Cinema-Television Ltd.

7411 Valensi, G. "Television in colors." U.S. 2,375,966, Jan. 14, 1939, May 15, 1945. Br. 524,443, Jan. 16, 1939. In France Jan. 17, 1938. Assigned: Alien Properties Custodian.

7412 Weiss, G. "Television transmitter." Br. 523,862, Jan. 17, 1939. Convention Jan. 17, 1938.

7413 Baird Television and V.A. Jones. "Discharge apparatus." Br. 513,628, Jan. 19, 1938.

7414 Baird Television and T.C. Nuttall. "Television transmitter." Br. 493,279, Jan. 20, 1938.

7415 Geiger, M. "Saw-tooth current generator." U.S. 2,227,075, Jan. 19, 1939, Dec. 31, 1940. Br. 524,039, Jan. 20, 1939. In Germany Jan. 20, 1938 (Telefunken).

7416 Hickok, W.H. "Electrode structure." U.S. 2,189,985, Jan. 20, 1938, Feb. 13, 1940. Assigned: RCA. Camera tube and mosaic structure.

7417 (Shaw, H.J.) "Television: Some conclusions resulting from experiment of the high-definition service." ELECT. 120 (Jan. 21): 83. Report of demonstration and talk by H.J. Shaw at Magnet House on Jan. 11.

7418 Scophony and F. Okolicsanyi. "Television receiver." Br. 509,715, Jan. 21, 1938.

7419 Brüche, E., and A. Recknagel. "Electron beam defining circuits." U.S. 2,276,758, May 26, 1939, Mar. 17, 1942. In Germany Jan. 22, 1938. Electron multiplier.

7420 S.T.C. "Method for television signals." Br. 523,434, Jan. 6, 1939. Convention Jan. 25, 1938.

7421 Clark, T.H. "Electron multiplier." U.S. 2,150,317, Jan. 26, 1938, Mar. 14, 1939 (RCA).

7422 Du Mont, A.B. "Method and system for television communication." U.S. 2,186,634, Jan. 26, 1938, Jan. 9, 1940. Assigned: A.B. Du Mont Labs, Inc.

7423 Rinia, H. "Device for scanning continuously moving film." U.S. 2,292,481, Jan. 24, 1939, Aug. 11, 1942 (RCA). In Netherlands Jan. 26, 1938 (N.V. Philips).

7424 Telefunken. "Television, valve generator circuits." Br. 525,680, Jan. 25, 1939. Addition to Br. 483,999. In Germany Jan. 26, 1938.

7425 Baird Television and T.C. Nuttall. "Television transmitter." Br. 510,171, Jan. 27, 1938.

7426 Henroteau, F.C.P. "Cathode-ray tube." Br. 488,605, Jan. 27, 1938. Signal multiplier.

7427 Hughes, L.E.C. "Television: Nearly 9,000 receivers now in use." ELECT. 120 (Jan. 28): 111.

7428 Lubcke, H.R. "System of television synchronization." U.S. 2,201,295, Jan. 28, 1938, May 21, 1940. Assigned: Don Lee Broadcasting System.

7429 Telefunken. "Electron multiplier." Br. 524,417, Jan. 30, 1939. In Germany Jan. 28, 1938.

7430 Adam, M. "Les caractéristiques des nouvelles émissions de télévision de la Tour Eiffel" [Characteristics of the new television transmitters at the Eiffel Tower]. GENIE CIVIL 112 (Jan. 29): 104-7. References to the systems used by Compagnie Française de Télévision, Compagnie Radio-Industrie, Grammont, and Thomson-Houston.

7431 Below, F. "Electron multiplier." U.S. 2,245,895, Feb. 4, 1939, June 17, 1941. In Germany Jan. 29, 1938.

7432 Grundmann, G.L., and Horace Clifford Allen. "Television receiver." U.S. 2,157,170, Jan. 29, 1938, May 9, 1939. Assigned: RCA.

7433 Nicolson, —., and Communication Patents. "Photoelectric device." U.S. 2,220,115, Jan. 29, 1938, Nov. 5, 1940. Photo-emissive cathode between two anodes and optical assembly. Divided from original July 7, 1930 (2479); U.S. 2,108,827, Feb. 22, 1938.

7434 S.T.C. "Electron multiplier." Br. 522,359, Dec. 6, 1938. Convention Jan. 29, 1938.

7435 Zworykin, V.K., and Richard L. Snyder, Jr. "Electron multiplier." U.S. 2,231,697, Jan. 29, 1938, Feb. 11, 1941 (RCA).

7436 Guanella, G. "Television system." U.S. 2,266,194, Jan. 23, 1939, Dec. 16, 1941. Assigned: Radio Patents Corp. In Switzerland Jan. 30, 1938.

7437 Strieby, M.E. "Television over coaxial cable." BELL LAB RECORD 16 (Feb.): 188-95.

7438 Bowie, R.M. "Cathode-ray wave form distortion at ultra-high frequencies." ELECTRONICS 11 (Feb.): 18-9.

7439 Mezger, G. Robert. "Single-unit video converter." ELECTRONICS 11 (Feb.): 31-4, 74.

7440 Duncan, J.R. "Paragraphs on television synchronization." ELECTRONICS 11 (Feb.): 51.

7441 Gernsback, H. "Visual broadcasting." RADIO-CRAFT 9 (Feb.): 453.

7442 "Television lights and shadows." RADIO-CRAFT 9 (Feb.): 454-5.

7443 "Preview of 1938 fashions successfully televised!" RADIO-CRAFT 9 (Feb.): 456-7, 490. 6 photos. Demonstration by RCA at 441 lines in New York on Nov. 18, 1937, using cathode-ray screens 7 1/2 by 10 in.

7444 "Let's peek in at television with two of its leaders." RADIO-CRAFT 9 (Feb.): 457, 495-6. Problems of American television discussed by A.N. Goldsmith; British and American systems compared by David Sarnoff.

7445 Sanabria, U.A. "Television students learn by making cathode-ray tubes." RADIO-CRAFT 9 (Feb.): 462, 492-3. 2 diags.

7446 Jewett, F.B. "Television 'piped' 100 miles." RADIO-CRAFT 9 (Feb.): 463, 497. 6 photos, 2 diags. Single-sideband transmissions over coaxial cables between New York and Philadelphia.

7447 Cockaday, L.M. "Firing the opening guns of television in the New York area." RADIO N. 19 (Feb.): 455-6.

7448 Ring, F. "Das deutsch Fernsehverfahren" [German television]. T.F.T. 27 (Feb.): 64-7.

7449 Baird Television, V.A. Jones, and T.C. Nuttall. "Television transmitter." Br. 510,530, Feb. 2, 1938.

7450 Baird Television and L.R. Merdler. "Valve generator." Br. 510,531, Feb. 2, 1938.

7451 Scophony, G. Wikkenhauser, and E.E. Thomson. "Television transmitter." Br. 504,668, Feb. 3, 1938.

7452 Rosenthal, A.H. "Television receiving system." Br. 513,776, Feb. 3, 1938; U.S. 2,330,171, Jan. 27, 1939, Sept. 21, 1943. Assigned: Scophony. U.S. 2,273,384, Mar. 19, 1946.

7453 "Television developments." ELECT. 120 (Feb. 4): 159.

7454 Faudell, C.L., R.E. Spencer, and Ivanhoe John Penfound James. "Television system." Br. 513,205, Feb. 4, 1938; U.S. 2,218,067, Feb. 4, 1939, Oct. 15, 1940. Assigned: EMI

7455 Smyth, Charles Norman. "Television receiver." U.S. 2,295,059, Dec. 30, 1938, Sept. 8, 1942. In Britain Feb. 4, 1938. Assigned: International Standard Electrical Corp.

7456 Kolster-Brandes and C.N. Smyth. "Amplifier for television receiver." Br. 510,715, Feb. 4, 1938.

7457 Möller, R., and H. Bähring. "Saw-tooth wave generator." U.S. 2,218,764, Feb. 4, 1939, Oct. 22, 1940. In Germany Feb. 4, 1938.

7458 Möller, R., and Werner Hartmann. "Image storage tube." U.S. 2,250,721, Feb. 4, 1939, July 29, 1941. In Germany Feb. 8, 1938.

7459 Percival, W.S. "Delay device for use in transmission of oscillations." U.S. 2,263,902, Feb. 2, 1939, Nov. 25, 1941. In Britain Feb. 8, 1938.

7460 Mitchell, Irvin Smith. "Television system and scanning apparatus." U.S. 2,247,030, Feb. 9, 1938, June 24, 1941.

7461 Rose, A. "Electron discharge device." U.S. 2,175,702, Feb. 9, 1938, Oct. 10, 1939. Assigned: RCA.

7462 Henderson, S.T. "Fluorescent screen." U.S. 2,243,097, Jan. 31, 1939. In Britain Feb. 10, 1938.

7463 Law, R.R. "Cathode-ray tube, electronic structures." U.S. 2,179,097, Feb. 10, 1938, Nov. 7, 1939.

7464 Baird Television. "Cathode-ray tube." Br. 511,048, Feb. 11, 1938.

7465 Deichmann, G.A. "Cathode-ray tube." U.S. 2,232,098, Feb. 11, 1938, Feb. 18, 1941.

7466 Schlesinger, K. "Amplitude limiter." U.S. 2,309,258, Feb. 11, 1938, Jan. 26, 1943 (RCA). Divided from U.S. 2,190,504, Feb. 26, 1937, Feb. 13, 1940.

7467 Brewer, R.W.A. "Electron multiplying device." U.S. 2,232,900, Feb. 15, 1938, Feb. 25, 1941 (RCA).

7468 G.E.C. and D.C. Espley. "Television." Br. 511,200, Feb. 15, 1938.

7469 Hollmann, H.E. "Oscillation generator." U.S. 2,245,670, Dec. 31, 1938, June 17, 1941. In Germany Feb. 16, 1938 (Telefunken).

7470 Baird Television and V.A. Jones. "Cathode-ray tube." Br. 511,362, Feb. 16, 1938.

7471 Marconi's and G.B. Banks. "Electron multiplier." Br. 511,449, Feb. 17, 1938; U.S. 2,164,892, Feb. 23, 1939, July 4, 1939. Secondary emission tube.

7472 Broadway, L.F., and O. Klemperer. "Cathode-ray tube." Br. 511,444, Feb. 17, 1938; U.S. 2,213,688, Feb. 16, 1939, Sept. 3, 1940. Assigned: EMI

7473 Guanella, G. "Synchronizing system for television." U.S. 2,231,998, Feb. 10, 1939, Feb. 18, 1941. In Switzerland Feb. 17, 1938.

7474 Guanella, G. "Television." Br. 525,342, Feb. 17, 1939. Convention Feb. 17, 1938.

7475 Klemperer, O., and W.D. Wright. "Cathode-ray tube." Br. 513,157, Feb. 17, 1938. Addition to Br. 480,857.

7476 "Television in colour: Demonstration of Baird 120-line mechanical scanning system at Dominion Theatre." ELECT. 120 (Feb. 18): 197.

7477 Kolster-Brandes, C.N. Smyth, and R.J. Berry. "Television receiver." Br. 511,519, Feb. 18, 1938.

7478 Faudell, C.L. "Valve generator circuit." Br. 511,847, Feb. 19, 1938; U.S. 2,248,975, Feb. 11, 1939, July 15, 1941 (EMI). Sawtooth generator.

7479 Hefele, J.R., and G.K. Teal. "Electronic discharge device." U.S. 2,217,168, Feb. 19, 1938, Oct. 8, 1940. Camera tube.

7480 Schlesinger, K., and D.S. Loewe. "Electronic tube." U.S. 2,185,135, Feb. 19, 1938, Dec. 26, 1939.

7481 Cackett, F.W. "Cathode-ray tube." Br. 512,933, Feb. 19, 1938 (Telefunken).

7482 Farnsworth, P.T. "Multipacitor amplifier." Br. 525,243, Feb. 21, 1938; U.S. 2,172,152, Sept. 5, 1939. Electron multiplier.

7483 Ferranti and M.K. Taylor. "Valve generator." Br. 493,142, Feb. 24, 1938. Saw-tooth generator.

7484 Oettingen, D. von. "Television receiver." Br. 517,181, July 21, 1938. Convention Feb. 25, 1938.

7485 Rose, A. "Cathode-ray tube." U.S. 2,214,973, Feb. 25, 1938, Sept. 17, 1940. Assigned: RCA.

7486 Scophony and A.H. Rosenthal. "Television transmitter." Br. 511,796, Feb. 25, 1938.

7487 Telefunken. "Automatic volume control for television." Br. 525,629, Feb. 24, 1939. In Germany Feb. 25, 1938.

7488 Telefunken. "Valve generator." Br. 525,701, Feb. 27, 1939. In Germany Feb. 25, 1938.

7489 Nittick, Kenneth A. "Television receiver." U.S. 2,261,795, Feb. 26, 1938, Nov. 4, 1941. Assigned: RCA.

7490 Grundmann, G.C., and RCA. "Wide-band amplifier." U.S. 2,217,839, Feb. 28, 1938, Oct. 15, 1940.

7491 Morton, G.A., and E.G. Ramberg. "Electro-optical device." U.S. 2,249,025, Feb. 28, 1938, July 15, 1941. Assigned: RCA.

7492 Beal, R.R. "Current field work in television." ELECT. ENG. 57 (Mar.): 118-9.

7493 Fink, D.G. "Television without synchronizing signals." ELECTRONICS 11 (Mar.): 33-4, 68. Photo, 2 diags. On a new system developed at Du Mont Laboratories. Waveforms of the sweep voltage generator are transmitted as modulating signals on a separate carrier; interlaced 4:1 at 15 frames per second.

7494 "Grid-type multiplier phototube introduced in England." ELECTRONICS 11 (Mar.): 38. 3 diags. Baird Co. types ML and MS.

7495 "Radio progress during 1937, part 4." PROC. IRE 26 (Mar.): 298-301.

7496 Banneitz, F., and F. Ring. "Fortschritte der Fernsehtechnik im Jahre 1937" [Progress of television techniques in 1937]. FERN. U. TON. 9 (Mar.): 22.

7497 Loeb, J. "Un nouveau principe d'exploration électronique des images en télévision" [A new principle of electronic exploration of television images]. ONDE ELECT. 17 (Mar.): 128-34.

7498 "Mileposts in television." RADIO-CRAFT 9 (Mar.): 576-9, 607.

7499 "Television waits on standards." RADIO-CRAFT 9 (Mar.): 597, 648.

7500 "Baird colour television." TELEV. & S.W.W. 11 (Mar.): 151-2.

7501 Levy, L., and D.W. West. "Luminescence and its applications to television." J. TELEV. SOC. 2 (Mar.): 337-44. Third annual Kerr Memorial Lecture.

7502 West, S. "Home-constructed receivers." J. TELEV. SOC. 2 (Mar.): 345-51. No illustrations. Report of discussion at monthly meeting, Jan. 19, 1938.

7503 Humphreys, T.D. "A commercial television receiver employing a small cathode-ray tube." J. TELEV. SOC. 2 (Mar.): 352-62. 3 photos, 6 diags. Demonstration of receiver made by Ultra Electric Ltd. at University College, London, Feb. 9, 1938.

7504 Espley, D.C., and G.W. Edwards. "Television receivers." J. TELEV. SOC. 2 (Mar.): 363-76. 5 photos, 20 graphs and diags.

7505 West, S. "Reception of BBC television at 100 miles." J. TELEV. SOC. 2 (Mar.): 388-9. Reception in Woolingham, Suffolk.

7506 "Colour television. Invention of Mr. J.L. Baird." J. TELEV. SOC. 2 (Mar.): 392.

7507 Cock, G. "British television." J. TELEV. SOC. 2 (Mar): 393. The BBC's director of television reviews the achievements of 1937.

7508 "Eiffel Tower transmissions." J. TELEV. SOC. 2 (Mar.): 394. Signal data.

7509 Jonker, J.L.H., and A.J.W. Overbeck. "Secondary emissions in amplifying." W. ENG. (Mar.).

7510 Baird Television. "Television transmitter." Br. 512,421, Mar. 1, 1938.

7511 Baird Television and T.C. Nuttall. "Valve generator circuits." Br. 512,519, Mar. 2, 1938.

7512 Geiger, M. "Circuit arrangement for electrostatic definition of cathode rays." U.S. 2,227,076, Feb. 24, 1939, Dec. 31, 1940. In Germany Mar. 2, 1938 (Telefunken).

7513 Schlesinger, K. U.S. 2,306,663, Nov. 5, 1938, Dec. 29, 1942 (Alien Properties Custodian). In Germany Mar. 2, 1938.

7514 Rothe, H. "Circuit for the amplification of ultra-high frequencies." U.S. 2,230,546, Feb. 16, 1939, Feb. 4, 1941. In Germany Mar. 3, 1938.

7515 Telefunken. "Television, valve generator circuits." Br. 526,032, Mar. 3, 1939. Convention Mar. 3, 1938. Addition to Br. 483,999, Oct. 28, 1935. Reference to Br. 525,680.

7516 Andrieu, R., and Heinrich Brändle. "Circuit arrangement for television receivers." U.S. 2,244,230, Mar. 11, 1939, June 3, 1941. In Germany Mar. 4, 1938.

7517 Fewings, D.J. "Television synchronizing impulse separator circuit." Br. 514,509, Mar. 4, 1938; U.S. 2,215,175, Feb. 28, 1939, Sept. 17, 1940. Assigned: RCA.

7518 Murphy, —.,and H.F. Wedge. "Television receiver." Br. 512,116, Mar. 5, 1938.

7519 Klatzow, L. "Phototube." U.S. 2,254,073, Aug. 26, 1941. In Britain Mar. 7, 1938.

7520 Klatzow, L. "Photo-electric cells." Br. 513,523, Mar. 7, 1938.

7521 White, E.L.C. "Valve generator." Br. 514,940, Mar. 7, 1938.

7522 Myers, L.M. "Television reproducer apparatus." U.S. 2,219,872, Apr. 13, 1938, Oct. 29, 1940. In Britain Mar. 8, 1938. Assigned: RCA.

7523 N.V. Philips and H. Rinia. "Television receiver." Br. 509,234, Mar. 6, 1939; U.S. 2,218,720, Mar. 18, 1939, Oct. 22, 1940. In Germany Mar. 8, 1938.

7524 Browne, C.O. "Optical tuning apparatus for television." U.S. 2,243,084, Aug. 30, 1938, May 27, 1941. In Britain Mar. 9, 1938.

7525 Ives, R.L. "Pictures through a pipe: Coaxial cable." SCI. N. LETTER 33 (Mar. 12): 170-2.

7526 Batchelor, J.C. "Image analyzer." U.S. 2,238,381, Mar. 12, 1938, Apr. 15, 1941.

7527 Dorsman, C. "Central television receiving system." U.S. 2,241,586, Mar. 11, 1939, May 13, 1941. In Netherlands Mar. 12, 1938. Assigned: RCA.

7528 Farnsworth, P.T. "Dissector tube." U.S. 2,235,477, Mar. 12, 1938, Mar. 18, 1941. Original Dec. 31, 1935. Camera tube.

7529 Goldsmith, Thomas T., Jr. "Method and system for television communication." U.S. 2,164,176, Mar. 12, 1938, June 27, 1939. Assigned: A.B. Du Mont Labs. See 7530.

7530 S.T.C. "Television." Br. 526,211, Mar. 10, 1939. Convention Mar. 12, 1938. Reference to Br. 526,226.

7531 Baird Television and D.V. Ridgeway. "Television receiver." Br. 512,798, Mar. 15, 1938.

7532 Clothier, S.L., and H.C. Hogencamp. "Motion picture film scanning." U.S. 2,163,539, Mar. 15, 1938, June 20, 1939. Assigned: Kolorama Labs. Recording television signals on film.

7533 Clothier, S.L., and H.C. Hogencamp. "Television communication." U.S. 2,268,523, Mar. 15, 1938, Dec. 30, 1941. Divided Dec. 30, 1941. U.S. 2,330,682, Sept. 28, 1943.

7534 Nelson, —. "Automatic control of television receiving systems." U.S. 2,240,533, Mar. 15, 1938, May 6, 1941 (Hazeltine).

7535 Hazeltine. "Automatic control of television receiving apparatus." Br. Feb. 16, 1939. Convention Mar. 15, 1938.

7536 Browne, C.O., by Margaret Winifred Browne and Ernest William Tole, administrators, and Henry William Hobbs. "Television system." U.S. 2,404,030, Mar. 7, 1944, July 16, 1946. In Britain Mar. 17, 1938. Deflector yoke and disk for cathode-ray tube.

7537 "Big screen television." ELECT. 120 (Mar. 18): 338. Report on BBC's prohibition on reproducing telecast from White City, Mar. 12. Baird Cinetel in Gaumont-British cinemas; Scophony in Odeon cinemas.

7538 Scophony and A.H. Rosenthal. "Television transmitter." Br. 512,903, Mar. 18, 1938.

7539 Scophony, J. Sieger, and R.E. Dryden. "Modulated light." Br. 512,085, Mar. 18, 1938.

7540 Scophony and A.H. Rosenthal. "Television receiver." Br. 514,155, Mar. 18, 1938; U.S. 2,306,407, Mar. 11, 1939, Dec. 29, 1942. Reissued Dec. 27, 1944, Apr. 10, 1945. Assigned: Scophony Corp. of America. Picture tube and optical system.

7541 Baird Television. "Television transmitter." Br. 512,855, Mar. 22, 1938.

7542 Schlesinger, K. "Dividing frequency." U.S. 2,252,442, Nov. 5, 1938, Aug. 12, 1941. In Germany Mar. 22, 1938. See Br. 526,584, Mar. 21, 1939. Applications to television.

7543 Lubcke, H.R. "Television apparatus." U.S. 2,185,640, Mar. 23, 1938, Jan. 2, 1940. Assigned: Don Lee Broadcasting System. Scanning disk.

7544 Andrieu, R. "Television receiver circuit." U.S. 2,266,731, Apr. 11, 1939, Dec. 23, 1941. In Germany Mar. 24, 1938. Assigned: Telefunken.

7545 N.V. Philips. "Electron multiplier." Br. 508,778, Mar. 22, 1939. Convention Mar. 25, 1938.

7546 Zworykin, V.K., H.W. Leverenz, and John E. Ruedy. "Secondary electron emissive electrode." U.S. 2,233,276, Mar. 25, 1938, Feb. 25, 1941 (RCA).

7547 Hickok, W.H. "Method of making mosaic electrodes." U.S. 2,189,986, Mar. 26, 1938, Feb. 13, 1940. Assigned: RCA.

7548 Baird Television. "Television." Br. 512,999, Mar. 28, 1938. Reference to Br. 504,460, Oct. 26, 1936.

7549 Ardenne, M.v. "Television system." U.S. 2,265,657, Apr. 18, 1939, Dec. 9, 1941. In Germany Mar. 29, 1938. Assigned: Fernseh A.-G.

7550 Lubszynski, H.G., and L. Klatzow. "Image dissectors." Br. 515,301, Mar. 29, 1938; U.S. 2,258,294, June 21, 1939, Oct. 7, 1941 (EMI). Photo-cathode in camera tube.

7551 George, R.H. "Electronic system." U.S. 2,289,493, Mar. 30, 1938, July 14, 1942. Divided July 16, 1940.

7552 Heimann, Walter. "Cathode-ray scanning device." U.S. 2,277,101, Mar. 1, 1939, Mar. 24, 1942. In Germany Mar. 20, 1938. Assigned: C. Lorenz A.-G.

7553 Gray, F. "Cathode-ray device." U.S. 2,251,332, Mar. 31, 1938, Aug. 5, 1941; Br. 526,534, Mar. 20, 1939. Assigned: B.T.L.

7554 Morton, G.A. "Electro-optical device." U.S. 2,222,181, Mar. 31, 1938, Nov. 19, 1940. Assigned: RCA.

7555 Ramberg, E.J., and George A. Morton. "Electron-image device." U.S. 2,249,041, Mar. 31, 1938, July 15, 1941. Assigned: RCA.

7556 Engstrom, E.W., and R.S. Holmes. "Television receivers." ELECTRONICS 11 (Apr.): 28-31, 63-6. Photos, 7 diags. Technical survey.

7557 "High definition." ELECTRONICS 11 (Apr.): 32. 5 photos of 441-line television images, selected by the editors as among the first images ever photographed. 4 of Fernseh, 1 of Philco.

7558 Banneitz, F. "Zur Normung des deutschen Fernsehrundfunks (On the standardization of the German television network)." FERN. U. TON. 9 (Apr.): 27.

7559 Pressler, H. "Fernsehen in natürlichen Farben" [Television in natural colors]. T.F.T. 27 (Apr.): 137-41.

7560 "Television gets a trial. Modern transmitting methods tested in new studio." POP. SCI. 132 (Apr.): 38-9.

7561 "American technique in the television studio." RADIO-CRAFT 9 (Apr.): 665. Photo. NBC studio.

7562 Du Mont, A.B. "The Du Mont television system." RADIO-CRAFT 9 (Apr.): 674-5, 705. 3 photos, table.

7563 Sanabria, U.A. "Television students learn by making cathode-ray tubes. Part 5." RADIO-CRAFT 9 (Apr.): 683, 708-9.

7564 "Is television here? Opposing opinions." RADIO N. 19 (Apr.): 16-7.

7565 Kowalewski, A. "Amateur's television transmitter." RADIO N. 19 (Apr.): 32-5.

7566 Burnett, C.E. "The Monoscope and its uses." RCA REV. 2 (Apr.): 414-20. 5 illus.

7567 Preisman, A. "Some notes on video amplifier design." RCA REV. 2 (Apr.): 421-32.

7568 Seeley, S.W. "Effect of the receiving antenna on television reception fidelity." RCA REV. 2 (Apr.): 433-41.

7569 Baird Television, A.K. Denisoff, and V.A. Jones. "Cathode-ray tube." Br. 513,099, Apr. 1, 1938.

7570 "Radio amateurs will attack home television problem." SCI. N. LETTER 33 (Apr. 2): 211-2.

7571 Sukumlyn, T.W. "Cathode-ray television receiver." U.S. 2,281,637, Apr. 2, 1938, May 5, 1942.

7572 B.T-H., J.T. Anderson, D. Gabor, H.W.H. Warren, and R.S. Wells. "Cathode-ray tube." Br. 513,332, Apr. 5, 1938. High-voltage tube for projecting a high-intensity image onto a large screen.

7573 Schlesinger, K. "Cathode-ray tube." U.S. 2,233,299, Nov. 5, 1938, Feb. 26, 1941; Br. 527,209, Apr. 4, 1939. In Germany Apr. 5, 1938.

7574 Lindemann, F.A. "Television." Br. 513,486, Apr. 6, 1938.

7575 "Ideal Home Exhibition: Television exhibits." ELECT. 120 (Apr. 8): 456.

7576 Messner, M. "Televising system." U.S. 2,248,772, Mar. 29, 1939, July 8, 1941. In Germany Apr. 8, 1938. Assigned: C. Lorenz A.-G.

7577 Paehr, Hans Werner. "Modulating device." U.S. 2,265,669, Apr. 10, 1939, Dec. 9, 1941. In Germany Apr. 8, 1938. Fluorescent cathode-ray tube.

7578 Knick, U. "Centering circuit for cathode-ray tubes." U.S. 2,216,273, Apr. 10, 1939, Oct. 1, 1940. In Germany Apr. 9, 1938.

7579 White, E.L. "Electrical oscillation generator." Br. 513,536, Apr. 11, 1938; U.S. 2,266,526, Apr. 11, 1939, Dec. 16, 1941 (EMI).

7580 Rosenthal, A.H. "Color television." Br. 513,693, Apr. 12, 1938; U.S. 2,330,172, Apr. 8, 1939, Sept. 21, 1943. Assigned: Scophony.

7581 White, E.L., and A.D. Blumlein. "Television receiver." Br. 514,825, Apr. 13, 1938; U.S.

2,222,427, Apr. 11, 1939, Nov. 19, 1940. Protective device.

7582 Rust, N.M., and Joseph Douglas Brailsford. "Negative circuit arrangement." Br. 514,304, Apr. 14, 1938; U.S. 2,274,347, Apr. 10, 1939, Feb. 24, 1942.

7583 "A new vacuum tube for use in television devised by P.T. Farnsworth." SCIENCE 87 (Apr. 15).

7584 Dome, R.B. "Electron discharge device." U.S. 2,234,691, Apr. 18, 1938, Mar. 11, 1941.

7585 "Television." ELECT. 120 (Apr. 22): 508-9. Discussion continued in 120 (Apr. 29): 534.

7586 Hughes, L.E.C. "Television. The Scophony receiver system." ELECT. 120 (Apr. 22): 515-6. 1 illus.

7587 Pye Ltd., William Jones, and Baden John Edwards. "Television" Br. 515,302, Apr. 22, 1938; U.S. 2,295,346, Apr. 21, 1939; Sept. 8, 1942.

7588 Schroeder, Willy. "Electron focusing system." U.S. 2,218,725, May 5, 1939, Oct. 22, 1940. In Germany Apr. 22, 1938.

7589 Warnecke, R. and André Briot. "Secondary electron emitter." U.S. 2,189,972, Apr. 19, 1939, Feb. 1, 1940. In France Apr. 22, 1938 (Compagnie sans Fil). Electron multiplier.

7590 Wolff, H.-H. "Cathode-ray tube." U.S. 2,342,778, Apr. 17, 1939, Feb. 29, 1944; Br. 527,843, Apr. 21, 1939. In Germany Apr. 22, 1938.

7591 "May spot airplanes with television receivers." SCI. N. LETTER 33 (Apr. 23): 269.

7592 S.T.C. "Television, retardation lines." Br. 527,104, Mar. 31, 1939. Convention Apr. 23, 1938.

7593 Blumlein, A.D. "Television." Br. 514,065, Apr. 25, 1938; U.S. 2,265,996, Apr. 22, 1939, Dec. 16, 1941 (EMI). Pulse generator or mixer for television; thermionic valve circuits.

7594 N.V. Philips. "Cathode-ray tube." Br. 527,892, Apr. 22, 1939. Convention Apr. 25, 1938.

7595 N.V. Philips. "Cathode-ray tube." Br. 527,893, Apr. 22, 1939. Convention Apr. 25, 1938.

7596 B.T.-H. and D.J. Mynall. "Cathode-ray tube." Br. 514,170, Apr. 27, 1938.

7597 Goldsmith, A.N. "Television control device." U.S. 2,244,251, Apr. 28, 1938, June 3, 1941. Assigned: RCA.

7598 Rust, N.M., and —. Goode. "Electrical filter." U.S. 2,244,022, Apr. 27, 1939, June 3, 1941. In Britain Apr. 28, 1938.

7599 "Television in Paris." ELECT. 120 (Apr. 29): 532. High-definition television transmissions inaugurated from the Eiffel Tower, Apr. 8 (15 kw, 46 MHz—to be increased to 30 kw, the most powerful in existence).

7600 Hughes, L.E.C. "Electron optics 1: General requirements of electron beams." ELECT. 120 (Apr. 29): 553-4.

7601 Baird Television and A.K. Denisoff. "Cathode-ray tube." Br. 514,270, Apr. 29, 1938.

7602 Baird Television and T.C. Nuttall. "Television and like receiver." Br. 514,271, Apr. 29, 1938; U.S. 2,200,009, Apr. 17, 1939, May 7, 1940.

7603 Herbst, P.J. "Television signal reproducing tube." U.S. 2,169,838, Apr. 29, 1938, Aug. 15, 1939, May 2, 1941, June 16, 1942; Br. 527,886, Apr. 22, 1939. Assigned: Hazeltine.

7604 Lewis, H.M. "Television synchronizing system." U.S. 2,231,829, Apr. 29, 1938, Feb. 11, 1941. Assigned: Hazeltine.

7605 Okolicsanyi, Ferenc. "Television receiver." Br. 515,304, Apr. 29, 1938; U.S. 2,313,286, Apr. 28, 1939, Mar. 9, 1943. Assigned: Scophony.

7606 Wilhelm, K. "Amplifier." U.S. 2,216,465, Feb. 24, 1939, Oct. 1, 1940. In Germany Apr. 29, 1938 (Telefunken).

7607 Herbst, P.J. "Video-frequency signal translating system." U.S. 2,243,599, Apr. 30, 1938, May 27, 1941 (Hazeltine).

7608 Snyder, R.L. Jr. "Electron multiplier." U.S. 2,231,692, Apr. 30, 1938, Feb. 11, 1941 (RCA).

7609 Marconi's. "Electron multiplier." Br. 527,870, Apr. 21, 1939. Convention Apr. 30, 1938.

7610 Everest, F.A. "Wideband television amplifier II." ELECTRONICS 11 (May): 24-7. Continued from January.

7611 Bachmann, C.H., and C.W. Carnahan. "Negative-ion components in the cathode-ray beam." PROC. IRE 26 (May): 529-39.

7612 Wheeler, Harold A., and A.V. Loughren. "The fine structure of television images." PROC. IRE 26 (May): 540-75.

7613 Wilder, M.P. "The construction of television receivers." QST 22 (May): 39.

7614 Shrage, W.E. "Television—here and abroad." RADIO-CRAFT 9 (May): 742-3, 768, 776. 8 diags.

7615 Sanabria, U.A. "Television students learn by making cathode-ray tubes, Part 6." RADIO-CRAFT 9 (May): 748, 757, 759, 761. 5 diags. Conclusion of the series.

7616 Schnurmacher, E.C. "What television means to you." RADIO N. 19 (May): 19. Interview with G. Seldes.

7617 "The world's most powerful television station." TELEV. & S.W.W. 11 (May): 261-4.

7618 Miller, H., and J.W. Strange. "The electrical reproduction of images by the photoconductive effect." PROC., PHYS. SOC. 50 (May 2): 374-84. 3 diags. Explains methods and results with various substances, especially zinc selenide.

7619 Pike, E.W., J.A. Rajchman, and R.L. Snyder, Jr. "Electron multiplier." U.S. 2,198,227, May 3, 1938, Apr. 23, 1940. Assigned: RCA.

7620 Marconi's. "Electron multiplier." Br. 527,996, Apr. 25, 1939. Convention May 3, 1938.

7621 Baird Television and T.C. Nuttall. "Amplifier." Br. 514,401, May 4, 1938.

7622 Beatty, William Arnold. "Television." Br. 515,474, May 4, 1938.

7623 Beatty, W.A. "Television." Br. 515,475, May 4, 1938.

7624 Pierce, J.R. "Electron discharge device." U.S. 2,207,354, May 4, 1938, July 9, 1940 (B.T.L.). Electron multiplier.

7625 Pierce, J.R. "Electron discharge apparatus." U.S. 2,207,356, May 4, 1938, July 9, 1940 (B.T.L.). Electron multiplier.

7626 Pierce, J.R. "Electron discharge device." U.S. 2,274,092, May 4, 1938, Feb. 24, 1942 (B.T.L.). Electron multiplier.

7627 Pierce, J.R., and G.K. Teal. "Electron discharge device." U.S. 2,200,722, May 4, 1938, May 14, 1940 (B.T.L.). Electron multiplier.

7628 Hughes, L.E.C. "Electron optics, 2: Ordinary optics." ELECT. 120 (May 6): 581-2.

7629 D.S. Loewe. "Television." Br. 528,424, May 6, 1939. In Germany May 6, 1938.

7630 McClintock, Raymond K. "Television tube." U.S. 2,243,041, May 7, 1938, May 20, 1941. Assigned: Hygrade Sylvania.

7631 Philips Lamps Ltd. "Television." Br. 528,354, May 4, 1939. In Netherlands May 7, 1938.

7632 Philips Lamps Ltd. "Television." Br. 528,355, May 4, 1939. In Netherlands May 7, 1938.

7633 Mullard, —. "Electron multiplier." Br. 510,232, May 6, 1939. Convention May 9, 1938.

7634 Baird Television and T.C. Nuttall. "Television." Br. 514,554, May 10, 1938.

7635 Bedford, L.H., Lionel Jofeh, and W.H. Stevens. "Cathode-ray tube." Br. 519,668,

May 10, 1938; U.S. 2,336,837, May 8, 1939, Dec. 14, 1943 (A.C. Cossor). Reference to 7636, 7637, 7638, 7639.

7636 A.C. Cossor, L.H. Bedford, L. Jofeh, and W.H. Stevens. "Cathode-ray tube." Br. 519,714, May 10, 1938. For television. Divided from 7635.

7637 A.C. Cossor, L.H. Bedford, L. Jofeh, and W.H. Stevens. "Cathode-ray tube." Br. 519,715, May 10, 1938. Divided from 7635.

7638 A.C. Cossor, L.H. Bedford, L. Jofeh, and W.H. Stevens. "Cathode-ray tube." Br. 520,723, May 10, 1938. Divided from 7635.

7639 A.C. Cossor, L.H. Bedford, L. Jofeh, and W.H. Stevens. "Cathode-ray tube." Br. 520,824, May 10, 1938. Divided from 7635.

7640 Kaufmann, H.W. "Luminescent screen." U.S. 2,219,929, May 10, 1938, Oct. 29, 1940 (RCA).

7641 Schlesinger, K. "Television transmission arrangement." U.S. 2,227,401, May 10, 1938, Dec. 31, 1940. Assigned: Loewe Radio Inc. Original in Germany Nov. 18, 1935.

7642 Baird Television and P.W. Willans. "Television." Br. 514,643, May 11, 1938.

7643 Collard, J. "Resistance element." Br. 514,997, May 12, 1938; U.S. 2,246,293, May 6, 1939, June 17, 1941 (EMI).

7644 Comp. Gaz. "Cathode-ray tube." Br. 541,872, May 11, 1939. In France May 12, 1938.

7645 Paumier, André Paul. "Electron screen device for television." U.S. 2,387,608, May 6, 1939, Oct. 23, 1943. In France May 12, 1938.

7646 S.T.C. "Modulation system for television." Br. 527,102, Mar. 31, 1939. Convention May 12, 1938.

7647 Hughes, L.E.C. "Electron optics, 3: Lens calculations." ELECT. 120 (May 13): 611-2. Diag.

7648 Mullard, —., and C.C. Eaglesfield. "Valve circuit." Br. 512,173, May 13, 1938.

7649 Mullard, —. "Electron multiplier." Br. 525,595, May 10, 1939. Convention May 13, 1938. Reference to Br. 500,356, Aug. 7, 1937.

7650 Adam, M. "Le nouveau centre émitteur de télévision de la Tour Eiffel à Paris" [The new television transmitter center at the Eiffel Tower in Paris]. GENIE CIVIL 112 (May 14): 413-6.

7651 IMK Syndicate and P. Nagy. "Television." Br. 518,210, May 14, 1938.

7652 EMI and E.L.C. White. "Television." Br. 515,208, May 17, 1938; U.S. 2,287,334, May 5, 1939, June 23, 1942. Elimination of undesired electrical signals.

7653 Schlesinger, K., and M. von Ardenne. "Picture transmission." U.S. 2,175,033, May 18, 1938, Oct. 3, 1939. Television receiver.

7654 EMI and E.L.C. White. "Television." Br. 515,209, May 18, 1938; U.S. 2,303,968, May 10, 1939, Dec. 1, 1942. Addition to Br. 476,935, May 15, 1936.

7655 Goldsmith, A.N. "Composite-delineation television." U.S. 2,236,502, May 19, 1938, Apr. 1, 1941.

7656 Rinia, H. "Synchronizing circuit." U.S. 2,226,260, May 18, 1939, Dec. 24, 1940 (RCA). In Netherlands May 19, 1938 (N.V. Philips). Electron multiplier, for television.

7657 Philips Lamps Ltd. "Television." Br. 528,894, May 16, 1939. In Netherlands May 19, 1938.

7658 White, E.L.C. "Circuit arrangement for separating electric pulses." Br. 515,210, May 19, 1938; U.S. 2,227,052, May 17, 1939, Dec. 31, 1940 (EMI).

7659 Hughes, L.E.C. "Electron optics, 4: Application to television." ELECT. 120 (May 20): 643-4. Diag.

7660 Cosmocolor Corp. "Color television." Br. 532,382, May 20, 1939. Convention May 21, 1938.

7661 Miller, H., and H.E. Kallmann. "Cathode-ray tube." Br. 515,308, May 25, 1938; U.S.

2,259,531, May 19, 1939, Oct 21, 1941 (EMI). Magnetic electron lens.

7662 Hughes, L.E.C. "Electron optics, 5: Deflection of electron beams." ELECT. 120 (May 27): 694. Diag.

7663 Lubszynski, H.G. "Image intensifier." Br. 515,264, May 27, 1938; U.S. 2,305,179, May 24, 1939, Dec. 15, 1942 (EMI). Electron multiplier; picture tube with image intensifier. Reference to Br. 457,493, May 30, 1935.

7664 Beers, G.L. "Television apparatus." U.S. 2,223,983, May 28, 1938, Dec. 3, 1940. Assigned: RCA.

7665 Holmes, R.S. "Television receiver." U.S. 2,246,939, May 28, 1938, June 24, 1941. Assigned: RCA.

7666 Philips Lamps Ltd. "Television." Br. 525,870, May 25, 1939. Convention May 28, 1938.

7667 Blumlein, A.D., F. Blythen, and J. Hardwick. "Television." Br. 515,362, May 30, 1938; U.S. 2,307,375, May 23, 1939, Jan. 5, 1943 (EMI). Transmission of electrical signals having a direct-current component.

7668 Blumlein, A.D. "Television, automatic volume control." Br. 515,364, May 30, 1938; U.S. 2,303,909, May 23, 1939, Dec. 1, 1942 (EMI). Transmission of electrical signals.

7669 EMI and A.D. Blumlein. "Television." Br. 515,361, May 30, 1938. Addition to Br. 458,585, Mar. 20, 1935.

7670 Blumlein, A.D. "Television or other signal-transmission system." U.S. 2,295,330, May 24, 1939, Sept. 8, 1942 (EMI). In Britain May 30, 1938.

7671 Blumlein, A.D. "Transmission of electrical signals having a direct-current component." U.S. 2,307,387, May 26, 1939, Jan. 5, 1943 (EMI). In Britain May 30, 1938.

7672 Blumlein, A.D. "Television." Br. 515,360, May 30, 1938.

7673 Ferranti, M.K. Taylor, and Hubert Wood. "Television receiver." Br. 494,502, May 30, 1938.

7674 Ferranti, M.K. Taylor, and H. Wood. "Television receiver video circuit." Br. 515,426, May 30, 1938; U.S. 2,258,370, May 31, 1939, Oct. 7, 1941. Assigned: Hazeltine.

7675 Hardwick, J. "Television." Br. 515,363, May 30, 1938; U.S. 2,307,218, May 27, 1939, Jan. 5, 1943 (E.M.I.). Thermionic valve circuits.

7676 Hewson, Bertram Tom, and A. Locan. "Color television." Br. 518,761, May 30, 1938.

7677 Hewson, B.T., and A. Locan. "Color television." Br. 518,811, May 30, 1938. Divided from 518,761 (above).

7678 Hewson, B.T., and A. Locan. "Television." Br. 518,816, May 30, 1938.

7679 Hewson, B.T., and A. Locan. "Television." Br. 518,813, May 30, 1938.

7680 Bouwers, A., and Aart van den Berg. "Electronic discharge tube." U.S. 2,299,792, May 26, 1939, Oct. 27, 1942. In Germany May 31, 1938 (N.V. Philips).

7681 Faudell, C.L. "Television." Br. 515,427, May 31, 1938; U.S. 2,297,612, May 26, 1939, Sept. 29, 1942.

7682 Hickok, W.H. "Television transmitting tube." U.S. 2,204,250, May 31, 1938, June 11, 1940. Assigned: RCA. Iconoscope and film.

7683 Marconi's. "Photoelectric cells, cathode-ray tube." Br. 529,410, May 30, 1939. Convention May 31, 1938. Camera tube.

7684 Marconi's. "Cathode-ray tube for television." Br. 529,411, May 30, 1939. Convention May 31, 1938. Film transmission.

7685 Iams, H.A. "Television transmitting tube." U.S. 2,213,548, May 31, 1938, Sept. 3, 1940. Assigned: RCA.

7686 Schlesinger, K. "Cathode-ray tube." U.S. 2,348,853, Nov. 5, 1938, May 16, 1944. In Germany May 31, 1938. See Br. 529,341.

7687 D.S. Loewe. "Cathode-ray tube." Br. 529,341, May 30, 193. In Germany May 31, 1938.

7688 Barber, A.W. "Video amplifier design." COMM. 18 (June): 13, 20.

7689 Strieby, M.E. "Television transmission by coaxial cable." ELECTRICAL ENGINEERING 57 (June): 249-56. Also B.S.T.J. 17 (July 1938): 438-57. Transmission from New York to Philadelphia.

7690 Engstrom, E.W., and R.S. Holmes. "Television I-F amplifiers." ELECTRONICS 11 (June): 20-3. Photo, 9 diags. Third part published in July.

7691 Faust, G. "Die Gleichlaufregelung in der Fernsehtechnik (Synchronization in television technique)." FERN. U. TON. 9 (June): 41.

7692 Wilson, J.C. "Channel width and resolving power in television systems." J. TELEV. SOC. 2 (June): 397-420. 26 diags. and graphs.

7693 Shmakoff, P. "The photo-electric properties of caesium cathodes when simultaneously excited by light and electron bombardment." J. TELEV. SOC. 2 (June): 421-4. 7 graphs and diags.

7694 Blumlein, A.D. "The Marconi-E.M.I. television system. Part 1: The transmitted waveform." J. TELEV. SOC. 2 (June): 430-6. 2 photos, diag. Abstract from J. IEE 83 (Dec. 1938): 758-92.

7695 Browne, C.O. "The Marconi-E.M.I. television system. Part 2: Vision input equipment." J. TELEV. SOC. 2 (June): 437-44. Photo, 7 diags. Abstract from J. IEE 83 (Dec. 1938): 758-92.

7696 Date, W.H. "Education of the television engineer." J. TELEV. SOC. 2 (June): 445-53.

7697 Selényi, P. "Application of electrography in television." W. ENG. 15 (June): 303-9.

7698 Ardenne, M. von. "Cathode-ray tube." Br. 529,480, June 1, 1939. Convention June 1, 1938.

7699 Van den Bosch, F.J.G. "Cathode-ray tube." U.S. 2,237,065, June 1, 1939, Apr. 1, 1941. In Britain June 2, 1938. Assigned: Vacuum-Science Products Ltd.

7700 Van den Bosch, F.J.G. "Electron multiplier." U.S. 2,254,128, June 1, 1939, Aug. 26, 1941. In Britain June 2, 1938. Assigned: Vacuum-Science Products Ltd.

7701 Hughes, L.E.C. "Electron optics, 6: Focusing electron beams." ELECT. 120 (June 3): 722-3.

7702 Philips Lamps Ltd. "Electron multiplier." Br. 529,433, May 31, 1939. Convention June 3, 1938.

7703 "The BBC working for the viewer. The only daily television service." ILLUS. LONDON NEWS (June 4): 1004-7. 12 photos, full-page color painting of a television studio.

7704 IMK Syndicate, P. Nagy, and D.H. Byron. "Television." Br. 519,515, June 4, 1938. Phonic wheel driving a scanning mirror, with control circuits.

7705 Weiss, G. "Electron multiplier." U.S. 2,243,178, June 4, 1938, May 27, 1941. Divided from original Germany patent of Jan. 8, 1935.

7706 Pye Ltd. and G. Liebmann. "Cathode-ray tube." Br. 519,111, June 6, 1938.

7707 Comp. Gaz. "Television." Br. 544,542, June 7. 1939. In France June 8, 1938.

7708 Schnitger, Herbert. "Electron multiplier." U.S. 2,238,607, Jan. 24, 1939, Apr. 15, 1941. In Germany June 8, 1938. Assigned: Fides Gessel.

7709 Loughren, A.V. "Television broadcast system." U.S. 2,254,435, June 9, 1938, Sept. 2, 1941; Br. 529,320, May 26, 1939. Assigned: Hazeltine.

7710 Hughes, L.E.C. "Electron optics, 7: Refraction of electron beams." ELECT. 120 (June 10): 751-2.

7711 Zworykin, V.K., and J.A. Rajchman. "Electron multiplier." U.S. 2,231,698, June 10, 1938, Feb. 11, 1941 (RCA).

7712 Marconi's. "Electron multiplier." Br. 528,818, May 15, 1939. Convention June 10, 1938.

7713 S.T.C. "Television." Br. 529,011, May 19, 1939. Convention June 11, 1938. Transmitter circuits.

7714 Telefunken. "Cathode-ray tube." Br. 530,523, June 12, 1939. In Germany June 11, 1938.

7715 Baird Television and V.A. Jones. "Cathode-ray tube." Br. 515,801, June 13, 1938.

7716 Baird Television and T.C. Nuttall. "Television." Br. 515,843, June 13, 1938.

7717 de Gier, Johannes. "Arrangement of cathode-ray tubes." U.S. 2,267,083, May 24, 1939, Dec. 23, 1941 (RCA). In Germany June 13, 1938 (N.V. Philips). Television receiver.

7718 Farnsworth, P.T., and Richard L. Snyder. "Shielded anode electron multiplier." U.S. 2,203,048, June 13, 1938, June 4, 1940. Assigned: Farnsworth Television and Radio Corp. Br. 529,496, June 2, 1939.

7719 Farnsworth, P.T. "Image projector." U.S. 2,233,887, June 13, 1938, Mar. 4, 1941. Divided from original of Feb. 6, 1935. Assigned: Farnsworth Television and Radio Corp.

7720 Baird Television and C.F. Chapter. "Image intensifier." Br. 517,514, June 14, 1938.

7721 Tingley, G.R. "Cathode-ray tube arrangement." Br. 515,947, June 14, 1938; U.S. 2,220,303, May 22, 1939, Nov. 5, 1940. Assigned: Baird Television.

7722 Knick, U. "Television transmitting system." U.S. 2,278,283, June 14, 1939, Apr. 7, 1942. In Germany June 14, 1938. Assigned: Fernseh A.-G.

7723 Flory, L.E. "Picture transmitting tube." U.S. 2,251,992, June 15, 1938, Aug. 12, 1941 (RCA).

7724 Marconi's. "Cathode-ray tube." Br. 529,277, May 24, 1939. Convention June 15, 1938. Camera tube screen.

7725 Schlesinger, K. "Television tube." U.S. 2,197,899, June 15, 1938, Apr. 23, 1940. Assigned: Loewe Radio Inc. Divided from German patent of Mar. 3, 1934. Original U.S. 2,137,353, Feb. 28, 1835, Nov. 22, 1938.

7726 Weiss, G. "Electron multiplier." Br. 527,230, Apr. 4, 1939. Convention June 15, 1938.

7727 Hughes, L.E.C. "Electron optics, 8: The equivalent focal length." ELECT. 120 (June 17): 788-9.

7728 Seeley, S.W. "Electrical circuits." U.S. 2,197,024, June 17, 1938, Apr. 16, 1940 (RCA). Television apparatus.

7729 Parker, L.W. "Television apparatus." U.S. 2,236,578. June 18, 1938, Apr. 1, 1941. Assigned: C.T. Allen.

7730 Baird Television and V.A. Jones. "Cathode-ray tube." Br. 516,351, June 20, 1938.

7731 Hazeltine. "Television receiver." Br. 529,319, May 26, 1939. In U.S. June 21, 1938.

7732 Marconi's. "Cathode-ray tube." Br. 530,138, June 17, 1939. Convention June 21, 1938.

7733 Wilson, J.C. "Television automatic amplification system." U.S. 2,214,846, June 21, 1938, Sept. 17, 1940. Assigned: Hazeltine.

7734 van der Mark, J. "Television scanning apparatus." U.S. 2,281,893, June 21, 1939, May 5, 1942. Assigned: RCA. In Netherlands June 23, 1938 (N.V. Philips).

7735 Hughes, L.E.C. "Electron optics, 9: Thin electron lenses." ELECT. 120 (June 24): 815-6.

7736 Scophony, A.F.H. Thomson, and A.H. Rosenthal. "Television receiver." Br. 516,247, June 24, 1938.

7737 Kodak Ltd. and R.S. Morse. "Television." Br. 531,262. Convention June 25, 1938.

7738 Blumlein, A.D., H.E. Kallmann, and W.S. Percival. "Impedance networks." Br.

517,516, June 28, 1938. For television, with cathode-ray tube.

7739 Lewis, H.M. "Signal transmitting system." U.S. 2,228,725, June 28, 1938, Jan. 14, 1941 (Hazeltine). Video-frequency circuit.

7740 Miller, H., and J.E.I. Cairns. "Cathode-ray tube." Br. 516,478, June 28, 1938; U.S. 2,294,123, May 16, 1939, Aug. 25, 1942 (EMI). Magnetic electron lens.

7741 Lewis, H.M. "Television combining amplifier." U.S. 2,191,796, June 29, 1938, Feb. 27, 1940 (Hazeltine). Divided from original U.S. 2,052,183, Oct. 5, 1934.

7742 S.T.C. "Electron multiplier." Br. 529,183, May 24, 1939. Convention June 29, 1938.

7743 White, E.L. "Thermionic valve circuits." Br, 515,864, June 30, 1938; U.S. 2,235,414, June 28, 1939, Mar. 18, 1941 (EMI).

7744 Strieby, M.E., and C.L. Weiss. "Coaxial cable system in television transmission." B.S.T.J. 17 (July): 438.

7745 Wild, R.F. "Notes on new television standards." COMM. 18 (July): 5-8, 34-6.

7746 (I.R.E.) "13th annual meeting." ELECTRONICS 11 (July): 12-5. Abstracts of papers read at New York meeting.

7747 "The image Iconoscope." ELECTRONICS 11 (July): 12.

7748 Fink, D.G. "Laboratory television receiver." ELECTRONICS 11 (July): 16-20. Continued in (Aug.) 26-9, (Sept.) 22-5, (Oct.) 16-9, (Nov.) 26-9, (Dec.) 16-9.

7749 Bamford, H.S. "A new television film projector." ELECTRONICS 11 (July): 25.

7750 Murray, A.F. "Radio Manufacturers Association completes television standards." ELECTRONICS 11 (July): 28-9, 55.

7751 "25 kw television transmitter at Eiffel Tower goes into operation." ELECTRONICS 11 (July): 45.

7752 Kirschstein, F. "Zur Frage der Zeilenzahl bei Fernsehübertragungen (On the question of the number of lines in television transmissions)." E.N.T. 15 (July): 218-34.

7753 Reusse, W. "Elektronenoptische Fragen der Fernsehtechnik" [Electron optical questions of television technique]. FERN. U. TON. 9 (July): 51.

7754 Belus, R. "Les cables coaxiaux, leur emploi en haute fréquence, en particulier pour la télévision" [Coaxial cables, their application at high frequency, particularly for television]. ONDE ELECT. 17 (July): 325-37, 409-16.

7755 "Television comes along." RADIO-CRAFT 10 (July): 6-7.

7756 "Tiny television-news camera." RADIO-CRAFT 10 (July): 8. Made by Fernseh, 2 photos.

7757 Sanabria, U.A. "Television without scanning?" RADIO-CRAFT 10 (July): 12, 57-8. 5 diags.

7758 Goldsmith, A.N. "Looking ahead to television occupations." RADIO-CRAFT 10 (July): 61-2, 64.

7759 "Television approaches the rural home." RADIO N. 20 (July): 24.

7760 Priess, W.H. "Television by resonance." RADIO N. 20 (July): 31.

7761 "How television tubes are made." RADIO N. 20 (July): 32-3.

7762 Bedford, A.V. "Figure of merit for television performance." RCA REV. (July).

7763 Ardenne, M. von, and H. Pressler. "Zum Problem des Farbfernsehens" [On the problem of color television]. T.F.T. 27 (July): 264-73.

7764 Cocking, W.T. "Television intermediate frequency amplifiers." W. ENG. 15 (July): 358-62.

7765 Kolster-Brandes and C.E. Lock. "Television receiver." Br. 516,631, July 1, 1938.

7766 S.T.C. and C.W. Earp. "Television." Br. 516,630, July 1, 1938.

7767 Baird Television and L.R. Merdler. "Cathode-ray tube." Br. 516,651, July 2, 1938.

7768 Baird Television. "Electron multiplier." Br. 516.785, July 7, 1938.

7769 S.T.C. "Oscillator." Br. 530, 956, July 7, 1939. Convention July 7, 1938.

7770 Lee, H.W. "The Scophony television receiver." NATURE 142 (July 9): 59-62. See also PROC. IRE 27 (Aug. 1939): 483-500.

7771 Flechsig, W. "Color television transmitter." U.S. 2,264,748, July 11, 1939, Dec. 2, 1941. Assigned: Fernseh A.-G. In Germany July 11, 1938. Camera tube.

7772 Richards, C.L., and H. Rinia. "Electron beam deflector apparatus." U.S. 2,260,725, July 6, 1939, Oct. 28, 1941 (RCA). In Netherlands July 12, 1938. Magnetic yoke assembly.

7773 Philips Lamps Ltd. "Cathode-ray tube." Br. 520,374, July 10, 1939. Convention July 12, 1938.

7774 S.T.C. "Television." Br. 531,104, July 11, 1939. Convention July 13, 1938. Addition to 523,434.

7775 B.T.-H. "Cathode-ray tube." Br. 531,148, July 13, 1939. Convention July 15, 1938.

7776 Philco. "Receiver." Br. 530,794, June 19, 1939. Convention July 16, 1938.

7777 G.E.C. and D.C. Espley. "Receiver network." Br. 516,252, July 19, 1938.

7778 White, E.L.C., and Reginald Philip Chasmar. "Television." Br. 517,170, July 20, 1938; U.S. 2,286,450, July 18, 1939, June 16, 1942 (EMI). Television receiving system.

7779 Clay, R.S. "Television." Br. 516,335, July 25, 1938.

7780 Schlesinger, K., and Loewe Radio. "Scanning disk for television transmission." U.S. 2,248,559, July 26, 1938, July 8, 1941. Divided from German patent of June 11, 1935. For film.

7781 Baird Television and Lawrence Cranmer Bentley. "Television receiver." Br. 517,428, July 27, 1938; U.S. 2,268,104, June 27, 1939, Dec. 30, 1941. Assigned: Cinema-Television Ltd.

7782 Espley, D.C. "Receiver." U.S. 2,270,652, July 22, 1939, Jan. 20, 1942. In Britain July 27, 1938. Includes television.

7783 Lewis, H.M. "Television receiver including black-level control." U.S. 2,249,533, July 27, 1938, July 15, 1941; Br. 530,426, June 23, 1939. Assigned: Hazeltine.

7784 Krenzien, O. "Secondary electron emitter and method of modulating it." U.S. 2,204,252, July 8, 1939, June 11, 1940. In Germany July 28, 1938.

7785 S.T.C. and D.N. Corfield. "Television." Br. 532,718, July 28, 1938.

7786 Baird Television and V.A. Jones. "Cathode-ray tube." Br. 517,482, July 29, 1938. Camera tube.

7787 Baird Television and V.A. Jones. "Cathode-ray tube." 517,483, July 29, 1938.

7788 Brett, G.F. "Electron beam tube." U.S. 2,256,311, July 8, 1939, Sept. 16, 1941 (RCA). In Britain July 29, 1938 (Marconi's).

7789 "Television in color covered by new patent." SCI. N. LETTER 34 (July 30): 90. R.G. Goldmark, U.S. 2,109,773.

7790 Bedford, A.V. "Television system." U.S. 2,223,812, July 30, 1938, Dec. 3, 1940. Assigned: RCA.

7791 Rose, A. "Television transmitting tube." U.S. 2,213,174, July 30, 1938, Aug. 27, 1940; Br. 530,409, June 22, 1939. Assigned: RCA.

7792 Snyder, R.L., Jr. "Electron-multiplying system." U.S. 2,198,233, July 30, 1938, Apr. 23, 1940. Assigned: RCA.

7793 Marconi's. "Electron multiplier." Br. 530,408, June 22, 1939. Convention July 30, 1938.

7794 Mallein, S. "La télévision française doit entrer dans le domaine pratique" [French television to enter the practical stage]. ANN. POSTES 28 (Aug.): 587-617.

7795 Engstrom, E.W., and R.S. Holmes. "Television voice-frequency circuits." ELECTRONICS 11 (Aug.): 18-21.

7796 Ring, F. "Eröffnung der Fernsehsprechverbendung Berlin-München" [Opening of the Berlin-Munich television-telephone connection]. FERN. U. TON. 9 (Aug.): 58.

7797 Parker, W.N. "A unique method of modulation for high-fidelity television transmitters." PROC. IRE 26 (Aug.): 946-62.

7798 "Where is television now?" POP. MECH. 70 (Aug.): 178-83.

7799 Gernsback, H. "The television age." RADIO-CRAFT 10 (Aug.): 69.

7800 Seeley, S.W. "Television antenna for good reception." RADIO-CRAFT 10 (Aug.).

7801 "French television." RADIO-CRAFT 10 (Aug.): 71.

7802 "Anent BBC video." RADIO-CRAFT 10 (Aug.): 71, 116. Photo.

7803 "Television pictorial." RADIO-CRAFT 10 (Aug.): 72. 6 photos. Philco, BBC, Cossor, Dieckmann and Glage apparatus (1906) in Deutsches Museum.

7804 Eichberg, R. "$125 television receiver now on the market?" RADIO-CRAFT 10 (Aug.): 74, 119. 3 photos. Developed by Louis W. Parker, chief engineer, Communicating Systems, Inc. 3-inch tube.

7805 "U.S. television stations." RADIO-CRAFT 10 (Aug.): 80, 111. Table of 19 stations with details and notes.

7806 "$500,000 television system!" RADIO-CRAFT 10 (Aug.): 81. GE plans for a four-station semi-network, including a relay station.

7807 "Latest continuous-film television." RADIO-CRAFT 10 (Aug.): 83, 112. 2 photos. Farnsworth apparatus.

7808 "Domestic television." RADIO-CRAFT 10 (Aug.): 116-7. Kolorama Labs demonstration of large screens. International Television Radio Corp.'s Priess system. Scophony has sales of 3,000 receivers in England. Other news items.

7809 Ferranti and M.K. Taylor. "Television." Br. 516,946, Aug. 3, 1938.

7810 Pietzsch, Herbert. "Electron multiplier." U.S. 2,280,449, July 29, 1939, Apr. 21, 1942. In Germany Aug. 3, 1938.

7811 C. Lorenz A.-G. "Electron multiplier" Br. 531,780, Aug. 1, 1939. In Germany Aug. 3, 1938.

7812 Snyder, R.L., and Farnsworth Television. "Power multiplier." U.S. 2,257,985, Aug. 3, 1938, Oct. 7, 1941. Br. 531,508, July 25, 1939.

7813 Soller, W. "Television system." U.S. 2,231,961, Aug. 3, 1938, Feb. 18, 1941. Half assigned to W.H. Woodin, Jr.

7814 Deserno, P. "Television receiver." U.S. 2,248,815, July 22, 1939, July 8, 1941. In Germany Aug. 4, 1938. Assigned: C. Lorenz A.-G.

7815 Deserno, P., and M. Messner. "Television receiver." U.S. 2,297,205, July 29, 1939, Sept. 29, 1942. In Germany Aug. 4, 1938.

7816 B.T.-H., and D.J. Mynall. "Valve generator." Br. 523,831, Aug. 5, 1938.

7817 Goldsmith, A.N. "Television scanning device." U.S. 2,227,080, Aug. 6, 1938, Dec. 31, 1940. Assigned: RCA.

7818 Shockley, William. "Electron discharge device." U.S. 2,236,012, Aug. 6, 1938, Mar. 25, 1941. Electron multiplier.

7819 Tingley, G.R. "Cathode-ray deflection apparatus." Br. 517,597, Aug. 8, 1938; U.S. 2,259,233, May 18, 1939, Oct. 14, 1941. Assigned: Cinema-Television Ltd.

7820 G.E.C. and D.C. Espley. "Television." Br. 517,602, Aug. 10, 1938. Disk construction.

7821 Lewis, H.M. "Television scanning system." U.S. 2,198,969, Aug. 10, 1938, Apr. 30, 1940. Assigned: Hazeltine.

7822 "Television here and in Germany." ELECT. 121 (Aug. 12): 172. Editorial note.

7823 Bingley, F.J., and Philco. "Synchronizing system." U.S. 2,231,792, Aug. 12, 1938, Feb. 11, 1941; Br. 535,331, June 29, 1939.

7824 Ferranti, J.L. Miller, and H. Wood. "Cathode-ray tube." Br. 518,221, Aug. 12, 1938.

7825 Hergenrother, R.C. "Electron discharge device." U.S. 2,206,954, Aug. 13, 1938, July 9, 1940. Assigned: Hazeltine.

7826 Baird Television and C.E. Maitland. "Receiver system." Br. 517,888, Aug. 15, 1938.

7827 Miller, W.E. "The radio exhibition." ELECT. REV. 123 (Aug. 19): 247, 248. Continued in 123 (Sept. 2): 318-20.

7828 Kolster-Brandes, C.N. Smyth, and P.A. Tiller. "Television receiver." Br. 518,615, Aug. 23, 1938. Reference to 7829. Cabinet construction.

7829 Kolster-Brandes and C.N. Smyth. "Television receiver." Br. 518,616, Aug. 23, 1938. Cabinet construction.

7830 White, —. "Valve generator circuits." Br. 518,378, Aug. 23, 1938; U.S. 2,230,819, Aug. 4, 1939, Feb. 4, 1941. Saw-tooth oscillations; thermionic valve circuits. References to Br. 424,221 (Oct. 3, 1933), 443,952 (July 4, 1934).

7831 Gray, F. "Electro-optical apparatus." U.S. 2,248,985, Aug. 25, 1938, July 15, 1941. Assigned: B.T.L.

7832 "The new television drive." ELECT. 121 (Aug. 26): 225, 226.

7833 "The radio exhibition." ELECT. 121 (Aug. 26): 227, 228. The London exhibition opened at Olympia Aug. 24, 1938, and closed Sept. 5.

7834 Banks, G.B. and Marconi's. "Electron multiplier." Br. 518,553, Aug. 26, 1938. Addition to 7471.

7835 Nicoll, F.H. "Cathode-ray tube." Br. 518,580, Aug. 26, 1938. Reference to Br. 431,327, Oct. 3, 1933.

7836 A.A. Thornton (Philco). "Television." Br. 518,434, Aug. 26, 1938.

7837 Wilson, J.C. "Electronic timing system." U.S. 2,188,970, Aug. 26, 1938, Feb. 6, 1940 (Hazeltine); Br. 531,712, July 29, 1939. Filter, timing pulses, time delay. Reference to 7602.

7838 Wilson, J.C. "Scanning-wave generator synchronizing system." U.S. 219,983, Aug. 26, 1938, Apr. 30, 1940; Br. 531,765, July 29, 1939. Assigned: Hazeltine.

7839 Wilson, J.C. "Automatic amplification and black level control for television receivers." U.S. 2,214,847, Aug. 26, 1938, Sept. 17, 1940; Br. 531,711, July 29, 1939. Assigned: Hazeltine.

7840 Wilson, J.C. "Periodic wave generator." U.S. 2,221,665, Aug. 26, 1938, Nov. 12, 1940 (Hazeltine). Saw-tooth wave generator.

7841 Gebauer, Rudolf, H.F.R. von Traubenberg, and Heinrich Rausch. "Electron multiplier." U.S. 2,283,004, Aug. 30, 1939, May 12, 1942. In Germany Aug. 30, 1938 (C. Lorenz A.-G.).

7842 Holmes, R.S. "Television receiver." U.S. 2,230,295, Aug. 31, 1938, Feb. 4, 1941. Assigned: RCA.

7843 Lewis, H.M. "Television video-frequency signal-translating system." U.S. 2,247,512, Aug. 31, 1938, July 1, 1941; Br. 535,413, Aug. 8, 1939. Assigned: Hazeltine.

7844 Shockley, W. "Electron discharge device." U.S. 2,207,355, Aug. 31, 1938, July 9, 1940 (B.T.L.). Electron multiplier.

7845 "Developments in television." COMM. 18 (Sept.): 20, 21. Pictorial review.

7846 Wilder, M.P. "European television." ELECTRONICS 10 (Sept.): 13.

7847 Lipfert, Kurt. "Fernsehen auf der 15. Grossen Deutschen Rundfunkausstellung in Berlin 1938" [Television at the 15th great German radio fair in Berlin, 1938]. FERN. U. TON. 9 (Sept.): 65.

7848 "Simplified television demonstration." POP. MECH. 70 (Sept.): 417.

7849 "Television." RADIO-CRAFT 10 (Sept.): 134, 135. 4 photos.

7850 Tuthill, C.A. "When television comes around!" RADIO-CRAFT 10 (Sept.): 148, 149, 168, 169. 9 photos. "Commercial television will rely much more upon movie technique than upon radio technique for staging video shows."

7851 "Television's here—in the same old way." RADIO-CRAFT 10 (Sept.): 160, 170. Comments on Communicating Systems, Inc.

7852 Rosen, H. "Have you a television face?" RADIO N. 20 (Sept.): 16.

7853 Ives, H.E. "The transmission of motion pictures over a coaxial cable." J. SMPE 31 (Sept.): 256-72. New York City to Philadelphia.

7854 "Television prospects." ELECT. 121 (Sept. 2): 250. Editorial note on statements by Sir Frank Smith, chairman of the Television Advisory Committee, that there are less than 10,000 sets in use in Britain. During the next 12 months, 295,000 pounds will be spent on the television service.

7855 "Television conference." ELECT. 121 (Sept. 2): 269.

7856 "The television organization behind the 'viewing' at Radiolympia: Making an Alexandra Palace broadcast." ILLUS. LONDON NEWS (Sept. 3): 410-3. Photo of the studio at Radiolympia; diagrams of the operation at Alexandra Palace.

7857 Berry, R.J. (C. Lorenz A.-G.). "Television receiver." Br. 506,709, Sept. 6, 1938. No German date given.

7858 Zworykin, V.K., and L. Malter. "Electron discharge device." U.S. 2,189,305, Sept. 8, 1938, Feb. 6, 1940 (RCA). Oscillation multiplier. Divided from U.S. 2,150,573, Jan. 31, 1936.

7859 Ardenne, M.v. "Television image projection device." U.S. 2,276,359, Aug. 26, 1940, Mar. 17, 1942. In Germany Sept. 10, 1938.

7860 Farnsworth, P.T. "Image analyzing system." U.S. 2,254,140, Sept. 10, 1938, Aug. 26, 1941 (Farnsworth Television). Camera tube.

7861 Bronk, O.v. "Color television device." U.S. 2,297,444, Oct. 5, 1939, Sept. 29, 1942 (Telefunken). In Germany Sept. 14, 1938.

7862 Ges. Tech. Hochschule. "Television." Br. 539,740, Sept. 11, 1939. In Germany Sept. 14, 1938.

7863 Winckel, F.W. "Fernsehen 1938" [Television 1938]. Z.F. FERN. 19 (Sept. 15): 137–42.

7864 "Television as a career." ELECT. 121 (Sept. 16): 304. Comment on Baird's remarks at Foyles literary luncheon; current demand for researchers and servicemen; plans to expand television in cinemas.

7865 Ges. Tech. Hochschule. "Television." Br. 547,285, Sept. 13, 1939. Convention Sept. 16, 1938.

7866 Diels, K., and M. Knoll. "Electron device." U.S. 2,218,702, Dec. 9, 1939, Oct. 22, 1940 (Telefunken). In Germany Sept. 20, 1938. Cathode-ray tube.

7867 Kolster-Brandes and W.A. Beatty. "Cathode-ray tube." Br. 519,330, Sept. 20, 1938. Receiver tube.

7868 Kolster-Brandes and W.A. Beatty. "Television receiver." Br. 519,631, Sept. 22, 1938.

7869 Taylor, M.K. "Television scanning system." U.S. 2,253,355, Sept. 23, 1939, Aug. 19, 1941. In Britain Sept. 24, 1938. Assigned: Hazeltine.

7870 Kolster-Brandes and W.A. Beatty. "Cathode-ray tube." Br. 519,653, Sept. 27, 1938.

7871 Bedford, A.V. "Television receiver." U.S. 2,207,775, Sept. 30, 1938, July 16, 1940. Assigned: RCA.

7872 Epstein, D.W. "Television receiver apparatus." U.S. 2,251,786, Sept. 30, 1938, Aug. 5, 1941 (RCA).

7873 Mandel, P. "Réponse des amplificateurs pour télévision aux signaux périodiques de courte durée et aux phénomènes transitoires" [Response of television amplifiers to periodic signals of short duration and to transitory phenomena]. ONDE ELECT. 17 (Oct.): 425-45.

7874 Barthélemy, R. "Les détecteurs de pointes" [Point detectors]. ONDE ELECT. 17 (Oct.): 446-48.

7875 Rinia, H. "Television with Nipkow disc and interlaced scanning." PHIL. TECH. REV. 3 (Oct.): 285-91.

7876 Sherman, J.B. "Building television receivers with standard cathode-ray tubes." QST (Oct.).

7877 Sicuranza, Charles. "Construction details of a 441-line teleceiver." RADIO-CRAFT 10 (Oct.): 202-5, 240, 242. 3 photos, 4 diags., list of parts. 5-inch cathode-ray tube.

7878 Lescarboura, A.C. "Electricity writes its own story: A.B. Du Mont and the cathode-ray tube." RADIO N. 20 (Oct.): 12, 13.

7879 Goldsmith, A.N. "Looking ahead to television occupations." RADIO N. 20 (Oct.): 44.

7880 "Progress report." SCI. AM. 159 (Oct.): 177.

7881 Berham, W.E. "Aerial coupling systems for television." W. ENG. 15 (Oct.): 555-61.

7882 Dillenburger, W. "Image analyzing tube." U.S. 2,264,624, Oct. 20, 1939, Dec. 2, 1941. In Germany Oct. 1, 1938.

7883 B.T.-H., L. Rushforth, and J.T. Anderson. "Cathode-ray tube." Br. 519,854, Oct. 4, 1938.

7884 Strange, J.W., and W.H. Connell. "Electron discharge device." U.S. 2,227,042, Oct. 4, 1938, Dec. 31, 1940. Assigned: EMI Picture tube. Original July 31, 1937; in Britain Aug. 1, 1936.

7885 Cawein, M. "Television synchronizing and control system." U.S. 2,240,490, Oct. 5, 1938, May 6, 1941 (Hazeltine).

7886 Lewis, H.M. "Television synchronizing and control system." U.S. 2,240,507, Oct. 5, 1938, May 6, 1941; Br. 541,005, Sept. 16, 1939. Assigned: Hazeltine.

7887 Wilson, J.C. "Television synchronizing and control system." U.S. 2,240,593, Oct. 5, 1938, May 6, 1941. Assigned: Hazeltine. See 7885.

7888 Fewings, D.J., and R.J. Kemp. "Saw-tooth wave generator circuit arrangement." Br. 519,897, Oct. 6, 1938 (Marconi's); U.S. 2,258,752, Oct. 3, 1939, Oct. 14, 1941 (RCA).

7889 Seeley, S.W. "Synchronized signal separator circuit." U.S. 2,256,529, Oct. 6, 1938, Sept. 23, 1941 (RCA).

7890 Marconi's. "Television." Br. 535,578. Convention Oct. 6, 1938.

7891 Seeley, S.W. "Synchronization system." U.S. 2,256,530, Oct. 6, 1938, Sept. 23, 1941 (RCA).

7892 Mountjoy, Garrard. "Television receiver." U.S. 2,221,104, Oct. 7, 1938, Nov. 12, 1940. Assigned: RCA.

7893 Smyth, C.N. "Television receiver." Br. 520,235, Oct. 11, 1938 (Kolster-Brandes); U.S. 2,236,222, Oct. 25, 1939, Mar. 25, 1941. Assigned: International Standard Electrical Corp.

7894 Kolster-Brandes, C.N. Smyth, and P.A. Tiller. "Wave receiving apparatus." Br. 520,234, Oct. 11, 1938.

7895 Coeterier, F. "Image converter tube." U.S. 2,235,831, Oct. 3, 1939, Mar. 25, 1941. In Netherlands Oct. 13, 1938 (N.V. Philips).

7896 Wilson, J.C. "Television-receiving system." U.S. 2,240,534, Oct. 13, 1938, May 6, 1941 (Hazeltine); Br. 545,245, Sept. 15, 1939.

7897 Goldsmith, A.N. "Color television system." U.S. 2,259,884, Oct. 18, 1938, Oct. 21, 1941.

7898 Adams, Albert Ernest. "Scanning method." U.S. 2,258,311, Oct. 19, 1938, Oct. 7, 1941 (Scophony). Film scanning.

7899 Collard, J. "Correcting television signals." Br. 521,744, Oct. 19, 1938; U.S. 2,284,085, Oct. 26, 1939, May 26, 1942 (EMI). Electric signal transmission system. References to Br. 422,906 (Apr. 13, 1933); 449,242 (Sept. 18, 1934); 471,913 (Mar. 12, 1935); 458,585 (Mar. 20, 1935); 464,828 (Oct. 23, 1935); 490,205 (Nov. 10, 1936); 507,239 (Nov. 6, 1937); 512,109 (Dec. 24, 1937).

7900 Scophony and A.F.H. Thomson. "Television." Br. 520,349, Oct. 19, 1938.

7901 Bedford, A.V. "Film projector for television." U.S. 2,227,054, Oct. 20, 1938, Dec. 31, 1940. Assigned: RCA.

7902 Wheeler, H.A., and J.C. Wilson. "Periodic wave repeater." U.S. 2,212,173, Oct. 21, 1938, Aug. 20, 1940 (Hazeltine). Synchronized source, time-delay circuit.

7903 Hazeltine. "Relaxed oscillations." Br. 538,553, Oct. 12, 1939. In U.S. Oct. 21, 1938.

7904 Kolster-Brandes and C.N. Smyth. "Cathode-ray tube." Br. 520,412, Oct. 21, 1938.

7905 Ardenne, M.v. "Television projection tube." U.S. 2,277,008, Dec. 5, 1939, Mar. 17, 1942. In Germany Oct. 24, 1938.

7906 Bedford, A.V., and RCA. "Frequency control circuits." U.S. 2,201,978, Oct. 26, 1938, May 28, 1940.

7907 Dome, R.B., and Robert E. Moe. "Television synchronizing system." U.S. 2,229,964, Oct. 26, 1938, Jan. 28, 1941. Assigned: G.E.

7908 Blumlein, A.D. "Television transmission tube." Br. 520,646, Oct. 27, 1938. References to 7663; Br. 457,493 (May 30, 1935).

7909 Jones, W.I., and Pye Ltd. "Television." Br. 520,709, Oct. 28, 1938.

7910 Compton, Robin D. "Television system." U.S. 2,237,655, Oct. 29, 1938, Apr. 8, 1941. Assigned: RCA.

7911 Hazeltine. "Television receiver." Br. 535,078, Oct. 12, 1939. Convention Oct. 29, 1938.

7912 G.E.C., E.C. Cherry, and R.J. Clayton. "Valve generator." Br. 520,460, Oct. 31, 1938.

7913 Villeneuve, R. "Sur un programme d'épreuves de qualité destiné à définir objectivement la valeur d'une installation de télévision" [A quality approval program made to define objectively the value of a television installation]. ANN. POSTES 27 (Nov.): 909-14.

7914 "Empire State television antenna." ELECTRONICS 10 (Nov.): 18.

7915 Engstrom, E.W., and R.S. Holmes. "Television synchronization." ELECTRONICS 10 (Nov.): 18-20.

7916 Banneitz, F. "Die neue Fernsehnorm der Deutschen Reichpost" [New television standards from the German Post Office]. FERN. U. TON. 9 (Nov.): 85.

7917 Bingley, F.J. "The problem of synchronization in cathode-ray television." PROC. IRE 26 (Oct.): 1327-39.

7918 "Television." RADIO-CRAFT 10 (Nov.): 262, 296. Photo. Fernseh 11-inch picture tube receiver.

7919 "Television—goes to high school." RADIO-CRAFT 10 (Nov.): 270–96. 2 photos. Technical High School, Dallas.

7920 "Television—pops on and off air." RADIO-CRAFT 10 (Nov.): 270, 305. Photo. NBC station resumed broadcasting Aug. 23.

7921 "Television activity increases." RADIO-CRAFT 10 (Nov.): 292, 308.

7922 Bamford, H.S. "A non-intermittent projector for television film transmission." J. SMPE 31 (Nov.): 453-61.

7923 Otterbein, G. "Ein Farblichtrelais" [Transmission in color]. T.F.T. 27 (Nov.): 550, 551. Special issue.

7924 Benham, W.E. "Asymmetric side-band phase distortion." W. ENG. 15 (Nov.): 616.

7925 Collard, J., and J.E. Best. "System for the transmission of oscillations." Br. 522,004, Nov. 4, 1938; U.S. 2,242,879, Jan. 11, 1940, May 20, 1941 (EMI).

7926 Wheeler. H.A. "Periodic wave generator." U.S. 2,242,934, Nov. 4, 1938, May 20, 1941; Br. 535,661, Oct. 12, 1939 (Hazeltine).

7927 Marconi's and E.W.B. Gill. "Electron multiplier." Br. 520,973, Nov. 5, 1938.

7928 Goldsmith, T.T., Jr. "Mosaic screen." U.S. 2,190,020, Nov. 7, 1938, Feb. 13, 1940. Assigned: A.B. Du Mont Labs. Br. 538,753, Nov. 7, 1939 (S.T.C.).

7929 A.B. Du Mont and Alfred J. Hinck. "Cathode-ray tube." U.S. 2,186,635, Nov. 7, 1938, Jan. 9, 1940.

7930 Harries, —. "Electron lens and deflecting system." U.S. 2,288,239, Nov. 2, 1939, June 30, 1942. In Britain Nov. 9, 1938.

7931 Hickok, Willard. "Television system." U.S. 2,258,762, Nov. 10, 1938, Oct. 14, 1941. Assigned: RCA. Camera tube and circuit.

7932 Jones, W., and Pye Ltd. "Television." Br. 521,028, Nov. 10, 1938.

7933 Philpott, L.R., and R. LaVerne. "Cathode-ray sweep circuit." U.S. 2,218,549, Nov. 10, 1938, Oct. 22, 1940.

7934 "Future of television." ELECT. 121 (Nov. 11): 558. Comment on Sir Noel Ashbridge's lecture to the Institute of Mechanical Engineers, Nov. 4, 1938. Brief history of television and London television station. Mention of different standards in Britain, U.S., Germany, and France.

7935 Ashbridge, Sir Noel. "Television." ENGINEER 166 (Nov. 11): 526-9. Lecture to the Institute of Mechanical Engineers, Nov. 4. Abstract appears in ENGINEERING 146 (Nov. 11): 565. Also in PROC. IME 140: 25-60, 4 plates.

7936 Cawein, M. "Modulated-carrier wave signal-translating system." U.S. 2,203,521, Nov. 12, 1938, June 4, 1940. Assigned: Hazeltine. Television receiver circuit.

7937 Ardenne, M.v. "Storage projection tube." U.S. 2,277,007, Nov. 29, 1939, Mar. 17, 1942. In Germany Nov. 14, 1938. Television receiver.

7938 Snyder, R.L. "Electron multiplier." Br. 521,347, Nov. 14, 1938.

7939 Gebauer, R. "Television transmitter." U.S. 2,265,365, Nov. 9, 1939, Dec. 9, 1941. Assigned: C. Lorenz A.-G. In Germany Nov. 15, 1938. Camera tube.

7940 Kolster-Brandes and W.F. Tedham. "Valve generator." Br. 521,409, Nov. 15, 1938.

7941 Jones, W., and Pye Ltd. "Television." Br. 521,367, Nov. 16, 1938.

7942 "Antenna systems: Feeder attenuation." ELECT. 121 (Nov. 18): 599, 600.

7943 Kolster-Brandes and C.N. Smyth. "Cathode-ray tube." Br. 521,439, Nov. 18, 1938.

7944 Scharfnagel, Rudolf. "Electron discharge device." U.S. 2,225,465, Oct. 24, 1939, Dec. 17, 1940. In Germany Nov. 18, 1938 (C. Lorenz A.-G.).

7945 Felgel-Farnholz, Richard Ritter. "Television transmission system." U.S. 2,268,001, Nov. 13, 1939, Dec. 30, 1941. Assigned: Fernseh. In Germany Nov. 19, 1938.

7946 Ardenne, M.v. "Television projection tube." U.S. 2,276,360, Nov. 29, 1939, Mar. 17, 1942. In Germany Nov. 21, 1938.

7947 Günther, J. "Cathode-ray deflecting device." U.S. 2,255,039, Nov. 22, 1939, Sept. 9, 1941. Assigned: Fernseh A.-G. In Germany Nov. 22, 1938.

7948 Kolster-Brandes and C.N. Smyth. "Television." Br. 521,522, Nov. 22, 1938. Addition to 7892.

7949 Hazeltine. "Receiver." Br. 535,313, Oct. 24, 1939. Convention Nov. 223, 1938. Filter circuit.

7950 Hinsch, W. "Cathode-ray tube." U.S. 2,228,958, Feb. 24, 1940, Jan. 14, 1941 (Fides). In Germany Nov. 23, 1938.

7951 Sukumlyn, T.W. "Television image pickup system." U.S. 2,262,123, Nov. 23, 1938, Nov. 11, 1941.

7952 "Progress of television." ELECT. 121 (Nov. 25): 616.

7953 Dillenburger, W. "Television transmission system." U.S. 2,297,461, Aug. 9, 1940, Sept. 29, 1942 (Alien Properties Custodian). In Germany Nov. 25, 1938 (Fernseh).

7954 Kolster-Brandes and W.A. Beatty. "Television." Br. 521,814, Nov. 25, 1938.

7955 Zworykin, V.K. "Television system." U.S. 2,280,877, Nov. 26, 1938, Apr. 28, 1942. See Br. 535,834 (Nov. 27, 1939), wide-band amplifier.

7956 Lewis, H.M., and R.C. Hergenrother. "Cathode-ray signal-generating tube." U.S. 2,169,840, Nov. 28, 1938, Aug. 15. 1939. Assigned: Hazeltine.

7957 Ardenne, M.v. "Television image-projection system." U.S. 2,297,442, Mar. 18, 1940, Sept. 29, 1942 (Alien Properties Custodian). In Germany Nov. 29, 1938.

7958 Kolster-Brandes and W.A. Beatty. "Television." Br. 521,873, Nov. 29, 1938. Reference to Br. 486,377.

7959 S.T.C. "Electron multiplier." Br. 533,807, Nov. 28, 1939. Convention Nov. 29, 1938.

7960 Ardenne, M.v. "Television image-projection system." U.S. 2,276,750. Mar. 18, 1940, Mar. 17, 1942. In Germany Nov. 30, 1938.

7961 Bähring, H. "Scanning current generator." U.S. 2,265,620, Dec. 21, 1939, Dec. 9, 1941. In Germany Nov. 30, 1938. Saw-tooth wave generator for television receiver.

7962 Bedford, A.V. "Synchronized signal generator." U.S. 2,258,943, Nov. 30, 1938, Oct. 14, 1941 (RCA).

7963 G.E. and G.W. Edwards. "Television." Br. 521,984, Nov. 30, 1938. References to Br. 484,412; 514,807.

7964 Edwards, G.W. "Synchronizing signal separating apparatus." U.S. 2,269,524, Nov. 17, 1939, Jan. 13, 1942 (Hazeltine). In Britain Nov. 30, 1938.

7965 Günther, J. "Deflecting device." U.S. 2,264,567, Nov. 22, 1939, Dec. 2, 1941. In Germany Nov. 30, 1938. Yoke and coil assembly.

7966 Iams, H.A. "Electron discharge device." U.S. 2,240,186, Nov. 30, 1938, Apr. 29, 1941. Assigned: RCA. Br. 535,866, Nov. 29, 1939. Camera tube, mosaic screen.

7967 Marconi's. "Television." Br. 537,375, Nov. 30, 1939. Convention Nov. 30, 1938.

7968 Aguillon, L. "Les ondes de réflexion sur les lignes quasi-homogenes. Cas des transmissions de télévision par cable coaxial" [Reflected waves on quasi-homogeneous lines. Case of television transmissions by coaxial cable]. ANN. POSTES 27 (Dec.): 997-1019. Continued in 28 (Mar. 1939): 143-74.

7969 Farnsworth, P.T., and B.C. Gardner. "Image amplifier pick-up tubes." ELECTRONICS 11 (Dec.): 8, 9. Abstract.

7970 Maloff, I.G. "Gamma and range in television." ELECTRONICS 11 (Dec.): 9, 10. Abstract.

7971 Goldman, Stanford. "Television detail and selective-sideband transmission." ELECTRONICS 11 (Dec.): 10, 11. Abstract. See PROC. IRE (Nov. 1939).

7972 Lyman, H.T. "Input circuits for television receivers." ELECTRONICS 11 (Dec.): 12. Abstract.

7973 Baker, W.R.G. "Economics of television." ELECTRONICS 11 (Dec.): 13. Abstract.

7974 Wheeler, H.A. "Interpretation of amplitude and phase distortion in terms of paired echoes." ELECTRONICS 11 (Dec.): 13. Abstract.

7975 Jupe, J.H. "High-speed synchronous motor employed in British television." ELECTRONICS 11 (Dec.): 38.

7976 Pressler, H. "Uber die Bildfeldzerlegung bei der Farbenfernsehübertragung" [Resolving the field of the image in color television transmission.]. FERN. 9 (Dec.): 89-93.

7977 MacNamara, T.C., and D.C. Birkinshaw. "The London television service; with station layout." J. IEE 83 (Dec.): pp. 729-57. 4 plates. Discussion pp. 793-800 and in J. IEE 85 (Aug. 1939): 271-9. Part I: "Transmitted wave form" by A.D. Blumlein, pp. 758-66. Part II: "Vision input equipment" by C.O. Browne, pp. 767-82. Part III: "Radio transmitter" by N.E. Davis and E. Green, pp. 782-92; discussion pp. 793-801.

7978 Shumard, C.C. "A practical television receiver for the amateur." QST (Dec.).

7979 "10 x 12 foot, 441-line scan-disc television!" RADIO-CRAFT 10 (Dec.): 341, 376. 3 photos, 2 diags. Report by M.P. Wilder (National Union Radio Corp.) on his visit to the 1938 Berlin Radio Exposition and Fernseh exhibits.

7980 "Scanning the telly field." RADIO-CRAFT 10 (Dec.): 354, 370, 371. NBC tours, Garod's kit, FCC's committee, RMA standards, news from Germany and Britain, films in U.S. television.

7981 Traub, E.H. "English and continental television." J. TELEV. SOC. 2 (Dec.): 457-68. 1938 Berlin Radio Exposition and London's Olympia show. 6 photos, diag. Four-page list of items with details.

7982 Robinson, D.M. "The optical system of the Scophony television receivers." J. TELEV. SOC. 2 (Dec.): 469-74.

7983 Wheeler, H.A., and A.V. Loughren. "Fine structure of television images." J. TELEV. SOC. 2 (Dec.): 489-94.

7984 Goldmark, P.C. "Television station W2XAX." J. TELEV. SOC. 2 (Dec.): 494-6. 2 diags.

7985 Ardenne, M.v. "Methods and arrangements for 'storage' in television reception." J. TELEV. SOC. 2 (Dec.): 497.

7986 Kolster-Brandes, C.N. Smyth, and D.S.B. Shannon. "Valve generator." Br. 522,165, Dec. 2, 1938.

7987 Ardenne, M.v. "Television image projection tube." U.S. 2,277,009, June 6, 1940, Mar. 17, 1942. In Germany Dec. 6, 1938.

7988 Henneberg, W. "Electron multiplier." U.S. 2,272,841, Nov. 15, 1939, Feb. 10, 1942 (A.E.G., G.E.C.). In Germany Dec. 6, 1938.

7989 Wheeler, H.A. "Television receiver with automatic shade-level control." U.S. 2,259,538, Dec. 6, 1938, Oct. 21, 1941. Assigned: Hazeltine. Br. 534,718, Nov. 4, 1939.

7990 Baird Television and K.A.R. Samson. "Cathode-ray tube." Br. 522,139, Dec. 7, 1938.

7991 Ferranti, M.K. Taylor, and —. Wood. "Cathode-ray tube." Br. 522,377, Dec. 7, 1938. Reference to Br. 472,165.

7992 G.E.C., E.C. Cherry, and R.J. Clayton. "Valve generator." Br. 522,443, Dec. 8, 1938.

7993 McGee, J.D., and H.G. Lubszynski. "Transmission of television." ELECT. 121 (Dec. 9): 697. Photo, diag. Super-Emitron tube. See also ELECT. REV. 123 (Dec. 9): 828, 829.

7994 Kolster-Brandes and D.S.B. Shannon. "Cathode-ray tube." Br. 522,227, Dec. 9, 1938.

7995 Klemperer, O. "Cathode-ray tube." Br. 522,317, Dec. 10, 1938. Reference to Br. 494,791 (Oct. 10, 1936).

7996 Lubszynski, H.G. "Cathode-ray tube." Br. 522,458, Dec. 10, 1938.

7997 Goldsmith, A.N. "Television system." U.S. 2,221,091, Dec. 13, 1938, Nov. 12, 1940.

7998 Graefe, K.H. "Method for producing luminescent screens." U.S. 2,253,426, Dec. 13,

1939, Aug. 19, 1941. In Germany Dec. 13, 1938 (D.S. Loewe).

7999 Kolster-Brandes and C.N. Smyth. "Cathode-ray tube." Br. 522,533, Dec. 13, 1938.

8000 Manson, Ray H. "Combined television and radio receiving system." U.S. 2,232,399, Dec. 13, 1938, Feb. 18, 1941. Assigned: Stromberg-Carlson Telephone Mfg. Co.

8001 Marconi's and D.J. Fewings. "Amplitude-limiting valve." Br. 522,709. Dec. 13, 1938. Circuits; television.

8002 Mahl, H. "Electron discharge device." U.S. 2,264,541, Dec. 14, 1938, Dec. 2, 1941. Assigned: G.E. (New York). Original German patent June 30, 1937 (A.E.G.).

8003 Murphy Radio Ltd. and K.S. Davies. "Thermionic valve for television." Br. 522,737, Dec. 14, 1938.

8004 G.E. and D.C. Espley. "Television." Br. 522,545, Dec. 15, 1938.

8005 Harnett, D.E. "Periodic wave repeater." U.S. 2,212,420, Dec. 15, 1938, Aug. 20, 1940 (Hazeltine).

8006 Heimann, W., and K. Wemheuer. "Cathode-ray tube." U.S. 2,306,881, Mar. 2, 1940, Dec. 29, 1942 (Alien Properties Custodian). In Germany Dec. 15, 1938 (Fernseh). For converting optical image to electronic impulse.

8007 Hirshman, C.L., and Metropolitan-Vickers. "Thermionic valve generator circuits for television." Br. 523,780, Dec. 15, 1938.

8008 Sommer, Alfred, and Baird Television. "Manufacture of photoelectrically sensitive layers." Br. 522,752, Dec. 15, 1938; U.S. 2,192,418, June 5, 1939, Mar. 5, 1940.

8009 Bull, E.W. "Valve generator." Br. 522,637, Dec. 16, 1938.

8010 Cawein, M. "Television synchronizing system." U.S. 2,294,072, Dec. 17, 1938, Aug. 25, 1942.

8011 G.E. and D.C. Espley. "Television transmitter." Br. 522,903, Dec. 20, 1938.

8012 Lubszynski, H.G. "Electron discharge device." Br. 522,951. Dec. 20, 1938; U.S. 2,256,460, Dec. 20, 1939, Sept. 16, 1940 (EMI). Image tube.

8013 Nicoll, F.H. "Cathode-ray tube." Br. 522,952, Dec. 20, 1938. References to Br. 489,028 (Nov. 16, 1935); 491,573 (Dec. 2, 1935).

8014 Poch, W.J. "Cathode-ray tube apparatus." U.S. 2,261,776, Dec. 20, 1938, Nov. 4, 1941. Assigned: RCA.

8015 Zworykin, V.K. "View transmission system." U.S. 2,285,551, Dec. 20, 1938, June 9, 1942.

8016 "Wins basic patent in television field. Dr. V.K. Zworykin gains rights covering electronic system." N.Y.T. 38 (Dec. 22):6. Concerns Zworykin's patent of 1923. The Patent Office tribunals had decided against him, but the District of Columbia Court of Appeals reversed the decision.

8017 "Television receivers: Recommendations for marking of controls." ELECT. 121 (Dec. 23): 749. A list of 14 items, with descriptions, from the RMA Technical Section.

8018 Kolster-Brandes and P.M. Brand. "Television receiver." Br. 523,075, Dec. 23, 1938.

8019 "Notes on television." N.Y.T. (Dec. 25): IX, 12: 7. Comment on the Zworykin patent, involved in 11 Patent Office interferences.

8020 Hergenrother, R.C. "Video-frequency signal-generating apparatus." U.S. 2,242,952, Dec. 29, 1938, May 20, 1941 (Hazeltine).

8021 S.T.C. "Electron multiplier." Br. 537,276, Dec. 22, 1939. Convention Dec. 29, 1938.

8022 Landis, Daniel O. "Television receiver." U.S. 2,273,801, Dec. 30, 1938, Feb. 17, 1942. Assigned: RCA.

8023 Poch, W.J. "Television circuit." U.S. 2,296,050, Dec. 30, 1938, Sept. 15, 1942. Assigned: RCA.

8024 Wendt, K.R. "Amplifier for television receiver." U.S. 2,261,787, Dec. 30, 1938, Nov. 4, 1941 (RCA).

8025 BBC. AND NOW—THE BBC PRESENTS TELEVISION TO THE WORLD. London: British Broadcasting Corporation, 1938. 32 pp.

8026 BBC HANDBOOK 1938. London:BBC, 1938. "Television to-day" (pp. 40-48), "The television service" (pp. 94-95).

8027 Baden, Anne L. TELEVISION: A SELECTED LIST OF RECENT WRITINGS. Washington, D.C.: Library of Congress, Bibliography Division, 1938. 25 pp. (typed).

8028 Boltz, Cecil Leonard. WIRELESS FOR BEGINNERS. WITH A CHAPTER ON TELEVISION. Second edition. London: Harrap, 1938. The first edition came out in 1933. A third edition appeared in 1942. 254 pp.

8029 Chauvièrre, M. LA TELEVISION: LES PROBLEMES THEORIQUES ET PRATIQUES DE LA TELEVISION ET LEUR SOLUTION [Television: Theoretical problems and practices of television and their solution]. Paris: Dunod, 1938. vi + 267 pp., illus.

8030 Lipfert, K. DAS FERNSEHEN: EINE ALLGEMEINVERSTANDLICHE DARSTELLUNG DES NEUESTEN STANDES DER FERNSEHTECHNIK [Television: A popular description of the newest television techniques]. Berlin/Munich: J.F. Lehmanns, 1938. 115 pp.

8031 Maloff, I.G., and D.W. Epstein. ELECTRON OPTICS IN TELEVISION: WITH THEORY AND APPLICATION OF TELEVISION CATHODE-RAY TUBES. New York: McGraw-Hill, 1938. xi + 299 pp., 306 illus.

8032 Marconi-E.M.I. Television. MOBILE TELEVISION UNIT. Pamphlet No. M.E.M.I.-2. London: Marconi-E.M.I. Television Co. Ltd., 1938. v + 19 pp.

8033 Moseley, S.A., and H.J.B. Chapple. A SIMPLE GUIDE TO TELEVISION. London: Pitman, 1938. 43 pp., 13 photos, 4 diags.

8034 Reyner, J.H. TESTING TELEVISION SETS. London: Chapman and Hall, 1938. viii + 128 pp., 12 plates, 49 diags.

8035 Waldrop, F.C., and Joseph Borkin. TELEVISION: A STRUGGLE FOR POWER. New York: Morrow, 1938. 299 pp, bibl. Useful and critical study focusing on RCA role and other major players and their business interactions.

8036 Walker, R.C., and T.M.C. Lance. PHOTOELECTRIC CELL APPLICATIONS. 3rd edition. x + 245 pp. The first edition appeared in 1933 (193 pp.); the second in 1935 (245 pp.).

CHAPTER 19

THE VIDEO ART: 1939

8037 Gray, F. "Electrostatic electron optics." B.S.T.J. 18 (Jan.): 1

8038 Engstrom, E.W., and R.S. Holmes. "Deflection circuits in television receivers." ELECTRONICS 12 (Jan.): 19-21, 32.

8039 Barber, A.W. "Resistors at video frequencies." ELECTRONICS 12 (Jan.): 38.

8040 Sallow, H. "Storage-type camera tubes with conducting dielectric." FERN. UND TON. 10 (Jan.): 1-4.

8041 Bartlett, G. "Electrical developments of 1938: Research and laboratory investigations." G.E. REV. 42 (Jan.): 2, 51.

8042 Kaar, I.J. "The road ahead for television." J. SMPE 32 (Jan.): 18-40.

8043 Strutt, M.J.O. "Etages à haute fréquence, étages changeur de fréquence et détecteur des récepteurs de télévision" [High-frequency stages, frequency changing stages, and detectors for television receivers]. ONDE ELECT. 18 (Jan.): 14-26, 83-91. Continued in Feb. issue.

8044 Barthélemy, R. "Télévision, les signaux de synchronisation" [Synchronizing signals in television]. ONDE ELECT. 18 (Jan.): 27-37.

8045 "Video signal generator tube." PROC. IRE 27 (Jan.): supp. 6.

8046 George, R.W. "A study of ultra-high frequency wide-band propagation characteristics." PROC. IRE 27 (Jan.): 28-35. Tests on transmissions from the Empire State Building in New York City at 81-86 and 140-145 mc.

8047 Shumard, C.C. "Construction and alignment of television receiver." QST (Jan.).

8048 Gernsback, H. "The television racket." RADIO-CRAFT 10 (Jan.): 389.

8049 "Television." RADIO-CRAFT 10 (Jan.): 391. BBC, Don Lee, Du Mont, and their receivers, one with a 14-inch picture tube. 3 photos.

8050 "A television kit." RADIO-CRAFT 10 (Jan.): 399, 441. Garod receiver with 5-inch tube gives good detail in a 3-by-4-inch picture. 2 photos, diags., table, list of parts.

8051 "The proposed television standards—are they fair to all?" RADIO-CRAFT 10 (Jan.): 402, 403, 432. With comments by William H. Priess. 3 diagrams.

8052 "Dilatory U.S. manufacturers may lose television market." RADIO-CRAFT 10 (Jan.): 417, 436. Comments by 18 companies.

8053 Kaufman, S. "Television preparations in New York." RADIO N. 21 (Jan.): 6, 7.

8054 Kaar, I.J. "Outstanding problems which face television stations both from financial and technical ends." RADIO N. 21 (Jan.): 16, 17.

8055 Kauzmann, A.P. "New television amplifier receiving tubes." RCA REV. 3 (Jan.): 271-289.

8056 Seeley, S.W., and C.N. Kimball. "Analysis and design of video amplifiers, Part 2." RCA REV. 3 (Jan.): 290-308.

8057 Ardenne, M.v. "The problem of stereoscopic television." T.F.T. 28 (Jan.): 26.

8058 Jackson, D., and Pye Ltd. "Television and wireless receivers." Br. 523,372, Jan. 3, 1939.

8059 Collins, Lee A. "Television." U.S. 2,354,199, Jan. 3, 1939, July 25, 1944.

8060 Jackson, L., and Pye Ltd. "Cathode-ray tube." Br. 523,439, Jan. 3, 1939.

8061 IMK Syndicate, P. Nagy, and M.J. Goddard. "Light modulating." Br. 526,875, Jan. 4, 1939.

8062 "Keeping lines in step." W.W. 44 (Jan. 5): 9-11.

8063 "Television in cinemas." ELECT. 122 (Jan. 6): 2. Editorial note concerning Scophony.

8064 "Television across the Atlantic." ELECT. 122 (Jan. 6): 2. Editorial note.

8065 Kolster-Brandes and W.A. Beatty. "Cathode-ray tube, electron multiplier, television." Br. 523,575, Jan. 6, 1939. See Br. 535,384, Oct. 6, 1939.

8066 Kolster-Brandes and W.A. Beatty. "Wireless transmitter system for television, automatic control system." Br. 523,604, Jan. 6, 1939. References to Br. 520,082, 521,710.

8067 Kolster-Brandes and D.S.B. Shannon. "Television receiver." Br. 528,444, Jan. 6, 1939.

8068 Edwards, B.J., and Pye Ltd. "Television." Br. 523,611, Jan. 9, 1939.

8069 Christaldi, Peter S. "Cathode-ray tube." U.S. 2,225,099, Jan. 10, 1939 (Du Mont).

8070 Kolster-Brandes and D.S.B. Shannon. "Cathode-ray tube." Br. 523,616, Jan. 10, 1939.

8071 Paehr, H.W. "Magnetic electron lens." U.S. 2,284,227, Dec. 29, 1939, May 26, 1942. In Germany Jan. 10, 1939.

8072 Carpmael, A. "Cathode-ray tube." Br. 522,860, Jan. 11, 1939 (Telefunken). Camera tube, mosaic screen.

8073 Thöm, K. "Electro-optical system." U.S. 2,293,521, Dec. 29, 1939, Aug. 18, 1942. Assigned: Fernseh G.m.b.H. In Germany Jan. 11, 1939.

8074 Ridgeway, D.V. and Baird Television. "Electro-magnetic focusing coil." U.S. 2,202,505, June 27, 1939, May 28, 1940. In Britain Jan. 13, 1939.

8075 Wilson, J.C. "Periodic saw-tooth wave repeater." U.S. 2,177,162, Jan. 14, 1939, Oct. 24, 1939 (Hazeltine).

8076 Wilson, J.C. "Television signal-translating system." U.S. 2,255,691, Jan. 14, 1939, Sept. 9, 1941 (Hazeltine); Br. 536,436, Dec. 18, 1939.

8077 Hazeltine. "Television." Br. 535,633, Dec. 18, 1939. Convention Jan. 17, 1939.

8078 "Progress in television." MAN. GUARD. (Jan. 19): 12.

8079 Baird Television and T.C. Nuttall. "Circuit arrangement for television." Br. 524,038, Jan. 20, 1939.

8080 Scophony and A.H. Rosenthal. "Cathode-ray tube." Br. 524,230, Jan. 22, 1939.

8081 Jones, W., and Pye Ltd. "Television." Br. 524,286, Jan. 25, 1939.

8082 "Television sales drive." ELECT. 122 (Jan. 27): 86. Promotional drive with posters, lectures, and demonstrations to begin Feb. 1. Slogan: "Television is here—you can't shut your eyes to it." Comments also on talk by H.L. Kirke (BBC) to the Royal Society of Arts on Jan. 18 in London; he said there are too few receivers in use; the public does not realize what they are missing.

8083 Hughes, L.E.C. "Television progress." ELECT. 122 (Jan. 27): 110.

8084 Wheeler, H.A. "Periodic wave generator." U.S. 2,226,648, Jan. 27, 1939, Dec. 31, 1940 (Hazeltine). Saw-tooth generator.

8085 Wilson, J.C. "Television signal translating system." U.S. 2,255,692, Jan. 27, 1939, Sept. 9, 1941 (Hazeltine).

8086 Holman, H.E. "Cathode-ray tube." Br. 524,354, Jan. 28, 1939. Mosaic screen.

8087 Poch, W.J., and RCA. "Synchronizing picture generator." U.S. 2,212,648, Jan. 28, 1939, Aug. 27, 1940.

8088 Kolster-Brandes and W.A. Beatty. "Television, cathode-ray tube, telephone system." Br. 527,904, Jan. 31, 1939.

8089 Marconi's. "Cathode-ray tube." Br. 538,412, Jan. 31, 1940. Convention Jan. 31, 1939.

8090 Nelson, Herbert. "Image transmitting tube." U.S. 2,258,791, Jan. 31, 1939, Oct. 14, 1941 (RCA).

8091 Goldsmith, A.N. "Television economics." COMM. 19 (Feb.): 18-20, 45-7. Continued in Mar., Apr., May, June, July, Aug. issues.

8092 Perkins, W.M. "Television receiver design factor." COMM. 19 (Feb.): 32, 34, 36, 47, 48.

8093 Goldsmith, Jr., T.T. "The Du Mont television system." COMM. 19 (Feb.): 38, 39, 42, 44, 45. IRE paper.

8094 Sheffield, B. "The television image." ELECTRONICS 12 (Feb.): 56, 57.

8095 Köpping, A. "Problems in transmission of wide-frequency bands over wires." FERN. U. TON. 10 (Feb.): 9-12.

8096 Ramberg, E. "Simplified derivation of the general properties of an electron-optical image." J. OSA (Feb.).

8097 Beers, G.L., E.W. Engstrom, and I.G. Maloff. "Some television problems from the motion picture standpoint." J. SMPE 32 (Feb.): 121-36.

8098 Rinia, H., and L. Leblans. "Nipkow disc." PHIL. TECH. REV. 4 (Feb.): 42-7.

8099 "Tests on street speed coming of television." POP. MECH. 71 (Feb.): 199.

8100 "Television receiver kit for students." POP. MECH. 71 (Feb.): 257.

8101 Iams, H. "A fixed-focus electron gun for cathode-ray tubes." PROC. IRE 27 (Feb.): 103.

8102 Finke, Herbert A. "A television pickup tube." PROC. IRE 27 (Feb.): 144-7.

8103 Sherman, J.B. "Using electromagnetic deflection cathode-ray tubes in the television receiver." QST (Feb.).

8104 "U.S. televising shows to beat Britain's best, says Sagall." RADIO-CRAFT 10 (Feb.): 479, 508. Photo. Comments by Solomon Sagall of Scophony Ltd.

8105 Thompson, M.W. "Introduction to modern television." RADIO N. 21 (Feb.): 6-8. Article continued in Mar., Apr., May, June, July issues.

8106 Dorf, W.C. "Video reporter." RADIO N. 21 (Feb.): 9. Continued in Mar., Apr., May issues.

8107 Webster, H. "Build your own television receiver." RADIO N. 21 (Feb.): 22-4.

8108 Ardenne, M.v. "Storage methods in television reception." TELEV. & S.W.W. 12 (Feb.): 67.

8109 de Nemos, T. "Colour television with electrical colour filters." TELEV. & S.W.W. 12 (Feb.): 73, 75.

8110 B.T.-H. "Cathode-ray tube." Br. 534,343, Jan. 30, 1940. Convention Feb. 1, 1939. Mosaic screen.

8111 "Television." ELECT. 122 (Feb. 3): 153. Discusses BBC, RMA.

8112 Kirke, H.L. "Recent progress in television." J. RO. ARTS 87 (Feb. 3): 302-25. British developments in television.

8113 S.T.C. and A.I. Vangeen. "Electron multiplier." Br. 524,658, Feb. 3, 1939.

8114 Kolster-Brandes and W.A. Beatty. "Television, cathode-ray tube." Br. 524,671, Feb. 7, 1939.

8115 Kolster-Brandes and C.N. Smyth. "Television receiver, valve amplifier circuits." Br. 524,672, Feb. 7, 1939.

8116 Kolster-Brandes and C.N. Smyth. "Wireless receiver with applications to television." Br. 524,776, Feb. 7, 1939.

8117 Gray, F. "Cathode-ray tube." U.S. 2,260,313, Feb. 8, 1939, Oct. 28, 1941. Assigned: B.T.L.

8118 Otterbein, G. "Das Ultraschall-Lichtrelais beim Fernsehen" [The ultrasonic light relay in television]. E.T.Z. 60 (Feb. 9): 161-3. Ultrasonic light relay and control for opto-mechanical apparatus.

8119 Paehr, H.W. "Cathode-ray tube." U.S. 2,297,429, Jan. 26, 1940, Sept. 29, 1942. In Germany Feb. 9, 1939.

8120 IMK Syndicate, P. Nagy, and M.J. Goddard. "Light modulating device for television receivers." Br. 526,742, Feb. 10, 1939. Cathode-ray tube. See next entry.

8121 IMK Syndicate, P. Nagy, and M.J. Goddard. "Light modulating device for television receivers." Br. 527,009, Feb. 10, 1939. Divided from the above.

8122 S.T.C. "Electron multiplier." Br. 538,760, Feb. 9, 1940. Convention Feb. 11, 1939.

8123 G.E., R.J. Clayton, and G.W. Edwards. "Television." Br. 525,049, Feb. 13, 1939. Reference to Br. 494,677.

8124 Wheeler, H.A. "Periodic wave generator." U.S. 2,250,170, Feb. 13, 1939, July 22, 1941 (Hazeltine); Br. 536,153, Jan. 15, 1940. Saw-tooth generator, receiver circuit.

8125 Campbell, R.L. "Synchronizing generator." U.S. 2,209,507, Feb. 15, 1939, July 30, 1940 (Du Mont).

8126 Wilson, J.C. "Periodic wave generator." U.S. 2,221,015, Feb. 16, 1939, Nov. 12, 1940 (Hazeltine); Br. 538,064, Jan. 25, 1940. Saw-tooth generator for magnetic scanning.

8127 Bowie, R.M. "Cathode-ray tube." U.S. 2,250,622, Feb. 17, 1939, July 29, 1941.

8128 Guanella, G. "Television, valve generator circuit, automatic control system." Br. 525,342, Feb. 17, 1939.

8129 Kolster-Brandes and C.N. Smyth. "Cathode-ray tube." Br. 525,181, Feb. 17, 1939.

8130 Bernstein, Philip. "Electron-optical method and apparatus." U.S. 2,199,066, Feb. 21, 1939, Apr. 30, 1940. Assigned: Press Wireless, Inc.

8131 Teal, G.K. "Electron discharge device." U.S. 2,250,283, Feb. 21, 1939, July 22, 1941 (B.T.L.). See Br. 534,318 (E.R.P.), Jan. 25, 1940. References to Br. 468,483 (S.T.C.), Aug. 3, 1935; 498,867 (Farnsworth), Nov. 2, 1936; 510,696 (EMI), Nov. 4, 1937.

8132 Strecker, F. "Telephone, facsimile, and television transmission over wires." E.T.Z. 60 (Feb. 23): 214.

8133 Cocking, W.T. "Television output circuits." W.W. 44 (Feb. 23): 174-7.

8134 Marconi's, L.M. Myers, and A.T. Starr. "Television, cathode-ray tube." Br. 525,616, Feb. 23, 1939. Reference to Br. 513,776 (Scophony), Feb. 3, 1938.

8135 Nagy, P., and M.J. Goddard. "Light modulating device for use in television receivers." Br. 528,734, Feb. 23, 1939 (IMK Syndicate); U.S. 2,290,569, Sept. 4, 1940, July 21, 1942.

8136 Kallmann, H.E. "Television, duplex with signalling." Br. 525,628, Feb. 24, 1939. References to Br. 489,102, Jan. 19, 1937; 505,079, Oct. 4, 1937.

8137 Blumlein, A.D. "Television, thermionic valve circuit." Br. 528,310, Feb. 25, 1939; U.S. 2,266,154, Mar. 1, 1940, Dec. 16, 1941 (EMI).

8138 Branson, H. "Cathode-ray tube." U.S. 2,274,586, Feb. 25, 1939, Feb. 24, 1942; Br. 538,684, Feb. 12, 1940. Assigned: Philco Radio & Television Corp.

8139 Goldsmith, A.N. "Color television system." U.S. 2,253,292, Feb. 27, 1939, Aug. 19, 1941.

8140 Beers, G.L. "Cathode-ray tube apparatus." U.S. 2,276,455, Feb. 28, 1939, Mar. 17, 1942. Assigned: RCA.

8141 Grundmann, G.L. "Wide-band amplifier." U.S. 2,261,803, Feb. 28, 1939, Nov. 4, 1941 (RCA).

8142 Kolster-Brandes, W.A. Beatty, and Profulla Kumar Chatterjea. "Electron multiplier." Br. 525,758, Feb. 28, 1939.

8143 Everest, F.A. "Practical aspects of wide-band television amplifier design." COMM. 19 (Mar.): 21, 22, 24, 38, 39, 48, 49.

8144 Barber, A.W. "Safety in television receivers." COMM. 19 (Mar.): 26, 27.

8145 Smith, T.A. "Radio transmission considerations: Sound vs. picture." COMM. 19 (Mar.): 30.

8146 "Television receivers in production." ELECTRONICS 12 (Mar.): 23-5, 78-81. Plans of six manufacturers for May 1.

8147 "Television transmitters." ELECTRONICS 12 (Mar.): 26-9, 47.

8148 Fink, D.G. "Television formulary: Definitions, equations, and design formulas." ELECTRONICS 12 (Mar.): 33-5. Abstract from his book to be published.

8149 "High-definition television stations in the United States." ELECTRONICS 12 (Mar.): 47.

8150 "Television bibliography: Articles selected from ELECTRONICS, from 1934 to the present." ELECTRONICS 12 (Mar.): 47.

8151 Günther, J. "Generation of saw-tooth currents for magnetic deflection in television tubes." FERN. U. TON. 10 (Mar.): 17.

8152 Murray, D.K. Woolfe [of BBC-TV]. "Production problems of television." J. TELEV. SOC. 3 (Mar.): 1-7. A BBC producer, Murray presented this paper Mar. 8, 1939, at the Television Society's 11th annual general meeting in London. Discusses general studio problems and procedures, together with a sample of script. 2 photos, diag.

8153 Valentine, P.W.S. [of Philips Lamps Ltd.] "The Philips large screen television receiver." J. TELEV. SOC. 3 (Mar.): 7-14. 2 photos, 8 diags. Tel 61, with a mirror in the lid, projected a picture 18 x 14 1/2 inches (considered the largest desirable for the living room).

8154 Parratt, D.W. [of Murphy Radio Ltd.]. "Servicing in relation to television receivers." J. TELEV. SOC. 3 (Mar.): 14-28. 6 photos and diags.

8155 "Television Society's new premises." J. TELEV. SOC. 3 (Mar.): 28-30. Floor plan. The Society had moved to 17 Featherstone Buildings, High Holborn, London—an early 18th-century house converted into offices.

8156 "Television for the provinces." J. TELEV. SOC. 3 (Mar.): 31. Extension from London via radio link or coaxial cable.

8157 "Eleventh annual report of the current membership." J. TELEV. SOC. 3 (Mar.): 32-4. Membership reported as: 1 Honorary Fellow (Baird), 148 Fellows, 164 Associates, 14 students, 20 others—total 347 members at the end of Dec. 1938 (total in Dec. 1937—402). Lord Selsdon died Dec. 24, 1938. Report on television from Alexandra Palace: 957 hours broadcast through 1938, plus 300 hours of film for trade demonstrations. 25% drama, 23% light entertainment, 11% obituaries, 9.5% features and topical, 6.4% talks, 3.5% music, 2.4% ballet.

8158 Bingley, F.J. "Sync problems in television." J. TELEV. SOC. 3 (Mar.): 34, 35.

8159 "Radio progress during 1938: Television." PROC. IRE 27 (Mar.): 174-6. Includes bibliography of 46 titles.

8160 (number not used)

8161 Sherman, J.B. "Electrostatic deflection kinescope unit for the television receiver." QST (Mar.).

8162 "Television antenna, 1939 model." RADIO-CRAFT 10 (Mar.): 523. NBC, Empire State Building. 2 photos.

8163 "World-wide television progress—a review." RADIO-CRAFT 10 (Mar.): 528, 529, 572, 573. 5 photos. Companies and receivers in England, Germany, France, and U.S.

8164 "Andrea in television with kits and sets." RADIO-CRAFT 10 (Mar.): 545. 2 photos.

8165 "Two national television networks rumored for spring." RADIO-CRAFT 10 (Mar.): 546, 560.

8166 Thompson, M.W. "Magic of the Iconoscope." RADIO N. 21 (Mar.): 6-8.

8167 "Photo-electric cell for television: Federal court holds that Zworykin is inventor." SCI. AM. 160 (Mar.): 199.

8168 Moulton, F.R. "Television in Washington." SCI. MON. 48 (Mar.): 289, 290.

8169 Skellett, A.M. "Narrow-band transmission system for animated line images." TRANS. AIEE 58 (Mar.): 124-6.

8170 Baird Television and G.A.R. Tomes. "Television, cathode-ray tube." Br. 525,791, Mar. 1, 1939.

8171 Hansen, Siegfried. "Television scanning." U.S. 2,274,366, Mar. 1, 1939, Feb. 24, 1942. Assigned: GE.

8172 Wilson, J.C. "Television signal-reproducing system." U.S. 2,253,312, Mar. 2, 1939, Aug. 19, 1941 (Hazeltine).

8173 "Television makes headway." ELECT. 122 (Mar. 3): 272. Comments on the televised Boon-Danahan fight and large-screen television at Marble Arch cinema and elsewhere in London. Baird sees ahead some ten years when central stations will televise programs to cinemas as well as homes. Report on the television sales drive: good results, with sales now of 500 sets a week. Estimates that some 40,000 sets will be sold during 1939.

8174 Kolster-Brandes, R.E. Prichard, and C.N. Smyth. "Television." Br. 525,967, Mar. 3, 1939. Addition to Br. 520,235. Reference to Br. 491,502.

8175 Blue, A.H., and R.D. Wood. "Television." Br. 530,777, Mar. 6, 1939.

8176 Rosenthal, A.H. "Secret television system." Br. 530,776, Mar. 6, 1939; U.S. 2,251,525, Apr. 29, 1940, Aug. 5, 1941.

8177 Faudell, C.L. "Television." Br. 526,111, Mar. 7, 1939; U.S. 2,303,924, Mar. 7, 1940, Dec. 1, 1942. Assigned: EMI Television, valve generator circuits.

8178 D.S. Loewe. "Television transmitter." Br. 537,352, Mar. 9, 1940. In Germany Mar. 9, 1939.

8179 Hardwick, J. "Thermionic valve circuit arrangement." Br. 527,628, Mar. 9, 1939; U.S. 2,267,095, May 18, 1940, Dec. 23, 1941 (EMI).

8180 Busch, Vern W. "Television apparatus." U.S. 2,224,287, Mar. 10, 1939, Dec. 10, 1940.

8181 "Television station has radically designed antenna." SCI. N. LETTER 35 (Mar. 11): 159.

8182 Mulert, Theodor, and F. Rudert. "Saw-tooth current generator." U.S. 2,284,337, Mar. 11, 1940, May 26, 1942. In Germany Mar. 11, 1939.

8183 Kolster-Brandes, C.N. Smyth, and R.E. Prichard. "Television." Br. 526,361, Mar. 14, 1939. Addition to Br. 520,235. Reference to Br. 520,234.

8184 S.T.C. (A.B. Du Mont). "Television." Br. 526,226, Mar. 14, 1939. Reference to Br. 526,211, Mar. 12, 1938.

8185 S.T.C. (A.B. Du Mont). "Cathode-ray tube, television." Br. 526,364, Mar. 14, 1939.

8186 Mullard, —., and C.C. Eaglesfield. "Cathode-ray tube." Br. 526,382, Mar. 14, 1939.

8187 Freeman, Robert L. "Television receiving apparatus." U.S. 2,259,520, Mar. 15, 1939, Oct. 21, 1941; Br. 538,103, Feb. 19, 1940. Assigned: Hazeltine.

8188 Sommer, A. "Method of manufacturing secondary emitting electrodes." Br. 522,774, Mar. 15, 1939; U.S. 2,206,372, June 14, 1939, July 2, 1940. Assigned: Baird Television Ltd.

8189 Puckle, O.S. "Cathode-ray tubes." W.W. 44 (Mar. 16): 242. A history of cathode-ray tubes. Continued in Mar. 23 issue.

8190 Browne, C.O. "Television." Br. 527,912, Mar. 16, 1939; U.S. 2,272,043, Mar. 30, 1940, Feb. 3, 1942 (EMI). Plurality of cameras.

8191 Hazeltine. "Television synchronization." Br. 537,878, Feb. 19, 1940. Convention Mar. 16, 1939.

8192 Kenyon, Franklin P. "Electron beam deflection means." U.S. 2,229,977, Mar. 16, 1939, Jan. 28, 1941. Deflection yoke assembly.

8193 "Finance of television." ELECT. 122 (Mar. 17): 332. Comments on the high cost of relaying programs from London. Cinemas should contribute if they receive BBC transmissions. Retailers of sets are opposed to cinema television.

8194 Campbell, R.L. "Television communication." U.S. 2,227.822, Mar. 17, 1939, Jan. 7, 1941. Assigned: A.B. Du Mont Labs.

8195 Lewis, H.M. "Television receiver synchronizing system." U.S. 2,252,599, Mar. 20, 1939, Aug. 12, 1941; Br. 540,014, Feb. 27, 1940. Assigned: Hazeltine.

8196 Bowman-Manifold, M. "Cathode-ray tube." Br. 526,954, Mar. 22, 1939. References to Br. 442,666, May 12, 1934; 457,493, May 30, 1935; 495,338, May 13, 1937.

8197 Goldsmith, T.T., Jr. "Method and system for television communications." U.S. 2,201,309, Mar.22, 1939, May 21, 1940. Assigned: A.B. Du Mont Labs. Divided from original of Mar. 12, 1938.

8198 Hanson, O.B. "Television system." U.S. 2,286,540, Mar. 22, 1939, June 16, 1942. Assigned: RCA.

8199 Percival, W.S. "Thermionic valve amplifier." Br. 528,179, Mar. 22, 1939; U.S. 2,302,798, Apr. 20, 1940, Nov. 29, 1942 (EMI). Shows amplifier with camera tube.

8200 Baird Television and V.A. Jones. "Image dissemination." Br. 526,622, Mar. 23, 1939. Reference to Br. 524,038, Jan. 20, 1939.

8201 Wheeler, H.A. "Periodic wave generator." U.S. 2,264,781, Mar. 29, 1939, Dec. 2, 1941 (Hazeltine). Saw-tooth wave generator.

8202 Wald, G. "Optical television." U.S. 2,306,656, Mar. 30, 1939, Dec. 29, 1942.

8203 Wheeler, H.A. "Periodic wave repeater." U.S. 2,255,403, Mar. 30, 1939, Sept. 9, 1941 (Hazeltine). Television receiver circuit.

8204 Poch, W.J. "Protective circuits." U.S. 2,227,603, Mar. 31, 1939, Jan. 7, 1941 (RCA). For cathode-ray tube.

8205 Schlesinger, K. "Television receiving arrangement." U.S. 2,265,780, Mar. 31, 1939, Dec. 9, 1941. Assigned: Loewe Radio Corp. Divided from U.S. 2,163,216, Oct. 19, 1935 (in Germany Oct. 25, 1934).

8206 Everest, F.A. "Television engineering." COMM. 19 (Apr.): 17-9, 34, 35. Continued in May, June, July, Aug., and Sept. issues.

8207 Waller, L.C. "Kinescopes for television receivers." COMM. 19 (Apr.): 20.

8208 Schmidling, G.T. "Fluorescent materials for television tubes." COMM. 19 (Apr.): 30.

8209 Eddy, W.C. "Miniature staging: The technical side of video effects." COMM. 19 (Apr.): 22.

8210 Mallein, S., and G. Rabuteau. "The Eiffel Tower television transmitter." ELECT. COMM. 17 (Apr.): 382-97.

8211 "Telesurgery." ELECTRONICS 12 (Apr.): 8.

8212 Engstrom, E.W., and R.S. Holmes. "Power for television receivers." ELECTRONICS 12 (Apr.): 22-4.

8213 "Cubical television antenna for G.E. station at Albany." ELECTRONICS 12 (Apr.): 51.

8214 "Television." ELECTRONICS 12 (Apr.): 51.

8215 Raeck, F. "Die geschichtliche Entwicklung des Zeilensprungverfahrens" [Historical development of the line jump procedure]. FERN. U. TON. 10 (Apr.): 25.

8216 "Television 1: A $13,000,000 'if.'" FORTUNE 19 (Apr.): 52-9, 168, 172-82. Continued in 19 (May): 69-74.

8217 Baker, W.R.G. "Television now ready for public participation. Brief review of some problems facing it." G.E. REV. 42 (Apr.): 167-9.

8218 Turnbull, I.L., and H.A.M. Clark. "Marconi-E.M.I. audio-frequency equipment at the London television station." J. IEE 84 (Apr.) 448.

8219 Cork, E.C., and J.L. Pawsey. "Long feeders for transmitting wide side-bands, with reference to the Alexandra Palace aerial-feeder system." J. IEE 84 (Apr.): 448-67. Discussion reported pp. 475-82.

8220 McGee, J.D., and H.G. Lubszynski. "E.M.I. cathode-ray television transmission tubes." J. IEE 84 (Apr.): 468-75. Discussion reported pp. 475-82. See also ELECT. 121 (Dec. 9, 1938): 697, and ELECT REV. (Dec. 9, 1938).

8221 "Iconoscopes: Technical information." PROC. IRE 27 (Apr.): Supp. 2.

8222 Bedford, A.V., and G.L. Fredendall. "Transient response of multistage video-frequency amplifiers." PROC. IRE 27 (Apr.): 277-84.

8223 "Television continues advance—except in opinion of the FCC." RADIO-CRAFT 10 (Apr.): 609, 626.

8224 Thompson, M.W. "Building television skywires." RADIO N. 21 (Apr.): 6-9, 44.

8225 Lindenblad, N.E. "Television transmitting antenna for the Empire State Building." RCA REV. 3 (Apr.): 387-408.

8226 Maloff, I.G. "Gamma and range in television." RCA REV. 3 (Apr.): 409-17.

8227 Seeley, S.W., and C.N. Kimball. "Transmission lines as coupling elements." RCA REV. 3 (Apr.): 418-30. Applications to television.

8228 Barco, Allen A. "Measurement of phase shift in television amplifiers." RCA REV. 3 (Apr.): 441-52.

8229 Hanson, O.B. "Here comes television! Technical equipment has limitations, standards laid down to prevent obsolescence of receivers." SCI. AM. 160 (Apr.): 207-9.

8230 Preisach, F. "Noise reduction in television receivers by means of photoelectric multipliers." W. ENG. 16 (Apr.): 169-73. Illus.

8231 Strutt, M.J.O. "High frequency mixing and detection stages of television receivers." W. ENG. 16 (Apr.): 174-87. Illus., bibliography.

8232 "Obsolescence is no worry to purchaser of radio; television and static-free broadcasting both for the future." SCI. N. LETTER 35 (Apr.): 205.

8233 Mullard, —. "Cathode-ray tube." Br. 539,496, Apr. 1, 1940. Convention Apr. 3, 1939. Mosaic screen assembly.

8234 Beatty, W.A., and P.K. Chatterjea. "Television system." Br. 527,310, Apr. 3, 1939 (Kolster-Brandes); U.S. 2,295,023, Mar. 26, 1940, Sept. 8, 1942. Assigned: International Standard Electrical Corp. References to Br. 443,896, (8065).

8235 Ballard, R.C. "Background control." U.S. 2,240,281, Apr. 4, 1939, Apr. 29, 1941 (RCA). Receiver circuit.

8236 Ballard, R.C. "Separating circuit." U.S. 2,246,659, Apr. 4, 1939, June 24, 1941 (RCA).

8237 Broadway, L.F. "Cathode-ray tube." Br. 527,313, Apr. 4, 1939; U.S. 2,264,274, Apr. 4, 1940, Dec. 2, 1941. Assigned: EMI

8238 Farnsworth, P.T., and Farnsworth Television and Radio Corp. "Image amplifier." U.S. 2,257,942, Apr. 5, 1939, Oct. 7, 1941.

8239 Farnsworth, P.T. "Cold cathode electron-discharge tube." U.S. 2,263,032, Apr. 5, 1939, Nov. 18, 1941 (Farnsworth Television and Radio Corp.). Divided from original of Nov. 4, 1936.

8240 West, S. "Television IF amplifier." W.W. 44 (Apr. 6): 319-22.

8241 Bingley, F.J. "Timing signal circuit." U.S. 2,230,926, Apr. 13, 1939, Feb. 4, 1941 (Philco). Saw-tooth generator circuit.

8242 "Extension of the television service." ELECT. 122 (Apr. 14): 464. Comments on letter by Lord Hirst in the TIMES. Plans to extend television to Birmingham and then to two other centers. Television financed by all holders of wireless licenses.

8243 "Television and the R.M.A." ELECT. 122 (Apr. 14): 483. Note that the RMA will stand the loss if the BBC extends television to Birmingham. Cost estimated at less than 100,000 pounds.

8244 G.E. and L.C. Jesty. "Cathode-ray tube." Br. 527,547, Apr. 14, 1939.

8245 Adam, M. "Démonstration officielle de télévision sur grand écran au Théatre Marigny, Paris, 31 mars 1939" [Official demonstration of large-screen television at the Théatre Marigny]. GENIE CIVIL 114 (Apr. 15): 324-35.

8246 Hadfield, B.M. "Amplifier." Br. 529,441, Apr. 17, 1939. Deflector plate amplifier.

8247 Van den Bosch, F.J.G., and Vacuum-Science Products Ltd. "Electron multiplier." Br. 527,978, Apr. 17, 1939.

8248 Kemp, R.J. "Navigation-aiding radio band system." Br. 527,841, Apr. 19, 1939; U.S. 2,284,873, Apr. 19, 1940, June 2, 1942 (RCA). Includes television.

8249 "Television for the Midlands." ELECT. 122 (Apr. 21): 494. Note on RMA's push to get television at Birmingham via a cable link. Also notes that Baird's large-screen units are to be sent to cinemas in New York on Apr. 22.

8250 Barthélemy, R. "Le centre expérimental de télévision de Montrouge." REV. GEN. 45 (Apr. 22): 503-16.

8251 Kolster-Brandes and W.A. Beatty. "Television." Br. 528,192, Apr. 22, 1939.

8252 Kolster-Brandes, D.S.B. Shannon, and P.K. Chatterjea. "Electron multiplier." Br. 529,837, Apr. 22, 1939.

8253 Farnsworth, P.T. "High-efficiency amplifier." U.S. 2,223,001, Apr. 24, 1939, Nov. 26, 1940. Cathode-ray tube.

8254 Farnsworth, P.T. and Farnsworth Television and Radio Corp. "Electron multiplier." U.S. 2,260,613, Apr. 25, 1939, Oct. 28, 1941. Divided from original of May 18, 1936.

8255 S.T.C. and P.A.J. Visschers. "Television receiver." Br. 528,324, Apr. 25, 1939.

8256 Jackson, D., and Pye Ltd. "Wireless receiver (for television)." Br. 528,198, Apr. 26, 1939. Reference to Br. 523,372.

8257 Wolff, I. "Cathode-ray deflector apparatus." U.S. 2,300,189, Apr. 26, 1939, Oct. 27, 1942 (RCA). Sweep circuit for picture tube.

8258 G.E. and L.C. Jesty. "Television." Br. 528,090, Apr. 27, 1939. References to Br. 443,896, 508,037, 527,547.

8259 Knoop, W.A. "Electro-optical image production." U.S. 2,274,710, Apr. 28, 1939, Mar. 3, 1942. Assigned: B.T.L.

8260 Parce, L. "Paires concentriques pour hautes fréquences" [Concentric pairs for high frequencies]. ANN. POSTES 28 (May-June): 262-289, 432-50.

8261 Eddy, William C. "Television lighting." COMM. 19 (May): 17.

8262 Maurer, J.A. "Sound motion picture films in television." COMM. 19 (May): 28, 30, 32. Continued in June, July, and Aug. issues.

8263 "Television components for receivers." ELECTRONICS 12 (May): 18-22. Illus.

8264 "Big screen television, by Baird Television, Ltd." ELECTRONICS 12 (May): 52.

8265 Rudert, F. "Points in design of home receivers." FERN. U. TON. 10 (May): 33-6.

8266 "How television works." MAN. GUARD. (May 1).

8267 "Sight and sound receivers." POP. MECH. 71 (May): 737.

8268 "Television grows up!" RADIO N. 21 (May): 6-10.

8269 Lubcke, H.R. "With the West Coast televisors: Station W6XAQ, Los Angeles." RADIO N. 21 (May): 11.

8270 Thompson, R.T. "Build your own video-audio set." RADIO N. 21 (May): 12, 13.

8271 Thompson, M.W. "Television receiver's heart—the intermediate frequency amplifier." RADIO N. 21 (May): 18-20.

8272 Rowe, W.S. "The Du Mont receiver." RADIO N. 21 (May): 21.

8273 "Andrea video-audio receiver." RADIO N. 21 (May): 24.

8274 Golby, J. "Constructing the Don Lee video receiver." RADIO N. 21 (May): 25, 26.

8275 Farrier, C.W. "NBC television sets the pace." RADIO N. 21 (May): 28, 29.

8276 "Television stations in the U.S. licensed by the FCC." RADIO N. 21 (May): 32. List of stations in the U.S.

8277 "Television system standards." RMA ENG. 3 (May): 14. See also 4 (Nov.): 24.

8278 G.E. and W.H. Aldous. "Oscillation generator." Br. 528,228, May 1, 1939. Saw-tooth wave generator.

8279 Okolicsanyi, F. "Optical system for television receivers." Br. 528,685, May 1, 1939 (Scophony); U.S. 2,296,943, Apr. 29, 1940, Sept. 29, 1942.

8280 Davisson, C.J. "Electron discharge device." U.S. 2,250,927, May 2, 1939, July 29, 1941 (B.T.L.). Television camera tube.

8281 "Television topics." W.W. 44 (May 4): 425. Continued in 44 (May 18): 473-5.

8282 Philco. "Television receiving circuit." Br. 542,639, Apr. 18, 1940. In U.S. May 4, 1939.

8283 Smith, Newland F. "Synchronizing circuit." U.S. 2,240,422, May 4, 1939, Apr. 29, 1941 (Philco).

8284 S.T.C. "Cathode-ray tube." Br. 528,801, May 5, 1939. Deflection coils.

8285 Campbell, R.L. "Television transmission system." U.S. 2,245,428, May 9, 1939, June 10, 1941 (Philco).

8286 Philco. "Television." Br. 542,436, Apr. 25, 1940. In U.S. May 11, 1939.

8287 Van den Bosch, F.J.G., and Vacuum-Science Products. "Electron multiplier." Br. 531,541, May 11, 1939; U.S. 2,285,848, Mar. 29, 1940, June 9, 1942.

8288 Scophony and A.H. Rosenthal. "Light valve." Br. 529,099, May 12, 1939.

8289 Deserno, P. "Television receiver." U.S. 2,282,992, May 11, 1940, May 12, 1942. In Germany May 13, 1939. Assigned: C. Lorenz A.-G.

8290 Nelson, H. "Phenomenon of secondary electron emission." PHYS. REV. (May 15).

8291 White, E.L.C. "Thermionic valve circuits for the generation of saw-tooth currents." Br. 529,383, May 15, 1939; U.S. 2,280,990, May 15, 1940, Apr. 28, 1942. References to Br. 400,976, 482,740.

8292 Gray, F. "Electro-optical system." U.S. 2,248,986, May 16, 1939, July 15, 1941. Assigned: B.T.L. Divided from U.S. 2,150,159, Mar. 4, 1936, Mar. 14, 1939.

8293 "Extension of television to the provinces." ELECT. 122 (May 19): 621. Comment on a television station in the Midlands and the benefit to the industry in promoting sales, both for home use and for export, and in maintaining Britain's lead in the television field.

8294 "Television and the provinces." ELECT. 122 (May 19): 632. Need for extended service to stimulate sales at home and abroad. There will be 20 stations in the U.S. by Sept. Italy has ordered German equipment for three stations.

8295 Reichel, W. "Color television." U.S. 2,289,457, May 13, 1940, July 14, 1942. In Germany May 19, 1939.

8296 Philco. "Cathode-ray tube." Br. 541,910, May 14, 1940. In U.S. May 20, 1939.

8297 Pietschack, Ernst. "Method of producing mosaic electrodes." U.S. 2,337,569, May 14, 1940, Dec. 28, 1943. In Germany May 20, 1939.

8298 "First report of Television Committee." Public Notice 34168, Washington, D.C. (May 22). The second report was issued Nov. 15, 1939.

8299 B.T.-H. and D. Gábor. "Cathode-ray tube." Br. 532,106, May 24, 1939. Including use in television receivers.

8300 Bingley, F.J. "Wide-band amplifier." U.S. 2,240,605, May 24, 1939, May 6, 1941 (Philco). For television receiver.

8301 Kolster-Brandes and W.A. Beatty. "Cathode-ray tube for television." Br. 529,648, May 24, 1939. Addition to (8065).

8302 Philco. "Television amplifier." Br. 544,403, May 14, 1940. Convention May 24, 1939.

8303 Van den Bosch, F.J.G., and Vacuum-Science Products. "Electron multiplier." Br. 531,821, May 25, 1939; U.S. 2,295,919, May 20, 1940, Sept. 15, 1942. Electron discharge device.

8304 A.C. Cossor and E.E. Shelton. "Cathode-ray tube." Br. 529,523, May 26, 1939.

8305 Lewis, H.M. "Wave-signal transmission system." U.S. 2,217,957, May 26, 1939, Oct. 15, 1940 (Hazeltine).

8306 Kolster-Brandes and C.N. Smyth. "Television." Br. 529,790, May 26, 1939.

8307 Iams, H.A., and A. Rose. "Television transmitting tube and system." U.S. 2,213,175, May 27, 1939, Aug. 27, 1940. Assigned: RCA. Br. 542,219, May 27, 1940 (Marconi's).

8308 Skellett, A.M. "Electron discharge apparatus." U.S. 2,217,774, May 27, 1939, Oct. 15, 1940.

8309 Kolster-Brandes and C.N. Smyth. "Television." Br. 529,985, May 30, 1939.

8310 Loughren, A.V. "Television signal-translating system." U.S. 2,269,540, May 31, 1939, Jan. 13, 1942. Assigned: Hazeltine.

8311 Naumberg, W. "Insulation in television." COMM. 19 (June): 24.

8312 "Television in the field. Brief report of its problems and accomplishments in the initial period of growth." ELECTRONICS 12 (June): 12-5, 90-2. Television in New York is one month old.

8313 "Art advances: Report of progress during the past twelve months on all fronts of electronic endeavor." ELECTRONICS 12 (June): 23-7.

8314 "Television receiver production at the RCA Victor plant." ELECTRONICS 12 (June): 36, 37. Illus.

8315 "Sync impulse generator for television deflection circuits." ELECTRONICS 12 (June): 48.

8316 "Radiator for Empire State television transmitter." PROC. IRE 27 (June): Supp. 2, 3.

8317 Wheeler, H.A. "The interpretation of amplitude and phase distortion in terms of paired echoes." PROC. IRE 27 (June): 359-85. Report on discussion pp. 384, 385.

8318 Carter, P.S. "Simple television antennas." PROC. IRE 27 (June): 410, 411. Abstract.

8319 Maloff, I.G. "Functions of electron bombardment in television." PROC. IRE 27 (June): 414. Abstract.

8320 Zworykin, V.K. "Electron optics in television." PROC. IRE 27 (June): 417. Abstract.

8321 Gernsback, H. "Television angles." RADIO-CRAFT 10 (June): 709. Comments on color, networks, transmitters, motion pictures, prices of receivers.

8322 "Television." RADIO-CRAFT 10 (June): 710.

8323 West, S. "Servicing television receiver faults." RADIO-CRAFT 10 (June): 714, 715, 746. 5 photos, 2 diagrams. Reprinted from TELEV. & S.W.W.

8324 "American teleceivers for 1939." RADIO-CRAFT 10 (June): 723, 744. 6 photos. Discusses Du Mont, G.E., Pilot, RCA Victor, Stewart-Warner, and Westinghouse.

8325 "Business preparing for boom as television makes its bow." RADIO-CRAFT 10 (June): 739, 760. Photo.

8326 Ragsdale, C.L. "Do your own televising: Television camera and receiver." RADIO N. 21 (June): 6-8.

8327 Goldsmith, A.N. "Opportunities in television." RADIO & TELEV. (June).

8328 Hanson, O.B. "How NBC television evolved." RADIO & TELEV. (June).

8329 Campbell, R.L. "Television transmitting system." U.S. 2,207,048, June 1, 1939, July 9, 1940. Assigned: A.B. Du Mont Labs. Circuits.

8330 Scophony. "Television." Br. 536,720, June 1, 1939. Addition to Br. 513,776, Feb. 3, 1938.

8331 Jefferson Electric Co. "Cathode-ray tube." Br. 539,122, Mar. 26, 1940. Convention June 2, 1939. Deflection coils.

8332 Jefferson Electric Co. "Cathode-ray tube." Br. 540,554, Mar. 26, 1940. Convention June 2, 1939. Divided from above. Deflection coils.

8333 Kolster-Brandes, D.S.B. Shannon, and P.K. Chatterjea. "Modulator." Br. 530,115, June 3, 1939. For television.

8334 Thornton, A.A., and Philco. "Synchronizing circuit." Br. 530,378, June 5, 1939.

8335 Baird Television and G.E.G. Graham. "Electron multiplier." Br. 530,260, June 6, 1939.

8336 Grenfall, Alexis René. "Deflecting circuit for cathode-ray tubes." Br. 530,259, June 6, 1939; U.S. 2,271,070, June 4, 1940, Jan. 27, 1942 (EMI).

8337 Poch, W.J. "Fluorescent lamp (television receiver)." U.S. 2,254,855, June 6, 1939, Sept. 2, 1941 (RCA).

8338 Rose, A. "Television transmitting tube." U.S. 2,213,176, June 6, 1939, Aug. 27, 1940. Assigned: RCA. Br. 540,034, June 6, 1940 (Marconi's).

8339 S.T.C. and C.N. Smyth. "Cathode-ray tube." Br. 530,263, June 6, 1939. For television, focus.

8340 Wheeler, H.A. "Television synchronizing system." U.S. 2,251,966, June 7, 1939, Aug. 12, 1941 (Hazeltine). Television receiver.

8341 Hazeltine. "Television." Br. 545,440, June 5, 1940. In U.S. June 7, 1939.

8342 Hazeltine. "Television." Br. 545,411, June 5, 1940. In U.S. June 7, 1939.

8343 Philco and A.A. Thornton. "Television amplifier." Br. 530,319, June 8, 1939.

8344 Thornton, A.A., and Philco. "Television amplifier." Br. 534,457, June 8, 1939. Reference to Br. 530,319, above.

8345 Thornton, A.A., and Philco. "Television receiver." Br. 534,839, June 8, 1939.

8346 Moore, Robert C., and Philco. "Synchronizing circuit." U.S. 2,294,341, May 31, 1940, Aug. 25, 1942. In Britain June 8, 1939. For television.

8347 Moore, R.C., and Philco. "Wide-band amplifier." U.S. 2,289,291, May 27, 1940, July 7, 1942. In Britain June 8, 1940. Television video circuit.

8348 "Television in cinemas." ELECT. 122 (June 9): 756.

8349 Marconi's and D.C. Plaistowe. "Synchronizing circuit for television." Br. 530,519, June 9, 1939.

8350 Wilson, J.C. "Video frequency signal translating system." U.S. 2,254,114, June 9, 1939, Aug. 25, 1941 (Hazeltine). Br. 537,599, June 5, 1940. Television receiver circuit.

8351 Van den Bosch, F.J.G., and Vacuum-Science. "Electron multiplier." Br. 532,025, June 12, 1939.

8352 Thornton, A.A., and Philco. "Valve generator." Br. 532,110, June 13, 1939. Saw-tooth wave generator. Reference to Br. 485,999 (Nov. 23, 1935).

8353 Ridgeway, D.V. "Line deflectors." W.W. 44 (June 15): 550-53. Magnetic deflectors; survey of receivers at the 1938 Olympia exhibition in London.

8354 "Radial scanning." W.W. 44 (June 15): 555.

8355 West, S. "Noise in television receivers." W.W. 44 (June 15): 563.

8356 Hewson, B.T., and A. Locan. "Color television." Br. 533,993, June 15, 1939; U.S. 2,328,145, Aug. 20, 1941, Aug. 31, 1943.

8357 Clothier, S.L., and H.C. Hogencamp. "Television apparatus." U.S. 2,260,559, June 16, 1939, Oct. 28, 1941. Assigned: Kolorama Labs. Divided from U.S. 2,163,538 (July 17, 1937).

8358 Moore, R.C. "Electron-beam deflector circuit." U.S. 2,251,851, June 16, 1939, Aug. 5, 1941 (Philco). Br. 542,994, May 16, 1940.

8359 S.T.C. and D.S.B. Shannon. "Television." Br. 530,095, June 16, 1939. Receiver cabinet arrangement.

8360 Iams, H.A. "Television transmitting tube." U.S. 2,213,177, June 24, 1939, Aug. 27, 1940. Assigned: RCA. Br. 543,890, June 24, 1940.

8361 Bull, C.S., and S. Hill. "Electron multiplier." Br. 534,208, June 26, 1939 (EMI).

8362 Seeley, S.W. "Television shading-control circuit." U.S. 2,271,876, June 27, 1939, Feb. 3, 1942. Assigned: RCA.

8363 Baird Television and P.W. Willans. "Television." Br. 530,591, June 28, 1939. Camera tube.

8364 Iams, H.A. "Television transmitting tube and system." U.S. 2,213,178, June 29, 1939, Aug. 27, 1940. Assigned: RCA.

8365 Grundmann, G.L. "Television receiver." U.S. 2,223,822, June 29, 1939, Dec. 3, 1940. Assigned: RCA.

8366 Bedford, A.V., and Felix E. Cone. "Cathode-ray deflector yoke." U.S. 2,234,038, June 30, 1939, Mar. 4, 1941 (RCA).

8367 Shelby, R.E. "Electron discharge tube." U.S. 2,193,539, June 30, 1939, Mar. 12, 1940 (RCA).

8368 Marconi's. "Valve generator circuit." Br. 542,032, June 20, 1940. Convention June 30, 1939. Saw-tooth wave generator.

8369 Goldsmith, T.T. "Pioneering television receiver engineering." ELECT. MFG 24 (July): 51-4, 68, 74. Du Mont.

8370 Rose, A., and H.A. Iams. "The Orthicon." ELECTRONICS 12 (July): 11.

8371 "The Orthicon: A new and improved form of the Iconoscope uses low-velocity electrons for scanning." ELECTRONICS 12 (July): 11-4. Cover illus., diags.

8372 Barthélemy, R. "Point detectors: Applications to television." ELECTRONICS 12 (July): 54, 55.

8373 Gehrts, A. "Die technische Ausrüstung von Fernsehaufnahmeräumen" [The technical equipment of television studios]. FERN. U. TON. 10 (July): 49.

8374 Wheeler, H.A. "Wide-band amplifiers for television." PROC. IRE 27 (July): 429-38. Bibliography, illus.

8375 Hollywood, J.M. "Single-sideband filter theory with television applications." PROC. IRE 27 (July): 457-72.

8376 Sarnoff, D. "Probable influences of television on society." J. APP. PHYS. 10 (July): 426-31.

8377 McIlwain, Knox. "Survey of television pickup devices." J. APP. PHYS. 10 (July): 432-42. 7 illus. Image dissector, Iconoscope, theory, construction, and technical details.

8378 Mertz, P. "High-definition television." J. APP. PHYS. 10 (July): 443-6.

8379 Goldmark, P.C. "Problems of television transmission." J. APP. PHYS. 10 (July): 447-54.

8380 Engstrom, E.W. "Television receiving and reproducing systems." J. APP. PHYS. 10 (July): 455-64. 18 diags. and photos.

8381 Ramberg, E.G., and G.A. Morton. "Electron optics." J. APP. PHYS. 10 (July): 465-78.

8382 Leverenz, H.W., and F. Seitz. "Luminescent materials." J. APP. PHYS. 10 (July): 479-93.

8383 Jacob, L. "Electron distribution in electron-optically-focused electron beams." PHIL. MAG. 28 (July): 81-98.

8384 "Television lets students watch operation." POP. SCI. 135 (July): 94.

8385 "Television." RADIO-CRAFT 11 (July): 6, 7. News items, 2 photos.

8386 West, J. "Servicing television receiver faults. Pt. 2." RADIO-CRAFT 11 (July): 24, 25, 61, 62. 5 photos, 6 diags.

8387 "Television boom starts." RADIO-CRAFT 11 (July): 35, 62. Scophony ad for cinema television.

8388 "More television." RADIO-CRAFT 11 (July): 44, 45.

8389 "1939 commercial teleceiver. Pt. 1." RADIO-CRAFT 11 (July): 60, 61. Photo, diag. RCA Victor models TRK 9 (9-inch) and TRK 12 (12-inch). Technical data, specifications, controls.

8390 Hutchinson, Thomas H. "Planning programs for television." RADIO & TELEV. (July).

8391 Sarnoff, David. "The birth of an industry." RCA REV. 4 (July).

8392 Castle, Donald H. "A television demonstration system for the New York World's Fair." RCA REV. 4 (July): 6-13.

8393 Kell, R.D., and G.L. Fredenhall. "Selective side-band transmission in television." RCA REV. 4 (July): 83.

8394 Barco, A.A. "An Iconoscope pre-amplifier." RCA REV. 4 (July): 89-107.

8395 "Television problems." SCI. AM. 161 (July): 2.

8396 "Screen of television." SCI. AM. 161 (July): 28.

8397 Engstrom, E.W., G.L. Beers, and A.V. Bedford. "Application of motion picture film to television." J. SMPE 33 (July): 3-16. See also RCA REV. 4 (July): 48-61.

8398 Goldmark, P.C. "A continuous type television film scanner." J. SMPE 33 (July): 18-25.

8399 Protzman, Albert W. "Television studio technic." J. SMPE 33 (July): 26-40. See also RCA REV. 4 (Apr. 1940): 399-413.

8400 Eddy, W.C. "Television lighting." J. SMPE 33 (July): 41.

8401 Lubcke, H.R. "An introduction to television production." J. SMPE 33 (July): 54-65. Don Lee station W6XAO.

8402 Du Mont, A.B. "Design problems in television systems and receivers." J. SMPE 33 (July): 66-73. Refers to RMA standards.

8403 Gladenbeck, F. "Successes of community work in television." T.F.T. 28 (July): 245. In German. Gladenbeck was president of the German Post Office. Abstract in J. TELEV. SOC. 3 (Mar. 1940): 110.

8404 Weiss, J.G. "On the development of the 'standard' television receiver E.1." T.F.T. 28 (July): 246-49. In German. Developed by the research institute of the German Post Office and five firms, beginning in Nov. 1938, with a working prototype in Feb. 1939. Cathode-ray tube 20 by 23 cm; magnetic focus and deflection. Abstract in J. TELEV. SOC. 3 (1940): 110.

8405 Andrieu, R., and F. Rudert. "The standard television receiver E.1." T.F.T. 28 (July): 249-57. In German.

8406 Mulert, T., and R. Urtel. "Beam deflection and high-voltage generator in the standard television receiver E.1." T.F.T. 28 (July): 257-64. In German.

8407 Knoblauch, H. (Telefunken), and E. Schwartz (Fernseh A.-G.). "The cathode-ray tube used in the standard television receiver

E.1." T.F.T. 28 (July): 264-7. In German. Abstract in J. TELEV. SOC. 3 (1940): 130-2.

8408 Deserno, P., and M. Messner. "A testing tool for measuring the frequency characteristics of the standard television receiver E.1." T.F.T. 28 (July): 267-71.

8409 Roosenstein, H.O. "The standard television broadcast receiving antenna." T.F.T. 28 (July): 271-6.

8410 "Traveling television exhibit." T.F.T. 28 (July): 288.

8411 Bingley, F.J. "Television transmission." U.S. 2,171,537, July 1, 1939, Sept. 5, 1939 (Philco). Divided from U.S. 2,171,536 (Nov. 23, 1935). (8412, 8413)

8412 Okolicsanyi, F. "Television receiver." Br. 536,289, July 3, 1939; U.S. 2,296,944, June 24, 1940, Sept. 29, 1942 (Scophony).

8413 Bingley, F.J. "Signal amplifier." U.S. 2,252,612, July 5, 1939, Aug. 12, 1941 (Philco). (8410)

8414 Bingley, F.J. "Signal transmitting system." U.S. 2,252,613, July 5, 1939, Aug. 12, 1941. (8410)

8415 Van den Bosch, F.J.G. "Electron multiplier." Br. 531,558, July 5, 1939.

8416 G.E.C. and W.H. Peters. "Cathode-ray tube." Br. 530,914, July 5, 1939. For television receiver; focus.

8417 Philco and F.J. Bingley. "Signal-driving circuit." U.S. 2,226,459, July 5, 1939, Dec. 24, 1940. Divided from U.S. 2,171,536 (Nov. 23, 1935). Pulse generator.

8418 "Radio and television." ELECT. 123 (July 7): 2. Lord Hirst's remarks on the future of radio and television manufacturing at a General Electric Co. meeting.

8419 Holman, H.E. "Cathode-ray tube." Br. 533,213, July 7, 1939.

8420 Baird Television and P.W. Willans. "Television." Br. 531,828, July 10, 1939.

8421 Marconi's and L.M. Myers. "Cathode-ray tube." Br. 531,760, July 12, 1939. Receiver tube.

8422 G.E.C. and D.C. Espley. "Electron multiplier." Br. 531,219, July 13, 1939. For television.

8423 G.E.C. and D.C. Espley. "Television." Br. 531,220, July 14, 1939. Transmission with electron multiplier. References to (8421), 492,662 (Mar. 23, 1937), 493,048 (Mar. 30, 1937), 519,757 (Oct. 5, 1937).

8424 "New television tube improves detail of image." SCI. N. LETTER 36 (July 15): 41.

8425 Poole, R.B. "Television." Br. 527,967, July 15, 1939.

8426 B.T.-H. and D.J. Mynall. "Television." Br. 531,295, July 17, 1939. Receiver.

8427 G.E.C. and D.C. Espley. "Television." Br. 531,159, July 19, 1939. Transmission.

8428 Scophony and A.H. Rosenthal. "Television receiver." Br. 531,306, July 18, 1939.

8429 Baird Television and A. Sommer. "Photoelectrically sensitive electrode." Br. 532,259, July 20, 1939; U.S. 2,285,062, May 9, 1940, June 2, 1942 (Cinema-Television).

8430 Thöm, K. "Circuit arrangement with secondary emission electron multipliers." U.S. 2,310,883, July 16, 1940, Feb. 9, 1943 (Fernseh; Alien Properties Custodian). In Germany July 20, 1939.

8431 Gottier, Thomas L. "Television transmitter modulator." U.S. 2,262,139, July 21, 1939, Nov. 11, 1941. Assigned: RCA.

8432 Baird Television and K.A.R. Samson. "Cathode-ray tube." Br. 532,525, July 24, 1939. Mosaic electrode.

8433 Okolicsanyi, F., and Alfred John Gale. "Television system and scanner." Br. 536,803, July 24, 1939; U.S. 2,320,380, June 10, 1940, June 1, 1943 (Scophony).

8434 Heimann, W. "Electronic television transmitter." U.S. 2,310,782, July 24, 1940, Feb.

9, 1943 (Alien Properties Custodian). In Germany July 25, 1939.

8435 Blumlein, A.D. "Amplifier." Br. 536,089, July 28, 1939; U.S. 2,269,001, Aug. 6, 1940, Jan. 6, 1942. For film transmission; thermionic valve amplifier. Reference to Br. 456,450 (Apr. 3, 1935).

8436 Blumlein, A.D., and F. Blythen. "Magnetic focusing arrangement for cathode-ray tubes." Br. 534,465, July 28, 1939; U.S. 2,291,682, Aug. 6, 1940, Aug. 4, 1942 (EMI).

8437 G.E.C. and T.R. Cowley. "Television." Br. 531,653, July 28, 1939. Receiver.

8438 Klemperer, O. "Cathode-ray tube." Br. 534,215, July 28, 1939; U.S. 2,367,130, July 25, 1940, Jan. 9, 1943 (E.M.I.). References to Br. 470,004 (Feb. 3, 1936), 505,751 (Sept. 13, 1937).

8439 Rajchman, J.A., and R.L. Snyder, Jr. "Electron multiplier." U.S. 2,285,126, July 28, 1939, June 2, 1942 (RCA).

8440 S.T.C. and A.I. Vangeen. "Electron multiplier." Br. 532,717, July 28, 1939.

8441 Gehrts, A. "Fernsehen." V.D.I.Z. 83 (July 29): 881-84. On the introduction of regular television service in Germany.

8442 Iams, H.A. "Television transmitting device." U.S. 2,213,179, July 29, 1939, Aug. 27, 1940. Assigned: RCA. Br. 542,332, July 29, 1940 (Marconi's).

8443 G.E.C. and B.J. O'Kane. "Television." Br. 531,724, July 31, 1939.

8444 Reichel, W. "Der Mehrfachzeilenspring" [Multiple interlacing]. FERN. 15 (Aug.): 171, 179.

8445 Baker, W.R.G. "Extending our horizons— with television." G.E. REV. 42 (Aug.): 335.

8446 Robinson, D.M. "The supersonic light control and its application to television, with special reference to the Scophony television receivers." PROC. IRE 27 (Aug.): 483-6.

8447 Sieger, J. "The design and development of television receivers using the Scophony optical scanning system." PROC. IRE 27 (Aug.): 487-92.

8448 Wikkenhauser, G. "Synchronization of Scophony television receivers." PROC. IRE 27 (Aug.): 492-6.

8449 Lee, H.W. "Some factors involved in the optical design of a modern television receiver using moving scanners." PROC. IRE 27 (Aug.): 496-500. Discusses the Scophony receiver.

8450 Vance, A.W. "A high-efficiency modulating system." PROC. IRE 27 (Aug.): 506.

8451 Law, R.R. "Contrast in kinescopes." PROC. IRE 27 (Aug.): 511-24.

8452 "Synchronizing-signal generator developed by Allen B. Du Mont Laboratories." PROC. IRE 27 (Aug.): Supp. 2.

8453 "Sound and picture receiver for experimenters." POP. MECH. 72 (Aug.): 295.

8454 "1939 commercial teleceiver, Pt. 2." RADIO-CRAFT 11 (Aug.): 74, 75, 110, 111.

8455 "—and with 441-line definition. Telly piped over phone wires!" RADIO-CRAFT 11 (Aug.): 82, 118. Photo, 2 diags. Demonstration by NBC and Bell Labs.

8456 West, S. "Servicing television receiver faults, Pt. 3." RADIO-CRAFT 11 (Aug.): 86, 87, 112. 5 photos, 3 diags.

8457 "Will phone lines stop worries about national television net?" RADIO-CRAFT 11 (Aug.): 99, 122.

8458 Bohlke, W. Hollander. "Television antennas and their installation." RADIO & TELEV. (Aug.).

8459 Cin. El. Comm. and P. Eisler. "Television." Br. 534,466, Aug. 2, 1939.

8460 Lewis, H.M., and J.C. Wilson. "Signal-transmission system and method of operation." U.S. 2,269,590, Aug. 2, 1939, Jan. 13,

1942 (Hazeltine). Receiver circuit with scanning disk.

8461 Maybank, N.W. (Report on Baird's color demonstration at Dominion Theatre, Feb. 4, 1938.) W.W. 44 (Aug. 3). (8472)

8462 Okolicsanyi, F. "Television receiver." Br. 536,290, Aug. 3, 1939; U.S. 2,349,298, July 31, 1940, May 23, 1944. Assigned: Scophony.

8463 "Television in color." ELECT. 123 (Aug. 4): 118. On demonstration by Baird from Crystal Palace to his laboratory two miles away.

8464 Calbrick, Chester J. "Cathode-ray device." U.S. 2,168,760, Aug. 8, 1939, Dec. 30, 1939 (B.T.L.).

8465 Schlesinger, K., and D.S. Loewe. "Low-frequency amplification of television pickup." U.S. 2,248,561, Aug. 8, 1939, July 8, 1941. Divided from German patent of Jan. 25, 1934.

8466 S.T.C. and C.N. Smyth. "Cathode-ray tube." Br. 533,301, Aug. 9, 1939. Television receiver.

8467 Wilson, J.C. "Signal translating channel." U.S. 2,253,313, Aug. 9, 1939, Aug. 19, 1941 (Hazeltine).

8468 De Tar, Donald R. "Electron discharge device." U.S. 2,234,720, Aug. 10, 1939, Mar. 11, 1941 (G.E.C.). Cathode-ray tube.

8469 Baird Television and D.V. Ridgeway. "Valve generator." Br. 532,074, Aug. 16, 1939.

8470 Gray, F. "Electron discharge device." U.S. 2,293,539, Aug. 16, 1939, Aug. 18, 1942. Assigned: B.T.L.

8471 M-O Valve Co. and G.W. Warren. "Electron multiplier." Br. 532,082, Aug. 16, 1939.

8472 Maybank, N.W. "Colour television: Baird television system described." W.W. 45 (Aug. 17): 145, 146. (8461)

8473 "Large-screen television." ELECT. 123 (Aug. 18): 191. Remarks of Isidore Ostrer, chairman of the Gaumont-British Pictures Corp. Ltd., at the annual meeting. The Baird Television Co. had recently demonstrated large-screen sets in America, "acclaimed a wonderful feat and one of vital importance to the cinema industry of that country."

8474 S.T.C., D.S.B. Shannon, and P.K. Chatterjea. "Valve generator." Br. 536,215, Aug. 18, 1939.

8475 "Television at Olympia." TIMES (Aug. 23, 1939): 13c, d. Comment on the poor reception of the opening of Alexandra Palace; few buyers of television receivers.

8476 Van den Bosch, F.J.G., and Vacuum-Science. "Electron multiplier." Br. 534,474, Aug. 23, 1939.

8477 Cooper, Arthur Henry. "Television receiver." Br. 534,973, Aug. 24, 1939; U.S. 2,298,870, Dec. 12, 1940, Oct. 13, 1942. Assigned: EMI.

8478 "Radiolympia, 1939." ELECT. 123 (Aug. 25): 203.

8479 Batchelor, J.C. "Television receiver." U.S. 2,264,172, Aug. 25, 1939, Nov. 25, 1941.

8480 Hepp, G. "Electronic generator." U.S. 2,292,835, Jan. 8, 1941, Aug. 11, 1942 (N.V. Philips). In Netherlands Aug. 29, 1939.

8481 Baird Television. "Television contrast amplifying system." Br. 542,820, Aug. 28, 1940. Convention Aug. 29, 1939.

8482 Langmuir, D.B. "Electron discharge device." U.S. 2,219,107, Aug. 29, 1939, Oct. 22, 1940 (RCA).

8483 "New television aerial." W.W. 45 (Aug. 31): 206.

8484 Hickok, W.H., and RCA. "Magnetic field neutralizing system." U.S. 2,214,729, Aug. 31, 1939, Sept. 17, 1940. Deflector coils on cathode-ray tube.

8485 Kell, R.D. "Method and apparatus for picture transmission." U.S. 2,298,796, Aug. 31, 1939, Oct. 13, 1942 (RCA). Camera tube.

8486 Kell, R.D. "Television." U.S. 2,299,328, Aug. 31, 1939, Oct. 20, 1942. Assigned: RCA. Br. 540,281, Aug. 31, 1940 (Marconi's).

8487 Marconi's. "Image converter, electron multiplier." Br. 543,710, Sept. 2, 1940. Convention Aug. 31, 1939.

8488 Morton, G.A. "Electronic image device." U.S. 2,255,801, Aug. 31, 1939, Sept. 16, 1941 (RCA). Includes electron multiplier, electron mirror, image intensifier.

8489 Rose, A., and RCA. "Image converter tube." U.S. 2,213,180, Aug. 31, 1939, Aug. 27, 1940.

8490 Fink, D.G. "Television receiver for the home." ELECTRONICS 12 (Sept.): 16-22. Model of "E.1" receiver; $262 or less.

8491 "Demonstration of Baird large-screen television." ELECTRONICS 12 (Sept.): 48.

8492 "Television symposia." ELECTRONICS 12 (Sept.): 60.

8493 Strutt, M.J.O., and A. van der Ziel. "Kurzwellen-Breitband-Ver-staerkung" [Short-wave wide-band amplification]. E.N.T. 16 (Sept.): 229-40.

8494 Turnbull, I.L., and H.A.M. Clark. "Marconi-E.M.I. audio-frequency equipment at the London television station." J. IEE 85 (Sept.): 439-62, 462-7.

8495 Janes, R.B., and W.H. Hickok. "Recent improvements in the design and characteristics of the Iconoscope." PROC. IRE 27 (Sept.): 535-40. Illus.

8496 Iams, H.A., G.A. Morton, and V.K. Zworykin. "The image Iconoscope." PROC. IRE 27 (Sept.): 541-7. Illus. (7747)

8497 Rose, A., and H. Iams. "Television pick-up tubes using low-velocity electron beam scanning." PROC. IRE 27 (Sept.): 547-55. Illus.

8498 Zworykin, V.K., and J.A. Rajchman. "The electrostatic electron multiplier." PROC. IRE 27 (Sept.): 558.

8499 Brown, G.H. "Vestigial-sideband filter for use with a television transmitter." PROC. IRE 27 (Sept.): 608. Abstract.

8500 Haeff, A.V. "Development of a 20-kilowatt ultra-high-frequency tetrode for television service." PROC. IRE 27 (Sept.): 610, 611. Abstract.

8501 Hartley, L.J. "Production alignment apparatus for television receivers." PROC. IRE 27 (Sept.): 612. Summary.

8502 Herold, Edward W. "Superheterodyne first-detector considerations in television receivers." PROC. IRE 27 (Sept.): 612. Abstract.

8503 Kallmann, H.E. "Transient response in television." PROC. IRE 27 (Sept.): 613. Abstract.

8504 Sarnoff, D. "Future of television." POP. MECH. 72 (Sept.): 321-5.

8505 "Fingerprints transmitted by television." POP. SCI. 135 (Sept.): 111.

8506 "How to install a television antenna." POP. SCI. 135 (Sept.): 200, 201.

8507 "Television." RADIO-CRAFT 11 (Sept.): 135. News items.

8508 West, S. "Servicing television receiver faults, Pt. 4." RADIO-CRAFT 11 (Sept.): 148, 149, 174, 175. 6 photos, 5 diags.

8509 Sicuranza, C. "Getting into television servicing." RADIO-CRAFT 11 (Sept.): 158, 159, 178, 179. 9 photos, diag.

8510 "Television tips." RADIO-CRAFT 11 (Sept.): 166, 183. News items.

8511 Marchant, F.W. "New Baird colour television system." TELEV. & S.W.W. 12 (Sept.): 541, 542.

8512 "Our lead in television." ELECT. 123 (Sept. 1): 230. Sir Stephen Tallent's remarks on the opening of Radiolympia; "unbounded optimism in regard to the future of television" and Great Britain's lead in the field.

8513 "Television convention." ELECT. 123 (Sept. 1): 232, 233.

8514 Morton, G.A. "Electron discharge device." U.S. 2,271,985, Sept. 1, 1939, Feb. 3, 1942. Assigned: RCA.

8515 Ruedy, J.E. "Electron discharge device." U.S. 2,264,717, Sept. 1, 1939, Dec. 2, 1941 (RCA).

8516 Marconi's. "Valve generator." Br. 543,550, Sept. 2, 1940. Convention Sept. 1, 1939.

8517 Rappold, Armin. "Television transmitter." U.S. 2,297,499, Aug. 22, 1940, Sept. 29, 1942 (Alien Properties Custodian). In Germany Sept. 5, 1939.

8518 Knick, U. "Broad-band amplifier." U.S. 2,265,291, Aug. 29, 1940, Dec. 9, 1941. In Germany Sept. 7, 1939.

8519 "Electron optics and television." ELECT. 123 (Sept. 8): 256. Summary of V.K. Zworykin's remarks at the British Association meeting in Dundee, Aug. 30, 1939. The meeting was terminated on Sept. 1, because of the European situation.

8520 Broadway, L.F. "Electron focusing system." Br. 534,627, Sept. 7, 1939; U.S. 2,283,041, Aug. 30, 1940, May 12, 1942. Assigned: EMI Reference to Br. 472,539 (Feb. 22, 1935).

8521 Rabuteau, G. "L'émetteur de télévision de la Tour Eiffel" [The television transmitter at the Eiffel Tower]. REV. GEN. 46 (Sept. 9): 291-305.

8522 B.T.-H. "Cathode-ray tube." Br. 543,499, Sept. 9, 1940. Convention Sept. 9, 1939.

8523 Tyers, P.D. "Scanning coil construction." W.W. 45 (Sept. 14): 248, 249. Continued (Sept. 21): 279, 280.

8524 Moore, R.C., and Philco. "Saw-tooth wave generator." Br. 534,705, Sept. 18. 1939; U.S. 2,296,727, Aug. 7, 1940, Sept. 22, 1942. Deflecting output circuits for cathode-ray tubes; television receiver circuits.

8525 Hepp, G., and J.v.d. Mark. "Cathode-ray tube device." U.S. 2,325,676, Feb. 2, 1942, Aug. 3, 1943 (N.V. Philips). In Netherlands Sept. 22, 1939. Camera tube.

8526 Peck, W.H. "Television system." U.S. 2,290,651, Sept. 26, 1939, July 21, 1942.

8527 S.T.C., D.S.B. Shannon, and P.K. Chatterjea. "Electron multiplier." Br. 532,920, Sept. 26, 1939.

8528 Levy, H.R. "Image reproduction." Br. 541,959, Sept. 28, 1939.

8529 Hergenrother, R.C. "Cathode-ray signal-reproduction unit." U.S. 2,280,191, Sept. 30, 1939, Apr. 21, 1942. Assigned: Hazeltine. Television receiver.

8530 Kell, R.D. "Television transmitter." U.S. 2,298,797, Sept. 30, 1939, Oct. 13, 1942. Assigned: RCA. Br. 543,474, Sept. 30, 1940.

8531 Snyder, R.L., Jr. "Electron multiplier." U.S. 2,231,693, Sept. 30, 1939, Feb. 11, 1941 (RCA).

8532 Peirce, J.R. "Limiting current densities in electron beams." J. APP. PHYS. 10 (Oct.): 715-24.

8533 Weis, C.L. "Television transmission over telephone cables." BELL LAB RECORD 18 (Oct.): 34-7. CBS.

8534 Smyth, C.N. "The implosion of cathode-ray tubes." ELECT. COMM. 18 (Oct.): No. 2. 3 photos; shows television console screen shattering with rifle fire.

8535 Deskey, D. "If I were a maker of television sets." ELECT. MFG 24 (Oct.): 76, 77, 118, 120.

8536 Hartley, L.J. "Production alignment apparatus for television receivers." ELECTRONICS 12 (Oct.): 17. Abstract.

8537 Larson, C.C., and B.C. Gardner. "The image dissector." ELECTRONICS 12 (Oct.): 24-7, 50.

8538 "Water-cooled lighting for television." ELECTRONICS 12 (Oct.): 48, 49.

8539 Nergaard, Leon S. "A theoretical analysis of single sideband operation of television transmitters." PROC. IRE 27 (Oct.): 666-77.

8540 "Television, three varieties." POP. MECH. 72 (Oct.): 615.

8541 Jarvis, R.F.J., and E.C.H. Seaman. "The effect of noise and interfering signals on television transmission." P.O. EE J. 32 (Oct.): 193-9. Abstract in J. TELEV. SOC. 3 (1940): No. 6, 155-9. 8 photos, diag.

8542 "Television." RADIO-CRAFT 11 (Oct.): 198. News items.

8543 West, S. "Servicing television receiver faults, Pt. 5." RADIO-CRAFT 11 (Oct.): 216-8, 237. 8 photos. Conclusion.

8544 Hutchinson, T.H. "Programming the television mobile unit." RCA REV. 4 (Oct.): 154-61.

8545 Carter, P.S. "Simple television antennas." RCA REV. 4 (Oct.): 168-85.

8546 Rose, A., and H.A. Iams. "The Orthicon, a television pickup tube." RCA REV. 4 (Oct.): 186-99. Reprinted in J. TELEV. SOC. 3 (Dec. 1939): 57-64. 9 diags.

8547 Mountjoy, G. "Television signal frequency circuit considerations." RCA REV. 4 (Oct.): 204-30.

8548 "The wireless exhibition, 1939: A technical survey." W. ENG. 16 (Oct.): 500-2.

8549 Gilmore, Otto C. "Television tube." U.S. 2,232,322, Oct. 5, 1939, Feb. 18, 1941. Assigned: Cosmocolor Corp.

8550 S.T.C., W.A. Beatty, and C.T. Scully. "Television." Br. 535,384, Oct. 6, 1939. References to 8065, 8114.

8551 Strübig, H. "Producing television images." U.S. 2,351,889, Sept. 26, 1940, June 20, 1944 (Alien Properties Custodian). In Germany Oct. 7, 1939.

8552 Baird Television and D.V. Ridgeway. "Cathode-ray tube." Br. 535,477, Oct. 9, 1939.

8553 Smith, Lester Harsen. "Cathode-ray image projecting device." U.S. 2,231,960, Oct. 16, 1939, Feb. 18, 1941. Receiver tube with vibrating screen carrying fine opaque particles.

8554 Campbell, R.L. "Television system and synchronization means therefor." U.S. 2,249,942, Oct. 19, 1939, July 22, 1941. Assigned: A.B. Du Mont.

8555 S.T.C. "Television." Br. 542,258, Oct. 16, 1940. Convention Oct. 19, 1939.

8556 Scophony, G.W. Walton, and G. Wikkenhauser. "Image converter." Br. 535,081, Oct. 19, 1939.

8557 Winckel, F.W. "Fernsehen 1939." Z. FERN. 20 (Oct. 20): 150-61.

8558 Bobb, Lloyd J. "Electron beam deflector yoke." U.S. 2,240,606, Oct. 21, 1939, May 6, 1941 (Philco); Br. 545,414, Aug. 15, 1940.

8559 S.T.C., D.S.B. Shannon, and P.K. Chatterjea. "Valve generator." Br. 535,905, Oct. 24, 1939.

8560 Vance, A.W. "Electrical network." U.S. 2,255,805, Oct. 25, 1939, Sept. 16, 1941 (RCA).

8561 Wheeler, H.A., and Hazeltine Corp. "Pulse circuits." U.S. 2,235,131, Oct. 25, 1939, Mar. 18, 1941; Br. 543,504, Oct. 5, 1940. Saw-tooth wave generator.

8562 Rappold, A. "Television device." U.S. 2,297,500, Sept. 6, 1940, Sept. 29, 1942 (Alien Properties Custodian). In Germany Oct. 26, 1939.

8563 Bedford, A.V. "Television system." U.S. 2,275,026, Oct. 27, 1939, Mar. 3, 1942. Assigned: RCA.

8564 Adam, M. "La réception des images de télévision" [The reception of television images]. REV. GEN. 46 (Oct. 28): 413-24.

8565 Epstein, D.W. "Cathode-ray tube." U.S. 2,287,906, Oct. 31, 1939, July 14, 1942. Assigned: RCA.

8566 Kallmann, H.E. "Stroboscopic light source." PROC. IRE 27 (Nov.): 690.

8567 Goddard, D.R. "Transatlantic reception of London television signals." PROC. IRE 27 (Nov.): 692-5. At Riverhead, Long Island, N.Y., from Sept. 1938.

8568 Goldman, S. "Television detail and selective-sideband transmission." PROC. IRE 27 (Nov.): 725-32.

8569 "Television shown in theaters." POP. SCI. 135 (Nov.): 87.

8570 "Television." RADIO-CRAFT 11 (Nov.): 262. News items.

8571 Sicuranza, C. "Converting a 5-inch telly kit for receiving a 9-inch image, Pt. 1." RADIO-CRAFT 11 (Nov.): 264, 265, 304. 3 photos, diag. Continued Jan. 1940.

8572 "Two-way telly demonstration." RADIO-CRAFT 11 (Nov.): 270, 316, 319. 3 photos. RCA at Atlantic City, N.J.

8573 "Review of FCC allocations of ultra-short-waves." RADIO-CRAFT 11 (Nov.): 274, 311, 312.

8574 "Big images needed to boom television?" RADIO-CRAFT 11 (Nov.): 289, 312.

8575 Goldman, S. "Dipole arrays as television receiving antennas." RMA ENG. 4 (Nov.): 2-8.

8576 Lubszynski, H.G., and H. Miller. "Image intensifier." Br. 536,417, Nov. 3, 1939. References to 7791, 8307, 8487.

8577 Flechsig, W. "Cathode-ray tube." U.S. 2,320,582, Oct. 16, 1940, June 1, 1943 (Fernseh A.-G., Alien Properties Custodian). In Germany Nov. 8, 1939.

8578 Ges. Hochschule. "Television." Br. 543,485, Jan. 22, 1940. In Germany Nov. 8, 1939.

8579 Davis, W. "Airplane passengers see their own plane in flight." SCI. N. LETTER 36 (Nov. 11): 318.

8580 James, I.J.P. "Electron image-dissecting arrangement." Br. 538,054, Nov. 13, 1939; U.S. 2,289,500, Nov. 22, 1940, July 14, 1942. Assigned: EMI.

8581 S.T.C., D.S.B. Shannon, and P.K. Chatterjea. "Valve generator." Br. 536,453, Nov. 14, 1939.

8582 S.T.C. and W.A. Beatty. "Television." Br. 536,588, Nov. 17, 1939.

8583 S.T.C. and Nat. Tel. Soc. Anon. "Electron multiplier." Br. 533,732, Nov. 17, 1939.

8584 Case, Nelson P. "Television signal-translating channel." U.S. 2,291,277, Nov. 18, 1939, July 28, 1942. Assigned: Hazeltine.

8585 "Electric and Musical Industries." TIMES (Nov. 23): 13d. Brief company report.

8586 Colborne, Ronald Henry. "Electron discharge device including fluorescent screen." Br. 536,730, Nov. 23, 1939; U.S. 2,325,110, Nov. 22, 1940, July 27, 1943. Assigned: EMI.

8587 Lubcke, H.R. "Television receiver." U.S. 2,282,487, Nov. 25, 1939, May 12, 1942. Assigned: Don Lee Broadcasting System.

8588 Dillenburger, W. "Dissector tube arrangement." U.S. 2,287,298, Oct. 31, 1940, June 23, 1942. In Germany Nov. 28, 1939. Image dissector.

8589 Homrighous, John H. "Television communication." U.S. 2,309,393, Nov. 28, 1939, Jan. 26, 1943.

8590 Law, R.R. "Fluorescent screen assembly and method." U.S. 2,233,786, Nov. 29, 1939, Mar. 4, 1941 (RCA).

8591 Rajchman, J.A. "Electron multiplier." U.S. 2,292,847, Nov. 30, 1939, Aug. 11, 1942 (RCA).

8592 Kallmann, H.E. "The gradation of television pictures." ELECTRONICS 12 (Dec.): 25. Abstract.

8593 Brown, W.J. "British vision receivers." ELECTRONICS 12 (Dec.): 26-9. Continued 13 (Mar. 1940): 26-9.

8594 Mountjoy, G. "Television signal frequency circuit considerations." ELECTRONICS 12 (Dec.): 58.

8595 Ashbridge, N. "Broadcasting and television." J. IEE 584 (Dec.): 380-7.

8596 "Television receivers." PHIL. TECH. REV. 4 (Dec.): 342-50.

8597 "Television." RADIO-CRAFT 11 (Dec.): 326, 327.

8598 Skellett, A.M. "Transmission system of narrow band-width for animated line images." J. SMPE 33 (Dec.): 670-6.

8599 Campbell, R.L. "Television control equipment for film transmission." J. SMPE 33 (Dec.): 677-89.

8600 Myers, L.M. "Electron optics." J. TELEV. SOC. 3 (Dec.): 37-49. 2 photos, 5 diagrams. Fourth Kerr Memorial Lecture, delivered to the IEE on Apr. 19, 1939.

8601 "In praise of television." J. TELEV. SOC. 3 (Dec.): 49-51. Reprinted from W.W. 44 (July 6, 1939). Discusses programs, etc. Only serious criticism: it wastes too much time.

8602 Bell, C.H. "Television—facts and problems." J. TELEV. SOC. 3 (Dec.): 51-4. Discusses Baird, EMI, Scophony.

8603 "Motor-car interference and the Murphy noise-limiting circuit." J. TELEV. SOC. 3 (Dec.): 74-6.

8604 Wikkenhauser, G. "Synchronisation of Scophony television receivers." J. TELEV. SOC. 3 (Dec.): 77-81. 3 photos. The Scophony pulse generator is described pp. 80-1.

8605 Pierce, —. "Electron discharge device." U.S. 2,268,196, Dec. 2, 1939, Dec. 30, 1941. Electron gun.

8606 E.R.P. "Cathode-ray tube." Br. 545,835, Nov. 8, 1940. Convention Dec. 2, 1939. Electron gun assembly.

8607 Freeman, R.L., and H.L. Blaisdell. "Television control system." U.S. 2,251,929, Dec. 8, 1939, Aug. 12, 1941. Assigned: Hazeltine. Br. 542,626, Oct. 29, 1940.

8608 Ges. Hochschule. "Television." Br. 543,565, Apr. 9, 1940. In Germany Dec. 9, 1939. Addition to 8578.

8609 Burnett, C.E. "Cathode-ray signal generator." U.S. 2,287,415, Dec. 15, 1939, June 23, 1942. Assigned: RCA.

8610 Dome, R.B. "Television receiver." U.S. 2,255,485, Dec. 15, 1939, Sept. 9, 1941. Assigned: G.E.

8611 George, R.H. "Electron device." U.S. 2,307,209, Dec. 21, 1939, Jan. 5, 1943. Image intensifier.

8612 Campbell, R.L. "Synchronizing system." U.S. 2,249,943, Dec. 22, 1939, July 22, 1941. Television.

8613 S.T.C. "Television." Br. 542,259, Oct. 24, 1940. Convention Dec. 22, 1939.

8614 West, A.G.D. "Television over phone lines." KINE. WKLY (Dec. 28). G.P.O. lines in England. Abstract in J. TELEV. SOC. 3 (1940): 106.

8615 Mertz, P. "Two-way television transmission." U.S. 2,308,381, Dec. 29, 1939, Jan. 12, 1943. Assigned: B.T.L.

8616 Tolson, W.A. "Television system." U.S. 2,299,361, Dec. 29, 1939, Oct. 20, 1942. Assigned: RCA.

8617 Hazeltine. "Receiver." Br. 546,830. Convention Dec. 30, 1939.

8618 Ardenne, M.v. CATHODE-RAY TUBES. Translated from the 1935 edition by G.S. McGregor and R.C. Walker. London: Sir Isaac Pitman Sons, 1939. xiii + 530 pp., 465 illus.

8619 Beitman, Morris N. CYCLOPAEDIA OF TELEVISION FACTS. Chicago: Supreme Pubs., 1939. 58 pp., illus., diags.

8620 Camm, F.J. TELEVISION AND SHORT-WAVE HANDBOOK. 4th ed. New York: Fortuny's, 1939. Dictionary of television terms, pp. 211-69. 271 pp., illus.

8621 Corbishley, Harold (ed.). TELEVISION AND SHORT-WAVE WORLD PRACTICAL HANDBOOK. London: Television and Short-Wave World, 1939.

8622 Federal Communications Commission. FIRST REPORT OF TELEVISION COMMITTEE. (FCC Mimeo 34168) Washington, D.C., May 22, 1939.

8623 Federal Communications Commission. SECOND REPORT OF TELEVISION COMMITTEE. (FCC Mimeo 37460) Washington, D.C., Nov. 15, 1939.

8624 Harding, Charles Francis, R.H. George, and H.J. Heim. THE PURDUE UNIVERSITY EXPERIMENTAL TELEVISION SYSTEM. (Engineering Bulletin, Purdue University Engineering Bulletin, Vol. XXIII, No. 2.) Lafayette, Ind.: Purdue University Engineering Experimental Station, 1939. 53 pp., illus., diags.

8625 Kirby, Philip. THE VICTORY OF TELEVISION. New York: Harper & Bros., 1939. 120 pp., 20 photos. Chapters on early inventors, studios, lighting, music, sponsors' problems, public service programs, etc. Appendices on FCC regulations and glossary of television terms.

8626 Klemperer, O. ELECTRON OPTICS. By the research staff of Electric and Musical Industries, Ltd. London: Cambridge University Press, 1939. x + 107 pp. An updated edition (471 pp.) appeared in 1953.

8627 Legg, Stuart, and Robert Fairthorne. THE CINEMA AND TELEVISION. (March of Time Series, Physics, No. 2.) London: Longmans, Green, 1939. 78 pp., plates. A "new improved edition" by Arthur Elton also appeared in 1939 (80 pp., 32 photos, diags.).

8628 Myers, L.M. ELECTRON OPTICS, THEORETICAL AND PRACTICAL. London: Chapman & Hall; New York: D. Van Nostrand, 1939. xviii + 618 pp.

8629 RADIO AND TELEVISION RECEIVER SERVICING WITH CATHODE-RAY OSCILLOGRAPHS GM 3152 AND GM 3155. London: Mullard Wireless Service Co., 1939. 46 pp.

8630 Sleeper, William Blake. THE TELEVISION HANDBOOK: LOOK AND LISTEN. New York: Norman W. Henley, 1939. 96 pp., more than 100 illus. Describes 1939 television practice for repairmen, set-builders, and students; status of television as of Apr. 30, 1939.

8631 Thomas, L. MAGIC DIALS: THE STORY OF RADIO AND TELEVISION. New York: Lee Furman, 1939. 142 pp. Popular picture treatment (with some color photos).

8632 Taylor, F. Sherwood. SCIENCE FRONT 1939. London: Cassell, 1939. 301 pp., 8 plates, diags. Television is discussed on pp. 167-210.

8633 West, S., and D.E. Osman. BUILDING TELEVISION RECEIVERS AT HOME. London: Television and Short-Wave World; Toronto: McClelland, 1939. 112 pp., illus. Articles reprinted, with revisions, from TELEVISION AND SHORT-WAVE WORLD, edited by H. Corbishley. The cover carries the subtitle "A practical home-constructor handbook for everybody."

CHAPTER 20

DISTANT VIEW: 1940–1995

Note: Before his death, George Shiers had collected scattered post-1940 historical references, hoping to fill out the history of television. Those citations, by no means as complete a listing as is provided for earlier years, and limited largely to books plus a few important periodicals, are included here. Arrangement, as with prior chapters, is chronological. Annotations have often been added or expanded by C.H. Sterling, who provided the annotated list of books published since 1978 which concludes the chapter.

1940–45

8634 "Radio progress during 1939: Cathode-ray and television tubes." PROC. IRE 28 (Mar. 1940): 103. Bibliography. "Part 6: Television," pp. 120–24.

8635 Town, G.R. "Television: History and principles of operation, and present status reviewed." ELECT. ENG. 59 (Aug. 1940): 313–22.

8636 BIBLIOGRAPHY OF PHOTOELECTRICITY. New York: B.T.L., 1940. 218 pp. 1,698 items arranged chronologically and alphabetically by author. Theoretical arts.

8637 DEVELOPMENT OF TELEVISION: HEARINGS ON S. RES. 251. Washington, D.C.: Government Printing Office, 1940. 81 pp. Hearings in U.S. Senate, Committee on Interstate Commerce, Apr. 10–11, 1940. Oversight of FCC policymaking.

8638 Cameron, J.R. TELEVISION FOR BEGINNERS: THEATRE TELEVISION. Woodmont, Conn.: Cameron Pub. Co., 1940. 94 pp., illus. Later edition: Coral Gables, Fla.: Cameron Pub. Co., 1947, 318 pp.

8639 Cocking, W.T. TELEVISION RECEIVING EQUIPMENT. London: Wireless World/Iliffe & Sons, 1940. 298 pp., illus., diags. Second edition 1947, 380 pp., includes advertisements).

8640 Fink, D.G. PRINCIPLES OF TELEVISION ENGINEERING. 1940. xii + 541 pp., 313 photos and diags. Appendix (pp. 517–21) lists transmission standards, recommended practices, definitions, and names of controls. Revised in 1947 to conform to the 525-line standard. Second edition (721 pp.), 1952. Long the definitive treatment of the National Television System Committee standards.

8641 Lohr, Lenox R. TELEVISION BROADCASTING: PRODUCTION, ECONOMICS, TECHNIQUE. Foreword by D. Sarnoff. New York: McGraw-Hill, 1940. xiv + 274 pp., 86 illus. Includes typical script (pp. 225–65) and FCC rules of June 18, 1940 (pp. 266–69). Useful for details on pioneering production methods. Lohr was network president.

8642 NBC. TELEVISION'S FIRST YEAR. New York: National Broadcasting Co., 1940. 48 pp., illus. Promotional booklet useful for studio and remote truck photographs.

8643 Porterfield, John, and Kay Reynolds, eds. WE PRESENT TELEVISION. New York: W.W. Norton, 1940. 298 pp., 16 plates, 4 diags. 12 chapters by specialists on different aspects of the new industry for the layman.

8644 Zworykin, V.K., and G.A. Morton. TELEVISION: THE ELECTRONICS OF IMAGE TRANSMISSION. New York: John Wiley; London: Chapman & Hall, 1940. xi + 646 pp., 495 illus. A basic and important text, based largely upon developments by RCA. Second edition (1,037 pp.), 1954.

8645 Engstrom, E.W. "Recent developments in television." ANNALS 213 (Jan. 1941): 130–7.

8646 Glover, Alan M. "A review of the development of sensitive phototubes." PROC. IRE 29 (Aug. 1941): 413–23. 12 illus. 73 references. Bibliography of 10 items.

8647 Du Mont Labs. PIONEERING THE CATHODE-RAY AND TELEVISION ARTS. Passaic, N.J.: Allen B. Du Mont Laboratories, 1941. 32 pp., illus.

8648 Hylander, Clarence J., and R. Harding, Jr. AN INTRODUCTION TO TELEVISION. New York: Macmillan, 1941. xviii + 207 pp., illus. Popular, semi-technical treatment.

8649 Stranger, Ralph. DICTIONARY OF RADIO AND TELEVISION TERMS. London: Newnes, 1941. 252 pp., diags.

8650 CBS. RADIO AND TELEVISION BIBLIOGRAPHY. New York: CBS, 1942. 62 pp. Lists books, pamphlets, articles, and early CBS radio publications.

8651 Camm, F.J. NEWNES TELEVISION MANUAL. London: Newnes, 1942; Brooklyn, N.Y.: Chemical Pub. Co., 1943. 224 pp., 94 illus. Fifth edition of TELEVISION AND SHORT-WAVE HANDBOOK, first published 1934.

8652 de Forest, Lee. TELEVISION TODAY AND TOMORROW. New York: Dial Press, 1942; London: Hutchinson, 1945. 361 pp., 77 illus. Later reprinted as TELEVISION NOW AND ONWARDS. 176 pp., illus. London: Hutchinson, 1946. The radio inventor's only book.

8653 Dunlap, O.E., Jr. THE FUTURE OF TELEVISION. New York: Harper & Bros., 1942. Revised 1947. xi + 194 pp., 8 plates. List of commercial stations (11 items). A 7-page appendix, "Historic steps in television," lists 100 items.

8654 Hubbell, Richard W. 4000 YEARS OF TELEVISION: THE STORY OF SEEING AT A DISTANCE. New York: G.P. Putnam's Sons, 1942. xvi + 256 pp., 8 diags. English edition (191 pp.) prepared by C.L. Boltz. London: Harrap, 1946.

8655 BIBLIOGRAPHY ON PHOTOELECTRIC CELLS. New York: B.T.L., 1943.

8656 Rettenmeyer, Francis X. RADIO-ELECTRONIC BIBLIOGRAPHY. 12: TELEVISION. 1943.

8657 Fink, D.G., ed. TELEVISION STANDARDS AND PRACTICE: SELECTED PAPERS FROM THE PROCEEDINGS OF THE NATIONAL TELEVISION SYSTEM COMMITTEE AND 15 PANELS. New York: McGraw-Hill, 1943. x + 405 pp., 116 illus., tables.

8658 Puckle, O.S. TIME BASES (SCANNING GENERATORS): THEIR DESIGN AND DEVELOPMENT, WITH NOTES ON THE CATHODE-RAY TUBE. Foreword by E.B. Moullin. London: Chapman & Hall; New York: John Wiley, 1943. Later edition, 1951. xii + 204 pp., 124 illus.

8659 Dunlap, O.E., Jr. RADIO'S 100 MEN OF SCIENCE: BIOGRAPHICAL NARRATIVES OF PATHFINDERS IN ELECTRONICS AND TELEVISION. New York: Harper & Bros., 1944. 294 pp., 16 plates. Useful details in brief biographies.

8660 Kellaway, Francis W. TELEVISION FOR EVERYMAN: HISTORY AND PRACTICE. London: John Crowther, 1944. 55 pp., illus.

8661 Lee, Robert Edwin. TELEVISION: THE REVOLUTION. Foreword by Dr. Lee de Forest. New York: Essential Books, 1944. xv + 230 pp. Panoramic view of the current status; nontechnical.

8662 McLean, F.C. TELEVISION IN FRANCE. London: HMSO, 1944. 6 pp. Report of the Combined Intelligence Objectives Subcommittee.

8663 RCA. TELEVISION. New York: RCA, Dept. of Information, 1944. 24 pp., illus.

8664 REPORT OF THE TELEVISION COMMITTEE. London: HMSO, March 1945. 26 pp. Lord Hankey, Chairman. Appointment announced in the House of Commons, Jan. 18, 1944; members included J.L. Baird, I. Shoenberg.

8665 Fink, D.G. "Television broadcasting practice in America." J. IEE 92 (Sept. 1945): 145–64.

8666 Eddy, W.C. TELEVISION: THE EYES OF TOMORROW. New York: Prentice-Hall, 1945. ix + 330 pp., 138 illus. General account covering all aspects of television, especially production methods.

8666a Dupuy, Judy. TELEVISION SHOW BUSINESS: A HANDBOOK OF TELEVISION PROGRAMMING AND PRODUCTION BASED ON FIVE YEARS OF OPERATION OF GENERAL ELECTRIC'S TELEVISION STATION, WRGB, SCHENECTADY, NEW YORK. Schnemectady, New York: General Electric, 1945. 246 pp., illus.

1946–50

8667 Smith-Rose, R.L. "John Logie Baird." NATURE 158 (July 20, 1946): 88, 89.

8668 BBC. TELEVISION AGAIN. Wembley, Middlesex: British Broadcasting Corp., 1946. 35 pp., illus.

8669 Federal Communications Commission. STANDARDS OF GOOD ENGINEERING PRACTICE CONCERNING TELEVISION BROADCAST STATIONS. Washington, D.C.: Government Printing Office, 1946. 27 pp.

8670 Goldsmith, T.T. THE TRUTH ABOUT COLOR TELEVISION. New York: Allen B. Du Mont Laboratories, 1946. 31 pp., illus.

8671 Hutchinson, T.H. HERE IS TELEVISION: YOUR WINDOW TO THE WORLD. New York: Hastings House, 1946. xvi + 366 pp., 94 illus. Revised in 1948, 1950. 368 pp.

8672 Kiver, Milton S. TELEVISION SIMPLIFIED. New York: D. Van Nostrand, 1946. vii + 375 pp., illus. Later editions 1948, 1950.

8673 RCA. TELEVISION: A BIBLIOGRAPHY OF TECHNICAL PAPERS BY RCA AUTHORS, 1926–1946. Princeton, N.J.: RCA Reviews, 1946. ii + 10 pp. 275 entries. See also 8680, 8681.

8674 Sarnoff, D. PIONEERING IN TELEVISION: PROPHECY AND FULFILLMENT. New York: RCA Technical Institutes Press, 1946. 119 pp., illus. Excerpts from speeches and statements. Reprinted in various subsequent editions.

8675 Tyler, Kingdon S. TELECASTING AND COLOR. New York: Harcourt, Brace, 1946. viii + 213 pp. General introduction for the layman. Section on color television (pp. 145–79) is primarily on the CBS system. A book list (pp. 202–4) contains 39 entries.

8676 Zworykin, V.K. "Television—retrospect and prospect." TECH. REV. 49 (Apr. 1947): 333–6, 354. 2 illus.

8677 Ives, H.E. "Television: 20th anniversary." BELL LAB RECORD 25 (May 1947): 190–3.

8678 Aschen, R., and Robert Gondry. THEORIE ET PRATIQUE DE LA TELEVISION [Theory and practice of television]. Paris: L.E.P.S., 1947. 171 pp., diags.

8679 Bettinger, Hoyland. TELEVISION TECHNIQUES. New York/London: Harper & Bros., 1947. 237 pp., illus. Drawings by the author.

8680 Goldsmith, A.N., et al., eds. TELEVISION: VOL. III (1938–1941). Princeton, N.J.: RCA Laboratories Division, 1947. xii + 486 pp., illus. 28 papers by RCA authors, and 13 summaries. Also summaries of papers in Vol. I (1936) and Vol. II (1937).

8681 Goldsmith, A.N., et al., eds. TELEVISION: VOL. IV (1942–1946). Princeton, N.J.: RCA Laboratories Division, 1947. xiv + 510 pp., illus. 32 papers by RCA authors, and 9 summaries. A "Television Bibliography" is given as an appendix, pp. 499–510.

8682 Hallows, Ralph W. TELEVISION SIMPLY EXPLAINED. London: Chapman & Hall, 1947. xvi + 198 pp., 16 plates, 97 diags. Foreword by Commander A.B. Campbell. 2nd edition 1954.

8683 McGee, J.D. "Electronic generation of television signals." Chapter 4 (pp. 135–211) in Bernard Lovell, ELECTRONICS AND THEIR APPLICATIONS IN INDUSTRY AND RESEARCH. 1947.

8684 Norris, Roy C. TELEVISION TO-DAY: A CONSTRUCTIVE GUIDE TO ITS PRINCIPLES AND PRACTICE. London: Rockliff, 1947. viii + 255 pp., 11 photos, 189 diags.

8685 Pedrick, Gale, ed. THE WORLD RADIO AND TELEVISION ANNUAL: JUBILEE ISSUE. Circa 1947. 192 pp., illus.

8686 Rose, O., ed. RADIO BROADCASTING AND TELEVISION: AN ANNOTATED BIBLIOGRAPHY. New York: The H.W. Wilson Co., 1947. 120 pp. History and general summary (pp. 9–21), 86 entries. Television (pp. 93–7), 26 entries.

8687 Sposa, Louis A. TELEVISION PRIMER OF PRODUCTION AND DIRECTION. New York: McGraw-Hill, 1947. viii + 237 pp., illus. Immediate post-war production methods.

8688 Willingham, G.A. HALF A CENTURY OF PROGRESS. London: A.C. Cossor Ltd., 1947. 32 pp., illus.

8689 "RCA's television." FORTUNE 38 (Sept. 1948): 80–5, 194–204.

8690 Lankes, L.R. "Historical sketch of television's progress." J. SMPE 51 (Sept. 1948): 223–9. Includes a bibliography of 22 items. (also in 8781)

8691 Lewis, G., and F.J. Mann. "Ferdinand Braun—inventor of the cathode-ray tube." ELECT. COMM. 25 (Dec. 1948): 319–27.

8692 Chauvièrre, M. LES RECEPTEURS DE TELEVISION [Television receivers and reception]. 284 pp., illus. Paris: Dunod, 1948.

8693 Dunlap, O.E., Jr. UNDERSTANDING TELEVISION: WHAT IT IS AND HOW IT WORKS. New York: Greenberg, 1948. 128 pp. Nontechnical introduction.

8694 Folwell, A. INTRODUCTION TO TELEVISION. London: Chapman & Hall, 1948. 120 pp., illus.

8695 Kempner, Stanley. TELEVISION ENCYCLOPEDIA. New York: Fairchild Pub. Co., 1948. 415 pp., 82 illus. Chronology, short biographies of key people past and present, and semi-technical dictionary.

8696 Newnham, John K. TELEVISION: BEHIND THE SCENES. London: Convoy Publishers, 1948. 103 pp., illus.

8697 Yates, R.F. NEW TELEVISION, THE MAGIC SCREEN. New York: Didier, 1948. 174 pp., illus.

8698 Everson, George. THE STORY OF TELEVISION: THE LIFE OF PHILO T. FARNSWORTH. New York: W.W. Norton & Co., 1949. 266 pp., 4 plates. Reprinted by Arno Press, 1974. One of the inventor's long-time backers details his life.

8699 Gable, Luther S. THE MIRACLE OF TELEVISION. Chicago: Wilcox & Follett, 1949. 151 pp., illus.

8700 Gorham, Maurice A.C. TELEVISION: MEDIUM OF THE FUTURE. London: Percival Marshall, 1949. xiv + 142 pp., illus. By a former head of BBC television.

8701 Maclaurin, William R., and R. Joyce Harmon. INVENTION AND INNOVATION IN THE RADIO INDUSTRY. New York: Macmillan, 1949. xxi + 304 pp., illus. Bibliography of 140 items from 1902 to 1945. Essential study, primarily of radio and wireless. Television and FM are covered in the last chapter. Reprinted by Arno Press, 1971.

8702 RCA. THIRTY YEARS OF PIONEERING. New York: RCA, 1949.

8703 Tilsley, Frank. TELEVISION STORY. London: BBC, no date (circa 1949). 68 pp., 31 photos, 4 diags. Includes 28 full-page advertisements by television manufacturers, some with photos of contemporary receivers.

8704 Zworykin, V.K., and E.G. Ramberg. PHOTOELECTRICITY AND ITS APPLICATIONS. New York: John Wiley, 1949. xii + 494 pp., illus.

8705 Maclaurin, W.R. "Patents and technical progress—a study of television." J. POLITICAL ECONOMY 58 (Feb.–Dec. 1950): 142–57. Based on his book (8701).

8706 McGee, J.D. "Distant electric vision." PROC. IRE 38 (June 1950): 596–608. Reprinted from PROC. IRE (Australia) 10 (Aug. 1949): 211–23. 18 illus.

8707 McGee, J.D. "A review of some television pick-up tubes." PROC. IEE 97 (Pt. 3) (Nov. 1950): 377–92.

8708 THE PRESENT STATE OF COLOR TELEVISION: REPORT OF THE ADVISORY COMMITTEE ON COLOR TELEVISION. Senate Doc. 197, 81st Cong., 2d Sess. Washington, D.C.: Government Printing Office, (July) 1950. 63 pp. Details competing CBS (mechanical) and RCA (electronic) as well as other systems.

8709 BBC. A PICTURE BOOK OF TELEVISION, 1930–1950. London: BBC, 1950. 60 pp., illus.

8710 Korn, Terry, and Elizabeth P. Korn. TRAILBLAZER TO TELEVISION: THE STORY OF ARTHUR KORN. New York: Charles Scribner's Sons, 1950. 144 pp., illus. Narrative, no documentation, no index.

8711 Percy, J.D. JOHN L. BAIRD: THE FOUNDER OF BRITISH TELEVISION. London: Television Society, 1950. 16 pp., 13 illus. Revised 1952.

8712 Reyner, J.H., et al. THE ENCYCLOPAEDIA OF RADIO AND TELEVISION: A COMPLETE ALPHABETICAL REFERENCE TO ALL ASPECTS OF MODERN RADIO TECHNOLOGY. London: Odhams, 1950. 768 pp., illus. Reprinted 1957.

8713 Siepmann, Charles A. RADIO, TELEVISION, AND SOCIETY. New York: Oxford University Press, 1950. vii + 410 pp. Critical analysis of the American industry by a British expert. Television is discussed in Chapter 13 (pp. 317–58). Includes map of television facilities in the U.S.

8714 Swift, John. ADVENTURE IN VISION: THE FIRST TWENTY-FIVE YEARS OF TELEVISION. 223 pp., 32 plates. London: John Lehman, 1950. Story of BBC television.

1951–60

8715 Zworykin, V.K. "Some prospects in the field of electronics." J.F.I. 251 (Jan. 1951).

8716 Fink, D.G. "Television broadcasting in the United States, 1927–1950." PROC. IRE 39 (Feb. 1951): 116–23.

8717 Herold, E.W. "Methods suitable for television color kinescopes." PROC. IRE 39 (Oct. 1951): 1177–85. 9 illus.

8718 "Color television issue." PROC. IRE 39 (Oct. 1951): 1123–1360. See also second issue, 1954 (8725a).

8719 Dunlap, O.E., Jr. DUNLAP'S RADIO AND TELEVISION ALMANAC. New York: Harper & Bros., 1951. 211 pp., 68 illus. Chronology.

8720 Horton, Derek. TELEVISION'S STORY AND CHALLENGE. London: Harrap, 1951. 183 pp., 14 plates, 22 diags.

8721 Garratt, G.R.M., and A.H. Mumford. "The history of television." PROC. IEE 99 (Pt. 3A) (May 1952): 25–42. 16 illus.

8722 Williams, R.C.G. "Industrial and professional applications of television technique." PROC. IEE 99 (1952): 651–64. Early survey of applications in industry and medicine. 14 references from 1949–52.

8723 Goebel, Gerhart. "Das Fernsehen in Deutschland bis zum Jahre 1945" [Television in Germany up through 1945]. ARCH. POSTFERNMELD. 5 (Aug. 1953): 259–393. 150 illus. Bibliography of 549 entries.

8724 Preston, S.J. "The birth of a high-definition television system." J. TELEV. SOC. 7 (July–Sept. 1953): 115–26. Covers the subject to 1949.

8725 TELEVISION: A WORLD SURVEY. Paris: UNESCO, 1953. 184 pp. Supplement published in 1955. 49 pp. Details on initial television development in most countries of the world—information often hard to find elsewhere. Both reprinted by Arno Press, 1972.

8725a "Second color television issue." PROC. IRE 42 (Jan. 1954): 1–357.

8726 Hogan, J.V.L. "The early days of television." J. SMPTE 63 (Nov. 1954): 169–73. 3 illus. (incl. in 8781)

8727 Jensen, Axel G. "The evolution of modern television." J. SMPTE 63 (Nov. 1954): 174–88. 29 illus. Later reprinted as Bell System Monograph 236. (incl. in 8781)

8728 Bourton, K. BIBLIOGRAPHY OF COLOUR TELEVISION. London: Television Society, 1954.

8729 Nottingham, Wayne Buckles. BIBLIOGRAPHY IN PHYSICAL ELECTRONICS. Cambridge, Mass.: Addison-Wesley, 1954. ix + 428 pp. Prepared by the staff of the Research Laboratory of Electronics, Massachusetts Institute of Technology. Wide coverage of books and articles in classified groups, 1930–50.

8730 Abramson, Albert. "A short history of television recording." J. SMPTE 64 (Feb. 1955): 72–6. 27 references. (incl. in 8781)

8731 Bells, Francis. "Color TV: Who'll buy a triumph?" FORTUNE 52 (Nov. 1955): 136–9, 201, 202, 204, 206. 10 illus.

8732 Barstow, J.M. "The ABC's of color television." PROC. IRE 43 (Pt. 1) (Nov. 1955): 1574–9. Reprinted as Bell System Monograph 2529.

8733 Abramson, A. ELECTRONIC MOTION PICTURES: A HISTORY OF THE TELEVISION CAMERA. Berkeley: University of California Press, 1955. 212 pp., 93 illus. Reprinted by Arno Press, 1974.

8734 Fink, D.G., ed. COLOR TELEVISION STANDARDS: SELECTED PAPERS AND RECORDS OF THE NATIONAL TELEVISION SYSTEM COMMITTEE. New York: McGraw-Hill, 1955. xiv + 520 pp., illus.

8734a Gouriet, G.G. AN INTRODUCTION TO COLOUR TELEVISION. London: Norman Price, 1955. 72 pp., illus. Two 1954 Royal Television Society technical lectures on the newly approved U.S. NTSC systems.

8735 Head, Sydney W. BROADCASTING IN AMERICA: A SURVEY OF TELEVISION AND RADIO. Boston: Houghton Mifflin, 1956. xvi + 502 pp., illus. Later editions 1972, 1976, (with Christopher H. Sterling) 1982, 1986, 1990 (and with Lemuel B. Schofield), 1994. A standard university text including history, economics, impact and policy.

8736 Paulu, Burton. BRITISH BROADCASTING: RADIO AND TELEVISION IN THE UNITED KINGDOM. Minneapolis: University of Minnesota Press, 1956; London: Oxford University Press, 1957. xii + 457 pp. Basic scholarly survey, primarily on BBC radio.

8737 Rotha, Paul, ed. TELEVISION IN THE MAKING. London: Focal Press, 1956. 216 pp. Discusses current means of television production.

8738 Shunaman, Fred. "30 years of television." RADIO-ELECTRONICS 28 (Jan. 1957): 50–3. 7 illus.

8739 "Television: 30 years of progress." BELL LAB RECORD 35 (Apr. 1957): 150–2. 5 photos. Highlights of Bell contributions from 1927.

8740 "The engineering origins of television." ENGINEERING 184 (Nov. 1, 1957): 546–8. 7 illus.

8741 Harvey, E. Newton. A HISTORY OF LUMINESCENCE FROM THE EARLIEST TIMES UNTIL 1900. Philadelphia: American Philosophical Society, 1957. xxiii + 692 pp., 50 illus. Extensive bibliography.

8742 Crozier, Mary. BROADCASTING: SOUND AND TELEVISION. London: Oxford University Press, 1958. 236 pp. Social survey.

8743 Sturmey, S.G. THE ECONOMIC DEVELOPMENT OF RADIO. London: Duckworth, 1958. 284 pp. Details history of the British industry including television (Chapter 11), pp. 214–35.

8744 Zworykin, V.K., E.G. Ramberg, and L.E. Flory. TELEVISION IN SCIENCE AND INDUSTRY. New York: John Wiley, 1958.

8745 THE TWENTIETH CENTURY, Vol. 166 (Nov. 1959). Special issue on television, various contributors.

8746 Blum, Daniel. A PICTORIAL HISTORY OF TELEVISION. Philadelphia: Chilton, 1959. 278 pp. Primarily stills from commercial programs.

8747 Ardenne, M.v. "Evolution of the cathode-ray tube: A survey of developments over three decades." W.W. 66 (Jan. 1960): 28–32. 7 illus.

8748 "The evolution of television: 1927–1943. As reported in the Annual Reports of the Federal Radio Commission and the Federal Communications Commission." J. BROADCASTING 4 (Summer 1960): 199–240. Excerpts from FRC/FCC Annual Reports.

8749 Scroggie, M.G. "The genius of A.D. Blumlein." W.W. 66 (Sept. 1960): 451–6. 12 illus. Numerous patent numbers given in the text.

8750 THE BBC TELEVISION CENTRE. London: British Broadcasting Corporation, 1960. 47 pp., 28 photos and diags. (many in color). Plus A NEW LONDON LANDMARK...A MILESTONE IN THE HISTORY OF TELEVISION, 46 pp. of photos and diags., with captions. Details design and layout of "White City."

8751 Moseley, S.A. THE PRIVATE DIARIES OF SYDNEY MOSELEY. London: Parrish, 1960. 567 pp., illus. See Chapter 20: "The amazing history of television" (pp. 204–21).

8752 "The evolution of television: 1944–1948, as reported in the Annual Reports of the Federal Communications Commission." J. BROADCASTING 5 (Winter 1960–61): 23–37.

1961–70

8753 Gorokhov, P.K. "The origins of modern television." RADIO ENG. 16 (June 1961): 71–80, 104–16. Translated from the Russian by O.M. Blumm from RADIOTEKHNIKA 16 (1961): 70–9.

8754 Pawley, Edward L.E. "BBC television 1939–60: A review of progress." PROC. IEE 108 (Pt. B) (July 1961): 375–97. 2 maps, 2 charts, table of BBC television stations. List of chief dates in television: 31 entries from Sept. 1, 1939; 49 references from 1938.

8755 "BBC television: 25th anniversary." W.W. 67 (Nov. 1961): 557. Illus.

8756 "25th anniversary of television." BR. INST. RAD. ENG. J. 22 (Dec. 1961): 526. The BBC's anniversary.

8757 "25th anniversary of television." ELECT. ENG. 33 (Dec. 1961): 797. The BBC's anniversary.

8758 BBC TELEVISION: A BRITISH ENGINEERING ACHIEVEMENT. London: British Broadcasting Corporation, 1961. 64 pp., 55 photos, diags., and maps (some in color). Useful historical survey.

8759 TELEVISION CLOSE-UP: ON THE 25TH ANNIVERSARY OF THE BBC TELEVISION SERVICE WE PRESENT THIS PICTURE BOOK OF SOME LEADING PROGRAMMES, EVENTS, AND PEOPLE YOU SEE ON BBC-TV. 98 pp., illus. London: British Broadcasting Corporation, no date (1961).

8760 Eckert, Gerhard. KNAURS FERNSEHBUCH [Knaur's television book]. 384 pp., 150 illus. Munich/Zurich: Droemer-Knaur, 1961.

8761 Ross, Gordon. TELEVISION JUBILEE: THE STORY OF 25 YEARS OF BBC TELEVISION. 224 pp., 33 plates. London: W.H. Allen, 1961. An informal history.

8762 Eckersley, P.P. "The achievement and failure of John Logie Baird." J. IEE 8 (Apr. 1962): 197–9. See also letter from P.V. Reveley in response to this article.

8763 Bingley, F.J. "A half century of television reception." PROC. IRE 50 (May 1962): 799–805.

8764 Owen, C.H. "Television broadcasting." PROC. IRE 50 (May 1962): 818–24. 7 illus.

8765 Schlesinger, K., and E.G. Ramberg. "Beam deflection and photo devices." PROC. IRE 50 (May 1962): 991–1005. 19 illus.

8766 Clarke, Basil. "The first live transatlantic link." INT. TELEV. TECH. REV. 3 (Nov. 1962): 498–501.

8767 Clarke, B. "The quest for high definition." INT. TELEV. TECH. REV. 3 (Nov. 1962): 546–9.

8768 Zworykin, V.K. "The early days: Some recollections." TELEV. QUARTERLY 1 (Nov. 1962): 69–73.

8769 Dunlap, O.E., Jr. COMMUNICATIONS IN SPACE: FROM MARCONI TO MAN ON THE MOON. New York: Harper & Row, 1962. Revised editions 1964, 1970. A popular history.

8770 Bitting, Robert C. "Creating an industry." J. SMPTE 74 (Nov. 1965): 1015–23. Part I: Formation and growth of RCA. Part II: Television development within RCA.

8771 Briggs, Asa. THE HISTORY OF BROADCASTING IN THE UNITED KINGDOM. Vol. 2: THE GOLDEN AGE OF WIRELESS. 688 pp, illus., biblio. London: Oxford University Press, 1965. Second volume of the definitive history of the BBC details the emergence of pre-war television.

8772 Kurylo, Friedrich K. FERDINAND BRAUN: LEBEN UND WIRKEN DES ERFINDERS DER BRAUNSCHEN ROHRE. NOBELPREISTRAGER 1909 [Ferdinand Braun: The life and work of the inventor of the cathode-ray tube, Nobel Prize-winner 1909]. Munich: Heinz Moos, 1965. 288 pp., 16 plates, illus. (see 8854 for English translation)

8773 [Michelis, Anthony.] FROM SEMAPHORE TO SATELLITE. Geneva, Switzerland: International Telecommunication Union, 1965. 342 pp., 365 illus., bibl. Official history published for ITU centennial.

8774 Dizard, Wilson P. TELEVISION: A WORLD VIEW. Syracuse, N.Y.: Syracuse University Press, 1966. 349 pp., 16 plates. Bibliography on pp. 321–33.

8775 Lyons, Eugene. DAVID SARNOFF. New York: Harper & Row, 1966. 372 pp., 30 photos. The first biography but lacks perspective.

8776 Rowland, John. THE TELEVISION MAN: THE STORY OF JOHN LOGIE BAIRD. London: Lutterworth Press, 1966. 144 pp. A popular treatment.

8777 Shulman, Arthur, and Roger Youman. HOW SWEET IT WAS: TELEVISION, A PICTORIAL COMMENTARY. New York: Shorecrest/Bonanza Books, 1966. 448 pp., 1,435 illus. Primarily programming.

8778 Bridgewater, T.H. "Baird and television." J. BR. KINE. 49 (Mar. 1967): 60–8. 7 illus. A paper read before the Society on Nov. 2, 1966. Based on the John Logie Baird Memorial Lecture, Royal College of Science and Technology, Glasgow, Mar. 1959.

8779 Ives, R.L. "Television's 40th birthday." RADIO-ELECTRONICS 38 (Apr. 1967): 55–6. 4 illus. 40 years since the B.T.L. demonstration of Apr. 7, 1927.

8780 THE BELL SYSTEM'S ROLE IN TELEVISION. Pamphlet PE 160. New York: AT&T, 1967.

8781 Fielding, Ray. A TECHNOLOGICAL HISTORY OF MOTION PICTURES AND TELEVISION: AN ANTHOLOGY FROM THE PAGES OF THE JOURNAL OF THE SOCIETY OF MOTION PICTURE AND TELEVISION ENGINEERS. Berkeley:

University of California Press, 1967. 255 pp., illus., bibl.. "Historical Papers—Television," pp. 227–54 includes four papers: 8691, 8726, 8727, 8730.

8782 Paulu, B. RADIO AND TELEVISION BROADCASTING ON THE EUROPEAN CONTINENT. Minneapolis: University of Minnesota Press, 1967. xii + 290 pp.

8783 "The work of Alan Blumlein." J. BR. KINE. (July 1968).

8784 Carson, David N. "The evolution of picturephone service." BELL LAB RECORD 46 (Oct. 1968): 282–91. 8 photos. From 1956, with mention of the picture transmission experiments of Apr. 1927.

8785 Shiers, G. "The first electron tube." SCI. AM. 220 (Mar. 1969): 104–12. 11 illus., including double-page chart showing the chronology of invention from 1879 to 1907. Reprinted in Gene I. Rochlin (compiler), SCIENTIFIC TECHNOLOGY AND SOCIAL CHANGE. San Francisco: W.H. Freeman & Co., 1974.

8786 Settel, Irving, and William Laas. A PICTORIAL HISTORY OF TELEVISION. New York: Grosset & Dunlap, 1969. xiv + 210 pp., illus. Primarily programming.

8787 Shiers, George. "Early schemes for television." IEEE SPECTRUM 7 (May 1970): 24–34. 11 illus. Also printed in PROC. IREE (Australia) 31 (Dec. 1970): 407–16.

8788 Baker, W.J. A HISTORY OF THE MARCONI COMPANY. London: Methuen, 1970; New York: St. Martin's Press, 1972. 413 pp. 24 plates, 28 illus. Only overall history of the firm available; includes television.

1971–80

8789 Shiers, George. "The induction coil." SCI. AM. 224 (May 1971): 80–8.

8790 McGee, J.D. "The life and work of Sir Isaac Shoenberg, 1880–1963." J. TELEV. SOC. 13 (May–June 1971): 207–16.

8791 Tucker, John D. "Sir Isaac Shoenberg." INT. BRD. ENG. (Supplement, Dec. 1971): 4–6, 8, 9. Illus.

8792 "John Logie Baird." INT. BRD. ENG. (Dec. 1971): 10–3. 4 illus.

8793 Turk, Walter E. "35 years of television pickup tubes." INT. BRD. ENG. (Dec. 1971): 16–8, 20, 21. 5 illus.

8794 Baker, W.J. "The Marconi Company and television." INT. BRD. ENG. (Dec. 1971): 22, 24, 25. 4 illus. Based on 8788.

8795 "Years of ideas and evolution." INT. BRD. ENG. (Dec. 1971): 50–2, 54, 56, 58. 10 illus.

8796 Shiers, G. "On the origins of electron devices." IEEE SPECTRUM 9 (Nov. 1972): 70–6.

8797 Pawley, E. BBC ENGINEERING 1922–1972. London: BBC Publications, 1972. xiv + 569 pp., 79 photos on 32 plates. Definitive history incorporates television throughout.

8798 Shiers, G., with May Shiers. BIBLIOGRAPHY OF THE HISTORY OF ELECTRONICS. Television and facsimile, pp 256–84. Annotated and indexed. Metuchen, N.J.: Scarecrow Press, 1972. 323 pp.

8799 Abramson, A. "A short history of television recording: Part II." J. SMPTE 82 (Mar. 1973): 188–97. 5 illus.

8800 Baird, Margaret. TELEVISION BAIRD: THE STORY OF THE MAN WHO INVENTED TELEVISION. Cape Town: H.A.U.M., 1973. 160 pp., 10 illus.

8801 Goldmark, P.C., with Lee Edson. MAVERICK INVENTOR: MY TURBULENT YEARS AT CBS. New York: Saturday Review Press/E.P. Dutton & Co., 1973. v + 278 pp. Autobiography of the long-time head of CBS labs and key figure in the CBS mechanical color TV system.

8802 Taylor, C.T., and Z.A. Silberston. THE ECONOMIC IMPACT OF THE PATENT SYSTEM: A STUDY OF THE BRITISH EXPERIENCE. London: Cambridge University Press, 1973. Chapter 12: "Electronics. C: The development of television," pp. 304–12.

8803 Shiers, G. "Ferdinand Braun and the cathode-ray tube." SCI. AM. 230 (Mar. 1974): 92–101.

8804 Herold, E.W. "History and development of the color picture tube." PROC. SOC. INFO. DISPLAY 15/4 (Fall 1974): 141–9.

8805 Layer, Harold A. "From radiovision to video . . . and television between." AV INST. 20 (May 1975): 6–11. 12 illus., bibl.

8806 Heightman, D.W. "Television reception 1925–1975." RADIO & ELECT. ENG. 45 (Oct. 1975): 559–69.

8807 Burns, R.W. "The first demonstration of television." ELECT. & POWER 21 (Oct. 9, 1975): 953–6. 7 illus. On J.L. Baird and his experiments, and his first success with half-tube images on Oct. 2, 1925.

8808 Shiers, G. "Television 50 years ago." J. BROADCASTING 19 (Fall 1975): 387–400. Also "Television" in J. TELEV. SOC. 16 (Jan.–Feb. 1976): 6–10, 13. Account of J.L. Baird's activities from 1923 to the end of 1926, with mention of the work of C.F. Jenkins.

8809 Barnouw, Erik. TUBE OF PLENTY: THE EVOLUTION OF AMERICAN TELEVISION. New York: Oxford University Press, 1975. viii + 518 pp., illus., bibl. Revised editions 1982, 1990.

8810 Lichty, Lawrence W., and Malachi C. Topping, eds. AMERICAN BROADCASTING: A SOURCE BOOK ON THE HISTORY OF RADIO AND TELEVISION. New York: Hastings House, 1975. 723 pp. Bibliography, pp. 693–708. Includes many articles on television.

8811 Waddell, Peter. "Television's eccentric pioneer." ILLUS. LONDON NEWS (Jan. 1976): 32–4. 3 illus. On J.L. Baird.

8812 Waddell, P., W.V. Smith, and J. Sanderson. "John Logie Baird and the Falkirk transmitter." W.W. 82: 43–6. 7 illus. The activities of the pioneer of television between 1925 and 1928.

8813 Fisk, Jim, and Dave Ingram. "50 years of television." HAM RADIO (Feb. 1976): 36–46. 23 illus.

8814 "Television Society honours Baird." W.W. 82 (Mar. 1976): 70.

8815 "The first 50 years of NBC." BROADCASTING (June 21, 1976): 29–92.

8816 Weimer, Paul K. "A historical review of the development of television pickup devices (1930–1976)." IEEE TRANS. (Electron Devices) 23 (July 1976): 739–52. 25 illus.

8817 Law, Harold B. "The shadow mask color picture tube: How it began—an eyewitness account of its early history." IEEE TRANS. (Electron Devices) 23 (July 1976): 752–9. 4 illus.

8818 O'Brien, Richard S., Robert B. Monroe, Charles E. Anderson, and Steven C. Runyon. "101 years of television technology." J. SMPTE 85 (July 1976): 457–80. 33 illus., chronological chart, bibl.

8819 Fink, D.G. "Perspectives on television: The role played by the two NTSC's in preparing television service for the American public." PROC. IEEE 64 (Sept. 1976): 1322–31. 4 illus.

8820 Herold, E.W. "A history of color television displays." PROC. IEEE 64 (Sept. 1976): 1331–8. 7 photos.

8821 Sandilands, John "Boys, we're doing the Coronation." OBSERVER MAGAZINE (Oct. 31, 1976): 46–8. 6 illus.

8822 Barthel, V.K., and H. Keil. "40 years of television transmission on coaxial cables. Pt. 1." FREQUENZ 30 (Oct. 1976): 288–90. Part 2 in FREQUENZ 30 (Nov. 1976): 307–13. In German.

8823 Caccia, G.G. "Color television: A little of the history." RADIO INDEX 43 (Nov. 1976): 27–30.

8824 "40 years' television from the BBC." J. TELEV. SOC. 16 (Nov.–Dec. 1976): 16, 17.

4 photos. Conversation between the editor, Denis Austin, and T.H. Bridgewater.

8825 Waddell, P. "Seeing by wireless." NEW SCIENTIST 72 (Nov. 11, 1976): 342–4. 3 illus.

8826 Davis, Anthony. TELEVISION: THE FIRST FORTY YEARS. London: Severn House, Independent Television Publications, 1976. 159 pp., illus.

8827 Exwood, Maurice. JOHN LOGIE BAIRD: 50 YEARS OF TELEVISION. London: Institution of Electronic and Radio Engineers, 1976. 31 pp., 7 illus., bibl.

8828 Shiers, G. "Historical notes on television before 1900." J. SMPTE 86 (Mar. 1977): 129–37. 6 illus., chronological table. List of errata published in July issue, p. 500.

8829 McGee, J.D. "The contribution of A.A. Campbell Swinton, F.R.S., to television." NOTES AND RESEARCHES ROY. SOC. 32 (July 1977): 91–105.

8830 Runyon, S. "Television." ELECT. DES. 25 (Sept. 1, 1977): 70–9.

8831 Dobriner, R. "The man who was sure television would work: An interview with Vladimir Zworykin." ELECT. DES. 22 (Sept. 1, 1977): 112–5.

8832 "CBS: The first five decades." BROADCASTING (Sept. 19, 1977): 45–116.

8833 Shiers, G. "Television in prospect, 1873–1927." J. ROY. TELEV. SOC. 16 (Sept.–Oct. 1977): 8–12. 3 illus., 21 references from 1828 to 1925. Prophecies and opinions about the possibilities for seeing by electricity, and its applications.

8834 Vil'dgrube, G.S., I.K. Malekhov, R.M. Stepanov, and V.A. Urvalov. "New Soviet television camera tubes." TEKH. KINO I TELEV. 10 (Oct. 1977): 42–9. Brief history of developments in Russia from the first use of the Iconoscope in 1933. In Russian.

8835 Rosselevich, I.A., E.I. Farber, and R.S. Kharchikyan. "The development of the engineering resources of studio and outside television broadcasting in the U.S.S.R." TEKH. KINO I TELEV. 10 (Oct. 1977): 49–61. The history of television broadcasting from the first 240-line system in Leningrad and 343-line system in Moscow, both in 1937, to the 1970s. In Russian.

8836 Dreher, C. SARNOFF: AN AMERICAN SUCCESS. New York: Quadrangle, 1977. 282 pp.

8837 Shiers, G., ed. TECHNICAL DEVELOPMENT OF TELEVISION: AN ANTHOLOGY OF 30 PAPERS COVERING THE YEARS 1878 TO 1973. New York: Arno Press, 1977. 8-page introduction. 9 pages of references, 64 entries, many multiple items. Book list, 91 items from 1925 to 1975.

8838 Knapp, J. George, and Julian E. Tebo. "The history of television. Part 1: Mechanical and semi-mechanical systems." IEEE COMM. 16 (May 1978): 8–22. 15 photos, 17 diags. Emphasis on American work patented by Bell Labs. Otherwise a skimpy treatment with numerous errors.

8839 Sterling, C.H., and John M. Kittross. STAY TUNED: A CONCISE HISTORY OF AMERICAN BROADCASTING. Belmont, Calif.: Wadsworth Publishing Co., 1978. xiv + 562 pp., photos, diags., extracts, tables. Includes chronology (pp. 471–81), glossary (pp. 483–508), historical statistics (pp. 509–36), bibliography (pp. 537–50). Revised ed. 1990, 705 pp.

8840 Broadway, L.F. "J.D. McGee and the Emitron." J. ROY. TELEV. SOC. 17 (July–Aug. 1979): 23.

8841 "Bosch Company has had a good nose." FUNKSCHAU 51 (Aug. 3, 1979): 913–5. History of the television work of Robert Bosch GmbH since 1929, when it became one of the founder members of Fernseh A.-G. In German.

8842 Burns, R.W. "J.L. Baird: Success and failure." PROC. IEE 126 (Sept. 1979): 921–8. 8 illus.

8843 50 YEARS OF FERNSEH, 1929–1979. (Bosch Technische Berichte, Vol. 6.) Stuttgart: Robert Bosch GmbH, 1979. 188 pp., illus. Includes Gerhart Goebel, "From the history of television—the first fifty years" (pp. 3–27) and F. Rudert, "Fifty years of Fernseh, 1929–1979" (pp. 28–58).

8844 McGee, J.D. "The history of electronic imaging" (pp. 11–54) in T.P. McLean and P. Schagen, eds., ELECTRONIC IMAGING. New York/London: Academic Press, 1979. Papers read at conference at the Royal Society, London, Sept. 11–13, 1978.

8845 Hallett, Michael. "Baird: The master of mechanical television." J. ROY. TELEV. SOC. 18 (Jan.–Feb. 1980): 10, 11.

8846 Roizen, Joe. "David Sarnoff: Father of American television." J. ROY. TELEV. SOC. 18 (May–June 1980): 26, 27.

8847 Birkinshaw, D. "Shoenberg: Faith in electronic television." J. ROY. TELEV. SOC. 18 (Sept.–Oct. 1980): 56.

8848 Flamm, Donald. "Baird in America: What was and what might have been." J. ROY. TELEV. SOC. 18 (Mar–Apr. 1981): 21–3. 6 photos.

8849 Hillier, James. "Vladimir Zworykin: Pioneer of electronic television." J. ROY. TELEV. SOC. 18 (May–June 1981): 43.

8850 Shiers, G. "The rise of mechanical television, 1901–1930." J. SMPTE 90 (June 1981): 508–21.

8851 Abramson, A. "Pioneers of television—Vladimir Zworykin." J. SMPTE 90 (July 1981): 579–90. 12 photos, 7 diags., table of patents (1927–65), Zworykin bibliography (74 items), list of honors and awards.

8852 Bridgewater, T.H. "Campbell Swinton: The man who conceived electronic television." J. ROY. TELEV. SOC. 18 (Sept.–Oct. 1981): 27–9. 4 photos, diag. A profile condensed from a monograph published later (see 8856).

1981–95

8853 Hallett, Michael. JOHN LOGIE BAIRD AND TELEVISION: PIONEERS OF SCIENCE AND DISCOVERY. Hove, England: Priory Press, 1978. 95 pp. illus. For young readers.

8854 Kurylo, F., Charles Susskind. FERDINAND BRAUN: A LIFE OF THE NOBEL PRIZE-WINNER AND INVENTOR OF THE CATHODE-RAY OSCILLOSCOPE. Cambridge: MIT Press, 1981. 289 pp., 51 illus., chronol., bibl.English translation of 8772.

8855 Udelson, Joseph H. THE GREAT TELEVISION RACE: A HISTORY OF THE AMERICAN TELEVISION INDUSTRY 1925-1941. University: University of Alabama Press, 1981. 197 pp., 26 illus., bibl. Analaysis focuses on both technology and business aspects of pre-war U.S. entities and inventors.

8856 Bridgewater, T.H. A.A. CAMPBELL SWINTON.London: Royal Television Society, 1982. 32 pp., 10 illus, bibl. Monograph 1 of the society, authored by a retired head of BBC television engineering, expands on his article (8852) and is the most complete survey of the inventor's life.

8857 Varian, Dorothy. THE INVENTOR AND THE PILOT: RUSSELL AND SIGURD VARIAN. Palo Alto, Calif.: Pacific Books, 1983. 314 pp. illus. Dual biography of the brothers; Russell worked with Farnsworth, then developed the klystron tube and together the two brothers founded Varian Associates.

8858 Norman, Bruce. HERE'S LOOKING AT YOU: THE STORY OF BRITISH TELEVISION 1908–39. London: BBC, 1984. 224 pp., 85 illus., bibl.Popular narrative, relying heavily on oral history, of pre-war developments, focusing on the 1930s.

8859 Burns, R.W. BRITISH TELEVISION: THE FORMATIVE YEARS. London: Peter Peregrinus/Science Museum, 1986. 488 pp., illus., refs.The definitive history of British efforts, based on primary documentation, of work through 1939. Well documented.

8860 THE HISTORY OF TELEVISION FROM EARLY DAYS TO THE PRESENT. London: Institution of Electrical Engineers,

1986. 185 pp., illus., refs. Its Conference Publication No. 271 includes 41 papers.

8861 Abramson, A. THE HISTORY OF TELEVISION, 1880–1941. Jefferson, N.C.: McFarland, 1987. 354 pp. 50 illus., refs. Definitive treatment of the period covered in the present bibliography, by a long-time expert (see, for example, 8733, an earlier version of the material found here).

8862 Bilby, Kenneth. THE GENERAL: DAVID SARNOFF AND THE RISE OF THE COMMUNICATIONS INDUSTRY. New York: Harper & Row, 1986. 326 pp., bibl. The best biography to date, as the author worked closely with Sarnoff but assesses many old myths and sets the story straight.

8863 Graham, Margaret B.W. RCA AND THE VIDEODISC: THE BUSINESS OF RESEARCH. New York: Cambridge University Press, 1986. 258 pp., illus. Valuable and detailed study of decision-making on what became an industrial debacle.

8864 Lardner, James. FAST FORWARD: HOLLYWOOD, THE JAPANESE, AND THE VCR WARS. New York: Norton, 1987. 344 pp., sources. Rise of the videocassette recorder from initial work here and in Japan to the legal battles over copyright.

8865 Yanczer, Peter F. THE MECHANICS OF TELEVISION: THE STORY OF MECHANICAL TELEVISION. St. Louis: the author, 1987. 170 pp., illus. Detailed assessment of the many mechanical systems, clearly explained and illustrated with diagrams.

8866 Baird, John Logie. SERMONS, SOAP AND TELEVISION: AUTOBIOGRAPHICAL NOTES. London: Royal Television Society, 1988. 147 pp., illus. Publication of a manuscript long in the society's archives. Introduction by the inventor's son Malcolm.

8867 Singleton, Thomas. THE STORY OF SCOPHONY. London: Royal Television Society, 1988. 152 pp., illus. Details the 1930s' story of a projection system of video designed for home use but applied only in theaters before the war stymied development.

8868 Dowsing, James. TV LONDON. London: Sunrise Press, nd. 109 pp., maps. Details of dozens of locations in the city related to television history.

8869 Farnsworth, Elma G. DISTANT VISION: ROMANCE AND DISCOVERY ON AN INVISIBLE FRONTIER—PHILO T. FARNSWORTH, INVENTOR OF TELEVISION. Salt Lake City: Pemberly Kent, 1990. 360 pp., illus., bibl., patent list. The inventor's wife details their life and his innovations.

8870 DEDICATION OF THE STATUE OF PHILO T. FARNSWORTH PRESENTED BY THE STATE OF UTAH: PROCEEDINGS IN THE ROTUNDA OF THE UNITED STATES CAPITOL. House Document 101-188, 101st Cong., 2d Sess. Washington: Government Printing Office, 1991. 72 pp., illus., bibl. Useful essay on the inventor's life plus appendices on his inventions.

8871 Inglis, Andrew F. BEHIND THE TUBE: A HISTORY OF BROADCASTING TECHNOLOGY AND BUSINESS. Stoneham, Mass.: Focal Press, 1990. 527 pp., illus., gloss., bibl. A former RCA engineer details the development of (in a chapter each): monochrome television, color television, broadcast video recording, and other technologies.

8872 Nwungwun, Aaron Foisi. VIDEO RECORDING TECHNOLOGY: ITS IMPACT ON MEDIA AND HOME ENTERTAINMENT. Stoneham, MA: Focal Press, 1990. 289 pp., illus., bibl. Details the multi-nation rise of audio and then video recording technologies.

8873 McArthur, Tom, and P. Waddell. VISION WARRIOR: THE HIDDEN ACHIEVEMENT OF JOHN LOGIE BAIRD. Kirkwall, Scotland: Orkney Press, 1990. 315 pp., illus. Somewhat breathless biography of the inventor, with considerable new material on his World War II work on radar and related devices. Updates and expands 1986 publication.

8874 Finn, Bernard S. THE HISTORY OF ELECTRICAL TECHNOLOGY: AN ANNOTATED BIBLIOGRAPHY. New York: Garland,

1991. 342 pp., 1,559 items, illus. Includes television.

8875 Marlow, Eugene, and Eugene Secunda. SHIFTING TIME AND SPACE: THE STORY OF VIDEOTAPE. New York: Praeger, 1991. 174 pp., bibl. First book devoted to the subject, including discussion of videotape's impact on advertising, programs, and the home market.

8876 Hilliard, Robert L., and Michael C. Keith. THE BROADCAST CENTURY: A BIOGRAPHY OF AMERICAN BROADCASTING. Stoneham, Mass.: Focal Press, 1992. 296 pp., illus, bibl. Chronological telling of the story, including television.

8877 Brittain, James E. ALEXANDERSON: PIONEER IN AMERICAN ELECTRICAL ENGINEERING. Baltimore: Johns Hopkins University Press, 1992. 381 pp., illus. Definitive biography, including the G.E. engineer's work with mechanical and projection television systems in the 1920s.

8878 Kraeuter, David W. RADIO AND TELEVISION PIONEERS: A PATENT BIBLIOGRAPHY. Metuchen, N.J.: Scarecrow Press, 1992. 319 pp. Over 3,000 patents are cited from the work of 40 inventors including Alexanderson, Baird (both Hollis and John Logie), Du Mont, Farnsworth, Jenkins, Tarzian, and Zworykin.

8879 Kraeuter, D.W. BRITISH RADIO AND TELEVISION PIONEERS: A PATENT BIBLIOGRAPHY. Metuchen, N.J.: Scarecrow Press, 1993. 206 pp. Some 1,100 patents from 29 inventors are included, among them such television pioneers Baird and Crookes.

8880 Ritchie, Michael. PLEASE STAND BY: A PREHISTORY OF TELEVISION. Woodstock, NY: The Overlook Press, 1994. 247 pp., illus., bibl. Informal history of American television to 1948 (with a chapter on the BBC), concentrating on programming and personalities.

8881 Abramson, Albert. ZWORYKIN: PIONEER OF TELEVISION. Urbana: University of Illinois Press, 1995. 319 pp., illus. Definitive biography of the Westinghouse and later RCA researcher/inventor that carefully weighs his accomplishments against those of (among others) Philo Farnsworth. Photos, extensive notes, index.

8882 Kisseloff, Jeff. THE BOX: AN ORAL HISTORY OF TELEVISION, 1920–1961. New York: Viking Press, 1995. 592 pp., bibl. Based on hundreds of interviews, this includes some material on pre-war American television experimenting and broadcasting, especially by DuMont, CBS, and NBC.

Name Index

Abbot, W. Barrie 2091, 2271, 2999, 3147, 3389
Abelli, A. A. 1002
Abrahamsohn, Max 6093
Abramson, Albert 8730, 8732, 8799, 8851, 8861
Abria, Jérémie Joseph Benôit 12; *2*
Adam, M. 5118, 5498, 6547, 7430, 7650, 8245, 8564
Adamian, Johannes 359, 393, 470
Adams, Albert Ernest 7898
Adams, Clayton Loftin 3679
Adams, D.S.F. 1878
Adams, Harold A. 3182
Adams, William Grylls 59, 65, 69, 73
Addink, N.W.H. 5833
Adsit, Frank W. 1180; *232*
A.E.G. *See* Allgemeine Elektricitäts Gesellschaft
Affel, Herman A. 1891
Agate, C.S. 4402, 4419, 4422, 4569
Agricola, A. 7311
Aguillon, L. 7968
Ahronheim, Albert Alexander 2037, 2420, 2591, 3303, 3734
Aigner, Franz 648
Aisberg, Eugène 2703, 2882, 3753
Alberti, Egon 3754
Aldous, H.W. 6073, 6085, 6117, 6435, 6436, 6626, 6801, 7007, 8278
Alexander, Frank 3502
Alexanderson, Ernst Fredrik Werner 826, 829, 832, 853, 867, 868, 870, 886, 888, 920, 926, 929, 956, 1110, 1111, 1115, 1116, 1119, 1151, 1187, 1190, 1194, 1222, 1429, 1455, 1616, 1631, 1899, 2278, 2391, 2455, 2588, 2778, 2990, 3227, 3320, 3473, 6629, 8877, 8878
  patents 803, 1361, 1949, 2354, 3107, 3156, 3223, 3635, 3675, 3918
Alexandra Palace. *See under* British Broadcasting Corporation
Alien Properties Custodian 7411, 7513, 7953, 7957, 8006, 8430, 8434, 8517, 8551, 8562, 8577
Allen, C.T. 7729
Allen, Herbet Stanley 432
Allen, Horace Clifford 7432
Allen, John Gillespie 530
Allgemeine Elektricitäts Gesellschaft (A.E.G.) 3212, 3215, 3369, 3460, 3484, 3491, 3638, 3868, 3869, 4004, 4193, 4571, 4686, 4687, 4892, 5023, 5071, 5121, 5228, 5333, 6013, 6040, 6041, 6054, 6096, 6145, 6151, 6185, 6266, 6513, 6929, 6993, 7014, 7988, 8002
Allgemeiner Deutscher Fernsehverein (German Television Society) 1033, 2265, 2368
Allingham, Garry 3202, 4132
Allouard-Carny, Paul 584
Alvess, P. 6585
American Telephone & Telegraph Company (AT&T). *See also* Bell Telephone Laboratories. 446, 594, 604, 610, 612, 719, 722, 821, 919, 966, 997, 1045, 1052, 1074, 1341, 1365, 1396, 2032, 2285, 2299, 2343, 2349, 2359, 2422, 3418, 3663, 4070, 5100, 5373, 5586, 5712, 5727, 7045
American Television Institute 7274
American Television Laboratories Inc. 2880, 3052, 3088, 3114, 3409, 5776, 6316
Ampthill, Lord 1328, 1702, 2325
Amstutz, Noah W. 238
Andersen, Anders Christian 369, 396, 412, 460, 840
Andersen, E. 2557, 5795, 6317
Andersen, Lauritz Sophus 369, 396, 412, 460, 840
Anderson, Charles E. 8818
Anderson, E. G. O. 7177
Anderson, John Spence 2704
Anderson, J.T. 7572, 7883
Anderson, Wilfred 1655
Anderson, W.P. 5307
Andrade, E.N. da Costa 2062
Andrea 8164, 8273
Andrieu, Robert 4817, 4946, 4989, 5036, 5194, 5280, 5294, 5424, 5444, 5499, 5527, 5676, 5680, 5687, 5714, 5766, 5779, 5787, 5859, 5888, 6649, 6822, 6862, 6990, 7516, 7544, 8405
Angwin, Arthur Stanley 3243, 4466, 4691, 4711, 4796
Anson, H. St. George 504
Antranikian, Haig 1146
Applebaum, David 3507
Appleton, W.A. 3442
Arapu, R. 443

Arathoon 6412
Archer 7048
Arco, Georg Wilhelm Alexander Hans von, 419
Ardenne, Manfred von 2322, 2360, 2553, 2585, 2717, 2793, 2841, 2940, 2979, 3061, 3095, 3146, 3269, 3452, 3630, 3730, 4103, 4245, 4264, 4490, 4591, 4794, 4878, 5108, 5437, 5513, 5575, 5648, 5723, 6024, 6026, 6139, 6232, 6241, 6308, 6570, 7268, 7763, 8057, 8108, 8618, 8747
  patents 2357, 2441, 2653, 2657, 2806, 2827-30, 2838, 2879, 2892, 2893, 2913, 2926, 2929, 2965-7, 3012, 3065, 3120, 3151, 3152, 3161, 3206, 3241, 3338, 3344, 3345, 3541, 3563, 3572, 3644, 3684, 3706, 3707, 3714, 3807, 3821, 3824, 3825, 3901, 3902, 3956, 3960, 3961, 3999, 4014, 4097, 4182, 4213, 4223, 4283, 4372, 4456, 4503, 4531, 4547, 4667, 4921, 5030, 5304, 6258, 6677, 6813, 7549, 7653, 7698, 7859, 7905, 7937, 7946, 7957, 7960, 7985, 7987
Aretz, E. 2556
Argentina 4085
Armagnac, J.P. 887, 1192, 2005
Armagnat, Henri 360
Armengaud, Jules 361, 362, 365, 368, 412
Armstrong, Edwin Howard 427, 436
Armstrong, Ralph W. 2398
Arnaud, Joseph John 1133
Arni, Hans 6669
Arnold, Frank Atkinson 4079
Arnold, John P. 1087, 1488, 1555, 1627, 1726, 1862 2050
Arvin, W.B. 703
Aschen, Robert 3753, 8678
Ashbridge, Noel 4466, 4691, 4711, 5954, 6919, 7934, 7935, 8595
Ashdown, E.S. 6449
Aspden, Ralph Leonard 977, 1719, 2611, 2915
Associated Electric Laboratories 587, 1105, 1606, 2288, 2689
Associated Telephone and Telegraph Co., Inc. 1282, 1283
A/S Telocle 463

Atkinson, Llewelyn Birchall 169, 204, 205, 586, 1804, 1832
Atkinson, Noel 5702, 7291
Atkinson, Sidney 4437, 5376, 5378
Atlantic Broadcasting Co. 2540
AT&T. *See* American Telegraph & Telephone Company
Austin 6149
Austin, Denis 8824
Australia 2023, 2243, 3947, 5161
Automatic Electric Co. 4304, 5373
Avey, Albert Franklin 5860
Aylesworth, Merlin Hall 2615, 2779, 2961, 3005, 3306
Ayrton, William Edward 74, 100, 127, 128, 130, 135, 156, 168, 292, 412

Babits, Victor A. 5260, 7080
Bachmann, C.H. 7611
Baden, Anne L. 8027
Baden-Powell, Fletcher Smyth 468, 2858
Bähring, Herbert 5393, 5397, 5809, 6069, 7252, 7457, 7961
Baethelmans 5133
Baier, Otto 6693
Bailey, F.G. 956
Bailey, Leslie 4132
Bailey, L.W.A. 1060
Bailey, W.C. 5965, 5172, 6449
Bain, Alexander 11, 40
Bainbridge-Bell, L.H. 3907
Baird, Horace (Hollis) Semple 1897, 2103, 2294, 2886, 2936, 2990, 3011, 3473, 8878
Baird, John Logie 400, 544, 548, 554, 583, 593, 599, 643, 644, 650, 651, 659, 675, 676, 680, 683, 690, 736, 739, 741, 742, 759, 768, 774, 777, 778, 783, 787, 789, 790, 793, 794, 796, 806-9, 811, 812, 815, 816, 831, 834, 836, 840, 841, 846-8, 857, 858, 862, 864, 866, 869, 871, 880, 881, 886, 892, 898-900, 914, 940, 968, 1016, 1038, 1043, 1049, 1098, 1100, 1112, 1115, 1116, 1120, 1128, 1129, 1136, 1137, 1147, 1171, 1174, 1179, 1183, 1217, 1222, 1238, 1246, 1261, 1270, 1273, 1275, 1276, 1288, 1303, 1311, 1316, 1320, 1321, 1325, 1328, 1333, 1353, 1360, 1366, 1378, 1404, 1438, 1444, 1475, 1487, 1518, 1538, 1578, 1582, 1587, 1589, 1590, 1643, 1649, 1666, 1682, 1685, 1692, 1698, 1699, 1706, 1733, 1738, 1766, 1772, 1773, 1805, 1899, 1918, 1988, 2011, 2018, 2022, 2030, 2035, 2045, 2057, 2079, 2082, 2102, 2121, 2126, 2136, 2140, 2143, 2155, 2157, 2159, 2209, 2223, 2267, 2271, 2277, 2281, 2300, 2312, 2319, 2323, 2235, 2331, 2348, 2371, 2458, 2464, 2470, 2488, 2497, 2524, 2595, 2670, 2766, 2770, 2798, 2857, 2858, 2937, 2995, 3044, 3099, 3101, 3154, 3162, 3174, 3178, 3203, 3272, 3280, 3480, 3600, 3702, 3942, 4113, 4116, 4415, 4588, 4704, 4814, 6509, 6928, 7316, 7377, 7506, 7864, 8157, 8173, 8664, 8667, 8711, 8762, 8776, 8778, 8792, 8800, 8808, 8811, 8812, 8814, 8827, 8839a, 8842, 8845, 8866, 8873, 8878, 8879
demonstrations and tests 585, 662, 664, 733, 740, 769, 772, 773, 776, 786, 788, 802, 818, 827, 839, 852, 865, 873, 874, 913, 915, 928, 932, 939, 955, 981, 986-8, 1028, 1030, 1041, 1124-7, 1129, 1130, 1134, 1161, 1178, 1240, 1277, 1329, 1352, 1403, 1404, 1503, 1512, 1523, 1535, 1543, 1549, 1551, 1556, 1569, 1587, 1594, 1595, 1648, 1781, 1787, 1790, 1805, 1812, 1821, 1825, 1906, 1933, 1940, 1988, 1991, 1992, 2010, 2017, 2021, 2025, 2045, 2087, 2347, 2365, 2367, 2374, 2432, 2489, 2491, 2505, 2526, 2529, 2563, 2565, 2567, 2636, 2638, 2640, 2671, 2735, 2741, 2764, 2848, 2924, 2938, 2939, 2995, 2996, 2999, 3288, 3433, 3438, 3459, 3461, 3476, 3486, 3487, 3489, 3614, 3917, 8461, 8463, 8807
patents 565, 579, 580, 640, 699, 704-7, 711, 712, 737, 761, 797-80, 814, 820, 821, 833, 860, 863, 876, 893, 946, 953, 976, 982, 989, 1011, 1018, 1025, 1064, 1082, 1083, 1106, 1213-5, 1225, 1252, 1257, 1267, 1268, 1284-7, 1297-1300, 1335-7, 1409, 1477, 1521, 1522, 1527-30, 1544, 1600, 1601, 1659, 1721, 1722, 1747, 1759, 1892, 1961, 2197, 2199, 2203, 2233, 2240, 2509, 2536, 2573, 2650, 2780, 2781, 2791, 2804, 2857, 2858, 3289, 3403, 3419, 3464, 3662, 3665, 3819, 3833, 3930, 3950, 3953, 4009-11, 4110, 4208, 4209, 4211, 4222, 4265, 4293, 4294, 4306, 4339, 4343, 4514, 4566, 4607, 4621, 4639, 4734, 4735, 4978, 4979, 5054, 5154, 5175, 5218, 5236, 5241, 5538, 5630, 5677, 5678, 5725, 5824, 5825, 5848
Baird vs BBC (request for transmission facilities) 1486, 1532, 1535, 1540, 1543, 1556, 1596, 1608, 1645, 1649, 1710, 1774, 1777, 1969, 1978, 2016, 2023, 2029, 2138
first broadcast with BBC station 2LO 2029, 2031, 2034, 2062, 2268, 2372
first play broadcast with BBC 2467, 2471, 2487-9, 2497, 2525, 2530, 2631

Baird Company (often used generically to refer to apparatus, etc.) 1665, 2325, 2367, 2519, 2726, 2761, 2795, 3041, 3071, 3078, 3174, 3235, 3288, 3331, 3362, 3370, 3439, 3447, 3482, 3508, 3514, 3527, 3538-40, 3573, 3577, 3595, 3615, 3624, 3656, 3743, 3769, 3782, 3800, 3835, 3839, 3887, 3915, 3942, 3980, 3991, 4063, 4072, 4104, 4125, 4137, 4197, 4368, 4385, 4386, 7393, 4410, 4426, 4452, 4453, 4525, 4574, 4821, 4865, 5103, 5113, 5204, 5279, 5314, 5373, 5518, 5523, 5575, 6192, 6197-9, 6311, 6325, 6504, 6656, 7476, 7494, 7500, 8249, 8472, 8491, 8511
dropped by BBC, barred from Britain 6656, 6667
Baird International Television Ltd. (founded Fernseh A.-G. in Germany) 1328, 2332, 2333, 2335, 2432
Baird-Nathan Company 3447
Baird Parent Inc. 1366
Baird Television 1496, 2332, 2525, 2635, 2681, 2852, 2853, 2900, 2935, 2943, 2953, 2960, 2995, 3083, 3116, 3143, 3145, 3148, 3149, 3173, 3269, 3291, 3400, 3475, 3526, 3578, 3639, 3841, 3848, 3979, 4032, 4062, 4073, 4122, 4147, 4157, 4259, 4370, 4718, 4788, 4808, 4861, 4888, 5079, 5128, 5142, 5145, 5146, 5164, 5272, 5381, 5382, 5956, 6154, 6195, 6239, 6328, 6329, 6345, 6346, 6662, 6850, 6928, 7326, 7361, 8264, 8473, 8602, 8848
patents 2483, 2486, 2568, 2573, 2780, 2781, 2804, 2854, 2857, 2858, 2951, 2969, 3010, 3070, 3216, 3226, 3289, 3299, 3363, 3373, 3395, 3403, 3419-21, 3464, 3537, 3550, 3662, 3665, 3744, 3819, 3833, 3849, 3930, 3950, 3953, 3962, 4009-11, 4040, 4041, 4047, 4048, 4057, 4061, 4067, 4105, 4107, 4110, 5154, 4162, 4189, 4202, 4208, 4209, 4211, 4222, 4265, 4280, 4282, 4293-5, 4299, 4306, 4309, 4339, 4343, 4347, 4377, 4382, 4425, 4451, 4514-7, 4538, 4541, 4553, 4556, 4562, 4566, 4575-7, 4581, 4582, 4587, 4604, 4607, 4621, 4639, 4640, 4679, 4682, 4734, 4735, 4744, 4766, 4825, 4826, 4857, 4924, 4927, 4951, 4978-81, 4987, 4988, 4996, 4997, 5026, 5028, 5037, 5047, 5048, 5054, 5061, 5062, 5073, 5086, 5110, 5111, 5154, 5155, 5175, 5176, 5207, 5212, 5218-20, 5222, 5281-3, 5288, 5307, 5317, 5337, 5338, 5347, 5388-90, 5394, 5410, 5411, 5425, 5446, 5447, 5465, 5466, 5481, 5493, 5524, 5537, 5538, 5595,

5614, 5630, 5677, 5678, 5691, 5693, 5697, 5698, 5708, 5718, 5738-43, 5746, 5750, 5772, 5773, 5778, 5785, 5788, 5810, 5818, 5823-6, 5835, 5848, 5861, 5866, 5880, 5886, 5893, 5899, 5900, 5930, 5937, 5939, 5991, 5992, 6010, 6011, 6037, 6038, 6056, 6060, 6065, 6070, 6149, 6156, 6157, 6177, 6178, 6193, 6267, 6324, 6417, 6418, 6484, 6544, 6621, 6628, 6650, 6651, 6673, 6748, 6749, 6753, 6773, 6777-9, 6800, 6839, 6841, 6842, 6864, 6871, 6932, 6935, 7022, 7046, 7049, 7052, 7085, 7130, 7138, 7154, 7168, 7177, 7226, 7227, 7244, 7285, 7410, 7413, 7414, 7425, 7449, 7450, 7464, 7470, 7510, 7511, 7531, 7541, 7548, 7569, 7601, 7602, 7621, 7634, 7642, 7715, 7716, 7720, 7721, 7730, 7767, 7768, 7781, 7786, 7787, 7826, 7990, 8008, 8074, 8079, 8170, 8188, 8200, 8335, 8363, 8420, 8429, 8432, 8469, 8481, 8552. *See also* Television Ltd.
Baird Television Corporation 1366, 1496, 2023, 2497
Baird Television Development Company, Ltd. 914, 946, 953, 976, 989, 1157, 1511, 1523, 1529, 1532, 1535, 1540, 1543, 1549, 1586, 1722, 1753, 1762, 1872, 1900, 2062, 2063, 2147, 2332, 2333, 2335
Baird Television Development Corporation, N.Y. 1325, 1356, 1392, 1394, 2196
Baird, Malcolm 8866
Baird, Margaret 8800
Baker, Donald Jerome 3404
Baker, L.S. 1222
Baker, Thomas Thorne 383, 390, 398, 524, 616, 840, 985, 1353, 2732, 3176, 3180, 3327
Baker, Walter R.G. 4481, 4495, 4560, 4627, 4699, 5571, 7973, 8217, 8445
Baker, W.J. 8788, 8794
Bakewell, Frederick Collier 15, 16, 112, 154, 625, 3324
Bakhmet'yev, P.I. 192
Baldwin, Millard Warner, Jr. 6205
Baldwin, M.W. 2446
Ballard, Harry W. 1400
Ballard, Jack F. 1400
Ballard, Randall Clarence 3057, 3253, 3553, 4467, 4473, 6089, 7346, 8235, 8236
Bamford, Harry S. 5041, 6175, 7749, 7922
Banca, Maggio C. 4076
Bandringa, Menge 6726, 6962, 7234
Banfi, A. 4225, 4364
Banfield, A.C. 4067

Banks, George Baldwin 2483, 2638, 2797, 2951, 3070, 3363, 3395, 3931, 4040, 4162, 4347, 4377, 5122, 5181, 5263, 5473, 5617, 5618, 5666, 6008, 6012, 6071, 6350, 6531, 6811, 6937, 7024, 7035, 7328, 7396, 7471, 7834
Banneitz, Fritz 2368, 2860, 3483, 5200, 5506, 6301, 7270, 7496, 7558, 7916
Barber, A.W. 7688, 8039, 8144
Barco, Allen A. 8228, 8394
Barnard, George P. 2272, 2705
Barnecut, William John 2811
Barnes, Allen C. 1615
Barnouw, Erik 8809
Barstow, J.M. 8732
Bartel, V.K. 8822
Bartelink, E.M 7306
Bartels, Bernhard 5556, 5769
Barthélemy, René 2041, 2237, 2389, 2672, 2675, 2690, 2720, 2891, 2985, 3001, 3006, 3032, 3509, 3631, 3803, 4204, 4310, 4321, 4406, 4548, 5015, 5102, 5118, 5119, 5163, 5259, 5348, 5383, 5497, 5508, 5575, 5775, 5799, 5803, 5869, 5883, 6215, 6639, 6815, 6920, 7031, 7147, 7874, 8044, 8250, 8372
Bartholomew, H.G. 668
Bartlane 668
Bartlett, G. 8041
Bartlett, T.W. 1157
Barz, G. 7076
Bassoli, Federico S. 3579
Batchelor, John C. 2104, 2977, 3058, 3254, 3259, 4732, 4739, 4769, 4789, 4810, 4823, 4841, 4844, 4933, 5006, 5014, 7101, 7102, 7110, 7160, 7526, 8479
Batcher, Ralph R. 3427
Batstone, L.F. 2574
Battig, R. 6493
Baxter, Charles E. 751, 3155
Bayer, H.M. 1633
Bayer, Joseph Verne 2687
Baynes, J.D. 5362
BBC. *See* British Broadcasting Corporation
Beal, Ralph R. 6587, 6596, 7078, 7492
Beatty, William Arnold 7622, 7623, 7867, 7868, 7870, 7954, 7958, 8065, 8066, 8088, 8114, 8142, 8234, 8251, 8301, 8550, 8582
Beatty, William Edward 984, 1080, 1229
Becker, Carol W. 2872
Becker, Franz August 4835
Becquerel, Alexandre Edmond 9, 10, 20, 44
Bedford, Alda V. 2576, 3462, 3670, 3792, 3892, 4467, 4505, 4584, 4622, 4659, 4671, 4706, 4942, 5017, 5227, 5431,

5564, 5565, 5637, 5801, 5896, 6486, 7192, 7306, 7342, 7762, 7790, 7871, 7901, 7906, 7962, 8222, 8366, 8397, 8563
Bedford, Leslie Herbert 3270, 3311, 3811, 4075, 4093, 4094, 4150, 4266, 4296, 4331, 4332, 4338, 4482, 4529, 4701, 4774, 4780, 7890, 4897, 5953, 6717, 7011, 7635-9
Beers, George L. 4231, 6699, 7664, 8097, 8140, 8397
Begrich, H. 6230
Behne, Rudolf 6612, 6759
Beitmen, Morris N. 8619
Belgium 2102, 2798, 3728, 4115, 7272
Belin, (Claude Joseph) Edouard 348, 365, 473, 477, 479, 480, 487, 489, 492, 495, 498, 523, 534, 536, 538, 541, 543, 547, 555, 563, 572, 574, 578, 599, 605, 723, 724, 739, 742, 744, 749, 771, 775, 813, 815, 817, 830, 884, 895, 901, 1033, 1037, 1039, 1040, 1071, 1085, 1086, 1098, 1159, 1187, 1701, 2703
  patents 305, 525, 633
Belin, François Xavier Edouard Marcel 305
(Etablissements) Belin et F. Holweck 1258, 2404
Bell, Alexander Graham 66, 71, 75, 81, 82, 84, 126, 127, 137-40, 146-8, 151, 153
Bell, C.H. 8602
Bell, J. 5034, 5814, 5822
Bell Telephone Laboratories (B.T.L., Bell Labs) 941, 960, 965, 969, 973, 974, 984, 990, 1003, 1026, 1036, 1052, 1068, 1143, 1170, 1187, 1239, 1272, 1353, 1388, 1899, 1949, 1971, 2007, 2050, 2299, 2351, 2430, 2449, 2458, 2495, 2515, 2732, 2767, 2818, 2875, 2884, 2924, 3482, 3616, 3697, 4967, 5375, 5575, 6084, 6188, 7307, 7380, 8739, 8779, 8780
  demonstrations and tests 909-13, 921, 923, 924, 939, 950, 961, 963, 966, 987, 988, 990, 1007, 1074, 1142, 1189, 1340, 1344, 1345, 1352, 1359, 1434, 1436, 1490, 1929, 1933, 1934, 1950, 1953, 2343, 2345, 2401, 2446
  patents 763, 764, 795, 890, 903-8, 959, 995, 998, 1010, 1046, 1047, 1065, 1076, 1080, 1081, 1140, 1141, 1229, 1338, 1363, 1364, 1422, 1534, 1536, 1676, 1742, 1859, 1860, 1894, 1895, 1930, 1968, 2048, 2071, 2073, 2146, 2148, 2202, 2229, 2280, 2295, 2298, 2328, 2330, 2338-41, 2445, 2478, 2547, 2582, 2603, 2606, 2608, 2646, 2654, 2682, 2699, 2742, 2923, 2927, 2972, 3105, 3255, 3301, 3436, 3929,

4064, 4251, 4276, 4277, 4365, 4420, 4470, 4476, 4518, 4572, 4580, 4719, 4992, 5094-6, 5448, 5472, 6095, 6183, 6205, 6244, 6245, 6331, 6466-8, 6557, 6564, 6910, 6936, 6986, 7144, 7242, 7553, 7624-7; 7831, 7844, 8131, 8259, 8280, 8292, 8455, 8464, 8470, 8615, 8838

Bellows, Henry A. 902
Bells, Francis 8731
Below, Fritz 5642, 6540, 6728, 7107, 7431
Belus, M. 1783
Belus, R. 7754
Benford, Frank A. 3923
Benham, Wilfrid Earnshaw 4396, 4408, 6351, 7924
Benjamin, Mark 6248
Benn, J. 3801
Benn, John A. 1486, 1549, 3477, 3885
Bennett 6459
Benson, Thomas William 466, 1975, 2706
Bentley, Jetson O. 1989
Bently, Lawrence Cranmer 7781
Berengaria, S.S. *See under* demonstrations and tests, Mar. 1928
Berham, W.E. 7881
Berjonneau 360, 365
Berliner, Emile 198
Berndt, Georg 341
Bernerd, Jeffrey 5831
Bernsley, J.T. 4714
Bernstein, Philip 8130
Berry, R.J. 7477, 7857
Berthollet, Claude Louis 1
Bertolotti, S. 5579
Berthon, R. 4163
Berzelius, Jöns Jakob 1, 2, 636
Beslin 6805
Besson, M. 1405
Besson, P. 4879, 5507
Best, Frank Ellison 732, 1063
Best, J.E. 7925
Best, J.F. 5894
Bettinger, Hoyland 8679
Beverage, Harold H. 3370, 7316
Biddle, A.J. Drexel, Jr. 1658
Bidwell, D.L. 691
Bidwell, Shelford 147, 155, 157, 158, 162, 173, 188, 350, 365, 366
Biedermann, F. 3483
Bigley 7306
Bilby, Kenneth 8862
Binder, V. 1622
Bingley, C.I. 1366, 2497
Bingley, Frank James 2854, 3226, 5482-6, 7823, 7917, 8158, 8241, 8300, 8411, 8413, 8414, 8417, 8763
Birch, A.F. 2088, 2225

Birch-Field, Charles A. 2028, 2974, 3020, 3560
Bird, P.R. 675, 683
Birkinshaw, Douglas C. 7977, 8847
Bishop, Roy N. 1453
Bissiri, Augusto 1107
Bitting, Robert C. 8770
Black, D.H. 3876, 5403
Blackwell, Otto B. 674, 2032
Blain, Albert 6991, 7262, 7293
Blair, Russell M. 792, 6556
Blaisdell, H.L. 8607
Blake, George Joseph 577
Blattner, D.G. 2448
Bligh, Jasmine 5907, 5950
Bligh, N.R. 6282
Bliss, H.N. 2521
Bloch 6423
Block, I. 3470
Blondin, Jules 233
Blue, A.H. 8175
Blum, Daniel 8746
Blumlein, Alan Dower 7694, 7977, 8749, 8783
 patents 3396, 3965, 3998, 4279, 4329, 4427, 4561, 4599, 4600, 4613, 4653, 4660, 4934, 4972, 5016, 5188-90, 5274, 5863, 5912, 6042, 6208, 6246, 6281, 6347, 6434, 6519, 6657, 6724, 6938, 6944, 6945, 6948, 7237, 7286, 7287, 7339, 7354, 7355, 7581, 7593, 7667-72, 7733, 7908, 8137, 8435, 8436
Blumm, O.M. 8753
Blythen, Frank 3818, 4468, 4469, 4613, 4692, 6624, 7404, 7667, 8436
Bobb, Lloyd J. 8558
Bocchi, R. 2852, 2944, 3140
Bodroux, D. 4003, 4546
Boersch, Hans 6145
Bohlke, W. Hollander 8458
Bohringer, Arthur John 635
Bolton, H.E. 132
Boltz, Cecil Leonard 8028, 8654
Bonelli, Gaetano 31, 36, 41
Bonfante, J. 2404
Bonham-Carter, Maurice 6285, 6292
Bonovision 3631
Borkin, Joseph 8035
Borries, B. von 6169, 6224
(Robert) Bosch A.-G. 8841
Bostwick, L.G. 2448
Bouck, Zeh 1562, 1811
Bourquin, H. 1843
Bourton, K. 8728
Bouwers, Albert 4790, 4880, 6357, 6361, 6429, 6710, 7680
Bowen, E.A. 3430
Bowen, J.P. 3414
Bower, D. 1020, 4746

Bowie, Robert M. 6167, 6978, 7129, 7306, 7538, 8127
Bowman, G. 2878
Bowman-Manifold, Michael 2074, 2075, 2101, 3455, 3456, 3511, 3536, 3777, 3817, 4000, 4005, 4135, 4184, 4519, 4532, 4585, 4586, 4641, 4644, 4653, 4770, 4984, 4985, 5091, 5494, 5732, 6246, 8196
Bowtell, G.M. 2204, 2812, 2822
Boyer, Jacques 273, 407, 492
Bozer, J. 438
Braddock 6490
Bradly, Harold 2268, 2470
Brady, William A. 4855
Brändle, Heinrich 7516
Bragg, William H. 3761
Brailsford, Joseph Douglas 7582
Brake and Saxby Signal 3841
Brand, P.M. 8018
Branson, Harry 3893, 4475, 6736, 8138
Brauer, Gerhard 5686
Braun, (Karl) Ferdinand 258, 263, 377, 8691, 8772, 8803, 8854
Bray, T. 3043
Bray, T.E. 3962, 4061, 4575, 4924, 5219
Bredow, Hans 2166
Brett, George Fairburn 3738, 5615-7, 5651, 5652, 5667, 5699, 6105, 7089, 7788
Brewer, R.W.A. 7467
Bridgewater, Thornton H. 3731, 4273, 5358, 8778, 8824, 8852, 8856
Briggs, Asa 8771
Briggs, Joseph A. 3260, 3261
Brillouin, Louis Marcel 219, 412
Briot, André 7589
British Broadcasting Corporation (BBC). *See also under* Baird, John Logie. 1342, 1347, 1349, 1439, 1486, 1532, 1535, 1540, 1543, 1596, 1598, 1645, 1699, 1710, 1724, 1787, 2009, 2019, 2155, 2239, 2277, 2432, 2776, 3147, 3157, 3202, 3235, 3283, 3285, 3392, 3477, 3580, 3693, 3702, 3743, 3747, 3835, 3887, 3888, 3915, 4033, 4063, 4071, 4083, 4090, 4147, 4157, 4174, 4259, 4353, 4389, 4595, 4745, 4788, 4799, 4802, 5002, 5003, 5105, 5113, 5308, 5372, 5594, 5954, 6051, 6405, 6409, 6419, 6420, 6427, 6440, 6447, 6478, 6492, 6507, 6711, 6734, 6775, 6792, 6867, 7212, 7366, 7505, 7507, 7537, 7703, 7802, 7803, 8025, 8026, 8049, 8082, 8111, 8152, 8193, 8243, 8668, 8700, 8709, 8714, 8736, 8750, 8754-9, 8761, 8797, 8824
 Alexandra Palace transmitting station 4898, 4976, 4977, 5113, 5114, 5135, 5144, 5278, 5279, 5285, 5332, 5373,

5381, 5523, 5605, 5907, 5958, 6103, 6187, 6189-92, 6197, 6198, 6210, 6212, 6213, 6223, 6239, 6240, 6311, 6325, 6328, 6344, 6368, 6369 ("Ally Pally"), 6405-8, 6411, 6536, 6599, 6667, 6683, 6712, 7145, 7366, 7856, 8157, 8219, 8475
Brookmans Park station 2300, 2317, 2324, 2325, 2331, 2333, 2344, 2372, 2566, 2848, 2900, 2953, 2999, 3745
first broadcasts from station 2LO (Oxford St.) 2029, 2031, 2034, 2062, 2063, 2067, 2079, 2122
first broadcasts from Studio 10 (near Waterloo Bridge) 3064, 3080
late evening broadcasts from Broadcasting House 3362, 3371, 3574, 3595, 3600, 3610, 3650
decision to drop Baird in favor of EMI-Marconi 6656, 6667
British Kinematography, Sound and Television Society 8778
British Thomson-Houston Company, Ltd. (B.T.-H.) 3841
patents 1181, 1266, 1361, 1414, 1849, 1856, 1955, 1956, 1989, 1993, 2049, 2105, 2108, 2115, 2302, 2326, 2354, 2356, 2387, 2427, 2428, 2576, 3107, 3223, 3417, 3635, 3638, 3675, 3846, 3918, 4457, 4571, 4687, 4896, 5071, 5121, 5153, 5228, 5333, 5426, 5429, 5629, 5639, 5854, 5967, 6096, 6112, 6116, 6145, 6186, 6266, 6384, 6481, 6539, 6654, 6745, 6843, 6857, 6858, 6877, 7390, 7407, 7572, 7596, 7775, 7816, 7883, 8110, 8299, 8426, 8522
Brittain, James 8877
Brittain, William J. 1033, 1057, 1086, 1101, 1119, 1193, 1398, 1589, 1618, 1700, 1775
Brittin, Frank L. 1625
Briza, J. 6616
Broadway, Leonard Francis 4397-9, 4685, 4727, 5000, 7472, 8237, 8520, 8840
Broderip, J.Y.M. 736
Brodie, Benjamin C. 30
Brolly, Archibald West 4152, 4557, 5256, 7347
Bronk, Otto von 291, 295, 409, 412, 420, 694, 863, 1750, 2183, 2198, 2236, 2287, 2291, 5321, 6322, 6604, 7861
Bronson, Harry 3716
Brott, J.F. 2127
Browde, Hirsh 4609
Brown 6650
Brown, A.J. 5086, 5222, 5317
Brown, Bradner 3570
Brown, Charles H. 7188
Brown, G.H. 8499

Brown, Jesse E. 5262
Brown, O.F. 4466, 4656
Brown, Reynolds D., Jr. 2819
Brown, Stanley W. 1167, 1168, 1186
Brown, William Steward 4811, 5112, 7086
Brown, W.J. 8593
Browne, Cecil Oswald 2290, 2476, 2656, 2934, 3134, 3256, 3316, 3349, 3535, 3813-5, 3820, 3856, 3871, 3998, 4051, 4058, 4099, 4145, 4427, 4511, 4533, 4585, 4610, 4613, 4643, 4644, 4692, 6434, 6624, 7055, 7524, 7536, 7695, 7977, 8190
Browne, Margaret Winifred 7536
Bruce 6800
Brüche, Ernst 3215, 4502, 4571, 4686, 4687, 4749, 4833, 5023, 5334, 5505, 5627, 5765, 6151, 6482, 6511, 6807, 6914, 7014, 7419
Bruining, Hajo 6780, 6781, 6798
Brun, Etienne (Stephane) Julian 754
Bruni, R. 1226
B.T.-H. *See* British Thomson-Houston
B.T.L. *See* Bell Telephone Laboratories
Buckley, Annette 1911
Büchner 779
Buecker, Heinrich 2161
Buecker, Hubert 2161
Bünger, Walter 6442, 6658, 7037
Bull, Cabot Seaton 4402, 5622, 5275, 5276, 7115, 8361
Bull, Eric William 6527, 8009
Bullard, W.H.G. 902
Bullimore, William Richard 3270, 3311, 3811, 4075, 4296
Bumstead, Ralph W. 5012
Buol, C.J. 1966
Burch, J.A. 2327
Burke, N. 682
Burnap, R.S. 7389
Burnett, Carlos E. 7062, 7306, 7566, 8609
Burns, R.W. 8807, 8842, 8859
Burrows, Arthur Richard 459
(Emil) Busch A.-G. 6537
Busch, Hans 823, 1048, 3294, 6510, 6583
Busch, Vern W. 8180
Buschbeck, Werner 5404, 5405, 7112
Bush Radio, Ltd. 3979, 3980, 4062, 4073, 4104, 4574
Bush, Vannevar 1603
Busse, Ernst 2585, 2717, 3132, 3379, 3529, 4856, 5004, 5223
Busson, Louis Palmella. *See* Dumaurier, George
Byrne, Louis 1383
Byron, D.H. 2568, 3826, 3948, 4060, 7704

Caccia, Giacomo 4750, 8823
Cackett, F.W. 5887, 7103, 7481
Cadman, John 4466
Cadzow, Robert 2877, 3004, 3293, 3457, 3604, 3661, 3829, 4661, 4741, 4742
Cairns, John Edwin Islington 6552, 6984, 7740
Calbrick, Chester J. 8464
Calcaterra, Joseph 2896, 2936, 2992, 3037
Caldwell, Orestes H. 902, 1222, 1255, 1466, 1473, 1525
Calfas, P. 538
Callan, Nicholas Joseph 5
Calloghan, George H. 6975
Cameron, James Ross 4284, 8638
Camm, Frederick James 4285, 4751, 7367, 8620, 8651
Campbell, A.B. 8682
Campbell, Desmond Robert 2423, 2463, 2565, 2729, 3084, 3175
Campbell, George Ashley 446
Campbell, Norman Robert 2163, 4752, 5180, 5568
Campbell, Richard L. 3688, 3793, 3932, 3951, 5115, 5116, 5139, 5140, 5237, 8125, 8194, 8285, 8329, 8554, 8599, 8612
Canada 3505, 3526, 5120, 5161, 5254, 5315
Canadian Television, Ltd. 3410
Cannell, John Clucas 6571
Carbonnelle 360, 365
Carey, George R. 115, 133-5, 249, 412, 1197, 1918
Carlson, Wendell L. 3232, 4322, 4672
Carnahan, Chalon W. 5439, 7284, 7611
Carpendle, Charles Douglas 4466
Carpmael, A. 7169, 8072
Carr, J. 1626, 1687
Carroll 2334
Carson, David N. 8784
Carter, Alva J. 1307, 1415, 1465, 1848
(A.J.) Carter Co. 1476, 1784
Carter Electric Co. 1637
Carter, P.S. 8381, 8545
Case, Nelson P. 8584
Case Research Laboratory 490, 702
Case, Theodore Willard 469, 484, 490, 566, 624, 702
Caselli, Giovanni 14, 23, 32, 36, 37
Caselli, Luigi 14
Castellani, A. 6376, 6377
Castle, Donald H. 8392
Castro, Cesar A. 4762
Cato, George C. 2142, 2321
Cauley, C.L. 1816
Cauley, S.H. 1816
Cavanagh, D. 933

Cavein, Madison 4632, 5297, 5385, 6555, 7228, 7260, 7299, 7331, 7885, 7936
Cawley, Aloysius J. 1964, 2026, 2227, 2393, 2425, 2537, 2770, 2916, 3025, 3076, 3504, 5417, 5733, 6803, 8010
CBS. *See* Columbia Broadcasting System
Centeno V, Melchor, 952, 1708, 1977, 2246, 2867, 3582
Chalfin, Benjamin 1331
Chalfin, Philip 1331
Chaplin, William Watts 2365
Chapman, Ernest Hall 6572
Chappell, Alan 6637
Chapple, Harry John Barton 2060, 2180, 2323, 2375, 2464, 2528, 2693, 2762, 2917, 3044, 3138, 3174, 3179, 3286, 3325, 3330, 3331, 3429, 3447, 3624, 3641, 3653, 3654, 3695, 3799, 3917, 3942, 3945, 4124, 4242, 4415, 4588, 5249, 8033
Chapter, C.F. 5048, 7720
Chasmar, Reginald Philip 7778
Chatterjea, Profulla Kumar 8142, 8234, 8252, 8333, 8474, 8527, 8559, 8581
Chauvièrre, Marc 5575, 6137, 8029, 8692
Cherry, E.C. 7912, 7992
Cheshire, F.J. 1569, 1704
Chevallier, Pierre Emile Louis 2072, 3601
Chilowsky, C. 934
Chouguet, C. 6906
Christaldi, Peter S. 8069
Chrysler Building transmitter 6797
Church, A.G. 2062
Church, Archibald 1378, 1707, 4113, 4125, 5341
Cin. El. Comm. 8459
Cinema-Television, Ltd. 7410, 7781, 7819, 8429
Cioffari, Bernard 1833
Cisin, H.A. 3276
Clapp, Benjamin 1125, 1366
Clarendon, Earl of 2239
Clark 7295
Clark, A.B. 658
Clark, Alexander Melville 46
Clark, Alfred 3703, 3704, 4207, 4471, 6453
Clark, H.A.M. 8218, 8494
Clark, Latimer 50
Clark, Paul Loveridge 532, 549, 596, 725, 859, 1233, 1265, 1731, 2175, 2757
Clark, T.H. 7421
Clarke, Basil 8766, 8767
Clarke, B.R. 3882
Clarkson, R.P. 1314, 1318, 1369
Clarostat Mfg. Co. 1633
Claude, Georges 270, 393
Claudy, C.H. 520

Clavier, André Gabriel 6976
Clay, Reginald Stanley 743, 1871, 3054, 7047, 7779
Clayton, R.J. 7912, 7992, 8123
Clement, L.M. 6033
Clothier, Stewart L. 5468, 5895, 5941, 6039, 6072, 6318, 6319, 6335, 6336, 6902, 7027-9, 7139, 7187, 7229, 7245, 7532, 7533, 8357
Coblyn, J.H. 296, 412
Cock, Gerald 5576, 6821, 7507
Cockaday, Laurence M. 2456, 2990, 3472, 7447
Cocking, N.T. 7764
Cocking, Walter Tusting 5019, 5035, 5134, 8133, 8639
Codel, Martin 5204
Codelli, Anton 1898, 2256
Coeterier, Frederik 5563, 5585, 6106, 7895
Coffey, Douglas F.W. 701
Cohan, Edwin K. 3017, 3022, 3795, 4815, 5823
Colberg, Rolf 6256, 6337, 6462, 6613, 7090
Colborne, Ronald Henry 8586
Colgate, Samuel Bayard 3233
Collard, John 5695, 5732, 6680, 7203, 7643, 7899, 7925
Collier, T.W. 2568, 3744, 4040
Colins, Archie Frederick 3756
Collins, Lee A. 8059
Colston, A.L. 5994
Columbia Broadcasting System (CBS) 1793, 2540, 2607, 2866, 2873, 3014, 3017, 3068, 3090, 3092, 3094, 3163, 3575, 3628, 3639, 3655, 3691, 5522, 6711, 6797, 6808, 6999, 7157, 7380, 8533, 8650, 8675, 8708, 8801, 8832
Columbia Graphophone Company 2824
Columbia Phonograph Broadcasting System 2042
Combihed Intelligence Objective Subcommittee 8662
Communicating Systems, Inc. 7804, 7851
Communication Patents, Inc. (Comm. Pats.) 1044, 1056, 1061, 1066, 1254, 2066, 2383, 2385, 2397, 2403, 2442, 2479, 2484, 2503, 2533, 2601, 2702, 2774, 2952, 3252, 3268, 3531, 3967, 4092, 4111, 4330, 4369, 4384, 4440, 4537, 4540, 4612, 7433
Compagnie des Compteurs 5869
Compagnie pour la Fabrication des Compteurs et Matériel d'Usines à Gaz (Comp. Gaz) 1766, 1842, 1946, 2041, 2116, 2237, 2336, 2337, 2389, 2617, 2643, 2659, 2675, 2690, 2807, 3006, 3073, 3126, 3266, 3290, 3509, 4204,

4310, 4321, 4381, 4406, 4454, 4512, 4548, 4950, 4994, 5295, 5383, 5384, 5462, 5566, 5608, 5933, 6215, 6216, 6663, 6700, 7031, 7050, 7644, 7707
Compagnie sans Fil 7589
Compagnie Française pour l'Exploitation des Procédés Thomson-Houston 5491, 7430
Compagnie Française de Télévision 7430
Compagnie Générale de Télégraphie sans Fil 6360, 6378
Compagnie Générale de Télévision (Procédés H. de France) 2962
Compagnie Radio-Industrie 7430
Compton, Arthur Holly 1942
Compton, Robin D. 7910
Condliffe, George Edward 3062, 4046, 4136, 4388, 5827, 7183
Cone, Felix E. 8366
Conklin, J.W. 7044
Conkling, R.W. 3134
Connell, William Horace 6141, 7884
Connelly 126
Conrad, Frank 1395, 1407, 1488, 1505, 1558, 1568, 1579, 1712, 1718
Conto, Armando 3219, 3318
Cook, Edward Cecil 3817, 4000
Cook, Gerald 6428, 6508
Cook, W.W. 3066
Cooking, R.W. 3458
Cooley, Austin C. 670, 1901
Cooper, Arthur Henry 8477
Cooper, H.J. 3533
Cooper, William Ranson 449
Corbett, Lawrence W. 1342, 1666
Corbishley, Harold 8621, 8633
Corfield, D.N. 7785
Cork, E.C. 4585, 4586, 4644, 4770, 6553, 7178, 8219
Corkling, R.W. 2348, 4214, 4246
Cornell, Elizabeth 5907, 5950
Cosens, C.R. 1421
Cosmocolor Corp. 7660, 8549
Cossor, A.C. 3270
(A.C.) Cossor Ltd. 3311, 3811, 3821, 3824, 3825, 3902, 3919, 3960, 3961, 3999, 4014, 4075, 4093, 4094, 4150, 4266, 4296, 4305, 4332, 4338, 4368, 4372, 4456, 4531, 4547, 4701, 4718, 4774, 4780, 4890, 4897, 5290, 5575, 5896, 6717, 7011, 7017, 7018, 7145, 7635-9, 7803, 8304
Coursey, Philip R. 476
Cowley, T.R. 8437
Cowper, Edward Alfred 110, 111, 118, 121, 122, 336
Cox, Howard Havelock 2270
Cox, William F. 3295
Coyne Electrical School 385
Craig, T.J.D. 3499

Crawley, C. 1242, 1322, 1516
Critesco, G. 1611
Crocker Research Laboratories 1453
Crocker, W.W. 1453
Crookes, William 99, 114, 120, 136, 150, 177, 218, 8879
Crosley Radio Corp. 1346
Crowe, Frederic C. 1816
Crowther, B.M. 6967
Crozier, Mary 8742
Cruse, Andrew W. 5210, 5311, 5544, 5546
Crystal Palace transmitter 4814, 4821, 4827, 4861, 4865, 5179, 5314, 6711, 8463
Culley, Richard Spelman 37
Cummings, Bryan Y. 3626
Cummings, Byron R. 1767
Cummings, Merle S. 4121
(E.T.) Cunningham Inc. 1095
Cunningham, Henry 2678
Cunningham-Reid 4465
Czechoslovakia 2143, 2376, 5161, 5254
Czudnochowski, W. Biegon 380

d'Ailly, G.H. 1771
Dall, H.E. 2743
Dallugge, Rudolph A. 499
Dalpayrat, H.F. 2989, 3199
Damas, Léon 5109, 5133
Dantin, C. 1187
d'Arlincourt, Ludovic Charles Adrien Joseph Guyot 46, 107
Dastouet, P. 602
Date, W.H. 7696
Dauvillier, Alexandre 557, 780, 1089, 1108, 1163, 1187, 1533, 1918, 2556, 2757
Daven Radio Corp. 1394, 1410, 1476, 1493, 1633, 1637
Davies, K.S. 4239, 5117, 5762, 7322, 8003
Davies, Lawrence E. 6164
Davis, Anthony 8826
Davis, Chester Leslie 2158, 2431, 2444, 2475, 2501, 2504, 2633
Davis, H.C. 1236
Davis, H.P. 1468, 1579, 2642, 4079
Davis, N.E. 7977
Davis, Robert F. 5437
Davis, Robert L. 1306, 1788
Davis, W. 8579
Davis, Watson 534, 558, 562
Davisson, Clinton J. 6564, 7242, 8280
Dawson, Leo H. 1970
Dawson, Wilfred 891
Day, Richard Evan 73
Day, Wilfred Ernest Lytton 548, 565, 579, 580

De Amicis, Domenic Sicari 2550
Dean, Basil 4901
Debenham, Nancy 2276
de Boer, Jan Hendrick 4325, 5087, 5833, 5834, 6781, 6798, 6946, 6949
de Forest, Lee 339, 346, 428, 434, 791, 1143, 1222, 1315, 1467, 1642, 1755, 1851, 1976, 2070, 2334, 2496, 2507, 2880, 2987, 3052, 3088, 3114, 3302, 3409, 4761, 4881, 5253, 5776, 6129, 6316, 7023, 8652, 8661
De Forest Radio Co. 2459, 2545, 2546, 2769, 2789, 3169, 3258, 3696, 4534
De France 5575
de Gier, Johannes 7717
Dehn, F.B. 7176
Deichmann, G.A. 7465
Deisch, Noel 2499, 2578
De Lacy, B. 1123
De la Forge, L. 1900, 2258
Delano, F.M. 742
De la Rive, August Arthur 35, 42, 43, 47, 49
De la Rue, Warren 57, 80, 97, 117, 119, 175
Dellinger, J.H. 1222, 1315
de Nemos, T. 8109
Denham, Alfred M. 4340
Denisoff, A.K. 7569, 7601
Denison, V. 6856, 7312
Denmark 3702, 3769, 3877
Dennis, A.J. 1205
Denny, Ludwell 2795
Dent, R.H. 3356, 3357
Denton, John J. 1651, 1704, 1738, 1780, 1832, 1910, 1980, 2019, 2061, 2183, 2272, 3697, 3773, 3804, 3884
de Paiva, Adriano 88, 89, 142, 143, 192, 412
De Quincey, Thomas 1741
Derby. *See under* sports
Deserno, Peter 4700, 4705, 4834, 6052, 6755, 7814, 7815, 8289, 8408
Deskey, D. 8535
Desmond, Shaw 1381, 1445, 1510, 2013
De Tar, Donald R. 8468
Deutsch, Ernest 1879
De Varigny, Henry 378
De Vendenil 389
De Wet, Pieter Justinus 1385, 3725
Dewhirst, Thornton P. 1427
Dicker, S.G.S. 1717, 1743, 1854
Dieckmann, Max 336, 337, 373, 374, 404, 412, 505, 599, 613, 665, 1033, 1086, 1235, 7803
Diehl, Phillip H. 1658
Diels, Kurt 4707, 5521, 5545, 5781, 6951, 6979, 7866
Dill, C.C. 2752; 461
Dillenback, Garrett Vander Veer, Jr. 2388

Dillenburger, Wolfgang 6678, 7882, 7953, 8588
Dillon, John F. 902
Diner-Dines, P. 720
Dinsdale, Alfred 762, 788, 811, 816, 841, 926, 935, 968, 975, 985, 1053, 1062, 1100, 1152, 1156, 1249, 1380, 1682, 1734, 1796, 1918, 2055, 2506, 2634, 2665, 2725, 2817, 2899, 3078, 3119, 3181, 3411, 3482, 3616, 5080
Dionne quintuplets 6818
Dippy, R.J. 5419, 5993
Discrola Inc. 481–3
Dizard, Wilson P. 8774
Dobke, Günther 3869
Dobriner, R. 8831
Dodge, J.S. 1355
Dodington 6845, 6846
Doering, U.W. 2579
Dolbear, Amos Emerson 98, 118
Dome, Robert B. 3846, 7584, 7907, 8610
Donisthorpe, H. de A. 776, 802, 858
Donle, Harold P. 1350, 1471, 1620, 1679, 2230, 2283, 2538, 2963, 2990, 3007, 3055, 3067, 3089, 3393, 3498
Dorf, W.C. 8106
Dorsman, Cornelis 6709, 7527
Dosai, M. 402
Doty, Marion Foster 766
Dovraston, George 5772, 7285
Dowd, Andrew D. 4365
Dowing, George Victor 4866, 5572
Dowsett, Henry Melville 2771, 2772, 2791, 2823, 2877, 2912, 2919, 2920, 3002-4, 3026, 3134, 3187, 3249, 3415, 3453, 3454, 3457, 3524, 3578, 3604, 3615, 3622, 3661, 3737, 3786, 3829, 3880, 3903, 3921, 4001, 4252, 4253, 4640, 4649, 4661, 4771, 4772, 4894, 5005
Dowsing, James 8868
Draper, H.N. 54, 116
Dreher, Carl 1006, 1015, 1772, 8836
Drewanz, Irwin 3215
Dryden, R.E. 7539
Dubois, Louis 370
DuBridge, Lee Alvin 3760
Duddell 1780
Dudding, Bernard Phineas 4268, 4862, 4941
Dufour 713
Dumaurier, George (Louis Palmella Busson) 100
Dumert, V. 2850
Du Moncel, Théodose Achille Louis 22, 36, 135, 143, 159
Du Mont, Allen Balcom 2459, 2876, 2988, 2990, 3722, 4614, 4756, 5255, 7095, 7272, 7402, 7422, 7562, 7878, 7929, 8184, 8185, 8402, 8554, 8878

(A.B.) Du Mont Laboratoris, Inc. 7402, 7422, 7493, 7529, 7928, 8049, 8093, 8215, 8194, 8197, 8272, 8324, 8329, 8369, 8452, 8647

Dumont, M. 1159

Duncan, Justin R. 3312, 7440

Dunham, C.R. 4159, 4192

Dunlap, Orrin E., Jr. 745, 748, 809, 870, 900, 2331, 2380, 2391, 2435, 2539, 2583, 2700, 3108, 3192, 3505, 3506, 3588, 3612, 3672, 3673, 3776, 3795, 3851, 3969, 3987, 4021, 4050, 4479, 4495, 4699, 4832, 5039, 5832, 5847, 5852, 5885, 5951, 6017, 6102, 6278, 6455, 6475, 6601, 6610, 6671, 6806, 6889, 6958, 7030, 8653, 8659, 8693, 8719, 8769

Dunod, A. 7370

Dunsheath, J. 3322

Dupuy, Judy 8666a

Dussaud, Frantz 271, 297, 412, 460, 820

Dyck, Joseph Géréberne Regina van 3757, 3758

Eade, S.R. 6168

Eaglesfield, Charles Cecil 6549, 7048, 7648, 8186

Earp, C.W. 7766

Eaton, Roland D. 4650, 5449

Eccles, William Henry 586

Eckersley, Peter Pendleton 1342, 1479, 1661, 1706, 1735, 2046, 2153, 2524, 2561, 3672, 8762

Eckert, Gerhard 8760

Eckhardt, George H. 6573

Edison, Thomas Alva 85, 86, 100, 123, 124, 176, 183

Edison Bell 4704

Edison Swan Electric Company 3841, 3952, 3983, 4073, 6521

Eddy, William C. 6790, 8209, 8261, 8400, 8666

Edson, Lee 8801

Edward VIII. coronation of 6492, 6698, 6711, 6821, 6861, 6867, 6869, 6879, 6883, 6886

Edwards 6722

Edwards, Baden John 7587, 8068

Edwards, George William 5442, 5528, 5535, 5692, 6097, 7504, 7963, 7964, 8123

Edwards, Norman 739, 1483, 1556, 1652, 1706, 2561

Egerton, Henry Clifford 475, 719

Egger, Paul R. 2293

Egyesült Izzólámpa és Villomosági Reszveny-Tarsasag 4390

Ehrenberg, Werner 7053, 7111

Eichberg, R. 7804

Eichhorn, Gustav 394, 842, 875

Eiffel Tower transmitter 5345, 5497, 5498, 5883, 6084, 6757, 6891, 7430, 7508, 7599, 7650, 7751, 8210, 8521

Einstein, Albert 324

Eisler, Paul 5171, 8459

Ekco-Scophony 6645

Ekström, Alfred 384

Electrical and Musical Industries, Ltd. (EMI) *See also* Marconi-EMI Television Co. 2824, 3682, 3683, 3703, 3704, 4147, 4157, 4168, 4207, 4368, 4471, 4472, 4888, 5108, 5148, 5204, 5272, 5279, 5523, 5575, 6195, 6293, 6294, 6452, 6453, 6718, 6850, 6923, 8585, 8602, 8626

patents 2476, 3188, 3349, 3396, 3455, 3456, 3488, 3511, 3535, 3536, 3602, 3666, 3705, 3708, 3748, 3777, 3785, 3813-5, 3817, 3818, 3820, 3828, 3856, 3871, 3896, 3897, 3920, 3965, 3998, 4000, 4005, 4046, 4051, 4058, 4099-101, 4135, 4136, 4145, 4184, 4185, 4257, 4279, 4329, 4383, 4397, 4398, 4402, 4419, 4452, 4453, 4464, 4532, 4536, 4561, 4585, 4600, 4610, 4613, 4641, 4653, 4654, 4660, 4685, 4692, 4693, 4770, 4829, 4867, 4929, 4931, 4934, 4937, 4972, 4975, 4985, 5000, 5016, 5074, 5091, 5092, 5112, 5190, 5195, 5196, 5206, 5225, 5239, 5274, 5296, 5335, 5350-2, 5402, 5428, 5453, 5494, 5602–4, 5656, 5702, 5827, 5927, 5929, 6006, 6007, 6042, 6079, 6098, 6114, 6141, 6208, 6246, 6262, 6271, 6281, 6297, 6431, 6434, 6527, 6532, 6552-4, 6558, 6623, 6657, 6679, 6682, 6724, 6730, 6741, 6742, 6744, 6750, 6758, 6762, 6795, 6827, 6859, 6878, 6885, 6893, 6905, 6944, 6945, 6948, 6984, 7026, 7053, 7082, 7084, 7086, 7115, 7163, 7165, 7166, 7178, 7183, 7233, 7236, 7237, 7241, 7259, 7276, 7279, 7282, 7283, 7286, 7287, 7289, 7291, 7294, 7295, 7333, 7334, 7336, 7339, 7354, 7395, 7404, 7454, 7472, 7478, 7550, 7579, 7593, 7643, 7652, 7654, 7658, 7661, 7663, 7667-71, 7675, 7740, 7743, 7778, 7884, 7925, 8012, 8131, 8137, 8177, 8179, 8190, 8199, 8220, 8237, 8336, 8361, 8436, 8438, 8477, 8520, 8580, 8586

Electrical Research Products, Inc. (E.R.P.)

patents 890, 903, 904, 906, 908, 959, 995, 998, 1010, 1047, 1141, 1338, 1341, 1365, 1675, 1894, 1930, 2073, 2229, 2299, 2328, 2330, 2338-41, 2445, 2478, 2547, 2582, 2603, 2660, 2682, 2699, 2923, 2927, 3105, 3255, 3929, 4251, 4470, 5744, 5745, 6469-71, 6557, 6565, 6684, 7130, 7142, 7143, 7216, 7240, 7298, 8131, 8606

Electronic Television Company, Ltd. 2570, 2751, 4297

Elektro-Physikalische Ges. 1840

Elton, Arthur 8627

Elster, Johann Philipp Ludwig Julius 172, 178, 185, 191, 194, 202, 206, 207, 210, 211, 214-6, 225-7, 230-2, 242, 243, 246, 250, 251, 260, 268, 339, 385, 408, 424

Elway, Thomas 962

Elwell, C.F. 624

EMI. *See* Electrical and Musical Industries, Ltd.

EMI Service Ltd. 6446

Empire State Building transmitter 3005, 3015, 3021, 3024, 3192, 5042, 5051, 5487, 6017, 6019, 6021, 6304, 6497, 6523, 6630, 7000, 7914, 8046, 8162, 8225, 8316

Emyradis Soc. A.R.L. 5191

Engstrom Elmer William 4227, 4228, 4449, 4484, 4670, 4966, 6033, 6597, 7556, 7690, 7795, 7915, 8038, 8097, 8212, 8380, 8397, 8645

Ente Italiano per le Audizioni Radiofoniche 3519

Epstein, David William 4712, 6124, 6488, 6595, 6965, 6985, 7248, 7267, 7872, 8031, 8565

E.R.P. *See* Electrical Research Products, Inc.

Erzold, Hellmuth 5938

Espenschied, Lloyd 804, 1891, 4625

Espley, D.C. 4568, 4900, 4903, 4925, 4930, 5052, 5406, 5413, 5419, 5442, 5471, 5479, 5495, 5535, 5598, 5638, 5661, 5684, 5692, 6090, 6094, 6097, 6161, 6286, 6696, 6904, 7238, 7278, 7290, 7292, 7391, 7392, 7468, 7504, 7777, 7782, 7820, 8004, 8011, 8422, 8423, 8427

Essig, Sanford F. 3310, 3567

Eugène Ltd. 2635, 2671

Evans, Earl R. 576

Evans, J.C. 600

Everest, F. Alton 7379, 7381, 7610, 8143, 8206

Everett, A. 1034

Everson, George 8698

Ewest, H. 2208

Exwood, Maurice 8827

Faerber, W. 2143

Fahrney, Callo D. 1800, 1801, 2355, 3087

Fairhurst, H.A. 6416

Fairthorne, Robert 8627

Faraday, Michael 6, 8, 13, 21, 24, 3761

(I.G.) Farben 4203, 4323
Farber, E.I. 8835
Farnsworth, Elma G. 8869
Farnsworth, Philo Taylor 665, 1453, 1694, 1695, 2123, 2311, 2472, 2548, 2549, 2558, 2662, 2674, 2685, 2800, 2801, 2817, 2845, 2897, 2899, 2924, 3225, 3286, 3616, 4053, 4579, 4589, 4713, 4717, 4718, 4845, 5246, 5312, 5749, 6005, 6018, 6138, 6573, 7583, 8698, 8857, 8869
  patents 566, 850, 1079, 1109, 1216, 1227, 1619, 2279, 2381, 2382, 2434, 2477, 2676, 3008, 3009, 3405, 3812, 3889, 3905, 4139, 4457, 4535, 4627, 4628, 4680, 4681, 4906, 4907, 5040, 5041, 5169, 5170, 5182-5, 5211, 5273, 5327, 5328, 5343, 5432, 5567, 5597, 5670, 5673, 5700, 5701, 5715, 5758, 5760, 5780, 5889, 5915, 5916, 5959, 5960, 6067, 6075, 6173, 6174, 6387, 6388, 6400-2, 6415, 6432, 6763-9, 6771, 6832-6, 6840, 6873, 6884, 7398, 7482, 7528, 7718, 7719, 7860, 7969, 8238, 8239, 8253, 8254, 8870, 8878
Farnsworth Television 4557, 4558, 4676, 4889, 5142, 5145, 5256, 5373, 5441, 5509, 5511, 5575, 6182, 6237, 6386, 6497, 6499, 6518, 6534, 6575, 6611, 6642, 6711, 6792, 7045, 7119, 7275, 7807
  patents 2381, 2434, 3009, 3348, 3812, 3889, 4139, 4152, 4191, 4263, 4681, 4910-7, 5040, 5041, 5169, 5170, 5182-5, 5273, 5327, 5328, 5343, 5626, 5670, 5759, 5780, 5889, 5916-9, 5925, 5959, 5961, 6067, 6082, 6083, 6171-5, 6387-9, 6400-3, 6415, 6432, 6687, 6763-70, 6772, 6832-6, 6872, 6939-42, 6973, 6974, 7058, 7108, 7175, 7256, 7812, 7860, 8131
Farnsworth Television and Radio Corporation 2382, 3405, 3603, 3905, 4535, 4680, 5567, 6075, 7256, 7301, 7718, 7719, 8238, 8239, 8254
Farren, L.I. 6494
Farrier, C.W. 8275
Faudell, Charles Leslie 4770, 5655, 5656, 5702, 5881, 6079, 6623, 6750, 7233, 7279, 7291, 7454, 7478, 7681, 8177
Faust, G. 7691
Federal Communications Commission (FCC) 4691, 5373, 5492, 5554, 5586, 5712, 5727, 5820, 5914, 5923, 5951, 5988, 5994, 5997, 6023, 6049, 6068, 6079, 6102, 6103, 6111, 6182, 6280, 6287, 6386, 6442, 6499, 6603, 6610, 6670, 6792, 7980, 8223, 8276, 8573, 8622, 8623, 8625, 8637, 8641, 8669, 8748, 8752

Federal Radio Commission (FRC; Radio Board, Commission) 902, 936, 970, 1255, 1310, 1372, 1435, 1473, 1487, 1492, 1495, 1546, 1597, 1629, 1668, 1670, 1672, 1677, 1709, 1728, 1752, 1755, 1758, 1761, 1785, 1794, 1841, 1863, 1920, 2038, 2100, 2459, 2602, 2610, 2658, 2680, 2684, 2758, 2759, 2835, 3021, 3072, 3102, 3164, 3220, 3322, 3342, 3343, 3400, 3463, 3475, 3616, 4079, 4151, 8748
Federal Telegraph Company 1023, 2151
Federmann, Wolfgang 2980, 3597, 3701, 4018, 4947
Feingold, Samuel 1211
Felgel-Farnholz, Richard Ritter 7945
Felgenstreu, S. 4172, 4181
Felix, Edgar H. 888, 1370, 1546, 1561, 1874, 2511, 2559, 3237, 3364
Felshin, Judah B. 1839
Felstern, Nathan 1217, 1223
Ferguson, Joseph B. 1223
Ferguson, William A. 1203
Fernseh A.-G. 2045, 2055, 2068, 2085, 2222, 2265, 2333, 2584, 2595, 2598, 2623, 2727, 3139, 3146, 3210, 3240, 3517, 3519, 3576, 3596, 3618, 3630, 3643, 3909, 4103, 4213, 4245, 4591, 4963, 5145, 5164, 5319, 5513, 5575, 5731, 6851, 7088, 7145, 7320, 7557, 7918, 8841, 8843
  patents 2078, 2097, 2098, 2205, 2232, 2813, 2831-3, 2839, 2855, 2860, 2871, 2881, 3028, 3030, 3049, 3051, 3097, 3098, 3183, 3217, 3300, 3309, 3336, 3365, 3372, 3515, 3544, 3621, 3709, 3710, 3713, 3719, 3735, 3740, 3749, 3816, 3850, 3853, 3854, 3870, 3924, 3925, 3927, 3937, 3957, 3964, 4054, 4055, 4067, 4078, 4108, 4212, 4303, 4316, 4370, 4474, 4498, 4510, 4513, 4647, 4709, 4725, 4730, 4731, 4824, 4986, 4991, 5001, 5069, 5070, 5077, 5078, 5137, 5141, 5214, 5224, 5269, 5353, 5369, 5393, 5397, 5398, 5414, 5443, 5464, 5525, 5557, 5558, 5671, 5682, 5703, 5816, 5830, 5839, 5884, 5901, 5949, 6069, 6108, 6113, 6165, 6179, 6242, 6256, 6257, 6261, 6270, 6337, 6462, 6522, 6540, 6562, 6612, 6613, 6655, 6657, 6658, 6665, 6678, 6687, 6688, 6774, 6804, 6809, 6812, 6814, 6824, 6828, 6863, 6864, 6868, 6881, 6896, 6982, 7012, 7090, 7105, 7107, 7150, 7252, 7360, 7549, 7722, 7756, 7771, 7945, 7947, 7953, 7979, 8006, 8073, 8430, 8577
FERNSEHEN (journal of Allgemeiner Deutscher Fernsehverein, German Television Society) 2166, 2265, 2368

Ferranti 4062, 4437, 4605, 4999, 5359, 5376-9, 5427, 5761, 5795, 5955, 5989, 6109, 6217, 6317, 6338, 6458, 6980, 7483, 7673, 7674, 7809, 7824, 7991
Fessenden, Helen M. 856, 1208
Fessenden, Reginald Aubry 507, 851, 856, 1208
Fewings, David John 5864, 6086, 6495, 6754, 7123, 7517, 7888, 8001
Feyerabrend 2368
Fides Gessel 7708, 7950
Fielding, Ray 8781
Fielding, Thomas James 5159
Filica, Enache 897
Filippo, Hendrik 5998
Fink, Donald G. 6917, 7493, 7748, 8148, 8490, 8640, 8657, 8665, 8716, 8734, 8819
Fink, G.A. 7306
Finke, Herbert A. 8102
Finn, Bernard S. 8874
Firmin, L. 3388
Fischel, Paul J.G. 810
Fischer, F. 5968
Fisk, Jim 8813
Fitch, Clyde J. 2414
Fitch, William A. 3417
Fitzgerald, George Francis 240, 267
Flaherty, Mark 3530, 6390, 6538
Flamm, Donald 8848
Flanze, G. 6848
Flechsig, Werner 6287, 6522, 6759, 6823, 6863, 6982, 7771, 8577
Fleisher, Richard 3759
Fleming, (John) Ambrose 174, 187, 209, 210, 220, 257, 261, 265, 294, 319, 323, 331, 339, 393, 428, 1241, 1279, 1321, 1582, 1682, 1787, 1905, 2009, 2062, 2132, 2216, 2231, 2289, 2318, 3841, 4353, 4379, 4394, 4887, 5954
Fleming-Williams, B.C. 7017, 7018
Flory, Leslie E. 4349, 4873, 4945, 5231, 5305, 6568, 6622, 6631, 6702, 7066, 7383, 7723, 8744
Flügge, Johannes 6537
Fluge, Werner 5445
Flynn, H. 4551
Foden-Pattinson, E.H. 5155
Folwell, A. 8694
Ford, D'Arcy 6574
Forman, J.R.H. 5037, 5347
Fournier, Lucien 578, 771, 815, 817, 889, 1008
Fournier d'Albe, Edmund Edward 343, 378, 382, 412, 586, 621, 636, 652, 667, 753, 840, 985
Fowler, J.B. 334, 338
Fox, Marshall 124

Fox, William C. 740, 1125, 1941, 2015, 2056, 2184, 2219, 2273, 2314, 2320, 2372, 2376
France 2106, 2667, 2798, 3447, 3526, 3631, 3696, 3745, 3803, 3947, 4003, 4115, 4129, 4133, 5118, 5161, 5210, 5254, 5259, 5345, 5348, 5497, 5498, 5805, 5838, 5869, 6181, 6255, 6264, 6547, 6921, 7272, 7275, 7430, 7801, 8163, 8662. *See also* Eiffel Tower transmitter
Francis, B.A. 3679
Francis, J.S. 3679
Francis, Oliver T. 4636
Frankenstein, A. 316, 412
Franklin, Charles Samuel 422, 804, 1891
A. Franks, Ltd. 2347
FRC. *See* Federal Radio Commission
Fredendall, G.L. 8222, 8393
Free, E.E. 886, 1003
Freed Television and Radio Corporation 3200
Freeman, George Stanley Percival 4654, 5112, 6905
Freeman, R.C. 7057
Freeman, Robert L. 8187, 8607
(Charles) Freshman Company 1844
Freundlich, H.F.W.J. 5117
Friebus, Reginald T. 2042
Friedel, Walter 727, 779, 819, 2168, 2303, 2451, 3382
Friedman, L.B. 3883
Fries, F. 1716
Fries, G. 1967, 2591
Fries, Peter Paul 3556
Frost, Herbert H. 1519
Frowde, Claude 583
Fry, D.W. 6073, 6146
Fuchs, F. 5580, 6584
Fuchs, Gerhard 843
Fulton, Otto 1311
Furse, M.B. 1176

Gable, Luther S. 8699
Gábor, Dennis 5937, 5939, 5940, 5967, 6116, 6384, 6844, 7390, 7572, 8299
Gabrilovitch, L. 4163
Gaede, Wolfgang 355, 379, 417, 437
GaisenBand, Palmyre 958
Gale, Alfred John 8433
Galileo 3697
Galle, J.B. 5807
Gallup, John L. 6528, 7303
Gander, L. Marsland 3101, 5013, 5158, 5523, 6143, 6187
Gandtner, V. 6647
Gannet, Danforth K. 993, 1220, 1396

Gardiner, Ernest L. 2241, 2784, 2945, 3884, 3978, 4035, 4062, 4087, 4128, 5108, 6696
Gardiner, H.W.B. 5463
Gardner, Bernard C. 3348, 3794, 4263, 5889, 5925, 6171, 6172, 6872, 7108, 7175, 7969, 8537
Gardner, Delamere B. 1472, 2296, 2436, 5533, 6312
Gardner, John Edward 556
Garner, Lloyd Preston 1432, 2027
Garod 7980, 8050
Garratt, Gerald R.M. 7368, 8721
Garside, Colin P. 1914, 2594
Garside, James W. 1658, 2254
Garvin, J.L. 848
Gassiot, John Peter 24, 25, 29, 34
Gaumont-British Pictures Corporation 3291, 7537, 8473
G.E. *See* General Electric Company (U.S.)
Gearing 3464
Gebauer, Rudolf 7841, 7939
G.E.C. *See* General Electric Company, Ltd. (U.K.)
Gehrts, A. 6848, 8441
Geiger, Max 5303, 5356, 5444, 5704, 5817, 5851, 5902, 5963, 5985, 6061, 6104, 6375, 6686, 6760, 6822, 6959, 6960, 6970, 6990, 7036, 7415, 7512
Geitel, Hans Friedrich Karl 172, 178, 185, 191, 194, 203, 206, 207, 210, 211, 214-6, 225-7, 230-2, 242, 243, 246, 250, 251, 260, 268, 339, 385, 408, 424
Geloso, John 1567, 1678
General Electric Company (U.S.) (G.E.) 504, 1102, 1110, 1114, 1204, 1260, 1308, 1391, 1457, 1461, 1462, 1469, 1476, 1478, 1557, 1559, 1631, 1638, 1779, 1944, 2015, 2036, 2178, 2307, 2391, 2392, 2402, 2432, 2455, 2516, 2517, 2520, 2559, 2588, 2602, 2752, 2776, 2788, 2925, 3841, 6629, 7306, 7806, 8324
patents 353, 433, 678, 679, 803, 896, 1107, 1181, 1266, 1361, 1414, 1767, 1849, 1856, 1955, 1956, 1960, 1989, 1993, 2049, 2105, 2108, 2115, 2302, 2326, 2354, 2356, 2387, 2427, 2428, 2576, 2613, 3107, 3156, 3212, 3215, 3223, 3417, 3422, 3460, 3465, 3484, 3491, 3486, 3918, 3923, 4004, 4571, 6286, 6384, 6426, 6482, 6542, 6993, 7014, 7131, 7362, 7907, 7963, 8002, 8004, 8011, 8123, 8171, 8213, 8244, 8258, 8278, 8610, 8666a, 8877
General Electric Company, Ltd. (U.K.) (G.E.C.) 789, 1980, 3841, 6247, 6263, 6410, 8418

patents 4159, 4187, 4188, 4192, 4268, 4307, 4434, 4435, 4544, 4550, 4565, 4568, 4570, 4634, 4812, 4813, 4862, 4900, 4903, 4904, 4925, 4930, 4941, 5052, 5055, 5058, 5060, 5180, 5406, 5413, 5419, 5442, 5460, 5463, 5471, 5479, 5495, 5528, 5531, 5535, 5555, 5568, 5598, 5612, 5638, 5657, 5661, 5684, 5692, 5993, 6073, 6085, 6090, 6094, 6097, 6117, 6146, 6161, 6248, 6282, 6289, 6423, 6435, 6436, 6494, 6520, 6652, 6696, 6722, 6801, 6808, 6858, 6877, 6898, 6904, 6914, 7007, 7032, 7159, 7230, 7238, 7249, 7278, 7290, 7292, 7391, 7392, 7403, 7468, 7777, 7820, 7912, 7988, 7992, 8416, 8422, 8423, 8427, 8437, 8443, 8468
General Radio Company 517
George, E.P. 6494
George, Roscoe Henry 3086, 5365-7, 5370, 7551, 8611, 6642
George, R.W. 8046
Gerard, François Joseph 4839
Germany 63, 1463, 1906, 1922, 1932, 2065, 2068, 2082, 2085, 3102, 2118, 2257, 2265, 2368, 2422, 2518, 2566, 2584, 2595, 2636, 2638, 2727, 2762, 2980, 2982, 3039, 3085, 3095, 3129, 3210, 3328, 3482, 3483, 3502, 3526, 3534, 3596, 3613, 3618, 3630, 3642, 3655, 3696, 3755, 3768, 3837, 3886, 3913, 3982, 4017, 4037, 4085, 4103, 4113, 4115, 4117, 4133, 4148, 4149, 4166, 4175, 4177, 4245, 4314, 4364, 4489, 4591, 4597, 4611, 4631, 4646, 4674, 4675, 4718, 4757, 4758, 5760, 4877, 4879, 5053, 5081, 5089, 5090, 5144, 5161, 5166, 5210, 5249, 5254, 5271, 5286, 5287, 5293, 5302, 5318-20, 5342, 5363, 5506, 5513, 5872, 6084, 6122, 6134, 6148, 6320, 6334, 6343, 6461, 6591, 6707, 6810, 6918, 7088, 7118, 7146, 7310, 7313, 7558, 7796, 7822, 7980, 8163, 8441, 8723
annual radio exhibition, Berlin (1928): 1450; (1929):1826, 2055, 2172; (1930): 2584, 2595, 2598, 2727; (1931): 3129, 3146, 3210; (1932): 3643 (1933): 4065, 4194, 4213, 4245 (1934): 4591, 4631, 4646 (1936): 5648, 6300, 6320, 6501-3, 6584 (1937): 7088, 7273, 7320 (1938): 7847, 7979, 7981
commencement of 180/25 broadcasting service, Berlin-Witzleben 4922, 4938, 4949, 4959, 4962, 4965, 5068, 5613
first telephone-television line, Berlin-Leipzig 5690, 5730, 5731, 5753, 5755, 5757, 5794, 5870, 6025, 6225, 6647

See also Manfred von Ardenne, Fernseh A.-G., D.S. Loewe, Kurt Schlesinger, Telefunken, 1936 Olympics (under sports), Reichspostzentralamt (German Post Office)
Gernsback, Hugo 376, 460, 472, 502, 559, 623, 671, 760, 967, 972, 1001, 1007, 1058, 1223, 1295, 1330, 1371, 1399, 1410, 1498, 1504, 1566, 1632, 3607, 4170, 4326, 4797, 5252, 6125, 7068, 7441, 7799, 8048, 8321
Gesellshaft Tech. Hochschule 7862, 7865, 8578, 8608
Gettinger, Joseph 3500, 4438
Gibos, H. 5872
Gibson, W.T. 3876
Gihring, H.E. 7004
Gilbert, A.H. 5337, 5338, 5900, 6037, 6056, 6267, 6748, 6841, 7226
Gill, A.J. 4656
Gill, E.W.B. 5083, 7927
Gillespie, Henderson C. 3252, 3967
Gilman, Ruth C. 7023
Gilmore, Otto C. 8549
Gimbel Brothers 3113, 3296
Gimbel, Richard 3113
Gimingham, Charles H. 99
Gladenbeck, F. 8403
Glage, Gustav 336, 337, 373, 374, 404, 412, 7803
Glass, L. 5150
Glass, Myron S. 6331
Glatzel, Bruno 412, 431
Gleason, C. Sterling 1692
Glew, F.H. 109
Globe Television and Phone Company 3468, 3469, 3696
Gloess, Paul François Marie 6272, 6976
Glover, Alan M. 8646
Goddard, D.R. 7201, 8567
Goddard, Marcus James 6348, 6353, 6719, 8061, 8120, 8121, 8135
Godefroy, Alexandre F. 2856
Goebbels, Josef 4757, 5287
Goebel, Gerhart 8723, 8843
Görlich, Paul 6043, 6443, 6545, 6551
Goerz, Paul 2085, 2169, 2222, 2636; *309*
Golby, J. 8274
Goldberg, Emmanuel 3627
Goldman, Henry 3502, 3534
Goldman, Stanford 7971, 8568, 8575
Goldmark, Peter Carl 3558, 3559, 5422, 5808, 5850, 5897, 6362, 6437, 7157, 7984, 8379, 8398, 8801
Goldmark, R.G. 7789
Goldsborough, Thaddeus R. 1000, 3699
Goldsmith, Alfred North 1143, 1470, 1495, 1668, 1813, 1817, 1847, 1883, 1902, 2000, 2541, 2542, 2641, 2821, 3699, 3900, 4079, 4815, 5167, 5253, 5440, 5510, 6133, 6382, 6477, 6659, 6915, 7019, 7020, 7054, 7197, 7243, 7357, 7444, 7597, 7655, 7817, 7879, 7897, 7997, 8091, 8139, 8327, 8680, 8681
Goldsmith, Thomas T., Jr. 7529, 7928, 8093, 8197, 8369, 8670
Goldstein, Eugen 70, 99, 150, 189, 193, 210
Gondry, Robert 8678
Goode 7598
Goodenough, Ernest Frederick 3668, 3786, 3903, 4407, 5474
Goodrich, E. 5790
Goottee, T.E. 7001
Gordon, George 3229
Gordon, James Edward Henry 60, 128, 130
Gorham, Maurice A.C. 8700
Gorokhov, P.K. 192, 8753
Goshaw, Iol R. 3441
Gosman, Thomas Andrew 3625
Gottier, Thomas L. 8431
Gould, Leslie A. 3165, 3267, 3501
Gould, Louis 2629
Gouriet, G.G. 8734a
Gouroff, W.A. 752
Grabovsky 718
Gradenwitz, Alfred 505, 770, 1649, 1826, 1906, 2143, 2420, 2595, 2727, 2902, 2940, 3146, 3328
Graefe, Kurt Heinz 6737, 7998
Grafton Radio 4062, 4073, 4127
Graham, George Edward Gordon 4857, 5595, 5878, 6544, 7285, 8335
Graham, Margaret B.W. 8863
(Etablissements) Grammont 6906, 7430
Gramophone Company 1754, 2074, 2075, 2101, 2228, 2290, 2342, 2426, 2476, 2571, 2656, 2736, 2738, 2739, 2747, 2748, 2749, 2790, 2824, 2898, 2924, 3062, 3191, 3256, 3316
Gray, Elisha 101
Gray, Frank 903, 904, 973, 991, 1065, 1148, 1536, 1624, 1675, 1742, 1859, 1860, 1930, 1968, 2048, 2202, 2280, 2295, 2338, 2445, 2446, 2547, 2654, 2682, 2699, 2742, 2923, 2972, 3105, 3183, 3255, 4420, 4470, 4476, 4528, 4580, 5448, 5705, 5739-43, 7553, 7831, 8037, 8117, 8292, 8470
Gray, J.A. 1861
Gray, Robert C. 5289
Great Britain. *Passim and see* Baird, BBC, British Thomson-Houston, EMI, General Electric Company, Gramophone Company, Marconi's, Television Society, 8736, 8743, 8754, 8758, 8761, 8859
Greece 4238
Green, E. 7977
Green, E.H.R. 1224
Green, Estil I. 993, 1220, 3418
Green, Herndon 1636, 7361
Greer, Henry 4385–7, 5145, 5146, 6346
Gregory, R. 5979
Grenfall, Alexis René 8336
Gretton, J.F. 2572, 3287
Griffin, J.W. 2820
Grimshaw, Robert 405, 426
Gripenberg, William Sebastian 395
Grisewood, Edgar Norman 1899, 1915, 2917
Gross, Gerald C. 3164
Grove, William Robert 18
Grundmann, G.C. 7490
Grundmann, Gustave L. 6829, 7432, 8141, 8365
Grutzmacher, M. 1852
Guanella, Gustav 5783, 7436, 7473, 7474, 8128
Gubb, Lawrence E. 5625
Gudden, Bernhard 1683
Günther, Johannes 4986, 6687, 7947, 7965, 8151
Guerbilsky, A. 934
Guibiansky, J. 3193, 4935, 5452
Gulliland, A.A. 1922, 1983
Gunther, Johannes 7107
Gutafson, Victor G. 1657

Haberle, Sumner Dudley 2095
Hadfield, B.M. 8246
Haefer, R. 3689
Haeff, A.V. 8500
Hague 2334
Haldane, Richard Burdon 1157
Hall, C.P. 4179, 4551
Hall, Howard 2071
Hall, Richard 784
Hall, Victor 5375
Hallett, Michael 8839a, 8845
Halloran, Arthur Hobart 2897, 6575
Hallows, Ralph W. 8682
Hallwachs, Wilhelm Ludwig Franz 200, 1942
Hammond, John Hayes, Jr. 550, 1055, 1660, 1949, 1990, 2093, 2435, 2539, 3505, 3711
Hankey, Lord 8664
Hankly, H.A. 4274
Hansell, Clarence 1022
Hansen, Edmund H. 668
Hansen, Siegfried 8171
Hanson, Oscar B. 6251, 6794, 8198, 8229, 8328
Harbord, James A. 4869
Harder, E. 3571
Hardie, K.F. 4373

Harding, Charles Francis 8624
Harding, Robert, Jr. 3184, 4269, 4318, 4375, 4376, 6080, 8648
Hardwick, John 3814, 3818, 3998, 4058, 4099, 4468, 4469, 4692, 5195, 5196, 7667, 7675, 8179
Hardy René 3975
Harker, Maurice Geoffrey 7251
Harman, M. 4776
Harmon, R. Joyce 8701
Harnett, Daniel E. 7300, 8005
Harries 7939
Harries, John Henry Owen 1713, 1866, 1943, 1981, 2014, 2144, 2437-9, 2731, 2826, 3134, 3209
Harriman, Oliver C. 6457, 6459, 6526
Harriman International Corporation 3502
Harris, Irvin 1234
Harris, Norman L. 3842
Harris, Percy W. 1184, 1315
Harrison, T.H., 2377
Hart, R.M. 1124, 1125
Hart, Russell 545
Hart, Samuel Lovington 435
Hartley, Lowell J. 2108, 8501, 8536
Hartley, Ralph Vinton Lyon 1047, 1422, 1534, 3183
Hartman, Hans 3185
Hartman, Werner 7458
Harvey, E. Newton 8741
Haskell, F.H. 2572, 3287
Hathaway, Kenneth A. 2262, 4286, 5573
Hatzinger, Hans 2296, 2535
Hauksbee, Francis 2
Hawking 7344
Hawking, G.F. 5762
Hayes, M.L. 1301
Haynes, F.H. 1948, 2157
Hazell, H.F. 3356, 3357
Hazeltine 7380
  patents 4632, 4635, 4828, 5297, 5385, 5681, 6059, 6487, 6530, 6555, 6874, 6903, 7015, 7016, 7132, 7134, 7228, 7260, 7299, 7300, 7331, 7332, 7534, 7535, 7603, 7604, 7607, 7674, 7709, 7731, 7733, 7739, 7741, 7783, 7821, 7825, 7837–40, 7843, 7869, 7885–7, 7896, 7902, 7903, 7911, 7926, 7936, 7949, 7956, 7964, 7989, 8005, 8020, 8075–7, 8085, 8124, 8126, 8172, 8187, 8191, 8195, 8201, 8203, 8305, 8310, 8340–2, 8350, 8460, 8467, 8529, 8561, 8584, 8607, 8617
Head, Sydney W. 8735
Headrick, Lewis Barnard 3939, 5751, 5920, 6907, 7122
Hefele, John R. 1742, 1859, 5094, 6244, 7479
Hehlgans, Fredrich W. 3212, 3422, 3460, 3484, 3491, 6246

Heightman, D.W. 8806
Heim, Howard John 3086, 5367, 8624
Heimann, W. 4795, 5069, 5070, 6165, 6261, 6516, 7382, 8006
Heimann, Walter 7552, 8434
Heinmann, Walter 3465, 5174
Hell, Rudolf 665
Heller, Alexander Gordon 2457, 3276
Hellings, G.M. 7025
Helmholtz, Hermann Ludwig Ferdinand von 181
Hémardinquer, Pierre 4115
Henderson, S.T. 5392, 7111, 7462
Henley, J.H. 6578
Henneberg, Walter 4571, 5071, 5853, 7988
Henroteau, A. 3757
Henroteau, François Charles Pierre 1884, 2570, 2751, 3741, 4297, 4344, 4601, 7426
Henry, Charles C. 670
Henry, Joseph 4
Hensel, Bernhard 4022, 4029
Hepp, Gerard 6837, 7124, 7393, 7394, 8480, 8525
Herbst, Philip J. 3926, 5049, 7603, 7607
Herd, J.F. 3907
Herdman, William J. 3222
Hergenrother, Rudolph C. 4717, 4761, 5256, 6487, 7015, 7016, 7134, 7825, 7956, 8020, 8529
Herman, Joseph 674, 2032, 3663
Hermann, Dietrich 6875, 7006, 7348
Herndon, Charles Allan 638, 696
Herold, Edward W. 8502, 8717, 8804, 8820
Herriott, E.G. 3922
Hertz, Heinrich Rudolf 150, 195, 196, 201, 229, 243, 1942
(Heinrich) Hertz Institute 3618, 4245, 5513
Hertzberg, Robert 1567, 1631, 1634, 1665, 1691, 3275
Hess, Kurt 4022, 4029
Hewel, Horst 2257, 2566, 2845, 3328, 5620, 6413
Hewitt, J.H. 4056
Hewitt, W.S. 4499
Hewson, Bertram Tom 7676–9, 8356
Heymann, Otto 6057
Hibberd, R.G. 5426
Hickok, Willard H. 4749, 6569, 6782, 7064, 7416, 7547, 7682, 7931, 8484, 8495
Hicks 126
Hill, S. 8361
Hilliard, Robert L. 8876
Hillier, James 8849
Hinck, Alfred J. 7929
Hinderer, Heinrich 6612

Hineline, Harris Dale 556
Hinsch, Wilhelm 6992, 7950
Hirshman, C.L. 8007
Hirst, Lord 8242, 8418
Hitchcock, William J. 2115
Hitler, Adolf 4757, 4760, 4938
Hittorf, Johann Wilhelm 17, 45, 99, 125, 179, 184, 210
Hobart, Arthur 965, 1036
Hobbs, Henry William 7536
Hodgson, Violet 3172
Hogan 4627
Hogan, I.V.C. 4627, 4761
Hogan, John Vincent Lawless 1984, 2399, 2473, 2773, 2990, 3037, 3056, 3089, 3171, 3936, 4539, 6005, 8726
Hogencamp, Harold C. 5468, 5895, 5941, 6039, 6072, 6318, 6319, 6335, 6336, 6902, 7027-9, 7139, 7187, 7229, 7245, 7532, 7533, 8357
Hoglund, Gustav E. 386, 460
Holland 1096, 1613, 2418, 3619, 5254, 5879, 6949, 7272. *See also* N.V. Philips
Holland, Walter E. 3124, 4627
Hollman, Hans Erich 3466, 5821, 5836, 5837, 5841, 5935, 6053, 6383, 7359, 7469
Hollywood, John M. 4171, 4352, 4417, 4448, 8375
Holman, Herbert Edward 4660, 4995, 5074, 5075, 5645, 5650, 6006, 6679, 7055, 7280, 8086, 8419
Holmes, E.J. 3326
Holmes, J.W. 3326
Holmes, Ralph S. 3834, 4250, 4350, 4522, 4672, 5368, 5789, 6538, 7113, 7556, 7665, 7690, 7795, 7842, 7915, 8038, 8212
Holst, Gilles 4325, 6385
Holweck, Fernand 815, 817, 884, 901, 1033, 1085, 1086, 1098, 1187, 1258, 1701
Holzer, Philip P. 3791, 6158
Homrighous, John H. 8589
Honoré, Fernand 382
Horii, K.T. 4630
Horn, Charles W. 3672, 5832
Horny, F. 2816
Horowitz, J. 269
Horton, Arthur W., Jr. 6095
Horton, Derek 8720
Horton, Joseph W., 658, 907, 974, 991, 995, 1076, 1141, 1894, 2001
Hough, Clinton W. 1023, 1291, 2500
Houston, Edwin James 183
Howard, Sydney 2062
Howe, George W.O. 4843, 4969
Howe, Marie 1125, 1126
Hoxie, Charles Alfred 615, 896

Hoyt, Karl Robert 7170
Hubbell. Richard W. 8654
Hudec, Erich 2649, 2716, 2933, 3131, 3196, 3207, 3308, 3380, 3467, 3492, 3545, 3894, 3908, 4351, 4666, 4768, 7005, 7200, 7309
Hudson-Essex 3994
Huffman, Charles Edgar 1998, 2096, 2193, 2609, 3035
Hughes, C.E. 1723
Hughes, David Edward 95
Hughes, L.E.C. 5634, 5689, 5713, 5754, 5763, 5771, 5786, 5812, 5829, 5845, 5911, 5932, 5946, 5972, 5977, 6633, 6683, 7266, 7427, 7586, 7600, 7628, 7647, 7659, 7662, 7701, 7710, 7727, 7735, 8083
Hughs, A. 3760
Hughs, Arthur Llewelyn 439
Humphreys, T.D. 7503
Hungary 4390
Hurd, Volney D. 6352
Hurst, W.N. 5475
Hutchinson, Oliver George 733, 735, 736, 739, 769, 802, 1075, 1112, 1125, 1126, 1131, 1136, 1166, 1167, 1173, 1325, 1328, 1356, 1358, 1697, 1772, 2102, 2878
Hutchinson, Robert William 2707, 5574, 7369
Hutchinson, Thomas H. 8390, 8544, 8671
Hygrade Sylvania 2109, 2110, 7630
Hylander, Clarence J. 8648

Iams, Harley A. 2282, 3416, 3878, 3879, 4357, 4477, 4521, 4759, 6309, 6548, 6566, 6701, 6880, 6907a, 6908, 6987, 7056, 7064, 7065, 7257, 7261, 7340, 7341, 7685, 7966, 8101, 8307, 8360, 8364, 8370, 8442, 8496, 8546
Ilberg, Wildemar 2150, 2255, 2394, 3483
IMK Syndicate 2868, 2869, 3448, 3717, 5975, 6353, 7651, 7704, 8061, 8120, 8121, 8135
Ingalls, Albert G. 1643
Inglis, Andrew F. 8871
Ingram, Dave 8813
Insuline Corporation of America 1493, 1564, 1633, 3276, 3278
International Carrier-Call & Television Corporation 5548
International General Electric 3369, 3465
International Standard Electrical Corporation 5264, 5562, 6272, 6363, 6424, 6976, 7455, 7893, 8234
International Telecommunication Union (ITU) 8773
International Telephone & Telegraph Corporation (ITT) 3295

International Television Corporation 4245, 4627, 5575
International Television Radio Corporation 3582, 4463, 7074, 7808
Interstate Electric Company 1493
Inverforth, Lord 4471, 5093
Ireland 2102
Irwin, G.C. 1415
Isakson, D.W. 503
Isnard, V. 4163
Italy 2852, 2944, 3140, 3519, 4175, 5161, 5254, 5721, 6135, 6715, 6850
Ives, Herbert Eugene 658, 936, 938, 966, 974, 984, 990, 1119, 1182, 1189, 1273, 1865, 1986, 2008, 2176, 2209, 2351, 2446, 2510, 2603, 2616, 2713, 2721, 2732, 2755, 2767, 2794, 3183, 7853, 8677
patents 567, 611, 763, 764, 795, 890, 903, 995, 1010, 1046, 1047, 1080, 1338, 1624, 1895, 1930, 2073, 2148, 2174, 2229, 2328, 2339, 2340, 2366, 2582, 2606, 2608, 2646, 2927, 3301, 3436, 3929, 4064, 4251, 4518, 4719, 4992, 5095, 5096, 5640, 5693, 5746, 6183
Ives, Ronald L. 7296, 7525, 8779
Izanstark, Charles 1217, 1223, 1325

Jackson D. 8058, 8060, 8256
Jackson, H. 3636
Jackson, S. 6338
Jacob, L. 8383
Jacomb, William Wykeham 2969, 3299, 3420, 3546, 3550, 3744, 4041, 4107
Jaeckel, George 6820
James, Ivanhoe John Penfound 7454, 8580
Jamieson, Andrew 151
Janes, Robert B. 7064, 7304, 8495
Jannes, H. 4527
Japan 3440, 3472, 4629, 4630, 5161, 5254, 5971, 6126, 6367, 6590, 8864
Japan Broadcasting Corporation 6367, 6533, 6733
Jarrard, W.J. 1325, 1665, 2023, 5026
Jarvis, Kenneth W. 792, 6556
Jarvis, R.F.J. 8541
Jaworski, Werner von 318, 412
Jefferson Electric Company 8331, 8332
Jeffree, John Henry 4308, 4360, 4428, 4747, 5476, 5600, 5623, 5624, 5934, 6315, 6723, 6747, 6826, 6953, 6955
Jeffries, Zay 2245
Jenkins, (Charles) Francis 245, 412, 425, 456, 496, 520, 534, 535, 540, 558, 568, 599, 602, 618, 627, 631, 634, 638, 639, 642, 647, 666, 672, 681, 685, 687, 689-91, 693, 696-8, 700, 703, 709,

716, 726, 728, 762, 815, 902, 1070, 1098, 1196, 1222, 1259, 1315, 1316, 1372, 1428, 1437, 1447, 1457, 1481, 1484, 1548, 1571, 1628, 1636, 1658, 1665, 1695, 1755, 1769, 1799, 1807, 1823, 1837, 1845, 1853, 1857, 1887, 1899, 1903, 1904, 1918, 1935, 1936, 1949, 1954, 1965, 1973, 1976, 2002, 2004, 2119, 2128, 2162, 2177, 2211, 2213, 2254, 2263, 2310, 2458, 2560, 2592, 2988, 2990, 3079, 3238, 3340, 3359, 3367, 3410, 3424, 3473, 3482, 3616, 8808, 8878
patents 464, 481-3, 493, 508, 509, 511-6, 518, 519, 529, 590, 620, 641, 653-6, 663, 673, 684, 686, 692, 757, 758, 767, 785, 948, 978, 996, 999, 1095, 1104, 1294, 1348, 1456, 1602, 1876, 2095, 2156, 2195, 2201, 2226, 2352, 2754
transmitting stations 1355, 1746, 1758, 1799, 2131, 2177, 2212, 2327, 2334, 2422, 2545, 2546, 2864, 2887, 2991, 3037, 3360
(C.F.) Jenkins, Inc. 2754
Jenkins Laboratories 515, 516, 518, 535, 559, 1104, 1294, 1348, 1456, 1602, 1633, 1658, 1876, 2156, 2195
Jenkins Television Corporation 1658, 1711, 1715, 1998, 2090, 2095, 2096, 2189, 2193, 2234, 2250, 2254, 2459, 2461, 2644, 2647, 2688, 3038, 3093, 3169
Jenkins, Ronald Osmond 6248
Jenkinson, Mark Webster 2333, 2335
Jensen, Axel G. 8727
Jesty, Leslie Connock 4187, 4188, 4268, 4307, 4434, 4435, 4544, 4550, 4565, 4570, 4634, 4812, 4813, 5055, 5058, 5060, 5180, 5460, 5531, 5555, 5568, 5657, 7032, 7249, 7325, 8244, 8258
Jevons, J.C. 1418, 1485
Jewett, Frank B. 936, 1222, 1315, 5727, 7446
Joers, Carl F. 2950
Jofeh, Lionel 7635-9
Johannessen, Jurg 6013
John Wesley Ernest 2069
Johnson, A.H. 5493
Johnson, H.C. 238
Johnson, John Bertrand 485, 510, 2478, 3197, 4276
Johnson, L.R.J. 6624
Johnsrud, A.L. 2174
Johnston, J. 1251
Johnstone, D.M. 4202, 4280, 4382, 4425, 4682, 4744, 5281, 5288, 5446, 5447, 5697, 5750, 5956, 5966, 6070, 6156, 6178, 6418, 6543, 7085
Jolliffe, C.B. 5832
Jolson, Al 6490

Jones 7190
Jones, E. Taylor 986
Jones, F.R. 6289
Jones, P.C. 1103
Jones, Robert B. 7191
Jones, V.A. 5282, 5283, 5691, 5718, 5738, 5773, 5788, 5810, 5818, 5826, 5861, 5899, 5930, 6010, 6070, 6178, 6193, 6417, 6628, 6651, 6673, 6749, 6753, 6773, 6871, 6932, 7046, 7052, 7227, 7413, 7449, 7470, 7569, 7715, 7730, 7786, 7787, 8200
Jones, W.I. 7909
Jones, William 7587, 7932, 7941, 8081
Jones, William Martin, Jr. 2358
Jonker, Johan Lodewijk Hendrik 5998, 6003, 7509
Joy, Henry William 1367
Joyce, Thomas F. 7075
Juhász, Béla 2301
Jupe, J.H. 7975

Kaar, I.J. 8042, 8054
Kaempffert, Waldemar Barnhard 835, 892, 921, 3100
Kakourin, S.N. 474
Kallmann, Heinz Erwin 5296, 6297, 7661, 7738, 8136, 8503, 8566, 8592
Kannenberg, Walter F. 2146
Kapella 5561
Karolus, August 606, 708, 755, 810, 840, 1097, 1187, 1388, 1424, 1485, 1514, 1590, 1760, 1875, 1890, 1906, 2249, 2490, 3146, 3271, 3483, 3547, 4300, 4301, 4400, 4401, 4429, 4432, 5242, 5342, 5890, 6708
Kassner, E. 1840
Kasson, C.L. 1027
Kaufman, S. 3171, 3691, 5104, 5259, 5441, 5511, 8053
Kaufmann, Henry W. 7140, 7640
Kautz, Robert J. 6200
Kauzmann, A.P. 8055
Keil, H. 8822
Keith, C.R. 2660
Keith, Michael 8876
Kell, Ray Davis 1181, 1266, 1361, 1616, 1849, 1856, 1955, 2049, 2105, 2326, 2356, 2428, 3107, 3121, 3127, 3778, 3779, 4230, 4584, 4671, 4942, 5801, 7343, 8393, 8485, 8486, 8530
Kellaway, Francis W. 8660
Keller-Dorian Colorfilm Corporation 3401
Kellog Switchboard & Supply 2117
Kemp, Lloyd A.W.E. 7403
Kemp, Ronald John 3221, 3454, 3668, 3737, 4515, 4773, 4777, 4945, 5329, 5864, 6983, 7123, 7330, 7888, 8248

Kempner, Stanley 8695
Kendall, G.P. 1165, 1538
Kendall, James M. 1993
Kennedy, Angus 2010, 2188, 2275, 4116
Kennedy, T.R., Jr. 2040, 2345, 2497
Kenyon, Franklin P. 8192
Keogan, Charles J. 2250
Kerber, K.H. 7162
Kerr, Alexander 2885
Kerr, John 13, 62, 74, 76, 91, 5289
Kessler, Jacob 6283, 6761, 6825, 7083
Kette, G. 2172, 2362, 2584, 2982, 3085, 3129, 3642, 4117, 4194, 4213, 4631, 6029, 6231, 6300, 6501
Keyston, John Edgar 4931, 4932, 5000, 5092, 5453
Kharchikyan, R.S. 8835
Kiepenheuer, K.O. 2983
Kimball, C.N. 7207, 8056, 8227
King (Sen.) 2909
King, C. 2062
King, E.B. 5614, 7244
King, J.B. 4217
King, R.W. 645, 960
Kinman, T.H. 5153
Kinne, Erich 2719, 4859, 5138, 5147, 5215, 5357, 5360, 5361, 5575, 5631, 5662-4, 5978, 6218, 6247
Kintner, Samuel Montgomery 801
Kirby, Philip 8625
Kirke, H.L. 4656, 8082, 8112
Kirschstein, F. 2210, 2450, 2514, 2622, 2843, 3378, 3643, 4324, 7752
Kirschstein, Morris 1604, 1839
Kishpaugh, Arthur W. 905
Kitroser, Issac 3401
Kittross, John M. 8839
Kiver, Milton S. 8672
Klatzow, Leonard 4617, 4936, 6007, 7519, 7520, 7550
Kleen, Warner 3764, 5391
Kleinberg, Ludwig 262
Klemperer, Otto 4931, 4932, 5296, 5402, 6114, 6859, 7026, 7082, 7084, 7163, 7395, 7472, 7475, 7995, 7438, 8626
Kliatchko, V. 4863, 4998, 5007-10, 5045, 5046, 5064-7, 5129-32, 5233, 5245, 5669, 6015, 6089, 6354, 6689
Klitscher, Gustav 273
Klüge, Werner 5938, 6438
Klugh, P.B. 1222
Knapp, Dorothy 2957
Knapp, J. George 8838
Knick, Ulrich 6655, 6665, 6725, 6729, 6774, 7360, 7578, 7722, 8518
Knickerbocker Broadcasting Company 3072, 3280
Kniepkamp, Heinrich 6977
Knipe, A.R. 2182, 3248

Knoblauch, Henning 4283, 5445, 6438, 8407
Knoeptke 1368
Knoll, M. 3860, 3863, 4023-8, 4042-5, 4288, 4317, 4328, 4891, 4909, 4918, 4919, 4923, 5192, 5380, 5521, 5556, 5768, 5769, 5819, 5938, 6514, 6849, 7866
Knoll, Max H. 3294
Knoofs, William A. 7211
Knoop, William A. 5472, 6245, 6464, 6557, 8259
Knothe, A. 375, 376, 731
Knudsen, H. 3941, 5683
Knudson, Hans 363, 398
Kober, Paul H. 1410
Koch, Earl L. 3297
(Earl L.) Koch Holding Corporation 3297
Koch, Winfield R. 3591, 4781, 7193
Kodak Ltd. 7737
Kodel Electric and Mfg. Co. 1691
Koempfner, R. 5969
König, Karl Rudolph 38
Koeppe, L. 3264
Köpping, A. 8095
Kollatz, C.W. 710, 879
Koller, Lewis R. 1191, 1500, 2693, 6900
Kolorama Laboratories 5468, 5895, 5941, 6039, 6072, 6335, 6336, 6902, 7027-9, 7139, 7187, 7229, 7245, 7532, 7808, 8357
Kolozsky, Louis W. 4404, 5020
Kolster-Brandes 2151, 2238, 7456, 7477, 7765, 7828, 7829, 7867, 7868, 7870, 7893, 7894, 7904, 7943, 7948, 7954, 7958, 7986, 7994, 7999, 8018, 8065-7, 8070, 8088, 8114-6, 8129, 8142, 8174, 8183, 8234, 8251, 8252, 8301, 8306, 8309, 8333
Konemann, H. 951
Konkle, Philip J. 3106, 6899
Korn, Arthur 293, 303, 314, 322, 345, 347, 350-2, 360, 365, 370, 398, 412, 423, 426, 506, 534, 547, 569, 599, 625, 1621, 1780, 1815, 8710
Korn, Elizabeth P. 8710
Korn, Terry 8710
Korshenewsky, Nicolai von 5213
Kosche, Erich 6442, 6658
Kowaleski, A. 7565
Kraak, Hajo Hubertus 6962
Kraeuter, David W. 8878, 8879
Kraus, John H. 1001, 1312
Krawinkel, Günther 2171, 2407, 2552, 2624, 3377, 3645, 4510, 5261, 5461, 5855–7
Krenzien, Otto 5948, 6529, 7784
Kröncke, H. 746
Kroker, A. 4172, 4182
Kroll, M. 4220

Kruckow, A. 2206
Kruesser 273
Kruh, Osias Otto 353, 393
Kubetsky 5515
Kursemeijer, H.J. 6681
Kurtz, Edwin Bernard 3843, 4247, 4455, 4593, 5520
Kurylo, Friedrich K. 8772, 8854
Kwal, Bernard 4232, 4753
Kwartin, Bernard 2914

Laas, William 8786
Labin, Emile 6255, 6363
Les Laboratoires de Matérie Téléphonique 6585
Lacault, Robert E. 536
La Cour, Poul 102, 103, 170
Laczay, T. von 2868
Lafount, H.A. 1263, 1466, 1473, 1629, 2100, 2440, 2834, 2835, 3251, 3463
Lamb, J. 4324
Lance, T.M.C. 3732, 3943, 4202, 4280, 4299, 4451, 4576, 4578, 4793, 4951, 5047, 5108, 5155, 5207, 5241, 5537, 5718, 5778, 5861, 6010, 6149, 6177, 6504, 6544, 8036
Landis, Daniel O. 8022
Lane, A.P. 1426
Lane, Henry M. 1684, 3384
Lang, Wilhelm 6044
Lange, Bruno 6576
Langenwalter, Hans-Wolfgang 5815, 6242, 6688, 6774
Langer, Nicholas 521, 531, 582, 592, 617
Langford-Smith, F. 2139
Langley, Ralph H. 882, 1009, 1346
Langmuir, David B. 7061, 8482
Langmuir, Irving 429, 433, 450, 451, 2387, 7281
Lankes, L.R. 8690
Lardeur, Alfred Edouard 275, 799
Lardner, James 8864
Larner, Edgar Thomas 1179, 1404, 1772, 2022
Larsen, Poul 3877
Larson, C.C. 8537
Latour, Marius 452, 747
Lattman, M. 5968
Laufer, Berthold 1581
LaVerne, R. 7933
La Via, Joseph 2808
Law, Harold B. 8817
Law, Russell R. 6876, 7060, 7149, 7463, 8590
Lawrence, William L. 3971
Layer, Harold A. 8805
Layzell, R.E. 3578, 3615, 3639
Leblanc, Maurice 145, 412, 820
Leblans, L. 8098

Le Boiteux, Henri Jean 6976
Le Duc, Jean 2041, 5883
Lee 6451
Lee, Don 6123
(Don) Lee Broadcasting System 3449, 3655, 3690, 6499, 6852, 6921, 7002, 7077, 7428, 7543, 8049, 8274, 8401, 8587
Lee, H.W. 7770, 8449
Lee, Robert Edwin 8661
Leeming, Harry Toyne 1269
Legg, Joseph W. 916
Legg, Stuart 8627
Lehmann, Otto 278
Leibman, Gerhard 5553
Leishman, Leroy J. 503, 2753, 2955
Leithäuser, G. 2368, 2714
Lemest, R.D. 7039
Lenard, Philipp Eduard Anton von 239, 241, 332, 1942
Lenier, H.R. 4272
Leonard J. 7349
Le Pontois, Leon 234, 389, 412
Le Queux, William 583
Lertes, Peter 844
Lescarboura, Austin C. 479, 2413, 2590, 2722, 2756, 7878
Lester, Mark 1648
Lester, Paul S. 7189
Leverenz, Humboldt W. 6588, 7546, 8382
Levin 6206
Levin, B. 4542
Levin, Nyman 2912, 2919, 3002, 3358, 4001, 4038, 4395, 4542, 5559, 5653, 5654
Levy, H.R. 8528
Levy, Leonard 1351, 6031, 7501
Levy, Rudolph 3502
Lewer, S.K. 2052
Lewin, E. George 2183
Lewis, Edwin John Godfrey 6577
Lewis, G. 8691
Lewis, Harold C. 2663
Lewis, Harold M. 4632, 4635, 4828, 5385, 5675, 6487, 6530, 6902, 6994, 7132, 7199, 7332, 7604, 7739, 7741, 7783, 7821, 7843, 7886, 7956, 8195, 8305, 8460
Liacos, Stavros J. 2890
Lichty, Lawrence W. 8810
Lieben, Robert von 329, 337, 397
Liebmann, Gerhard 5628, 7126-8, 7706
Liesegang, Raphael Eduard 221, 222, 412
Lindbergh kidnapping 3335
Lindemann, Frederick Alexander 6561, 7574
Lindenblad, N.E. 8225
Linder, Ernest G. 4871, 550, 5867, 7356
Lindner, Paul 6540
Ling, F.W. 1449

Lensell, Alfred Aubyn 4895, 4905, 5021, 5084, 6275, 6371, 7217
Lipfert, Kurt 7847, 8030
Lippincott, Donald K. 3603, 4676, 4845, 4846, 5243, 5529, 5530, 5701
Locan, A. 7676-9, 8356
Lock, C.E. 7765
Lodge, Oliver Joseph 152, 243, 302, 344, 1172
Loeb, J. 5943, 7497
Löpp, Edmund Heinrich 5998, 5999, 6003, 6243, 6780
D.S. Loewe 2979, 3146, 3210, 3630, 3768, 3790, 4017, 4103, 4591, 5319, 5513, 5575, 6122, 6712, 7320
  patents 2657, 2692, 2994, 2696, 2830, 2892, 2926, 3151, 3345-7, 3350, 3352-4, 3366, 3397, 3412, 3413, 3432, 3443-5, 3485, 3493, 3496, 3512, 3513, 3542, 3548, 3549, 3552, 3554, 3555, 3561, 3562, 3568, 3586, 3693, 3606, 3632, 3633, 3637, 3658-60, 3676, 3677, 3680, 3681, 3685, 3687, 3699, 3718, 3745, 3746, 3750, 3781, 3783, 3784, 3796, 3822, 3830-2, 3855, 3861, 3872-5, 3901, 3928, 3933, 3934, 3939, 3940, 3954, 3958, 3959, 3972, 3986, 3992, 3993, 3995, 3996, 4006-8, 4012, 4013, 4015, 4052, 4059, 4066, 4077, 4112, 4134, 4141-4, 4158, 4160, 4161, 4167, 4186, 4193, 4199-201, 4216, 4219-21, 4254-6, 4260, 4261, 4271, 4302, 4311, 4315, 4333-7, 4341, 4361-3, 4374, 4411-3, 4421, 4430, 4431, 4442, 4443, 4458-60, 4486, 4491, 4493, 4500, 4501, 4504, 4507, 4545, 4564, 4567, 4602, 4603, 4608, 4618, 4637, 4638, 4657, 4658, 4663, 4678, 4683, 4684, 4690, 4694-8, 4720, 4721, 4724, 4728, 4743, 4763, 4767, 4779, 4870, 4872, 4893, 4902, 4948, 4953, 4982, 5027, 5038, 5057, 5063, 5072, 5082, 5124, 5143, 5151, 5157, 5186, 5201, 5202, 5229, 5238, 5240, 5244, 5266, 5268, 5291, 5298, 5299, 5301, 5336, 5386, 5387, 5399-401, 5407, 5408, 5418, 5421, 5454, 5467, 5469, 5470, 5478, 5480, 5490, 5526, 5536, 5539, 5547, 5550, 5551, 5553, 5587, 5591, 5593, 5606, 5609, 5628, 5674, 5685, 5734, 5764, 5777, 5792, 5842-4, 5947, 5987, 6004, 6058, 6074, 6077, 6150, 6152, 6184, 6250, 6259, 6268, 6273, 6313, 6314, 6323, 6330, 6333, 6374, 6414, 6444, 6454, 6472, 6474, 6483, 6541, 6559, 6560, 6608, 6664, 6666, 6674-6, 6694, 6697, 6737, 6746, 6838, 6971, 7034, 7040, 7100, 7180, 7219, 7246, 7247, 7480, 7629, 7687, 7998, 8178, 8465

Loewe Radio 3397, 3398, 3618, 3730, 4198, 4245, 4342, 5981, 5986, 6076, 6162, 6625, 7034, 7097, 7136, 7137, 7250, 7297, 7351, 7641, 7725, 7780, 8205
Loewe, Siegmund 2085, 2694, 2913, 2926, 3556, 3594, 3605
Lofgren, Benjamin F. 2285
Lohr, Lenox R. 8641
Loiseau, Louis Marie Jean 1946, 2116
Lona, Luis A. 4095
C. Lorenz A.-G. 825, 1362, 1820, 1958, 3465, 3891, 4097, 4555, 4559, 4606, 4700, 4705, 4835, 4920, 4926, 5076, 5173, 5203, 5205, 5300, 5319, 5513, 5575, 5645, 5648, 6052, 6194, 6226, 6693, 6727, 6755, 6787, 6865, 7038, 7051, 7087, 7320, 7552, 7576, 7811, 7814, 7841, 7857, 7939, 7944, 8289
Lorenzen, Rolf 6975
Loughren, Arthur V. 7199, 7612, 7709, 7983, 8310
Lovell, Bernard 8683
Low, Archibald Montgomery 455, 542, 637, 729, 1098, 6685
Lowenstein, Fritz 414
Lubcke, Harry R. 2123, 2558, 2837, 3337, 3449, 3565, 3966, 5168, 5641, 5984, 6816, 7428, 7543, 8269, 8401, 8587
Lubin, Emile 3540
Lubszynski, Günther 2849, 2905
Lubszynski, H.A. 5092
Lubszynski, Hans Gerhard 4829, 4830, 5350, 5001-4, 5927, 6262, 6554, 6741, 6742, 6893, 6984, 7086, 7282, 7289, 7404, 7550, 7663, 7993, 7996, 8012, 8220, 8576
Lucas, William 167-9, 205, 6016
Lübcke, Ernst 2910
Lund, Johan Henrik L'Abée 388
Lupton, Bertha 1737
Lux, Friedrich 310, 342, 364, 412, 2787
Lux, Heinz 1082, 3483
Lyford, Elmore B. 4798
Lyle, A.E. 3426
Lyman, H.T. 7972
Lynch, Arthur H. 1976, 2459
Lyon, R. 3540
Lyon, T.S. 6269
Lyons, Eugene 8775

McArthur, Tom 8873
McCarger, Jesse B. 4053, 5142
McCarthy, James 6672
McClintock, Raymond K. 7630
McConnell, E.D. 5111, 6800
McCreary, Harold J. 566, 587, 1105, 1282, 1283, 1606, 1665, 2288, 2689

McDonald 6895
MacDonald, (James) Ramsay 3178
McFarlane, M.D. 668
McGee, James Dwyer 3488, 3602, 3708, 3748, 3785, 3828, 3920, 4101, 4383, 4536, 4561, 4616, 4617, 4829, 5112, 6340, 6356, 6885, 7121, 7258, 7259, 7282, 7289, 7333, 7336, 7404, 7993, 8220, 8683, 8706, 8707, 8790, 8829, 8840, 8844
McGill, William J. 2701
McGregor, G.S. 8618
MacGregor-Morris, John T. 714, 3205, 6578, 6922
McIlwain, Knox 8377
McKay, Helen 6368
McKay, Herbert 6579
McKay, John W. 3592, 3808, 5339
MacKay Radio and Telegraph Corporation 3295
Mackintosh, E.E.B. 7368
McLachlan, N.W. 6234, 6306
Maclaurin, William R. 8701, 8705
McLean, F.C. 8662
McLean, T.P. 8844
McLeod, A.E. 7203
McLoud, M.C. 601
MacLulich, J.M. 1926
MacNamara, T.C. 7977
MacPherson, E.R. 1873
McQuarrie, J.L. 3066
McTighe 126
Maddock, Alan Julian 2427
Madeira 4129, 5105
Magnavox 4928
Magnus 2368
Maguire, Irwin Leonard 3859, 3968, 4366, 4858, 7335
Mahl 6040
Mahl, Hans 6933, 6993, 8002
Maitland, C.E. 7826
Majorana, Quirino 248, 412
Malekhov, I.K. 8834
Mallein, S. 7794, 8210
Malm, William 979
Maloff, I.G. 4388, 4433, 4712, 5433, 5504, 5569, 5858, 6985, 7267, 7269, 7288, 7306, 7970, 8031, 8097, 8226, 8319
Maloff, Loury Gregory 4289
Malone, Cecil 1868
Maloney, Patrick Edward 2395, 2474
Malter, Louis 4782, 5234, 5247, 5571, 5643, 5722, 5790, 5868, 5945, 6091, 6100, 7858
Maly, Rolf 7096
The Man with the Flower in His Mouth, by Luigi Pirandello (first BBC-Baird play) 2467, 2471, 2487-9, 2497, 2525, 2530, 2631

Mandel, George 5497
Mandel, P. 7873
Manderfeld, Emanuel C. 1140
Mandolf, H.I. 1013
Mann, F.J. 8691
Manning, E.L. 2628
Manson, Ray H. 8000
Manville, Edward 1328, 1702, 1762, 2333, 2335
Marchant, E.W. 7171
Marchant, F.W. 8511
Marconi, Guglielmo 258, 263, 1129, 3672, 3900, 4140, 4151, 4471, 6441
Marconi's Wireless Telegraph Company, Ltd. 626, 3524, 3564, 3578, 3583, 3620, 3623, 3629, 3651, 3742, 3838, 3841, 4038, 4096, 4125, 4471, 4479, 5093, 5846, 6999, 8788, 8794
patents 422, 430, 954, 1022, 1833, 1834, 1921, 1931, 1962, 1963, 2194, 2494, 2541-3, 2580, 2698, 2771, 2772, 2791, 2823, 2865, 2877, 2912, 2919, 2920, 2928, 2964, 2977, 3002-4, 3026, 3057, 3058, 3106, 3121, 3127, 3187, 3221, 3232, 3249, 3250, 3253, 3254, 3259, 3261, 3293, 3310, 3312, 3358, 3370, 3414, 3415, 3423, 3442, 3453, 3454, 3457, 3462, 3530, 3553, 3567, 3591, 3604, 3622, 3640, 3661, 3668-71, 3688, 3699, 3716, 3720, 3737, 3738, 3778-80, 3786, 3793, 3834, 3847, 3878-80, 3892, 3893, 3895, 3903, 3906, 3921, 3922, 3932, 3951, 4001, 4102, 4206, 4252, 4253, 4345, 4349, 4357, 4395, 4396, 4407-9, 4445, 4446, 4467, 4473, 4475, 4477, 4480, 4482, 4494, 4505, 4515, 4522, 4542, 4554, 4583, 4584, 4623, 4624, 4645, 4648, 4649, 4659, 4661, 4740-2, 4771-3, 4777, 4782-5, 4842, 4871, 4873, 4894, 4895, 4905, 4942, 4945, 4970, 4971, 4990, 5005, 5021, 5022, 5050, 5083, 5084, 5098, 5122, 5149, 5152, 5181, 5231, 5234, 5247, 5263, 5309, 5322, 5329, 5415, 5420, 5430, 5473, 5474, 5500-2, 5529, 5530, 5559, 5560, 5564, 5565, 5615, 5618, 5651-4, 5668, 5716, 5719, 5784, 5864, 5865, 5892, 5903, 5944, 6008, 6009, 6012, 6071, 6086, 6092, 6099, 6101, 6105, 6159, 6166, 6206, 6227, 6228, 6275, 6299, 6350, 6371, 6495, 6531, 6566, 6634, 6704, 6705, 6743, 6830, 6887, 6937, 6983, 7024, 7035, 7091, 7114, 7123, 7144, 7191, 7217, 7304, 7328, 7396, 7471, 7609, 7620, 7683, 7684, 7712, 7724, 7732, 7788, 7793, 7834, 7888, 7890, 7927, 7967, 8001, 8089, 8134, 8307, 8338, 8349, 8368, 8421, 8442, 8486, 8487, 8516

Marconi-EMI Television Company, Ltd 4471, 4472, 4788, 4808, 5113, 5373, 5381, 5382, 5516, 5517, 5633, 5635, 5636, 6199, 6214, 6240, 6326, 6344, 6656 (decision over Baird in Britain), 6712, 7266, 7694, 7695, 8032, 8218, 8494
Marcotte, E. 1376
Marcus 7362
Mardy 5575
Marino, A. 416
Markia Corporation 5422, 5808, 5850, 5897, 6362, 6437
Marlowe, A.C. 389
Marlowe, Eugene 8875
Marlsch, F. 6805
Marris, J.C. 6520
Marrison, Warren A. 1141
Marsh, W.W. 5403
Martin 6756
Martin, E.V.R. 1778
Martin, Karl 6537
Martin, L.C. 3867
Martin, Louis Claude 4716
Martin, Marcus J. 442, 444, 453, 467, 492
Martin, Robert Henry 546
Martin, Thomas 3761
Marzin, P. 4527
Mason, C.P. 1433, 1693
Mason, J.J. 4773
Massa, E.A., Jr. 5430, 5796
Massa, Earnest A. 5247, 6756
Le Matériel Téléphonique 552
Mather, Frederick William 1880
Mathes, Robert C. 959, 974, 991, 1080, 1081, 1363, 1364
Matsuyama, K. 4490
Mattke, Charles F. 4572
Maurer, J.A. 8262
Maver, William, Jr. 258, 377
Mavis, Harry B. 3265
Maxwell, C.B. 1246
Maxwell, Herbert 781
Maxwell, James Clerk 237
May, Joseph 50, 67, 68
Maybank, N.W. 8461, 8472
Mayo, Bernard Joseph 7165, 7397
Mead, John Edward 6147
Meenaw, W.T. 1714
Meissner, Alexander 419
Memardinquer, P. 7370
Merdler, L.R. 4562, 4640, 4825, 4927, 4987, 5220, 5337, 5338, 5388, 5389, 5394, 5466, 5481, 5698, 5880, 5900, 5991, 6060, 7154, 7450, 7767
Mertz, Pierre 997, 1365, 4528, 8378, 8615
Mervyn Sound and Vision Co., Ltd. 3772, 3978, 3981
Mesney, René 4287

Messner, Maximilian 4559, 5205, 5300, 6052, 6755, 7576, 7815, 8408
Metcalf, H.E. 4676
Metcalf, Morris 2577
Metropolitan Vickers Electrical Company (Metro-Vicks) 667, 8007
Meyer, Eugene Carl 4651
Mezger, G. Robert 7439
Michaelis, E. 4859, 5138, 5147, 5215, 5357, 5360, 5361, 5631, 5662-4, 5978, 6218-21, 6274, 6288, 6290, 6332
Michelis, Anthony 8773
Michelssen, Fritz 3069, 3074, 3194, 3483, 3599, 3634, 4590
Middelraad, Franciscus Leonardus 1924
Middleton, Henry 129
Mierlo, Stanislas van 6424, 6585, 6586
Mihály, Denes von 462, 528, 551, 578, 582, 592, 599, 614, 720, 770, 819, 840, 845, 899, 1033, 1086, 1098, 1309, 1357, 1450, 1520, 1590, 1688, 1694, 1763, 1780, 1786, 1806, 1826, 1843, 1903, 1948, 1952, 2055, 2082, 2129, 2170, 2207, 2723, 2869, 3146, 3448, 3717, 4103, 4213, 4234, 4245
Mildenstein, W.R. 5894
Millen, James 1562
Miller, Harold 5335, 5351, 5352, 5428, 6552, 6742, 6762, 6795, 6984, 7618, 7661, 7740, 8576
Miller, James N. 2004
Miller, J.L. 7824
Miller, W.E. 7153, 7827
Millikan, Robert Andrews 458, 595
Mills, H.S. 497, 840
Mills, John 1188
Mills Novelty Co. 497
Milne 6740
Milner, David Morton 891
Mines, R. 714
Mitchell, Irvin Smith 7460
Mitchell, Leslie 6198
Mitchell, W.G.W. 1043, 1154, 1324, 1515, 1647, 1651, 1704, 1738, 1739, 1780, 1832, 1871, 1910, 1980, 2019, 2061, 2183, 2218, 2272, 2740, 2810, 2814, 2898, 2924, 3269, 3788, 4314, 6923
Mitchell-Thompson, William 1787. *See also* Lord Selsdon
Mobsby, E.G.H. 3339
Moe, Robert E. 7907
Möller, Hans Georg 2232, 3030, 3689
Möller, Rolf 2232, 2408, 2512, 2813, 2842, 3030, 3098, 3183, 3242, 3300, 3381, 3519, 4730, 4963, 4991, 5464, 5642, 6820, 7457, 7458
Moffett, Cleveland 283
Mohr, Franklin 906, 2183
Moir, J. 5426, 5639

Monroe, Robert B. 8818
Monteath, J. Darbyshire 1199, 1248, 1281, 1327, 1382, 1448
Moore, Daniel McFarlan 456, 703, 730, 1051, 1098, 1308, 1414, 1956, 2302
Moore, Robert C. 8346, 8347, 8358, 8524
Morecroft, John H. 1052
Morgan, R.B. 1754, 2228, 2290, 2342
Morlock, William J. 3720
Morris, G.C. 4930, 5612
Morris, R.M. 7003
Morrison, Frederick C. 1387
Morse, George H. 235, 1836, 2390
Morse, R.S. 7737
Morshed, W. 109
Morton, Edmund R. 908, 966, 992, 998, 2298
Morton, George A. 4783-5, 4873, 4954, 5231, 5305, 5420, 5501, 5570, 5578, 5722, 5803, 6238, 6379, 6498, 6631, 6702, 6888, 6909, 7066, 7383, 7491, 7554, 7555, 8381, 8488, 8496, 8514, 8644
Moseley, Sydney Alexander 1480, 1509, 1645, 1652, 1697, 1706, 1735, 1777, 1827, 1867, 1908, 1940, 1978, 2016, 2058, 2062, 2138, 2179, 2217, 2267, 2317, 2323, 2374, 2375, 2419, 2465, 2524, 2525, 2530, 2561, 2636, 2667, 2761, 2795, 2848, 2900, 2917, 2937, 2939, 2942, 2996, 3044, 3063, 3071, 3081, 3173, 4415, 6579, 8033, 8751
Moss, B.H. 2292, 3277
Moss, Richard Jackson 54, 61, 116
Moullin, E.B. 8658
Moulton, F.R. 8168
Moulton, John Fletcher 113, 149, 163, 164, 171
Mountjoy, Garrard 7892, 8547, 8594
M-O Valve Company 6626, 8471
Moyer, James Ambrose 6580
Müller 5513
Müller, C. 2954
Müller, Hugo W. 57, 80, 97, 117, 119
Mulert, Theodor 8182, 8406
Mullard 7048, 7633, 7648, 7649, 8186, 8233
Mullard, Stanley Robert 1443
Muller, E.N. 6310
Mumford, Albert H.M. 7202, 8721
Munro, John 236, 591
Murphy 7344, 7518
Murphy Radio Ltd. 5117, 5762, 6416, 7322, 8003, 8154, 8603
Murray, Albert F. 3128, 4627, 5592, 6394, 6609, 6636, 7073, 7265, 7306, 7750
Murray, D.K. Woolfe 8152
Murray, G.E.P. 1821, 1870
Murray, Howard J. 6176, 6339

Muth, H. 3483
Myers, Elman B. 3674, 3770
Myers Electrical Research Laboratory 3664, 3667
Myers, Leonard Morris 1877, 1878, 1885, 2235, 3715, 4248, 4274, 4480, 4741, 4742, 5022, 5106, 5149, 5474, 5668, 6009, 6159, 6581, 6887, 7329, 7522, 8134, 8421, 8600, 8628
Mynall, D.J. 5429, 6481, 6857, 6858, 6877, 7596, 7816, 8426

Nagashima, M. 5162
Nagy, Paul 6720, 7651, 7704, 8061, 8120, 8121, 8135
Nairne, Edward 12
Nakashima, Tomomasa 3376, 3472, 3712, 3739, 4068, 4629
Nakken, Theodorus Hendrik 478, 1256, 1262, 1295, 1316, 1317, 1370, 2651
Nakken Patent Corporation 2651
Nakken Television Corporation 1223, 1319
Nason, Charles H.W. 2189, 2234, 2260, 2308, 2664, 2895, 3034
National Association of Broadcasters 5311
National Broadcasting Company (NBC) 2615, 2802, 2961, 3000, 3005, 3021, 3037, 3192, 3616, 3672, 4320, 5187, 5302, 5487, 6084, 6397, 6422, 6433, 6440, 6456, 6497, 6500, 6535, 6643, 7156, 7182, 7204, 7213, 7316, 7561, 7920, 7980, 8162, 8275, 8328, 8455, 8642, 8815. *See also* Empire State Building transmitter
National Company 1493, 1501, 1633
National Electrical Manufacturers Association 1612
National Television Corporation 3184, 3569, 3590, 3592, 3808, 4069, 4269, 4275, 4317, 4375, 4376, 4552, 4702, 4703, 4993, 5339, 5554, 6080, 6103, 6111
Nat. Tel. Soc. Anon. 5125, 5344, 8583
National Television System Committee (NTSC) 8640, 8657, 8734, 8734a, 8819
National Union Radio Corporation 7979
Naumberg, W. 8311
NBC. *See* National Broadcasting Company
Neidhart, Peter 7087
Nelson 7534
Nelson, Edward L. 994, 1230
Nelson, Herbert 8090, 8290
Nelson, James 6063
Nentwig, K. 2718
Nergaard, Leon S. 8539

Nesper, Eugen 570, 750, 2409, 2556, 2757
Neuberger, A. 2209, 2306, 2322, 2515, 2588, 2723
Neugebauer, Hans 6669
Newberger, Albert 1514
Newnham, John K. 8696
Newton, Alfred Vincent 32
New Zealand 1698
Nicol, William 3
Nicoll, Frederick Hermes 4399, 4655, 4693, 4727, 4778, 4837, 4838, 4867, 4931, 4932, 5622, 5774, 6098, 6558, 6817, 7165, 7276, 7277, 7397, 7835, 8013
Nicolson 7433
Nicolson, Alexander McLean 457, 552, 1044, 1056, 1061, 1066, 1254, 2066, 2383, 2385, 2397, 2403, 2442, 2479, 2484, 2503, 2601, 2702, 2774, 2952, 3268, 3531, 4092, 4111, 4330, 4384, 4537, 4540, 4612
Nicolson, Norman J. 1913, 1979, 2021, 2054
Nield, J.H. 7321
Nielsen, Axel 3877
Nightingale, Harry C. 4267
Nind, Eric Arthur 4972
Nipkow, Paul Gottlieb 13, 181, 190, 412, 632, 2636, 4050, 5089. *See also* Nipkow disk *under* scanning
Nisco, Adriano 307, 338, 412, 560
Nittick, Kenneth A. 7489
Noack, Fritz 2118, 2411, 2452, 2518, 2589, 2591, 3495
Nobbs, W.J. 3752, 3963
Norman, Bruce 8858
Norris, Roy C. 8684
Nottingham, Wayne Buckles 8729
NTSC. *See* National Television System Committee
Nuttall, Thomas Cayton 6628, 6651, 6777, 6779, 6932, 7046, 7138, 7414, 7425, 7449, 7511, 7602, 7621, 7634, 7716, 8079
Nwungwun, Aaron Foisi 8872
Nymen, Alexander 3118
Nyquist, Harry 1341, 4070

Oakville, R. 5374
Oates, W.H. 2640
Obach, Eugen Friedrich August 87, 141
O'Brien, Richard S. 8818
Ochial, I. 4669
O'Connor, Sexton 599, 1212
Oettingen, D. von 7484
Ogloblinsky, Gregory N. 3355, 3640, 3780, 3906, 4114, 4874, 5364
O'Kane B.J. 8443

Okolicsányi, Franz von 1472, 2305, 2513, 2535, 2586, 2625, 2975, 3047, 3103, 3130, 3827, 4123, 4156, 4234, 4245, 5371, 5540-3, 5658, 5660, 5862, 7209, 7232, 7338, 7345, 7418
Okolicsanyi, Ferenc 7605, 8279, 8412, 8433, 8462
Olpe, Werner H. 1177
Olympia. *See* Radiolympia
O'Neil, Peggy 382
Oppenheim 6463
Orange Securities Corporation 3295
Orth, Richard Tempel 3939, 3940, 4494
Orthuber, Richard 5707, 5710, 5797, 6040, 6041, 6054
Orvin, Lars Jörgen 4487
Osawa, Juichi 5264
Osborne, Charles Percy 3897
Oskow, Louis 1604, 1839
Osman, D.E. 8633
Ostrer, Isidore 3291, 4814, 8473
Otterbein, G. 7923, 8118
Overbeek, Adrianus Johannes Wilhelms Marie van 5998, 5999, 6003, 7509
Owen, C.H. 8764

Paehr, Hans Werner 7577, 8071, 8119
Paffrath, Georg 5729
Page, Charles Grafton 4, 7, 220
Painter, William H. 4955, 5931, 7059
Pajes, Wolf S. 2683, 2805
Paley, William S. 2039, 3505, 5988, 7231
Palmer, Eric 3104
Papst, Hermann 3288, 3431
Parce, L. 8260
Parker, Louis W. 5020, 7729, 7804
Parker, Ralzemond D. 658, 719, 2229, 2339
Parker, W.N. 7306, 7797
Parr, A. 6648
Parr, Geoffrey 3983, 4313, 4327, 4355, 4884, 7368, 7372
Parratt, D.W. 8154
Parsons, Laurence (4th Earl Rosse) 55
Pattinson, R.J. 2744
Paulu, Burton 8736, 8782
Paumier, André Paul 7645
Pawley, Edward L.E. 8754, 8797
Pawsey, J.L. 6553, 7178, 8219
Pear, T.H. 6491
Pearson, S.O. 504
Peck, A.P. 1151, 1904, 2131, 3428, 3576, 3609, 3628, 3770, 4036, 4082
Peck Television Corporation 4234, 4627, 4633, 5315
Peck, William Hoyt 3213, 3375, 3471, 3866, 4074, 4237, 4589, 4598, 4627, 4714, 4761, 4882, 5120, 6136, 8526
Pedrick, Gale 8685

Peirce, J.R. 8532
Penning, Frans Michel 4378
Perchermeir, E. 2252, 2626, 3131, 3207, 3380
Percival, William Spencer 3897, 4005, 4051, 4135, 4184, 4185, 4569, 4836, 4985, 5225, 5226, 5239, 5275, 5276, 5694, 5828, 5928, 5929, 6271, 6291, 6380, 6404, 6431, 6615, 6624, 6758, 6878, 7166, 7179, 7283, 7334, 7459, 8199
Percy, James 1157
Percy, James D. 4538, 8711
Perkins, Theodore B. 6892
Perkins, W.M. 8092
Perosino, Carlo Mario 112, 412
Perrin, Jean Baptiste 252, 824; *41*
Perry, John 74, 100, 127, 128, 130, 135, 156, 160, 168, 292, 412
Perskyi, Constantin 288, 2902, 3579
Peters, H. 2554, 3133, 3521
Peters, W.H. 6929, 8416
Petersen, Axel Carol Georg 553
Peterson, E.L. 1406
Peterson, H.O. 7201
Peto-Scott Company 238
Pevny, F. 5171
Pfeiffer, George S. 2117
Phelps, Boyd 1177, 1630, 1690, 1729
Philadelphia Storage Battery Company (later Philco Radio and Television Corporation) 2819, 3225, 3295
Philco Radio and Television Corporation 3124, 4627, 4711, 5373, 5423, 6164, 6170, 6236, 6394, 6395, 6497, 6609, 6668, 6706, 6792, 6853, 7073, 7306, 7380, 7557, 7803
  patents 5115, 5116, 5139, 5140, 5482-6, 5592, 5625, 5706, 5908, 5909, 6899, 7776, 7823, 7836, 8138, 8241, 8282, 8283, 8385, 8286, 8300, 8302, 8334, 8343-7, 8352, 8358, 8411, 8413, 8417, 8524, 8558
Philip, Charles C. 2708
N.V. Philips (Naamlooze Vennootschap Philips' Gloeilampenfabrieken) 5319, 5513, 5581, 5879, 6170
  patents 1717, 1743, 1854, 2346, 4378, 4563, 4642, 4689, 4790, 4856, 5004, 5087, 5088, 5127, 5136, 5156, 5216, 5223, 5396, 5563, 5589, 5834, 5835, 5980, 5983, 5998-6003, 6106, 6107, 6243, 6357-9, 6361, 6385, 6429, 6430, 6546, 6567, 6726, 6739, 6946, 6949, 6962, 7092, 7124, 7125, 7135, 7218, 7234, 7235, 7393, 7423, 7523, 7545, 7594, 7595, 7656, 7680, 7717, 7734, 7895, 8480, 8525
Philips Lamps Ltd. 7631, 7632, 7657, 7666, 7702, 7773, 8153

Phillips, F.W. 4466, 4691, 4711
Phillips, Stephen 922
Philpott, L.R. 7933
Phinney, Edward D. 1145, 4418
Pickard, S. 1222, 1466
Pictet, August Oswald 371
Picture Page 6370
Pieplow, H. 6995
Pierce 8605
Pierce, J.R. 7624–7
Pietschack, Ernst 8297
Pietzsch, Herbert 7810
Pike, Eugene W. 7263, 7619
Pilot Electric Mfg. Co. 1432, 1499, 1567, 1633, 1640, 1678, 1758, 8324
Pine, Emmanuel R. 5945, 6703, 6704
J. Pintsch A.-G. 3437
Pioneer Mercantile Company 4175
Pioneer Television Company 3279
Piskounoff 718
Plaistowe, Donald Leopold 2920, 3002, 3249, 3250, 3442, 3453, 4945, 5865, 6166, 6495, 7091, 8349
Planck, Max 324
Plessner, Maximilian 273
Plew, F. 4298
Plew Television, Ltd. 4574, 4596, 5079
Ploke, Martin 5891, 5942, 6044, 6450, 6465, 6551, 6619
Plücker, Julius 26, 27, 30, 45, 99, 714
Poch, Waldemar J. 4478, 5097, 5098, 5248, 5306, 5434, 5791, 5936, 6488, 6595, 8014, 8023, 8087, 8204, 8337
Pohl, Robert Wichard 399, 440
Poland 6084
Pollack, Justin Erwin 1282, 1283
Pollak, A. 3319
Pollard, Hugh B.C. 659
Pollock 7011
Polumordvinov, A.A. 285
Poole, R.B. 8425
Poole, Ronald R. 1780, 1910, 1937
Pooler, Louis G. 2809
Poore, Charles G. 2247
Poperwell, F. 7159
Popoff 713
Porter, B.H. 6593
Porterfield, John 8643
Portugal 88, 89
Post Office, General (GPO) (U.K.) 1869, 3771, 3841, 4353, 4450, 5135, 8614
  and Baird 1805, 1821, 1827, 1869, 1870, 2023, 2029
  Postmaster General (P.M.G.) 1532, 1787, 1846, 1870, 2029, 3771, 4385, 4387, 4450, 4452, 4453, 4465, 4466, 5279, 6447, 6448
Postal Telegraph-Cable Company 1145
Poulsen, Arnold 553
Poulsen, Vlademar 281, 287, 289

Pratt, Harry P. 5265
Preece, William Henry 90, 139, 161, 186, 310
Preisach, F. 8230
Preisman, A. 7567
Prescott, Charles M., Jr. 6986
Press Wireless, Inc. 8130
Pressler, H. 7559, 7763, 7976
Pressler, M.A.E. 3886
Preston, S.J. 8724
Preston, T.W. 4313, 4327, 4335, 4884
Price, Clair 898, 2344
Prichard, R.E. 8174, 8183
Priess, William H. 4463, 4589, 4627, 4798, 5208, 5209, 6132, 7074, 7760, 7808, 8051
Pringsheim, Peter 440
Prinz, Dietrich 2329, 2686, 2803, 3236
Prisner, S. 2024
Proctor, Mary 1157
Protzman, Albert W. 8399
Pruscino, William Vincent 1727
Poste Télégraphes et Téléphones Française 7275
Puckle, Owen Standige 3919, 4093, 4094, 4266, 4305, 4331, 4332, 4338, 4529, 4867, 5033, 5957, 6570, 8189, 8658
Pugh, David W. 4189, 4576, 4577, 5061, 5062
Pullas, C.A. 6586
Pullin, V.E. 1623, 1724
Pulvari-Pulvermacher, K. 4224, 4441
Pupin, Michael Idvorsky 1222, 1315, 3434, 3435
Purdue University 8624
Pye 7126-8
Pye Ltd. 7587, 7706, 7909, 7932, 7941, 8058, 8060, 8068, 8081, 8256
Pye Radio 3558, 3559, 6645

Rabourdin 244
Rabuteau, Guy 6363, 8210, 8521
Radio Board. *See* Federal Radio Commission
Radio City 2779, 7003
Radio Corporation of America (RCA) 626, 628, 756, 1185, 1470, 1495, 1616, 1668, 1813, 1822, 1902, 1935, 1974, 2124, 2130, 2247, 2433, 2498, 2502, 2738, 2821, 2911, 3072, 3111, 3295, 3446, 3450, 3971, 4290, 4718, 4869, 5042, 5051, 5080, 5158, 5164, 5204, 5271, 5373, 5477, 5487, 5534, 5575, 5647, 5847, 6033, 6050, 6055, 6064, 6304, 6501, 6575, 6582, 6587, 6596, 6643, 6889, 6999, 7075, 7078, 7186, 7204, 7239, 7306, 7373, 8035, 8572,

8644, 8663, 8673, 8680, 8681, 8689, 8702, 8708, 8770, 8863
patents 708, 765, 954, 1022, 1097, 1145, 1289, 1348, 1424, 1760, 1817, 1818, 1833, 1834, 1921, 1931, 1962, 1963, 2077, 2190, 2191, 2194, 2201, 2226, 2249, 2297, 2352, 2388, 2490, 2492, 2494, 2541-3, 2569, 2580, 2683, 2698, 2805, 2823, 2865, 2876, 2919, 2920, 2928, 2964, 2973, 2977, 3026, 3057, 3058, 3086, 3096, 3118, 3121, 3127, 3186, 3232, 3253, 6254, 3259-61, 3310, 3312, 3313, 3355, 3370, 3394, 3408, 3423, 3451, 3462, 3510, 3530, 3551, 3553, 3567, 3584, 3585, 3587, 3591, 3640, 3670, 3671, 3688, 3699, 3711, 3716, 3720, 3741, 3778, 3780, 3792, 3793, 3834, 3878-80, 3892, 3893, 3903, 3906, 3921, 3926, 3932, 3938-40, 3951, 3956, 3960, 4014, 4076, 4102, 4114, 4206, 4250, 4253, 4300, 4301, 4322, 4346, 4349, 4350, 4378, 4388, 4392, 4395, 4400, 4401, 4405, 4407-9, 4414, 4429, 4432-4, 4446, 4467, 4473, 4475, 4477, 4478, 4480, 4482, 4494, 4505, 4508, 4515, 4520-4, 4554, 4578, 4583, 4584, 4615, 4622, 4624, 4652, 4659, 4661, 4664, 4665, 4707, 4733, 4740, 4748, 4772, 4777, 4781-5, 4792, 4842, 4871, 4873-5, 4894, 4895, 4905, 4942, 4954, 4955, 4957, 4958, 4990, 5005, 5024, 5025, 5049, 5084, 5085, 5097, 5098, 5122, 5152, 5181, 5227, 5228, 5231, 5234, 5237, 5247, 5248, 5263, 5305, 5306, 5309, 5329, 5365-8, 5370, 5415, 5420, 5430, 5431, 5433, 5434, 5451, 5473, 5474, 5500-2, 5504, 5529, 5530, 5564, 5565, 5569, 5570, 5616, 5637, 5666, 5667, 5699, 5790, 5858, 5864, 5865, 5867, 5868, 5931, 6012, 6014, 6022, 6086, 6089, 6091, 6100, 6101, 6105, 6159, 6166, 6275, 6298, 6309, 6350, 6357, 6361, 6371, 6379, 6385, 6390, 6429, 6486, 6495, 6528, 6538, 6548, 6549, 6556, 6563, 6566-9, 6602, 6622, 6625, 6631, 6634, 6677, 6699, 6701-4, 6726, 6736, 6738, 6756, 6782-4, 6798, 6813, 6829, 6837, 6876, 6880, 6888, 6892, 6897, 6907-9, 6937, 6946, 6949, 6962, 6965, 6969, 6972, 6983, 6985, 6989, 6991, 7024, 7056, 7091, 7092, 7109, 7113, 7122, 7140, 7181, 7184, 7188-92, 7194, 7219, 7234, 7248, 7261-3, 7288, 7303-5, 7328-30, 7340-3, 7356, 7358, 7405, 7416, 7421, 7423, 7432, 7435, 7443, 7461, 7566, 7467, 7485, 7489-91, 7517, 7522, 7527, 7546, 7547, 7554, 7555, 7597, 7619, 7640, 7656, 7664, 7665, 7682, 7685,
7711, 7717, 7723, 7728, 7734, 7772, 7788, 7790-2, 7817, 7842, 7858, 7871, 7872, 7888, 7889, 7891, 7892, 7901, 7906, 7910, 7931, 7962, 7966, 8014, 8022-4, 8087, 8090, 8140, 8141, 8198, 8204, 8235, 8236, 8248, 8257, 8307, 8337, 8338, 8360, 8362, 8364-7, 8431, 8439, 8442, 8482, 8484-6, 8488, 8489, 8514, 8515, 8530, 8531, 8560, 8563, 8565, 8590, 8591, 8609, 8616, 8871
RCA Communications 1928
RCA-Victor Company 2604, 2627, 3018, 3045, 3072, 3188, 4120, 4140, 4228, 4484, 4488
RCA-Victor Television Laboratories 4627, 5463, 6488, 8314, 8324, 8389
Radio Inventions 1471, 1620, 1984, 2230, 2283, 2399, 2473, 2538, 2773, 2963, 3007, 3055, 3056, 3067, 3089, 3165, 3267, 3364, 3393, 3498, 3501, 4539
Radio-Keith Orpheum (RKO) 2433, 3949
Radio Manufacturers Association (RMA) 1210, 1293, 1401, 1459, 1519, 1545, 1656, 1665, 1999, 2051, 2577, 3321, 3322, 3342, 3425, 3463, 5996, 6447, 6448, 6475, 6592, 7265, 7306, 7380, 7750, 7980, 8017, 8111, 8243, 8249, 8402
Radiolympia (radio exhibits, Olympia, London) 789, 973, 794, 1475, 1511, 1587, 2367, 2640, 3116, 3148, 3611, 4034, 4063, 4072, 4073, 4083, 4573, 4574, 4596, 6198, 6199, 6201-4, 6209, 6211, 6223, 6249, 6252-4, 6307, 6499, 6927, 7152, 7153, 7158, 7210, 7827, 7833, 7856, 7981, 8353, 8475, 8478, 8512
Radio Patents Corporation 3466, 4095, 4503, 5783, 7436
Radio Pictures Corporation 508, 509, 512–4, 519, 3171
Radio Reconstruction 3841, 4060
Radio Research Station 3907
Radio-Vision Corporation of America 7170
Raeck, F. 8215
Rag 6735, 6952
Ragsdale, C.L. 8326
Rajchman, Jan A. 5790, 7263, 7619, 7711, 8439, 8498, 8591
Ramberg, Eduard G. 6498, 7491, 8381, 8704, 8744, 8765
Ramberg, Edward J. 6381, 6901, 7555, 8096
Ramsay, William 270, 320, 393
Ramsey, A. 3406
Ramsey, George 561, 3211
Ranger, Richard Howland 626, 628, 631, 756
Rappold, Armin 8517, 8562
Rathbun, John B. 2534
Rausch, Heinrich 7841
(W.C.) Rawls & Company 3608
Raycroft, L.B.F. 1612, 1838
Rayleigh, Lord (John William Strutt) 94, 270
Ray-O-Television Manufacturing Company 3787
Ray-O-Vision Corporation of America 1406, 3787
Raytheon Manufacturing Company 1369, 1375, 1377, 1420, 1458, 1493, 1603, 1925
RCA. *See* Radio Corporation of America
Re, Filippo 308, 412
Reader, E. 5150
Recknagel, Alfred 5853, 7419
Redmond, Denis D. 108, 109, 131, 132
Reeve, A.S. 1741, 2599
Reichel, Wilhelm 5703, 6462, 8295, 8444
Reichspostzentralamt (RPZ) (German Post Office) 1843, 2055, 2065, 2173, 2368, 2552, 2584, 2595, 2598, 3039, 3131, 3146, 3207, 3210, 3377, 3618, 3630, 3768, 4103, 4166, 4175, 4194, 4213, 4245, 4492, 4591, 4883, 5053, 5217, 5251, 5318, 5513, 5575, 5731, 6025, 6103, 6144, 6231, 6848, 7145, 7270, 7320, 7916, 8404
Reick, J. 6930
Reimann, Ernst 7350
Reis, Christoph 461
Reisman, Mildred S. 2028, 2974, 3020, 3229
Reisser, Walter 2082
Reisz, Eugen 397, 434
Reith, John Charles Walsham 3477
Rennie, J. Cameron 1155, 1200, 1439, 1583, 1705, 1872
Replogle, Delbert E. 1377, 1430, 1574, 1665, 1808, 1925, 2006, 2094, 2099, 2177, 2213, 2252, 2259, 2297, 2363, 2522, 2647, 2688, 2864, 2990, 2991, 2994, 3036, 3079, 3137, 3473, 3523
Ressler, Hugh C. 5962
Rettenmeyer, Francis X. 8685
Reusse, W. 7753
Reveley, P.V. 3848, 4581, 5154, 5893, 8762
Reyner, John Hereward 4447, 5346, 5514, 7374, 8034, 8712
Reynolds, Frederick W. 566, 722, 797, 821, 2359
Reynolds, Kay 8643
Rhea, Robert 5790
Rhein, E. 2304
Rhodes, Howard E. 1493
Ribbe, Paul 316, 321, 840
Rice, M.P. 1222, 1264, 1466, 1469
Richards, Amyle P. 3315

Richards, Claude Langdon 2197, 3373, 6567, 6640, 7772
Richards, Vyvyan 1685
Richardson, H.A. 4195, 4506, 4853, 5221, 5503, 5811
Richardson, Owen Willans 304, 441, 454, 2152
Richardson, William J. 2185, 2224, 2264, 2371, 2757, 3142, 3246, 3281
Richmond, H.B. 1210, 2076, 2138
Richter, Johann 3194, 4018, 4022, 4029
Richter, Otto Schriever 3597
Ridgeway, Denis V. 7168, 7351, 8074, 8353, 8469, 8552
Rieder, H.J.R. 2670
Riesz, Robert 6910
Rife, M.W. 7206
Rigby, E.J. 5475
Righi 1942
Rignoux, Georges M. 328, 378, 382, 384, 412, 443, 815
Ring, F. 6027, 6225, 7337, 7448, 7496, 7796
Ring, Friedrich 6372, 6373
Rinia, Herre 5456, 6709, 7423, 7523, 7656, 7772, 7875, 8098
Risdon, P.J. 5435
Roberts, Coryton Ernest Carr 1304, 2348, 3208
Roberts, J.H.T. 676, 744, 1042, 1164
Roberts, J.J. 4656
Roberts, J. Varley 4466, 4485
Roberts, T.S. 2057
Robey, George 1992
Robida, Albert 180
Robinson, D.M. 7982, 8446
Robinson, E.H. 2529, 5576, 5955
Robinson, F.H. 585
Robinson, Gordon D. 3944
Robinson, I.E. 1466
Robinson, J. 1360, 1390, 1402, 1438, 1460, 1482, 1506, 1584, 1644, 1699, 1872, 2053, 2068
Robinson, J.A. 5257
Robinson, James 2506
Robinson, James Michael 3625, 5659
Rochlin, Gene I. 8785
Rodda, Sidney 4464, 4830, 6505
Rodwin, George 1818, 2003
Röntgen, Wilhelm Konrad 254-6
Rogan, John J. 2109, 2110
Rogers, Donald S. 1658
Rogers, F.H. 1334
Rogers, K.D. 742, 2035
Rogowski, Walter 4700, 4705, 4835
Rohde, L. 3647
Roizen, Joe 8846
Roll, Hans Georg 6537

Roosenstein, Hans Otto 4367, 5305, 5438, 5610, 5620, 5644, 5679, 5688, 5729, 5781, 5851, 7098, 7350, 8409
Rose, Albert 6783, 7065, 7181, 7194, 7461, 7485, 7791, 8307, 8338, 8370, 8489, 8546
Rose, O. 8686
Rosen, Herbert 3039, 7852
Rosenberg, H. 3214, 3678, 3806, 3864, 3974
Rosenberg, K. 3806, 3864
Rosenfelder, R.I. 2284
Rosenthal, Adolf Heinrich 5752, 7408, 7409, 7452, 7486, 7538, 7540, 7580, 7736, 8080, 8176, 8288, 8428
Rosenthal, Henry 3502
Rosing, Boris (L'vovich) 349, 400, 401, 403, 405-7, 411, 412, 460, 599, 649, 688, 815, 1032, 1098, 2145, 2858, 3407
Ross, Albion 5756
Ross, Gordon 8761
Ross, John King 5754
Ross, Oscar A. 2647
Rosse, 4th Earl (Laurence Parsons) 55
Rosselevich, I.A. 8835
Rotha, Paul 8737
Rothe, Horst 5391, 7514
Rothschild, Sidney 335, 460
Round, Henry Joseph 460, 765
Rowe, Cyril Leslie 1054
Rowe, James Jesse 1054
Rowe, W.S. 8272
Rowland, John 8776
Royal, John F. 5302
Royal Television Society 8734a, 8856
RPZ. See Reichspostzentralamt
RR 5513
RRG 4591, 5513
Rtcheouloff, Boris 500, 501, 863, 2183
Rudert, Frithjoh 7096, 8182, 8265, 8405, 8843
Rudkin, E.P. 6968, 7025
Rüdenberg, Reinhold 2929, 2965
Ruedy, John E. 7546, 8515
Ruff, H.R. 4592
Ruhmer, Ernest Walter 298, 372, 376, 396, 406, 411, 815, 840, 2732, 2902
Ruhmkorff, Heinrich Daniel 18, 21, 22
Rump, A. 3388
Runyon, Steven C. 8818, 8830
Rupp, H. 6988
Rushforth, Leonard 6843, 6844, 7883
Ruska, Ernst 4316, 4725, 4731, 4736, 5077, 5078, 5141, 5214, 5224, 5269, 5353, 5369, 5398, 5414, 5455, 5464, 5558, 5703, 5748, 6066, 6169, 6224, 6242, 6257, 6462, 6655
Ruska, Ernst August Friedrich 3294
Russel 6696

Russell, Alexander 772, 874, 1404
Russell, A.V.F.V. 2265
Russell, W.O. 5463
Russia (U.S.S.R.) 660, 3333, 3407, 3526, 4133, 5254, 5583, 5726, 6393, 6590, 6860, 8834, 8835
Rust, N.M. 4952, 5050, 7582, 7598
Rutherford, Robert E. 4191
Ruzicka, C. 1228
Ryde, J.W. 564
Ryftin, J. 5512

Sabbah, Camile A. 566, 678, 679
Sabine, Robert 92, 93
Sagall, Solomon 8104
St. John, Ancel 6576
Saint-René, H.C. 392, 412, 758
Sale, M.L. 53
Sallow, H. 8040
Samson 7052
Samson, K.A.R. 7990, 7432
Sanabria, Ulysses (Ulises) A. 1293, 1301, 1431, 1565, 1634, 1917, 2959, 2970, 3078, 3108, 3109, 3115, 3117, 3119, 3122, 3150, 3153, 3159, 3181, 3275, 3277, 3378, 3473, 3616, 3997, 4002, 4121, 6131, 7274, 7317, 7324, 7387, 7445, 7563, 7615, 7757
Sanchez, Alberto 1727
Sandell, Henry K. 497
Sanders, A.W. 1646
Sanderson, J. 8812
Sandilands, John 8821
Sangor, B.W. 1325
Sarasin, Edouard 47, 49
Sardina, Camille Casimir Antoine 598
Sarnoff, David 937, 1110, 1222, 1315, 1466, 1720, 1744, 2247, 2350, 2480, 2911, 2930, 3111, 3112, 3125, 4620, 4761, 4814, 4869, 5042, 5043, 5051, 5059, 5080, 5235, 5534, 5997, 6366, 6433, 6440, 6441, 7075, 7205, 7231, 7444, 8376, 8391, 8504, 8641, 8674, 8775, 8836, 8846, 8862
Sawyer, William Edward 134, 135, 412
Schade, Otto H. 6989
Schadow, R. 2454
Schaffernicht, Walter 4686, 4687, 4868, 4892, 5505, 6151, 6513
Schagen, P. 8844
Schantz, J.D. 7057
Scharfnagel, Rudolf 7944
Scheppmann, Wilhelm 4920
Scherzer, O. 4749, 6512
Schewe, E. 381
Schienemann, Rudolf 4946
Schiff, Ludwig 3051, 4423, 4424
Schiffenbauer, R.G. 5583
Schildenfeld, Rudolf 782

Schiller, Saul 6751
Schleede, Arthur 4016, 4270
Schlesinger, Kurt 2361, 4017, 4245, 8765
 patents 2357, 2921, 3053, 3189, 3230, 3262, 3346, 3347, 3350, 3352-4, 3366, 3397, 3398, 3412, 3413, 3432, 3443-5, 3485, 3493, 3512, 3513, 3542, 3548, 3549, 3552, 3554, 3555, 3561, 3562, 3568, 3586, 3606, 3632, 3633, 3658-60, 3676, 3677, 3680, 3681, 3685, 3687, 3700, 3718, 3745, 3746, 3750, 3783, 3784, 3822, 3862, 3872-5, 3933, 3934, 3954, 3958, 3972, 3986, 3992, 3996, 4006-8, 4013, 4015, 4059, 4112, 4134, 4144, 4158, 4160, 4161, 4167, 4193, 4198, 4200, 4216, 4256, 4260, 4271, 4302, 4312, 4333-7, 4341, 4342, 4361, 4411, 4421, 4430, 4431, 4442, 4458, 4459, 4500, 4507, 4545, 4564, 4602, 4608, 4637, 4638, 4657, 4658, 4678, 4683, 4695-8, 4720, 4728, 4743, 4763, 4767, 4779, 4786, 4870, 4893, 4948, 4953, 4982, 5027, 5038, 5063, 5072, 5124, 5143, 5151, 5157, 5186, 5230, 5238, 5240, 5244, 5266, 5268, 5291, 5386, 5407, 5408, 5421, 5467, 5469, 5480, 5526, 5551, 5587, 5588, 5590, 5591, 5596, 5606, 5628, 5674, 5685, 5735, 5770, 5777, 5792, 5842, 5843, 5882, 5921, 5973, 5981, 5986, 6058, 6074, 6076, 6152, 6162, 6184, 6250, 6259, 6260, 6284, 6323, 6330, 6374, 6414, 6439, 6454, 6483, 6541, 6550, 6559, 6560, 6674, 6694, 6697, 6746, 6971, 7040, 7097, 7136, 7137, 7219, 7247, 7250, 7297, 7351, 7466, 7480, 7513, 7542, 7573, 7641, 7653, 7686, 7725, 7780, 8205, 8465
Schloemilch, Wilhelm 420, 4919
Schmidling, Gilbert T. 1784, 2614, 8208
Schmierer, M. 387, 412
Schnabel, W. 4729, 5584, 6088
Schneider et Cie 1751
Schneider, R. 309, 412
Schnitger, Herbert 7708
Schnurmacher, E.C. 7616
Schöffler, B. 279
Schoenberg, I. 5409
Schoenberg, Virgil A. 1674
Schofield, Lemuel B. 8735
Scholz, Werner 3646, 4489, 4758, 5081, 5313, 5800
Schoultz, Edvard Gustav 488, 1271, 1871
Schraeder, Frank J., Jr. 619
Schrage, Wilhelm E. 4968, 5032, 5166, 5254, 5582, 6127, 7071
Schriever, O. 3483, 3701, 3733, 4031
Schroeder, Willy 7588
Schröter, Fritz 810, 840, 2080, 2167, 2316, 2406, 2417, 2466, 2531, 2666, 2777, 2787, 2849, 2905, 2997, 3042, 3483, 3775, 4619, 4815, 6233, 6302, 6849, 7375
 patents 943, 949, 980, 1090, 1617, 2581, 2737, 2815, 2861, 3013, 3074, 3218, 3543, 3597, 3857, 4016, 4019, 4020, 4045, 4049, 4146, 4262, 4270, 4281, 4543, 4908, 5242, 5267, 5284, 5340, 5354, 5380, 5457, 5556, 5665, 5938, 6229
Schubert, A. 3515
Schubert, Georg 2623, 2813, 2844, 2860, 2881, 2981, 3028, 3098, 3183, 3217, 3240, 3517, 4078, 4118, 5250, 5619, 6655
Schütz, W. 4379
Schulz'sche A.-G. 1024
Schunack, Johannes 5001, 5557, 5599, 6066, 7096
Schuster, Arthur 182, 197, 212
Schwartz Erich 3309, 4498, 4709, 5101, 5137, 5141, 5455, 5672, 6540, 6598, 6820, 8407
Science Museum, London
 Baird apparatus presented 796
 television exhibition (1937) 6923, 6957, 6964, 6966, 7145, 7368
Scophony Television 4033, 4718, 5575, 5720, 6285, 6292, 7537, 7586, 7770, 7808, 7982, 8063, 8104, 8387, 8602, 8604, 8867
 patents 1542, 4308, 4360, 4428, 4747, 5018, 5362, 5476, 5488, 5600, 5622, 5623, 5658, 5709, 5862, 5934, 6314, 6451, 6525, 6723, 6747, 6826, 6845, 6846, 6953-5, 7209, 7232, 7275, 7338, 7345, 7408, 7409, 7418, 7451, 7452, 7486, 7538-40, 7580, 7605, 7736, 7898, 7900, 8080, 8134, 8279, 8288, 8330, 8412, 8428, 8433, 8446-9, 8462, 8556
Scophony Corporation of America 7540
Scotland 2275, 2369
Scott, Walter Dill 2386
Scott, W.J. 6654
Scroggie, Marcus Graham 5160, 8749
Scully, C.T. 8550
Seager, G.W. 4570, 4904
Seaman, E.C.H. 8541
Secor, Henry Winfield 969, 973, 1001, 1239, 1312, 2126
Secrest, J.D. 2648
Secunda, Eugene 8875
Seeley, Stuart W. 7207, 7358, 7568, 7728, 7800, 7889, 7891, 8056, 8227, 8362
Seguin, Augustin 575
Seguin, Laurent 575
Seitz, F. 8382
Seldes, G. 7616
Selényi, Paul 4390, 7697
Selfridges (demonstrations in department store) 662, 664, 675, 1137, 1139, 1275, 1648, 3614
Sellers, Gilbert 367, 5437
Selsdon, Lord (William Mitchell-Thompson) 4466, 4656, 4691, 4711, 4761, 4805, 4818-20, 4886, 4960, 5104, 5113, 8157. *See also* Selsdon report *under* Television Advisory Committee
Selvey, Dora 1167, 1168, 1177, 1186, 1207
Senlecq, Constantin 104-6, 154, 165, 192, 354, 360, 412
Sensicle, Laurence Henry 571
Settel, Irving 8786
Sewall, Charles Henry 290
Shannon, D.S.B. 5489, 7986, 7994, 8067, 8070, 8252, 8333, 8359, 8474, 8527, 8559, 8581
Sharma, Devendra Nath 1393, 1417
Sharpe 7032
Shaw, H.J. 7417
Shaxby, J.H. 600
Sheffield, B. 8094
Shelby, Robert Evart 7003, 7405, 8367
Sheldon, H. Horton 1899, 1915, 2917
Shelton, E.E. 7017, 7018, 8304
Sherman, J.B. 7876, 8103, 8161
Shiers, George 95, 98, 323, 339, 8785, 8787, 8789, 8796, 8798, 8803, 8808, 8828, 8833, 8837, 8850
Shiers, May 8798
Shinton, Joseph Sidney 1423
Shmakoff, P. 7693
Shmakov, Paul 3333, 5515, 5726
Shockley, William 7818, 7844
Shoenberg, Isaac 4136, 4471, 4814, 5409, 7183, 8664, 8790, 8791, 8847
Shorney, A.B. 4710
Short, Donald William 2644, 3031, 3408
Short Wave & Television Laboratory, Inc. 1897, 1928, 2103, 2294, 2458, 2460, 2886, 2896, 2935, 2970, 2993, 3011, 3094
Shrage, W.E. 7614
Shrewsbury, John B. 1592
Shulman, Arthur 8777
Shumaker, E.E. 2604, 2627
Shumard, C.C. 7978, 8047
Shunaman, Fred 8738
Sicuranza, Charles 7877, 8509, 8571
Siebertz, Karl 6496
Sieger, J. 5488, 6315, 6845, 6846, 7345, 7539, 8447
Siemens, Charles William (or Carl Wilhelm) 67
Siemens, (Ernst) Werner 56, 63, 64
Siemens & Halske A.-G. 717, 1809, 1947, 2910, 5870, 6057, 6496, 6529, 6669, 6977

Siemens-Schuckertwerke A.-G. 2929
Siepmann, Charles A. 8713
Sieveking, Lance 2525
Silberstein, Ludwik 1756, 1893
Silberston, Z.A. 8802
Silver, W.D. 6653
Simms, C.H. 6073, 6652, 6808, 6898
Simon 412
Simon, H. 3762
Simpson, L.M. 4304
Sinding-Larsen, Alf 388, 460, 463
Singleton, Thomas 8867
Skala, Ljubomir William 619, 1334
Skala Research Laboratories 1334
Skaupy, Franz 465, 1923, 2485, 5355
Skellett, Albert M. 6789, 6936, 7363, 8169, 8308, 8598
Skinner, G.D. 4928
Skinner, James M. 5996
Skorstad, James B. 1180
Slaby 181
Sleeper, M.B. 1770
Sleeper, William Blake 8630
Sloane, Thomas O'Conor 730
Smith, Alfred E. 1559
Smith, C.G. 1377
Smith, Frank 7854
Smith, H.E. 1959
Smith, John Paul 3451, 4875
Smith, Lester Harsen 8553
Smith, Newland F. 8283
Smith, S.B. 1425
Smith, Theodore A. 1818, 1834, 1921, 1931, 1962, 1963, 2003, 8145
Smith, Willoughby 50-2, 68, 83, 228, 636, 2705
Smith, W.V. 8812
Smith-Rose, R.L. 8667
Smyth, Charles Norman 7455, 7456, 7477, 7828, 7829, 7893, 7894, 7904, 7943, 7948, 7986, 7999, 8115, 8116, 8129, 8174, 8183, 8306, 8309, 8339, 8466, 8534
Snow, Harold A. 3551
Snowden, Mrs. Philip 2942
Snyder, Richard L. 6081, 6387, 6432, 6847, 6939-41, 6973, 7301, 7302, 7305, 7812, 7938
Snyder, Richard L., Jr. 7435, 7608, 7619, 7792, 8439, 8531
Société Indépendente de Télégraphie sans Fil 1412, 1413
Société Anonyme 5943
Sofar 5575, 6376, 6377
Sohnemann, K. 2714
Soller, Walter 4526, 4791, 7116, 7214, 7813
Solzberg, Bernard 4759
Somers, Frank J. 6402, 7058, 7198
Sommer, Alfred 8008, 8188, 8429

Sommer, P. 1716
Sommerfeld, Ernest 4028
Soundie, L.H. 4373
South Africa 1385, 1698, 2010, 2023, 2087, 2188, 2670, 5254
Soward, Alfred W. 168
Spain 5254
Sparks, William 3303
Spencer, Rolf Edmund 5091, 6297, 6945, 7475
Spengler, Otto 5769
Spiegel, Felix 6975
Spindler, H. 1858
Spooner, Henry John 577
Sposa, Louis A. 8687
Spottiswoode, William 57, 58, 72, 77-9, 96, 113, 149, 163, 164, 171
Sprague, Carlton S. 5370
Spratt, Hector Gordon Merson 6147
Sprayberry, F.L. 7388
Sprengel, Hermann Johann Philipp 39, 166
Stacho, Michel 2378
Stager, A. 6139
Stalnecker, Edward L. 2701
Standard Television and Electric Corporation 3278, 3876
Stanley, Lulu 2062
Stark, Johannes 300, 471
Starr, Arthur T. 4517, 8134
Statz, Willi 6805
S.T.C. patents 1891, 5096, 5123, 5125, 5344, 5403, 5562, 5922, 6095, 6118-21, 6180, 6207, 6272, 6276, 6355, 6364, 6365, 6424, 6788, 6866, 6894, 6911, 6912, 7161, 7158, 7220, 7420, 7434, 7530, 7592, 7646, 7713, 7742, 7766, 7769, 7774, 7785, 7928, 7959, 8021, 8113, 8122, 8131, 8184, 8185, 8255, 8284, 8339, 8359, 8440, 8466, 8474, 8527, 8550, 8555, 8559, 8581-3, 8613
Stepanov, R.M. 8834
Stephan, Walther 217, 333, 358
Stephenson, William Samuel 527, 537, 661
Sterling, Christopher H. 8735, 8839
Sterling, Louis 4471
Stern, Milton M. 4348
Steudel, Eberhard 5707, 5710, 5765, 5797, 6013, 6041, 6054, 6185, 6542
Stevens, S.T. 5896, 6791, 7636–9
Stevens, Walter Henry 4890, 5290, 7635
Stewart-Warner 8324
Stille, Curt 421
Stocker, Arthur C. 2613, 4508, 4652, 4748, 5024, 7063
Stokes, George Gabriel 19
Stolëtov, Aleksandr Grigorjevic 208, 1942

Stoll, Oswald 6614
Stoller, Hugh M. 966, 974, 992, 998, 2298, 2341, 2447
Stone, Thomas E., Jr. 2499, 2578
Stoney, George Johnstone 223, 247, 343
Stoyanowsky, A.T. 3540, 3910
Strachan, James 603
Strafford, F.R.W. 6716
Strange, John William 6141, 7618, 7884
Strange, Robert William 1117
Stranger, Ralph 2709, 8649
Strauss, Siegmund 397
Strecker, F. 8132
Strieby, M.E. 4625, 7437, 7689, 7744
Stromberg-Carlson Telephone Mfg. Co. 8000
Strübig, Heinrich 5672, 5898, 5990, 6337, 6613, 6796, 8551
Strupf, F. 7337
Strutt, John William. See Rayleigh
Strutt, M.J.O. 8043, 8231, 8493
Stumf, F. 4492
Sturmey, S.G. 8743
Subrizi, Victor 2340
Süddeutsche Telefon-Apparate-, Kabel-, und Drahtwerke. See Tekade
Suhomann, R. 3762
Sukumlyn, Thomas W. 2922, 7571, 7951
Susskind, Charles 8854
Sutcliffe, W. 1249
Sutton, Henry 181, 213, 391, 412
Suzuki, S. 4490
Swan, Joseph Wilson 20, 23
Sweden 253
Sweeney, William H. 3158
Swift, F.G. 3916
Swift, John 8714
Swinton, (Alan Archibald) Campbell 255, 259, 261, 264, 286, 366, 410, 413, 414, 566, 586, 587-9, 718, 805, 840, 1271, 1314, 1318, 1354, 1360, 1390, 1391, 1402, 1408, 1474, 1483, 1550, 1556, 1623, 1701, 1724, 1739, 1815, 1871, 1918, 1949, 2155, 2710, 2924, 3324, 6340, 6923, 8829, 8852, 8856
Switzerland 3728
Sykes, Eugene O. 902, 4151
Sylven, Gustaf 6110
Sylvester, Cyril 1442, 1508, 1588, 1650, 1703, 1740, 1776, 1830, 1907, 1909, 1938, 2269
Syphrit, Samuel Thomas 1465
Szczepanik, Jan 262, 269, 272-4, 282, 283, 330, 412, 815
Szegho, C. 5212, 5236, 5241, 5307, 5750, 5835, 5866, 6011, 6157, 6178, 6935
Szenyovsky, Ladislaus 1024
Tainter, Charles Sumner 126
Tait, Robert W. 1232
Takahashi, S. 4669

Takayanagi, Kenjiro 1667, 3376, 3440, 3472, 3712, 3739, 3751, 4068, 4490, 4629, 4630, 4668, 4669, 6126, 7033
Tallent, Stephen 8512
Tambert, Elmer A. 1764
Tanimoto, Frank Ryozo 1451
Tanner, R.W. 3136, 3170
Tarzian 8878
Tate, Alfred Orde 1526, 1664, 1680, 1889, 2111, 2493, 2508
Tawil, E.P. 3304
Taylor, A. Hoyt 2114
Taylor, C.T. 8802
Taylor, F. Sherwood 8632
Taylor, G.R.R. 3282
Taylor, Maurice Kenyon 4437, 4605, 4999, 5359, 5377, 5378, 5761, 5955, 6109, 6338, 6503, 6980, 7483, 7673, 7674, 7809, 7869, 7991
Taylor, S. Gordon 6853
Taynton, William 733, 1329, 1781
Teal, G.K. 6466-8, 7130, 7144, 7479, 8131
Teale, E. 6235
Tebo, Julian E. 8838
Tedham, William Francis 3602, 3705, 3785, 4100, 4136, 4257, 4397-9, 7183, 7940
Teichmann, Horst 3759
Tekade (TKD) (Süddeutsche Telefon-Apparate-, Kabel-, und Drahtwerke A.-G.) 2975, 3047, 3048, 3103, 3146, 3207, 3210, 3269, 3618, 3630, 3655, 3827, 3858, 3904, 3935, 3973, 3990, 4103, 4123, 4190, 4196, 4245, 4591, 4611, 4877, 5319, 5513, 5575, 7320
Telefunken Gesellschaft für Drahtlose Telegraphie m.b.H. 810, 1187, 1514, 1890, 2726, 2776, 2777, 2980, 3630, 3732, 4103, 4213, 4234, 4245, 4591, 4879, 5319, 5342, 5438, 5507, 5513, 5575, 5644, 5679, 6590, 6591, 6645, 7145, 7273, 7320
  patents 420, 734, 943, 949, 980, 1077, 1090, 1091, 1221, 1617, 1750, 1795, 1802, 1820, 1916, 1919, 2150, 2192, 2198, 2200, 2236, 2291, 2329, 2354, 2394, 2581, 2686, 2737, 2803, 2815, 2861, 3013, 3050, 3059, 3069, 3074, 3194, 3195, 3218, 3231, 3236, 3292, 3305, 3307, 3402, 3466, 3532, 3543, 3597, 3599, 3634, 3686, 3701, 3733, 3809, 3810, 3857, 3860, 3863, 3989, 4016, 4019, 4020, 4022-30, 4042-5, 4049, 4098, 4109, 4146, 4153, 4164, 4258, 4262, 4270, 4281, 4300, 4301, 4317, 4319, 4328, 4367, 4391, 4436, 4543, 4549, 4707, 4708, 4722, 4737, 4738, 4787, 4817, 4877, 4908, 4909, 4918, 4923, 4940, 4943, 4944, 4946,
4973, 4974, 4989, 5036, 5056, 5192-4, 5232, 5242, 5267, 5277, 5280, 5284, 5292, 5294, 5303, 5321, 5330, 5340, 5349, 5354, 5356, 5380, 5391, 5404, 5405, 5424, 5444, 5445, 5457, 5458, 5499, 5527, 5545, 5552, 5556, 5621, 5665, 5676, 5680, 5687, 5688, 5714, 5767, 5769, 5779, 5840, 5859, 5890, 5904, 5905, 5924, 5976, 5985, 6053, 6061, 6093, 6104, 6163, 6229, 6258, 6375, 6383, 6413, 6438, 6479, 6604, 6649, 6686, 6760, 6802, 6822, 6862, 6882, 6951, 6959, 6960, 6963, 6970, 6979, 6990, 7006, 7013, 7103, 7112, 7350, 7401, 7415, 7424, 7429, 7469, 7481, 7487, 7488, 7512, 7515, 7544, 7606, 7714, 7861, 7866, 8072
Telefunken-Karolus 810, 1187, 1514, 1890, 2055
TELEVISION (official journal of the Television Society until 1930)
  first issue 1152
Television Inc. 3295
Television Ltd. (Baird) 676, 736, 2332
  patents 704, 706, 737, 761, 797, 798-800, 814, 833, 860, 863, 893, 982, 1011, 1018, 1025, 1064, 1082, 1083, 1106, 1213-5, 1225, 1252, 1257, 1267, 1268, 1284-7, 1297-1300, 1335-7, 1409, 1477, 1521, 1522, 1527-30, 1544, 1600, 1601, 1659, 1721, 1722, 1747, 1759, 1892, 1961, 2197, 2199, 2203, 2233, 2240, 2509, 2536, 2650
Television Advisory Committee (to GPO, U.K.) 4450, 4452, 4453, 4465, 4466, 4485, 4509, 4595, 4656, 4688, 4691, 4711, 4745, 4775, 4799, 4818, 4976, 5272, 7854, 8664
  report of the committee (1935; Selsdon report) 4788, 4801-7, 4819, 4820, 4822, 4886, 4888, 4960, 4964, 5039, 5104, 5113, 5145, 5146
Television-Baird-Nathan 2738
Television Committee (U.S.) 8298, 8622, 8623
  Committee on Color Television 8708
Television and Electric Corporation of America 4404
Television Laboratories, Inc. 850, 1079, 1109, 1216, 1227, 1619, 2279, 2477, 2548, 2549, 2676, 3008, 3794, 4053
Television Manufacturing Company of America 3201, 3319
Television Society (of Great Britain) 1043, 1152, 1154, 1157, 1201, 1449, 1515, 1582, 1585, 1651, 1704, 1738, 1780, 1792, 1804, 1832, 1872, 1910, 1980, 2009, 2019, 2061, 2089, 2139, 2183, 2272, 2318, 2348, 2368, 2370, 2377, 2733, 2859, 2870, 2883, 2901,
3174, 3845, 4177, 4354, 4380, 4595, 4885, 8155, 8157, 8814
  first formal meeting 1247, 1277
  became Royal Television Society in 1966 8856
Television Supplies Ltd. 238
Tellegen, Bernardus Dominicus Hubertus 5459
Tenny, Lloyd S. 2768
Termen, L.C. 1035
Terrell, W.D. 1466
Terry, V.J. 7161
Tervo, Oscar 1662
Tetzman, Carl 6134
Teves, Marten Cornelis 4325, 5087, 5563, 5585, 6726, 6798, 6962, 7092, 7234
Theile, Richard 3245, 5031, 7401
Thilo, Hans Georg 1809
Thöm, Kurt 6678, 8073, 8430
Thomas, Albert B. 6947
Thomas, L. 8631
Thompson, Harry C. 5152
Thompson, M.W. 8105, 8166, 8224, 8271
Thompson, R.T. 8270
Thompson, Silvanus Phillips 199, 202
Thompson, William H. 338
Thomsen, Paul H. 1237
Thomson, A.F.H. 7736, 7900
Thomson, E.E. 6762, 7451
Thomson, Joseph John 224, 237, 247, 266, 267, 280, 311, 315, 340, 357, 1942
Thornton, A.A. 7836, 8334, 8343-5, 8352
Thuau, Urbain Jules 1146
Thun, Rudolph 1886, 2244, 2410, 2587, 2621, 2978, 3239, 3383, 3518, 3520, 3644, 3730, 4754, 5437
Thurm, Leon 863, 876, 958, 1014, 1088, 1292, 1313, 1554, 1689
Tierney, Clarence 1154, 1157, 1352, 1379, 1733, 2087, 2140, 2181, 2188, 2357
Tihanyi, Kalman (Koloman) 1289, 1290, 1339, 7167
Tiller, P.A. 7828, 7894
Tilsley, Frank 8703
Tiltman, Ronald Frank 872, 1059, 1098, 1160, 1278, 1503, 1507, 1517, 1569, 1587, 4116
Tingley, George Richard 4988, 5061, 5062, 5073, 5338, 5390, 5785, 5991, 6484, 6839, 6842, 7410, 7721, 7819
Tival 360
TKD. *See* Tekade
Todd, Leonard Pierce 1541, 2745
Toepler, August Joseph Ignaz 33, 39
Tole, Ernest William 7536
Tolson, William A. 1960, 2492, 2973, 3312, 3423, 4392, 4405, 4444, 4520,

4454, 4664, 4672, 4733, 5025, 5085, 5504, 5716, 6289, 8616
Tomes, G.A.R. 6011, 6935, 8170
Topping, Malachi C. 8810
Torrabadella, Pedro 861
Torres, H.Z. 5068
Toulon, Pierre Marie Gabriel 5197, 5450, 5451, 5496, 5632, 5913, 5995, 6059, 6062, 6950, 6961, 7399
Towers, Natalie 2957
Town, G.R. 8635
Townsend, Henry 1641
Townsend, John Sealy Edward 448
Trainer, Merril A. 2602, 3510, 3587, 4671, 5801
Traub, E. 4106, 4662, 4723, 4726, 4956, 5549, 5711, 5964, 6348, 6349, 7221-4
Traub, Ernest H. 3131, 3207, 3210, 3618, 3730, 4148, 4156, 4177, 4245, 4591, 4646, 5108, 5513, 6502, 7320, 7981
Traubenberg, H.F.R. von 7841
Trav-Ler Manufacturing Corporation 3474
Travers, Morris William 270
Treadwell, Louis L. 974
Treloar, L.R.G. 6652, 6801
Trenton, Leslie 2135
Triggs, W.W. 2484, 2548, 2549, 4369, 4440
Tringham, W.S.L. 4990, 5415
Troller, A. 638
Trouant, Virgil E. 1749
Truefitt, E.V. 7353
Truell, John 6969
Trutolife 5489
Tryon, G.C. 6051, 6447, 6448
Tschernyschev A.A. 573, 660, 721
Tschörner, Ludwig 1384, 2106
T.T.S. 3838
Tucker, John D. 8791
Tuczek, F. 3483
Turk, Walter E. 8793
Turnbull, I.L. 8218, 8494
Turner, F.S. 4847-52
Turner, Norman 2369
Tuthill, C.A. 7850
Twain, Mark 274
Tyers, Paul D. 7376
Tyler, Kingdon S. 8675

Udelson, Joseph H. 8855
Ullswater, Lord 5002, 6051
Ultra Electric Ltd. 7503
United Research 1756, 1893
United States. *Passim and see, e.g.,* B.T.L., G.E., RCA, Farnsworth, Jenkins, Zworykin, 3237, 8748, 8752, 8810, 8855

United States Radio and Television Corporation 1896
Universal and General Radio Company Ltd. 1877, 1878, 1885, 2235
Uralov, V.A. 8834
Urtel, Rudolf 4258, 4436, 4737, 4738, 4940, 4943, 4944, 4973, 4974, 5056, 5192, 5194, 5277, 5280, 5349, 5444, 5458, 5871, 5905, 5924, 5976, 6163, 6391, 6882, 6960, 6963, 6990, 7352, 8406
U.S.S.R. *See* Russia

Vacuum-Science Products Ltd. 7699, 7700, 8247, 8287, 8303, 8351, 8476
Valensi, Georges 526, 822, 983, 1069, 1149, 1187, 4961, 5029, 5099, 7411
Valentine, P.W.S. 8153
Vance, Arthur W. 2104, 2964, 3394, 3671, 4414, 4445, 4473, 4475, 4523, 4578, 4615, 4624, 4665, 4785, 4957, 4970, 4971, 5719, 6014, 6295, 6784, 8450, 8560
van den Berg, Aart 7680
Van den Bosch, François Joseph Gerard 4839, 4840, 5198, 5199, 5736, 6913, 7008, 7009, 7093, 7155, 7699, 7700, 8247, 8287, 8303, 8351, 8415, 8476
Van de Velde, H.R.C. 4471, 7169
van der Mark, Jan 5004, 5126, 5581, 6392, 6738, 7384, 7734, 8525
van der Ziel, A. 8493
Vangen, A.I. 8113, 8440
Van Mierlo, Stanislas 5562
van Overbeek. *See* Overbeek
Van Schie, J.W.A. 2018
Varian Associates 8857
Varian, Dorothy 8857
Varian, Russell H. 3348, 4911-7, 8857
Varian, Sigurd 8857
Varley, Cromwell Fleetwood 48
Veenemann, C.F. 6780, 6781
Veernemans, Cornelius Frederik 4325
Venis, Adolph 5004
Verbeek, Henri Petrus Johan 5459
Ver. Gluh. A.-G. 6222, 7195
Vermillion, Charles O. 2605
Verne, Denison A. 1444
Verrals, J.M. 2134
Vestergren, Harry Einar Maurits 6110
Vierl, Hermann 4403
Vil'dgrube, G.S. 8834
Villeneuve, R. 7913
Vinogradov, C.N. 1688
Vipond, L.C. 2846
Visrschers, P.A.J. 8255
Vogel, T. 7275
Vol'fke, M. 276, 393
von Ardenne. *See* Ardenne

von Bronk. *See* Bronk
von Lieben. *See* Lieben
von Mihály. *See* Mihály
von Okolicsányi. *See* Okolicsányi
von Traubenberg. *See* Traubenberg
Vorobieff, A. 2396
Voss, August 607, 731
Voulgré, Andre Denis Joseph Antoine 447
Vrabely, T. 4439

Wade, Clem F. 2863
Wade, Harold 497
Waddell, Peter 8811, 8812, 8825, 8873
Wagner, Carl J. 1067
Wainwright, Lawrence 2746
Wald, George 1810, 1927, 1997, 2443, 2630, 6752, 8202
Waldrop, F.C. 8035
Walker, Jack L. 1607
Walker, John (Jimmy) 2159, 3017, 3022
Walker, Louis Edward Quintrell 2919, 2928, 3003, 3187, 3358, 3415, 3457, 3622, 3668, 3669, 3880, 3921, 4088, 4130, 4252, 4253, 4408, 4648, 4649, 4894, 5005
Walker, R. 3083
Walker, Ronald Claude 3943, 4793, 8036, 8618
Wall, Charles A. 4320
Wallace, Richard Edgar 2190, 2191, 2569
Waller, L.C. 8207
Walsh, J.W.T. 2705
Walter, Derek Oscar 5535, 6286, 7238
Walters, Douglas 2575, 2600
Walton, George William 527, 537, 661, 1542, 1748, 2612, 2652, 2750, 2782, 2783, 2785, 2786, 2792, 3160, 3351, 3368, 3598, 3694, 3727, 3970, 4155, 4210, 5018, 5269, 5323, 6525, 6954, 8556
Waltz, G.H. 2986, 3033, 3077, 3135, 3168, 3198, 3244, 3317, 3386
Warmisham, A. 5561
Warnecke, Robert 6360, 6378, 7589
Warren, G.W. 8471
Warren, H. 5271, 5310
Warren, H.W.H. 7572
Warschauer, Frank 1590
Washburne, R.D. 4120, 5254, 6128, 7073
Waters, A.A. 1910, 1912, 1939, 1982, 2012, 2059, 2086, 2137, 2186, 2220, 2242, 2266, 2313, 2655
Watson, Arthur H. 1789, 1791, 1855, 2262
Watson, D.S. 5135, 6745
Watson, G.H. 6718
Watson-Watt, Robert A. 3907
Weald, Geoffrey 2277
Webster, H. 8107
Wedge, H.F. 7518

Wehnelt, Artur Rudolph Barthold 299, 301, 306, 312, 317, 325-7
Wehnert, Waldemar 3236
Weiller, Jean Lazare 204, 412, 2842
Weiller, P.A. 3323
Weimer, Paul K. 8816
Weinberger, Julius 1817, 1818, 2003, 2194
Weinhart, Howard W. 2071, 2330, 4276, 4277
Weiss, C.L. 7744, 8533
Weiss, E.H. 1118
Weiss, G. 4764, 4765, 5251, 5798, 6480, 6515
Weiss, Georg 6372, 6918, 7406, 7412, 7705, 7726
Weiss, J.G. 8404
Wellman, Fred C. 2534
Wells, H.G. 937
Wells, R.S. 7572
Wemheuer, K. 7382, 8006
Wendt, Karl R. 6022, 6563, 6985, 8024
Wenstrom, William H. 3324, 3387, 4080
Werner, Richard W. 4651
Wertz, Hugh S. 6910
West, A.G.D. 4047, 4048, 4105, 4541, 4556, 5110, 5177, 5179, 5324-6, 5341, 5416, 8614
West, Donald W. 6031, 7501
West, J. 8386
West, S. 7308, 7502, 7505, 8240, 8323, 8355, 8456, 8508, 8543, 8633
Westcott, C.H. 1647
Western Electric Company (W.E.) 457, 473, 552, 567, 713
Western Electric Company, Ltd. 1676
Western Television Corporation 1917, 2027, 2458, 2481, 2677, 2863, 2976, 3219, 3257, 3318
Westinghouse Electric and Manufacturing Company (W.E.&M.) 556, 566, 695, 801, 916, 947, 1000, 1050, 1306, 1395, 1407, 1457, 1468, 1488, 1505, 1558, 1568, 1579, 1712, 1718, 1749, 1757, 1788, 1819, 1864, 1951, 1995, 2092, 2104, 2107, 2282, 2379, 2398, 2642, 2847, 3190, 3416, 3841, 6129, 8324
  patent suit against RCA over Zworykin's inventions 6064
Westman, Harold P. 1368
Wheeler, Harold A. 7612, 7902, 7926, 7974, 7983, 7989, 8084, 8124, 8201, 8203, 8314, 8340, 8374, 8561
Whilems, C.J. 4983
Whipple, R.R. 4247
Whiston, Ernest William 486
Whitaker, Alfred 2426, 2476, 2571
White, 6208, 6532, 6744, 6758, 7355, 7830

White, Edwin Lee 3765, 6682, 7286, 7287, 7579, 7581
White, Eric Lawrence Casling 3897, 4051, 4239, 4692, 4929, 4937, 4975, 5148, 5195, 5196, 5206, 5331, 5655, 5656, 5881, 6750, 6827, 7233, 7236, 7241, 7251, 7286, 7287, 7521, 7652, 7654, 7658, 7743, 7778, 8291
White, G.W. 5086, 5465, 5524
White, H.A. 4471
White, Hardwick 6730
Whitten, William Henry 677, 1000, 2183
Wiedemann, Eilhard Ernst Gustav 150, 246
Wiedemann, F. 2620, 2175
Wienecke, Bruno 3496
Wikkenhauser, E. 5108
Wikkenhauser, Gustav 1996, 2535, 4428, 5362, 5488, 5709, 7451, 8448, 8556, 8604
Wild, R.F. 7745
Wilder, Marshall P. 4171, 4352, 4417, 4448, 7145, 7315, 7613, 7846, 7979
Wiley, H.W. 1332
Wilhelm, K. 7606
Wilhelmy, H.J. 5342
Wilkerson, Dan C. 669
Wilkins and Wright 4056
Willans, Peter William 3896, 3897, 4679, 5086, 5207, 5410, 5411, 5886, 5899, 5992, 6038, 6065, 6324, 6621, 6778, 6779, 7022, 7642, 8363, 8420
Williams, P.W. 5718, 5773
Williams, R.C.G. 8722
Williams, Robert 1829
Williams, W.E. 2544, 5607, 5611, 5970, 6524
Willingham, G.A. 8688
Wilson, Earl De Witt 2712, 3763, 4755
Wilson, Harold Albert 418
Wilson, John Charles 3729, 3914, 4089, 4176, 4243, 4461, 4462, 4525, 5519, 5955, 7377, 7692
  patents 2486, 3010, 3216, 3363, 3421, 3537, 3849, 4057, 4061, 4154, 4162, 4282, 4295, 4309, 4516, 4553, 4587, 4604, 4766, 4826, 4980, 4981, 4996, 5026, 5028, 5379, 5427, 5989, 6109, 6217, 6458, 7733, 7837-40, 7887, 7896, 7092, 8075, 8076, 8085, 8126, 8172, 8350, 7460, 8467
Wilson Laboratory 3715
Wilson, R. 3884
Wilson, R.G. 1910, 2241, 2242, 2655, 2743, 2775, 6653
Wilson Stuart Leader Tringham 4206
Wimbledon. *See under* sports
Winch, George Bluett 1328
Winch, G.T. 7325

Winckel, Fritz Wilhelm 2711, 3522, 3557, 5363, 6334, 6461, 7174, 7863, 8557
Windred G. 4356
Winfield, Bernard 652
Winters, S.R. 535, 647, 672, 715, 1695
Wired Radio 1291, 2158, 2431, 2444, 2475, 2500, 2501, 2504, 2605, 3222, 3295, 3441
Wireless Pictures 1464
Witsenberg, H.E. 3619
Witts, Alfred T. 7378
Wolf, Menno 6385, 7067
Wolff, Frederik 170
Wolff, Hans-Heinz 3781, 3993, 5301, 5490, 5536, 5553, 7034, 7099, 7100, 7590
Wolff, I. 8257
Wolfson, H. 1441, 1513, 1591, 1653, 1701, 1736, 1782, 1828, 1942, 2020, 2765, 2799, 3391
Wood 7991
Wood, A.B. 713
Wood, Howard Kingsley 3771, 4452, 4465, 4804, 5002, 5113
Wood, Hubert 7673, 7674, 7824
Wood, R.D. 8175
Woodford, John W. 2187, 2221, 2274, 2315, 2373, 2416, 2468, 2523, 2564, 2596, 2639, 2669
Woodin, William H., Jr. 4526, 4791, 7116, 7214, 7813
Woodroffe, M. 2348
Woodruffe, H. 292
Worlitz, Daniel E. 3110
Worrall, Robert H. 3589
Worthington, W.S. 5034, 5814, 5822
Wostel, John F. 6580
Wotton, E. 2618, 2619, 3566
Wraight, W.L. 5105
Wright, E.E. 3216, 4530, 4582, 4997, 5107, 5425, 5878
Wright, E.H. 4298
Wright, George Maurice 954, 1425, 5560
Wright, H.R. 2847
Wright, W.D. 2790, 3191, 3617, 3666, 6114, 7082, 7475

Yamaguchi, K. 4630, 4668
Yamashita, A. 4630, 4668
Yanczer, Peter F. 8865
Yates, Raymond Francis 2165, 2917, 8697
Yelf, J.R. 815, 1043, 1154
Youman, Roger 8777
Young, Arthur James 4345, 4396, 4583, 4623, 4742, 4842, 5309
Young, Charles J. 4673

Zeiss, Carl 6160, 7196

Zeiss Ikon A.-G. 3139, 3596, 3627, 5395, 5696, 5782, 5891, 5926, 5442, 6043-6, 6450, 6465, 6473, 6545, 6551, 6607, 6619, 7104, 7176

Zeitline, Appolinar 3502, 4863, 4998, 5007-10, 5045, 5046, 5064-7, 5129-32, 5233, 5245, 5669, 6015, 6087, 6354, 6689

Zeitline, Vladislaw 3502, 4863, 4998, 5007-10, 5045, 5046, 5064-7, 5129-32, 5233, 5245, 5669, 6015, 6087, 6354, 6689

Zenith 6895

Ziebig, K. 3377, 3645

Zillger, Arno 3569, 3590, 4275, 4589, 4627, 4702, 4703

Zimber, Raymond M. 2077

Zworykin, Vladimir Kosma 679, 702, 821, 850, 1271, 1739, 2112, 2113, 2183, 2214, 2215, 2253, 2309, 2712, 2847, 2931, 2984, 3166, 3763, 3852, 3909, 3969, 3971, 3977, 3987, 3988, 4002, 4036, 4081, 4082, 4119-21, 4169, 4229, 4290, 4291, 4368, 4497, 4589, 4755, 5051, 5158, 5412, 5436, 5477, 5578, 5649, 5722, 5804, 5873, 5877, 6030, 6034, 6393, 6500, 6855, 6870, 6889, 7059, 7066, 7184, 7208, 7275, 7383, 8016, 8019, 8320, 8496, 8498, 8519, 8644, 8676, 8704, 8715, 8744, 8768, 8831, 8849, 8851, 8878

patents 566, 581, 695, 947, 1050, 1757, 1819, 2092, 2107, 2125, 2379, 2494, 2543, 2580, 2698, 2865, 2977, 3186, 3190, 3313, 3355, 3584, 3585, 3895, 4114, 4346, 4446, 4524, 4792, 4874, 4958, 5234, 5364, 5430, 5643, 5868, 6100, 6101, 6602, 6972, 7109, 7435, 7546, 7711, 7858, 7955, 8015

court case over inventions 6064, 8016, 8019, 8167

Subject Index

acoustic resonator 621, 652
advertising (*see also* commericial television) 2635, 2671, 2834, 3612, 4079
banned by Britain 6047
aircraft and television 1853
  airborne television 1405, 1845, 1853, 1963, 1965, 6130, 8579
  airborne military surveillance 405
  aircraft detection 6166
  aircraft landing via television 2435
  control of aircraft 623, 111
  navigational aid to aircraft 1990
  transmission to aircraft 3449
amateurs and television 672, 1487, 1904, 2418, 3619, 4495, 5160, 6303, 6579, 7570
  home construction of equipment 1123 1158, 1165, 1184, 1202, 1237, 1253, 1274, 1326, 1330, 1368, 1499, 1548, 1562, 1564, 1565, 1571, 1572, 1574, 1577, 1625, 1626, 1637, 1641, 1687, 1729, 1823, 1824, 1899, 1910, 1912, 1939, 1941, 1982, 2012, 2051, 2059, 2086, 2137, 2165, 2182, 2186, 2187, 2220, 2265, 2286, 2313, 2457, 2469, 2521, 2907, 2968, 2992, 3035, 3037, 3077, 3135, 3167, 3168, 3179, 3248, 3282, 3385, 3654, 3756, 3877, 3942, 3978, 3983, 4131, 4180, 4244, 4285, 4588, 4595, 4751, 5572, 5575, 6005, 6396, 6592, 6644, 6714, 6793, 6852, 7069, 7274, 7387, 7389, 7445, 7502, 7563, 7565, 7613, 7615, 7876, 7877, 8107, 8265, 8270, 8274, 8326, 8633
  reception by amateurs 1177, 2219, 2273, 2314, 2376, 2418, 2469, 2575, 3328, 3728, 4124
  sale of components and kits for amateurs 1137, 1139, 1238, 1260, 1275, 1308, 1493, 1633, 1637, 2312, 2325, 2371, 2461, 2469, 2595, 2853, 2896, 2935, 2936, 3033, 3036, 3038, 3116, 3145, 3154, 3200, 3201, 3276, 3278, 4032, 4122, 4899, 7978, 7980, 8050, 8100, 8164, 8263, 8571
apartment buildings, special problems of television 4418, 6445, 6446
audience (*see also* receivers, numbers of) 2789, 6507
Audion 339, 428, 436, 452, 4006

bandwidth. *See* frequency bandwidth
black-level control 4145, 4613, 7783, 7839
black-light. *See* infrared and Noctovision
black-spot correction 5859, 5905
Braun tube (earlier called indicator tube; *see also* cathode-ray tube, picture tube) 211, 263, 301, 326, 336, 373, 411, 805, 1048, 2167, 2360, 2361, 2451, 2793, 3131, 3132, 3380, 3467, 3754, 4502, 4666, 4667, 4768, 4833, 4834, 4878, 6516
  patents 349, 465, 2657, 2696, 2829, 2966, 2967, 3030, 3053, 3230, 3262, 3345, 3354, 3466, 3496, 3541, 3555, 3556, 3594, 3605, 3658, 3676, 3680, 3681, 3685, 3714, 3746, 3860, 3863, 3873, 3894, 3901, 3908, 3933, 3958, 3972, 3992, 3995, 3996, 4007, 4134, 4223, 4260, 4316, 4430, 4498, 4709, 4725, 4731, 5023, 5078, 5137, 5214, 5269, 5334, 5398, 5490, 5162

cables 6721, 6931
  coaxial 804, 1891, 4625, 4967, 5050, 5187, 5586, 6084, 6711, 6792, 6943, 7296, 7437, 7525, 7744, 7754, 7968, 8156, 8249, 8822
  Birmingham - Manchester 6447
  London - Birmingham 6448, 6819, 7202, 7203
  N.Y. - Philadelphia 5100, 5712, 5717, 5727, 5793, 6188, 6517, 7264, 7307, 7446, 7689, 7853
  distribution system 2441, 2507, 4175, 5177, 5179, 5344, 5897
  electronic 5695, 6519
  optical 1022, 4638, 5100, 5344, 5375, 5870
  submarine telegraph 50, 68, 228
camera tube (*see also* cathode-ray tube, electron tube, image dissector tube) 366, 413, 805, 2348, 3971, 4002, 4081, 4119, 4121, 4671, 5271
  patents 488, 501, 566, 577, 581, 587, 665, 678, 679, 702, 718, 821, 850, 1105, 1227, 1282, 1304, 1339, 1949, 2379, 2494, 2549, 3190, 3253, 3310, 3567, 3602, 3640, 3699, 3778, 3780, 3792, 3793, 3829, 3878, 3920, 3932, 3951, 4114, 4329, 4464, 4468, 4475, 4477, 4482, 4491, 4505, 4524, 4532, 4543, 4561, 4584, 4610, 4616, 4617, 4622, 4636, 4654, 4659, 4662, 4664, 4681, 4692, 4706, 4811, 4829, 4830, 4836, 4837, 4844, 4853, 4862, 4874, 4875, 4929, 4936, 4942, 4958, 5000, 5045, 5046, 5074, 5148, 5228, 5231, 5243, 5288, 5292, 5597, 5601-4, 5611, 5665, 5718, 5738, 5782, 5818, 5819, 5827, 5835, 5848, 5859, 5899, 5927, 5969, 5970, 5976, 5986, 5988, 6014, 6093, 6110, 6157, 6165, 6272, 6480, 6486, 6561, 6613, 6624, 6655, 6701-4, 6753, 6762, 6774, 6782, 6783, 6795, 6903, 7015, 7083, 7084, 7086, 7108, 7134, 7176, 7189, 7234, 7235, 7401, 7416, 7479, 7528, 7550, 7771, 7786, 7787, 7860, 7931, 7939, 7966, 8040, 8072, 8199, 8280, 8363, 8485, 8525
career possibilities in television 2632, 2663, 3027, 7758, 7864, 7879, 8327
  training 8508, 8509, 8630
cathode, oxide-coated 306, 326, 327, 329
"cathode ray" 70
cathode rays, research 45, 48, 70, 99, 114, 136, 145, 150, 182, 193, 197, 229, 239-41, 252, 259-61, 265-7, 306, 332, 404, 714, 823, 1179, 1701, 1871, 4923, 5511, 7348, 7611, 8647
  research by Swinton 259, 264, 286, 366, 413, 1314, 1550, 1556, 1701, 1871, 5532
cathode-ray tube (*see also under* scanning; *see* Braun tube, camera tube, electron tube, picture tube) 167, 326, 336, 373, 485, 510, 1085, 1212, 1235, 1701, 1739, 1871, 2125, 2214, 2215, 2218, 2253, 2322, 2674, 2685, 2725, 2800, 2817, 2845, 2924, 2940, 2968, 3061, 3095, 3134, 3146, 3166, 3205-7, 3241, 3314, 3429, 3446, 3449, 3452, 3468, 3482, 3521, 3572, 3696, 3886, 3907, 3952, 3983, 4084, 4120, 4169, 4171, 4182, 4249, 4278, 4283, 4313, 4314, 4327, 4352, 4355, 4417, 4447, 4490, 4573, 4590, 4611, 4619, 4646, 4666, 4668, 4718, 4860, 4884, 4959, 5101, 5146, 5260, 5573, 5679, 5723, 5812, 5953, 6031, 6124, 6224, 6233, 6241, 6500, 6516, 6570, 6593, 6648,

6922, 7061, 7306, 7317, 7372, 7387, 7389, 7445, 7503, 7563, 7615, 7878, 8031, 8189, 8220, 8407, 8618, 8658, 8691, 8747, 8772, 8803

patents 329, 337, 397, 457, 525, 526, 550, 556, 573, 702, 983, 1056, 1089, 1097, 1226, 1304, 1491, 1606, 2049, 2104, 2115, 2244, 2543, 2579, 2689, 2690, 2692, 2737, 2751, 2806, 2838, 2841, 2877, 2879, 2892, 2914, 2926, 2929, 3004, 3051, 3059, 3069, 3074, 3151, 3152, 3161, 3195, 3212, 3215, 3231, 3254, 3270, 3292, 3305, 3307-9, 3311, 3352, 3353, 3369, 3374, 3394, 3412, 3413, 3422, 3443-6, 3465, 3484, 3488, 3491, 3492, 3507, 3511, 3532, 3542, 3544, 3545, 3551, 3552, 3554, 3563, 3584, 3597, 3599, 3602, 3621, 3634, 3644, 3659, 3670, 3677, 3687, 3706, 3708, 3712, 3718-20, 3722, 3730, 3745, 3748, 3784, 3785, 3794, 3810, 3816, 3821, 3824, 3825, 3828, 3850, 3857, 3869, 3872, 3876, 3891, 3893, 3895, 3902, 3924, 3925, 3934, 3938, 3939, 3940, 3956, 3957, 3959-62, 3966, 3989, 3993, 4004, 4008, 4010, 4014, 4015, 4018-20, 4023, 4025-7, 4029, 4042-5, 4052, 4055, 4066, 4077, 4093, 4097, 4100, 4101, 4109, 4112, 4114, 4136, 4161, 4164, 4199, 4206, 4220, 4221, 4229, 4258, 4261, 4263, 4270, 4277, 4281, 4288, 4289, 4303, 4317, 4334, 4346, 4347, 4361-3, 4373, 4383, 4384, 4388, 4391, 4396-9, 4412, 4413, 4423, 4424, 4435, 4456, 4474, 4491, 4494, 4508, 4512, 4513, 4532, 4539, 4547, 4549, 4555, 4570, 4583, 4604, 4605, 4614, 4616, 4617, 4623, 4624, 4634, 4639, 4642, 4647, 4655, 4685, 4689, 4690, 4693, 4694, 4700, 4705, 4707, 4722, 4727, 4732, 4733, 4735, 4736, 3741, 4748, 4756, 4774, 4778, 4790, 4791, 4801, 4813, 4823, 4824, 4835, 4837-41, 4851-3, 4867, 4904, 4909, 4911-3, 4918, 4919, 4954, 4955, 4973, 4980, 4986, 4989, 4995, 4996, 4999, 5007-10, 5014, 5015, 5026, 5045, 5046, 5055, 5060, 5088, 5110, 5141, 5143, 5147, 5156, 5192, 5198, 5199, 5212, 5213, 5236, 5242, 5255, 5262, 5273, 5282, 5283, 5290, 5307, 5317, 5338, 5340, 5349, 5353, 5366, 5379, 5380, 5391, 5392, 5396, 5403, 5415, 5460, 5467, 5493, 5545, 5552, 5555, 5587, 5588, 5591, 5593, 5606, 5615, 5616, 5622, 5627, 5631, 5653, 5654, 5657, 5674, 5677, 5678, 5682, 5685, 5699, 5705, 5734, 5742, 5745, 5751, 5758, 5759, 5761, 5768, 5774, 5781, 5853,
5854, 5903, 5931, 5936, 5938, 5942, 5943, 5959, 5962, 5968, 5983, 5987, 5991, 6007, 6011, 6013, 6015, 6022, 6037, 6052, 6053, 6061, 6065, 6069, 6077, 6089, 6098, 6105, 6116, 6141, 6150, 6158, 6166, 6167, 6178, 6182, 6183, 6193, 6194, 6206, 6207, 6220, 6221, 6226, 6248, 6267, 6268, 6273, 6283, 6284, 6298, 6314, 6317, 6324, 6347, 6355-8, 6373, 6377, 6384, 6390, 6402, 6417, 6443, 6458, 6462, 6493, 6527, 6530, 6542, 6543, 6545, 6551, 6563, 6565, 6632, 6635, 6664, 6666, 6673, 6677, 6678, 6684, 6689, 6693, 6705, 6738, 6804, 6809, 6812-4, 6816, 6817, 6825, 6828, 6838, 6840, 6843, 6844, 6858, 6865, 6873, 6877, 6887, 6893, 6894, 6910-2, 6914, 6935, 6947, 6951, 6962, 6965, 6967, 6969, 6972, 6977-9, 6984, 6987, 6992, 6993, 7012-4, 7017, 7018, 7022, 7026, 7037, 7040, 7082, 7085, 7090, 7098, 7111, 7114, 7115, 7121, 7122, 7126-8, 7137, 7138, 7155, 7163, 7165, 7167, 7183, 7184, 7242, 7246, 7248, 7269, 7282, 7293, 7336, 7347, 7362, 7408, 7463-5, 7470, 7472, 7475, 7481, 7485, 7536, 7553, 7569, 7571-3, 7578, 7590, 7594-6, 7601, 7635-9, 7644, 7661, 7684, 7686, 7687, 7698, 7699, 7714, 7715, 7730, 7732, 7740, 7767, 7773, 7775, 7824, 7835, 7866, 7867, 7870, 7883, 7904, 7929, 7933, 7943, 7950, 7990, 7991, 7994-6, 7999, 8006, 8013, 8014, 8060, 8065, 8069, 8070, 8080, 8088, 8089, 8110, 8114, 8117, 8119, 8127, 8129, 8134, 8138, 8140, 8170, 8185, 8186, 8196, 8204, 8237, 8244, 8296, 8299, 8301, 8304, 8339, 8416, 8419, 8421, 8438, 8464, 8466, 8468, 8522, 8552, 8565, 8577

cesium cathodes 2673, 3602, 5515, 7693

cinemas and theaters, television in 2405, 2505, 2527, 2565, 2567, 3153, 3159, 3275, 3277, 3489, 5145, 5179, 5440, 5510, 7323, 8173, 8193, 8249, 8348, 8387, 8569, 8867

cinematography (*see also* telecine) 305, 426, 435, 447, 547, 983, 1014, 1786, 3806, 8627, 8781

Cinetel 7537

color systems 145, 334, 416, 645, 687, 1352, 1382, 1404, 1418, 1441, 1446, 1503, 1512, 1551, 1556, 1692, 1738, 1828, 1933, 1934, 1950, 1953, 1957, 1971, 1986, 2005, 2007, 2008, 2037, 2050, 2052, 2174, 2176, 2209, 2323, 2348, 2420, 2507, 2591, 2616, 2708, 2721, 2732, 2762, 3176, 3199, 4247, 4447, 4461, 4462, 4525, 5109, 5133,
5261, 5646, 6485, 6998, 7080, 7147, 7306, 7476, 7500, 7506, 7559, 7763, 7789, 7923, 7976, 8109, 8321, 8461, 8463, 8472, 8511, 8670, 8675, 8717, 8718, 8725a, 8727, 8731, 8732, 8734, 8735, 8801, 8804, 8817, 8820, 8823, 8871

patents 285, 295, 318, 369, 468, 537, 550, 587, 695, 704, 707, 764, 859, 1024, 1046, 1083, 1106, 1181, 1282, 1283, 1285, 1287, 1298, 1335, 1337, 1339, 1367, 1385, 1541, 1615, 1859, 1860, 1930, 2073, 2116, 2204, 2229, 2284, 2297, 2302, 2385, 2395, 2403, 2431, 2509, 2582, 2603, 2606, 2608, 2611, 2647, 2744, 2745, 2774, 2782, 2785, 2786, 2812, 2929, 2955, 2965, 3165, 3180, 3259, 3264, 3303, 3356, 3357, 3401, 3503, 3589, 3658, 3790, 3853, 3854, 3918, 3930, 3990, 4064, 4217, 4307, 4390, 4403, 4516, 4723, 4853, 5045, 5094-6, 5155, 5216, 5659, 5752, 5824, 5825, 6604, 6975, 7411, 7580, 7660, 7676, 7677, 7771, 7861, 7897, 8139, 8295, 8356

commercial television (*see also* advertising) 2160, 2590, 2635, 2671, 2834, 7326, 7850

copying telegraphy. *See* facsimile

costs of equipment. *See* prices

Crookes tube (*see also* discharge tube) 255, 259, 261

dark space
  Crookes dark space 99
  Faraday dark space 6, 27

daylight television (outdoor pickup and transmission) 1344, 1345, 1352, 1359, 1379, 1380, 1383, 1389, 1340, 1434, 1436, 1481, 1490, 1503, 1551, 1605, 1636, 1880, 1913, 1952, 2323, 2685, 2938, 2939, 2953, 2960, 2995, 2996, 3093, 3696, 3909, 4558, 4671, 5852, 7064, 7182, 7213

deaf, television for the 6924

definition. *See also* line transmissions
  low 4309, 4751, 4899, 5575, 7370
  high (*see also* ultra-short-wave transmission) 2123, 2305, 4147, 4157, 4309, 4314, 4452, 4471, 4472, 4573, 4588, 4595, 4745, 4899, 4938, 5145, 5179, 5441, 5517, 5679, 6080, 6123, 6241, 6419, 6633, 7088, 7370, 8149, 8378, 8767

deflection 850, 4153, 5620, 5729, 5858, 5969, 6162, 6687, 7390, 7410, 7819, 7930, 7947, 8765
  amplifier 3513, 5429

circuits 4229, 4447, 4668, 4672, 4959, 8038, 8315
  patents 2381, 2696, 2837, 3058, 3127, 3253, 3311, 3929, 3932, 3954, 4014, 4061, 4296, 4013, 4014, 4307, 4319, 4345, 4406, 4434, 4444, 4473, 4474, 4486, 4493, 4505, 4508, 4550, 4554, 4559, 4575, 4665, 4701, 4705, 4706, 4725, 4859, 4875, 4942, 4957, 4970, 4984, 5024, 5025, 5036, 5097, 5150, 5227, 5393, 5462, 6014, 6414, 6562, 6862, 7352, 8257, 8336, 8358, 8524
  coils 413
  patents 336, 337, 349, 566, 665, 743, 1304, 1836, 2580, 3004, 3058, 3096, 3127, 3396, 3532, 3553, 3584, 3739, 3785, 3873, 3934, 4258, 4433, 4477, 4555, 4561, 4571, 4578, 4606, 4624, 4640, 4733, 4946, 4947, 4996, 5037, 5077, 5115, 5122, 5132, 5192, 5194, 5269, 5369, 5390, 5401, 5414, 5427, 5443, 5494, 5504, 5715, 6052, 6281, 6295, 6486, 7965, 8284, 8331, 8332, 8484
  electrostatic 3597, 3972, 4109, 4276, 4382, 4383, 4736, 5125, 5227, 5385, 7247, 8161
  magnetic and electromagnetic 182, 500, 613, 3416, 3793, 3889, 3972, 4068, 4109, 4185, 4382, 4383, 4647, 4652, 4736, 4737, 4744, 4748, 5061, 5097, 5141, 5214, 5276, 5295, 5385, 5445, 5569, 5618, 5706, 5716, 5789, 5993, 6022, 6323, 8103, 8151, 8353
  oscillator (*see also* saw-tooth wave oscillator) 3687, 5072, 5336, 5466
  plates 465, 510, 577, 587, 1819, 2291, 2478, 2829, 3004, 3051, 3053, 3194, 3397, 3512, 3513, 3532, 3545, 3552, 3555, 3563, 3584, 3686, 3785, 3828, 3873, 3925, 4014, 4198, 4199, 4391, 4435, 4456, 4458, 4513, 4640, 4731, 4741, 4774, 4931, 4998, 5009, 5010, 5076, 5150, 5304, 5309, 5558, 6013, 8246
  sharp-edge 6838
  yoke 3511, 3670, 3671, 3688, 4258, 5294, 5337, 5433, 5706, 7536, 7772, 7965, 8192, 8366, 8558
department stores, television demonstrations in 1410, 1573, 1896, 6536 (*and see* Gimbels, Selfridges)
diaphote 126, 135
direction-finding (navigational) systems 1482, 1516, 1990, 2054, 2093, 3453, 3454, 3457, 3661, 3711, 3880, 3907, 3921, 4777, 4945, 7330, 8248
discharge tube (also called Crookes, Geis-sler, and Hittorf tubes) 295, 299, 303, 314, 335, 353, 359, 435, 526, 615, 719, 909, 983, 1145, 1252, 1520, 1717, 1747, 1749, 1754, 2198, 2202, 2438, 3217, 3576, 3841, 4069, 4159, 4198, 4515, 4703, 4776, 5038, 5225, 5744, 5797, 5998
glow discharge tube 2501, 2799, 3293, 5038
disks. *See under* scanning
disk recording 198
distributor, early applications of 15, 154, 291, 295, 307, 342, 367, 378, 387, 554, 891, 903-5, 909, 943, 944, 977, 980, 982, 1056, 1080, 1081, 1091, 1294, 1536, 2117, 2198, 2199, 2203, 2249, 2393, 2425, 2537, 2544, 2578, 2699, 3052, 3076, 3088, 4155, 4400
double-beam tube 2291, 3658, 3768
drums, *See under* scanning
duplex system 1024, 1742, 1860, 2395, 2403, 2474, 2572, 2804, 4419, 8136

E.1 (standard German receiver) 8404-8, 8490
Edison effect 174, 178, 183, 184, 186, 210, 257, 304
educational uses of television 2132, 6280, 7041, 7173
electrical discharges in rarefied gases. *See* rarefied gases
electric telescope. *See* telescopy
electric valve-tube (Wehnelt) 312, 313, 325
electrography 7697
electroluminescence 278, 598
electromagnetism 43, 47, 49, 91, 95, 237, 259, 343
"electron" 223, 247
electron, discovery of 266, 267
electrons 302, 304, 343, 344, 458, 595, 7208
electron amplifier 5152, 7398
electron beam 823, 5829, 4277
electron gun 4397, 4475, 4543, 4561, 4708, 4712, 4727, 4742, 4765, 4903, 4979, 4981, 5000, 5170, 5185, 5243, 5267, 5273, 5282, 5292, 5351, 5399, 5400, 5418, 5443, 5473, 5601, 5632, 5818, 5835, 5925, 5969, 6975, 6985, 7060, 7129, 7397, 8101, 8605, 8606
electron lens 3294, 4277, 5849
electron multiplier (*see also* secondary emission multiplier) 4676, 5412, 6709, 7186
  patents 4139, 4535, 4628, 4764, 4765, 4782, 4792, 4836, 4853, 4871, 4873, 4889, 4896, 4906, 4997, 5040, 5083, 5092, 5145, 5146, 5149, 5202, 5225, 5231, 5234, 5296, 5322, 5347, 5402, 5420, 5430, 5436, 5453, 5500, 5515, 5525, 5562, 5589, 5607, 5608, 5614, 5619, 5626, 5642, 5651, 5652, 5667-9, 5670, 5673, 5700, 5701, 5707, 5710, 5765, 5778, 5813, 5815, 5816, 5830, 5840, 5856, 5857, 5915-9, 5926, 5937, 5939, 5940, 5994, 5949, 5960, 5961, 5989, 5999-6002, 6008, 6009, 6012, 6041, 6044-6, 6054, 6066, 6071, 6073, 6082, 6085, 6091, 6092, 6096, 6099, 6107, 6112, 6113, 6117-21, 6146, 6173, 6177, 6215, 6216, 6222, 6242, 6255, 6256, 6282, 6330, 6333, 6338, 6350, 6360, 6364, 6365, 6371, 6381, 6387, 6388, 6432, 6435, 6436, 6464, 6466, 6468-72, 6474, 6494, 6496, 6515, 6522, 6529, 6531, 6544, 6556, 6613, 6626, 6631, 6632, 6652, 6655, 6674-6, 6688, 6695, 6697, 6759, 6763-7, 6769, 6770, 6772, 6777, 6801, 6808, 6811, 6823, 6824, 6832, 6834, 6836, 6847, 6863, 6864, 6866, 6892, 6898, 6901, 6913, 6932, 6937, 6939-42, 6973, 6974, 6982, 7007-9, 7016, 7024, 7035, 7086, 7093, 7104, 7129, 7142, 7143, 7177, 7188, 7195, 7218, 7227, 7230, 7259, 7263, 7298, 7301, 7302, 7305, 7328, 7356, 7364, 7395, 7406, 7407, 7419, 7421, 7426, 7429, 7431, 7434, 7435, 7467, 7471, 7482, 7545, 7589, 7608, 7609, 7619, 7620, 7624-7, 7633, 7649, 7656, 7663, 7700, 7702, 7705, 7708, 7711, 7712, 7718, 7726, 7742, 7768, 7792, 7793, 7810, 7811, 7818, 7834, 7841, 7844, 7927, 7938, 7959, 7988, 8021, 8065, 8113, 8122, 8142, 8247, 8252, 8254, 8287, 8303, 8335, 8351, 8361, 8415, 8422, 8423, 8430, 8439, 8440, 8471, 8476, 8487, 8488, 8498, 8527, 8531, 8591
electron optics 3909, 4274, 4712, 4716, 4749, 5334, 5505, 5804, 6169, 6505, 6510-4, 6575, 6581, 6583, 7375, 7600, 7628, 7647, 7659, 7662, 7701, 7710, 7727, 7735, 7753, 8031, 8037, 8096, 8320, 8381, 8519, 8600, 8626, 8628
electro-optical apparatus 2028, 7491, 7831, 8073, 8130, 8292
electro-optical image device 6742, 8259
electro-optical light-valve 6662
electro-optical reproducer 7110
electron theory of matter 340, 357, 441
electron tube (*see also* cathode-ray tube) 306, 366, 410, 433, 475, 497, 527, 550, 556, 566, 581, 586, 615, 719, 907, 959, 983, 1076, 1409, 2249, 2601, 3069, 3194, 3597, 3599, 3634, 4015, 4018, 4019, 4028, 4061, 4281, 4317, 4328, 4388, 4402, 4494, 4909, 5092, 5748, 5861, 6805, 6888, 6909, 7480, 7788, 8785

electrostatic birefringence (*see also* Kerr effect, Kerr cell) 62
electrostatic system 1993
Emitron camera 6326, 7294, 8840
  Super-Emitron tube 7993
Ethovisor 4127

facsimile (or copying telegraphy; *see also* Fultograph, phototelegraphy, telectroscopy) 14, 16, 36, 37, 40, 107, 108, 112, 115, 126, 129-34, 154, 298, 348, 398, 412, 416, 445, 453, 479, 626, 634, 647, 668, 669, 672, 693, 728, 756, 779, 1001, 1070, 1311, 1901, 2000, 2712, 2984, 4754, 4761, 4797, 8132, 8798
  patents 11, 15, 23, 31, 32, 41, 46, 305, 455, 983, 989, 1022, 1622, 1916, 1951, 2354, 2613, 3303, 6437
Faraday cell 333, 378, 493, 499, 561
Faraday effect. *See* magneto-optic effect
Felkirk transmitter 8812
"Fernsehen" (television) 221
FE IV receiver (Telefunken) 5438, 5507, 5644
film. *See under* scanning *and under* transmission systems
firsts in television
  first advertisement 2635
  first living image photographed from a television screen 769
  first news event (Gov. Smith accepting nomination for presidency, Aug. 1928) 1559
  first televised plays
    U.K.:"The Man with the Flower in His Mouth" 2467 *et al.*
    U.S.:"The Maker of Dreams" 2825
  first public performance of television in a theater 2567
  first use of telelvision in a political campaign (Oct. 1932) 3664, 3673
  first broadcasting of election results 382, 385
fluorescence (*see also under* screen) 19, 259, 432, 4549, 4639, 4729, 4772, 4823, 6872, 8208
flyback 162, 167, 5150, 5263, 5336, 5446, 6665
focusing electron beams 823, 1048, 3634, 4276, 4289, 4423, 4424, 4558, 4824, 5212, 5455, 6635, 7277, 7855, 8436
Foto-Cell 1377
frequency bandwidths 902, 1310, 1435, 1487, 1492, 1563, 1583, 1597, 1692, 1734, 1755, 1770, 1790, 1808, 1815, 1841, 1860, 2090, 2210, 2308, 2553, 2653, 2674, 2684, 3321, 3322, 3361, 3387, 3425, 3430, 3616, 3766, 4205, 4289, 4314, 4857, 5179, 6154, 6597

methods for reducing transmission bandwidths 1860, 2144, 2611, 2962, 3010, 4253, 4304
frequency interleaving 1860
frequency multiplier 4142, 4473
Fultograph facsimile system 1464, 1486, 1547

galvanometer. *See under* modulation of light
Geissler tube (*see also* discharge tube) 276, 295, 359, 393, 470
glow lamp (*see also* discharge tube) 186, 244, 245, 257, 387, 456, 558, 703, 730, 943, 1095, 1221, 1750, 1757, 1921, 1930, 2002, 2148, 2194, 2208, 2287, 2296, 2303, 2330, 2338, 2346, 2406, 2453, 2555, 2557, 2622, 2699, 2799, 3052, 3750, 4144, 4160, 4272, 5573
glow discharge lamp 2485, 2544, 2573, 2608, 2690, 2890, 3098, 3448, 3543, 3647, 4070
Moore glow lamp 456, 703, 730, 1308, 1780
Gramovision 5079

Iconophone, Ikonophone 2818, 2343
Iconoscope, iconoscope 3939, 3971, 3977, 3987, 3988, 4036, 4082, 4091, 4119, 4291, 4368, 5171, 5578, 5877, 5911, 6034, 6393, 6500, 6855, 7066, 7186, 7383, 7386, 7682, 7747, 8166, 8221, 8371, 8377, 8394, 8495, 8496, 8834
image amplifier 5184, 5230, 6465, 8238
image analyzer 5327, 6613, 7526, 7882
image converter 4487, 5629, 6160, 6558, 6761, 6885, 7895, 8489, 8556
image dissector/image dissector tube (*see also* camera tube) 2801, 4557, 4628, 4889, 5174, 5806, 5932, 6238, 6391, 6498, 8377, 8537
  patents 665, 850, 1109, 1216, 1619, 2382, 2434, 2477, 2548, 2922, 3355, 3405, 3603, 3905, 4139, 4190, 4457, 4686, 4687, 4845, 4846, 4849, 4850, 4910, 4914, 4931, 4933, 4951, 5170, 5182, 5183, 5185, 5211, 5224, 5328, 5343, 5350, 5351, 5364, 5567, 5691, 5703, 5780, 5782, 5826, 5891, 6151, 6174, 6400, 6401, 6403, 6450, 6473, 7108, 7289, 7550, 8012, 8580, 8588
image intensifier 1339, 4912, 5138, 5305, 6546, 7663, 7720, 8488, 8576, 8611
image pickup tube (*see also* camera tube) 4457, 5069, 5070, 5264, 5267, 5399, 5418, 5431, 5443, 5454, 5464, 5501,

5503, 5536, 5547, 5553, 5570, 5581, 7951, 7969, 8102
image plate 566, 575, 577, 665, 718, 4682
image projection system 6581, 6820, 6870, 7175, 7719, 7859
image storage tube 7458
image transmission 6849, 7170
image transmitting tube 5065, 5066, 8090
induction coil, early uses of 4, 5, 7, 18, 21, 22, 25, 46, 220, 235, 271, 276, 334, 348, 358, 2287, 8789
infrared (*see also* Noctovision *and also see under* scanning) 798, 827, 834, 836, 839, 858, 871, 874, 890, 932, 940, 1058, 1059, 1120, 1130, 1199, 1279, 1280, 1516, 1738, 4272, 4325, 4487, 4933, 5473, 6238
interlaced scan. *See under* scanning

Karolus cell (*see also* Kerr cell) 755, 1042, 1077, 1386, 1491, 1695, 2391
Kerr cell (*see also under* modulation of light) 62, 213, 755, 810, 1491, 1514, 1780, 1906, 2255, 2391, 2594, 2903, 3134, 3514, 3577, 3755, 4032, 4176, 4243, 5106, 5289, 5725
  patents 493, 525, 606, 633, 694, 708, 721, 734, 803, 820, 954, 983, 1097, 1351, 1361, 1367, 1413, 1423, 1885, 1919, 1923, 1955, 2235, 2284, 2326, 2356, 2428, 2499, 2578, 2656, 2683, 2790, 2854, 2877, 3088, 3191, 3299, 3395, 3546, 3598, 3738, 3744, 3867, 3904, 3922, 4001, 4106, 4196, 4315, 4407, 4542, 4581, 4582, 4726, 4773, 4894, 4978, 5022, 5468, 5658, 6902
Kerr effect 74, 76, 127, 128, 606, 2559, 2903, 6581
keystone distortion 3671, 3828, 5060, 5291, 5638
kinescope, Kinescope (cathode-ray tube) 2072, 2107, 2125, 2306, 3312, 3601, 4119, 4229, 5877, 6034, 6855, 7062, 8161, 8207, 8451, 8717
  projection kinescope 6889, 7059, 7060, 7072, 7149
Kino lamp (Raytheon neon tube) 1375, 1377, 1458, 1497

lens disk. *See under* scanning
light-chopper disk. *See under* scanning
light pipe 134, 388, 392, 640, 758, 765, 767, 797, 821, 1025, 1294, 1721
light-spot. *See under* scanning
light-valve 508, 561, 567, 810, 850, 1675, 2805, 2950, 2954, 2974, 3301, 3593, 3598, 3744, 3848, 4077, 4196, 4210, 4224, 4315, 4441, 4480, 4542, 4581,

4582, 4718, 4726, 4902, 5315, 5476, 5540, 5547, 5752, 5814, 6176, 7345, 8288
supersonic light-valve 5658, 5709, 5892, 6342, 6353
line transmissions (scanning lines; definition) per frames/second 3743, 4080, 4205, 4227, 4358, 4462, 4573, 4857, 6585, 7071, 7752
12 lines 313
24 lines 1461
25 lines 7070
30 lines 2029, 2735, 3742, 3952, 3980, 4033, 4137, 4174, 4259, 4358, 4359, 4389, 4574, 4595, 5079, 5308, 5105, 5435
30 lines/12.5 2055, 2065, 4197
48 lines/15 313, 315
48 lines/20 2391
50 lines 3623, 3651, 3742, 4125
60 lines 3884, 4137, 4598
60 lines/20 1902, 2003, 4417
60 lines/25 5118, 5348, 6137
72 lines 2343
80 lines/15 3690
80 lines/16.6 3139
80 lines/25 4245
84 lines/25 3146
90 lines 4175
90 lines/20 4175
90 lines/25 3139, 3655, 4245, 4591, 5513
96 lines/25 4245
100 lines 4033, 4629, 4669
100 lines/25 5513
120 lines 4137, 4157, 4368, 4452, 5346, 5514, 6606, 7426
120 lines/24 4228
120 lines/25 3917, 4083, 4125, 4175, 4245, 4314, 4591
150 lines 5179
180 lines 4157, 4227, 4821, 4877, 4883, 5120, 5346, 5679, 6122, 6170
180 lines/24 4671
180 lines/25 4017, 4037, 4065, 4166, 4245, 4385, 4410, 4591, 4595, 4718, 4938, 4959, 4963, 4965, 5068, 5302, 5497, 5513, 5581, 5731, 5870, 6025, 6144
240 lines 4227, 4314, 5113, 8835
240 lines/24 5246, 5312, 7307
250 lines 2123
270 lines/30 4558
300 lines 2674
320 lines/25 5513
343 lines/60 5051, 5204, 6600, 8835
345 lines 6706
360 lines 4227
400 lines 5179, 6585
405 lines 5692, 5879, 6170, 6719

405 lines/50 5093, 5108, 5113, 5158
441 lines 6475, 6476, 6600, 6630, 6706, 6792, 6854, 7073, 7088, 7204, 7386, 7443, 7557, 7877, 7979, 8455
450 lines 6170
525 lines 8640
729 lines 7088
luminescence (*see also under* screen) 2625, 2626, 6506, 7501, 8382, 8741

magnetic recording 281, 291, 501, 863, 876, 1014
magneto-optic effect (Faraday effect) 13, 74, 76, 91, 181
magnetron 4988
manometric flame. *See under* modulation of light
matrix systems 222, 372, 387, 1221, 1481, 1636, 1810, 2198, 2199, 2201, 2249, 2352, 2442, 2544, 2878, 3026, 3437, 4400, 4429, 4432
mercury vapor lamp 3170, 3592, 3646, 3667, 3674, 3770, 6129
message tape system 3524, 3564, 3578, 3583, 3615, 3624, 3656, 3668, 3669
mirrors: disk, drum, screw, vibrating, wheel, etc. *See under* scanning
mobile units 6618, 6792, 7206, 7314, 7316, 8032, 8544
modulation of light, methods 301, 1981, 2255, 2720, 2989, 3001, 3722, 3727, 3765, 4278, 4332, 7306, 7493, 7797
  patents 457, 953, 1925, 2192, 2543, 2871, 2951, 3531, 3749, 3875, 3928, 3973, 4206, 4322, 4398, 4510, 4551, 4556, 4567, 4693, 5027, 5172, 5499, 5503, 6550, 6560, 6723, 6953, 6954, 7185, 7196, 7214, 7219, 7539, 7646, 7784, 8061, 8135, 8333, 8431, 8450
  arc 309, 328, 386, 486, 3044, 3662
  bimetallic strips 6607
  cathode-ray tube 526, 3308, 4345, 7577, 8120, 8121
  cell 620, 3222, 5376, 6335, 6336
  Faraday cell 333, 493, 499, 3560
  Karolus cell 1077
  Kerr cell 213, 493, 606, 640, 737, 820, 1923, 3107, 3662, 5658
  deflection 234, 413, 499, 2291
  diaphragm 4693
  differential of two signals 4366
  discharge tube 526
  dual radio frequency 556
  electrode 3365, 5000
  electro-optical 6315
  filament lamp 4300, 4301
  film 4295
  galvanometer 354, 359, 368, 376, 384, 392, 468, 537, 576, 752, 2660

  mirror galvanometer 219, 368, 803
  graded or shaded screen 368, 530, 611
  graded transparency 369, 536
  light valve 181, 674
  liquid, changing opacity of 2483
  manometric flame 38, 151, 204, 234, 371, 571, 2436
  mirror, moving 367, 1035
  neon tube 1417, 3662
  oscillograph, mirror 1731
  oscillograph, moving coil 546
  photo 545
  picture and sync signals 5222
  picture tube 141
  piezoelectric crystals 677, 694, 4274, 5600
  prism 3715
  reflector and apertured plate 532
  screen, apertured 2542
  shutter 233, 474, 507, 820
  telephone 66, 145, 204, 571
  telephone-actuated pressure chamber 389
  telephone-actuated shutter 145, 820
  telephone-actuated spark gap 318
  telephone-mirror 321
  ultrasonic vibrations 4360
  variable frequency 1406
  variable apertures 145, 219, 376, 497, 567, 820
Monoscope 7306, 7566
mosaic structures (*see also under* screen) 108, 127, 129, 154, 235, 245, 365, 392, 455, 566, 598, 797, 821, 1695, 1903, 3310, 3531, 3602, 4081, 4095, 4257, 4326, 4440, 4464, 4477, 4487, 4494, 4543, 4465, 4785, 4874, 5464, 5986, 6171, 6704, 7416
  electrode 5819, 6524, 6528, 6569, 6628, 6726, 7547, 8297, 8432
  electromagnetic 1107
  multiwire 127, 133, 211
  plates 4475, 4477, 4708, 5990, 6552
  selenium 455, 502
multiplex systems 342, 2633, 3499, 4866, 4903, 4930, 5012

navigational systems. *See* direction-finding systems
neon, discovery of 270
neon lamps or tubes 393, 504, 564, 643, 730, 909, 991, 1203, 1232, 1260, 1308, 1369, 1491, 1574, 1647, 1653, 1780, 1903, 1977, 1979, 2015, 2056, 2308, 2323, 2343, 2528, 2559, 2594, 2666, 3141, 3538, 4183
  patents 580, 706, 743, 767, 876, 903, 904, 906, 907, 958, 959, 977, 980, 995, 1014, 1076, 1088, 1091, 1117, 1140,

1141, 1229, 1251, 1252, 1294, 1306, 1338, 1351, 1409, 1417, 1721, 2071, 2342, 2537, 2689, 3259, 3503, 3903, 4058, 4648
news, first television broadcast 1559; *237*
Nicol prism 3, 167, 181, 378, 550, 561, 619, 640, 734, 755, 850, 1077, 1078, 1412, 3593, 4001, 4032, 4224, 4726
Nipkow disk. *See under* scanning, disks
Noctovision 798, 827, 839, 932, 1028, 1043, 1120, 1160, 1279, 1321, 1516, 1738, 2011, 2054, 2323, 2708
Noctovisor 1988, 2054, 2083, 2196, 2277

Ormatron 1308
Orthicon 8370, 8371, 8546
oscillation generator (*see also* relaxation oscillation generator, saw-tooth wave oscillator, deflection oscillator) 3366, 4372, 4535, 5233, 5263, 5275, 5656, 5902, 7112, 7334, 7359, 7469, 7579
oscillation multiplier 5643, 7858
oscillation valve 319, 331, 339
oscillator 6828, 6983, 7348
 crystal oscillator 1142
 electron oscillator 6771
Oscillight receiver 5509
Oscillite picture tube 2801, 3009
oscillographs 1701, 3572, 3658, 6495, 6768
 cathode-ray oscillograph 485, 510, 713, 817, 1739, 1780, 3133, 3197, 3975, 4263, 4344, 4368, 4379, 4661, 4729, 4917, 5033, 5837, 6578, 8629, 8854
 mirror oscillograph 850, 894, 916, 1079, 1886, 2983
Oscillophone 3631
Osglim lamp 504, 600, 1158
Osram photoelectric cell 1944
outdoor pickup and transmission. *See* daylight television

Phantoscope 1918
phonic wheel. *See under* synchronization
phongraph 85, 86, 90
phonograph recording 275, 435, 799, 871, 940, 1269, 1405, 2513
Phonoscope 238, 1028
Phonovision 799, 1120, 1321, 1358, 1738, 2323, 5079
Phoroscope 204
phosphorescence (*see also under* screen) 99, 306, 432, 4549
 phosporescent belt 719
photoelectric cell (photocell; *see also* phototube *and see under* scanning) 408, 484, 624, 683, 938, 966, 1153, 1179, 1191, 1232, 1241, 1432, 1500, 1624, 1636, 1914, 1944, 1986, 2020, 2163, 2323, 2628, 2704, 2712, 2720, 2732, 2799, 2849, 2863, 2905, 2984, 2997, 3042, 3208, 3242, 3727, 3759, 3762, 3763, 3804, 3943, 3971, 4183, 4352, 4447, 4592, 4752, 4755, 4910, 5159, 5573, 8036, 8167, 8655
 patents 388, 556, 640, 655, 656, 684, 765, 1292, 1300, 1348, 1351, 1393, 1412, 1423, 1425, 1760, 2117, 2231, 2744, 2751, 2781, 3025, 3127, 3156, 3740, 3955, 4057, 4163, 4217, 4269, 4297, 4305, 4400, 4423, 4454, 4548, 4565, 4584, 4585, 4648, 4762, 4787, 5069, 5229, 5288, 5346, 5547, 5566, 5677, 5739, 5740, 5744, 5745, 5835, 6741, 7520, 7683
photoelectric effect 195, 196, 200, 201, 260, 324, 1441, 1591
photoelectric mosaic 2379, 3602, 4487, 4494, 4762, 4783, 4784, 4912, 5264, 5267, 5443, 5501, 5718, 5457, 6685, 6988
photoelectric surface 6172, 8008
photoelectricity 208 432, 439, 440, 463, 469, 478, 622, 1087, 1179, 1513, 1683, 1726, 1942, 2377, 2765, 2799, 3391, 3760, 4356, 7433, 7693, 8230, 8636, 8704
 research by Elster and Geitel 207, 214-6, 225-7, 230-2, 242, 243, 246, 250, 251, 260, 268, 385, 408, 424
photoluminescence 324
photophosphorescence 4639
Photophone 126, 137-40, 146-8, 151, 153, 157, 161, 820
photoradiogram 626, 628, 631, 756
photo recording 638, 647, 669, 983, 1716, 4011
phototelegraphy (*see also* facsimile *and* telectroscopy) 112, 155, 157-9, 162, 211, 213, 253, 279, 291, 293, 322, 341, 360, 363, 381, 383, 390, 391, 398, 399, 404, 412, 416, 423, 438, 443, 445, 477, 479, 480, 491, 503, 534, 547, 616, 710, 727, 843, 870, 926, 1001, 1098, 1187, 2053, 2703, 4528
 patents 321, 353, 358, 447, 500, 528, 545
 research by Bidwell 155, 157, 158, 162, 365, 366
 Korn phototelegraph 298, 303, 347, 350-2, 360, 365, 370, 426, 547, 569
phototube (*see also* photoelectric cells) 211, 215, 424, 536, 810, 991, 1102, 2020, 2377, 4759, 8646
 patents 349, 400, 433, 474, 546, 550, 557, 615, 719, 722, 734, 764, 792, 907, 959, 983, 1417, 1603, 1884, 2190, 2202, 2445, 2479, 2490, 2503, 2542, 2606, 2608, 3233, 3364, 3395, 3584, 3705, 3741, 3822, 3833, 3857, 4155, 4262, 4272, 4293, 4329, 4344, 4378, 4425, 4427, 4482, 4503, 4506, 4531, 4602, 4892, 5354, 5355, 5664, 5742, 5743, 5948, 6697, 6986, 7494, 7519
photovoltaic effect 9, 10, 5335
photovoltaic target 6880
pickup tube 500, 4682, 5284, 5480, 6487, 7065, 8497, 8707, 8793, 8816
picturephone 8784
picture tube (*see also* Braun tube, cathode-ray tube) 413, 805, 2112, 2113, 2309, 2801, 2979, 3512, 3800, 4119, 4121, 4628, 5319, 6247
 patents 465, 499, 501, 556, 557, 566, 577, 581, 587, 613, 1227, 1282, 1339, 1819, 1951, 2072, 2107, 2150, 2282, 2291, 2329, 2357, 2381, 2394, 2478, 2490, 2548, 2580, 2649, 2653, 2657, 2686, 2693, 2694, 2696, 2698, 2803, 2830, 2861, 2910, 2964, 2973, 3008, 3009, 3013, 3054, 3057, 3058, 3086, 3096, 3121, 3127, 3188, 3194, 3218, 3259, 3261, 3270, 3309, 3312, 3338, 3345, 3348, 3352, 3365, 3376, 3397, 3423, 3460, 3462, 3492, 3511, 3530, 3536, 3554, 3555, 3565, 3591, 3676, 3677, 3680, 3681, 3684, 3685, 3687, 3707, 3739, 3746, 3807, 3818, 3834, 3894, 3931, 3933, 3934, 3954, 3958, 3962, 3999, 4007, 4008, 4010, 4013, 4014, 4016, 4030, 4048, 4054, 4055, 4058, 4061, 4134, 4136, 4146, 4152-4, 4161, 4164, 4187, 4188, 4190, 4193, 4250, 4254, 4258, 4268, 4276, 4293, 4302, 4316, 4335, 4336, 4350, 4383, 4391, 4405, 4433, 4442-4, 4446, 4468, 4474, 4478, 4519, 4520, 4521, 4523, 4526, 4544, 4555, 4568-70, 4583, 4604, 4607, 4632, 4636, 4641, 4652, 4658, 4664, 4683, 4684, 4689, 4695, 4735, 4738, 4742, 4767, 4837, 4847, 4848, 4851, 4856, 4863, 4866, 4872, 4893, 4895, 4905, 4913, 4925, 4926, 4928, 4931, 4941, 4943, 5057, 5058, 5072, 5084, 5085, 5097, 5115, 5130-2, 5151, 5157, 5180, 5186, 5197, 5237, 5239, 5248, 5303, 5348, 5365, 5385, 5401, 5406, 5432, 5434, 5451, 5466, 5491, 5531, 5538, 5550, 5560, 5568, 5589, 5609, 5612, 5617, 5632, 5664, 5715, 5750, 5825, 5850, 5866, 5920, 5966, 5967, 5978, 6110, 6159, 6246, 6359, 6426, 6857, 7053, 7540, 7884
piezoelectric crystal (*see also under* scanning *and under* modulation of light) 4315, 4323, 5476
politics and television

first use of television in an election campaign (Oct. 1932) 3664, 3673
election results broadcast (1930) 382, 385
portable equipment (*see also* mobile units)
portable camera 1559, 3093
portable installation 7384
portable receiver 4012
portable scanner 3408
portable transmitter 2900, 2943, 3157, 7156
prices of components, kits, sets, service 739, 816, 1453, 2312, 2325, 2461, 3071, 3145, 3154, 3201, 3278, 3279, 3608, 4104, 4534, 4560, 4821, 4922, 6410, 6690, 6799, 7804, 7806, 8321, 8490
programming 6776, 6831, 6890, 7042, 8104, 8601, 8666a, 8746, 8759, 8777, 8786
projection tube 5252, 5842, 5860, 5890, 6590, 6591, 7032, 7067, 7905, 7937, 7946, 7987
push-pull amplifier 5809
push-pull circuit 3874, 5426, 5465
push-pull detector 4006, 4143, 4158, 4199, 4200, 4201, 4431, 5973
push-pull modulator 5086

radio movies, radiomovies (Jenkins) 245, 456, 464, 472, 540, 558, 568, 642, 666, 691, 701, 759, 853, 948, 999, 1259, 1372, 1397, 1416, 1468, 1548, 1568, 1571, 1658, 1768, 1823, 2002, 2263, 2592, 2754, 3037, 3238
radiophot 502, 112
radio photography 442
radio or wireless transmissions 467, 474, 486, 489, 492, 493, 505, 506, 513, 516, 524, 536, 542, 544, 548, 554, 1395, 1820
radio vision, radiovision (Jenkins) 568, 681, 685, 716, 726, 728, 1272, 1416, 1484, 1614, 1665, 1695, 1823, 2546, 3424, 7370, 8805
Radiovisor 1416, 1628, 1695, 1823, 2213, 2259, 2334, 2461, 3038, 3079
rarefied gases, electric discharges in 6, 8, 12, 24-7, 29, 30, 34, 35, 42, 43, 45, 48, 49, 70, 125, 149, 150, 171, 179, 182, 184, 197, 209, 212, 216, 224, 237, 259, 280, 299, 300, 311, 429, 448, 3761, 4880
conduction with heated filament in a vacuum 186, 187, 191, 194, 203, 206, 209

molecular physics of high vacua, research by Crookes 99, 114, 136, 177, 218
striated discharges 12, 25, 27, 29, 34, 44, 45, 57, 58, 70, 72, 77-80, 96, 117, 119
research by De la Rue and Müller 57, 80, 97, 117, 119, 175
research by Spottiswoode 57, 58, 72, 77-9, 96
research by Spottiswoode and Moulton 113, 163, 164
raster. *See under* scanning
Rayphoto 1901
receivers, numbers of (*see also* viewers, numbers of) 1399, 2325, 2497, 2789, 2907, 3787, 7427, 7808, 7854, 8173
regenerative circuit 420, 422, 427, 430
super-regenerative circuit 4425, 4895
relaxation oscillation, relaxation oscillation generator (*see also* deflection oscillattor, saw-tooth oscillator and generator) 1743, 3346, 3350, 3548, 3549, 3586, 3632, 3633, 3637, 3638, 3660, 3700, 3701, 4049, 4054, 4059, 4280, 4336, 4367, 4458, 4470, 4532, 4697, 4741, 4842, 5024, 5038, 5057, 5082, 5091, 5298, 5300, 5306, 5383, 5421, 5792, 6074, 6481, 7228, 7903
relay systems 734, 1899, 3313, 5930, 6548, 7806
radio relay link 1820, 4673, 6304
repeater stations 4789
repeater systems 5930
remote control 435, 674

saw-tooth wave generator (*see also* relaxation oscillation generator) 504, 3207, 4229, 8151
patents 3312, 3344, 3432, 3455, 3456, 3536, 3751, 3817, 3897, 3918, 4005, 4342, 4392, 4433, 4477, 4486, 4624, 4635, 4665, 4706, 4817, 4937, 4953, 4970, 4978, 4998, 5004, 5025, 5085, 5115, 5280, 5356, 5357, 5393, 5424, 5596, 5663, 5676, 5697, 5714, 5766, 5851, 5887, 5963, 6104, 6205, 6258, 6295, 6375, 6532, 6649, 6686, 6754, 6760, 6822, 6875, 6959, 6960, 6970, 7048, 7124, 7125, 7415, 7457, 7478, 7483, 7840, 7888, 7961, 8075, 8124, 8126, 8182, 8201, 8241, 8278, 8291, 8352, 8368, 8524, 8561
saw-tooth oscillator (*see also* deflection) patents 2921, 3396, 3423, 4046, 4061, 4135, 4185, 4382, 4409, 4454, 4467, 4468, 4520, 4554, 4587, 4737, 4744, 4828, 4875, 4900, 5052, 5062, 5125, 5127, 5181, 5203, 5276, 5295, 5361, 5384, 5427, 5527, 6963, 7830

scannerless systems 1228, 1840, 1858, 3604, 7757
scanning methods (transmitters and receivers) 1246, 1872, 1937, 2720, 2897, 3272, 3483, 3598, 4119, 4165, 4809, 5437, 5754, 5771, 5941, 6015, 6039, 6665, 6725, 6729, 6751, 7198, 7300, 7460, 7734, 7817, 7821, 7869, 8171
apartment houses, scanner for individual rooms 4418
apertured disks. (*see also* disks, perforated) 316, 321, 486, 1879, 1880, 1924, 2026, 2390, 3941
bank of lamps 548, 1601, 2240, 2491, 3214, 3864
belt, endless 1897
bubble, moving 953
cathode-ray tube 366, 1393, 1417, 2394, 2437, 2827, 2837, 3311, 3317, 3433, 3777, 3781, 4075, 4076, 4084, 4211, 4257, 4349, 4445, 4454, 4531, 4549, 4575, 4601, 4853, 4889, 4950, 5005, 5200, 5215, 5284, 5292, 5346, 5445, 5448, 5489, 5514, 5584, 5739, 5808, 5827, 5976, 6024, 6088, 6139, 6261, 6555, 7023, 7065, 7252, 7552
cross-scanning 475, 800
cylinders
apertured cylinder 1400
concentric cylinders 285, 2227, 2811
eccentric cylinders 2242
slotted cylinder 3636
diagonal 5176
discharge with magnetic deflection 1061
discharges between movable electrodes 1066
disks 909, 1232, 1234, 1431, 1433, 1434, 1580, 1584, 1628, 1939, 2142, 2161, 2182, 2184, 2321, 2362, 2457, 2628, 2723, 3242, 3507, 3653, 3915, 4242, 4278, 4574, 4751, 5105, 5513, 6137
patents 906, 907, 995, 998, 1076, 1090, 1140, 1141, 1181, 1229, 1306, 1338, 1526, 1531, 1603, 1607, 1718, 1749, 1750, 1759, 1859, 1860, 1947, 1960, 1961, 1998, 2048, 2074, 2075, 2190, 2202, 2204, 2228, 2242, 2387, 2428, 2452, 2493, 2500, 2508, 2576, 2609, 2644, 2678, 2683, 2688, 2754, 3106, 3373, 3401, 3587, 3921, 3963, 4040, 4041, 4105, 4439, 4506, 4538, 4588, 5028, 5094, 5395, 5463, 5472, 5693, 5740, 5747, 5808, 5848, 5924, 6259, 6286, 6559, 6767, 7543, 7780, 7820, 8460
coaxial disks 561, 754
concentric disks 1888, 2191, 2395
contact disks 1602, 2074
double disks 1024, 1064, 1719

double disks with neon lamps 3249
lens disks 219, 512, 565, 590, 641, 643, 673, 684, 686, 692, 699, 725, 737, 996, 999, 1064, 1082, 1106, 1146, 1767, 1823, 1833, 1955, 1970, 2356, 2650, 3025, 3375, 3379, 3427, 3469, 3470, 3608, 3819, 3950, 3981, 4110, 4209, 4572, 5513
  lens disk coacting with mirror drum 2745
  lens disk with spiral tracks 5659
  disk with double spiral of lenses 675
light-chopper disk 400, 579, 590, 593, 598, 615, 619, 859, 1233, 1385, 1541, 1884, 2092, 2490, 3675
light-transmitting points on a disk 3211
mirror disk 801, 1035, 1064, 1424, 1716, 1801, 2569, 4343, 4514, 5172, 5359, 5468
mirror-lens disk 4714
multiple disk 747
Nipkow disk (perforated spiral) 213, 271, 308, 333, 354, 389, 593, 1918, 2303, 2408, 2409, 2512, 2623, 2843, 3196, 3269, 3522, 3689, 3742, 5348, 6709, 7875, 8098
  patents 181, 276, 336, 359, 470, 548, 557, 580, 640, 704, 708, 797, 833, 1092, 1622, 1663, 1673, 1786, 1814, 1835, 1850, 1854, 2771, 2860, 2915, 2920, 2962, 2964, 2973, 3049, 3097, 3098, 3180, 3300, 3627, 4146, 4251, 5330, 5528
perforated or apertured disks 354, 536, 554, 1501, 1579, 3279
  patents 316, 321, 369, 499, 615, 705, 751, 761, 795, 800, 822, 860, 890, 977, 978, 984, 1064, 1285, 1297, 1298, 1335, 1341, 1365, 1367, 1405, 1521, 1541, 1617, 1676, 1678-80, 1719, 1751, 1921, 1962, 2027, 2096, 2097, 2101, 2111, 2328, 2337, 2358, 2388, 2431, 2474, 2478, 2569, 2744, 3002, 3233, 3260, 3261, 3293, 3339, 3741, 3859, 3968, 4110, 4293, 4298, 4482, 4505, 4564, 4602, 4637, 4648, 4657, 4720, 4994, 5047, 5124, 5154, 5638
  heart-shaped aperture pattern 2041, 2398
  spiral apertured disk (*see also* Nipkow disk) 2175, 2742, 3127, 3139, 3156, 3181, 3196, 3289, 3303, 3543, 5386, 5526
    with two or more spirals 2574, 2753, 3385, 5339
      semi-spiral 3421
      two semi-spirals 2041, 2826
      three continuous partial spirals 2509
    staggered aperture or lens 1931
    zigzag apertured 1018

platinum foil with contacts on disk 1528
polished studs on disk 2231
prismatic disk 481-3, 493, 534, 590, 638, 653, 655, 673, 801, 1864, 1949, 3265
double-spiral prism disk 2445, 2646
rotating and reciprocating disks 358, 549, 550, 732, 757, 983, 1063, 2205
rotating disk with light pipes 758
spiral rotating disk 2819
shutter disk 2119, 3856, 3865, 3871, 4584
slotted disks 248, 275, 285, 386, 447, 532, 537, 567, 584, 611, 615, 674, 711, 743, 784, 983, 1054, 1265, 1351, 1385, 1405, 1423, 1529, 1809, 1839, 1989, 2378, 2574, 3007, 3055, 3193, 3406, 3533, 3819, 3930, 4340, 4511, 4734, 5630
  concentric slotted disks 1024
  overlapping slotted disks 2962
  overlapping slotted and apertured disks 3625
  radially slotted disk 2189, 2191, 2287, 2537, 2538, 3929, 4366, 5659
  radially slotted disk coacting with helically arranged lenses on cylinder 2916
  slotted disk coacting with slotted drum 2230
  slotted disk with rotary mirror 182
  slotted disks rotating in opposite directions 386
  spirally slotted disk 3929, 4343
  spirally slotted disk coacting with apertured disk 4566
  spirally slotted disk coacting with disk 3436, 5692
spiral disks (see also Nipkow disk, perforated or apertured disks, slotted disks) 2605, 2650, 2651, 3031, 6260
  single spiral 4269, 4743, 5520
  double spiral 897, 1945, 1968, 1987, 2614, 3003, 3408, 3635, 4603, 4685
  multispiral 3858, 4282, 5520
  triple spiral 3791
spiral of discharge tubes 2241
spiral of photocells or neon lamps 980, 1336, 1930, 3357
spiral of points 1477, 1757
toothed disk 4061
disk in vacuum chamber 743
displaced line scanning 2692
double-image scanning 5595
double scan 737
drums 1628, 1823, 1855, 1887, 1904, 1916, 2002, 2119, 2355, 2890, 3963, 4040, 4278, 4438, 4751
  coaxial drums 2156
  concentric drums 2077

  double drum with light pipe 1721, 1886
  helical drums 767, 1196, 1294, 1966
  lens drum 435, 512, 752, 2301, 2791, 2919, 3011, 3087, 3564, 3737, 3742, 4649
    with helically arranged lenses 2656
    with multispiral lens 2611
  light-pipe drum 2213
  mirror drum 204, 213, 721, 731, 1388, 2362, 2735, 3842, 2938, 3149, 3170, 3514, 3538, 3577, 3654, 3695, 3729, 3742, 3755, 3914, 3915, 3948, 3978, 3980, 4035, 4084, 4087, 4104, 4122, 4128, 4179, 4215, 4552, 4574, 4588, 5513, 6645, 6719
    patents 295, 318, 367, 468, 497, 532, 537, 571, 859, 1063, 1265, 1406, 1662, 1721, 1833, 1834, 1919, 1949, 2078, 2233, 2284, 2483, 2486, 2568, 2643, 2650, 2743, 2746, 2772, 2786, 2823, 2831, 2839, 2857, 2858, 2919, 2962, 2963, 3056, 3062, 3067, 3070, 3089, 3226, 3266, 3271, 3301, 3349, 3351, 3395, 3419, 3421, 3431, 3533, 3535, 3537, 3558, 3566, 3622, 3662, 3665, 3717, 3737, 3752, 3815, 3826, 3833, 3856, 3865-7, 3891, 3930, 3950, 4000, 4056, 4058, 4106, 4195, 4208, 4222, 4262, 4265, 4293, 4308, 4343, 4348, 4360, 4366, 4483, 4506, 4511, 4514, 4533, 4553, 4585, 4607, 4662, 4723, 4935, 4956, 4978, 5018, 5105, 5422, 5452, 5540, 5549, 5658, 5934, 5964, 5965, 6449
    conical mirror drum 3222
    helical mirror drum 1180, 6080
    polyhedral mirror drum 349, 400, 725, 856, 958, 1014, 1208, 4204
    three-zone mirror drum 2760
    triple mirror drum 3953
    mirror drum with apertured disk 2574
    mirror drum with lenses 2536
    mirror drum coacting with spirally slotted disk and rocking mirror 3464
    drum with oscillating mirrors 7386
    mirror drum with rocking mirrors 6449
    mirror drum with projected arc light 4208
    drum with stacked plates 4318
    mirror drum, reflecting mirror, and rotating mirror 6653
  perforated or apertured drum 560, 767, 1117, 1800, 2103, 2156, 2474, 2772, 2791, 2919, 3679
    helically apertured drum 3448
    helically apertured drum with mirror drum 5475
    spirally apertured drum 2868, 2869

Subject Index

perforated drum with lamps inside 2550
rotary drums with mirrors 2812
rotating drum with helical glow tube 3267
slotted drum 296, 336, 782, 2156, 2285, 2572, 3055, 3287, 4217
echelon assemblies 1542, 1748, 2782, 2785, 2786, 3351, 3368, 4155
electron beam 678, 679, 702, 1289, 3853, 3854, 5066, 5092, 5474, 5927, 7382
  double-beam 3833
  multiple-beam 1862, 2912, 6907
  multiple-beam, 7-spot 803, 829, 832, 835, 867, 868, 870, 926, 1151
electrostatic 694
film scanning (*see also* film *under* transmission systems) 4175, 4230, 6139, 6241, 8398
  patents 673, 684, 903, 1962, 1963, 1984, 2069, 2104, 2108, 2189, 2190, 2234, 2283, 2437, 2609, 2654, 2688, 2767, 2773, 2786, 2880, 2892, 2963, 3152, 3182, 3184, 3233, 3300, 3305, 3311, 3349, 3364, 3401, 3498, 3535, 3777, 3781, 3813, 3825, 3830, 3856, 4047, 4060, 4075, 4076, 4110, 4211, 4251, 4265, 4275, 4329, 4428, 4445, 4454, 4533, 4564, 4575, 4602, 4680, 4747, 4991, 5124, 5378, 5448, 5450, 5528, 5808, 5827, 5934, 6010, 6076, 6559, 7028, 7029, 7031, 7423, 7532, 7780, 7898
generator (*see also* saw-tooth generator, relaxation oscillation generator, deflection oscillator) 3633, 3637, 3889, 3919, 4009, 8658
helical 1067
honeycomb lens with light pipes 797, 821, 940
infrared 798, 827, 834, 836, 839, 858, 871, 874, 890, 932, 2650, 3447, 5228, 5330
interlaced, intermeshed, interleaved 5381, 6131, 6137, 6170, 6706, 7875, 8444
  patents 435, 537, 699, 747, 949, 1788, 1833, 1917, 3464, 3553, 3861, 3950, 3951, 4222, 4265, 4293, 4343, 4467, 4470, 4473, 4482, 4483, 4505, 4511, 4514, 4533, 4553, 4566, 4585, 4602, 4605, 4634, 4637, 4643, 4680, 4690, 4723, 4734, 4984, 4994, 5047, 5054, 5124, 5154, 5218, 5238, 5240, 5268, 5368, 5447, 5526, 5536, 5779, 5827, 5895, 6101, 6374, 6483, 6694, 6971, 7324
lens 2144, 4209, 4657, 5386, 5934
  cylindrical lens 4428

spirally twisted lens 2618
lens turret 2492
light beam 3742, 4506
light-spot (or spot-light) 384, 566, 907, 991, 995, 1321, 1738, 1913, 1979, 2595, 2614, 3139, 4566, 4991, 5743, 6192
  flying light-spot 328, 737, 977, 1573, 1593, 2827, 3093, 3623
linear 11, 15, 145, 162, 167
line-by-line 316, 1816
mask, apertured 3930, 3970
mirrors 2955, 3242, 4195, 4657
  coacting mirrors 4651
  double mirror 328
  endless band of canted mirrors 3403
  fixed mirrors, multiple 3290
  helical mirror 3146, 5191, 5640
  mirror cylinder 2535
  moving mirror 305, 384, 519, 576, 663, 2437, 2832, 3066
  oscillating or vibrating mirror 145, 296, 309, 447, 502, 536, 817, 819, 1780, 4798
  patents 367, 388, 457, 475, 518, 525, 528, 550, 633, 640, 677, 708, 719, 722, 725, 752, 952, 1089, 1258, 1708, 1893, 1951, 2246, 2396, 2476, 2500, 2534, 2659, 2679, 2783, 2785, 2786, 2867, 3158, 3351, 3503, 4215, 4343, 4463, 4514, 5218, 5468, 5548, 5862, 5894
  mirrors on pivoted levers 2822
  ring of mirrors 4245, 4252
  rotary mirror 384, 6072
  mirror screw 1472, 2296, 2436, 2535, 2586, 2923, 2927, 2975, 3047, 3048, 3103, 3130, 3569, 3590, 3646, 3655, 3732, 3904, 3935, 4196, 4215, 4234, 4375, 4376, 4404, 4476, 4511, 4611, 4702, 4719, 5105, 5218, 5319, 5513, 5533, 6312
  multiple mirror screw 3858
  spiral mirror 2619
  mirror wheel 1423, 1657, 1875, 2771, 2843, 2877, 2912, 3049, 3134, 3221, 3228, 3358, 3420, 3786, 3950, 5354
  double-sided mirror wheel 2972
moving arc 2479, 2484, 2702, 4369
multiple-beam or multibeam. *See under* scanning, electron beam
multispot 4279
one-shot 154
optical system 3968
  optical lever 699
  optical slots 1946
photocell 684, 980, 1600, 1795, 3501, 3970, 4978, 5346
piezoelectric crystals 677, 694, 934, 1023, 2238, 3304
pin-hole 3066

plates, overlapping spirally apertured 3626
prism
  prism lens 513, 690
  prism, moving 916, 947
  prism, rotary 2396, 3968
radial 5776, 7023, 8354
raster 336, 373, 5763
reflectors
  fixed 4978
  rotating 4252
  rotating and oscillating 4858
remote control of 674
ribbon, perforated 369, 416, 743
ring with spiral of apertures 2872
roller 455
rotary scanning 3713, 3808, 4267, 4308
rotary screw 4580
sequential 982, 5447
single-line 4845, 4846, 5970
spherical 1465
spiral 133, 192, 488, 699, 860, 947, 1742, 1849, 1856, 1862, 1871, 1876, 1898, 2256, 2386
split 2682
spot-light. *See* light-spot
tape with apertured drum 3524
trapezoidal 5076
tuning fork with mirror 584
tube, slotted, with photocell or lamp, rotating inside another rotating tube 4403
two-way 6856, 7312
variable-area 1713, 1759, 1898, 1989
variable-rate 2437, 3161, 4264, 4330
vertical 162
wheel with conductor rods 2226
wheel with light pipes 2195
zigzag 262, 526, 546, 817, 1018, 3264, 6316
zone 516, 640, 1011, 1529, 2735, 2760, 2898, 2924, 2937, 3011, 3044, 4978
screen 809, 2878, 2952, 3050, 3134, 3996, 4321, 4355, 4549, 5726, 7267, 7645
  antidazzle 2508
  apertured 3856, 4572
  cathode-ray tube 2965, 3957, 4797, 5768, 5769, 6588, 6619, 6669, 6679, 7140, 7443
  colored 1946, 4941
  concave 4604
  curved 5232
  electroluminescent 598
  fine-gauge 3829
  fluorescent 263, 375, 731, 4325, 5845, 6031
    patents 465, 566, 577, 587, 702, 1226, 1290, 1964, 2580, 2581, 2828, 2885, 2966, 2977, 3230, 3584, 3604, 3666,

3714, 3785, 3824, 3850, 3876, 4257, 4270, 4328, 4457, 4487, 4494, 4503, 4563, 4605, 4639, 4684, 4739, 4742, 4787, 4890-2, 4933, 5064-7, 5129, 5213, 5241, 5245, 5355, 5400, 5501, 5550, 5618, 5632, 5750, 5751, 5833-5, 5866, 5899, 6372, 6612, 6975, 7462, 8586, 8590
frosted 3139
glass 794
glow discharge 2444, 2475
graded, graduated, shaded 354, 361, 5503
ground glass 368, 386, 675, 695, 1395, 2753, 2748, 3066, 3084, 3904, 4772, 7067
helix wire 5758
illuminated 4941
incandescent 4010, 4735, 4851, 5041, 5136, 5184, 5216, 5968, 6175, 7119, 7141
intermediate 5750, 5866
Karolus 5513
large 2491, 2507, 2588, 2667, 2924, 2939, 2959, 2970, 3044, 3108, 3111, 3117, 3119, 3122, 3153, 3159, 3181, 3206, 3424, 3476, 3514, 3538, 3614, 4002, 4038, 4096, 4125, 4245, 4591, 5145, 5179, 5342, 5513, 6343, 6606, 6629, 6719, 7088, 7149, 7239, 7537, 7808, 8153, 8173, 8245, 8249, 8264, 8473, 8491
patents 2509, 4684, 5422, 7572
luminescent 1095, 2158, 3794, 3812, 4018, 4841, 4847, 5087, 5273, 5627, 5657, 5678, 5833, 5834, 5866, 5889, 6011, 6141, 6151, 6275, 6946, 7160, 7329, 7640, 7998
metal mesh or gauze 413, 4303, 4660, 5074, 6539
mosaic 160, 413
patents 695, 891, 3879, 3920, 4349, 4491, 4523, 4561, 4584, 4601, 4616, 4617, 4622, 4654, 4740, 4811, 4829, 4830, 4862, 4908, 4931, 4936, 5283, 5292, 5329, 5355, 5399, 5409, 5418, 5469, 5470, 5480, 5556, 5601, 5604, 5618, 5650, 5696, 5899, 5901, 5927, 5966, 5968, 6004, 6418, 6554, 6905, 7115, 7244, 7333, 7928, 7966, 8072, 8086, 8110, 8233
multicell 5329
oblique 3956, 3960, 4456, 4663, 5076, 5715
phosphorescent 571, 5228
screen phosphors 814, 2827, 2929, 3012, 3658, 3854
photoconductive 5351, 5428
photomosaic 4475, 4983, 4995, 5065, 5501

photosensitive 5129
projection 3026, 6598, 7055
photoelectric 4682, 4710, 5064-7, 5092, 5245, 5260, 5292, 5399, 5490, 5601
resistive 4650
selenium 1226, 5351
spark detector 893
translucent 2808, 3184, 5252
transparent 5172
vibrating 8553
secondary electron emission. *See* electron gun, electron amplifier, secondary emission multiplier
secondary emission multiplier (*see also* electron multiplier) 2279, 3705, 4139, 4536, 5152, 5182, 5477, 5722, 5780, 5782, 5790, 5868, 6947, 6976
secret signaling system 856
secret transmission 1341, 1949, 2539, 4012, 8176
selenium
 allotropy of 17, 116
 applications of 88, 106, 108, 112, 130, 138, 142, 147, 151, 155-8, 213, 234, 235, 238, 262, 275, 288, 334, 378, 575, 577, 636, 1098, 1179, 1780, 3066
 cells 162, 291, 295, 303, 305, 308, 309, 318, 328, 330, 345, 347, 348, 354, 358, 359, 369, 371, 375, 386, 389, 392, 449, 462, 466, 497, 499, 554, 571, 580, 607, 621, 625, 897, 1284, 1738, 2443, 2705, 5159
 discovery of 1, 2
 general research 60, 61, 87, 144, 161, 461, 579, 766
 inertia of (slow response to light changes) 134, 291, 345, 347, 553, 712, 946
 photoconductivity and photosensitivity of 50, 51, 53-5, 66, 92, 93, 116, 141, 173, 188, 297, 2272, 7618
 research by W.G. Adams 59, 65, 69, 73
 research by E.W. and C.W. Siemens 56, 63, 64, 67
 research by W. Smith 50, 52, 68, 83, 228
signal generating and transmitting systems 7603, 7607, 7667, 7668, 7670, 7671, 7739, 7843, 7899, 7936, 8020, 8305, 8414, 8460
signal reproducing system 8172
signal storage 765, 1145, 1251, 1348, 1363
signal translating system 8076, 8085, 8350
single-beam tube 3853, 3854
sound film, sound and vision transmission. *See under* transmission systems
sports on television
 boxing 3296, 4071, 4090

Derby 554, 2953, 2960, 2995, 2996, 2999, 3489, 3490, 3494, 3497, 3516, 3648
football 7212
Olympics (1936) 5089, 5090, 5756, 6028, 6144, 6148, 6155, 6499
standards (*see also* definition and line transmission) 899, 1656, 1665, 1669, 1691, 1866, 1943, 1999, 2000, 2003, 2051, 2055, 2118, 2123, 2620, 2621, 2715, 2719, 2734, 2981, 3034, 3134, 3206, 3210, 3387, 3799, 4149, 4227, 4237, 4314, 4358, 4471, 4472, 5030, 5108, 6251, 6994, 7071, 7265, 7306, 7499, 7745, 7750, 7916, 7934, 7980, 8051, 8229, 8277, 8640, 8657, 8734
quality of image in British television 6792
stations. *See* transmission stations
Stenode Radiostat 2506, 2784, 2945
stereoscopic systems (stereo; duplicate) 388, 550, 704, 859, 1024, 1335, 1403, 1440, 1444, 1448, 1512, 1518, 1569, 1578, 1719, 1738, 1742, 1859, 1860, 1945, 2246, 2284, 2323, 2395, 2403, 2474, 2572, 2708, 2781, 2782, 3356, 3357, 4102, 4634, 4771, 4853, 5055, 5155, 5171
stroboscopic effect in television 529, 2729
stroboscopic light source 8566
submarine television 3185
superheterodyne circuit 3136, 4216, 4312, 4698, 4825, 4926, 4959, 5153, 8502
surgery and television 8211, 8384
synchronization (synchronism, synchronous control, sync) 899, 1244, 1246, 1428, 1470, 1471, 1906, 1910, 1975, 2170, 2207, 2308, 2323, 2511, 2522, 2714, 2724, 2844, 3001, 3032, 3134, 3272, 3483, 3907, 4088, 4119, 4130, 4138, 4149, 4194, 4239, 4669, 4672, 5579, 5779, 7440, 7691, 7915, 7917, 8044, 8158, 8448, 8604
patents 457, 725, 859, 1213, 1620, 1663, 1664, 1743, 1842, 2104, 2149, 2193, 2232, 2290, 2382, 2389, 2426, 2427, 2429, 2447, 2473, 2509, 2613, 2804, 3008, 3126, 3252, 3337, 3347, 3349, 3350, 3423, 3493, 3504, 3830, 3856, 4000, 4005, 4068, 4098, 4153, 4154, 4310, 4339, 4437, 4439, 4585, 4586, 4982, 4991, 5056, 5124, 5599, 6059, 6161, 6184, 6621, 6625, 6746, 7006, 7096, 7107, 7187, 7331, 7332, 7360, 7428, 7473, 7604, 7885-7, 7891, 7907, 8010, 8191, 8195, 8340, 8554, 8612
air jet with musical note 571
armature bars 1679

automatic 349, 711, 2057, 2454, 2672, 3665, 5015, 5119, 5508, 5799
auxiliary light source 4602
blacker-than-black 4696, 5173
circuits 475, 527, 537, 550, 580, 615, 632, 643, 908, 2649, 2855, 3733, 3814, 3817, 3820, 3834, 3871, 3893, 3928, 3998, 4093, 4266, 4377, 4505, 4519, 4562, 4576, 4577, 4644, 4721, 4767, 4934, 4948, 4988, 4990, 5388, 5444, 5447, 5496, 5535, 5888, 6094, 6608, 6841, 7517, 7656, 8283, 8315, 8334, 8346, 8349
delay network 3892
disks
  apertured 3260, 3261, 3553
  Nipkow 1964, 3160
  slotted 4451 5244, 5692, 6483
eddy-current brake 825, 1362, 1766, 2336
electric clockwork 305, 369
electric motors 367, 976, 983, 992, 998, 1100, 1140, 1555, 2341, 2447, 2522, 2655, 2783, 2928, 3415, 3608, 4204, 4212, 5876, 7975
electromagnetic 366, 1266, 2378, 2962
generator 5240, 5281, 5469, 5537, 5981, 6022, 6728, 7838, 7962, 8087, 8125, 8452
hysteresis motor 3006
inductor 349
interrupted wave trains 1751
interrupter 335, 785
light siren 5479
light-spot registration 462, 561
line frequency signals 2969, 4411
neon lamp 743, 3250
periodic voltage 4381, 4645, 7306, 7902
phonic wheel 94, 102, 103, 170, 190, 213, 528, 717, 763, 764, 825, 1357, 1622, 1835, 1885, 1996, 2074, 2098, 2427, 2522, 2535, 2664, 2723, 3558, 3665, 3783, 4197, 4204, 7704
photoelectric 5924
pulse 731
quartz crystal oscillator 1142, 1170, 1239
rotary resistance and circuit 309, 2439
(sync) separation 4184, 4576, 4679, 4683, 4770, 5117, 5442, 5481, 7889, 7964
shaded optical filters 3160
spark discharges 751
start-stop, on-off 303, 347, 435
stroboscope 983, 1362, 2521
toothed wheel 1743, 1766, 1961, 2045, 3248
tuning fork 46, 102, 170, 190, 213, 234, 295, 328, 335, 528, 529, 557, 571, 719, 743, 763, 764, 785, 983, 1141, 1142,

1227, 1292, 1579, 1835, 2074, 3250, 3564
watch 2204

Tel 61, 8153
telautogramme 543
telautograph 110, 298, 336, 364, 381, 398, 412
Telautophote 335
telecine or telecinematography 633, 734, 903, 1313, 1554, 1689, 1715, 1719, 1843, 2021, 2323, 2813, 3039, 3139, 6442, 6906, 7370
Telectrograph 398
telectroscopy (*see also* electric telescopy, facsimile, phototelegraphy) 88, 89, 102, 110, 115, 133, 134, 167-9, 180, 234, 238, 290, 619
  research by Senlecq 104-6, 154, 165, 354
  research by Szczepanik 262, 269, 272-4, 282, 283, 330
Telegraphone 281, 287, 289, 291
telegraphy (*see also* facsimile, Fultograph, phototelegraphy, telectroscopy) 88, 101, 102, 228, 342, 390
  copying telegraphy. *See* facsimile and phototelegraphy
  sight telegraphy, "seeing by electricity," "seeing by telegraph," "electric vision at a distance" (*see also* facsimile *and* phototelegraphy) 307, 308, 359, 361, 362, 366, 368, 410, 413, 8706
  wireless telegraphy 258, 339, 377, 390, 422, 423, 430, 459, 875, 3243
  writing or autographic telegraphy (*see also* telautography) 110, 111, 118, 412
  research by Cowper 110, 111, 121, 122, 236
Telehor 551, 570, 592, 614, 617, 720, 845, 1780, 3146
téléscope 271
Telephane 213
telephone, telephony 66, 71, 75, 81, 82, 84, 88, 95, 98, 100, 101, 181, 323, 334, 460, 890, 984, 2000, 2412, 2446, 3243, 3895, 4163, 6027, 7357, 8533
  telephone relay 415, 465
Telephonioscope 100, 180
Telephonovision 2443
telephot 376, 460
téléphote 126, 135, 233, 236, 378, 382, 780
telephotography. *See* phototelegraphy
Tele-Radio receiver 3138
telescopy, electric (*see also* telectroscopy) 88, 89, 108, 109, 131, 142, 143, 190, 349, 358, 400, 401, 403, 405-7, 411, 530, 596, 4050
telestereograph 348, 480, 538

Teletalkies 1991, 1992, 2023, 2025, 2121, 2323, 2565, 3044
Televidascope 2348
"television" 142, 288, 348, 376, 1013, 1332, 2902, 3579, 5003
television, definition by RMA 1545
Televisor 411, 740, 741, 768, 769, 783, 789, 793, 794, 809, 816, 846, 848, 881, 900, 940, 1035, 1043, 1049, 1060, 1071, 1125, 1126, 1167, 1202, 1217, 1253, 1275, 1276, 1303, 1420, 1444, 1511, 1523, 1538, 1586, 1636, 1778, 2126, 2129, 2178, 2278, 2312, 2325, 2333, 2335, 2460, 2529, 2882, 2936, 2938, 2995, 3145, 3178 (in 10 Downing St.), 3201, 3527, 3539, 3577, 3888, 3979, 3980, 4104, 6504, 6928
(Hollis) Baird Universal Televisor 376
Televue 334, 338
"telly" 7980
terminology 781, 1570, 1618, 2552, 3246, 4751, 6577, 6917, 6928, 7058, 7146, 7378, 8620, 8625, 8640, 8649, 8695
tests, demonstrations, and early transmissions (in order by date)
  Lyons - Paris, Belin, photo by wire (Jul. 1920) 473, 494
  N.Y. - St. Louis, Belin, photo by wire (Nov. 1920) 480
  N.Y. - Paris, Belin, photo by wire (Aug. 1921) 487
  Annapolis - Malmaison and Croix d'Hino - Bar Harbor, Belin, photo by wire (May 1922) 495
  Italy - U.S., Korn, photo by radio (June 1922) 506
  Washington, D.C., Jenkins, photo by radio (Apr. 1923) 534, 535
  Hastings, Baird, shadowgraph demonstration (Apr. 1924) 585
  Cleveland - N.Y., AT&T, pictures by wire (May 1924) 594, 604
  London - N.Y., Marconi/RCA, photoradiograms (Nov. 1924) 626, 628, 646
  Selfridge's (London), Baird shadowgraph (Apr. 1925) 662, 664, 675, 8807
  Washington, D.C., Jenkins, "radio vision" (May and June 1925) 681, 685
  Frith St. (London), Baird, moving halftone images (Jan. 1926) 733, 740
  Motograph House (London), Baird, moving halftone images (June 1926) 769, 772, 874
  Washington, D.C. - N.Y., RCA/B.T.L., image and sound transmission by wire (Apr. 1927) 909-13, 919, 921, 923, 939, 966, 988, 990, 8779

Whippany, N.J. - N.Y., RCA/B.T.L., image and sound transmission by radio (Apr. 1927) 910, 924, 966, 1007

London - N.Y., Baird, secret transmission (Apr. 1927) 915, 928, 1112, 1116

N.Y., B.T.L., demonstration to AIEE and IRE (May 1927) 950

London - Glasgow, Baird, transmission by wire (May 1927) 955, 981, 986

London - Leeds, Baird, transmission by wire (Sept. 1927) 1028, 1043

Schenectady, Alexanderson, receiver tests in homes (Jan. 1928) 1110, 1111, 1113, 1114, 1116, 1194

London - Hartsdale, N.Y., Baird (Feb. 1928) 1124-7, 1129, 1134, 1161, 1178, 1179, 1240, 2365

London, Baird, infrared searchlight (Feb. 1928) 1130

London - S.S. Berengaria (Mar. 1928) 1167-9, 1175, 1178, 1186, 1205-7, 1249, 1273

B.T.L., daylight pickup (Jul. 1928) 1340, 1345, 1352, 1436, 1490

Long Acre, Baird stereoscopic television (Aug. 1928) 1403, 1569

Bamberger's store (Newark, N.J.), Daven Co., puppet show televised (Aug. 1928) 1410, 1473

N.Y. University, Gernsback, television over WRNY (Aug. 1928) 1411

San Francisco, Farnsworth, demonstration of electronic system (Sept. 1928) 1453

Schenectady, G.E., play broadcast over WGY (Sept. 1928) 1461, 1462, 1478

Glasgow at BAAS meeting, Baird, color and stereo images (Oct. 1928) 1512

N.Y. - Johannesburg, images over 2XAL (Dec. 1928) 1671

London, Baird, official demonstration to BBC and GPO (Mar. 1929) 1787, 1805, 1821, 1825

Bamberger's store (Newark, N.J.), U.S. Radio & Television Corp., transmission by light beam (May 1929) 1896, 2084

B.T.L., color transmission by wire (June 1929) 1933, 1934, 1950, 1953

London, Baird, demonstration of Noctovisor (Aug. 1929) 1988

South Africa, Baird, demonstration (Sept. 1929) 2010

London, Baird and BBC, first broadcast over 2LO (Sept. 1929) 2062, 2063, 2079, 2333

Schenectady - Australia and back, G.E. (Feb. 1930) 2243

N.Y., B.T.L., two-way with telephone (Apr. 1930) 2343, 2345, 2401, 2446

Manchester, Sunderland, Southampton, Bournemouth, New Castle, Baird, demonstrations (Apr. /May 1930) 2347, 2367, 2376, 2421

Schenectady, G.E., theater screen demonstration (May 1930) 2391, 2392, 2402, 2432, 2559, 2561, 2628

Long Acre studio to Coliseum large screen, Baird, talking film (Jul. 1930) 2489, 2491, 2505, 2526, 2527, 2563, 2565, 2567

New York, Jenkins and de Forest, outdoor radio vision demonstration (Aug. 1930) 2545, 2546

N.Y. - London, first transatlantic reception by amateur (Sept. 1930) 2575

Schenectady - Leipzig, Berlin, London, G.E. (Feb. 1931) 2776

Boston and Washington - S.S. Leviathan, CBS (Jul. 1931) 2971, 3016, 3019

N.Y. - S.S. Vulcania, CBS, Jenkins, Short Wave & Television Corp. (Sept. 1931) 3075, 3090, 3094

Madison Square Garden, Sanabria, large-screen demonstration (Sept. 1931) 3108, 3111, 3117, 3119, 3122, 3123, 3181

Brookmans Park (London) - express train, Baird (Feb. 1932) 3288, 3298, 3330

Long Acre studio to Selfridge's, Baird, ultra-short-wave transmission (Apr. 1932) 3433, 3438, 3641

Empire State Building, RCA (May 1932) 3446, 3450

Paris, Baird, two-way demonstration (May 1932) 3447, 3459, 3461, 3479, 3540

L.A. to airplane, movie via W6XAO (May 1932) 3449, 3479, 3655, 3690

Derby from Epsom Downs to Metropole Cinema, London, Baird (June 1932) 3476, 3486, 3487, 3489, 3490, 3494, 3497, 3516, 3648

Chelmsford - York, Marconi's, transmission by radio (Sept. 1932) 3623, 3629, 3651

Leicester at BAAS meeting, Marconi's, transmission by light beam to 4-foot receiver (Sept. 1933) 4096, 4125

Crystal Palace, Baird, direct pickup and intermediate film (Feb. 1935) 4821, 4865

London, demonstration "theatres" in department stores (Dec. 1936) 6536

N.Y., RCA, 441-line transmission of fashion show (Nov. 1937) 7443

Thalofide cell 469

thermionic valve (*see also* saw-tooth wave oscillator)
 amplifier 6291, 6615, 6730, 6948, 7179, 7251, 7287, 8199, 8435
 circuits 3903, 4185, 4407, 4409, 4975, 5863, 5928, 6042, 6079, 6271, 6431, 6532, 6657, 6938, 7593, 7675, 7743, 7830, 8003, 8007, 8137, 8179, 8291

three-electrode tube (triode) 346, 409, 419, 433, 434, 436, 452, 2485, 2544

time modulation 7005

transmission systems 2720, 3273, 3414, 4089
 single-channel 1227, 1239, 1254, 1534, 2190, 2650, 2682, 3161, 3503, 3932, 5595, 6101
 two-channel 959, 1080, 2146, 2682, 2699, 2781, 2913, 3156, 3363, 3395, 3404, 3675, 3986, 4068, 4146, 4158, 4190, 4202, 4229, 4992, 5472, 5557
 three-channel 613, 1010, 1046, 1930, 2032, 2354, 2608, 2713, 2735, 2912, 3476, 4064
 four-channel 1010, 2073
 five-channel 2656, 2736, 3256, 3316
 multichannel 245, 803, 867, 876, 1211, 1338, 1364, 1894, 2284, 2582, 3216, 3626, 3663, 4155, 4163, 4518, 4537, 4719, 5094-6, 5323, 6557

film, transparencies (*see also* film *under* scanning) 309, 1992, 2065, 2362, 2411, 2457, 2514, 2565, 2595, 2721, 2841, 2981, 3452, 3518, 3643, 3655, 4233, 4368, 4671, 6709, 7386
 patents 275, 447, 470, 546, 633, 652, 979, 996, 1014, 1090, 1146, 1291, 1351, 1393, 1786, 1788, 1819, 1876, 1886, 1951, 2041, 2101, 2144, 2151, 2162, 2244, 2287, 2297, 2395, 2399, 2656, 2682, 2921, 2965, 3062, 3073, 3106, 3114, 3120, 3214, 3253, 3370, 3372, 3378, 3395, 3503, 3509, 3510, 3553, 3640, 3736, 3778, 3780, 3792, 3796, 3864, 3867, 3871, 4000, 4051, 4058, 4078, 4107, 4114, 4145, 4146, 4414, 4421, 4447, 4499, 4505, 4551, 4637, 4657, 4680, 4704, 4720, 4730, 4924, 4950, 4980, 5045, 5047, 5063, 5268, 5291, 5299, 5312, 5386, 5395, 5413, 5536, 5561, 5658, 6024, 6154, 7684, 7749, 7807, 7901, 7922, 8435, 8599

double-film system 3219, 3318, 3495, 3515, 3870, 3910

intermediate film system 1047, 1894, 2295, 3183, 3300, 3517, 3596, 3636, 3709, 3710, 3719, 3927, 3937, 3964, 4067, 4072, 4108, 4118, 4203, 4304, 4306, 4309, 4368, 4390, 4541, 4589, 4591, 4621, 4821, 4971, 5103, 5145,

Subject Index

5219, 5250, 5302, 5364, 5513, 6325, 6906, 7396
frequency
  frequency-selective 342, 372
  interleaved frequency 1860
  multifrequency 342, 497, 502, 598, 705, 861, 977, 1282, 1292, 2200, 2744, 3118, 5123, 5541
  varied frequency 2431
halftone images 707, 733, 740, 1221, 1799
light-beam transmission 1896, 2084, 3223, 3227, 4096, 4125
light-spot transmitter 2595, 3139, 4965
luminous images 108, 130, 145, 152, 154, 156, 158, 160, 222, 297
moving images 388, 685, 733, 772, 3303
shadowgraphs 558, 662, 664, 1238, 1447, 1778, 1912, 2004, 3326
silhouettes 691, 696, 1259, 1372, 1484, 1799, 1837, 2457
simultaneous sound and image, sound film (*see also* transmission, two-way) 700, 1992, 2300, 2324, 2325, 2372, 2443, 2598, 2712, 3575, 3609, 3628, 3691, 4283, 4598, 4677, 5133, 6545
  patents 501, 3261, 3368, 3409, 3862, 3926, 3937, 4058, 4333, 4533, 4632, 4633, 4781, 4930, 5006, 5153, 5368, 5495, 5688, 5926
single-wire 133, 181, 192, 291, 305, 372, 378
two-way 295, 333, 386, 388, 581, 795, 890, 984, 1064, 1254, 1341, 1609, 1880, 2299, 2339, 2343, 2349, 2351, 2353, 2364, 2366, 2401, 2407, 2415, 2446-9, 2495, 2510, 2515, 2650, 2755, 2794, 2865, 2884, 2894, 2924, 3447, 3459, 3941, 4537, 5251, 8615
transmitters. *See* Alexandra Palace, Chrysler Building, Crystal Palace, Eiffel Tower, Empire State Building
transmitting stations 734, 735, 739, 783, 1250, 1492, 1493, 1614, 1627, 1630, 1691, 1728, 1761, 1844, 1920, 1972, 3060
list of stations (in order by date)
  11 U.S. stations (Oct. 1928) 1493
  26 U.S. stations (June 1929) 1920
  26 U.S. stations (Aug. 1929) 1972
  8 U.S. stations on regular schedules (Sept. 1929) 1999
  8 U.S. stations (Jul. 1930) 2462
  19 U.S. stations (Dec. 1930) 2684
  19 U.S. stations (Feb. 1931) 2759
  U.S. and Canadian stations (1932) 3505
  35 U.S. stations (Feb. 1933) 3797
  27 "experimental" stations (Dec. 1934) 4715
  27 U.S. stations (Sept. 1935) 5316
  20 U.S. stations (Feb. 1937) 6670
  18 U.S. stations (Sept. 1937) 7172
  19 U.S. stations (Aug. 1938) 7805
  U.S. stations (May 1939) 8276, 8294
  11 commercial U.S. stations (1942) 8653
  map of U.S. facilities (1950) 8713
  table of BBC stations (1939-60) 8754
by call letters (including sound stations)
2L0 (London) 2029, 2031, 2034, 2062, 2063
2TV (Motograph House, London) 783, 790, 802, 818
2TW (Harrow) 783, 786, 809
2XAD 1745
3XK 1355, 1484
3XN (Whippany, N.J.) 910, 924, 994
5XX (BBC) 1547
G2BS (Chelmsford) 3623
IXAY 1355
JOAK (Tokyo) 3440, 3472
KDKA (Pittsburgh) 1395, 1568, 1995
MOSPS (Moscow) 454, 464
VE9AK (Montreal) 5315
VKZME (Sydney) 2243
WAAM (Newark) 1758
WABC (N.Y.) 2540, 2691, 3296
WCFL (Chicago) 1301, 1307, 1431, 1565, 1674
WCSH (Portland, Maine) 3045
WEEL (Boston) 2294
WGAR 3343
WGBS 2864, 2888, 2889, 2906, 2908, 2918, 2991
WGXAO 6921
WGY (Schenectady) 1110, 1111, 1113, 1114, 1260, 1264, 1296, 1302, 1308, 1316, 1369, 1461, 1462, 1557, 1559, 1631, 1677, 1745
WIBO (Chicago) 1634, 1677
WJR 3343
WJZ 2502
WLEX (Lexington, Mass.) 1296, 1373, 1758
WLTH (Jenkins) 2327
WLWL 3091
WMAQ (Chicago) 1634, 2482, 2551, 2825
WMCA (N.Y.) 3071, 3154, 3203, 3280, 3400, 3475
WOR 1410, 1573
WPCH (N.Y.) 3203
WRGB (Schenectady) 8666a
WRNY (N.Y.) 1223, 1256, 1295, 1317, 1319, 1330, 1370, 1374, 1399, 1411, 1432, 1539, 1560, 1565-7, 1640, 1671, 2334
WXBZ (Saranac Lake) 3072
W1XAV (Boston) 2896, 2935, 3019, 3046, 3094
W1XAY (Boston) 1635
W2XAB (N.Y.) 2866, 2873, 3014, 3017, 3068, 3094, 3163, 3171, 3224, 3335, 3399, 3575, 3588, 3613, 3664, 3795
W2XAJ (RCA Victor) 3072
W2XAP (Washington) 3360
W2XAV (Washington) 3019
W2XAX 7984
W2XB (Long Island City) 3072
W2XBA 2038
W2XBB (RCA) 3072
W2XBJ 2038
W2XBS (N.Y.) 1813, 1902, 1974, 2124, 2130, 3072, 3171
W2XBW (N.Y.) 1765, 2038
W2XBY (N.J.) 1765
W2XCD (Passaic) 2212, 2334, 2546, 2769, 2789, 3094, 3171, 3258
W2XCL 1811
W2XCR (N.Y.) 1799, 1881, 2120, 2177, 2212, 2334, 2461, 2546, 2769, 2862, 2864, 2887, 2889, 2906, 2908, 2918, 2991, 3046, 3171
W2XCW (Schenectady) 2391
W2XDV (N.Y.) 5522
W2XR (Radio Pictures) 3171
W3XAD (RCA-Victor) 3018
W3XE 6497
W3XK (Washington) 1635, 1715, 1765, 1823, 2131, 2461
W3XPF (Philadelphia) 6711
W6XAH (Bakersfield, Calif.) 4175
W6XAO (L.A.) 3449, 3479, 3690, 6130, 6499, 7094, 8401
W6XAQ (L.A.) 8269
W6XE 4175
W8XAY (Westinghouse) 1995
W9XAA (Chicago) 314
W9XAO (Chicago) 2386, 2863, 2907
W9XAP (Chicago) 2551, 2645, 2677, 2825, 2863, 2907, 3257
W9XK (Univ. of Iowa) 3843, 4455
X2XAF (Schenectady) 2243
X2XBU (Mt. Beacon, N.Y.) 1959
XZXE (Philadelphia) 7073
tuning fork. *See under* synchronization
two-electrode tube (diode) 174, 319, 339, 2675
two-way. *See under* transmission systems

ultra-high frequencies (UHF) 2589, 2758, 6023, 6915, 7004, 7438, 7514, 8046, 8500
ultra-short-wave television 2123, 2553, 2717, 2758, 3377, 3433, 3438, 3439, 3478, 3641, 3643, 3747, 3991, 4072,

4083, 4103, 4124, 4137, 4147, 4149, 4166, 4174, 4175, 4214, 4246, 4278, 4385, 4588, 4758, 4788, 4921, 4922, 4938, 4969, 5144, 5179, 5313, 5582, 5879, 6570, 6599, 6925, 8573
  patents 2441, 2913, 3855, 3874, 3986, 4186, 4411, 4698, 6362
ultra violet 196, 324, 734, 798, 890, 1280, 1896, 4344, 4549, 5473

vacua. *See* rarefied gases
vacuum pump 27, 28, 33, 39, 99, 166, 199, 202, 355, 379, 417, 437, 450, 451
  Bunsen's pump 166
  Sprengel's pump 39, 166
vacuum tube (*see also* picture tube) 70, 99, 120, 490, 500, 1927, 2750, 4981, 6616, 7583

valve amplifier 5207, 5226, 5844, 6874, 8115
valve generator circuit (*see* saw-tooth wave oscillator, relaxation oscillator) 3485, 4159, 4299, 4645, 5125, 5795, 5881, 5886, 5887, 5896, 6070, 6086, 6156, 6217, 6270, 6276, 6484, 6842, 7283, 7344, 7424, 7450, 7488, 7511, 7515, 7912, 7940, 7986, 7992, 8009, 8128, 8177, 8469, 8474, 8516, 8559, 8581
velocity modulation 400, 1886, 1981, 2244, 3311, 3644, 3811, 4093, 4150, 4264, 4278, 4295, 4331, 4332, 4529-31, 4794, 4859
videocassette recorder 8864
videodisk 8863
video recording 8871, 8872
videotape 8875

viewers, names for 971, 1973, 2552, 2836, 2874, 4865
viewers, numbers of 1973, 3915, 4132, 4174

Wehnelt cylinder 301, 2967, 3241, 3292, 3764, 5379
wireless telegraphy. *See under* telegraphy
women announcers 2957, 5906, 5907, 5950

X rays 255, 560, 1701, 2757
  discovery of 254, 256
X-ray tube 375, 731, 2885, 3507

zinc sulfide crystal 3827, 4123, 4156